WORLDCOMP'13
July 22-25, 2013
Las Vegas Nevada, USA
www.world-academy-of-science.org

PROCEEDINGS OF THE 2013 INTERNATIONAL CONFERENCE ON SOFTWARE ENGINEERING RESEARCH & PRACTICE

SERP 2013

Editors

Hamid R. Arabnia
Leonidas Deligiannidis
George Jandieri

Associate Editors

Vince Schmidt
Ashu M. G. Solo
Fernando G. Tinetti

(An Imprint of Laxmi Publications Pvt. Ltd.)
An ISO 9001:2008 Company
BENGALURU • CHENNAI • COCHIN • GUWAHATI • HYDERABAD
JALANDHAR • KOLKATA • LUCKNOW • MUMBAI • RANCHI • NEW DELHI
BOSTON (USA) • ACCRA (GHANA) • NAIROBI (KENYA)

This volume contains papers presented at The 2013 International Conference on Software Engineering Research & Practice (SERP'13). Their inclusion in this publication does not necessarily constitute endorsements by editors or by the publisher.

Branches

Branch	Telephone	
Bengaluru	080-26 75 69 30	
Chennai	044-24 34 47 26,	24 35 95 07
Cochin	0484-237 70 04,	405 13 03
Guwahati	0361-254 36 69,	251 38 81
Hyderabad	040-27 55 53 83,	27 55 53 93
Jalandhar	0181-222 12 72	
Kolkata	033-22 27 43 84	
Lucknow	0522-220 99 16	
Mumbai	022-24 91 54 15,	24 92 78 69
Ranchi	0651-220 44 64	

PUBLISHED IN INDIA BY

An ISO 9001:2008 Company
113, GOLDEN HOUSE, DARYAGANJ,
NEW DELHI - 110002, INDIA
Telephone : 91-11-4353 2500, 4353 2501
Fax : 91-11-2325 2572, 4353 2528
www.laxmipublications.com info@laxmipublications.com

C—
Printed at: Repro Knowledgecast Limited, Thane

Foreword

It gives us great pleasure to introduce this collection of papers to be presented at the 2013 International Conference on Software Engineering Research and Practice (SERP'13), July 22 through 25, 2013, at The New Tropicana Hotel, Las Vegas, USA.

An important mission of the World Congress in Computer Science, Computer Engineering, and Applied Computing (a federated congress to which this conference is affiliated with) includes *"Providing a unique platform for a diverse community of constituents composed of scholars, researchers, developers, educators, and practitioners. The Congress makes concerted effort to reach out to participants affiliated with diverse entities (such as: universities, institutions, corporations, government agencies, and research centers/labs) from all over the world. The congress also attempts to connect participants from institutions that have* ***teaching*** *as their main mission with those who are affiliated with institutions that have* ***research*** *as their main mission. The congress uses a quota system to achieve its institution and geography diversity objectives."* By any definition of diversity, this congress is among the most diverse scientific meeting in USA. We are proud to report that this federated congress has authors and participants from 82 different nations representing variety of personal and scientific experiences that arise from differences in culture and values. As can be seen (see below), the program committee of this conference as well as the program committee of all other tracks of the federated congress are as diverse as its authors and participants.

The program committee would like to thank all those who submitted papers for consideration. About 57% of the submissions were from outside the United States. Each submitted paper was peer-reviewed by two experts in the field for originality, significance, clarity, impact, and soundness. In cases of contradictory recommendations, a member of the conference program committee was charged to make the final decision; often, this involved seeking help from additional referees. In addition, papers whose authors included a member of the conference program committee were evaluated using the double-blinded review process. One exception to the above evaluation process was for papers that were submitted directly to chairs/organizers of pre-approved sessions/workshops; in these cases, the chairs/organizers were responsible for the evaluation of such submissions. The overall paper acceptance rate for regular papers was 31%; 10% of the remaining papers were accepted as poster papers (at the time of this writing, we had not yet received the acceptance rate for a few individual tracks.)

We are very grateful to the many colleagues who offered their services in organizing the conference. In particular, we would like to thank the members of the Program Committee of SERP'13, members of the congress Steering Committee, and members of the committees of federated congress tracks that have topics within the scope of SERP. Many individuals listed below, will be requested after the conference to provide their expertise and services for selecting papers for publication (extended versions) in journal special issues as well as for publication in a set of research books (to be prepared for publishers including: Springer, Elsevier, BMC, and others).

- *Dr. Alireza Abbasi; School of Engineering and Information Technology, University of New South Wales (UNSW), Canberra, Australia*
- *Prof. Afrand Agah (FECS); West Chester University of Pennsylvania, Pennsylvania, USA*
- *Dr. Selim Aissi (World Congress Steering Committee); formerly, Chief Strategist - Security, Intel Corp., USA; Senior Business Leader & Head of Global Enterprise Security Architecture, Visa Corporation, USA*
- *Prof. Babak Akhgar (World Congress Steering Committee); Fellow of the British Computer Society, CITP; Professor of Informatics; Co-Director of CENTRIC (Centre of Excellence in Terrorism, Resilience, Intelligence & organised Crime research), Sheffield Hallam University, Sheffield, UK*
- *Prof. Nizar Al-Holou (World Congress Steering Committee); Professor and Chair, ECE Department; Vice Chair, IEEE/SEM-Computer Chapter; University of Detroit Mercy, Detroit, Michigan, USA*
- *Dr. Haider M. AlSabbagh (FECS); University of Basra, Iraq*
- *Prof. Hamid R. Arabnia (World Congress Steering Committee); Professor, Computer Science; Editor-in-Chief, The Journal of Supercomputing (Springer); Elected Fellow, Int'l Society of Intelligent Biological Medicine (ISIBM); The University of Georgia, Department of Computer Science, USA*
- *Peyman Arebi; Assistant Professor, Department of Computer Engineering, Technical and Vocational University, Bushehr, Iran*

- *Prof. Ezendu Ariwa (Publicity Vice-Chair); Chair, IEEE Consumer Electronics Chapter, UK&RI; Visiting Professor, Gulf University, Bahrain*
- *Dr. Azita Bahrami (Session Chair, FECS); President, IT Consult, USA*
- *Mehdi Bahrami; Senior Software Analyst and Software Manager, Lian Processor Co.; BISC member, University of California, Berkeley, California, USA*
- *Prof. Juan Jose Martinez Castillo; Director of The Acantelys Research Group and Coordinator of the Computer Engineering Department, Universidad Gran Mariscal de Ayacucho, Venezuela*
- *Dr. Hsi-Ya (Jerry) Chang (PDPTA); Division Chief, National Center for High-Performance Computing, Taiwan; Secretary General of ACCTA; Member, Council of the Taiwan Association of Cloud Computing (TACC); Taiwan, ROC*
- *Prof. Juan Cuadrado-Gallego; Universidad de Alcala, Edificio Politecnico, Madrid, Spain; Ecole de technologie superieure, University of Quebec, Canada*
- *Prof. Kevin Daimi (World Congress Steering Committee, SAM Chair); Director, Computer Science and Software Engineering Programs; Department of Mathematics, Computer Science and Software Engineering; University of Detroit Mercy, Detroit, Michigan, USA*
- *Prof. Leonidas Deligiannidis; Professor, Computer Science, Wentworth Institute of Technology, MA, USA*
- *Somdip Dey (FCS); St. Xavier's College (Autonomous), Kolkata, India*
- *Prof. George A. Gravvanis; Democritus University of Thrace, Greece*
- *Dr. Bing He (PDPTA); Cisco System Inc., San Jose, California, USA*
- *Prof. George Jandieri (World Congress Steering Committee); Georgian Technical University, Tbilisi, Georgia; Chief Scientist, The Institute of Cybernetics, Georgian Academy of Science, Georgia; Editorial Board Member: International Journal of Microwaves and Optical Technology, The Open Atmospheric Science Journal, American Journal of Remote Sensing, Georgia*
- *Prof. Seifedine Kadry (PDPTA); School of Engineering, American University of the Middle East, Kuwait*
- *Prof. Dong Hwa Kim; Department of Electronic and Control Engineering, Hanbat National University, Korea; Visiting Professor, Budapest University of Technology and Economic, Hungary; International Einstein awardee for Scientific achievement (2010)*
- *Prof. Dattatraya V. Kodavade (World Congress Steering Committee); Head of Computer Science and Engineering, D.K.T.E Society's Textile & Engineering Institute, Ichalkaranji, Maharashtra State, India*
- *Prof. Raghu Korrapati; Elected Fellow, Information Systems, Walden University, Minneapolis, MN, USA*
- *Prof. B. Raja Sarath Kumar; Principal, Lenora College of Engineering, Andhra Pradesh, India*
- *Dr. Vitus S.W. Lam; Chartered Member of The British Computer Society; Senior IT Manager, Information Technology Services, The University of Hong Kong, Hong Kong*
- *Prof. Kun Chang Lee (World Congress Steering Committee); Prof. of MIS and WCU Prof. of Creativity Science, Business School & Department of Interaction Science, Sungkyunkwan University, South Korea*
- *Prof. Zhongyu (Joan) Lu; University of Huddersfield, Huddersfield, UK*
- *Muhammad Naufal Bin Mansor; Intelligent Signal Processing Group (ISP), University Malaysia Perlis, Kangar, Perlis, Malaysia*
- *Arshad Mansoor; Pakistan Aeronautical Complex, Pakistan*
- *Dr. Tao Mao (ICAI); Oracle America, Inc., Santa Clara, California, USA*
- *Prof. George Markowsky (World Congress Steering Committee and SAM Session Chair); Professor and Associate Director, School of Computing and Information Science; Chair International Advisory Board of IEEE IDAACS; Director 2013 Northeast Collegiate Cyber Defense Competition; Cooperating Professor Mathematics and Statistics Department UMaine; Cooperating Professor School of Policy & International Affairs UMaine; University of Maine, Orono, Maine, USA*
- *Suzanne Kranjac McIntosh; Team Lead & Senior Software Engineer, IBM T. J. Watson Research Center, Yorktown Heights, New York, USA; Adjunct Professor, NYU Courant Institute of Mathematical Sciences, Graduate School, USA*
- *Dr. Sara Moein; Editorial Board, International Journal of Science and Technology; Faculty of Engineering, MultiMedia University, Malaysia*
- *Dr. Ali Mostafaeipour; Industrial Engineering Department, Yazd University, Iran*
- *Dr. Saurabh Mukherjee; Associate Professor, Department of Computer Science, Banasthali University, Banasthali, Rajasthan, India*
- *Prof. Prashant R. Nair (FECS); Vice-Chairman, Information Technology & Accreditation; Faculty, AMRITA-TIFAC Centre of Excellence in Cyber Security; Amrita University, Tamil Nadu, India*
- *Prof. G. N. Pandey (World Congress Steering Committee); Vice-Chancellor, Arunachal University of Studies, Arunachal Pradesh, India; Adjunct Prof., Indian Institute of Information Technology, India*
- *Prof. James J. (Jong Hyuk) Park (World Congress Steering Committee); Professor of Computer Science and Engineering, Seoul National University of Science and Technology (SeoulTech), Korea; President, KITCS; President, FTRA; Editor-in-Chiefs: HCIS, JoC and IJITCC Journals*

- *Dr. Satish Penmatsa; Computer Science, University of Maryland - Eastern Shore, Maryland, USA*
- *Prof. R. Ponalagusamy; Department of Mathematics, National Institute of Technology, Tiruchirappalli, India*
- *Prof. Junfeng Qu; Clayton State University, Morrow, Georgia, USA*
- *Prof. B. V. A. N. S. S. Prabhakar Rao; School of Computing Science and Engineering, VIT University, Chennai Campus, India*
- *Prof. Abd-El-Kader Sahraoui; LAAS-CNRS and Toulouse University, Toulouse, France*
- *Dr. Vince Schmidt (Session Chair, SERP); Battlespace Visualization Branch, Human Effectiveness Directorate of the United States Air Force Research Laboratory (AFMC 711 HPW / RHCVE), Wright Patterson Air Force Base, Ohio, USA*
- *Dr. Salva Sebastien; Fellow, Limos laboratory (CNRS), France; Associate Professor, University of Auvergne (UdA), LIMOS Complexe scientifique des Cezeaux, Aubiere, France*
- *Dr. Liang Shi; Senior Researcher, McAfee, USA*
- *Dr. Kok Swee Sim; Faculty of Engineering and Technology, Jalan Ayer Keroh Lama, Melaka, Malaysia*
- *Ashu M. G. Solo, (Publicity Chair); Fellow of British Computer Society, Principal/R&D Engineer, Maverick Technologies America Inc., USA*
- *Prof. Fernando G. Tinetti (World Congress Steering Committee); School of CS, Universidad Nacional de La Plata, La Plata, Argentina; Co-editor, Journal of Computer Science and Technology (JCS&T)*
- *Dr. Predrag Tosic (World Congress Steering Committee); Microsoft, Washington, USA*
- *Prof. Vladimir Volkov (World Congress Steering Committee & Vice-Chair of IPCV); The Bonch-Bruevich State University of Telecommunications, Saint-Petersburg, Russia*
- *Prof. Patrick Wang (MSV); Fellow of IAPR, ISIBM, WASE; Zijiang Chair Professor, ECNU, Shanghai and NTUST, Taipei, Taiwan; Founding President and CEO, Wang Teknowlogy Lab.; MIT Research Consultant; Harvard University, Adj. Faculty, USA; Northeastern University, Boston, MA, USA*
- *Dr. Wei Wei (GCA); School of Computer Science & Eng., Xi'an University of Technology, Xi'an, P. R. China*
- *Dr. Alexander Wohrer (ICOMP + GCA); Program Manager ICT at Vienna Science and Technology Fund, Schlickgasse, Vienna, Austria*
- *Prof. Jongwook Woo; Director, High-Performance Information Computing Center (HiPiC), Computer Information Systems Department, California State University, Los Angeles, California, USA*
- *Dr. Qiang Xu; Senior Lecturer, School of Science and Engineering, Teesside University, England, UK; UMIST (Institute of Science and Technology), The University of Manchester, England, UK; University of Huddersfield, UK*
- *Prof. Jane You (CGVR + MSV + Vice-Chair of IPCV); The Hong Kong Polytechnic University, Hong Kong*

As Sponsors-at-large, partners, and/or organizers each of the followings (separated by semicolons) provided help for at least one track of the World Congress: Aldebaran Robotics Inc., USA (http://www.aldebaran-robotics.com); Altera Corporation, USA (http://www.altera.com/); Computer Science Research, Education, and Applications Press (CSREA); Impulse Accelerated Technologies, Inc., USA (http://www.impulseaccelerated.com/); NVIDIA Corporation, USA (http://www.nvidia.com/object/about-nvidia.html); Parallella Community, Supercomputing for Everyone, USA (http://forums.parallella.org/); Pico Computing, Inc., USA (http://picocomputing.com/); SemiWiki.com, The Semiconductor Wiki Project, USA (http://www.semiwiki.com/); Solarflare Communications, Inc., USA (http://www.solarflare.com/); Stream Computing, Performance Engineers, The Netherlands (http://streamcomputing.eu/); Taylor & Francis, UK (http://www.taylorandfrancis.com/); US Chapter of World Academy of Science (http://www.world-academy-of-science.org/) ; and WEBestSOL & Webest Solutions Ltd, UK (http://webestsol.com/). In addition, a number of university faculty members and their staff (names appear on the cover of the set of proceedings), several publishers of computer science and computer engineering books and journals, chapters and/or task forces of computer science associations/organizations from 5 countries, and developers of high-performance machines and systems provided significant help in organizing the conference as well as providing some resources. We are grateful to them all.

We express our gratitude to keynote, invited, and individual conference/tracks and tutorial speakers - the list of speakers appears on the conference web site. We would also like to thank the followings: UCMSS (Universal Conference Management Systems & Support, California, USA) for managing all aspects of the conference; Dr. Tim Field of APC for managing the printing of the proceedings; and the staff of the New Tropicana Hotel in Las Vegas for the professional service they provided. Last but not least, we would like to thank the Co-Editors and Associate Co-Editors of SERP'13: Prof. Hamid R. Arabnia, Prof. Leonidas Deligiannidis, Prof. George Jandieri, Dr. Vince Schmidt, Ashu M. G. Solo, and Prof. Fernando G. Tinetti.

We present the proceedings of SERP'13.

Steering Committee, 2013
http://www.world-academy-of-science.org/

Contents

SESSION: NOVEL APPLICATIONS, METHODOLOGIES AND CASE STUDIES + INTELLECTUAL PROPERTY ISSUES + EDUCATION

Principles for Profiling Healthcare Data Communication Standards 3
Robert Snelick, Frank Oemig

A Model Driven Serious Games Development Approach for Game-based Learning 10
Stephen Tang, Martin Hanneghan

Rocket Aiming Project: A Service Learning Study 17
Johnny Carroll, Chao Zhao, Feridoon Moinian, Mike Estep

Concurrent Collaborative Captioning 23
Mike Wald

Dynamic Adaptation of Business Process Models: Application to the Healtcare Process in the AP-HM 29
Renaud Angles, Philippe Ramadour, Corinne Cauvet, Sophie Rodier

Research Trends and Open Issues in Mobile Application Software Engineering 38
Mark Rowan, Josh Dehlinger

Strategies to Improve Development in Brazilian Financial Institution Integrating Distinct Environments 45
Claudio Goncalves Bernardo, Paulo Roberto Chineara Batuta

Advocation Over Investigation: Comments on Robert Glass' Fact #55 51
James Neilan

Senior Citizens in Interaction with Mobile Phones: A Flexible Middleware Approach to Support the Diversity 56
Vinicius Goncalves, Vania Neris, Jo Ueyama, Sibelius Seraphini, Teresa Dias, Geraldo Filho

Semantic Obfuscation and Software Intention 63
Sheryl Duggins, Frank Tsui, Orlando Karam, Zoltan Kubanyi

Simulation Software Generation using a Domain-Specific Language for Partial Differential Field Equations 69
Ken A. Hawick, Daniel P. Playne

A Component-Based Architecture for Ginga 76
Marcio Ferreira Moreno, Luiz Fernando Gomes Soares, Renato Cerqueira

Managing User Accounts Across Heterogeneous Information Systems In The University 83
Askar Boranbayev, Mikhail Mazhitov, Rinat Yamalutdinov

Teams using Real World Projects in a Software Engineering Course 88
Nasser Tadayon

An Investigation into Mobile Based Approach for Healthcare Activites Occupational Therapy System 95
Sardasht Mahmood, Joan Lu

Teaching Software Engineering Through a Real-World Project: A New Approach 102
Chao Zhao, Mike Estep, Kenneth Smith

Why to Research in Knowledge Management in Software Engineering Processes? 108
Ernesto Galvis-Lista, Marcela Sanchez-Torres

SESSION: SOFTWARE SYSTEMS, REQUIREMENTS + MIDDLE-WARE + SOFTWARE DEVELOPMENT PROCESS + MODELING AND ARCHITECTURE DESCRIPTION LANGUAGES

Systems on Abstract Network 117
Kazutaka Nakamura, Kiyofumi Tanaka, Yasushi Hibino

XCD A Design-by-Contract Architecture Description Language 124
Mert Ozkaya, Christos Kloukinas

A Quantitative Approach to the Evolution of Domain-Specific Modeling Languages. 131
Kiyotaka Ota, Kenji Hisazumi, Weiqiang Kong, Tsuneo Nakanishi, Akira Fukuda

Using Productivity Measure and Function Points to Improve the Software Development Process 138
Eduardo Alves de Oliveira, Ricardo Choren Noya

Scaffolding the Software Design Process: Fine-Grained Specifications from Design Tactics 144
Abdel Ejnioui, Carlos Otero, Abrar Qureshi

SESSION: SOFTWARE ARCHITECTURE + DESIGN PATTERNS

Building Information Technology Based on a Human Behavior-Oriented Approach to Enterprise Architecture 153
Dominic M. Mezzanotte, Sr., Josh Dehlinger

Applying Design Patterns in Game Programming 160
Junfeng Qu, Yinglei Song, Yong Wei

New Paradigms for Software Application Development: Software Architectures and Component-based Development 166
Sergio David Villarreal, Guillermo Villasana, Juan Carlos Lavariega

SESSION: UNIFIED MODELING LANGUAGE / UML, OBJECT ORIENTED METHODS, AND CASE STUDIES

A QoS Driven Web Service Selection Methodology Using UML and UML Profiles 175
Rashmi Phalnikar, B. Devesh Jinwala

Generation of Efficient Embedded C Code from UML/MARTE Models 182
Luis Felipe Lennis, Jose Edinson Aedo

An Object-Oriented Framework for Digital Voting 189
Patricia Dousseau, Ricardo Pereira, Roberto Silvino

Towards Improving Object-Oriented Software Maintenance during Change Impact Analysis 196
Bassey Isong, Obeten Obi Ekabua

SESSION: USABILITY STUDIES + COST ESTIMATION AND MANAGEMENT + SOFTWARE TESTING, ANALYSIS, VALIDATION, AND VERIFICATION + RFORMANCE STUDIES

Evaluating the Effectiveness of a Collaborative Requirements Engineering Modeling Notation for Planning Globally Distributed Projects 205
Paula Laurent, Adam Steele, Jane Cleland-Huang, Patrick Maeder

Analysis and Application of Earned Value Managment in Software Development 212
Frank Tsui

On Acceptance Testing 218
Jean-Pierre Corriveau, Wei Shi

A Framework for Maturity Assessment in Software Testing for Small and Medium-Sized Enterprises 225
Adailton F. Araujo, Cassio L. Rodrigues, Auri R. M. Vincenzi, Celso G. Camilo, Almir F. Silva

Constructing Verifiably Correct Java Programs Using OCL and CleanJava 231
Yoonsik Cheon, Carmen Avila

An Open Source Platform for Collaborative Remote Usability Studies 238
Daniel Lyng Roder, Erik Frokjær

Study of Data Imputation on the Predictive Value of Software Attributes in the ISBSG-10 Data Set 243
Adrian Barb, Kailasam Satyamurthy

Finding The Relationship Between Software Testing Effort And Software Quality Metrics 249
Nurhan Yagci, Kursat Ayan

Examining the Performance of Java Static Analyzers 256
Kevin Daimi, Shadi Banitaan, Kathy Liszka

Verification and Validation Experience of Safety-grade Optical Modem for Core Protection Calculator (CPC) 263
Jang Yeol Kim, Kwang Seop Son, Young Jun Lee, Se Woo Cheon, Kyoung Ho Cha, Jang Soo Lee, Kee Choon Kwon

Findings of Expert Validation and Review of the Technology Enhanced Interaction Framework 268
Kewalin Angkananon, Mike Wald, Lester Gilbert

An Approach to Configuration-based Generation of Validation Rules for Shipdex 275
Youhee Choi, Jeong-Ho Park, Byungtae Jang

Experimental Evaluation of Static Source Code Analysis tools 281
Khalid Alemerien, Kenneth Magel

An Efficient Regression Testing Technique For Test Case Prioritization 288
Prem Jacob T, Ravi T

Security Requirements Engineering: Analysis and Prioritization 292
Daya Gupta, Shruti Jaiswal, Anupriya Tewari

Empirical Evaluation of Software Development Methodology Selection Consistency: A Case Study Using Analytical Hierarchy Process 299
Benson Moyo, Peeps Gonde, Ndabezinhle Soganile, Gilbert Dzawo, Kudakwashe Madzima

The Impact of Non-Functional Attributes on the Analysis Operations of Feature Models 306
Ines Achour, Lamia Labed, Henda Ben Ghazela

Determining Software System Type from Software Requirement Specification 312
Suneeta H. Angadi, S. Mohan, G. T. Raju

SESSION: SOFTWARE ENGINEERING AND MANAGEMENT + CODE REUSE + SOFTWARE MAINTENANCE METHODS + RELEASE PLANNING + SOFTWARE PRODUCTIVITY AND QUALITY

On-Demand Source Code Generation & Scheduling Optimised Parallel Applications on Heterogeneous Platforms 317
Ken A. Hawick, Daniel P. Playne

Lights on the Impact of Requirements Interdependencies on Priorities during Release Planning Decisions 324
Bassey Isong, Obeten Obi Ekabua, Ifeoma Ohaeri

Towards a Software Domain Metric based on Semantic Web Techniques 330
Francisco Castillo-Barrera, Hector Perez-Gonzalez, Masoud Sadjadi

A Template-Based Approach to Modeling Variability 336
Soheila Bashardoust Tajali, Jean-Pierre Corriveau, Wei Shi

Software Maintenance Risk Management Process - A Case Study 343
Vinicius Miana, Calebe Bianchini, Selma Melnikoff, Marcelo Martins

Test Case Prioritization Related to Code Quality 349
Savas Ozturk, Nurhan Yagci, Mehmet Aktas, Mehmet Ozbek, Furkan Paligu

An Eclipse Plug-In for Generating Database Access Documentation in Java Code 356
Paul Bergstein, Aditya Gade

A Decision Model for Monitoring Project Status with Earned Value Management Indicators. 362
Maria Teresa Baldassarre, Nicola Boffoli, Danilo Caivano, Giuseppe Visaggio

Software Engineering Practices for Minimizing Technical Debt 369
Vinay Krishna, Anirban Basu

SESSION: AGILE SOFTWARE METHODS

Agile Project-Based Teaching and Learning 377
Dagmar Monett

Study of Agility in Mobile Application Development 384
Vanessa Cooper, Hisham Haddad

A Model-Based Agile Process for DO-178C Certification 391
David Coe, Jeffrey Kulick

IEEE std 829-2008 and Agile Process Can They Work Together? 397
Ning Chen

Managing a Global Software Project under an Agile and Cloud Perspective 403
Giulio Concas, Katiuscia Mannaro, Luisanna Cocco

SESSION: SOFTWARE ENGINEERING AND EMBEDDED SYSTEMS

Video Processing for Motion Tracking of Safety Critical Systems 413
Travis Cleveland, David Coe, Jeffrey Kulick

Strengthening Interrupt Controls in Embedded Systems by Cooperation between Windows CE and REMON 419
Shigeki Nankaku, Hisao Koizumi, Akira Fukuda

Independent Verification and Validation of Software for Weapon Management System of a High Performance Aircraft 426
Sudha Srinivasan, Rekha R, Karunakar Kundapur

SESSION: POSTERS AND SHORT PAPERS

An Effective Method to Test Sensor Applications 433
Hwan-Cheol Joeng, Jang-Wu Jo

Towards Cycle-Accurate Performance Predictions for Real-Time Embedded Systems 435
Konstantinos Triantafyllidis, Egor Bondarev, Peter H.N. de With

A Study on Traceabilty for Model-based Testing of Automotive Embedded System 437
Kabsu Han, Insick Son, Jeonghun Cho

SESSION: LATE BREAKING PAPER: SOFTWARE ENGINEERING + MAINTENANCE, LEGACY CODES, METRICS, COLLABORATIVE WORK, SOFTWARE PROCESS IMPROVEMENT AND MODELS, SOA, CASE STUDIES

Emerging and Innovative Techniques and Methodology in Software Engineering for Systems Maintenance and Development 441
Maureen Ann Raley

Novel Visual and Analytical Methods in Repurposing Legacy Scientific Code A Case Study 448
Christopher Oehmen, Darren Curtis, Aaron Phillips, Elena Peterson

Use of Closures to Engineer Software for a Family of Numerical Simulation Models 455
Ken A. Hawick, Elliot Clarkson

A Case Study in the Model-Driven Development of CorkBoard a WebApp for Collaborative Work **462**

Andrew Harnage, Doug Flagg, Amber Whittemore, Devon Simmonds

An Object Oriented Runtime Complexity Metric based on Iterative Decision Points **468**

Amr Desouky, Letha Etzkorn

The Influence of Human Aspects in Software Process Improvement: a Brazilian Public Company Study **473**

Regina Albuquerque, Andre Bibiano, Rosilene Fernandes, Daniel Araujo, Andreia Malucelli, Sheila Reinehr

Methodology for Ontology Development in Support to the MPS Model for Software **479**

Alessandro Viola Pizzoleto, Hilda Carvalho de Oliveira

A Method and a Tool for Evaluating the Quality of an SOA **486**

R. Belkhatir, M. Oussalah, A. Viguier

Training Users of Accounting Information Systems for their Satisfaction, Decision-making, and Competitiveness **491**

Jose-Melchor Medina, Yolanda Loera, Karen Gonzalez, Alberto Mora

Dynamic Registration Forms **496**

Troy Johnson, Joshua Edinborough, Matthew Binder, Andrew Bryant, Blayne Dennis, Roger Lee

Software Reuse: The State of Art **501**

Abdullah A. Al-Baity, Kanaan Faisal, Moataz Ahmed

Empirical Validate C&K Suite for Predict Fault-Proneness of Object-Oriented Classes Developed Using Fuzzy Logic **508**

Mohammad Amro, Moataz Ahmed, Kanaan Faisal

Template Generation in a Tiered Architecture - Practical C# class templates from DDL statements **513**

James duPuis, Daniel Riehl, Roger Lee

The Proposal of Smart Phone Camera Application Which Realize a Person's Super Deformation **520**

Hideaki Hashimoto, Takayuki Fujimoto

An Interface Generator For Customizable Fuzzy Expert System **524**

Tongjun Ruan, Robert Balch

Lessons Learned: Porting Java Applications to Android **530**

G. Hsieh, D. Paruchuri, C. Steward, E. Nwafor, D. Gadam

SESSION

NOVEL APPLICATIONS, METHODOLOGIES AND CASE STUDIES + INTELLECTUAL PROPERTY ISSUES + EDUCATION

Chair(s)

TBA

Principles for Profiling Healthcare Data Communication Standards

R. Snelick[1] **and F. Oemig**[2]
[1]National Institute of Standards and Technology (NIST), Gaithersburg, MD, USA
[2]Agfa Healthcare, Bonn, Germany

Abstract - *Healthcare organizations often have many proprietary heterogeneous information systems that must exchange data reliably. Seamlessly sharing information among systems is complex. The widely adopted HL7 version 2 messaging standard has helped the process of systems integration. However, using the HL7 standard alone does not ensure system interoperability. The HL7 standard offers a wide range of options. Trading partners, without prior agreement, are not likely to implement options that are compatible. As a result, interoperability is hindered and organizations are left to employ their own ad hoc solutions. Message profiles provide a solution to this problem. Message profiles define a standard template that provides a precise definition of the data exchanged between applications in a common format. Defining a set of message profiles for controlling message exchanges establishes a well-defined communications interface among organizations and facilitates interoperability. However in order to be effective, message profiles must be designed and applied correctly. Additionally, with efficient design, a family of message profiles can be developed which leverage existing message profile components. Such a strategy is employed in the development the United States EHR certification family of standards for laboratory ordering and results reporting. This paper presents a methodology and best practices for designing a set of related message profiles. Although the methodology is applied to the healthcare messaging standards it has broad applicability for the class of communication standards.*

Keywords: Conformance; Communication Standards; Interoperability; Message Profiles; Messaging Systems.

1 Introduction

A major challenge for the healthcare industry is achieving interoperability among proprietary applications provided by different vendors. For example, each hospital department may use one or more applications to share clinical and administrative information. Each application may support multiple communication interfaces that must be modified and maintained. This is a difficult way to achieve interoperability. Alternatively, interoperability can be achieved through the use of standardized interfaces; the definition of which can remove the cost of building a separate interface for each associated application. Developers can build applications that conform to the standardized interface definition, increasing the likelihood of interoperability and reducing cost. Maintenance cost is also reduced because the number of interfaces to maintain decreases.

The Health Level Seven (HL7) *Application Protocol for Electronic Data Exchange in Healthcare Environments* Version 2.x standard (hereafter HL7) is the de facto standard for moving clinical and administrative information between healthcare applications [1]. The standard is based on the concept of application-to-application message exchange. An HL7 *message* is an atomic unit of data transferred between systems [1]. Typical HL7 messages include admitting a patient to a hospital or requesting a laboratory order for a blood test. HL7 describes an *abstract message definition* for each real world event (*e.g.*, admitting a patient). The abstract message definition is comprised of a collection of segments in a defined sequence. Rules for building an abstract message definition are specified in the HL7 message framework, which is hierarchical in nature and consists of building blocks generically called *elements*. These elements are *segment groups*, *segments*, *fields*, *components*, and *sub-components*. Each element has associated attributes that further defines and constrains the element. These include optionality, cardinality, value set, length, and data type attributes. Segment groups and segments can contain additional elements, fields and components can contain additional elements or be primitive elements; sub-components are strictly primitive elements. Primitive elements are those that can hold a data value and have no descendant structure.

When originally developed, HL7 was designed to accommodate the many diverse business processes that exist in the healthcare industry. This universal design was necessary to gain broad industry support. However, such broad accommodations resulted in a standard with many optional elements, thus aligning interface implementations presented difficulties.

Applications using HL7 are generally connected in two ways, point-to-point or via middleware, typically communication server products. Point-to-point entails connecting each pair of applications independently of other applications. In the communication server approach, all applications are connected to a centrally located message broker. A set of HL7 message definitions specifies the requirements between the communicating applications. Although the message definitions are specific there are many ways to specify a given HL7 transaction. In practice, vendor-provider specifications may not quite match, therefore differences need to be accounted for in each connection. In point-to-point architectures, each new combination will require a separate implementation. With communication servers, a new mapping transformation definition needs to be defined. In both cases, the breadth of the specification leads to cumbersome and *ad hoc* interface implementations. System implementations are prone to error, difficult to maintain, and do not scale easily.

To help alleviate this shortcoming, the HL7 standard introduced the concept of *conformance message profiles* (also commonly referred to as conformance profiles, message profiles, or profiles—hereafter message profile or profile). Message profiles by defining processing rules and which optional elements in the standard a message might include provide an unambiguous description of HL7 messages.

2 HL7 Message Profile Defined

Message profiles[1] constrain HL7 message structure and requirements for a particular interaction. A message profile provides a mechanism for specifying a single message definition. An implementation guide is often created to organize a collection of message profiles for specifying a set of related HL7 V2.x interactions described by a use case or use cases. Implementation guides typically describe broader conformance requirements such as a use case model, a dynamic definition, a static definition, and application functional requirements. IHE integration profiles can be characterized as implementation guides [7].

The use case model provides a description, defines actor responsibilities, and describes a sequence of actions performed by the sending and receiving applications. The dynamic definition describes the interaction between the sender and the receiver in terms of the expected acknowledgments (or other transactions such as query/response). The static model provides a precise definition of the message structure and constraints for a single message; this is the message profile. Functional requirements describe the application (or actor) level requirements. Such requirements may include how a set of messages are to be used to enact certain application functionality. The message profile definition, use, and organization within an implementaiton guide are key issues addressed in this paper.

A message profile can be represented as an XML document, Figure 1 shows an example XML profile snippet. Each element in the message profile is listed along with its associated attributes. For a more detailed description of a message profile refer to the HL7 standard [1]. It is important to note that the attributes and the constraints a profile places on a message provide a clear and unambiguous definition, thereby, facilitating the design, implementation, and testing of interfaces [3,4,5].

Fig. 1. Snippet from a Message Profile

```
...
&lt;Segment Name="PID" LongName="Patient Identification"
      Usage="R" Min="1" Max="1"/>
   <Reference>3.4.2</Reference>
 <Field Name="Set ID - PID" Usage="R" Min="1" Max="1"
      Datatype="SI" MaxLength="4" MinLength="1">
 </Field>
...
 <Field Name="SSN Number - Patient" Usage="X" Min="0"
    Max="0" Datatype="ST" MaxLength="16" MinLength="1" />
 <Field Name="Driver's License Number - Patient" Usage="R"
      Min="0" Max="0" Datatype="DLN" MaxLength="66"
      MinLength="1">
   <Component Name="License Number" Usage="R"
      Datatype="ST" MaxLength="20" MinLength="1" />
   <Component Name="Issuing State, Province, Country"
      Usage="R" Datatype="IS" Table="0333" MaxLength="20"
      MinLength="1" />
   <Component Name="Expiration Date" Usage="O"
      Datatype="DT" MaxLength="24" MinLength="1" />
 </Field>
...
```

The rules for constructing a message are described by the message framework [1]. In addition, for each real world event, for example "Admitting a Patient", a specific abstract message structure (ADT_A01) is defined. The message structure defines a template or structure in which the message must comply; it explicitly defines the elements and the order the elements must appear in a message instance. For example, in Figure 1, the "PID" segment contains the field "Set ID – PID", and so on. The usage attribute refers to the circumstances in which an element appears in a message [1]. For example, the "Driver's License Number" component in the profile snippet is required (Usage="R") and must be present in a valid message instance. Cardinality refers to the minimum and maximum number of occurrences an element may have [1]. An example of an element cardinality is [0..1]; the element may not appear in the message instance, but can only have one occurrence if it does. A table of allowable values can be defined and associated with a certain element. For example, see the

[1] Message profiles are not to be confused with the Integrating the Healthcare Enterprises (IHE) integration profiles. Often IHE integration profiles will use HL7 message profiles.

"Issuing State, province, country" component in Figure 1; this element must be populated with a data value that is defined in Table 0333. The length attributes define the minimum and maximum allowable lengths a value can have for a particular element. The data type defines the allowable data values an element can contain. For primitive data types, such as string (ST), interpretation is straightforward and requirements for each data type are specified in the standard [1]. Complex data types, such as the Extended Person Name (XPN), may be composed of primitive types or other complex data types. For example, an XPN contains a family name (FN), which itself is a complex data type that is composed of five primitive elements, all of type string (ST). All complex data types are ultimately composed of primitive data types.

A message profile is distinguished from a specification by application of the conformance rules, the openness permitted by the base standard is ultimately removed to such an extent that the interface specified by the profile may be directly implemented (Figure 2). The HL7 standard allows for numerous ways to define an interface; profiles reduce the number of possibilities to a manageable set, and their use helps to ensure that systems attempting to communicate with each other implement compatible sets of possibilities. It is important to recognize that profiles do not eliminate possibilities allowed by the standard; they select a specific group from the total set of those allowed. In this regard, a profile defines a constraint on the standard, such that the resultant constrained specification may be used to implement the interface. The profile also imposes a discipline upon the interface partners. This ensures harmony in the actual implementation which is necessary to fulfill a certain use case.

A key development for promoting interoperability was the codification of a means to express message profiles in a standardized way. While natural language documentation of a message profile acceptably facilitates interoperability at the message implementation level, the standardization of the message profile documentation itself adds a new dimension to the promotion of interoperability. The standardized conformance profile is an XML document specified in terms of a normative schema. This standardized form aids in many aspects in documentation, implementation, and testing. The NIST EHR certification conformance test tools use the XML message profile as the basis for validation [5].

2.1 Message Profile Hierarchy

HL7 V2 message profiles have three levels of specification:

- HL7 Standard Profile Level
- Constrainable Profile Level
- Implementation Profile Level

The HL7 Standard Profile (hereafter standard profile) represents the base standard definitions and constraints for a specific message structure (e.g., ORU_R01 for laboratory results reporting). At this level, the overall structure including the data type definitions are fully defined, however many element attributes are not. The standard profile can be more precisely defined by adding constraints to the elements attributes.

Fig. 2. Message Profile Hierarchy

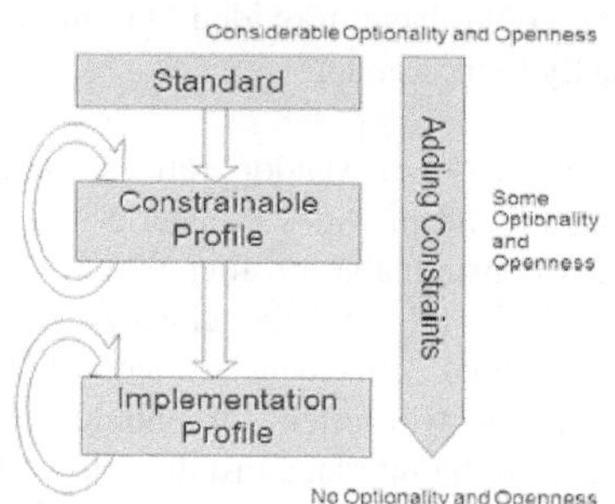

Other message profile levels are derived from the standard profile. A Constrainable Profile (hereafter constrainable profile) is derived from either the standard profile or another constrainable profile and further constrains the message definition attributes. For example, an element with a usage of "*optional*" may be changed to "*required*", however, the data type structure for that element cannot be changed. In a constrainable profile, analogous to the standard profile, not all element attributes are fully constrained. An Implementation Profile (hereafter implementation profile) defines all elements such that all *optionality* and *openness* is removed. All deployed interfaces are implementation profiles whether they are documented (explicitly) or not (implicitly). It is highly recommended that interfaces are completely documented to the implementation profile level using the profiling mechanisms described in this paper and the HL7 V2.x Conformance Chapter [1]. An implementation profile may also be derived from another implementation profile. In this case all openness has been removed. However, further constraints on attributes can be applied; for example, the usage of "*required, but may be empty*" can be strengthened to "*required*".

As described, constraints can be added iteratively, thereby forming a hierarchy of messages profiles. As such, a certain set of rules must be followed. A message profile is prohibited to further refining certain requirements defined in the *parent* message profile. For example, if an element (e.g. field) is "*required*" in the parent profile it can't be profiled to "*optional*" in the *child* profile as the requirement is relaxed (The allowable derivations are described in HL7 V2.x Conformance

Chapter [1]). Figure 2 illustrates the concept of profile hierarchy and acceptable derivations.

Two possible real world scenarios for using the profile hierarchy model are presented in Figure 3. In the first case a national level constrainable profile is developed. A hospital (chain) adopts and refines the national level guidance provided in the realm specific constrainable profile. The hospital procures a vendor that has a product that can be configured to satisfy the requirements. The hospital and the vendor finalize the requirements and the software is installed. The resultant interface is documented as an implementation profile. Alternatively, the hospital could have provided the implementation profile directly to the vendor.

In the second case, a vendor refines national level guidance profile and provides a generic implementation based on this constrainable profile. When working with clients in which this profile closely satisfies their requirements a final refinement is made at the specific sites. The vendor will often (or should) provide the documentation of the interface installed in the form of an implementation profile. These examples can be nested and refined to any depth as appropriate (See Figure 2).

Fig. 3. Use of Profile Examples

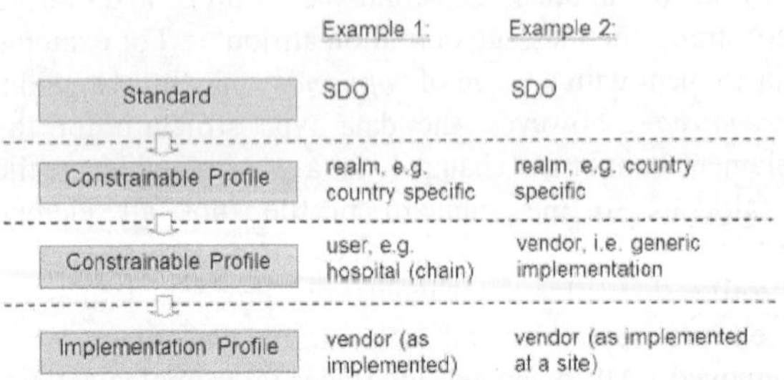

The concept and use of constrainable profiles is important in practice as this level is often (and should be) what standard organizations (e.g., IHE or the HL7 affiliates [9]) specify. Constrainable profiles can be thought of as a set of harmonized requirements and are useful at a national or any intermediate level down to the local site implementation. Employing implementation profiles at a high-level such as nationally often precludes widespread adoption because of their restrictiveness. Therefore, this practice is not recommended and should be avoided.

Use of the message profile hierarchy is the strategy employed in the United States by the Office of the National Coordinator (ONC) Meaningful Use (MU) electronic health records (EHR) certification program. The named standards in the certification criteria specify "*national level*" requirements—although they are not explicitly named as such. For the HL7 V2 messaging standards these requirements are published in implementation guides and realized as constrainable message profiles—meaning that a selected set of elements are fully specified while others are yet to be determined. This approach guarantees that certified EHR technologies (CEHRT) have a certain level of common capabilities while providing flexibility for local customization. However, these implementation guides are independent, so no harmonization among the profiles is guaranteed. For example, specification of patient demographics does not necessarily coincide in the transmission to immunization registry and laboratory results reporting implementation guides.

Local installations are likely to complete trading-partner agreements. That is, they will further refine the national level requirements to satisfy their local requirements within the framework established by the constrainable profile. It is important that the local trading-partner agreements do not relax or conflict with the national level requirements. The certification of the EHR products seeks to ensure a minimum level of capabilities that will not necessarily meet all local requirements (and often will not). Once local trading-partner agreements are put in place, the EHR technology and partner systems will need to be implemented and configured accordingly. For example, a provider and their state immunization registry will coordinate exchange requirements. The referenced Meaningful Use interoperability standard (i.e., the constrainable profile) provides the basis, but additional requirements may be necessary for this jurisdiction (specified in an implementation profile derived from the constrainable profile). In this case, the system receiving the HL7 V2 messages (i.e., the immunization registry) must be able to consume and understand the state-level information according to CEHRT to achieve the desired interoperability. To ensure accuracy and integrity for this exchange of information, local site testing must be performed. At present, this aspect of testing is not part of the Meaningful Use program; however, using CEHRT provides a shorter pathway to achieving site-specific interoperability.

2.2 Message Profile Component Defined

A message profile component (hereafter profile component) defines a part or a certain aspect of a profile and is used to differentiate requirements from another profile or profile component. A profile component can be applied to any construct or section of a profile. A profile component in a family of profiles can be used to identify different levels of requirements for the same use case or to identify the differences in requirements for different, but closely related, use cases.

In the first case, a specification may want to express different levels of conformance. For example, a profile may be written to require the use of Object Identifiers

(OIDs) for all identifiers. Another profile may be written in which this is a not requirement. An intermediate profile may be written which requires certain identifiers to support the use of OIDs but not all. This specification is describing three levels of conformance. These three levels can be described using a base profile definition and three profile components. The profile components describe the differences in the requirements. A similar scheme as described here is employed in the HL7 V2 2.5.1 Laboratory Results Interface (LRI) implementation guide's laboratory results message profiles (ORU_R01 message structure) [6].

In the second case, a profile component is employed to express requirements for a different, but closely related, use case. Here the profile component is used to leverage the requirements of an existing profile since this profile contains many common requirements. The HL7 V2.5.1 Electronic Laboratory Reporting (ELR) to Public Health Revision 2 implementation guide uses the concept of a profile component in this manner [8].

In the first case, the use case is the same; however, the requirements in which it can be achieved are different. The profile component is expressing a different level of conformance. In the second case, the use case is similar but different, therefore the requirements are different. The profile component concept is used to leverage the common requirements defined by the profile and to express the differences in requirements by defining them in a profile component.

Profile components can express missing requirements for a base profile component, common requirements, additional requirements, or replace requirements in a profile or profile component.

The description of the different conformance levels, profiles, and profile components are expressed in the conformance clause section of a specification. Subsequently an implementer makes a conformance claim as to which level of conformance they support.

3 Profile Design and Management

This section presents an approach for designing and managing profiles such that profiles and profile components can be leveraged. When writing a set of related profiles (or a family of profiles such as those in IHE or for a particular domain such as laboratory orders and results) it is important to reuse the profile and profile components, to harmonize the requirements and to gain efficiency.

Figure 4 illustrates a sample of possible configurations for composing a family of related profiles. The design principle is to develop a common or base profile component that applies across a family of profiles with the intent of using the profile component concept to specify profiles.

In the first depiction, a base profile component is developed that expresses all of the common requirements for a related set of profiles. Profile component 1 and profile component 2 are also created for aspects that are not defined in the base profile component. Combined the three profile components are used to describe a complete specification, Profile 1. For the second depiction, the base profile component and profile component 1 are reused and combined with profile component 3 to specify Profile 2. In the third depiction, Profile 1 is combined with profile components 4 and 5 to create Profile 3.

Fig. 4. Profiling Design Principles

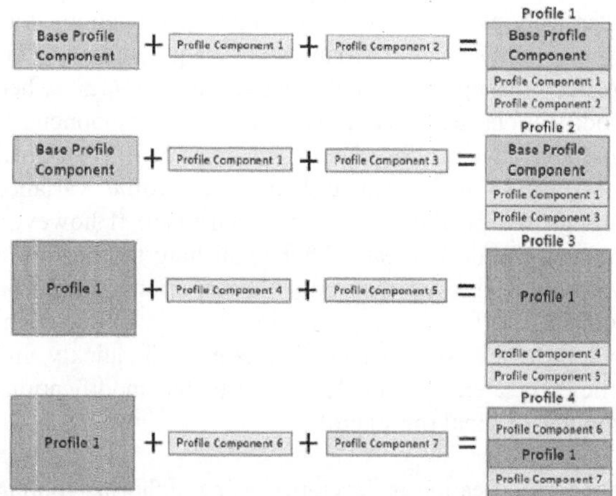

Profile components can also express requirements that replace requirements established in a base profile component or profile. This may often be the case when different levels of profiles are developed or the profile provides utility outside the original set of related profiles. The fourth depiction illustrates such a case where a subset of requirements for an existing profile is overridden. Here Profile 1 is used. However, certain aspects are redefined according to the rules and documented in profile components 6 and 7 which results in Profile 4. For each of the complete specifications illustrated in Figure 4 the resulting profile can be a constrainable or an implementable profile.

The key design principles for developing a family of related specifications is to leveraged existing profiles or design/create base profiles that are a harmonization of requirements for a related set of use cases. The profile components can be developed at any level of granularity. However, caution should be exercised when creating profile components at the fine grain level. Often creating and managing too many building block artifacts will start to outweigh the benefits. If tooling is available then fine granularity of profile components is attainable. A good practice is to introduce an orthogonal structure of the individual requirements, e.g., data type constraints in one regard and value set definitions in another. This allows for easy integration, combinations, and management.

Unfortunately, often in practice, a related set of profiles are each fully specified that duplicate sizeable sections of the document. These profiles are not harmonized and unnecessarily lead to maintenance issues. It is also important not to confound requirements targeted for different use cases (interactions) within a single profile definition. This also occurs in practice and should be avoided. For each interaction, a separate message profile needs to be defined. The use of profile components as described facilitates this approach.

3.1 Publishing the Specification

An important design principle for publishing the specifications is not to copy entire specifications that express only small variances in requirements. This creates management and maintenance issues when modifications are made in the base profile component. If possible, the profile should be part of the original specification and distinguished as a profile variance through the profile component mechanism. If however, the new profile is created after publishing the profile in which it is derived then only the variations should be published in the new specification. Often this document will be a few short pages. This approach quickly and efficiently alerts the implementers to the modifications from the original (base) profile.

If the specification is developed using authoring tooling then the user is afforded various options for publishing since the tool handles the rendering and maintenance. The National Institute of Standards and Technology (NIST) is developing a tool to enable manipulation of profiles for HL7 V2. This tool builds upon the concepts developed in the Messaging Workbench (MWB) [2,3]. The NIST tool is being designed to allow for the development of profile components. Since all artifacts related to the profile are machine process-able within the tool, the user will have the option to publish a specification that expresses the variance of a profile, the complete profile, or other artifacts such as the XML representation of the profile.

4 Information Mapping

This section describes an approach for system developers for mapping information in their systems to HL7 interface data requirements. This technique provides a flexible and universal methodology to a systematically account for variations in interface requirements of trading partners. Figure 5 illustrates a proposed information mapping approach to support multiple interfaces with varying requirements, which are expressed in a related set of message profiles.

The basic principle is that specifications are not to be influenced by implementation design or by trying to accommodate different use cases (interactions) within a single profile definition. This approach is not recommended because requirements are confounded when they should not be. A profile needs to be written in a manner to express the requirement for a single interaction and nothing more. The profile design principle section describes how one can accommodate similar uses cases (which require different interactions). If this strategy is employed, there can be a gain in efficiency by accommodating the various use cases and without having to rewrite or create entirely new specifications. This approach allows for more choices in implementation design and support. If multiple use cases are comingled into a single specification, then those who choose not to support certain components are forced to deal with the unwanted components. The profile design mechanism proposed in section 3 also provides a clean and flexible avenue for implementers, as they are not tied to implementation choices dictated in the specification.

Fig. 5. Information Mapping to Support Multiple Interfaces

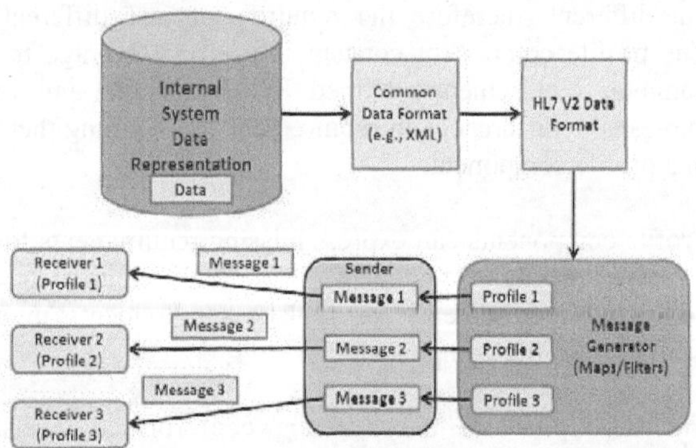

Figure 5 proposes a possible approach that a system might implement to support various profiles to interact with a multitude of systems with similar but different requirements. Internally the system maintains a database containing the information necessary for the application. It is necessary that this application communicate with a number of different trading partners. The trading partner interfaces have slightly different requirements. Various profiles are created that express the requirements for each of the interfaces. The methodology described in section 3 is used to create the profiles. When communicating, the sending system extracts data from the database and transforms it into a common representation (e.g., an XML specification). For each interface, the data is used to populate the message using the message profile as a map (i.e., template).

In the example depicted in Figure 5 there are three HL7 V2 interfaces that have to be supported. Depending on the interface, the application creates a message based on the given requirements expressed in the profile. The profile is represented in XML and acts as a filter of the complete data known to the system. Depending on the trading partner, a different "filter" (profile) is utilized. For each interface, a specific message is created with the necessary requirements. There is no need to disambiguate requirements for different trading partners or interface requirements.

This is a simplification of the process and does not account for all the complications (especially the mapping of the data). However, it does illustrate a simple and straightforward approach to interfacing with multiple trading partners where the requirements are clearly defined in isolation although built upon a common foundation. That is, the requirements of an interface are separated from the implementation and operational aspects of the system. This design is scalable since many more trading partners could be added that have different interface requirements and the only additional artifact needed is a profile. Of course, the above illustration describes an interaction with nearly the same set of requirements, for example, reporting immunization records to an Immunization Information System (IIS). The vendor product will often need to support all or many of the state's IISs each with slightly different reporting requirements.

5 Summary

The ability to share relevant information among diverse healthcare systems and provide consistent data across applications will help improve the quality of care. It will also improve patient safety and reduce the cost of healthcare. HL7 defines the specification for interfaces that allow both centrally located and distributed information systems to communicate. The standard establishes rules for building interfaces and provides many optional features to accommodate the disparate needs of the healthcare industry. However, for interfaces to be reliably implemented, a precise and unambiguous specification must be defined. HL7 introduced the concept of message profiles that precisely declare the structure and constraints of a message. The use of message profiles promotes interoperability by providing trading partners a common format for documenting interface specifications.

There are three levels of profiles that form a hierarchy including the standard level, the constrainable level, and implementation level. A message profile component defines a part or a particular aspect of a profile and is used to differentiate requirements from another profile or profile component. A profile component can be applied to any construct or section of a profile. Combining the concepts of profile levels and profile components provide implementation guide authors with the tools to effectively create and manage a set of related profiles. A profile can be represented in a standardized XML form that enables automatic processing of many facets including publishing and message validation. System developers can take advantage of message profiles to simplify implementations that support many similar or disparate interface requirements.

To ensure interoperability among healthcare systems, installations must be implemented correctly—conformance testing is essential [3,4,5]. Using and specifying well defined message profiles facilitates and promotes more rigorous testing. Employing an implementation and testing strategy based on message profiles and the tools to support them will improve interoperability among healthcare systems. This ultimately leads to more reliable systems and reduced costs.

6 References

[1] Health Level 7 (HL7) Standard Version 2.7, ANSI/HL7, January, 2011, http://www.hl7.org.

[2] Messaging Workbench (MWB). Developed by Peter Rontey. http://www.hl7.org.

[3] *Towards Interoperable Healthcare Information Systems: The HL7 Conformance Profile Approach.* R. Snelick, P. Rontey, L. Gebase, L. Carnahan. Enterprise Interoperability II: New Challenges and Approaches. Springer-Verlag, *London Limited 2007 pp.* 659-670.

[4] *A Framework for testing Distributed Healthcare Applications.* R. Snelick, L. Gebase, G. O'Brien. 2009 Software Engineering Research and Practice (SERP09), WORLDCOMP'09 July 13-16, 2009, Las Vegas, NV.

[5] *NIST Laboratory Results Interface (LRI) EHR Tool.* http://hl7v2-lab-testing.nist.gov/mu-lab/

[6] *HL7 Version 2.5.1 Laboratory Results Interface (LRI) Implementation Guide.* Draft Standard for Trail Use. July 2012. http://www.hl7.org.

[7] *Integrating the Healthcare Enterprises (IHE) Technical Framework.* http://www.ihe.net

[8] *HL7 Version 2.5.1 Electronic Laboratory Reporting (ELR) to Public Health Implementation Guide, Release 2.* Work in Progress. http://www.hl7.org.

[9] *German Message Profile Architecture.* 2004-2007. http://www.hl7.de/download/documents/Profile_2.1.zip.

A Model Driven Serious Games Development Approach for Game-based Learning

Stephen Tang[1] and Martin Hanneghan[2]
School of Computing and Mathematical Sciences,
Liverpool John Moores University
Byrom Street, L3 3AF Liverpool, UNITED KINGDOM.
Email: {[1]o.t.tang, [2]m.b.hanneghan} @ljmu.ac.uk

Abstract - *Computer games, predominantly a form of interactive entertainment, are having some success being repurposed for educational use. However, this approach is hindered by the lack of availability of experience in serious games tools. Much research is already underway to address this challenge, with some who choose to use readily available commercial-off-the-shelf games and others attempted to develop serious games in-house or collaboratively with industry expertise. These approaches present issues including educational appropriateness of the serious game content and its activities, reliability of serious games developed and the (often high) financial cost involved. Developments in software engineering that enable automatic generation of software artefacts through modelling or Model Driven Engineering (MDE) promises new hope for game-based learning adopters, especially those with little or no technical knowledge, to produce their own serious games for use in game-based learning. In this article, we present our model-driven approach to aid non-technical domain experts in serious games production for use in games-based learning.*

Keywords: Model Driven Serious Games Development, Model Driven Engineering, Model Driven Development, Serious Games, Game-Based Learning.

1 Introduction

Game-based learning (GBL) refers to both the innovative learning approach derived from the use of computer games that possess educational value and other software applications that use games for learning and education purposes (e.g. learning support; teaching enhancement; assessment and evaluation of learners etc.) [1]. These computer games are also referred to as educational games or in a more popular term known as *serious games*. As computer gaming becomes a digital culture deeply rooted amongst the new generation of learners, many educational researchers and practitioners agree that it is now appropriate to exploit gaming technologies in order to create engaging interactive learning content to motivate learners to learn through game-playing using the GBL approach [2].

The preliminary results of GBL have shown some positive impact towards students' learning [3]. However, the adoption rate of GBL still remains low. One of the barriers to the adoption of GBL is the extremely steep learning curve required to create serious games. Most of the computer games available in the market are designed for entertainment purposes and the majority of content is not fit for educational purposes. This has led some domain experts to create serious games through bespoke in-house development, using open source or royalty-free game engines in collaboration with a team of developers and 'modding' (or *modifying*) commercial-off-the-shelf games by utilising a game editor application. Many of these tools and technology platforms for producing serious games are readily available but most of these tools require substantial technical knowledge in games development which hinders non-technical domain experts from adopting games-based learning. We believe by addressing the absence of high-level authoring environments and support for non-technical domain experts (i.e. teachers) to create custom serious games will be a major factor in the rise of serious games.

Advancements in software engineering are making the creation of high-level serious games authoring environments for non-technical domain experts viable. The MDE (Model Driven Engineering) approach uses abstract models to formally represent aspects of serious games software which is then automatically transformed into more refined software artefacts and subsequently into serious game software applications. This approach provides non-technical domain experts the tools to produce serious games easily and quickly (and possibly at a lower cost) through the use of Domain Specific Modelling Languages (DSML). This therefore lowers the barriers that hinder the production of these applications. MDE offers an increase in productivity, promotion of interoperability and portability among different technology platforms, support for generation of documentation, and easier software maintenance [4]. In addition, it can produce better code quality and improves reliability of the code [5]. From the non-technical domain experts' perspective, an MDE's ability to encapsulate the technical aspects of development via a DSML massively lowers the barriers that hinder the production of applications. We believe by marrying games development and the MDE approach, we can provide a technological solution to the aforementioned issues.

In this paper, we present our model-driven serious games development approach. In Section 2, we briefly introduce our model-driven serious games development framework and the underlying models designed to formally represent serious

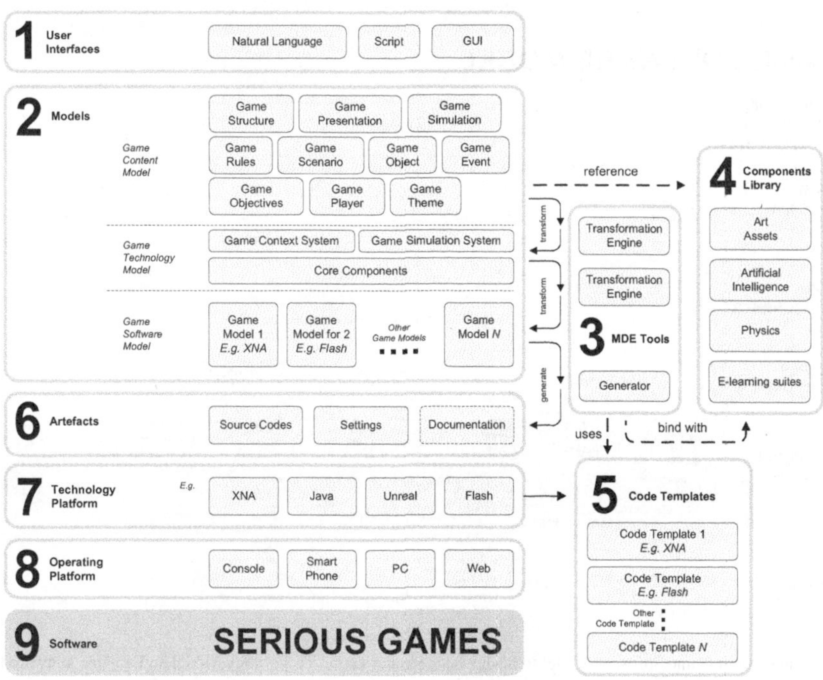

Figure 1: Model-driven Serious Games Development Framework.

games. We then explain our model-driven approach and describe our model driven technologies in Section 3. In Section 4, we present a case study to demonstrate the design and production of a serious game using our model-driven approach and follow with a discussion in Section 5. Finally, we draw conclusions on the future of this exciting field of research in Section 6.

2 Model Driven Serious Games Development Framework

Our novel model-driven serious game framework (see Figure 1) is designed to support the production of a variant of serious game software that covers a wide range of technology platforms as well as operating platforms. It consists of nine parts namely: (1) User Interface (UI), (2) Models, (3) MDE Tools, (4) Components Library, (5) Code Templates, (6) Artefacts, (7) Technology Platform, (8) Operating Platform and (9) Software. This configuration loosely couples the modules allowing the framework developer to flexibly substitute modules while maintaining the integrity of relationships among the modules via well-defined interfaces. It also clearly divides the views of entities while promoting structured and systematic workflow [6]. At the core of the framework are three models namely the Game Content Model, Game Technology Model and Game Software Model.

2.1 Game Content Model

Our novel Game Content Model improves on the existing work Game Ontology Project (GOP) [7], Rapid Analysis Method (RAM) [8] and Narrative, Entertainment, Simulation and Interaction (NESI) [9]. It combines our study on game design, game development and serious games with a selection of concepts from the aforementioned existing works to form a robust formal model. Our Game Content Model covers all the essential game design concepts for documenting serious game design in the role-playing and simulation genres initially (but this can be easily expanded upon to support other genres). The top level of our game content model consists of ten interrelated key concepts that best represent the rules, play and aesthetic information of a computer game. These are *Game Structure, Game Presentation, Game Simulation, Game Rules, Game Scenario, Game Event, Game Objective, Game Object, Game Player* and *Game Theme* [10].

In brief, the game structure provides the form and organises the game into segments of linked game presentations and game simulations. The interactions between a game object and the results of an interaction in a game simulation are defined using game rules. A game simulation can be used to host multiple game scenarios aligned with the storyline. Each game scenario is set up using a selection of game objects to create an environment, a sequence of game events and a set of game objectives that challenges the game player's skills and knowledge about the game domain. The game player can control game object(s) and interact with others via hardware controllers or a graphical user interface. And finally, the game theme describes the "look and feel" of the game. Detail on our Game Content Model is available in our previous work in [10].

2.2 Game Technology Model

Our Game Technology Model is based on a data-driven architecture and includes the essential game specific systems and core components of software which facilitates the operation of serious games. The Game Context System handles the transitions between contexts and works cooperatively with the Game Simulation System to simulate a scenario. For ease of processing, a scene graph is used to organise renderable and updatable objects such as media components, GUI components, front-end display components, game objects and lights. These objects are processed using

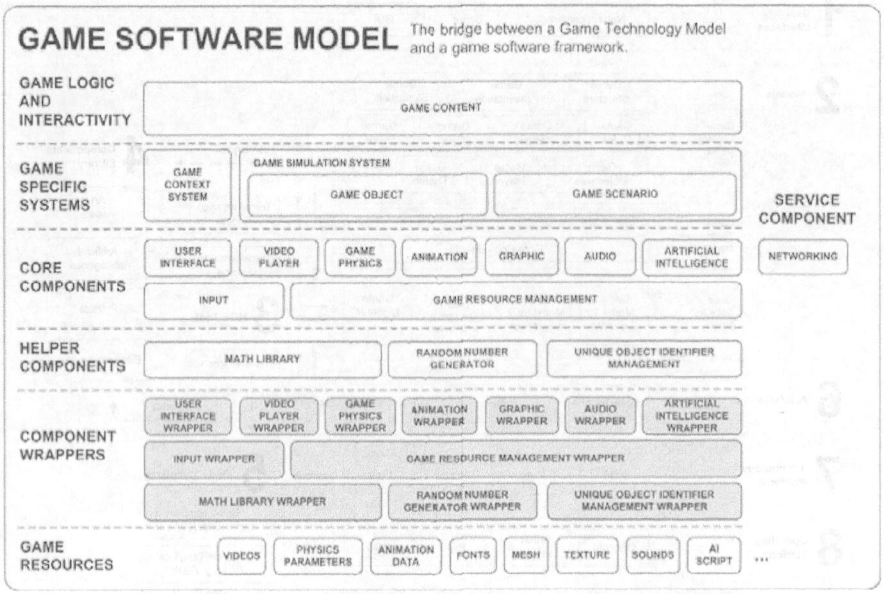

Figure 2: Overview of our Game Software Model to bridge between our Game Technology Model and a game software framework.

the platform independent core components such as renderer, animation, audio, input, game physics, user interfaces, video player, game resource manager, networking and artificial intelligence [11].

Supporting these core components are the helper components namely the math library, random number generator and unique object identifier management. The functionality of each component defined in the Game Technology Model are specified as interfaces that each wrap a different implementation of a game technology. This allows serious games software to be produced on different technology platforms through code generation which reads the Game Technology Model and translates it into software artefacts. More details on our Game Technology Model can be found in [11].

2.3 Game Software Model

Our Game Software Model is the platform specific software representation of the game software. The Game Software Model is designed by a technical person who possesses great understanding of the model driven framework and the technology platform. Developers of the Game Software Model may choose one of the two different perspectives; (1) to bridge the Game Technology Model to an existing game software framework (e.g. Microsoft's DirectX) or (2) to implement game software from scratch for an intended technology platform. Both these exercises may require platform specific details or components to be added which has been omitted in the Game Technology Model.

Implementing the Game Software Model for an existing game software platform will require framework developers to map the components presented in the Game Technology Model to the chosen game software framework. Often it is likely to achieve a one-to-one mapping of Game Technology Model components with game software framework components with possible inclusion of information that is required by the game software framework. Figure 2 illustrates the overview of Game Software Model with component wrappers (shaded in grey colour) which map components of Game Technology Model to the appropriate component in a game software framework.

Unlike the former approach described above, designing a Game Software Model for a specific software technology platform will require the addition of certain platform specific components which are used by the core components. These are identified by Gregory [12] as *window management*, *file system*, *timer*, *graphics wrapper* and *physics wrapper*. Most game software frameworks would have these platform specific components implemented in low level code that is coupled to a specific operating platform to ensure it delivers the performance required of the game software. In our approach, these platform specific components have been omitted from the Game Technology Model and are only added in the final stage of the model transformation to achieve true operating platform independence. Implementers of our Game Software Model will have to define these platform specific components so they can be mapped to the right implementation during the generation of program code. This makes the Game Software Model structure differ from the earlier version described above as the component wrapper is replaced with platform specific components (shaded grey in Figure 3).

3 Model Driven Serious Games Development Approach

Our model-driven serious game development approach, based on our framework presented in Section II, is made-up of a modelling environment, model translators and an artefacts generator. An overview of this is shown in Figure 4. In the following subsections, we briefly discuss the implementation of our model-driven approach.

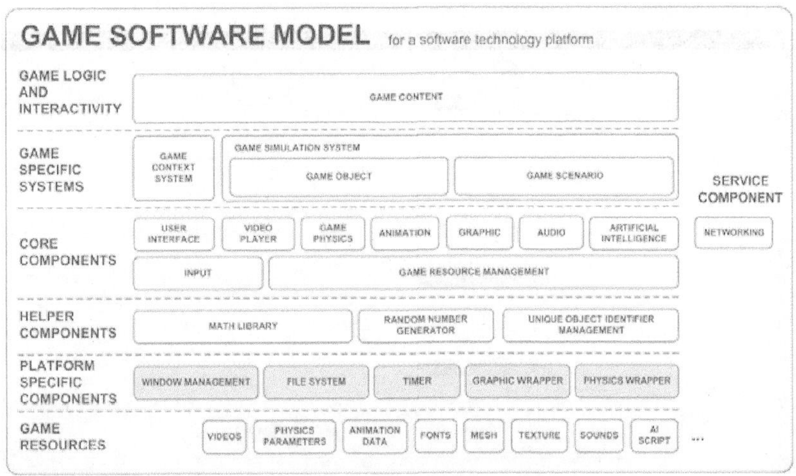

Figure 3: Overview of Game Software Model that includes platform specific components for a software technology platform.

3.1 Serious Games Modelling Environment (SeGMEnt)

Our modelling environment, referred to as Serious Games Modelling Environment (SeGMEnt), is designed to allow non-technical domain experts to model a serious game using both graphical notations and step-by-step guides. We have chosen to develop a web-based modelling environment due to the wide-access the web can offer to the game-based learning community. This approach can also lower the barrier of entry for adoption of game-based learning as practitioners don't necessarily require a high-performance multimedia computer to produce serious games. We have chosen the Adobe Flash platform as our initial development platform of the modelling environment as it has a rich range of facilities to support our requirements. Non-technical domain experts will use this modelling tool to author serious game content, collating the art assets and defining the necessary game mechanics that make up the serious game.

We have implemented five unique user interface (UI) components that can assist non-technical domain experts when modelling the aspects serious games design in the SeGMEnt modelling environment. These UI components are:

- *Flow visualisation* – this provides visual tools to represents the flow of states within the serious game using a state diagram notation that has been extended to include additional information;
- *Dynamic option interface* – this is a list of options generated from data fetched from within SeGMEnt to simplify the data entry process and to prevent error in data entry;
- *What-you-see-is-what-you-get (WYSIWYG) visualisation* – this aids users to visually position media, graphical user interface (GUI), front-end display (FED) and game objects strategically on a 2D space through drag-and-drop interaction and edit properties of media, GUI, FED and game objects via a simple data entry interface;
- *Statement construction interface* – this guides users in constructing an acting statement, which is an English-like sentence that defines a game act, by selecting the verb, noun or conjunction from the options presented in dynamic option interface; and
- *Guided data entry interface* – this provides a step-by-step guide for users to document aspects of serious games systematically via common GUI components to avoid overloading requests for information from users.

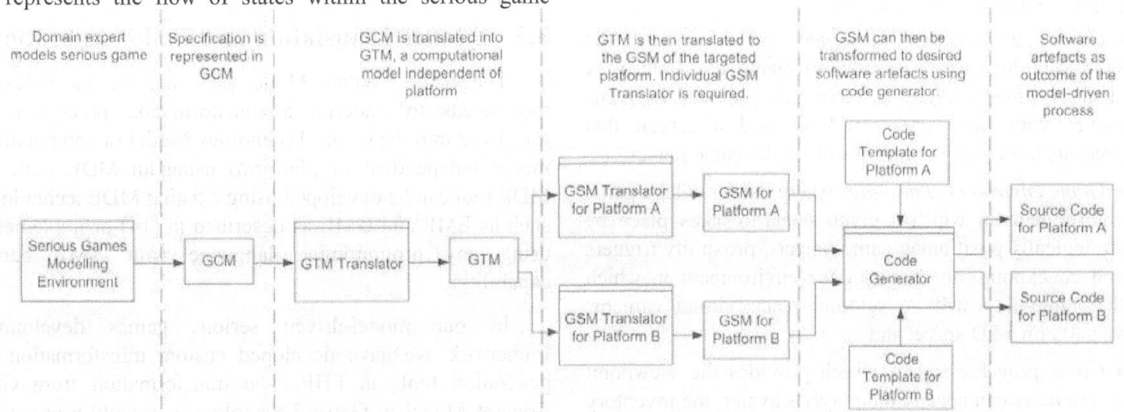

Figure 4: Model-driven pipeline for the prototype

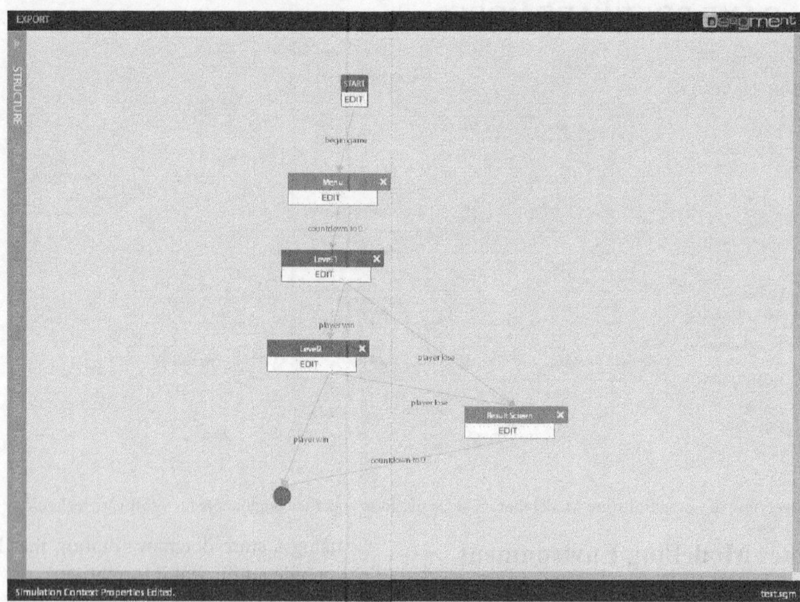

Figure 5: Modelling Game Structure in Game Structure Designer.

Our SeGMEnt tool consist of seven different viewpoints designed to separate ten aspects of serious games design described in our Game Content Model into smaller and more manageable clusters of data. Each of the viewpoints uses a combination of UI components described earlier to aid users in visualising aspects of serious game design. These design viewpoints are:

- *Game structure designer* which allows users to model the flow and the structure of a serious game (see Figure 5);
- *Game scenario designer* where users specify the flow of events in a scenario through the definition of game scenario, game events and game objectives;
- *Game object designer* which provides the interface to define a game object's identity, specify the associated attributes, assign an appearance, define actions and define associated intelligence; *Game simulation designer* which provides the facilities for users to specify game simulation concepts by adding and positioning FEDs on the virtual canvas and defining the game tempo and physics via a data entry interface;
- *Game presentation designer* which offers the viewpoint for users to model off-game user interfaces such as a menu screen, a screen that presents the game player with the game objectives and a screen that presents the victory or loss results to the game player;
- *Game environment designer* where users model a game environment in which a given scenario takes place by strategically positioning game objects, proximity triggers and checkpoints to construct the environment in which the game-play will be set and place virtual cameras visually on a 2D space; and
- *Game player designer* which provides the viewpoint where users can specify the player's avatar, the inventory size which limits the storage of virtual items, the game attributes associated, the data to be tracked and the mapping of game controls to a game object's action.

Our SeGMEnt tool only serves as an interface aid for domain experts to document the design of a serious game that is compliant with our Game Content Model. Underlying the UI is the data which needs to be saved, processed and exported into eXtensible Markup Language (XML) format which are then transformed into more refined models using our MDE tools.

3.2 Model representation

In our model driven approach we have chosen to use XML as the format for representing our models. This offers great flexibility for defining the data format for representing models. In addition, XML can easily accept additional information from the automated transformation process between the models for MDE. Furthermore it is also well supported by MDE technologies such as Eclipse Modelling Framework (EMF) and Generic Modelling Environment (GME) [13] making it the ideal choice for representing our data-model.

3.3 Model Translation and Code Generation

The Game Content Model generated by our SeGMEnt tool needs to undergo a transformation process to be translated into the Game Technology Model (a computational model independent of platform) using an MDE tool. The MDE tool can be developed using existing MDE technologies such as EMF and GME as described in [14] or implemented using any programming language with XML parsing capability.

In our model-driven serious games development framework, we have developed custom transformation and generation tools in PHP. The transformation from Game Content Model to Game Technology is mainly a process of refining data and reformatting it into a computation independent model by reorganisation of data into programmatic structures. This also involves the addition of programmatic statement calls to the relevant Game Technology Model component's function to process the relevant data. The transformation from Game Technology Model to Game Software Model further refines the data by adding in platform specific data.

Our implementation follows a simple approach by traversing through the entire source model to locate the required token of information (XML element) and a new target model is composed by structurally reformatting data in the source model and adding in the additional information. This approach does not constrain us to the structure of the source model. A similar approach is used to transform the Game Technology Model to the Game Software Model by appending additional tokens of information that mark the interfaces of the components to be included to enable code pairing during the software artefact generation process.

Our basic code generation tool is also implemented using an approach similar to that described for the transformation tool. Each of the marked tokens are located and then translated into code for a specific platform. Each token of information either maps to a single line of code or a segment of codes defined in some code template. The final code is built up based on the structure of Game Software Model and generated as a textual artefact.

4 Producing Serious Games for Games-based Learning using A Model-Driven Approach

The production of serious games for game-based learning is centred on design for learning where rules and game-play are design to support the defined learning objectives. In our previous work [15], we proposed an educational game design methodology consisting of thirteen activities that are grouped into three phases:

- *Planning Phase:* (1) Define learning objectives and design goals, (2) understand learners, (3) identify learning activities for learning objectives defined in activity 1, (4) Sequence learning activities in increasing complexity order, (5) design the story to set the scene and link learning activities defined in activity 3;
- *Protoyping Phase:* (6) design game mechanics for learning activities defined in activity 3, (7) Design game components and associated behaviours, (8) Design scenarios and game-play for learning activities defined in activity 3 using activity 4 and activity 5, (9) prototype game level, (10) evaluate prototype against learning objectives, (11) refine the game level;
- *Finalising Phase:* (12) finalise educational game and (13) quality assurance test on educational game.

The model-driven approach follows the same process where non-technical experts conduct the design activities 1 to 7 on paper. Once the details of the serious game have been decided, domain experts can then model the serious game in our SeGMEnt tool. Modelling in SeGMEnt follows a bottom-up approach in which it requires a modeller to model basic elements with a view to creating more complex composite elements from these basic elements later on. There are seven successive stages to follow when modelling a serious game in SeGMEnt (see Figure 6). The first stage involves modelling of game objects and this is done using the game object designer. Once all game objects have been defined the game environment can be set up using the game environment designer. This is followed by modelling of the game scenarios and definition of game rules and game objectives using the game scenario designer. The next stage involves the modelling of various game presentation contexts using the game presentation designer. Then the domain expert can model the game simulation parameters via the game simulation designer. The order of stage 4 and stage 5 can swapped as there is no precedence dependency. Once the game presentation context, game simulation context and game scenarios have been modelled, domain experts can now focus on modelling the game flow. The final stage of modelling of the serious game involves the definition of the game player via the game player designer.

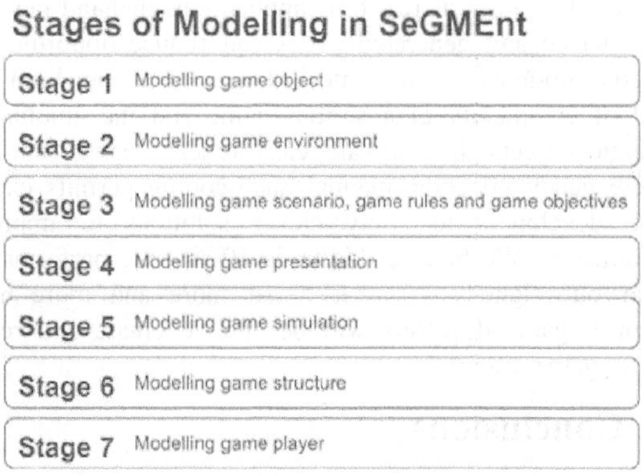

Stages of Modelling in SeGMEnt

Stage 1	Modelling game object
Stage 2	Modelling game environment
Stage 3	Modelling game scenario, game rules and game objectives
Stage 4	Modelling game presentation
Stage 5	Modelling game simulation
Stage 6	Modelling game structure
Stage 7	Modelling game player

Figure 6: Stages of serious game modelling in SeGMEnt.

The transformation of models and generation of code in our model driven approach is automatic and can be initiated through the "Export" command in the SeGMEnt tool. This will first generate an XML file compliant with the Game Content Model by passing the data from SeGMEnt to Game Content Model Creator. After the file has been created, the Game Content Model Creator will pass the control to Game Technology Model Translator which will read the Game Content Model and transform it into a programmable format which is also in XML file format. Once the Game Content Model has been transformed to Game Technology Model, the control is then passed to the Game Software Model translator which will read the Game Technology Model and add in platform specific information to the Game Technology Model to form the Game Software Model. Once the transformation is complete, the control is then passed to the code generator which generates code in the form of text output presented on a web interface. At present, our code generator supports the generation of ActionScript 2.0 code for execution on the Adobe Flash platform.

5 Discussion

This model-driven approach changes how serious games are developed traditionally. Instead of developing software based on a set of given design requirements, our model-driven approach demands software developers to produce assets and tools which non-technical domain expert can use to produce serious games without worrying the technical aspects of games development. The complexity of serious games development is now hidden behind the SeGMEnt tool and driven by the models and MDE tools that interprets and refine the models for generation of software artefacts.

Using the model-driven approach in serious games development does not imply that every aspect of serious games production is automated. Domain experts are expected to understand serious game design and required to adhere to the methodical approach of serious game modelling in SeGMEnt to ensure that the Game Content Model produced by experts using our SeGMEnt tool is valid. We acknowledge that serious games design is still a creative process and it demands specialised skill despite the tools being a guide and aid for non-technical domain experts. Therefore we cannot expect our model-driven approach to instantly transform a novice tutor to a serious game designer capable of designing interesting and creative problems for game players.

Serious games as real-time applications demand lag-free performance and generated codes can reduce opportunities for code optimisation in some instances. This can limit the level of complexity of a serious game and the amount of dynamic objects the software can process during runtime. Unlike generated code, manual hand-coding permits expert game developers to apply clever solutions to improve performance. We believe this trade-off in code performance is far outweighed by the fact that more and more non-technical game designers will be able to create and reuse serious game resources.

6 Conclusions

Game-based learning is a highly desirable learning approach for the "PlayStation-driven" generation of learners. However, it lacks technological solutions that can help non-technical domain experts to author custom interactive learning content to support this innovative learning approach. Our model-driven framework supports the development of serious games through the use of our MDE tools. The model-driven approach helps non-technical domain experts to produce serious games quickly, easily and affordably (in the long term). Our vision is for our model-driven serious game development framework and our model driven approach to serve as a basis for more implementation of high-level serious game authoring tools designed specifically for non-technical domain experts who wish to produce serious games. We look forward to a future where serious game artefacts are published freely and openly by non-technical practitioners around the world to build upon and improve opportunities for learning.

7 References

[1] S. Tang, M. Hanneghan, and A. E. Rhalibi, "Introduction to Games-Based Learning," in *Games-Based Learning Advancements for Multi-Sensory Human Computer Interfaces: Techniques and Effective Practices*, T. M. Connolly, M. H. Stansfield, and L. Boyle, Eds., ed Hershey: Idea-Group Publishing, 2009, pp. 1-17.

[2] FAS. (2006). *Harnessing the power of video games for learning, Summit on Educational Games 2006*. Available: http://fas.org/gamesummit/Resources/Summit%20on%20Educational%20Games.pdf

[3] H. Jenkins, E. Klopfer, K. Squire, and P. Tan. (2003, October 2003) Entering The Education Arcade. *Computers in Entertainment (CIE)* [Applications]. 17-17.

[4] A. G. Kleppe, J. B. Warmer, and W. Bast, *MDA Explained: The Model Driven Architecture : Practice and Promise*: Addison-Wesley, 2003.

[5] S. Kelly and J.-P. Tolvanen, *Domain-Specific Modeling: Enabling Full Code Generation*. Hoboken, New Jersey: Wiley-IEEE Computer Society Press, 2008.

[6] S. Tang and M. Hanneghan, "A Model-Driven Framework to Support Development of Serious Games for Game-based Learning," presented at the 3rd International Conference on Developments in e-Systems Engineering (DESE2010), London, UK, 2010.

[7] J. P. Zagal, M. Mateas, C. Fernández-Vara, B. Hochhalter, and N. Lichti, "Towards an Ontological Language for Game Analysis," in *DiGRA 2005 - the Digital Games Research Association's 2nd International Conference, Selected Papers*, Simon Fraser University, Burnaby, BC, Canada, 2005, pp. 3-14.

[8] A. Järvinen, "Introducing Applied Ludology: Hands-on Methods for Game Studies," presented at the Digra 2007 Situated Play: International Conference of the Digital Games Research Association, Tokyo, Japan, 2007.

[9] V. Sarinho and A. Apolinário, "A Feature Model Proposal for Computer Games Design," presented at the VII Brazilian Symposium on Computer Games and Digital Entertainment, Belo Horizonte, 2008.

[10] S. Tang and M. Hanneghan, "Game Content Model: An Ontology for Documenting Serious Game Design," in *Proceedings of 4th International Conference on Developments in e-Systems Engineering (DESE2011)*, Dubai, UAE, 2011, pp. 431-436.

[11] S. Tang, M. Hanneghan, and C. Carter, "A Platform Independent Model for Model Driven Serious Games Development," in *6th European Conference on Games Based Learning (ECGBL 2012)*, Cork, Ireland, 2012, pp. 495-504.

[12] J. Gregory, *Game Engine Architecture*. Natick, Massachusetts: A K Peters, Ltd., 2009.

[13] A. Ledeczi, M. Maroti, A. Bakay, G. Karsa, J. Garrett, C. Thomason, G. Nordstrom, J. Sprinkle, and P. Volgyesi, "The Generic Modeling Environment," in *Workshop on Intelligent Signal Processing*, Budapest, Hungary, 2001.

[14] S. Tang and M. Hanneghan, "State-of-the-Art Model Driven Game Development: A Survey of Technological Solutions for Game-Based Learning," *Journal of Interactive Learning Research,* vol. 22, pp. 551-605, 2011.

[15] S. Tang and M. Hanneghan, "Designing Educational Games: A Pedagogical Approach," in *Design and Implementation of Educational Games: Theoretical and Practical Perspectives*, P. Zemliansky and D. Wilcox, Eds., ed Hershey, PA: IGI Global, 2010, pp. 108-125.

Rocket Aiming Project: A Service Learning Study

J. Carroll, C. Zhao, F. Moinian, and M. Estep
Computing & Technology Department, Cameron University, Lawton, OK, USA

Abstract – *The Rocket Aiming Project was introduced to the Computer Science program at Cameron University in the fall semester, 2011. The mission of this project was to develop an unclassified rocket aiming algorithm for the Guided Multiple Launch Rocket System (GMLRS) Program. This project provided the Computer Science students a unique opportunity to apply what they gained from classroom teaching in solving a real-world problem. There is discussion on how students were instructed to complete the project following government software development procedures. The authors concluded that a service learning approach not only enriched the learning environment and enhanced the students' problem-solving abilities, but also established a healthy relationship between Cameron University and the Fires Center of Excellence at Fort Sill.*

Keywords: Service Learning, Rocket Aiming, Problem Solving

1 Introduction

It is a crucial task in a Computer Science program to enhance students' problem solving ability. Traditional classroom teaching may be insufficient due to a lack of connection to the real world [1]. Service learning may increase current student satisfaction [2, 3]. The Rocket Aiming Project was introduced to the Computer Science Program at Cameron University in the fall semester, 2011. The purpose of the project was to develop an unclassified rocket aiming algorithm for the Guided Multiple Launch Rocket System (GMLRS) program to optimize aim point distribution when attacking area targets. The algorithm supports circular and rectangular targets distributing aim points to maximize area coverage while weighing the center of the target at a higher priority. The Rocket Aiming project provided the authors' CS students with a unique opportunity to apply what they gained from classroom teaching in solving a real-world problem. The CS4003 Rocket Aiming seminar was created to complete this project. In this article, the software development process, algorithm development and implementation, and testing management is discussed. The rocket aiming project created an enticing learning environment where students were motivated to use their knowledge to solve a real problem. The students also had an opportunity to learn the software development process from U.S. government computer scientists. This project not only enriched the students' learning environment and enhanced their creative problem-solving ability [4], but also established a healthy relationship between Cameron University and the Fires Center of Excellence at Fort Sill [5]. As a result, the completion of this project benefited both student learning and U.S. armed forces.

2 Methods and Procedures

2.1 Forming Teams and Signing Team Contracts

Ten students were enrolled in the rocket aiming class. They were divided into two even teams. Each team consisted of a captain, a lead programmer, a lead algorithm developer, testing designer, and systems analyst. Team members first signed a team contract to clearly define each member's responsibilities and then worked together to make a project management plan that included: milestones of the project, Gantt chart, algorithm development strategies, work log, and leaders for each task (Figure 1). The two teams worked on the same project in competition against each other, vying to produce the winning project chosen by the client.

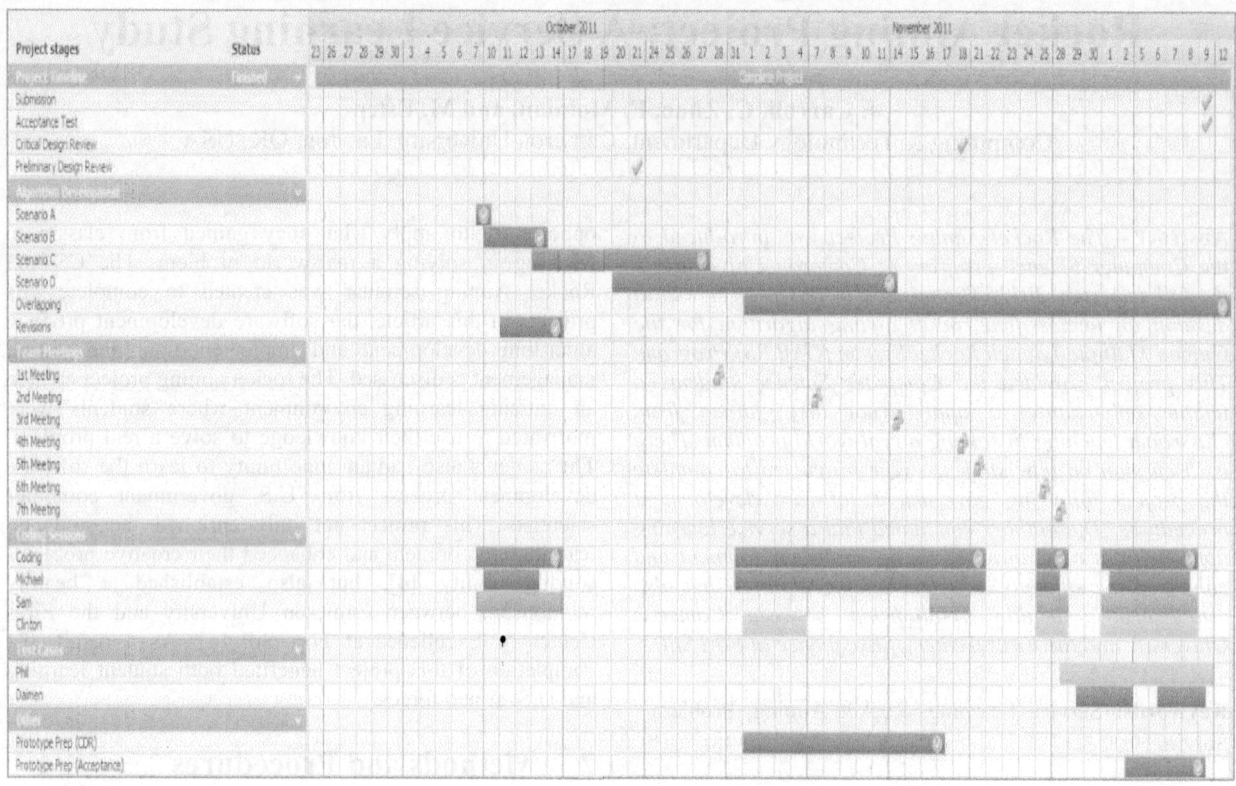

Figure 1. Project Management (Gantt Chart)

2.2 Determining System Requirements

The student teams met with the computer scientists, mathematicians, and government agents to conduct a Primary System Review. During this meeting, the students asked questions that were prepared before the meeting to determine the system requirements [6]. The resulting requirements are shown in Figure 2.

Requirements

- Develop an aiming algorithm that supports both Circular and Rectangular target geometries
- Develop an aiming algorithm that minimizes the deviation from a given point regardless of the number of aim points
- Develop an aiming algorithm that minimizes the unaffected area within a target area regardless of the number of aim points
- Develop an aiming algorithm that does not affect areas outside the boundaries of a designated target area unless the X value is larger than the target dimensions given
- Provide to the government at no cost an aiming algorithm in C or C++ format
- Provide to the government software documentation of the developed code consisting of definitions, etc.

Requirements (cont.)

- Provide to the government a test plan and testing procedures for the developed software
- Provide to the government the internal testing results leading up to the acceptance test
- Provide to the government a text file detailing off-set (from target center) aim point locations, minimum requirement. Desired: a GUI depicting impact locations
- Provide an aiming algorithm capable of computing impact locations (off-sets) for up to 12 aim points
- Provide an aiming algorithm capable of returning from 1 to 12 aim points from as many as 12 aim points
- Software shall employ a numbering convention (1-12) from left to right, top to bottom
- Software shall return the specific aim point number with associated aim point (offsets)

Figure 2. System Requirements

2.3 Conducting System Analysis and Design

Based on the information obtained in the interview, each team completed their system analysis and created a system information flow chart [6]. An example chart is shown in Figure 3.

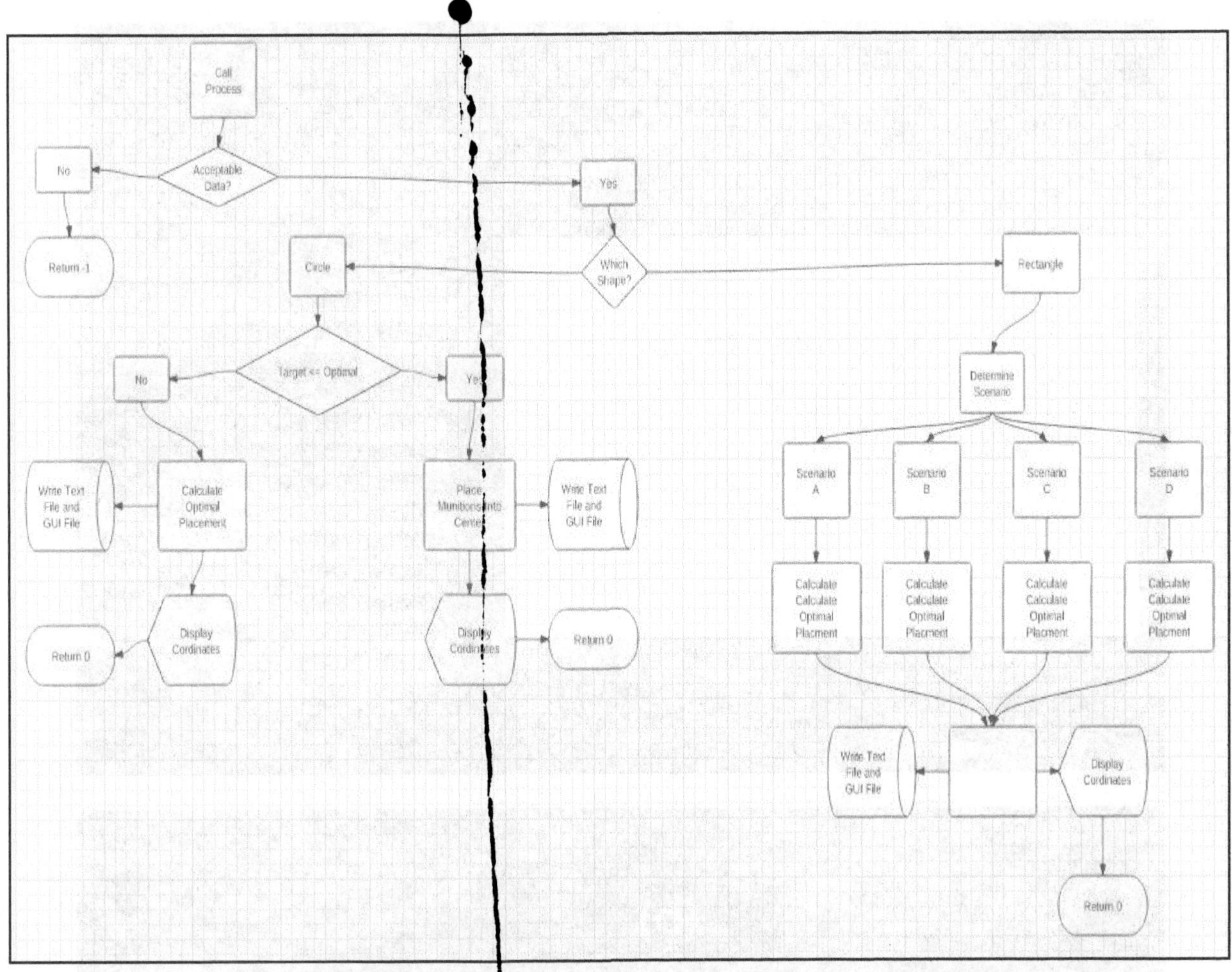

Figure 3. Rocket Aiming System Information Flow Chart

2.4 Algorithm Development and Implementation

Based on the approved system design, the teams started their algorithm development to solve the problem [6]. After finishing algorithm development, the teams presented their algorithms to the clients in a Critical System Review meeting. In their presentations, they had to prove that their algorithm was correct mathematically and show some basic functionality of the system using prototypes. After the Critical System Review, the algorithm was coded in C, and then the output of the program execution was imported in a GUI display program to show the graphic result. Two implementation samples are shown in Figure 4.

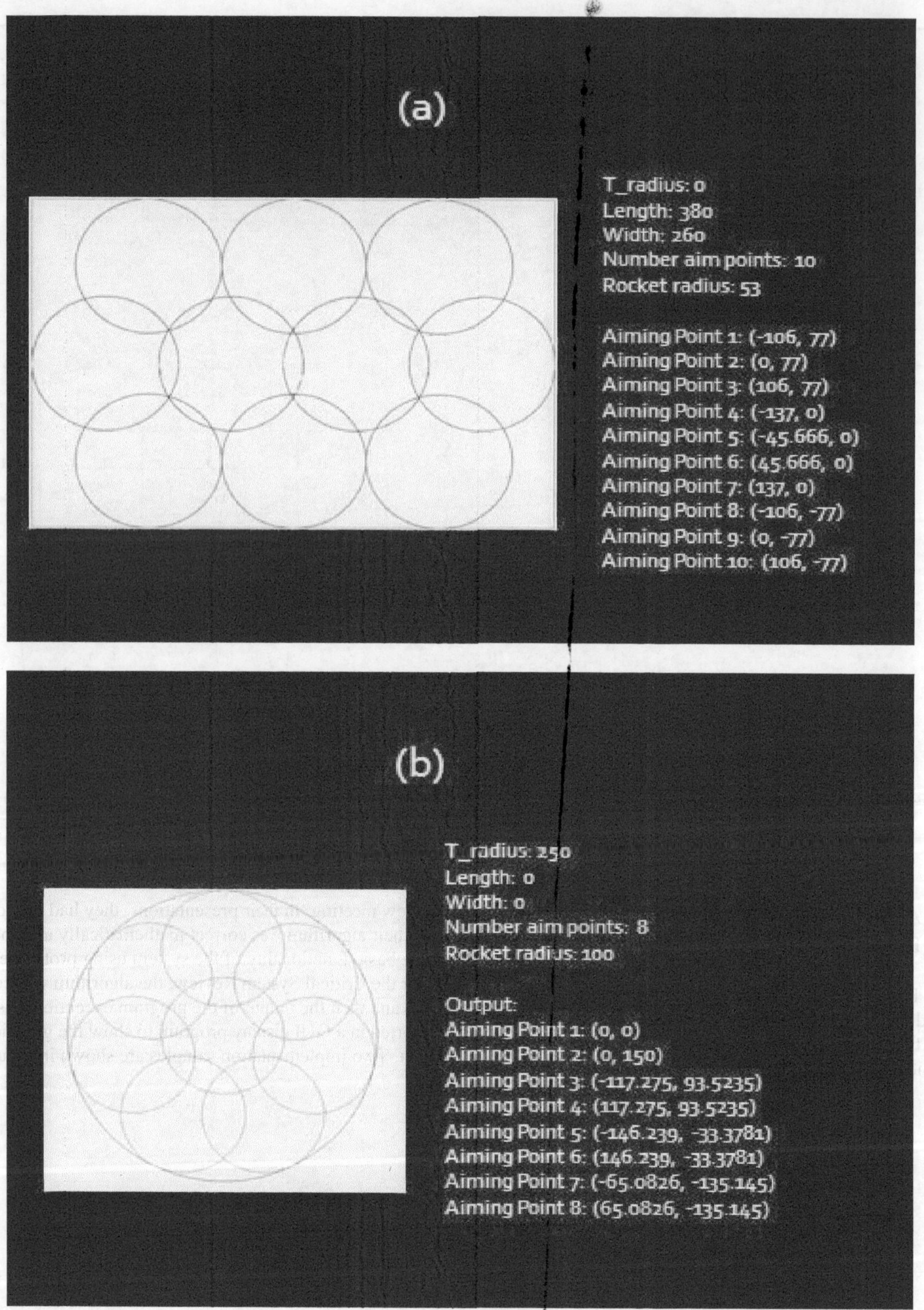

Figure 4. Implementation Results: (a) Rectangular Target, (b) Circular Target

2.5 Testing

Each team was required to make a testing plan that included, but was not limited to, testing strategies, testing data set, and testing methods [6]. A team testing plan is shown in Figure 5. The test data was generated by a random number generator, and millions of cases were tested. The results of testing met the satisfaction of the clients.

Testing Plan

The purpose of testing these algorithms is to ensure each of them, when properly used, is capable of producing accurate aim points for any combination of length/width or radius. Also, testing ensures that any invalid data entries are taken care of properly to ensure there are no errors from the start and only valid output is given. Testing was split into three main parts to provide more accurate results overall.

1. The first mode of testing was in-bounds testing. The in-bounds testing was done by starting at 0 for the width and length or radius and incrementing them one at a time for each test run all the way to 9999. When these numbers are entered into the program, the program runs and gives results; those results are the (x,y) coordinates of all the rockets. When the results are analyzed they are checked to see if the rocket radius lies outside the bounds of the target. If so, then the dimension(s), number of rockets, and the X value are documented so that a tester could go back and replicate the error and find out what went wrong.
2. The second mode of testing was the out-of-bounds testing. This testing was done to validate that the program would deny any unwanted or invalid data. This was achieved by starting at -9999 for the width, length, and/or radius as well as X and incrementing them one at a time for each individual test case all the way to 0. The results would come out to be all the test cases and if they failed or not. If a test run failed, that means that it was correct because every time a test case is run the input was incorrect which should return invalid results. If a test run completed then that means the invalid data entered was accepted; they were documented then reviewed and corrected.
3. The final mode of testing was done manually. A tester would hard code numbers into the variables, compile and run, then check the GUI to visually verify that the results gave valid aim points that are within the bounds of the target and properly spaced within the target. All numbers entered into the program manually were randomly thought of by the tester to try to push the limits of the program for errors. If errors occurred they were documented then submitted for review and correction.

Figure 5. Sample of a Testing Plan

2.6 Acceptance Test & Results

The final project was presented to Fort Sill Fires Center of Excellence personnel, including the Commanding General David Halverson and Lockheed Martin [5], at Cameron University. Both student teams passed the acceptance test and Fort Sill is in the process of integrating the rocket aiming algorithms into their systems. Client comments included the following...

- "It was apparent that both teams have dedicated a lot of time into software development and briefing products. You should be extremely proud of their efforts. A project like this would have cost the government an extreme amount of money and would not be any better."
- "From my perspective, both groups were excellent. It was evident that a great deal of work was put into both the briefings as well as into the products themselves. In fact, all of the government people present were impressed by the amount, quality, and creativity of the work. As you know, the ultimate goal of the CDR phase is to get a "green light" to complete the work package. In the cases of both groups, that approval was given."

3 Discussion & Findings

A real-world project provides a unique opportunity for students to apply what they gain from classroom teaching in solving a real-world problem. During this problem solving process, the students are motivated significantly and are willing to work harder than when taking a regular lecture-based class. First, on-site job training provides students with valuable lessons in personal responsibility, citizenship, team work, and product quality, which can be helpful to improve the quality of these future computing professionals. Second, student learning outcomes are enhanced, especially the ability to "learn by doing." Third, this approach builds a bridge between higher education and community that benefits both parties. Finally, the instructors teaching practices are enhanced as a byproduct of working with students on a real-world project.

4 References

[1] ***Teaching Software Development vs. Software Engineering***, Gary Pollice, Worcester Polytechnic Institute, http://www.ibm.com/developworks/rational/library/dec05/pollice/index.html

[2] ***Making Service Learning Accessible to Computer Scientists***, Brian J. Rosmaita, http://academics.hamilton.edu/computer_science/brosmait/talks

[3] **The Cameron University Green Website Project-Part 1: Service Learning in the Fall 2009,** Mike Estep, David Kenneth Smith, Chao Zhao, and Tom Russell, International Journal of Education Research, Volume 5 No. 2, Summer 2010

[4] ***Blooms Taxonomy***, Vanderbilt University, http://cft.vanderbilt.edu/teaching-guides/pedagogical/blooms-taxonomy/

[5] ***Cameron University Announces Winners of "University Choice Awards,"*** Cameron University, http://www.cameron.edu/media-releases2012/University-Choice-Awards

[6] ***Object-Oriented and Classical Software Engineering***, 8th Edition, Stephen R. Schach, McGraw Hill, 2011.

Concurrent Collaborative Captioning

M. Wald
ECS, University of Southampton, UK

Abstract - *Captioned text transcriptions of the spoken word can benefit hearing impaired people, non native speakers, anyone if no audio is available (e.g. watching TV at an airport) and also anyone who needs to review recordings of what has been said (e.g. at lectures, presentations, meetings etc.) In this paper, a tool is described that facilitates concurrent collaborative captioning by correction of speech recognition errors to provide a sustainable method of making videos accessible to people who find it difficult to understand speech through hearing alone. The tool stores all the edits of all the users and uses a matching algorithm to compare users' edits to check if they are in agreement.*

Keywords: Accessibility, Speech recognition, Captioning, Collaborative editing

1. Introduction

As more videos are becoming available on the web these require captioning/(subtitling) if they are to benefit hearing impaired people, non-native speakers, anyone if no audio is available (e.g. watching TV at an airport) and also anyone who needs to search, review recordings of what has been said (e.g. at lectures, presentations, meetings etc.) or translate the recording.

The provision of synchronized text captions with video also enables all their different communication qualities and strengths to be available as appropriate for different contexts, content, tasks, learning styles, learning preferences and learning differences. For example, text can reduce the memory demands of spoken language; speech can better express subtle emotions; while images can communicate moods, relationships and complex information holistically.

Professional manual captioning is time consuming and therefore expensive[i] (e.g.180$/hour). Automatic captioning is possible using speech recognition technologies but this results in many recognition errors requiring manual correction [1]. With training of the software and experience some speakers can sometimes achieve less than 10% word error rates with current speech recognition technologies for conversational speech using good quality microphones in a good acoustic environment. With conversational speech however the accuracy can drop as the speaker speeds up and begins to run the ends of words into the beginnings of the next word. Speakers also use fillers (e.g. ums and ahhs) and sometimes hesitate in the middle of a word. People do not speak punctuation marks aloud when conversing normally but speech recognition technologies designed for dictation use dictated punctuation to indicate the end of one phrase or sentence and the beginning of another to assist the statistical recognition processing of which words are likely to follow other words. However, often it is not possible to train the speaker or the software and in these situations, depending on the speaker and acoustic environment, word error rates can increase to over 30% [2] even using the best speaker independent systems and therefore extensive manual corrections may be required. If close to 100% accuracy is required then a human editor will be required and even if the Word Error Rate is very low, unless a human editor checks it nobody can be certain of the accuracy.

In this paper, further details of the development of a tool is described that facilitates collaborative correction of speech recognition captioning errors to provide a sustainable method of making audio or video recordings accessible to people who find it difficult to understand speech through hearing alone [3]. If there is no correct version of the transcript in existence there is no simple way of knowing whether the person creating or correcting the captions is making errors or not. The new approach described in this paper therefore is to allow many people to edit the captions at the same time and automatically compare their edits to verify they are correct. The term 'Social Machines'[ii] has been used to describe such large scale collaborative problem solving by humans and computers using the web.

Section 2 reviews other approaches, section 3 describes Synote and its captioning method, section 4 describes the new collaborative caption creation tool while section 5 summarises the conclusions and future planned work.

2. Review of other approaches

There are many web based captioning tools some which only allow captioning of videos they host (e.g. YouTube[iii], overstream[iv], dotsub[v]) while others allow manual captioning of web based videos hosted elsewhere (e.g. Amara[vi], originally a Mozilla Drumbeat project called

Universal Subtitles; CaptionTube[vii]; Subtitle Horse[viii]; Easy YouTube Caption Creator[ix]).

There are also many examples of desktop captioning/ subtitling software (e.g. magpie[x], MovieCaptioner[xi], Subtitle Workshop[xii] etc.) but these cannot normally be used with web hosted video and would involve transferring files between captioners if more than one person was involved in captioning.

None of the captioning systems are designed to allow more than one person at a time to create the captions or edit the captions.

Transcription is not only used for hearing impaired and non native speakers. Speech recognition scientists need transcribed speech to build and improve their acoustic speech models but the accuracy of the transcriptions is less important as Novotney and Chris Callison-Burch [4] showed that the accuracy of speech recognition models could be improved more cheaply using more lower accuracy transcriptions by Amazon Mechanical Turk to transcribe speech for 3% of the cost of more accurate professional transcription. Lee & Glass [5] used workers on the Amazon Mechanical Turk[xiii] with two stages of transcription each using ASR to filter out poor quality. The first stage presented each worker with five, five to six second clips created automatically by silence detection. A 15% word error rate (WER) was achieved by proving feedback using an automatic quality detector measuring both the range of words used (e.g. to detect lots of 'ums') and how closely it matched the n best words and phoneme sequences (e.g. to detect random corrections) rejecting poor quality transcripts with a WER greater than 65%. The second stage joined together clips to make 75 seconds of audio synchronised with the first stage transcripts to provide more audio context. Feedback on performance quality (with 80% being the acceptance threshold) was given by comparing the number of corrections made with the number of corrections needed estimated by using ASR word confidence scores. Their trained support vector machine classifier was able to judge 96.6% of the submitted transcripts correctly, reducing poor quality transcripts by over 85% and WERs to 10%.

3. Synote

Synote[xiv] [6] is a cross browser web based application that can use speaker independent speech recognition[xv] for automatic captioning of recordings. Synote also allows synchronization of user's notes and slide images with recordings and has won national[xvi] and international awards[xvii] for its enhancement of education and over the past four years has been used in many countries[xviii]. Figure 1 shows the Synote interface with the video in the upper left panel, the synchronized transcript in the bottom left panel with the currently spoken words highlighted in yellow and the individually editable 'utterances' in the right panel. While Synote provides an editor to correct speech recognition errors in the synchronised transcript in the bottom left panel, the whole transcript rather than individual corrections are saved to the Synote server which can take a substantial time (many seconds). If two people edit the same transcript then the most recently saved version will overwrite the previously saved version. It is therefore only possible to use collaborative editing in this way by only permitting one person to edit at a time. While this approach can be used for professional editing, that is not an affordable solution for editing of lecture recordings in universities. The individual captions in the right hand panel are however saved individually and so it may be possible to motivate students to correct some of the errors while reading and listening to their lecture recordings by providing rewards, for example in the form of academic credits. Some short experiments using a few students have indicated that students who edit the transcript of a recorded lecture do better on tests on the content of that lecture than students who just listen to and watch the lecture. The top right hand 'Synmark' (*SYN*chronised book*MARKS*) panel was originally designed for creating synchronized notes rather than captions although it does also allow for multimedia captions as shown in Figure 2. where each caption has a picture of the speaker and a different colour for what they are saying which is very helpful to identify which speaker a caption refers to. The pictures of the speaker are not stored on Synote's server but can be stored anywhere on the web (e.g. imdb.com). A 'parser' was developed (Figure 3) to automatically split the transcript into utterances which could be uploaded as 'Synmarks'. This enables the best way of automatically splitting the synchronized transcript into editable utterances/captions to be investigated; including the number of words in an utterance, total time length of utterance, the length of silence between words or by the commas inserted by the default silence setting of the IBM speaker independent speech recognition system [7]. The best way of automatically presenting the utterances for correction is also being investigated including separating utterances with commas or full stops or spaces and capitalizing the first word of each utterance. The system can produce both a standard text format SRT file for use with most captioning systems or an XML file for use with Synote.

Figure 4 shows some of a transcript created using speech recognition without splitting into utterances while Figure 5 shows the same transcript split into utterances using silences.

The transcript file format uploaded to the parser could be Synote XML (the native format of the IBM speech recognition used by Synote) , Synote Print preview (Synote's output format and so allowing uploading of Synote's manually edited and/or transcribed synchronized

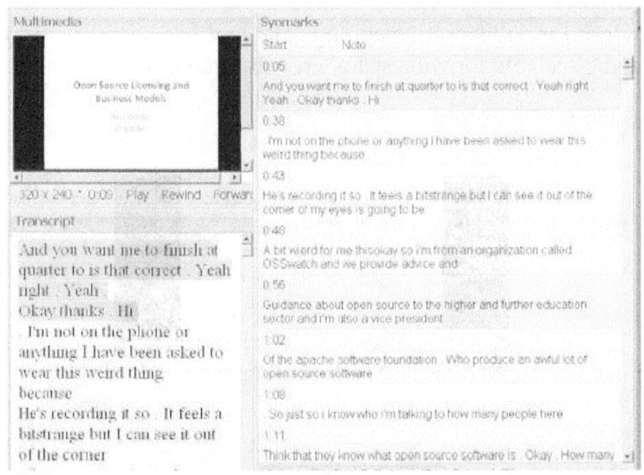

Figure 1. Synote Player Interface

Figure 2. Captioning in Synmarks

transcripts) or SRT (A common video captioning format). Although Synmarks are saved to the server when they are created by a user any changes to Synmarks by users will only be updated in other users' Synmark panels when they choose to refresh the browser. This was a decision made when Synote was being designed as updating all the Synmarks whenever one Synmark was edited or created took a few seconds and so detracted from the user experience. This means that if users are editing the captions in the Synmark panel, they must regularly refresh the browser to check if any other users have edited or corrected any Synmarks. Synote only stores the most recent edit to a Synmark and keeps no record of previous edits. Synote also allows multiple users to concurrently manually caption or correct the errors in the speech recognition transcript. If two users concurrently select the same time period to caption (i.e. without realizing the other user is captioning Synmarks) this could create an unsatisfactory user experience of seeing multiple captions. If two users concurrently edit the same speech recognition utterance in a Synmark then the first person to save their correction will have their correction overwritten by the second person saving their corrections. A research tool was therefore developed to investigate what would be the best design for a collaborative editing tool.

Parser

Select a file to upload:

[Browse...]

Which type of file will you be uploading?

- (•) XML
- ( ) Print Preview
- [ ] Output in SRT format

How do you wish to split the utterances?

- (•) by Number of Words
- ( ) by Utterance Length
- ( ) by Pause Length
- ( ) by Comma

Number of words:

Additional Options:

- (•) Keep Commas
- ( ) Remove Commas
- ( ) Convert Commas to Full Stops

- [ ] Capitalise First Letter

[Submit]

Figure 3. Transcript Parser

This is a demonstration of the problem of the readability of text created by commercial speech recognition software used in lectures they were designed for the speaker to dictate grammatically complete sentences using punctuation by saying comma period new paragraph to provide phrase sentence and paragraph markers when people speak spontaneously they do not speak in what would be regarded as grammatically correct sentences as you can see you just see a continuous stream of text with no obvious beginnings and ends of sentences normal written text would break up this text by the use of punctuation such as commas and periods or new lines by getting the software to insert breaks in the text automatically by measuring the length of the silence between words we can improve the readability greatly

Figure 4. Transcript without splitting into utterances

This is a demonstration of the problem of the readability of text created by commercial speech recognition software used in lectures

they were designed for the speaker to dictate grammatically complete sentences using punctuation by saying comma period new paragraph to provide phrase sentence and paragraph markers

when people speak spontaneously they do not speak in what would be regarded as grammatically correct sentences

as you can see you just see a continuous stream of text with no obvious beginnings and ends of sentences

normal written text would break up this text by the use of punctuation such as commas and period or new lines

by getting the software to insert breaks in the text automatically by measuring the length of the silence between words we can improve the readability greatly

Figure 5. Transcript split into utterances

4. Collaborative Captioning Tool

The collaborative correction tool shown in Figure 6 stores all the edits of all the users and uses a matching algorithm to compare users' edits to check if they are in agreement before finalizing the 'correct' version of the caption. This improves the captioning accuracy and also reduces the chance of 'spam' captions. The tool allows contiguous utterances from sections of the transcript to be presented for editing to particular users or for users to be given the freedom to correct any utterance. The idea of the tool is that students could watch recordings of lectures that have captions created by automatic speech recognition and they could correct as many or as few of the recognition errors as they choose. Administrator settings (Figure 7) allow for different matching algorithms based on the closeness of a match and the number of users whose corrections must agree before accepting the edit. Contractions are accepted (e.g. I'm) as meaning the same as the full version (i.e. 'I am') and to enable these 'rules' to be easily extended a substitution rules XML file uploader is provided (Figure 8). As shown in Figure 6, the red bar on the left of the utterance and the tick on the right denote that a successful match has been achieved and so no further editing of the utterance is required while the green bar denotes that the required match for this utterance has yet to be achieved. Various display and editing modes are provided for users. Users are awarded points for a matching edit and it is also possible to remove points for corrections that do not match other users' corrections (Figure 9). A report is available showing users' edits (Figure 10). Investigations are currently underway using this research tool in order to determine the most sustainable approach to adopt for collaborative editing. The tool has been designed to be scalable for wide scale 'crowdsourcing' of captioning.

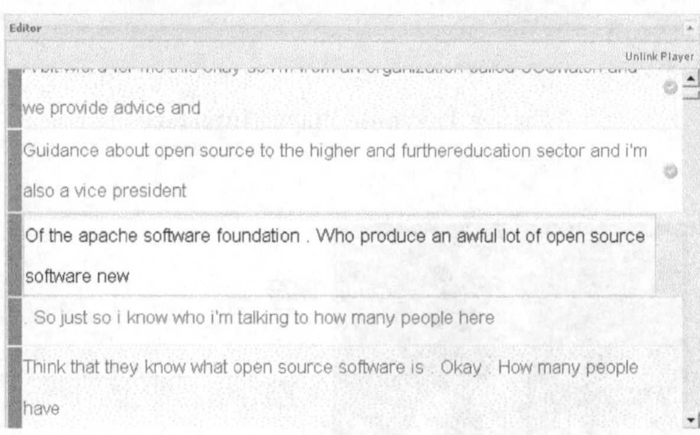

Figure 6. Collaborative correction tool

Settings

6 users - Interactive guide to using Synote (full)	
videos/mike0.wmv	
Transcript ID	5
Original Transcript's Accuracy	99.3 %
Editing method	sections
Number of users editing one section	3
Matching Method	close
Required minimum similarity of edits	75 %
Scoring Method	rewards

Figure 7. Collaborative Tool Settings

Substitution Rules Uploader

Upload an XML file containing substitution rules: [ ] Browse... Upload

Figure 8. Substitution Rules Uploader

Scores

First Name	Last Name	Rewards	Penalties	Score
Alexander	Kilcoyne	0	0	0
dmk106	dmk106	0	0	0
Mike	Kanani	1	0	1
M	W	7	2	5
m	w	8	1	7
Alex	Kilcoyne	0	0	0
Stanley	Kubrick	0	0	0

Figure 9. Rewards and penalty scores

User	Final	Similarity	Word Changes	Utterance
				50001
				welcome to this brief interactive guide to using senate , what is senate ,
u1	◎	92	1	welcome to this brief interactive guide to using Synote , what is senate ,
u2	-	83	2	welcome to this brief interactive guide to using Synote , what is Synote ,
u3	◎	92	1	welcome to this brief interactive guide to using synote , what is senate ,
u4	-	-	-	NOT EDITABLE
u5	-	-	-	NOT EDITABLE
u6	-	-	-	NOT EDITABLE

Figure 10. Report showing users' edits

5. Conclusion

The use of collaborative correction of speech recognition errors offers a promising approach to providing sustainable captioning and Synote and its associated parser and collaborative correction tool provide the opportunity to investigate the best approach for both making it as easy as possible for users to correct the transcripts and also for providing the motivation for them to do so. Future work will involve further user trials of the system. A wmv format video demonstration of the systems tools described in this paper is available for downloading[xix] and is also available on Synote[xx] captioned using Synote's speech recognition editing system. If users wish to annotate the recording on Synote they need to register before logging in with their registered user name and password, otherwise they can go to the "Read, Watch or Listen Only Version". The panels and size of the video can be adjusted up to full screen and the size of the text can also be enlarged.

6. Acknowledgments

Dawid Koprowski is the collaborative tool's lead developer and other ex ECS students Mike Kanani, Karolina Kaniewska, Stella Sharma were also involved in the tool's development and Alex Kilcoyne conducted the user trials

7. References

[1] Bain, K., Basson, S., Wald, M. (2002) Speech recognition in university classrooms. In: *Proceedings of the Fifth International ACM SIGCAPH Conference on Assistive Technologies.* ACM Press, 192-196

[2] Fiscus, J., Radde, N., Garofolo, J., Le, A., Ajot, J., Laprun, C., (2005) The Rich Transcription 2005 Spring Meeting Recognition Evaluation, National Institute Of Standards and Technology

[3] Wald, M. (2011) Crowdsourcing Correction of Speech Recognition Captioning Errors. In, *W4A: 8th International Cross-Disciplinary Conference on Web Accessibility, Hyderabad, India,* W4A.

[4] Novotney, S. Callison-Burch, C. (2010) "Cheap, fast and good enough: automatic speech recognition with non-expert transcription," in Proc. HLT-NAACL, pp. 207-215.

[5] Lee, C. Y., Glass, J. (2011) A transcription task for crowdsourcing with automatic quality control. *Proc. Interspeech2011, Florence.*

[6] Wald, M. (2010) Synote: Designed for all Advanced Learning Technology for Disabled and Non-Disabled People. In, *Proceedings of the 10th IEEE International Conference on Advanced Learning Technologies, Sousse, Tunisia,* pp 716-717.

[7] Soltau, Hagen; Saon, G.; Kingsbury, B. (2010) "The IBM Attila speech recognition toolkit," *Spoken Language Technology Workshop (SLT), 2010 IEEE* , pp.97-102

[i] http://www.automaticsync.com/caption/
[ii] http://gow.epsrc.ac.uk/NGBOViewGrant.aspx?GrantRef=EP/J017728/1
[iii] www.youtube.com
[iv] http://www.overstream.net/
[v] http://dotsub.com/
[vi] http://www.amara.org
[vii] http://captiontube.appspot.com

[viii] http://www.subtitle-horse.com/

[ix] http://accessify.com/tools-and-wizards/accessibility-tools/easy-youtube-caption-creator/

[x] http://ncam.wgbh.org/invent_build/web_multimedia/tools-guidelines/magpie

[xi] http://www.synchrimedia.com/#movcaptioner

[xii] http://www.urusoft.net/products.php?cat=sw&lang=1

[xiii] https://www.mturk.com/

[xiv] http://www.synote.org

[xv] http://www.liberatedlearning.com/news/AGMSymposium2009.html

[xvi] http://www.ecs.soton.ac.uk/news/3874

[xvii] http://www.eunis.org/activities/tasks/doerup.html

[xviii] http://www.net4voice.eu

[xix] http://users.ecs.soton.ac.uk/mw/recordings/Mike%20Wald/webaccessibilitycompetitionsubmit/webaccessibilitycompetitionsubmit.wmv

[xx] http://www.synote.org/synote/recording/replay/55564

Dynamic Adaptation of Business Process Models

Application to the healthcare process in AP-HM

Renaud ANGLES[1,2], Philippe RAMADOUR[2], Corine CAUVET[2], Sophie RODIER[1]

[1]Assistance Publique – Hôpitaux de Marseille
Direction des Systèmes d'Information et de l'Organisation
147, Boulevard Baille
13 005 MARSEILLE, FRANCE
{firstname.lastname}@AP-HM.fr, http://fr.AP-HM.fr

[2]AMU (Aix-Marseille University), LSIS (UMR CNRS 7 296)
Domaine Universitaire de Saint-Jérôme
Avenue Escadrille Normandie-Niemen
13 397 MARSEILLE cedex 20, FRANCE
{firstname.lastname}@lsis.org, http://www.lsis.org

***Abstract*— Healthcare organizations, which are facing the challenge of delivery personalized services to their patients, are obviously affected by the problems of flexibility and adaptability of their processes. This research is applied to healthcare processes in the context of AP-HM hospitals (Assistance Publique - Hôpitaux de Marseille). In this paper, we consider specifically the drug circulation process where the complexity and the high level of variability are critical issues and important in practice. The paper introduces the V-BPMI approach for process variability and it presents how dynamic adaptation can be carried out for delivering process models that satisfy actor's business requirements. The paper focusses on both the steps of the adaptation cycle and the adaptation trees dynamically produced on business actors' demand.**

Keywords—Process flexibility, Process adaptation, Adaptation trees, Variability trees

I. Introduction

Companies have identified enterprise information systems agility as a competitive advantage required for increasing product and service customization, for improving quality of products and services delivered and for adapting their business rules to highly dynamic working environments. Healthcare organizations, which are facing the challenge of delivery personalized services to their patients, are obviously affected by the problems of flexibility and adaptability of their processes. Many reports in the healthcare field state that there is an *"absence of real progress towards applying advances in information technology to improve administrative and clinical processes"* [1]. Furthermore, in healthcare organizations, the lack of flexibility of enterprise information systems is considered as a major obstacle in improvement of organizational and medical treatment processes.

This research is applied to healthcare processes in the context of AP-HM hospitals (Assistance Publique - Hôpitaux de Marseille). In this paper, we consider specifically the drug circulation process where the complexity and the high level of variability are critical issues and important in practice.

Our research is based upon a recent information system paradigm known as PAIS (Process-aware Information Systems): a PAIS is defined as *"a software system that manages and executes operational processes involving people, applications and/or information sources on the basis of process models"*. Flexibility requirement for PAIS therefore raises two issues: *(i)* how to express and manage variability in process models at design-time [2], [3] and *(ii)* how to take into account the business environment for adapting business process models at run-time [1], [4], [5].

The proposal advocates V-BPMI, an approach where process models emphasize variability and are supported by services. V-BPMI provides a process modeling language (so-called V-BPMN). Goal and context are the main concepts introduced to support process variability and adaptation. Process models are memorized in a process repository statically structured with arborescent links (variability trees). Dynamic adaptation of process models consists in discovering and composing available process models to satisfy actor's business requirements. The paper focusses on dynamic adaptation of process models. It introduces both the steps of the adaptation method and the adaptation trees dynamically produced on business actors' demand.

The remainder of the paper is organized as follows. In section 2, we introduce the requirements of variability and adaptability in the drug circulation process of AP-HM hospitals that have motivated this research. Section 3 presents an overview of V-BPMI approach. Section 4 introduces the V-BPMI base. Section 5 describes the dynamic adaptation method and explains dynamic adaptation trees for producing context-dependent process models. Section 6 presents operators supporting dynamic adaptation in V-BPMI. Section 7 presents related work and section 8 concludes this paper.

II. Process variability requirements for The Drug Circulation in the AP-HM

This section introduces the drug circuit process in the AP-HM organization and it highlights the highly dynamic environment of this process. Such a process requires a very flexible approach to adapt its execution on the fly in order to deal with constraints in front of which this process is executed.

A. *Overview of the drug circuit process*

The process of circulation of the drugs is complex. But, at high level, it is generally accepted that it can be specified with three phases as shown in Fig. 1.

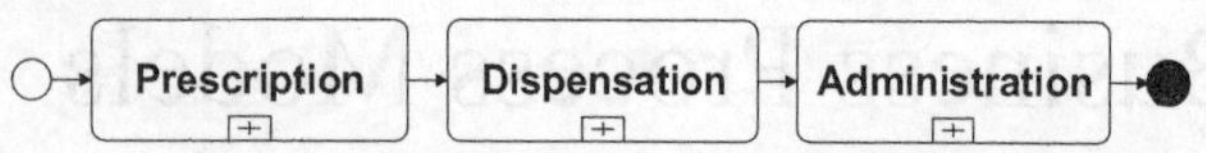

Fig. 1. High level BPMN description of the drug circulation process

The **prescription** is performed by a doctor in a medical unit, according to a diagnostic. The **dispensation** consists in the preparation and the delivery of the prescribed drugs. Pharmacists are responsible for validating prescribed drugs and carrying out the preparations in the pharmacy. Nurses are in charge of the **administration** phase, so they are responsible for giving the adequate drugs and monitor the patients.

B. Process variability

If we consider now in details the sub-process prescription, it is a loosely specified process which has to be refined by end-users during run-time, for example taking into account that if the doctor is a senior the prescription is send immediately, whereas if he is a junior the prescription has to be validated by a senior. In this example, there is a predefined constraint leading to execute or not some validation activities. In practice, due to the high number of choices, not all of them can be anticipated and hence pre-defined in a unique process model.

The AP-HM organization manages 4 different hospitals with their own pharmacy. Each of them is concerned with the dispensation phase of the drug circulation process. However, due to available resources which differ from one pharmacy to another, each one performs a specific variant of the drug circuit process to satisfy the same business requirement.

Most of healthcare processes are complex and they are partially realized by existing legacy applications which can be shared among different processes. In addition, the benefits of process automation from within a single hospital can be transferred to other hospitals. Moreover, some process activities are similar in all cases and there are some differences regarding the involved software components. Nowadays, the service paradigm seems to be a further step in process flexibility due to "late biding" possibility of services. So, services registries must be defined, managed and maintained.

C. Drug circuit process and its working environment

In practice, there are a large variety of constraints which impact process definition and deployment as shown in Fig. 2. The law around the drug circulation process is highly fluctuative and revisions of the way the process has to be run are often required, so **legal constraints** impact processes. The pharmacy size and the available storage space have an impact on the storage policy. Every constraint linked to the resources and the environment is considered as an **environmental constraint**. It is possible to perform a task with different strategies: the storage policy or the period of the day devoted to the dispensation, for example, are **organizational constraints**. To finish, the same technologies are not available in every pharmacy: the Wi-Fi coverage or the used software are not the same for example. These are **technical constraints**.

The constraints where a process is deployed influences the way it has to be modeled and the way it will be run [6], [7].

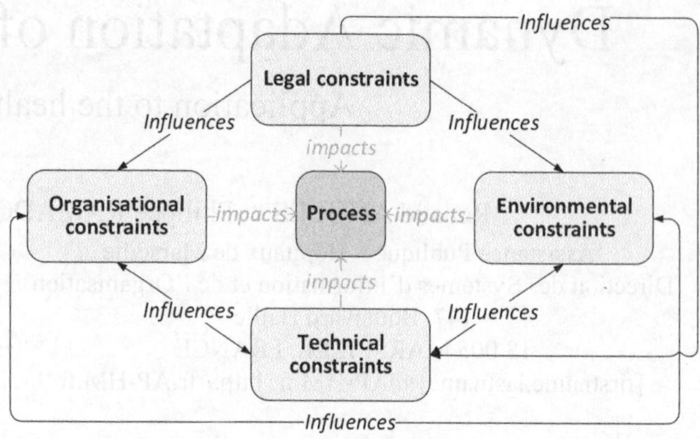

Fig. 2. Process constraints and their interactions

Our proposal introduces a methodology, V-BPMI, to model and manage process variability. Taking into account the specificity of each deployment context, V-BPMI provides a dynamic adaptation approach to produce a process suitable to this context. In this paper, we only consider a simplified representation of the dispensation phase of the drug circulation process to illustrate V-BPMI.

III. V-BPMI OVERVIEW

The V-BPMI approach introduces concepts to model and produce flexible processes in alignment with the business requirements. This section presents the architecture of V-BPMI and the main conceptual tools supporting it (Fig. 3).

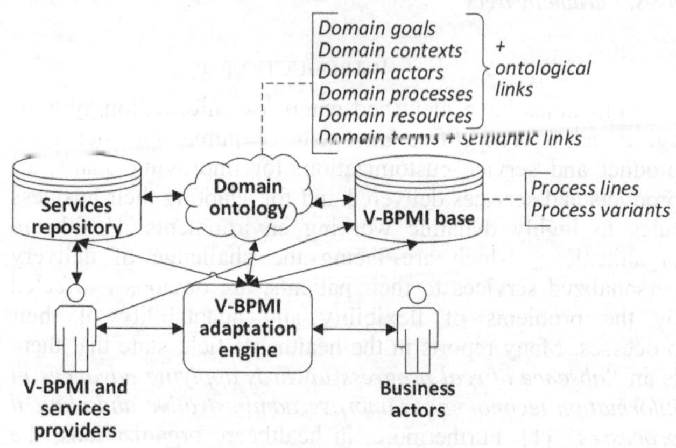

Fig. 3. V-BPMI overview for process adaptation

V-BPMI is mainly supported by:

- *A V-BPMI base:* this repository contains V-BPMI process lines and process variants, which support process variability modelling and dynamic production of adapted processes (cf. IV and V).
- *A services repository:* due to the services orientation of processes in V-BPMI, the service repository is used to implement such processes.
- *A domain ontology:* this ontology is used both for the production and the usage of V-BPMI concepts (process

lines and process variants). This domain ontology contains the goals, contexts, actors, processes, resources of the domain and ontoligical links. It also contains the domain terms with semantic links (mainly synonymy, paronymy, hypernymy and hyponymy). The Fig. 3 underscores the central role of the domain ontology.

- A V-BPMI adaptation engine: this is the core of the V-BPMI adaptation approach. This engine is used by business actors (in our case, healthcare actors) to produce dynamically adapted processes.

The V-BPMI approach adopts a dual orientation:

- This is an *intentional* approach: the notion of goal is one of the main concepts supporting V-BPMI. Goals allows to define variable processes, thus information systems, in alignment with the strategy of the enterprise. According to this orientation, we consider that the deployement of a business process allows satisfying a business goal.
- This is a *contextual* approach: due to the process constraints interaction (cf. Fig. 2), we consider that a goal can be satisfied in several ways, depending on the situation in which it has to be satisfied. The contextual orientation is powerful for describing several processes satisfying the same goal, each one being discriminated by the context in which its deployment is the more relevant.

IV. The V-BPMI base

We define the V-BPMI approach to model, store and manage flexible processes. According to the dual orientation of V-BPMI, we consider that a business process satisfies a goal in a relevant specific context.

There are several languages for business process modeling. One of the most common is BPMN [8]. This language mainly allows expressing activities and their scheduling. Despite the notion of *ad-hoc* processes, BPMN unfortunately doesn't focus on the variability. That's why V-BPMI introduces the V-BPMN language, which encapsulates BPMN and allows modeling new concepts introduced in V-BPMI. One of the reasons of the choice of a language encapsulating BPMN is the service approach for the operationalization of the processes. It introduces a first level of flexibility, allowing choosing the way to operationalize a BPMN service task with a "late binding" possibility. An advantage of this choice is that a BPMN process is also a V-BPMN process.

This section presents the different concepts related to the variability before introducing the V-BPMI base used to store the variable processes.

A. V-BPMI Concepts Supporting the Variability

V-BPMI introduces some concepts for the process variability modeling and management. We describe here the main V-BPMI concepts supporting this dual orientation.

- A **goal** allows describing the finality of a business process. Its expression is based on domain ontology. Goals introduce a way for supporting the alignment between the strategy of the enterprise and the process deployed. Inspired by [9], we propose to formally express a goal with an *action* and an *object* concerned by the action: $(To\ do)_{Action}\ (Something)_{Object}$.

  For example, $(Pick\ up)_{Action}\ (Drugs)_{Object}$ is an healthcare goal.

- A **context** is the formal expression of specific situation in which the deployment of a process is relevant. A context is a set of *contextual assertions* supported by the domain ontology. The assertions are typed and logically linked in a context with an AND operator (a context is a conjunction of contextual assertions). Some of them can be negated with a NOT operator.

  For example, $(Dispensation\ type = emergency)_{Environmental}$ AND $(Storage\ mode = Robot)_{Resource}$ is an healthcare context.

- A **process line** abstracts all the ways (*i.e.* business processes) for satisfying a business goal. A process line is identified by a business goal. Each business goal to be satisfied in the domain is associated with a process line in the V-BPMI base. Thus, in a V-BPMI base, all the business processes satisfying a business goal *G* are associated with the process line identified by *G*. (cf. Fig. 4).

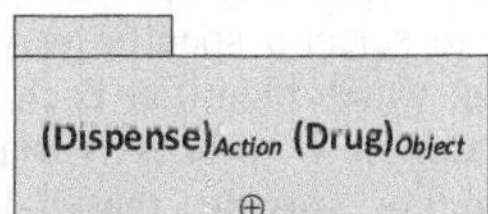

Fig. 4. V-BPMN notation of the collapsed view of the process line of the drug dispensation

- A **process variant** contains the description of a business process in which the variability can be emphasized (thus, this is a V-BPMN process, as shown in Fig. 5). So, a process variant provides one of the ways for satisfying a business goal in a specific context.

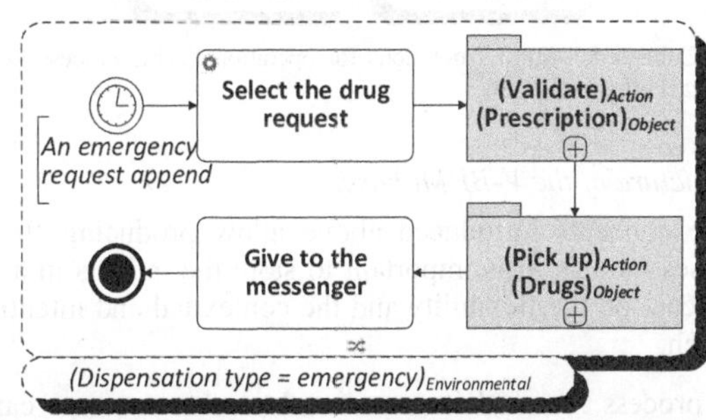

Fig. 5. V-BPMN notation of the expanded view of a process variant

A process variant is always associated with a process line: the one identified by the goal satisfied by the V-BPMN process contained in the process variant. Several process variants can then be associated with the same process line, each one providing a V-BPMN process satisfying the goal that identifies the process line. That's why we discriminate each process variant by a context which identifies it (cf. Fig. 6).

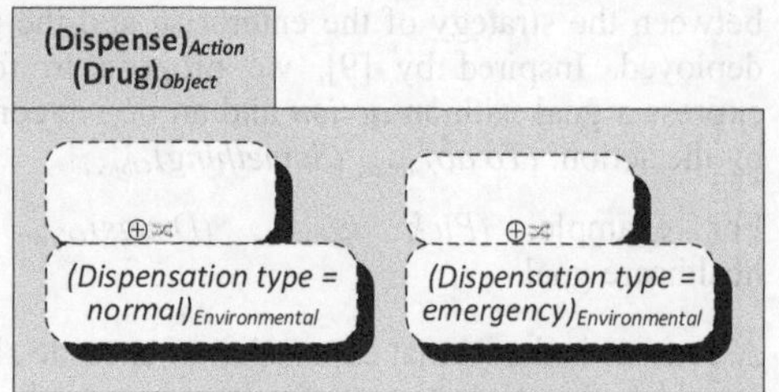

Fig. 6. V-BPMN notation of the expended view of the process line of the drug dispensation associated with 2 collapsed process variants

The V-BPMN process included in a process variant can contain one or more references to process lines. Such references allow expressing that a business requirement has to be satisfied here and it can be satisfied in several ways. This leads us to identify 2 types of process variants:

- *Operationalizable process variants* contain no reference to any process line. In this case, the business process included in the process variant is an usual BPMN process which can be operationalized (for example in BPEL [10], [11]).
- *Abstract process variants* contain at least one reference to a process line. In this case, the business process included in the process variant is a V-BPMN process that can't be immediately operationalized: a choice has to be made to select a specific way for satisfying the business goal which identifies each referenced process line. The example of process variant in Fig. 5 is an abstract process variant: the V-BPMN process it contains refers 2 process lines.

The language V-BPMN defines 2 symbols to identify operationalizable process variants and abstract process variants (cf. Fig. 7).

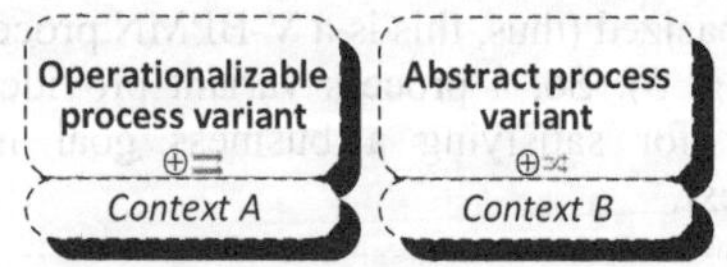

Fig. 7. Collapsed V-BPMN notations for operationalizable process variants and abstract process variants

B. Structure of the V-BPMI base

The concepts introduced above allow producing flexible processes models. It is important to store the models in a base taking care on the flexibility and the contextual and intentional approach.

A process line and its associated process variants can be structured in a two-level tree. The process line is the tree root and they are as many leaves in the trees as process variants, either operationalizable or abstract, associated with the process line. The link between the process line and the process variants is a *selection link* (*i.e.* an XOR link). This kind of tree is called a *variability tree* in the V-BPMI approach.

Fig. 8 presents an example of a variability tree. Its root is the process line identified by the goal *(Pick up)$_{Action}$ (Drugs)$_{Object}$* and its leaves are 3 process variants (the first one is operationalizable and the second and the third ones are abstract) discriminated by their context.

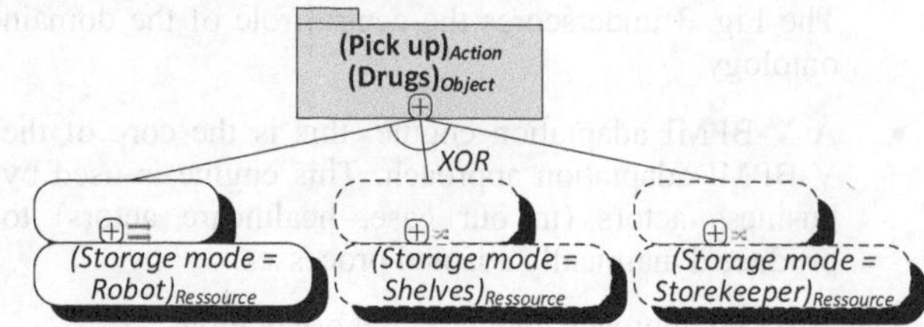

Fig. 8. An example of variability tree

Such trees statically structure the V-BPMI base. Thus, the V-BPMI base can be seen as a forest of variability trees (cf. Fig. 9), each one containing all the managed ways (process variants which are the leaves of the tree) which can satisfy a managed goal (the one of the process line which is the root of the tree).

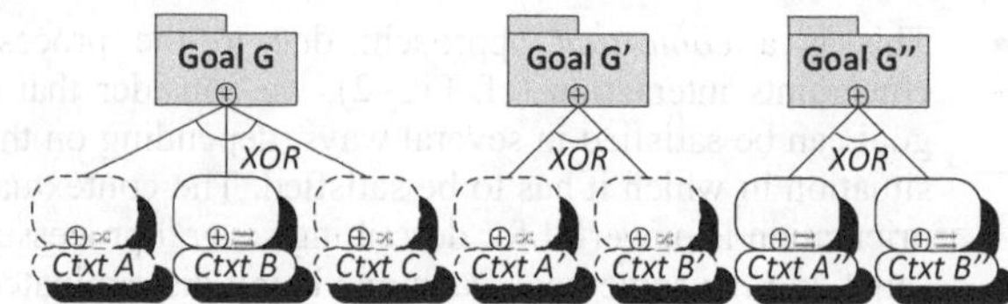

Fig. 9. Forest of variability trees structuring the V-BPMI base

Leaves of the variability trees are process variants. Thus, they can be operationalizable or abstract. Let's remember that operationalizable process variants are BPMN processes whereas abstract process variants are V-BPMN processes in which at least one reference to a process line appears.

So, due to abstract process variants, which can reference process lines, it can be interesting to dynamically link some of the variability trees. This is the role of dynamic adaptation trees presented below.

V. Dynamic Adaptation of Processes

We introduce in this section the concept of *dynamic adaptation trees* and their usage during the production of adapted processes. This production is conducting according with the *cycle of dynamic adaptation*.

A. Dynamic adaptation trees

The abstract variants associated with a process line refer to other process lines contained in the V-BPMI base. Thus, it is possible to dynamically link an abstract process variant to the process lines it references. This can be done by linking the variability tree of which the process variant is a leaf with the variability tree of which the referenced process line is the root.

For example, the process line *(Dispense)$_{Action}$ (Drug)$_{Object}$* presented in Fig. 6 is the root of a variability tree which has 2 leaves corresponding to the 2 abstract process variants appearing in Fig. 6. One of these variants, which is detailed in Fig. 5, refers 2 process lines: *(Validate)$_{Action}$ (Prescription)$_{Object}$*

and *(Pick up)$_{Action}$ (Drugs)$_{Object}$*. It means that, to operationalize this process variant, both referenced process lines have to be satisfied. Thus, it is possible to dynamically link the process variant of the process line *(Dispense)$_{Action}$ (Drug)$_{Object}$* relevant in the context *(Dispensation type = emergency)$_{Environmental}$* with the process line *(Validate)$_{Action}$ (Prescription)$_{Object}$* and the process line *(Pick up)$_{Action}$ (Drugs)$_{Object}$*.

This kind of link is a *dynamic composition link* (*i.e.* an AND link). Fig. 10 illustrates that link.

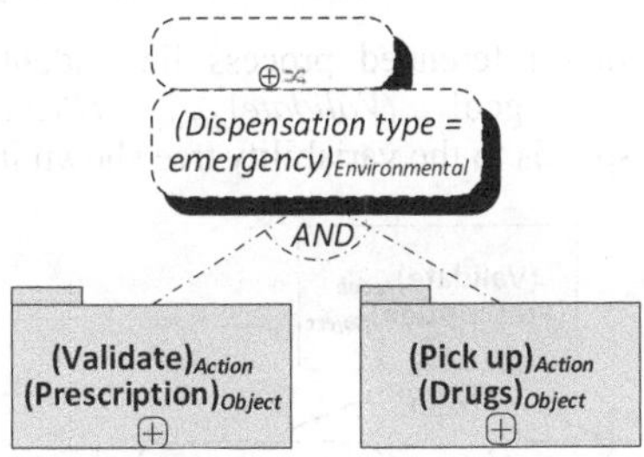

Fig. 10. An example of composition links between an abstract process variant and referenced process lines

With such dynamic composition links, and existing static selection links structuring the V-BPMI base, it is possible to compose variability trees. The result of the composition of variability trees is called a *dynamic adaptation tree*. The root of an adaptation tree is a process line and the leaves are process variants. Nodes of odd levels are process lines while nodes of even levels are process variants (either operationalizable or abstract). The links from process lines of an odd level *n* to process variants of the even level *n+1* are XOR links (selection links). This links are static and are those which structure the V-BPMI base throughout the variability trees. The links from the process variants of an even level *n* to process lines of the odd level *n+1* are AND links (composition links). This links are dynamic.

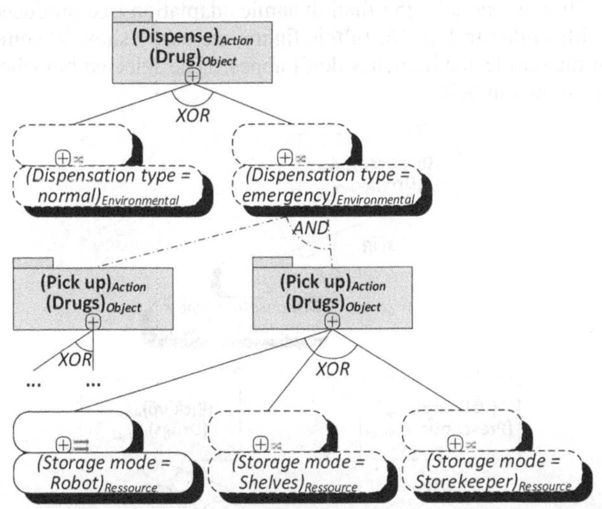

Fig. 11. Dynamic adaptation tree (partial view)

For example, the dynamic adaptation tree shown in Fig. 11 is the composition of 3 variability trees: the one in which the process variant of the Fig. 10 is a leaf, the one in which the process line *(Validate)$_{Action}$ (Prescription)$_{Object}$* is the root and the one in which the process line *(Pick up)$_{Action}$ (Drugs)$_{Object}$* is the root.

Adaptation trees are useful to support the cycle of dynamic adaptation during which adapted processes are produced.

B. Cycle of dynamic adaptation

This cycle of dynamic adaptation is triggered when a business requirement is expressed. A business requirement is formally structured with a business goal (the one to be satisfied) and a business context (the one in which the goal has to be satisfied).

For example, a healthcare business requirement can be:

((Give)$_{Action}$ (A drug)$_{Object}$)$_{Goal}$
((Dispensation type = emergency)$_{Environmental}$
AND
(Storage mode = Robot)$_{Resources}$))$_{Context}$

The output of the cycle of dynamic adaptation is an operationalizable BPMN process which satisfies the goal of the business requirement in the expressed context.

The cycle of dynamic adaptation is made of 4 phases.

The **research** phase requires a goal specification. The V-BPMI adaptation engine determines the more relevant process line, according to the domain ontology. If there is no process line satisfying this goal, the user can dynamically create one which then will be stored in the V-BPMI base.

For example, when the preceding business requirement is expressed, the adaptation engine will search in the V-BPMI base the more relevant process line. If the domain ontology defines the terms *"Dispense"* and *"Give"* as synonyms, the engine will select the variability tree (cf. Fig. 12) associated with the process line introduced in Fig. 4.

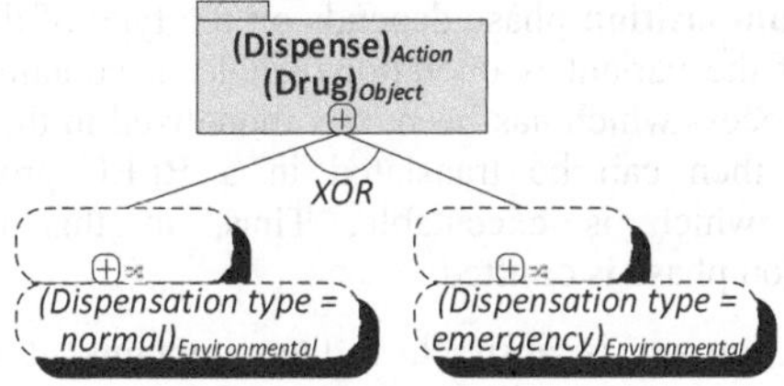

Fig. 12. Output of the research phase

The **selection** phase requires both a process line and a context specification. The first is provided by the research phase and the second is given by the business requirement. During this phase, the adaptation engine selects the more relevant variant of the selected process line. This selection is based on the ontology. At this step, a process variant is selected. According to the business requirement expressed above, the context compatibility will identify the convenient variant.

In our example, the more relevant variant in front of the initial business requirement is the second one (on the right). Thus, the right-branch of the variability tree is selected, as shown in Fig. 13.

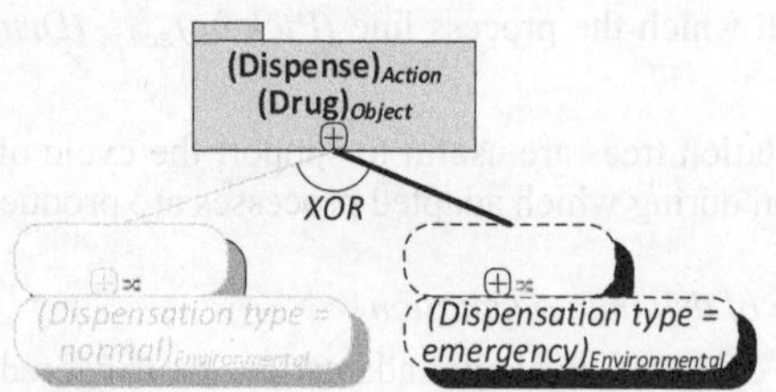

Fig. 13. Output of the selection phase: only one of the branches of the initial variability tree is selected

The **operationalization** phase aims at specifying the way of operationalizing all of the BPMN activities of the selected variant. For example, for BPMN service tasks, the binding of services has to be done. The adaptation engine will check in the service base an adequate service for each BPMN service task.

In our example, the selected process variant contains a BPMN service task (identified by *"Select the drug request"*). This service task can be bind with a specific web service, as shown in Fig. 14.

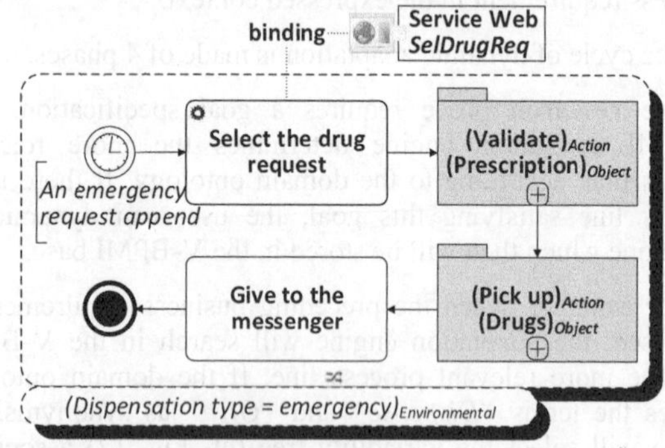

Fig. 14. Output of the operationalization phase

The **composition** phase depends on the type of the current variant. If the variant is operationalizable, it contains a usual BPMN process which has been operationalized in the previous phase. It then can be translated in a BPEL process (for example) which is executable. Thus, in this case, the composition phase is omitted.

If the variant is abstract, it then contains at least one reference to process lines. Such references have to be operationalized. This is the objective of the composition phase. This stage aims at composing variability trees, which results in a dynamic adaptation tree:

- The one in which the abstract process variant appears as a leaf: it will be at the top of the dynamic adaptation tree resulting from the composition,
- The ones in which the referenced process lines appear as roots: they will be sub-trees in the dynamic adaptation tree resulting from the composition.

The sub-trees have to be produced with new iterations in the cycle of adaptation: input of these new iterations is a business requirement expressed as following: the goal is the one identifying a referenced process line and the context is the actual context.

Thus, recursively, a dynamic adaptation tree is produced. The iterations are stopped when all leaves of the dynamic adaptation tree are operationalizable process variants, *i.e.* when whole the variability has been "frozen". All BPMN processes appearing in all leaves are then composed and the result is a classic BPMN process which can be translated in a BPEL process [10] to be executed.

In our example, the abstract process variant refers to 2 process lines, each one associated with a variability tree:

- The first referenced process line, identified by the business goal $(Validate)_{Action}$ $(Prescription)_{Object}$, corresponds to the variability tree shown in Fig. 15.

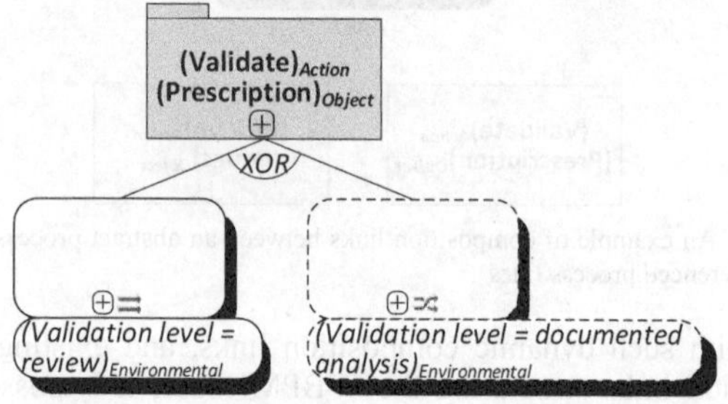

Fig. 15. Variability tree to be composed

- The second referenced process line, identified by the business goal $(Pick\ up)_{Action}$ $(Drugs)_{Object}$, corresponds to the variability tree shown in Fig. 8.

For each of those referenced process lines, a new iteration has to be done in the cycle of dynamic adaptation, *i.e.* research of the more relevant variability trees, selection of a unique branch in those trees, operationalization of the produced V-BPMN process and, possibly, composition with other variability trees.

In our example, the final dynamic adaptation tree produced is illustrated in Fig. 16. In this figure, we partly show it: some of the unselected branches don't appear. The selected branches are shown in bold.

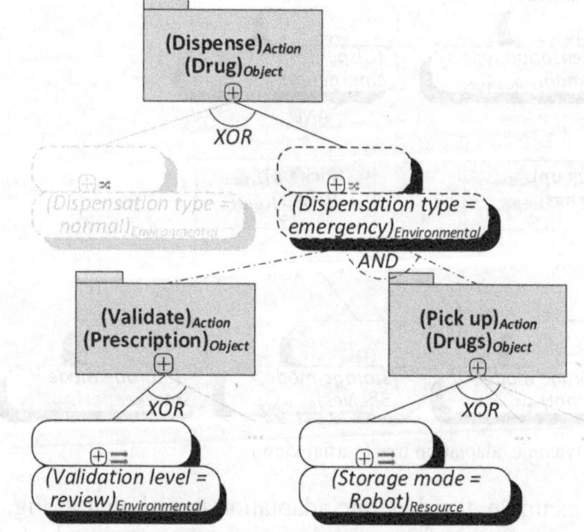

Fig. 16. Output of the composition phase: final dynamic adaptation tree

All leaves of this dynamic adaptation tree are operationalizable process variants, which then contain BPMN processes. These BPMN processes can be composed according to the selected branches of the dynamic adaptation tree. This results in a BPMN business process satisfying the goal of the initial business requirement and relevant in the context specified in this business requirement.

Dynamic adaptation trees are conceptual tools supporting the cycle of dynamic adaptation. This cycle is also supported by a set of operators described in the next section.

VI. OPERATORS SUPPORTING DYNAMIC ADAPTATION

We define a set of operators inspired of [12] supporting the production of dynamic adaptation trees, *i.e.* the cycle of dynamic adaptation. Three classes of operators are defined: ontological operators for terms and contextual assertions equivalence evaluation, similarity operator defined on goals and compatibility operator defined on contexts and adaptation cycle operators (selection, composition…).

A. *Ontological equivalence operators*

These operators support comparison between terms and comparison between assertions by exploiting semantic links (mainly synonymy, paronymy, hypernymy and hyponymy) defined in the domain ontology.

The ≡ operator evaluates the rate of semantic equivalence between 2 terms or 2 groups of terms T_1 and T_2. The result of this operator is a float in [0..1] which corresponds to the rate of semantic equivalence between T_1 and T_2 calculated as a distance, in the domain ontology, throughout semantic links between T_1 and T_2.

The ≊ operator is an operator which defines the rate of semantic equivalence between contextual assertions. Let's remember that a contextual assertion is typed and has a formulation. Thus, we can formally express a contextual assertion with a couple *(T, F)*, where *T* is the type of the contextual assertion and *F* is its formulation. Let's consider two assertions $A_1 = (T_1, F_1)$ and $A_2 = (T_2, F_2)$. The rate of semantic equivalence between A_1 and A_2 is null (0) if $T_1 \neq T_2$ and returns $(F_1 \equiv F_2)$ otherwise (the ≡ operator is the same as presented before). Thus, the result of this operator is a float in [0..1] which corresponds to the rate of the semantic equivalence between F_1 and F_2 *if* $T_1 = T_2$ (0 otherwise).

B. *Similarity and compatibility operators*

These operators are mainly defined for matching goal and context within a business requirement:

- *goalsSimilarity(G_1, G_2):* the goal similarity is evaluated as following: the goal G_1 is composed of $Action_{G1}$ and $Object_{G1}$, the goal G_2 is composed of $Action_{G2}$ and $Object_{G2}$. Then, the similarity between G_1 and G_2 is calculated as following: $similarity(G_1, G_2) = (Action_{G1} \equiv Action_{G2}) \times (Object_{G1} \equiv Object_{G2})$.
- *contextsCompatibility(C_1, C_2):* the context compatibility is described as following: we define $Pos(C_1)$ as the set of the assertions contained in C_1 and which are not operand of a NOT operator. We define $Neg(C_1)$ as the set of the assertions contained in C_1 and which are operand of a NOT operator. $Pos(C_2)$ and $Neg(C_2)$ are defined in the same way. $Pos(C_1)$ and $Neg(C_1)$ are disjoined and it is the same for $Pos(C_2)$ and $Neg(C_2)$. Then, the compatibility between C_1 and C_2 is calculated as fallowing:

$$\forall A \in Pos(C_1), \exists A' \in Pos(C_2) \mid (A \approxeq A') \text{ returns } P_i$$

$$\forall A \in Neg(C_1), \exists A' \in Neg(C_2) \mid (A \approxeq A') \text{ returns } N_i$$

$$compatibility(C_1, C_2) = \prod P_i \times \prod N_i$$

C. *Adaptation cycle operators*

We introduce here 5 operators: the first one supports whole the cycle of dynamic adaptation, and the 4 other ones support the 4 stages of this cycle.

- *adaptationCycleIteration(businessRequirement(Goal G, Context C)):* this operator implements an algorithm triggering iteration(s) of the adaptation cycle. Its input is a business requirement and its output is a V-BPMN process satisfying the goal *G* in the context *C*. This operator is based on the 4 next ones.
- *processLineResearch(Goal G):* input of this operator is a goal *G*. It researches in the V-BPMI base all process lines identified by a goal similar to the goal *G*. If several process lines are returned, they can be ordered by similarity value with the goal *G*. Output of this operator is in fact a variability trees *VT* corresponding to the process line identified by the goal *G'* the most similar to the goal *G*. This operator is used during the research phase of the cycle of dynamic adaptation.
- *processVariantSelection(Context C, Variability Tree VT):* inputs are the variability tree *VT* produced beforehand and the context *C* of the business requirement. It research in the process variants of *VT* the one discriminated by the context *C'* the most compatible with the context *C*. This process variant is called *PV*, has a type *T* (operationalizable or abstract) and contains a V-BPMN process *Proc*. This operator is used during the selection phase of the cycle of dynamic adaptation.
- *processVariantOperationalization(processVariant PV):* input is a process variant *PV*, which has a type *T* (operationalizable or abstract) and contains a V-BPMN process *Proc*. For each activity in *Proc* marked as a service task (according to BPMN definition), bind a convenient service referenced in the service repository. This operator is used during the operationalization phase of the cycle of dynamic adaptation.
- *processVariantComposition(processVariant PV):* input of this operator is a process variant *PV*, which has a type *T* (operationalizable or abstract) and contains a V-BPMN process *Proc*. If *PV* is operationalizable, then this operator returns *Proc*, which is a BPMN process. If *PV* is abstract, then, the following algorithm is executed:

for each process line PL referenced in Proc
PL is identified by the goal G
BR is a business requirement (G, current context C)
subProc ← adaptationCycleIteration
subProc is integrated in PV instead of the reference to PL
end for each

This set of operators supports all the phases of the cycle of dynamic adaptation. They allow a business actor to express a business requirement and get back a BPMN process in which service tasks are bind with available web services.

VII. Related Work

Several approaches address variability in process modeling [13], [14]. These approaches often consider variability capture in process models. C-EPC [15] is an extension of the language EPC and of the ARIS method [16]. It introduces the notion of *configurable nodes*, *configurable functions* and the *guidelines* to support the flexibility of the processes. PROVOP [17] starts with a generic model that contains some *adjustment points* to identify the variability zone in the process. It is possible to define some sets of actions called *options* to modify (add, delete, or modify) the activities to build an adapted process. BPCN [18], [19] is a hybrid approach, blending a declarative and descriptive definition of the process. There is a static part of the process, and an *ad-hoc* part. In this part some non-scheduled available activities are defined. BPCN introduce two kinds of constraints networks to describe the way to use the non-scheduled available activities. The notion of constraints network is used in the DECLARE/YAWL framework [20], [21]. The language DECLARE permits to describe a process only with sets of constraints. They can be mandatory or optional according to the need. It is possible to define *constraints templates* to aggregate some sets of constraints under a conceptual high level constraint.

Even if the existing methods propose powerful concepts for variability capture they consider a little the *intention* and the *context* of a process. In [22] the authors propose to link a context and a goal to every process version, and in [23] it is possible to link an intention to a process description to support the variability of the organizational dimension of the process. These approaches are concerned with process variability modeling and they little exploit goal and context for guiding process adaptation. In [24], the authors consider run time adaptation by allowing the user to modify the process model. Process adaptation guidance and process adaptation automating are yet research issues. V-BPMI dynamic adaptation cycle based on process lines and process variants reuse is a step further in process adaptation.

VIII. Conclusion

We introduce the V-BPMI approach to model process variability and provide tools and methodology for contextualized processes production. The V-BPMI adaptation cycle allows selecting process variants and composing the relevant process lines in order to construct a process satisfying a business requirement. Dynamic adaptation trees and operators have been defined to support the adaptation cycle.

We actually address the definition of an architecture for V-BPMI implementation. This architecture is service-oriented: in particular, it involves user's interface services, ontology services (for the manipulation of the domain ontology) and services for management of the V-BPMI base.

In the future, dynamic adaptation trees should be used at design-time to evaluate the consistency of the V-BPMI base and help the process designer in process lines and process variants production.

In the AP-HM context, memorizing dynamic adaptation trees should be an interesting issue for traceability of the drug process design.

IX. Bibliography

[1] B. Weber, M. Reichert, and S. Rinderle-Ma, "Change Patterns and Change Support Features - Enhancing Flexibility in Process-Aware Information Systems," *Data & knowledge engineering*, vol. 66, no. 3, pp. 438–466, 2008.

[2] M. Rosemann and J. Recker, "Context-aware Process Design: Exploring the Extrinsic Drivers for Process Flexibility," in *The 18th International Conference on Advanced Information Systems Engineering. Proceedings of Workshops and Doctoral Consortium*, 2006, pp. 149–158.

[3] M. Vervuurt, "Modeling Business Process Variability," University of Twente, 2007.

[4] M. Weske, "Business Process Management Architectures," in *Business Process Management*, Springer Berlin Heidelberg, 2012, pp. 333–371.

[5] E. Andonoff, C. Hanachi, and S. Nurcan, "L'adaptation des processus d'entreprise," Cépaduès., P. Lopisteguy, D. Rieu, and P. Roose, Eds. 2012.

[6] GMSIH, *Informatisation du circuit du médicament et DMS - architecture cible et son intégration dans le système d'information de production de soins*. 2008.

[7] ANAP, "Sécuriser la prise en charge médicamenteuse du patient. La délivrance nominative des médicaments dans les établissements de santé." 2012.

[8] OMG, "Business Process Model and Notation (BPMN)," 2011.

[9] N. Prat, "Goal Formalisation and Classification for Requirements Engineering," Paris I - Panthéon-Sorbonne, 1997.

[10] S. A. White, "Using BPMN to Model a BPEL Process." 2005.

[11] C. Ouyang, E. Verbeek, W. M. P. van der Aalst, S. Breutel, M. Dumas, and A. H. M. ter Hofstede, "Formal semantics and analysis of control flow in WS-BPEL," *Science of Computer Programming*, vol. 67, no. 2–3, pp. 162–198, 2007.

[12] P. Ramadour and M. Fakhri, "Modèle et langage de composition de services," in *INFORSID*, 2011.

[13] C. Ayora, V. Torres, and V. Pelechano, "Dealing with Variability in Business Process models: An Evaluation Framework." p. Technical Report, ProS–TR–2011–05, 2011.

[14] R. Denekere, E. Kornyshova, and I. Rychkova, "Des lignes de processus aux familles de processus," *INFORSID*, 2011.

[15] J. Mendling, J. Recker, M. Rosemann, and W. M. P. van der Aalst, "Generating correct EPCs from configured C-EPCs," in *Proceedings of the 2006 ACM Symposium on Applied Computing (SAC'06)*, 2006, pp. 1505–1510.

[16] A. W. Scheer, *ARIS: Business Process Modelling, 3rd Edition*, Springer-V. Berlin: , 2000.

[17] A. Hallerbach, T. Bauer, and M. Reichert, "Capturing Variability in Business Process Models : The Provop Approach," *Journal of Software Maintenance and Evolution: Research and Practice*, vol. 22, no. 6–7, pp. 519–546, 2010.

[18] L. Ruopeng, S. Shazia, and G. Guido, "Using a Temporal Constraint Network for Business Process Execution," in *ADC '06 Proceedings of the 17th Australasian Database Conference*, vol. 49, G. Dobbie and J. Bailey, Eds. Australian Computer Society, Inc. Darlinghurst, 2006, pp. 157–166.

[19] L. Ruopeng, S. Shazia, and G. Guido, "On managing business processes variants," *Data & Knowledge Engineering*, vol. 68, no. 7, pp. 642–664, 2009.

[20] W. M. P. van der Aalst and A. H. M. ter Hofstede, "YAWL: Yet Another Workflow Language," *Information Systems*, vol. 30, no. 4, pp. 245–275, 2005.

[21] M. Pesic, H. Schonenberg, and W. M. P. van der Aalst, "DECLARE: Full Support for Loosely-Structured Processes," in *Enterprise Distributed Object Computing Conference, 2007. EDOC 2007. 11th IEEE International*, 2007.

[22] M. A. Chaabane, E. Andonoff, R. Bouaziz, and L. Bouzguenda, "Modélisation multidimensionnelle des versions de processus," *Ingénierie des systèmes d'information*, vol. 15, no. 5, pp. 89–114, 2010.

[23] S. Nurcan and M.-H. Edme, "Intention-driven modeling for flexible workflow applications," *Software Process: Improvement and Practice*, vol. 10, no. 4, pp. 363–377, 2005.

[24] M. Rosemann, J. Recker, and C. Flender, "Contextualisation of business processes," *International Journal of Business Process Integration and Management*, vol. 3, no. 1, pp. 47–60, Jan. 2008.

Research Trends and Open Issues in Mobile Application Software Engineering

Mark Rowan and Josh Dehlinger
Department of Computer and Information Sciences
Towson University, Towson, MD USA

Abstract—*Mobile development is becoming an increasingly critical area of software engineering as more users are integrating mobile devices into the fabric of their daily lives. As an evolving field, it is important to identify the research trends and challenges in order to assess if the open issues are receiving the requisite research and if any gaps exist. Some of the challenges involve improving user interfaces, software development processes, tools, and education programs. This paper presents the results of a literature review analysis that identified research work in mobile application software engineering and subsequently classified papers by topic to identify trends in relation to open issues. Results include an analysis into the distribution of 103 classified publications, to include identifying common research questions. It was discovered that progress is being made on some of the open challenges to mobile application software engineering.*

Keywords—mobile application, software engineering, literature review

1 Introduction

Mobile application software engineering is an emerging field and presents fresh software engineering challenges (e.g., location-sensitivity or context-awareness, usability, power consumption, etc.) [1, 2]. The development of meaningful and functional mobile applications is important to multiple stakeholders to include end users, businesses, and organizations as they all try to interface with one another in an increasingly mobile and networked environment.

It is difficult to precisely describe how mobile application software engineering is different than traditional software engineering. One earlier perspective by Roman, Pico, and Murphy stated that "mobility represents a total meltdown of all the stability assumptions" made in software engineering [3]. A more moderate view by Wasserman, points out that mobile applications offer some unique requirements that are less commonly found in traditional software engineering [1], including: interaction with other applications; sensor handling; native versus hybrid applications; families of hardware and software platforms; user interfaces; and complexity of testing. Wasserman also offers a research agenda for software engineering research in the development of mobile applications in the following areas: user experience, non-functional requirements, portability, and processes, tools, and architecture [1]. While mobile application software engineering has been active, the research community needs a better research agenda to enable the design and development of more meaningful, usable and robust mobile applications. To catalyze a research agenda in mobile application software engineering, this work presents a literature review analysis that was conducted with the goal of identifying current trends and exploring the relationship between published research and some previously observed challenges in mobile application software engineering. This paper helps to improve understanding of the current trends and challenges with mobile application software engineering as well as the research currently being conducted. In this analysis, mobile application software engineering trends were identified by reviewing 103 full-text, peer-reviewed publications published between 2008 and 2012 that were acquired from the IEEE and ACM digital libraries [4–106]. Specifically, this paper provides the following contributions:

- An analysis of current mobile application software engineering research trends.
- A discussion of the open issues or least reported topics related to mobile application software engineering research.

The culmination of these contributions will enable mobile application software engineering researchers to focus their efforts in solving open research challenges in this area. This work is part of a larger effort to better understand the current trends and the open issues in mobile application software engineering. The results will inform mobile application developers with an overview of trends in software engineering techniques and tools to design and develop high-quality mobile applications as well as existing open issues.

2 Research Methodology

The research goal of this work is to improve the understanding of the current trends in mobile application software engineering research and exploring the gap between published research and some open issues in mobile application software engineering. Specifically, the research questions addressed in this study are:

- *What are the common topics and nature of the publications reporting on mobile application software engineering?*
- *What are the open issues or least reported topics within related to mobile application software engineering?*

Answering these questions may inform mobile application developers with an overview of trends in software engineering techniques and tools to design and develop high-quality mobile applications as well as existing open issues that warrant further research. Prior to article collection, explicit inclusion and exclusion criteria were established as parameters for the literature review performed in this work. The inclusion criteria were as follows:

1. The publication was in English.
2. Mobile applications as a part of a software engineering context.
3. The literature was current, which we defined as being published between January 2008 and December 2012.
4. The literature was peer-reviewed and presented in a scholarly ACM or IEEE conference/journal.

Similarly, the established exclusion criteria were as follows:

1. Publications prior to January 2008 since we were solely focused on identifying current trends.
2. Literature that was considered non-scholarly reviewed: unpublished working papers, conference tutorials, workshops or abstracts, news reports and editorials.
3. Topics unrelated to mobile applications in a software engineering context.
4. Summaries or other situations in which the full-text publication could not be acquired.

The papers in this literature review were collected in February 2013 from the ACM and IEEE digital libraries, and most were drawn from conferences. Table 1 illustrates the ten conferences that were found to have published the most articles related to mobile application software engineering. An advanced keyword search was completed for *software engineering* in the ACM digital library using the keywords *mobile* AND *application*, and published as a journal, proceeding OR transaction for full-text publications since 2008. This resulted in an initial capture of 73 possible articles that was subsequently reduced to 64 possible articles based on a closer review of titles and abstracts utilizing our selection criteria.

Similarly, in the IEEE digital library for Conference Proceedings, an advanced keyword search was conducted for *software engineering* in Conference Name using the exact phrase *mobile application* in full-text publications since 2008. This resulted in an initial acquisition of 44 possible articles that was subsequently reduced to 39 possible articles based on closer review of titles and abstracts.

Table 1. Popular Conferences

Conference Title	Count	%
Software Engineering, Artificial Intelligence, Networking and Parallel/Distributed Computing	5	4.9%
International Conference on Software Engineering	5	4.9%
Software Engineering and Advanced Applications	5	4.9%
Symposium on Applied Computing	4	3.9%
Computer Science and Software Engineering	4	3.9%
Advances in Mobile Computing and Multimedia	4	3.9%
Mobile and Ubiquitous Multimedia	4	3.9%
MobileHCI	3	2.9%
Australian Software Engineering Conference	3	2.9%
Brazilian Symposium on Software Engineering	3	2.9%

After eliminating papers out of context, the remaining 103 papers were classified and the following data was recorded: primary author, title, venue published, year and the 1998 ACM Computing Classification System (CCS) tags and a brief summary of the research. The papers were classified with the relevant ACM CCS tags by the reviewer; if the publication did not already have classifications. If there was any uncertainty, the entire full-text publication was reviewed. There were 55 different ACM CCS tags used to describe the publications overall. Many publications had more than one ACM CCS classification. Table 2 shows a breakdown of 194 classifications within the ACM CCS Level 2 for the set of 103 papers.

Table 2. ACM Second Level Classification Breakdown

ACM CCS Level 2	Count	%
C2 Computer Communications Networks	16	8.2%
C3 Special Purpose and Application-Based Systems	1	0.5%
C4 Performance of Systems	6	3.1%
C5 Computer System Implementation	2	1.0%
D1 Programming Techniques	3	1.5%
D2 Software Engineering	79	40.7%
D3 Programming Languages	8	4.1%
D4 Operating Systems	2	1.0%
F2 Analysis of Algorithms and Problem Complexity	1	0.5%
F3 Logics and Meanings of Programs	3	1.5%
H1 Models and Principles	3	1.5%
H2 Database Management	2	1.0%
H3 Information Storage and Retrieval	11	5.7%
H4 Information Systems Applications	6	3.1%
H5 Information Interfaces and Presentation	26	13.4%
I2 Computing Methodologies	2	1.0%
I6 Simulation and Modeling	1	0.5%
J1 Administrative Data Processing	1	0.5%
J3 Life and Medical Sciences	3	1.5%
K3 Computers and Education	8	4.1%
K4 Computers and Society	7	3.6%
K6 Management of Computing and Information Systems	3	1.5%
	194	100.0%

Table 3. Temporal Distribution

Year	Count	%
2008	25	24.2%
2009	20	19.4%
2010	20	19.4%
2011	15	14.6%
2012	23	22.4%

Data analysis of the 103 publications found the temporal distribution as follows: 2008 (25), 2009 (20), 2010 (20), 2011 (15), and 2012 (23), as seen in Table 3.

Initially a bottom-up classification system was considered, so the papers could create their own classification system. After trial and error it was determined that a top-down classification methodology using an already established hierarchical classification system would be a better approach to identify trends and to prevent any gaps in information.

3 DISCUSSION

Table 4 illustrates that one of the most frequently discussed mobile application software engineering categories involved Design Tools and Techniques (D.2.2). Reoccurring topics involved software libraries, modules, interfaces and computer aided software engineering. Examples can be found in [13, 20, 33, 36, 44, 47, 49, 69, 74, 77, 89, 93, 98, 101, 103].

As Wasserman suggests, the challenge of making the best possible use of limited screen space, user interface design takes on greater importance than ever for software engineering [1]. The findings reflected mobile-related software engineering based on User Interfaces (H.5.2), human computer interaction, user-centered design, screen design, creating user interfaces for differently-abled people and improving usability were prevailing themes. Examples can be found in [4, 7, 13, 40, 41, 43, 47, 67, 69, 75, 77, 86].

Table 4. Popular ACM Classifications

ACM CCS Level 3	Count	% of Total
D.2.2 Design Tools and Techniques	17	8.8%
H.5.2 User Interfaces	17	8.8%
D.2.5 Testing and Debugging	13	6.7%
D.2.11 Software Architectures	11	5.7%
C.2.1 Network Architecture and Design	8	4.1%
D.2.8 Metrics	8	4.1%
C.2.4 Distributed Systems	7	3.6%
C.4 Performance of Systems	6	3.1%
D.2.4 Software/Program Verification	6	3.1%
H.3.5 Online Information Services	6	3.1%
K.3.2 Computer/Information Science Education	6	3.1%

Publications related to Testing and Debugging (D.2.5) covered tracing, code inspections, walk-throughs, debugging aides, distributed debugging and error handling and recovery. Examples can be found in [12, 24, 38, 70, 87, 94, 96].

Software Architecture (D.2.11) related publications discussed interoperability, domain-specific architectures, patterns, distributed objects and service-oriented architecture. Examples can be found in [11, 27, 42, 57, 66, 73, 78, 99].

This paper is an initial attempt at identifying trends and open issues with software engineering related to mobile applications. The overwhelming majority of articles in the final data set represented qualitative research. There was a lack of publications discovered during this literature analysis that dealt with the following ACM CCS areas: Processor Architectures (C.1), Coding Tools and Techniques (D.2.3), Distribution, Maintenance, and Enhancement (D.2.7). There is a need for more quantifiable data, empirical studies and industry experience on the trends in mobile application software engineering. These gaps may be reflective of the early stage of technology adoption or the fragmented nature of mobile computing technologies. The following limitations were also noted for this study:

- Different keyword searches may lead to different findings. So the keywords were chosen to provide a focused overview of current trends within the mobile application software engineering community.
- The same keyword search in the same libraries at a different date could lead to different findings (e.g., due to search engine or library updates). We were satisfied with selecting 2008, because it signified the beginning of broader acceptance of smartphones and mobile applications in the general population, which were influenced by the iPhone AppStore and Android Market (now called Google Play).

These noted limitations were addressed and mitigated as best as possible.

4 CONCLUSION

This paper briefly describes the findings of a limited literature review and analysis conducted using research articles published in the IEEE and ACM digital libraries. The ACM CCS was used to classify 103 publications with a top-down approach. Although this review was not exhaustive, it indicates that progress is being made to address some of the identified research challenges with mobile application software engineering.

Future work is geared towards further investigating the open issues and lack of publications involving the following categories: privacy related issues, coding tools and techniques, software distribution, maintenance, and enhancement. More extensive investigation can be accomplished with a manual citation review of identified publications as well as expanding into journals and other digital libraries. There is a need for more quantifiable data, empirical studies and industry experience in mobile application software engineering.

5 ACKNOWLEDGEMENTS

This material is based upon work supported by the National Science Foundation under Grant No. 1140781.

6 REFERENCES

[1] A. Wasserman. 2010. Software engineering issues for mobile application development. In Proceedings of the FSE/SDP workshop on Future of software engineering research (FoSER '10). ACM, New York, NY, USA, 397-400.

[2] J. Dehlinger and J. Dixon, Mobile Application Software Engineering: Challenges and Research Directions, in Proceedings of the Workshop on Mobile Software Engineering. Springer, 2011, pp. 29-32.

[3] G. Roman, G. Picco, and A. Murphy. 2000. Software engineering for mobility: a roadmap. In Proceedings of the Conference on The Future of Software Engineering (ICSE '00). ACM, New York, NY, USA, 241-258.

[4] A. Hussain and E. Ferneley. 2008. Usability metric for mobile application: a goal question metric (GQM) approach. In Proceedings of the 10th International Conference on Information Integration and Web-based Applications & Services (iiWAS '08), Gabriele Kotsis, David Taniar, Eric Pardede, and Ismail Khalil (Eds.). ACM, New York, NY, USA, 567-570.

[5] M. Aleksy and B. Stieger. 2010. Supporting service processes with semantic mobile applications. In Proceedings of the 8th International Conference on Advances in Mobile Computing and Multimedia (MoMM '10). ACM, New York, NY, USA, 167-172.

[6] C. Hu and I. Neamtiu. 2011. Automating GUI testing for Android applications. In Proceedings of the 6th International Workshop on Automation of Software Test (AST '11). ACM, New York, NY, USA, 77-83.

[7] S. Mirisaee. 2010. A human-centred context-aware approach to develop open-standard agile ridesharing using mobile social networks. In Proceedings of the 22nd Conference of the Computer-Human Interaction Special Interest Group of Australia on Computer-Human Interaction (OZCHI '10).

[8] A. Altaf,. M. Javed, A. Ahmed, "Security Enhancements for Privacy and Key Management Protocol in IEEE 802.16e-2005," Software Engineering, Artificial Intelligence, Networking, and Parallel/Distributed Computing, 2008. SNPD '08. Ninth ACIS, pp.335-339, 6-8 Aug. 2008.

[9] M. Maia, J. Filho, C. Filho, R. Castro, R. Andrade, and F. Toorn. 2012. Framework for building intelligent mobile social applications. In Proceedings of the 27th Annual ACM Symposium on Applied Computing (SAC '12). ACM, New York, NY, USA, 525-530.

[10] C. Quinton, S. Mosser, C. Parra, and L. Duchien. 2011. Using multiple feature models to design applications for mobile phones. In Proceedings of the 15th International Software Product Line Conference, Volume 2 (SPLC '11), Ina Schaefer, Isabel John, and Klaus Schmid (Eds.). ACM, New York, NY, USA, Article 23, 8 pages.

[11] N. Ali, C. Solís, and I. Ramos. 2008. Comparing architecture description languages for mobile software systems. In Proceedings of the 1st international workshop on Software architectures and mobility (SAM '08).

[12] F. Balagtas Fernandez and H. Hussmann. 2009. A Methodology and Framework to Simplify Usability Analysis of Mobile Applications. In Proceedings of the 2009 IEEE/ACM International Conference on Automated Software Engineering (ASE '09).

[13] A. Lorenz and M. Jentsch. 2010. The ambient media player: a media application remotely operated by the use of mobile devices and gestures. In Proceedings of the 9th International Conference on Mobile and Ubiquitous Multimedia (MUM '10).

[14] X. Zhang, A. Kunjithapatham, S. Jeong, and S. Gibbs. 2011. Towards an Elastic Application Model for Augmenting the Computing Capabilities of Mobile Devices with Cloud Computing. Mob. Netw. Appl. 16, 3 (June 2011), 270-284.

[15] V. Rivera-Pelayo, V. Zacharias, L. Müller, and S. Braun. 2012. Applying quantified self-approaches to support reflective learning. In Proceedings of the 2nd International Conference on Learning Analytics and Knowledge (LAK '12), Simon Buckingham Shum, Dragan Gasevic, and Rebecca Ferguson (Eds.). ACM, New York, NY, USA, 111-114.

[16] J. Ayres and S. Eisenbach. 2009. Stage: Python with Actors. In Proceedings of the 2009 ICSE Workshop on Multicore Software Engineering (IWMSE '09). IEEE Computer Society, Washington, DC, USA, 25-32.

[17] N. Bencomo. 2009. On the use of software models during software execution. In Proceedings of the 2009 ICSE Workshop on Modeling in Software Engineering (MISE '09). IEEE Computer Society, Washington, DC, USA, 62-67.

[18] A. Bertolino, G. De Angelis, F. Lonetti, A. Sabetta, "Let The Puppets Move! Automated Testbed Generation for Service-oriented Mobile Applications," Software Engineering and Advanced Applications, 2008. SEAA '08. 34th Euromicro Conference, pp.321-328.

[19] D. Brooker, T. Carey, I. Warren., "Middleware for Social Networking on Mobile Devices," Software Engineering Conference (ASWEC), 2010, pp.202-211.

[20] N. Cacho, F. Dantas, A. Garcia, F. Castor, "Exception Flows Made Explicit: An Exploratory Study," Software Engineering, 2009. SBES '09, pp.43-53.

[21] B. Cafeo, F. Dantas, A. Gurgel, E. Guimaraes, E. Cirilo, A. Garcia, C. Lucena, "Analysing the Impact of Feature Dependency Implementation on Product Line Stability: An Exploratory Study," Software Engineering (SBES), 2012, pp.141-150.

[22] F. Chen, J. Chen, K. Chen, C. Shui, "Smart Energy Management of Multi-threaded Java Applications on Multi-core Processors," Software Engineering, Artificial Intelligence, Networking and Parallel & Distributed Computing (SNPD), 2012, pp.260-265.

[23] T. Clear, W. Hussain, S. MacDonell, "The Many Facets of Distance and Space: The Mobility of Actors in Globally Distributed Project Teams," Global Software Engineering (ICGSE), 2012, pp.144-148.

[24] C. Colombo, G. Pace, G. Schneider, "LARVA --- Safer Monitoring of Real-Time Java Programs (Tool Paper)," Software Engineering and Formal Methods, 2009, pp.33-37.

[25] K. Gama, W. Rudametkin, D. Donsez, "Resilience in Dynamic Component-Based Applications," Software Engineering (SBES), 2012, pp.191-195.

[26] M. Girolami, S. Lenzi, F. Furfari, S. Chessa, "SAIL: A Sensor Abstraction and Integration Layer for Context Awareness," Software Engineering and Advanced Applications, 2008. SEAA '08. 34th Euromicro Conference, pp.374-381.

[27] M. Gomez-Rodriguez, V. Sosa-Sosa, I. Lopez-Arevalo, "An External Storage Support for Mobile Applications with Scare Resources," Software Engineering Artificial Intelligence Networking and Parallel/Distributed Computing (SNPD), 2010, pp.109-114.

[28] B. Hao, Y. Liu, D. Wei, Y. Sun, Z. Fang, "Research on the Interconnection Model between Vehicular CAN Network and Internet Based on In-vehicle Gateway," Software Engineering, Artificial Intelligence, Networking and Parallel & Distributed Computing (SNPD), 2012, pp.615-620.

[29] G. Hislop, "Teaching Programming to the Net Generation of Software Engineers," Software Engineering Education and Training Workshop, 2008. CSEETW '08, pp.5-8.
[30] S. Kumar, A. Raj, S. Rabara, "A Framework for Mobile Payment Consortia System (MPCS)," Computer Science and Software Engineering, 2008, vol.2, pp.43-47.
[31] E. Lee, K. Seo, "Code Generation of an XForms Client for Service Integration," Future Generation Communication and Networking Symposia, 2008. FGCNS '08. vol.5, pp.75-80.
[32] L. Lima, J. Iyoda, A. Sampaio, E. Aranha, "Test case prioritization based on data reuse an experimental study," Empirical Software Engineering and Measurement, 2009. ESEM 2009. pp.279-290.
[33] T. Bultan. 2010. Software for everyone by everyone. In Proceedings of the FSE/SDP workshop on Future of software engineering research (FoSER '10). ACM, New York, NY, USA, 69-74.
[34] R. Erikson, V. Rosa and V. Lucena, Jr.. 2011. Smart composition of reusable software components in mobile application product lines. In Proceedings of the 2nd International Workshop on Product Line Approaches in Software Engineering (PLEASE '11). ACM, New York, NY, USA, 45-49.
[35] C. Scharff and R. Verma. 2010. Scrum to support mobile application development projects in a just-in-time learning context. In Proceedings of the 2010 ICSE Workshop on Cooperative and Human Aspects of Software Engineering (CHASE '10). ACM, New York, NY, USA, 25-31.
[36] J. Roth. 2011. Context-aware apps with the Zonezz platform. In Proceedings of the 3rd ACM SOSP Workshop on Networking, Systems, and Applications on Mobile Handhelds (MobiHeld '11). ACM, New York, NY, USA, Article 10, 6 pages.
[37] X. Xiao, N. Tillmann, M. Fahndrich, J. De Halleux, and M. Moskal. 2012. User-aware privacy control via extended static-information-flow analysis. In Proceedings of the 27th IEEE/ACM International Conference on Automated Software Engineering (ASE 2012). ACM, New York, NY, USA, 80-89.
[38] L. Zhang, M. Gordon, R. Dick, Z. Morley Mao, P. Dinda, and L. Yang. 2012. ADEL: an automatic detector of energy leaks for smartphone applications. In Proceedings of the eighth IEEE/ACM/IFIP international conference on Hardware/software codesign and system synthesis (CODES+ISSS '12). ACM, New York, NY, USA, 363-372.
[39] L. Yan, T. Wong., "Component Architecture and Modeling for Microkernel-Based Embedded System Development," Software Engineering, 2008. ASWEC 2008, pp.190-199
[40] G. D'Amico, A. Del Bimbo, A. Ferracani, L. Landucci, and D. Pezzatini. 2012. Indoor and outdoor profiling of users in multimedia installations. In Proceedings of the 20th ACM international conference on Multimedia (MM '12). ACM, New York, NY, USA, 1197-1200.
[41] F. T. Balagtas-Fernandez and H. Hussmann. 2008. Model-Driven Development of Mobile Applications. In Proceedings of the 2008 23rd IEEE/ACM International Conference on Automated Software Engineering (ASE '08). IEEE Computer Society, Washington, DC, USA, 509-512.
[42] C. Challiol, A. Fortier, S. Gordillo, and G. Rossi. 2008. Model-based concerns mashups for mobile hypermedia. In Proceedings of the 6th International Conference on Advances in Mobile Computing and Multimedia (MoMM '08), Gabriele Kotsis, David Taniar, Eric Pardede, and Ismail Khalil (Eds.). ACM, New York, NY, USA, 170-177.
[43] J. Suárez, A. Trujillo, M. de la Calle, D. Gómez-Deck, and J. Santana. 2012. An open source virtual globe framework for iOS, Android and WebGL compliant browser. In Proceedings of the 3rd International Conference on Computing for Geospatial Research and Applications (COM.Geo '12). ACM, New York, NY, USA , Article 22, 10 pages.
[44] T. Mikkonen, A. Taivalsaari, and M. Terho. 2009. Lively for Qt: a platform for mobile web applications. In Proceedings of the 6th International Conference on Mobile Technology, Application & Systems (Mobility '09). ACM, New York, NY, USA, Article 24, 8 pages.
[45] B. Gil and P. Trezentos. 2011. Impacts of data interchange formats on energy consumption and performance in smartphones. In Proceedings of the 2011 Workshop on Open Source and Design of Communication (OSDOC '11). ACM, New York, NY, USA, 1-6.
[46] M. Mohsin Saleemi, J. Bjorkqvist, and J. Lilius. 2008. System architecture and interactivity model for mobile TV applications. In Proceedings of the 3rd international conference on Digital Interactive Media in Entertainment and Arts (DIMEA '08). ACM, New York, NY, USA, 407-414 [47] J. Seifert, B. Pfleging, C. Valderrama, M. Hermes, E. Rukzio, and A. Schmidt, "MobiDev : A Tool for Creating Apps on Mobile Phones," in Human computer interaction with mobile devices and services, 2011, pp. 109–112.
[48] C. Siebra, P. Costa, R. Miranda, F. Silva, and A. Santos. 2012. The software perspective for energy-efficient mobile applications development. In Proceedings of the 10th International Conference on Advances in Mobile Computing & Multimedia (MoMM '12), Ismail Khalil (Ed.). ACM, New York, NY, USA, 143-150.
[49] Y. Maki, G. Sano, Y. Kobashi, T. Nakamura, M. Kanoh, K. Yamada, "Estimating Subjective Assessments Using a Simple Biosignal Sensor," Software Engineering, Artificial Intelligence, Networking and Parallel & Distributed Computing (SNPD), 2012, pp.325-330.
[50] T. Miettinen, D. Pakkala, M. Hongisto, "A Method for the Resource Monitoring of OSGi-based Software Components," Software Engineering and Advanced Applications, 2008. SEAA '08. 34th Euromicro Conference, pp.100-107.
[51] L. Nascimento, E. de Almeida, S. de Lemos Meira, "A Case Study in Software Product Lines - The Case of the Mobile Game Domain," Software Engineering and Advanced Applications, 2008. SEAA '08. 34th Euromicro Conference, pp.43-50.
[52] U. Nikula, P. Oinonen, L. Hannola., "Extending Process Improvement into a New Organizational Unit," Software Engineering Conference, 2009. ASWEC '09, pp.267-276.
[53] Z. Pingping, J. Shiguang, C. Weihe, "A Location-Based Secure Spatial Audit Policy Model," Computer Science and Software Engineering, 2008, vol.4, pp.619-622.
[54] W. Premchaiswadi, S. Pattanavichai, "Pricing Model and Real Options in 4G LTE Mobile Network," Software Engineering, Artificial Intelligence, Networking and Parallel & Distributed Computing (SNPD), 2012, pp.54-59.
[55] J. Reed, D. Janzen, "Contextual Android education," Software Engineering Education and Training (CSEE&T), 2011, pp.487-491.
[56] S. Agarwal, R. Mahajan, A. Zheng, and V. Bahl. 2010. Diagnosing mobile applications in the wild. In Proceedings of the 9th ACM SIGCOMM Workshop on Hot Topics in Networks (Hotnets-IX). ACM, New York, NY, USA, Article 22 , 6 pages.
[57] G. Cugola, C. Ghezzi, L. Pinto, and G. Tamburrelli. 2012. SelfMotion: a declarative language for adaptive service-oriented mobile apps. In Proceedings of the ACM SIGSOFT 20th International Symposium on the Foundations of Software Engineering (FSE '12). ACM, New York, NY, USA, Article 7 , 4 pages.
[58] W. Du and L. Wang. 2008. Context-aware application programming for mobile devices. In Proceedings of the 2008

C3S2E conference (C3S2E '08). ACM, New York, NY, USA, 215-227.

[59] A. De Lucia, R. Francese, M. Risi, and G. Tortora. 2012. Generating applications directly on the mobile device: an empirical evaluation. In Proceedings of the International Working Conference on Advanced Visual Interfaces (AVI '12), Genny Tortora, Stefano Levialdi, and Maurizio Tucci (Eds.). ACM, New York, NY, USA, 640-647.

[60] S. Casteleyn, W. Van Woensel, and O. De Troyer. 2010. Assisting mobile web users: client-side injection of context-sensitive cues into websites. In Proceedings of the 12th International Conference on Information Integration and Web-based Applications & Services (iiWAS '10). ACM, New York, NY, USA, 443-450.

[61] D. Singh and H. Lee. 2009. Database design for global patient monitoring applications using WAP. In Proceedings of the 2nd International Conference on Interaction Sciences: Information Technology, Culture and Human (ICIS '09). ACM, New York, NY, USA, 25-31.

[62] C. Safran and B. Zaka. 2008. A Geospatial Wiki for m-Learning. In Proceedings of the 2008 International Conference on Computer Science and Software Engineering - Volume 05 (CSSE '08), Vol. 5. IEEE Computer Society, Washington, DC, USA, 109-112.

[63] B Bergvall-Kåreborn and S. Larsson. 2008. A case study of real-world testing. In Proceedings of the 7th International Conference on Mobile and Ubiquitous Multimedia (MUM '08). ACM, New York, NY, USA, 113-116.

[64] N. Huy and D. vanThanh. 2012. Evaluation of mobile app paradigms. In Proceedings of the 10th International Conference on Advances in Mobile Computing & Multimedia (MoMM '12), Ismail Khalil (Ed.). ACM, New York, NY, USA, 25-30.

[65] A. Lago and I. Larizgoitia. 2009. An application-aware approach to efficient power management in mobile devices. In Proceedings of the Fourth International ICST Conference on COMmunication System softWAre and middlewaRE (COMSWARE '09). ACM, New York, NY, USA, Article 11 , 10 pages.

[66] A. Lorenz. 2010. Research directions for the application of MVC in ambient computing environments. In Proceedings of the 1st International Workshop on Pattern-Driven Engineering of Interactive Computing Systems (PEICS '10). ACM, New York, NY, USA, 28-31.

[67] F. Balagtas-Fernandez, Max Tafelmayer, and Heinrich Hussmann. 2010. Mobia Modeler: easing the creation process of mobile applications for non-technical users. In Proceedings of the 15th international conference on Intelligent user interfaces (IUI '10). ACM, New York, NY, USA, 269-272.

[68] Q. Mahmoud, S. Zanin, and T. Ngo. 2012. Integrating mobile storage into database systems courses. In Proceedings of the 13th annual conference on Information technology education (SIGITE '12). ACM, New York, NY, USA, 165-170.

[69] B. Biel and V. Gruhn. 2010. Usability-improving mobile application development patterns. In Proceedings of the 15th European Conference on Pattern Languages of Programs (EuroPLoP '10). ACM, New York, NY, USA, Article 11 , 5 pages.

[70] E. Boix, C. Noguera, T. Van Cutsem, W. De Meuter, and T. D'Hondt. 2011. REME-D: a reflective epidemic message-oriented debugger for ambient-oriented applications. In Proceedings of the 2011 ACM Symposium on Applied Computing (SAC '11). ACM, New York, NY, USA, 1275-1281.

[71] Q. Mahmoud, T. Ngo, R. Niazi, P. Popowicz, R. Sydoryshyn, M. Wilks, and D. Dietz. 2009. An academic kit for integrating mobile devices into the CS curriculum. In Proceedings of the 14th annual ACM SIGCSE conference on Innovation and technology in computer science education (ITiCSE '09). ACM, New York, NY, USA, 40-44.

[72] H. Truong, A. Manzoor, and S. Dustdar. 2009. On modeling, collecting and utilizing context information for disaster responses in pervasive environments. In Proceedings of the first international workshop on Context-aware software technology and applications (CASTA '09). ACM, New York, NY, USA, 25-28.

[73] I. Giurgiu, O. Riva, D. Juric, I. Krivulev, and G. Alonso. 2009. Calling the cloud: enabling mobile phones as interfaces to cloud applications. In Proceedings of the 10th ACM/IFIP/USENIX International Conference on Middleware (Middleware '09). Springer-Verlag New York, Inc., New York, NY, USA, Article 5, 20 pages.

[74] J. Cardoso and R. José. 2012. Creating web-based interactive public display applications with the PuReWidgets toolkit. In Proceedings of the 11th International Conference on Mobile and Ubiquitous Multimedia (MUM '12). ACM, New York, NY, USA, Article 55, 4 pages.

[75] A. Khambati, J. Grundy, J. Warren, and J. Hosking. 2008. Model-Driven Development of Mobile Personal Health Care Applications. In Proceedings of the 2008 23rd IEEE/ACM International Conference on Automated Software Engineering (ASE '08). IEEE Computer Society, Washington, DC, USA, 467-470.

[76] S. Ashmore and S. Kami Makki. 2011. IMISSAR: an intelligent, mobile middleware solution for secure automatic reconfiguration of applications, utilizing a feature model approach. In Proceedings of the 5th International Conference on Ubiquitous Information Management and Communication (ICUIMC '11). ACM, New York, NY, USA, Article 58, 7 pages.

[77] B. Pfleging, E. del Carmen Va.Bahamondez, A. Schmidt, M. Hermes, and J. Nolte. 2010. MobiDev: a mobile development kit for combined paper-based and in-situ programming on the mobile phone. In CHI '10 Extended Abstracts on Human Factors in Computing Systems (CHI EA '10). ACM, New York, NY, USA, 3733-3738.

[78] D. Sollenberger and M. Singh. 2009. Koko: engineering affective applications. In Proceedings of The 8th International Conference on Autonomous Agents and Multiagent Systems - Volume 2 (AAMAS '09), Vol. 2. International Foundation for Autonomous Agents and Multiagent Systems, Richland, SC, 1423-1424.

[79] J. Kaasila, D. Ferreira, V. Kostakos, and T. Ojala. 2012. Testdroid: automated remote UI testing on Android. In Proceedings of the 11th International Conference on Mobile and Ubiquitous Multimedia (MUM '12). ACM, New York, NY, USA, Article 28, 4 pages.

[80] C. Scharff, "Guiding global software development projects using Scrum and Agile with quality assurance," Software Engineering Education and Training (CSEE&T), 2011, pp.274-283.

[81] C. Schuster, M. Appeltauer, and R. Hirschfeld. 2011. Context-oriented programming for mobile devices: JCop on Android. In Proceedings of the 3rd International Workshop on Context-Oriented Programming (COP '11). ACM, New York, NY, USA, Article 5, 5 pages.

[82] N. Seyff, G. Ollmann, M. Bortenschlager, "iRequire: Gathering end-user requirements for new apps," Requirements Engineering Conference (RE), 2011 19th IEEE International, pp.347-348.

[83] S. She, S. Sivapalan, I. Warren, "Hermes: A Tool for Testing Mobile Device Applications," Software Engineering Conference, 2009. ASWEC '09. pp.121-130.

[84] Q. Sheng, S. Pohlenz, J. Yu, H. Wong, A. Ngu, and Z. Maamar. 2009. ContextServ: A platform for rapid and flexible development of context-aware Web services. In Proceedings of

the 31st International Conference on Software Engineering (ICSE '09). IEEE Computer Society, Washington, DC, USA, 619-622.

[85] E. Stroulia, D. Chodos, N. Boers, J. Huang, P. Gburzynski, and I. Nikolaidis. 2009. Software engineering for health education and care delivery systems: The Smart Condo project. In Proceedings of the 2009 ICSE Workshop on Software Engineering in Health Care (SEHC '09). IEEE Computer Society, Washington, DC, USA, 20-28.

[86] P. Ackermann, C. Velasco, and C. Power. 2012. Developing a semantic user and device modeling framework that supports UI adaptability of web 2.0 applications for people with special needs. In Proceedings of the International Cross-Disciplinary Conference on Web Accessibility (W4A '12). ACM, New York, NY, USA, Article 12, 4 pages.

[87] Z. Ding and K. Chang. 2008. Issues related to wireless application testing. In Proceedings of the 46th Annual Southeast Regional Conference on XX (ACM-SE 46). ACM, New York, NY, USA, 513-514.

[88] M. Kovács, P. Lollini, I. Majzik and A. Bondavalli. 2008. An integrated framework for the dependability evaluation of distributed mobile applications. In Proceedings of the 2008 RISE/EFTS Joint International Workshop on Software Engineering for Resilient Systems (SERENE '08). ACM, New York, NY, USA, 29-38.

[89] T. Pohjola, P. Tolppanen, and V. Kaksonen. 2008. Movial IXS mobile internet device. In Proceedings of the 10th international conference on Human computer interaction with mobile devices and services (MobileHCI '08). ACM, New York, NY, USA, 511-513.

[90] M .Tanuan, "Design and delivery of a modern mobile application programming course — An experience report," Software Engineering Education and Training (CSEE&T), 2011, pp.237-246.

[91] H. Truong, L. Juszczyk, S. Bashir. A. Manzoor, S. Dustdar, "Vimoware - A Toolkit for Mobile Web Services and Collaborative Computing," Software Engineering and Advanced Applications, 2008. SEAA '08. 34th Euromicro Conference, pp.366-373.

[92] C. Wang, J. Li, J. Chen, Z. Zhuang, Y. Zhou, "A Novel Strategy Enhancing Location Cloaker for Privacy in Location Based Services," Computer Science and Software Engineering, 2008, vol.3, pp.651-655.

[93] J. Winter, K. Ronkko, M. Hellman, "Reporting usability metrics experiences," Cooperative and Human Aspects on Software Engineering, 2009. CHASE '09. ICSE Workshop, pp.108-115.

[94] H. Kim, B. Choi, and S. Yoon. 2009. Performance testing based on test-driven development for mobile applications. In Proceedings of the 3rd International Conference on Ubiquitous Information Management and Communication (ICUIMC '09). ACM, New York, NY, USA, 612-617.

[95] J. Huang, Q. Xu, B. Tiwana, Z. Morley Mao, M. Zhang, and P. Bahl. 2010. Anatomizing application performance differences on smartphones. In Proceedings of the 8th international conference on Mobile systems, applications, and services (MobiSys '10). ACM, New York, NY, USA, 165-178.

[96] Y. Ridene, N. Belloir, F. Barbier, and N. Couture. 2010. A DSML for mobile phone applications testing. In Proceedings of the 10th Workshop on Domain-Specific Modeling (DSM '10). ACM, New York, NY, USA, Article 3, 6 pages.

[97] R. Scandariato and J. Walden. 2012. Predicting vulnerable classes in an Android application. In Proceedings of the 4th international workshop on Security measurements and metrics (MetriSec '12). ACM, New York, NY, USA, 11-16.

[98] A. Wasserman. 2010. Software engineering issues for mobile application development. In Proceedings of the FSE/SDP workshop on Future of software engineering research (FoSER '10). ACM, New York, NY, USA, 397-400.

[99] Q. Zhang, L. Zhang, "Aspect Oriented Middleware for Mobile Real-Time Systems," Advanced Software Engineering and Its Applications, 2008. ASEA 2008, pp.138-141.

[100] H. Ziv, S. Patil, "Capstone Project: From Software Engineering to "Informatics"," Software Engineering Education and Training (CSEE&T), 2010, pp.185-188.

[101] R. Honken, K. Janz, Z. Boudreau, and J. Yearous. 2012. Building a sustainable mobile device strategy to meet the needs of various stakeholder groups. In Proceedings of the 40th annual ACM SIGUCCS conference (SIGUCCS '12). ACM, New York, NY, USA, 41-48.

[102] H. Liu, B. Krishnamachari, and M. Annavaram. 2008. Game theoretic approach to location sharing with privacy in a community-based mobile safety application. In Proceedings of the 11th international symposium on Modeling, analysis and simulation of wireless and mobile systems (MSWiM '08). ACM, New York, NY, USA, 229-238.

[103] J. Silva and M. Aparicio. 2011. Community sharing platform for mobile devices. In Proceedings of the 2011 Workshop on Open Source and Design of Communication (OSDOC '11). ACM, New York, NY, USA, 7-11.

[104] A. Girardello and F. Michahelles. 2010. AppAware: which mobile applications are hot?. In Proceedings of the 12th international conference on Human computer interaction with mobile devices and services (MobileHCI '10). ACM, New York, NY, USA, 431-434.

[105] M. Maia, Claysson Celes, R. Castro, and R. Andrade. 2010. Considerations on developing mobile applications based on the Capuchin project. In Proceedings of the 2010 ACM Symposium on Applied Computing (SAC '10). ACM, New York, NY, USA, 575-579.

[106] T. Mikkonen and A. Taivalsaari. 2009. Creating a mobile web application platform: the lively kernel experiences. In Proceedings of the 2009 ACM symposium on Applied Computing (SAC '09). ACM, New York, NY, USA, 177-184.

Strategies to Improve Development in Brazilian Financial Institution Integrating Distinct Environments

Claudio Gonçalves Bernardo
MSc. Computer Engineering
Universidade Paulista
Brasilia – Brazil
claudiogbernardo@ig.com.br

Paulo Roberto Chineara Batuta
MBA Software Quality
Centro Universitário de Araraquara
São Paulo - Brazil
pbatuta@hotmail.com

Abstract **– With every release of financial solution IT organizations invest heavily in new technologies with the goal of providing quality software products that meet customer requirements. By this solution often requires processing functionality in environments with totally different from one another. Without the integration of these processes in different environments can not meet the functional and nonfunctional requirements such as integrity, performance, reliability, transparency and inclusiveness. This article presents a solution developed in Brazilian financial institution that was only possible due to environmental Mainframe integration with distributed platforms, manipulated in Eclipse Platform products through Rational Developer for System z and Rational Team Concert. We proposed a collaborative setting that allowed it was tapped what each can provide a better environment without losing its fundamental characteristics. The direct beneficiaries are the end customers and the financial institution responsible for the project.**

Keywords: Tool Integration, Mainframe, Eclipse, Collaborative Platform, Financial Industry.

I. INTRODUTION

Many financial institutions are improving its technology with the goal of increasing their income and contemplate the new regulatory requirements of the global market. The requirements of each business point to a trend more customers focused, that directs your needs for a corporate infrastructure, unlike the former departments that possessed particular structure and separated from other environments. This requirement presents challenges as tools integration, transparency in this integration, solutions for the end customer. The difficulty of integrating different business models with different hardware supporting software becomes a big challenge, because it is complex and carries a big risk involved. This requires a large technical effort both in IT and in the business area [4].

Reference [11] laims that this situation is worsened by the fact that there is an increase in the share of the budget allocated for this purpose because a large sum of capital spending is also in the maintenance of current applications, since businesses can not stop. Integrated tools provide a modern development platform that enables high productivity both individually and as a team, extending the benefits of collaborative management lifecycle for developers completely different environments. This integration allows speed up the "Time to Market" with high quality solutions and increase the development of applications by managing collaborative lifecycle development with integrated planning, task tracking, version control, builds and management reports.

This strategy reduces the capital investment required for reconstruction or development of systems, taking advantage of the business opportunities that arise every day. Thus presents significant opportunities for solutions that previously were either impossible to put into practice many features demanded or presenting few results.

II. ENVIRONMENTS INTEGRATION

For the integration of environment totally different from each other as insurmountable challenges arise. You must create compatibility between interfaces and standardized data structures, business rules must have the same goal, without which it is impossible to bring a result that pleases the consumer. Financial institutions are increasingly trying to create this integration and to invest heavily in this technology. Must meet the requirements of the financial market and it is also necessary to integrate the technology infrastructure.

A. Mainframe Development Environment

A Mainframe operating system is a collection of programs that manage a computer system's internal workings— its memory, processors, devices, and file system. Mainframe operating systems are robust products with substantially different characteristics and purposes. Although an operating system cannot increase the speed of a computer, it can maximize use of resources, thereby making the computer seem faster by allowing it to do more work in a given period of time. A computer's architecture consists of the functions the computer system provides. The architecture is distinct from the physical design, and, in fact, different machine designs might conform to the same computer architecture. In a sense, the architecture is the computer as seen by the user, such as a system programmer. Part of the architecture is the set of machine instructions that the computer can recognize and execute. In the mainframe environment, the system software and hardware comprise a highly advanced computer architecture, the result of decades of technological innovation. Principal operational system is z/OS [2], which is IBM's foremost operating system. To edit programs and manipulate files professionals use the product ISPF - Interactive System Productivity Facility [13] which includes a screen editor. It provides a terminal interface with a set of panels and each of them include menus and dialogs to run tools[5]. These panels provide an interface to run tasks and jobs in batch processing. ISPF is used to manipulate data sets. In Figure 1 is possible to see a normal screen used to edit programs and access a data set.

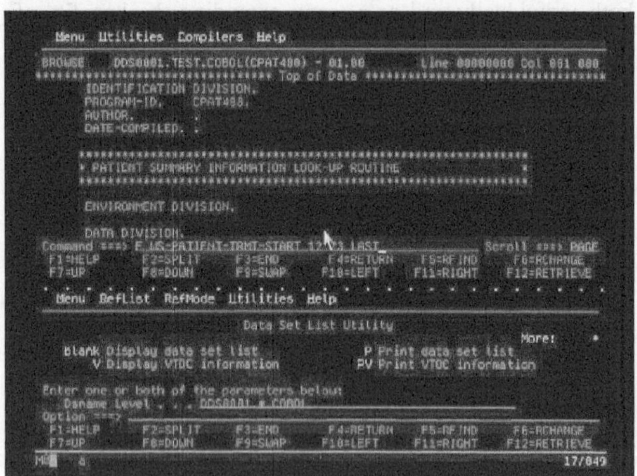

Figure 1 – Use of ISPF product Font: authors

It is useful for mainframe developers to have a working knowledge of other mainframe operating systems. One reason is that a given mainframe computer might run multiple operating systems [7].

B. Eclipse Platform

Eclipse is an open source software that consists of a software development platform extensible Java-based. Presents a framework and a set of services to application development components, accompanied by standardized plug-ins, including the Java development tools and a PDE - Plug-in Development Environment, which allows developing tools that integrate seamlessly into your environment.

The Platform defines the set of frameworks and common services that collectively make up infrastructure required to support the use of Eclipse as a component model, as a RCP - Rich Client Platform and as a comprehensive tool integration platform. These services and frameworks include a standard workbench user interface model and portable native widget toolkit, a project model for managing resources, automatic resource delta management for incremental compilers and builders, language-independent debug infrastructure, and infrastructure for distributed multi-user versioned resource management [8].

Like presented in figure 2 the Eclipse Architecture is divided into some component areas as Workspace, Debug Framework, Text Editor, User Assistance, Release Engineering, Ant integration, Search Facility, Standard Widget Toolkit, User Interface and others.

Java developers use Eclipse SDK - Software Development Kit which includes the Java development tools [10]. Users can extend its abilities by installing plug-ins written for the Eclipse Platform, such as development toolkits for other programming languages, and can write and contribute their own plug-in modules [9]. Figure 3 presents this kit.

In this environment all the tools developers have a level playing field to offer extensions to the Eclipse IDE and provide a unified and consistent users. Although Eclipse is written in the Java programming language, its use is not limited to it. Its structure can also be used as a basis for other applications not related to software development, to content management systems.

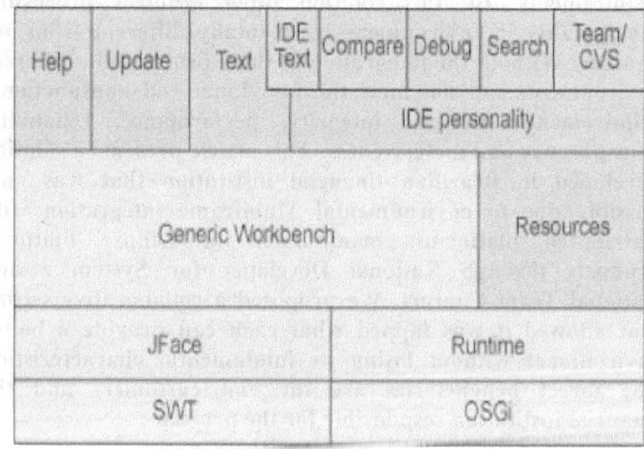

Figure 2 –Architecture of Eclipse Platform Font: [8]

Being an open source Eclipse has a community of volunteers who focus on creating an open development platform comprised of frameworks, tools and runtimes extensible for developing, deploying and managing software across the lifecycle. Call Eclipse Foundation [8] is a nonprofit corporation held by his associates that hosts the Eclipse projects and helps cultivate an open source community and an ecosystem of complementary products and services.

The Eclipse Project was originally created by IBM in November 2001 and supported by a consortium of software vendors. Eclipse Foundation was created in January 2004 as an independent nonprofit organization to act as the organizer of the Eclipse community.

It was created to allow the emergence of a community around the Eclipse independent supplier, with intention to be open and transparent. It manages and directs its continued development by providing services to the community.

C. RD/z – Rational Developer For System z

The Workbench is a graphical RDZ IDE - Integrated Development also environment containing common configuration tools to assist the developer in major mainframe languages such as COBOL, C/C + + and PL/I but being based on Eclipse platform. Applying this environment runs on Windows and Linux Operating System, integrating application development tools for the operating system z/OS [2][6]. See these workbench in figure 4.

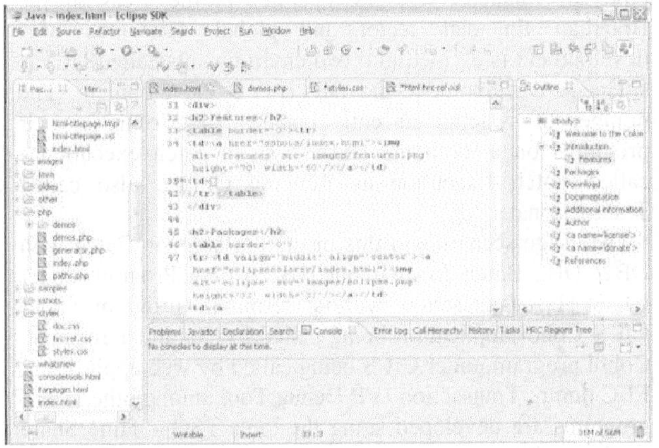

Figure 3 – Eclipse SDK Font: [10]

RDz has a debug session, whose functions with monitored expressions, dynamic data update, breakpoints, access to source tools like program analysis, flow diagram and navigation, real-time access to edit and browse DB2 table values, IMS database values, VSAM files and QSAM files. Figure 4 shows how the interaction happens in RD/z. It is proposed mainly in the financial services industries such as banking, financial and similar. Its architecture described in figure 5 allows a client software interact with z/OS resources through a host-installed listener (a task) and interact through JDBC drivers to data sources. The principals Mainframe security software acts in RDz tasks as the same politics.

D. RTC – Rational Team Concert for System z

RTC is a software innovation through collaboration [11]. Functions in real time, in-context team collaboration, make software development more automated, transparent and predictive. Acts in an integrated planning, source control, work item, build management and project visibility, assess real-time project health, capture data automatically and unobtrusively, automate best practices, dynamic processes accelerate team workflow, out-of-the-box choice of agile processes or customize, unify software teams, integrate a broad array of tools and clients, support for System z and System i servers, Visual Studio Client and integrate document collaboration.

Rational Team Concert for System z is a Jazz Team Server whose can runs on System z/OS, taking advantage of the quality of service, integrates with RACF, relies on DB2 on z/OS, Linux for System z. Support server consolidation initiative and LDAP can be under RACF control [14]. RTC Build Engine can runs on system z/OS, it has access to the z/OS Unix System Services commands, Rexx commands, JCL submission and it allows interact with your existing assets.

III. Need For Collaborative Solution in Organizations

The integration of the organizations keeping all operations working has been presented as a necessity and some of these organizations have a project to standardize infrastructure outsourcing your IT environment. The integration is performed by steps and systems of each area/unit are migrated separately, the operations in operation and without loss of information. This unification requires alignment technology infrastructure in order to support the increasing operation before smelting and growth for the next activities.

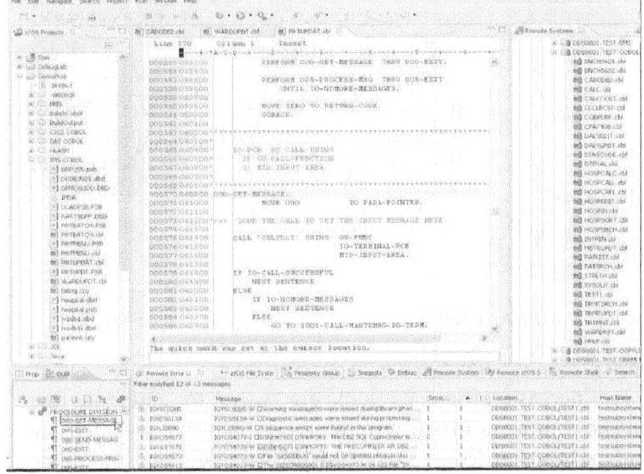

Figure 4 – A graphical IDE Based on Eclipse Font: [10]

It is important to note that you should consider security issues with low impact, overseeing the operation, maintenance and security of the entire IT infrastructure which are the servers, operating systems, storage, network devices, software and ERP.

IV. Integration of Rational Team Concert to Mainframe Development

This paper presents an enterprise modernization solution which has the intention of construct a smarter way to maximize the value of applications, people and teams by reducing application maintenance costs, increase agility to respond to changes and increase overall quality. Its intention is consolidate team infrastructure to increase efficiency, collaboration, and governance across software lifecycle. Achieve greater business agility and productivity by leveraging existing domain knowledge and new talent.

For this goal was designed a platform for the business process of software delivery aligning with evolving business priorities and stakeholder constituencies. To improve coordination and visibility, look for ways to collaborate across the software delivery process broader and richer participation in software projects virtualizes "team memory" to overcome geographic and temporal gaps in the software lifecycle, enable flexible, global resourcing and energy-saving workplace models [11][12].

Collaborate means to drive organizational consensus on priorities and improve workforce productivity, to ensure progress towards business outcomes and look at how to report on the software delivery process; make better informed decisions by leveraging the real-time instrumentation of the software delivery process; leverage metrics for continuous individual and team capability improvement; gain insight into a projects which span organizational and geographic boundaries with minimal disruption.

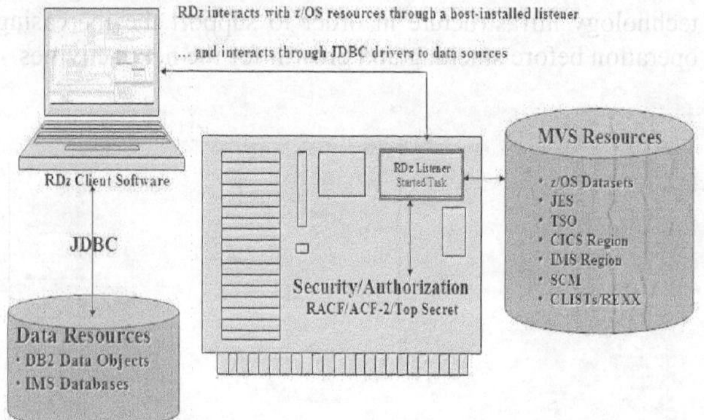

Figure 5 – RD/z Architecture Font: [11]

To increase efficiency look for ways to automate the business process of software delivery, improve productivity and reduce headcount, standardize processes and automate repetitive tasks to improve team efficiency while reducing time to value and enhance regulatory compliance through self documenting data and workflows.

The Jazz Team Server [3] can run on System z/OS, it takes advantage of the quality of service because integrates with RACF, relies on DB2 on z/OS, run Linux for System z, support server consolidation initiative. The Build Engine can run on system z, on z/OS, it has access to the z/OS USS - Unix System Services commands. Runs Rexx commands and JCL submission. It allows RTC to interact with your existing assets. Collaborate and unify software teams across platforms, z/OS and distributed developers. Specialized support for developing and building applications in z/OS languages such as COBOL, PL/I and Easytrieve[12].

Rational Team Concert supports development teams in the following roles: By analysts, define and managing change requests, where are generated work items of requirements, by team planning and assigning work items, where are generated releases and iterations, estimating tasks linked to work item assignments. By developer, design code and unit test, track work item, define and initiate builds linked to change sets and work items; By tester, tests functional, integration, system, performance. Test definitions defects are linked to work items, builds and change sets. A common repository provides seamless transitions of all artifacts between all activities and team roles, promoting traceability throughout the lifecycle.

V. Development in Brazilian Financial Institution using RDz

The organization where this research was applied is a publicly traded financial institution, large and providing all types of financial services, operates in the areas of the Brazilian financial sector and global. His area of development is divided into two environments called DEVA - The A Development and DEVB – B Development. The number of systems currently reaches 1400 running their programs on a 24 hours basis, both in batch execution - called Batch Execution as Running Online, also called Transactional.

The usage scenarios in this institution are: Job Batch with DB2; DB2 Batch Job without DB2; Cobol Program under CICS [1]; Transaction without terminal; program under CICS Cobol application being called by Natural Language; Cobol program under CICS being called by web application; EEC dump; Transaction IVP Debug Tool among others. The programs are developed suing the tools TSO - Time Share Option and Roscoe.

Some data of customer are: 54 million customers, 15 k Service Points, 40 k ATM, 5 k Banking Agencies, 110 k employees, 2 centuries of foundation, 1st in financial assets (USD 438 bilions), present in 21 countries, revenues of Brazilian Credit Card Market : 20%, market value (USD 31 bilions), profit in 2011 (USD 5,4 bilions), implementation plan at financial institution, implementation at 3 LPARS – 1 lab & 2 production environment, implementation of license server, elaboration of instillation guide, installation in workstations, definition of user model, validation of development environment (compilation, tests and more), workshop for knowledge transfer, hands on coaching.

From the current working scenario was presented a proposal for modernization solution delivering collaborative integrating RTC - Rational Team Concert and RDZ - Rational Developer for System z, with options for station development programs, local syntax, compiling, building debugs and delivery. Figure 6 shows this configuration. The scenery presented solution for the development environment is as follows:

{1}Program Sources controlled by RTC and Maintained in RTC

{1}Developer work controlled by RTC process and Work Items

{2}Debugging and Remote Syntax Check with RDz connected to Mainframe z/OS

{3}Coding and Local Syntax Check at Developer workstation with RDz

Scenario Options for Compilations (for Development and Builds) before delivery made to the development environment is as follows:

{2}{1}RTC Build (Smart Build) or full Build

{2}{1}Personal Build with RTC/RDz

{1}{2} Build submitting Dynamic JCL

{2} Submit JOBs with RDz

The Option is Delivered to Build Code submitted to the development environment is as follows:

{2} {1} RTC Build (Smart Build) or full Build.

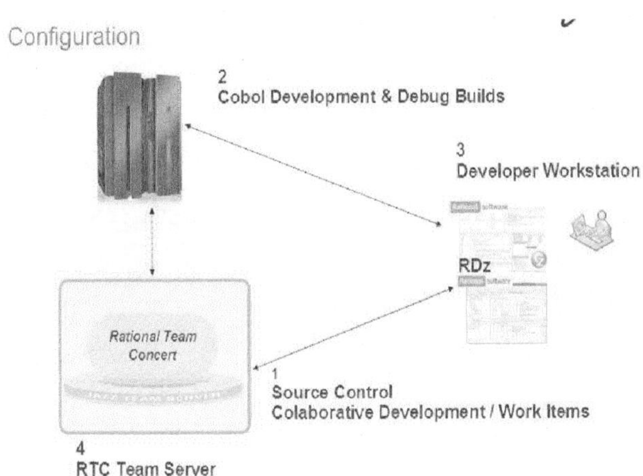

Figure 6 – Solution Configuration Font: [11]

The scenario generated for development with builds and jobs and showed in figure 7 has the following activites:

1 - Create work item to manage a development task;

2 - Developer assigned for the work item starts work, in RDz loads the project in local workspace;

3 - In RDz developer makes changes/codings to the programs and local syntax check;

4 - Load zFiles to z/OS with RTC Client;

5 - Do compile/link with JCL / JOB's;

6 - On z/OS and RDz Test / Debug application;

7 - Deliver the changes to RTC repository;

8 - Do a normal Build to create the final executable, RTC records the change;

The scenario generated for build using JCL has the following activities:

1 - Dependent build with following configuration - translator defined just to support upload of source files; command post processor with a Rexx Program that will build the JCL (for all sources) and with .submitJCL command to execute the Job .

2 - Build definition executes in the following steps: RTC uploads the source files (language definition in z/OS dependent build); Rexx program in post-processing command creates the JCL (parse buildableFiles.xml to find the files) – correlation is buildRequesterUserId. Needs to include customization required by the customer; .submitJCL in port-processing executes the JOB created before in Rexx.

VI. Conclusion

This research proposed a solution to integrate environment Mainframe is the product RDZ - Rational Developer for System z environment with distributed developers, represented by the product RTC – Rational Team Concert, which collaborates and unifys software teams across platforms. Found issues and dependences are: local syntax check is limited if the developer workstation does not have all SW installed (DB2 Connect, TX Series); to do syntax check on programs with DB2 and CICS commands, all workstations need to have DB2 and TX Series installed (developer can do Remote Syntax Check and Syntax by Editor); use debug perspective on RDz , CICS Explorer to manage CICS transactions (Newcopy, Debug Profiles); compilation of programs with JCL is not registered on RTC; alternative to load zFiles, copy and paste from local workspace to PDS using RDz; customer has his own compiling Jobs that is dynamically created. So the build process with RTC will need considerable customization to create and submit Jobs.

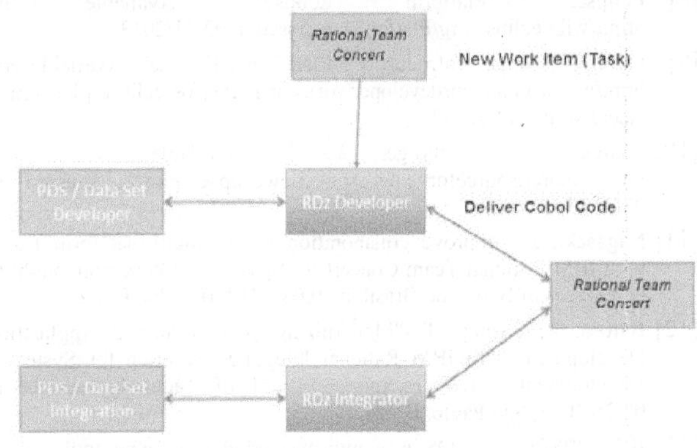

Figure 7 – Scenario for development Font: [11]

It can be concluded from this research that the demands of financial businesses that have a tendency more customer focused, directs your needs for a corporate infrastructure. To meet this need as tools integration challenges must be overcome, introducing transparency and with solutions for the end customer. The difficulty of integrating different business models with different hardware supporting software becomes a major barrier, poser be complex and bring great risk. Some strategies to improve development in financial institution like presented in this paper can be made from using RD/z - Rational Developer for System z integrated with RTC – Rational Team Concert.

VII. Acknowledgments

Authors of this paper would like to acknowledge:

1 – FAPDF – Fundo de Apoio à Pesquisa do Distrito Federal – A Brazilian fund to support research located in Brasilia city, Distrito Federal state.

VIII. References

[1] IBM. "CICS Transaction Server Glossary. CICS Transaction Server for z/OS V3.2". IBM Information Center, Boulder, Colorado, USA. September, 2010. http://publib.boulder.ibm.com/infocenter/cicsts/v3r2/index.jsp. Acessed in 02/06/2011.

[2] IBM. "IBM previews z/OS Version 1 Release 13 and z/OS Management Facility Version 1 Release 13". IBM Corporation, Armonk, New York, USA. February, 2011. Available in: http://www-03.ibm.com/systems/z/os/zos/. Acessed in 05/05/2012.

[3] Jazz Foundation. "Jazz Team Server". Available em: https://jazz.net/products/jazz-foundation/jazz-team-server/ Acessed in 04/06/2013.

[4] PRESSMAN, R. S. "Software Engineering", McGraw-Hill International Editions, Artmed, 2006.

[5] IBM. "Modern development tools for mainframe application development". Available em: http://www-01.ibm.com/software/rational/products/developer/systemz/. Acessed in 09/03/2013.

[6] IBM. "Rational System z Development and Testing Hub". Available in:https://www.ibm.com/developerworks/mydeveloperworks/groups/service/html/communityview?communityUuid=5d4610cf-76f1-46d9-806f-88f157367222. Acessed in 09/03/2013.

[7] IBM. "What are mainframe operating systems?". Available em: http://publib.boulder.ibm.com/infocenter/zos/basics/index.jsp?topic=/com.ibm.zos.zmainframe/zconc_opsysintro.htm. Acessed in 03/30/2013.

[8] Eclipse. "Platform Eclipse". Available in: http://wiki.eclipse.org/Platform. Acessed in 03/31/2013.

[9] Developerworks. "Introdução à Plataforma Eclipse". Available em: http://www.ibm.com/developerworks/br/library/os-eclipse-platform/. Acessed in 03/31/2013.

[10] Source Forge. Available in: http://colorer.sourceforge.net/sshots/neweclipse4.png Acessed in 03/31/2013.

[11] Nagasaki, J. "Improve collaboration across multi-plataform teams with IBM Rational Team Concert for System z". Workshop taught to employees of Banco do Brasil in 10/08/2012. Brasília, Brazil.

[12] Barosa, R; Feeney, T. "Modernizing your System z Application Development with IBM Rational Integrated Solution for System z Development - Lab Exercises". Proof of Technolgy taught in 03/26/2013, São Paulo, Brazil.

[13] IBM. "ISPF for z/OS is a multifaceted development tool set for System z". Available in: http://www-01.ibm.com/software/awdtools/ispf/. Acessed in 04/06/2013.

[14] IBM. "RACF - Resource Access Control Facility. Available in: http://www-03.ibm.com/systems/z/os/zos/features/racf/. Acessed in 04/06/2013.

Advocation Over Investigation

Comments on Robert Glass' Fact #55

James Neilan
Department of Computer Science
Northern Kentucky University
Highland Heights KY
neilanj1@nku.edu

Abstract *– Robert Glass, in "Facts and Fallacies of Software Engineering" [1], states clearly his view on research in software engineering (SE). SE research in the empirical sense does not adequately support current SE practice as it is generally believed. Glass supports his statement and provides a "fact" explaining that SE researchers advocate more than they investigate. It is agreed that the "fact" accurately describes the current state of the field. In this paper, support for Glass' statement and opinions on the two resulting components are given. Marketing resources are provided which detail the use of hype for targeted marketing strategies, possibly contributing to advocating new tools rather than investigating the viability of these tools in the SE research paradigm.*

Keywords—Software Engineering; Research; Investigation; Advocation

I. Introduction

There is a belief that a chasm exists between software theory and practice [1]. This chasm or lack of theoretical correlation with software engineering practices exists due to the inability of current SE researchers to supply practitioners with a valuation of current computing technologies. This leads to practitioners being unable to determine which new technologies can provide substantial benefit. Researchers cite varied reasons as to the cause of the chasm. A primary belief is that SE research does not contain empirical methods that define how research should be carried out for SE projects [2][3] [7]. This belief is supported by Glass in [1] and [6] stating that software engineering research is only 14% evaluative; and computer science research, given the entire field, is only 11% evaluative.

Other researchers have attempted to address the disconnection by first evaluating the types of research papers in the SE field and then presenting methods to improve and better develop the communication of research results to other researchers. In [3], Shaw presents an analysis of the types of questions found in SE, types of research results, and the types of research validations used to substantiate the results. Shaw also goes on to validate the maturation of software architecture research as the principle study of the overall structure of software systems [4]. Shaw identifies six typical phases:

- *Basic Research*
- *Concept Formulation*
- *Development and Extension*
- *Internal Enhancement and Exploration*
- *External Enhancement and Exploration*
- *Popularization*

Software engineering is defined in [7] as developing, maintaining and managing high quality software systems in a cost effective and predictable way. Researchers who study theoretical phenomena of SE generally consider two main activities:

- *Development of new, or modification of existing technologies.*
- *Evaluation and comparison of the effect of using such technology in complex interaction of individuals, teams, projects and organizations.*

Sjoberg, Dyba, and Jorgensen [7] also defined the means to approach the disconnection between theory and practice by stating that the need for increased competence in application and combination strategies for empirical methods, tighter links between academia and industry, and development of common research agendas, focusing on empirical methods and resources for those methods.

The general view in the computing community is that software research and software development are mutually exclusive. Engineers agree that this exclusivity creates greater subsequent problems, leading to software development cost overruns, project failures, and market release failures. Wind and Mahajan [6] give a review of the use of marketing hype in product research and market introduction. Wind and Mahajan state that despite advances in concept testing and pre-launch product testing, the percentage of new product failure is alarmingly high.

Though [7] defines marketing hype and develops a model for using it correctly and effectively, the use of hype in a market strategy can adversely affect the end product market outcome, ending in product acceptance failure as shown in Bresciani and Eppler [8].

A consistent point is made in [1][2][3][6] and [7] that the core inability of theory to support development in positive ways stems from ill-defined methods of SE research and the slow adoption of empirical, scientifically valid research paradigm(s) in the field of software research and development. This is expressed in Glass' research fact #55.

II. ANALYSIS – FACT #55

Robert Glass presents his research "fact" in [1] stating:

"Many Software researchers advocate rather than investigate. As a result, (a) some advocated concepts are worth far less than their advocates believe, and (b) there is a shortage of evaluative research to help determine what the value of such concepts really is."

Glass presents his fact in a somewhat backward manner. He first claims that software researcher's advocate, assuming tools and techniques, a viable product solution rather than researching the solution to determine true viability. In part (a), Glass gives a result of the facts premise; advocated concepts are worth much less than what is believed by the researcher responsible for the recommendation. Glass poses a cause and effect from his main statement and part (a) of his results.

There seems to be a circular argument in part (b) of the statement. Glass is emphasizing that because software engineers advocate rather than investigate, a deficiency of evaluative research exists in the field. However, it could be equally valid to state that a deficiency of evaluated research techniques gives rise to SE researchers advocating more than investigating due to a lack of research methodologies. It is clear that (a) follows from Glass' main statement, however, it is not clear the (b) is also a result.

Glass seems to be stating that SE researcher unwillingness to investigate concepts prior to advocating them leads to potentially misleading technology promotion, instilling misplaced product confidence, and leading to eventual concept failure. Is it the result of the field's lackadaisical attitude towards research? Or is it that SE researchers simply do not have the tools and training to perform valid, meaningful concept investigation?

It is true that when researchers do not do the research, there is little for developers to review prior to making judgments on new technology and concepts. If product valuations are not done by other researchers, than the only other source of product information comes from the product developers and marketing groups. If product information and evaluation stems only from groups who can gain from product adoption, than the information is inherently skewed and presented in a way that promotes the product or concept over others and not necessarily providing all of the relevant information to the customer base.

Three questions present themselves from Glass' statement:

1. Do researchers have the tools to effectively evaluate software concepts?
2. Does marketing hype sway researcher opinions when the tools for evaluation are absent or at best ill defined?
3. Do SE researchers perform pseudo-research to promote their own concepts or methods?

III. THE HYPE CYCLE

Bresciani and Eppler describe the hype cycle and how it characterizes the relative maturity of market technologies [8]. The Gartner hype cycle [9] characterizes the progression of emerging technologies, starting from a technology trigger and traveling through five distinct phases.

1. *Technology Trigger*
2. *Peak of Inflated Exceptions*
3. *Trough of Disillusionment*
4. *Slope of enlightenment*
5. *Plateau of Productivity*

The first phase, Technology Trigger, represents a product launch or announcement such that it garners significant press coverage and domain interest. The second phase, Peak of Inflated Expectations, represents the frenzied public enthusiasm and unrealistic expectations typically generated [8]. The next phase, Trough of Disillusionment, characterizes the state when a technology fails to meet expectations and quickly becomes "unfashionable" [8]. This phase is then followed by the Slope of Enlightenment, representing a technology's period of practical benefit through experimentation by individuals or organizations that adopted to continue with the product through the Trough of Disillusionment. This leads into the final stage, Plateau of Productivity, where the benefits of the product become widely demonstrated and accepted [8]. This phase also represents the stage when the product obtains mainstream adoption.

Bresciani and Eppler give a graphic representation of the hype cycle. Figure 1 depicts the cycle as represented in [8].

Figure 1 The Hype Cycle

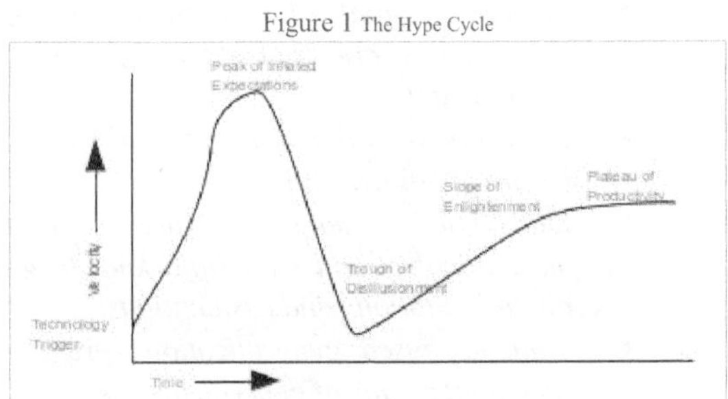

Feen, Bresciani and Eppler go onto explain that the rationale behind the hype cycle, stating that the cycle is more about human attitudes towards innovation rather then to a given technology [8][9]. Public perception of value in regards to technology arises in part from speculation or promises and from real engineering data or business maturity results [8]. The cycle is the result of combining the initial excitement of a product and the gradual maturity of the technology. These two concepts describe the cycle of hype that is present in novel or enhanced product release.

Regarding Wind [5], Feen [9], and Brasciani [8], there exists support for the use of hype for initial market investment, hype as a natural phenomenon in new technology perception, and the understood model of product maturity. Taken together, the hype cycle provides insight into how hype and product maturity impact consumer perception.

IV. DISCUSSION

Glass gives nine major categories of research focus in the computer science field. Research can be of many forms as well, such as informational, observational, or literature report based. Research can also be analytical or evaluative [1]. Giving the types of research and the numerous combinations possible, Ramesh, Glass, and Vessey [6] provide a formal analysis on topic types, research approaches and methods.

Glass' nine categories are:

- *Problem solving concepts*
- *Computer concepts*
- *Systems/software concepts*
- *Data/information concepts*
- *Problem-domain specific concepts*
- *Systems/software management concepts*
- *Organizational concepts*
- *Societal concepts*
- *Disciplinary issues*

Ramesh, Glass, and Vessey [6] surveyed 595 articles from both the ACM and IEEE journals covering the above nine categories. They found that the top topic, with 28.67% of the papers representing computer concepts covering hardware architecture, inter-computer communication, operating systems, and machine/assembly-level data/instructions. The next highest topic was problem-domain specific concepts at 21.50% covering scientific/engineering, information systems, systems programming, real-time systems and robotics, and computer graphics. Systems/software concepts was third at 19.11% with the major focus, 5.25%, on software tools, with life cycle and design reuse trailing closely behind at 3.82% each. The remaining categories received 14.65% for problem solving, 15.45% for data/information concepts, 0.32% for systems/software management and organizational concepts, with no hits for societal and disciplinary issues.

Another interesting finding from [6] is the research methods used in the study. Ramesh et al. found that 73.41% of the papers where conceptual analysis/mathematically based, 15.13% strictly conceptual analysis based, and 2.87% proof of concept implementation based. The remaining methods where case study and data analysis with 0.16% respectively, field study another 0.16%, laboratory experiment with humans 1.75%, literature review 0.32%, mathematical proof with 2.39%, simulation with 1.75%, and software experiment at 1.91%.

Table I shows the top two and bottom two categories with the representative number of papers.

TABLE I. TOP AND BOTTOM CATEGORIES

	Top 2 and Bottom 2 Categories		
	Category	***Percentage***	***Number of papers(of 595)***
Top	Computer Concepts	28.67	171
Top	Problem-Domain Specific	21.5	128
Bottom	Systems/Software Management	0.32	2
Bottom	Organizational	0.32	2

a. Note: Not considering the topics of societal concepts nor Disciplinary issues.

We can also look at the top and bottom research methods used, shown in Table II.

TABLE II. TOP AND BOTTOM RESEARCH METHODS

	Top 2 and Bottom 2 Research Methods		
	Methods	*Percentage*	*Number of papers(of 595)*
Top	Conceptual Analysis/Mathematical	73.41	437
Top	Conceptual Analysis	15.13	90
Bottom	Literature Review	0.32	2
Bottom	Case Study	0.16	1

Considering the issue of software research, sitting at 1.91%, or 11 papers out of the 595, we can see where issues lie in the field. What the study in [6] shows is the level of interest in the categories and what methods are most popular in working with in the nine categories. It is clear that mathematically based analysis and conceptual analysis in computer concepts and problem domain specific topics dominate the computer science field. We also see that case studies and literature review methods are used infrequently and that systems/software management and organizational research lacks significantly. Coupled with the 1.91% of papers concerned with software experimentation, it seems clear that the interest in such topics is considerably low.

Further support from a marketing view comes from Wind and Mahajan [5]. They provide a good review of the use of hype in product promotion. Concept adoption is influenced by the number of people and the amount of hype initially generated to create favorable and supportive environments for the product. Wind and Mahajan go on to state the given that most product concepts and models are not based on the concept of hype, it is important to modify the models and research instruments to accommodate the concept.

From a marketing perspective, we have a documented source stating that hype should be used. What is not clear is how hype should be used and what checks should be used in ensuring that what is advertised accurately represents the product's capabilities. The hype cycle, however, gives guidance to the practitioner and can aid in navigating the viability of a new software product.

Additional evidence pointing to the lack of scientific rigor in SE is given in [7]. Sjoberg et al. state very clearly the current state in quality of the SE researcher:

- *Researchers frequently do not build sufficiently on previous research results.*
- *Research methods and included design elements are frequently applied without careful consideration of alternative study designs.*
- *Study results are frequently not robust due to lack of replication.*
- *Studies frequently conducted by researchers with a vested interest in study outcome, with insufficient precautions to prevent bias.*
- *Reference points for comparisons of technologies are frequently not stated, nor relevant.*
- *The scope of validity of empirical studies is rarely defined explicitly.*
- *Statistical methods are used mechanically, and with little knowledge about limitations and assumptions.*
- *Statistics-based generalizations are the dominant means of generalizations.*

Out of 5453 scientific articles published in 12 major SE journals and conferences spanning from 1993 to 2002, Sjoberg et al. identified only 113 controlled experiments in which humans performed SE tasks [7]. This analysis, coupled with Ramesh et al. in [6], it is easy to claim that, with the lack of empirical rigor, an SE researcher would tend towards advocation over investigation, trusting market hype to provide the functional support and benefit of a product or concept. Whereas the SE researcher should first consider the hype cycle to better investigate prior to advocation.

There were no publications that directly argue against Glass' fact. Glass states that SE researchers will back their own claims by denying that advocation happens more often and in place of investigation. Coupled with the results from [3][4][6], it is hard to conclude that SE researchers can do anything more than advocate. The results shown [6] and [7] clearly point to the lack of research focus.

V. CONCLUSIONS

What are the reasons behind the lack of scientific rigor in software engineering? Is it that the field is to young as eluded to by Shaw [4]? It is because the SE industry pushes for re-using rather then re-inventing? When SE researchers hear of a new, novel, and seemingly beneficial product, do they jump on board due to development time constraints? Is it time constraints that cause researchers to rush to unsound judgments? Are they swayed by personal reasons? Should we blame the marketing hype as described by Wind [5]? Many more questions can be asked as to the whys of the seeming failure of SE research in computer science.

However, considering the three questions posed earlier and given the fact that empirical methods have yet to be fully adopted as stated in [2][3][4] and [7], it is sound to answer the following:

1. *Do researchers have the tools to effectively evaluate software concepts?*

Yes. It seems that the empirical tools and techniques have been developed though not popularized nor taught as fully as they are needed [2][3][7].

2. *Does marketing hype sway researcher opinion when the tools for evaluation are absent or at best ill defined?*

Yes. Marketing hype is a valid technique in raising product awareness and angling market foot hold [5]. This can be used for both good and bad. Also, the study by Feen and Bresciani clearly shows that hype is an integral part new product release and reception. From excitement, disillusionment and finally product maturity, SE researchers must be aware of the product Hype Cycle; and how to maneuver through it.

3. *Do SE researchers perform pseudo-research to promote their own concepts or methods?*

Glass and Sjoberg believes that this is true [1][8]. Researchers want to publish and show valid, novel improvements over known and more traditional methods. Academic dishonesty, plagiarism, and number fudging have always been an unfortunate component of scientific publication. It is left to the research community to study the findings and ensure that the inherent self-checking mechanism in the scientific method succeeds. However, the initial hype curve, evident in the Hype Cycle, is a powerful motivating factor in early, inadequately researched, adoption of technologies that are destined to fail meeting expectations.

It seems correct to state that researchers agree that a chasm exists between theory and practice. Though attempts have been made to bridge it, given the literature, fact #55 models the actual state of SE research. With the promise of better designed approaches, higher quality results, and better empirical analysis in SE, the tools exist to change the fact into a fallacy. Yet, until further research proves otherwise, each SE researcher must guard against quick adoption of novel concepts and practices. It is up to the individual SE researcher to understand the empirical methods available to her such that a concept advocation carries with it the full content of fact, utilizing level headed scientific approaches that are required.

VI. REFERENCES

[1] Glass, R., "Facts and Fallacies of Software Engineering", Addison Wesley publishing. ISBN978-0-321-11742-7. 2003, pp.147-150.

[2] Perry, D., Porter, A., Votta, L., "Empirical Studies of Software Engineering: A Roadmap". Association for Computing Machinery, 2000.

[3] Shaw, M., "What makes Good Research in Software Engineering?", International journal of Software Tools for Technology Transfer. 2002, vol. 4, no. 1, pp.1-7

[4] Shaw, M., "The Coming-of-Age of Software Architecture Research", ICSE 2000.

[5] Wind, J., Mahajan, V., "Marketing Hype: A New Perspective for New Product Research and Introduction". J Prod INNOV MANAG 1987, vol 4, pp.43-49

[6] Ramesh, V., Glass, R., Vessey, I., "Research in computer science: an empirical study"., Journal of Systems and Software, 2004, pp165-176.

[7] Sjoberg, D., Dyba, T., Jorgensen, M., "The Future of Empirical Methods in Software Engineering Research". IEEE FOSE, 2007.

[8] Bresciani, S., Eppler, M., "Gartner's Magic Quadrant and Hype Cycle", Institute of Marketing and Communication Management , Univerita' Della Svizzera Italiana. Collaborative Knowledge Visualization Case Study Series Case Nr. 2, 2008

[9] Feen, J., "Understanding Gartner's Hype Cycle", Gartner Research ID Number G00144727, 2007.

Senior Citizens in Interaction with Mobile Phones: A Flexible Middleware Approach to Support the Diversity

Vinícius P. Gonçalves[1], Vânia P. A. Neris[2], Jó Ueyama[1], Sibelius Seraphini[1], Teresa C. M. Dias[3], and Geraldo P. R. Filho[1]

[1]*Institute of Mathematics and Computer Science, University of São Paulo, 13566-590, São Carlos-SP, Brazil*
[2]*Department of Computing, Federal University of São Carlos, 13565-905, São Carlos-SP, Brazil*
[3]*Department of Statistics, Federal University of São Carlos, 13565-905, São Carlos-SP, Brazil*
{vpg, joueyama, geraldop}@icmc.usp.br, vania@dc.ufscar.br, sibelius@grad.icmc.usp.br, dtmd@ufscar.br

Abstract - *The elderly population grows and it is necessary to develop appropriate technologies to them. Although many elderly afford a mobile phone, several of them only receive calls and do not benefit from other mobile phones' functions due to interaction problems. The current design of mobile devices applications favor young audience, instead of also considering the elderly different interaction needs. The elderly population has different educational levels, experience with technology, cognitive skills and physical dexterity. This paper presents the designs of user interfaces that are flexible to meet the diverse requirements of elderly when interacting with smartphones. A framework for the design of flexible user interfaces was applied, and interaction requirements were formalized considering syntactic, semantic and pragmatic aspects. A set of rules defining the design of the system adaptable behavior was specified. A middleware was adopted and customized, and flexible user interfaces to a commercial Android smartphone were developed. The flexible solution was evaluated by elderly users. The results suggest a reduction in the interaction time with the use of flexible user interfaces and an increase in users' satisfaction.*

Keywords: Reconfigurable middleware, mobile devices, tailorable interfaces, elderly, evaluation, framework.

1 Introduction

According to the United Nations [19], there are currently 893 million people over the age of 60 in the world. This number will nearly triple to 2.4 billion by the middle of this century. "All countries - rich or poor, industrialized or developing - are seeing their populations age in one degree or another" [19].

Even in the elderly population, there are differences regarding educational levels, experience with technology, cognitive skills and physical dexterity [8][9][17]. Many of the solutions in information and communication technologies (ICTs) are currently developed focusing on young users and not including the elderly population that has specific interaction needs [3][5][6][20]. Studies show a negative association between age and interaction skills [8][9][11][16] and a significant reduction in the number of people over 45 that benefits from current ICTs [13].

However, the design solutions for mobile devices that target the elderly public should not offer solutions that discriminate or cause embarrassment [9][17]. This paper argues for the design of interfaces that are flexible to meet the diverse requirements of the elderly in the interaction with mobile phones. The solutions should be tailorable, respecting diversity in the group of users, adjusting to each profile, considering differences related to experience with technologies, cognitive skills, education and physical abilities and minimizing the fears arising from user inexperience or lack of knowledge [7][15].

Flexibility refers to changes regarding the presentation of the interface elements, namely changes in color, size and window position, as well as changes in the order of interaction actions [12]. It is therefore important to emphasize that such interfaces should provide the user an updated layout, subjectively interesting, with relevant information, and with size and setting that is appropriate to the context and that corresponds directly with the users' requirements and preferences.

Aiming to offer adaptable mobile interfaces to the elderly, this paper applied a framework for the design of flexible user interfaces named Plu*R*aL [14]. Interaction requirements were formalized considering syntactic, semantic and pragmatic aspects. The design proposal was also supported by the observation of a group of elderly interacting with a commercial version of a mobile phone agenda. To support the development of a flexible mobile user interface solution, we have adapted a middleware named OpenCom [4][18] and developed a framework called FlexInterface.

The flexible solution was evaluated with 21 elderly users. The results suggest a reduction in the interaction time with the use of flexible user interfaces and an increase in users' satisfaction.

This paper is organized as follows: Section 2 presents the related works; Section 3 describes the design of flexible interfaces for mobile phones focusing on the elderly diversity; Section 4 presents the FlexInterface approach for tailorable interfaces; Section 5 describes the evaluation with the elderly and compares the results of a flexible approach with the commercial one which is non-flexible and Section 6 presents the conclusion and suggests future works.

2 Flexible Interface Design For Elderly People

The first results of this research report the outcomes of a case study with older users, in order to support the formalization of a flexible interface design for mobile phones to meet the interaction requirements of the elderly public [7]. The case study considered the application of the PLu*R*aL [14][15] framework for the design of flexible interfaces. See Figure 1.

The PLu*R*aL is organized in three pillars. The first one is to clarify the differences among the potential users, devices and environments in which the system can be used. Therefore, this step is to clarify the problem and identify possible solutions.

To support the definition of the users' need, elderly people interacting with a commercial version of a phonebook were observed. After that, some cards were filled in. These cards consist in one of artifacts that PLu*R*aL proposes. The aspects listed consider, for instance, eyesight impairment as a physical characteristic, ease of use as a use purpose and user satisfaction regarding the cell phone.

Moreover, the form has a general specification, from the simplest to the most essential characteristics. In the "emotional issues", for example, impatience for the restless users that use the mobile phone, and also the lack of curiosity, and also some user's fear of breaking something new is highlighted. After filling in the cards for different users' profiles, devices and environments where interaction may occur, interaction requirements are specified considering six layers, including semantic and pragmatic requirements.

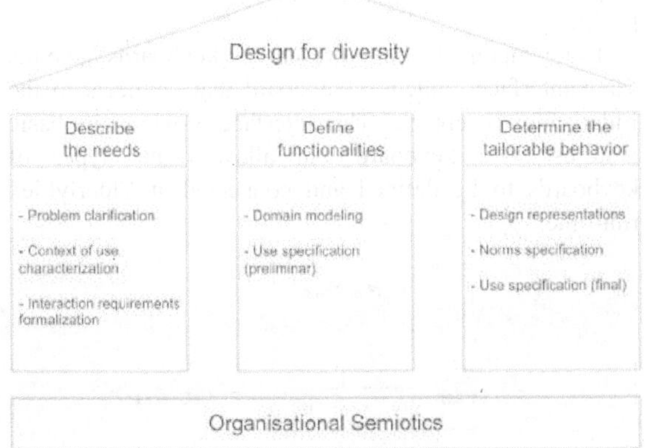

Fig. 1. PLu*R*aL framework [15].

The second pillar is the formalization of functional requirements, which is constructed upon a consistent view of the domain, and that includes rules that oversee the users' behavior. Finally, the third pillar addresses an approach that defines the design of flexible interfaces through the formalization of norms for the tailored behavior of the system, as can be seen in the Table 1.

Considering an approach that emphasizes the Universal Design [1], it is important to design systems that allow access to knowledge and information, without physical and social segregation and also that makes sense to the largest possible number of users according to their different sensory, physical, cognitive and emotional abilities. Thus, it is necessary to approach the elderly users and understand their interaction requirements in order to generate tailored interfaces that meet the preferences and needs of this target audience.

Therefore, unlike conventional applications, the development of a tailor-made system requires designers to consider in their interfaces the different potential uses, including the progress of users and their experience with technology.

In order to meet the many interaction requirements of the elderly public in a flexible approach that is aligned with the Universal Design principles [1], this paper adopted the PLu*R*aL as a reference to guide the design process and OpenCom [10][18] to support the implementation of these flexible interfaces. However, perceiving that the literature emphasizes the interaction problems faced by elderly users and brings little on the various requirements of this population of users, a practical observation activity was performed, to learn more about the interaction diversity of elderly users [7].

The observation of the elderly corroborated with the characterization of the public in question, which guided and enriched the formal interaction requirements with mobile phones in six different aspects, starting with those regarding the physical aspect of the device, up to the impact of this interaction with the real world and the adjustable behavior of a cellular system to meet the interaction requirements of the elderly [7].

For this research, the development of systems that adapt to various needs is highlighted; meeting the requests of different users, distinctive devices and changes in environmental conditions. Given the aforementioned considerations, this study did not consider in its implementation only average needs, but primarily the differences, as described in the next section.

3 Implementation Issues

Using the set of rules that were defined in Section 3, for the design of flexible interfaces for elderly users, we developed a functional prototype which provides the interfaces that can adapt to the older public during run-time. The FlexInterface is a framework that assists in implementing flexible interfaces and was developed by Adaptive Middleware OpenCom [10][18]. With the aid of this resource, it is possible to have mobile phone interfaces that adapt to different older user profiles.

Table 1. Examples of norms representing a the tailorable behavior of a phonebook for different elderly users.

Context			Condition		Tailorable behavior
Device	*Environment*	*Users*	*Functionality*	*Representation*	*Element and mode*
mobile phone	any	elderly with education level less than 4 year	search contact	contact List / index	remove scrollbar
mobile phone	any	elderly with memory deficit	save	form	polychromatic
mobile phone	any	elderly with education level more than 4 year	buttons	save / cancel	more significant
mobile phone	any	Elderly inexperienced in the use of mobile phones	save	form	fewer fields to fill
mobile phone	any	Elderly with physical motor deficit	dial	key	greater distance between the keys
mobile phone	any	elderly experienced in the use of mobile phones	buttons	save / cancel	monochrome
mobile phone	any	elderly deficit of vision	dial	keyboard	increase keyboard

3.1 The FlexInterface Approach

This research adopts a generic approach to build adaptive applications for mobile devices. Thus, [9][18] show that run-time reconfiguration is a key feature to handle the heterogeneous hardware that is inherent in mobile devices.

Thus, by defining the design of flexible interfaces so that they meet the many interaction requirements of the elderly with mobile phones [7] [17], it was possible to develop a software layer called FlexInterface based on the OpenCom component model [4][18].

FlexInterface is generic and has a flexible and extensible architecture that is not dependent on language. It is based on a microkernel, where the functions are incremented upon request. In this context, there is FlexComp, which is a generic and reflective component of FlexInterface that has two receptacles called FlowScreen and ProfileChecker, as shown in Figure 2.

The FlowScreen component is responsible for storing the sequence of actions/screens that a given older user profile possesses, so that it can carry out a task in the device. Thus, with the FlowScreen it is possible, for example, to determine a sequence of specific screens, for older adults with a low level of education, to record a contact in the cell phone's agenda (Example: flow of actions / screens: Record Name > Record Phone > Save Contact).

Additionally, the ProfileChecker component receives the user's interaction data and based on this information, it can set the most appropriate type of profile, and then determine whether it is necessary to reconfigure the FlexInterface components.

3.2 Flexinterface for Older Users

FlexInterface is a framework supported by the development of adaptive interface designs that allows the application to adapt to the needs of the user during his interaction with it. Considering the results of the design process specified in the set of norms (see Table 1), two different profiles for elderly people were selected: seniors with up to fourth-grade schooling (low education) and those with education beyond the fourth grade (high education).

Given the range of requirements, we used FlexInterface to provide flexibility to the interfaces. This meant that, as well as a change of actions/screen flow and of the interface elements, changes in the structure and size of the keyboard were also necessary. In view of this, the ElderlyFlex has been created, which is an extension of the FlexComp of the FlexInterface. This extension includes a new receptacle that can load the keyboard component and is suitable for the profile determined by the ProfileChecker, as shown in Figure 3.

Thus, the keyboard is represented by three components to meet the requirements of elderly users: a) the default, b) for the elderly with low education and c) for those with high education (DefaultKeyboard, LowEducationKeyboard and HighEducationKeyboard, respectively). Depending on how the user interacts with the application, the ProfilerChecker sets the most suitable profile at runtime and enables the ElderlyFlex to connect to the keyboard component that is better suited to the profile.

The components that represent the keyboards have the same interface, called Ikeyboard that connects to the ElderlyFlex receptacle. This interface provides the basic features of a keyboard and allows other types of keyboards to be defined and connected at ElderlyFlex run-time.

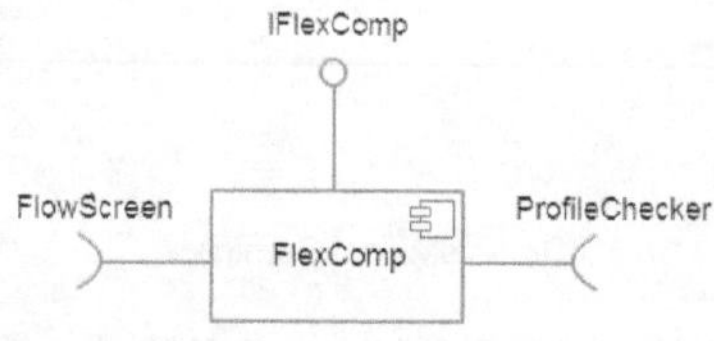

Fig. 2. ElderlyFlex Component and its receptacles.

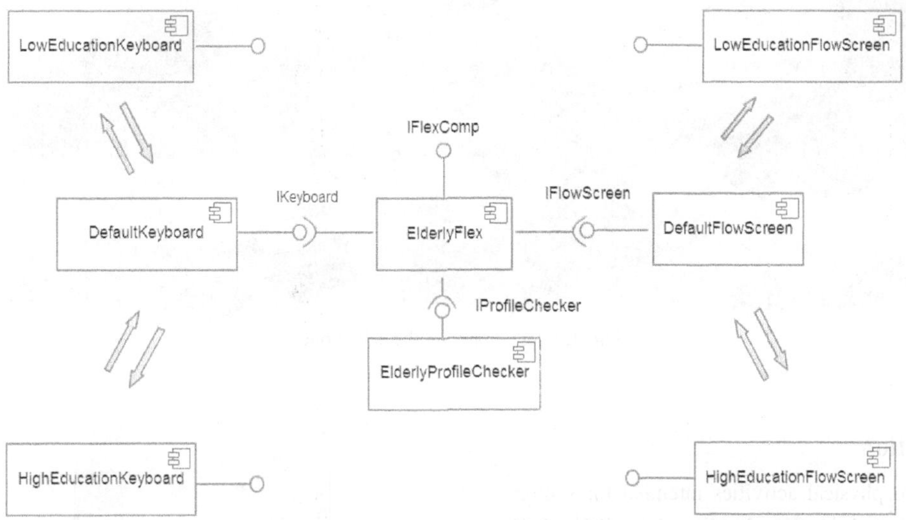

Fig. 3. Our FlexInterface Components along with implemented Plugable Extensions.

The FlexInterface architecture is organized in components. The component which implements the screen flow is called FlowScreen. For this particular scenario, it was possible to explore the reconfiguration of the actions/screen flow. In this case, the ProfileChecker defines the interaction profile and analyzes the use of a new layout with a different action flow that can be used for the interface at the appropriate time.

Thus, owing to the change in the user´s standard interaction, in the scenario in which the default screens/actions flow component (DefaultFlow) is loaded the ProfilerChecker can,for example, set the low education as the most appropriate default for this older user. As a result, the default flow component will be disconnected and destroyed, freeing up the memory; following this, the screens/actions flow component for lower education (LowEducationFlow) will be created and connected to ElderlyFlex, making the application suitable for the new interaction default.

It should be noted that when the screens/actions flow reconfiguration is added, the screens of each flow establish the interface layout formatting, the position of the keys, the colors and the voice access, by strictly adhering to the rules defined by [7][9] and using the PLu*R*aL framework.

4 Evaluation with Elderly People

For the case study, thirty one elderly above 60 years old were observed while interacting with flexible user interfaces for a mobile phonebook.

4.1 Planning

The proposal was applied in places with activities geared to the target audience. Two factors were instrumental in obtaining the sample. (1) find places with activities for the elderly and (2) invite elderly people to interact with a smartphone. Finally, the sample size was determined by considering the locations and the number of users who accepted the invitation. The study was conducted in sessions during 4 days. Thus, the sample has 31 participants.

Hypothesis: based on the different interaction requirements of the elderly with cell phones, we believe it makes sense to develop software solutions that address the existence of specific situations, taking into consideration the standards defined by (Gonçalves, Neris and Ueyama, 2011) for the tailored behavior of the interfaces.

Purpose of the case study: observe and analyze elderly user interaction with smartphone flexible interfaces and verify if there is an interaction improvement, using as a parameter the practice (Gonçalves, Neris and Ueyama, 2011) of elderly interacting with smartphone non-flexible interfaces.

Methodology applied: in order to analyze the elderly user interaction using mobile phone flexible interfaces, a senior user group was invited to participate in a practice using cell phones. **The purpose of the activity was for the users to save a contact in the cell's phonebook and then place a call**. With the data obtained in the observation, it was possible to see whether FlexInterface had facilitated the interaction.

Support Material: To conduct the case study, a Term of Consent, a Profile Survey Questionnaire and a Participant Observation Form were prepared. The Term of Consent elucidated the participants regarding the research objective, the voluntary participation and its scientific nature. The Profile Questionnaire Survey had social and cultural questions that allowed profiling these elderly users. The Participant Observation Form was designed to help observe the user during his interaction with the cell phone.

Devices used: Each elderly people received a smartphone Samsung Galaxy mini with Android with OS version 2.3. The cell phone had the battery charged and with prepaid credits to make calls.

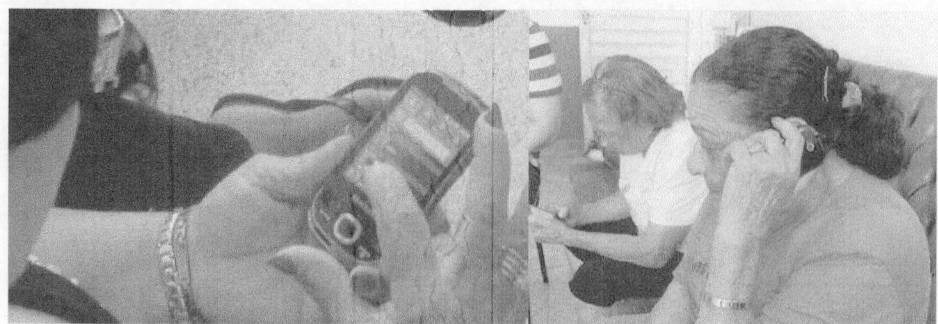

Fig. 4. Interaction with the cell phone.

4.2 Execution

In parallel to physical activities intended for seniors, such as dance and theater, twenty one people were invited to participate in some interaction tasks with the cell phones, as described below.

First, the users were profiled. Furthermore, users who did not have schooling, or never used cell phones, or just used them to answer calls could be identified. However, users with higher or secondary education besides making calls, also send messages, take pictures, edit contacts and play on their phones.

It should also be noted that there was a user who had Alzheimer's, which according to the teacher of the group, was in an advanced stage.

For this application scenario a concept test that allowed adapting the interface to two user profiles was considered, defined by [7][9]: the elderly with low education (studied up to fourth grade), and educated elderly (studied beyond the fourth grade). It was correlated that the low education profile was characterized by having poor mobile phone experience. Thus, for each such user profiles had a type of tailorable interfaces, as seen in Figure 4

Also, these users were shown a paper that had the name and phone number of a person they had to save in the cell's phonebook and then call the number in question, as seen in Figure 5.

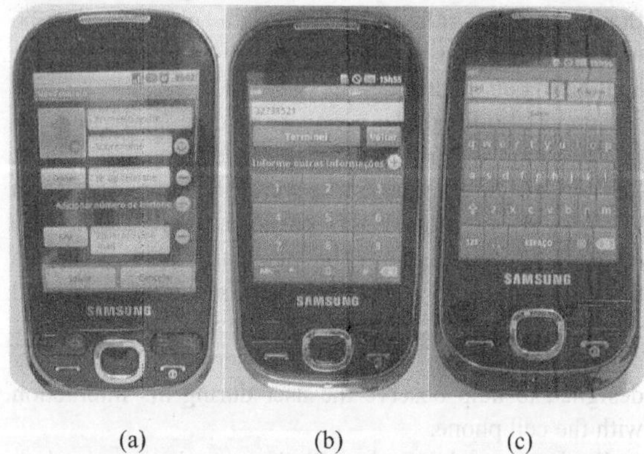

(a) (b) (c)

Fig. 5. Examples of flexible and non-flexible interfaces. (a) Non-flexible interfaces, (b) flexible interfaces for non-educated users, (b) flexible interfaces for educated users.

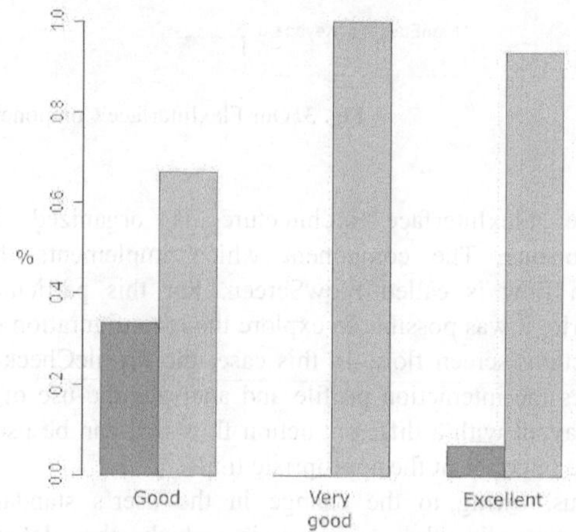

Fig. 6. Satisfaction second task completion With flexible interaction (green = yes, red = no).

While the users performed the task with the cell phone, the researchers conducting the case study filled out an observation form with questions such as: Needed help to start the task? The screen size is adequate for the items? Besides these data, the interaction time was observed and the users' comments were annotated.

After completing the task, the authors performed a discussion session with the elderly people, raising issues related to flexibility, the requirements met and the difficulties encountered during the cell phone interaction.

4.3 Observation Results

For users in the sample, 68% participated in the group that interacted with the flexible interface. Considering both groups, the average age is approximately 69 years (standard deviation of about 8 years). The level of education of the elderly in both groups ranging from no education (19%) pos-graduation (10%), with the majority (45%) is from 1st to 4th grade.

The task described in Section 5 was held for approximately 90% of users. A variable degree of satisfaction (measured by the positive and negative spoken sentences) in the statistical analysis, was classified in levels (Very low: 0 a 19; Low: 20 a 39;

Good: 40 a 59; Very good: 60 a 79 e Excellent: 80 a 100).

Figure 6 and 9 shows the levels of user satisfaction when performing the task with the flexible interface (Figure 6) and non-flexible (Figure 7). Regardless of whether or not completing the task flexible degree of user satisfaction varies from 67% to 100% if the task is non-flexible degree of user satisfaction varies from 33% to 67%.

A variable degree of satisfaction (measured by the positive and negative spoken sentences) in the statistical analysis, was classified in levels (Very low: 0 a 19; Low: 20 a 39; Good: 40 a 59; Very good: 60 a 79 e Excellent: 80 a 100). Figure 6 and 9 shows the levels of user satisfaction when performing the task with the flexible interface (Figure 6) and non-flexible (Figure 7). Regardless of whether or not completing the task flexible degree of user satisfaction varies from 67% to 100% if the task is non-flexible degree of user satisfaction varies from 33% to 67%.

To compare the execution times of task between flexible and non-flexible proposal we applied the Mann-Whitney test. This is a nonparametric test often used when the assumption for applying a parametric test, as for example, normal observations, it is not checked and when the sample size is small. This test compares two sets of data [2].

The Mann-Whitney variable is applied in the runtime task, flexible and non-flexible. In this case, the hypothesis H0 considers that, on average, the two interaction times (flexible and non-flexible) are iqual and H1 is the assumption that the interaction time with the flexible solution is smaller than the interaction time with the non-flexible solution, on average. The hypothesis H_0 is rejected (p-value = 0.001). That is, the runtime task proposed for flexible on average is less than the time of the proposed non-flexible. The graph of Figure 8 shows the behavior of this variable in each situation. Note that 50% of users performed the task in the flexible solution up to 5 minutes and in the non-flexible interface, the task was performed within 10 minutes.

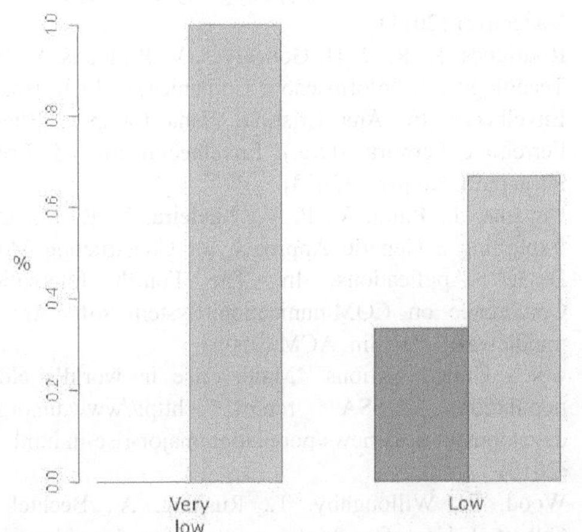

Fig. 7. Satisfaction second task completion without flexible interaction (green = yes, red = no).

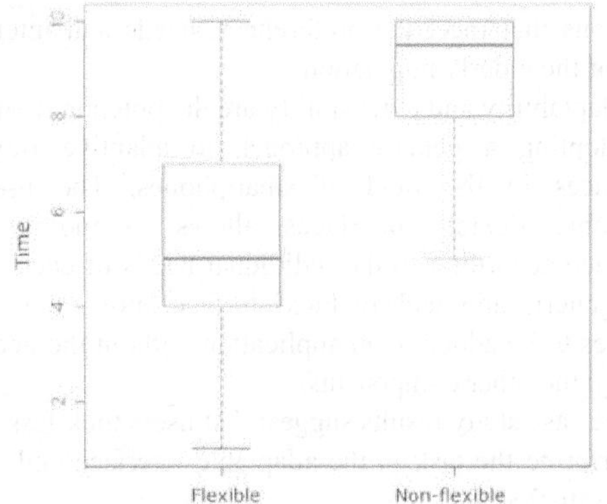

Fig. 8. Boxplot of the task execution times.

Similarly, the Mann-Whitney test is applied to the variable degree of satisfaction of tasks, flexible and non-flexible. In this case, the hypothesis H_0 is equal, on average, between the degrees of satisfaction for both proposed and H_1 is the hypothesis that the degree of satisfaction of the proposal is less flexible than the flexible proposal on average. The hypothesis H_0 is rejected (p-value < 0.001). That is, the satisfaction to execute the task is higher when it is flexible. The graph of Figure 11 shows the behavior of this variable for both tasks. Note that 50% of users of the proposal presented a flexible satisfaction between 83% and 100% for the proposal and there is non-flexible satisfaction between 14% and 29%.

The results suggest that elderly users, while interacting with the flexible user interfaces, took less time to perfume the tasks and were more satisfied.

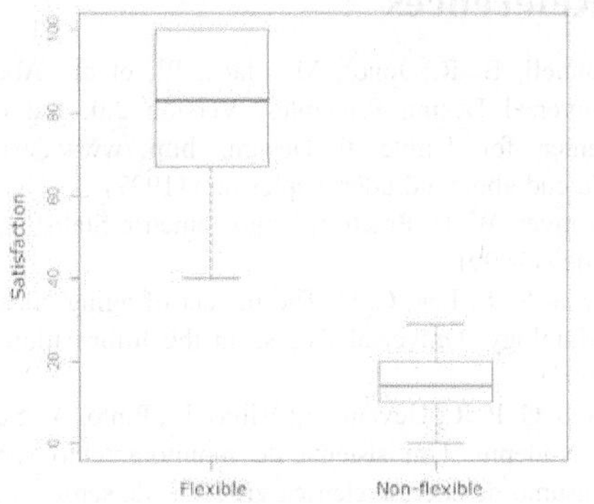

Fig. 9. Boxplot of the degrees of satisfaction, in each situation.

5 Conclusions and Further Work

Population aging is a widespread reality and must be taken into account when designing "future" technologies and services. Technological innovations are not just comfort gadgets, but play an increasingly essential role in people's routines. The elderly, in particular, who represent a significant portion of society can benefit from the use of technological innovations. Therefore, it is important to improve the development process of user interfaces, adding quality to the design of tailorable solutions that meet the preferences, needs and intended uses of the elderly population.

Adaptability and extensibility are the potential benefits of adopting a generic approach to adaptive flexible interfaces in the field of smartphones. The use of adaptable flexible interfaces allows to modify the interface according to the individual needs of each user. The generic approach of FlexInterface allows new user profiles to be added to an application without the need to change the other components.

The case study results suggest that users took less time to performe the task in the adaptable interface and were more satisfied.

In future work, we will better describe user behavior collecting a greater amount of user interaction data (touch screen clicks, keys, duration, etc.). This interaction detail will also allow an element of the screen to be reconfigured independently of the others. For example, if a user takes too long to click the Save key having already entered all the contact data. The color of the key changes so that the user perceives what action he should do to finish the task.

Accordingly, the detailed behavior together with the reconfiguration of interface elements may allow these interfaces to adapt to a wider range of features and skills of elderly users.

6 Acknowledgements

The authors of this paper would like to thank FAPESP for funding their research project (Process ID 2008/05346-4).

7 References

1. Connell, B. R., Jones, M. Mace, R., et al., About UD: Universal Design Principles. Version 2.0. Raleigh: The Center for Universal Design. http://www.design.ncsu.edu/cud/about_ud/udprinciples.htm (1997)
2. Conover, W. U. Practical Nonparametric Statistics. 3a. ed. Wiley (1999)
3. Czaja, S. J.; Lee, C. C. The impact of aging on access to technology. Universal Access in the Information Society (2007)
4. Filho, G. P. R., Ueyama, J.; Villas, L.; Pinto, A.; Seraphini, S. Nodepm: Um sistema de monitoramento remoto do consumo de energia elétrica via redes de sensores sem fio. In: Simpósio Brasileiro de Redes de Computadores e Sistemas Distribuídos (SBRC 2013), 2013, Brasília. Anais do SBRC 2013,v. 31. p. 17-30 (2013)
5. Gonçalves, V. P.; Leite, B. C. S.; Carvalho; J. R.; Gomes, M. D. S. Inspeção de Usabilidade: Um Processo Informatizado para Melhor Satisfazer os Objetivos do Usuário. In: Escola Regional de Informática (ERIN 2010), 2010, Manaus. ISSN: 2178375-6-9-772178-375006. Anais do ERIN 2010, v. 1. p. 157-166 (2010)
6. Gonçalves, V. P.; Neris, V. P. A.; Morandini, M.; Nakagawa, E. Y.; Ueyama, J. Uma Revisão Sistemática sobre Métodos de Avaliação de Usabilidade Aplicados em Software de Telefones Celulares. In: IHC+CLIHC 2011, 2011, Porto de Galinhas. ISBN: 978-85-7669-257-7. Anais do IHC+CLIHC 2011, v. 1. p. 197-201 (2011)
7. Gonçalves, V. P.; Neris, V. P. A.; Ueyama, J. Interação de Idosos com Celulares: Flexibilidade para Atender a Diversidade. In: IHC+CLIHC 2011, 2011, Porto de Galinhas. ISBN: 978-85-7669-257-7. Anais do IHC+CLIHC 2011, v. 1. p. 343-352 (2011)
8. Gonçalves, V. P.; Neris, V. P. A.; Ueyama, J.; Seraphini, S. An Analytic Approach to Evaluate Flexible Mobile Phone User Interfaces for the Elderly. In 14th International Conference on Enterprise Information Systems (ICEIS 2012), 2012, Wrolaw. ISBN: 978-989-8565-12-9. In Proc. ICEIS 2012, v. 3, p. 91-96 (2012)
9. Gonçalves, V. P.; Neris, V. P. A. ; Ueyama, J. ; Seraphini, S. ; Dias, T. C. M. Providing Flexibility to Mobile Devices: An Approach to Meet the Diverse Requirements of the Elderly. Journal of the Brazilian Computer Society, Rio de Janeiro, RJ, Brasil. No prelo (2013)
10. Gonçalves, V. P.; Seraphini, S.; Neris, V. P. A.; Ueyama, J. FlexInterface: a Framework to Provide Flexible Mobile Phone User Interfaces. In 15th International Conference on Enterprise Information Systems (ICEIS 2013), 2013, Angers. In Proc. ICEIS 2013. No prelo (2013)
11. Hellman, R. Universal Design and Mobile Devices. Proceedings of the 4th international conference on Universal access in human computer interaction: coping with diversity. Beijing (2007)
12. Henricksen, K.; Indulska, J. Adapting the web interface: an adaptive web browser. In: Australasian User Interface Conference (AUIC 2001), 4, 2001, Gold Coast, Queensland, Austrália. Proceedings AUIC 2001. Gold Coast, Queensland Austrália: IEEE (2001)
13. MT - Minister of Industry. Learning a Living - First Results of the Adult Literacy and Life Skills Survey. OECD, Paris. http://www.nald.ca/fulltext/learnliv/learnliv.pdf (2005)
14. Neris, V. P. A.; Baranauskas, M. C. C. Making interactive systems more flexible: an approach based on users' participation and norms. In Simpósio de Fatores Humanos em Sistemas Computacionais (IHC 2010): Belo Horizonte (2010)
15. Neris, V. P. A.; Baranauskas, M. C. C. Designing tailorable software systems with the users participation, 09/2012, Journal of the Brazilian Computer Society, v. 18, p. 213-227, Rio de Janeiro, RJ, Brasil (2012)
16. Olwal, A., Lachanas, D., Zacharouli, E. OldGen: Mobile Phone Personalization for Older Adults. In: Conference on Human Factors in Computing Systems (CHI 2011), Vancouver (2011)
17. Rodrigues, K. R. D. H; Gonçalves, V. P.; Neris, V. P. A. Tecnologias de Informação e Comunicação Inclusivas e o Envelhecer. In: Ana Cristina Viana Campos; Efigênia Ferreira e Ferreira. (Org.). Envelhecimento. ed. Érica - Iátria (SP). No prelo (2013)
18. Ueyama, J., Pinto, V. P. V., Madeira, E. R. M., et al. Exploiting a Generic Approach for Constructing Mobile Device Applications. In: The Fourth International Conference on COMmunication System softWAre and middlewaRE, Dublin. ACM (2009)
19. UN - United Nations. 'Major' rise in world's elderly population: DESA report. http://www.un.org/en/development/desa/news/population/major-rise-in.html (2010)
20. Wood, E., Willoughby, T., Rushing, A., Bechtel, L., Gilbert, J. Use of computer input devices by older adults. The Journal of Applied Gerontology (2005)

Semantic Obfuscation and Software Intention

Sheryl Duggins, Frank Tsui, Orlando Karam, and Zoltan Kubanyi
Department of Computer Science and Software Engineering, Southern Polytechnic State University, Marietta, Georgia, 30060 USA

Abstract - *Software protection (SP) research on intellectual property (IP) protection has primarily focused on entertainment media such as games, music and videos, using Digital Rights Management (DRM) systems [1]. Today SP research has broader goals, and includes all types of software with the aim of preventing tampering, reverse engineering and illegal redistribution. In this paper we propose an approach to protect software IP by increasing its complexity to prevent reverse engineering. We introduce four Conjectures for SP through obfuscation and provide rationale for why these four Conjectures make logical sense. We also discuss the results of an experiment verifying our conjectures.*

Keywords: Obfuscation, Security, Software Protection, Software Complexity, Intellectual Property

1 Introduction

While many software solutions are provided through open source, the question of proprietary interest still remains. Much of the key intellectual property is often still hidden and protected. In this paper we explore one potential approach to protect software IP based on complexity. Software complexity [2, 3, 4, 5] has traditionally been studied with the goal of reducing complexity such that software quality and software development productivity may be improved. In this paper we propose the reverse, namely, that increasing complexity may also have some positive effects for the software industry.

With the explosion of outsourcing software development, there came the potential of one's outsourcing partners becoming competitors; if we give them access to certain components, even with source code for some of them, what would stop them from eventually reverse-engineering those components and incorporating them into a competing product? However, the scope of potential adversaries who may try to attack the intellectual property of our software is far greater than one's outsourcing partners. As Colberg and Thomborson [6] identified, there are three types of attack: software piracy, malicious reverse engineering, and tampering.

Software piracy is a $58.8 billion dollar per year industry [7] and is simply the illegal copying and resale of software. Reverse engineering is increasingly being utilized due to the prevalence of tools to aid in this task and the fact that software is frequently distributed in forms like Java bytecode that are easy to decompile and reverse engineer. Tampering deals with the extraction or modification of software that contains encryption keys like e-commerce applications. Therefore, the question of how can we protect the IP of our software component is becoming an issue of much greater importance [8, 1, 9, 10, 11, 12] and can be handled either legally through patents and copyright or technically through techniques like syntactic obfuscation and encryption. We show that protection through increasing the complexity via semantic obfuscation may be another avenue of protection.

This paper will begin with a brief introduction to obfuscation for security, and explore the types of obfuscation used for defenses against malicious attacks. We then present an example to illustrate our approach in the Simple Scenario section. Then we pose a number of Conjectures and demonstrate the merits of these Conjectures. Conjectures (a) and (b) are discussed in the Syntactical and Enumeration Analysis section and Conjectures (c) and (d) are discussed in the Semantic Analysis section. We then discuss the results of an experiment designed to verify our conjectures and follow with conclusions.

2 Obfuscation Overview

The term obfuscation means attempting "to transform a program into an equivalent one that is harder to reverse engineer" [6, p.737]. The earliest work on this was done two decades ago by Cohen [13], who suggested increasing the complexity of a system to a level such that the difficulty of attack is too high to be worth the effort. He called this "security through obscurity" and advocated program evolution as the technique to increase complexity. This was the first of many techniques for syntactic, or code obfuscation. Code obfuscation involves a number of transformations that change a given program into an equivalent program such that obscurity is maximized and execution time is minimized. Researchers today are still developing techniques for syntactic obfuscation, including recent work done on instruction embedding [14] and cloud protection [15]. In addition to software developers using code obfuscation to protect their products from reverse engineering, writers of viruses and malware are also using code obfuscation to hide their work from virus scanners [16]. Regardless of the technique being utilized, all researchers in SP realize that the attacker is human and therefore has creativity and motivation, and thus will eventually be able to circumvent any defense in some period of time [1].

Our work is unique in that we consider transformations based on both the syntax and the semantics of the code. Semantic obfuscation utilizes the fact that the attacker is human, and therefore has a predefined set of background knowledge. This background will determine whether or not the true intention of a program will be discovered and the attack successful. We posit that semantic transformations will take longer to decipher and could therefore be a new direction for SP research.

3 Simple Scenario

We first describe a very simple scenario to demonstrate the approach. Suppose we are asked to write a program that will provide the sum of 1 to n consecutive integers, where n is a non-zero, positive integer. A likely pseudo-code solution, *Solution A*, may be the following.

1. initialize sum, n as integers of value zero
2. initialize counter as integer of value 1
3. ask for and read in the value of n
4. validity check the input value of n
5. if the input n is valid then repeatedly perform { (sum= sum + counter) and increment counter by 1}while the counter is still less than n; then print out sum and terminate
6. if the input n is invalid then issue a message and return to step 3

An alternative approach, and perhaps a less likely one, is to use a mathematical formula to calculate the sum of the numbers 1 through n as follows. Call this *Solution B*.

1. initialize sum, n as integers of zero value
2. ask for and read in the value of n
3. validity check the input value of n
*4. if the input n is valid then compute (sum = (n * (n+1))/2); print out sum and terminate*
5. if the input n is invalid then issue a message and return to step 2

Even for such a simple problem, the two solutions look very different. *Solution A* has 6 statements, and *Solution B* has 5 statements. Let the cardinality of Solution X, |X|, represent the number of statements in Solution X. Then we not only have $|B| \leq |A|$, but also $|A|/|B| = 6/5$, showing that |A| is a 20% increase over |B|. However, this expansion may be worse than it seems. We will see later that if we consider the permutations of 5 statements versus the permutations of 6 statements, the increase is significantly more.

Now consider a third approach, using recursion, to add the numbers 1 through n. Call this *Solution C*.

1. ask for and read in the value of n
2. validity check the input value of n
3. if the input n is zero then return 0; print out sum and terminate
4. if the input n is not equal to zero return n + C(n-1)
5. if the input n is invalid then issue a message and return to step 1

Furthermore, note that the "crux" of the solution is in statement 5 of *Solution A* and is in statement 4 of *Solution B*. Statement 4 in *Solution B* is a straightforward arithmetic computational assignment followed by print and termination. On the other hand, statement 5 in *Solution A* involves a loop which iteratively performs an arithmetic computational assignment while a certain condition is true, then prints and terminates when that condition is no longer true. Let us look at the different types of activities involved in these two statements. Both statements have an arithmetic computation, a print, and a termination. But statement 5 of *Solution A* includes a loop-structural statement with a terminating condition. Thus statement 5 of *Solution A* includes one more computational task type, a loop structure. If we compare both of these two solutions with *Solution C*, we see that statement 4 of *Solution C* involves recursion, which is quite a bit more complicated than a simple loop structure, even though the cardinality of *Solution A* is greater than that of *Solution C*.

In terms of these syntactical measurements, cardinality of solution and number of different computational task types, *Solutions A* and *C*'s source statements, as represented with the pseudo-code, will be considered more complex. If more complex implies its intention is less likely to be discovered, then one might believe that *Solution A* or *C* is the better solution. Thus *Solution A* or *C* may be thought, by some, as more protective of the intent of the solution than *Solution B*. Now, let's review what a perpetrator may do to ascertain the intent of these solutions. One obvious and commonly used procedure is to observe the behavior of the three solutions by feeding different inputs to the solutions, similar to black-box testing approach. For illustrative purpose, we will ignore the small potential problem of integer division by 2 in statement 4 of *Solution B*. Then all 3 solutions will behave alike in terms of what they output. Since all 3 solutions will behave alike with the same inputs, one may conclude that the intent of all solutions will either never be cracked or cracked simultaneously. Under such black-box analysis, the effort required to discover the intent behind the three solutions will essentially be equal. If the pseudo-code or the actual source code were not available, black-box approach may be the only available approach.

Consider the scenario where the source code or the pseudo-code became available (as in by reverse engineering or from a partner). Then would there be a difference in the effort expended for the discovery? According to the earlier syntactical analysis, *Solution A* should be more difficult, or take more effort, to analyze. On the other hand, if one is not familiar with the term (n*(n+1))/2, then statement 4 in *Solution B* may present quite a challenge. Similarly, for those who are unfamiliar with recursion, *Solution C* may be even more challenging. We also note that the variable name, "sum", may be a give-away. Thus we replace the variable name "sum" with some arbitrary, possibly misleading name such as "product." The two respective statements, 5 in *Solution A* and 4 in *Solution B*, would look as follows.

5. if the input n is valid then repeatedly perform { (product = product + counter) and increment counter by 1}while the counter is still less than n; then print out product and terminate

4. if the input n is valid then compute (product = (n * (n+1))/2); print out product and terminate

This purposeful renaming of a variable further from its contextual intent may make statement 4 in *Solution B* even more difficult to analyze. The confusion introduced by this purposeful renaming in statement 5 of *Solution A* may not be as much as that in *Solution B*. But it opens a window into what semantics behind the syntax may bring, and the topic will be discussed in the section on semantic analysis.

We have illustrated several Conjectures with this simple example, and they are presented below.

(a) Cardinality of solution, in terms of number of statements should make a difference in the effort required to discover the real intention.

(b) Syntactical complexity, measured by some volume of syntax whether it is cardinality of solution or number of different operational types, should contribute to the effort needed for discovery of the solution intent or purpose.

(c) Unfamiliar semantics behind a simple syntactical term such as ((n * (n+1)) /2) may be a deterrent to discovery of solution intent.

(d) Picking syntactical terms, such as "product" as opposed to "sum," which have less affinity to the real, semantic intent also contributes as a deterrent to discovery of the real intention.

4 Syntactical and Enumeration Analysis

First, let us explore Conjecture (a) and the impact due to the increase in cardinality of solution or the increase in the number of programming or pseudo-code statements. The simple example above of 5 statements versus 6 statements, without considering the content of each statement, showed an increase of 20% in cardinality of solution. Now, let us consider the permutations of 5 statements. There are 5! different ways the statements may be ordered, of which, there may be several that would suffice as the solution. For example, the order of the last two statements of *Solution A* may be interchanged, and the solution would still be the same. So there is more than one permutation of sequence of statements that would suffice. We, as author of the statements, may keep and hide the real order and then re-order the statements to protect the solution and confuse the perpetrator.

If we employ the reordering of the sequence of statements as one of the methods of obfuscation, then even a small increase in cardinality of the solution may make a large difference. The example of |A|/|B| = 6/5 with a 20% increase is minor compared to 6!/5!. Note that the number of permutations for *Solution A* is 6 times more than the number of permutations for *Solution B*. Thus by increasing the cardinality of solution, one can disproportionately increase the permutations of the statements. For example, we can take *Solution B* and expand it by splitting statement 4 into three statements as follows:

- if the input n is valid, then compute y = n*(n+1)
- sum = y/2
- print out sum and terminate

We can further add one more initialization statement for variable y into *Solution B* and further increase its cardinality. Obviously, there are many more ways to increase the number of statements, resequence and confuse the potential perpetrator.

If the cardinality of solution, |Z|, is x, then adding one more statement to the solution to get |Z| = x+1 would increase the permutations by a factor of x+1. Adding two more statements would increase the permutations by a factor of (x+1)*(x+2) or an order of x^2. Thus the following general proposition may be stated.

- If k more statements are added to a list of source code statements that has cardinality of solution of x, then the number of permutations of those statements increases by an order of x^k.

This is a tremendous increase in the possibilities of confusing the potential code-pirate. Thus we believe Conjecture (a) has a high potential in protecting the intellectual property.

Introducing confusion with additional syntactical terms and unfamiliar terms is one of the primary types of code obfuscation. We have introduced one more variable, y, in the above discussion when we split statement 4 of *Solution B* into three statements. In software engineering, many studies of different complexity metrics [3, 17, 18, 5] exist. A classical one that counts distinct syntactical terms and occurrences of the terms as a contributor to complexity is Halstead's metric. If n is the number of distinct operators and operands and N is the sum of the occurrences of distinct operators and operands, then Halstead's volume is defined as $V=N*(Log_2 n)$. Thus an increase of k new terms increases the Halstead volume to at least $(N+k)*(log_2 n+k)$. We say "at least" because k distinct terms may have more than k occurrences. While this increase is not as dramatic as the increase in permutations of statements, it is still greater than a linear increase in number.

Thus introducing more syntactical terms into the solution also provides more opportunity for confusion. We, thus, believe Conjecture (b) also has a high potential for software protection.

Next we examine Conjectures (c) and (d) via the relation of syntax to the intended semantics.

5 Semantic Analysis

In this section, we explore the relationship of syntax to the intended semantics and the resulting possibility of obfuscation. Hitherto we have focused on the syntax and the enumeration of the syntactical statements except when the term "sum" was purposely changed to "product." Although it was a simple syntactical change and the semantics of the statement in terms of syntactical arithmetic assignment rule was preserved, it was meant to purposely elicit some confusion in semantics.

While Conjectures (a) and (b) dealt with syntactical obfuscation, Conjectures (c) and (d) are related to semantics and intentions. We know from complexity studies and previous work on syntactical obfuscation [1, 2, 4, 5, 6, 13, 14, 17, 18] that adding more terms or introducing misleading terms increases complexity, thus more obfuscation. However, the value of semantic obfuscation is virtually unexplored. We believe that discovering the intention of a piece of code requires not only semantic knowledge, but specific semantic knowledge in the correct background. Therefore, the more difficult statement to analyze in our code solutions is the intention of statement 4 of *Solution B*, if one is not familiar with the mathematics. Thus the interpretation function requires both the semantics of the syntactical terms and the correct background to properly map to the intention as shown below.

Interpretation (semantics, background) → Intention

The semantics of the term "(sum = (n * (n+1))/2);" in statement 4 of *Solution B* can be analyzed by following the syntactical rules which parse the variables, n and sum, and the constant 2 along with the operators of +, *, /, (,), and =. Combining the specific meanings of each token and following the syntactical rules allows us to develop the semantics of the expression. However, even with clear syntactical rules, for those who are unfamiliar with the mathematical equation, it may still not be obvious that the intention here is to add the sequence of integers from 1 through n. So, while the semantics of the syntactical term may be clear and the computational result is correct, the intention behind the semantics may continue to be a mystery. That is, the term (n * (n+1))/2 may still not be clear to a human reader. Thus we further need the concept of interpreting the semantics to intention. In order to determine the intention, we need the "correct" background for the Interpretation function to realize the intention of the semantics as shown in the Figure 1.

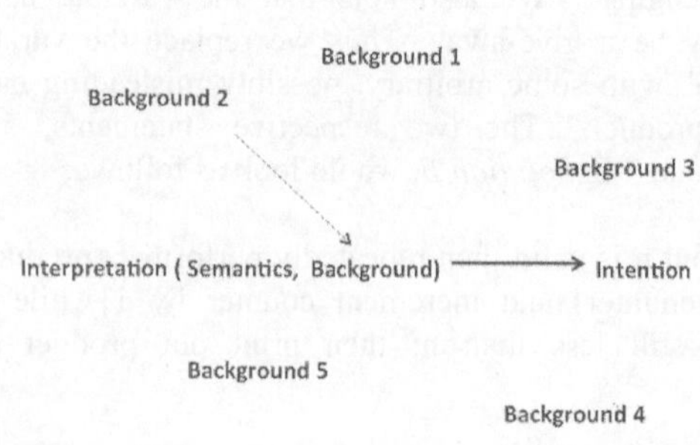

Figure 1: Interpretation and Picking Correct Background

We now turn our attention to statement 5 in *Solution A* above. We realize that, loosely speaking, it has the same intention as statement 4 in *Solution B*, though the semantics are different. It includes the following: "repeatedly perform {(sum= sum + counter) and increment counter by 1} while the counter is still less than n." If we used Halstead's measure of volume to count the number of operators and operands according to $V=N^*(\text{Log}_2\ n)$, then this segment of statement 5 from *Solution A* will certainly have more volume and thus be considered more complex than the "compute (sum = (n * (n+1))/2);" segment in statement 4 of *Solution B*. However, to computer programmers, the intent of this seemingly more complex looping statement is quite clear. That is because when we read pseudo-code, we are already using the background knowledge of computer programming. Within the programming background, the loop statement's intent becomes very clear. Thus to bring confusion (and protect the software), it would be more powerful to move as far away from the real intention as possible. Although for this solution, the background of mathematics and the background of programming would both satisfy the intention; many programmers are less familiar with the background of mathematics. Changing the background and causing confusion on intention is a viable way to bring obfuscation. Conjectures (c) and (d) both address this notion of obscuring the real intent and thus are also high potentials for IP protection.

6 Experimental Results

We developed an experiment to assess the validity of our assumptions and gave the experiment to students of our Software Engineering (SWE) Capstone course, which is taken by both undergraduate and graduate SWE students. These students had taken all of the core software engineering courses as well as all of the required math courses (e.g., Calculus and Discrete Math) required for the BSSWE or the MSSWE. It should be noted that our BSSWE is an ABET accredited program and our MSSWE is based on the Model Curriculum for Graduate Programs in Software Engineering. Thus, all Capstone students had also completed programming courses through Data Structures. While our sample size was small, we believe it was representative of typical practicing software engineers, since about half of the participants were already practicing software engineers and the rest were in the process of looking for a SWE position. Capstone is taken during the final term, so all of the students were graduating at the end of the term. Our sample size was 14, of which 4 were graduate students, and 10 were undergraduate students.

We created two versions of the test, each containing three versions of the code samples; each version contained either the formula-based or the recursive-based solution, followed by the semantically challenged version using "product" instead of "sum", and ending with the straightforward loop version of sum. We built a program to administer the tests and collect the data. The students were presented with the code while a timer was going, and were asked to click "Got it!" when he/she understood what the code was doing. At that point the timer was stopped, and an input box was displayed asking for a brief explanation of what the code was doing. This was repeated for the three code samples, and there was also an option to "Give Up" for each code version. Our findings were very encouraging and supported our intuition on the benefits of semantic obfuscation.

6.1 Findings

Most students took significantly longer trying to decipher the formula-based and the recursive-based solutions, indicating that they did not appear to have the mathematical background needed to understand the semantics of those methods. For the formula-based solution, most students described the intent by simply writing out the code – doing a literal translation; for example: "a (recursive?) method taking in a number, multiplying it by one greater than it and then dividing it by 2." Recall this solution wasn't recursive and due to the lack of semantic knowledge in math, the students missed the true intent, which was successfully obfuscated. In the recursive solution, the common response was similar, again the students typically gave a literal translation of the code; for example: "if n equals to zero then return zero, else return n plus class name n minus 1". The whole idea of recursion was missed, seemingly indicating a lack of semantic knowledge of recursion, and an obfuscation of the true intent of the code. Again it should be mentioned that all students had passed Data Structures, Calculus, and Discrete Mathematics, and should have had the requisite semantic knowledge to understand all of the code samples. So why didn't they figure it out?

We believe that the true intent of the code was obfuscated both by the semantics as well as the students' inability to select the correct background knowledge for the Interpretation function to realize the intention of the semantics. While each student in the experiment had learned the requisite knowledge to be able to decipher the true intention of each code sample, that correct background knowledge was not successfully utilized, and the intention was hidden.

As shown in the table below, the discovery of the true intention in these samples was very low – no one deciphered the formula-based solution and only one student (who was a professional software engineer) figured out the recursive solution. The "product" term also confused the students as the semantics interfered with their understanding, and consequently this code sample took longer than the "sum" version to process and several students came up with the wrong explanation of the intent. For example, a fairly common response was "determines if the product value is equal to the int", which means the students were unable to figure out the true intention due to the semantic interference caused by the term "product". This was precisely what we were expecting to happen, and it illustrates the potential of semantic obfuscation for IP protection. Finally, the students were familiar with the straightforward loop structure that had no obfuscation since the term "sum" was used. Consequently this code sample yielded the shortest time for comprehension as well as the greatest accuracy of explanation and intention.

While this was an informal experiment, it was certainly encouraging enough that we are planning on a more formal experiment in our Usability Lab with a larger pool of students and a more thorough set of tools. It need also be mentioned that to utilize this style of obfuscation in a real-world setting, one would need to use automated tools to facilitate the semantic obfuscation: tools capable of inserting semantic obfuscation as well as reverting back to the original code.

Table 1: Experimental Results

Code Sample	% Correct	Time Range in Sec.s	Mean in Sec.s	Rationale
Version 1				
Recursion	20	7-33	9	Lacking math semantics background
Prod Loop	40	6-63	25.8	Semantic obfuscation of "product"
Sum Loop	100	8-18	11.8	Known syntax & correct background
Version 2				
Formula	0	8-138	50	Lacking math semantics background
Prod Loop	40	9-61	33	Semantic obfuscation of "product"
Sum Loop	80	5-36	9.6	Known syntax & correct background

While this was an informal experiment, it was certainly encouraging enough that we are planning on a more formal experiment in our Usability Lab with a larger pool of students and a more thorough set of tools. It need also be mentioned that to utilize this style of obfuscation in a real-world setting, one would need to use automated tools to facilitate the semantic obfuscation: tools capable of inserting semantic obfuscation as well as reverting back to the original code.

7 Summary and Conclusions

Software complexity study and the desire to simplify software originated from the needs of reducing development effort and reducing error and defect rates in software. In this paper we explored the reverse; we looked at introducing complexity and the potential leveraging of complexity to protect our intellectual property. Four Conjectures for protecting our software through obfuscation were introduced. We explored and provided rationale of why these four Conjectures make logical sense and should be considered for further formal experiments. We believe that complexity, especially used with semantic obfuscation, may be considered a positive tool besides the legal channels for protecting our software intellectual property. Our Conjectures were also demonstrated by the results of our student experiment.

8 References

[1] C. Colberg, J. Davidson, R. Giacobazzi, Y. X. Gu, A. Herzberg, and F. Wang. Toward Digital Asset Protection, IEEE Intelligent Systems, November/ December 2011.

[2] J. M. Bieman and B. K. Kang, "Measuring Design-Level Cohesion," IEEE Transactions on Software Engineering, vol. 24, no. 2, February, 1998.

[3] M. H. Halstead, Elements of Software Science, Elsevier, 1977.

[4] R. Subramanyan and M.S. Krishnan, "Empirical Analysis of CK Metrics for Object-Oriented Design Complexity: Implications for Software Defects," IEEE Transactions on Software Engineering, vol. 29, no 4, April 2003.

[5] E. J. Weyuker, "Evaluating Software Complexity Measures," IEEE Transactions on Software Engineering, vol.14, no. 9, September 1988.

[6] C. Colberg and C. Thomborson, Watermarking, Tamper-Proofing, and Obfuscation – Tools for Software Protection, IEEE Transactions on Software Engineering, vol 28, no 8, August 2002.

[7] Business Software Alliance, Eighth Annual BSA Global Software 2010 Piracy Study, May 2011. Portal.bsa.org/globalpriacy2010/downloads/study_pdf/2010_BSA_Piracy_Study-Standard.pdf , accessed March 2012.

[8] C. Colberg, CSc 620 lecture notes, http://www.cs.arizona.edu/~colberg/Teaching/620/2002/Handout_13.ps retrieved February, 2012.

[9] E. S. Freibrun, "Intellectual Property Rights in Software: What They Are and How the Law Protects Them," http://www.freibrun.com/articles/articl2.htm, accessed 2012.

[10] Software and Information Industry Association, http://www.siia.net, accessed 2011.

[11] U.S. Department of Justice, Report of the Department of Justice's Task Force on Intellectual Property, October 2004. http://www.justice.gov/criminal/cybercrime/IPTaskForceReport.pdf, accessed 2011.

[12] M.H. Webbink, "A New Paradigm for Intellectual Property Rights In Software," Duke Law & Technology Review, May, 2005, http://www.law.duke.edu/journals/dltr/articles/2005dltr0012.html, accessed 2012.

[13] F. Cohen, "Operating System Protection through Program Evolution", 1992. https://all.net/books/tech/evolve.pdf , accessed March 2012.

[14] C. LeDoux, M. Sharkey, C. Miles, and B. Primeaux, "Instruction Embedding for Improved Obfuscation," in Proceedings of the ACM SE 2012, Tuscaloosa, Alabama, 2012.

[15] M. Hataba and A. El-Mahdy, "Cloud Protection by Obfuscation : Techniques and Metrics," Proceedings of the 2012 Seventh Intenational Conference on P2P, Parallel, Grid, Cloud and Internet Computing, Victoria, Canada, November 12 – 14, 2012.

[16] A. Balakrishnan and C. Schulze, "Code Obfuscation Literature Survey," http://pages.cs.wisc.edu/~arinib/writeup.pdf , retrieved May 2013.

[17] T.J. McCabe, "A Complexity Measure," IEEE Transactions on Software Engineering, vol 2, no 4, December 1976.

[18] F. Tsui, O.Karam, S. Duggins, and C. Bonja, "On Inter-Method and Intra-Method Object-Oriented Class Cohesion, International Journal of Information Technologies and System Approach, 2(1), June 2009.

Simulation Software Generation using a Domain-Specific Language for Partial Differential Field Equations

K.A. Hawick and D. P. Playne
Computer Science, Massey University, North Shore 102-904, Auckland, New Zealand
email: {k.a.hawick, d.p.playne }@massey.ac.nz
Tel: +64 9 414 0800 Fax: +64 9 441 8181

April 2013

ABSTRACT

Domain-specific language techniques can considerably lower the software development effort and time required for problems in computational science and engineering. We describe our domain specific language for field-based partial differential equation simulations and show how it can address a whole family of such problems. Our system requires minimal effort to generate C++ software for a new equation model, but also dramatically lowers the effort needed to generate code in a different output language. We report on the lines of code for several example problems discuss software engineering implications of this automatic code generation approach.

KEY WORDS
generative programming; DSL; partial differential equation.

1 Introduction

Many problems in computational science and engineering can be formulated in terms of partial differential equations (PDEs). A common simulation pattern involves the time-integration of an initial value model where the system is defined on a spatial mesh with spatial calculus operators in the equation. Although the mathematical and numerical methods for solving such problems are well known, it is still a tedious and error-prone task to write correct and efficient software for a new problem.

Although a great deal of techniques [1] are known for building optimising compilers [12, 15, 30] the goal of automatic parallelising compilation remains elusive. Some important progress was made for some data-parallel constructs [5, 29]. However it seems likely that there are some general problems that compiler generators will probably never be able to solve completely, without programmer assistance [32]. More optimistically however it is feasible to look at some specific classes of application domain problems and use application domain-specific languages and tools to address them.

In this paper we report on how modern compiler-level tools and technology can be used to make a generative programming system that can create fast and readable data-parallel software for solving some PDE based problems. Four example PDEs that fit into the example category are introduced - the Heat, Cahn-Hilliard, Ginzburg-Landau and Spatial Lotka-Volterra equations. These PDEs are first-order in the time derivative but contain second- or fourth-order spatial calculus operators. Example illustrations of the Cahn-Hilliard, Ginzburg-Landau and Lotka-Volterra equations are shown in Figure 1. We explain how a plain ASCII expression of these mathematical equations can be parsed and used to generate software in a language like C or C++. This is our domain-specific language for formulating field-based PDE applications.

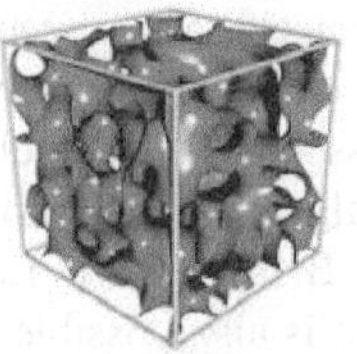
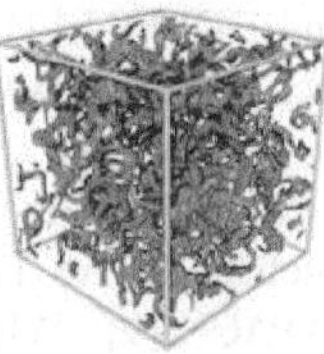

Figure 1: Three-dimensional segments of field solutions of the Cahn-Hilliard (left), Ginzburg-Landau (center) and Lotka-Volterra (right) equations.

We show how a relatively minor change to the mathematical specification of the equation allows a whole new code to be generated relatively trivially. These approaches combined in saving on: programmer time; testing effort; and production run time. This system supports the investigation of whole families of problems that would hitherto have taken a lot longer to tackle.

A number of software systems and algebraic problem solving environments allow users to automatically generate solver source code in standard programming languages such as Fortran [10, 11, 23]. A number of systems also address the problem of generating parallel code [35]. Research projects [3, 24] and commercial problem solving systems such as Matlab [31] or Mathematica [34] also support code generation from a mathematical formulation of equations. We are interested however in combining all these.

Although there are a number of mathematical and numerical approaches such as finite-elements that can be expressed using this approach to code generation, we focus in this paper on regular mesh problems that can be solved using finite-difference methods. We defer a detailed discussion on different numerical time integration techniques and different stencil operators for the spatial calculus to another work [28].

The idea of generating PDE solver software is not new. As long ago as 1970, Cardenas and Karplus experimented with manually written programs that combine both translation and generation in a single *ad hoc* stage [8] partial differential equation language (PDEL) based on PL/1 syntax. Some important work is being done by Logg and collaborators on the semi-automatic generation of **Finite Element** algorithms. The FENICS [20] and DOLFIN [21] projects take a somewhat different approach to the one we do, making more heavy use of linear algebraic methods and the associated separately-optimised software for solving linear algebra and matrix-oriented problems such as BLAS [13], BLACS [14], LAPACK [4] and ScaLAPACK [9]. While it is also possible to formulate the Finite Difference methods that we employ using full matrix methods too, we focus here on direct methods and formulations for regular meshes that do not need full matrices and that make use of explicit sparse data storage methods. This allows us the luxury of worrying less about storage space for the spatial calculus and thus being able to experiment more readily with higher-order time-integration methods which themselves require multiple copies of the field data for intermediate fractional time steps.

In this article we discuss the general form of applicable partial differential field equation problems in Section 2. The structure and operation of our parser and code generator is given in Section 3. We present some generated code examples and associated run-time performance data in Section 6 and discuss associated issues in Section 7. We offer some conclusions in and ideas for future work in Section 8.

2 Solving Field PDEs

Many interesting problems in physics, chemistry, biology and other areas of science can be formulated as partial differential field equations that evolve over time. These formulations fall into the general pattern:

$$\frac{du(\mathbf{r},t)}{dt} = \mathcal{F}(u,\mathbf{r},t) \quad (1)$$

where the time dependence is first order and the spatial dependence in the right hand side is often in terms of partial spatial derivatives such as $\nabla_x, \nabla_y, \nabla_z, \nabla^2, \nabla^2 \cdot \nabla^2, ...$ Some well-known problems that fit this pattern are:

The **Heat equation** which models how heat is distributed through a material over time. The heat distribution can be defined in terms of the scalar field u and α which is a positive constant representing the thermal diffusivity.

$$\frac{\partial u}{\partial t} = \alpha \nabla^2 u \quad (2)$$

The **Cahn-Hilliard equation** [7, 17] which models a quenching binary allow and is expressed in terms of a scalar field u:

$$\frac{\partial u}{\partial t} = \mathrm{m}\nabla^2\left(-\mathrm{b}u + \mathrm{U}u^3 - \mathrm{K}\nabla^2 u\right) \quad (3)$$

where it is usual to truncate the series in the free energy [6] at the u^4 term, although some work has used up to the u^6 term [33].

The **Time-Dependent Ginzburg Landau equation** [22] which can be used to describe the macroscopic behavior of superconductors can be defined in terms of a complex scalar field u:

$$\frac{\partial u}{\partial t} = -\frac{p}{i}\nabla^2 u - \frac{q}{i}|u|^2 u + \gamma u \quad (4)$$

The **Lotka-Volterra** equation is often written as:

$$\frac{d\mathbf{P}}{dt} = \mathcal{F}(\mathbf{P}) \quad (5)$$

where $\mathbf{P}$ might be vector of several population variables for predator and prey species and $\mathcal{F}$ might incorporate a matrix of cross-coupling terms and spatial calculus operators. This equation can be formulated as a two-species predator-prey model using the Laplacian operator for spatial coupling [16]. This can be defined as:

$$\begin{aligned} \frac{du_0}{dt} &= D_0\nabla^2 u_0 + Au_0 - Bu_0u_1 \\ \frac{du_1}{dt} &= D_1\nabla^2 u_1 + Du_0u_1 - Cu_1 \end{aligned} \quad (6)$$

where u_0 is the prey population and u_1 is the predator population.

In some cases the full details of the right-hand sides of these sort of equations are known and are immutable parts of the field model. In other cases a family of equations can be generated by using different expansions or approximates. A good example is the Cahn-Hilliard equation where the free-energy term is usually approximated by a polynomial with second and fourth order terms, but alternatives such as including higher order terms make sense but are hard (tedious and error-prone) to implement.

A powerful idea to address implementation difficulties is therefore a software tool that can help generate lines of code in a standard programming language like C, C++, D, Java, Fortran, that implements one of the standard numerical approaches to solving the equation in question. There are some well known lines of approach to solving the numerical integration in time - storing the state of the entire model field that expresses the right hand side and applying second order methods such as the midpoint method (aka second-order Runge-Kutta) or higher-order methods such as the well-known Runge-Kutta Fourth-order method as appropriate.

3 Parser and Generator Structure

In this section we describe the various components of our generative programming prototype - known as "Simulation Targeted Automatic Reconfigurable Generator of Abstract Tree Equations (STARGATES)." This system assembles simulation code of partial-differential field equation(s) from different simulation components. It is important to make the distinction between the model, the simulation and the implementation. The model is the equation(s) and the parameters of the model. The simulation is the specific combination of a model and the methods used to simulate it - the lattices, spatial stencils, boundary conditions and numerical methods. The implementation is the target specific code that can be compiled into machine code to compute that simulation.

The system will take the different components of the simulation and use them to construct an abstract "simulation" object that contains all the relevant information. To construct this object all the components must be combined together in an appropriate way. The stencils used by the equation must be supplied and matched with the type of lattice the simulation is using. The integration method must be combined with the equation to form the calculations of each step of the integration. The final combination of components forms the simulation object.

This object can be then queried by an output generator to produce code that performs the simulation using a desired target programming language. Some additional configuration information about the simulation must also be supplied to define properties of the simulation such as system size, parameter values etc. Different output generators will produce different code which represents the different possible implementations of the same simulation. The architectural structure of the generative system prototype is shown in Figure 2.

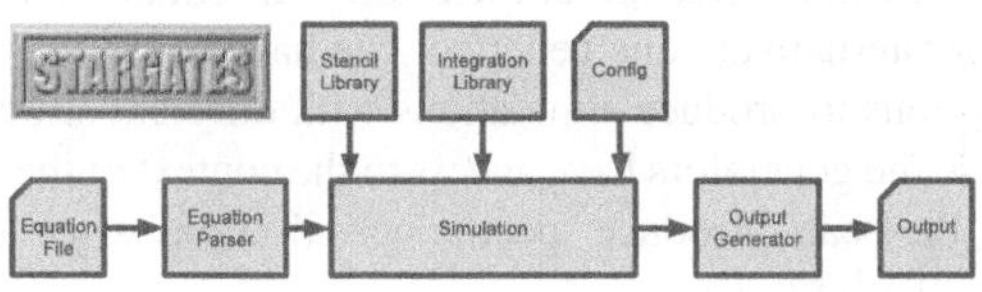

Figure 2: Structure and logical flow of STARGATES. The system takes an equation description and a configuration file as input and the output generator produces an output file.

A major advantage of this approach is the ability to separate the simulation from the implementation. The simulations can be defined and experimented with separate from the specific code used to compute them. Migrating simulations to a new computing architecture is as simple as writing a new output generator. When developing a new simulation it is simply the equation that must be defined which can make use of the other components and immediately make use of optimised parallel code. In this present paper we focus on the generation of CPU serial C/C++ code but other output generators that produce code using GPU CUDA, MPI, Pthreads and Intel's Threading Building Blocks have also be written. Additional generators could also be written to produce implementations using FORTRAN, OpenMP, OpenCL etc.

4 Equation Parser

The system allows the user to write the equation(s) that define the model in a mathematical form using ASCII. The **Equation Parser** reads this ASCII and constructs a tree representing the equation. The equation tree will contain all the information required by the rest of the system to generate output code for that simulation. Parsing mathematical equations is a potentially open ended problem but as indicated we are able - for our prototype tool - to restrict the equation forms we are addressing to some specific patterns, and make the problem tractable.

To write the **Equation Parser**, we have made use of the compiler generator technology ANTLR [25]. ANTLR is a relatively modern tool building upon historical developments [2] including the well known lexing/parsing tools: lex/yacc [19] and flex/bison [18, 26]. ANTLR allows us to specify a simple grammar from which ANTLR will automatically generate a Lexer and a Parser. The grammar shown here supports the declaration of parameters, lattices and equations with simple mathematical operators $+, -, *, /$. The advantage of using ANTLR is that it is very easy to extend and change the grammar as necessary. A simple version of the grammar is shown in Listing 1.

Listing 1: Simple equation ANTLR grammar.

```
DIGIT        : '0'..'9';
CHAR         : 'a'..'z'|'A'..'Z'|'_';
ID           :  CHAR (CHAR|DIGIT)*;
NUM          : (DIGIT)+ ('.' (DIGIT)+ )?;
DERIVATIVE   : 'd/dt';
FUNC         : ('ABS' | 'SQRT' |    );
...

file         : (statement)+ EOF!;
statement    : (declaration | equation);
declaration  : ID '[' ']' ID ';'
             | ID ID ';' ;
equation     : DERIVATIVE ID '=' additive ';' ;
additive     : mult (('+' ^ | '-' ^) mult)*;
multi        : unary (('*' ^ | '/' ^) unary)*;
unary        : atom
             | MINUS atom;
atom         : NUM
             | ID
             | '(' additive ')'
             | ID '{' additive '}' ;
```

This grammar is sufficient to parse equations such as the Cahn-Hilliard model (see equation 3) in the form:

```
floating M;
floating B;
```

```
floating U;
floating K;
floating[] u;
d/dt u =M*Laplace{(-B*u+U*(u*u*u)-K*Laplace{u})};
```

where the "equation" start-point defines a first order time-differential equation, whose right hand side has a number of spatial calculus operators as well as algebraic combinations of the fundamental field and parameters.

This equation is processed by the ANTLR generated parser which will construct a tree representing the model. This tree includes the types, parameters, fields and equations of the model. For example the tree created for the Cahn-Hilliard equation (See equation 3) is shown in Figure 3.

After the initial equation is parsed, the tokens are converted into a tree which can then be parsed by a ANTLR tree parser. This tree parser constructs a tree representing the equation out of objects that are each equivalent to a component of the equation (parameters, operators, stencils etc). Given the example of the Cahn-Hilliard equation (See equation 3), when this equation is parsed, the ANTLR tree parser generates the tree shown in Figure 3.

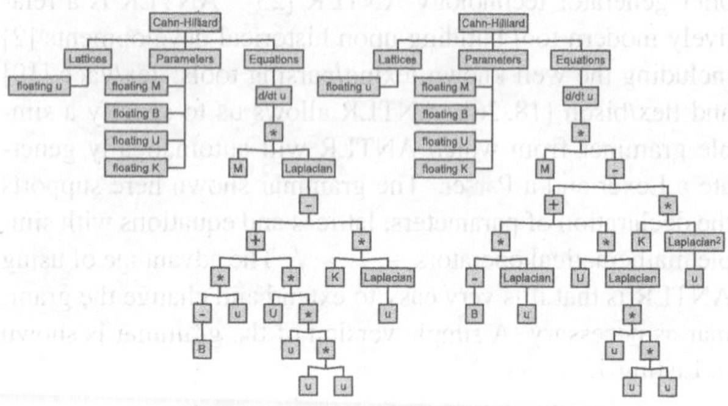

Figure 3: Two equation trees representing the Cahn-Hilliard Equation. The initial tree created by the ANTLR parser (left) and the tree after it has been rearranged by the Stencil Library to contain no nested stencil nodes (right).

The tree contains all of the information about the equation needed by the system. To form a simulation objection, this equation tree must be combined with an integration method. However, before this is done, the stencils used by the equation must first be resolved. The **Stencil Library** provides the necessary stencils and in some cases may manipulate the equation tree. This is best performed before the tree is combined with an integration method.

This equation parser is capable of processing equation files that contain multiple fields and multiple equations. This is necessary for equations such as the Lotka-Volterra model which has a field for each of the multiple species populations and equations governing their interactions. The spatial predator-prey form of the Lotka-Volterra model can be described in ASCII form as follows:

Algorithm 1 C++ code structure template.

generate integration function
for all *stage* in Steps **do**
  generate iteration code
  generate neighbour access code
  for all *equation* in *stage* **do**
    traverse *equation* to **generate** calculation
  end for
end for
generate function end

generate main function
  generate parameter allocation
  generate parameter initialisation
  generate lattice allocation
  generate lattice initialisation code
  generate time step iteration code
  generate call integration function
  generate end iteration code
generate main end

```
float A;
float B;
float C;
float D;
float D0;
float D1;
float[] u0;
float[] u1;

d/dt u0 =  A*u0 - B*u0*u1 + D0 * Laplace{u0};
d/dt u1 = -C*u1 + D*u0*u1 + D1 * Laplace{u1};
```

5 Output Generator

The output generators are responsible for querying the simulation object and creating language-specific output code. These generators glean the information they need from the simulation object and combine that information with language specific code templates to produce an implementation of the simulation. There is very little restriction placed by the system on output generators. Multiple generators can be created to target the same language but use different simulation structures or alternatively one generator can have many configuration options to produce simulations with different structures. Because the generators have access to the context of the simulation, they can introduce specific optimisations when appropriate.

Code generators can be constructed for many different sequential and parallel programming languages [27]. The generators will differ in terms of the instructions they produce and the general code structure. The syntax of the generators will depend on the target language, but generators based on the same syntax will often share similar components. For example, both the C++ and CUDA generator use C-style syntax so several elements of the target code will be the same. The high-level structure of the code will be dependent on the type of implementation they are producing. The example code structure template for a C++ implementation is shown in Algorithms 1.

The generators also have many operation templates which are populated with data from the simulation object to perform operations required by the generator. These operations include - allocating memory for a lattice, initialising parameters, calling functions etcetera. Some examples of the instructions produced by this output generators are shown in Section 6.

The advantage of this approach is that the front-end parsing and simulation object construction for the simulations remains the same regardless of the output generator used. When a new architecture or language is released, a new generator can be written that will allow all existing simulations to be migrated to make use of that new architecture or language. This makes it much easier to adopt a new language or architecture without the need to rewrite the entire simulation base. This is a far easier and more extensible programming model than maintaining separate code versions for each simulation and computing architecture.

6 Results

The system currently has a number of output code generators that can produce target code of simulations for a number of computing architectures. The main code generator discussed in this work is for single-threaded C++ code generation. However, the system can also generate code for multi-core CPUs using TBB or pThreads, for distributed machines using MPI and for Tesla, Fermi or Kepler generation GPU devices using CUDA.

Listing 2: Generated code sample produced by the C++ generator.

```
int main(){
  float *u, *u0, *u1, *u2;
  u = new float[Y * X];
  ...
  for(int t = 0; t < 1024; t++){
    rk2(u0, u1, u2, h);
    swap(u0, u2);
  }
  memcpy(u, u0, Y * X * sizeof(float));
}

void rk2(float *u0,float *u1, float *u2,float h){
  for(int iy=0; iy < Y; iy++) {
    for(int ix=0; ix < X; ix++) {
      ...
    }
  }
  ...
}
}
```

Here we present the code generated by the two output generators for the Cahn-Hilliard equation (see Equation 3). One of the generators builds a single-threaded C++ program and the other generates a CUDA program optimised for Fermi architecture GPUs. Sample generated code can be seen in Listing 2 which shows the general structure of main function and integration method for a C++ simulation of the Cahn-Hilliard model using the Runge-Kutta 2nd order integration method. The generator creates and initialises the main mesh of the equation u. It also creates the three meshes required by the RK2 method $u0$, $u1$ and $u2$. Also shown in Listing 2 is the function to perform the integration steps, in this code both of the RK2 steps are performed in one C++ function.

Since both the C++ and CUDA generator stages use C-like syntax, the code to perform the actual equation is the same for both generators. This code (with whitespace formatted for ease of reading) is shown in Listing 3. This code calculates the change in one spatial cell for the Cahn-Hilliard equation $u(x, y)$. We have tried to make the variable names and code layout closer to human readable choices than some code generators do since the programmer may decide to adopt the generated code and include it in a code package that is subsequently human-maintained rather than regenerated.

Listing 3: The same equation calculation code generated by both the C++ and CUDA generators.

```
M*(
-B*(            u_ym1x      +
     u_yxm1 + (-4*u_yx) + u_yxp1 +
                u_yp1x) +
U*(         (u_ym1x*u_ym1x*u_ym1x)   +
            (u_yxm1*u_yxm1*u_yxm1)   +
            (-4*u_yx*u_yx*u_yx)+
            (u_yxp1*u_yxp1*u_yxp1)   +
           (u_yp1x*u_yp1x*u_yp1x))   -
K*(              u_ym2x   +
      (2*u_ym1xm1) + (-8*u_ym1x) + (2*u_ym1xp1) +
u_yxm2 +(-8*u_yxm1) + (20*  u_yx) + (-8*u_yxp1)
+ u_yxp2 +
      (2*u_yp1xm1) + (-8*u_yp1x) + (2*u_yp1xp1) +
                  u_yp2x))
```

One of the major advantages of a code generator is the reduced effort required to produce an implementation of a simulation. Programmer effort is difficult to measure but the number of lines of code required to define a simulation can be used as an approximation. To define a simulation the programmer must define both the model (fields, parameters and equations) and the configuration (parameter values, integration method, lattice geometry etcetera). Table 1 shows the number of lines of code defined by the programmer (definition) and the number of generated lines of code for a number of different simulations.

The code that the generator produces obviously does not contain every possible optimisation as humans are usually much better at identifying which optimisations are applicable for particular simulations. However, if the pattern of possible optimisation is identified, it could subsequently be incorporated into an output generator. The generator can identify optimisations that cannot easily be found by compilers due to the higher level of information available to the generator.

	Heat		Cahn-Hilliard		Ginzburg-Landau		Lotka-Volterra	
Definition (lines)	12		18		21		23	
Generated Code (lines)	C	CUDA	C	CUDA	C	CUDA	C	CUDA
2D Rectilinear Euler	50	55	69	80	71	86	72	89
2D Rectilinear RK2	71	79	106	120	101	120	102	123
2D Rectilinear RK4	127	141	234	238	189	216	190	219
2D Hexagonal Euler	56	61	83	94	79	94	80	97
2D Hexagonal RK2	83	91	134	148	117	136	118	139
2D Hexagonal RK4	157	171	292	312	233	260	234	263
3D Rectilinear Euler	61	66	94	102	86	101	87	104
3D Rectilinear RK2	90	98	153	167	126	145	127	148

Table 1: Lines of code defined by the programmer compared to the number of lines of code generated by the system.

7 Discussion

The optimisations that allow the hand-written simulations to perform faster could be incorporated into the output generator and are not fundamental changes to the model. It is possible to build optimisations into the output generators that are either always applied or applied to some simulations based on input from the configuration file. Even so, these simple output generators still produce code that performs efficiently and have performance comparable to hand-written code.

This generative programming system can significantly accelerate the process of simulation development. By allowing the user to simply define a new model and construct it using existing components, the development effort of creating a simple implementation and optimising it is significantly reduced.

The design of this system allows language-specific optimisations to be incorporated with ease. Because the output generators are purely responsible for traversing the simulation tree and generating output code, optimisations can be added without affecting any other part of the system. This means that if a method of identifying when an optimisation is applicable (or an option is added to the configuration file) then it can be included into the generated code.

In general our design philosophy is to defer decisions that the programmer might want to make about details for a particular "run" as far down the generation process as possible, and associated with this, to separate as far as possible the different specifications. So the equation parsing language should be separable from the particular equation parameters, and the code generation options and optimisation choices are also separated as much as possible. We have been through various early stage software prototypes where a monolithic architecture was used and as we have learned more about the processes involved we have managed to aim at a cleaner more separable set of components for our system.

ANTLR has helped considerably in providing a higher level parser generator apparatus. In particular the concept of separating out the tree walker generation stages is much easier using ANTLR.

We have deferred discussion of code generation for parallel platforms to [28]. There is scope for applying the approach we have outlined to many other members of this class of time-integrated partial differential equation fierld equations.

8 Conclusions and Future Work

In summary, we have described how a staged parser and tree-walking code generator can produce device agnostic software for modern platforms, where the software is optimized, human-readable and maintainable. This is possible as we have focused on a very specific form of application domain problem - solving regular partial differential equations using finite difference equations. The speed performance of the generated code is very close to that attainable by expert hand-generated software but with considerably less time required to develop and test a new equation or indeed to deploy for a new platform.

One important outcome of this work for us is the ability to investigate whole families of problems rather than having to focus on just one hand-coded one. Problems like the Cahn-Hilliard equation or the Time-Dependent Ginzburg-Landau equation have a number of choices embedded in them that, while compactly expressible in mathematics, lead to quite different software formulations. A tool like this opens up a number of feasible investigations in computational physics that would otherwise be quite time consuming - and in the past have consumed a whole PhD-worth of research effort each in terms of coding, testing and general experimental effort.

A more general outcome of this work is the software architecture for scientific problem domain specific languages that can be parsed and can have output code generated in a number of different target languages and associated platforms. We note the promise of modern compiler generator tools such as ANTLR and the benefits of using them rather than attempting a monolithic single stage parser-generator tool.

The domain-specific language approach is a powerful one for lowering the software engineering effort required for investigating problems in computational science. There is considerable scope for expanding the simulation model-driven approach we have taken to other problems and platforms.

References

[1] Aho, A.V., Sethi, R., Ullman, J.D.: Compilers Principles, Techniques, and Tools. Addison-Wesley (1986), iSBN 0-201-10194-7

[2] Aho, A.V., Ullman, J.D.: Principles of Compiler Design. No. ISBN 0-201-00022-9, Addison-Wesley (1977)

[3] Benson, T., Milligan, P., McConnell, R., Rea, A.: A knowledge based approach to the development of parallel programs. In: Parallel and Distributed Processing, 1993. Proceedings. Euromicro Workshop on. pp. 457–463 (Jan 1993), iSBN 0-8186-3610-6

[4] Bischof, C.H., Dongarra, J.J.: A linear algebra library for high-performance computers. In: Carey, G.F. (ed.) Parallel Supercomputing: Methods, Algorithms and Applications, chap. 4, pp. 45–55. Wiley (1989)

[5] Bozkus, Z., Choudhary, A., Fox, G.C., Haupt, T., Ranka, S.: Fortran 90D/HPF compiler for distributed-memory MIMD computers: design, implementation, and performance results. In: Proc. Supercomputing '93. p. 351. Portland, OR (1993)

[6] Cahn, J.W., Hilliard, J.E.: Free Energy of a Nonuniform System. I. Interfacial Free Energy. The Journal of Chemical Physics 28(2), 258–267 (1958)

[7] Cahn, J., Hilliard, J.: Free energy of a non-uniform system III. Nucleation in a two point compressible fluid. J.Chem.Phys. 31, 688–699 (1959)

[8] Cardenas, A.F., Karplus, W.J.: PDEL - A Language for Partial Differential Equations. Comm. of the ACM 13(3), 184–191 (March 1970)

[9] Choi, J., Dongarra, J.J., Pozo, R., Walker, D.W.: Scalapack: A scalable linear algebra library for distributed memory concurrent computers. In: Proc. of the Fourth Symp. the Frontiers of Massively Parallel Computation. pp. 120–127. IEEE Computer Society Press (1992)

[10] Cook, G.O.: Code Generation in ALPAL Using Symbolic Techniques. In: Int. Conf. on Symbolic and Algebraic Computation. pp. 27–35. ACM/SIGSAM, Berkeley, CA, USA. (1992), ISBN:0-89791-489-9

[11] Cook, G.O., Painter, J.F., Brown, S.A.: How symbolic computation boosts productivity in the simulation of partial differential equations. Journal of Scientific Computing 6(2), 193–209 (June 1991), ISSN: 0885-7474

[12] Cooper, K.D., Torczon, L.: Engineering a Compiler. No. ISBN 1-55860-698-X, Morgan Kaufmann (2004)

[13] Dongarra, J.J., Croz, J.D., Duff, I.S., Hammarling, S.: A set of level 3 basic linear algebra subprograms. ACM Trans. Math. Soft. 16, 18–28 (1990)

[14] Dongarra, J.J., Whaley, R.C.: A users' guide to the BLACS v1.1. Tech. rep., Univ of TN, Knoxville (1997), http://www.netlib.org/blacs

[15] Grune, D., Bal, H.E., Jacobs, C.J.H.: Modern Compiler Design. No. ISBN 0-471-97697-0, Wiley (2000)

[16] Hawick, K.A.: Spectral analysis of growth in spatial lotka-volterra models. In: Proc. International Conference on Modelling and Simulation. pp. 14–20. No. 685-030, IASTED, Gabarone, Botswana (6-8 September 2010)

[17] Hawick, K.A., Playne, D.P.: Modelling, Simulating and Visualizing the Cahn-Hilliard-Cook Field Equation. International Journal of Computer Aided Engineering and Technology (IJCAET) 2(1), 78–93 (2010), inderscience

[18] Levine, J.: flex and bison: Text Processing Tools. O'Reilly Media (2009), iSBN: 978-0-596-15597-1

[19] Levine, J.R., Mason, T., Brown, D.: LEX and YACC. O'Reilly, 2nd edn. (1992), iSBN 1-56592-000-7

[20] Logg, A.: Automating the finite element method. Arch. Comput. Methods Eng. 14(2), 93–138 (2007), http://home.simula.no/~logg/pub/papers/Logg2007a.pdf

[21] Logg, A., Wells, G.N.: Dolfin: Automated finite element computing. ACM Trans. Math. Soft. 37(2), 1–28 (April 2010)

[22] M.A.Carpenter, E.Salje: Time dependent Landau theory for order / disorder processes in minerals. Mineralogical Magazine 53, 483–504 (Sep 1989)

[23] McMullin, P., Milligan, P., Corr, P.: Knowledge assisted code generation and analysis. In: High-Performance Computing and Networking. LNCS, vol. 1225, pp. 1030–1031. Springer (1997)

[24] Milligan, P., McConnell, R., Benson, T.: The Mathematician's Devil: An Experiment In Automating The Production Of Parallel Linear Algebra Software. In: Proc. Second Euromicro Workshop on Parallel and Distributed Processing. pp. 385–391 (Jan 1994), ISBN: 0-8186-5370-1

[25] Parr, T.: The Definitive ANTLR Reference - Building Domain-Specific Languages. No. ISBN 978-0-9787392-5-6, Pragmatic Bookshelf (2007)

[26] Paxson, V., Estes, W., Millaway, J.: The Flex Manual - Lexical Analysis with Flex, version 2.5.35 edn. (Spetember 2007)

[27] Playne, D.P., Hawick, K.A.: Auto-generation of parallel finite-differencing code for mpi, tbb and cuda. In: Proc. International Parallel and Distributed Processing Symposium (IPDPS); Workshop on High-Level Parallel Programming Models and Supportive - HIPS 2011. pp. 1163–1170. IEEE, Anchorage, Alaska, USA (16-20 May 2011), in conjunction with IPDPS 2011, the 25th IEEE International Parallel & Distributed Processing Symposium

[28] Playne, D.P., Hawick, K.A.: Stencil methods and graphical processing units for simulating field equations in parallel. In: Proc. 9th Int. Conf. on Foundations of Computer Science (FCS'13). p. FCS3958. No. CSTN-173, WorldComp, Las Vegas, USA (22-25 July 2013)

[29] Polychronopoulos, C.D.: Parallel Programming and Compilers. Parallel Processing and Fifth Generation Computing, Kluwer Academic Publishers (1988)

[30] Srikant, Y., Shankar, P. (eds.): The Compiler Design Handbook - Optimizations and Machine Code Generation. No. ISBN 1-4200-4382-X, CRC Press, second edn. (2008)

[31] The MathWorks: Matlab. available at http://www.mathworks.com (2007), Availableathttp://www.mathworks.com

[32] Tofte, M.: Compiler Generators - What they can do, what they might do, and what they will probably never do. No. ISBN 0-387-51471-6 in EATCS Monographs on Theoretical Computer Science, Springer-Verlag (1990)

[33] Tuszynski, J., Skierski, M., Grundland, A.: Short-range induced critical phenomena in the Landau-Ginzburg model. Can.J.Phys. 68, 751–755 (1990)

[34] Wolfram Research: Mathematica. available at http://www.wolfram.com (2007), Availableathttp://www.wolfram.com

[35] Zima, H.: Automatic vectorization and parallelization for supercomputers. In: Perrott, R. (ed.) Software for Parallel Computers, chap. 8, pp. 107–120. Chapman and Hall (1991)

A Component-Based Architecture for Ginga

Marcio Ferreira Moreno, Luiz Fernando Gomes Soares, Renato Cerqueira
Departamento de Informática – PUC-Rio
Rua Marquês de São Vicente, 225 – Rio de Janeiro/RJ – 22453-900 – Brasil
{mfmoreno, lfgs, rcerq}@inf.puc-rio.br

Abstract — This paper discusses how component-driven development can be used in the design of the Ginga middleware architecture, including its Ginga-NCL presentation module. Presentation engines have an important facility, since they allow for previewing when each specific media player is needed. Therefore, to maintain temporal consistency during application presentations, instantiation time of media players can be computed. The paper describes how this approach has been considered in the design and implementation of Ginga, the middleware of ISDB-T terrestrial digital TV system and ITU-T Recommendation for IPTV services. The evaluations presented in the paper illustrate the benefits component-driven architecture can bring to digital TV middleware systems, such as decreasing the amount of needed resources and improving their dynamic evolution capability.

Keywords- component-driven architecture, NCL, Ginga, Multimedia Synchronism, Digital TV, Interactive TV.

I. INTRODUCTION

In digital TV (DTV) systems, middleware is the software layer that gives support to application execution and makes them independently from receiver platforms.

The middleware design and implementation must take into account some special constraints. Usually, receivers have scarce resources offered to applications, due to cost limitations: low power CPU and limited memory. However, they usually provide specialized hardware targeting TV content presentation.

Component-based development [1] can be an interesting approach in this scarce resource scenario, in which a given set of functionalities must be present, only when they are required at presentation time. However, a critical issue must be stressed, the delay imposed in loading a component may not impair the temporal synchronization among media content during DTV application presentation. To find a strategy that enables multimedia presentations with the minimum software components in memory during application running without breaking the spatiotemporal relationships specified by application authors is thus a key issue.

Another key issue in DTV middleware design that can also take profit of component-based approach is the real time support to software updates. Dynamic middleware evolution support allows for integrating new functionalities, for replacing old ones, and for architectural redefinitions coming from unpredictable changes in the original project [1].

This paper discusses how component-driven development can be used in the design of the Ginga middleware architecture, including its Ginga-NCL presentation module. Ginga is the middleware of the ISDB-T (International Standard for Digital Broadcasting) standard [2]. Ginga-NCL supports the presentation of applications developed using the NCL (Nested Context Language) declarative language and its Lua scripting language [2] [3]. Ginga-NCL and NCL are also ITU-T H.761 Recommendation for IPTV services [3]. The component-driven approach proposed has been used in the Ginga reference implementation [4].

The paper is organized as follows. After this introduction, Section II presents some related work. Section III describes the modular architecture of Ginga in its support to declarative applications. Section IV discusses the component-driven implementation applied to Ginga architecture. Section V presents and comments performance measures coming from the Ginga monolithic and the Ginga component-driven implementations. Finally, Section VI concludes the paper.

II. RELATED WORK

Restraining our discussion to middleware systems, several component-driven solutions aiming at providing high-degree of adaptability and better control of computational resources have been discussed in the literature.

Coulson et al. [5] present OpenCom as a software component model to design low-abstraction-level systems, e.g. middlewares, trying to provide the same reconfiguring facilities other component infra-structures provide for the final application levels. OpenCom has been used in middleware systems for different application domains, such as programmable network processors, reflexive communication middleware systems, and routing systems for mobile ad-hoc networks [6] [7].

The Fractal component model [8] has also been used to design middleware systems. Layaida et al. [9] present an archetype based on this fractal model for multimedia application design, named PLASMA. In their paper, they show how the architecture provides real time adaptations with low performance impact, even if it is used by mobile devices with scarce computational resources.

Souza Filho et al. proposed the FlexCM model [10] aiming at the automatic composition of middleware architectures by explicitly representing component connections using an XML file to specify the middleware architecture. In the specification, component interfaces are identified by Globally Unique Identifiers (GUID) that guarantees the global individuality. Each component can declare the required and provided GUID. An execution environment is then able to compose the final architecture. FlexCM was used in the design of FlexTV [10] middleware for DTV Java applications.

Although there are reports about component-driven designs for DTV imperative middleware systems, like those previously introduced, to the best of our knowledge our proposal is the first one targeting DTV declarative middleware engine. DTV presentation engines have an important facility, since they allow for previewing when each specific media player is needed. Therefore, to maintain temporal consistency during application presentations, instantiation time of media players can be computed. If these players are not yet present in the presentation platform, a prefetching plan for loading them can be built.

The experimental results obtained for Ginga component-driven implementation reinforce the advantages raised in works presented in this Section II. However, it must be stressed that the Ginga implementation was developed based on services directly provided by the operating system, that is, without using any software infra-structure for component-driven design, as is the case of all previously mentioned approaches. This feature is significant for our purpose since it can contribute to reduce memory and CPU consumption, which are important constraints for DTV receivers, as aforementioned.

Table 1 shows some central key points regarding the work efforts mentioned in this section. Note that all proposals, apart from Ginga, do not have temporal synchronization in their requirements. This means that delay problems coming from component loading are neglected. However, this is a very important requirement for multimedia presentations by low cost receivers, as those provided for DTV systems.

TABLE I. COMPARISON OF COMPONENT-DRIVEN APPROACHES

	Dynamic Evolution	Resource Management	Infra-structure Independency	Temporal Synchronization
OpenCom	✓	✓		
Fractal	✓	✓		
FlexCM	✓	✓		
Ginga	✓	✓	✓	✓

III. GINGA COMPONENT-DRIVEN ARCHITECTURE

Figure 1 shows the Ginga modular architecture divided into two main subsystems: Ginga-NCL presentation engine and Ginga Common Core (Ginga-CC).

Ginga-CC provides basic media transmission/reception and decoding services to Ginga-NCL and Ginga's optional extensions (not discussed in this paper). Ginga-CC is the single part of Ginga that depends on the receiver hardware and the operating system platform. It allows Ginga-NCL to be platform independent.

Ginga-NCL is the logical subsystem of Ginga that controls the entire life cycle of an NCL DTV application.

In presenting the Ginga architecture, a module is defined as a set of software components that provides a specific functionality. Software component is defined as in Szyperski [1]: a unit of composition with contractually specified interfaces and explicit context dependencies only.

There are two types of components: permanent and temporary. The first ones are those that are used uninterruptedly, while the device is in operation. Therefore, they must be kept all time in memory. Updates in these components should be done when the receiver is in the stand-by mode. On the other hand, temporary components are those only needed in specific moments of the presentation. They should be kept in memory only when needed.

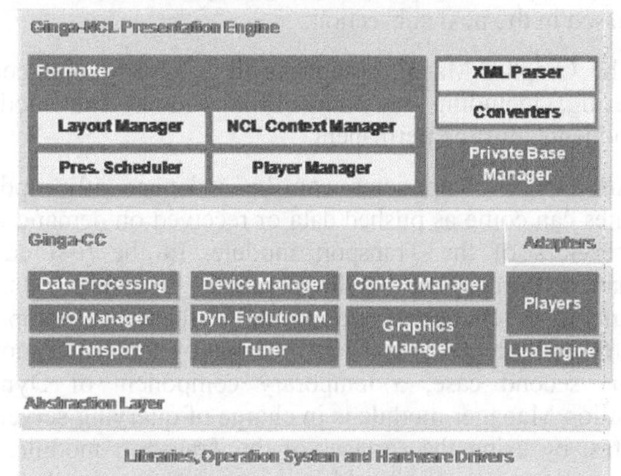

Figure 1. Ginga Architecture

A. Ginga-CC Componentization

The Tuner module of Ginga-CC is responsible for identifying the set of services that compounds a DTV channel, and for receiving these services' content pushed by DTV content providers. The Tuner components must be permanent, since content presentations are usually interrupted only by viewer actions.

DTV applications can be received from the Tuner module or from other network interface. In this last case, the Transport module is in charge of controlling the appropriate communication protocols and network interfaces. If DTV applications are received on demand, Transport components can be kept in memory only during the data reception.

The Data Processing Module monitors information that signalize DTV application transmissions and which are their sources. The monitor components must be permanent since it is impossible to determine when signalizing events will take place. Applications multiplexed in DTV service data received by the Tuner module are passed to the Data Processing temporary components. These temporary components demultiplex and generate application data files. These components can be withdrawn from memory when the generation process finishes.

The I/O module manages the temporary storage of DTV applications, including their media content. The module's components can be temporary but must remain in memory during all application life cycle.

The Players module is in charge of decoding and rendering each media content type that compounds a DTV application. Each media player component is temporary. The time interval these components are kept in memory is defined by the Player Manager, discussed in the next subsection. Ginga-NCL defines an API that shall be followed by all media players, in order to standardize the communication between the NCL Player and the media players. If third party media player components are integrated to Ginga, it can need the service of Adapters modules. Content to be exhibited by media players can come from the Data Processing module, if it comes multiplexed in the service transport flow, or can be received from the Transport module.

A special media player is the Lua engine for Lua code execution. Like other media players, Lua engine is kept in memory only during periods defined by the Player Manager, discussed in the next subsection.

The Graphic Manager controls the global spatial content rendering, including the main DTV video. The module's components must be permanent.

All Ginga components can be independently updated. Updates can come as pushed data or received on demand using the services of the Transport module. In the first case, a permanent component of the Dynamic Evolution Manager module is in charge of monitoring if there are component updates multiplexed in the data received by the Tuner module. In the second case, a temporary component of Dynamic Evolution Manager module is in charge of querying servers for updates, by using the services of the Transport module. This temporary component should be kept in memory only during query resolutions. Update query polices can be determine by viewers. The other Dynamic Evolution Manager components are responsible for the updating process, without interrupting the middleware execution. These components are temporary and should be kept in memory only during the updating process.

The Device Manager module deals with tasks related to distributed presentation on multiple exhibition devices: device registering, device intercommunication, distributed-media synchronization control, etc. [2] [3]. The module's components should be kept in memory only during distributed presentations.

Finally, the Context Manager module administers information about viewers and devices profiles, used in content and content presentation adaptations. Since this information is persistent, the module's components can be kept in memory only during information updating and access.

B. Ginga-NCL Componentization

The main module of the Ginga-NCL subsystem shown in Figure 1 is the Formatter, or NCL Player. This module is in charge of receiving and running NCL applications, no matter if they are resident applications or if they are applications received from Ginga-CC. The Formatter's components can be kept in memory only if there is an application to run.

Upon receiving an NCL application, the Formatter requests the services of the XML Parser module that translates the NCL textual specification into data structures that represents the NCL conceptual data model, called NCM [2] [3]. The XML Parser's components are only needed during the translation process and to compute NCL live editing commands discussed ahead. Therefore, they may be all temporary components.

The resulting NCM entities are grouped in a data structure called Private Base. Ginga-NCL associates at least one private base with each TV channel (assembling a set of channel services). Other private bases can be opened (or created), but at most one to each service in a tuned channel. NCL documents in a private base may be started, paused, resumed, stopped and may refer to each other.

As soon as the XML Parser ends its translation process, the Formatter calls the Scheduler to orchestrate the NCL application presentation. The Scheduler interprets the NCM data structures, using the services of the Converter module, in a second translation step done during application presentation, step by step. The Converter's components are needed during all the application presentation, differently from the XML Parser's components that do their job before presentations begin. This is one of the reasons why two-step conversion has been used.

During the presentation, the Scheduler requests the Play Manager module to instantiate players according to the content type being presented. When a content presentation finishes, the media player notifies the Scheduler. If there is no other content of the same type to be exhibited, the Scheduler commands the Player Manager to destroy the media player instantiation. The same procedure can happen if the Scheduler needs to stop a media presentation. Therefore, the Player Manager is in charge of loading and freeing media player components.

Media content in exhibition must be placed in a display area in agreement with the NCL application specification. The Layout Manager module associates content rendered by media players to display regions of one or more device screens. If multiple exhibition devices are used, the Layout Manager calls the Device Manager's services to transmit content to be presented to appropriate devices and to control their presentation. The Layout Manager's components must be kept in memory during the whole presentation.

The Private Base Manager must control all created private bases. This module's components shall be kept in memory while there is at least one active private base. The Private Base Manager is also responsible for processing live editing commands that allow for private base control (activation, open, close, etc.), for controlling of NCL application life cycles, and for changing applications during runtime. Changes on NCL application requested by NCL editing commands may be specified as XML parameters. Therefore, when needed, the Private Base Manager module calls the XML Parser's services to translate these changes into NCM data structures.

Finally, the NCL Context Manager adapts NCL applications, according to information provided by Ginga-CC and NCL instructions programmed by application authors.

IV. Component-Driven Implementation of Ginga

From version 0.10.1 on, the Ginga reference implementation has added a new optional module called Component Manager. At compile time the instantiation or not of this module defines if middleware libraries will result in a component-driven Ginga implementation or in a monolithic version. The two versions are provided to allow for implementing Ginga in platforms that do not offer support to component-driven development. These two versions are compared in Section 5.

The Component Manager module, shown in Figure 2, has the necessary functionalities to load and to release each component of the Ginga architecture. These operations are accomplished by the *ComponentManager* permanent component through the libdl library, which is the single introduced dependency to allow for loading and unloading components into system memory, by using the *IComponentManager* interface. The code for handling components is kept centralized to make easier the middleware embedment into receiver platforms that need an alternative to *libdl* library.

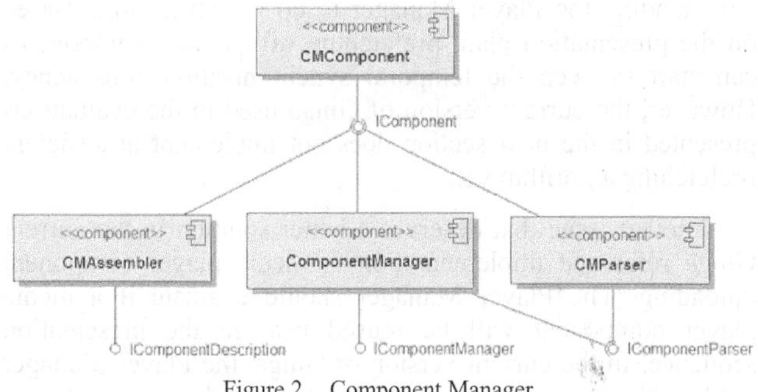

Figure 2. Component Manager

The architecture specification is defined in an XML document created by a script on component compilation and installation. When the receiver device starts its operation, the *ComponentManager* initiates and calls the services of the *CMParser* component, through the *IComponentParser* interface, to interpret the XML document. As a result, a set of directives on component loading and unloading are represented by the *IComponent* interface for all Ginga components.

If the middleware must be updated, the Dynamic Evolution Manager module receives the updates and changes the XML document by means of the *IComponentDescriptor* interface. The Dynamic Evolution Manager module is also responsible for notifying the *ComponentManager*, by means of the *IComponentManager* interface, that the update took place.

Figure 3 shows the DTD (document type definition) of the Ginga architecture XML specification. The <middleware> element is defined as the parent element of one or more <component> elements. To assist the Dynamic Evolution Manager, the required attributes of the <middleware> element define the receiver platform (identifier, operating system - OS, OS kernel version) where Ginga will be embedded.

The <component> element defines the necessary information to load and to unload the component represented by the element. Its *package*, *name* and *version* attributes define the architecture module the component pertains, the name of the component and its version, respectively. The <component> element may contain one or more <symbol> elements, zero or more <dependency> elements, the <location> element, and zero or more <repository> elements.

The <location> element gives the exact site of the component, which can be remote or local, depending on the value of the *type* attribute. The *uri* attribute defines the component address. When a component is loaded from a remote location, the *uri* contains its new local address, the remote address is set to the *uri* attribute of the <repository> element.

The <repository> element allows the Dynamic Evolution Manager to deal with more than one repository of components. In case of local component fails or loses, these repositories can be accessed, as in the case of component updates.

To allow for using the component functionalities after its loading, symbols that can be found during runtime must be defined. The <symbol> element allows for defining the *creator, destroyer* and *object* attribute. The *object* defines the component functionality to be found; its creator and destroyer are set to attributes of same names. The *interface* attribute allows the *ComponentManager* to know all objects that implement the same interface. For example, a middleware component can use the *ComponentManager* to check all platform network interfaces.

```
<?xml version="1.0" encoding="UTF-8"?>
<!ELEMENT middleware (component+)>
<!ATTLIST middleware
  platform CDATA #REQUIRED
  system CDATA #REQUIRED
  version CDATA #REQUIRED>
<!ELEMENT component (
  (symbol, location) |
  (dependency+, location, repository) |
  (dependency+, symbol+, location, repository))>
<!ATTLIST component
  package CDATA #REQUIRED
  name CDATA #REQUIRED
  version CDATA #REQUIRED>
<!ELEMENT location EMPTY>
<!ATTLIST location
  type CDATA #REQUIRED
  uri CDATA #REQUIRED>
<!ELEMENT repository EMPTY>
<!ATTLIST repository
  uri CDATA #REQUIRED>
<!ELEMENT symbol EMPTY>
<!ATTLIST symbol
  object CDATA #REQUIRED
  creator CDATA #REQUIRED
  destroyer CDATA #REQUIRED
  interface CDATA #REQUIRED>
<!ELEMENT dependency EMPTY>
<!ATTLIST dependency
  name CDATA #REQUIRED
  version CDATA #REQUIRED>
```

Figure 3. DTD for XML component descriptions of the Ginga architecture

The <dependency> element specifies the dependency that a component has of another component (its name and version). This is used by the Dynamic Evolution Manager to update not only a component but also all its dependencies.

The Component Manager and the Dynamic Evolution Manager modules are also useful when applications need components that were not predicted in the original implementation. As an example, Figure 4 shows a fragment of an NCL application in which the content type (DivX), not required in a conformant Ginga implementation [2] [3], is referred for presentation (line 4). To present this application, the Ginga-NCL Player Manager will be called by the Presentation Scheduler (see Section 3.2) to create the DivX player.

In the Ginga monolithic implementation, when there is no player able to display some content type, the Player Manager notifies the failure to the Presentation Scheduler that tries to maintain the presentation temporal consistency. However, in the component-driven implementation, the player must be downloaded from the location specified in the *player* attribute (see Figure 4). A failure is reported only if the player instantiation cannot be succeeded. In the example of Figure 4, the Player Manager calls the Dynamic Evolution Manager to analyze the "videoMM" media object and the corresponding information specified (line 4). From the *<media>* element, it infers that there is a description for a player adapter component addressing the content type with the "avi" extension in the set of component descriptions whose address is specified in the *player* attribute.

```
1: <?xml version="1.0" encoding="UTF-8"?>
2: <ncl id="unknownContent"
       xmlns="http://www.ncl.org.br/NCL3.0/EDTVProfile">
3:  ...
4:    <media id="videoMM" src="bolinha.avi"
       player="http://www.gingancl.org.br/plugins/avi.xml"/>
5:  ...
6:  </ncl>
```

Figure 4. NCL application with a non-predicted media type

If the remote XML document describing the component is the one shown in Figure 5, the Dynamic Evolution Manager module then knows that the "avi.xml" file has the DivX player component targeting many platforms and operation systems.

```
1: <middleware platform="ST7100" system="stlinux"
              version="2.4">
2:   <component package="gingancl"
              name="gingancldivxadapter" version="1.0.1">
3:     <dependency name="divxplayer" version="1.0.1"/>
4:     <dependency name="gingancladapter" version="0.13.5"/>
5:     <location type="remote"
          uri="http://www.gingancl.org.br/plugins/st7100/"/>
6:     <symbol object="DivXPlayerAdapter"
              creator="createDivXAdapter"
              destroyer="destroyDivXAdapter"
              interface="IPlayerAdapter"/>
7:   </component>
8: </middleware>
9: <middleware platform="AOpen" system="Windows"version="7">
10: ...
```

Figure 5. avi.xml file: remote description of components

The Dynamic Evolution Manager is responsible for analyzing the XML file to get the receiver platform description. In this example the module will get the following descriptions for its platform "ST7100": the operation system is "stlinux" in its version "2.4" (line 1); the "gingancldivxadapter" component, in its "1.0.1" version, pertains to the "gingancl" module (line 2); the location of this component is given in line 5; the component depends on "divxplayer" ("1.0.1" version) and "gingancladapter"("0.13.5" version) components (lines 3 and 4), so, all of them must be updated together. The symbols for creating and destroying the "DivXPlayerAdapter" player are also defined in the figure (line 6). In line 9 begins the description of the DivX player for another platform.

As soon as a component and its set of dependencies are downloaded using the Transport or Tuner modules, they are stored in a local memory. Before any operation, the Dynamic Evolution Manager verifies the possibility of running out of resources. If there is no risk, the Dynamic Evolution Manager updates the XML document that describes the middleware architecture, adding or updating the new downloaded components, and then notifies the *ComponentManager*.

While new components are being downloaded, the Player Manager keeps the Presentation Scheduler informed that the download process is in progress, and assures that the application presentation continues even if the component downloads fail. It should be stressed that using the solution proposed in this paper the Ginga reference implementation may be updated on-the-fly, and not only when it is halted in background.

The Presentation Scheduler and Player Manager modules assure that download delays do not impair the temporal synchronization among content that compounds DTV applications. For this sake, the Presentation Scheduler keeps a presentation data structure (presentation plan [11]) knowing in advance each content type to be presented and thus commanding the Player Manager to do its job in time. Based on the presentation plan, prefetching of updating components can start to keep the temporal synchronization consistency. However, the current version of Ginga used in the evaluations presented in the next section does not implement an efficient prefetching algorithm yet.

Another issue that deserves a better solution in the current Ginga reference implementation is media player component unloading. The Player Manager should evaluate if a media player component will be reused near in the presentation sequence. In the current version of Ginga, the Player Manager holds a player component idle in memory for one second after it has completed its job. If after this short period of time the player component is still not needed, it will be unloaded by the Player Manager.

V. SOME EVALUATIONS BASED ON MEASURES

This section presents some measures comparing the Ginga monolithic and component-driven implementations (referred as Mono and Comp in all figures, respectively), with regards to resource usage, CPU consumption and delays, both implementations have the same base platform: the Fedora Core 15 distribution of Linux operating system is used, all decoding and rendering processes are implemented in software (there are no specific hardware codec for any media content type); the DirectFB library [12] is used to handle graphical interfaces, to decode and to render text, images, audio and video content types; media objects with Lua code and HTML code are implemented using public libraries controlled by Ginga itself; the RAM memory was limited to 256 MB, with only 144 MB free memory (112 MB are used by Linux OS and other processes); the swap partition and disk cache policy was disabled.

Our first test document (document A) starts presenting in sequence an image, a text, an object running Lua language code, an audio, and an HTML page. The sequence is repeated twice. In a pure monolithic implementation all players are loaded from the beginning of the document presentation. However, it should be stressed that the DirectFB library implements the dynamic loading of media codecs without any Ginga control. So, the Mono version used in the evaluations indeed is not a pure monolithic case. To be more realistic, the Comp version presenting document A should be compared with the Mono version using document B, which contains the same media objects, but all of them starting at the same time. Note that when we load all media object of the document B, we are not using the dynamic loading characteristics of DirectFB library, which is more real for the Mono version evaluation. Of course the presentation duration of both A and B documents must be the same.

However, although taking care of simulating correctly the component loading of the Mono and Comp versions, our measures are still not precise due to another feature of DirectFB: when a player is loaded it is kept in memory until the end of the application presentation. Therefore, for the Comp implementation version, we are not considering the unloading of the image, text and audio codecs controlled by DirectFB. Therefore, even better results than those presented in this section could be obtained if unloading of those components could be done. As Lua and HTML players use libraries controlled by Ginga, the unloading problem does not happen. Even at a disadvantage, the measures presented have sufficient data for analysis.

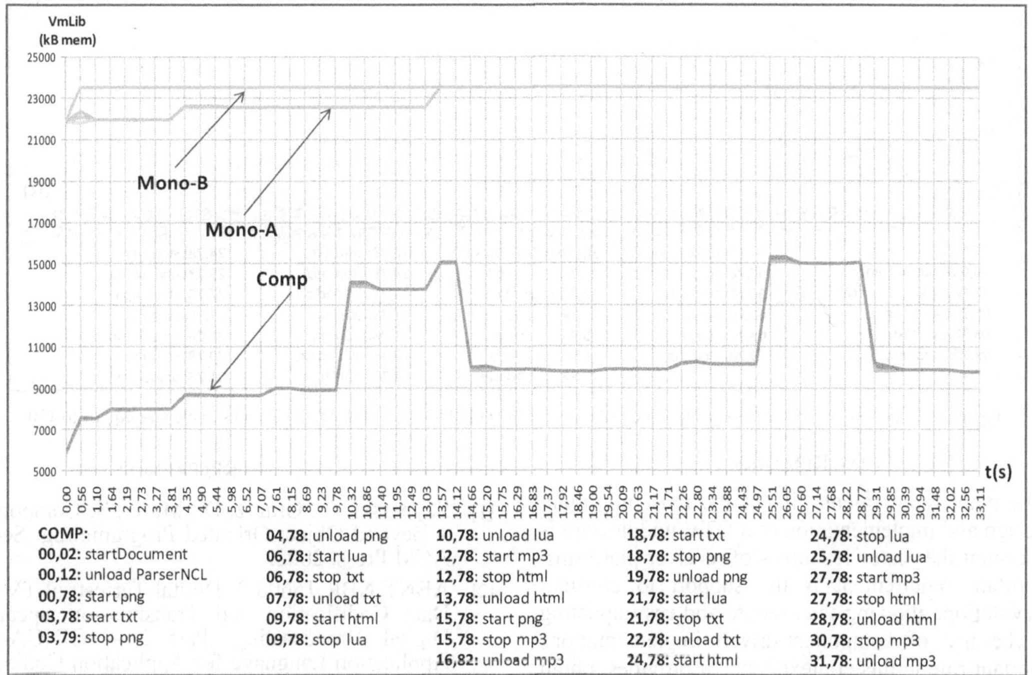

Figure 6. Memory use: max confidence interval equals to 174 kB, with 0.95 of confidence level and sample size equals to 100

It should also be mentioned that the absence of video content in the tests is due to the fact that this media type is usually implemented in hardware in DTV receiver platforms. The decoding and rendering of this content type in software require a lot of CPU and memory resources that would affect the scale of the evaluation graphs, making difficult to see the measured results. The exclusion of video type in the tests does not cause however any harm to the evaluations.

Figure 6 and 7 present the comparison between the Comp version running A document and the Mono version using A and B documents regarding amount of memory in use and regarding amount of used CPU, respectively.

Note in Figure 6 that near 0s, the amount of memory required by the Mono version is 3,7 times the one required by the Comp version. This is an important time instant since at this point only the Ginga implementation is in memory. During the [0,02 s, 0,78s[time interval the Mono version loads all DirectFB functionalities needed to run document B, while the Comp version loads only the components (see Section 3) needed to start the NCL application. When the first media content starts its presentation at 0,78s, the difference between the Comp version and the better case for the Mono version (Mono-A) is 14567 KB. At t=9,78s the HTML player is loaded and this is the moment at which the difference between the two versions is the least, remembering that DirectFB does not allow player unloading. This fact explains why at t=10,78s, t=13,78s, t=25,78s e t=28,78s we have a considerable reduction of memory use by the Comp version, since the HTML and Lua players are not controlled by DirectFB, but by the Ginga Component Manager, and these components are unloaded at these moments.

As it is predictable the efficiency in memory use is very high. Figure 7 confirms that this efficiency doesn't happen at great processing costs. Indeed, the Comp version demands less CPU use than Mono-A and Mono-B. Note the difference in CPU use required by the best case of the Mono version and the Comp version due to instantaneous loading of all Ginga libraries required by the Mono version. It is very important to note that the loading and unloading process do not demand relevant augments in CPU usage in the Comp version due to the Ginga component model, developed based on services directly provided by the operating system, that is, without using any software infra-structure for component-driven design.

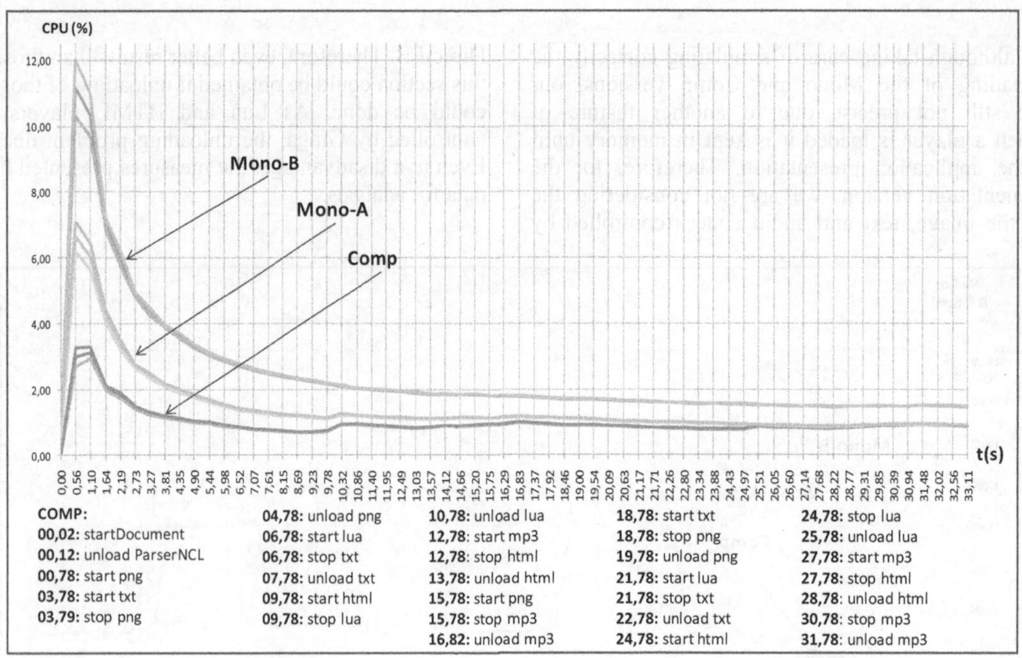

Figure 7. CPU use: max confidence interval equals to 0.28 %, with 0.95 of confidence level and sample size equals to 100

VI. Final Remarks

One of the main requirements, if not the most important one, in the design and implementation of a DTV middleware is to take into account the scarce resources of receiver platforms. Another important requirement is the support to constant middleware evolution, allowing fast, secure and easy updating procedures. The use of component-driven implementations plays an important role in this context, since it provides a high degree of adaptability and of computing resource control.

One of the main contributions of this work is to show how component-driven techniques can be used in DTV middleware architectures and implementations, presenting the Ginga implementation as an example. The proposal presented in this paper allows for DTV middleware updating during application runtime, without putting at risk the presentation in exhibition. The component-driven implementation favors the minimum waste of memory and CPU resources.

Ginga-NCL presentation engine, as other DTV declarative environments, allows for building a presentation plan (a hypermedia temporal graph - HTG) that allows for predicting when each media content type player is needed. In the case these players are not yet instantiated, a prefetching plan for loading them can be built. An intelligent prefetching algorithm should be devised to not impose any unnecessary memory burden of having a component in memory for a time longer than needed. Intelligent prefetching algorithms are in our future working plans.

We plan also to continue with performance measures using commercial receiver platforms, possibly without the limitations we have had (like the previously mentioned DirectFB characteristics) and possibly with other limitations coming from their hardware/software scarce resources. We intend to extend the evaluations to also take into account swap partition use.

References

[1] Szyperski, C., Gruntz, D., Murer, S. Component Software – Beyond Object-Oriented Programming. Second edition. ACM Press, 2002.

[2] ABNT NBR 15606-2. Digital Terrestrial TV Standard 06: Data Codification and Transmission Specifications for Digital Broadcasting, Part 2 – GINGA-NCL: XML Application Language for Application Coding, São Paulo, Brazil, 2007.

[3] ITU-T Recommendation H.761. Nested Context Language (NCL) and Ginga-NCL for IPTV Services. Geneva, 2009.

[4] Soares, L.F.G, Rodrigues, R. F., Moreno, M. F. Ginga-NCL: the Declarative Environment of the Brazilian Digital TV System. Journal of the Brazilian Computer Society, v. 12, p. 37-46, 2007.

[5] Coulson G. et al. A Generic Component Model for Building Systems Software. ACM Transaction on Computer Systems (TOCS), Volume 26, Issue 1, 2008.

[6] Ramdhany R. et al. MANETKit: supporting the dynamic deployment and reconfiguration of ad-hoc routing protocols. Proceedings of the 10th ACM/IFIP/USENIX International Conference on Middleware. Urbanna, Illinois. 2009.

[7] Gomes A.T.A. LindaX: a Language for Describing Adaptable Communication Systems. PhD Thesis. Departamento de Informática. PUC-Rio. August, 2005.

[8] Bruneton E. et al. The FRACTAL Component Model and Its Support in Java. Software, Practice and Experience. 36(11-12): 1257-1284. 2006.

[9] Layaïda O., Hagimont D. Designing Self-Adaptive Multimedia Applications through Hierarchical Reconfiguration, 5th IFIP DAIS, Athens, Greece, 2005.

[10] Filho S. M. et al. FLEXCM – A Component Model for Adaptive Embedded Systems. Proceedings of the 31st Annual International Computer Software and Applications Conference - Volume 01. Pages: 119-126. 2007.

[11] Costa, R. et al. DocEng, ACM Symposium on Document Engineering, "Intermedia Synchronization Management in DTV Systems", São Paulo, Brazil, 2008.

[12] DirectFB Library. www.directfb.org

Managing User Accounts Across Heterogeneous Information Systems In The University

Askar Boranbayev[1], **Mikhail Mazhitov**[1], **and Rinat Yamalutdinov**[1]
[1]Nazarbayev University, Astana, Republic of Kazakhstan

Abstract - *The present level of IT technologies provides the ability to automate much of the academic and administrative business processes of universities. With this said the park of information systems and services, often built using different technologies and architectures, in the universities is constantly expanding. In this regard, there are a number of issues related to the security of information, control of access to the information, as well as the optimization of the use of labor resources in the maintenance of information systems. To solve these issues qualitatively - the university must have an organized process for managing users of information systems and user privileges. This article shows an example of how to organize such a process with the use of modern IT means of automation.*

Keywords: Identity management, Identity and Access Management, information technology, information systems, authentication, authorization

1 Introduction

Management of user accounts and their privileges is an important part of the security of any information system (IS). Inefficient management of users and privileges in IS can lead to compromise, to incorrect functioning, and possibly even full paralysis of these IS. Moreover, this kind of incident to one or more IS belonging to a common IT infrastructure can completely paralyze the entire IT infrastructure. In this case, the less effective management of users and their privileges and the bigger the park of information systems included in the infrastructure, the correspondingly higher these risks.

Any large organization nowadays is actively using multiple IS to automate their processes. Each of these systems automates certain set of business processes of the organization and has pools of users with special privileges for each IS, which, in turn, may overlap. The larger the organization, and the more diverse its internal business processes, the greater the number of IS involved in the automation of the business processes of the organization, and the greater the degree of difference, and the area of intersection between pools of users of these information systems and their privileges.

The infrastructure for automation of business processes of a University, as an educational institution, is a fairly complex set (may depend on the size of the university) of information systems with associated structures of user privileges of different IS. We must be aware that these IS store and process important for the university and often confidential information, loss or compromise of which can lead to serious consequences and damage. Thus, the issue of increasing the efficiency of managing users of IS and their privileges for universities is an important task.

2 Choosing ways of solutions

2.1 Unique features of educational organizations in the management of users

As it was mentioned above, often the IT infrastructure for automating business processes of universities is represented by several interrelated IS, which actually is a standard pattern at the current level of IT development.

However, educational institutions can have a number of specific aspects of organizational type, which greatly complicate the management of users of IS and their privileges:

- Extensive network of subsidiaries with a very flexible organizational and staff structure. In this case, the same employee may work in various positions in various structural units and organizations of the university and at the same time to take different roles. For example, a person at a time can work as a professor at another school and be a member of the University Research Center, or even be a part time student in a different school, etc. in various ways.
- Presence of groups of people who are neither students nor staff, or have otherwise long-term formal association with the University, who at different times based on the non-recurring terms need to have access to information systems and services of the University. For example, third-party readers (outsiders) of the library, professionals of auditing firms, or teachers invited for short-term teaching, etc.

Such organizational issues impose additional constraints on the management of users and their privileges. Solving these issues by following standard techniques can lead to an undesirable increase in beurocratic procedures, and also greatly increases the risk of making an error by assigning incorrect use privileges with all the ensuing consequences. So when setting up a management of users and their privileges at the university people should especially pay attention to these aspects and take them into account when making organizational and technical decisions on these issues.

2.2 Possible Solutions

At its core, properly structured management of users and their privileges should be a strictly regulated process, deviations from which must be minimal. Privileges are assigned to users based on their position in the organizational structure of the organization and the role that the user plays in the organization, which is strictly regulated by the internal documents of the organization, as well as the hiring and firing a worker (creating a user account and blocking a user account). Therefore, for any organization, including the university, we can develop an algorithm for creation/blockage of user accounts in information systems of the organization and destination of privileges.

It is clear that the availability of a completed algorithm allows automating the process that the algorithm describes. The same applies to the management of users and their privileges - currently on the market there are a number of software systems of class IDM (Identity Management), or as they are called IAM (Identity and Access Management) intended for the centralized management of user access to information, user accounts, passwords, and other attributes in various information systems, thus reducing the risks of information security, and optimize the cost of administering IT infrastructure.

Currently there are two common approaches of automation of processes of management of user accounts and their privileges:

The ***first approach*** is to create a ***single point of authentication and authorization*** (shown schematically in Figure 1).

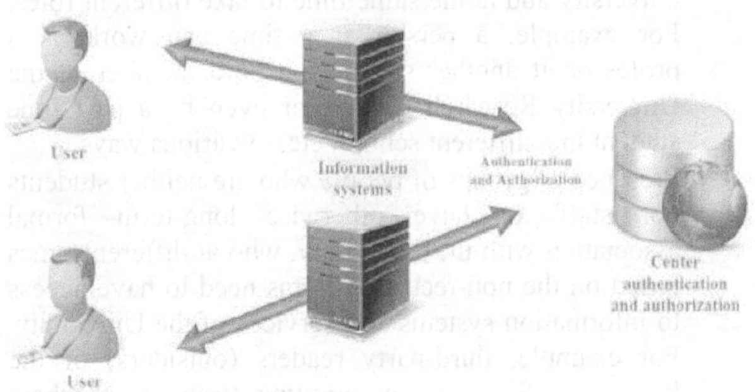

Figure 1. The single common center of authentication and authorization.

With such approach to the implementation:

- The authentication and authorization take place on the side of the center of authentication and authorization, and not on the side of information systems;
- User account credentials are stored only on the side of the center of the authentication and authorization;
- The change of the user account credentials is possible only on the side of the center of authentication and authorization.

The ***second approach*** is to create a single repository of user account information and their attribute information (schematically shown in Figure. 2).

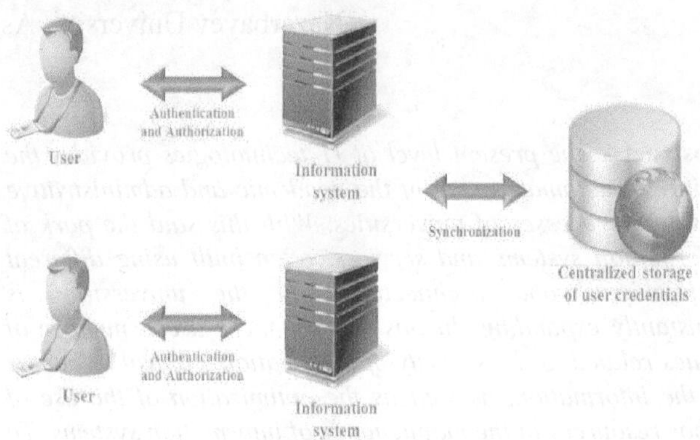

Figure 2. A single repository of user credentials

With such approach to the implementation:

- The authentication and authorization takes place only on the side of Information Systems (IS);
- User account credentials are stored on both the IS and on the side of the center of authentication and authorization;
- There is a periodic two-way synchronization of credentials between the center and the IS;
- The change of user account credentials is possible both on the side of the center of authentication and authorization and on the side of the IS.

3 The pros and cons of the various approaches

Let's consider the advantages and disadvantages of the above approaches to automate the user account management process.

The *advantage* of using a single center of authorization and authentication over other solutions is:

- Less time spent on data synchronization - the access to all of the systems and services (based on the user rights and privileges) are available to the user immediately after user registration;
- Low labor costs for the technical management and maintenance;
- There is a minimal risks of possible information theft and compromise a user's account.

The *disadvantages* of this approach are noted bellow:

- In the case of connecting various active information systems to this center we will required to make changes to the operation of authentication and authorization of these information systems, so it works with the common single center. Sometimes it is not possible to do this with the proprietary or out of the box application software, which is not easy to customize and adopt.
- the complexity of building and managing a single repository in the environment of production processes;
- a mandatory single common password to access all of the information systems;
- difficulty of implementing a number of business processes due to lack of synchronization of information between information systems;
- The failure in the operation of the single common center of authentication and authorization leads to failure in all of IS.

The advantages of the second approach over the first one (namely the creation of a single repository of user account information and their attributes) are:

- There is no need to revise or make major changes to an information system in order to connect to the center;
- The possibility of using the means of information systems for authentication, authorization and for control of additional parameters. Such ability gives an opportunity to manage pools of users for each information system separately (without being controlled by a single common center). Also it can simplify the granting of various privileges to users in various information systems, in the case when a user holds multiple occupations at the same time and plays different roles in the organization;
- We minimize the risk of the failure of the whole complex. In the case of failure of one central authentication and authorization - the work in the information systems will not be completely paralyzed;
- the ability to synchronize reference information;
- the ability to use different passwords for IS;

The shortcomings of this approach such as the need for duplication of user account information in the information systems, and the time spent on synchronization - are not critical. That is why we can tell for sure that the second approach to the automation of management of users and their privileges in the information systems is better than the first one.

4 Project Implémentation

Based on the information from above, in our university, in January 2012, we initiated a project to design and install a unified user management system, designed for a uniform and centralized management of registration of user accounts and user's identity, and management of access to information resources of the university by providing a transmission of user information in the target IS.

The main challenge for the system being created was to provide unified information about users in all of the IS of the university. That is, the system should automatically sync all user accounts (students, faculty and staff), and reference information between information systems - Figure 3. In particular, automatically, on the basis of the date from HR and Student Registrar systems, create new user accounts and block user accounts of dismissed or expelled students and staff.

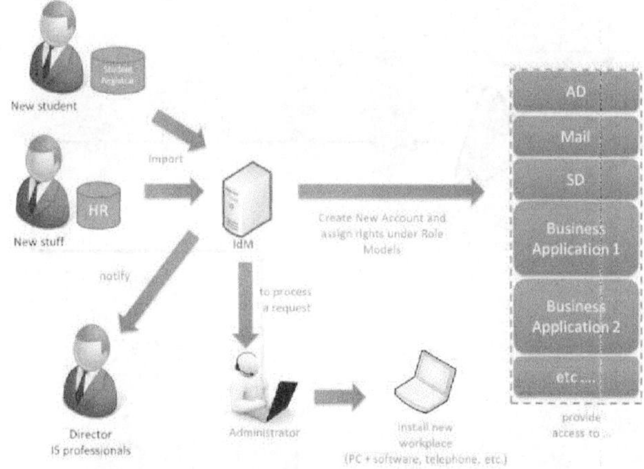

Figure 3 - The process of management of user accounts of information systems of the university and their privileges with MS FIM. [1]

The system implemented as part of the project consists of three functional blocks:

1. User Management - the main purpose is to manage directories, user registration data, user accounts, and connectors to different IS, and synchronization of data;

2. Self-service for users - the main purpose is to allow users to self-change their user account records and user registration data;

3. Managing user access rights - the main purpose is to provide access control to the system and the functionality to configure user access to system resources.

The system is built with the use of Microsoft products, such as:

- MS Forefront Identity Manager;
- MS SQL Server;
- MS IIS;
- MS Windows Server.

The major architectural design for this implementation is the availability of specialized connectors MS FIM to the technologies used to store information of users inside of third-party IS, with the ability to synchronize, with a pre-defined algorithm in the system, this information through SQL queries, or through using LDAP or specialized APIs. In summary, the system architecture is shown in Figure. 4 (see below).

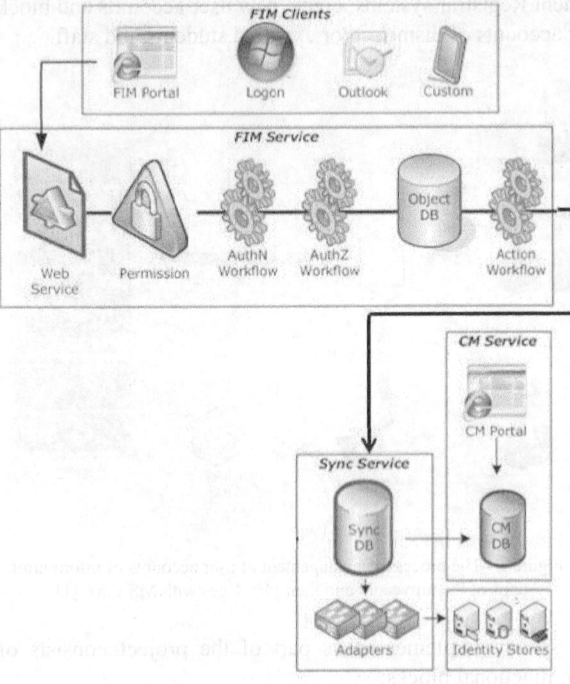

Figure 4. The overall architecture of the unified system of management of users. [2]

The project, which was successfully completed in four months, a single repository of user credentials with 14 information systems integrated together was created. It was built using various technologies such as Oracle DB, Oracle Portal and WebCenter Suite, IBM WebSphere Portal, EMC Documentum, Apache Tomcat and HTTP Server, MS IIS, MS Access, My SQL. The system automates the process of creating and managing user accounts of all information systems at the University and the process of synchronization of reference information, as well as registration information of students and employees of the University in all target systems.

The result of successful implementation of this system shows that in the IT department of the University there is a decline and optimization of the cost of labor for maintenance and keeping up to date a list of all the users of information systems and their privileges. Before the project implementation this work was performed by 6 employees working on part-time basis - after the implementation – one person is enough. We can see that the number of incidents of unauthorized access has greatly decreased. The transparency has increased. The process of getting a user access to information systems and services has become quicker.

The implementation of the project has allowed unifying user account information and to maintain the integrity of the personal data of users.

5 Conclusion

In this paper we have shown the process of automation of management of user accounts and their privileges at our university, with the approaches and techniques described above. The system and the process have shown its effectiveness technically and in terms of information security. And given the favorable pricing of Microsoft to academic institutions, compared with other producers of proprietary software (IdM systems in particular) led to greatly reduce the financial cost of the organization of an effective process of managing user accounts and their privileges and to greatly reduce the maintenance costs of the process in the future

6 References

[1] What is Microsoft FIM, and how does it work? Galust Shahbazyan. 10.05.2012. http://csbims.ru/about/publications/publications_9.html

[2] FIM 2010 Technical Overview, Updated: April 12, 2010. Applies To: Forefront Identity Manager 2010. http://technet.microsoft.com/en-us/library/ff621362%28v=ws.10%29.aspx

[3] Forefront Identity Manager 2010 R2: http://www.microsoft.com/en-us/server-cloud/forefront/identity-manager.aspx

[4] Forefront Identity Manager (FIM) Migration: Decisions and Steps Toward a Major Change. By Jim Cook, Ferris State University; Frank Drewes, Oxford Computer Group. http://www.merit.edu/events/mmc/abstracts.php?mamdate=2012&sp=Cook

[5] Private University Reduces Identity Management Workload by 320 Hours per Month. By Dan Cotterman, Director of IT Infrastructure, Grand Canyon University: https://images01.insight.com/media/pdf/insight-grand-canyon-university-case-study-sharepoint.pdf

[6] Enabling Business Opportunities with Identity Management: University of Iowa. By Robert Heitman & Randy Wiemer: https://www.brighttalk.com/webcast/8503/64991

[7] Georgia State University: Building an Identity Management Infrastructure for the eUniversity: http://www.nmi-edit.org/case_studies/GSU_nmiCaseIdMgtFinal16Oct2004.pdf

[8] FIM 2010 Product Site: http://go.microsoft.com/fwlink/?LinkId=187552

[9] FIM 2010 Web Forum: http://go.microsoft.com/fwlink/?LinkId=163230

[10] Technical Resources: http://go.microsoft.com/fwlink/?LinkId=187554

[11] N.Hritonenko and Yu.Yatsenko, Creative destruction of computing systems: Analysis and modeling, Journal of Supercomputing, 38(2006), pp. 143-154.

[12] Yu.Yatsenko and N.Hritonenko, Network economics and optimal replacement of age-structured IT capital, Mathematical Methods of Operations Research, 65(2007), pp. 483-497.

[13] Boranbayev A, Defining methodologies for developing J2EE web-based information systems, *Nonlinear Analysis (2009)*, doi: 10.1016/j.na.2009.02.002.

[14] Boranbayev A, Belov S, Data Center Design and Implementation at the University, *Proceedings of The 2012 International Conference on Computer Design (CDES'12)*, Las Vegas, Nevada, July 16-19, 2012, pp. 124-126.

Teams using Real World Projects in a Software Engineering Course

Nasser Tadayon, Associate Professor
Department of Computer Science and Information Systems, Southern Utah University, Utah, USA

Abstract: *For a Computer Science undergraduate degree program the topics in software engineering are among the core topics recommended by the joint task force in computing curricula 2005. There is a large area of literature supporting the concept of project-based learning in a team setting to enhance teaching in a software engineering course. This paper discusses the curriculum issues within a software engineering course and explores and analyzes some advantages/disadvantages of using a team based approach with a real world project. Using data collected through a software engineering course at Southern Utah University, the author examines the overall experience in having a real software project from a local company using the PBL (Problem Base Learning) style in a team setting.*

Keywords: Software Engineering, Team work, Real World Project, Education

1 Introduction

The main objective of an initial course in Software Engineering should be providing the students with knowledge and experience as well as some level of comprehension through practical application within the ten knowledge areas (KAs). These KAs are defined by the ACM/IEEE Computer Society in their 2004-SWEBOK (Software Engineering Body of Knowledge) [9]. However, due to the dynamic nature of the software engineering discipline, a new SWEBOK guide (V3) includes some adjustment/removal of non-relevant topics as well as the addition of new knowledge areas. The ACM/IEEE Computer Society has also provided a guideline within undergraduate degree programs in software engineering SEEK (Software Engineering Education Knowledge) which defines "Core Material" as the minimal knowledge for a program in software engineering [8].

Software engineering courses within Computer Science undergraduate programs can vary from one school to another. The most recent curriculum guideline for Computer Science programs CC2001 and CS2008 suggest coverage of several software engineering concepts within a total of 31 core hours as follows:

SE1. Software design (8)	SE7. Software evolution (3)
SE2. Using APIs (5)	SE8. Software project management (3)
SE3. Software tools and environments (3)	SE9. Component-based computing
SE4. Software processes (2)	SE10. Formal methods
SE5. Software requirements and specifications (4)	SE11. Software reliability
SE6. Software validation (3)	SE12. Specialized systems development

Table 1- Curriculum guideline for Computer Science

Within this list, SE1 – SE8 are considered as core and others SE9 – SE12 as elective. Computer Science curriculum 2013 (Ironman Draft) further divided the KA requirements into two sections (Tier 1 and Tier 2). It contains 6 hours in Tier1 (required core) and 21 hours in Tier2 (elective) within software engineering concepts. It also rephrased and changed the core requirement of the "Programming Fundamentals" which was 38 hours in CC2001 and 47 hours in CS2008 to SDF - Software Development Fundamentals (43 hours, all Tier 1). Amongst the SDF requirement several software engineering concepts were added (like Program Correctness or Refactoring). CS2013-ironman (v0.8) within software engineering requirement identifies the topics in tier1 and tier2 as follows:

CS2013 – Ironman (v 0.8)	Core Tier 1 hrs.	Core Tier 2 hrs.	Includes Electives
SE/Software Processes	2	1	Y
SE/Software Project Management		2	Y
SE/Tools and Environments		2	N
SE/Requirements Engineering	1	3	Y
SE/Software Design	3	5	Y
SE/Software Construction		2	Y
SE/Software Verification and Validation		3	Y
SE/Software Evolution		2	Y
SE/Formal Methods			Y
SE/Software Reliability		1	Y
Total	6	21	

Table 2- Ironman 2013 for Software Engineering Curriculum

This indicates that there are overall 6 core hours in the required section with 3 hours in Software Design, 2 hours in Software Processes, and 1 hour in Software Requirement. All other topics except Formal Methods are covered in 21 hours of the elective section. It is noteworthy that Software Design has remained one of the major topics within software engineering. SWEBOK is updating its guideline but in its 2004 version indicated the following ten knowledge areas (KAs):

1. Software Requirements
2. Software Design
3. Software Construction
4. Software Testing
5. Software Maintenance
6. Software Configuration Management
7. Software Engineering Management
8. Software Engineering Process
9. Software Engineering Tools and Methods
10. Software Quality

Although a software engineering course is a required course within many Computer Science programs, it was removed from the core degree requirement in Computer Science in Southern Utah University. Based on input from Department Industrial Advisory Board (IAB) members and students' interest, the proposal to offer the software engineering course as part of the elective requirement in the CS program was approved by the appropriate curriculum committees. This paper explains the process as well as pros and cons of team selection in the software engineering course offered through a hands-on practical approach using a real world project.

2 Software Engineering course

The main learning objectives of the software engineering course in a Computer Science program are to describe the major problems in large system development and to discuss issues, principles, methods, and technology associated with software engineering theory and practices (e.g. Planning, Requirement Analysis, Design, Coding, Testing, Quality Assurance, and Configuration Management). Other important performance objectives include providing an environment for students to work as part of a team and learning through hands-on experience with a real-world project. Through this method, students can learn how to use a software development process to develop high-quality software products in an effective manner.

In Southern Utah University, the software engineering course was offered in Fall 2012 as an elective course for CS majors with 11 students for the first time since 2004. The course started by defining software engineering and issues related to software quality as well as crises within software to give the students a deep understanding of the importance of characteristics related to software quality. To promote a habit of data collection among students, they were encouraged to follow incremental steps of PSP (Personal Software Process) as a simple individual developmental process. The students were tasked with specific instructions to keep track of their time, line of code (LOC), and defects within several relatively small programming assignments. Students were also instructed to use their previously collected data in order to create a plan for the next assignment using PSP-tool. The purpose of these exercises was to make students aware of their productivity and the quality of their programs. The other objective was for each student to gather some data that can be used for planning his or her team project. Unfortunately, students who undergo programming classes without following a specific process are accustomed to being assessed on the final delivery of their product with minimal testing on functionality. It has been a challenge to encourage students to plan for their small assignment tasks and collect correct data. One of the major problems in teaching software engineering is to convince students to use a planning tool to collect data as most students find this work redundant. Students at the senior level often develop a limited method for completing programming assignments, and tend to allocate insufficient time to complete their work. It was apparent that several students faked time data in order to meet the requirement of the assignment. One cause for this could be that overall the students are exposed to programming much earlier than software engineering [6]. While some individuals demonstrated skills in planning during team projects, the majority had missed this critical stage in their projects.

The external project used for the course was one from a local software development company that seemed to be feasible for the level of the class. Although the students had gone through several advanced programming classes

before taking this class, there were only six students who were familiar with web programming using PHP, a requirement for the project. There were several discussions with the customer to outline the scope and procedure to use in their class project. The customer was eager and interested in their involvement in the project.
The project was scheduled for completion within three cycles. After providing the need statement, which was coordinated with the customer for the project, the teams were guided through the launch activity. A milestone for the first two cycles of the project was given. Critical sections of the requirement were identified and required to be completed within the first two cycles.

Students in the teams went through all phases of the software development defined by TSP (Team Software Process). They were guided during each phase and developed an initial plan, CM (Configuration Management by defining base line and change process), SRS, SDS, and a test plan through each phase as well as postmortem at the end of each cycle.

3 Project Team Management

3.1 Background

One of the main problems in any team-oriented project, especially in a software engineering course, is creating teams with members that work well together. Although studies show that students learn more through participating in a team environment [1], it is a challenge to form the teams with an open (members able to switch position, support each other, and review each other's work) and random (independent thinking and less directive) team style. Team projects provide students with self-study skills in their programming and improve their written and oral communications skills, which are standard requirements within large software development. Expected benefits in team projects include gaining invaluable software development experience and providing problem solving and critical thinking skills for students as well as training in teamwork coordination skills [1]. One other advantage of a group project is the obligation and responsibility that some members of the team feel towards other members, a sentiment that has proven in many occasions to be a driver that motivates students in contributing further toward a project's success. The author has noticed in several occasions that students with initially low interest spend time and effort in order to demonstrate their abilities and to impress their teammates. The group project concept is also among the largest problems in management within education as well as the real world in ensuring a collaborative environment among the members working on a project [2].

A study has shown that the dominant personality type of software engineers has undergone a transition from introversion to extroversion. This change could be associated with the increasingly diverse activities in the software industry over the last thirty years and the ubiquity of software. [7]

3.2 Group Formation

Selection of team members for a project is a sensitive step which requires careful study. One proposed approach is to use dynamic group management; however, this approach lacks many of the advantages of traditional group projects, such as students' motivation and dedication to teams. However, there are advantages in changing the composition of each student group at each phase of the software lifecycle [5]. Another approach is to organize students into an actual software development company and conduct activities that mimic real-world operations in that company [3] [10]. This seems to work well as students are provided with training experience on the job. Although there are many benefits to this approach, the educational aspect of software engineering should go beyond a specific company's process.

In order to get the best team members possible in a group and to ensure the success of all teams in the class, a first step is to collect relevant information from the students in the class. In industry the team members are often selected based on their familiarity and experience in similar projects; however, for a class environment there may not be any useful information available.

Better results may be achieved if the roles and responsibilities of the team members are well-defined. Students need to be given a brief description of different team members' roles and responsibilities. These roles were defined by TSP (Team Software Process) as:

1. Team Leader: leads the team and ensures that engineers report their process data and complete their work as planned.

2. Development Manager: leads and guides the team in designing and developing the product.
3. Requirement/Support Manager: leads the team in developing the software requirements and helps the team meeting its technology and administrative support needs.
4. Planning Manager: supports and guides the team in planning and tracking their work.
5. Quality/Process Manager: supports the team in defining their process needs and establishing and managing the quality plan.

This set of team roles seems relevant and appropriate for a group project in a software engineering class. The process of selection started with a survey to collect the information related to the students' familiarity and experiences with the programming languages. Additional information related to their experience on any other team roles as well as their leadership or management practice, their weekly schedule, and their preference for team role in the project were collected. The students were asked to indicate if there was anyone they would prefer to team up with for the project. Typically, it is best to group students who know one another well and want to work together on a project. They were told to indicate at most two other students in order of preference and they were assured that every effort will be made to include at least one of these selections in their team.

The information gathered helped in forming the three teams and identifying their members, and the roles were suggested and left to be decided among the team members during their first team meeting. The main driving force for forming a team was student preference; however, in order to make sure all teams succeed and included at least one experienced programmer, not all of the preferences in team selection were met for some students.

During the team's launch meeting, all the team members adapted to their suggested role in the teams. Each team had at least two competent programmers in the language used (PHP) to ensure their success. All team leaders had indicated some experience in leadership positions at different levels (some in work and some in other team projects). However, based on the size of the teams, there were some students who had to take several less demanding roles. During the launch phase, teams were also asked to set up their weekly meeting time and place and to indicate some measureable goals related to the project, both individually and as a team. The teams were encouraged to maintain regular meetings at least once every week. The team leader was the main contact point and was encouraged to inform the instructor of any problems or foreseeable issues.

As always, several students had a busy schedule and did not have (or did not wish to allocate) time to meet, but were persuaded to make time by their team members. The team members were encouraged to be involved and participate in all tasks while paying special attention to their role(s) and responsibilities. Although team members were warned of common team problems, it was apparent that some teams experienced poor communication, ineffective leadership, and poor planning. In the worst cases, some team members had weak participation, lack of discipline, and no interest or motivation.

3.3 Survey Results

A survey[1] was conducted to assess different aspects of teams as part of their postmortem from all students. The teams had 4, 3, and 4 members consecutively and not all of the members participated in the survey. The ranking was from 1 to 5 where 1 was the lowest ranking and 5 the highest. The following is the average of rankings from each team based on team assessment that shows the number of participants:

Rating after Cycle 1	Team 1 (4/4)	Team 2 (2/3)	Team3 (4/4)	Average
Team spirit	3.5	3.5	4.25	3.75
Overall effectiveness	4.25	3.5	4.25	4
Rewarding experience	3.75	4	3.75	3.83
Team productivity	4.25	2.5	3.25	3.33
Process and product quality	4	4	4	4
Overall Average	**3.95**	**3.5**	**3.9**	**3.78**

Table 3- Cycle 1 Teams Evaluation

[1] Acknowledgement: The survey was developed by Dr. Thomas Hilburn

The same questions after cycle 2 results are as follow:

Rating after Cycle 2	Team 1 (3/4)	Team 2 (3/3)	Team3 (4/4)	Average
Team spirit	3.67	4.33	4	4
Overall effectiveness	4	4	3.75	3.92
Rewarding experience	4	4.67	3.5	4.06
Team productivity	4.33	3.67	3.75	3.92
Process and product quality	4.33	4	4.25	4.19
Overall Average	**4.07**	**4.13**	**3.85**	**4.02**

Table 4- Cycle 2 Team Evaluation

There were small improvements on all overall averages for teams except Team 3. One reason for this problem was the fact that the software company that the students were working with hired three members of Team 3 and paid them to do the project or other side projects at the same time. The hired students were exposed to different processes which caused some dysfunction and confusion as well as loss of interest in the process used in the class. This was the main catalyst for creating a lack of motivation among some other students in the class who were aware of the hiring. Some students complained and felt that they were being used by the company to do their job. The customer from the company hiring the students was using a process that did not require students to keep track of their time and the primary objective was to get the job done within the shortest time. The average results of the survey rating the student in each role for their overall contribution on a similar scale (1-5) is shown below:

Rating after Cycle 1	Team 1 (4/4)	Team 2 (2/3)	Team3 (4/4)	Average
Team Leader	3.75	4.5	4.75	4.33
Development Manager	4.25	5	4.75	4.67
Planning Manager	4.75	3.5	3.75	4
Quality/Process Manager	3.75	3.5	4.25	3.83
Support Manager	3.75	3	4.25	3.67
Overall Average	**4.05**	**3.9**	**4.35**	**4.1**

Table 5- Cycle 1 Overall Contribution

Rating after Cycle 2	Team 1 (3/4)	Team 2 (3/3)	Team3 (4/4)	Average
Team Leader	4	4.33	4.5	4.28
Development Manager	5	5	4.25	4.75
Planning Manager	5	4	3.5	4.17
Quality/Process Manager	4.67	4.33	4.25	4.42
Support Manager	4.67	4	4	4.22
Overall Average	**4.67**	**4.33**	**4.1**	**4.37**

Table 6- Cycle 3 Overall Contribution

This demonstrates the moderate decrease in contribution of Team 3 members to the project based on the data they provided. As shown, the data for Team 1 and 2 has a moderate increase for all team members from Cycle 1 to 2.

The results of student ratings in each role for helpfulness and support are as follows:

Rating after Cycle 1	Team 1 (4/4)	Team 2 (2/3)	Team3 (4/4)	Average
Team Leader	4.25	4.5	4.5	4.42
Development Manager	4.5	5	4.25	4.58
Planning Manager	4.75	4.5	3.75	4.33
Quality/Process Manager	4	4	3.5	3.83
Support Manager	4	4	3.75	3.92
Overall Average	**4.3**	**4.4**	**3.95**	**4.22**

Table 7- Cycle 1 Helpfulness and Support

Rating after Cycle 2	Team 1 (3/4)	Team 2 (3/3)	Team3 (4/4)	Average
Team Leader	4.33	4.67	4.25	4.42
Development Manager	5	5	4.25	4.75
Planning Manager	4.67	4.67	4	4.44
Quality/Process Manager	4.67	5	4	4.56
Support Manager	4.67	4.33	3.5	4.17
Overall Average	**4.67**	**4.73**	**4.00**	**4.47**

Table 8- Cycle 2 Helpfulness and Support

Parallel results can be observed in helpfulness and support for Teams 1 and 2; however, Team 3 indicates an increase in rating for helpfulness/support from the Planning Manager and Quality/Process Manager, who happened to be the same person. All other members had no increase in their ratings.

Finally, the results of the survey for each role performance are as follows:

Rating after Cycle 1	Team 1 (4/4)	Team 2 (2/3)	Team3 (4/4)	Average
Team Leader	4.25	4	4.75	4.33
Development Manager	4.5	4.5	4.25	4.42
Planning Manager	4.25	4	4	4.08
Quality/Process Manager	4.25	3.5	4	3.92
Support Manager	4	4	4	4
Overall Average	**4.25**	**4**	**4.2**	**4.15**

Table 9- Cycle 1 Performance

Rating after Cycle 2	Team 1 (3/4)	Team 2 (3/3)	Team3 (4/4)	Average
Team Leader	4.33	4.67	4.5	4.5
Development Manager	5	5	4	4.67
Planning Manager	5	4.67	3.75	4.47
Quality/Process Manager	4.67	4.67	4.25	4.53
Support Manager	4.67	4.33	3.75	4.25
Overall Average	**4.73**	**4.67**	**4.05**	**4.48**

Table 10- Cycle 2 Performance

The results of the performance survey ratings again emphasize the same concept. By end of Cycle 2, all teams and their members had increased in their performance except Team 3. All members of Team 3 decreased in their performance except the Quality/Process Manager.

4 Conclusion

The basis of having a team-based real-world project is that it is both effective and an essential tool for teaching software engineering. The data clearly shows a decrease in the functionality of team members if they are paid to work in the same company. It is essential to keep a professional and consistent relationship between students and customers. In this project, the customer was a manager for the company and an alumnus of our program and held a close friendship with some of the students. This caused a conflict of interest and some confusion about the seriousness of the project. During the elicitation and final presentations, the owners were invited to attend with the customer, which helped to ease the situation.

Among other issues, there were also complaints based on the inability of some members to contribute to the development of project due to restrictions on the programming language. In addition, students provided generally negative feedback on the paperwork and pace of the project.

5 References

[1] J. Guo, "Group Projects in Software Engineering Education," *Consortium for Computing Sciences in Colleges,* pp. 194-202, 2009

[2] P. Y. Priyatham Anisetty, "Collaboration Problems in Conducting a Group Project in a Software Engineering Course," *Consortium for Computing Sciences in Colleges,* pp. 45-52, 2011

[3] K. R. Jay-Evan J Tevis, "Using Industry-Style Software Engineering and Project Management in a Project," *Consortium for Computing Sciences in Colleges,* pp. 77-82, 2010

[4] S. Davis, "Appointing Team Leads for Student Software Development Projects," *Consortium for Computing Sciences in Colleges,* pp. 92-99, 2009

[5] K. Anewalt, "Dynamic Group Management in a Software Projects Course," *Consortium for Computing Sciences in Colleges,* pp. 146-151, 2009

[6] K. Garg, "People Issues Relating to Software Engineering Education and Training in Idia,"

in *ISEC*, Hyderabad, India, 2008

[7] D. Varona, "Evolution of Software Engineers' Personality Profile," *ACM SIGSOFT*, pp. Vol 37, No1 , 2012

[8] ACM, "Computing Curricula 2005," ACM, [Online]. http://www.acm.org/education/curricula-recommendations

[9] IEEE Computing Society, "Guide to the Software Engineering Body of Knowledge," http://www.computer.org/portal/web/swebok/v3guide

[10] L. Jaccheri, "On the Importance of Dialogue with Industry about Software Engineering Education," *SSEE 06 - ACM*, pp. 5-8, 2006

An Investigation into Mobile Based Approach for Healthcare Activites Occupational Therapy System

Sardasht Mahmood, Joan Lu
School of Computing and Engineering, University of Huddersfield, UK

Abstract — **This research is to design and optimize the high quality of mobile apps, especially for iOS. The objective of this research is to develop a mobile system for Occupational therapy specialists to access and retrieval information. The investigation identifies the key points of using mobile-D agile methodology in mobile application development. It considers current applications within a different platform. It achieves new apps (OTS) for the health care activities.**

Keywords-component; Mobile Apps; Health care; Agile Methodology; Mobile-D; Design; Optimzation; Testing.

I. INTRODUCTION

Mobile application development has progressed rapidly in the recent years to provide a better performance for the users. Mobile technology has developed in terms of technology 'Data communication' and real world apps 'Mobile apps'. Mobile apps have increased and improved in different aspects such as health sector. Having more demands on mobile apps from the users and organizational needs made the numbers of different platforms and tools to increase significantly in order to improve mobile applications for various purposes [16]. Mobile computing is a 'computing that allows continuous access to remote resources, even to small computing devices such as laptops and digital cell phones' [6: p.2]. Then, Occupational Therapy (OT) enables 'people to achieve health well-being and life satisfaction through participation in occupation' [20: p.761].

II. AIMS AND OBJECTIVES

This research is to deploy an advanced methodology in mobile apps. It is aimed to develop Occupational Therapy System (OTS) mobile application for the heath sector, which establishes the communication channel between the patients and therapists. To access of the resources, information and healthcare service delivery through wireless technology [22]. Improving patient safety and reducing costs are increasingly recognized and emphasized [22]. Design of the application within this research is based on using mobile computing and software development. It is a multi-tire iOS mobile application to improve some issues within the health sector. It consists of the two main sections which are server side and client side (user interface). Furthermore, the vision behind this application is to provide core functionalities to the patients and then improving the health sector through identifying different functionalities.

Usability, recovery error (robust), clear navigation and minimum number of views are the main fundamental functionalities within the application. Other functionalities are delivery services in short time and secure process (Authentication). Moreover, Data storage on the server side (cloud) is one of the essential functionality, which leads to increasing the performance of the application. Furthermore, significant differences in mobile applications especially within OTS are a design and optimization. This research concentrates on the design and optimization within the application to improve the usability and user interface design. There are some specifications that identify what OTS mobile application exactly does:

- The OTS application consists of three essential sections as a tab bar style. It includes login, registration and support for the patients and therapists.
- Only registered users (patients or therapists) can access to the main view of the OTS application.
- The main view includes different services such as create assessment, view assessment and access to therapist feedback.

Figure 1 OTS Mobile Application

Besides, OTS has been designed based on some of the issues within mobile applications design.

III. BACKGROUND

The background of this research is categorized into some crucial sections which are Employed Method, Mobile Apps Design, Implementation and Testing.

A. Employed Method 'Mobile-D Agile Methodology'

Methodology is defined as a sequence process or 'road map to execute the processes to achieve the result' [9: p.27]. The agile methodologies are designed based on reduction and customization within the development process and being more flexible [15]. Another definition for agile development methodology is 'incremental (multiple releases), cooperative (a strong cooperation between developer and client), straightforward (easy to understand and modify) and adaptive (allowing for frequent changes)' [1: p.17].

'4-DAT' is an analytical framework which is based on the four elements to analyse the agility of methodology for instance, method scope, agility characterization, agile values characterization and Software Process Characterization [13]. The core functionality and fundamental elements in agile methodology for developing mobile application consist of the 'simple design principles, a large number of releases in a short time frame, extensive use of refactoring, pair programming, test-driven development' [12: p.2].

Mobile-D is defined as 'the method is based on agile practices, drawing elements from well established agile methods such as Extreme Programming and Crystal Methodologies [2: p.4]. Meanwhile, the mobile-D is adopted from the different methodologies such as XP practices, scrum and RUP phases [12]. Test-Driven Development (TDD) is defined as XP method for developing an application based on reducing the iterations [17]. It is one of the techniques or approaches to develop software which is based on writing test code (Unit test) before beginning to write coding for the application (program) [3][11].

There are some of the advantages of Mobile-D agile methodology for mobile application development, for instance 'increased progress visibility, earlier discovery and repair of technical issues, low defect density in the final product, and a constant progress in development' [2: p.175].

Having more advantages of using agile methodology are crucial to identify the way how to manage and create a plan during the development processes of the application. However, having more complexity during the combination of different plans and lacking 'scientific validation' are some of the arguments against agile methodologies generally [16].

Adaptability of mobile development and each of the Mobile-D phases have been identified clearly in detail to simplify the whole processes during the development. In addition, Mobile-D is providing the software documentation completely [16]. Then, short iterations support changing user requirements frequently which makes more agility rather than to be fixed with the requirements. Having more efficiency because of pair programming which allows the maintenance and development easily. Stability is one of the vital advantages between the stakeholder requirements and developers [16].

On the other hand, Mobile-D is not perfect for the complex or large system. Then, it has other weak points in terms of testing an application. For that reason, mobile-D should be adjusted with TDD to test different sections within the project [16][17].

B. Mobile Apps Design

The backbone of mobile and software applications is based on having a good design [10]. There are some of the basic principles to design mobile application, for instance readability, navigation, hotspots, pagination, button and call to action [5]. Useful, desirable, accessible, credible, findable and usable are different aspects that increase the value of mobile applications [5]. Furthermore, user interface design is a set of command or key navigation which can be used by users to use the application [4][19]. Pettini (2007) indicates that context is the main concept to design the application which is divided into three elements which are context of use (analyse requirements), context of medium (deign) and context of evaluation (testing /evaluation) [4].

The rationale behind using MVC is critical to decrease the limitation and expand the advantages of mobile application by providing full functionality on the server to be accessed by the clients [7]. For that reason, model, view and controller might be reused repeatedly which leads to produce another application [8].

One of the advantages of using MVC is to minimize or optimise the architecture of mobile applications [8]. Then, it is to provide a better maintenance for the functionalities of an application separately. Moreover, reusability is another advantage of MVC in terms of writing less programming code.

However, some of the most important classes which are absent within iOS to develop dual-platform mobile applications [19]. That is why it is one of the weak points of iOS to use MVC effectively because those classes are responsible of controlling data management and user interface design.

C. Implementation

Implementation of the OTS mobile application includes both sides of the OTS application, which are patients and therapists. Furthermore, it explains that how OTS mobile application has been implemented based on Model View Controller (MVC).

D. Testing

Testing mobile application is one of the essential parts within developing mobile applications [14]. Unlike software development, testing mobile application is difficult and more complex [14][18]. The life cycle of testing mobile application includes 'Testing Environment', 'Levels of Testing', 'Testing Techniques' and 'Scope of the Testing'.

White box testing and black box testing are fundamental classes to test applications [21]. White box testing (structural testing) is defined as 'testing that takes into account the internal mechanism of a system or component' [14: p.36]. Furthermore, it is called structural testing which includes Unit test. This type of test is inside the test level of the mobile application testing. Unit test is defined as a 'smallest testable piece of software that can be compiled, linked, loaded for example functions/procedures, classes, and interfaces' [14: p.1455].

However, Black box is defined testing as 'testing that ignores the internal mechanism of a system or component and focuses solely on the outputs generated in response to selected inputs and execution conditions' [21: p.36]. Furthermore, it is called functional testing which includes the test scope within the mobile application testing.

IV. Employed Methodo (Case Study)

The research method employed based on comparisons between some of the agile methodologies and assessing them. The ability of continuous changes during the development, improving the quality of the product and customer satisfaction, reducing wasting time by completing the development in short periods and predictability are several key factors lead to increasing the practicality of using agile methodology from some organizations.Having different software development methodologies makes it difficult to indicate the appropriate methodology within the project.

Several agile methodologies are described and compared in terms of their strength as well as weakness based on key points, characteristics and limitations such as Extreme programming (XP), Crystal methodologies and Rational Unified Process (RUP). However, none of them are specified separately to develop and implement mobile applications. That is why a suitable agile methodology for mobile application development called Mobile-D which supports the agility of mobile application.

The Mobile-D agile methodology consists of the five main phases which are Explore, Initialize, Productionize, Stabilize, and System Test & Fix. Each phase includes different iterations which are identified in Figure 2.

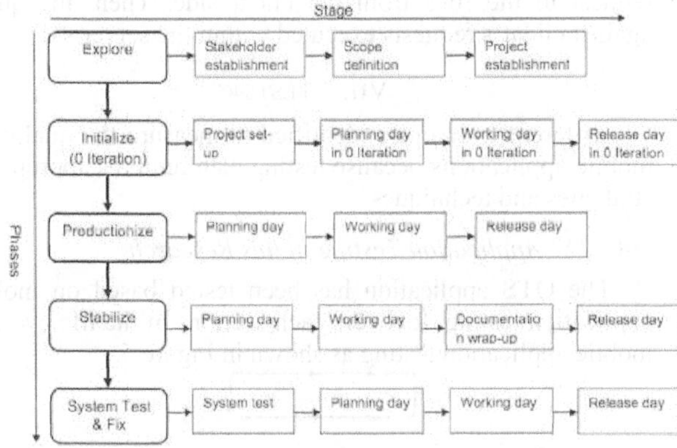

Figure 2 Mobile-D Agile Methodology Phases and Stages

A. Explore

Explore means to setup initial characteristics version of the project requirements and establishing the project plan. The main purpose of explore phase is to highlight the scopes and requirements within the project.

B. Initialize (0 Iteration)

When the initial requirements and plans of the project are well-organised and established, then, the Initialize phase begins which requires from the developer to build the first iteration within the project. Identifying the resources within the project technically and physically is one of the key points of this phase. Then, providing the communication channel between the developer and stakeholders is another important point during the application development.

C. Productionize

It means the implementation of functionalities that are collected within the Explore and Initialize phases of the project. In addition, it is divided into three stages. Firstly, the purpose of the planning day stage is to analyse the gathered requirements and prioritizing them to identify the core functionalities within the project. Then, it is providing iterations planning for implementation of the application development process which is called pre-established plan with compromising the test plan.

Secondly, working days step begins heading towards the pre-established plan which is provided to complete the core functionalities by using Test-Driven Development. Finally, when the testing process has been done perfectly release days step is the working version of the application which is produced successfully.

D. Stabilize

It means to collect and combine iterations together to finalise the product. To stabilise the application, one of the vital stages is to integrate all parts and putting them together as each system divided to different parts.

E. System Test & Fix

System Test & Fix is the final phase of Mobile-D agile methodology which based on the application testing frequently, fixing errors and finalises, complete the documentation of the application.

Having more characteristics and advantages of using agile methodology in terms of software development makes the agile methods more popular. Then, Mobile-D has been chosen because it is an agile methodology which is specified to develop mobile application.

V. System Design

To maximize the value of application, designers and developers should be concerned about different aspects and principles in mobile application development. In addition, it is important to make a comparison between some of the implemented user interfaces and then design the new interface with more efficiency.

This research consists of designing OTS architecture and diagrams based on using Model View Controller (MVC). Designing interface for the mobile application is about the achievements of the application and how it looks to produce the high quality interface design of an application. Usability and accessibility are two vital elements to obtain acceptable design. User experience which means utilizing the applications with features/services from users. Furthermore, Button sound (audible), standard fonts, zoom and alert vibration and background colours are some features in mobile applications.

Flowchart, wireframes and stylization/skinning are some of the essential ways to design the applications to create an intuitive application interface and to produce fixed overall design of the applications. User interface design is one of the challenges for mobile application.

High quality of user interface design of the applications can be achieved through making an attractive application user interface, usability which is simplicity of screen size, limitation which provides different keyboards based on the input information. Some functionality should be considered and applied in designing the applications such as user input format, use of context and present minimum information on the screen.

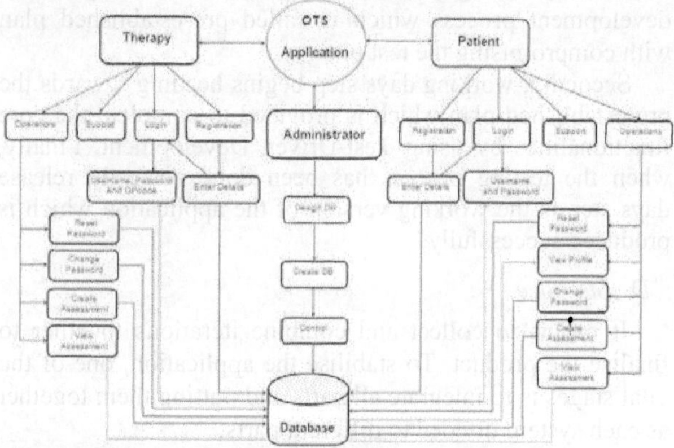

Figure 3 OTS Screen Design and User Interface

VI. Implementation

A. Classes and Operations (Model)

In this project, different operations are implemented to meet the OTS requirements and specifications. Each of the operations within the application consists of the two classes with the graphical user interface. Classes are implemented to store and manage the information within the application.

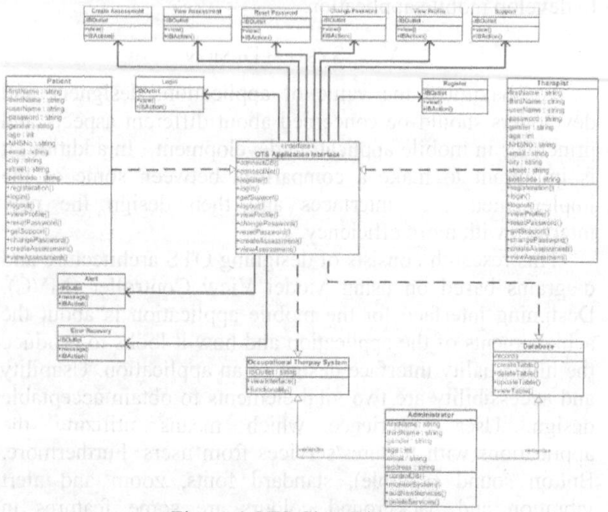

Figure 4 OTS Class Diagram

B. Graphical User Interfae (View)

It allows users to do various operations on the OTS application. The application user interfaces (views) are related to the View layer within the MVC. The OTS consists of tab bar navigation to switch between login; registration process and support as shown in Figure 1. Figure 2 illustrates the other views of the application.

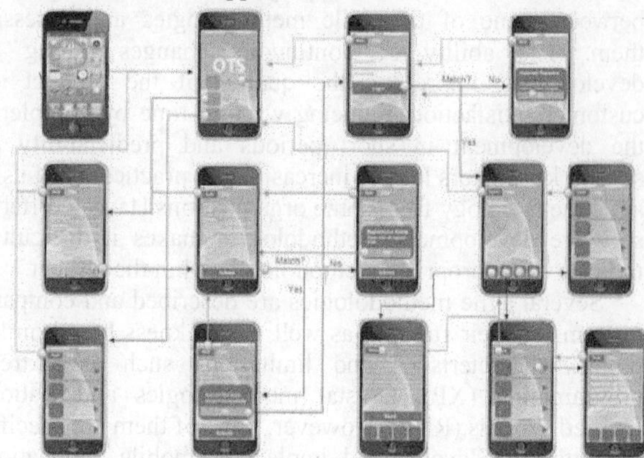

Figure 5 OTS Screen Design and User Interface

C. Appication Control (Control)

The final section within the MVC is a Control. The OTS application controls the connection between more views and models. The OTS database is uploaded to the indicated server, the connection is established through access and request to the files from the client side. Then, the query against client's requests executed within the server side.

VII. Testing

Different techniques identified to measure the quality of mobile applications because testing plan requires appropriate strategies and techniques.

A. The Application Testing in this Research

The OTS application has been tested based on mobile application testing. It covers each sections of the life cycle of mobile application testing as shown in Figure 5.

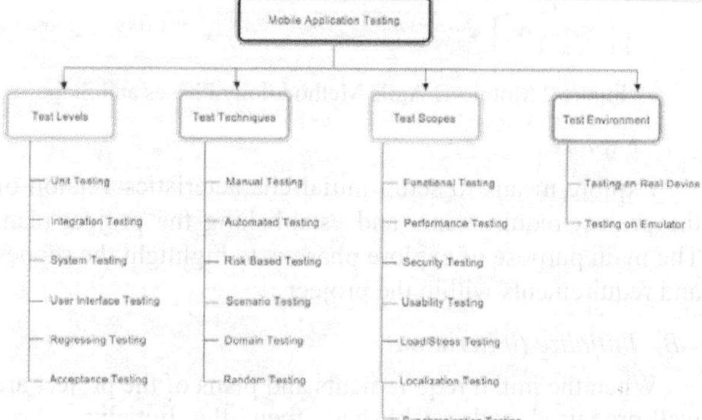

Figure 6 Life Cycle of Testing Mobile Application

In Testing Environment, during the development, the simulator used to test each actions and steps of the OTS application. In Levels of Testing, the application tested through White box testing (Unit testing). When the implementation phase of the application has been completed successfully, then unit testing begins by the developers. Then, the OTS application has been tested by a developer, post graduated graduate student and the supervisor, which is an Acceptance testing.

In Testing Techniques, Automated testing used within the project, the automated test case allows unit testing performs within the iOS platform. In Scope of the Testing, the application has been tested through Black box testing which includes different areas such as Functional Testing, Security Testing and Usability Testing.

Rational behind testing mobile application is that developers focus on and concern about the functionalities of the applications rather than testing applications on the real device. Moreover, lack of specific software to test mobile applications. Different types, techniques and tool of testing are given in order to improve the design of OTS application, to provide run able application. There are some crucial points behind testing application. Firstly, it is to verify that the source codes works perfectly. Then, it is to ensure that the application is stabilised and ready to use.

VIII. Results

It seems that there are some mobile applications which are designed for the purpose of a healthy life. Different tools and languages used within this project to create OTS mobile application for iOS platform. In this research, NHS direct and Epocrates iPhone applications are disciplined and analysed based on the principles of mobile application design. Lists of current issues in the health sector are identified. Furthermore, new designs of the mobile application achieved which minimizing some issues within those applications, OTS mobile application obtained which works on the iOS platform.

It is a multi-tire mobile application (client and server sides) which will be used within the health sector. The communication channel obtained through the application between the patients and therapists. In addition, the application optimized and minimized the number of views for different purposes such as easy to use, more user friendly and clear navigation.

IX. Evaluation and Analysis

This research is to create a mobile application for iOS platform. The aim was to organise, obtain and collect valuable resources within this research. Document design is one of the crucial steps before applications development begins. For that reason, the appropriate methodology (MVC) to design the OTS application was given. Then, functionalities of the application had been identified.

Furthermore, the OTS application had been designed technically such as architecture of user interface and server side, UML diagrams for the functionalities and screen designs. Theoretically, designing document consisted of the outlines of the application which include different sections on the application identification in detail. Moreover, designing document provided the initial document to clarify goals and overall ideas about the application. After that, it is possible to restructure or modify the outlines within the application. One of the views was well structure planning at the beginning of the project. Furthermore, analysing requirements specification, establishing communication channels and designing functionalities within the project are other successful aspects.

The connection between the background of this research and the OTS project is based on different views such as user interface design, usability and functionality. Furthermore, NHS Direct, Epocrates applications have been chosen because of compatibility with OTS project. Both of applications had been used for the purposes that they are related to the health sector. OTS application comes out based on those existed applications and other systems, which operated on different platforms. Furthermore, OTS application is reviewed and strengthened in terms of readability, navigation, pagination, hotspots, buttons, and call to action.

This project was managed through using agile methodology to develop mobile application. Furthermore, it considered choosing specific methods for mobile application development, which is Mobile-D agile methodology. Mobile-D is a combination of different agile methodologies in software development such as XP, Crystal and RUP. Mobile-D phases and stages had been applied within OTS project.

Despite efforts to identify Mobile-D advantages and disadvantages, there are some points require to be extended to improve of the Mobile-D methodology in mobile application development. One of the Mobile-D weak points is testing. Besides, to minimize disadvantages of Mobile-D methodology, different approaches to test the application are given.

If you take the advantages of Mobile-D methodology through iterations or reviews, Iterations in each phase of the Mobile-D made the application more robust (error free), reliable in terms of functionality. In terms of usability, it made the OTS application easy to use and simple. Those positive observations had been achieved through the OTS application. Solving the issues technically and efficiently extended the advantages of Mobile-D methodology within the mobile application development.

X. Conclusion and Future Work

To sum up, this research proposed to use appropriate methodology for OTS mobile application. In the research method, it disciplined agile methodologies such as XP, Crystal and RUP. Mobile-D agile methodology had been chosen because it is a combination of those declared methodologies. Furthermore, all phases of the Mobile-D are explained with Mobile-D advantages and disadvantages in mobile application development. The research conduct explains how different phases of Mobile-D are applied within this research.

Some applications and existing systems for iOS platform had been taken into account. Different tools and software are discussed in terms of mobile application for iOS platform. The fundamental features of usability are stated in OTS application such as effectiveness, efficiency and satisfaction.

In the design section, this research explained a brief background and some principles of design mobile applications. It presented each layers of Model View Controller (MVC) with advantages and disadvantages in mobile application development. The Architecture of the application outlined in design section such as functionality architecture and system architecture.

The implementation and testing of mobile application are organised in a different sections. Implementation part explains how OTS application is implemented. Furthermore, testing section includes a background of testing mobile application. It identified different types of testing mobile application such as Black box and White box testing. Both types of testing are applied within the OTS mobile application. In evaluation section, project evaluation, theoretical evaluation of the project and methodology evaluation had been analysed.

REFERENCES

[1] Abrahamsson, P., Salo, O., Ronkainen, J., & Warsta, J. (2002). 'Agile Software Development Methods: Review and Analysis'. Finland: VTT Electronics VTT Publications 478.

[2] Abrahamsson, P., Hanhineva, A., Hulkko, H., Ihme, T., Jäälinoja, J., Korkala, M., Koskela, J., Kyllönen, P. & Salo, O. (2004). 'Mobile-D: An Agile Approach for Mobile Application Development'. In *Proceeding OOPSLA '04 Companion to the 19th annual ACM SIGPLAN conference on Object-oriented programming systems, languages, and application,* Vancouver. ACM Press, pp. 174-175

[3] Astels, D. (2003). 'Test Driven Development: A Practical Guide'. New Jersy: Prentice Hall.

[4] Ayob, N. Ab. Hussin, R. & Dahlan, H. (2009). 'Three Layers Design Guideline for Mobile Application'. *Information Management and Engineering*. IEEE Computer Society, ICIME '09. International Conference on. pp.427-431 .

[5] Finck (2010). 'Mobile Information Architecture & Interaction Design.' *Design For Mobile.* Chicago.

[6] Garg, K. (2010). *Mobile Computing: Theory and Practice*. Delhi: Pearson Education.

[7] La, H. Lee, H. & Kim, S. (2011). 'An Efficiency-centric Design Methodology for Mobile Application Architectures'. *Wireless and Mobile Computing, Networking and Communications* (WiMob), 2011 IEEE 7th International Conference on. pp.272-279 .

[8] Lezama, A. (2010). *Introduction to Mobile Application Development with an example of a "PhraseBook App"*. (MSc) University Politècnica de Catalunya [Available online] http://upcommons.upc.edu/pfc/handle/2099.1/10994 [Accessed on 1st July 2012].

[9] Mainardi, R. (2011). *Harnessing the Power of Continuous Auditing : Developing and Implementing a Practical Methodology*. New Jersy: Wiley.

[10]Mark, D. (ed.) (2009). *iPhone User Interface Design Projects*. New York: Apress.

[11]Panc˘ur, M. & Ciglaric˘, M. (2011). 'Impact of test-driven development on productivity, code and tests: A controlled experiment'. *Information and Software Technology*. 53, pp.557- 573.

[12]Puolitaival, O. (2008). 'Adapting model based testing to agile context'. Finland: VTT Electronic Publications 694.

[13]Qumer, A. & Henderson-Sellers B. (2008). 'A framework to support the evaluation, adoption and improvement of agile methods in practice'. In *The Journal of Systems and Software.* vol.81 (11) pp.1899-1999.

[14]Selvam, R. & Karthikeyani, V. (2011). 'Mobile Software Testing – Automated Test Case Design Strategies'. *International Journal on Computer Science and Engineering (IJCSE),* Vol. 3 (4), pp. 1450-1461.

[15]Soundararajan, S. (2011). *A Methodology for Assessing Agile Software Development Approaches.* (Doctor of Philosophy) Virginia Polytechnic Institute and State University [Available online] http://arxiv.org/ftp/arxiv/papers/1108/1108.0427.pdf [Accessed on 13th July 2012].

[16]Spataru, A. (2010). *'Agile Development Methods for Mobile Applications'* (MSc) University of Edinburgh [Available online] www.inf.ed.ac.uk/publications/thesis/online/IM100767.pdf [Accessed on 15th June 2012].

[17]Tort, A., Olivé, A. & Sancho, M. (2011). 'An approach to test-driven development of conceptual schemas'. *Data & Knowledge Engineering*, vol.70 (12), pp. 1088-1111.

[18] Tracy, K. (2012). 'Mobile Application Development Experiences on Apple's iOS and Android OS'. IEEE. vol.31. (4), pp.30-34.

[19] Uther, M. (2002). 'Mobile Internet usability: what can 'mobile learning' learn from the past?'. *Wireless and*

Mobile Technologies in Education. Proceedings. IEEE International Workshop on. pp. 174- 176.

[20] Watson, M., Lucas, C., Hoy, A. & Wells, J. (2009). *Oxford Handbook of Palliative care* (2nd ed.) New York: Oxford University Press.

[21] Williams, L. (2008). 'A (Partial) Introduction to Software Engineering Practices and Methods'. (5th Ed.) NCSU CSC326 Course Pack, 2008-2009.

[22]Yu, P., Wu, M., Yu, H. & Xiao, G.(2006). 'The Challenges for the Adoption of M- Health'. *IEEE International Conference*. pp.181-186.

Teaching Software Engineering Through a Real-World Project: A New Approach

C. Zhao, M. Estep, and K.D. Smith
Computing & Technology Department, Cameron University, Lawton, OK, USA

Abstract – *Software Engineering is a commonly required course in the Computer Science degree curriculum. It can be a challenging task to teach the course in a way that is relevant to what students will experience in industry upon graduation. In this article, the authors discuss the use of a real-world project to teach Software Engineering. This new approach promotes a fresh and creative learning environment in which students apply their knowledge to engineer a real product for a real client. During the process, basic principles, methods, and CASE tool usage of Software Engineering are addressed. Student learning outcomes are enhanced as well.*

Key Words: Software Engineering, Real-world project, Web Development, PHP, SQL, UML

1 Introduction

Software Engineering (SE) is a required core course in the Computer Science (CS) B.S. curriculum at Cameron University. This course is designed to provide CS students with necessary skills, techniques, and tools to develop and manage complex programming projects. The way SE is taught affects not only the quality of CS academic programs, but also the quality of future software professionals [1]. The traditional teaching method of covering basic SE principles and general applications can be insufficient to communicate the complexity and dynamics of software development that is experienced beyond the classroom [2]. In order to improve the quality of the SE course, the authors have been exploring a new approach – the use of interdisciplinary combined capstone classes. Recently, the authors have combined CS SE and Information Systems (IS) capstone classes to complete real-world projects. Such projects provide students with an opportunity to apply knowledge learned in class to solve real problems for real clients. This in turn promotes a fresh and creative learning environment where student learning outcomes and problem-solving abilities are enhanced. Moreover, completed projects have also benefited some non-profit organizations, and therefore social impact was positive [3]. In this article, the authors introduce basic concepts and procedures on how this new approach was recently conducted for CETESjobs.com, in the creation of a job search engine designed to bring together a local metropolitan business community with retired veterans seeking employment [4].

2 Initial Methods

2.1 Class Arrangement

The 16-week SE class was divided into two 8-week parts: the first 8-week focus was on teaching students basic principles, processes, and methods of SE and completing analysis and design of the targeted project; the second 8 week emphasis was on coding, testing, and validation of the project.

2.2 Forming Teams

At the beginning of the semester, students turned in two copies of resumes and job application letters, one with identifying information and the other without identifying information. Two teams were established with the team captain being chosen by the instructors. Then captains selected team members by using the blind resumes. Once formed, teams acted as a unit to complete the project. A typical CS team consisted of a captain, a lead programmer, a lead algorithm developer, a testing designer, and a coordinator.

2.3 Project Components

The authors have completed four real-world projects to date. A typical real-world project usually contains three components, as shown in Figure 1:

(1) Front end Web pages that are coded in HTML/CSS/JavaScript
(2) Middleware PHP code that fetches data from web forms, processes it, and then sends data to…
(3) Back end system that consists of a MySQL database and database management system

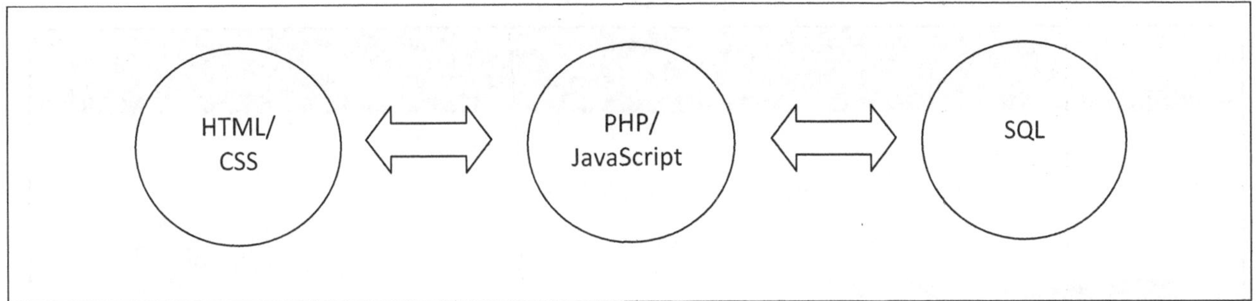

Figure 1. Web Project Components

2.4 Requirements

In order to determine client needs, the authors scheduled an interview between the client and students. Before the interview, student developers developed an interview question list. After interviewing the client, student development teams were required to send a summarized needs list back to the client for verification. As necessary, this process was repeated until the client need was clear and verified. At the same time, student developers also collected forms from the client to obtain useful system information.

2.5 Analysis

Once system requirements were determined, each team developed a system information flow chart and UML class diagram/Use Case Diagram using System Architect to show system components and relationships among the system components. An example flow chart is shown in Figure 2.

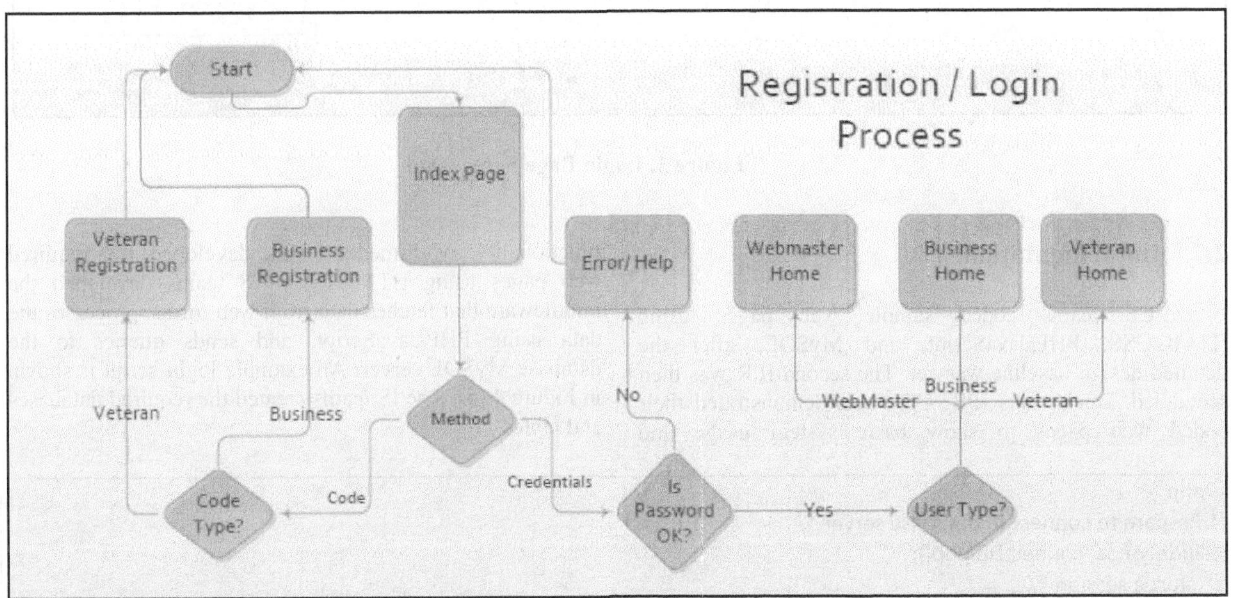

Figure 2. System Information Flow Chart

2.6 Design

After obtaining instructor approval, each team refined their basic system design using stepwise techniques to develop a detailed system design, where each class entity contained attributes and methods. After completing the detailed design, the first in-process review (IPR) was presented to the client. During the IPR, each team gave a PowerPoint presentation demonstrating their basic system design and how the system works. Client representatives asked questions and verified their needs. After the first IPR, system requirements and design were then modified to meet the client needs. A screenshot of an example login page is shown in Figure 3.

Figure 3. Login Page Screenshot

2.7 Implementation

CS teams coded sample web pages using HTML/CSS, PHP/JavaScript, and MySQL, after the detailed design baseline was set. The second IPR was then scheduled. During this IPR, CS teams demonstrated their coded web pages to show basic system usage and functionality. Multimedia teams developed the required web pages using HTML/CSS. CS teams developed the middleware that fetches data from web forms, processes the data using PHP/JavaScript, and sends queries to the database MySQL server. An example login script is shown in Figure 4 [5]. The IS teams created the required databases and tables.

```
<?php
/* Prepare to connect to database server */
include_once('connectDB.php');
/* start a session */
 session_name('cameron');
 session_start();
 ob_start();
 /* connect function */
$conn = mysql_connect($host, $user, $pass)or die (' Database connection cannot be established.');
/* select the database */
$selectDB = mysql_select_db($database, $conn);
/* SQL injection protection function */
 include ('clean.php');
 /* Data validation Section */
 if ( $_POST['submit'] )
```

```
{       $u_username = $_POST['username'];
        $u_password = $_POST['password'];
        /*check if data has been inputed properly */
        if ( !$u_username || !$u_password ){
                printf(" Username or password field is empty.");
        }
        else{ /* input data was validated*/
                $val = mysql_query("SELECT * FROM `user` WHERE `u_username` = '".$u_username."'");
                $num = mysql_num_rows($val);

                /* if u_username do not macth with database */
                if($num==0)
                {
                        printf("username doesn't match with database.");
                }
                else{ /* if u_username matches,and then check for u_password */
                        $val = mysql_query("SELECT * FROM user WHERE u_username = '".$u_username."' AND
                        u_password = '".$u_password."'");
                        $num = mysql_num_rows($val);
                        /* if u_username and u_password both match */
                        if($num==0)
                        printf("password doesn't match with database.");
                        else
                        {       /**** USER HAS AUTHENTICATED FROM HERE ****/
                                /* fetch the matched user row into a associative array */
                                $array=mysql_fetch_assoc($val);
                                /* check for if account has been activated */
                                if($array['active'] == 0)
                                printf(" Account is still not activated. Please check your email. ");
                                else {
                                /*** ACCOUNT ACTIVATED MODE FROM HERE ****/
                        /* store the login session. This is used to check if the user is logged in or not*/
                                $_SESSION['u_id'] = $array['id'];
                                printf(" You have successfully logged in. ");
                                /* Set the timestamp of last login of the user */
                                mysql_query("UPDATE `members` SET `stamp` '".$time."' WHERE `id` =
                                '".$_SESSION['u_id']."'");
                                printf(" You have successfully logged in ");
                                // count current logged in user
                                $_SESSION['count'] = 0;
                                 //setting a variable so that later i know that this user i logged in
                                $_SESSION["isLoggedIn"] = 1;
                                $_SESSION["user"] = $u_username;
                                $currentCookieParams = session_get_cookie_params();
                                $rootDomain = '.subedi.us';
                                session_set_cookie_params (
                                        $currentCookieParams["life"],
                                        $currentCookieParams["path"],
                                        $rootDomain,
                                        $currentCookieParams["secure"],
                                        $currentCookieParams["httponly"]
                                        );
                                session_name('cameron');
                                session_start();
                                setcookie($cookieName, $cookieValue, time() + 3600, '/', $rootDomain);
```

```
                    header('Location: ../retiree/profile.php');
                }
            }
        }
    }
?>
```

Figure 4. Login.php Supporting Login Page

2.8 Testing

The students did two kinds of testing: (1) non-executable testing of analysis and design. This kind of testing was conducted using team walk-throughs, and (2) executable testing to detect code artifacts. This testing was carried out by team lead programmers and test data designers to fix any syntax and logic errors.

2.9 Validation

After completing the entire project, deliverable products were presented to the client in a final meeting. The client watched team presentations and assessed whether deliverables were acceptable or not. The client then selected the team project that best fit client needs. Once the chosen deliverable passed validation, it was installed on a client machine, after the chosen team completed necessary modifications.

3 Discussion

- **Software development is a two dimensional process, rather than a linear process [6]:** During developing software to solve a real-world problem, the authors can see there are generally five work flows – requirement, analysis, design, implementation, and testing. However, one work flow may be dominant over others. Seeing this in a real-world project can help students truly understand the complexity of the software development process.
- **Real software development experience:** Each real-world project development process offers students an excellent opportunity to be engaged in all phases of software development, which may benefit their professional practice in the future.
- **Ability to develop and manage a larger project:** The completed real-world projects may be considered as mid-sized software development that needs to integrate multiple programming languages HTML, CSS, PHP, JavaScript, and SQL to have a working system. A completed project may contain hundreds of PHP modules and hundreds of analysis and design documents.
- **Communication skills:** To complete a real-world project, much oral and written communication has to take place between the client and student development teams, between different student teams, and within a student team. This offers students a chance to improve and enhance their professional communication skills.
- **Student learning:** Student learning is one of the core values at Cameron University. The students from different disciplines worked together and not only learned professional knowledge from each other, but also learned how to work with others.
- **Benefits to society:** Because deliverable projects are provided pro-bono to clients, a beneficial service is provided, which is especially helpful if the clients are also non-profit organizations. This results in a positive social impact on the southwestern area of Oklahoma.

4 Conclusion

The real-world project approach changed the way the authors teach SE at Cameron University. This approach provides our students with a great opportunity to apply their knowledge to solve a real-world problem. It also creates an enjoyable learning environment that motivates the students to go further and dig deeper in their professional field [7]. This practice can improve the quality of SE and student learning outcomes. Moreover, the approach allows the authors' department and students to reach out to diverse organizations in society, thereby providing significant positive social impact.

5 References

[1] ***Teaching Software Development vs. Software Engineering***, Gary Pollice, Worcester Polytechnic Institute, http://www.ibm.com/developworks/rational/library/dec05/pollice/index.html

[2] ***Teaching Software Engineering through Simulation***, Oh, Emily, http://www.ics.uci.edu/~emilyo/papers/ICSEDS02.pdf

[3] **The Cameron University Green Website Project-Part 1: Service Learning in the Fall 2009,** Mike Estep, David Kenneth Smith, Chao Zhao, and Tom Russell, *International Journal of Education Research*, Volume 5 No. 2, Summer 2010

[4] ***CETES Jobs, Bridging Opportunities***, http://www.cetesjobs.com

[5] ***PHP and MySQL Web Development***, Fourth Edition, Luke Weling, Laura Thomson, Addison Wesley, 2009

[6] ***Object-Oriented and Classical Software Engineering***, 8th Edition, Stephen R. Schach, McGraw Hill, 2011

[7] ***How We Teach Software Engineering,*** Christine Mingins, Jan Miller, Martin Dick, and Margot Postema, Monash University, Melbourne, Australia, http://citeseerx.ist.psu.edu/viewdoc/summary?doi=10.1.1.102.1045

Why To Research in Knowledge Management in Software Engineering Processes?

E.A. Galvis-Lista[1], J. M. Sánchez-Torres[2]
[1]Facultad de Ingeniería, Universidad del Magdalena, Santa Marta, Colombia.
Doctoral Student, Universidad Nacional de Colombia, Bogotá Colombia
[2]Facultad de Ingeniería, Universidad Nacional de Colombia, Bogotá, Colombia

Abstract – *Knowledge Management is a young discipline that nowadays it is important for software development organizations (SDO). For this reason, this paper presents a review about the form knowledge management has been included in several Software Process Reference Models. For this study, five software process reference models, broadly used in Latin-American countries, were analyzed. The findings of this study show that in all models there are elements of knowledge management processes, and there are two models with a process area named Knowledge Management. Nevertheless, the knowledge management aspects included in these models is grounded in statements from Earl's systems and engineering schools. Likewise, in terms of Gold's knowledge management capabilities, the technology, knowledge acquisition and knowledge conversion capabilities are broadly covered but elements for others capabilities are not included in these reference models.*

Keywords: Knowledge management in software engineering, Knowledge management processes, Software process reference models, Knowledge management in software organizations.

1 Introduction

In recent years, Knowledge Management (KM) has become an important set of processes in Software Engineering (SE). Several publications have developed this topic from diverse perspectives. One synthesis of the scientific work about KM in SE [1] identified the predominant interest in topics such as knowledge codification, IT-based knowledge storage and retrieval. However, knowledge creation, knowledge transfer and knowledge application, are processes that have had little coverage. Furthermore, the authors concluded that most of the empirical research works are focus on KM in software process improvement (SPI).

In this regard, KM in software processes and KM in SPI were identified by [2] as important research topics, because KM is the main component of SPI initiatives. Also, the application of KM in SE is useful in software process definition, the application of a process approach in software engineering, and the adaptation of software process for future uses. However, in a deeper review of papers in which the main topic is KM in SPI, published in the last five years, we found out that the predominant approach is knowledge codification, as can be seen in [3]–[9]. In addition, there are works about knowledge mapping by the construction of organizational knowledge directories [5], [10] and the creation and empowerment of organizational structures to promote knowledge sharing [10]–[13].

After the review we identified that the research on KM in SPI has been focused in the application of KM as a tool in SPI initiatives. However, KM does not be conceived as an integral process within the scope of SPI. For that reason, the purpose of this paper is to present a review about how KM has been included in several SPRM. It is important to say that the SPRM are the basis for SPI initiatives because they contain the process definitions that a SDO could implement and improve to gain process capability and organizational maturity.

The remainder of this paper is organized as follows. Section 2 presents the theoretical background about KM. Section 3 describes the methodology used for the review. Section 4 presents the results of the review according to our chosen theoretical background. Section 5 concludes.

2 Theoretical Background

This section presents a synthesis of two theoretical statements needed for the later analysis of the selected SPRM. In the first part, a classification of KM work into schools of thought that was proposed by [14] is presented. In the second part, a complementary perspective, composed by a set of KM organizational capabilities, proposed by Gold, Malhotra and Segars [15], is described.

The first referent is a "KM strategies taxonomy" proposed by Earl in 2001 [14]. The used methodology and the variety of data sources make this classification one of the most detailed. Further classifications can find in [16]–[24], but Earl's taxonomy is considered the most complete, because It was constructed based on descriptive data from: (1) six case studies in companies; (2) interviews with 20 chief knowledge officers; (3) Workshops about KM programs in organizations; and (4) a review of publications about KM from research and practice. The identified KM schools are categorized as "Technocratic", "Economic" and "Behavioral".

The technocratic schools are focused on IT tools to support employees in their knowledge-based tasks. The technocratic schools are the systems school, the cartographic school and the engineering school. The systems school is focused on technology for knowledge codification and sharing using knowledge bases. The cartographic school is focused on the creation and maintenance of knowledge maps using knowledge directories. The engineering school is focused on knowledge processes and knowledge flows within organizations.

The economic schools are focused on the exploitation of knowledge as intellectual capital to create revenues streams. In the economic schools Earl identified only the commercial school.

The behavioral schools are focused on the promotion and encouragement of knowledge creation and sharing and all organizational and personal issues to use knowledge as an organizational resource. In the last category there are three schools identified as organizational school, spatial school and strategic school. The organizational school is focused on the creation of networks for sharing knowledge. The spatial school is focused on the design of work spaces to promote knowledge sharing. The strategic school is focused on the development of the organizational strategy based on knowledge as its essence. A synthesis of Earl's taxonomy is showed in Table 1.

Table 1 Knowledge management schools **[14]**

Category	School	Focus	Aim
Technocratic	Systems	Technology	Knowledge bases
	Cartographic	Maps	Knowledge directories
	Engineering	Processes	Knowledge flows
Economic	Commercial	Income	Knowledge assets
Behavioral	Organizational	Networks	Knowledge Pooling
	Spatial	Space	Knowledge exchange
	Strategic	Mindset	Knowledge Capabilities

The second referent is the work of Gold, Malhotra and Segars that was published in 2001 [15]. In this work, the authors argue that organizations must leverage their knowledge and create new knowledge to compete in their markets. In order to accomplish this, organizations must develop two types of KM capabilities: knowledge infrastructure capabilities and knowledge process capabilities. Knowledge infrastructure capabilities enable maximization of social capital, understood as "the sum of actual and potential resources embedded within, available through, and derived from the network of relationships possessed by a social unit" [15]. Complementary, knowledge process capabilities are the dynamic elements that leverage the infrastructure capabilities to make knowledge an active organizational resource.

The three infrastructure capabilities are technology, structure and culture. The technological dimension addresses the tools and means that enable knowledge flows in an efficient way. The structural infrastructure focuses on the existence of norms, and trust mechanisms, as well as, formal organizational structures, which enable and encourage people to create and share knowledge. The cultural dimension refers to the presence of shared contexts within organization.

The four process capabilities are knowledge acquisition, knowledge conversion, knowledge application, and knowledge protection. The knowledge acquisition process is oriented toward obtaining knowledge from diverse sources both within and outside organizations. The knowledge conversion process is focused on making existing knowledge useful based on knowledge encoding, combination, coordination and distribution. The knowledge application process is oriented toward the actual use of knowledge, and the knowledge protection process is designed to protect the organizational knowledge from illegal or inappropriate use or theft. As illustrated in Figure 1, in terms of Gold et al, infrastructure and process dimensions reflect an additive capability to launch and sustain a program of change through KM in order to gain organizational effectiveness.

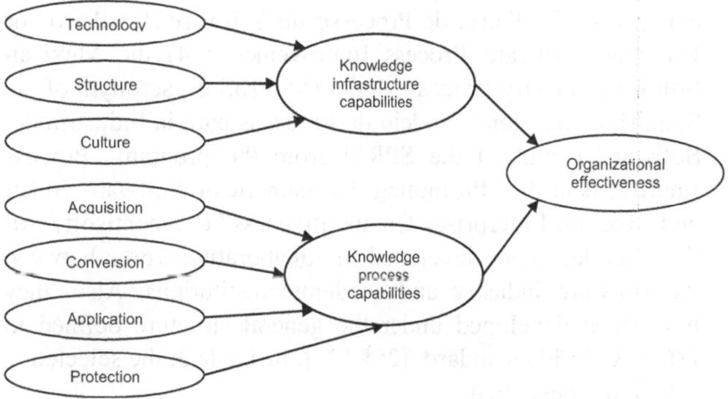

Figure 1 Knowledge management capabilities and organizational effectiveness. **[15]**.

3 Methodology

The methodology designed for this work consists of three stages:

1. **SPRM selection**: The purpose of this stage was to select a set of SPRM used at Colombian and Latin American levels. To do this, a set of publications of the last decade, which main topic was SPI in Latin America's SDO was reviewed. The five most mentioned SPRM were selected.

2. **Analysis of SPRM Processes and KM:** The description of each process within each SPRM was analyzed to find aspects related to KM. The review was focused on the statement of process purpose and the descriptions of process outcomes. A subset of KM-related processes was selected.

3. **Mapping of SPRM process and KM:** In this stage, the KM-related processes selected in the second stage were analyzed in relation to the KM schools proposed by [14] and the organizational KM capabilities, proposed by [15]. To do this, a single mention of some idea from KM schools or KM capabilities, was enough to map the process.

4 Results

The main results of this work were: 1) the selection of five SPRM; 2) the identification of 19 processes related to KM within SPRM; and 3) the mapping of the 19 processes to KM schools and KM organizational capabilities. In the next three subsections the detailed results of each stage are described.

4.1 SPRM selection

The first result was the selection of five SPRM from a set of 155 documents from SCOPUS database. The selected models were: 1) the ISO/IEC 122007 standard; 2) the Capability Maturity Model Integration for Development (CMMI-DEV); 3) the Brazilian SPRM (MPS.BR, acronym of the Portuguese expression "Melhoria de Processo do Software Brasileiro" or Brazilian Software Process Improvement); 4) the Mexican Software Industry Process Model (MoProSoft, acronym of the Spanish expression "Modelo de Procesos para la Industria del Software"); and 5) the SPRM from the program "Process Improvement for Promoting Iberoamerican Software Small and Medium Enterprises Competitiveness" (Competisoft). All these models were developed in collaborative works between the software industry and academic institutions. Also, they have been developed under the general structure defined in ISO/IEC 15504 standard [25]–[27]. In Table 3, the selected SPRM are described.

4.2 Analysis of SPRM Processes and KM:

The analysis of the processes to identify those with some KM ideas resulted in a set of 19 processes from the 101 processes included in the five selected models. In Table 2, the selected processes, for each SPRM, are presented.

Table 2 Processes related to KM ideas.

Model	Process related to KM
ISO 12207	1. Software Configuration Management 2. Software Problem Resolution Process 3. Life Cycle Model Management 4. Human Resource Management 5. Reuse Asset Management 6. Domain Engineering
CMMI-DEV	1. Configuration Management 2. Organizational Process Definition 3. Organizational Training
MPS.BR	1. Configuration Management 2. Organizational Process Definition 3. Human Resource Management 4. Development for reuse
MoProSoft	1. Process Management 2. Human Resources and Work Environment Management 3. Organizational Knowledge
Competisoft	1. Process Management 2. Human Resources and Work Environment Management 3. Organizational Knowledge

4.3 Mapping of SPRM process and KM

Related to the analysis of SPRM and KM schools, we found out that most of the KM aspects are related to systems school. In other words, the predominant approach is knowledge codification. In fact, even in several SPRM there is an explicit reference to KM or to organizational knowledge (MoProSoft, Competisoft), the scope of this process is limited to keep available and manage a knowledge repository. The content of this knowledge repository is, mainly, best practices, lessons learned, knowledge work products, and knowledge about process definitions. Also, ISO/IEC 12207, CMMI-DEV and MPS.BR included the concept of an organizational knowledge repository as part of two processes: configuration management process and organizational process definition process.

In addition, all SPRM include aspects related to engineering school. In particular, this school appears in the form of training activities and the provision of qualified personnel to do knowledge activities. These statements are part of human resource management processes. In Table 4, the relations between the selected SPRM and the KM schools are presented.

Table 3 Description of selected SPRM.

Model	Last update	Institution	Country	Processes	Used References
ISO/IEC 12207	2008	International Organization for Standarization	International	43	[28];[29]; [30]; [31];[32];
CMMI-DEV	2011	Software Engineering Institute	USA	22	[33]; [34]; [35]
MPS.BR	2011	Association for Promoting the Brazilian Software Excellence	Brazil	19	[36]; [37]; [38]; [39]
MoProSoft	2005	Mexican Association for Software Engineering Quality	Mexico	8	[40]; [41]; [42]; [43]
Competisoft	2008	An Ibero American Research Network on Software Quality	Spain – Latin America	9	[44]; [45]; [46]; [47]; [48]

Table 4 Relations between SPRM's process and KM schools.

Model	Process related to KM	KM Schools						
		Systems	Cartographic	Engineering	Commercial	Organizational	Spatial	Strategic
ISO 12207	Configuration Management	X	-	-	-	-	-	-
	Software Problem Resolution Process	X	-	-	-	-	-	-
	Life Cycle Model Management	-	-	X	-	-	-	-
	Human Resource Management	X	-	X	-	-	-	-
	Reuse Asset Management	X	-	-	-	-	-	-
	Domain Engineering	X	-	-	-	-	-	-
CMMI-DEV	Configuration Management	X	-	-	-	-	-	-
	Organizational Process Definition	X	-	-	-	-	-	-
	Organizational Training	-	-	X	-	-	-	-
MPS.BR	Configuration Management	X	-	-	-	-	-	-
	Organizational Process Definition	X	-	-	-	-	-	-
	Human Resource Management	-	-	X	-	-	-	-
	Development for reuse	X	-	-	-	-	-	-
MoProSoft	Process Management	X	-	-	-	-	-	-
	Human Resources and Work Environment Management	-	-	X	-	-	-	-
	Organizational Knowledge	X	-	-	-	-	-	-
Competisoft	Process Management	X	-	-	-	-	-	-
	Human Resources and Work Environment Management	-	-	X	-	-	-	-
	Organizational Knowledge	X	-	-	-	-	-	-

The analysis of the SPRM in relation to KM capabilities found out that most of the KM aspects are related to technology infrastructure capability and knowledge conversion process capability. These findings are coherent with the emphasis on Systems School. Another important element is that all SPRM have at least a process concerning to the design and implementation of a process-based organizational structure. Likewise, the acquisition and application process capabilities are covered explicitly within the models. The relations between the processes from SPRM and the KM capabilities are presented in Table 5.

5 Conclusions

From an Earl's KM schools perspective, the topics included in SPRM are limited to the content of two schools: systems and engineering. Hence, any software organization involved in a SPI initiative cannot include KM strategies from another KM schools in the implementation, evaluation and improvement of its processes. For instance, the physical design of workspaces to promote knowledge creation and knowledge sharing, from spatial school, are not include in the studied SPRM, even though a grown number of companies have been applied it. In addition, many authors have argued, in many publications, that the software industry is, by definition, a knowledge-intensive industry. Hence it is surprising that the statements of commercial school are not explicitly included in the studied SPRM. Also, it is remarkable that the statements of organizational and strategic schools have a closed relation to the principles and practices of agile methods to software development, but these schools are not included in the studied SPRM too, even though, the agile methods have an important influence in software industry, especially in small and medium SDO.

In terms of the organizational KM capabilities, the studied SPRM do not include explicitly the cultural knowledge management capability. Nevertheless, in recent years the research literature in software engineering process design and improvement, especially all "agile" movement, has emphasized the crucial role of organizational culture in SDO. For this reason, this absence is a big gap to fill soon. Moreover, the studied SPRM do not include two crucial process capabilities: knowledge application and knowledge protection.

Along these lines, this work has showed that the studied SPRM include, within their scope, some aspects related to KM. This fact reaffirms the importance of KM for SDO, and, in particular, the importance of KM in SPI. Mainly, the topics of interest about KM in SPRM are: 1) knowledge codification, 2) use of knowledge repositories, and 3) organizational training. These interest topics are located, in terms of Buono and Poulfelt [49], in a first generation KM. In this type of KM, knowledge is considered as a possession or something that could be caught and stored in IT-based knowledge repositories. On contrary, in the second generation KM, knowledge is considered a complex phenomenon concerning to socio-cultural, politic and technological aspects. Hence, a gap is evidenced in the content of the analyzed SPRM because they do not take into account elements from the second generation KM.

These arguments allow us to formulate three questions that serve as a source of motivation for future research: 1) what KM outcomes and purposes should be included in the existing SPRM to have a more complete reference in processes design, implementation, evaluation and improvement within a SDO?; 2) is it possible to incorporate the KM purposes and outcomes

Table 5 Relations between SPRM's process and KM capabilities.

Model	Process related to KM	KM Capabilities						
		Technology	Culture	Structure	Acquisition	Conversion	Application	Protection
ISO 12207	Configuration Management	X	-	-	-	X	-	-
	Software Problem Resolution Process	X	-	-	-	X	-	-
	Life Cycle Model Management	-	-	X	X	-	-	-
	Human Resource Management	-	-	-	X	-	-	-
	Reuse Asset Management	X	-	-	-	X	X	-
	Domain Engineering	X	-	-	X	X	-	-
CMMI-DEV	Configuration Management	X	-	-	-	X	-	-
	Organizational Process Definition	X	-	X	-	X	-	-
	Organizational Training	-	-	-	X	-	-	-
MPS.BR	Configuration Management	X	-	-	-	X	-	-
	Organizational Process Definition	X	-	X	-	X	-	-
	Human Resource Management	-	-	-	X	-	-	-
	Development for reuse	X	-	-	-	X	X	-
MoProSoft	Process Management	X	-	X	-	X	-	-
	Human Resources and Work Environment Management	-	-	-	X	-	-	-
	Organizational Knowledge	X	-	-	-	X	-	-
Competisoft	Process Management	X	-	X	-	X	-	-
	Human Resources and Work Environment Management	-	-	-	X	-	-	-
	Organizational Knowledge	X	-	-	-	X	-	-

as a new KM process within existing SPRM? Or, maybe is it necessary a KM process reference model for SDO?; 3) if the resultant KM process reference model would be used in an process capability determination initiative, how could be the correspondent KM process evaluation model?. The answers of all these questions have high value in KM research and would constitute a contribution aligned to the KM research trends identified by [50]. They argue that future research in the field of KM requires studies related to unifying different KM models in the existing literature and understanding the determinants of the evolution of KM in organizations. Also, studies pertaining to KM effectiveness and associated organizational and IT support are needed.

Summing up, this work constitutes an important reference for research and practice because it presents a synthesis of the knowledge management topics included in software process reference models, and helps practitioners, from software development organization, to identify the foundations and the options to implement knowledge management initiatives within their organizations. Likewise, this study helps researchers to identify trends and topics to formulate new research projects about include the different "flavors" of knowledge management in software process reference models or to develop a knowledge management process reference model relevant for software development organizations.

6 References

[1] F. O. Bjørnson and T. Dingsøyr, "Knowledge management in software engineering: A systematic review of studied concepts, findings and research methods used," Information and Software Technology, vol. 50, no. 11, pp. 1055–1068, Oct. 2008.

[2] A. Aurum, F. Daneshgar, and J. Ward, "Investigating Knowledge Management practices in software development organisations - An Australian experience," Information and Software Technology, vol. 50, no. 6, pp. 511–533, May 2008.

[3] K. Alagarsamy, S. Justus, and K. Iyakutti, "The knowledge based software process improvement program: A rational analysis," in 2nd International Conference on Software Engineering Advances - ICSEA 2007, 2007.

[4] K. Alagarsamy, S. Justus, and K. Iyakutti, "On the implementation of a knowledge management tool for SPI," in Proceedings - International Conference on Computational Intelligence and Multimedia Applications, ICCIMA 2007, 2008, vol. 2, pp. 48–55.

[5] K. Alagarsamy, S. Justus, and K. Iyakutti, "Implementation specification for software process improvement supportive knowledge management tool," IET Software, vol. 2, no. 2, pp. 123–133, 2008.

[6] J. Capote, C. J. Llantén, C. Pardo, A. Gonzalez, and C. Collazos, "Gestión del conocimiento como apoyo para la mejora de procesos software en las micro, pequeñas y medianas empresas," Ingenieria e investigacion, vol. 28, 2008.

[7] M. A. Montoni, C. Cerdeiral, D. Zanetti, and A. R. Cavalcanti da Rocha, "A Knowledge Management Approach to Support Software Process Improvement Implementation Initiatives," in Software Process Improvement, vol. 16, R. V. O'Connor, N. Baddoo, K. Smolander, and R. Messnarz, Eds. Berlin, Heidelberg: Springer Berlin Heidelberg, 2008, pp. 164–175.

[8] R. Cruz Mendoza, M. Morales Trujillo, M. Morgado C, H. Oktaba, G. E. Ibarguengoitia, F. J. Pino, and M. Piattini,

"Supporting the Software Process Improvement in Very Small Entities through E-learning: The HEPALE! Project," in 2009 Mexican International Conference on Computer Science (ENC), 2009, pp. 221–231.

[9] M. Ivarsson and T. Gorschek, "Tool support for disseminating and improving development practices," Software Qual J, May 2011.

[10]Z. Li, S. Huang, and B. Gong, "The knowledge management strategy for SPI practices," Chinese Journal of Electronics, vol. 17, no. 1, pp. 66–70, 2008.

[11]J. Capote, C. J. Llantén, C. Pardo, and C. Collazos, "Knowledge management in a software process improvement program in micro, small and medium-sized enterprises: KMSPI Model," Revista Facultad de Ingenieria, no. 50, pp. 205–216, 2009.

[12]P. A. Nielsen and G. Tjørnehøj, "Social networks in software process improvement," Journal of Software Maintenance and Evolution: Research and Practice, vol. 22, no. 1, pp. 33–51, Jan. 2010.

[13]S. B. Basri and R. V. O'Connor, "Knowledge Management in Software Process Improvement: A Case Study of Very Small Entities," in Knowledge Engineering for Software Development Life Cycles: Support Technologies and Applications, IGI Global, 2011, p. 273.

[14]M. Earl, "Knowledge Management Strategies: Toward a Taxonomy," J. Manage. Inf. Syst., vol. 18, no. 1, pp. 215–233, 2001.

[15]A. H. Gold, A. Malhotra, and A. H. Segars, "Knowledge management: An organizational capabilities perspective," Journal of Management Information Systems, vol. 18, no. 1, pp. 185–214, 2001.

[16]S. Sieber and R. Andreu, "La gestion integral del conocimiento y del aprendizaje. (With English summary.)," Economia Industrial, no. 2, pp. 63–72, 1999.

[17]R. McAdam and S. McCreedy, "A critical review of knowledge management models," The Learning Organization, vol. 6, no. 3, pp. 91–101, 1999.

[18]D. Apostolou and G. Mentzas, "Managing corporate knowledge: a comparative analysis of experiences in consulting firms. Part 1," Knowledge and Process Management, vol. 6, no. 3, pp. 129–138, Sep. 1999.

[19]M. Alvesson and D. Kärreman, "Odd Couple: Making Sense of the Curious Concept of Knowledge Management," Journal of Management Studies, vol. 38, no. 7, pp. 995–1018, Nov. 2001.

[20]H. Takeuchi, "Towards a Universal Management Concept of Knowledge," in Managing industrial knowledge, Sage, 2001, p. 315.

[21]B. Choi and H. Lee, "An empirical investigation of KM styles and their effect on corporate performance," INFORMATION & MANAGEMENT, vol. 40, no. 5, pp. 403–417, May 2003.

[22]N. K. Kakabadse and A. Kakabadse, "Reviewing the knowledge management literature: towards a taxonomy," Journal of Knowledge Management, vol. 7, no. 4, pp. 75–91, 2003.

[23]D. Rodríguez Gómez, "Modelos para la creación y gestión del conocimiento : una aproximación teórica," Educar, no. 37, pp. 25–39, Apr. 2007.

[24]A. Barragán Ocaña,, "Aproximación a una taxonomía de modelos de gestión del conocimiento," Intangible Capital, vol. 5, no. 1, pp. 65–101, 2009.

[25]ISO/IEC, ISO/IEC 15504-2:2003, Software engineering - Process assessment - Part 2: Performing an assessment. Ginebra, Suiza: International Organization for Standardization, 2003.

[26]ISO/IEC, ISO/IEC 15504-1:2004, Information technology - Process assessment - Part 1: Concepts and vocabulary. Ginebra, Suiza: International Organization for Standardization, 2004.

[27]ISO/IEC, ISO/IEC 15504-3:2004, Information technology - Process assessment - Part 3: Guidance on performing an assessment. Ginebra, Suiza: International Organization for Standardization, 2004.

[28]F. J. Pino, F. García, F. Ruiz, and M. Piattini, "Adaptación de las normas ISO/IEC 12207: 2002 e ISO/IEC 15504: 2003 para la evaluación de la madurez de procesos software en países en desarrollo.," in Proceedings of JISBD'05, 2005, pp. 187–194.

[29]F. J. Pino, F. Garcia, F. Ruiz, and M. Piattini, "Adaptation of the standards ISO/IEC 12207:2002 and ISO/IEC 15504:2003 for the assessment of the software processes in developing countries," IEEE Latin America Transactions, vol. 4, pp. 85–92, Apr. 2006.

[30]ISO/IEC, ISO/IEC 15504-5:2006, Information technology - Process Assessment - Part 5: An exemplar Process Assessment Model. Ginebra, Suiza: International Organization for Standardization, 2006.

[31]ISO/IEC, ISO/IEC 12207:2008, Standard for Systems and Software Engineering - Software Life Cycle Processes. 2008.

[32]M. T. Baldassarre, M. Piattini, F. J. Pino, and G. Visaggio, "Comparing ISO/IEC 12207 and CMMI-DEV: Towards a mapping of ISO/IEC 15504-7," in Proceedings of the ICSE Workshop on Software Quality, 2009. WOSQ '09, 2009, pp. 59–64.

[33]CMMI Product Team, CMMI® for Development, Version 1.3, CMU/SEI-2010th-TR-033 ed. Pittsburgh, PA, USA: Carnegie Mellon University, 2010.

[34]M. B. Chrissis, M. Konrad, and S. Shrum, CMMI for Development®: Guidelines for Process Integration and Product Improvement (3rd Edition), 3rd ed. Addison-Wesley Professional, 2011.

[35]SCAMPI Upgrade Team, Standard CMMI® Appraisal Method for Process Improvement (SCAMPI SM) A, Version 1.3: Method Definition Document, CMU/SEI-2011th-HB-001 ed. Pittsburgh, PA, USA: Carnegie Mellon University, 2011.

[36]K. C. Weber, E. E. R. Araújo, A. R. C. Rocha, C. A. F. Machado, D. Scalet, and C. F. Salviano, "Brazilian Software Process Reference Model and Assessment Method," in Computer and Information Sciences - ISCIS 2005, vol. 3733, pInar Yolum, T. Güngör, F. Gürgen, and

C. Özturan, Eds. Berlin, Heidelberg: Springer Berlin Heidelberg, 2005, pp. 402–411.

[37]G. Santos, M. Kalinowski, A. R. Rocha, G. H. Travassos, K. C. Weber, and J. A. Antonioni, "MPS.BR: A Tale of Software Process Improvement and Performance Results in the Brazilian Software Industry," 2010, pp. 412–417.

[38]SOFTEX, MPS.BR - Mejora de Proceso del Software Brasileño - Guía de Evaluación. Brasil: SOFTEX, 2011.

[39]SOFTEX, MPS.BR - Mejora de Proceso del Software Brasileño - Guía General. Brasil: SOFTEX, 2011.

[40]H. Oktaba, C. Esquivel, A. Su Ramos, A. Martínez, G. Quintanilla, M. Ruvalcaba, F. López, M. Rivera, M. Orozco, and Y. Fernández, Modelo de Procesos para la Industria de Software MoProSoft Version 1.3. México: Secretaría de Economía, 2005.

[41]H. Oktaba, C. Esquivel, A. Su Ramos, A. Martínez, G. Quintanilla, M. Ruvalcaba, F. López, M. Rivera, M. Orozco, and Y. Fernández, Modelo de Procesos para la Industria de Software MoProSoft Version 1.3 Por Niveles de Capacidad de Procesos. México: Secretaría de Economía, 2005.

[42]H. Oktaba, C. Esquivel, A. Su Ramos, A. Martínez, G. Quintanilla, M. Ruvalcaba, F. López, M. Rivera, M. Orozco, and Y. Fernández, Software Industry Process Model MoProSoft Version 1.3. 2. México: Ministry of Economy, 2006.

[43]H. Oktaba, "MoProSoft®: A Software Process Model for Small Enterprises," in Proceedings of the 1st International Research Workshop for Process Improvement in Small Settings, 2006, pp. 93–110.

[44]H. Oktaba, F. García, M. Piattini, F. Ruiz, F. J. Pino, and C. Alquicira, "Software Process Improvement: The Competisoft Project," Computer, vol. 40, pp. 21–28, Oct. 2007.

[45]Competisoft, "COMPETISOFT. Mejora de Procesos para Fomentar la Competitividad de la Pequeña y Mediana Industria del Software de Iberoamérica," 2008.

[46]Competisoft, "COMPETISOFT. Mejora de Procesos de Software para PEqueñas Empresas," 2008. [Online]. Available: http://alarcos.inf-cr.uclm.es/Competisoft/framework/. [Accessed: 20-Aug-2011].

[47]H. Oktaba, Competisoft : mejora de procesos software para pequeñas y medianas empresas y proyectos, 1a ed. México D.F.: Alfaomega, 2009.

[48]A. F. Aguirre, C. J. Pardo Calvache, M. F. Mejía, and F. J. Pino, "Reporte de experiencias de la aplicación de Competisoft en cinco mipymes colombianas," Revista EIA, no. 13, pp. 107–122, 2010.

[49]A. F. Buono and F. Poulfelt, Challenges and issues in knowledge management, vol. 5. Information Age Pub Inc, 2005.

[50]Y. K. Dwivedi, K. Venkitachalam, A. M. Sharif, W. Al-Karaghouli, and V. Weerakkody, "Research trends in knowledge management: Analyzing the past and predicting the future," Information Systems Management, vol. 28, no. 1, pp. 43–56, 2011.

SESSION

SOFTWARE SYSTEMS, REQUIREMENTS + MIDDLE-WARE + SOFTWARE DEVELOPMENT PROCESS + MODELING AND ARCHITECTURE DESCRIPTION LANGUAGES

Chair(s)

TBA

Systems on Abstract Network

Kazutaka NAKAMURA*, **Kiyofumi TANAKA and Yasushi HIBINO**
School of Information Science, Japan Advanced Institute of Science and Technology, Ishikawa, Japan.

Abstract— *The authors developed a new system abstraction method, "Abstract Network Framework", implemented its prototype, ANetFW, and confirmed feasibility of the new method. In this paper, the method is proposed by explaining the implementation and behavior of ANetFW. This method does only abstraction of operations for inter-component connection and the components directly communicate each other at run-time without any intervention of the framework. Therefore the method is easier to introduce than the method of replacing the whole abstraction layers such as operating systems, while it does not cause any run-time overheads due to abstraction that overlay approaches such as middle-wares would cause.*

Keywords: Network Distributed System, Network Operating System, Middle-ware, System Abstraction Method, Abstract Network

1. Introduction

A system is a set of inter-communicating components. Therefore system development is regarded as selection of appropriate components for the system from available components and connection of them.

Each component is prepared as a suitable form for its requirements. Therefore, different components have different interfaces and communicate by different communication methods. This fact makes some pairs of components not communicable, which raises a necessity of facilities to make it possible.

There is another problem in system development. To connect components, the developer needs to follow the connection procedures according to the details of the implementation. If he or she does it by himself/herself, he or she needs to know about the details of the procedures for all components used, which raises knowledge cost for system development. Abstraction is the way of reducing this cost by hiding differences in implementations of components and allows users to handle various components and inter-component connections in a single manner.

1.1 Conventional approaches

The most popular conventional method of solving the problems has been provided as an abstraction layer, where communication functions with protocol stacks or device drivers are provided on the layer. The example productsof this method are operating systems or middle-wares [1].

But in some cases, the rich protocol stacks or device drivers can not be installed. For example, the environment has very limited resources, or the target system requires very high performance. In other cases, the target system requires some special functions and the existing abstraction products do not have such functions, such as network distributed environment support [2] or high security facility or advanced error recovery. To solve such problems, there are two typical approach.

The first is overlay approach which lay new abstraction layer providing specific function on an existing layer. For example, a network system based on RPC(Remote Procedure Call) [3] consists of a middle-ware which provides RPC function and is laid on a stand alone operating system. Grid computing [4] provides substantial functionalities for network distributed computing. The WWW which consists of HTTP servers [5], [6] working on operating systems is another example of this approach. Overlay approach is easy to introduce but ad hoc. Thus it requires run-time overhead and another new knowledge cost for the overlay itself. Overlay approach provides some functionality and abstraction in exchange for performance but is not for knowledge cost reduction.

On the other hand, there is replacement approach which makes whole new abstraction layer providing all functionality for new requirement and replaces the existing layer. Embedded operating systems and network distributed operating systems [7], [8] are the products based on this approach. Replacement approach causes no problems after introducing a product into the target system and learning about new abstraction layer. Unfortunately, replacement approach causes serious spreading or applicable area problem. In fact, network distributed operating systems have not spread in popular or distributed their benefits, and embedded operating systems adopts only for embedded systems. Replacement approach is an ideal solution but requires high cost for introduction and could not spread in popular.

Due to these problems, Real systems is constructed on patchwork approach and consit of various abstraction layer. The example is web service. It uses some IPC(Inter-Process Communication) or RPC mechanisms in their site and uses HTTP to provide an interface for the user, since HTTP clients, web browsers, have already spread widely and allow to avoid the spreading problem.

* Presently, the author is with Universal Shell Programming Laboratory, Ltd, Tokyo, Japan.

As saw above, conventional approaches lead chaos of abstraction layers and have not achieve their goal, reduction of knowledge cost.

1.2 The problems and The idea

This chaos is not desirable. To solve this, the authors focused that the conventional approaches are trying to provide two function at a time, connection between components of different implementation and abstraction of different operation, and tryed to separate them.

At first, The authors recognized that there is no communication method which satisfies all of possible requirements and each components adopts suitable communication methods or develop new one to satisfy the system requirements. Therefore, the unification of communication method is impossible. Communication methods are also important parts of systems. As a system requires various components, a system requires various communication methods. Therefore, if an abstraction layer also try to provide communication method, the abstraction layer can not be a general purpose abstraction layer.

Fortunately, the success of patchwork systems shows us that system development does not require unified communication method. On the other hand, patchwork systems causes very high knowledge cost. But every communication methods makes a set of components communicable each other. Thus, various communication methods can be abstracted and be handled in single manner.

The replacement approach does this abstraction of communication methods but has spreading problem. The authors thought it is causes the problem that the conventional abstraction layer is developed as a foundation for component development, especially software component development. For this purpose, software components on the layer expects be able to execute all operation for every real communication methods. This task is difficult and requires run-time conversion, in other words interpretation, in many cases.

But if a new abstraction layer does not try to be a foundation for component development and does only abstractions for component connection, the conversion can be completed beforehand, in other words can be compile. In this solution, the new abstraction layer does only designation of communication partner and then each components communicates with its communication partner directly by their own natural communication method. Therefore, there is no need for whole replacement like conventional approach, only need for laying a compiling layer like overlay approach. This solves spreading problem.

Based on these idea, the authors developed new abstraction layer which does only abstraction of operation for inter-component connection. This means the abstraction layer does not provide communication functions and just connects components by existing communication methods. While using this new abstraction layer, since each component can choose most suitable communication methods, their requirements of communication methods will never be a problem of abstraction layer functionality. And since every operations for connection is converted beforehand to native operations, there is no abstraction cost in run-time, is only connection cost which is fundamentally necessary, and will never be a problem of abstraction layer performance or environment resource limit.

On this abstraction layer, a user chooses components and connect them to construct a target system. And if a set of real connections is derived from the set of abstract connections for the target system, a set of command sequence for the real connections is generated and executed, the target system on abstraction layer is embodied as a real runnable system. If this process, deriving, generate and execute, can be done by abstraction environment, our new method can be realized.

1.3 The structure of this paper

The authors developed a new system abstraction method, "Abstract Network Framework", implemented its prototype, ANetFW(*A*bstract *Net*work *F*rame*W*ork), and confirmed that the prototype works correctly. Then the authors concluded that Abstract Network Framework is feasible and propose it in this paper. In the section below, the overview of the method is explained. Next, through describing about an use-case of the prototype, ANetFW, the implementation of the method is illustrated. Finally, the authors discuss about current problems, future opportunity and related works.

2. Overview of Abstract Network Framework

Abstract Network Framework abstracts available components and inter-component connections(Fig. 1-c) and provides a consistent view(Fig. 1-a) whose name is "Abstract Network". An abstract network is a conceptual communication network which connects between abstract function [1]. A user can connects necessary functions without being bothered by implementation and operation differences(Fig. 2-a). And the abstract functions and connections between them are converted to, or embodied as real components and real inter-component connections respectively by the framework(Fig. 2-c), then the system on the abstract network becomes a real runnable system.

2.1 Construction of Abstract Network

In order to construct an abstract network, all available components and their inter-component connections(Fig. 1-1) are described in "Base Network" definition(Fig. 1-b). And the base network definition is abstracted(Fig. 1-2) as an abstract network definition. Abstract Network Framework abstracts connection operations of various components while abstracting real resources to base networks and abstracts

[1] This method is based on various idea of network technology

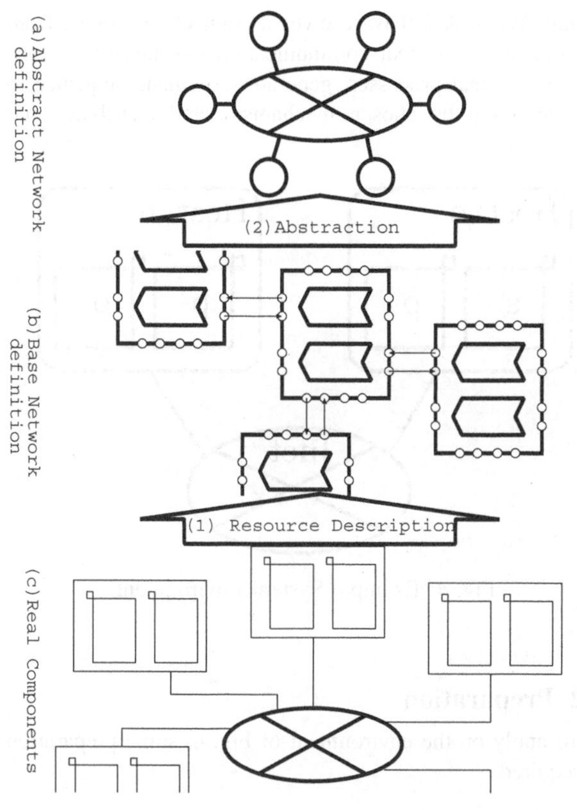

Fig. 1: Abstract Network Construction

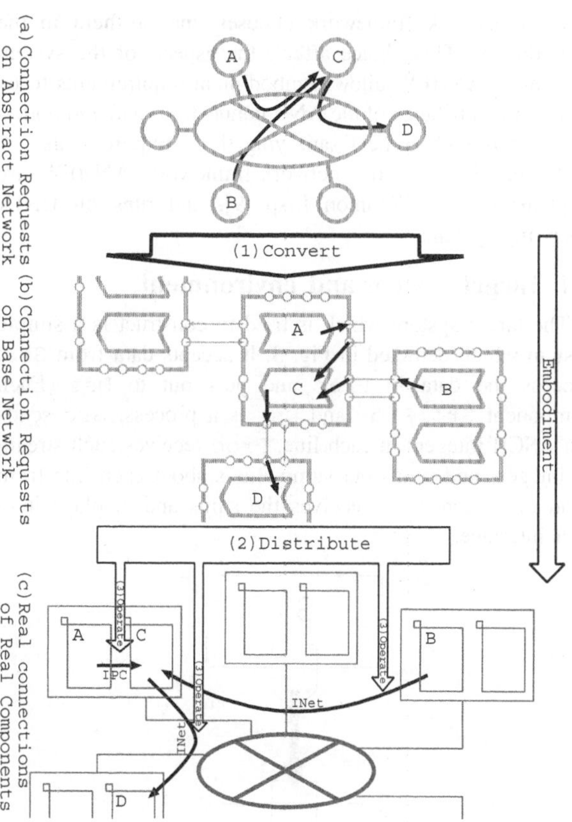

Fig. 2: Flow of Embodiment

inter-component connections while abstracting a base network to an abstract network.

Ideally, an abstract network should be automatically constructed for given environment like device detection of operating systems. But in this time, the authors defined abstract networks by our hands.

2.2 Connection and Embodiment

Abstract Network Framework converts operations on an abstract network to operations on base network(Fig. 2-1), and converts operations on base network to real command sequences for real components. And it sends them to and executes them in appropriate components(Fig. 2-2,3). In Abstract Network Framework, these process is called "Embodiment". Abstract Network Framework is a framework for and does embodiment process by referring abstract network definition and base network definition.

2.3 Advantages

Abstract Network Framework abstracts system components and their inter-component connections, does no any operations on the target system during run-time and let the components communicate each other directly. Therefore, Abstract Network Framework is easier to introduce than the products of replacement approach and cause no run-time overheads due to abstraction that the products of overlay approaches would generate.

3. Overview and Behavior of the prototype, ANetFW

The authors implemented a prototype based on Abstract Network Framework and named it ANetFW. And the authors constructed an abstract network from a simple system environment, embodied a simple system by ANetFW, and confirmed that ANetFW works correctly. In this section, the overview of ANetFW and how to implement Abstract Network Framework are explained while a construction process of an abstract network and an embodiment process of a system on the abstract network are illustrated.

In ANetFW, an abstract network is ANet, a base network is BNet. There can be more than one possible embodiment result for a system description on an abstract network. The abstract network framework chooses one of them in the embodiment. This choice affects the aspects of the system embodied. ANetFW allows embodiment requirements to be attached in attributes of the ANet connections and end nodes. It conducts embodiment satisfying those requirements. A prototype of the abstract network framework, ANetFW, are implemented by Common Lisp [9], and runs on UNIX operating systems.

3.1 Target system and environment

The target system which is tried to construct is a simple system which depicted in Fig. 3. It accepts data from `Src`, process the data in `Proc` and puts out to `Dst`. Each component `Src`, `Proc` and `Dst` is a process. `Src` sends out ASCII integers in each line. `Proc` receives such stream of integers and sends out summations about each line from head of stream. `Dst` receives the sums and displays it in user interface.

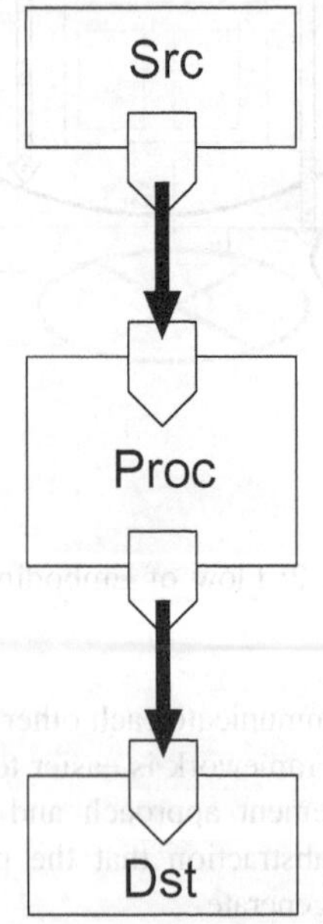

Fig. 3: Target System

The authors constructed the target system in a test environment with ANetFW. The environment is depicted in Fig. 4. In the environment, there are two Internet node `n` and `m`, and processes `s`, `p` and `d` which is running in the nodes and corresponding to `Src`, `Proc` and `Dst` respectively. These processes can communicate each other by TCP/IP network. some of them can uses IPC(Inter-Process Communication) mechanisms [2].

ANetFW abstracts this environment as an ANet. An user constructs the target system(Fig. 3) without caring about whether each process can use a communication mechanisms or not. When ANetFW receives a connection request from an user, it selects real communication mechanism for corresponding real processes, generates command sequence to connect them by chosen mechanism, and distributes and executes it.

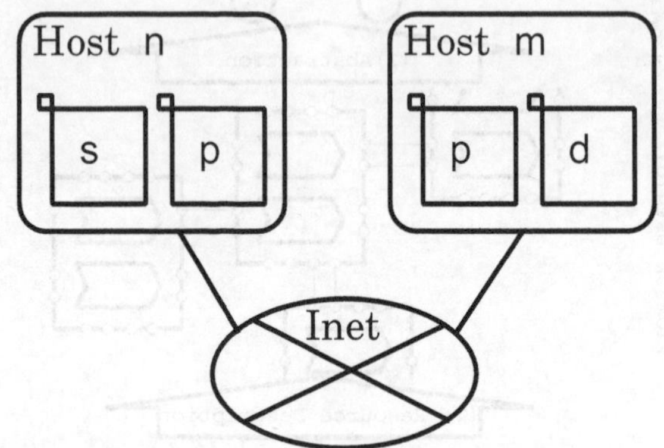

Fig. 4: Example System Environment

3.2 Preparation

To apply on the environment of Fig. 4, some preparation is required.

3.2.1 BNet definition

At first, all available real components and their available real inter-component connections must be described as BNet definition. On a BNet, available components and their connections are described and managed as nodes and links. From the environment of Fig. 4, a BNet is defined like Fig. 6 which can be depicted like Fig. 5.

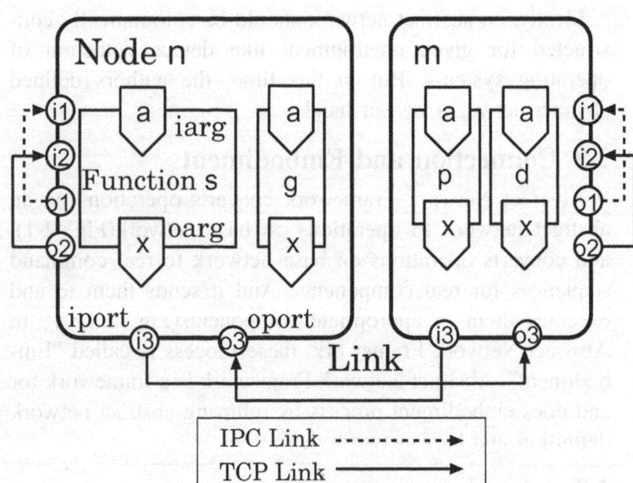

Fig. 5: BNet Definition Image

[2]This prototype uses Unix Domain Socket as IPC

```
;; default port assignment constraint
;; == ``(:p tcp)''
(node n (i1 i2 i3) (o1 o2 o3)
  (:fn (s () ((x(:p ipc tcp))))
       (p ((a(:p ipc tcp))) (x)) ))

(node m (i1 i2 i3) (o1 o2 o3)
  (:fn (p ((a(:p ipc tcp))) (x))
       (d (a) ()) ))

;; inner loop of node n
(link (n o1) (n i1) (:p ipc) (:e (b 10)))
(link (n o2) (n i2) (:p tcp) (:e (b 1)))
;; inner loop of node m
(link (m o1) (m i1) (:p ipc) (:e (b 10)))
(link (m o2) (m i2) (:p tcp) (:e (b 1)))
;; inter link between n and m
(link (n o3) (m i3) (:p tcp) (:e (b 1)))
(link (m o3) (n i3) (:p tcp) (:e (b 1)))
```

Fig. 6: BNet Definition

BNet definition is a directed acyclic graph and consists of nodes and links. On this BNet, each Internet node is defined as a BNet node and each process in the Internet nodes is defined as a BNet function in a BNet node. In the description(Fig. 6), each clause which starts from `(node ...` is BNet node definition. And in a clause of a node definition which starts from `(:fn ...`, each clause is a BNet function definition. For example, the clause which starts from `(node n ...` is a BNet node definition about BNet node `n`. And in the clause of the definition of BNet node definition `n` which starts from `(:fn ...`, the clause which starts from `(s ...` is a BNet function definition about BNet function `s` of BNet node `n`.

Each process needs to distinguish communication partners. On a BNet it is treated as arguments of BNet function, iarg(*I*nput *ARG*ument) and oarg(*O*utput *ARG*ument).

On a BNet, each available connection is described as unidirectional links between BNet nodes. Many of connections are provide bidirectional communication transport function. On a BNet, such bidirectional connection is described as two unidirectional links. Each contact point of a links to a node is described as a BNet port which belongs to the contacting BNet node. a point which contacts to inbound link is called iport(*I*nput *PORT*), and a point which contacts to outbound link is called oport(*O*utput *port*). A link is described as a pair of an iport and an oport. For example, in the clause which starts from `(node n ...`, the clause, `(i1 i2 i3)` and `(o1 o2 o3)`, is a clause of iport and oport of BNet node `n` respectively. Each clause which starts from `(link ...` is a BNet link definition. For example, `(link (n o1)(n i1) ...)` is a BNet link definition which transports data from port `o1` of node `n` to port `i1` of node `n`.

Each clause of BNet link definition which starts from `(:e ...` is description about performance of the link. For example, bandwidth(`b`) of BNet link `(link (n o1)(n i1) ...` is `10`. Each clause of BNet link definition which starts from `(:p ...` is description about protocol of the link. For example, protocol of BNet link `(link (n o1)(n i1) ...` is IPC(`ipc`).

A BNet function distinguishes communication partner by its own argument and communicates with each partner through a link. This is depicted as assigning a port to the argument and called "Port Assignment". What protocols the function can use for an argument is described as constraints of port assignment. In this example, the default port assignment constraint is `(:p tcp)` and the identical description of constraint is omitted. For example, the oarg `x` of function `s` of node `n` is described as `(x(:p ipc tcp))` which means the oarg can use both protocol identified by `ipc` and `tcp` for its communication.

These information for performance and protocol is used to select appropriate connection for each connection request on ANet.

3.2.2 ANet definition

BNet definition is direct description of available components and their inter-component connections. Therefore, connection operation on BNet, port assignment, is direct designation which connection is used.

ANet is constructed by abstracting BNet to hide specific real connections and allow users to focus on the functions and their abstracted connections.

An ANet is defined like Fig. 7 which can be depicted like Fig. 8. BNet functions `s` and `p` of BNet node `n` and BNet functions `p` and `d` of BNet node `m` are abstracted as ANet nodes(function) `s`, `p1`, `p2` and `d` respectively. BNet links which can actually connects a pair of BNet arguments are abstracted as an ANet link.

```
(node s  ()  (x) (n s))
(node p1 (a) (x) (n p))
(node p2 (a) (x) (m p))
(node d  (a) ()  (m d))

(link s p1  ((n o1)(n i1)) ((n o2)(n i2)))
(link s p2  ((n o3)(m i3)))
(link s d   ((n o3)(m i3)))
(link p1 p2 ((n o3)(m i3)))
(link p1 d  ((n o3)(m i3)))
(link p2 p1 ((m o3)(n i3)))
(link p2 d  ((n o1)(n i1)) ((n o2)(n i2)))
```

Fig. 7: ANet Definition

And finally, the processes which does embodiment actually are deployed on the environment.

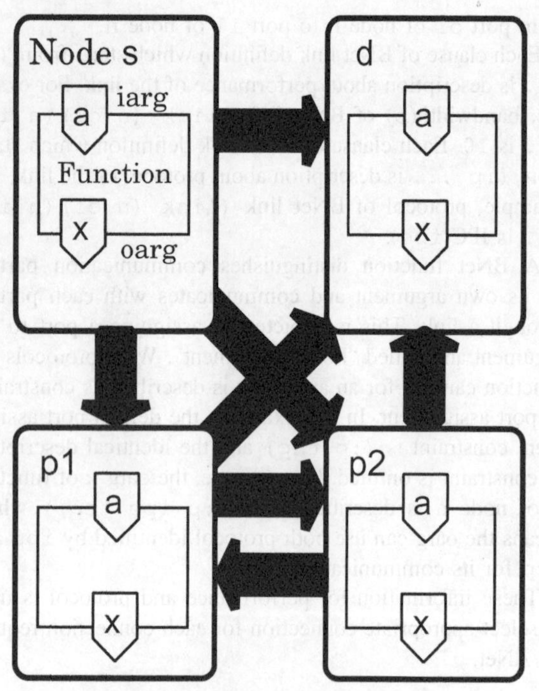

Fig. 8: ANet Definition Image

3.3 Embodiment Process

On the ANet which is constructed like above, the authors constructs the target system depicted in Fig. 3 by connecting ANet functions. The connection request is like below.

```
(connection(s x) (p1 a)(:e(<= 10 b))); (1)
(connection(p1 x)(d a))              ; (2)
```

In this request, ANet connection `(connection(s x)(p1 a)...)` is attached a clause, `(:e(<= 10 b))`, which is called embodiment constraint description. ANetFW tries to embody this connection by using a link whose bandwidth(b) is at least 10.

The authors gave ANetFW this ANet connection request and ANetFW converted the requests to BNet port assignments like below.

```
(assign n s x o1) ; (1)
(assign n p a i1) ; (1)
(assign n p x o3) ; (2)
(assign m d a i3) ; (2)
```

From an ANet connection requests marked by (1), ANetFW generates two BNet port assignment requests marked by (1). It is same about (2). In this case, BNet link `(link(n o2)(n i2)...)` can connect between the arguments which specified by the ANet connection marked by (1). But since the BNet link `(link(n o2)(n i2)...)` does not satisfy the embodiment constraint `(:e(<= 10 b))`, ANetFW selected BNet link `(link(n o1)(n i1)...)`.

These generated BNet port assignment requests are distributed to each node and executed corresponding real operation.

3.4 Behavior of the target system

And the authors made the embodied target system run. The data whom the process s sends out is like below.

```
540
670
924
684
374
```

The user interface whom the process d controlling showed data like below.

```
540
1210
2134
2818
3192
```

4. Discussion

From the behavior of ANetFW, the followings are drawn. A system described as a set of ANet connection requests was embodied and the system worked correctly. In the conversion step, ANetFW correctly dealt with graph constraints, port assignment constraints and embodiment requirements, and chose relevant communication paths. In the operation step, ANetFW correctly distributed port assignment requests, and did setup for each BNet function. These facts show that ANetFW is working correctly. Therefore Abstract Network Framework is feasible.

Since the aim of this prototype is feasibility verification for the basic idea of Abstract Network Framework, some problems have been left in this time. A big problem is that the construction of abstract network is done by hand. This should be hidden to reduce knowledge cost which is the goal of abstraction.

This prototype focused on the basic idea which consists of management, abstraction and choice of available components, their inter-component connections and their operations, and did not treat the content of communication that is data format or protocol. Some functions which treat component protocols will make system development easier on Abstract Network Framework.

Abstract Network Framework gives us more opportunities. This prototype equips the basic function of Abstract Network Framework, choosing appropriate inter-components connection from available connections. Since this was feasible, It must be also feasible to choose appropriate components for given target system. And if it was include connection macro and able to treat composed function as link or function, it can does automatic system construction in limited area, such like insertion of compression or encryption functions into communication paths.

4.1 Related works

Abstract Network Framework provides an abstract view for whole computer system environment. The products of conventional methods, such like operating systems and middle-wares [1], [4], try to provide this but have problems described in section 1.2. Facing on this situation, Abstract Network Framework is focused on their goal, the function of abstraction and choice for components and inter-component connections, and avoid the problems of conventional methods. In other words, the conventional methods seek compilers or interpreters and Abstract Network Framework seeks powerful make [10] or linker [11]. From this design, the products of Abstract Network Framework is easier to introduce and does not cause any run-time overhead for abstraction.

On the other hand, since Abstract Network Framework is not a foundation for component development, it does not provide various functions which is communication functions, unified interface for various protocols or protocol stacks for some protocols, and other additional functions, resource multiplexing or fault tolerance. The authors think that the functions can handle as one of functions of component or inter-component connections, choose them and use them.

As system development environment, Abstract Network Framework is component oriented technologies whose examples of existing products are object oriented frameworks [12] or Service Oriented Architecture [13]. The existing products base on middle-ware technologies which uses specific inter-component communication mechanisms and cause some problems. Abstract Network Framework trying to solve the problems.

Since described target system on an abstract network is embodied as real system, Abstract Network Framework seems to be system generation technology from specification whose examples of existing products are Model Driven Architecture [14] or LOTOS [15], the protocol description language. While system generation technology is top down approach and aims to generate whole system from connections to component itself, but it does not aim to reuse of generated components. Abstract Network Framework is bottom up approach and just a kind of abstraction method for existing components, their inter-communication connections and their connecting operations.

5. Conclusion

In this paper, the authors introduced a new abstraction method, "Abstract Network Framework", and illustrated its implementation and behavior with the prototype implementation, ANetFW. Abstract Network Framework abstracts available components, their inter-component connections and their operations, and the components directly communicate each other at run-time without any intervention of the framework. Therefore Abstract Network Framework is easier to introduce than the replacement approach, such as operating systems, while it does not cause any run-time overheads due to abstraction that overlay approaches such as middle-wares would generate. Abstract Network Framework provides various opportunity which can be implemented as additional feature. The feature which is implemented in this prototype is automatic choice of component for given request and allows users to construct systems without choice from the components providing same function in his environment.

This prototype has some problems, but the authors try to solve them and realize opportunities of Abstract Network Framework.

References

[1] S. Tanenbaum, Andrew, *Modern operating systems*. Pearson Prentice Hall, 2008. [Online]. Available: http://books.google.co.jp/books?id=y22rPwAACAAJ

[2] S. Tanenbaum, Andrew and M. van Steen, *Distributed Systems: Principles and Paradigms (2nd Edition)*. Upper Saddle River, NJ, USA: Prentice-Hall, Inc., 2006.

[3] D. Birrell, Andrew and J. Nelson, Bruce, "Implementing remote procedure calls," *ACM Transactions on Computer Systems*, vol. 2, no. 1, pp. 39–59, 1984.

[4] I. Foster and C. Kesselman, *The Grid: Blueprint for a New Computing Infrastructure*. Morgan Kaufmann, 2004.

[5] The Apache HTTP Server Project, "Apache http server documentation." [Online]. Available: http://httpd.apache.org/docs/

[6] R. Fielding, J. Gettys, J. Mogul, H. Frystyk, L. Masinter, P. Leach, and T. Berners-Lee, "Rfc 2616: Hypertext transfer protocol–http/1.1," *RFC*, no. 2616, 1999.

[7] S. Tanenbaum, Andrew, R. van Renesse, H. van Staveren, J. Sharp, Gregory, and J. Mullender, Sape, "Experiences with the amoeba distributed operating system," *Communications of the ACM*, vol. 33, no. 12, pp. 46–63, Dec. 1990. [Online]. Available: http://doi.acm.org/10.1145/96267.96281

[8] R. Pike, D. Presotto, S. Dorward, B. Flandrena, K. Thompson, H. Trickey, and P. Winterbottom, "Plan 9 from bell labs." [Online]. Available: http://plan9.bell-labs.com/sys/doc/9.html

[9] L. Steele Jr., Guy, *Common LISP. The Language. Second Edition*. Digital Press, June 1990.

[10] I. Feldman, Stuart, "Make–a program for maintaining computer programs," *Software: Practice and experience*, vol. 9, no. 4, pp. 255–265, 1979.

[11] R. Levine, John, *Linkers & Loaders*, ser. Operating Systems Series. Morgan Kaufmann, 2000. [Online]. Available: http://books.google.co.jp/books?id=Id9cYsIdjIwC

[12] Object Management Group, *Common Object Request Broker Architecture(CORBA) Specification, Version3.2*. http://www.omg.org/spec/CORBA/3.2/, 2011.

[13] The Open Group, *SOA Source Book*. Van Haren Publishing, 2009.

[14] R. Raman and F. Paige, Richard, "Process-centered review of object oriented software development methodologies," *ACM Computing Surveys*, vol. 40, pp. 3:1–3:89, February 2008. [Online]. Available: http://doi.acm.org/10.1145/1322432.1322435

[15] International Organization for Standardization, "Information processing systems-open systems interconnection-lotos-a formal description technique based on the temporal ordering of observational behaviour," *ISO*, no. 8807:1989, 1989.

XCD – A Design-by-Contract Architecture Description Language

Mert Ozkaya and Christos Kloukinas
Department of Computer Science, City University London, London, EC1V 0HB, UK

Abstract—*Software architecture description languages (ADL) have been proposed as a way to properly specify the architectures of complex software systems, in a way that allows both communication among the different stakeholders and an early analysis of these systems for a number of properties. However, practitioners seem to have shunned the ADL developed in academia and mainly use other modeling languages, that were not originally created for describing architectures. In a recent survey, practitioners have expressed a wish for analyzing their architectures (esp. for non-functional properties) and at the same time expressed their dissatisfaction with existing ADL, finding that the formal notations they use have a learning curve that they perceive as being too steep.*

In this paper we propose a new ADL, called XCD, *that attempts to address these issues. To this end,* XCD *is a formal language, allowing the formal analysis of systems. In its current form, it focuses on safety and liveness properties (deadlocks, etc.), leaving support for non-functional properties, such as reliability or performance, for later. In order to avoid imposing a steep learning curve on practitioners,* XCD *follows a Design-by-Contract (DbC) approach. DbC has the advantage of allowing practitioners to express formal models in a notation that resembles the programming languages they use. DbC has in fact already been embraced by practitioners, who so far use it mainly for improving their testing methods.*

1. Introduction

There has been significant work on architectural description languages (ADL) from the early nineties as a way of specifying the architecture of complex software systems [15], [30]. Rapide [21], Wright [1], Darwin [22], UniCon [34], ACME [14], XADL [10], and C2 [25] are widely-known early ADLs; LEDA [7], AADL [11], Koala [35], COSA [28], SOFA [31], RADL [32], PRISMA [29], π-ADL [27], PiLar [9], and Connect [18] are ones developed more recently. These languages have explored different ways of representing architectures, using component and connector abstractions or just component abstractions. Many among them have been designed to facilitate formal analysis of safety and liveness properties, for which they require architects to specify the behaviors of system elements using some formal language, usually a form of a process algebra.

A recent survey by Malavolta et al. [24] on the needs of the industry with respect to architectural specification, indicates that the languages developed in academia so far have not been very successful in practice. Practitioners remarked that they need to analyze their systems for non-functional properties like performance or reliability, which are not usually supported by ADL and their related tools. They also considered the formal notations used in ADL as imposing a learning curve that is too steep and having a low return on investment in their eyes.

We take the view that both these issues are important but we cannot resolve the former without first resolving the latter. This is because safety and liveness properties, like deadlock-freedom, are of a more basic nature than performance and reliability analyses – after all, a deadlocked system has zero performance and zero reliability. Therefore we need to design an ADL that allows practitioners to specify behaviors in a way that allows for formal verification but without imposing upon them a notation that is unfamiliar to them. For this reason we have developed XCD, a new ADL that follows a Design-by-Contract (DbC) approach [26]. XCD allows architects to specify the behaviors of their systems in a language that resembles a programming language, which should render the investment required in learning the new notation small enough for it to become a reasonable approach to consider.

1.1 XCD Language Design Considerations

Table 1 shows a number of ADL, covering both the major early ones (Darwin to XADL) and more recent ones (PRISMA to CONNECT). It compares them against three characteristics that we believe to be important for supporting the architectural specification of complex systems, namely whether they allow formal behavior specification, whether they support complex connectors as first-class elements and whether the architectures expressed in them are realisable. Most of these ADL do allow *formal behavior specification,* albeit in notations that practitioners have found to require a steep learning curve. The ones that do not support formal behavior specification do so because they focus more on direct code production from architectural descriptions. Interestingly, practitioners surveyed in [24] did not rate code production as an important feature.

Then we see that the ADLs in Table 1 are more or less divided between those that do support *complex connectors* as first-class elements and those that do not, either allowing a limited set of connectors only or requiring that architects simulate these through components. We acknowledge that this is somewhat a question of taste, just like Java requires

Table 1: Some important ADL characteristics

ADLs	Formal behaviour specification	First-class complex connectors	Realisable
Darwin [22]	FSP	No	Yes
Wright [1]	CSP	Yes	Potentially no (glue centralised controller element)
ACME [14]	Possible with annotations	Yes	Potentially no (when Wright connectors employed)
Rapide [21]	Event patterns	No	Potentially no (global architectural constraints pattern)
UniCon [34]	No	No	Yes
C2 [25]	Z	No	Yes
LEDA [7]	pi-calculus	No	Yes
OLAN [2]	No	No	Yes
XADL [10]	Possible with schema extension	Yes	Potentially no (when Wright connectors employed)
PRISMA [29]	pi-calculus	Yes	Potentially no (when connector aspects are employed)
RADL [32]	Finite State Machine	No	Yes
PiLar [9]	process algebraic notation	Yes	Potentially no (when constraints are employed)
π-ADL [27]	pi-calculus	Yes	Potentially no (when connector protocols are employed)
AADL [11]	Automata	No	Yes
Koala [35]	No	No	Yes
COSA [28]	No	Yes	Potentially no (glue centralised controller element)
SOFA [31]	Behaviour Protocols (simplified CSP)	No	Yes
CONNECT [18]	FSP	Yes	Potentially no (glue centralised controller element)

that every procedure is specified as a method of some class while C++ allows independent procedures too. As we do not like having to write `Math.sqrt()` in Java to call the square root function, we believe that it is better to not try to fit everything into a single element and offer a separate notion to characterize protocols – connectors.

Indeed, when (complex) connectors are implicit entities embedded in components (as is, for instance, the case with Darwin, Rapide, OLAN, LEDA, and RADL), they cannot be re-used in different contexts. Furthermore, components become less re-usable too being specific to certain interaction protocols. Worse, when interaction protocols are omitted entirely in architectures, this results in architectural mismatch [13] That is, it is not documented how the components are to behave in their environment and interact with other components; thus, it is very likely that those components are unable to be composed successfully to a whole system.

Having mentioned the importance of explicit complex connectors in design, a careful reader will notice that in Table 1 each referred ADL supporting connectors as a first-class entity have a *realisability* problem. That is, *centralised global* constraints are allowed (if not forced) to be specified that coordinate the behaviour of components – which however can never exist in distributed (i.e., decentralised) systems. In such a case, specifications would become unrealisable that cannot easily be implemented in reality. Separating the global constraints into distributed protocols for the participating components may avoid this, which may however be impossible to do. Worse yet, no tool can warn designers that their design is potentially unrealisable, as the realisability problem is undecidable in general.

Therefore, connectors in XCD are not specified with glue-like centralised units. Instead, as depicted in Figure 1, we consider connectors as abstractions of *decentralised roles*, which represent the interaction behaviour of participating components, and *connector channels* between the roles. Thus, architectural design of distributed systems is specified in a decentralised manner without the restriction of using centralised glues rendering them realisable by construction.

In cases where glue-like centralised choreographers are desired, they are specified as explicit connector roles too.

2. Architecture Specification with Design by Contract

Design by Contract (DbC) invented by Bertrand Meyer [26] is considered as an approach for specifying the behaviour of software in terms of contracts consisting essentially of pre-conditions and post-conditions. A contract herein imposes on software units that if the required pre-condition is satisfied by the caller of the unit, then the unit is executed and is ensured to meet certain post-condition.

In this section, we focus on the idea of adopting and extending DbC for specifying software architectures that can be easily developed and formally analyzed.

2.1 Why Design-by-Contract (DbC)

Formal specification DbC essentially promotes a formal specification of software behaviour in that the notion of contracts has its formal semantics based on Hoare's logic [16] and VDM's rely-guarantee [3] specification approach.

Familiar to developers DbC has been supported by various programming languages and thus already known and used by many developers. This highly aids in contractual specifications being more familiar among developers, compared with process algebras requiring unusual concurrency operators such as parallel composition and (non)deterministic choice operators. DbC has been widely utilized in test-driven

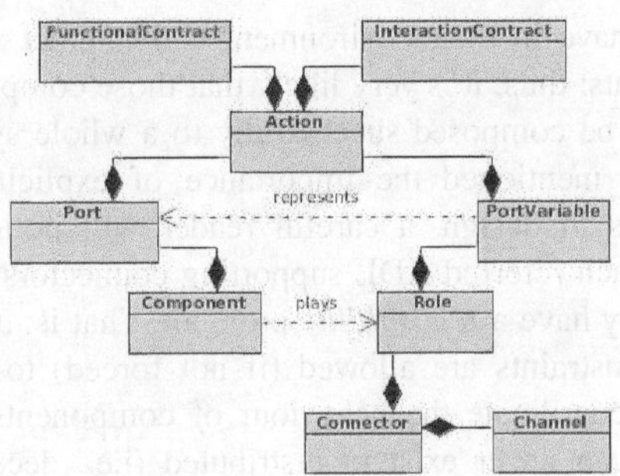

Fig. 1: Meta-model of XCD

developments with the purpose of improving fault detection in software units. Indeed, there are ever-increasing attempts put on this field, e.g., [4], [6], [33]. Java Modeling Language (JML) [8] is one of most well-known work on DbC. Intended for Java language, JML allows for specifying the behaviour of Java modules (e.g., Java classes, methods, or interfaces) with executable contracts. Hence, the behaviour of Java units can be formally specified using JML and further formally verified [12]. Moreover, JML is found easy to use by the software engineering community in that it has been used in teaching for undergraduates [19].

Gap in the field of software architecture Although DbC has been widely considered for the implementation stage of software development, the situation is the contrary for the software architecture level of design stage. To our knowledge, there is only a couple of ADLs developed so far, i.e., RADL [32] and CBabel [5], which include in their focus the DbC. However, their support is rather limited, or, just like other ADLs, suffer from the above mentioned problems. Given the advantages of DbC in specifying formal behaviours and the importance of early formal verification, we believe that this is a crucial gap not thoroughly addressed so far. Indeed, if there was a DbC-based ADL providing comprehensive support to specifying software architectures, designers would be highly attracted enabling the formal verification of their architectures early on in the design stage.

2.2 XCD– A DbC-based ADL

With the main intent on specifying the behaviour of implementation components, DbC contracts are, in general, considered for methods provided by classes, just like JML does. Though this is enough for specifying and verifying the implementation components, it is certainly not so at the level of software architecture design. Indeed, architectural components includes not only the explicit specification of provided services but also that of required services. Moreover, components in software architectures may communicate explicitly by emitting/receiving asynchronous events too.

Therefore, following our initial attempt in [20], XCD extends DbC to apply the notion of contracts to the software architecture design. Component behaviour is specified with contracts constraining the event/method actions performed via component ports. Likewise, the connector roles played by components are specified with contracts constraining their port-variables (representing the participating component ports – see section 2.2.2). Contracts, as depicted in Figure 1, are separated into functional and interaction units: the former is used to represent the functional behaviour of components and the latter represents either the interaction behaviour of components or the interaction protocols of connectors. The rest of this section further elaborates on contractual component and connector specifications.

Listing 1: Generic component structure

```
component Name {
  data;*
  provided port Name {
   @interaction{
    accepts: pre-condition
    rejects: pre-condition
    ***OR***
    waits: pre-condition }
   @functional{
    requires: pre-condition
    ensures: post-condition }
   method;+
  };*
  required port Name {
   @interaction{
    promises: pre-condition }
   @functional{
    promises: pre-condition
     requires: pre-condition
    ensures: post-condition }
   method;+
  };*
  emitter port Name {
   @interaction{
    promises: pre-condition }
   @functional{
    promises:  pre-condition
    ensures: post-condition }
   event;+
  };*
  consumer port Name {
   @interaction{
    accepts: pre-condition
    rejects: pre-condition
    ***OR***
    waits: pre-condition }
   @functional{
    requires: pre-condition
    ensures: post-condition }
   event;+
  };*
}
```

2.2.1 Contractual Component Specifications

Components are used to specify at a high-level the *functional* units in software systems. Unlike AADL, XCD allows designers to describe high-level components without imposing on them lower-level notions (e.g., threads, process).

Component types are essentially specified in terms of (i) *ports* representing the points of interaction with their environment and (ii) *data* representing the component state.

As depicted in Listing 1, four types of ports can be specified for a component: provided and required ports for receiving and making method calls respectively; emitter and consumer ports for emitting and receiving asynchronous events respectively from the component's environment. Herein we extend DbC to allow for contractual specification of not only provided ports, but also required ports and event ports. Furthermore, contracts are split into *functional* and *interaction* contracts, allowing to distinguish between the functional and interaction behaviour. Both contract types are specified over component data and method/event action parameters.

The interaction contracts have precedence over functional; the former states when an event/method action can be taken by a port, and the latter the functional behaviour that is the case upon successful execution of the action.

Provided ports – Provided ports are specified as a set of synchronous method signatures, composed of return type, id, parameters, and exceptions. Each method, as shown in Listing 1, is specified using *@interaction* and *@functional* contract pair. *@interaction* is defined with a pre-condition that can take two alternative forms. In the first form, it specifies when a call can be immediately accepted (*accepts*) or rejected (*rejects*), while in the second form it specifies *wait* condition which delays the caller before its method-call is accepted. *@functional* is specified with pre- and post-conditions, *requires* and *ensures* respectively. Herein, they are used to specify what actual parameters are required in the pre-state of the component that ensures certain specific values for result/exception returned by the method-call.

Required ports – Likewise, required ports are specified with method signatures and contracts attached to the methods. *@interaction* contract for a method herein is specified with a *promised* pre-condition that needs to be satisfied before making the method-call. *@functional* contract herein is specified with *promises*, *requires*, and *ensures* clauses: *promises* states the promised condition on the actual parameters for the method to be called, *requires* states the pre-condition on the response received for the method-call (e.g., whether exception or result is expected), *ensures* states the post-condition on the received response.

Emitter ports – Emitter port are specified similarly to required ports. *@interaction* contract for an event herein is specified with a *promised* pre-condition stating what needs to be met before the event is emitted. *@functional* is specified with *promises* and *ensures* clauses: the former states the pre-condition on the actual parameters of the event, the former states the condition on the component data after the event emission with the promised actual parameters. Note that unlike required ports emitter port does not wait for a response.

Consumer ports – Consumer ports are specified similarly to provided ports. *@interaction* contract for an event is specified just like that of provided ports with the same semantics. They state the acceptance (*accepts*) and rejection (*rejects*) conditions on an event receipt or the *wait* condition for an event to be received. *@functional* contract is specified with *requires* pre-condition and *ensures* post-condition. *requires* states the condition on the received actual parameters of the event whose satisfaction leads to the *ensures* condition being met. Note that consumer ports receive event asynchronously and do not send responses, as is the case with required ports communicating synchronous methods.

Listing 2: Generic connector structure

```
connector Name {
  role Name {
    data;*
    required/provided port_variable Name {
      @interaction{
       waits: pre-condition
       ensures: post-condition }
       method;+
    };*
    emitter/consumer port_variable Name {
       @interaction{
       waits: pre-condition
       ensures: post-condition }
       event;+
    };*
  }
  channel;+
}
```

2.2.2 Contractual Connector Specifications

As aforementioned, connectors in XCD are introduced to represent high-level *complex interaction protocols* which the components interacting through connectors adhere to.

Connector types are specified via *roles* and *channels.* A role acts as a component wrapper representing the interaction behaviour of the participating component. It is described with *data* and *port-variables.* The role port-variables essentially represent the respective ports of the components adopting the role. Channels of a connector represent the communication links between interacting roles and are described with a pair of communicating role port-variables.

As depicted in Listing 2, connector behaviour is specified at the role port-variable level. Port-variables are specified with *@interaction* contracts attached to the event/method actions. These interaction contracts are specified to constrain port-variable actions so that the respective component ports behave in a particular manner (i.e., through execution of certain action order) that meet desired interaction protocols. In doing so, it can be avoided that components get involved in unexpected interactions with other components associated with the same connector. The end result is then a set of components interacting with their environments successfully to compose the whole system.

As shown in Listing 2, *@interaction* contract for a port-variable action is specified uniformly for each port-variable type, with *waits* and *ensures* clauses. Herein, *waits* defines a pre-condition which delays the execution of a port-variable action, namely the respective action of the matching component port. When the wait condition is satisfied, the method/event action may be executed. and the *ensures* post-condition is then to be satisfied too. Note that when the interaction contracts for an action imposed via port-variable are met, then the interaction contracts of component ports are evaluated before executing the action.

2.2.3 Shared-Data Access Case Study

Listing 1 below illustrates XCD's DbC-based behavioral specification on shared-data access. Two component types are specified, *user* between lines 1-21 and *memory* between lines 22-44. User comprises a *required* port, $puser_r$ (lines 4-12), through which its instances call method *get* from the *memory* and an *emitter* port, $puser_e$ (lines 13-20), through which event *set* is emitted. Memory comprises a *provided* port, *pmem_p* (lines 25-34), through which its instances accept calls for method *get* from users and a *consumer* port, $pmem_c$ (lines 35-43) through which event *set* is received.

a) User Component Type: User's *required* port $puser_r$ is used to make a call for method *get*. These calls are delayed until the *promised* condition specified in *@interaction* is met. Since it is *true* in line 6, *get* can be called immediately. Next, the *@functional* in lines 7-10 is evaluated; since *get* has no parameters, there is no promised actual parameters (*promises* condition in line 8 is *true*). Upon receiving the response after calling *get* without parameters, if the *requirement* that an exception is not thrown by the memory is *true*, then the received result are *ensured* to be stored in the *data*.

The user components emit event *set* through its *emitter* port $puser_e$. Note that events are specified without return types – they can only have identifier and parameters. The emission of event *set* is delayed until the promised condition of *@interaction* in lines 14-15 is met. Since it is specified as *true*, emission is made immediately with the promised actual parameters specified in *@functional* (line 17). This then *ensures* that *initialised_u* is set to *true*.

b) Memory Component Type: Memory's *provided* port $pmem_p$ receives calls for method *get*. These calls are accepted when the *accepts* condition in *@interaction* is met, *initialised_m* evaluating to *true* (line 27). Otherwise, the call is *rejected* when *initialised_m* is *false* (line 29) leading to chaos. If the call is accepted, then *@functional* in lines 30-32 is evaluated. There, it is *ensured* that the result value to be responded is equal to the *sh_data*.

The memory components receive event *set* via the *consumer* port $pmem_c$. The receipt of the event *set* is delayed until the promised condition is met in *@interaction*. Since it is specified as *true* in line 37, the *set* is received immediately. Upon successful receipt of the event *set*, *@functional* in lines 38-41 is evaluated. If the *requirement* that the received actual parameter *data_arg* is greater than or equal to zero, then $initialised_m$ is ensured to be *true* and *sh_data* is assigned to *data_arg*.

c) Shared-Data Connector Type: Connector type, *sharedData*, is specified in lines 45-90 which serves as a mediator between users and memory. It essentially avoids memory from performing a chaotic behaviour. In the *sharedData*, three roles are specified, *userRole* in lines 47-53, *initialiserRole* in lines 55-69, and *memoryRole* in lines 71-85, where the *userRole* and *initialiserRole* are played by the *user* component instances and the *memoryRole* by the *memory* instances.

Users playing the *userRole* can call method *get* or emit event *set* in any orders. Indeed, the role port-variables pv_user_r and pv_user_e in lines 48-53 do not include contracts specified for the actions.

However, users playing the *initialiserRole* have to emit event *set* before calling *get*, thus first initialising the memory. The port-variable pv_init_r in lines 57-62 includes *@interaction* contract for method *get* stating that it cannot be called until the role data *initialised_i* is *true*; the pv_init_e in lines 63-68 also includes *@interaction* allowing event *set* to be emitted immediately which then ensures that the role data *initialised_i* is *true*.

The *memoryRole* has two port-variables, pv_mem_p in lines 73-78 and pv_mem_c in lines 79-85. The former includes an *@interaction* contract for method *get* so that received method calls are delayed until the shared data is initialized; the latter includes *@interaction* for event *set* so that when an event *set* is received, *initialised_m* is set to *true*. Therefore, memory components playing the *memoryRole* cannot accept calls for method *get* until they receive event *set* first. The end result is a set of users playing either *userRole* or *initialiserRole* interacting with a memory component that would not cause chaos.

In lines 86-89, there are four channels specified to indicate which role port-variable communicates with which other role port-variable.

The matching between connector roles and components are performed via the connector parameters, as specified in lines 45-46. At configuration time, when the *sharedData* is instantiated, the user and memory component instances are passed to first and last parameters respectively.

```
1 component user{
2   bool initialised_u = false;
3   int data;
4   required port puser_r {
5     @interaction{
6      promises : true; }
7     @functional{
8      promises : true;
9       requires : !\exception
10      ensures : data = \result; }
11    int get();
```

```
  };
  emitter port puser_e {
    @interaction{
     promises: true; }
    @functional{
     promises: data_arg = 7;
     ensures: intialised_u = true;  }
    set(int data_arg);
  };
};
component memory {
  bool initialised_m = false;
  int sh_data = 0;
  provided port pmem_p{
    @interaction{
     accepts: initialised_m;
    also:
     rejects: !initialised_m; }
    @functional{
     requires: true;
     ensures: \result = sh_data;}
    int get();
  };
  consumer port pmem_c{
    @interaction{
     accepts: true; }
    @functional{
     requires: data_arg ≥ 0;
     ensures: intialised_m = true
           && sh_data = data_arg; }
    set(int data_arg);
  };
};
connector sharedData(userRole{pv_user_r/e},
  initialiserRole{pv_init_r/e}, memoryRole{pv_mem_p/c})
  role userRole{
    required port_variable pv_user_r{
      int get();
    };
    emitter port_variable pv_user_e{
      set(int data_arg);
    };
  };
  role initialiserRole{
    bool initialised_i = false;
    required port_variable pv_init_r{
      @interaction{
       waits: when(intialised_i);
       ensures: true; }
      int get();
    };
    emitter port_variable pv_init_e{
      @interaction{
       waits: true;
       ensures: initialised_i = true; }
      set(int data_arg);
    };
  };

  role memoryRole{
    bool initialised_m = false;
    provided port_variable pv_mem_p{
      @interaction{
       waits: when(intialised_m);
       ensures: true; }
      int get();
    };
    consumer port_variable pv_mem_c{
      @interaction{
       waits: true;
       ensures: initialised_m = true; }
      set(int data_arg);
    };
  };
  channel user2memory_m(pv_user_r, pv_mem_p);
  channel user2memory_e(pv_user_e, pv_mem_c);
  channel init2memory_m(pv_init_r, pv_mem_p);
  channel init2memory_e(pv_init_e, pv_mem_c);
};
```

Listing 3: Shared-data Access in XCD

3. Formally Defined Semantics with FSP

The semantics of XCD are based on Finite State Process (FSP) [23]. FSP is essentially a process algebra allowing to specify system behaviour formally with interacting processes. In this way, specifications with XCD can be transformed into formal FSP specifications which can further be analyzed for safety and liveness properties (e.g., deadlock). This section gives an initial flavor of the FSP mappings for XCD component and connector specifications in terms of parallel interaction (||) of FSP processes.

Component Semantics The semantics of a component with data D and ports $p1$,..., pn is the composite process:

$$P_{D_c} \;||\; P_{p1} \;..\; ||\; P_{pn} \qquad (1)$$

where P_{D_c} is the data process and P_{p1},..., P_{pn} each is a port process whose definition is:

$$P_{IC} \;||\; P_{FC_{a1}} .. \;||\; P_{FC_{am}} \qquad (2)$$

where P_{IC} is the interaction constraints process and $P_{FC_{a1}}$..,$P_{FC_{am}}$ each is a process for a functional constraints imposed on a single method/event action taken via the port.

Connector Semantics The semantics of a connector with roles r_1,..., r_n channels ch_1,..., ch_n is the composite process:

$$P_{r1} \;..\; ||\; P_{rn} \qquad (3)$$

where P_{r1}..., P_{rn} each is a role process whose definition is:

$$P_{D_r} \;||\; P_{pv_1} \;..\; ||\; P_{pv_n} \qquad (4)$$

where P_{D_r} is the data process and P_{pv_1},..., P_{pv_n} each is a port-variable process that represents the interaction constraints imposed on method/event actions taken by the port-variable.

Channels of a connector are mapped to *FSP relabeling function* employed in the composite process corresponding to the connector. The relabeling function, for each channel, re-names the actions taken by the provided/consumer port-variable in one end of the channel to the names of the respective actions taken by the required/emitter port-variable in the other end. Therefore, corresponding FSP processes can synchronize on the actions they have been re-named to.

4. Conclusion and Future Work

In this paper, we presented a new ADL, XCD, which resolves three main problems either of which seems to be suffered by current ADLs: unfamiliar notations adopted in specifying architectural behaviours, lack of support for complex connector specifications, and potentially unrealisable designs.

In response to these problems, XCD is based on Design-by-Contract approach in specifying the behaviour of software architectures, instead of more abstract formal notations (e.g., process algebras). Thus, software architectures can be specified with contracts that many developers are already familiar with. Furthermore, architectural connectors in XCD can be used to specify either simple interconnection mechanisms or complex interaction protocols. So, large and complex systems can be specified at a high level as components interacting via complex interaction protocols improving their development and analysis. Connectors are specified in terms of decentralised roles played by the participating components; there is no glue-like centralised units forced in connector specifications. This leads to architectural designs that are realisable by construction.

To allow for formal analysis, we define the semantics of XCD using Finite State Process (FSP). We are currently exploring a definition of XCD semantics based on Promela [17], so as to take advantage of the SPIN model checker and better control the state-space explosion problem.

5. Acknowledgements.

This work has been partially supported by the EU project FP7-257367 IoT@Work – "Internet of Things at Work".

References

[1] R. Allen and D. Garlan. A formal basis for architectural connection. *ACM Trans. Softw. Eng. Methodol.*, 6(3):213–249, 1997.

[2] L. Bellissard, N. De Palma, and D. Féliot. The olan architecture definition language. Technical report, C3DS Technical Report, 2000.

[3] D. Bjørner and C. B. Jones, editors. *The Vienna Development Method: The Meta-Language*, volume 61 of *Lecture Notes in Computer Science*. Springer, 1978.

[4] C. Boyapati, S. Khurshid, and D. Marinov. Korat: automated testing based on java predicates. In *ISSTA*, pages 123–133, 2002.

[5] C. Braga and A. Sztajnberg. Towards a rewriting semantics for a software architecture description language. *Electr. Notes Theor. Comput. Sci.*, 95:149–168, 2004.

[6] L. C. Briand, Y. Labiche, and H. Sun. Investigating the use of analysis contracts to improve the testability of object-oriented code. *Softw., Pract. Exper.*, 33(7):637–672, 2003.

[7] C. Canal, E. Pimentel, and J. M. Troya. Specification and refinement of dynamic software architectures. In P. Donohoe, editor, *WICSA*, volume 140 of *IFIP Conference Proceedings*, pages 107–126. Kluwer, 1999.

[8] P. Chalin, J. R. Kiniry, G. T. Leavens, and E. Poll. Beyond assertions: Advanced specification and verification with JML and ESC/Java2. In *FMCO'05 – Formal Methods for Comp. and Obj.*, volume 4111 of *LNCS*, pages 342–363. Springer, 2006.

[9] C. E. Cuesta, P. de la Fuente, M. Barrio-Solórzano, and M. E. B. Gutiérrez. An "abstract process" approach to algebraic dynamic architecture description. *J. Log. Algebr. Program.*, 63(2):177–214, 2005.

[10] E. M. Dashofy, A. van der Hoek, and R. N. Taylor. A highly-extensible, xml-based architecture description language. In *WICSA*, pages 103–112. IEEE Computer Society, 2001.

[11] P. H. Feiler, D. P. Gluch, and J. J. Hudak. The Architecture Analysis & Design Language (AADL): An Introduction. Technical report, Software Engineering Institute, 2006.

[12] C. Flanagan, K. R. M. Leino, M. Lillibridge, G. Nelson, J. B. Saxe, and R. Stata. Extended static checking for java. In J. Knoop and L. J. Hendren, editors, *PLDI*, pages 234–245. ACM, 2002.

[13] D. Garlan, R. Allen, and J. Ockerbloom. Architectural mismatch or why it's hard to build systems out of existing parts. In *ICSE*, pages 179–185, 1995.

[14] D. Garlan, R. T. Monroe, and D. Wile. Acme: An architecture description interchange language. In *Proceedings of CASCON'97*, pages 169–183, Toronto, Ontario, November 1997.

[15] D. Garlan and M. Shaw. An introduction to software architecture. In V. Ambriola and G. Tortora, editors, *Advances in Software Engineering and Knowledge Engineering*, pages 1–39, Singapore, 1993. World Scientific Publishing Company.

[16] C. A. R. Hoare. An axiomatic basis for computer programming. *Commun. ACM*, 12(10):576–580, 1969.

[17] G. J. Holzmann. *The SPIN Model Checker - primer and reference manual*. Addison-Wesley, 2004.

[18] V. Issarny, A. Bennaceur, and Y.-D. Bromberg. Middleware-layer connector synthesis: Beyond state of the art in middleware interoperability. In M. Bernardo and V. Issarny, editors, *SFM*, volume 6659 of *Lecture Notes in Computer Science*, pages 217–255. Springer, 2011.

[19] J. R. Kiniry and D. M. Zimmerman. Secret ninja formal methods. In J. Cuéllar, T. S. E. Maibaum, and K. Sere, editors, *FM*, volume 5014 of *Lecture Notes in Computer Science*, pages 214–228. Springer, 2008.

[20] C. Kloukinas and M. Ozkaya. Xcd - Modular, realizable software architectures. In C. S. Pasareanu and G. Salaün, editors, *FACS*, volume 7684 of *Lecture Notes in Computer Science*, pages 152–169. Springer, 2012.

[21] D. C. Luckham. Rapide: A language and toolset for simulation of distributed systems by partial orderings of events. Technical report, Stanford University, Stanford, CA, USA, 1996.

[22] J. Magee and J. Kramer. Dynamic structure in software architectures. In *SIGSOFT FSE*, pages 3–14, 1996.

[23] J. Magee, J. Kramer, and D. Giannakopoulou. Analysing the behaviour of distributed software architectures: a case study. In *FTDCS*, pages 240–247. IEEE Computer Society, 1997.

[24] I. Malavolta, P. Lago, H. Muccini, P. Pelliccione, and A. Tang. What industry needs from architectural languages: A survey. *IEEE Transactions on Software Engineering*, 99, 2012.

[25] N. Medvidovic, P. Oreizy, J. E. Robbins, and R. N. Taylor. Using object-oriented typing to support architectural design in the c2 style. In *SIGSOFT FSE*, pages 24–32, 1996.

[26] B. Meyer. Applying "Design by Contract". *IEEE Computer*, 25(10):40–51, 1992.

[27] F. Oquendo. π-adl: an architecture description language based on the higher-order typed π-calculus for specifying dynamic and mobile software architectures. *SIGSOFT Softw. Eng. Notes*, 29(3):1–14, May 2004.

[28] M. Oussalah, A. Smeda, and T. Khammaci. An explicit definition of connectors for component-based software architecture. In *ECBS*, pages 44–51. IEEE Computer Society, 2004.

[29] J. Pérez, I. Ramos, J. J. Martínez, P. Letelier, and E. Navarro. Prisma: Towards quality, aspect oriented and dynamic software architectures. In *QSIC*, pages 59–66. IEEE Computer Society, 2003.

[30] D. E. Perry and A. L. Wolf. Foundations for the study of software architecture. *SIGSOFT Softw. Eng. Notes*, 17(4):40–52, Oct. 1992.

[31] F. Plasil and S. Visnovsky. Behavior protocols for software components. *IEEE Trans. Software Eng.*, 28(11):1056–1076, 2002.

[32] R. Reussner, I. Poernomo, and H. W. Schmidt. Reasoning about software architectures with contractually specified components. In A. Cechich, M. Piattini, and A. Vallecillo, editors, *Component-Based Software Quality*, volume 2693 of *Lecture Notes in Computer Science*, pages 287–325. Springer, 2003.

[33] D. S. Rosenblum. A practical approach to programming with assertions. *IEEE Trans. Software Eng.*, 21(1):19–31, 1995.

[34] M. Shaw, R. DeLine, D. V. Klein, T. L. Ross, D. M. Young, and G. Zelesnik. Abstractions for software architecture and tools to support them. *IEEE Trans. Software Eng.*, 21(4):314–335, 1995.

[35] R. C. van Ommering, F. van der Linden, J. Kramer, and J. Magee. The koala component model for consumer electronics software. *IEEE Computer*, 33(3):78–85, 2000.

A Quantitative Approach to the Evolution of Domain-Specific Modeling Languages

Kiyotaka Ota, Kenji Hisazumi, Weiqiang Kong, Tsuneo Nakanishi, and Akira Fukuda
Graduate School of Information Science and Electrical Engineering, Kyushu University
Fukuoka-city, Japan

Abstract - *Domain-Specific Modeling Languages (DSMLs) are modeling languages that are effective only for particular domains, and DSMLs can make software development much simpler. It is often desirable for DSMLs to be usable repeatedly and for a long time since developing DSMLs is costly and time-consuming. However, this is not easy because it is difficult to evolve existing DSMLs. Conventional evolution of DSMLs is usually conducted based on the information obtained from domain experts (i.e., the interview results of domain experts). However, the DSML problems understood by domain experts can be incomplete, which makes it difficult for DSML developers to judge how to evolve DSMLs and whether an evolution is effective or not. In this paper, we propose an approach to the evolution of DSMLs using quantitative information such as the application data of DSMLs.*

Keywords: Domain-Specific Modeling Languages; Evolution; Metrics;

1 Introduction

In recent years, software development meets many problems that are caused by increase in software scale, the complexity of software design, the reduction of development schedule and cost and so on. Domain-Specific Modeling (DSM)[1] as a method to solve these problems has been attracting attention.

DSM is to design by domain-specific languages (DSLs) [1], the languages that are applicable only to particular domains, so as to make software development small-scale. Since DSLs are defined by concepts and terminologies particularly used in specific software development, DSLs facilitate the software development by domain experts, who have much knowledge of the domain and are also end users themselves. DSLs using graphical notations are called Domain-Specific Modeling Languages (DSMLs) [1]. DSMLs cannot be used for developing the software of other domains, and additionally, the development of DSMLs takes much cost and time before putting them into practical usages. Therefore, it is desirable for a DSML to be usable for more software development repeatedly and be used for a long time [1]. However, this is difficult because DSML developers must evolve DSMLs in accordance with the changes of the requirements of DSMLs. Conventional maintenance of DSMLs employs qualitative information such as dissatisfaction and needs from domain experts, and the quantitative information is seldom used [2]. It is difficult to show the validity and efficacy of DSML evolution to domain experts because the DSML problems domain experts understand are incomplete. Since it is difficult to assess the efficacy of DSML evolution by the incomplete information, DSML developers cannot evaluate DSML evolution.

In order to improve this situation, we propose to maintain DSMLs by quantitative information collected during software development with DSMLs, and we call such quantitative information *DSMLs application data*. With our proposal, DSML developers can quantitatively analyze the problems of DSMLs and decide possible options for solving the problems. As a result, DSML developers can show the validity and efficacy of DSML evolution to domain experts.

In this paper, our purpose is to evolve abstract syntax and concrete syntax of DSMLs. A DSML is comprised of three components: abstract syntax, concrete syntax, and semantics. The abstract syntax defines modeling concepts and their relationships and the concrete syntax defines physical appearance of the abstract syntax. The semantics is the meaning that a model described by a DSML has, and is used to translate the model. The target of our proposal is the evolution of the concepts or the appearance of DSMLs, and we are not concerned with the evolution of the translation of DSMLs.

2 Process of DSML maintenance

Figure 1 is the DSML maintenance process. In order to make DSMLs usable for a long time, DSMLs are maintained in the four phases except the *Deployment Phase*. These phases are explained in detail below:

1) Deployment Phase: Domain experts develop software with DSMLs. DSML developers collect DSML application data for the purpose of the maintenance during domain experts develop software. If fixed time passed or requirements to DSMLs change DSML developers move to the *Evaluation Phase*.

2) Evaluation Phase: DSML developers evaluate, based on the collected data, DSMLs' quality, efficacy, efficiency or the achievement level of requirements. If there are problems, they move to the *Analysis Phase*, otherwise, they move to the *Deployment Phase*.

3) Analysis Phase: DSML developers analyze possible options for solving the problems identified in the *Evaluation Phase*. After analysis, a decision on choosing which options is made.

4) Design Phase: DSML developers re-design the DSMLs newly.

5) Implementation Phase: DSML developers implement the DSMLs designed in the *Design Phase* and enable domain experts to use the DSMLs.

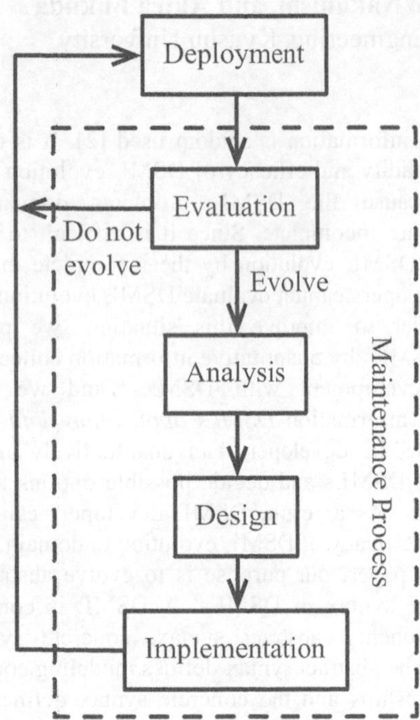

Figure 1. The process of DSML maintenance

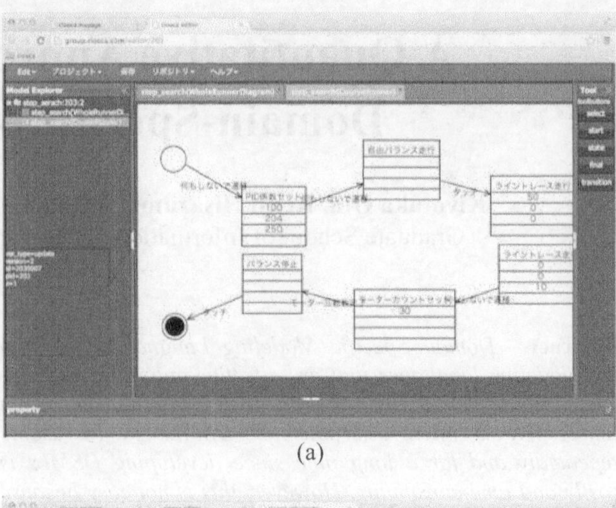

(a)

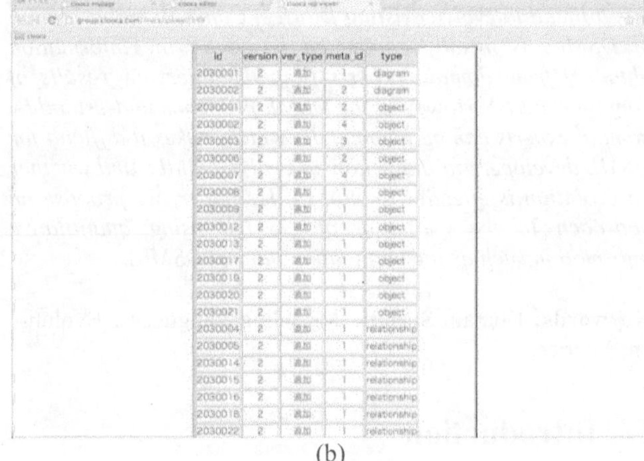

id	version	ver_type	meta_id	type
2030001	2	追加	1	diagram
2030002	2	追加	2	diagram
2030001	2	追加	2	object
2030002	2	追加	4	object
2030003	2	追加	3	object
2030006	2	追加	2	object
2030007	2	追加	4	object
2030008	2	追加	1	object
2030009	2	追加	1	object
2030012	2	追加	1	object
2030013	2	追加	1	object
2030017	2	追加	1	object
2030019	2	追加	1	object
2030020	2	追加	1	object
2030021	2	追加	1	object
2030004	2	追加	1	relationship
2030005	2	追加	1	relationship
2030014	2	追加	1	relationship
2030015	2	追加	1	relationship
2030016	2	追加	1	relationship
2030018	2	追加	1	relationship
2030022	2	追加	1	relationship

(b)

Figure 2. (a) A screen snapshot of the clooca operation window. (b) A screen snapshot of clooca repository.

3 Environment for collecting data of the DSML application

A software development environment to collect DSML application data is required by our proposal. In this study we utilize *clooca* [3] to collect DSML application data. *clooca* is a web-based development environment to develop software by DSMLs and data of described models can be accumulated on servers. DSML developers can measure the quality of DSMLs and analyze possible options for DMSL evolution because they can use the available data for metrics. Moreover, since clooca is under development, it is possible to expand clooca so that we can collect DSML application data. Figure. 2a is a screen snapshot of clooca operation window and Figure. 2b is a screen snapshot of clooca repository. (Note that, as you can see from the snapshots, clooca supports Japanese input as well as English input.)

4 Metrics for DSML evolution

In this section we show the metrics required for the evolution of DSMLs. There are two metrics in our proposal, which are the metrics for DSML quality, and the metrics for problem solving. They are computed from the data collected during domain experts develop software by the DSMLs in the *Deployment Phase* and are used by DSML developers for the maintenance of the DSMLs. We explain them in detail below:

4.1 The metrics for DSML quality

The metrics for DSML quality are used to measure the quality of the DSMLs used in the *Deployment Phase*. DSML developers can identify whether the evolution of DSMLs is necessary or not by measurement their quality. If the DSMLs are effective, it is then not necessary to evolve the DSMLs, and the DSMLs should continue to be used. Moreover, the measurement of DSML quality can make the objectives of the evolution of DSMLs clearer. DSML developers can identify the problems DSMLs have and can realize the quality that should be improved by them.

Table 1 is an example of the metrics for the DSML quality. The targets of measurement by metrics of DSML quality are classified in three kinds, which are the quality of DSML definitions, the quality of DSMLs usages and the quality of DSML products. The quality of DSML definitions is the degree of the excellence of the characteristics that DSMLs themselves have and the RDD in Table. 1 corresponds to it. The RDD demonstrates the degree of the dissatisfaction that domain experts have. The RDD is calculated by Equation (1). The ND in Equation (1) is the number of domain experts who press a dislike button, a button which clooca has to show dissatisfaction of a DSML; the DE in Equation (1) is the number of domain experts who use a DSML. The quality of DSML usages is the degree of usability and efficiency when domain experts use a DSML and the TMD in Table. 1 corresponds to it. The TMD demonstrates the degree of the length to develop with a DSML and the TMD is obtained by measuring time until a model is completed. The quality of DSML products is the degree of the excellence of the characteristics that DSML products have and the CCM and the RSI in Table. 1 corresponds to it. The CCM demonstrates the quality of the models described by a DSML and is calculated by the data of the model in the database server of clooca. The RSI demonstrates the conversion efficiency of source code. The RSI is calculated by Equation (2). The SS in Equation (2) is the size of source code and the MI in Equation (2) is the number of model instances. The quality of DSML is measured by these metrics.

$$RDD = \frac{ND}{DE} \quad (1)$$

$$RSI = \frac{SS}{MI} \quad (2)$$

Table 1. Example of metrics for DSML quality

Metric	Description
CCM	The cyclomatic complexity [3] of the model described by a DSML.
RSI	The ratio of the size of source code and the number of instances of DSMLs.
RDD	The proportion of domain experts who have dissatisfaction to a DSML.
TMD	The time spent for a model description.

4.2 The metrics for problem solving

The metrics for problem solving are used to analyze possible options for solving the problems DSMLs have. They are used by DSML developers to design a DSML that do not have the problems identified by using the metrics for DSML quality. The evolution of DMSLs is classified under eight patterns (Table 2). The options analyzed by the metrics have one or more functions of these patterns.

Table 3 is an example of the metrics for problem solving. The DER measures the connection and the dependence of DSML elements, the elements that are the words to describe models, and is used for the union of DSML elements or the addition of DSML constraint in Table 2. The DER is obtained by calculating combination of DSML elements and frequency of it by the database of clooca. The DEU measures utilization of each DSML element and is used for the deletion of DSML elements. The DEU is calculated by Equation (3). The EI in Equation (3) is the number of model instances of a DSML element and the AI in Equation (3) is the number of all model instances. The NDE measures the dissatisfaction to each DSML elements and is used for the deletion of DSML elements, the modification of DSML elements, the union of DSML elements, or the separation of DSML elements. The NDE is measured by the dislike button of each DSML elements.

$$DEU = \frac{EI}{AI} \quad (3)$$

Table 2. The eight patterns of the DSML evolution

Pattern	Description
Addition of DSML elements	To add new elements to a DSML.
Deletion of DSML elements	To delete elements from a DSML.
Modification of DSML elements	To modify elements of a DSML.
Union of DSML elements	To unite elements of a DSML.
Separation of DSML elements	To separate elements of a DSML.
Addition of constraint	To add new constraint to a DSML.
Deletion of constraint	To delete constraint from a DSML.
Modification of constraint	To modify constraint of a DSML.

Table 3. Example of metrics for problem solving

Metric	Description
DER	DSML elements relevance.
DEU	DSML elements utilization.
NDE	The number of votes of dissatisfaction to DSML elements.

5 Case study

In this section we show an evolution of a DSML for line trace robots. Domain experts can command this robot to run either following a line drawn in a course or run freely. This DSML have a diagram like activity diagrams and domain experts can describe the run scenarios of the robots. Figure 3a is a simple metamodel of the DSML and Figure 3b is a model described by the DSML. The model describes the following things:

- After a robot runs following a line at speed 60 until 100 encoders counts pass, it stops for 10 seconds.
- It runs straight at speed 30 until 50 encoders counts pass or 20 seconds pass.

We evolved this DSML by metrics.

First, we measured the quality of the DSML by metrics. The results of quality measurement by the CCD and the RDD are as follows:

- The cyclomatic complexity of all models described by the DSML is less than 10 (Figure 5).
- 92.9% of domain experts voted to dissatisfaction.

These results showed us the followings facts:

- Models described by this DSML are not complex.
- Many domain experts have dissatisfaction to the DSML.

We understood from the facts that we must make a re-design to reduce dissatisfaction to this DSML.

Then, using the results of the quality measurement, we analyzed the possible options for a DSML evolution. In order to reduce dissatisfaction, we must identify the points to which domain experts have dissatisfaction. The results we analyzed by the NDE in Table 3 are as follows:

- Much dissatisfaction is caused by the concepts of the *Time Setting*, the *Distance Setting*, the *Complete Time* and the *Complete Distance* (Table 4).

This result made us realize that we must modify the four DSML elements. As a result of interview with domain experts we obtained an opinion that it was bothersome to describe the transitions caused by time or distance. Therefore, we decided to analyze whether we can implement one or more of the three patterns so as to achieve a simple description. We used the DER in Table 3 to analyze options for describing the transitions more easily. The results are as follows:

- The *Time Setting* and the *Complete Time* are mostly used in combination such as shown in Figure 4a.
- The *Distance Setting* and the *Complete Distance* are mostly used in combination such as shown in Figure 4b.

The results showed that we could unite these elements. Thus, we decided to create the Time that unites the *Time Setting* and the *Complete Time*, and the Distance that unites the *Distance Setting* and the *Complete Distance.* Figure 6a is a simple metamodel of the evolved DSML and Figure 6b is a model that is described by the evolved DSML.

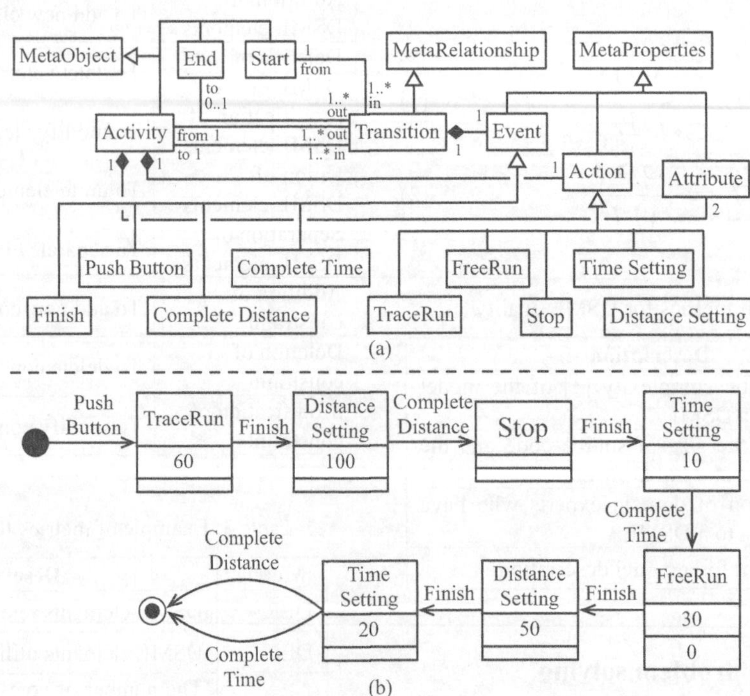

Figure 3. (a) A simple metamodel of the DSML for Line Trace Robot. (b) A model described by the DSML.

We compared the two DSMLs by considering the RSI and the RDD of the metrics for DSML quality to evaluate the efficacy of the evolution. The results are as follows:

- The proportion of domain experts, who have dissatisfaction to the DSML, becomes 42.9%.
- Source code could be generated by fewer instances (Figure 7).

We understood from these results that the DSML evolution is effective.

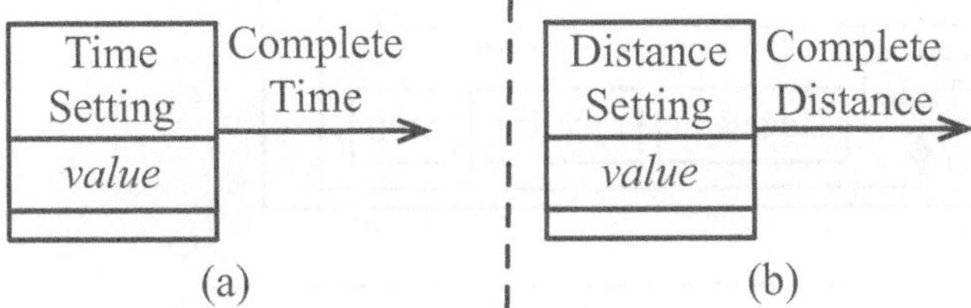

Figure 4. (a) A combination of the *Time Setting* and the *Complete Time*. (b) A combination of the *Distance Setting* and the *Complete Distance*.

Table 4. The number and the proportion of votes of dissatisfaction to the DSML elements

Analysis Item		Vote	Proportion
DSML Element Appearance	Run	4	6.8
	Stop	1	1.7
	Time Setting	3	5.1
	Distance Setting	3	5.1
	Push	0	0
	Complete Time	0	0
	Complete Distance	0	0
DSML Element Concept	Run	0	0
	Stop	0	0
	Time Setting	13	22
	Distance Setting	13	22
	Push	0	0
	Complete Time	11	18.6
	Complete Distance	11	18.6
Total		59	

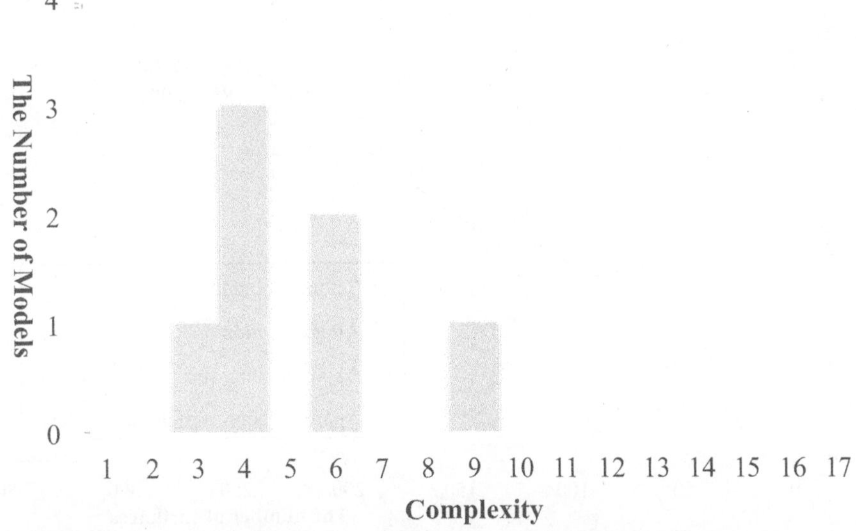

Figure 5. A histogram of cyclomatic complexity described by the DSML.

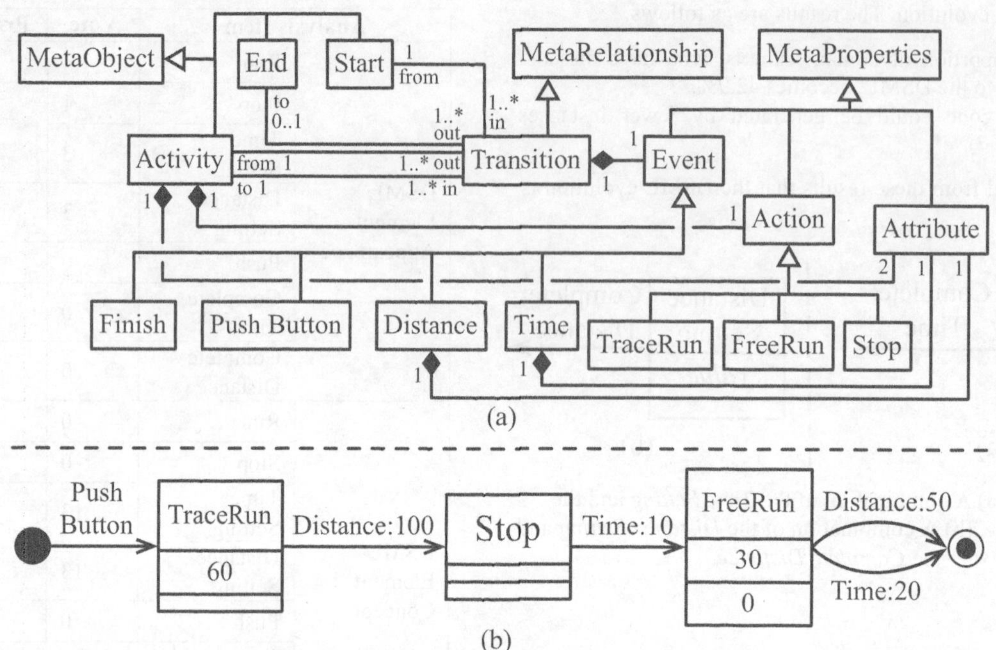

Figure 6. (a) A simple metamodel of the evolved DSML. (b) A model described by the evolved DSML.

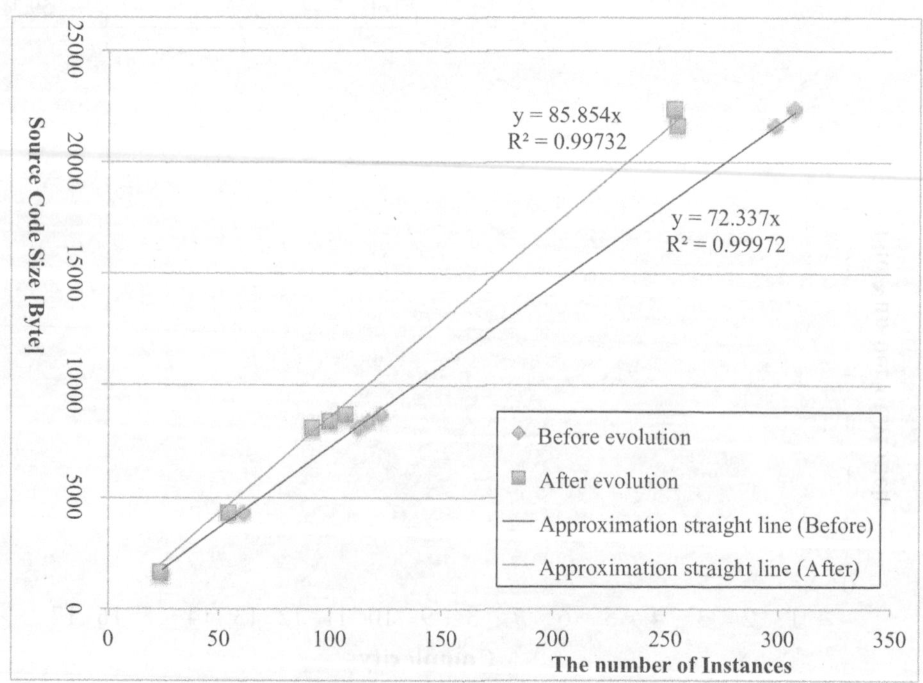

Figure 7. Trends of source code size by the number of model instances.

6 Related work

The work in [5] demonstrates a method to develop DSMLs by *community* and a supporting tool. The community means the group of DSML developers and domain experts. The assessment by domain experts is carried out in each phase of a DSML development process because the domain experts participate in the whole development process. As a result, DSML developers can analyze and design by using the idea from domain experts, and they can reduce rework and improve the quality. In this proposal, although the problems of DMSLs are analyzed by qualitative information such as proposals from a community, the design is evaluated by the quantitative information such as the number of affirmative votes to the proposals.

The work in [6] proposes a systematic approach to assess the efficacy of the introduction of DSLs. The usability of a DSL for High Energy Physics (HEP) called Pheasant is assessed by the data (i.e., the ratio of correct uses and the training time). The purpose of this study is not the evolution of DSLs but the assessment.

In [7], the metamodel of UML is assessed by object-oriented design metrics. The changes of UML are analyzed by assessing the five metamodels of UML (i.e., UML 1.1, UML 1.3, UML 1.4, UML 1.5 and UML 2.0). In this work, it is argued that the method for assessing UML metamodels can be used to control and predict the evolution of UML. The purpose of this study is to assess the quality of UML metamodels. However, the quality of usage is not assessed and the evolution of UML is not proposed.

7 Conclusion and future work

In this paper, we proposed a quantitative approach to the evolution of DSMLs by DSML application data. This approach requires two kinds of metrics: the metrics for measuring the quality of DSMLs and the metrics for solving the problem of DSMLs. The metrics for DSML quality are used to find the problems of DSMLs and decide to evolve DSMLs and the metrics for problem solving are used to analyze the possible options for solving the problems DSMLs have. The DSML application data for the metrics is collected by clooca during domain experts develop software.

We have to identify two problems, which are to define the metrics for the DSML quality and the problem solving and to further evaluate the results of our studies. Some definitions of metrics will be provided by a survey of existing researches. These researches will give us definitions of metrics for DSML quality. With regard to metrics for problem solving, we will be able to obtain them by not only the survey of the researches to evaluate DSMLs, but also the survey of the researches on the occurrence and the relation of the DSML elements, for example, co-occurrence or model clone. In addition to these researches, we will also analyze necessary metrics for DMSL evolution from the DSML deployment problems to software development problems. Our proposed method must be evaluated by many DSMLs, therefore, we will evaluate our studies by DSMLs designed for the software development of agricultural robots or airships. Moreover, we will use the application data of DSMLs for quantitative evaluation.

8 References

[1] S. Kelly and J-P. Tolvanen, "Domain-Specific Modeling: Enabling Full Code Generation", Wiley-IEEE Computer Society Press, 2008.

[2] A. van Deursen and P. Klint, "Little languages: Little maintenance?", In Journal of Software Maintenance, pp.75-92, 1998.

[3] Thomas J. McCabe, "A Comlpexity Measure", In the Proceedings of the 2th International Conference on Software Engineering, pp.308-320, 1976.

[4] S. Hiya, clooca educational version, http://www.clooca.com/, (Accessed 2013-03-18).

[5] J.L.C. Izquierdo and J. Cobot, "Community-Driven Language Development", In the Proceedings of the International Workshop on Modeling in Software Engineering, pp.29-35, 2012.

[6] Ankica Barišić, Vasco Amaral, Miguel Goulão, and Bruno Barroca, "Quality in Use of Domain Specific Languages: a Case Study", In the Proceedings of the 3rd ACM SIGPLAN Workshop on Evaluation and Usability of Programming languages and tools, pp.65-72, 2011.

[7] Haohai Ma, Weizhong Shao, Lu Zhang, Zhiyi Ma and Yanbing Jiang, "Applying OO Metrics to Assess UML Metamodels", <<UML>> 2004 - The Unified Model ing Language. Modeling Languages and Applications, pp.12-26, 2004.

Using Productivity Measure and Function Points to Improve the Software Development Process

Eduardo Alves de Oliveira and Ricardo Choren Noya

Computer Engineering Section, Military Engineering Institute, Rio de Janeiro, Brazil

Abstract *- Usually, cost and time estimations are done at the beginning of a software project for budget planning purposes. Such estimations are used at the end of the project to verify if the initial planning was followed or if there were any deviations. In this sense, these estimations can only be used as an input to improve the process for other projects. This paper presents an iterative method, which uses productivity and function points metrics, to identify possible deviations in the amount of time and effort needed to carry out the process tasks, thus continuously updating the estimations in order to cope with the current project needs. It is presented a real case study of how this process can be applied.*

Keywords: *Function Point Analysis, Indicator of Productivity, Software Development Process, Project Management.*

1 INTRODUCTION

Software development companies are getting more and more competitive. To understand how competitive a company is, it must measure the productivity and quality in their Software Development Processes (SDP) [9]. Knowing the productivity in the SDP, allows the company to improve the prediction of several projects parameters such as effort, time and cost. Both users and project managers want to know before a project starts its estimated cost and time to enhance performance with the best accuracy possible [14].

Currently, it is usual to calculate a productivity estimate at the initial planning phase of a project and then to verify the actual productivity yield at the end of the project. [11] The use of a measure at these two moments is extremely important because the estimates are based on historical productivity. However, measuring the productivity only at these two moments in a project is rather insufficient and may cause some difficulties, e.g., knowing throughout the development cycle if the time and cost estimates will be met; monitoring the productivity of medium and large projects; detecting the factors that impact the productivity of a SDP; providing ongoing adjustments to the SDP, and; controlling whether the scope of the project is being met or not.

There already are some techniques for monitoring the productivity of a SDP [11]. Nevertheless such techniques do not assess productivity through a functional measurement. This makes it difficult for managers to compare the productivity of the development of a given functionality to the productivity of other functionalities and to the estimated productivity of project as a whole.

A functional measurement standardizes the estimation of the functional size of any project [8]. Thus it can be used as the unit to be used to measure productivity. Moreover, by using function units managers can assess the project productivity throughout the project and not only at its end.

Changes in the scope of project requirements are a good example of how the use of a functional measure can give further information to managers. Such changes can present a growth rate of 2% per month from the time the project moves from specification to codification [4]. If some functionality had its scope changed it is likely to have its functional size changed thus impacting on productivity. If managers only measure productivity at the end of the project they will probably find the reason why it presented a downside in productivity: changes in the scope. However they missed the opportunity to respond to such changes in order to keep or even enhance productivity during the project execution. The functional measurement could show the productivity rate of function development required for managers to cope with the difficulty to meet the estimated productivity.

This paper presents a method for productivity monitoring all along an iterative SDP execution. Each iteration should have its size measured using a functional measurement of the project use cases. The manager will give a percentage of size of the iteration to each SDP phase. This will allow for effort and productivity division and monitoring in every process iteration. This work uses Function Point Analysis (FPA) [8] as functional measurement.

This article is structured as follows. Section 2 presents how project planning should be done using a productivity indicator. Section 3 describes the method proposed in this paper, i.e. the SDP productivity monitoring. Section 4 illustrates a simple example and, finally, section 5 concludes this paper.

2 PLANNING PROJECTS USING PRODUCTIVITY

The productivity indicator is an important information for planning a project, since it improves the performance in the production of software [12]. Productivity is measured to monitor production, reduce costs and improve the quality of the delivered product [7].

It is considered a complex project measure, which relies on over a hundred known factors [3]. Productivity is a ratio of production output to what is required to produce it. The measure of productivity is defined as a total output per one unit of a total input. [6]. A production output unit in software can be represented by lines of code, components, artifacts or function points. Inputs can be effort (time) or financial (this paper consider inputs as effort measured in hours).

Figure 1 shows a simplified diagram of productivity [5]. It shows how resources are consumed by a particular process or sub process for the generation of a particular software product.

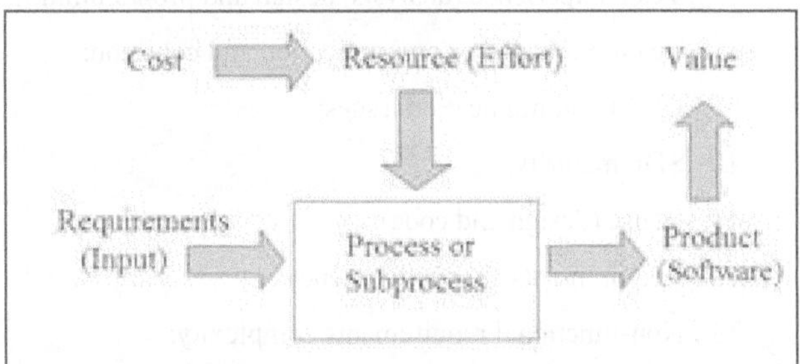

Figure 1: Simplified Model for Productivity [5]

The productivity indicator is calculated using a simple mathematical equation (1).

$$Productivity = Resource / Product \qquad (1)$$

This paper uses the measure of hours of effort (H). The product is represented by the number of function points (FP) produced. Thus productivity is calculated as:

$$Productivity = H / FP \qquad (2)$$

There are other ways to measure the size of a project, such as lines of code (LOC) [1, 10] and use case points. The function point (FP) metric was chosen because it is currently the most used measure for functional measurement software in the market. Besides it is independent of the technology of the format of the unit. This technique has emerged as a result of studies at IBM in the 70s [2].

FP considers the functions that store data and the transactions that manipulate such data. The FPA is described in a manual that describes how to calculate the functional size of a software project or improvement of software [8]. The technique does not define, among other things, how to treat indicator of productivity or costs (pricing).

This paper uses FP as a basic measure in the calculation of productivity. FPA can be used to parameterize the functional size of software systems and projects regardless of the technology that will be used to build it [8]. It lets all functional requirements, recognized and specified by the user, to be sized as a number of function points. Thus it is possible for the project manager measure all user functional requirements in a standardized and objective way.

3 A METHOD FOR MONITORING PRODUCTIVITY

This paper proposed a method to monitor the productivity of a project in every iteration during its life cycle. The idea is to allow for adjustments between iterations so that the project does not suffer from delays, increased costs or loss of product quality. It is important to mention that adjustment actions made by managers will impact the project SDP. For these impacts to enhance productivity, it is essential for the manager to know which activities, sub processes or phases are presenting poor (or downslope) productivity.

The method is presented as a set of steps. Each step indicates an action that should be performed side by side with the SDP activities. The main purpose is to allow the manager to compare the actual current productivity with the previously estimated project productivity, done at early project planning phases.

Step1: Dividing the Development Cycle by Phase and Iteration

The development cycle corresponds to the total (i) effort consumed, and (ii) software size (FP) produced in a project. The project should divide the development in iterations (or sprints for agile methods). Each iteration should correspond to a sub cycle of the SDP. It is important to mention that the management does not change the phases (add or drop) in an iteration in order to increase or decrease the effort spent.

Each phase in an iteration is responsible for a share of the total effort estimated for the iteration. The project manager should establish such share to distribute the effort that will be employed in each phase. Such distribution should be done by using historical data or by experience. It is important that this distribution be realistic.

Step 2: Estimating the size of an iteration in Function Points

After the preparation of the iteration, the project manager will have the requirements approved by the client, and these are described in a specification. The method proposed here was used in projects that specified its requirements using use cases. The method to estimate the FP count by use case is as follows:

1) Finding the Elementary Processes: the manager should find the elementary processes in the use case flows. An elementary process is the smallest unit of meaningful activity for the user to specify the requirement [8]. For each elementary process found in the use case, there should be a corresponding transactional function. After finding the transactional functions, the manager can identify the functions that manipulate data.

2) Finding the Data Functions: during the analysis of transactional functions it is possible to identify the data that is manipulated by these functions. The presence of a logical data model is important for a more precise identification of the data, but this model is not always present at the moment the project. Each data function has a complexity that corresponds to an amount of FPs. However a data function can be used by transactional functions from different use cases. In this scenario, the manager can follow two approaches:

2.1) select an owner Use Case: an owner use case is the use case that is the most important (from the client prioritizing point of view) or that uses the data function more. Then the data function should contribute to the FP size of the owner use case.

2.2) divide the contribution of Function Data: each use cases that manipulate the data function should get a slice of its size in FP. This slice is decided by the manager.

3) Finding the estimated FP size of the Use Case: the sum of transactional functions and data functions found in a use case results in the estimated size FP of the use case.

Step 3: Calculating Estimated Effort of an Iteration

The project manager must, through a history of similar projects or a historical company base, find the estimated productivity of the project. This estimated productivity should take into consideration the particular aspects of the project. The iterations of the project refer to the estimated productivity of the project. The productivity of the iteration cannot be far from the productivity of the project, because it will increase the risk of non-compliance (time and cost).

To reach the estimated effort, in hours, of an iteration, the manager should multiply the estimated size of all use cases of iteration by iteration the estimated productivity.

Step 4: Calculating the Real Productivity of an Iteration

At the end of the iteration the project manager calculates the total hours of actual effort (final), expended by the iteration development. Besides calculating the actual effort, the project manager should make the final FP count of the iteration. These will allow the manager to calculate the actual productivity of the iteration (H / FP).

If there is a deviation in the productivity, the project manager should take actions to adjust the SDP execution. Otherwise the project will be at the risk of delays and/or increase costs. These can impact the product quality.

Step 5: Assessing Impacts on the Actual Productivity

At the end of each iteration, the project manager must answer a checklist of questions to evaluate factors that impacted the actual productivity of the iteration. In doing so, the manager will be able to define the actions to be taken in subsequent iterations, aiming to adjust in real productivity of the next iterations.

The checklist should include questions that allow the evaluation of each SDP phase. The organization using the proposed method can define its own set of questions. Below, we present a set of aspects that can be used in the checklist. All of them are related to aspects found in productivity literature [7, 13]:

1. Project complexity;
2. Project type (e.g. real time, distributed);
3. Innovation support;
4. Development infrastructure ;
5. Work environment;
6. Application integration (to other applications);
7. Team experience (analysis, design and programming);
8. Team motivation, communication and cohesion;
9. Client communication issues;
10. SDP maturity;
11. Reuse (design and code);
12. Requirements change frequency;
13. Non-functional requirements complexity;
14. Programming language complexity;
15. Verification (testing and defect removal);
16. Re-work (change management);
17. Quality standards and issues;
18. Client approval issues;
19. Evolution (maintenance aspects, refactoring, etc.);
20. Changes in the team (inclusion, drops, etc.).

The manager should verify if there were positive or negative impacts of each aspect in the iteration productivity. These will aid the manager to analyze possible process improvements.

4 Case Study

This section presents a case study to show the proposed productivity monitoring approach. The goal is to show that the method allows the project manager to monitor the productivity of the project and give indications of the reasons that are leading to deviations of productivity in phases and iterations.

The example portrayed here refers to a project developed by the energy organization and its development process was divided into three phases, namely: Requirements, Construction and Testing. The distribution of percentage of effort per phase was: 21% for Requirements; 53% for Construction, and; 26% for Testing. These percentages were reported by the project manager. The project was planned to be done in 9 (nine) iterations with a total of fifty five use cases and a team of six persons. At the time of this paper, six iterations have already been performed.

The iteration analysis should include a set of questions, such as:

1. Was the productivity of each iteration better or worse than the initial productivity? Why was that?
2. Has the project manager defined actions to adjust the SDP after each iteration (if necessary)?
3. Did the actions have any effects in the subsequent iterations?

Table 1 presents the distribution, by iteration, of the number of use cases, the FP size and the effort hours for each of the six iterations already carried out. For the sake of simplicity, this study did not present the FP count by use case. The size in FP is presented by iteration. Table 2 shows the actual productivity per iteration and phase. All phases of the development process of this project were estimated at 17.92 H / FP.

If at the end of an iteration, the phase of the process had productivity lower than the estimated productivity, there is a deviation that can cause higher costs and increased time to deliver the project. If productivity has been better than planned, it should be a review to see if there was over estimation of resources hours, or if all activities of the SDP were properly executed. This may result in product quality decrease, leading to user dissatisfaction.

The project manager created a checklist of questions based on the aspects listed in section 3. The responses to these questions were used as input to perform the analysis of the factors impacting positively and negatively on the productivity of each iteration. Thus it revealed the factors that impact the productivity of iterations along the development cycle of the project.

The description of the six iterations in this study is below.

- First iteration (productivity 10.55 H/FP)
  - Strengths:
    - Team: motivated to learn a new technology and a new domain, and; trained before the iteration began;
    - Functionality: CRUD use cases; reuse.
  - Weaknesses:
    - Team: only one member on testing team (unfamiliar with testing tool); requirements team working on different site.
  - Actions taken for second iteration
    - Weekly meetings with all members;
    - Peer reviewing (done by senior analyst).
- Second iteration (productivity 5.56 H/FP)
  - Strengths:
    - Team: testing team increased to two members;
    - Functionality: continued CRUD use cases; reuse.
  - Weaknesses:
    - Team: testing team still unfamiliar with testing tool; weekly meetings did not include requirements members (as they were in another site).
  - Actions taken for third iteration
    - Hire analyst familiar with testing tool;
    - Space provision to move requirements members.
- Third iteration (productivity 15.26 H/FP)
  - Strengths:
    - Team: two new requirement analysts added; another senior analyst added;
    - Functionality: other core use cases (three of the biggest (in size) use cases included).
  - Weaknesses:
    - Team: changes impacted on communications; part of the team was idle;
    - Workplace: not yet completed for all team members;
    - Testing: not automated;
    - Functionality: difficulties with the development of specific functions.
  - Actions taken for fourth iteration
    - Improve workplace (mainly equipments) for team.
- Fourth iteration (productivity 29.99 H/FP)
  - Strengths:
    - None in special.
  - Weaknesses:
    - Team: (workplace impacts related) requirements, development and testing teams worked on different sites; project manager shared time with another project;
    - Testing: not automated;
    - Functionality: intense internal reworking.
  - Actions taken for fifth iteration

Table 1: Distribution of Use Cases, FP and Effort of each iteration.

Iteration	Number of UCs	Size (FP)	Effort (Hours)
1st	8	167	1,761.25
2nd	11	181.5	1,027.50
3rd	12	129.5	1,976.35
4th	10	78.5	2,354.50
5th	10	71.5	1,782.50
6th	4	36	1,429.25

Table 2: Productivity Calculation for Phase and Iteration

Iteration	Productivity (H/FP) – Initial Productivity = 17,92 H/FP				
	Requirement	Construction	Test	Iteration	Difference
1st	9.69	14.49	3,20	10.55	-7.38
2nd	7.12	5.23	5.36	5.66	-12.26
3rd	15.45	16.45	12.69	15.26	-2.66
4th	31.73	37.81	12.67	29.99	+12.07
5th	15.92	19.23	43.83	24,93	+7.01
6th	50.60	15.59	79.99	39.70	+21.78

•

▪ None in special.

- Fifth iteration (productivity 24.93 H/FP)
  - o Strengths:
    - ▪ None in special.
  - o Weaknesses:
    - ▪ Team: new members were added (but were not experienced); project manager still shared time with another project;
    - ▪ Testing: not automated; number of defects increased (including the detection of defects related to previous iterations).
  - o Actions taken for sixth iteration
    - ▪ Team training.
- Sixth iteration (productivity 39.70 H/FP)
  - o Strengths:
    - ▪ None in special.
  - o Weaknesses:
    - ▪ Team: requirements, development and testing teams still worked on different sites; project manager shared time with another project;
    - ▪ Testing: not automated; defect complexity increased.

Iterations 1 and 2 present a productivity rate above the project estimation and they deliver the best productivity in the whole project (iterations 1 through 6). This was mainly because the functionality comprised CRUD use cases (with more simple testing), there was a high rate of reuse and the team was highly motivated.

On the other hand, iterations five and six presented the worst productivity rate – way below the first estimate. This increased the risk of deviations from the costs and scheduled previously planned for the project. This was mainly motivated due to the development of more complex use cases, higher fault detection (including faults from previous iterations); higher defect complexity; change in the team, and; a somewhat loose of project management control (the project manager was also assigned to another project).

Such information allows for the assessment of factors impacting the project productivity. The checklist was used to detect these factors. Indeed, the factors were used to devise actions to improve the productivity. Nonetheless, it is important to mention that, although the management tried to take actions in-between the iterations, the productivity did not improve along the project.

5 CONCLUSION

Knowing the actual (final) productivity is key to evaluate the process of a development organization. It serves as input for calibration of the estimated productivity indicator. But measuring and analyzing the real productivity (final) is insufficient to monitor a project.

The use of Function Points to calculate the productivity of a particular project allows it to be compared to other projects. It parameterizes the size of the functionalities and enables the use of historical productivity information to better estimate the schedule and the budget of new projects.

Failure to follow a project can cause serious problems to a software project. Regarding productivity, problems may occur to the time and the cost initially established for the project. It also impacts in the quality of the delivered product. Usually, the project manager only estimates the productivity at the beginning of the project and then calculates actual delivered productivity at the end of the project. If the project manager awaits the completion of the project to evaluate the actual productivity, only the next project may benefit from measures to improve the development process.

When the project manager monitors the productivity of the project, by iteration, it is possible to detect which process phases present lower productivity. With such information, the manager can attempt to take actions to improve the process on-the-fly in order to increase the project productivity. Even if it is not possible to take such actions, the management will have more accurate information about the possible causes of productivity decrease. This information will have an important role in estimating and negotiating new projects.

This paper presented a proposal for defining a process for monitoring the productivity of software projects through the use of productivity indicator monitoring. This indicator is used to assess whether the estimated productivity is being fulfilled during the iterations of the development cycle of the project. The calculation of this indicator is done using the size of the use cases performed in function points, and effort in hours for its completion. This calculation is dismembered by phases, allowing a detailed analysis of what steps need to be improved.

With the implementation of this monitoring process the project manager will able to take actions in the process of adjustment of project development in order to adjust it before it ends. Analyzing the indicator by use case and phase can be used to try to identify the pitfalls of a development process with more accuracy.

6 REFERENCES

[1] A. Albrecht, J. Gaffney. "Software Function, Source Lines of Code, and Development Effort Prediction: A Software Science Validation" – IEEE Transactions on Software Engineering, SE-9, 6, 1983.

[2] A. Abran, P. N. Robillard, "Function Point Analysis: An Empirical Study of Its Measurement Processes", IEEE Transaction on Software Engineering, Vol. 22, Nº. 12, December 1996.

[3] C. Jones, "Positive and Negative Factors that Influence Software Productivity", versão 2.0. Software Productivity Research, Inc, 1998.

[4] C. Jones, "Software Estimating Rules of Thumb", version 3, 2007.

[5] D. N. Card, "The Challenge of Productivity Measurement". Pacific Northwest Software Quality Conference, 2006.

[6] G. Karner, "Resource Estimation for Objectory Projects", Objective Systems SF AB, 1993.

[7] G. P. Sudhakar, A. Farooq, S. Patnaik, "Measuring Productivity of Software Development Teams". Serbian Journal of Management, 2012.

[8] International Function Point Users Group (IFPUG), "Counting Practices Manual (CPM)", versão 4.3.1, publicado em Janeiro de 2010.

[9] J. T. Joseph, "Role of Function Point as a Reuse Metric in a Software Asset Reuse Program", International Conference on Software Engineering Research and Practice (SERP) – Las Vegas – Nevada - USA, 2011.

[10] J. Schofield, "The Statistically Unreliable Nature of Lines of Code". Sandia National Laboratorie, Albuquerque – USA, 2005.

[11] PMI - Project Management Institute, "PMBOK – Guia do Conjunto de Conhecimentos em Gerenciamento de Projetos – Official Portuguese". 4ª Edição". São Paulo: Project Management, 2008.

[12] S. Han, S. Lee, "Quantified Comparison and Analysis of Different Productivity Measurements". Journal of Asian Architecture and Building Engineering, November 2008.

[13] S. Walt, "Understanding Software Productivity", Software Engineering and Knowledge Engineering: Trends for the Next Decade, D. Hurley (ed.), Vol. 4, World Scientific Press, 1995.

[14] W. W. Agresti, W. M. Evanco, W. M. Thomas, "Models for Improving Software System Size Estimates during Development". J. Software Engineering & Applications, 2010.

Scaffolding the Software Design Process: Fine-Grained Specifications from Design Tactics

A. Ejnioui[1], **C. E. Otero**[1], **and A. A. Qureshi**[2]
[1]Dept. of Information Technology, University of South Florida, Lakeland, Florida, USA
[2]Dept. of Mathematics and Computer Science, University of Virginia's College at Wise, Wise, Virginia, USA

Abstract–*Software projects define requirements to describe what the system does. In some cases, these requirements are not available. Instead, customers demand that the system meet specific quality goals. Experience shows that domain experts use design tactics to meet quality goals for several application domains. Because most engineers are not domain experts, they may experience difficulties in understanding and implementing these tactics as effective solutions to design problems related to quality attributes. In these situations, a significant amount of trial-and-error work takes place during design to ensure a particular goal is met. In some cases, this valuable knowledge can be lost throughout the life cycle or hard to reuse in future projects. This paper proposes a two-step approach in which fine-grained specifications can be extracted from design tactics. To address this problem, design tactics are modeled as activity diagrams. The Unified Modeling Language provides these diagrams as effective representations for conveying system behavior in terms of what actions the system performs. Action and control nodes of these diagrams are examined in order to generate specifications expressed in natural language based on subject-verb-object templates.*

Keywords: requirements; design tactics; activity diagrams; natural language; templates

1 Introduction

After a few decades of experience in engineering software, the software community considers requirements to be the cornerstone of any software project. Because requirements express the needs and interests of different stakeholders, they can impact the success or failure of a software system. Determining the correct requirements for a software system can be fraught with pitfalls. This is understandable since requirements analysis always starts with a project with unclear vision and scope [1]. Contrary to software architecture and implementation, determining requirements is a task that has to be performed in an unconstrained space. In fact, the attempt to determine the requirements results in a constrained space in which a design solution can be elaborated. These difficulties make requirements determination highly iterative in nature, time-consuming, and resource-intensive.

Practice on the field shows that requirements are sometimes not elicited in a systematic fashion. In some cases, determining requirements becomes urgent only when architects are about to develop the architecture of the software system under construction [2]. What is common in practice is for customers and users to demand that the system meets specific quality attributes or goals. These quality attributes can be system, business or architecture-specific qualities [2]. Specifically, system attributes are critical as they can be the foundation for system requirements. Many times, customers express a system quality attribute as a goal while leaving the derivation and specification of requirements related to this goal for engineers to deal with. For instance, a customer may require that the software system meet the goal of availability. In this context, availability can be viewed as the minimization of system failures and their associated consequences [2]. This goal can be met using several design approaches depending on the target application domain. In embedded systems for instance, availability can be met by integrating a watchdog timer in the system architecture. On the other hand, this goal can be met by using a server process to monitor the state of the network and other related protocols such as HTTP in a web server. In many software organizations, it is not uncommon to encounter engineers who are not domain experts as they are not sufficiently knowledgeable about specific design approaches to meet specific goals in specific application domains. If an engineer never worked on an embedded system, he/she will unlikely be aware of watchdog timers as a possible design approach to meet the goal of availability. In this case, as long as the engineer does not see any documented requirements specific to a watchdog timer, he/she will not integrate it in the system. In the worst case, customers and management expect the engineer to generate the requirements to meet their specific goal and sign up on these requirements as they are being implemented. Even if the engineer was aware of watchdog timers as a way to support availability, he/she may not have a full understanding of the architecture and design of the timer. In addition, he/she may have difficulty integrating the timer in the overall design of the system. As a result, there is an urgent need to (i) make engineers aware of the existence of a number of design approaches to meet well-defined goals, (ii) expose engineers to design issues related to these approaches, and (iii) assist engineers with elaborating the requirements appropriate to meet a specific quality goal considering the target application domain.

In practice, experienced architects and domain experts use design tactics as a means to meet quality goals. A design tactic is a design decision intended to control a single quality attribute [2, 3]. Design tactics are building blocks for design and analysis during the software architecture activity. They have been used on the field and shown to produce consistent results [2, 3, 4]. Design tactics can be refined into other design tactics that are more specialized for a given target system. As design artifacts, design tactics may not be easy to understand by inexperienced engineers and consequently may not be easy to implement. Although design tactics are somewhat fine-grain representations when integrated in software architecture, they are still too abstract at the conceptual level for engineers to translate from design to implementation. Through experience, engineers develop a number of tailored solutions to specific problems that can be summarized as lists of ready-to-use how to's recipes. In some instances, these solutions have been tested and proven on the field in numerous projects. Based on this field experience, technical leaders are able to develop technical requirements derived from these tested solutions. From this perspective, one can easily understand how beneficial it is to capture a snapshot of a solution model, extract technical requirements from it, and use the requirements to hold developers accountable for their implementation. In fact, it is not unreasonable to see how technical requirements specifying how to do something, may be sometimes required to build a high-quality system. This problem has been raised in projects with stringent security goals. Because there are few security experts available at this moment, engineers will be relieved to have a list of how to's technical requirements to help them with designing solid solutions to meet security goals. In this context, it would be helpful to inexperienced engineers if design tactics can be transformed into sets of requirements intended to meet a quality goal. These requirements are the foundation on which most engineers will build the system. Because design tactics have been developed and tested on the field for some time, several catalogs of these tactics have been already assembled to meet quality goals such as availability, modifiability, performance, testability and usability [2]. These catalogs can be the starting point for generating sets of requirements for each quality attribute where these requirements are grouped by design tactics. However, numerous other design tactics employed in successful systems may still exist and may be hidden in design details that have not yet been catalogued to benefit the rest of the software engineering community.

Considering these difficulties, we propose a method intended to generate specifications from a design tactic in order to meet a quality attributes. This method can take as input a formal model of a design tactic and produces in return a set of requirements specified in natural language. The modeling of design tactics into a formal language is necessary in the method to ensure a systematic and predictable way for generating requirements in natural language expression. This method can help in reducing the effort of manually deriving requirements from design tactics and facilitating traceability between requirements and formal models of design tactics. Such a method can be readily integrated in an automated requirements engineering environment.

2 Related work

One of the earliest attempts to generate natural language specifications from class diagrams in UML using the GenLangUML tool has been presented in [5]. The tool relies on WordNet as ontology to form the phrases in the natural language text. In this attempt, the authors intended to offer stakeholders two different views of the same model in class diagrams and natural language specification. In addition, the authors tried to provide stakeholders with a reverse engineering tool that allow them to track changes in natural language as the system evolves. The authors acknowledge that it would be far effective to generate natural language specification if the models include activity, sequence, collaboration and state diagrams as well as statements in Object Constrained Language (OCL) [6].

A second attempt in formulating natural language descriptions from class diagrams is presented in [7]. This attempt was intended to help students and teachers describe classroom-scale models using class diagrams and textual specification for pedagogical purposes. The authors have developed the m2n tool to generate text descriptions based on sentence templates by analyzing class diagrams. The authors recognize that sentence templates are limited in their power to generate a natural text.

In [8], the authors propose a two-step approach to transform a class diagram into a natural language specification. The class diagram follows the semantics of xtUML [9] while the generation of specification in natural language relies on the Grammatical Framework [10] to define the linguistic model of the generated text. In this attempt, the authors intended to capture the requirements of the Computational Independent Model to validate the Platform Independent Model (PIM). The authors acknowledge that dynamic aspects of the PIM cannot be all captured by class diagrams. To this end, the Action language code of the diagrams can be translated to textual comments.

In [11], the author proposes an algorithm to automatically extract requirements from use case diagrams. This algorithm focuses rather on extracting a tree representing the hierarchy of the requirements as well as the project tasks and test cases that need to be generated for the use cases. In this attempt, there is less emphasis on natural text generation of the extracted requirements. The author claims that the extraction algorithm is fairly robust since it can process models of over 800 use cases.

While these works generate textual descriptions form class or use case diagrams, they do mostly as an aid to help different stakeholders link design and implementation. In this regard, they are intended as reverse engineering tools to help stakeholders acquire requirements when they are not available. Our approach goes a step further by assisting engineers at the behavioral modeling level during the elaboration of a non-trivial solution to a specific quality goal. This requires the use of modeling diagrams such activity diagrams that offer a process view showing the dynamic aspects of what the system is intended to do. Because understanding and integrating well-designed and tested solutions such as design tactics require extensive domain knowledge, developing their requirements becomes a tedious and time-consuming task. These requirements are necessary for management and engineers to keep track on which parts of the system have been implemented and tested. Without such requirements checklists, there is no way to show progress in implementation. In addition, these requirements provide an information-rich view of the decisions made about a specific design tactic, but may have been lost throughout the design phase.

3 Passive redundancy tactic

In order to transform design tactics into an intermediate form of representation, it would be convenient if design tactics were specified in some formalism that is as precise as possible and easily amenable to analysis. In addition, it would help if this formalism were widely adopted in the software engineering community. UML provides different diagrams for modeling and designing purposes [12]. Most studies in software engineering using UML diagrams focused mostly on class diagrams since these diagrams are arguably the most practical diagrams in UML for object-oriented software. Although they can play a role in modeling and designing software systems by capturing structural relationships between software components, they are widely preferred because they can be used to support code generators instead. On the other hand, other behavioral diagrams, such as activity and sequence diagrams, can provide the behavioral constructs necessary to model the steps involved in meeting functional requirements at different levels of abstractions, which cannot be readily expressed by class diagrams. Specifically, activity diagrams are considered critical in the process view because they can illustrate system behavior in terms of what actions the system must perform as well as the relationships between these actions [13].

In order to show the importance of deriving requirements from design tactics, this paper uses the passive redundancy tactic as an example that can be used to meet the goal of system availability. Availability refers to a property of software that is there and ready to carry out its task when it is needed [2]. As such, availability can be viewed as the ability of a system to mask or repair faults such that the cumulative service outage period does not exceed a required value over a specified time interval [2]. Among the tactics used to repair faults in a system is the passive redundancy tactic shown in Fig. 1 [14]. The design of this tactic consists of the following components:

- The log receives all input coming to the system and directs them to the primary. In addition, it replays an input when asked by the manager, which occurs in the presence of errors.
- The primary receives inputs from the log before processing them into outputs. In the presence of errors, this component forwards its state to the storage when requested by the manager.
- The backup becomes active when an error occurs on the primary. In that case, the manager instructs the primary to import the last state from storage and waits to receive the last input from the log, after which it processes that input to produce an output, thus taking over the role of the primary.
- The storage records the state exported by the primary and the last input received from the log.
- The manager detects errors on the primary. When an error occurs, the manager activates the backup, then instructs the storage to forward the last state recorded to the backup and the log to replay the last input.

This tactic is modeled as a data flow model in the activity diagram shown in Fig. 2.

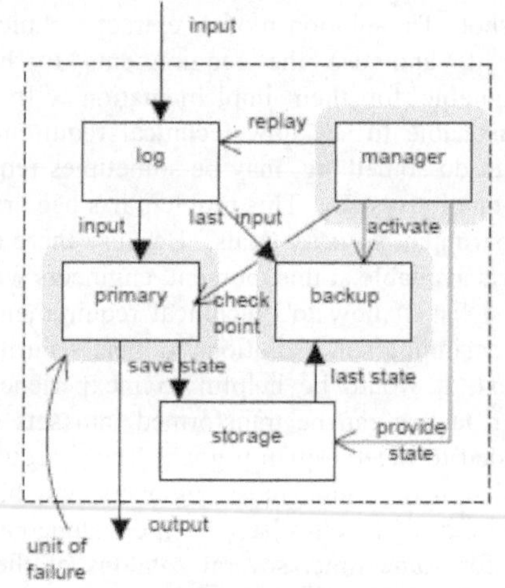

Figure 1. Structure of the passive redundancy tactic.

4 Proposed approach

The method proposed in this paper consists primarily of a transformation engine, which takes as input a formal specification of a design tactic and produces the technical specification of a set of related functional and system requirements in natural language as shown in Fig. 3. To simplify the transformation process, it is broken down into two main steps where the first step converts the specification of the design tactic into an intermediate format while the second step translates the intermediate format into simple statements in natural language. In this paper, focus will be on the second step.

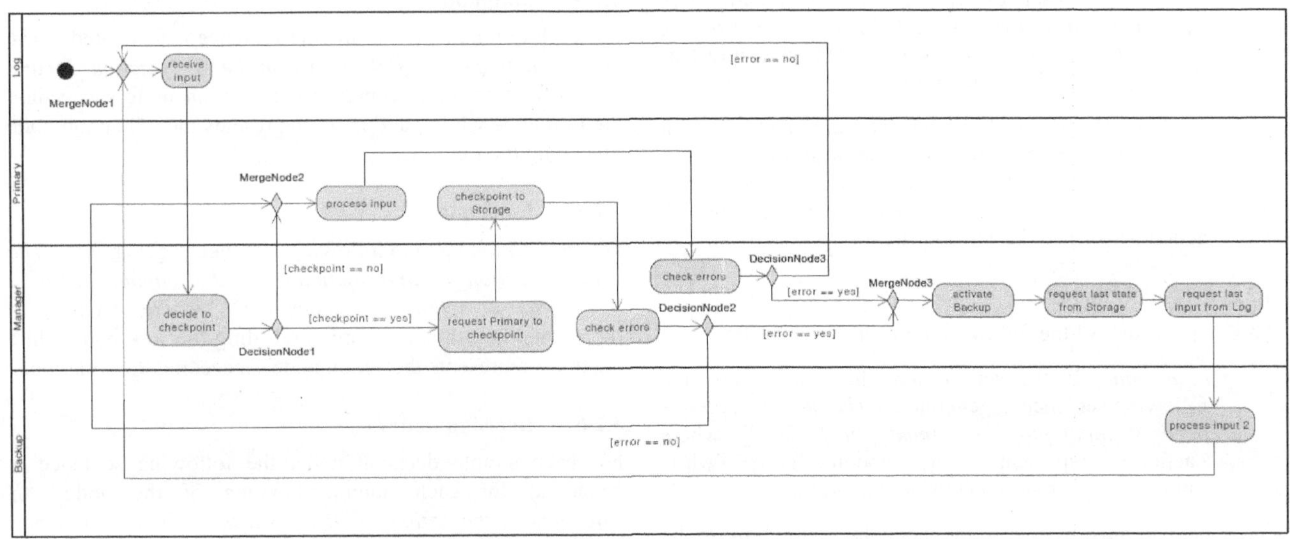

Figure 2. Activity diagram of the passive redundancy tactic.

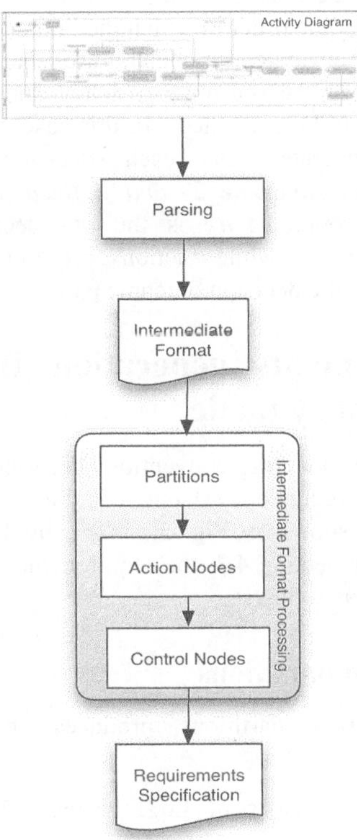

Figure 3. Overview of the requirements generation process.

4.1 Appropriate modeling in activity diagrams

In this approach, it is assumed that modeling of a design tactic using activity diagrams must follow a set of conventions in order to facilitate the task of requirements generation as follows:

- Partitions: Each partition or lane in the activity diagram should be reserved for a principal actor or component that plays an important role in the tactic. The main actors in the passive redundancy tactic are the manager, primary, backup, and log.
- Actions nodes: Actions in action nodes are expressed as verbs followed by complements. It is implied that the subject of an action is the owner of the lane in which the action node is located.
- Decision nodes: Each decision node must have a guard condition. The outgoing branches of the node must all be labeled with the evaluation of the condition.
- Data flow: Data flow is generally represented as input or output pins attached to action nodes. The pins attached to action nodes must be labeled with input or output names.
- Object flow: Object flow is represented as object nodes. Such nodes must be clearly labeled with their appropriate names.

4.2 Requirements generation

This paper adopts a simple requirements language similar to the Requirements Specification Language [15]. In essence, this language keeps a constrained structure in order to express the derived requirements in a more precise and less ambiguous way. This constrained structure mandates that sentences follow the subject-verb-object (SVO) form [16]. Additional types of sentences can be used to address constrained forms for handling pre-condition and post-condition scenarios. This paper uses the following steps to extract requirements from an activity diagram using the SVO form.

4.2.1 Diagram partitions

This step consists of the following:

- The actor in each diagram partition is identified to generate the following sentence: *"The tactic consists of <actor_1> <actor_2>..."* where <actor_n> represents the *n*th partition in the diagram.
- The actions performed by each actor are identified. For each actor, the following sentence is generated: *"The <actor> performs the following actions: <action_1> <action_2>..."* where <action_n> represents the *n*th action performed the actor <actor>.

4.2.2 Action nodes

This step consists of the following for each action node:

- *Input pins*: If the action node has input pins, the following sentence is generated: *"The action <action> needs <input_pin_1> <input_pin_2> ..."* where <action> represents the action node while <input_pin_n> represents its *n*th input pin.
- *Output pins*: If the action node has output pins, the following sentence is generated: *"The action <action> produces <output_pin_1> <output_pin_2> ..."* where <action> represents the action node while <output_pin_n> represents its *n*th output pin.
- *Exceptions*: If the action node has exception output pins, the following sentence is generated: *"If the action <action> fails, it produces <exception_1> <exception_2> ..."* where <action> represents the action node while <exception_n> represents its *n*th exception output.
- *Preceding object nodes*: If the action node has preceding object nodes, the following sentence is generated: *"The action <action> needs <object_1> <object_2> ..."* where <action> represents the action node while <object_n> represents its *n*th incoming flow object.
- *Succeeding object nodes*: If the action node has succeeding object nodes, the following sentence is generated: *"The action <action> produces <object_1> <object_2> ..."* where <action> represents the action node while <object_n> represents its *n*th outgoing flow object.
- *Control Flows*: If the action node has a preceding action nodes connected by an control flow edge, the following sentence is generated: *"The action <action_1> follows the action <action_2>"* where <action_1> represents the action node that follows the action node <action_2>.

4.2.3 Merge nodes

For each merge node, the following sentence is generated: *"The action <action> starts after <action_1> or <action_2> or ... is completed."* where <action> represents the action node succeeding the merge node while <action_n> represents the *n*th action node preceding the merge node.

4.2.4 Join nodes

For each join node, the following sentence is generated: *"The action <action> starts after <action_1> and <action_2> and ... "* where <action> represents the action node succeeding the join node while <action_n> represents the *n*th action node preceding the join node.

4.2.5 Fork nodes

For each fork node, the following sentence is generated: *"The actions <action_1> and <action_2> and ... cannot start until the action <action> is complete."* where <action_n> represents the *n*th action node preceding the fork node while <action> represents the action node succeeding the fork node.

4.2.6 Decision nodes

For each simple decision node, the following sentence is generated for each outcome branch of the node: *"If <outcome>, the action <action> starts."* where <outcome> represents the outcome of the evaluation of the guard condition on that branch while <action> represents the action node succeeding the decision node. Because UML does not say anything about the order in which the branch of a decision node should be evaluated, modelers use chained decision nodes to indicate a specific order in which the outcomes of the decision should be evaluated. In this case, the following sentence is generated for each decision path: *"If <outcome_1> and <outcome_2> and ..., the action <action> starts."* where <outcome_n> is the *n*th decision in the decision outcome path while <action> represents the action node at the end of the decision outcome path.

5 Requirements generation from passive redundancy tactic

By following the modeling conventions described in section 4.1, the passive redundancy tactic can be modeled in an activity diagram shown in Fig. 3. Also, by following the rules described in section 4.2, the requirements of this tactic can be generated as follows:

5.1 Diagram partitions

Processing diagram partitions produces the following sentences:

- This tactic consists of Log, Primary, Manager and Backup.
- The Log performs the action "receive input".
- The Primary performs the actions "process input" and "checkpoint to Storage".
- The Manager performs the actions "decide to checkpoint", "request primary to checkpoint", "check errors", "activate Backup", "request last state from Storage", and "request last input from Log".
- The Backup performs the action "process input 2".

5.2 Action nodes

Processing action nodes produces the following sentences related to control flows:

- The action "decide to checkpoint" follows the action "receive input".
- The action "check errors" follows the action "process input".
- The action "checkpoint to Storage" follows the action "request Primary to Backup".
- The action "check errors" follows the action "checkpoint to Storage".
- The action "request last state from Storage" follows the action "activate Backup".
- The action "request last input from Log" follows the action "request last state from Storage".
- The action "process input 2" follows the action "request last input from Log".

5.3 Merge nodes

Processing merge nodes produces the following sentences:

- MergeNode1: The action "receive input" starts after "process input 2" is complete or "error == no".
- MergeNode2: The action "process input" starts after "checkpoint == yes" or "error == no".
- MergeNode3: The action "activate Backup" starts after "error == yes".

5.4 Decision nodes

Processing decision nodes produces the following sentences:

- DecisionNode1:
  - If "checkpoint == yes", the action "request Primary to checkpoint" starts.
  - If "checkpoint == no", the "process input" starts.
- DecisionNode2:
  - If "error == yes", the action "activate Backup" starts.
  - If "error == no", the action "process input" starts.
- DecisionNode3:
  - If "error == yes", the action "activate Backup" starts.
  - If "error == no", the action "receive input" starts.

The sentences generated above provide a basic requirement specification showing what the tactic is intended to do. While these requirements are listed following the steps in the requirement generation process, these requirements can be re-organized along different perspectives related to input-output and precedence relationships among actions in the activity diagram. Such re-organization can enhance the structure of the document containing these requirements specification. Although templates are used to generate the sentences in the specification text, the resulting text is sufficiently expressive to give an idea of what the design tactic accomplishes as a solution to meet a quality goal.

6 Conclusions

This paper presents an approach to generate requirements specification from an activity diagram. This approach is intended to help engineers develop requirements for design tactics meant to solve specific problems for meeting well-defined quality goals. This is a significant contribution, since requirements are the main elements used to hold developers accountable for meeting desired functionality. This is perhaps one of the most significant implications of presenting design tactics as requirements rather than design diagrams. Moreover, when presented this way, these requirements checklists can be used by other, non-programmers in the team to verify that the desired behavior to meet a quality goal is implemented and that the final solution meets the expected level of quality, as defined by the design tactic.

This work is by no means complete, and as such a number of extensions can be considered to make the approach in this paper very practical and useful. Since activity diagrams are in essence graphs, special structures such as cycles can appear in these diagrams. In this perspective, cyclical activity must be viewed as part of what the modeled tactic does. Hence, specifications of cyclical actions must be included in the requirements specification of the modeled tactic. Also, this approach can be applied to meet specific security goals since it is widely believed that security is a people problem. In [17], it is clearly stated that security is a people problem, not a machine problem, and ultimate responsibility lies with management. In this context, one can develop security-oriented design tactics from which technical requirements can be extracted to assist engineers in building highly secure systems.

7 References

[1] B. H. C. Cheng and J. M. Atlee, "Research directions in requirements engineering," *IEEE Future of Software Engineering*, pp. 285-303, 2007.

[2] L. Bass, P. Clements and R. Kazman, *Software Architecture in Practice*, Third Edition, Addison-Wesley, 2013.

[3] J. Scott and R. Kazman, "Realizing and refining architectural tactics: Availability." Technical Report CMU/SEI-2009-TR-006, Software Engineering Institute, August 2009.

[4] L. Bass, J. Ivers, M. Klein and P. Merson, "Reasoning Frameworks," Technical Report CMU/SEI-2005-TR-007, Software Engineering Institute, July 2005.

[5] F. Meziane, N. Athanasakis, and S. Anniadou, "Generating natural language specifications from UML class diagrams," *Requirements Engineering*, vol. 13, no. 1, 2008, pp. 1-18.

[6] Object Management Group, *Object Constraint Language Specification*, available at

http://www.omg.org/technology/documents/modeling_spec_catalog.htm#OCL, February 2013.

[7] P. Brosch and A. Randak, "m2n: Translating models to natural language descriptions," *Proc. 6th Educator's Symposium: Software Modeling in Education at MODELS*, vol. 34, 2010.

[8] H. Burden and R. Heldal, "Natural language generation from class diagrams," *Proc. *th International Workshop on Model-Drive Engineering, Verification and Validation*, Wellington, New Zealand, October 2011.

[9] S. J. Mellor and M. J. Balcer, *Exceutable UML: A Foundation for Model-driven Architecture*, Addison-Wesley, 2002.

[10] A. Ranta, *Grammatical Framework: Programmign with Multilingual Grammars*, CLSI Publications, Stanford, 2011.

[11] B. Berenbach, "The automated extraction of requirements from UML models," *Proc. 11th International Conference on Requirements Engineering*, Monterey, California, 2003.

[12] Object Management Group, "Introduction to OMG's Unified Modeling Language," available at http://www.omg.org/gettingstarted/what_is_uml.htm, February 2013.

[13] C. Bock, "UML 2 activity and action models," *Journal of Object Technology*, vol. 2, no. 4, July-August 2003, pp. 43-53.

[14] T. Saridakis, "A system of patterns for fault tolerance," *Proc. 7th European Conference on Pattern Languages of Programs*, Irsee, Germany, July 2002, pp. 535-582.

[15] M. Smiatek, A. Ambroziewicz, J. Bojarski, W. Nowakowski, and T. Straszak, "Introducing a unified requirements specification language," *Proc. CSEE-SET*, Software Engineering in Progress, Nakom, 2007, pp. 172-183.

[16] K. Wolter, T. Krebs and L. Hotz, "A combined similarity measure for determining similarity of model-based and descriptive requirements," *Workshop on Artificial Intelligence Techniques in Software Engineering,* Patras, Greece, July 2008, pp. 11-15.

[17] M. R. Smith, *Commonsence Computer Security*, Second Edition, McGraw-Hill, New York, 1994.

SESSION

SOFTWARE ARCHITECTURE + DESIGN PATTERNS

Chair(s)

TBA

Building Information Technology Based on a Human Behavior-Oriented Approach to Enterprise Architecture

Dominic M. Mezzanotte, Sr. and Josh Dehlinger
Department of Computer and Information Sciences
Towson University
{dmezzanotte, jdehlinger}@towson.edu

Abstract

Enterprise Architecture (EA) frameworks (EAF) define a comprehensive step-by-step process with an expected outcome an EA plan that details the guidelines for governing and aligning an enterprise's strategic business plan with it's information technology (IT) capabilities. The process attempts to simplify the capture and validation of the design artifacts used to implement new information systems. Yet, many EA projects fail. In analyzing failure, EA changes the culture, character, and structure of an enterprise that often manifests itself in new stakeholder behavioral patterns (i.e., organizational transformation). Existing EAFs, though technically comprehensive, fail to acknowledge non-technical factors such as stakeholder behavior which may have more influence on EA than technology. This paper progresses earlier work assessing the affect of stakeholder behavior and organizational transformation on EA. Our approach to EA encourages a more holistic, humanistic, and behavior-driven process using Giddens' Theory of Structuration as a lens guiding EA design.

Keywords: Enterprise architecture, organizational change, stakeholder behavior

1. Introduction

In today's increasingly competitive economic landscape, many organizations are looking to improve operational efficiency and effectiveness by implementing new and/or enhanced technology [13]. Enterprise Architecture (EA) represents the first step towards this goal using a framework (EAF) and modeling techniques that specifies high-level, macro-oriented abstraction of functional and non-functional requirements that will drive subsequent information technology (IT) design, development, and implementation. In its simplest form, EA provides a layered view of desired enterprise-wide systems [18][23][27]. Usually tiered as a series of architectural views of the enterprise's information assets and needs, the layers define the business, application, data, and technology requirements needed for IT [28][37].

In literature, EA is defined as the alignment of an enterprise's strategic business plan and operational model with its IT capabilities [26][28][37]. In reality, EA organizes into a single, easy to understand, and neatly documented plan called an EA plan (EAP) that contains the guidelines to manage and govern the alignment process. The EAP thus represents both an aggregation of design requirements derived from both explicit and tacit organizational knowledge and descriptions of the systems, subsystems, resources and infrastructure needed to progress IT. In effect, *EA defines what IT is to do* and *IT is doing EA*.

Collectively, the requirements input to EA represent the foundation for guiding, managing, governing, controlling, and building IT [3][27]. As can be seen, failure to capture and validate design requirements not only jeopardizes EA, it can also doom IT. The EAF, usually under the direction of an Enterprise Information Architect(s) (EIA), provides a comprehensive set of techno-centric processes to elicit and document EA requirements [28][37]. To be effective, the requirements gathering and analysis process must capture and analyze both explicit and tacit organizational knowledge [24][26].

As inclusive as the EAF and modeling processes appear to be, EA design and implementation remains difficult and often confronted with obstacles with many EAs being either partially implemented or completely abandoned [3][6]. Statistics support this assertion claiming that between 20-30% of all private sector EA and IT projects are completely abandoned with an additional 30-60% ending in partial implementation [17][33]. Public sector projects, on the other hand, fare even worse with a success rate of only 16% [8][9]. The cost for failure is even more significant with expenditures of money and resources estimated annually into the billions of dollars [8][33].

Failed EA is often attributed to erroneous requirements and is commonly referred to as "poor architecture" [24]. Poor architecture, in this context, means [8][9][19][31]:

- The requirements do not meet the expectations of the stakeholder(s)
- The requirements are inconsistent or incomplete
- Changing the requirements is too costly after they have been agreed upon

With stakeholders responsible for the input to the EA requirements engineering process, "poor architecture" might have more to do with their reaction to and acceptance of EA rather than any technological concern. In essence, an analysis of stakeholder behavior can be traced to:

- The impact new technology has on organizational transformation reflected in both organizational/stakeholder behavior [1][2] [24]
- The manner in which the EA is being introduced by management into the enterprise [7][18][20][29]
- The either covert and/or overt stakeholder resistance and/or reluctance to change [2][12]
- The intentional and/or unintentional miscommunication and/or providing misleading information related to design requirements needed for the EAP [10][24]

Solving these issues, however, can be difficult, perhaps requiring a major shift in the way EA is approached. This may require adopting practices from the fields of psychology and sociology to mitigate negative stakeholder behavior and thus enhance the traditional processes and procedures found in existing EAFs and modeling schemes. This paper treats stakeholder behavior as a major factor in EA design. It focuses on technology and organizational transformation recognizing stakeholder behavior and the risks to management from the inherent uncertainties surrounding projects such as EA. This paper specifically progresses our earlier research [22][24][25] by expanding our knowledge in human behavior and it's effect on the design of large, complex, and multi-faceted system/entities of EA [22][24][25].

This work builds on our earlier communicative approach to EA proposing, as a first step in recognizing stakeholder behavior, an Architectural Design Plan (ADP) that formulates how EA should be approached. The communicative aspect of the ADP encourages stakeholder collaboration and participation by allowing stakeholders an active role in EA design throughout the EA life-cycle. From this position, potential EAF and modeling solutions can be planned for and implemented that facilitate verification and validation of design requirements.

2. Stakeholder Behavior and Organizational Transformation

Stakeholder behavior may be influenced by several factors such as: technology, the cognitive capacity of stakeholders to contribute to, and the way EA is introduced into an organization [2][13][24][29]. In most instances, management expects stakeholders to learn, accept, adapt to, and use without question new technology and processes [2][29]. What management forgets is that today, stakeholders frequently question the rationale and need for new technology. In the case of EA, these factors alone can play a significant role in acceptance or rejection of EA. Given this perspective, the behavior of project stakeholders, who have the capacity to act for or at odds with the enterprise's desires, must be taken into account during EA design [2][10][29].

If we analyze the manner in which EA is introduced into the enterprise, we find many EAs are unexpectedly initiated without any stakeholder input [2][29]. This affects EA in several ways. First, this kind of management behavior works only in organizations where a tightly controlled and constrained environment is the norm. Second, in other organizations, some stakeholders may accept the new technology and simply move on while others may resent the way change was introduced and thus resist EA. Third, stakeholders may actively threaten and jeopardize EA either overtly or covertly perhaps even resorting to sabotage. Two factors that influence this kind of stakeholder behavior are their perception of and reaction to how EA will affect:

- The environment in which they currently function [10][35]
- Their future status and their new assigned roles, duties, and responsibilities [2][12][29]

Stakeholder attitudes towards and use of technology has long been recognized as a key ingredient to EA success [4][5]. In fact, stakeholder acceptance is often considered the pivotal factor in determining the success or failure of an EA [5]. Thus, stakeholders may accept, reject, and, in some cases, modify the technology to suit their own self interests [24][29]. In the most extreme situations, stakeholders may intentionally misuse (and/or sabotage) the technology and thus EA [10][13][20][29]. In most cases, stakeholder reluctance or resistance to change usually follows some action that has the potential to affect the enterprise's equilibrium/status quo [2][12][16]. Given behavior alone, resistance to change follows human action caused by stakeholder [1][2][4][10]:

- Parochial self-interests – some stakeholders are more interested in "what's in it for them" rather than the good of the enterprise
- Fear of change – some stakeholders operate from a personality position that fears change
- Low tolerance for change – some stakeholders feel more secure maintaining a sense of stability and security in their work
- Misunderstanding of the situation – some stakeholders may disagree with the rationale for change

Table 1. Comparison of Enterprise Architecture Requirements Modeling Schemes

Modeling Approach	Definition Documentation	Ease of Use	Stakeholder Behavior
Unified Modeling Language (UML)	Well defined, industry-standard notation lending itself to several automated modeling tools.	The present version is overly complex, though Version 2.0 may be addressing this issue. It does not lend itself alone to modeling business requirements as needed in EA.	UML is not used extensively in EA development. It does not take into consideration stakeholder behavior in its scheme for modeling specifications and requirements.
Model-Driven Architecture (MDA)	Provides guidelines for structuring system specifications. Typically just as much as model-driven automation as it is about model-driven architecture.	Uses XML and UML to generate and produce modeling diagrams, notation, and semantics for the system. Often used with other modeling schema such as EUP and RUP. Encourages developers and architects to work at higher levels of abstraction.	The primary focuses of MDA are mapping documents, transformation, and UML profiles. A review of various works published on MDA methodologies does not highlight any issues on the process regarding human or organizational related to this approach.
Zachman Framework (Z|FA)	Uses rows and columns to define an EA. The notation used within Z|FA represents various/ different views of stakeholders.	The framework consists of thirty-six cells each of which supports one or more artifacts. It can lead to a personalized biased approach to an EA solution.	In Zachman's EAF , human behavior is not a part of the Zachman Modeling Scheme though each cell is considered a modeling point.
Enterprise Unified Process (EUP)	An instantiation of the Unified Process (UP) and RUP.	Explicitly brings EA into the RUP arena.	Human behavior not considered as part of this approach.
Rational Unified Process (RUP)	Defined for software development and follows the Unified Process (UP). It reflects business "best practices" and typically does not codify approaches until they are well established in the field.	IBM's approach to software Development, a well-defined and rigorous process. Divides the development process into phases with each concluded with a project milestone.	Provides for agreement with stakeholders on lifecycle objectives for the project and the design and implementation focusing on a viable marriage of essential business requirements and the technical architecture.

In addition, change affects people differently and may be the product of insecurity brought about by internal organizational influences. Though all of the these factors are well known, there are no provisions for mitigating these negative influences in either existing EAFs [25] and/or the modeling schemes (see Table 1). To succeed, EA requires a well-designed EAP that adequately defines design requirements produced by the right kind of tool sets, EAFs and modeling schemes [16][26].

Design requirements elicited from stakeholders lie at the heart of EA providing the building blocks that define the system specifications needed for IT [3][7][16][31][34]. Thus, the capture of design specifications is critical to EA success and if incorrect, they can plant the seeds for EA failure. Supporting this line of reasoning, most EA literature blames failure on the requirements used describing the requirements as "poor architecture" [24]. Extending our analysis of "poor architecture" allows us to take into account stakeholder behavior and miscommunication. This is most prevalent in eliciting tacit, undocumented knowledge known only to a single or group of select stakeholders.

EA design today relies on an EAF and modeling schemes to capture and validate design requirements [28][37]. The procedures found in each framework establish the enterprise's goals and objectives aiming to ensure adequate documentation for the EAP [16][26][37]. However, the organizational goals and objectives desired of EA are not always those shared by stakeholders responsible for doing work.

In today's environment, existing EAFs and modeling schemes follow generally accepted software engineering and requirements engineering principles and practices with the expected outcome a documented set of requirements that includes the resources and infrastructure, necessary for IT [26][27]. The frameworks and modeling schemes are comprehensive, disciplined, and designed to handle large volumes of complex and interdependent system and subsystem requirements from a purely technological perspective [26][27][31]. State-of- the-practice EAFs formulate EA aimed at maintaining business continuity and the alignment of the enterprise's strategic business plans, business operations with its IT infrastructure and resources [7][11][26]. These are the strengths of existing EAFs.

Conversely, the inherent weakness of each EAF centers on the techno-centric and techno-oriented solutions they prescribe producing only a desired set of technical deliverables for the EA [7][26]. This process satisfies the high-level abstraction of design requirements needed for EA identifying, in detail, the proposed organizational structure, business processes, desired information systems, design requirements, implementation plan, and associated IT infrastructure. However, the processes discount the importance of the intersection of technology with human behavior, the inevitable organizational transformation that takes place as a result of EA, and their potential effect on the quality of the work effort delivered, specifically the design requirements [24].

For example, the key element around which all design activity takes place in The Open Group Architecture Framework (TOGAF) Version 9.1, the Application Development Method (ADM), describes a purely technical perspective and detailed series of step-by-step processes and procedures for EA [28]. Stakeholder roles, responsibilities, and contribution to EA are identified through the ADM based on what is termed "Stakeholder Management". This process consists of four concepts: Stakeholders, Concerns, Views, and Viewpoints. The process essentially identifies who will be involved and needed in EA design [28]. The process analyzes stakeholder role, decision-making, and resource control. Though these questions by themselves sound relevant, the process itself fails to ask questions that would improve good decision-making and problem-solving such as "why?" and "why not?" For example, questions not asked by this and other EAFs are:

- Why is one stakeholder assigned to EA while another is not?
- What is the cognitive capacity of the stakeholder to contribute?
- What will be the impact on stakeholder behavior caused by EA and/or organization transformation?

In general, little attention or recognition is given to stakeholder behavior and the consequences of either positive or negative influence on EA.

There are some modeling approaches with the inclusion of stakeholder behavior in validating EA requirements. For example, the *i** modeling scheme [36] recognizes human input and their respective behavioral patterns to the requirements elicitation process. We will study *i** in more depth in the future.

3. The Theory of Structuration Applied to Enterprise Architecture

The large-scale development of IT systems planned for in EA expects change to take place in an orderly and controlled manner. With the introduction of new EA technology, a transformation of the enterprise's culture, aimed at improving operational effectiveness and employee productivity is expected by management [29][30]. This transformation however affects stakeholder in several ways as the result of learning new processes and procedures and the change is their respective roles, duties, and responsibilities. Thus, an EA initiative that incorporates psychological and sociological principles and practices to facilitate a dynamic behavior-driven view of an enterprise would be Giddens' *Theory of Structuration* [24][29]. The *Theory of Structuration* uses the term *structuration* to refer to the conditions governing the continuity or transformation of *structures* and social systems indicating that structure represents the codes for social action. *Agency*, on the other hand, indicates the activities of individual members of the system existing in a recursive manner and relationship [10]. Simply, agents draw on structures during their processes of interactions, they perform social activities and continually reproduce the actions that make these practices possible [10][29][30].

In previous work [22][24][25], we described, in detail, the concepts and principles underlying Giddens' theory describing the sociological aspects of Giddens' theory applied to technology. Giddens' theory in it's original formulation pays little attention to technology. However, if we examine the pervasiveness of IT on everyday life, especially in the workplace, we can apply Giddens' theory to any organization's everyday operation and the reality of technology in contemporary organizations.

Given this perspective, the *Theory of Structuration* does not merely provide a means to understand the nature of an organization but can be applied to gain insight on the impact of the use of technology [34]. Orlikowski [29] proposed the *Structurational Model of Technology (SMT)* based on Giddens' theory to provide a more complete model of understanding of how technology affects organizations. This theory is predicated on the perceptions of the *Duality of Technology* and the

Interpretive Flexibility of technology. The *Duality of Technology* posits that the socially created view and the objective view of technology is intertwined and are differentiated because of the temporal distance between the creation and use of technology. *Interpretive Flexibility* defines the degree to which users of a technology are engaged in its constitution (physically and/or socially) during its development.

SMT has three components – the Human Agents, Technology and Institutional Properties of Organization. The model specifies an interactive recursive relationship between these in that each of these components influences and is at the same time influenced by the others. Technology is created by and exists through ongoing human action. Humans constitute technology by using it, while at same time making it an outcome of human actions such as design, development, appropriation and modification. However once technology is implemented, it both facilitates human action through the provision of interpretive schemes, facilities and norms.

From an organizational perspective, institutional properties influence humans in their interaction with technology, through, by constituting: professional norms; rules of use – design standards and available resources (time, money and skills). There is a consequence of the institutional interaction with technology and are manifested by impacting the institutional properties of an organization through reinforcing or transforming Giddens' structures of signification, domination and legitimization that characterize the institutional realm.

In summary, the theoretical premise of the *Theory of Structuration* [10] and the *SMT* [29] is an acknowledgement that organizational structures, technology, and human action are not distinct but are intertwined such that each is continually reinforced and transformed by the other. We can therefore conclude that an initiative such as the formulation of EA remains incomplete if it does not explicitly take into account human action. The *Theory of Structuration* provides a framework which, if adopted, could form the basis for a more inclusive, holistic, humanistic, and behavior driven approach to formulating an EA. Specifically, this theory provides a lens for the EIA to take advantage of understand the dynamics of an organization and use that information to formulate an EA that is contextual to that enterprise and advocated by the stakeholders.

In this context, stakeholders are recognized as purposely able to provide reasons for their activities, including perhaps even lying about them. However, this behavior can be managed by promoting an environment that encourages stakeholder collaboration and participation in the decision-making process. Successful implementation of new technology is the product of navigating human behavior and the resultant influence on organizational change. In this context, the actions of EIAs leads to changes in the way people behave and in a business context, human behavior and organizational factors contribute more to the success or failure of an EA than technical factors. Simply stated, stakeholders are affected by IT change and may be resistant if the change is forced upon them without warning and input from them.

4. Building and Modeling Enterprise Architecture

Stakeholder requirements represent one of the essential elements for managing, governing, and controlling the complexity, risk, project magnitude scope and boundary, and ambiguity associated with the elicitation of stakeholder requirements. These requirements form the basis for defining the goals and objectives of EA and what IT is to do and therefore are critical to EA success. However in a typical EA, it is not a matter of choosing which requirements to meet but of trying to meet all practical requirements.

In earlier work [22][24][25], several causal factors leading to EA failure are identified and addressed. From that work, we propose a solution and approach where management, the EIA, and key stakeholders collectively define, establish, and execute a management system that manages and governs EA that also includes a reliability plan that better ensures the quality of EA design requirements.

The solution establishes an Architectural Design Plan (ADP) put together by all stakeholders, an analysis of the *"as is"* environment, management style, organizational knowledge base, available skill sets, and the overall capabilities of the enterprise from a stakeholder behavior point-of-view. As currently envisioned, the ADP consists of two components: a Development Plan (DP) and a Control Plan (CP). The DP documents and establishes how the overall conduct of the EA is to be progressed, stakeholders selected and assigned to the project, the kinds of procedures to be used in eliciting design requirements, the communications and feedback loop(s) needed to verify design requirements, and the measurement, monitoring, and governance techniques needed to ensure the validity of the design requirements. The primary purpose of the plan is twofold:

- Provide the mechanism for the EIA to learn the existing organizational environment and identify areas of potential concern

- Provide the basic scheme for eliciting information (i.e., requirements) from which to design the EA

This process provides an excellent opportunity for the EIA to learn not only what needs to be done but also who is to participate along with their personalities, how the project is to be managed and governed, and why it needs to be done.

The second step in this process, the CP, defines and describes the specific design handles and control processes that are to be used to ensure stakeholder requirements are met. In this step, factors such as organizational capabilities, skill sets, organizational reaction to nonconformance to either the DP or CP, and the exact critical in-design parameters that control the quality attributes of the design are established, documented, assessed, and agreed-upon to ensure that exact stakeholder expectations are met focused on the *"to be"* state of the enterprise.

Giddens' *Theory of Structuration* can be used to establish and formulate the ADP primarily because it recognizes stakeholders as individuals that have the ability to act in ways other than those that support the existing organization or social structure. Therefore the ADP must be cognizant, structured, and designed to identify, and perhaps anticipate, adverse influences before they can seriously affect EA. A final and complete definition of the ADP would be made on an enterprise-to-enterprise situation as each enterprise has it's own character, culture, and structure. Finally, EA should begin only upon completion of the ADP.

5. Discussion, Concluding Remarks, and Future Directions

Systems of coordinated activities represent work embedded in complex networks of technology-centric relations and boundary-spanning exchanges. The by-product of EA and the introduction of new technology into the workplace is a transformation of the organization's character, culture, and structure as well as a change in the hierarchical sociological and political structure of the enterprise. This latter change should not be discounted but rather expected and planned for as it manifests itself in new stakeholder behavioral patterns.

Giddens' *Theory of Structuration* [10] recognizes and addresses how relationships between human agents and structures can be both beneficial and at odds with each other. The theory also states that individuals have the ability to act in ways other than those that support the existing organization or social structure. In other words, their actions may be counterproductive. Orlikowski's *Structurational Model of Technology (SMT)* [29] recognizes the impact of technology on human behavior and organizations postulating Giddens' theory and providing more insight into the human behavioral aspects of and new technology in the organization.

The factors contributing to EA failure can be minimized by providing an environment where stakeholders become active participants and are receptive to change. A work atmosphere where stakeholders are encouraged to share ideas and information, communicate and collaborate whenever and however they need to in order to solve problems and exchange knowhow and knowledge. The possibility and prospect of EA success becomes more realizable if an enhanced working environment where participation in the design and implementation of new EA technology is welcomed and not perceived as a threat to stakeholder well–being. As can be envisioned, the derivable benefits from such an environment surely would include improved workforce morale and productivity.

In conclusion, the *Theory of Structuration* and it's relationship to human behavior and organizational change [10], *SMT's* approach to the effects of technology on human behavior [29] coupled with a well designed Architectural Design Plan, conceptualize unique opportunities for successful EA implementation. Finally, to address modeling schemes, future research will include an in-depth analysis of Yu's *i** agent oriented approach to EA to better ensure the validity of EA design requirements.

6. References

[1] I. Bakan, M. Tasliyan, I. Eraslan, & M. Coskun, *The Effect of Technology on Organizational Behavior and the Nature of Work*, IAMOT Conference, Washington, D.C., 2004.

[2] M. Beer. Organizational Behavior and Development. Harvard Business Review, Harvard University, 1998.

[3] Booz, Allen & Hamilton, *Getting IT Right: Maximizing Efficiency in Government IT Investments with IT Right*, www.boozallen.com/media/File/GettingITRight-RightIT-Brochure-2011.pdf.

[4] K. C. Carson, *Organization Theory*, BookSurge, 2008.

[5] F. D. Davis, *User Acceptance of Information Technology: System Characteristics, User Perceptions, and Behavioral Impacts*, Int. J. Man-Machine Studies, Academic Press Limited, 1993.

[6] C. Edwards, *Is Lack of Enterprise Architecture Partly to Blame for the Finance Industry Collapsing So Spectacularly*, www.AgileEA.com, Version 0.01, 29th, February, 2009.

[7] C. Ferreira and J. Cohen. "Agile Systems Development and Stakeholder Satisfaction: A South African Empirical Study." *Proceedings 2008 Conference of South African Institute Computer*

Scientists and Information Technologists on IT Research in Developing Countries, pp. 48-55, 2008.

[8] D. Galoraith. *Software Project Failures Costs Billions: Better Estimation & Planning Can Help*. Filed under Project Management, June 7, 2008.

[9] R. Gauld. "Public Sector Information System Failures: Lessons from a New Zealand Hospital Organization." *Government Information Quarterly*, 24(1):102-114, 2007.

[10] A. Giddens. The Constitution of Society: Outline of the Theory of Structuration. University of California Press, 1984.

[11] H. M. Hanza, *Separation of Concerns for Evolving Systems: A Stability Driven Approach*, Workshop on Modeling and Analysis of Concerns in Software, (MACS 2005), St. Louis, MO, May, 2005.

[12] Harvard Business Review, *On Human Relations*, Harper & Row, Publishers, New York, New York, 1979.

[13] F. Herzberg, B. Mausner, & B. Bloch Synderman, *The Motivation to Work*, Wiley Johns & Sons, Inc., January, 1959.

[14] B. Iyer and R. Gottlieb. *The Four-Domain Architecture: An Approach to Support Enterprise Architecture Design*. In IBM Systems Journal, 43(4):587-597, 2004.

[15] R. Kaur, J. Sengupta, Software Process Models and Analysis on Failure of Software development Projects, International Journal of Scientific & Engineering Research, Volume 2, Issue 2, February, 2011.

[16] M. Lankhorst & H. von Drunnen. *Enterprise Architecture Development and Modeling, Via Nova Architecture*. March, 2007.

[17] B. Lawhorn. *More Software Project Failures*. CAI, March 31, 2010.

[18] R. Lewin and B. Regine. "Enterprise Architecture, People, Process, Business, Technology." Institute for Enterprise Architecture Developments [Online], Available: http://www.enterprise-architecture.info/Images/Extended Enterprise/ExtendedEnterpriseArchitecture3.html.

[19] M. L. Markus, *Power, Politics, and MIS Implementation*, Communications of the ACM, Vol. 26, 6, June, 1983.

[20] D. McGregor. *The Human Side of Enterprise*. McGraw-Hill, 1960.

[21] N. Melville, K. L. Kraemer, and V. Gurbaxani. 2004 Review: *Information Technology and Organizational Performance: An Integrative Model of IT Business Value*. MIS Quarterly, Volume 28, Number 2, pp. 283-322, June 2004.

[22] D. M. Mezzanotte, Sr., J. Dehlinger, and S. Chakraborty. "Applying the Theory of Structuration to Enterprise Architecture Design." *2011 World Conference in Computer Science, Computer Engineering, and Applied Computing,* IEEE/WorldComp 2011, SERP 2011, July, 2011.

[23] D. M. Mezzanotte, Sr., and J. Dehlinger, "Enterprise Architecture: A Framework Based on Human Behavior Using the Theory of Structuration." *International Association of Computer and Information Science, 2012 IEEE/ACIS 10th International Conference on Software Engineering Research, Management, and Applications*, 2012.

[24] D. M. Mezzanotte, Sr. and J. Dehlinger, "Enterprise Architecture and Organizational Transformation: The Human Side of Information Technology and the Theory of Structuration," *2012 World Conference in Computer Science, Computer Engineering and Applied Computing*, IEEE/WorldComp 2012, SERP 2012. July, 2012.

[25] D. M. Mezzanotte, Sr., J. Dehlinger, and S. Chakraborty. "On Applying the Theory of Structuration in Enterprise Architecture." Computer and Information Science, 2010 IEEE/ACIS 9th International Conference on Software Engineering Research, pp. 859-863, 2010.

[26] D. Minoli, *Enterprise Architecture A to Z*, CRC Press, New York, 2008.

[27] F. Molina, J. Pardillo, C. Cachero, A. Toval, *An MDE Modeling Framework for Measureable Goal-Oriented Requirements*, International Journal of Intelligent Systems (IJIS), Wiley & Co., August, 2010.

[28] The Open Group. *TOGAF Version 9.1, 2011.*

[29] W. Orlikowski. "The Duality of Technology: Rethinking the Concept of Technology in Organizations." *Organization Science*, 3(3):398-427, 1992.

[30] M. S. Poole and G. DeSanctis. *Structuration Theory in Information Systems Research: Methods and Controversies*. Handbook for Information Systems Research, M. E. Whitman and A. B. Woszczynski (eds.), Hershey, PA., Idea Group Publishing, 2004.

[31] R. S. Pressman. *Software Engineering: A Practitioner's Approach*. 7th Ed., McGraw-Hill Series in Computer Science, New York, NY, 2010.

[32] D. Quartel, W. Engelsman, H. Jonkers, *ArchitMate Extension for Modeling and Managing Motivation, Principles and Requirements in TOGAF*, The Open Group, BiZZdesign, White Paper, October, 2010.

[33] Roeleven, Sven and J. Broer. "Why Two Thirds of Enterprise Architecture Projects Fail." *ARIS Expert Paper* [Online], Available: http://www.ids-scheer.com/set/ 6473/EA_-_Roeleven_Broer_-_Enterprise_Architecture _Projects_Fail_-_AEP_en.pdf.

[34] N. Rozanski and E. Woods. *Software Systems Architecture*. Addison-Wesley Professional, 2006.

[35] C. D. Wickensand J. G. Hollands, *Engineering Psychologyand Human Performance*, 3rd Ed., Prentice Hall, Inc., Upper Saddle River, NJ, 2000.

[36] E. Yu, *Agent-Oriented Modeling: Software Versus the World*, Faculty of Information Studies, University of Toronto, Toronto, Canada, No Date.

[37] J. Zachman, *Concepts of the Framework for Enterprise Architecture*. Information Engineering Services, Pty, Ltd., 1987.

Applying Design Patterns in Game Programming

Junfeng Qu[1], Yinglei Song[2], Yong Wei[3]
[1] Department of Computer Science & Information Technology, Clayton State University, Morrow, GA, 30260
[2] Department of Computer Science, Jiangsu University of Science and Technology, Zhenjiang, China, 212001
[3]Department of Computer Science, North Georgia State University, Dahlonega, GA 30597

***Abstract*—This paper discussed an object-oriented design for general game using C# and XNA using design pattern. We presented application of structural patterns, creational pattern and behavioral pattern to create game sprite, manage game state and game sprites, different collision and rewards among sprites or between sprites and map; we also discussed how to apply design patterns to handle communications between sprites and NPC by using observer pattern and mediator patterns. Although lots of design patterns are discussed, other design patterns might suitable as well because game programming are so complicated to separate each pattern independently.**

Keywords-Game, Programming, Design Patterns, UML, XNA, C#

I. Introduction

A. Computer Game and Development

The video games industry has undergone a complete transformation in recent years especially after mobile device and casual game have impact people's life greatly.

Computer programmers are writing game in the way, that cow boys are riding on wild west, wild and innovative. However, as the game is getting bigger, more complex, and changing during development. A well designed overall game program design and architecture that modulated and integrated with software development procedure are very important. Also, a well- designed game program should be able to extend easily, portal to other platform easily without deep revision of source code to minimize deliver time is also important.

A large size of program can be developed and organized better with Object-oriented Programming(OOP) because of its significant advances over procedure programming. A series of new techniques and packages have been proposed to handle the complexity and organization problems in game programming, for example, XNA from Microsoft, AndEngine for android mobile game, etc. These components are usually context insensitive and can be used to work on most general game related programming issues and programmers are able to concentrate on the part of the code that often defines the functionalities of game.

B. Design Patterns

Design patterns are proven solutions to well-established software engineering problems. In game programming, programmers are often tend to make sure the correctness of a program by evaluating its behavior of character, and overlooked the design aspect, such as open-close principle, scalability, maintainability, flexibility, extensibility, and robustness to changes, therefore, programmer has to rework or dispose their work complete in order to accommodate changes of algorithm, level, and game mechanics during the game development process.

Due to their well-known importance and usefulness, we proposed some example design pattern solutions to these commonly problems encountered during game development with Microsoft XNA such as handle sprite, communication, control, and collision.

It's not easy to find patterns that can be used as common solutions for common problems in game programming. There are two categories of design patterns in game development. One category of design pattern was introduced by Bjork[1], where a set of design pattern is used for describing(employing a unified vocabulary) the game mechanics(gameplay and game rules) during game development. It focuses on reoccurring interaction schemes relevant to game's story and core mechanics of game. After interviewed with professional game programmers, the authors analyzed the existing games and game mechanics and then proposed those patterns involving game design process. The authors said 'The way to recognize patterns is playing games, thinking games, dreaming games, designing games and reading about games'. For example *Paper-Rock-Scissor* pattern is commonly known in game as triangularity, and this pattern was used in game when there are three discrete states, or options as described in figure 1.

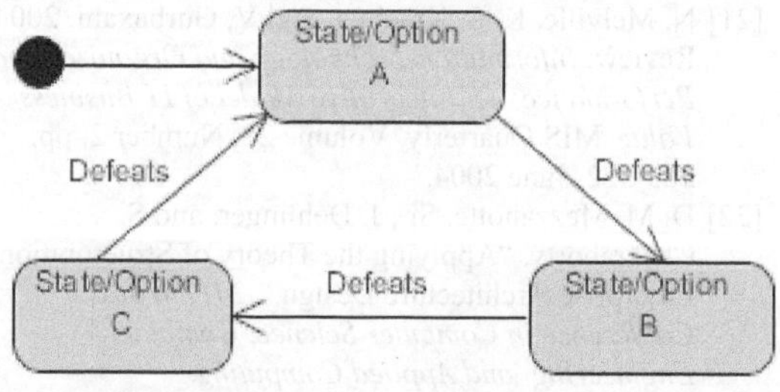

Figure 1. Triangularity design pattern in game

These patterns are not related to the software engineering , architecture or coding. So these are not discussed in this paper. The second category of design pattern in game is use of object-oriented design patterns in programming games, which are discussed and analyzed in the following sections.

One of the unique characteristics of game development and programming is rapidly evolutional modification and goal changing during game design and development, therefore it's very common that game programmers have to dispose their works that they have been working for months and to restart again. Once the game has been completed, it is often transformed into various game platform, such as PC, mobile devices (Android, iOS, Windows 8 etc), game console (PS3, Xbox 360 etc.). Therefore a well-designed game program would spend minimal efforts and changes to migrate. A well designed game programming that offer great flexibility, code reusability, extensibility, and low maintenance costs is highly desired.

Daniel Toll etc.[2] found that it is difficult to perform unit testing in computer game. Computer game often involves poor defined mathematical models, therefore it's difficult to produce expected results of unit under testing. On the other hand, computer game's rules of play needs to validated based on player's inputs, and new functions are unlocked as player makes progress, which in term makes it's difficult to perform testing in the complex interactions of varieties of game objects. For example, as player is making progress in Angry Birds, new challenges features are unlocked to entertain and challenge player, and player is able to perform more options and actions to overcome challenges presents. As these levels, new game items, and new features are added into game, even a small change of codes results a number of test and retest large part of the game. The difficulties of testing of game are also because the tight coupling of modules in game programming.

Most research works focus on teaching design patterns using game programming as examples, and show how effectively there are represented in case studies, such as computer game[3], the Game of Life[4], the Game of Set[5] and [6], which uses a family of games to introduce design patterns. Some researchers[7] had evaluated the usage of design patterns in game programming. It has proven that if design patterns are used properly and in appropriate cases, the programming maintainability, extensibility, flexibility and comprehensibility can be extremely beneficial and improved.

In this paper, we discuss some design patterns in the category of creational patterns, structural patterns and behavioral patterns, such as builder pattern, strategy pattern, mediator pattern, and state pattern, and how these are adapted into game programming info-structure such as C# and XNA.

II. Game Architecture and Loop

A. Game Architecture

Most computer games shares a similar architecture in regardless of languages used in game development. Bishop[8] etc. described a general software architecture of game as shown in Figure 2.

The slid-line ovals represent essential component of game architecture and the dashed-line ovals are modules that can be found in more complex games. The Even handler and the input provides player's action to game. The game logic renders game's core mechanics and story if any. The audio and graphics supplies sounds, images, game objects etc. in the game world to the player based on the level data module, where the details about static behaviors are stored. The dynamic module configures the dynamic behavior of game's character and objects. Most official games have all or partial components of above architecture, such as UnReal, Unity 3D, RPG Maker etc.

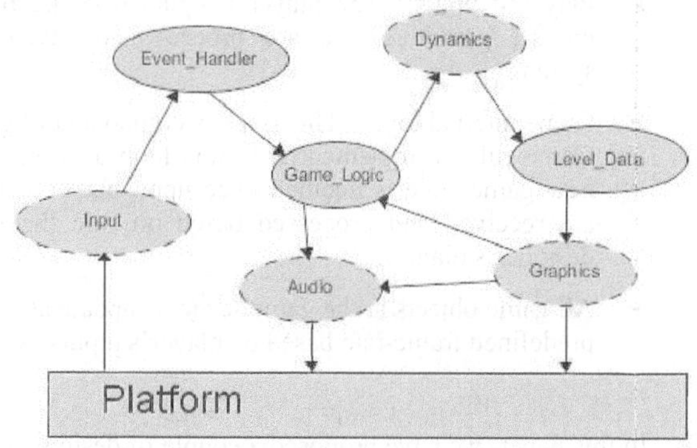

Figure 2. Common Game Architecture[8]

B. Game Loop in Game Programming

In general, most game programming can be viewed as an game loop. The player's inputs are process in each iteration, and the game states and the game world change based on internal game logics until the game is over. Of course the rendering and game logic processing can be coded with event thread, which leads to a simpler code. In small scale or turned-based game with little or no animation, this approach works perfectly. Visual C Sharp XNA provides a game loop that is driven by a control loop that similar to the event-processing loop described above. The game loop uses active rendering as shown in figure 3.

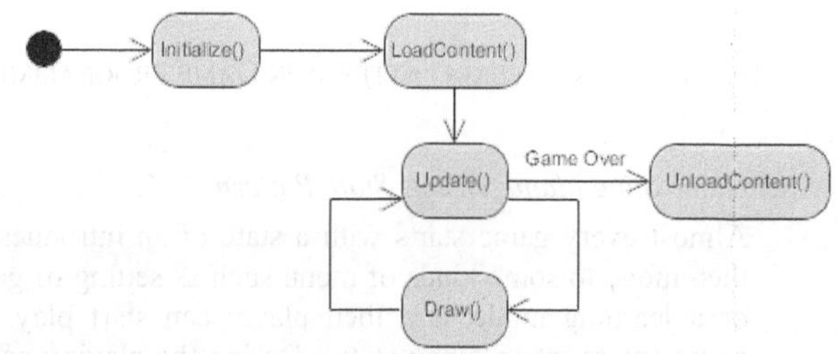

Figure 3. Game Loop Template in XNA

Game *initialization()* include nongraphics initialization. *LoadContent()* include graphics initialization, such as reading game object, sprite, texture etc. After that *Run()* is called to initiate game loop, which includes *Update()* and *Draw()* methods.

Update() method updates game objects, checking for collisions, game AI, game object movement, updating scores, checking for end-game logic etc. *Draw()* method is used to draw game objects on game scene. All logics that effects the gameplay will be done in the loop of *Update()* and *Draw()*. If game ending logic is satisfied, *UnloadContent()* is call to unload resources and memory allocated to game scene. In *Update()* and *Draw()* of the game loop following game related objects are handled:

- Player's inputs: The player's inputs from keyboard, mouse, game console are process and saved into system
- Game internal logic: This is a key component of game. Game rule is implemented in this loop as well. The new game state is decided once upon player's inputs are received and processed based on rule the game designer's plan.
- All game objects in the game scene is update at certain predefined frame-rate based on player's inputs as well.

In this paper, we have proposed a couple of design patterns that we have experienced during game development and design since it's very apparent in game development the common elements and mechanics that the games share are often handled with class abstraction, inheritance, polymorphism in code refactoring.

We use Microsoft XNA as a game development platform and try to integrated creational patterns, structural patterns and behaviors patterns into XNA game loop described above. Design patterns can be applied in design and coding of any game module, what we have illustrated here does not imply that these patterns are more suitable and applicable than other patterns or fields since game programming is so complicated to be included in all scenarios in the discussion, and it also does not mean no other design patterns can be used.

III. Applying Design patterns in Game Programming

A. Game State Management: State Pattern

Almost every game starts with a state of an introduction, then move to some kinds of menu such as setting of game or a learning mode, and then player can start play and game enters into playing state. During the playing of the game, the player will be able to jump back to main menu, set parameters, or pause the game until the player is finally defeated and the game moves to a game-over state, the player then may start from main menu again. In general, each state handles different events differently, from, and draw something different on the screen. Each state might handle its own events, update the game world, and draw the next frame on the screen differently from other game states. Figure 4 illustrated an example game state change from main entry to Play State, Pause state and End State respected to different button that pressed by the player.

Traditionally, the multiple states of game are handled with a serious of *if..else if..* statement, *switch..case* statement. Every time through the game loop, the game program must check current state of the game and display and draw game objects correspondingly, also, events are handled and checked to see player's input will trigger the change of game state. This programming approach results a highly coupled codes, therefore it's difficult to debug, testing and code maintain.

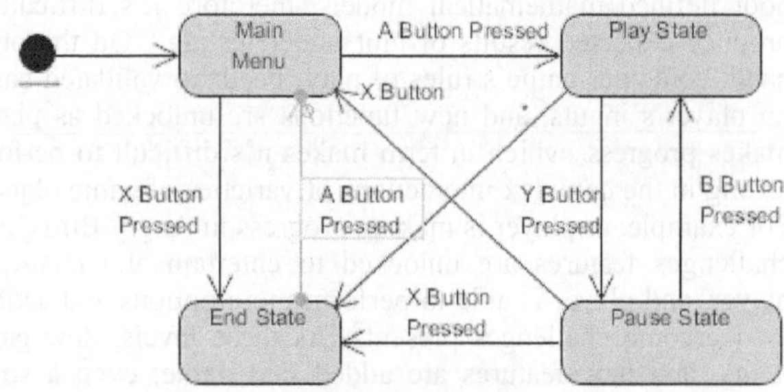

Figure 4. An Example of Game State Changes

State pattern is a natural solution to above problems as illustrated in Figure 5. The state pattern allows an object to alter its behavior when its internal state changes[9].

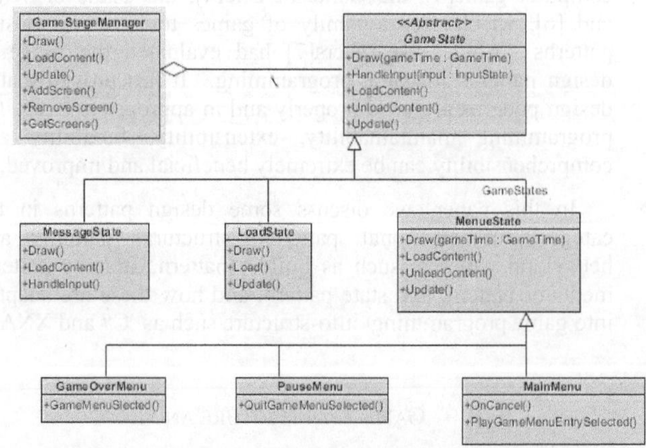

Figure 5. State Pattern for Game State Management

GameStateManager maintains a concrete state at any given time. The abstract *GameState* class encapsulates the behavior associated with a particular state of game. The concrete states of game such as *LoadState, MenuState, Pause, EndState, and Main* implement the behaviors associated with each state in regarding *Draw(), Update()* respectively.

With the use of state pattern, first, we avoided excessively and repetitively using of *switch .. case* or *if .. else*, therefore the complexity of the programming is reduced, secondly, the application of state pattern explained software engineering principles such as Open-Closed principle and single responsibility principle. Each game state is a subclass, in case more states are required during game development, the programmer simply adds a subclass, e.g. programmer will be able to create a subclass to manipulate background of game. In case the state requirements are changed, the programmer just modifies the corresponding class. Thirdly, the benefit of use state pattern is that the classes are well encapsulated, the change of state is implemented within each class, caller does not to need to know how changes of state and behavior are implemented internally. Lastly, the state objects can be shared if they have no instance variables. State objects protect the context from inconsistent internal states, because state transitions are atomic (the transition between states happen by changing only one variable's value, not several)[9]. Although state pattern brings so many benefits, the complicated game might produce too many subclasses quickly to be out of the control of the programmer and it might be so difficulty to manage these classes.

B. Creation and Behavior of Game Objects: Factory, Command , and State Patterns

In Microsoft XNA game programming, all graphics, sounds, effects, and other items are loaded in XNA thought content pipeline. A sprite in XNA is a flat, preloaded image that is used as part of a computer game, such as players, enemies, and projectiles. To draw a sprite on game world, programmer needs to specify location information that tells XNA where to draw the image as well as where the resource is located in the OS. In XNA, *Texture2D* is one of most commonly used sprite to render images in game world. The Sprite itself lend to object-oriented design: it has states and exhibits behaviors as well.

Sprites have state and they exhibit behaviors. The state of a sprite includes information of location, velocity, size and image. The behavior of sprites usually is based on external or internal game information and modified itself input for player sprites, or gameplay.

The program used nested loop with if or switch statements to explicitly detect the current state and take the appropriate behavior. This procedural approach carries with it all the usual baggage: State-dependent logic is distributed throughout the code and adding new state is error-prone.

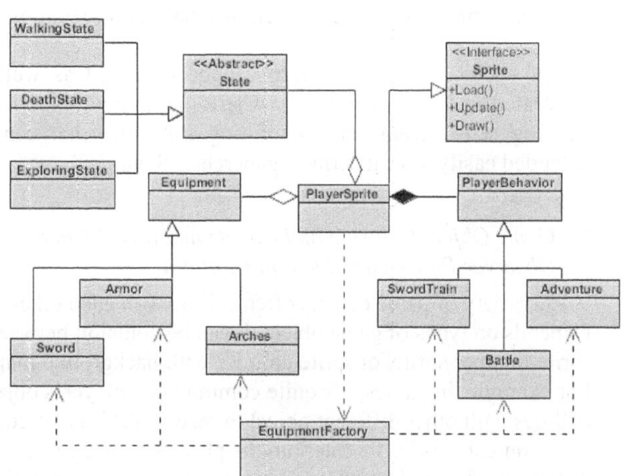

Figure 6. Factory, State and Command Patterns in RPG

In RPG game, a character, player or enemy is often represented by a sprite has to face difference challenges and act correspondingly with different behaviors, for example player may work on training to use sword, complete an mission or submission of a battle, or even adventure to hunt for treasure. Of course it's possible to implement above behaviors within sprite with loop and/or switch, the open-closed principles is not quite followed in above approach. Base on GoF, Command design pattern encapsulate a request as an object, thereby letting you parameterize clients with different requests, queue or log requests, and support undoable operations. A command object can have a lifetime independent of the original request, and can specify, queue, and execute request at different times[9]. The command pattern encapsulates the player's behavior as an object to facilitate extends of player's behavior. By specifically creating a behavior class to solve a variety of behaviors a player may have. We can deal with evaluation of game design easily. If a now behavior is needed for game development and story, a new class that inherits from behavior class can be added to implement concrete actions that player need to work on.

In RPG game, player also often equipped with different equipment based on game development and player's progression. It's natural to create and equipment superclass that can be concretely implemented with different equipment such as sword, armor etc. Factory pattern can have an object return an instance from a family of related classes[9]. The player behaves differently based on game development and game progression, for example, the sword and armor are used in training, arches is used during adventure, therefore, an *EquipmentFactory* class is introduced to determine what equipment are required according to different scenario, which is strategy pattern. The strategy patterns defines a family of algorithms, encapsulates each one, and make them interchangeable[9]. By employing these patterns, the program code can be maintained easily and it's more flexible to accommodate changes in game development such as behavior change, equipment adding and removal based on scenarios.

Of course, the state pattern can be deployed as well as illustrated in UML of figure 6, where player may experience walking state, death state, exploring state etc. that can be extended easily after inherits is superclass State.

C. Game Object Collision and Communication: Visitor, Observer Pattern and Mediator Pattern

A variety of game objects often collide with each other. Depends on types of game object, it can be collision between a sprite to other sprite, or sprite collides with background map. For example, in games, it's quite common that player's object collides with other different object to receive different credits based on game rule. To entertain the players better, game designers often add a variety of game objects to increase play of fun in game to reward players unexpectedly. The NPC is often introduced as well to work with player or fight against player, either case, the state of player is necessary to broadcast to the teammates or interest game objects based on game mechanics.

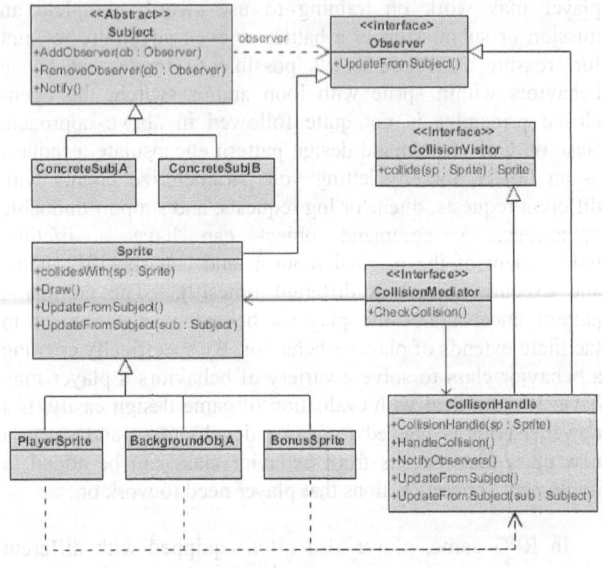

Figure 7. Visitor, Observer and Mediator for Collision and Communication

Visitor design pattern represents an operation to be performed on the elements of an object structure. Visitor lets programmer define a new operation without changing the classes of the elements on which it operates[9]. Visitor pattern is suitable when you want to be able to do a variety of different things to objects that have a stable class structure. Adding a new kind of visitor requires no change to that class structure, which is especially important when the class structure is large. By using of visitor pattern, different collision algorithms can be implemented and different rewarding rules of a variety of objects collision can be implemented while following open-closed principle of software design. The UML illustrated in figure 7 shows that CollisonVisitor interface handles different collision among different sprite in game world.

In RPG game, the character sprite changes states, for example, 'Live' and 'Dead', the domain must notify the graphical user interface to allow it to update itself. Likewise, when the user clicks on, or collides with other objects, the UI must notify the domain so that it can record the appropriate changes to its model.

To communicate among sprites of interests, observer pattern or mediator patter are illustrated in figure 7. Depends on communication is one-to-many or many to many, programmer could choose one or both to pass different subject to interested game elements. According to GoF, The observer pattern is applicable and appropriate in many situations including when (1) The application has two separate aspects that can be varied independently of one another, or (2)the application involves objects that when changed require changing other objects. In observer pattern, a list of watcher(observers) are notified any time the state of the subject changes. The observer pattern defines a one-to-many dependency between objects that when one object changes state, all its dependents are notified and updated automatically. The abstracting coupling between subject and observers make it easier to update notifications to be broadcasted and as a result the subject is not interested in which observers care about the changes, since it is their responsibility to react to it[9]. The observer pattern allows programmer vary subject and observers independently. The subjects can be reused without reusing their observers, and vice versa.

Mediator pattern promotes the many-to-many relationships between interacting peers to "full object status". The Mediator pattern defines an object that encapsulates how a set of objects interact. Mediator promotes loose coupling by keeping objects from referring to each other explicitly, and it lets you vary their interaction independently[9]. The communications between objects are encapsulated in mediator, and objects are no longer directly communicating with each other, but rather through the mediator. If mediator pattern is used for communication among game objects, the mediator will be responsible to update game objects. The mediator handles communications between all of these objects to reduce coupling between game objects when the sprite might collide with one another under certain circumstances as illustrated by the UML in figure 7.

IV. Conclusion

In this paper, we have presented the use of a family of design patterns in game development that can be integrated with XNA game development well during game programming. We have covered design patterns that could be used to create sprite, separate behaviors from sprite with strategy and command patterns, separate states from sprite by using state patterns, game state management with state design pattern, communication among sprite with observer or mediator patterns, and collision detection with the visitor pattern. Additionally, the applicability of other design patterns in game development should be also investigated as well.

To evaluate the benefits of object-oriented design patterns in game, we plan to conduct a software quality metrics analysis in terms of size, complexity, coupling and cohesion in near future.

REFERENCES

[1] S. Björk, S. Lundgren, H. Grauers, and S.- Göteborg, "Game Design Patterns," *Lecture Note of the Game Design track of Game Developers Conference*, 2003.

[2] D. Toll and T. Olsson, "Why is Unit-testing in Computer Games Difficult?," in *2012 16th European Conference on Software Maintenance and Reengineering*, 2012, pp. 373–378.

[3] P. V. Gestwicki, "Computer games as motivation for design patterns," *ACM SIGCSE Bulletin*, vol. 39, no. 1, p. 233, Mar. 2007.

[4] M. R. Wick, "Teaching Design Patterns in CS1 : a Closed Laboratory Sequence based on the Game of Life," in *SIGCSE*, 2005, pp. 487–491.

[5] S. Hansen, "The Game of Set – An Ideal Example for Introducing Polymorphism and Design Patterns," in *SIGCSE*, 2004, pp. 110–114.

[6] M. A. Gómez-Martín, G. Jiménez-Díaz, and J. Arroyo, "Teaching design patterns using a family of games," *ACM SIGCSE Bulletin*, vol. 41, no. 3, p. 268, Aug. 2009.

[7] A. Ampatzoglou and A. Chatzigeorgiou, "Evaluation of object-oriented design patterns in game development," *Information and Software Technology*, vol. 49, no. 5, pp. 445–454, May 2007.

[8] L. Bishop, D. Eberly, T. Whitted, M. Finch, and M. Shantz, "Designing a PC Game Engine," *Computer Graphics inEntertainment*, no. February, pp. 2–9, 1998.

[9] E. Gamma, R. Helm, R. Johnson, and J. Vlissides, *Design Patterns: Elements of Reusable Object-Oriented Software*, 1995.

New Paradigms for Software Application Development: Software architectures and component-based development

Sergio David Villarreal, Guillermo Villasana, Juan Carlos Lavariega
ITESM, Monterrey, Nuevo León, México

Abstract *In recent years several technologies and programming languages have appeared for developing software systems. Each one provides advantages and specific implementations to business applications. However, traditional approaches are still in use in many software projects, and therefore the software code was not initially developed with reuse in mind. This situation leads to delays in delivery times, production costs above budget, and possible generation of incomplete/defective software products. The architectures and the component-based development emerge as alternatives for traditional software development. The challenge is software with and for reuse, and interoperability between different technologies, platforms and applications. This paper provides a description of the component-based development and the uses of software architectures. Also, examples of program technologies that implement these concepts are given such as .NET, Web Services, OSGi, ICE, and SCA.*

Keywords
Software architecture, component-based development, CBSD, .NET, Web Services, OSGi, ICE, SCA.

1. Introduction

Software industry is moving away from the giant, monolithic, and hard development code-based practices. Software developers now have more variety of tools and methodologies to choose for building software products. But, despite the advances and alternatives available, during the design and development phase the software application may have several mishaps that can compromise the success of a software project: incomplete requirement analysis, use of technologies not suited to the type of problem to be solving, poor designs, and delays in delivery times, production costs above budget, or defective end products. Furthermore, the use of traditional approaches prior to object oriented programing (OOP) do not take into account concepts such as modularity, low coupling, information hiding, or encapsulation. These leads to develop new software projects from scratch. To overcome the aforementioned problems, the experts in the software industry have adopted the use of component-based solutions [19]. The component-oriented programming approach proposes a paradigm change in the process of software construction. The software needs to be conceived for and with reuse in mind to allowing previously developed components to be assembled and utilized in new projects. On the other hand, software architectures are useful to try to meet the necessities and requirements of customers. Roughly speaking, software architecture is a system design that includes high-level structures and sets the properties of interest that the system must meet.

Some actual technologies, like Microsoft .NET, Web Services, Open Services Gateway initiative (OSGi), Internet Communications Engine (ICE), and Service Component Architecture (SCA) are examples of technologies which implement the concepts above mentioned. SCA is an outstanding platform that incorporates and extends many of the features seen in the other technologies, and brings an easy interoperability implementation among different platforms/languages.

The use of software architectures and the component-oriented development approach seeks to provide a comprehensive solution that favors successful construction of software applications, with lower development costs and time, and a higher overall quality.

The organization of this work is as follows: Section 2 is a description of the concept of software architecture and its main features, such as high-level structures of a system and the relationships between them and their properties of interest (performance, reliability, security, and maintenance). Section 3 talks about Component-Based Software Development (CBSD) and its advantages to modify, extend, reuse and make language independence code. Section 4 gives a general description of how .NET, Web Services, OSGi, ICE, and SCA implement the concepts related to component-oriented development and software architectures. Finally, Section 5 presents a developed software project using SCA and software architecture.

2. Software Architecture

The software architecture comprises high-level structures of a system, the relationships between them and their environment [8]. An architectural design aims to facilitate the development of software applications, verifies the correct evolution of the system, aid in the detection of errors, contribute to the maintenance actions and help to reduce the associate costs. A well-designed architecture allows reasoning about satisfaction of customer´s key requirements and to make agreements on engineering principles and the properties of interest, such as performance, reliability, security, and maintenance. Also provides a clear allocation of functions to components establishes conceptual integrity principles and pursues to minimize rework applications during the life of the system [5].

A complex software system may comprise several structures of interest: modules, runtime entities, development teams, physical devices, and networks, to name a few. Therefore appropriate architectural design must be described in terms of different views. Each view represents an architectural perspective of the system. Each perspective shows certain structures and characteristics of the system to deal with a particular set of problems.

When designing software architectures is important to take into account the following aspects:

Requirements.- Software architectures are generated from the functional and non-functional requirements. A functional requirement specifies the actions that a system must meet, while a non-functional requirement establishes general limitations in existing solutions, like performance or design's constraints [12].

Complexity. - One of the design activities of software architecture is the decomposition of the system into subsystems (components). The purpose of decomposition is to reduce complexity into smaller and more manageable parts. While the complexity cannot be entirely eliminated, any reduction facilitates the development of the system [1].

Anticipation of changes. – Changes are very common during the software development. A single change may lead to new requirements or consider re-evaluating existing ones. The architecture should be flexible enough and reusable to adapt positively to the changes [12].

Performance and scalability. - The performance of a system is the largest and greatest risk to the success of a software project. Performance issues are caused generally by deficient architectures derived from poor design choices in the initial stages of the software life cycle [3].

Garlan & Schmerl (2006) suggest the use of execution structures, or views (or graphs) of component and connector (C & C) to deal with software architectures. The C&C views express more directly the critical features related to dependence, such as reliability, safety, performance. The C&C allows the employing of traditional lines and diagrams of boxes to represent software architectures. Also, C&C has a correspondence with the primitive building blocks of most architectural description languages (ADLs)[5].

3. Component-Based Software Development (CBSD)

The component-based software development (CBSD) tries to provide an effective approach for the construction of software products. Splitting up systems in its binary components it is possible to achieve a higher level of reusability, extensibility, and system maintenance compared to traditional object-oriented approach. An application in CBSD consists of a collection of one or more components in conjunction with the link calls to interact between them. The functionality of each component contributes to implement and execute the business logic of the application [14].

A component is an auto deployment self-contained entity that implements a business function and provides a high level of software reuse. Some components may be general purpose while other components may be highly specialized and / or built specifically for the application [21].

Some advantages of CBSD are:

- Modifiability. Components can be added or removed according to the requests of each application.
- Extensibility. When a new requirement needs to be implemented, if it can be incorporated using new components it is not necessary to modify existing ones that are not related to the implementation.
- The changes, if necessary, will apply only to the involved components. The components can be updated even while a client application is running, provided that the components are not being used.
- Improvements and arrangements made to a component can be immediately available to all applications that use the component.
- Component-oriented programming allows customer applications and components to be developed and evolve separately.
- The language independence promotes the exchange of components, their adoption and reuse. Developers using component-oriented development can focus on the decomposition of interfaces. The interfaces will be used as contracts between clients and services provided by the components.

Component-oriented programing (COP) takes the good methodologies of the OOP as it base, but it has the components as its basic programming elements [14]. Some of the principal characteristics in COP are: It is based in interfaces. It is a distribution technology and component packaging. It supports high-level reuse. COP, in principle, can be written in any language. They are loosely coupled components. Components have long granularity. Support for multiple interfaces, and a design-oriented interfaces. Have mechanisms that enhance the integration of third-party compositions. It supports multiple ways to link and dynamic discovery. Provides support higher order services like security and transactions.

In COP the basic application unit is an interface. An interface is a logical grouping of method definitions that act as a contract between the customer and the service provider. Each provider is free to give their own interpretation of the interface. The interfaces are implemented by a black box component that completely encapsulates the interior. To use the service offered by a component, it is not necessary to know how an interface is internally implemented. The client only needs to know the definition of the interface [14].

4. Component-Based Development Technologies

The current challenge of new technologies is to promote software reuse and component-based development. Interoperability and reusability not only represents a long-term challenge - because software is constantly evolving -, but also a great opportunity for improvement in terms of time and quality software development. In the following subsections we introduce various technologies, such as .NET, Web Services, OSGi, ICE, and SCA. These technologies, at different levels, implement the concept of component-based development and promoting software reuse.

4.1 Microsoft .NET

. NET is a technology designed to simplify the development and implementation of components, while providing interoperability between various programming languages such as Visual Basic, Visual C + +, C #, among others [14]. The .NET framework is made up of two main parts [21]: Common Language Runtime (CLR), and a set of unified libraries like ASP.NET Web Forms, Windows Form and ADO.NET.

The CLR provides a common context in which all .NET components are running, regardless of the language they are written [14]. The CLR consists of: Common Type System (CTS), Intermediate Language (IL) code, Just-In-Time (JIT) compiler, an execution unit, and some other management services. Figure 4.1 shows how the CLR works.

In .NET all compilers generate code in agreement to the common type system (CTS). Any .NET component is transformed to an intermediate common language infrastructure (CLI), also calling Microsoft Intermediate Language (MSIL), instead of a processor's specific object or platform. The MSIL instruction set is platform independent, and can be run in any environment that supports CLI. The use of MSIL helps to eliminate the necessity to distribute different executable for different platforms and CPU types.

The basic unit of packaging in .NET is the assembly. An assembly gets together multiple physical files into a single logical unit. The assembly can be a class library (DLL) or a standalone application (EXE) [14]. An assembly consists essentially of: MSIL code modules, a manifest, metadata modules, and several resources. A metadata is a comprehensive, standard, mandatory, and complete way to describe the content of the assembly. A manifest describes the assembly itself; provide the logical attributes shared by all modules and components within the assembly [14]. In .NET the component composition can be implemented in two ways: by aggregation (external exposure of the interface), or by containment (the process is performed internally and transparent to the user). .NET allows the use of code contracts. A code contract sets the preconditions, post conditions and invariant program objects codes. Contracts act as documentation for internal and external APIs, and are used to improve testing via runtime revisions. The composition of components, property inheritance, and methods of classes -written in different languages - allow reuse of components.

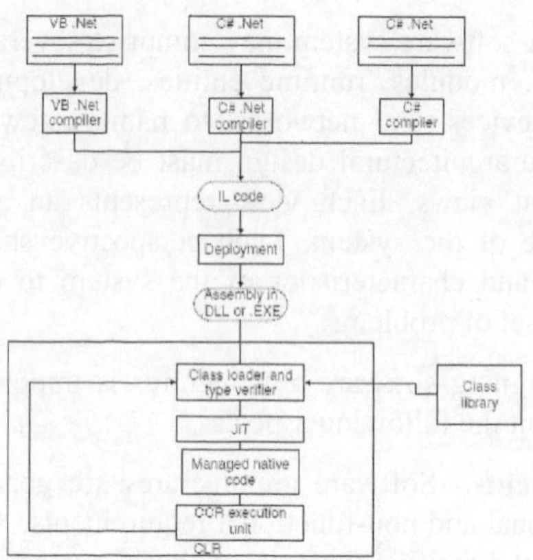

Figure 4.1. - CLR in .NET

The basic unit of packaging in .NET is the assembly. An assembly gets together multiple physical files into a single logical unit. The assembly can be a class library (DLL) or a standalone application (EXE) [14]. An assembly consists essentially of: MSIL code modules, a manifest, metadata modules, and several resources. A metadata is a comprehensive, standard, mandatory, and complete way to describe the content of the assembly. A manifest describes the assembly itself; provide the logical attributes shared by all modules and components within the assembly [14]. In .NET the component composition can be implemented in two ways: by aggregation (external exposure of the interface), or by containment (the process is performed internally and transparent to the user). .NET allows the use of code contracts. A code contract sets the preconditions, post conditions and invariant program objects codes. Contracts act as documentation for internal and external APIs, and are used to improve testing via runtime revisions. The composition of components, property inheritance, and methods of classes -written in different languages - allow reuse of components.

4.2 Web Services

A Web Service is a software system designed to support interoperability and interaction machine-to-machine over a network that has an interface described in a machine-process able format [16]. Laws et al. (2011) said Web Service is a term generally used to describe an interface provided by a software application that can be called via network. More recently, the term has been used to describe the services provided in a network using SOAP over HTTP protocol. By using SOAP a XML format is described for message passing from the client to server and server to the client. To describe the interfaces provided by a Web Service a Web Services Definition Language (WSDL) is used. WSDL is a XML language that defines the functionality of the interfaces in terms of the providing operations, and the physical details about where the Web Service is hosted.

The basic actions performed by a Web Service are [7]: publish a Web Service, and consume a Web Service. On the other hand, an application that consumes a Web Service has two components: a proxy object to interact with the Web

Service, and a client application to consume – by invoking methods on the proxy object - the Web Service.

The Web Service communication can be functionally made between two completely different environments by using standard protocols. The calls in Web Services are translated into a language and standard protocol that both computers can understand. Generally, a XML format is used. The XML language is a text-based format commonly understood among different applications. Also, the Web Services allows the calling of remote applications by remote procedure calls (RPC) [10].

Some characteristics of Web Services that promote software reuse design [11] are: open infrastructure (usage of widely documented and accepted protocols like HTTP and XML), transparency of language (interoperability between clients written in different programming languages), and modular design (aggregation services through integration and layering). These features distinguish Web Services from other distributed software systems.

There are several methods of Web Services. Some of them are: Simple Object Access Protocol (SOAP), Universal Description, Discovery and Integration (UDDI), Web Services Description Language (WSDL), Representational State Transfer (REST), and Action Message Format (AMF). Languages like C / C + +, C #, Java, Perl, Python, and Ruby provide libraries, utilities, and even frameworks that support Web Services.

Figure 4.2 shows a Web Service architecture with three elements: a client, a provider Web Service and UDDI Registry. The Web Service provider registers/publish its services in the UDDI register. The services are globally available to the customers who require them.

4.3 *Open Services Gateway initiative* (OSGi)

The alliance Open Services Gateway initiative (OSGi) emerged in 1999. Its purpose was to provide Java embedded technology to network gateways in households [6]. Currently, OSGi framework is a component specification that provides modularity to the Java platform. OSGi allows the creation of highly cohesive and loosely coupled modules which can be integrated into larger applications. Each module can even be independently developed, tested, implemented, updated, and managed with zero or minimal impact with respect to the other modules [20].

OSGi is built over the Java platform, and is made of several layers: module definition, lifecycle modules, service registration, services, and security layers. The OSGi framework and the Java platform are illustrated in Figure 4.3

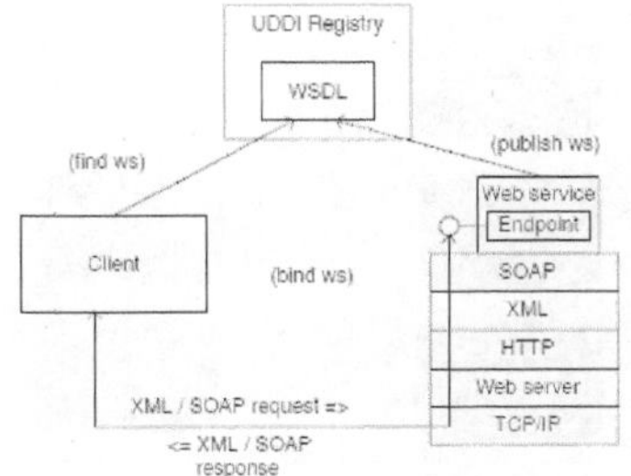

Figure 4.2. - Web Service Architecture

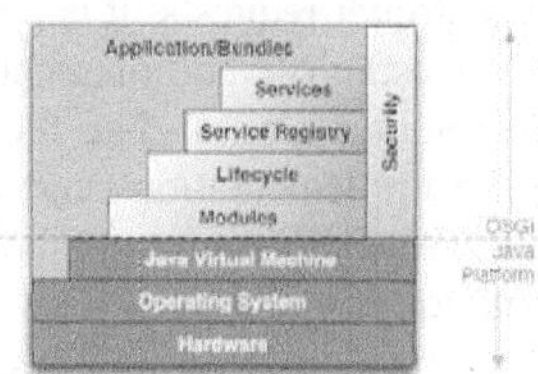

Figure 4.3.- OSGi framework

The module part defines a deployment model based on Java. In OSGi the implementation unit is the bundle. The OSGi bundles are very similar to JAR files, except that its META-INF/MANIFEST.MF file contains specific OSGi metadata, including a final name, version, dependencies, and some other implementation details. A bundle can be compared to a Web ARchive (WAR) in the context of a web container, or an Enterprise ARchive (EAR) in the context of Java Enterprise Platform[6].

A bundle can be installed, initialized, stopped or uninstalled from the framework according to the life cycle prescribed by the OSGi specification. The OSGi framework provides a service registry, in which bundles can be publish and/or consume services. However, unlike some interpretations of service oriented architecture (SOA) using Web Services, OSGi services are published and consumed within the same Java virtual machine. OSGi is also described as a "SOA JVM". OSGi, as well, defines an optional security layer to authenticate bundles to be deployed in a safe manner.

OSGi provides the following additional modular features to Java [20]: hiding content, service record (the services are known by their interfaces), parallel versions of bundles, dynamic modularity, strong naming (the bundles are identified by a symbolic name and version number).

4.4 *Internet Communications Engine* (ICE)

ICE is an object-oriented middleware that allows developers to build client-server applications in a distributed fashion with minimal effort. Similar in concept to CORBA, ICE provides a simpler and more powerful object model. ICE includes improvements such: user datagram protocol (UDP) support, sending asynchronous mode, security, automatic object persistence, and interface aggregation. The object model is a set of definitions about computational entities properties, like available types and their semantics, rules for type compatibility, and behavior in case of error [9].

ICE has tools, APIs, and support libraries to build client-server object oriented application. ICE can be used in heterogeneous environments, as clients and servers can be written in different programming languages. ICE can run on different operating systems and architectures, using a variety of network technologies to communicate [17]. ICE currently supports C++, Java, C #, Objective-C, Python, Ruby, and PHP languages, on Linux, Mac OS, Windows, Android and Solaris platforms.

ICE operation is based on RPC using TCP or UDP to invoke remote objects as if they were local. The objects are called

ICE objects, which are a local or remote entities responsible for responding to customer requests. It is necessary to have a client-side proxy to establish communication with remote objects hosted on remote servers. The local client needs a Servant to know the implementations and methods which a remote object has. The Servant will be responsible for explaining the behavior of operations.

Slice is the property of ICE that can transform objects written in different languages supported by the middleware in ICE objects. Each ICE object has an interface with a specific number of operations. The Slice language defines the interfaces, operations, and data types that are exchanged between the client and the server. Slice allows establishing the entity contracts between the client and server independently of the programming language.

The ICE architecture provides several benefits to software developers [18]: object-oriented semantics, asynchronous, synchronous messages, multithreading and multiple interfaces support; machine architecture, implementation, operating system, and transport independence; location and server transparency, and security.

4.5 *Service Component Architecture* (SCA)

SCA was originally created by a group of companies such as IBM, Oracle, SAP, and BEA. SCA is a programming model that abstracts standard business functions into software components [15]. The basic building block in SCA is the component. The components are then used as building blocks. The implementation of an SCA component can be performed in any technology, like Ruby, BPEL, Java, or even frameworks like Spring, Java EE and OSGi.

A SCA components consist of [2]: services (interfaces), references (also called interfaces, they are the required dependences to perform its task), properties (configuration), and intention policies (component's behavior). The SCA component´s parts are illustrated in Figure 4.4.

The unit of deployment in SCA is the composition. A composition is an aggregation of one or more components. A composition can provide externally the services and references provided by its internal components through promotions[4]. Applications can be built using one or more compositions. The components within a composition can use the same technology or be implemented in different technologies. This feature promotes the reuse of components [4].

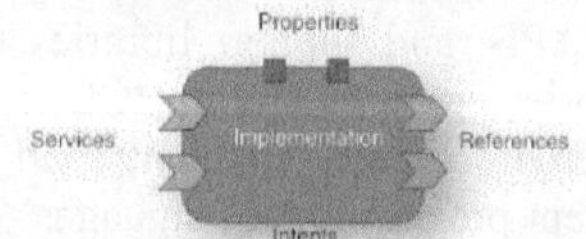

Figure 4.4. - SCA component's elements

An SCA composition is described in a configuration file with a .composite extension. The .composite file is build using a Service Component Definition Language (SCDL) based on XML. The SCDL describes the existing components within the composition and the relationships between them. An item package that is part of the business solution is known as contribution. A contribution is a unit of deployment, and may contain compositions, Java classes, and XSD or WSDL files.

One of the most important concepts in SCA is the bindings. A binding specifies the communication methods that a client can use to access a service, and the methods that a service can use to access other services, either within the same SCA domain or outside it. Services can be configured to use different types of bindings without have to change the component´s code. Therefore multiple bindings can be associated for the same service. For example, one software solution should have JMS bindings, Web Services bindings, Atom bindings, and Corba bindings. Through the use of bindings it is possible to focus on the business logic of the components, instead of the problems associated with communications and management protocols. This feature allows SCA compositions to be flexible, and grow and adapt without code changes.

5. Software Project

A software project was developed to illustrate how software architectures and component-based development contribute to build and reuse the software. The SCA was selected due is a component architecture platform that extends many of the features seen in the other technologies mentioned above.

5.1 Project description

A system with a Web application was built to provide available billboard information from several movie theaters within certain particular region. The application offers an online catalog service where users can query and evaluate the results according to their preferences.

5.2 Objectives

The main objectives of the project were: collection and processing of information in different formats, allow the use of different technologies to communicate components and services, using software architectural designs according to the project specifications, development of component-based software to implement system functionality, and software development with and for reuse.

5.3 Architecture

The selected pattern was a layered client-server approach. The server is always active and waiting for connections and queries from customers. The architecture of the project, seen from a general point of view, has five main components: Clients, Cinemas, Intelligent Agents, MovieCatalog, and Data Access. The five components and their respective relationships are illustrated in Figure 5.1.

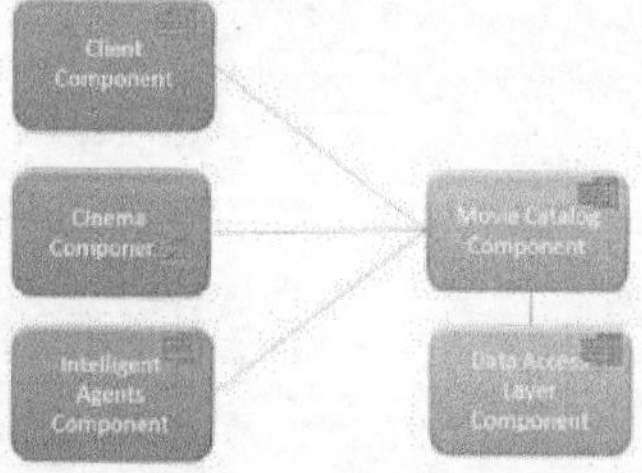

Figure 5.1. - General architecture

The description of each component of Fig 5.1 is as follows:

Customers. - Represent users who will use the service MoviesSCA.

Cinemas. – The movie theaters that will be recorded in the system. Each movie theaters will provide movie data from their billboards.

Intelligent Agents. - Perform search operations over Internet to collect billboard information. This mechanism is proposed to automate the data collection process periodically.

MovieCatalog. – This component offers the query and movie research services.

Data Access Layer. – This component directly communicates with the database engine to perform query and update operations. The data access layer component brings independence to the database from the other components.

Figure 5.2 shows a class diagram from an architectural perspective. The architectural view adds the interfaces and classes that compose each one of the components.

5.4 Implementation

For the exchange of information between components a scheme based on XML was created. The framework Tuscany was chosen to build the project. Tuscany is a lightweight infrastructure that implements the following technologies: Service Component Architecture (SCA), Service Data Objects (SDO), and Data Access Service (DAS). The My Structured Query Language (MySQL) was selected to implement the database of the software project. The MySQL is an open source relational database management system (RDBMS) widely used in software projects.

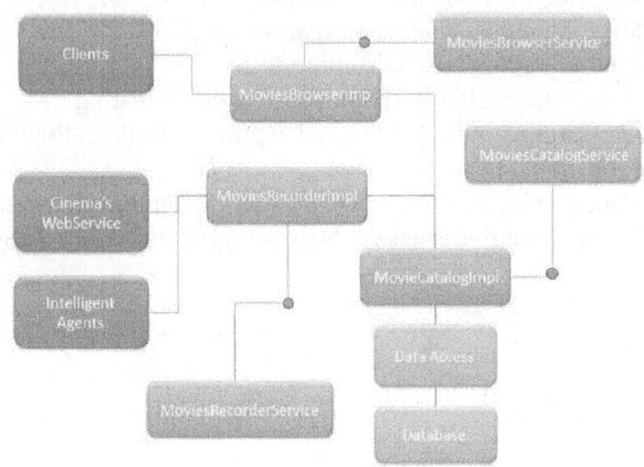

Figure 5.2.- Class Architecture Diagram

5.5 Results

A well-designed architecture provides system decomposition into several subsystems, specifies the role of each component, and helps to meet the key project requirements.

The SCA technology offers an excellent component based solution for software development with reuse in mind. The SCA diagrams make easier to understand the communication, dependency, and interaction between components within a system. The use of bindings allows interoperability among different technologies outside SCA in a transparently manner. To add a new communication protocol only is needed to aggregate a few lines in the .composite file, leaving the component´s code without any modification.

Finally, with SCA the reuse of software is feasible due the SCA components can be ported to other environments and can run without major complications, although the rest of the application was developed in a different language.

6. Conclusions

Nowadays, there are several platforms, technologies, and programming languages to build software systems. Each one offers different solutions and implementation to client´s business requirements. Unfortunately, traditional approaches prevent the reuse of previously developed software -mainly because of bad software practices -, deriving in the necessity to build new software from scratch every time.

The architectural designs and the CBSD are some of the latest tools available for software developers. The use of architectural designs facilitates the development of software applications. It provides system decomposition into several subsystems, specifies the assigned roles to each component, gives conceptual integrity principles, and tries to minimize rework applications during the lifetime of the system. Also, a well-designed architecture allows the verification of the correct evolution of a system, the satisfaction of key project requirements, helps to detect system errors, reduce associated costs, and contribute to the maintenance actions.

The component-oriented programming promotes the software development with and for reuse. The component-oriented technologies discussed in this paper bring different features and capabilities for software reuse. Some are easier to implement, as the case of Web Services, while others have a higher learning curve, such as OSGi. .NET is a good option if you work mostly on Microsoft´s platforms and programming languages. ICE offers many improvements over its predecessor, Corba, but it is still under development, so many of its features are not available. Finally, SCA is a component architecture that incorporates and extends many of the features seen in other technologies, thus SCA brings a more comprehensive and complete software solution.

The SCA's advantages found with this research are listed below:

- It is a component-based architecture.
- Using SCA diagrams it is easy to design the component architecture for the software project. During the implementation phase, a very close correspondence exists between the code and the different architectural elements.
- In SCA services and references can be developed and connected in a distributed fashion, using a variety of technologies and languages.
- SCA is a flexible and versatile platform that can interact with other applications outside SCA through the use of bindings.

- The bindings enable SCA interoperability with applications developed in other languages or using different communication protocols.
- To add a new binding to the SCA service it is not necessary to make changes to the component's code. Only a few lines in the .composite file are required to implement the communication service.
- The compositions and contributions promote the programming with and for software reuse.
- Using the SCDL simplifies the description of the components within a composition.

In general, the software architectures and the component-based development represents a long-term challenge - because the software is constantly evolving -, but also represents a great opportunity for design, time, cost, and software quality improvements.

7. 7 References

[1] AlSharif, M., Bond, W., & Al-Otaiby, T. (2004), "Assessing the complexity of software architecture", Proceedings of the 42nd annual Southeast regional conference. (ACM Digital Library).

[2] Apache, S. F. (2010), "SCA Introduction", Retrieved October 7, 2011, from http://tuscany.apache.org/documentation-2x/ sca-introduction.html

[3] Bondi, A. (2009), "The software architect as the guardian of system performance and scalability", *Proceedings of the 2009 ICSE Workshop on Leadership and Management in Software Architecture*. (ACM Digital Library).

[4] Chappell, D. (2007), "Introducing SCA", San Francisco, California: Chappell & Associates. Retrieved October 11, 2011, from http://www.davidchappell.com/articles/introducing_sca.pdf

[5] Garlan, D., & Schmerl, B. (2006), "Architecture-driven modelling and analysis", *Proceedings of the eleventh Australian workshop on Safety critical systems and software.* (ACM Digital Library).

[6] Gédéon, W. (2010), "OSGi and Apache Felix 3.0". Birmingham: Packt Publishing.

[7] Gonzalez, P., & Perez, O. (2011), "Servicios Web", Retrieved November 9, 2011 from http://cursos.itesm.mx/

[8] Gorton, I. (2006), "Essential Software Architecture", New York: Springer-Verlag.

[9] Henning, M (2004), "A new approach to object-oriented middleware". *Internet Computing, IEEE, V. 8, I. 9*, (IEEE Digital Library).

[10] James, T. (2010), "Drupal Web Services". Birmingham: Packt Publishing Ltd.

[11] Kalin, M. (2009), "Java Web Services: Up and Running". Sebastopol, CA: O'Reilly Media.

[12] Lakshminarayanan, V., Liu, W., L Chen, C., Easterbrook, S., & E Perry, D. (2006), "Software Architects in Practice: Handling Requirements", *Proceedings of the 2006 conference of the Center for Advanced Studies on Collaborative research.* (ACM Digital Library).

[13] Laws, S., Combellack, M., Feng, R., Mahbod, H., & Nash, S. (2011), "Tuscany SCA in Action". Stamford, CT: Manning

[14] Lowy, J. (2005), "Programming .NET Components", Sebastopol, CA: O'Reilly

[15] Marino, J., & Rowley, M. (2010), "Understanding SCA". Indiana: Addison-Wesley

[16] Richards, R. (2006), "Pro PHP XML and Web Services". New York: Apress©

[17] Spruiell, M. (2011 a), "Ice Architecture", Retrieved November 12, 2011 from http://doc.zeroc.com/display/Ice/Ice+Architecture

[18] Spruiell, M. (2011 b), "Architectural Benefits of Ice", Retrieved November 12, 2011 from http://doc.zeroc.com/display/Ice/Architectural+Benefits+of+Ice

[19] Vitharana, P., Zahedi, F., & Jain, H. (2003), "Design, retrieval, and assembly in component-based software development", *Communications of the ACM, Volume 46 Issue 11*. (ACM Digital Library).

[20] Walls, C. (2009), "Modular Java: Creating Flexible Applications with OSGi and Spring". Dallas: Pragmatic Bookshelf.

[21] Wang, A., & Qian, K. (2005), "Component-Oriented Programming", Hoboken, New Jersey: John Wiley & Sons.

SESSION

UNIFIED MODELING LANGUAGE / UML, OBJECT ORIENTED METHODS, AND CASE STUDIES

Chair(s)

TBA

A QoS Driven Web Service Selection Methodology Using UML and UML Profiles

A. Rashmi Phalnikar[1], **B. Devesh Jinwala**[2]
[1] MIT College Of Engineering , Paud Road, Kothrud ,Pune , India : 411038
[2] SV National Institute Of Technology , Ichchanath, ,Surat , India - 395007

Abstract - *Business process modeling and execution in SOA requires a set of methodologies and tools which support transition from analysis to execution level. Web services play a significant role in application development in SOA environment and publishing its functionality on registries to link their data and operations for different applications. Web service selection must satisfy not only the functional requirements but also the Non Functional Requirements (NFR) of the user. Based on our literature survey, we observe the need for improvement in current approaches so as to consider NFR during web service selection. Further, as number of users and their specific requirements increase, NFR conflicts are bound to rise and need to be understood. Detecting them and finding their impact on the system is the next rational step. Our work proposes to detect these conflicts using Ontology, Unified Modeling Language (UML) and UML Profile. The focus is on selecting an appropriate web service so that the Quality of Service (QoS) values are maintained. Our contribution is to develop a model driven approach so as to allow the designer to choose an appropriate web service. This is expected to greatly reduce the development and operational time besides providing transparency.*

Keywords: Web Service Selection, QoS, Ontology, UML Profiles. Non Functional Requirements

1 Introduction

Web services based on ubiquitously adopted internet standards and supporting interoperability across different platforms have introduced a new era in application development. With an ever increasing number of web services providing similar functionality, Quality of Service (QoS) is becoming an important criterion for selection of the best available web service. QoS becomes a significant concern for service consumers and providers during service selection. Users need to know QoS information, reliability of the information and also the performance impact of a wrongly chosen web service. However, representing, storing and understanding the interdependency of the QoS values is an issue and needs due attention.

When discovering web services, clients look for those web services that meet their functional requirements. The service descriptions are manually scanned and those services which satisfy user requirements are selected or composed. With an increasing number of web services providing similar functionalities, the discovery process now emphasizes on how to find the service that best fits the consumer's NFR.

NFR based service selection is not possible with the traditional mechanism as they do not consider user constraints. So the need of the hour is a system that assists the user to search and incorporate these capabilities that defines the QoS factors. QoS is defined as a set of quality requirements present in the collective behavior of one or more object parameters and are a set of non functional attributes like service response time, throughput, reliability and availability. They sometimes refers to the level of quality of service, i.e. the guaranteed service quality.

Our investigation raised certain issues:

i. What is an appropriate method of description of QoS values?
ii. After the filtering of web services what method is apt for non functional requirement based selection?
iii. How will the user know that the shortlisted web service will meet a distinctive non functional requirement?
iv. What is the best way to judge the extent to which QoS values of the user and provider agree?
v. How to associate the weights for each of the user's non functional requirements?
vi. Do the NFR conflict and if they do to what extent do they affect the working of the system and its QoS value?

The goal of this research is to investigate how dynamic web service selection can be realized to satisfy a customer's QoS requirements using a new model that can be accommodated within the existing web service selection methods. This paper focuses on study of the possibility of improving the proposed UML profile, including the OCL (Object Constraints Language) for the representation of user constraints during selection. This way the developers' whose knowledge does not extend beyond UML can develop applications that use semantic web services. We propose a method to detect these conflicts using Ontology, Unified Modeling Language (UML) and UML Profile. Even though matching of QoS factors have been understood, it is more important to understand how NFR conflicts and how it can affect the system.

The remainder of this paper is structured as follows. We outline the motivation in section 2. Section 3 expresses use of Model Driven development in web service selection. Section 4 describes the method of representing NFR in UML diagrams. Section 5 overviews verification of class diagram and OCL and Section 6 concludes the paper.

2 Motivation

The preface makes it evident that the first step for the support of QoS of web service is to provide a framework which considers the NFR of service provider and requester. The idea in the proposed design and implementation is to maintain all features with the standard web service selection mechanisms and expand them to support QoS characteristics. As a result, a web service user can pick among services the one that suits him/her most and further refine his options using quality criteria. To be widely adopted by users and to succeed in real-world applications, the development must catch up with mainstream software trends like Model Driven Development.

We can broadly classify web service selection methods into those discovered by functional requirements and those by non functional requirements as shown in Fig, 1.

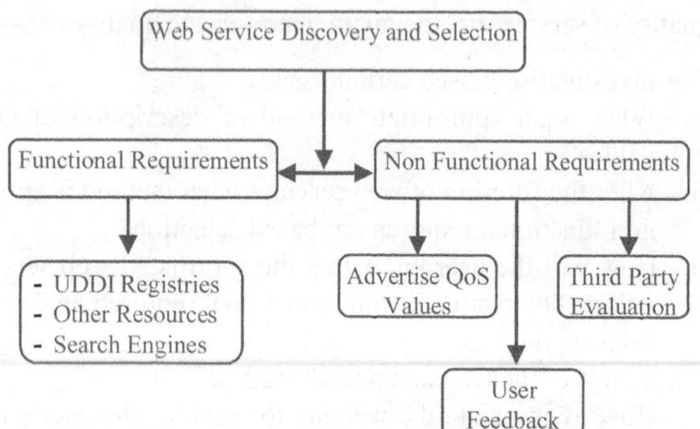

Fig. 1: Web Service Discovery Methods

During design time or static web discovery that concentrates only on functional description, the application designer makes use of service registries and service descriptions to select and test binding to a service.

As number of web services grows they share similar functionalities, but possess different non-functional requirements. The web service discovery and selection methods that use NFR have been investigated and a backdrop for motivation of our research is created. Solutions to service selection based on QoS problem can be roughly divided into three categories:

i. Self Advertising: Web service providers will describe their expected QoS information. A disadvantage is that provider may not be neutral in describing its own QoS information.
ii. Web service consumers experience about service quality: QoS data are collected by other user's feedback or by active monitoring. A drawback of this approach is its complexity and overhead implementation.
iii. Third party evaluation of a web service owner. It will test the web service and it's published QoS information. This method is expensive and inflexible to implement.

Kokash et.al [2] suggested adding QoS values to UDDI by adding properties to property bag. Use of Quality Requirements Language (QRL) for QoS information was described by Ran et.al. [3]. However it does not provide sufficient information on when and how to control and manage any specified QoS information. The paper further suggested the use of a QoS certifier. The new certifier's role is to verify service provider's QoS claims. The proposed extension to the current UDDI design may not be always feasible and the verification of QoS properties at the time of registration may not guarantees up-to-date QoS information.

Maximillen et.al. [4] suggests use of agents based on distributed reputation metric models. Rajendran et.al. [5] proposed the Multi-Agent based architecture for both services registration and service discovery. The architecture utilizes the services of response agent, certification agent and query agent. D'Mello et.al [6] presents a repository to store, retrieve and act with QoS information. Efshani et.al. [7] uses a QoS broker to manage the interaction of QoS information between service requester and service provider and further effort is being placed on how to find the service that most coordination the consumers' requirements. Al-Masri [8] proposes use of Web Service Relevancy Function used for measuring the relevancy ranking of a particular web service based on client's preferences, and QoS metrics.

Another approach suggests use of WS-Policy [9]. WS-Policy is a specification that allows web services consumers and producers to advertise their policy requirements. Certain solutions suggest a conceptual model that is based on web service reputation and user feedbacks [10][11]. They however suffer from the fact that service do not provide guarantee as to the accuracy of QoS values over time or having up-to-date QoS information. QoS Ontology based solutions [4] uses a multiagent framework based on ontology for QoS. The ontology provides a basis for providers to advertise their offerings, for consumers to express their preferences, and for ratings of services to be gathered and shared. Baocai et.al. [12] proposes a framework that supports the automatic discovery of web services using QoS ontology. However they suffer from performance problems due to the use of ontology reasoners.

Where matching of web services is concerned, work by Baocai et.al [12] and Kritikos et.al [13] draws attention to semantic similarity, so as to improve the precision of service discovery. However the interface of web service has difficulty to describe the service correctly. Moreover users also find it hard to exactly present their requirements.

In general, the widespread understanding and use of web services should be promoted to enable development of ubiquitous computing and for widespread adoption of web services. However, the learning curve for semantically rich languages can be steep. This fact provides a barrier to adoption and widespread use. So, development must catch up with mainstream software trends, as for example, the Model Driven Architecture.

We propose the use of UML profile and OCL constraints, to describe the NFR requirements and constraints of web service with the help of QoS Ontology. Note that the OCL is language familiar for the average software developer and such a selection process at design time could improve the overall performance by reducing conflicts at run time.

3. Model Driven Development for Web Service Selection

Model Driven Development (MDD) is a style of software development where the primary software artifacts are models from which code and other artifacts are generated. A model is a description of a system from a particular perspective, omitting irrelevant detail so that the characteristics of interest are seen more clearly. In MDD a model has to be machine-readable.

In MDD, models are used not just as sketches or blueprints but as primary artifacts from which efficient implementations are generated by the application of transformations. It has the potential to greatly reduce the cost of solution development and improve the consistency and quality of solutions. It does this by automating implementation patterns with transforms, which eliminates repetitive low-level development work. Rather than repeatedly applying technical expertise manually when building solution artifacts, the expertise is encoded directly in transformations. This has the advantage of both consistency and maintainability.

MDD shifts the emphasis of application development away from the platform allowing developers to design applications without concern of platform-level concepts. A software development project needs to produce many non-code artifacts and many of these are completely or partially derivable from models. The advantages of an MDD approach are as follows:

- Increased productivity:
- Maintainability
- Reuse of legacy
- Adaptability
- Consistency
- Repeatability
- Improved stakeholder communication
- Improved design communication

When designing a solution, we must consider non functional characteristics such as security and performance. In an MDD approach, it is often possible to capture many decisions related to non functional characteristics in transformations. However, it is not always possible or desirable to completely automate these aspects of a solution. Solution-specific design may be necessary. In such cases, we introduce modeling techniques relevant to specifying non functional characteristics. For example, we might introduce stereotypes that indicate the kind of traffic that is expected over a connection (frequent/infrequent, high volume/low volume). The transformations then use this information to generate implementation artifacts that are optimized for these performance characteristics.

4. Representing NFR Using UML Profiles

UML editors are ubiquitous in the software industry, and many can be updated to recognize new profiles. UML documentation of the requirements engineering process will sit more comfortably with all other UML documentation for a software project. A domain-oriented design approach that provides mechanisms for illustrating NFR using UML classes would facilitate the mapping from one domain to the other also.

Our work proposes to design a system which can assist in NFR based web service selection process in Service Oriented Architecture (SOA) environment. For illustration purpose, we have created a framework for UML profile corresponding to a Chronic Obstructive Pulmonary Disease (COPD) patient. This profile is meant to ease the work of software developers.

An important part of UML is the Object Constraint Language (OCL) – a textual language that allows to specify additional constraints on models in a more precise and concise way than it is possible to do with diagrams only. UML Profile contains stereotypes and tagged values. Stereotypes are attached to model elements to convey the meaning of those elements. Tagged values are name/value pairs. They are attached to model elements in order to supply additional information which is needed in the transformation process. We suggest the use of a a precise approach that allows an analysis and validation of UML models and OCL constraints.

i. Case Study: COPD Patient

In e-health Remote Patient Monitoring (RPM) refers to variety of technologies designed to manage and monitor health conditions of a patient. RPM come with many advantages like reduced cost, early intervention, integration of care and increased productivity. Chronic Obstructive Pulmonary Disease (COPD) is a slowly progressive disease of the airways characterized by a gradual loss of lung function. This leads to a limitation of the flow of air to and from the lungs, causing shortness of breath (dyspnea). The symptoms of COPD can range from chronic cough and sputum production to severe disabling shortness of breath.

These are the first signs of complications in the patient's condition and the risk associated with it. Many COPD patients monitor their vital capacities and peak flow rates at home. This monitoring helps them and their physician to monitor the patient's condition. The proposed model will be helpful to these COPD patients being monitored remotely to predict the onset of a spasm and alert the medical professional. Due to the prevalence and economic burden of hospitalized COPD patient, it is necessary to seek out methodologies that would facilitate the prevention, monitoring and treatment of them. Experts and researchers suggest monitoring and tracking patients' symptoms on an everyday basis in order to prevent emergencies.

We consider this setup in a Service Oriented Environment (SOA) where web services will be used to transfer data securely. The selection of web services is critical as each patient's NFR are unique. However they have to match the NFR offered by web service, and this is where our model comes into use. We try to select the most appropriate web service that delivers the highest QoS by matching the NFR or unique requirements of the user.

ii. System Design

Fig. 2 shows the data flow of the proposed system.

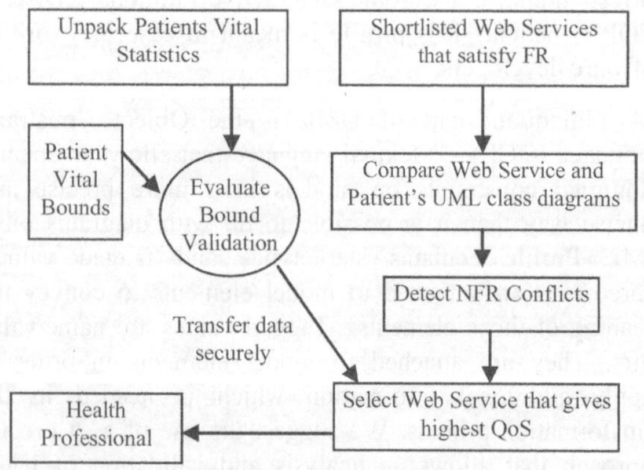

Fig. 2: Data Flow Diagram

The specifications of the present system are studied to determine what changes will be needed to incorporate the user needs. The input will consist of the user specifications, and the output will be the identity of the web service that can deliver highest QoS.

iii. Non Functional Requirements Diagram

NFR Diagram is used to understand how NFR are interrelated. For our discussion we consider two important NFR: security and response time. Later we will increase the scope of the NFR under consideration.

The NFR are different from the functional characteristics in the sense that they are not always completely satisfied. The set of NFR are interrelated and if they are conflicting, they affect the working of the system. To understand this, we draw NFR diagram, a visual representation of the decomposition of NFR. In this sense, the diagram shows how various NFR are rationalized. In analyzing NFR, one does not analyze them independent of each other, but rather in relation to each other. There can be looser relationships where one NFR considers, prevents or contributes towards the fulfillment of another.

a. **Security NFR Diagram:** The decomposition is shown in Fig. 3 below.When the patient's vital data is sent, it is recognized as normal or abnormal condition. In case it is abnormal, the login protocols are bypassed and the vital data validation is done. This is done to avoid any delays to authentication and authorization.

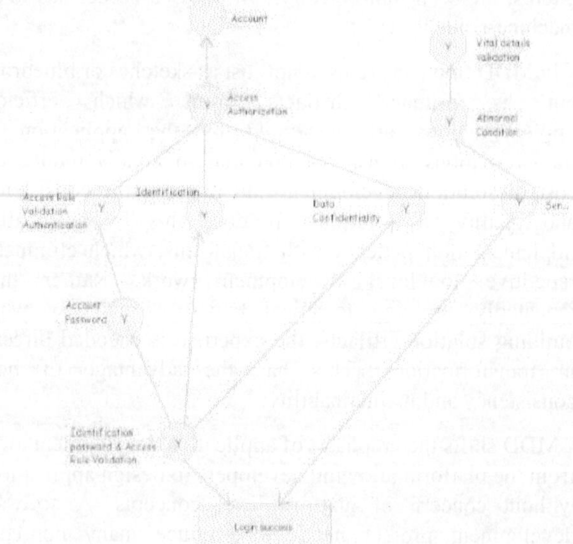

Fig. 3. Security NFR Diagram

However in normal conditions, the patient's data is validated through the Login Process. It consists of Access Rule validation, identification and data confidentiality. This figure shows that security NFR itself can be decomposed into several NFR.

b. **Response Time NFR Diagram:** Response Time is defined as the elapsed time between the end of an inquiry on a computer system and the beginning of a response. The total response time NFR consists of response time for validating data, logging in, response time for alert and then saving data.

All of the goals considered can be termed as soft goals, that is, they are yet too vague to be formalized. Since they are not sufficiently defined, it is also not yet clear what it would take to satisfy one of these goals. Ordinarily, a "reduces" relationship holds between a goal and a subgoal if satisfaction of the subgoal is sufficient for satisfaction of the goal it reduces. However, where a reduces relationship exists between goals in which any of the reduced goals are soft, we talk in terms of partially satisfying rather than satisfying.

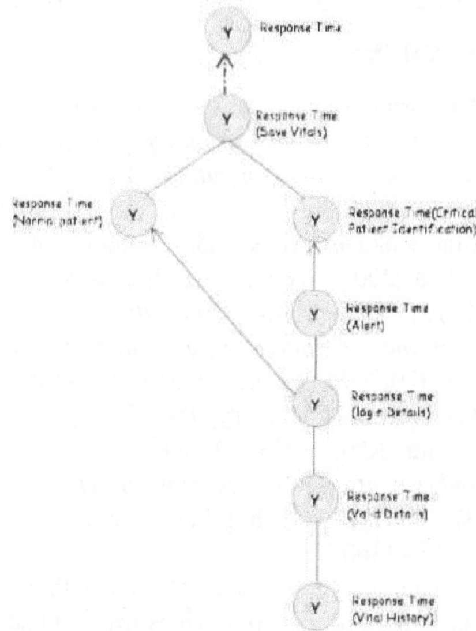

Fig. 4. Response Time NFR Diagram

c. **Class Diagrams for Patient:** Once the NFR decomposition is complete, it is evident that NFRs conflict as shown in Fig, 5.

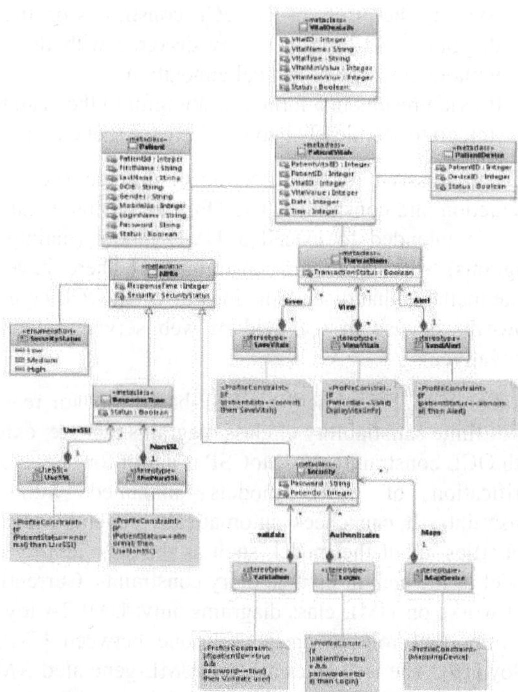

Fig. 5: Class Diagram for Patients NFR

The conflicts are evident and is shown in the the class diagram for patient which is mapped by traversing step-by-step through the WSDL file and identifying the most important UML concepts.To understand how NFR can conflict and hamper, we begin the process of mapping the patient's requirements and web service specifications to the UML metamodel. We define stereotype to handle transactions which include Save Vitals, View Vitals and Send Alerts. Further the NFR Security and Response time are also elaborated using stereotypes and constraints.

5. Verification of Class Diagrams and OCL

The idea of verification of web service suitability using MDD in the case of a COPD patient seems to be a promising idea. As a result it will be able to detect mismatch or a reduction in QoS values due to NFR conflicts. The approaches revolve around satisfiability property of a model, i.e. deciding whether it is possible to create a well-formed instantiation of the model.

A general outline for this work would be:

i. Depict the candidate web services in the form of a class diagram, making use of the WSDL file structure and its tags.
ii. Understand the input notation/ requirement of the user. These are the OCL constraints. If an internal formal notation is used, it should be transparent to the designer.

iii. Analyze the effect of the OCL constraints on the class diagrams and how they may disagree with the design without any type of manual annotation.
iv. Provide results in a format meaningful to the designer.
v. Integrate seamlessly into the designer tool chain.

The expressivity of class diagrams is limited to class level interaction and constraints. The Object Constraint Language OCL is intended to extend a UML model (mainly class diagrams) with symbolic constraints[14].There have been some methods that discuss the idea of UML/OCL constraint. However its use in the field of web service selection is innovative.

Cabot et al. [15] describe a CSP-based tool for reasoning about finite satisfiability of class diagrams that are extended with OCL constraints. UMLtoCSP is a tool for the automatic verification of UML models annotated with OCL constraints. It can check automatically several correctness properties about the model, such as the satisfiability of the model or the lack of contradictory constraints. Currently, the tool works on UML class diagrams only. UML2Alloy plays an important role to create a bridge between UML and Alloy.[16]. The tool takes an ArgoUML-generated XMI file in order to transform the UML model into Alloy code. It transforms the input into assertions, simulations, or invariants.

Nevertheless, there are a few obstacles that may prevent the introduction of WS provision. One of them is the inability to represent the non-functional features of WSs, i.e. their quality-of-service. To take care of this we second the use the formulation of a QoS ontology framework that is used to support QoS-aware web service selection [14]. A set of rules defined by Semantic Web Rule Language (SWRL) can also be described and designed for reasoning to acquire more advanced knowledge based on simple ones.

6. Conclusion and Future Work

This work elucidates the relevance of QoS during web service selection for a COPD patient remotely monitored. Remote monitoring involves critical data handling and data security keeping in mind the patients unique requirements. The report discusses the relevance of NFR during web service selection and the effect of conflicting NFR. The paper proposes use of Model Driven Development (MDD), UML Profiles and its extensions for ranking the most suitable web service from a list of functionally satisfying web services that are shortlisted. The benefits of MDD ranges from ease of understanding to its use during design stage to avoid conflicts during run time. The web service class diagrams and OCL constraints can be verified using a UML verification tool in future.

The proposed method is flexible and transparent and can be used along with any web service selection method. It also contributes to the improvement of service selection efficiency when service is retrieved in an automatic way. The major advantage of this approach is to decrease the complexity of web service selection to user as it can be included during design stage.

Our current interest as described in the paper focuses mainly in two directions:

i. Investigating the NFR conflicts and
ii. Understanding the effect of these conflicts on the QoS values.

In future, we would want to extend our experimental setup with additional scenarios. We also plan to extend QoS parameters to include information such as availability, reliability etc. Moreover, this approach may be extended to automatic service selection using multi-dimensional QoS.

7. References

[1] Latha Srinivasan and Jem Treadwell, 2005,"*An Overview of Service-oriented Architecture, Web Services and Grid Computing*" HP Software Global Business Unit.

[2] Natallia Kokash, Aliaksandr Birukou, and Vincenzo D'Andrea. 2007. Web service discovery based on past user experience. In *Proceedings of the 10th international conference on Business information systems* (BIS'07), Witold Abramowicz (Ed.). Springer-Verlag, Berlin, Heidelberg, 95-107.

[3] Shuping Ran. 2003. A model for web services discovery with QoS. *SIGecom Exch.* 4, 1 (March 2003), 1-10. http://doi.acm.org/ 10.1145/ 844357.844360.

[4] E. Michael Maximilien and Munindar P. Singh. 2004. Toward autonomic web services trust and selection. In *Proceedings of the 2nd international conference on Service oriented computing* (ICSOC '04). ACM, New York, NY, USA, 212-221. http://doi.acm.org/10.1145/1035167. 035198

[5] T. Rajendran, P. Balasubramanie, "An Efficient Multi-Agent-Based Architecture for Web Service Registration and Discovery with QoS", European Journal of Scientific Research, Vol.60 No.3 , 2011, Pgs. 421-432

[6] Demian Antony D'Mello, V. S. Ananthanarayana, and Santhi Thilagam. 2008. A QoS Broker Based Architecture for Dynamic Web Service Selection. In *Proceedings of the 2008 Second Asia International Conference on Modelling \& Simulation (AMS)* (AMS '08). IEEE Computer Society, Washington, DC, USA, 101-106. DOI=10.1109/AMS.2008.94

[7] Reihaneh Khorsand Motlagh Esfahani, Farhad Mardukhi, Naser Nematbakhsh, "Reputation Improved Web Services Discovery Based on QoS", Journal of Convergence Information Technology Vol. 5, No.9.

2010 , Pgs. 206-214. http://www.aicit.org/jcit/ppl/JCIT0509_21.pdf

[8] Al-Masri, E.; Mahmoud, Q.H.; , "QoS-based Discovery and Ranking of Web Services," *Computer Communications and Networks, 2007. ICCCN 2007. Proceedings of 16th International Conference on* , vol., no., pp.529-534, 13-16 Aug. 2007. DOI =: 10.1109/ICCCN.2007.4317873 .

[9] Web Service Policy, Available at: http://www.w3.org/ Submission/ WS-Policy/

[10] Ziqiang Xu; Martin, P.; Powley, W.; Zulkernine, F.; , "Reputation-Enhanced QoS-based Web Services Discovery," *Web Services, 2007. ICWS 2007. IEEE International Conference on* , vol., no., pp.249-256, 9-13 July 2007 DOI = 10.1109/ICWS.2007.152

[11] Youakim Badr, Ajith Abraham, Frrederique Biennier, and Crina Grosan. 2008. Enhancing Web Service Selection by User Preferences of Non-functional Features. In *Proceedings of the 2008 4th International Conference on Next Generation Web Services Practices* (NWESP '08). IEEE Computer Society, Washington, DC, USA, 60-65. DOI= http://dx.doi.org/10.1109/NWeSP.2008.39

[12] Yin Baocai; Yang Huirong; Fu Pengbin; Gu Liheng; Liu Mingli; , "A framework and QoS based web services discovery," *Software Engineering and Service Sciences (ICSESS), 2010 IEEE International Conference on* , vol., no., pp.755-758, 16-18 July 2010 , DOI = 10.1109/ICSESS.2010.5552261.

[13] Kyriakos Kritikos and Dimitris Plexousakis. 2007. A Semantic QoS-based Web Service Discovery Algorithm for Over-Constrained Demands. In *Proceedings of the Third International Conference on Next Generation Web Services Practices* (NWESP '07). IEEE Computer Society, Washington, DC, USA, 49-54,DOI=http://dx.doi.org/10.1109/NWESP.2007.5

[14] Rashmi Phalnikar, Devesh Jinwala,"Ontology Support For Detecting NFR Conflicts In SOA", In Proceedings Of *2nd Annual International Conference On Software Engineering & Applications (SEA 2011)*,Singapore 2011,Pp75-83.

[15] J Cabot, R Clarisó, D Riera, " UMLtoCSP: a tool for the formal verification of UML/OCL models using constraint programming", In *Proceedings of the twenty-second IEEE/ACM 2007.*

.[16] K. Anastasakis, B. Bordbar, G. Georg, and I. Ray. Uml2alloy: A challenging model transformation. In *ACM/IEEE 10th International Conference on Model Driven Engineering Languages and Systems*, pages 436-450, 2007.

Generation of Efficient Embedded C Code from UML/MARTE Models

L. Lennis[1] and J. Aedo[2]
[12]Department of Electronic Engineering, University of Antioquia, ARTICA, Medellín, Colombia

Abstract—*Nowadays, the increasing complexity of the embedded software development process, demands design techniques capable of addressing such complexity efficiently. In this article, a methodology that follows MDA guidelines for the design of real-time embedded software is presented. This methodology comprises two fundamental activities: application modeling and code generation. Our modeling strategy uses UML and MARTE extensions to elaborate models where the specification of the application functionality is decoupled from the platform execution support. This modeling approach is complemented by a code generation strategy that transforms the application model into efficient C code for execution on embedded systems. A sender-receiver application is used as a case study to illustrate the complete methodology workflow.*

Keywords: UML, MARTE, SRM, code generation, embedded systems, FreeRTOS.

1. Introduction

Due to the constantly increasing complexity of microprocessing ICs, the code-centric approach to design embedded, real-time, software is no longer an effective task. Given that about 80% of embedded systems development cost is attributed to software aspects of design [1], the demand for methods and design techniques that make it possible to address the complexity of the software design process is growing every day.

MDA (Model Driven Architecture) [2] is a design vision, proposed by the Object Management Group (OMG), that promises to reduce time and effort to develop portable and high quality software for execution platforms such as real time embedded systems. Modeling, aids in understanding software application functionality through the mechanism of abstraction, while the code that implements such functionality, in a specific platform, is automatically obtained "generated" from the models. Nonetheless, an effective approach to the practice of MDA is only possible with the support of tools that automatically transform the model into the application code. In MDA, models are constructed using the Unified Modeling Language (UML). Since UML was conceived as a general purpose modeling language, it lacks the expressive power to address the Real Time Embedded Systems (RTES) domain. This shortcoming was alleviated with the standardization of the profile for Modeling and Analysis of Real Time and Embedded systems (MARTE) [3]. SRM (Software Resource Modeling) is a profile contained within MARTE, that enables the description of real time operating system and framework APIs via UML model libraries. The purpose of the article is to illustrate a methodology for embedded software application modeling in sensor monitoring and control applications, using MDA and SRM guidelines, as well as our proposed code generation strategy by which C language code for a real time framework is obtained.

This paper is organized as follows: in section 2 previous work in this area of study is overviewed; section 3 introduces the SRM sub profile of MARTE; in section 4 the modeling and code generation strategies are described; section 5 presents the case study example and its code generation results and, finally, the article is concluded in section 6.

2. Related Work

Adopting the MDA design vision promises some advantages. One, is minimizing errors and coding effort to implement the application thanks to automatic code generation [4]. Nevertheless, research is needed to improve the results of the automatic generation process given that "source code generation is an immature technique that is either very restrained or very unoptimized" [5].

Two main approaches are identified in the literature for code generation in a model based design context: visitor based and template based code generation [6]. Templates are code fragments composed of static text (code) and parameterized text. The parameterized text is later replaced by expressions in the target language resulting in a source code file. It is remarked in [6] that the template based technique has advantages over the visitor based generation, since templates resemble closely the code to be generated and, besides, they are understandable and easy to design.

A generalized technique that uses template based code generation for embedded application design, is described in [7], [5] and [8]: since UML models are stored in a textual, standard, format, denominated XMI (XML Metadata Interchange) in order to be interchangeable between modeling tools, this technique uses an XMI to XML mapping through XSLT[1] transformations in order to extract key information

[1]XSLT (Extensible Style sheet Language Transformations): It is an XML based language that enables transformations of this kind of documents to other formats such as different XML schema, HTML and others.

from the UML models (e.g., variable names, class names, MARTE stereotypes and others). Then, the resulting XML file is used to build a tree structure, more precisely a Document Object Model (DOM), which is later used by a template engine (e.g., Freemaker) to generate the code according to pre-established templates for a given language (e.g., C++/SystemC, Java, etc). "Unfortunately, using XMI and XSLT has scalability limitations. Manual implementation of model transformations in XSLT quickly leads to non maintainable implementations because of the verbosity and poor readability of XMI and XSLT" [6].

Code generation frameworks that do not use XSLT are available, most notably Acceleo [9], JET [10] and Xpand [11] which are all part of the eclipse modeling tools ecosystem. Particularly, Acceleo is an implementation of the MOF Model to Text transformation language standard issued by OMG [12] and UML 2.x models built with various modeling tools are compatible with it. Code generators have been developed with Acceleo for the generation of Modelica code [13] from ModelicaML (UML profile for Modelica) and C++/SystemC from UML/MARTE models [14], however MARTE::SRM utilization in the models and C code generation for embedded prototypes using this framework is scarcely explored.

Commercial tools that provide support for MARTE and code generation for embedded systems are Rational Rhapsody Developer [15] and Artisan Studio [16] but these are closed source and are not available for most of researchers due to its high cost.

Compared to prior efforts and tools available, our work specifically aims to enable the UML modeling of RTES applications and its automatic transformation into C language source code according to MARTE::SRM and MDA guidelines. Moreover, since standard UML 2.x features and MARTE stereotypes are used, any tools that support those standards can be used to construct the models. Full code generation, for deployment on real embedded prototypes is achieved using eclipse integrated tools such as Papyrus [17] for modeling and Acceleo which implements the MOF Model to text transformation (code generation) standard.

3. SRM Overview

SRM is a sub profile of MARTE that provides facilities for building UML model libraries that describe software execution platforms (e.g., Real Time Operating Systems, RTOS, or real-time frameworks) APIs in a standard way. It provides standard stereotypes for addressing concerns such as concurrent execution contexts (e.g., tasks, interrupts), interaction between concurrent application components for communication or synchronization (e.g., mutexes, queues, semaphores, etc.) and hardware/software resource intermediation (e.g., driver or memory management) [3].

The SRM profile can be used in processes where platform modeling is important (e.g., the MDA Y-Chart) and it covers RTOS concerns with low level of details to enable generative approaches (code generation) from the models [18]. A complete review of the SRM profile is beyond the scope of this article. A thorough description is presented in [18] and [3].

4. Methodology

This embedded software application design workflow is based on the MDA Y-Chart process in which "a platform independent model of the software (PIM) is transformed into a platform specific model (PSM); given a platform description model (PDM)" [18]. In this scheme, the SRM sub profile of MARTE is used in the construction of the execution software platform model (PDM) in order to describe its resources and services. The automatically generated code, obtained from an application model is going to be executed in hardware platforms with restricted computational resources, i.e., with a few kilobytes of RAM and FLASH and limited processing power. For this reason, the target language chosen for the code generation was C, and the selected software execution platform was the FreeRTOS [19], which is a real-time and lightweight micro-kernel also written in C.

4.1 Modeling Strategy

In the rest of the article the PIM will be referred as the Analysis Model, the PDM as the Platform Model and the PSM as the Specific Application Model. The following subsections illustrate our approach for the construction of the aforementioned models (Analysis, Platform and Application models). Papyrus [17] is used as the tool for model construction, given its support for the MARTE stereotypes and integration with the Eclipse modeling tools ecosystem.

4.1.1 The Analysis Model

This model contains the functional specification of the embedded software application. It is designed to be independent of the platform[2], i.e., it can be ported between platforms without change [18]. In our case, the language chosen to specify the actions in the model was the C language (ANSI C), so this model remains independent among the platforms that support such language [4].

This model uses different but complementary UML views or diagrams. The structural view provides information of the elements conforming an application and specifies the relationships between them. The dynamic view defines the behavior and interaction between structural components. In our approach, the class diagram is used to specify attributes and operations for the structural entities of the application, while the dynamic aspect of the model is specified via the activity diagram which is used to define the body of class

[2]A platform is a set of technological resources that provide a specific functionality. Any application supported by the platform can make use of such functionality regardless of how it is implemented [2].

operations (methods) and the state machine diagram is used to model the behavior of reactive classes.

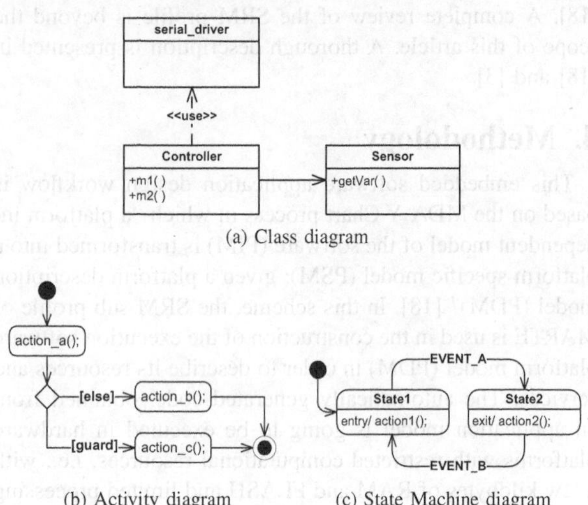

(a) Class diagram

(b) Activity diagram (c) State Machine diagram

Fig. 1: UML diagrams used in the Analysis Model

Figure 1a depicts an example class diagram. Empty classes mean that its code is available (legacy code), otherwise their attributes and operations should be specified as well. Usage relationships handle class dependencies with external (existing) libraries or data types. Alternatively, common association relationships between classes can be used. Class operation behavior is defined by means of an associated activity diagram to the operation (Figure 1b shows an example of an activity diagram). If the class has a reactive behavior it should be specified in an associated state machine diagram to the class. Figure 1c shows an example of a state machine diagram. In state machines, transitions between states are triggered by event occurrences. Entry or exit actions can be defined for a state, i.e., actions that execute at the moment of entering or exiting the state.

4.1.2 The Platform Model

This is the model library where all platform resources and APIs necessary to construct the application are defined [20]. In our proposed approach a decision was made to design a framework that better matches the application domain (sensor monitoring applications). Lee [21] defines a framework as a set of constraints on components of the execution platform such that a set of benefits result from those constraints. The framework designed is based on the active object design pattern which combines the benefits of preemptive multitasking operating systems and the event driven programming paradigm [22]. "Active objects are nothing more than individual tasks with their own event queues" [22]. The designed framework has the following concurrent components: reactive tasks, interrupts, and algorithmic tasks. The reactive task (a.k.a active object, i.e., it owns an event queue) is where state machine, reactive, behavior executes. Events, if present, are extracted from the queue in order of arrival (FIFO) and dispatched to the state machine, otherwise the reactive task enters a blocking state. There is also an algorithmic task resource in which periodic, real-time, behavior can be scheduled for execution. Algorithmic tasks and hardware interrupts can send asynchronous messages (events) to reactive tasks, and reactive tasks can communicate between them in a similar fashion, but not with algorithmic tasks or interrupts given that they do not own a queue for the reception of event messages. The benefits of constraining the software platform with the framework is improving application concurrency and simplifying synchronization complexity among tasks by using asynchronous message passing (events) instead of semaphores and mutexes, besides it also simplifies the process of code generation. A selection of SRM stereotypes was made in order to properly characterize the framework's resources. Table 1 shows the selected stereotypes and their semantic.

Table 1: Selected SRM stereotypes

Stereotype	Semantic
swSchedulableResource	encapsulated sequences of actions which execute concurrently.
messageComResorce	communication resource used to exchange messages.
interruptResource	computing context to execute user delivered routines.
EntryPoint	supplies the routine executed in the context of a concurrent resource.

Figure 2, depicts the UML model of the framework created using the SRM profile and the FreeRTOS API. The SRM stereotypes «`swSchedulableResource`», «`messageComResource`» and «`interruptResource`», are used to denote, respectively, concurrent, communication and interrupt resources of the software, FreeRTOS based, platform.

4.1.3 The Specific Application Model

In this model, the mapping of the functionality onto the platform takes place. First, the Platform Model needs to be imported, then the Specific Application model is constructed by instantiating and initializing the resources defined in the Platform Model. Also, the binding of the Application with the Analysis Model is realized by connecting instances (objects) of the Platform Model with instances of the Analysis Model by means of «`EntryPoint`» stereotyped dependency relationships [20]. The later step, specifies which function behavior (routine) from an object defined in the Analysis Model is going to be executed in a concurrent resource of the framework, i.e., reactive or algorithmic task. Figure 3 illustrates the process of linking Analysis and Application models using the «`EntryPoint`» stereotype.

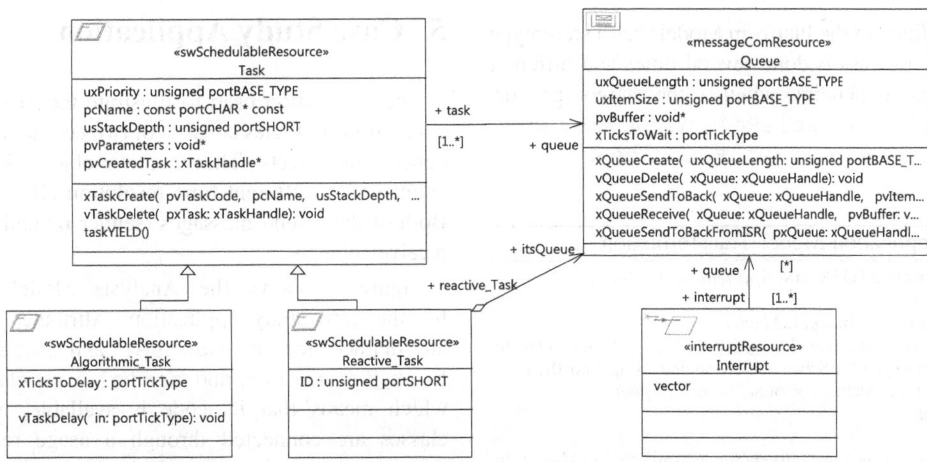

Fig. 2: Platform Model (Tagged Values not shown due to space limitations).

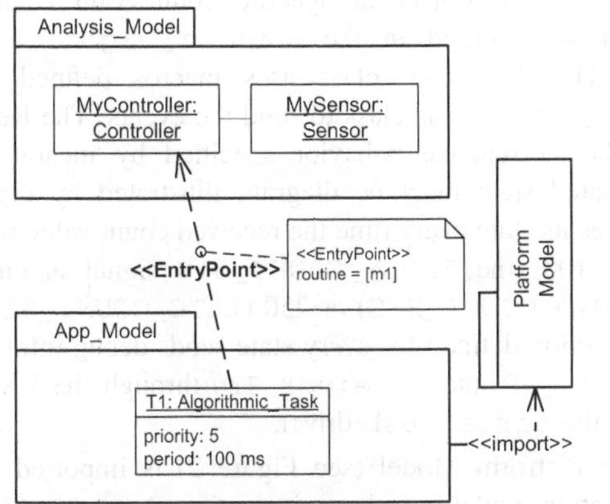

Fig. 3: Binding the Specific Application Model (bottom) with the Analysis Model.

4.2 Code Generation Strategy

The code generation strategy follows a template based approach using Acceleo. All models are transformed into code by executing a chain of Acceleo template scripts.

Algorithm 1 shows the pseudocode for the transformation of the Analysis Model into C code. The `GenerateStructure` template receives the Analysis Model as input parameter. Then, there is an iteration over all classes that are present inside the model and if attributes or associations are defined for that class, the `GenerateHeader` template is called with that class as an argument. Also, if class operations are defined the `GenerateImplementation` template is invoked in order to create the corresponding C file implementation of that class.

The `GenHeader` template is responsible for generating the necessary dependencies according to association and usage relationships for the particular class. It then generates a structure composed by the attributes and pointers to associated classes. Also, prototypes for the operations are generated. If the class has state machine associated behavior, an enumeration with the sate machine signals (event names) is created and the includes to auxiliary state machine libraries are also generated.

Algorithm 1 Analysis Model Transformation

```
template GENERATESTRUCTURE(AnalysisModel)
    for all Class ∈ AnalysisModel do
        if attributes or associations not empty then
            GENHEADER(Class)
        else if behavior not empty then
            GENIMPLEMENTATION(Class)
        end if
    end for
end template
```

The `GenImplementation` template generates the inclusion of the corresponding header files and the implementation for class owned operations (methods). The methods of a class, are generated by transforming a subset of the associated activity diagram into a sequence of statements in the C language. For the classes that have state machine defined behavior, a script is used to transform the associated state machine diagram into C code conforming to the finite UML state machine implementation proposed by Samek [23].

The Specific Application Model transformation, where the application main file is generated is illustrated by Algorithm 2. First, a file named "main.c" is opened for writing, then all application dependencies are included by calling the `GenIncludes` template, which selects the instantiated objects belonging to the Analysis Model and includes their header files. Then, an iteration takes place over all instances defined in the Application Model in order to ask if its classifier (the class defined in the Platform Model) has a stereotype application. This process is done several times and different actions are taken, depending whether the stereotype corresponds to «swSchedulableResource», «messageComResource» or «interruptResource».

Algorithm 2 Application Model Transformation

```
template GENERATERTOSMAIN(ApplicationModel)
    file ('main.c')
        GENINCLUDES(AnalysisModel)
        for all InstanceSpec.classifier ∈ ApplicationModel do
            if Stereotype 'swSchedulableResource' is applied then
                GENTASKPROTOCOLS(InstanceSpec)
            end if
        end for
        for all InstanceSpec.classifier ∈ ApplicationModel do
            if Stereotype 'MessageComResource' is applied then
                GENQUEUEHANDLES(InstanceSpec)
            end if
        end for
        INSTANTIATEOBJECTS(ApplicationModel)
        void main(void){
        for all InstanceSpec.classifier ∈ ApplicationModel do
            if Stereotype 'MessageComResource' is applied then
                GENQUEUECREATION(InstanceSpec)
            end if
        end for
        for all InstanceSpec.classifier ∈ ApplicationModel do
            if Stereotype 'swSchedulableResource' is applied then
                GENTASKCREATION(InstanceSpec)
            end if
        end for
        }
        GENALGTASKBODY(ApplicationModel)
        GENREACTIVETASKBODY(ApplicationModel)
        for all InstanceSpec.classifier ∈ ApplicationModel do
            if Stereotype 'interruptResource' is applied then
                GENINTERRUPTS(InstanceSpec)
            end if
        end for
    end file
end template
```

Note, that inside the main function, the creation of tasks and queues takes place, this is done by GenQueueCreation and GenTaskCreation, this templates extract the initialization values from the application model instances and generate the C statements that realize this task with the FreeRTOS APIs. Reactive and algorithmic task bodies are generated by GenAlgTaskBody and GenReactiveTaskBody respectively. Finally, any interrupts instantiated in the Application Model are generated by GenInterrupts.

Since the C language is not object oriented by design, the resulting code from the generation process was designed in an object oriented fashion, in the sense that every method of a class receives as input parameter a pointer to a structure containing all the attributes defined, for that specific class, in the class diagram, which results in a natural mapping from the UML diagrams to the code.

5. Case Study Application

The application used to illustrate the modeling and code generation strategies consists of two counter and two receiver concurrent objects. The counting objects keep an internal count with a different time resolution (10 ms and 100 ms). Both of them send messages (sender ID and count value) to receiver objects.

Figure 5 shows the Analysis Model class diagram for the case study application. Attributes and operations are defined for the Counter and Receiver classes. task_intercomm and serial_usb classes are empty which means that its code is available. Note, that both classes are connected through a usage relationship with the CountEvt data type. This means that this type definition is known by both classes. CountEvt represents the event message that a Counter object will send to a Receiver object at specific count values, this behavior is specified in the Counter_algorithm routine. The Counter class uses macros defined in the task_intercomm class to send the events. The Receiver, that has a reactive behavior specified by means of the associated state machine diagram illustrated by Figure 4, changes its state every time the received count value matches either 100 (the EARLY_COUNT_SIG signal is emitted), 150 (MID_COUNT_SIG) or 250 (LATE_COUNT_SIG). An entry action defined for every state sends debug information (Sender_ID and Receiver_ID) through the USB port using the serial_usb driver.

The Platform Model (see Figure 2) is imported by the application model in order to instantiate the resources of the framework. Then, as illustrated by Figure 6, two Counter and two Receiver objects are instantiated in the Analysis Model and four tasks are instantiated in the Application Model; two reactive tasks and two algorithmic tasks. The Receiver_Dispatch routine (this routine dispatches received events to state machines) is linked for execution inside reactive tasks and the Counter_Algorithm routine, that generates and sends count events to reactive tasks, is linked with both algorithmic tasks.

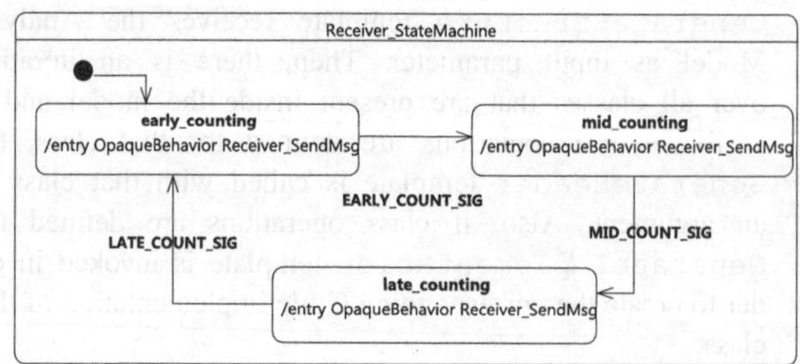

Fig. 4: Receiver state machine.

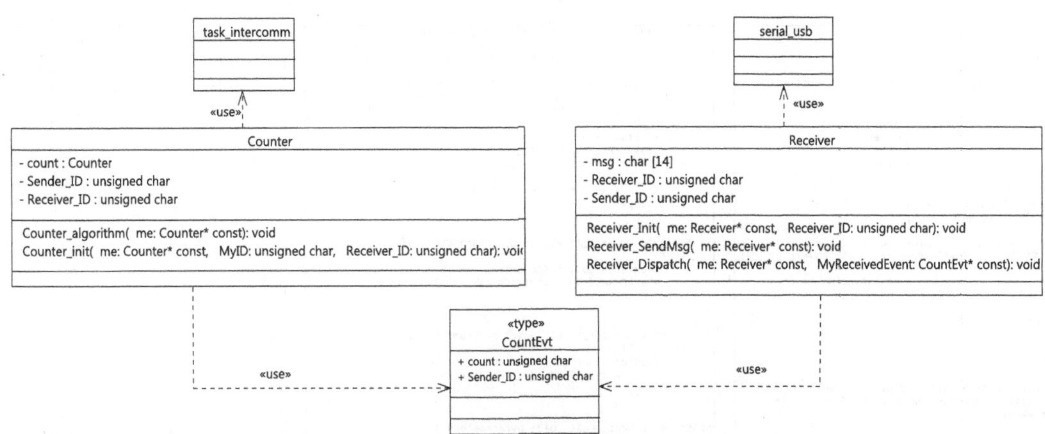

Fig. 5: Analysis model class diagram for the case study.

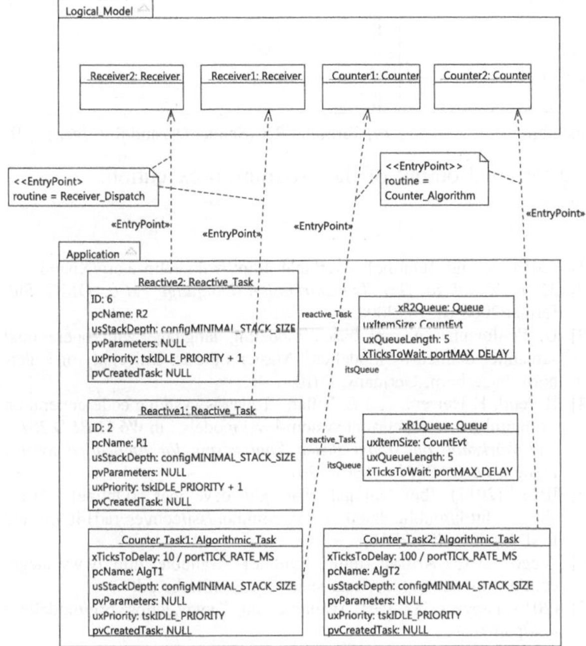

Fig. 6: Linking the Specific Application Model (bottom) with the Analysis Model for the case study.

5.1 Results

The generated code was compiled with the Code Composer Studio v4.2 compiler for the MSP430F5438A microcontroller from Texas Instruments, with no optimizations. The correct execution of the generated application was tested on the TI MSP-EXP430F5438 evaluation board. Figure 7, illustrates portions of the generated code, particularly, the main function, the implementation of algorithmic and reactive tasks and the reception of messages in a PC terminal.

The FLASH memory consumption obtained from analyzing the ".map" file, generated by the linker, reveals that the complete application takes 8414 bytes of which 1338 bytes correspond to the generated code and libraries (drivers) that provide application support while the remaining 7076 bytes correspond to the FreeRTOS execution support and msp430 support libraries. RAM consumption is 1550 bytes total of which 59 bytes are used by the main application file, 1026 bytes represent the user configured amount of heap and the rest is used by the FreeRTOS execution support.

6. Conclusions and Future Work

In this paper a methodology workflow for UML modeling of embedded systems applications, using SRM and MDA guidelines, was illustrated. Also, the subsequent process of automatic model transformation (code generation) into compilable C code was demonstrated. Both processes, application modeling and code generation, were carried out with open source tools, Papyrus and Acceleo, which are part of the eclipse modeling tools.

The main advantage of including the SRM profile in the design methodology is that execution platforms can be easily described independently of application functionality and a stereotype guided strategy for code generation can be implemented.

A framework was designed in order to restrict the platform model to the active object model of computation, this decision simplifies synchronization complexity of concurrent components of the framework but the application domain is limited to event oriented, reactive embedded applications such as sensor monitoring and control or sensor network systems. The memory footprint of the generated code is appropriate for execution in memory constrained microcontrollers generally used in sensor monitoring applications or wireless sensor nodes.

Future research involves the study of debugging strategies that can be incorporated into the methodology workflow,

```c
/* Application Includes */
#include "Receiver.h"
#include "Counter.h"

static void prvSetupHardware( void );

/* Task protocols */
static void Reactive1( void* pvParameters );
static void Counter_Task1( void* pvParameters );
static void Reactive2( void* pvParameters );
static void Counter_Task2( void* pvParameters );

/* Queue Handle Creation */
static xQueueHandle xR2Queue = NULL;
static xQueueHandle xR1Queue = NULL;

/*Automatically Generated Task_Queue Look Up Table*/
Task_Queue_LUT TQL[2] = { {&xR1Queue , 2} , {&xR2Queue , 6} };

/* Event(s) and object(s) (Structs) instantiation */
Counter Counter2;
Receiver Receiver1;
Receiver Receiver2;
Counter Counter1;

void main( void )
{
    /* Configure the peripherals used by this application
     * and initialize state machine objects.*/
    prvSetupHardware();

    /* Create the queues used by tasks and interrupts to
    interchange data*/
    xR2Queue = xQueueCreate( 5 , sizeof( CountEvt) );
    xR1Queue = xQueueCreate( 5 , sizeof( CountEvt) );

    /* If the queue could not be created then don't
    Create any tasks that might attempt to use the queue. */
    if( ( xR2Queue != NULL ) && ( xR1Queue != NULL ) ){

        /* Create the tasks*/
        xTaskCreate( Reactive1, ( signed char * ) "R1",
                     configMINIMAL_STACK_SIZE,      NULL,
                     tskIDLE_PRIORITY + 1,          NULL );

        xTaskCreate( Counter_Task1, ( signed char * ) "AlgT1",
                     configMINIMAL_STACK_SIZE,      NULL,
                     tskIDLE_PRIORITY,              NULL );
```

(a) task creation (continues in (b))

```c
        xTaskCreate( Reactive2, ( signed char * ) "R2",
                     configMINIMAL_STACK_SIZE,      NULL,
                     tskIDLE_PRIORITY + 1,          NULL );

        xTaskCreate( Counter_Task2, ( signed char * ) "AlgT2",
                     configMINIMAL_STACK_SIZE,      NULL,
                     tskIDLE_PRIORITY,              NULL );

        /* Start the scheduler. */
        vTaskStartScheduler();
    }

    /*If all is well then this line will never be reached.*/
    for( ;; );
}

static void Counter_Task1( void* pvParameters ){
    for( ;; ){
        Counter_algorithm(&Counter1);
        vTaskDelay( 10 / portTICK_RATE_MS );
    }
}

static void Counter_Task2( void* pvParameters ){
    for( ;; ){
        Counter_algorithm(&Counter2);
        vTaskDelay( 100 / portTICK_RATE_MS );
    }
}

static void Reactive1( void* pvParameters ){
    CountEvt ReceivedCountEvt;
    for( ;; ){
        xQueueReceive( xR1Queue,
                       &ReceivedCountEvt,
                       portMAX_DELAY );
        Receiver_Dispatch( &Receiver1 , &ReceivedCountEvt );
    }
}

static void Reactive2( void* pvParameters ){
    CountEvt ReceivedCountEvt;
    for( ;; ){
        xQueueReceive( xR2Queue,
                       &ReceivedCountEvt,
                       portMAX_DELAY );
        Receiver_Dispatch( &Receiver2 , &ReceivedCountEvt );
    }
}
```

(b) task implementation

```
Communication
ASCII | HEX | Decimal | Binary |

10:55:23.003 [RX] - R=2 S=1<LF>
R=6 S=2<LF>
R=2 S=1<LF>
R=2 S=1<LF>
R=2 S=1<LF>
R=6 S=2<LF>
R=2 S=1<LF>
R=2 S=1<LF>
R=2 S=1<LF>
R=6 S=2<LF>
R=2 S=1<LF>
R=6 S=2<LF>
R=2 S=1<LF>
R=2 S=1<LF>
R=2 S=1<LF>
R=2 S=1<LF>
R=6 S=2<LF>
R=2 S=1<LF>
R=2 S=1<LF>
R=2 S=1<LF>
R=6 S=2<LF>
R=2 S=1<LF>
R=2 S=1<LF>
R=6 S=2<LF>
R=2 S=1<LF>
R=2 S=1<LF>
R=2 S=1<LF>
R=6 S=2<LF>
R=2 S=1<LF>
R=2 S=1<LF>
R=2 S=1<LF>
```

(c) Terminal RX (Sender (S) and Receiver (R) IDs)

Fig. 7: Sections of the generated main application file and terminal output of the program in execution.

using the sequence diagram, in order to verify, in real-time the correctness of the generated application. One possible alternative is to generate instrumented code that can reproduce a sequence diagram by sending information of the application execution status to a PC application.

References

[1] ITRS, "International technology roadmap for semiconductors, design," ITRS, Tech. Rep., 2011. [Online]. Available: http://www.itrs.net/Links/2011ITRS/2011Chapters/2011Design.pdf

[2] OMG. (2003, June) Mda guide version 1.0.1. Object Management Group. [Online]. Available: http://www.omg.org/cgi-bin/doc?omg/03-06-01.pdf

[3] *UML Profile for MARTE: Modeling and Analysis of Real-Time Embedded Systems*, OMG Std. formal/2011-06-02, 2011.

[4] M. Maranzana, J.-F. Ponsignon, J.-L. Sourrouille, and F. Bernier, "Timing performances of automatically generated code using mda approaches," in *FDL*. ECSI, 2004, pp. 252–12.

[5] L. G. Murillo, "Bridging the Gap Between Model Driven Engineering and HW/SW Codesign," Master's thesis, University of Lugano, ALaRI Institute, Lugano, Switzerland, 2009.

[6] K. Czarnecki and S. Helsen, "Feature-based survey of model transformation approaches," *IBM Systems Journal*, vol. 45, no. 3, pp. 621–645, 2006.

[7] B. Correa, J. Eusse, and J. Vélez, "High level system-on-chip design using uml and systemc," in *Electronics, Robotics and Automotive Mechanics Conference, 2007. CERMA 2007*. IEEE, 2007, pp. 740–745.

[8] S. Villa, J. Villa, J. Yepes, and J. Aedo, "Virtual platform generation tool for embedded systems design." in *Engineering Research and Practice, The 11th International Conference on*, 2012.

[9] (2013) Acceleo. [Online]. Available: http://www.eclipse.org/acceleo/

[10] (2013) Jet. [Online]. Available: http://www.eclipse.org/modeling/m2t/?project=jet

[11] (2013) Xpand. [Online]. Available: http://wiki.eclipse.org/Xpand

[12] *MOF Model to Text Transformation Language, v1.0*, OMG Std. formal/2008-01-16, 2008.

[13] U. Pohlmann, "A uml based modeling language with operational semantics defined by modelica," Master's thesis, University of Paderborn, Paderborn, Germany, 2010.

[14] P. Penil, F. Herrera, and E. Villar, "Towards systemc code generation from uml/marte concurrent system-level models," in *W6 M-BED 2011: 2nd Workshop on Model Based Engineering for Embedded System Design. DATE 2011*. IEEE, 2011.

[15] IBM. (2013) Ibm rational rhapsody developer. [Online]. Available: http://public.dhe.ibm.com/common/ssi/ecm/en/rad14043usen/RAD14043USEN.PDF

[16] Atego. (2013) Artisan studio. [Online]. Available: http://www.atego.com/downloads/support/data-sheets/ArtisanStudio.pdf

[17] (2013) Papyrus. [Online]. Available: http://www.eclipse.org/modeling/mdt/papyrus/

[18] F. Thomas, S. Gérard, J. Delatour, and F. Terrier, "Software realtime resource modeling," *Embedded Systems Specification and Design Languages*, pp. 169–182, 2008.

[19] R. Barry. (2013) The freertos project. [Online]. Available: http://www.freertos.org

[20] F. Thomas, J. Delatour, F. Terrier, and S. Gérard, "Towards a framework for explicit platform-based transformations," in *Object Oriented Real-Time Distributed Computing ISORC, 2008 11th IEEE International Symposium on*. IEEE, 2008, pp. 211–218.

[21] E. Lee *et al.*, "Computing for embedded systems," in *IEEE Intrumentation and Measurement Technology Conference Proceedings*, vol. 3. IEEE; 1999, 2001, pp. 1830–1837.

[22] J. Kopjak and J. Kovacs, "Event-driven control program models running on embedded systems," in *Applied Computational Intelligence and Informatics (SACI), 2011 6th IEEE International Symposium on*. IEEE, 2011, pp. 323–326.

[23] M. Samek, *Practical UML statecharts in C/C++: event-driven programming for embedded systems*. Newnes, 2008.

An Object-Oriented Framework for Digital Voting

Patricia Dousseau Cabral
Graduate Program in Computer Science
Federal University of Santa Catarina
UFSC
Florianópolis, Brazil
dousseau@inf.ufsc.br

Ricardo Pereira e Silva
Department of Informatics and Statistics
Federal University of Santa Catarina
UFSC
Florianópolis, Brazil
ricardo@inf.ufsc.br

Roberto Silvino da Cunha
Labsoft
Federal University of Santa Catarina
UFSC
Florianópolis, Brazil
rsc@inf.ufsc.br

Abstract— Voting is a mechanism widely used in decision making and are commonly employed by governments and businesses. The confidence in the voting process is fundamental to the credibility of the result. Increasingly polls are conducted over the internet due to its practicality and ease of use. But this practice brings new challenges, such as denial of service, confidence in the system, and coercion of voters. Several online voting systems have been proposed, but implementing and evaluating them is a difficult and complex task. To facilitate the development and evaluation of these systems, as well as the idealization of new digital voting protocols, we developed an object-oriented framework. With it you can extend systems and protocols in an easier way, allowing focus on the most important points of development.

Digital voting, object-oriented framework, voting protocols, voting systems

I.Introduction

In recent years new vonting alternatives have emerged, such as online elections. It brings benefits such as a faster and more efficient tally, making it easier to cast the vote, eliminating the need of commuting to the polling station, possibility of process verification and reducing costs. But new threats can emerge, such as ease of coercion of voters and new opportunities for fraud. To reduce these risks, there are several safety requirements that the system must meet [1]:

- Accuracy: ensure that only valid ballots will be counted in the tally and cannot be changed or duplicated.

- Uniqueness: ensuring that only authorized voters participate in the voting, only voting once.

- Privacy: not allowing to link the vote to the voter (anonymity), not allowing knowing the option selected by the voter (non-coercion) and all ballots must be kept secret until the end of the tally (impartiality)

- Verifiability: there are two types of verifiability: individual, that allows the voter to verify that their vote was correctly determined; and universal, which shows that all the votes were counted correctly.

There is an inherent difficulty in meeting all these requirements since some tend to be self-exclusionary, such as the difficulty in proving that the vote of the voter was properly counted while not revealing their voting option. Or difficulty in allowing only authorized voters to cast a ballot without associating the vote with the voter.

Several voting protocols have been proposed in literature trying to satisfy the requirements mentioned above. Besides the difficulty of designing new protocols, there is the difficulty of implementing a complete system that uses it to be able to validate and analyze the proposed protocol. To facilitate this process, we developed an object-oriented framework for systems and digital voting protocols to simplify the deployment and management of online voting.

II. Comparative study

Several of the proposed protocols which are developed for specific situations did not meet all the requirements that make an election safe. This is due to the difficulty in meeting all requirements. An example is the Helios voting system [2], which is suitable for elections where voting should be secret, but where coercion is not a major threat. In this line of work we can cite polls for clubs, software communities and student communities. The system described by Chuan-Kun Wu and Ramesh Sankaranarayana [3] is suitable for coercion free elections, because the system surpasses this threat by allowing the voter to vote several times. Making it harder to force the voter to choose a particular option, since they can change it later. There are several proposed protocols and voting systems, as can be seen in [2] [7][8] [9] [10].Protocols structures are well formed and usually small changes in its logic can compromise system security. It is not an easy task to change a part of the protocol or extend it without considering the impact across its logic. Thus, typically they are not configurable, and neither the systems that use them, since they are dependent. So we have systems that are inflexible and difficult to reuse if you want to change their operating logic.

A. Voting primitives

According to Jörg Helbach and Jörg Schwenk [6] voting systems use different technologies for its implementation, the most used are:

- Homomorphic encryption: allows the sum of the votes and decryption of encrypted result as follows $E(x1) + E(x2) = E(x1 + x2)$ where x1 and x2 are ballots. By way of this technique is not necessary to decipher each vote individually, making it more difficult to associate the voter and their vote, making it easier to proof that all ballots were counted correctly, and all ballots received were counted.

- Mixnet: shuffles the order of arrival of the ballots guaranteeing anonymity of the voters, making it impossible to determine the order of voting.
- Blind signature: allows signing documents without knowing their contents. This is useful in validating ballots so that the system can validate it without knowing the choice of the voter.
- Bulletin Board: works like a mural of information, allowing sensitive data to be safely released. It can be used to publish the election results, because it ensures that only authorized entities publish information, and ensures that the data has not been changed or deleted. [11]
- Asymmetric encryption: allows encryption and signatures of the contents in a secure way. To facilitate the use of asymmetric cryptography, a repository of keys and digital certificates are used, which are both implemented in the framework.
- Symmetric encryption: allows secure encryption of content, using only one key instead of two.
- Hash: generates unique identifiers making it easy to identify objects and analyzing if changes were made.

In the developed framework these technologies were considered as different primitives that will be used in the protocol. You can insert and remove the primitives from the structure of the framework in specific places without major impacts.

B. Motivation

Given the fact there is a large number of proposed protocols and the difficulty to validate them, since a new system is required to be built whenever you want to validate a specific change, an object-oriented framework for protocols is a good idea. Nevertheless, there are not many documented proposals. David Lundin [4] proposes a digital voting system based on components that can be interchanged and audited, so that you can add and remove components without impacting other parts of the system. Such a system ends up being difficult to use, since it is necessary to create a new component every time you want to change something, being necessary to follow all the conventions of the component during its creation.

Stefan Popoveniuc and Poorvi L. Vora [5] propose a framework for voting systems using mixnet and paper ballots. They analyzed four systems whose front-end and back-end can be interchanged. Such a system is restricted to voting using paper ballots and mixnet, additionally in being completely necessary to build the back-end and front-end when you want something different.

The proposed object-oriented framework is more flexible than similar proposals, it allows you to implement specific changes rather than being required to build a component or a front / back end. Moreover, it is modularized and can make changes with little impact on other parts of the framework with a high code reuse, since most of the structure of the voting process is implemented in the framework, and reused every time a new voting system is developed. This is ideal for testing and evaluating new protocols and systems, since minor codes need to be written.

C. Vulnerabilities

Although there are several proposed protocols for digital voting that meet all or some of the requirements mentioned, none is used in a large scale election with high criticality [3]. The reason is that there are several difficulties in making a voting system reliable. According Chuan-Kun Wu and Ramesh Sankaranarayana [3] there are several aspects that make digital voting so complex and vulnerable: reliability in software, reliability on the internet, reliability of database system, confidentiality of electronic votes, detection of double voting, vote buying and internet terrorist attacks.

It is necessary that the authors of protocols and digital voting systems adhere to the above challenges, so that the system can be as reliable as possible. With the framework it is possible to reduce the development cycles and tests, and the maturation of the software becomes more reliable.

III. Framework

For the development of the object-oriented framework was considered the aspects that must be taken into account when envisioning the digital voting system: their vulnerabilities, technologies, potential threats to its integrity and the entire management of an election. Its structure consists of modules that interact with each other. One module is responsible for cryptographic primitives, another for the management of ballots and voting options, authentication, creating protocols, managing users and for managing elections (Figure 3).

A. Functionalities

A digital voting system should provide basic functionalities. Whereas there are in the system administrator, voter, register agent and auditor profiles, we can list the following roles associated with the use cases of Figure 1 and 2.

Administrator: The system administrator is responsible for registering elections and all information about it, such as voting date, title, voting options, etc. These steps are different use cases, since it can be performed at different times.

Voter: have the power to obtain a ballot, cast a ballot, verify that their ballot was counted correctly and check the result. Receiving the ballot and casting the ballot are parts of the voting process that are divided into two stages because they necessarily do not happen together. Checking if the ballot was properly audited takes place in the final stage of the voting which depends on the protocol.

Auditor: the system has two types of auditing. The configuration auditing and result auditing. Every election may or may not enable them, leaving it to the system administrator. If at least one is enabled, it is necessary that at least one auditor is registered in the election. The configuration auditing concerns the data analysis of the election, that is, if all the information registered by the administrator is correct: election title, voting date, voting options, etc. The election can only be made public after the approval of all auditors. Since the result auditing concerns the analysis of the ballot counting and other evidences that the election may issue depending on the protocol, such as evidence that the mixnet shuffle was done correctly. Only after this analysis is that the result can be revealed. If the auditing is rejected by some problem, the election should be canceled because it proves that there was some fault or fraud during the process.

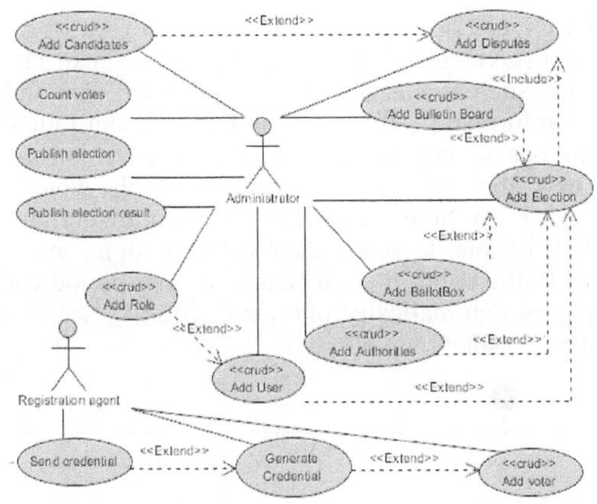

Figure 1. Administrator and register agent use cases

Register agent: Responsible for the registration of voters in a particular election. This function can also be assigned to the administrator, eliminating this role.

Besides the specific use cases for each role, they all have the ability to log into the system and list all elections that they are related.

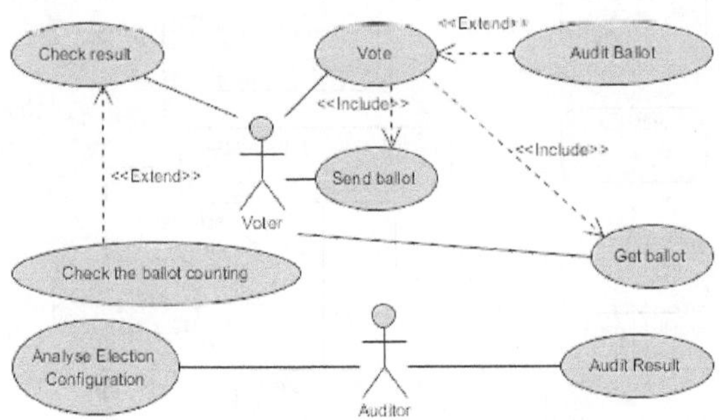

Figure 2. Voter and auditor use cases

B. Development methodology

The domain analysis to develop the framework started with the identification of similarities between different voting protocols described in the literature. For this, we selected the following protocols [2] [7] [8] [9] [10]. These choices have some characteristics relevant to voting systems and constitute a sample of the relevant field of voting protocols. In the case of Helios [2] it has both individual and universal verification. This allows the voter to verify that his vote was correctly casted and also allows the analysis of the vote count. In the case of Three-Ballot-based protocol [7], it was chosen because it makes use of three ballots for voting and three ballot boxes, and the most common is to use only one. Sensus protocol [8] was chosen because it requires three subsystems, validator, pollster and tallier. The Seas protocol [9] is based on the Sensus protocol, with minor modifications intended to eliminate the possibility of authorities voting in the place of voters who abstained from voting. It was an issue found in the Sensus protocol. Finally, the protocol proposed by Ray [10] makes use of three authorities, a ballot distributor, a certifying authority and a voter compiler.

From the domain analysis, it is concluded that it is possible to split a vote in four steps:

- Initialization: optional step, performed if there is need for some protocol initialization, such as the inclusion of previous blank ballots in the ballot box or mixnet creation servers.
- Obtaining a ballot: a step where the voter gets a ballot, and optionally performs the auditing. It is usually anticipated by the authentication process of voting, with some exceptions, as can be seen in [2], where the voter authenticates just in time to cast the ballot, allowing anyone to get a ballot and perform the auditing.
- Casting a ballot: it is the act of voting. A step after the voter selects their voting option, and then send their ballot to the system. Some protocols require that the voter authenticate themselves in this step, for example, Helios [2].
- Tally: a step started after the end of voting, where all votes are counted and the results are announced. This step can also contain the results of the auditing conducted by the auditors of the election.

All these steps may employ some common mechanisms, such as authentication, use of ballots, user profiles, etc.

A common factor was the use of ballots containing the voting options and the definition of roles a user can assume in the system, normally being voters, administrators, register agents, auditors and fiscals. Another key aspect is the role of the authorities. Some systems, such as Helios, use only a controlling authority, which manages the entire voting process: voter authentication, receiving the votes, counting and publishing the results.

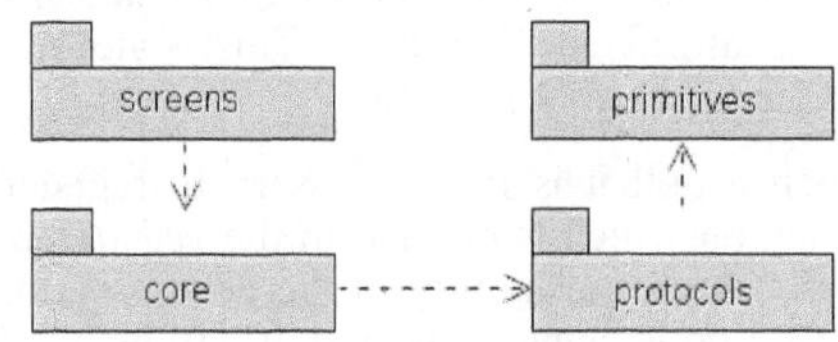

Figure 3. Framework modules

While others, such as [10] distributes the intelligence of the system between three authorities: one to identify the voter and to issue the ballot, another to verify that the ballot was cast and ensure that each voter submits only one ballot and the last for counting the votes and revealing the results.

C. Framework structure

The framework consists of four modules, each responsible for managing an aspect of the voting system, as shown in Figure 3. This division reduces the risk of errors in other modules of the system when performing any change in the framework.

1)Screen

Contains the screens that will be used by system users and a layer between the core system and screens. This middle layer is responsible for identifying which methods are available for each system profile, and it is through it that the screens will have access to features implemented.

2)Core

The system core is the main part of the framework. It manages the operation of the system. It is also responsible for the election, ballot boxes, disputes, voting options, user authentication and the management of user roles and ballots.

3)Protocols

Responsible for various implementations of the protocols that will be used by the elections. They are the heart of the election, being responsible, in large part, by the security of the electoral process. The protocol defines the structure of the ballot and how they will be obtained, how the votes will be counted, how the ballots will be casted, and which cryptographic operations the system will perform during the voting, among other things. You can extend the framework by adding new protocols.

4)Primitives

The framework contains several primitives already implemented, and others can be easily added to the system. They will help you compose a new protocol, and key points of its implementation. Often primitive structures are quite complex and its functioning is quite critical. If they do not work properly, the protocol will not work. An example of this is the mixnet, which requires several distributed servers working in a coordinated way. You can extend the framework by adding new primitives.

D.Electoral System Behavior

There are key stages in the electoral process, such as the period that is allowed to vote and the voting stage where the votes will be counted. A poll consists of 13 states, which can be better visualized in Figure 4. This state machines is included in the framework structure.

To launch a poll it is first necessary to register it in the system, an action which is defined in the *registered* state and that is usually the responsibility of the election administrator. While the election is being registered, it will be available only to the administrator and it is not possible to any other profile to view it. After completion of this step, there are two options: waiting for configuration auditing or not.

If it is not awaiting auditing, it can be published immediately, changing to the state *published* and becoming viewable to all profiles related to that election. In case it is awaiting auditing, after the registration completion the election will be available to the auditors registered in that election in order to check whether the registered data is correct. If all auditors approve its settings, it immediately goes to the state *published*. If at least one auditor reject its settings, then it should return to the state *registered* and once again become editable and corrected by the administrator, to then go back to the state *waiting configuration auditing*, and become non-editable again. These first steps concern the election registration and analysis of its configuration by persons registered in the system. This ensures that the information registered is correct when it is disclosed to the users.

When the election goes to the state *published*, it becomes visible to the voters of that election, so they can check its information such as election title, the election date and other important information. It remains in this state until the start of the voting period, automatically changing to the *started* state. In this new state the election can receive the votes of the voters, i.e., when the election really starts allowing the voters to get their ballots, to select their voting options and to send the ballot to the ballot box. When the voting period ends, the election goes automatically into state *finished*, which makes impossible for voters to vote.

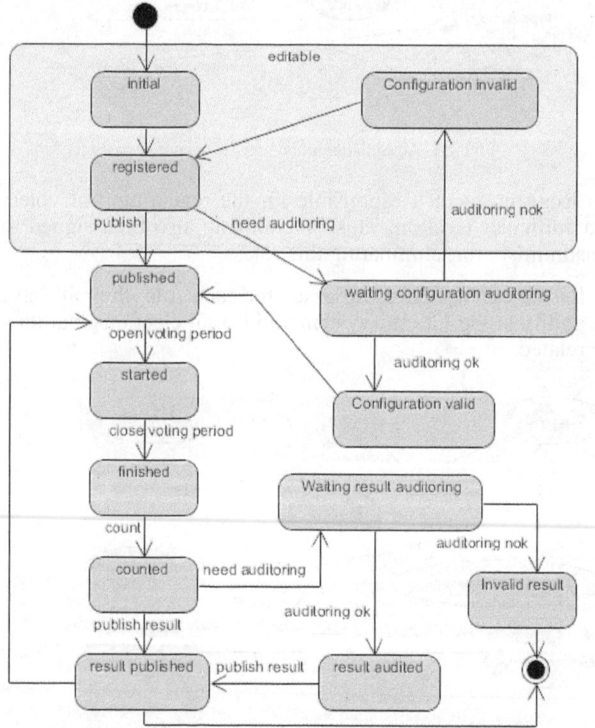

Figure 4. Election state machine

When the election is finished, it is necessary to count the votes, an operation that is performed at the request of the administrator, then changing into the state *counted*. From this state there are two possibilities depending on whether the election allows result auditing or not. If it does not allow, the administrator can publish your result straightaway, making it available to all users. If the election allows auditing of its result, it goes to the state *waiting configuration auditing* and remains there until all auditors have examined the proofs issued during the voting phase that prove that the operations have been performed correctly. This step is important to ensure that it did not occured any failures or frauds during the electoral process, being dependent on the protocol implemented. For example, a protocol that uses network mixture can provide evidence that the shuffle of the ballots took place correctly. If all auditors validate the integrity of the proofs, the results can be published. If at least one auditor rejects them, this indicates that there may have been some error or fraud during the voting, the result will not be published and the election will be terminated.

E.Core behavior

Besides the logic of the electoral process, there are other mechanisms in the system that work to make the framework flexible and reliable. These mechanisms are within the core package, as well as the election.

1)Authentication

Because there are multiple profiles, each has its own defined field of action, which is extremely important to know which events each user is allowed to run. Authentication can be done in different ways and at different times of the voting process. For example, the voter can authenticate himself by using a login and a password, via a valid certificate, a token or by a unique identifier which has been informed to the user. This authentication can also take place at different stages: when the user enters the system, the time they request a ballot or the time they cast a ballot. In the case of the framework it was implemented an authentication by login and password, but is flexible to use other authentication mechanisms.

2)User management

The election process can contain different types of users, each with different requirements and obligations. The most common are voters, administrators, auditors, fiscals and register agents who are responsible for registering voters. This is useful to delegate responsibilities and restrict the field of activity of users. You can, for example, create ballot box fiscals, which will shared a key to decipher the ballots. Thus, only when all fiscals act in a shared way, the tally can be initiated. More profiles and its responsibilities can also be added easily.

3)Ballot management

Ballots facilitate the voting process, because it contains the disputes and their voting options, and also the options selected by the voter. You can perform various operations with a ballot, such as blinding for blind signature, encryption, signing, storage, etc.

The ballot must be a structure flexible enough to allow its use in different ways to meet the needs of each protocol. Hence structure of the ballot is not always trivial, depending on how the disputes and its options are organized and which individual information can be added. To facilitate its creation, a ballot is created and others are copied from the original ballot. If any additional voter data has to be added, like a ballot identifier, it is inserted after the copy.

4)Disputes and voting options

The disputes relate to matters which are voted in the election, and which voting options are available for each subject. It was determined that there are two types of disputes, candidates and plebiscite. The framework allows the creation of new types of disputes and voting options without much impact on the rest of the system. Disputes like plebiscites are open questions with simple answers. Another kind of dispute are candidate ones, that requires a complex structure normally required for candidates. For example, the relationship between candidate, party, coalition and slate.

5)Ballot box

The ballot box is responsible for maintaining the ballots of a specific election, so only those authorized can retrieve them in the same way as physical ballots. They are kept encrypted by the ballot box, to prevent others from reading without permission.

IV. Discussions on experiments results

This section describes the implementation of three protocols, showing what was needed to modify and what was possible to reuse, as well as other aspects of the use of the framework for the creation of digital voting protocols and graphical part of the system.

A.Protocols and primitives

Three protocols have been implemented using the framework. A simplistic protocol, a protocol that makes use of blind signatures, and a protocol that makes use of mixnet [1]. If the developer wants to change some aspect of the system, they should override the responsible class and implement it following the structure of that class. Below is an example of protocols developed and what classes were necessary to create or override.

1)Simplistic protocol

For the implementation of the simplistic protocol it was necessary to override only the Protocol class and two of its methods. From 306 classes in the system, only one was overridden and 2 of its 25 methods were overridden and no new methods were created. Practically all the necessary infrastructure to implement the simplistic protocol is already developed. There is already all the basic structure of a digital voting system, including the administration, voting and presentation results screens.

2)Protocol with blind signature

The protocol that makes use of blind signature requires more interaction with the voting system, since it is necessary to blind and unblind the ballot on the user machine. For this it was necessary to implement an applet that perform these operations reliably.

To implement the protocol with blind signatures, it was necessary to override the Protocol class and two of its methods, besides being necessary to create three more. It was also necessary to create an applet to blind the voter ballot before sending it to the system to sign. In this case it was necessary to create a different interface with the voter, which was able to perform certain cryptographic operations on the users machine before sending it to the authority in order to increase confidence in the whole process.

The reuse in this case remains quite high. From 306 classes in the system, only one was overridden, with 4 of its 25 methods overridden and three new ones were created. Besides, it was necessary to create a new class with three new methods.

3)Protocol with mixnet

The protocol that uses mixnet was implemented so that the network servers were distributed between multiple machines. Before the start of the election, it was necessary to create the mixnet and start the servers. These actions were not required in other protocols. It was also necessary to encrypt the votes with the system key before sending them to the mixnet.

To implement the protocol with mixnet it was needed to override the protocol class and two of its methods. There was no need to create new classes or methods.

B.System screens

The screens are important channels of communication between users and the system. The framework contains the implementation of the main screens that will be used in the voting systems developed, and will allows developers to implement their own when necessary.

One of the main screens of the system is the election registration screen used by the administrator. It contains all necessary fields to complete registration for a full election, separated into different stages, as can be seen in Figure 5.

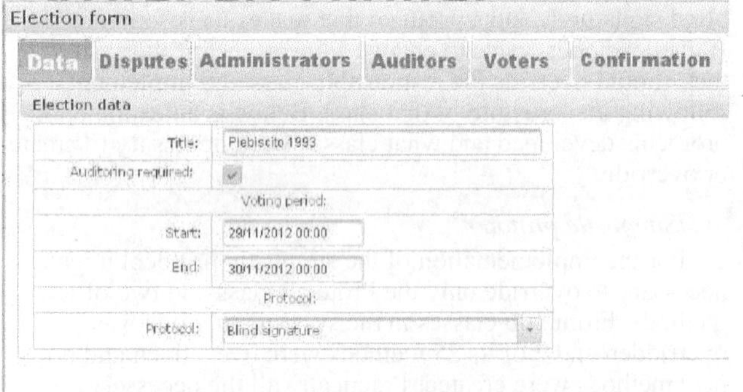

Figure 5. First screen of election registration

In the first step, the administrator registers the basic information of an election. After that, you can register disputes, administrators (if there are others besides him), auditors and voters. After entering all the data, it is necessary to view and confirm the inserted information.

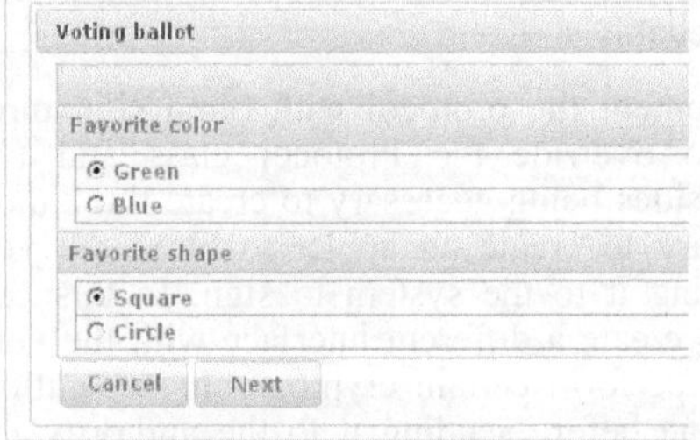

Figure 6. Screen where the voter selects its options

Another screen is the one that allows the voter to choose his voting options, as can be seen in Figure 6 and 7. All disputes are presented on the same screen, with their respective options. After the voter has select among the given options, a screen asking to confirm the vote will be shown, and only then, the vote will be counted. These screens were used in the three protocols implemented, but they may be unnecessary if the protocol requires the voter to download the ballot, check his voting option, and then upload his ballot in the system.

Apart from these, there is also a results screen that shows the result of the election and the winner option of each dispute, as shown in Figure 8.

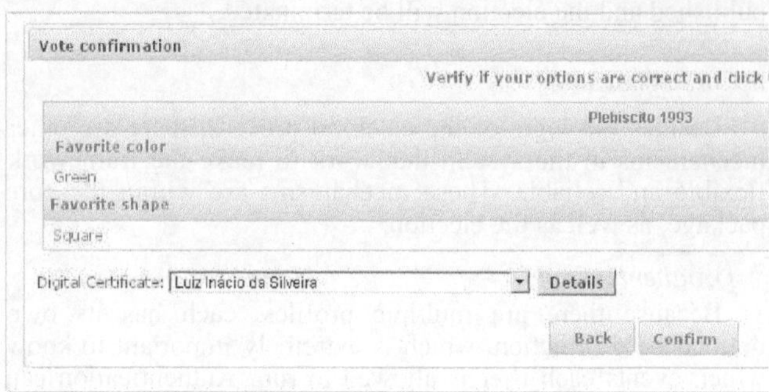

Figure 7. Voting confirmation screen

There is also an auditing screen, seen in Figure 9, which allows auditors to examine all configurations of the election and issue its opinion. This screen is used when the election is marked as requiring auditing. Every election is liable to have these options selected, which would require the entire process of settings election analysis conducted by the auditors and only then have its information disclosed to the voters.

Figure 8. Election result screen

Besides, there are several others ones used during the electoral process, such as display screens and screens for users and roles registration, etc. All the screens mentioned above were used in the implementation of the three protocols described.

C.Core

In all protocols implemented it was not necessary to modify the core of the framework, although this does not impossibility its alteration if necessary. For example, if it is desirable to implement another type of dispute that does not fit in the categories defined in the framework or to implement a different ballot that is not available. The framework is flexible in this regard, being able to implement new protocols easily, but not preventing changes in its structure if necessary.

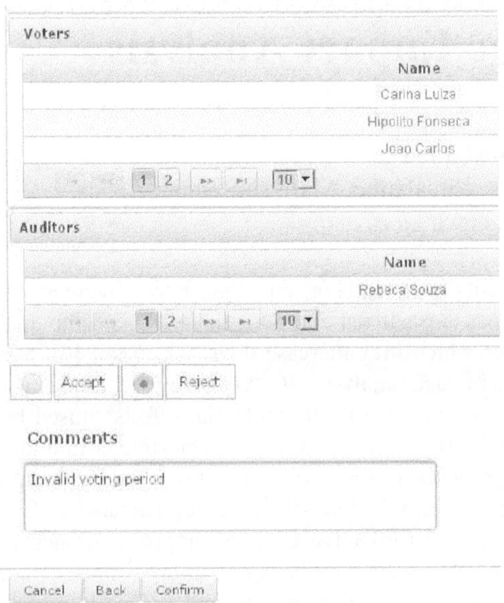

Figure 9. Auditing screen

D. Results

Through the implementation of the three protocols, it was possible to verify the feasibility of the framework to support the development of electoral systems, as well as to permit a considerable reuse in the development.

The three protocols implemented showed a reuse greater than 90%. This does not mean that any new voting system will have an equivalent reuse, but in any case the framework provides the infrastructure needed and allows the definition of new protocols and cryptographic primitives through the specialization of its classes.

V. Conclusion

Because of the importance of digital voting systems and the difficulty in implementing them and evaluate them, it is important to have a mechanism that facilitates ideation and development of new systems. The framework was able to show its usefulness through the implementation of three protocols, facilitating the development and evaluation of new systems, and presenting a high degree of reuse. This allows the developer to focus on the most important aspects of development, since the whole structure of a voting system is implemented in the framework. With respect to similar proposals, it proved to be more flexible, more comprehensive and greater reuse.

References

[1]*R. Samarone, "Protocolos Criptográficos para Votação Digital," Unpublished master's thesis for mater's degree, Universidade Federal de Santa Catarina, Florianópolis, Brazil, 2002*

[2]*B. Adida, "Helios: web-based open-audit voting,"* Proceedings of the 17th conference on Security symposium *(SS'08). USENIX Association, Berkeley, CA, USA, 2008, pp. 335-348.*

[3]*C. K. Wu, R. Sankaranarayana, "Internet voting: concerns and solutions," Cyber Worlds, 2002. Proceedings. First International Symposium on Cyber Worlds, 2002, pp. 261 – 266*

[4]*D. Lundin, "Component Based Electronic Voting Systems", In Towards Trustworthy Elections, David Chaum, Markus Jakobsson, Ronald L. Rivest, Peter A. Ryan, and Josh Benaloh (Eds.). Springer-Verlag, Berlin, Heidelberg pp. 260-273. 2010*

[5]*S. Popoveniuc, P. Vora, "A framework for secure electronic voting", In IAVoSS Workshop On Trustworthy Elections, 2008*

[6]J. Helbach, J. Schwenk "Secure internet voting with code sheets," In Proceedings of the 1st international conference on E-voting and identity (VOTE-ID'07), Ammar Alkassar and Melanie Volkamer (Eds.). Springer-Verlag, Berlin, Heidelberg, 2007, pp. 166-177.+

[7]A.O. Santin, R.G. Costa, C.A Maziero, "A Three-Ballot-Based Secure Electronic Voting System," Security & Privacy, IEEE , vol.6, no.3, May-June 2008, pp.14-21,

[8]L.F. Cranor, R.K. Cytron, "Sensus: a security-conscious electronic polling system for the Internet," System Sciences, 1997, Proceedings of the Thirtieth Hawaii International Conference on System Sciences - HICSS '97 , 7-10 Jan 1997, pp.561-570 vol.3

[9]F. Baiardi, A. Falleni, R. Granchi, F. Martinelli, M. Petrocchi, A. Vaccarelli, "SEAS: A Secure E-Voting Applet System," Lecture Notes in Computer Science pp. 318-329, January 2004

[10]I. Ray, I. Ray, N. Narasimhamurthi, "An Anonymous Electronic Voting Protocol for Voting Over The Internet," In Proceedings of the Third International Workshop on Advanced Issues of E-Commerce and Web-Based Information Systems (WECWIS '01) (WECWIS '01). IEEE Computer Society, Washington, DC, USA, pp. 188-. 2001

[11]J. Heather, D. Lundin, The Append-Only Web Bulletin Board. Guildford, Surrey, UK, University of Surrey, 2008.

Towards Improving Object-Oriented Software Maintenance during Change Impact Analysis

Bassey Isong[1] and Obeten Ekabua[2]
Department of Computer Science, North-West University, Mmabatho, Mafikeng, South Africa
{[1]24073008, [2]obeten.ekabua}@nwu.ac.za

Abstract - *Today, resources are geared towards modifying rather than developing new software systems. Changes are necessary during the system's lifetime to keep it useful but the major challenge is how these changes are controlled and managed. Software systems are complex with large dependency webs and components that are fault-prone. Modifying components without regard to its dependencies or its fault-proneness may have some unpredicted and potential effects on the quality or increase their risk to fail. Object-oriented software (OOS) systems are not exception. Identifying these components early may reduce system failure risks when implementing changes. Traditional researches on change impact analysis (CIA) of software code change and failure prediction are disjointed. Therefore, the main goal is to propose a change impact analysis framework that incorporates change and failure prediction while enhancing software quality and reducing maintenance time, cost and effort. By way of contribution and extension of existing knowledge, this research will explore and analyze OOS component's relationship for effective change impact analysis and predicting early, the failure associated with fault-prone components by utilizing OO metrics.*

Keywords: Change, impact analysis, Object-oriented, Failure, Metrics, Prediction.

1 Introduction

Software maintenance has been recognized as the most costly and difficult part of software development, accounting for at least 50% of the total software production cost in particular, object-oriented systems [1,2,3]. Software changes are necessary during software maintenance and software might need to be changed to fix defects, to change executing logic, to make the processing more efficient, or to introduce new features and enhancements [5]. However, when changes are made, there will unavoidably have some unpredicted and potential effects on the software and may cause the software to deteriorate. Though software does not deteriorate or change with age, it is believed that most software maintenance involves changes that potentially degrade the software unless it is proactively controlled [4].

Changing OOS in large software systems today is complex requiring a good understanding of the dependencies between software components. This is because a modification to components with little or no regard to dependencies may have some unpredicted and potential effects on the quality of the latter which may increase their risk to fail [6]. Software change impact analysis (CIA) is a technique used to understand and identify the potential effects caused by such changes [2,7]. Given software, the objective is to understand how a proposed change will affect the software components in order to allow more effective prioritization of change requests [1]. An effective CIA can improve the accuracy of required resource estimates, allow more accurate development schedules to be set, and reduce the amount of corrective maintenance by reducing the number of errors introduced as a by-product of the maintenance effort [3].

In the realm of OO maintenance, OO paradigm unlike the procedural paradigm introduce new concepts such as encapsulation, inheritance, polymorphism, and dynamic binding [3,8]. Such features frequently result to more complex relationship between classes and attributes, making it difficult to anticipate and identify the ripple effects of changes. The more a change affects classes, the more its realization cost escalate. In addition, empirical evidences in literature has shown that OO classes are not faults or failures free [9,10]. A software fault is a defect in a software system that may cause an executable product to fail. The intuitive reason is that if a change is implemented on a fault-prone component, software failure will be inevitable. Hence, the early identification of these components will allow mitigating actions to be employed before change can be implemented, if found desirable.

Though several CIA approaches for OOS and software failure prediction exist in the literature [3, 8, 11], the two approaches are disjoint which consequently, can be linked to failures of some OOS after maintenance. It is believed that improving the maintenance of OOS requires CIA approach that is effective at analysis and capturing the complex dependencies among components as well as predicting the early failure of the software, if changes are to be implemented. With this approach, maintenance effort and costs can be reduced while ensuring the quality of the software. In addition, good decisions can be taken before implementing changes. By identifying the potential impact of a modification and the early identification of potential failure, the risk to deal with expensive and unpredictable changes will be reduced. Therefore, the objective of this paper is to propose an approach for early failure prediction to support CIA in order to enhance the maintenance of OOS. The approach involves dependencies extraction and analysis, change impact analysis, early failure prediction which will lead to modification decision.

The rest of the paper is organized as follows: the introduction is in section 1, section 2 is a description of the related works, section 3 gives the research goal and approach, and section 4 is work in progress. Accordingly, the research contributions and conclusions are in given section 5 and 6 respectively.

1.1 Background Information

Software changes are inevitable in software development and evolution. Changes occur in every phase of software development like requirements, design, implementation, and maintenance. Thus, systems modification should be taken seriously and the effects of changes must be considered because changes in any phase will affect the behaviour of the delivered software product in another phase [4]. (See Fig. 1)

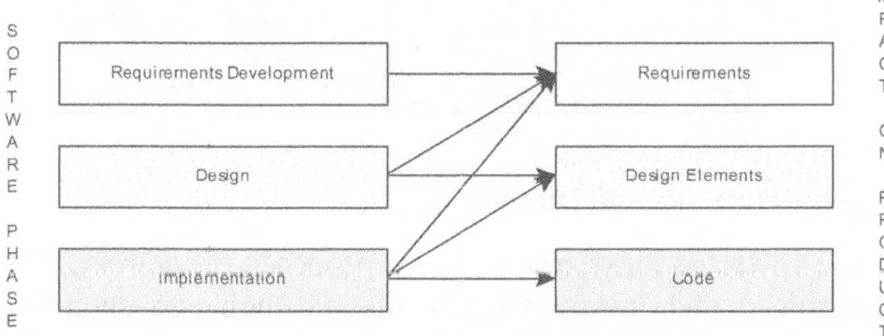

Figure 1: Impacts of change on software life-cycle objects

When changes made to software negatively affects the software, it may bring inconsistencies to other parts of the original software and the changed with the affected components may no longer fit for the rest of the software product – software deterioration [4,12]. Deterioration occurs in many ways because changes to software rarely have the small impact they are believed to have [4]. This stems from impact overlooking, impact underestimation to impact overestimation as a result of the complexity and size of current software applications. CIA is a process for controlling changes and avoids software deterioration if properly applied.

In today's software development world, OO approach is increasingly gaining momentum and widespread use. It is an approach where systems are described in terms of objects. OO approach has the benefits of producing a clean, well-understood design characterized by easier to understand, test, maintain, extend etc [3]. However, the application of the technology does not by itself ensure the quality of the software, guard against developer's mistakes, nor prevent faults. OO approach introduces new concepts whose features often lead to more complex relationships (i.e. use, invoke, member and inheritance [11]) as shown in Fig. 2. These complex dependencies frequently make it difficult to anticipate and identify the ripple-effects of changes [3,8].

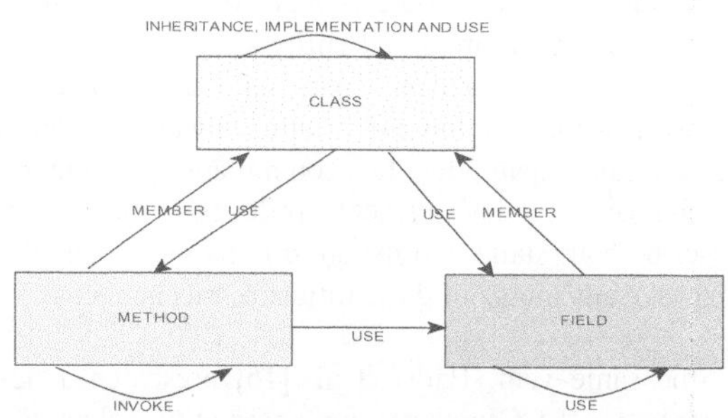

Figure 2: Dependencies between object oriented program components [11]

For instance, encapsulation promotes an intended functionality to be achieved by invoking several member functions from some classes and changes to a class may affect many classes. Inheritance implies that a class can reuse the data members and member functions of another class. Therefore, new dependencies are created between two classes and changes to a class may affect other classes which are related to it. Polymorphism allows many different implementations of the same specification. All these features make it difficult to define a cost-effective test and maintenance strategy for OOS [3]. With an effective CIA approach, one can determine for some level of granularity (e.g. statements, modules, features), whose components in the software can be affected by changes. In addition, empirical evidence indicates that most OO application components are fault-prone or failure-prone [9,10], though, believed to be found only on few of the system's components. During the course of maintenance, CIA in particular, if these faulty components are not known before changes are implemented, it could compound the risks and may lead to software failure. Thus, identifying these components prematurely allows mitigating actions, such as validation and verification activities to be focused on the high risk components so as to avoid software failures. Based on this, we intend to evolve a unique failure prediction model that will be incorporated into the CIA process for effective decision making during software changes.

2 Related Works

In this section, we introduce some related current works on CIA. Sharafat and Tahvildari [13] propose a probabilistic approach to predict changes in an OOS system using the dependencies obtained from UML diagrams, as well as source code of several releases of a software system using reverse engineering techniques. Abdi et al. [14] propose the calculation technique of change impact expressions using a meta-model approach to analyze and predict changes impacts in OO systems. Sun et al. [7] propose Object Oriented Class and Member Dependence Graph (OOCMDG) that represents the program to be analyzed based on static CIA. The objective was on the precision improvement of the impact sets which depends on the change types and the dependence types between the modified entity and other entities. Breech et al. [15] presented coarse-grained impact analysis algorithms that exploit information about how changes can actually propagate due to scoping and parameter passing mechanisms. They present influence mechanisms and describe both static and dynamic impact analysis algorithms that take advantage of these influence mechanisms.

In the same vein, Badri et al. [16] presented a new static technique (CCGImpact) for predictive change impact analysis based on control call graphs (CCG) which captures the control related to components calls and generates the different control flow paths in a program. The generated paths, in a compacted form are used to identify the potential set of components that may be affected by a given change. Oliveira et al. [17] present a hybrid impact analysis technique based on both static and dynamic analysis of OO source code to improve resulting impact estimates in terms of recall. Also, Shao et al. [18] present an approach in which the impact of a source code change can be analyzed by slicing with the variable def-use pairs. Data-flow and program slicing are combined to show data dependencies. Kagdi and Maletic [19] combined the estimated change sets computed from impact analysis techniques with the actual change sets that can be recovered from version histories will result in improved software-change prediction. In the above studies, different CIA approaches on OOS have been reported. All the approaches have been designed for change impact prediction and none employed failure prediction in any way. Therefore, in this research, our approach is unique and is aimed at amalgamating the two approaches in order to effectively calculate the ripple effects and rid or reduce the risks of software failures during and after change implementation.

3 Research Goal

One indispensable property of any software is change and is a key operation for maintenance. These changes are made to realize various change proposals for OOS. With the available change proposal, the maintainer responsible have to analyze and evaluate it in order to predict the impacts in terms of dependences, and failure-prone components, make a decision on the outcome, and give some modification advice to reduce the risk and cost of the change implementation. For in stance, if a change proposal is known to have significant ripple-effects over the entire system, or undesirable effects or affected classes are fault-prone, the best approach will be either to reject it, or consider an additional change plan, or redesign the system, or accept the change proposal. These activities are carefully carried out before the actual change is implemented and all form parts of the proposed change analysis framework. This research tries to provide an effective and comprehensive solution to the activities related to change analysis in order to improve software maintenance. Therefore, the overall goal of our research is to develop a CIA framework and model for early failure prediction of the impact of changes to OOS to enhance software quality and reduce the time, cost and effort associated with its maintenance.

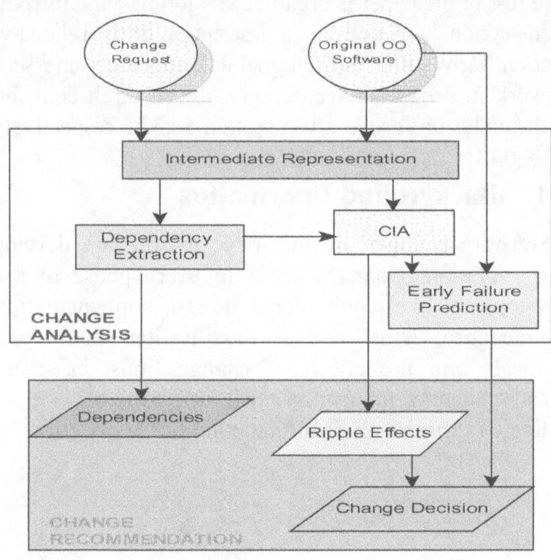

Figure 3: Proposed CIA framework

Fig.3. presents an overview of our proposed framework. The activities which are the focal points and their corresponding goals are discussed as follows:

1) Dependencies Analysis and Extraction: With the available change proposal and the original OO source code, the first step is to construct a representation for original OOS that is simple and effectively show all the possible dependencies among the components of the original software. The representation is aimed at providing full understanding of how components relates with each other and to facilitate the CIA activities in the next stage.

2) Change Impact Analysis: This step is to perform the actual CIA where the maintainer will have an overview of which parts in original OOS is truly affected by the change proposal, and consequently may bring inconsistence to the software. For effectiveness of this approach, accuracy and precision are top priorities for its evaluation and minimization of the predicted numbers of impact sets.

3) Early Failure Prediction: This is the prediction stage where the change proposal is evaluated from two perspectives - results of the impact analysis and the values of the OO design metrics extracted from the original software for a failure-free change implementation. To predict which of the classes affected by change proposal are fault-prone which in turn may result in system failure if change is implemented, the extracted OO design metrics and a suitable prediction model will be used and decision made accordingly.

4) Change Implementation: Implementing a change will depend on the results obtained from earlier analysis and evaluation. That is, a change is implemented if the risk is known to be low or after validation and verification activities have been performed on the affected faulty parts. Otherwise, it is rejected if known to have deteriorating effects on the whole system. The essence of the results is to reduce the maintenance time, cost, effort, change consequences and facilitation of regression testing.

4 Research Approach

As stated earlier, our objective is to analyze and predict changes impacts and failure in OOS before change implementation. The approach involves choosing an existing impact model and adjusts it afterward to meet our objective. The work uses both CIA and failure prediction techniques to support and enhance the maintenance of OOS. The approach takes OO components (i.e. field, methods, and classes) and the relationships that exist between them into account as well as the structural properties of the classes. The analysis will be centered on software systems written in Java language which is essential for computing impact of any possible change with our model. In addition, tools (such as Analyst4j) will be utilized to analyze the source code of the system and extract the design measures of every component (class) used for predicting the potential failures.

The approach begins with the construction of an intermediate representation of the original OOS where dependencies between OOS components are extracted and analyzed, and the impact sets are computed. With the impact results, OO design metrics are extracted from the original software and the values are use to predict which components are fault-prone that could result in failure if the change is implemented on such components. With results obtain, decision is then made if a change will be implemented or apply verification activities or reject the proposal if is known to cause huge negative impacts on the entire system.

5 Work in Progress

This section presents how far we have gone with this research. At this point, discussion is based on the investigated dependencies analysis and extraction, CIA techniques and failure prediction approach utilizing the source code change proposal.

5.1 Dependency Analysis and Extraction

Dependency analysis is a critical activity that is performed during CIA. It is an integral part of CIA framework as it assists in understanding how one entity relates to another through effective representation of the original software. Various dependency graphs exist which can be generated by statically extracting the relationships between types (i.e. classes or interfaces) in the source codes. System dependence graph (SDG) [3,20] is one of the commonly used representations for program analysis especially, OO source code. It represents OOS and analyses its elements as well as their relationships at very fine level of granularity [3]. The outcome of the representation is important information about the program elements and relationships between them. Nevertheless, constructing this representation requires much carefulness and good knowledge of OO design because wrong results can lead to over or under estimation of impact sets. Hence, understanding the system dependencies is essential for efficient software change.

Unlike the procedural program, in OO program, emphasis is placed on what the program does to data and their relationships, rather than the program's structure. In addition, software objects are related to each other by complex dependencies and constraints [11]. To emphasize on this, we use the labeled OO components dependency graph (OOComDG). The OOComDG describes dependencies in OOS while the software system components are viewed as classes, methods, and fields. In our OOComDG, the components are represented as the nodes and the dependences are represented as the edges. The dependences types are the label such as *inheritance (H)), invocation (V), uses (U)*, and *member (M)* on the edges. Once the original software has been represented as OOComDG, it is then transformed two adjacency matrices to ease the correct identification of the starting impact set (SIS). In our initial study, we have constructed a representation of the original system using OOComDG. The dependence between fields and methods, dependence between methods, dependence between classes, and dependence between classes and methods, can be revealed based on the concept analysis. Though some information may be missing in the representation, the representation is in line with various existing activities in the change analysis framework in literature. The initial investigation results show that dependencies between classes, methods and field are well covered, though it is a small sized program. In general, the representation is reasonable and may be applied to large programs.

5.2 Change Impact Analysis

CIA plays an important role in identifying the consequences or ripple-effects of proposed changes. Among other approaches, static and dynamic analysis are the most commonly used techniques [5,7]. Given the proposed change entities, the object of CIA technique is to find the parts of the software that are truly affected by the change. However, the impact sets produced may be inaccurate due to either underestimate (false-negatives) or overestimate (false-positives) change impact as a result of the problems the maintainer responsible may face in finding the parts affected by the change.

To guard against these inaccuracies and reduce the predicted impact sets, our research employed static CIA technique using concept of OO impact method to compute the potential impact set from the proposed changed. In view of this, we will introduce the *impact range* concept to obtain the impacted entities in a given change category based on movement along the program's OOComDG from the SIS of the changed entity obtained from the adjacency matrix. In OOS, different change types often have different impact methods. For instance, some changes made to programs do not affect other entities in programs regardless of some dependencies while some other changes may potentially impact other entities in programs [11]. The impact method of a change is based on the code change types of modified components and the dependencies between them (i.e. the modified and other components). In our approach, the SIS is computed using the adjacency matrices, while the potential impact set (PIS) is computed based on the SIS and *impact range*. Two types of adjacency matrices are introduced here: intra and inter-class member relation matrices. At this point, we have not validated our techniques on the real-world program to see its effectiveness. However, we are confident the technique will produce fewer impact sets with a reduction in false-positives and false negatives.

5.3 Early Failure Predictions

The early failure prediction is a stage where we evaluate the probability of failure occurrence if a change proposal is implemented. It is based on two aspects: results of the impact analysis and the values of the OO design metrics extracted from the original software which is then mapped onto the affected classes. It is true that when changes are made to software, they will inevitably have some unpredictable and undesirable ripple-effect on other parts of the software [21]. In the same way, the degree of the ripple-effect is proportional to the complexities of the structural properties of the software product which in turn affects the cognitive complexity of the maintainer. Cognitive complexity is known to constitute the mental burden of the maintainer who has to deal with the component [10]. Thus, high cognitive complexity of a system leads to components exhibiting undesirable external qualities, such as increased fault-proneness and reduced maintainability (see Fig. 4).

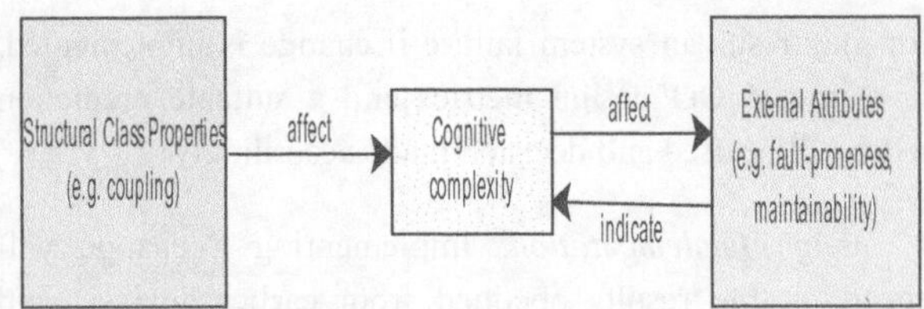

Figure 4: Effect of product's structural properties on maintenance

Several empirical evidences have shown that OOS applications are not fault-free, though found only on few of the system's components [9]. In addition, our perception in this research is that when changes are implemented on components that are fault-prone, they will complicate the situation and inevitably result in failure. Therefore, predicting the failure early before implementing change proposal can help maintainer responsible to answer whether a change proposal is accepted or to determine which change schedule is more suitable to employ (i.e. to focus verification actions on the high risk, failure-prone components) or to decide on rejecting the change proposal.

In the sphere of OOS, the construction of prediction models using OO design metrics is one approach aimed at discovering faulty classes early in development and maintenance. Such models usually uses historical data, design metrics which can used for identifying potentially faulty classes in future applications or releases [10]. With the result of such investigation, an organization can take actions prematurely aimed at alleviating the situation and consequently avoid costly rework. Several numbers of OO design metrics have been constructed such as the Chidamber and Kemerer [22], Li and Henry [23], Abreu and Carapuca [24], Briand et al. [25], etc. in literature. In addition, there are several empirical studies that validated and revalidated the relationship between the different OO design metrics and fault-proneness and their effect on cognitive complexity as well as the prediction models that utilize them in the literature [26,27,28,29].

In this research, we are going to employ the existing OO design metrics, particularly, the Chidamber and Kemerer [22]. Emphasis will be on extracting the design metrics that are positively associated with the fault-proneness of classes. However, the question is, "which metrics are suitable for OO failure prediction?" Though several prediction models associated with fault-proneness exist, the approach of this research will be unique and two-dimensional. This means that we will consider failure prediction based on the values of extracted measures for both *pre-release* and *post-release OOS*. For prediction based on design measures, the intuition is that higher values of these metrics represent structural properties that increase the probability that a class will have a fault that causes a field failure. At this point, we are still at the stage of identifying which OO design metrics are significantly associated with fault or failure-proneness.

6 Research Contributions

Understanding changes during CIA is essential for understanding the evolution of a software system. With our proposed approach, given a change proposal, the task is i) obtain the information about the dependencies in original system, ii) compute the potential ripple-effects induced by the change proposal based on the code change type and impact and dependency types, iii) perform the early failure prediction based on the design measures extracted from the original system to identify fault-prone components that could cause failure if change proposal is implemented, and iv) make modification based on the results. Consequently, the expected contributions of the research are as follows:

- Support maintainer in performing static CIA on OOS through:
  - A representation that is simple enough and reveal all the dependencies between the elements in the original software
  - Capture impact sets that are accurate, not large enough or difficult for practical use and with fewer false-negatives and false-positives to predict the ripple effects induced by the change proposal.
- To evolve software metrics (i.e. predictors) that is based on the structural properties of the product and which can accurately predict failure early enough that is assumed to occur when certain changes are made.
- CIA framework that support various change analysis activities by incorporates impact prediction and failure prediction in order to identify and reduce the cost and risks associated with change implementation.

In all, by identifying the potential impacts and failures before change implementation during maintenance, the risks associated with embarking on a costly change can be reduced drastically.

7 Conclusions

In this paper, we have proposed an approach to support the maintenance of OOS system during CIA through early failure prediction. The approach starts with dependencies analysis and extraction of the original software, impact analysis based on adjacency matrix analysis and their impact expression and early failure prediction based on extracted design metrics and historical data. Although, the research is still at its preliminary stage, we however conclude that, by identifying potential impacts and failures before committing a change, the risks associated with embarking on a costly change will be drastically reduced. This is because the cost of unforeseen problems generally increases when there are discovered lately. Furthermore, it will help management to choose between alternative changes when undesirable effects are known. The work is still in progress with emphasis on the CIA and failure prediction phases.

8 References

[1] P. Grubb and A.A. Takang. *Software Maintenance: Concepts and Practice*, 2nd ed. World Scientific Publishing Co. Pte. Ltd, Singapore, 2003

[2] Turver, R. J. and Malcolm, M. "An early impact analysis technique for software maintenance". *The Journal of software Maintenance, Research and Practice,* 18(12):35-52, January-February 1994.

[3] M. Lee et al. "Algorithmic analysis of the impacts of changes to object-oriented software" *34th International Conference on Technology of Object Oriented Languages and Systems.* August 2000. pp. 61-70.

[4] P. Jönsson and M. Lindvall. "Impact Analysis" *Engineering and Managing Software Requirements* Issue: 6, Springer-Verlag, pp. 117-142, 2005

[5] S. A. Bohner. "Extending software change impact analysis into COTS components" *Proceedings of the 27th Annual NASA Goddard Software Engineering Workshop*, Greenbelt, USA, 2002, pp.175 -182.

[6] T. Zimmerman, N. Nagappan, K. Herzig, R. Premraj and L. Williams. "An Empirical Study on the Relation between Dependency Neighborhoods and Failures" *Proceedings 2011 IEEE Fourth International Conference on Software Testing, Verification and Validation (ICST 2011),* pp. 347-56.

[7] X. Sun, B. Li, C. Tao, W. Wen, and S. Zhang. "Change Impact Analysis Based on a Taxonomy of Change Types" *2010 IEEE Proceedings of 34th Annual Computer Software and Applications Conference (COMPSAC 2010),* 2010. pp.373-82.

[8] J.K. Jang et al: "Change impact analysis for a class hierarchy" Proceedings *1998 Asia Pacific Software Engineering Conference (Cat. No.98EX240),* 1998, pp. 304-11

[9] Fenton, N., Ohlsson, N: Quantitative analysis of faults and failures in a complex software system. IEEE Transactions on Software Engineering, 2000

[10] K.E. Emam, W. Melo and J. C. Machado. "The prediction of faulty classes using object-oriented design metrics" *The Journal of Systems and Software*. Vol.56, pp. 63-75, 2001

[11] X. Sun, B. Li, C. Tao, W. Wen, and S. Zhang. "Change Impact Analysis Based on a Taxonomy of Change Types" *2010 IEEE Proceedings of 34th Annual Computer Software and Applications Conference (COMPSAC 2010)*, 2010. pp.373-82.

[12] C. Chen, C. She, and J. Tang. "An object-based, attribute-oriented approach for software change impact analysis" *IEEE International Conference on Industrial Engineering and Engineering Management*, 2007, pp. 577-81

[13] A.R. Sharafat and L. Tahvildari. "A Probabilistic Approach to Predict Changes in Object-Oriented Software Systems' *11th European Conference on Software Maintenance and Reengineering (CSMR'07)* March 2007, pp. 27-38

[14] M. K. Abdi, H. Lounis, and H. Sahraoui. "Analyzing change impact in object-oriented systems" *Proceedinds of 32nd Euromicro Conference on Software Engineering and Advanced*, 2006, pp.8

[15] B. Breech, M. Tegtmeyer and L. and Pollock, "Integrating Influence Mechanisms into Impact Analysis for Increased Precision," *Proceedings of the 22nd IEEE International Conference on Software Maintenance (ICSM06)*, 2006, pp.55-65

[16] Linda Badri, Mourad Badri, Daniel St-Yves, "Supporting Predictive Change Impact Analysis:A Control Call Graph Based Technique," Proceedings of the 12th Asia-Pacific Software Engineering Conference (APSEC'05), IEEE Press, 2005, pp.167-175

[17] M. Oliveira et al: "The Hybrid Technique for Object-Oriented Software Change Impact, Analysis" *Proceedings of the 14th European Conference on Software Maintenance and Reengineering (CSMR 2010)*, IEEE Press, 2010, pp.252-255

[18] S.Danhua , S. Khurshid, and D. E. Perry, "Semantic Impact and Faults in Source Code Changes: An Empirical Study," *2009 Proceedings of Australian Software Engineering Conference(ASWEC 2009)*, IEEE Press, 2009, pp.131-141

[19] H. Kagdi and J. L. Maletic. "Software-Change Prediction: Estimated+Actual" *Second International IEEE Workshop on Software Evolvability (SE'06)* , 2006.

[20] S. Horwitz, T. Reps, and D. Binkley, "Inter-procedural slicing using dependence graphs," ACM Transactions on Programming Languages and Systems, vol. 12, no. 1, pp. 27–60, 1990

[21] Arnold, R.S., and Bohner, S.A., "Impact analysis – towards a framework for comparison", The Intl Conf. on Software Maintenance, 1993.

[22] Chidamber, S., Kemerer, C.F.: A metrics suite for object oriented design. IEEE Trans. Softw. Eng. 1994, 20 (6), 476–493.

[23] Li, W., Henry, S.: Object oriented metrics which predict maintainability. J. Syst. Softw. 1993, 23 (2), 111–122.

[24] Abreu, F.B., Carapuca, R.: Object-oriented software engineering: measuring and controlling the development process. In: Proceedings of the Fourth International Conference on Software Quality, 1994

[25] Briand, L., Devanbu, P., Melo, W.: An investigation into coupling measures for C++. In: Proceedings of the 19th International Conference on Software Engineering, 1997

[26] Basili, V., Briand, L., Melo, W.: A validation of object-oriented design metrics as quality indicators. IEEE Transactions on Software Engineering. 1996, 22 (10), 751-761.

[27] Chidamber, S., Darcy, D., Kemerer, C.: Managerial use of metrics for object oriented software: an exploratory analysis. IEEE Trans. Softw. Eng. 1998, 24 (8), 629–639.

[28] Briand, L., Wuest, J., Daly, J., Porter, V.: Exploring the relationships between design measures and software quality in object oriented systems. Journal of Systems and Software 2000, 51, 245-273.

[29] Cartwright, M., Shepperd, M.: An empirical investigation of an object-oriented software system. IEEE Transactions on Software Engineering, to appear, 2000

SESSION

USABILITY STUDIES + COST ESTIMATION AND MANAGEMENT + SOFTWARE TESTING, ANALYSIS, VALIDATION, AND VERIFICATION + RFORMANCE STUDIES

Chair(s)

TBA

Evaluating the Effectiveness of a Collaborative Requirements Engineering Modeling Notation for Planning Globally Distributed Projects

P. Laurent[1], A. Steele[1], J. Cleland-Huang[1] and P. Mäeder[2]
[1]Systems and Requirements Engineering Center, DePaul University, Chicago, IL, USA
[2]Technical University of Ilmenau, Ilmenau, Germany

Abstract *- In many software projects, stakeholders are distributed across different time zones, organizations, and geographical locations. This creates challenges for conducting people-intensive activities such as requirements elicitation, analysis, and prioritization. To address these problems we previously introduced a visual modeling notation to help project managers plan the collaboration infrastructures needed to support requirements-related activities in globally distributed projects. In this paper we present a refined version of the notation and report on an observational study we conducted in which project managers used our notation to plan globally distributed projects. Results show that the modeling activity and the resulting diagrams helped the project managers to better understand the communication needs for the project, to identify potential communication and collaboration problems, and to proactively address the infrastructure and communication needs for the project.*

Requirements, global projects, visual notation

1 Introduction

In globally distributed projects stakeholders are often separated across time-zones and geographical boundaries. This creates numerous challenges for eliciting, analyzing, negotiating, specifying, and managing requirements [1], especially in conducting activities that are typically performed in face-to-face meetings. Herbsleb's study on communication problems identified several impedences in distributed projects, such as cultural differences, incompatible support environments, and disparities in domain expertise across sites [2], while Taweel observed that communication and coordination challenges resulted in delayed projects, poorly-defined requirements, and repetition in the software development effort [3]. Finally, Damien et al [4, 5] studied the ways in which development teams coordinated their efforts when working on interrelated requirements.

Results from a series of interviews we conducted with requirements engineers from six globally distributed projects [6] showed that failing to clearly identify critical stakeholders and their interactions, and to establish the necessary communication and tooling infrastructures negatively impacted the success of the project and led to disorganized stakeholder interactions, data overload, increased travel requirements, and inefficient processes for supporting specific requirements engineering tasks [7].

To address these challenges we developed the Collaborative Global Requirements Engineering Notation (CGREN) which equips project managers to plan, analyze, and optimize their distributed requirements engineering processes, so that they can better understand their existing processes, identify weaknesses and problems, and establish essential processes and infrastructures [6]. As an additional benefit, CGREN provides a common notation for modeling distributed requirements projects and activities, and thereby facilitates comparisons across projects. These comparisons make it possible to identify recurring patterns of collaboration, common obstacles, and best practices used for collaborative requirements engineering activities. Such observations enable researchers to propose new techniques or improve existing methods to handle the specific challenges of global requirements processes.

In this paper we present a refined version of the CGREN, and also describe a participatory study we conducted in which requirements analysts were asked to interactively use the CGREN to plan requirements engineering activities for distributed projects. The study was designed to evaluate the effectiveness of the CGREN taxonomy, notation, and process for supporting stakeholders in the process of planning distributed requirements engineering activities. The results of this study led to some improvements in the model and clearly show the benefits of using the CGREN.

The remainder of this paper is structured as follows. Sections 2 and 3 present the taxonomy and notation of the CGREN. Sections 4 and 5 describe the study we conducted and the subsequent modifications to CGREN. Section 6 describes related work and section 7 summarizes our findings.

2 CGREN Taxonomy

The initial CGREN taxonomy focused around entities of: *roles*, *sites*, and *artifacts*; as well as three general types of relations: *houses*, *accesses*, and *communicates*, that were observed between the entities.

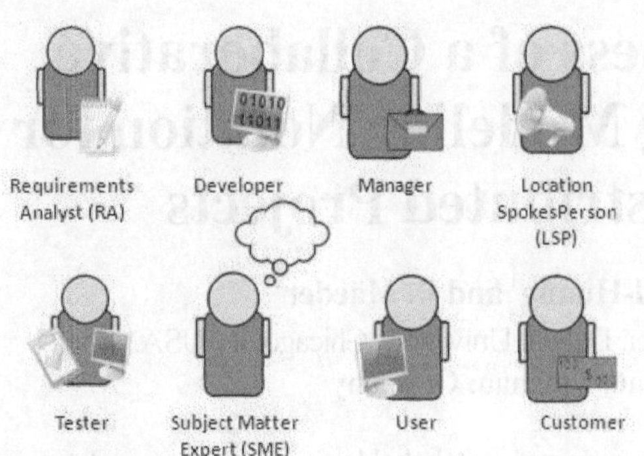

Figure 1. Specific Stakeholder Roles

Figure 2. Multiplicity of stakeholder roles (one, few, many)

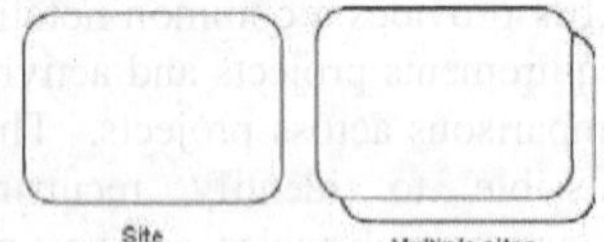

Figure 3. Site

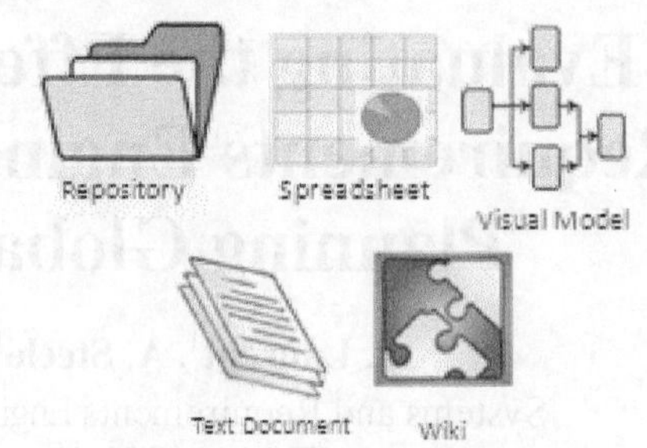

Figure 4. Stationary and traveling artifact types

Communicate co-located   Communicate distributed   Accesses

Figure 5. Relationships

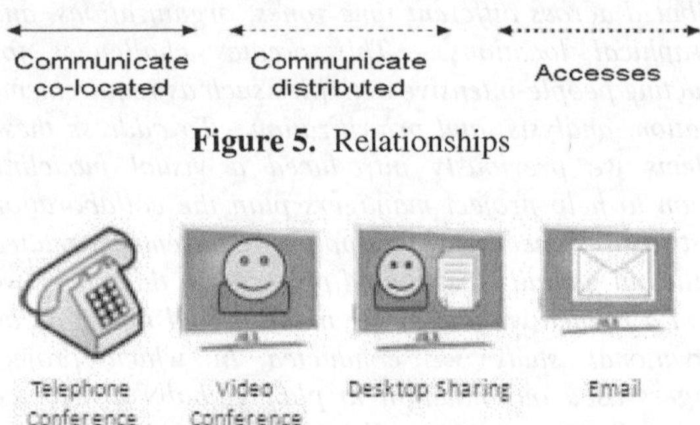

Figure 6. Relation types and Communication Media Stereotype for Distributed Communication

- **Roles:** The Rational Unified Process (RUP) defines a *role*, as a "hat" which can be worn either by an individual or a group of people [8]. Our study results identified a set of commonly occurring roles including a Subject Matter Expert (SME), Requirements Analyst (RA), Customer, Location Spokesperson (LSP), Project Manager (PM), Developer, Tester, and User. The SMEs took on a number of domain specific roles such as Artist and Sales Person. The most commonly identified roles were the SME, RA, and LSP. Most projects we investigated did not officially have RAs; however the RA responsibilities were assigned to a variety of job titles such as project managers and lead developers. The RA role is responsible for overall management of the requirements elicitation process. Several projects also included the LSP role, which was responsible for coordinating the requirements-related processes at a specific location. In some cases the LSP also served as a language translator between local and remote stakeholders. The LSP role was assumed by personnel holding a variety of job titles such as *technical lead* and *designated regional representative.*

The *role* entity has two attributes of *subtype* and *multiplicity.* The *subtype* attribute can be set to any predefined role type (i.e. SME, RA etc), while the *multiplicity* attribute documents the number of stakeholders assuming the given role. CGREN adopts the counting concept used by Amazon's Pirahã tribe by constraining multiplicity values to *one*, *few*, or *many*.

- **Locations:** By definition, a distributed project includes two or more distinct locations. We refer to each location as a **site**, and define it as a place at which at least one project stakeholder is situated. A site is characterized by the close proximity of stakeholders, and their ability to meet together frequently to engage in face-to-face meetings. Stakeholders at a single site are normally able to communicate using a shared primary language. The metamodel shows that a site is defined by location, (primary) language, and time zone attributes.

- **Artifacts:** An artifact is defined as the specification of a physical piece of information that is used or produced by a software development process, or by deployment and operation of a system [8]. The primary goal of the requirements elicitation process is to discover and document requirements for the system. These requirements may be represented textually in structured or unstructured formats and/or graphically. Documentation can therefore assume multiple formats including but not limited to: Word documents, databases, UML models, dataflow diagrams, and/or spreadsheets. Some artifacts are associated with a specific location and reside permanently on a shared drive, online library, or in a repository at a specific site; while other artifacts are frequently moved from stakeholder to stakeholder across multiple locations, primarily via email. As a result, the *artifact* entity in the meta-model is specialized into *Stationary* and

Travelling artifacts. A *Stationary artifact* belongs to exactly one site and is accessed at that site by both local and remote stakeholders, while a travelling artifact has no persistent site and is passed between distributed stakeholders using some kind of ownership token.

- **Means of Communication:** The study also identified three commonly occurring communication patterns involving various roles and artifacts. A **communicate distributed** relationship represents direct communication between two specific roles. For example, in one project, SMEs in North America communicated with SMEs in Asia primarily using email; while in another project the RA in North America held regular tele-conferences with developers in Europe. This type of communication was characterized by the medium used (i.e. telephone, web-conference, or email), and also by the multiplicity of participating roles (i.e. 1:N, N:M etc). The *Communicate distributed* relationship is represented in the meta-model as an association between roles, while the communication medium is represented in individual models as a stereotype. The multiplicity of participating roles is captured through the previously discussed multiplicity attribute.

A **communicate co-located** relationship also connects two roles; however it represents the case that the associated roles are co-located and can communicate face-to-face. Roles can engage in a communicate co-located relationship either by being situated at the same *Site*, or when one or more of the participating stakeholders travel to the other site. For example, in one project an RA was responsible for traveling to two North American sites and a European site in order to interview SMEs. Finally, the **accesses** relationship associates roles with artifacts and means that stakeholders adopting that role contribute to the construction or maintenance of the associated artifact. Access is defined as read (R), write (W), and read/write (RW). The meta-model depicts the accesses relationship as an association between role and artifact entities, while the type of access (R, W, or RW) is modeled as a stereotype and not visible in Figure 11.

3 Visual Notation

The purpose of our work was to develop a visual modeling notation that could be used by stakeholders to plan, evaluate, and manage the requirements process in a distributed project [6]. We evaluated the icons used to represent entities and communication in the meta-model through conducting online surveys of 50 Software Engineering students from DePaul University. In the first phase of the study, participants were given a description of the role or relationship and were presented with 3-5 icon options. They were then asked to select the most representative icon and to optionally provide a rationale for their choice. We conducted this phase of the study in two rounds, using the second round to present additional icons, and/or to narrow down choices for controversial elements

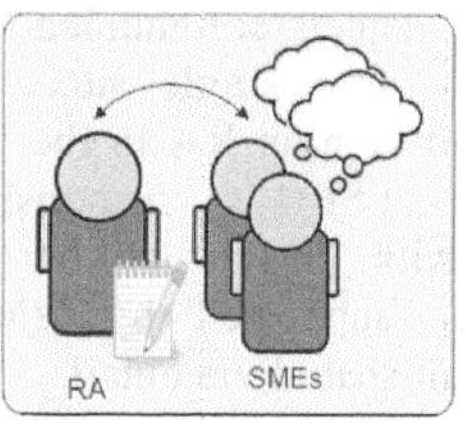

Figure 7. Modeling local collaboration

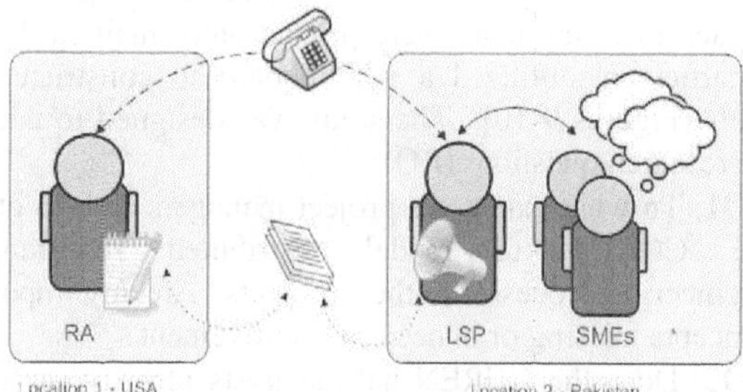

Figure 8. Modeling remote site communication with a local spokesperson at the remote site.

of the notation. In a second complimentary study we presented participants with the entire set of role icons and a list of the specific stakeholder roles, and asked them to associate each icon with a role. To increase the readability of our models we decided to label each role icon with the specific role. The notation, depicted in Figures 1-6, and presented throughout the remainder of this paper is the new notation developed as a result of this series of studies.

A. Basic Elements

Stakeholder roles are depicted as human shapes (Figure 1) and shown as one, few, or many stakeholders (Figure 2). Various adornments are used to represent specific roles, for example the RA is given a pencil, the LSP is assigned a bullhorn, and the customer is given a paper currency. Sites are depicted as containers (Figure 3). Artifacts are represented using well recognized symbols such as a file folder, spreadsheet, or text document (Figure 4). Finally, relationships are depicted intuitively using arcs (Figure 5). A solid line represents co-located communication between roles, a dashed line represents distributed communication between roles, and a dotted line represents the relationship between a role and an artifact. Arcs are adorned by symbols (Figure 6) representing various media of distributed communication, such as email or phone.

B. Examples

The CGREN notation can be used to model a variety of concepts at varying levels of abstraction. For example, a general view of the project may show sites, key roles, primary communication paths, and artifacts visible at the global level. In contrast a more concrete view might map out the specific communication and infrastructure needed to support the elicitation phase of the requirements process. Figure 7 depicts communication between an RA and a few SMEs at a single site. Figure 8 depicts communication between an RA in the USA and a LSP in Pakistan. The LSP is responsible for internal communication with SMEs at her site. Inter-site communication is supported by teleconferencing and through a document shared via email.

4 A Participatory Study

Our observatory study was conducted using a tactile approach in which icons were printed onto small cards, and the participants utilized a white board to construct their models (Figures 9-10). The study was designed to address three research questions (RQ):

- **RQ1**: To what extent are project managers able to utilize the CGREN to model distributed requirements engineering processes in their projects? Are any important concepts missing or in need of improvement?
- **RQ2**: Does the CGREN help analysts identify problems and/or improve the infrastructure of their projects?
- **RQ3**: What is an effective process model for utilizing CGREN to model a project?

C. *Study Design and Execution*

Each observation of a requirements analyst using CGREN involved a training and enactment phase.

- **Participants:** Three professional requirements analysts (RA), from technical consulting, research, and healthcare fields participated in this study. Their specific job titles were consultant, business analyst and director, respectively. Each observation was conducted individually with only the RA and one researcher present.
- **Training:** At the start of each session, the researcher presented several examples of CGREN models and demonstrated the modeling of a project at the whiteboard. Each participant was given a notation guide which included icons depicted in Figures 1-6 and was given the opportunity to ask clarification questions.
- **Design and Procedure:** Each participant created a CGREN model for a specific distributed requirements elicitation project in which they had recently engaged. Project meta-data such as domain, size, duration, and geographical locations, was also collected. The study involved a 'think-aloud' protocol augmented by specific questions from the researcher, and an exist survey based on the questions depicted in Table 1.

D. *Case Study Example*

To illustrate the kind of modeling activities that were conducted during the participatory study, we describe the diagrams that were constructed by the first RA.

RA1 worked as a requirements analyst for a technical consulting company that had been engaged to develop an epidemiology tracking tool. The consulting company had leased office space in the same city as their client. RA1 was one of several RAs who communicated with distributed SMEs and developers. The group of RAs collectively authored and managed the requirements using a commercially available requirements management tool. The RAs elicited and gathered requirements from the SMEs using a combination of individual phone calls and through email exchanges. Each of the RAs was assigned a specific topic area and interacted with the respective SME to elicit requirements. The lead developer and a couple of the managers had read and write access to the requirements repository. Specific project sites and stakeholder roles are depicted in Table 2.

Figure 9. The study was conducted using paper icons for each of the stakeholder roles.

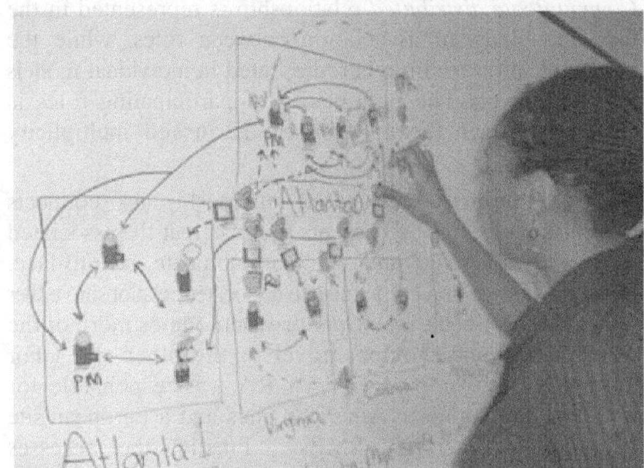

Figure 10. A participant constructs a CGREN model

E. *Evaluation*

Our study was qualitative in nature. Research questions were systematically answered as a result of observing the participants utilizing CGREN, reviewing transcripts of the sessions, and through evaluating the answers to the open-ended exit survey questions.

RQ1: To what extent can project managers use CGREN to model distributed requirements engineering processes? All of the participants were able to successfully model the roles, locations, communication methods, and artifacts of their selected projects. When asked "were you able to model all the concepts from your project?" all three participants responded positively. Furthermore the models produced during each of the three sessions demonstrated that all three RAs developed models which they claimed fully represented their projects, and which were correct with respect to the metamodel. However, when specifically asked if any graphical symbols were missing, two of the participants mentioned the need for the notation to allow stakeholders to assume multiple roles, sometimes simultaneously, and sometimes at different phases in the project. RA2 also pointed out the need to *"denote frequency of communication*" in order to differentiate between varying communication frequencies along different communication channels. In general, the results of this study confirmed that CGREN provided the ability to model most aspects of the distributed requirements engineering processes that the RAs were engaged in.

RQ2: Does the CGREN help analysts identify problems and/or improve the infrastructure of their projects? Each participant in our study was asked "what, if anything, did you gain from using CGREN?" RA1 stated that she gained *"A better understanding of the project (and a) better understanding of the stakeholders, the access they had, and ... their reach (impact in the project)."* Using the communication diagram (Figure 10) she identified a specific problem that occurred because of the distribution of the major stakeholders. In this case the lead developer was located in Knoxville, while most of the communication to establish requirements took place in Atlanta. As a result of modeling these interactions, the RA commented *"Wait a minute, all this communication is happening here (while) we have this one person who has to do all of these things, but they're doing it remotely."* She stated that if CGREN had been available to her earlier in the project, this observation would have led to restructuring of communication patterns.

RA2 noted that for their project *"the model is helpful for showing that ... in some of my locations I don't really have a Spokesperson. And so there's (sic) multiple SMEs that I'm going to... and (it is unclear) to what extent are they truly the authority.*" She also stated that as a result of modeling the stakeholder roles, this reinforced that it would be helpful for her to have a designated spokesperson for each site who would be responsible for identifying SMEs. She further commented that *"there's multiple SMEs that I'm going to. And so that's a lot of people I'm communicating with. ... I feel like it would be helpful to have fewer people and more people that were kind of designated as Spokespeople,*" which echoes the findings of Turner and Boehm that stress the importance of finding CRACK (Collaborative, Representative, Accountable, Committed, Knowledgeable) people during the requirements elicitation phase of project planning[9].

TABLE 1. EXIT SURVEY QUESTIONS

1. How useful was the modeling notation?
   a. Were you able to model all of the concepts from your project?
   b. Any problems using the graphical symbols? Any concepts missing?
   c. What was easy to model? What was difficult?
   d. Were the stakeholder types and roles sufficient? Was it helpful to differentiate the roles in this way?
   e. Was the one-few-concept effective?
2. What, if anything, did you gain from using CGREN?
3. Did CGREN help you identify any potential issues?
4. Would you use a software version of this tool during your next project? If so, at what phase?

TABLE 2. RA1'S PROJECT SITES AND STAKEHOLDERS

Site	Stakeholder Role
USA0 – Atlanta, GA Consulting company	1 PM/Lead RA and 5-7 RAs (from consulting company) 10+ Developers
USA1 – Atlanta, GA Customer site	1 Higher-level Manager 1 Manager/LSP 10+ SMEs
USA2 – Virginia/D.C area	1 Manager/executive 10+ Developers
USA3 – California	5+ Developers 10+ Testers
USA4 – Knoxville, TN	1 Lead Developer

Finally, RA3 pointed out that CGREN would *"shed some light on what some of the possible constraints and limitations could be" with respect to the* current project configuration. In particular she pointed out that in her project all communication was via email, and that planning in advance would enable better infrastructure setup that could include video-conferencing technology and other techniques to support communication between stakeholders.

One of the key results of the modelling activity for the RAs was that the method and quantity of communication during the planning and execution phase of the project was highlighted. For example, RA1 commented "...*I never really noticed that I didn't talk to the testers, even though they definitely wrote their test cases and complained sometimes about the way we wrote our requirements... after doing this [exercise] now I notice it.*" Both RA1 and RA2 noted that the exercise made them painfully aware of the complexity of their communication needs.

We noticed the paucity of different elicitation techniques used in the three projects. All of the RAs relied on individual interviews and group meetings either conducted in face-to-face meetings or using phone or video-conferencing technologies. There were no examples of more creative elicitation techniques such as Joint Application Design (JAD) sessions, creativity workshops, or even basic scenario-writing using storyboarding or other similar techniques [10].

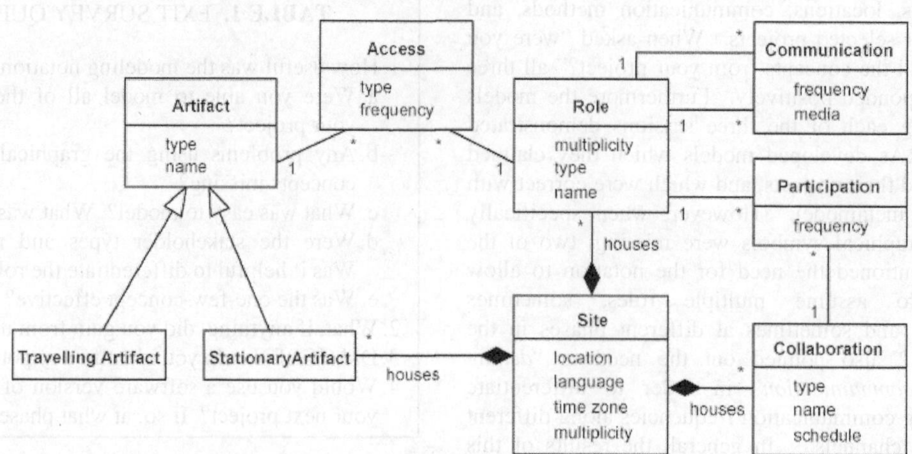

Figure 11. Updated CGREN Metamodel reflecting new concepts of communication frequency, roles, and collaboration.

As a result of this observation we noted that if CGREN were extended to include the notion of meeting types and/or elicitation techniques, it could serve to inspire and educate project stakeholders about new techniques, and encourage them to think beyond their previous planning experiences.

RQ3: What is an effective process model for utilizing CGREN to model a project? Based on our previous experiences and our observations during the participatory study we developed the following guidelines that can be used in conjunction with CGREN.

1. Identify primary locations and model them as sites.
2. Identify project-level organizational roles and assign them to specific sites as the organizational plan evolves.
3. For each site, identify key local roles and communication patterns between roles within the site.
4. Establish basic communication patterns between critical roles across sites and assign communication responsibilities to specific roles. In CGREN add appropriate relationship arcs and attach applicable communication media to each of the relationship arcs. Decide how each communication path will be supported by technology.
5. Determine the key artifacts that are to be created collaboratively, and model them along with each role's access and privileges. Include the applicable tooling/version control infrastructure.
6. Revisit project-level organizational structures and ensure that all roles are assigned to specific sites.
7. Model specific elements of the requirements engineering process by mapping task-specific roles, artifacts, and communication mechanisms onto the previously identified sites.

This process can be supported through the use of exemplar project templates from previous projects. Ideally the CGREN modeling exercise would be conducted as part of the kick-off event, but it can also be revisited throughout the project. One of the RA's in our study specifically mentioned that she saw the CGREN models as part of a "*living document*."

5 Refining the Model

As a result of the study we extended the meta-model to support the notions of communication volume, multiple hats, and elicitation techniques. Figure 11 presents the new meta-model uses classes to model *access* with associated *type* and *frequency* attributes, and the *communication* class with *frequency and media* attributes. The *frequency* attribute addresses our study participants' request to model the volume of communication between two roles. Three additional classes are added to the meta-model to depict the notion of elicitation techniques used with specific collaborative events. To this end, an event is modeled as a *collaboration* between *participants.* A collaboration is associated with meeting *type* (i.e. JAD, Storyboarding, etc), a meeting *name,* and an outlook-style schedule depicting actual meeting times and duration. The associated icons are shown in Figure 12.

Each *participant* has a *role* in the meeting and each *collaboration* is assigned to a primary *site. Communication* and *participation* elements are represented as associations in instantiated models, while the *collaboration* type is modeled using one of the meeting type entities in Figure 12. To support the extended taxonomy, we also added an additional "many hats" icon, and introduced the visual notation that the width of the communication arc is approximately proportional to the estimated communication frequency. In addition, we introduced the icons shown in Figure 12 to represent a variety of elicitation techniques.

Figure 13 provides an illustrated example of how the new taxonomy and related notation could be used to plan a globally distributed JAD session. In this session the JAD meeting is being organized at Location-1 by a project stakeholder wearing dual hats of JAD Facilitator and RA.

Figure 12. New Icons for multiple roles and Requirements Elicitation

Many participants, including SMEs, a developer, and a tester all physically participate in the JAD session, while SMEs from Location 2 and an LSP from Location 3 participate remotely using video-conferencing. The Location2 LSP communicates with local developers if issues arise during the JAD session. Finally, a report is sent to the manager at Location 4 at the end of the session.

6 Related Work

Other techniques exist for modeling stakeholders and their communication channels within an organization and/or project. Organizational charts identify project participants but are rather rigid in nature and often fail to capture the realities of how information is disseminated in an organization, and how roles and responsibilities are assigned in real projects [11]. Damian et al [4] described the communication paths between stakeholders in distributed projects using requirements-centered social network (RCSN) models. CGREN adopts several concepts from the RCSN, namely identifying stakeholders, and modeling communication paths between sites. However, the CGREN provides a more expressive approach for modeling com - munication media, stakeholder collaborations by role, artifact types, and other requirements engineering activities. Other visually oriented methods for describing large projects and their interactions fall short of capturing the details of a globally distributed requirements engineering project.

7 Conclusions

This paper describes our observations of the use of CGREN by requirements analysts to plan distributed requirements engineering processes. In general, CGREN helped the analysts to identify important locations, roles and communication mechanisms. Furthermore, new aspects of CGREN introduced in this paper, such as the inclusion of icons for specific elicitation activities, introduce the potential for stimulating greater creativity and improving the effectiveness of the requirements elicitation process. Our future work will involve augmenting our previously created CGREN tool with the new and modified icons, and testing CGREN in industrial settings.

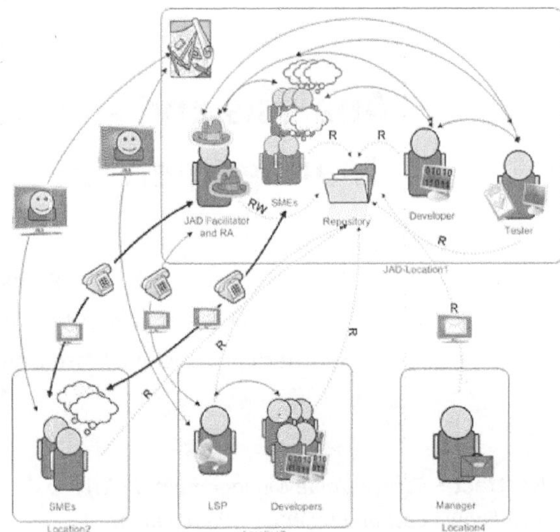

Figure 13. Utilizing the proposed new taxonomy and icons to model a Joint Application Design (JAD) session

8 References

[1] P. Sawyer, "The Context of Software Requirements," in *Software Engineering, Volume 1: The Development Process,* vol. 1, R. H. Thayer and M. J. Christensen, Eds., 3rd ed:John Wiley & Sons, 2005.

[2] J.D.Herbsleb. Global Software Engineering: The Future of Socio-technical Coordination. Future of Software Engineering, 2—7. FOSE'07, 23-25, May 2007, pp. 188-198.

[3] A. Taweel, B. Delaney, T.N.Arvanitis, L. Zhao, "Communication, Knowledge and Co-ordination Management in Globally Distributed Software Development: Informed by a Software Engineering Case Study," ICGSE, 2009, pp.370-375.

[4] D. Damian, "Stakeholders in Global Requirements Engineering: Lessons Learned form Practice," *IEEE Software,* vol 24, pp. 21-27,2007.

[5] D. Damian, S. Marczak, and I. Kwan, "Collaboration Patterns and the Impact of Distance on Awareness in Requirements-Centered Social Networks," presented at 15th IEEE International Requirements Engineering Conference (RE 2007), New Delhi, India, 2007.

[6] P.Laurent, P. Mader, J. Cleland Huang, and A. Steele, "A Taxonomy and Visual Notation for Modeling Globally Distributed Requirements Engineering Projects" presented at 5th IEEE International Confernece of Global Software Engineeting, (ICGSE '10), Princeton, USA, 2010.

[7] P. Laurent and J. Cleland Huang, "Requirements-Gathering Collaborative Networks in Distributed Software Projects," presented at Collaboration and Intercultural Issues on Requirement: Communication, Understanding and Softskills (CIRCUS '09), Atlanta, GA, USA.

[8] P. Kroll and P. Krutchen, *The Rational Unified Process Made Easy: A Practitioner's Guide to the RUP*, Addison-Wesley, 2003.

[9] R. Turner and B. Boehm, "Using Risk to Balance Agile and Plan-Driven Methods," *Computer*, vol. 36, pp. 57-66, 2003.

[10] Alan M. Davis, Óscar Dieste Tubío, Ann M. Hickey, Natalia Juristo Juzgado, Ana María Moreno: Effectiveness of Requirements Elicitation Techniques: Empirical Results Derived from a Systematic Review. RE 2006: 176-185.

[11] B. Berenbach, "Impact of Organizational Structure on Distributed Requirements Engineering Processes: Lessons Learned," International Workshop on Global Software Development for the Practitioner, New York, NY, USA, 2006, pp.15-19.

Analysis and Application of Earned Value Management in Software Development

Frank Tsui
School of Computing and Software Engineering
Southern Polytechnic State University, Marietta, Georgia, USA 30060

Abstract - *Earned Value Management (EVM) is a well-known cost and schedule management technique in government and defense industry projects. Its usage, however, is not as wide spread in the general software industry. In this paper we explore some of the shortcomings in EVM and suggest several improvements in the application of EVM in software development projects. In particular, we analyze the nature of software projects and offer improved ways to approximate Estimate of Completion for cost of software projects. Another area of special attention in this paper is demonstrating that EVM's metric such as Schedule Performance Index alone does not alert the project managers early enough on late task starting date and that the actual start date itself must be taken into account.*

Keyword: EVM, Cost, Schedule, Software Projects

1 Introduction

Earned Value Management (EVM) is a cost-schedule management and control technique. Since its inception in government financial management approximately fifty years ago, EVM has been used for project management in various government and defense industry related projects [1, 6, 7]. However, its usage is still relatively new in the software industry [5]. EVM has been adopted by some Agile software development projects [8], but it remains foreign to a large number of software project managers. In this paper we explore and analyze the applicability of this technique as it applies to software project management and to software engineering. Through this analysis, we will delineate some of the potential drawbacks in handling projections and show how one may cope with these in order to incorporate EVM as a project management technique for software engineering. In particular, at the macro level, we offer potential improvements to Estimate of Completion (EAC) for cost. We also offer suggestions at the micro level where examining only the numerical metrics such as Schedule Performance Index (SPI) and Cost Performance Index (CPI) of EVM alone may not be enough. We show that while EVM metrics are mostly task completion driven, project managers still need to guard against delay in task start date.

In the next section, Macro Level Definition and Application of EVM, we quickly review the familiar terms and the specific metrics employed in EVM. We then explain the forecasting problem of Estimate at Completion (EAC) as it is applied to software development projects. Some possible ways to improve on the EAC forecasting problem is offered in the Potential Improvements section. In the Micro Level Application of EVM section, we discuss ways to account for and to provide credits to tasks that have started and have completed part of the tasks. The need to be mindful of slippage in task start date and having to look beyond SPI and CPI metrics is discussed in Task Late Start Problem section. Lastly, we summarize the analysis of application of EVM to software projects in the Conclusion section.

2 Macro Level Definitions and Application of EVM

At the macro level, all large software development projects have a similar set of major activities: requirements analysis and specification, architectural design, detailed design, code implementation, build and integration, functional testing, system testing, and release for deployment. In a way, one may view this as the work breakdown structure (WBS) of macro tasks in software development [9]. For each of these macro tasks one may assign it an estimated amount of effort, or a Budgeted Cost (BC), along with an estimated start date and completion date. The sum of all the allocated cost of these tasks, or ∑BC, at project completion is called Budget At Completion (BAC). The major elements of EVM are composed of Budgeted Cost of Work Scheduled (BCWS), Budgeted Cost of Work Performed (BCWP), and Actual Cost of Work Performed (ACWP). At any project status check time, t, the sum of BCs of all those tasks that are scheduled to be completed is BCWS. For those tasks that are actually completed or performed at time t, the sum of those tasks' BCs is the BCWP. Both BCWS and BCWP use the estimated work effort, BCs, but they may contain different set of tasks because scheduled and actually completed tasks at time t may be different. The sum of the Actual Effort (AC) expended for those actually completed tasks at time t is ACWP. Thus, at time t, ACWP is the sum of ACs for those same tasks accounted for in BCWP.

Furthermore, one may now track and compare the planned versus the actual project status using a pair of measurements, Schedule Variance (SV) and Cost Variance (CV). An alternate, but similar, pair of Schedule Performance Index (SPI) and Cost Performance Index (CPI) may be used to monitor the project status and provide an indicator of how the project is performing relative to its planned schedule and cost. Note that SPI = BCWP/BCWS and CPI = BCWP/ACWP; thus when SPI > 1, we are ahead of schedule, but when CPI > 1, we are under-running the cost. When SPI and CPI are both equal to 1, then we are on target for both schedule and cost. When SPI < 1, we are behind schedule, but when CPI < 1 we have a cost over-run situation. As a project manager, one may ask for guidance on how much smaller than 1 does SPI need to be before one should be alarmed. Similarly, how much smaller than 1 does CPI needs to be before one should feel uneasy? These may be industry or enterprise specific, and there is no general guidance at this time.

EVM also includes a computational formula for prognosticating Estimate at Completion (EAC) for cost and for schedule as follows. Let EAC_S stand for EAC for Schedule and EAC_C stand for EAC for Cost. Then,

$$EAC_S = ACWP + (BAC - BCWP)/SPI \quad (1)$$
$$EAC_C = ACWP + (BAC - BCWP)/CPI \quad (2)$$

These forecasted numbers are based on two components. One part is the actual cost incurred to-date, or ACWP, and the other part is the estimated remaining work, or (BAC - BCWP). A vital part of estimating the remaining work utilizes a feed-back mechanism of in-project history, SPI and CPI, for estimating respectively the new schedule at project completion and the new cost at project completion. This method of predicting EAC has been shown to be relatively accurate for some projects [3]. An earlier study of differing EAC by varying the CPI and SPI indices was conducted by Christensen [4] and found that one still need to be cautious in EAC projection.

2.1 Forecasting Problem for Software Projects

For software development, especially for large software projects, the major tasks involving requirements, design, implementation, etc. are very different in nature and are often times performed by different people with varying levels of skills. For example, requirements solicitation and analysis work is very different from implementation work. It is also very different from design or testing tasks. These macro tasks in software development are each composed of different activities and thus require different skills sets. The different tasks of software development would present at least the following list of differences that will make productivity and actual performance information of any one major task practically non-applicable to another major task of software development for in-project feedback.

- Different set of sub-activities and skills required for any major task
- Different sets of people performing that major task
- Quality effects of one task on later tasks

For example, as we progress from completing the requirements task to the other tasks, the in-project history of requirements task for that project may not be appropriate for estimating the remaining effort, both cost and schedule, of implementation task or of testing task of the project. Thus using in-project SPI and CPI indices, at the completion of requirements task may actually be misleading in projecting task completions for other tasks because the other tasks are significantly different in nature. Therefore, the resulting EAC_S and EAC_C may create false hope or false alarm.

The quality effect in software development is an example that relates to the special situation of software development that EVM does not account for. Because software development tasks such as design, implementation and even testing still include many creative inventions, the likelihood of errors is high. The projection of defects from these errors, which must be corrected prior to release, is not very accurate. Thus the amount of extra work needed in down-stream activities, such as different testing and bug fixing tasks, resulting from these potential errors in earlier, upstream activities, can not be folded into the CPI or SPI indices. Thus EAC projections for schedule and cost, which do not take this quality effect into consideration, may be off the mark for software development projects. This notion of software development often taking longer than expected is also highlighted in [2].

2.2 Potential Improvements

We propose two categories of approaches to improve the projection for software projects. First category is to address the situation via using a different set of feedback mechanism than the generic in-project CPI and SPI. We need to recognize that each type of task in software development is markedly different from other types of tasks. The historical information relating to each different type of remaining task should be used as the new cost and schedule adjuster. This assumes an organization that either has historical data or has access to historical data. Let the remaining major tasks be E1, ---, En. Corresponding to each E_j, we will define BC_j, and AC_j to be the Budgeted Cost and Actual Cost of those efforts related only to that major task which is still remaining. Then define a $CPI_j = BC_j/AC_j$ from past data for each remaining major task j. Note that we use BC and AC of each task because we are interested in delineating each specific task. In the most simplified case, we would just use the average of these CPI_j 's as the new CPI'. Thus for the remaining n tasks, the new CPI' = $(\sum CPI_j)/ n$. The new Estimate at Completion for Cost will then be the following.

$$EAC_C' = ACWP + (BAC - BCWP)/ CPI' \quad (3)$$

Such a derived CPI' may be still too simplified. We may also look at each CPI_j for the remaining tasks and consider the following:

$$CPI'_{max} = \text{maximum } (CPI_j s) \quad (4)$$
$$CPI'_{min} = \text{minimum } (CPI_j s) \quad (5)$$
$$CPI'_{w} = w1xCPI_{j1} + w2xCPI_{j2} + \text{----} + wnCPI_{jn}, \text{ where } 0<wi<1 \text{ and } \sum wi = 1 \quad (6)$$

CPI'_{max} is the CPI' derived from the type of task whose historical BC/AC ratio is the largest among all the remaining tasks. Thus CPI'_{max} may be considered for an optimistic prognostication of EAC. CPI'_{min} is the reverse case and may be considered for a pessimistic prognostication. Finally, the project manager may place different weights on each of the remaining tasks' CPIs and create a weighted CPI', or CPI'_w. Using past projects' information closely related to the remaining tasks, when picking the appropriate CPI', brings an additional level of accuracy in the projections. The software project manager may consider each of the following for his or her Estimate at Completion:

$$EACc'1 = ACWP + (BAC-BCWP)/CPI'_{max} \quad (7)$$
$$EACc'2 = ACWP + (BAC-BCWP)/CPI'_{min} \quad (8)$$
$$EACc'3 = ACWP + (BAC-BCWP)/CPI'_{w} \quad (9)$$

The application of weights utilized in CPI'w may now take quality results of earlier tasks into consideration for the yet to finish tasks. Software project managers may also bring in other risk considerations in choosing which of the above projections to use. Aforementioned quality effects may be folded in as an additional risk consideration. If it is known from historical data that certain tasks such as design or implementation is more error prone for the particular set of developers of the project, then subsequent testing and fix tasks may require more effort than projected. Thus the project manager may choose to be more conservative and use EACc'2 for estimating the completion cost. EACc'3 may be most complicated, but it is the most flexible in that it allows the project manager to allocate different levels of concern for each of the different types of remaining tasks. Note that EACc' is just a special case of EACc'3 where the weights in CPI'w are all equal.

The above discussion is based on enterprises that have collected and kept historical data on software development. Moreover, these enterprises need to have monitored projects using EVM and kept the BCs and ACs for the major software development tasks. However, most of the enterprises have not used EVM nor kept such data related to past BC and AC by major task types. Hence, a different approach is needed for those enterprises who are new to EVM and do not have historical data. These organizations would still need to use the in-project data to estimate the remaining efforts for EAC.

A different category of approach to improving the projection of EAC is to modify the project management approach and choose the appropriate projects to fit the measurement, not modifying the projection formula. When the project is small, we often times use a small group of people of similar skills and have these same people involved in all aspects of the project. This management approach for small projects is sometimes a result of economic practicality where specialization by task type is just not possible. Such an approach will take out one of the earlier mentioned problems of different specialists performing different tasks and thus causing inaccurate prognostication of remaining tasks based on in-project data. Furthermore, apply EVM to not only small, but also simpler projects where less new innovation is required. This will ease the potential quality variance problem. Limiting the application of EVM to small, simple software project and employing the same set of people to perform all major tasks, should provide more stability to in-project data for estimating even different tasks. This approach should provide a partial improvement to using the original formulae of EAC_S and EAC_C.

3 Micro Level Application of EVM

Adoption of EVM for software engineering also needs some guidance at the micro level. One difficult area is the computation of BCWP. For project status analysis and report at time t, we accumulate all the BC's of the tasks that are completed by time t. That becomes the BCWP at time t and is used for CPI and SPI indices. However, at time t there may be tasks that are partially complete. Traditionally, these partially completed tasks are not included in the computation of BCWP. In other words, a task gets either 0% or 100% of the BC when computing the BCWP. In software development many tasks are performed in parallel, and these partially completed tasks need to be folded in the computation of BCWP to gain a more accurate account of the project status. Consider Figure 1 where multiple tasks are performed in parallel. The project of status of BCWP on March 15 would include those tasks that are completed, namely, requirement and design. Thus BCWP would be 100 + 76 = 176 person hours, ACWP would be 105 +65 = 170 person hours and BCWS would be 100 + 76 = 176 on the March 15 status report. The schedule performance index, SPI = BCWP/BCWS = 176/176, would be 1, and cost performance index, CPI = BCWP/ACWP = 176/170, would be greater than 1. This says that we are *right on schedule* and *under-run on cost*. But we also need to account for the other two major tasks, implementation and testing, that have started and have already expended some effort in our status report. Furthermore, we note that the testing activity actually started later than the estimated start date.

Figure 1: Project Status on March 15

Major Task	Estimated Effort (BC) In person hrs.	Actual Effort Expended (AC In person hrs.	Estimated Start date	Actual Start date	Estimated Completion date	Actual Completion date
Requirement	100	105	Jan 10	Jan 10	Feb 15	Feb 15
Design	76	65	Feb 10	Feb 10	March 10	March 5
Implement	150	55	March 1	March 1	April 15	-----
Test	90	35	Feb 10	Feb 15	May 1	-----
Integrate	8	0	May 2	-----	May 5	-----

Several approaches may be taken. If the software development project is laid out in broad chunks of requirements, design, implementation, test, integration and release, we can see that these tasks will overlap. For example, that part of testing which addresses test scenario and test case development may overlap with requirements and design tasks. Taking a project status at the end of the requirements phase and not allocate any credit to some sub-task completions within testing would create a false impression of the status. To evade this type of problem, partial task completion credit may be given with rules such as the following.

- Allocate 0% of the BC of the task if it has started but not reached 30% of the task BC.
- Allocate 25% of the BC of the task if it is started and has passed 30% of the task BC.
- Allocate 100% of the BC of the task only when it is completed.

Including the tasks' partial BCs and adding that into the computation of BCWP may provide a more accurate account of the project status. The above suggestion is a relatively conservative approach. Using this conservative credit allocation scheme, the new BCWP = 100 + 76 + (.25 x 150) + (.25 x 90) = 236. The new ACWP = 105 + 65 + 55 + 35 = 260. Utilizing the new BCWP and ACWP, we can recalculate for new SPI = 236/176 and new CPI = 236/260. The new SPI > 1, and the new CPI < 1; thus with partial credits, our project status on March 15 would be quite different from what was previously stated. We are now *ahead of schedule*, but has a slight *cost over-run.*

Clearly, one may vary the 25% to something lesser or larger, depending on past experiences and history with the project team and the nature of the current project. One may also add more increments and granularities such as allocating only 10% when the task is started, allocating 25% when the task is believed to be half way completed, and allocating 50% when it is believed to have past the half way mark. Since the adoption of EVM in software development has not been broad enough, no clear guidance on the percentage can be provided yet. However, we do know the binary case of 0% or 100% creates some problems projecting an accurate project status when there is more than one task that has already incurred some effort, including those tasks that started earlier than planned.

3.1 Task Late Start Problem

If a task is started earlier than planned, we can adopt some variation of the above suggested, partial credit approach. However, in our Figure 1 example, the testing activity actually started five days later than the planned start date of February 10th. While one can easily see this delay in test starting date in a tabular form such as Figure 1, there is no clear way to indicate this delay in task starting if one just looked at EVM metrics of SPI and CPI. The previously computed project SPI indicated that the project was on schedule on March 15. The newly computed SPI, with partial credits, even indicated that the project was ahead of schedule. Experienced software engineers and project managers know that a late starting task often results in late completion of that task and/or requires more effort and may even adversely affect other related tasks. Project managers may wonder whether they should have been alarmed on March 15 by the start date delay. Let us fast forward from March 15 status day to May 1, when the testing task is scheduled to compete. To keep the discussion focused, we will assume that the implementation task actually completed on target, both schedule and cost wise. Let us examine the two major possibilities for the testing task on May 1: (a) the testing task is completed and (b) the testing task is not completed. The amount of actual effort expended is also a variable. This is shown in Figure 2, where the completion date of test task is marked as XXX and the AC for test is marked as NN.

Figure 2: Project Status on May 1

Major Task	Estimated Effort (BC) In person hrs.	Actual Effort Expended (AC) In person hrs.	Estimated Start date	Actual Start date	Estimated Completion date	Actual Completion date
Requirement	100	105	Jan 10	Jan 10	Feb 15	Feb 15
Design	76	65	Feb 10	Feb 10	March 10	March 5
Implement	150	150	March 1	March 1	April 15	April 15
Test	90	NN	Feb 10	Feb 15	May 1	XXX
Integrate	8	0	May 2	----	May 5	-----

Consider the first case where the testing task is completed on May 1. Then there are three further sub-divisions: (i) the actual cost is NN= 90 person hours as planned, (ii) the actual cost is NN > 90 person hours, (iii) the actual cost is NN < 90 person hours. The best possibility is case (i) that NN = 90 as planned, in which case the SPI = 416/416 = 1 and CPI = 416/410 >1. The 5 days delay in test starting day caused no harm because the project is on schedule with a slight cost under-run. In case (ii) let us assume that we expended 100 person hours. Thus NN would be 100 and SPI = 416/416 = 1 and CPI = 416/420 <1. The delay caused a slight cost over-run, perhaps to make up for the schedule delay. For situation (iii), consider NN to be 80. Then SPI is still 1, but CPI = 416/400 > 1. The delay caused no harm in case (iii). Perhaps, the estimated BC for testing activity was a bit high to start with. The three scenarios demonstrated here show that in two of the three cases, the five day delay in starting the test task did not adversely affect the project.

Now consider the second case where the testing task is not complete on May 1 as planned. While we can not tell when the task will be complete and what the actual final effort would be, we can still look at the situation on May 1. We would have the same three sub-divisions of actual effort expended on May 1. First consider (i) where NN = 90 units expended. Now follow the strict EVM metric rule. Then BCWP is really 326 because test task is not complete on May 1, and BCWS is 416. Thus SPI is 326/416 < 1 and CPI = 326/410 <1. This says that the project is behind schedule with a cost over-run and potentially even higher cost over-run. This is bad, but it is the correct status on May 1. For situation (ii), again, assume that NN = 100 units expended even though the task is still incomplete. Then SPI = 326/416 <1 and CPI = 326/420 < 1. This says that the project is behind schedule but has an even higher cost over-run than case (i). This is also a negative status, but a correct one. Lastly, consider case (iii) where NN = 80. Again, SPI is the same less than 1, and CPI = 326/400 < 1. This project status report is pretty much the same as case (i) and (ii); that is, the project is behind schedule and over-run in cost.

When we fast forwarded from March 15 project status day to May 1, we saw that of the six possible scenarios four resulted in negative outcomes. For the three scenarios associated with the test task missing the May 1 completion date, the project was both behind schedule and over-budget. EVM, being a technique that is based mostly on effort at completion, does not readily provide a view into the potential problems of missing the task start date. The earlier a potential problem is squashed, the less likely will the problem mushroom into some uncontainable situation as shown in this example of test task missing the February 10th start date. Therefore, in using EVM, project managers can not just depend only on numeric figures such as SPI and CPI. One must still track not only the end dates, but also the actual start dates of the tasks and perform some forward projections when a task start date is missed.

4 Concluding Remarks

In this paper, we examined EVM as a project management technique for software development. In particular, we focused on its capability in portraying the current status and in projecting the future. As expected, future prognostication is a difficult task for most management techniques. We focused on two levels, macro and micro levels, of looking beyond just current status. Through this exploration we have proposed several improvements. One improvement at the macro level is a better in-project forecasting mechanism for Estimate at Completion of Cost (EACc) which allows one to vary the Cost Performance Index (CPI) depending on what and the nature of the remaining tasks. The other, at the micro level, is to look beyond just the SPI and CPI indices of EVM. Project managers must be mindful of the actual start and completion dates of tasks.

5 References

[1] W.F. Abba, "Earned Value Management-Reconciling Government and commercial Practices," Project Management, Special Issue, January/February 1997, pp 58-67.

[2] P.G. Armour, "The Business of Software - How We Build Things," Communications of ACM, January 2013, vol.56, No1, pp 32-33.

[3] I. Attarzadeh and O.S. Hock, "Implementation and Evaluation of Earned Value Index to Achieve an Accurate Project Time and Cost Estimation and Improve Earned Value Management System," International Conference on Information Management and Engineering, Kuala Lumpur, Malaysia, April, 2009.

[4] D. Christensen, "The Estimate At Completion Problem: A Review of Three Studies," Project Management Journal 24, March 1993, pp 37-42.

[5] H. Erdogums, "Tracking Progress through Earned Value," IEEE Software, September/October 2010, pp 2-7.

[6] Office of Secretary of Defense, Earned Value Management, www.acq.osd.mil/evm, accessed December, 2012.

[7] Q.W. Fleming and J.M. Koppelman, Earned Value Project Management, 4th Edition, Project Management Institute, Inc., 2010.

[8] T. Sulaiman, B. Barton, T. Blackburn, "AgileEVM – Earned Value Management in Scrum Projects," Proceedings of the AGILE 2006 Conference, Minneapolis, USA, July 2006, pp 7-16.

[9] F. Tsui, Managing Systems and IT Projects, Jones and Bartlett Learning, 2011.

On Acceptance Testing

Jean-Pierre Corriveau
School of Computer Science
Carleton University
Ottawa, CANADA
jeanpier@scs.carleton.ca

Wei Shi
Faculty of Business and Information Technology
University of Ontario Institute of Technology
Oshawa, CANADA
Wei.shi@uoit.ca

***Abstract*— Regardless of which (model-centric or code-centric) development process is adopted, industrial software production ultimately and necessarily requires the delivery of an executable implementation. It is generally accepted that the quality of such an implementation is of utmost importance. Yet current verification techniques, including software testing, remain problematic. In this paper, we focus on acceptance testing, that is, on the validation of the actual behavior of the implementation under test against the requirements of stakeholder(s). This task must be as objective and automated as possible. Our goal here is to review existing code-based and model-based tools for testing in light of what such an objective and automated approach to acceptance testing entails. Our contention is that the difficulties we identify originate mainly in a lack of traceability between a testable model of the requirements of the stakeholder(s) and the test cases used to validate these requirements.**

Keywords— Validation, Acceptance Testing, Model-Based Testing, Traceability, Scenario Models

Contact author for SERP 2013 paper: J-Pierre Corriveau

I. Introduction

The use and role of models in the production of software systems vary considerably across industry. Whereas some development processes rely extensively on a diversity of semantic-rich UML models [1], proponents of Agile methods instead minimize [2], if not essentially eliminate [3] the need for models. However, regardless of which model-centric or code-centric development process is adopted, industrial software production ultimately and necessarily requires the delivery of an executable implementation. Furthermore, it is generally accepted that the quality of such an implementation is of utmost importance [4]. That is, except for the few who adopt 'hit-and-run' software production [1], the importance of software verification within the software development lifecycle is widely acknowledged. Yet, despite recent advancements in program verification, automatic debugging, assertion deduction and *model-based testing* (hereafter MBT), Ralph Johnson [5] and many others still view software verification as a "catastrophic computer science failure". Indeed, the recent CISQ initiative [6] proceeds from such remarks and similar ones such as: "The current quality of IT application software exposes businesses and government agencies to unacceptable levels of risk and loss." [*Ibid.*]. In summary, software verification remains problematic. In particular, software testing, that is evaluating software by observing its executions on actual valued inputs [7], is "a widespread validation approach in industry, but it is still largely ad hoc, expensive, and unpredictably effective" [8]. Grieskamp [9], the main architect of Microsoft's MBT tool Spec Explorer [10], indeed confirms that current testing practices "are not only laborious and expensive but often unsystematic, lacking an engineering methodology and discipline and adequate tool support".

In this paper, we focus on one specific aspect of software testing, namely the validation [11] of the actual behavior of an *implementation under test* (hereafter IUT) against the requirements of stakeholder(s) of that system. This task, which Bertolino refers to as "acceptance testing" [8], must be as objective and automated as possible [12]. Our goal here is to survey existing tools for testing in light of what such an "objective and automated" approach to acceptance testing entails. To do so, we first discuss in section 2 existing code-based and, in section 3, existing model-based approaches to acceptance testing. We contend that the current challenges inherent to acceptance testing originate first and foremost in a lack of traceability between a testable model of the requirements of the stakeholder(s) and the test cases (i.e., code artifacts) used to validate the IUT against these requirements. We conclude by considering whether Model-Driven Development may offer an avenue of solution.

[1] according to which one develops and releases quickly in order to grab a market share, with little consideration for quality assurance and no commitment to maintenance and customer satisfaction!

II. CODE-BASED ACCEPTANCE TESTING?

Testing constitutes one of the most expensive aspects of software development and software is often not tested as thoroughly as it should be [8, 9, 11, 13]. As mentioned earlier, one possible standpoint is to view current approaches to testing as belonging to one of two categories: code-centric and model-centric. In this section, we briefly discuss the first of these two categories.

A code-centric approach, such as Test-Driven Design (TDD) [3] proceeds from the viewpoint that, for 'true agility', the design must be expressed once and only once, in code. In other words, there is no requirements model per se (that is, captured separately from code). Consequently, there is no traceability [14] between a requirements model and the test cases exercising the code. But such traceability is an essential facet of acceptance testing: without traceability of a suite of test cases 'back to' an explicitly-captured requirements model, there is no objective way of measuring how much of this requirements model is covered [11] by this test suite.

A further difficulty with TDD and similar approaches is that tests cases (in contrast to more abstract *tests* [11]) are code artifacts that are implementation-driven and implementation-specific. Consequently, the reuse potential of such test cases is quite limited: each change to the IUT may require several test cases to be updated. The explicit capturing of a suite of implementation-independent tests generated from a requirements model offers two significant advantages:

1) It decouples requirements coverage from the IUT: a suite of tests is generated from a requirements model according to some coverage criterion. Then, and only then, are tests somehow transformed into test cases proper (*i.e.*, code artifacts specific to the IUT). Such test cases must be kept in sync with a constantly evolving IUT, but this can be done totally independently of requirements coverage.

2) It enables reuse of a suite of tests across several IUTs, be they versions of a constantly-evolving IUT or, more interestingly, competing vendor-specific IUTs having to demonstrate compliance to some specification (e.g., in the domain of software radios).

Beyond such methodological issues faced by code-based approaches to acceptance testing, because the latter requires automation (e.g., [11, 12]), we must also consider tool support for such approaches.

Put simply, there is a multitude of tools for software testing (e.g., [15, 16]), even for specific domains such as Web quality assurance [17]. Bertolino [8] remarks, in her seminal review of the state-of-the-art in software testing, that most focus on functional testing, that is, check "that the observed behavior complies with the logic of the specifications". From this perspective, it appears these tools are relevant to acceptance testing. A closer look reveals most of these tools are code-based testing tools (e.g., JAVA's JUnit [18] and AutoTest [19]) that mainly focus on unit testing [11], that is, on testing individual procedures of an IUT (as opposed to scenario testing [20]). A few observations are in order:

1) There are many types of code-based *verification* tools. They include a plethora of static analyzers, as well as many other types of tools (see [21] for a short review). For example, some tackle design-by-contract [22], some metrics, some different forms of testing (e.g., regression testing [11]). According to the commonly accepted definition of software testing as "the evaluation of software by observing its executions on actual valued inputs" [7], many such tools (in particular, static analyzers) are not testing tools per se.

2) As argued previously, acceptance testing requires an implementation-independent requirements model. While possibly feasible, it is unlikely this testable requirements model (hereafter TRM) would be at a level of details that would enable traceability between it and unit-level tests and/or test cases. That is, typically the tests proceeding from a TRM are system-level ones [11], not unit-level ones.

3) Integration testing tools (such as Fit/Fitness, EasyMock and jMock, etc.) do not address acceptance testing proper. In particular, they do not capture a TRM per se. The same conclusion holds for test automation frameworks (e.g., IBM's Rational Robot [23]) and test management tools (such as HP Quality Centre [24] and Microsoft Team Foundation Server [25]).

One possible avenue to remedy the absence of a TRM in existing code-based testing tools may consist in trying to connect such a tool with a requirements capture tool, that is, with a tool that captures a requirements model but does not generate tests or test cases from it. However, our ongoing collaboration with Blueprint [26] to attempt to link their software to code-based testing tools has revealed a fundamental hurdle with such a multi-tool approach: Given there is no generation of test cases in Blueprint, traceability from Blueprint requirements[2] to test cases (be they generated or merely captured in some code-based testing tool) reduces to *manual* cross-referencing. That is, there is currently no automated way of connecting requirements with test cases. But a scalable approach to

---

[2] Blueprint offers user stories (which are a simple form of UML Use Cases [11, 27]), UI Mockups and free-form text to capture requirements. The latter are by far the most popular but the hardest to semantically process in an automated way.

acceptance testing requires such automated traceability. Without it, the initial manual linking of (e.g., hundred of) requirements to (e.g., possibly thousands of) test cases (e.g., in the case of a medium-size system of a few tens of thousands lines of code) is simply unfeasible. (From this viewpoint, whether either or both tools at hand support change impact analysis is irrelevant as it is the initial connecting of requirements to test cases that is most problematic.) At this point in time, the only observation we can add is that current experimentation with Blueprint suggests an eventual solution will require that a 'semantic bridge' between this tool and a code-based testing tool be constructed. But this is possible only if both requirements and test cases are captured in such a way that they enable their own semantic analysis. That is, unless we can first have algorithms and tools that can 'understand' requirements and test cases (by accessing and analyzing their underlying representations), we cannot hope to develop a semantic bridge between requirements and test cases. However, such 'understanding' is *extremely* tool specific, which leads us to conclude that a multi-tool approach to acceptance testing is unlikely in the short term (especially if one also has to 'fight' a frequent unfavorable bias of users towards multi-tool solutions, due to their over-specificity, their cost, etc.).

The need for an automated approach to traceability between requirements and test cases suggests the latter be somehow generated from the former. And thus we now turn to model-based approaches to acceptance testing.

III. MODEL-BASED TESTING

In her review of software testing, Bertolino [8] remarks: “A great deal of research focuses nowadays on model-based testing. The leading idea is to use models defined in software construction to drive the testing process, in particular to automatically generate the test cases. The pragmatic approach that testing research takes is that of following what is the current trend in modeling: whichever be the notation used, say e.g., UML or Z, we try to adapt to it a testing technique as effectively as possible [.]”

Model-Based Testing (MBT) [10, 28, 29] involves the derivation of tests and/or test cases from a model that describes at least some of the aspects of the IUT. More precisely, an MBT method uses various algorithms and strategies to generate tests (sometimes equivalently called 'test purposes') and/or test cases from a behavioral model of the IUT. Such a model is usually a partial representation of the IUT's behavior, ‘partial’ because the model abstracts away some of the implementation details.

Several survey papers (e.g., [8, 30, 31) and special issues (e.g., [29]) have addressed such model-based approaches, as well as the more specific model driven ones (e.g., [32, 33]). Some have specifically targeted MBT tools (e.g., [28]). While some MBT methods use models other than UML state machines (e.g., [34]), most rely on test case generation from such state machines (see [35] for a survey).

Here we will focus on state-based MBT tools that generate executable test cases. Thus we will not consider MBT contributions that instead only address the generation of tests (and thus do not tackle the difficult issue of transforming such tests into executable IUT-specific test cases). Nor will we consider MBT methods that are not supported by a tool (since, tool support is absolutely required in order to demonstrate the executability of the generated test cases).

We start by discussing Conformiq's Tool Suite [36, 37], formerly known as Conformiq Qtronic (as referred to in [35]). This tool requires that a system's requirements be captured in UML statecharts (using Conformiq's Modeler or third party tools). It "generates software tests [...] without user intervention, complete with test plan documentation and executable test scripts in industry standard formats like Python, TCL, TTCN-3, C, C++, Visual Basic, Java, JUnit, Perl, Excel, HTML, Word, Shell Scripts and others." [37]. This includes the automatic generation of test inputs (including structural data), expected test outputs, executable test suites, test case dependency information and traceability matrix, as well as support for boundary value analysis, atomic condition coverage, and other black-box test design heuristics" [*Ibid.*].

While such a description may give the impression acceptance testing has been successfully completely automated, extensive experimentation[3] reveals some significant hurdles:

First, Grieskamp [9], the creator of Spec Explorer [10], another state-based MBT tool, explains at length the problems inherent to test case generation from state machines. In particular, he makes it clear that the *state explosion problem* remains a daunting challenge for all state-based MBT tools (contrary to the impression one may get from reading the few paragraphs devoted to it in the 360-page User Manual from Conformiq [37]). Indeed, even the modeling of a simple game like Yahtzee (involving throwing 5 dice up to three times per round, holding some dice between each throw, to

[3] by the authors and 100+ senior undergraduate and graduate students in the context of offerings of a 4th year undergraduate course in Quality Assurance and a graduate course in Object Oriented Software Engineering twice over the last two years.

achieve the highest possible score according to a specific poker-like scoring algorithm) can require a huge state space if the 13-rounds of the game are to be modeled. Both tools offer a simple mechanism to constrain the state 'exploration' (or search) algorithm by setting bounds (e.g., on the maximum number of states to consider, or the "look ahead depth"). But then the onus is on the user to fix such bounds through trial and error. And such constraining is likely to hinder the completeness of the generated test suite. The use of 'slicing' in Spec Explorer [10], via the specification of a scenario (see Figures 1a and 1b), constitutes a much better solution (to the problem of state explosion) for it emphasizes the importance of *equivalence partitioning* [11] and rightfully places on the user the onus of determining which scenarios are equivalent (a task that, as Binder explains [*Ibid.*], is *unlikely* to be fully automatable).

```
// score 36 end states with 3, 3, 3 (as last dices)
// then score one end state for 2, 2, 1, 1, 3: must score 0
machine ScoreThreeOfAKind() : RollConstraint
{ (  NewGame;
     (RollAll(_, _, 3, 3, 3);
     Score(ScoreType.ThreeOfAKind)
   | RollAll(2, 2, 1, 1, 3);
     Score(ScoreType.ThreeOfAKind)))
   || (construct model program from RollConstraint)
}
```

Figure 1.a A Spec Explorer scenario for exploring scoring of three-of-a-kind rolls

```
//Sample hold test: should vary only 4th and 5th dice
// Gives 36 possible end states
machine hold1() : RollConstraint
{    (NewGame; RollAll(1,1,1,1,1);
     hold(1); hold(2); hold(3); RollAll)
   || (construct model program from RollConstraint)
}
```

Figure 1.b: A Spec Explorer scenario for holding the first three dice

Second, in Conformiq, requirements coverage[4] is only possible if states and transitions are manually associated with requirements (which are thus merely annotations superimposed on a state machine)! Clearly, such a task lacks automation and scalability. Also, it points to an even more fundamental problem: requirements traceability, that is, the ability to link requirements to test cases. Shafique and Labiche [35, table 4.b] equate "requirements traceability" with "integration with a requirements engineering tool". Consequently, they consider that both Spec Explorer and Conformiq offer only "partial" support for this problem. For example, in Conformiq, the abovementioned requirements annotations can be manually connected to requirements captured in a tool such as IBM RequisitePro or IBM Rational DOORS [37, chapter 7]. However, we believe this operational view of requirements traceability downplays a more fundamental semantic problem identified by Grieskamp [9]: a system's stakeholders are much more inclined to associate requirements to scenarios [20] (such as UML use cases [27]) than to parts of a state machine... From this viewpoint:

1) Spec Explorer implicitly supports the notion of scenarios via the use of "sliced machines", as previously illustrated. But slicing is a sophisticated technique drawing on semantically complex operators [10]. Thus, the state space generated by a sliced machine often may not correspond to the expectations of the user. This makes it all-the-more difficult to conceptually and then manually link the requirements of stakeholder's to such scenarios.

2) Conformiq *does* support use cases, which can be linked to requirements and can play a role in test case generation [37, p.58]. Thus, instead of having the user manually connect requirements to elements of a state machine, a scenario-based approach to requirements traceability could be envisioned. Intuitively this approach would associated a) requirements with use cases and b) paths of use cases with series of test cases. But, unfortunately, this would require a totally different algorithm for test case generation, one not rooted in state machines, leading to a totally different tool.

Third, test case executability may not be as readily available as what the user of an MBT tool expects. Consider for example, the notion of a "scripting backend" in Conformiq Designer. For example [37, p.131]: "The TTCN-3 scripting backend publishes tests generated by Conformiq Designer automatically in TTCN-3 and saves them in TTCN-3 files. TTCN-3 test cases are executed against a real system under test with a TTCN-3 runtime environment and necessary adapters." The point to be grasped is (what is often referred to as) 'glue code' is required to connect the generated tests to an actual IUT. Though less obvious from the documentation, the same observation holds for the other formats (e.g., C++, Perl, etc.) for which Conformiq offers such backends. For example, we first read [37, p.136]: "With Perl script backend, Perl test cases can be derived automatically from a functional design model and be executed against a real system." And then find out on the next page that this in fact

[4] not to be confused with state machine coverage, nor with test suite coverage, both of these being directly and quite adequately addressed by Conformiq and Spec Explorer [35, tables 2 and 3].

requires "the location of the Perl test harness module, i.e., the Perl module which contains the implementation of the routines that the scripting backend generates." In other words, Conformiq does provide not only test cases but also offers a (possibly 3rd party) test harness [*Ibid.*] that enables their execution against an IUT. But its user is left to create glue code to bridge between these test cases and the IUT. This manual task is not only time-consuming but potentially error-prone [11]. Also, this glue code is implementation-specific and thus, both its reusability across IUTs and its maintainability are problematic.

In Spec Explorer [10], each test case corresponds to a specific path through a generated state machine. One alternative is to have each test case connected to the IUT by having the rules of the specification (which are used to control state exploration, as illustrated shortly) explicitly refer to procedures of the IUT. Alternatively, an adapter, that is, glue code, can be written to link these test cases with the IUT. That is, once again, traceability to the IUT is a manual task. Furthermore, in this tool, test case execution (which is completely neatly integrated into Visual Studio) relies on the IUT inputting test case specific data (captured as parameter *values* of a transition of the generated state machine) and outputting the expected results (captured in the model as return *values* of these transitions). As often emphasized in the associated tutorial videos (especially, session 3 part 2), the state variables used in the Spec Explorer rules are only relevant to state machine exploration, not to test case execution. Thus any probing into the state of the IUT must be explicitly addressed through the use of such parameters and return values. The challenge of such an approach can be illustrated by returning to our Yahtzee example. Consider a rule called RollAll to capture the state change corresponding to a roll of the dice:

```
 [Rule]
 static void RollAll(int d1, int d2, int d3, int d4, int d5)
{     Condition.IsTrue(numRolls < 3);
      Condition.IsTrue(numRounds < 13);
      if (numRolls == 0) {
              Condition.IsTrue(numHeld == 0); }
      else  { Condition.IsTrue(!d1Held || d1 == d1Val);
              Condition.IsTrue(!d2Held || d2 == d2Val);
              Condition.IsTrue(!d3Held || d3 == d3Val);
              Condition.IsTrue(!d4Held || d4 == d4Val);
              Condition.IsTrue(!d5Held || d5 == d5Val);
      }
    /* store values from this roll */
      d1Val = d1;        d2Val = d2;    d3Val = d3;
      d4Val = d4;    d5Val = d5;    numRolls += 1;
}
```

Here numRolls, numRounds, numHeld, d_iHeld and d_iVal are all state variables. Without going in details, this rule enables all valid rolls (with respect to the number of rounds, the number of rolls and which dice are to be held) to be potential next states. So, if before firing this rules the values for d_iVal were {1, 2, 3, 4, 5} and those of the d_iHeld were {true, true, true, true, false}, then only rolls that have the first 4 dice (which are held) as {1, 2, 3, 4} are valid as next rolls. The problem is that {1, 2, 3, 4, 5} is valid as a next roll. But, when testing against an IUT, this rule makes it impossible to verify whether the last dice was held by mistake or actually rerolled and still gave 5. The solution attempted by students given this exercise generally consists in adding 6 more Boolean parameters to RollAll: each Boolean indicating if a die is held or not. The problem with such a solution is that it leads to state explosion (especially if the scenario under test addresses the 3 throws of a round!). One alternative, which is far less obvious, is to use the return value of this rule to indicate for each die if it was held or not...

The key point to be grasped from this example is that, beyond issues of scalability and traceability, one fundamental reality of all MBT tools is that their semantic intricacies can significantly impact on what acceptance testing can and cannot address. For example, in Yahtzee, given a game consists of 13 rounds to be each scored once into one of the 13 categories of the scoring sheet, a tester would ideally want to see this scoring sheet after each roll in order to ensure not only that the most recent roll has been scored correctly but also that previous scores are still correctly recorded. But achieving this is notoriously challenging unless it is explicitly programmed into the glue code that connects the test cases to the IUT; an approach that is quite distant from the goals of automated testing.

Finally, on the topic of semantics, it is important to emphasize the wide spectrum of semantics found in MBT tools. Consider, for example, Cucumber rooted in BDD [38], a user-friendly language for expressing scenarios. But these scenarios are extremely simple (nay simplistic) compared to the ones expressible using slicing in Spec Explorer [10]. In fact, most MBT tools cannot adequately address the semantic complexities (e.g., temporal scenario inter-relationships [20]) of a scenario-driven approach to test case derivation [*Ibid.*])[5]. The question then is to ask how relevant to acceptance testing other semantic approaches may be. We consider this issue next.

---

5 despite, we repeat, Grieskamp's [9] crucial observation that the stakeholders of a software system are much likelier to express their requirements using scenarios than state machines!

IV. DISCUSSION

There exists a large body of work on modeling 'specifications' in vacuum, that is, with no connection to an executable system. From Büschi automata to Formula [39], researchers have explored formalisms whose semantics enable objective (and possibly automated) 'model checking', which consists in deciding if a model is well-formed or not. The lack of traceability to an IUT disqualifies such work from immediate use for acceptance testing. In fact, because the semantic gap between such approaches and what can be observed from the execution of a system under test is so significant, it is unlikely such approaches will be reconcilable in the short or medium term with the demands of practical acceptance testing, especially with respect to traceability from requirements to test cases.

Because the lack of traceability between models and code is widely acknowledged as a common problem, we should consider modeling approaches not specifically targeted towards acceptance testing but that address traceability. More to the point, we must now ask if *model-driven design* (MDD) [40] may be the foundations on which to build a scalable traceable approach to acceptance testing. MDD's philosophy that "the model is the code" [*Ibid.*] certainly seems to eliminate the traceability issue between models and code: code can be easily regenerated every time the model changes[6]. And since, in MDD tools (e.g., [41]), code generation is based on state machines, there appears to be an opportunity to reuse these state machines not just for code generation but also for test case generation. This is indeed feasible with Conformiq Designer [36], which allows the reuse of state machines from third party tools. But there is a major stumbling block: while both code and test cases can be generated (albeit by different tools) from the same state machines, they are totally independent. In other words, the existence of a full code generator does not readily help with the problem of traceability from requirements to test cases. In fact, because the code is generated, it is extremely difficult to reuse it for the construction of the scriptends that would allow Conformiq's user to connect test cases to this generated IUT. Moreover, such a strategy defeats the intention of full code generation in MDD, which is to have the users of an MDD tool never have to deal with code directly (except for defining the actions of transitions in state machines).

One possible avenue of solution would be to develop an integrated generator that would use state machines to generate code and test cases for this code. But traceability of such test cases back to a requirements models (especially a scenario-driven one, as advocated by Grieskamp [9]), still remains unaddressed by this proposal. Thus, at this point in time, the traceability offered in MDD tools by virtue of full code generation does not appear to help with the issue of traceability between requirements and test cases for acceptance testing. Furthermore, one must also acknowledge Selic's [40] concerns about the relatively low level of adoption of MDD tools in industry.

In the end, despite the dominant trend in MBT of adopting state-based test and test case generation, it may be necessary to consider some sort of scenario-driven generation of test cases from requirements for acceptance testing. This seems eventually feasible given the following concluding observations:

1) There is already work on generating tests out of use cases [11, 42] and use case maps [43], and generating test cases out of sequence diagrams [44, 45]. Path sensitization [11] is the key technique typically used in these proposals. There are still open problems with path sensitization [*Ibid.*]. In particular, automating the identification of the variables to be used for path selection is problematic. As is the issue of path coverage (in light of a potential explosion of the number of possible paths in a scenario model). In other words, the fundamental problem of equivalence partitioning [*Ibid.*] remains and an automated solution for it appears to be quite unlikely. However, despite all of this, we remark simple implementations of this technique already exist (e.g., [43] for use case maps).

2) (Partial if not ideally fully) automated traceability between these three models can certainly be envisioned given their semantic closeness, each one in fact refining the previous one.

3) Traceability between sequence diagrams and an IUT appears quite straightforward given the low-level of abstraction of such models.

4) Within the semantic context of path sensitization, tests can be thought of as paths (i.e., sequences) of observable responsibilities (i.e., small testable functional requirements). Thus, because tests from use cases, use case maps and sequence diagrams are all essentially paths of responsibilities, and because responsibilities ultimately map onto procedures of the IUT, automated traceability between tests and test cases and between test cases and IUT seems realizable.

[6] As one of the original creators of the ObjecTime toolset, which has evolved in Rational Rose Technical Developer [41], the first author of this paper is well aware of the semantic and scalability issues facing existing MDD tools. But solutions to these issues are not as relevant to acceptance testing as the problem of traceability.

REFERENCES

[1] Kruchten, P.: The Rational Unified Process, Addison-Wesley, Reading, 2003.

[2] Rosemberg, D. and Stephens, M.: Use Case Driven Object Modeling with UML, APress, New York, 2007.

[3] Beck, K.: Test-Driven Development: By Example. Addison-Wesley Professional, Reading, 2002.

[4] Jones, C. and Bonsignour, O.: The Economics of Software Quality, Addison-Wesley Professional, 2011.

[5] Johnson, R.: Avoiding the classic catastrophic computer science failure mode, 18th ACM SIGSOFT International Symposium on Foundations of Software Engineering, 2010, Santa Fe, NM, USA, November 7-11, 2010.

[6] Surhone, M., Tennoe, M. and Henssonow, S.: Cisq, Betascript Publishing, 2010.

[7] Ammann P. and Offutt J.: Introduction to Software Testing, Cambridge University Press, 2008.

[8] Bertolino, A.: Software Testing Research: Achievements, Challenges and Dreams, Future of Software Engineering (FOSE '07), pp.85-103, IEEE Press, Minneapolis, May 2007.

[9] Grieskamp, W.: Multi-Paradigmatic Model-Based Testing, Technical Report, pp.1-20, Microsoft Research, August 2006.

[10] Spec Explorer Visual Studio Power Tool, http://visualstudiogallery.msdn.microsoft.com/271d0904-f178-4ce9-956b-d9bfa4902745

[11] Binder, R.: Testing Object-Oriented Systems, Addison-Wesley Professional, Reading, 2000.

[12] Corriveau, J.-P.: Testable Requirements for Offshore Outsourcing, SEAFOOD, Zurich, February 2007.

[13] Meyer, B.: The Unspoken Revolution in Software Engineering, IEEE Computer 39(1), pp.121-123, 2006.

[14] Corriveau, J.-P.: Traceability Process for Large OO Projects, IEEE Computer 29(9), pp.63-68, 1996.

[15] First list of testing tools: http://www.info.com/Tools%20Software%20Testing?cb=22&cmp=316574&gclid=CO7R4eeH1LICFaR9OgodYBsAmw

[16] Second list of testing tools: http://en.wikipedia.org/wiki/Category:Software_testing_tools

[17] Testing tools for Web QA: http://www.aptest.com/webresources.html

[18] JUnit, http://www.junit.org/

[19] Meyer, B. et al.: Programs that test themselves, IEEE Computer 42(9), pp.46-55, 2009.

[20] Ryser, J. and Glinz, M.: SCENT: A Method Employing Scenarios to Systematically Derive Test Cases for System Test., Technical Report. University of Zurich, 2003.

[21] Arnold, D., Corriveau, J.-P. and Shi, W.: Validation against Actual Behavior: Still a Challenge for Testing Tools, SERP, Las Vegas, July, 2010.

[22] Meyer, B.: Design by Contract. IEEE Computer 25(10), pp. 40-51, 1992.

[23] IBM: Rational Robot, http://www-01.ibm.com/software/awdtools/tester/robot/

[24] HP Quality Centre http://www8.hp.com/us/en/software-solutions/software.html?compURI=1172141&jumpid=ex_r11374_us/en/large/eb/go_qualitycenter#.UTEXSI76TJo

[25] TFS http://msdn.microsoft.com/en-us/vstudio/ff637362.aspx

[26] Blueprint https://documentation.blueprintcloud.com/Blueprint5.1/Default.htm#Help/Project%20Administration/Tasks/Managing%20ALM%20targets/Creating%20ALM%20targets.htm

[27] UML Superstructure Specification, v2.3, http://www.omg.org/spec/UML/2.3/

[28] Utting, M. and Legeard, B. 2007: Practical Model-Based Testing: A Tools Approach, Morgan Kauffmann

[29] Testing Experience, Model-Based Testing, March 2012, Díaz & Hilterscheid GmbH, Germany

[30] Prasanna, M. et al.: A survey on Automatic Test Case Generation, Academic Open Internet Journal, Volume 15, part 6, 2005

[31] Neto, A. et al.: A survey of Model-based Testing Approaches, WEASELTech'07, Atlanta, November 2007.

[32] Baker, P., Dai, Z.R., Grabowski, J., Schieferdecker, I. and Williams, C.: Model-Driven Testing: Using the UML Profile, Springer, 2007.

[33] Bukhari, S. and Waheed, T.: Model driven transformation between design models to system test models using UML: A survey, Proceedings of the 2010 National S/w Engineering Conference, article 08, Rawalpindi, Pakistan, October 2010.

[34] http://wiki.eclipse.org/EclipseTestingDay2010_Talk_Seppmed

[35] Shafique, M. and Labiche, Y.: A Systematic Review of Model Based Testing Tool Support, Technical Report, SCE-10-04, Carleton University, 2010

[36] Conformiq Tool Suite, http://www.verifysoft.com/en_conformiq_automatic_test_generation.html

[37] Conformiq Manual, http://www.verifysoft.com/ConformiqManual.pdf

[38] Chelimsky, D. et al.: The RSpec Book: Behaviour Driven Development with Rspec, Cucumber and Friends, Pragmatic Bookshelf , 2010.

[39] FORMULA, http://research.microsoft.com/en-us/projects/formula/

[40] Selic, B.: Filling in the Whitespace, http://lmo08.iro.umontreal.ca/Bran%20Selic.pdf

[41] Rational Technical Developer, http://www-01.ibm.com/software/awdtools/developer/technical/

[42] Nebut C., Fleury F., Le Traon Y., and Jézéquel J. M.: Automatic Test Generation: A Use Case Driven Approach. IEEE Transactions on Software Engineering, Vol. 32, 2006.

[43] A. Miga, Applications of Use Case Maps to System Design with Tool Support, M.Eng. Thesis, Dept. of Systems and Computer. Engineering, Carleton University, 1998.

[44] Zander, J. et al: From U2TP Models to Executable Tests with TTCN-3 - An Approach to Model Driven Testing. 17th International Conf. on Testing Communicating Systems TestCom 2005, Montreal, Canada, ISBN: 3-540-26054-4, May 2005.

[45] Baker, P. and Jervis, C.: Testing UML 2.0 Models using TTCN-3 and the UML 2.0 Testing Profile. LNCS 4745, pp. 86-100, 2007.

A Framework for Maturity Assessment in Software Testing for Small and Medium-Sized Enterprises

Adailton F. Araújo[1], **Cássio L. Rodrigues**[1], **Auri M.R. Vincenzi**[1], **Celso G. Camilo**[1] **and Almir F. Silva**[2]
[1]Institute of Informatics, Federal University of Goias, Goiania, Goias, Brazil
[2]Development Department, Decisão Sistemas, Goiania, Goias, Brazil

Abstract— *This paper proposes a framework for a software maturity assessment model for small and medium-sized enterprises (SMEs) based on the TMMi model. Our framework includes an evaluation questionnaire based on TMMi subpractices, support tools with examples of artefacts required to ensure the questionnaire is thoroughly completed, as well as an automated tool support for its application, enabling SMEs to carry out self-assessment. The model was applied to four SMEs.*

Keywords: Maturity Assessment of Test Process, Software Test Process Improvement, TMMi, TMM

1. Introduction

Small and medium-sized software enterprises play a major role in world economic development, representing 99,2% of the world's software companies [1]. In 2010, computer programs developed in Brazil had a 35% share in the country's software market. This market is explored by about 8,520 companies dedicated to software development, production and distribution, as well as to services. A total of 94% of all software development and production companies (2,117) are classified as SMEs [12]. Moreover, those with less than ten employees represent 93% of European companies and 56% of American companies [9]. Thus, most of the world's software development businesses are classified as SMEs [8], which shows their importance in the market.

The production of high-quality software is a challenge for SMEs. In general, they are known to develop good software quality in limited ways [9]. The software market has become more demanding and SMEs must continually improve their products to meet market demands. The quality of a system or product is usually determined by the quality of the process used and requires a foundation to maximize people's productivity as well as technology to enhance competition in the market [7]. A good process alone does not help an organization to develop a successful product, but a good process is necessary to create a successful one [9].

Considering the importance of the use of processes, the software industry seeks certifications in various models which highlight discipline, such as CMMI (Capability Maturity Model Integration) [7] and MPS.BR (Software Process Improvement in Brazil) [10]. Companies of different sizes need minimum financial requirements to start a software process improvement program. Such investment may be insignificant to a large company's income, but may not be feasible to an SME [2]. Furthermore, software process improvement in small businesses must give special attention to the applications of models and standards designed by large organizations [16].

Testing is an important part of the development cycle which leads to high-quality software production [15]. Test maturity models such as CMMI and MPS.BR present some problems in the way that they do not perceive the test as important, in addition to requiring testing only for high levels of maturity, which are not usually reached by SMEs. According to MPS.BR, which focuses on SMEs, only 8% of registered companies have high level certifications A, B, C and D [13], which require the verification and validation process.

The software industry has focused on process improvement to enhance its performance [15]. Therefore, test maturity models were created for such purpose, such as TMM (Test Maturity Model) [3] and TMMi (Test Maturity Model Integration) [4]. However, such models are not adequate for SMEs due to their high costs and the fact that they are originally created from the standpoint of large organizations. TMM is one of the most widely used models in the world, and TMMi is an upgraded version of it [3]. Up to the present, there are no free assessment questionnaires available for SMEs to use as a self-evaluation tool.

Thus, our work aims at defining a framework for a software maturity assessment model based on TMMi practices which may be applied by SMEs. Due to financial restrictions, these companies need a method that enables them to assess their test maturity process, for the investments required by a formal assessment are not compatible with the reality of SMEs. Also, they must deal with low maturity levels during both test and improvement processes. Therefore, we offer support by providing resources for companies to evaluate themselves without advanced knowledge of the model. Our main contribution is an objective questionnaire for maturity assessment which follows the TMMi model. For each question, examples are presented on how the company may meet the model's demands. Furthermore, an automated tool support was developed to help with the assessment and attainment of results. Such support may reduce assessment effort because it takes into consideration the relationships between the questions, therefore reducing the number of questions to be answered.

The benefits for SMEs would be numerous. According to the Tassey report [14], the lack of an appropriate test process would result in: 1) an increased number of faults due to its low quality; 2) higher development costs; 3) delay in production; and 4) rise in tool support costs.

The remaining part of this paper is organized as follows: Section 2 presents related works; Section 3 shows the steps taken to create our proposed framework; Section 4 describes the case study by setting the context in which the framework was applied; Section 5 exhibits the results and an assessment of the framework. Finally, the conclusions are shown in Section 6.

2. Related Works

Various works and tools have been developed to support the maturity assessment of development and test processes. Tayamanon et al. [15] propose a supporting tool based on TMM-AM, which enables each company to make its own test process evaluation. The first steps taken for its construction were the analysis of each question in the TMM-AM questionnaire and the registration of all products based on IEEE 730 and 829 standards, all of which would be necessary to answer each question. Tool assessment was carried out by comparing the standard product to the one produced by the organization. Ng et al. [11] suggest that the downside to the use of such approach in SMEs lies on the fact that most of them do not implement test documentation requirements and end up creating customized documents. Partial documentation would frequently be produced by the companies, a fact not taken into account by the tool, which would ultimately hinder its assessment as regards SMEs. This would result in a subjective assessment of the level of each product, which is not adequate for SMEs.

Appraisal Assistant is an assessment tool that was developed by Software Quality Institute (SQI) at Griffith University [6]. This support tool is used to assess an organization's capacity or maturity process, based on assessment models such as SCAMPI (CMMI) and ISO/IEC 15504. It uses multiple reference models, including CMMI V1.1, V1.2 and V1.3, ISO/IEC 12207 and others. Even though it is used to assess the maturity of the development process, tests carried out on it showed it can be used easily.

Höhn [5] shows a framework which aimed at gathering general knowledge on the test area and making it available for the community to facilitate its transfer, test process definition and improvement, also providing more quality. KITTool is a part of this framework, which carries out software maturity assessment based on the TMMi model. It provides two types of test process diagnostic procedures: one of them is based on TMMi goals and the other on its practices. In the first case, both the process areas and goals are identified. Each goal representing the test process is given a grade (0, 4, 6, 8, 10). The second approach uses SCAMPI assessment model in CMM and presents the goals and practices related to each objective. The assessor then gives a rate (0, 25%, 50%, 75%, 100%) based on a reference table, which shows how much practice has been implemented in the assessment process. However, applying this tool requires a high level of knowledge of the TMMi model and does not focus on SMEs.

Thus, considering the related works, our framework is different in the sense that:

- it provides support for SMEs to carry out maturity self assessment in test process;
- its automated support allows the association of the evidence provided to check whether each TMMi goal/practice has been met. It gives an overview on how the company is making use of the model, facilitating the process's reassessment as well as potential external auditing;
- the automated support promotes direct relationships between the questions from the assessment questionnaire, reducing the number of items that need checking and even revealing inconsistencies during the evaluation process;
- the framework was applied and assessed in a case study.

3. Creating the Framework

This section presents the steps taken to create the framework for software test maturity assessment based on the TMMi model.

3.1 Definition of the assessment questionnaire

There are five maturity levels in the TMMi model and each of them contains a set of process areas. Each process area has a set of goals, each goal has a set of practices and each practice has a set of sub-practices. The latter is a detailed description that provides guidelines for interpreting and implementing a specific practice [4]. For example, the first column of Table 1 shows some of the sub-practices associated with the practice Define Test Goals, the aim Establish Test Policies, and the process area Test and Policy Strategies, which is related to maturity level 2.

Table 1: Questions based on TMMi sub-practices

Sub-practice	Question
1. Study business needs and objectives;	OR
2. Allow feedback to clarify business needs and objectives, if necessary;	OR
3. Define test goals which trace back to business needs and objectives;	(3)Are test goals defined based on business needs and objectives?
4. Review test goals with the interested parties;	OR
5. Reassess test goals whenever necessary e.g. annually.	(5) Are test goals periodically reviewed?

This is the structure of all process areas related to levels 2, 3, and 4. Level 5 process areas do not contain practices or sub-practices; the generic practices, which may be applied to all process areas, do not have sub-practices. Höhn's work [5] provides two forms of assessment: 1) based on the goals; and 2) based on model practices. Assessing the TMMi model showed that the provision of details of sub-practices would be crucial for SME's self-assessment, for in this case the assessor does not know the detailed information required to achieve a certain goal/practice. Therefore, a questionnaire was created to assess the adherence to the TMMi model based on its sub-practices.

The questionnaire took into account the following criteria:

- Questions were created only for the sub-practices that represent a given result to be achieved by the model. The remaining sub-practices that are orientations for practice implementation did not have related questions. Table 1 shows examples of questions based on sub-practices 3 and 5. Sub-practices which did not have related questions (1, 2, and 4) were named OR (orientation);
- Model traceability among questions and sub-practices was maintained to facilitate questions' future improvements and maintenance. As shown in Table 1, the numbers in parentheses beside each question indicate such traceability;
- Whenever the model does not provide sub-practices (all the generic practices and some specific practices), a question was created based on the practice's description. For instance, the practice Distribute Test Policy to Interested Parties, with the description "Test policies and goals are presented and explained to the interested parties involved or not involved with the test activity", had the following question: Were test policies presented to the interested parties (that are involved or not with the test)?; and
- Whenever the model does not provide practices (level 5 process areas), a question was created based on goal description. For example, the goal Select Test Process Improvements, with the description "Test process improvements are chosen when they contribute to the achievement of product quality as well as process development goals", had the following question: Are test process improvements selected to achieve product quality and process development goals?

As a result, a questionnaire was created to cover all TMMi process areas with 261 questions. Twelve of them are related to generic model practices, which means they can be applied to all process areas. As for the questions based on sub-practices, each was associated to one or more sub-practices related to the same practice. Furthermore, there were sub-practices with no associated questions. Regarding the questions directly linked with the goals and practices, only one question was associated to each of them due to their greater specificity.

The maturity level is defined based on the answers given in the questionnaire, according to the TMM [3] assessment method. The answers predicted by this method are: Yes, No, Not Applicable, and Unknown.

3.2 Definition of the support material

In order to help SMEs carry out their self-assessment, even if the assessor does not have advanced knowledge of the TMMi model, each question provides examples of artefacts typical of works that are often used to prove the organization attends the result expected by the model. The TMMi model already provides examples for many of its sub-practices. Therefore, the examples were chosen according to the following criteria:

- For the practice-related questions, examples provided by the TMMi model were used. Some of these were extensive, so, to prevent the support material from disturbing the assessment, a maximum of five examples was established per item. All examples were read and then chosen when clearly related to the item;
- For the practice-related questions without examples in the TMMi model, examples were taken from other practices that showed details of model implementation; and
- For the questions that did not fit into any of the previous cases, experience and/or other references were used in the artifact's proposition.

Consequently, examples were produced for all 261 questions in the questionnaire, some of which are shown in Table 2. Questions (3) and (5) derived from Table 1, whereas the rest were created from other TMMi sub-practices. Question (1), "Were test project techniques selected to provide adequate test coverage regarding the risks of defined products?", the following examples were indicated: Equivalence Partitioning, Boundary Value Analysis, Decision Table, State Transition Testing and Use-Case Testing.

3.3 Definition of the automated support for assessment

An electronic spreadsheet made it possible to visualize each question's support material, attribute an answer (Yes, No, Not Applicable, or Unknown) and associate evidence from artefacts produced by the company that support "Yes" answers.

Results were based on the TMM [3] assessment method, which is also questionnaire-oriented. We were able to use this method because TMMi process areas are similar to TMM goals, and TMMi goals are similar to TMM sub-goals.

To carry out the assessment according to TMMi, each maturity goal has a set of related questions. The goal is regarded as achieved when the number of "Yes" answers is higher than or equal to 50% i.e. if its degree of satisfaction

Table 2: Some examples based on the TMMi model and on experience

Question	Support Material
(1)Were test project techniques selected to provide adequate test coverage regarding the risks of defined products?	*Typical work product:* Test Plans with test project techniques. *Examples of test techniques:* Equivalence Partitioning, Boundary Value Analysis, Decision Table, State Transition Testing, Use-Case Testing.
(3)Are test goals defined based on business needs and objectives?	*Typical work product:* Testing goals which trace back to business goals. *Examples of testing goals:* Validate product for use; Prevent faults during operation; Verify conformity to external standards; Provide information on product quality.
(4)Was documentation developed to support the implementation of the testing environment?	*Typical work product:* Support documentation for the implementation of the testing environment. *Examples:* Guide for environmental setup; Guide for environmental operation; Guide for environmental maintenance.
(5) Are testing goals periodically reviewed?	*Typical work product:* Review of testing goals. *Examples of reviews:* Meeting with the interested parties to review and discuss the need to make changes to testing goals (register in the meeting minute).

is medium, high or very high. Table 3 shows how a goal's degree of satisfaction was calculated.

Table 3: Goals' Degree of Satisfaction [3]

Degree of Satisfaction	Criteria
Very high	If "yes" answers are above 90%
High	If "yes" answers range between 70-90%
Medium	If "yes" answers range between 50-69%
Low	If "yes" answers range between 30-49%
Very low	If "yes" answers are below 30%
Not Applicable	If "Not Applicable" answers are 50% or more
Not Classified	If "Unknown" answers are 50% or more

Maturity classification in process areas relies on goal classification (see Table4). A satisfactory level indicates that all maturity goals were achieved. A spreadsheet was used to implement this method. Considering the answers given, it then automatically produced the results and establishes a maturity level for the company. Results are displayed in both summary and detailed versions. In the summary version, the satisfaction and maturity level of each process area are determined. The detailed version provides not only information listed in the summary version but also the degree of satisfaction of each goal related to the process areas, stating whether there are questions without any attributed answer.

3.4 Establishment of dependencies between questionnaire questions

A question X is considered dependent of Y when it is only possible to obtain a positive answer to X if Y was previously attributed a positive answer. An example that might represent this situation would be to attribute X="Was the test project monitored throughout its lifecycle by comparing what was planned and what was accomplished in relation to potential risks" and Y="Were test project risks identified and was each risk analyzed regarding its probability of occurrence, impact and priority?". Therefore, it is not possible to monitor the risks that were not defined previously.

Table 4: Satisfaction of Process Areas [3]

Satisfaction	Criteria
Achieved	If achieved goals are 50% or more
Not achieved	If achieved goals are below 50%
Not Applicable	If not applicable goals are 50% or more
Not Classified	If not classified goals are 50% or more

This relationship was established through the assessment of existing dependencies between questions, which created a dependency matrix among the questions. Establishing such dependency has two distinct aims:

1) *To detect inconsistencies in assessment answers* - use dependency relationships to find inconsistencies between questionnaire answers i.e. if there are "Yes" answers to questions that depend on another question which has "No" as an answer; and
2) *To eliminate dependent questions* - use dependency relationships to eliminate questions that depend on other questions which have a "No" answer, thus reducing the number of questions to be answered.

Our proposed framework will make both approaches available. If a company chooses to reduce assessment time by eliminating some questions, it will not be able to identify inconsistencies. The selection of the most adequate approach may be done in accordance with the company's maturity level. For example, companies with more mature testing processes may feel more secure to eliminate some questions.

4. Case Study

Framework analysis was carried out to assess its adaptability in four SMEs, here referred to as A, B, C, and D for secrecy issues. All of them are involved in a test process improvement project.

These companies required some feedback on the actual condition of their test process before implementing any improvements. To obtain such information, the first assessment was thus carried out:

- A TMM [3] questionnaire was applied;
- The questionnaire was answered by 2-3 collaborators from each company who were members of the development/test team;
- No evidence of attainment of model practices was required.

Results from the first assessment revealed a 67,8% rate of divergence among the answers given by collaborators from the same company. It was then concluded that the diagnostic results might not show the true level of maturity of the companies during test process. Also, the final results may have been affected by a combination of factors, such as the lack of knowledge of collaborators and lack of clarity in questions.

The diverging results contributed to the adoption of the TMMi model. Examples were then provided and evidence of practices was required. The second assessment was carried out as follows:

- The proposed framework contained the TMMi questionnaire and the support material;
- The questionnaire was answered by only one company collaborator, also a member of the test team;
- With each positive answer in the spreadsheet, evidence (artefacts) showed how the company puts into practice what is required by the model;
- Once all answers were concluded and evidence was associated, company representatives assessed the framework and raised the problems found as well as suggested improvements;
- Auditing was carried out to focus on the evidence shown on the spreadsheet, in order to check if the documentation adhered with the practices required by the model.

5. Results

Table 5 compares maturity level results from the first assessment, which used the TMM model, to the ones from the second assessment, which used our framework. Satisfaction of a certain maturity level by a company is represented by S and non-satisfaction by NS. Also, different results are highlighted in bold. Companies A and C showed different results, reaching a two-level difference in relation to company A. Comparison of both software testing evaluations also revealed a significant difference related to goal achievement (Table 6). Such difference reached 69% in company C and 41% in company A. Considering that the second assessment was audited, its results better represent the companies' current situation in software testing.

Table 5: Assessment Results

Company	Evaluation	Level2	Level3	Level4	Level5
A	1	S	**S**	**S**	NS
	2	S	**NS**	**NS**	NS
B	1	NS	NS	NS	NS
	2	NS	NS	NS	NS
C	1	**S**	NS	NS	NS
	2	**NS**	NS	NS	NS
D	1	NS	NS	NS	NS
	2	NS	NS	NS	NS

The questionnaire was used to assess our framework. Each question had four answer options, of which only one should be chosen, presented in the form of classification ratings. Table 7 shows the relationships between the applied questions and the options for each question. The company identifier (A, B, C, and D) represents the answer it attributed to a given classification range for each question. For example, company A selected the same range for all questions (76-100%), except for the third one

Table 6: Metas Satisfeitas

Company	Assessment	% of goals achieved	Variation
A	1	85%	41%
	2	44%	
B	1	8%	8%
	2	0%	
C	1	69%	69%
	2	0%	
D	1	0%	0%
	2	0%	

Results revealed that 80% of the answers ranged from 51-100%, and most of them ranged from 76-100%. Company A was the one that better assessed the framework and hence used it more frequently, as it was the only company that reached at least one maturity level. All answers ranging from 26-50% were attributed to company D (Table 7). As is shown in Table 6, the same company did not meet any goals according to TMMi assessment. The company's feedback also revealed that, since the beginning of the assessment, it had concluded that an ad hoc test was being carried out. Therefore, there would be no evidence for any of the questions in the questionnaire i.e. the company did not have the means to carry out a more detailed assessment of the framework due to the fact it was rarely used.

Despite being defined as part of the framework, as described in Section 3.4, the second assessment did not use the dependency relationship between the questions to eliminate dependent questions. Table 8 shows the percentage of questions that each company would not answer due to the elimination of some questions, based on the "No" answers. Company D showed a 65% rate, which represents the maximum reduction obtained by using a certain dependency relationship, seen that this company answered "No" to all the questions.

6. Conclusions

The present paper has shown that software development SMEs are important for world economy. These companies also have a constant need to improve their product quality to meet market demands. Considering the importance of software testing for high-quality software production, we created a framework to the assess maturity level in software testing based on the TMMi model, which is suitable to the reality faced by SMEs.

Results revealed that the objective questionnaire, the support material related to each question, and the spreadsheet which automatically processes assessment results contribute to SMEs' self-assessment of maturity levels in software

Table 7: Questionnaire Assessment

Question	0-25%	26-50%	51-75%	76-100%
1-What was the degree of clarity of questions?		D	C	A B
2-What was the degree of clarity of examples?			B C D	A
3-What was the level of importance of examples in understanding the questions?		D	A	B C
4-What was the level of importance of examples in associating the evidence with the questions?		D		A B C
5-What was the level of association between the vocabulary used in the questions and examples and your reality?		D	BC	A

Table 8: Reduction via Dependencies

Company	Reduction
A	26%
B	37%
C	60%
D	65%

testing, despite their low maturity levels. However, in order to make results more compatible with a company's reality, we suggest that: 1) the questionnaire be answered by only one company representative; 2) this person be a member of the test team or have a great knowledge of the company's test process and 3) the assessment be evidence-based.

Companies positively assessed the questionnaire. A total of 45% of assessed items was rated 76-100%, the largest range available, and 80% of all items was classified in the 51-100% range. The main obstacle faced by the companies was the large number of questions. This aspect may be improved by the use of better support material to implement the option to eliminate questions based on previously defined interdependent relationships between the questions. This would promote a 65% reduction on the number of questions.

By comparing the results from both assessments, we observed a 69% variation regarding goal satisfaction. Furthermore, we learned that wrong results may be generated if low maturity companies carry out a self-assessment without a material that supports the attribution of answers or without evidence association. However, our proposed framework aims at solving these kinds of problems, hence presenting more realistic results in software testing for SMEs.

The results of this assessment will be used as a basis for the development of a test process that is adequate for SMEs, one which considers its maturity level. The process will be implemented in all four companies through pilot project applications. Moreover, further assessment will be carried out using the proposed framework to identify the companies' maturity development. Finally, the framework will be available to the community free of charge.

7. Acknowledgement

Grateful thanks are owed to the four enterprises participants of the survey for their invaluable help in this study. This work was partially supported by FAPEG.

References

[1] M. Q. A. A., S. Ramachandram, and A. M. A. An evolutionary software product development process for small and medium enterprises (SMEs). pages 298–303. IEEE, Oct. 2008.

[2] J. Brodman and D. Johnson. What small businesses and small organizations say about the CMM. pages 331–340. IEEE Comput. Soc. Press, Aug. 2002.

[3] I. Burnstein. *Practical Software Testing: a process-oriented approach.* Springer-Verlag New York, Inc., Secaucus, NJ, USA, 2002.

[4] T. Foundation. Test maturity model integration - TMMi version 3.1.

[5] E. Höhn. *KITeste - A Framework of Knowledge and Test Process Improvement.* PhD thesis, USP, São Carlos - SP - Brazil, June 2011. (in Portuguese).

[6] S. Q. Institute. Appraisal assistant, 2007.

[7] S. E. Institute-SEI. Capability maturity model integration - CMMI version 1.3.

[8] M. Khokhar, K. Zeshan, and J. Aamir. Literature review on the software process improvement factors in the small organizations. pages 592 – 598. IEEE Comput. Soc. Press, May 2010.

[9] C. Laporte, S. Alexandre, and A. Renault. Developing international standards for very small enterprises. *Computer*, 41(3):98–101, Mar. 2008.

[10] M. A. Montoni, A. R. Rocha, and K. C. Weber. MPS.BR: a successful program for software process improvement in brazil. *Softw. Process*, 14(5):289–300, Sept. 2009.

[11] S. Ng, T. Murnane, K. Reed, D. Grant, and T. Chen. A preliminary survey on software testing practices in australia. pages 116–125. IEEE, 2004.

[12] B. A. of Software Companies. Brazilian software market - overview and trends. Technical report, June 2011. (in Portuguese).

[13] Softex. Evaluations published MPS.BR, Mar. 2012. (in Portuguese).

[14] G. Tassey. The economic impacts of inadequate infrastructure for software testing. May 2002.

[15] T. Tayamanon, T. Suwannasart, N. Wongchingchai, and A. Methawachananont. TMM appraisal assistant tool. pages 329–333. IEEE, Aug. 2011.

[16] T. Varkoi, T. Makinen, and H. Jaakkola. Process improvement priorities in small software companies. page 555. Portland Int. Conf. Manage. Eng. & Technol. PICMET, Aug. 2002.

Constructing Verifiably Correct Java Programs Using OCL and CleanJava

Yoonsik Cheon and Carmen Avila
Department of Computer Science
The University of Texas at El Paso
El Paso, Texas, U.S.A.
ycheon@utep.edu; ceavila3@miners.utep.edu

Abstract—**A recent trend in software development is building a precise model that can be used as a basis for the software development. Such a model may enable an automatic generation of working code, and more importantly it provides a foundation for correctness reasoning of code. In this paper we propose a practical approach for constructing a verifiably correct program from such a model. The key idea of our approach is (a) to systematically translate formally-specified design constraints such as class invariants and operation pre and postconditions to code-level annotations and (b) to use the annotations for the correctness proof of code. For this we use the Object Constraint Language (OCL) and CleanJava. CleanJava is a formal annotation language for Java and supports Cleanroom-style functional program verification. The combination of OCL and CleanJava makes our approach not only practical but also suitable for its incorporation into existing object-oriented software development methods. We expect our approach to provide a practical alternative or complementary technique to program testing to assure the correctness of software.**

Keywords: correctness proof, functional program verification, intended function, CleanJava, Object Constraint Language.

I. INTRODUCTION

A recent software development trend is a shift of focus from writing code to building models [1]. The ultimate goal is to systematically generate an implementation from a model through a series of transformations. One key requirement of this model-driven development is the availability of a precise model to generate working code from it. A formal notation such as the Object Constraint Language (OCL) [2] can play an important role to build such a precise model. OCL is a textual, declarative notation to specify constraints or rules that apply to models expressed in various UML diagrams [3]. Modeling and specifying design constraints explicitly is also said to improve reasoning of software architectures and thus their qualities [4].

A formal design model can also provide a foundation for correctness reasoning of an implementation. In this paper we propose one such a method that takes advantage of formal design models to construct verifiably correct programs. The key idea of our approach is to derive code-level annotations from a formal design and to prove the correctness of code using a Cleanroom-style functional program verification technique. We use OCL as the notation for formally documenting design decisions and constraints and CleanJava as the notation for writing code-level annotations. CleanJava is a formal annotation language for the Java programming language to support Cleanroom-style functional program verification [5] (see Section II-B for an overview of CleanJava). A functional program verification technique such as Cleanroom [6] [7] views a program as a mathematical function from one program state to another and proves its correctness by essentially comparing two functions, the function computed by the program and its specification [8] [9] [10]. Since the technique uses equational reasoning based on sets and functions, it requires a minimal mathematical background, and unlike Hoare logic [11] it supports forward reasoning, reflecting the way programmers informally reason about the correctness of a program.

It is a known fact that software contains defects. Defects are introduced during software development and are often found through testing. However, studies indicate that testing can't detect more than 90% of defects; 10% of defects are never detected through testing. As stated by a famous computer scientist, testing has a fundamental flaw in that it can show the existence of a defect but not its absence. We expect our approach to provide a practical alternative or complementary technique to program testing to assure the correctness of software. We believe that the combination of OCL and CleanJava make our approach more practical and approachable by practitioners.

There has been an approach proposed to combine Cleanroom methodologies and formal methods [12], however there is no work done on combining OCL and functional program verification. Stavely described an approach to integrating the Z specification notation [13] into Cleanroom-style specification and verification [14]. One interesting aspect of his work is that a Z specification is converted to a constructive form, expressing state changes in an assignment notation. In this way, a Z specification can serve as a specification function for the program code to be developed, and the development can proceeds in Cleanroom style by verifying every section of code. Our approach also takes advantage of OCL constraints written constructively by translating them automatically to CleanJava annotations using a set of translation rules. However, we also learned that such constraints raise some interesting questions (see Section VI). Another related work is the translation of OCL to JML [15]. JML is a behavioral interface specification language for Java [16] [17]. In this work, JML is used as an assertion language for Java in that a subset of OCL constraints is translated into JML assertions for both static reasoning and runtime checks. One important contribution of this work is the

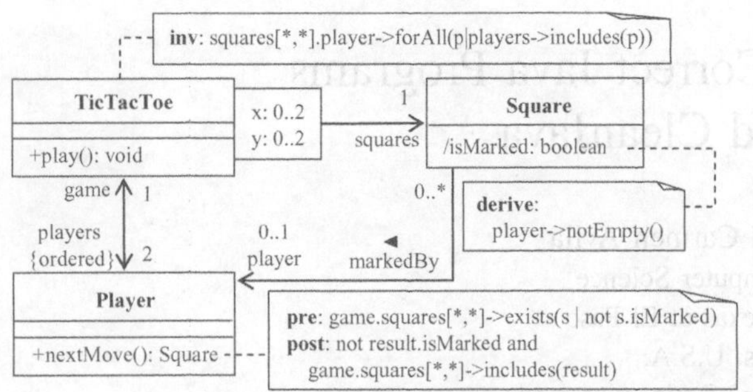

Fig. 1. UML class diagram with OCL constraints

```
//@ f0:[squares := Square[][]->any(sqs| isGameOver(sqs))]
  //@ f1:[p := nextPlayer()]
  Player p = nextPlayer();

  /*@ f2:[squares, p := Square[][]->any(sqs| isGameOver(sqs)
    @  && isSubState(squares, sqs)), anything] where
    @  isSubState(s1,s2) = (* s1 is substate of s2 *) @*/
  while (!isWonBy(p) && hasEmptySquare()) {
   /*@ f3:[sq.player, p := p, nextPlayer()]
     @  where sq = p.nextMove() @*/
    p = nextPlayer();
    Square sq = p.nextMove();
    sq.setPlayer(p);
  }
```

Fig. 2. Sample CleanJava code

translation rules from OCL to JML. Assertions are said to be more effective when derived from formal specifications, and several different techniques have been proposed for translating OCL constraints to runtime assertion checks [18].

The remainder of this paper is structured as follows. In Section II we briefly explain OCL and CleanJava using an example. In the subsequent two sections we first give an overview of our approach and then apply it to our running example. In Section V we describe our translation of OCL constraints to CleanJava annotations, and in Section VI we discuss some interesting aspects of our translation. In Section VII we provide a concluding remark.

II. Background

A. Object Constraint Language

The Object Constraint Language (OCL) [2] is a textual, declarative notation to specify constraints or rules that apply to UML models. OCL can play an important role in model-driven software development because UML diagrams lacks sufficient precision to enable the transformation of a UML model to complete code. In fact, it is a key component of OMG's standard for model transformation for the model-driven architecture [19].

A UML diagram alone cannot express a rich semantics of and all relevant information about an application. The diagram in Figure 1, for example, is a UML class diagram modeling the game of tic-tac-toe. A tic-tac-toe game consists of 9 places in a 3×3 grid, and two players take turns to mark the places and win the game by marking three places in a horizontal, vertical, or diagonal row. However, the class diagram doesn't express the fact that a place can be marked only by the two player participating in the game. It is very likely that a system built based only on diagrams alone will be incorrect. OCL allows one to precisely describe this kind of additional constraints on the objects and entities present in a UML model. It is based on mathematical set theory and predicate logic and supplements UML by providing expressions that have neither the ambiguities of natural language nor the inherent difficulty of using complex mathematics. The above-mentioned fact, for example, can be expressed in OCL as follows.

```
context TicTacToe
  inv: squares[*,*].player->forAll(p|players->includes(p))
```

This constraint, called an *invariant*, states a fact that should be always true in the model. The invariant is written using OCL collection operations such as `forAll` and `includes`; the `forAll` operation tests whether a given condition holds for every element contained in the collection, and the `includes` operation tests whether an object is contained in a collection.

It is also possible to specify the behavior of an operation in OCL. For example, the following OCL constraints specifies the behavior of an operation `Player::nextMove():Square` using a pair of predicates called *pre* and *postconditions*.

```
context Player::nextMove():Place
  pre: game.squares[*,*]->exists(s|not s.isMarked)
  post: not result.isMarked and
        game.squares[*.*]->includes(result)
```

The above pre and postconditions states that if invoked in a state that has at least one unmarked square the operation returns an unmarked square. In the postcondition, the keyword `result` denotes the return value.

B. CleanJava

CleanJava is a formal annotation language for the Java programming language to support Cleanroom-style functional program verification [5]. In the functional program verification, a program is viewed as a mathematical function from one program state to another. In essence, functional verification involves calculating the function computed by code, called a *code function*, and comparing it with the intention of the code written also as a function, called an *intended function* [8] [9] [10]. CleanJava provides a notation for writing intended functions. A *concurrent assignment* notation, $[x_1, x_2, \ldots, x_n := e_1, e_2, \ldots, e_n]$, is used to express these functions by only stating changes that happen. It states that x_i's new value is e_i, evaluated concurrently in the initial state—the state just before executing the code; the value of a state variable that doesn't appear in the left-hand side remains the same. For example, $[x, y := y, x]$ is a function that swaps the values of two variables x and y.

Figure 2 shows sample Java code annotated with intended functions written in CleanJava. It shows partial code of the `play` method of the TicTacToe class. Each section of code is annotated with its intended function. A CleanJava annotation is written in a special kind of comments either preceded by

`//@` or enclosed in `/*@` and `@*/`, and an intended function is written in the Java expression syntax with a few CleanJava-specific extensions. The first annotation labelled f_0 states that the new value of the `squares` field is an arbitrary value of a game-over state. In CleanJava, a type such as Square[][] can be used to denote the set of all values belonging to it, and `any` is a collection iterator that denotes an arbitrary value of a collection that satisfies a given condition; CleanJava defines several other collection iterators such as `forAll` and `exists`. The intended function labelled f_2 is interesting, as it shows several features of CleanJava. First, the keyword **anything** denotes an arbitrary value and its use indicates that one doesn't care about the final value of the local variable `p`. Second, a **where** clause introduces local definitions like the `isSubState` function. Third, in CleanJava one can escape from formality and mix a formal text such as a Java expression with an informal description, any text enclosed in a pair of `(*` and `*)`. For example, the notion of substate between two Square[][] objects—i.e., the `isSubState` function—is defined informally. The example also shows that one can omit the signature of a function introduced for use in annotations. It is automatically inferred by CleanJava and such a function typically defines a polymorphic function. The following is one possible formulation of the `isSubState` function with its signature completely specified.

```
boolean isSubState(Square[][] s1, Square[][] s2) =
  s1.length == s2.length &&
  CJSet{1..s1.length}->forAll(int i|
    s1[i].length == s2[i].length &&
    CJSet{1..s1[i].length}->forAll(int j|
      s1[i][j] == s2[i][j] &&
        (s1[i][j].isMarked ==>
          s1[i][j].getPlayer() == s2[i][j].getPlayer())))
```

If code is annotated with its intended function, its correctness can be proved formally. It would be instructive to sketch a correctness proof of the code shown in Figure 2. It requires the following proof obligations.

- Proof that the composition of functions f_1 and f_2 is correct with respect to, or a refinement ($\sqsubseteq$) of, f_0, i.e., $f_1; f_2 \sqsubseteq f_0$, where ";" denotes a functional composition.
- Proof that f_1, f_2, and f_3 are correctly refined by the corresponding code.

In functional verification, a proof is often trivial or straightforward because a code function can be easily calculated and directly compared with an intended function; for example, f_1 and f_3 are both code and intended functions. However, one often need to use different techniques such as a case analysis for an **if** statement and an induction for a **while** statement as in the proof of f_2 [9] [10]. Below we discharge the first proof obligation, where T is short for Square[][].

$f_1; f_2 \equiv$ [p := nextPlayer()];
[squares, p := $T \rightarrow$any(sqs| isGameOver(sqs) &&
isSubState(squares, sqs)), anything]
$\equiv$ [squares, p := $T \rightarrow$any(sqs| isGameOver(sqs) &&
isSubState(squares, sqs)), anything]
$\sqsubseteq$ [squares := $T \rightarrow$any(sqs| isGameOver(sqs) &&
isSubState(squares, sqs)]
$\sqsubseteq$ [squares := $T \rightarrow$any(sqs| isGameOver(sqs))]
$\equiv f_0$

III. Overview of Our Approach

The key idea of our approach is (a) to derive code annotations from formal designs and (b) to prove the correctness of code in Cleanroom-style functional verification by refining the derived annotations. We use OCL as the notation for formally documenting design decisions and details and CleanJava as the notation for writing code annotations. There are several advantages in using OCL as a formal design notation compared to more traditional formal specification languages such as Z [13]. It is a textual formal specification language that provide concise and precise expressions that have neither the ambiguities of natural language nor the inherent difficulty of using complex mathematics. As part of the standard modeling language UML, it allows one to specify and attach constraints and rules to various design models expressed in diagrams. From UML dynamic models with OCL constraints, e.g., state machine diagrams, it is also possible to derive working code (see Section IV for an example). There are also advantages in using CleanJava as the annotation notation and verification technique, compared to Hoare-style assertions. Unlike Hoare logic based on the first-order predicate logic, the technique requires a minimal mathematical background by viewing a program as a mathematical function from one program state to another and by using equational reasoning based on sets and functions. The reasoning in Hoare logic is backward in that one derives (weakest) preconditions from postconditions. This is similar to reading source code backward from the last line to the first. The functional program verification technique supports a forward reasoning by reflecting the way programmers reason about the correctness of a program informally. The combination of OCL and CleanJava will make our approach more approachable to Java programmers and practitioners.

The main steps of our approach are as follows.

1) Document a design using UML diagrams along with OCL constraints specifying design decisions and details.
2) Generate skeleton or working code from UML design models.
3) Translate OCL constraints to CleanJava intended functions to annotate the generated code.
4) Write algorithms to complete the skeleton code by refining the intended functions.
5) Verify the correctness of the algorithm code with respect to its intended function.

The last two steps may be performed simultaneously in a stepwise refinement fashion. In the next section, we will illustrate these steps in detail by applying them to our tic-tac-toe example.

IV. Illustration

In this section we illustrate our proposed approach by applying it to the running example. As sketched in the previous

```
context TicTacToe
  inv: squares[*,*].player->forAll(p|players->includes(p))

context TicTacToe::TicTacToe()
  post: squares[*,*]->forAll(s|not s.isMarked)

context TicTacToe::play():void
  pre: squares[*,*]->forAll(s|not s.isMarked)
  post: isWonBy(players->at(1)) or isWonBy(players->at(2))
        or not hasEmptySquare()

context TicTacToe::isWonBy(p: Player): boolean
  body: Set{0..2}->exists(i|Set{0..2}->
          forAll(j|getSquare(i,j).isMarkedBy(p)))
     or Set{0..2}->exists(i|Set{0..2}->
          forAll(j|getSquare(i,j).isMarkedBy(p)))
     or Set{0..2}->collect(i|getSquare(i,i))->
          forAll(s|s.isMarkedBy(p))
     or Set{0..2}->collect(i|getSquare(i,2-i))->
          forAll(s|s.isMarkedBy(p))

context TicTacToe::hasEmptySquare(): boolean
  body: squares[*,*]->exists(s|not s.isMarked)

context TicTacToe::getSquare(i: int, j: int): Square
  pre: 0 <= i and i <= 2 and 0 <= j and j <= 2
  post: result = squares[i,j]

context Square::isMarked: boolean
  derive: player.notEmpty()

context Square::isMarkedBy(p: Player): boolean
  body: player = p

context Player::Player(g: TicTacToe)
  post: game = g

context Player::nextMove(): Square
  pre: game.hasEmptySquare()
  post: not result.isMarked and
        game.squares[*,*]->includes(result)
```

Fig. 3. OCL constraints for tic-tac-toe

section, the first step is to document a detailed design using UML diagrams along with OCL constraints.

1) Detailed design in UML and OCL: We elaborate our class diagram model by adding OCL constraints to the model and documenting detailed design decisions. Figure 3 shows OCL constraints for classes TicTacToe, Square, and Player along with several new operations introduced. In OCL, we document class invariants, operation pre and postconditions, values for derived attributes (e.g., `isMarked` of class Square), and return values of query operations (e.g., the `isWonBy` operation of class TicTacToe and the `isMarkedBy` operation of class Square). In addition to class invariants and operation pre and postconditions, OCL provides several other constructs, some of which are used in the example. The **body** construct defines the result of a query operation, and the **derive** construct specifies the value of a derived attribute or association end. The collection operation `at` appearing in the postcondition of the `play` operation returns the element at the given index; OCL uses 1-based index. The notation `Sequence{0..2}` denotes a sequence consisting of numbers from 0 to 2, inclusive.

It is also possible to define detailed algorithms for important operations using a combination of UML diagrams and OCL. For example, we can define an algorithm for the `play()` operation of the TicTacToe class using a UML state machine diagram, as shown below.

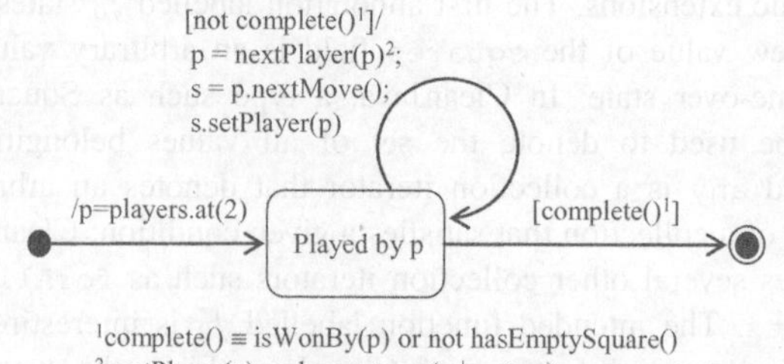

The state machine is called a *behavior state machine* and specifies that each player takes a turn to make a move—i.e., mark a square—until a play becomes completed. A play is complete if it is won by a player or there is no more empty square left. A behavior state machine can be used to derive implementation code (see below).

2) Skeleton code: The next step is to derive skeletal code from UML diagrams such as class diagrams. From a detailed class diagram, skeletal code such as shown below can be systematically or automatically generated.

```
public class TicTacToe {
  private Square[][] squares;
  private Player[] players;
  public TicTacToe() { ... }
  public void play() {... }
  public boolean isWonBy(Player p) { ... }
  public boolean hasEmptySquare() { ... }
  public Square getSquare(int i, int j) { ... }
}

public class Square {
  private Player player;
  public void setPlayer(Player p) { player = p; }
  public Player getPlayer() { return player; }
  public isMarkedBy(Player p) { ... }
  public boolean isMarked() { ... }
}

public class Player {
  private TicTacToe game;
  public Player(TicTacToe g) { ... }
  public Square nextMove() { ... }
}
```

For an association like `markedBy`, a pair of getter and setter methods (e.g., `getPlayer` and `setPlayer`) can also be automatically generated using the role names of the association ends (e.g., `player`). A derived attribute such as `isMarked` of class Square is translated to a query method.

This step may require making important implementation decisions such as deciding data structures. For example, we decided to represent the qualified association between TicTacToe and Square using a two-dimensional array. Such decisions often have impacts on the way we translate OCL constraints to CleanJava annotations in the following step, as CleanJava annotations are usually expressed in terms of concrete representation values.

3) OCL-to-CleanJava Translation: We next translate OCL constraints to CleanJava annotations and add them to the skeletal code. Figure 4 shows the skeletal code of class TicTacToe annotated in CleanJava. Most annotations are direct translations of the corresponding OCL constraints such as

```
public class TicTacToe {
  /*@ inv: [squares.length == 3 &&
    @       squares->forAll(Square[] sqs|sqs.length == 3)] @*/

  /*@ inv: [players.length == 2]

  /*@ inv: [squares->forAll(Square[] sqs|
    @         sqs->forAll(Square sq| !sq.isMarked() ||
    @         players->includes(sq.getPlayer()) @*/

   private Square[][] squares;
   private Player[] players;

  /*@ [square := Square[][]->any(Squares[][] sqs|
    @   isPristine(sqs))] @*/
   public TicTacToe() { ... }

   /*@ [isPristine(sqs) ->
     @   squares := Square[][]->any(Square[][] sqs|
     @     isGameOver(sqs))] @*/
   public void play() {... }

   /*@ [result : = isWonBy(squares, p)] @*/
   public boolean isWonBy(Player p) { ... }

   /*@ [result := squares->exists(Square[] sqs|
     @   sqs->exists(Square sq| !sq.isMarked()))] @*/
   public boolean hasEmptySquare() { ... }

   /*@ [0 <= i && i <= 2 && 0 <= j && j <= 2 ->
     @   result := squares[i][j]] @*/
   public Square getSquare(int i, int j) { ... }

   /*@ fun boolean isPristine(Square[][] sqs) =
     @   sqs->forAll(Square[] sq|
     @     sq->forAll(Square s| !s.isMarked())) @*/

   /*@ fun boolean isGameOver(Square[][] sqs) =
     @   isWonBy(sqs, players[0])
     @   || isWonBy(players[1])
     @   || sqs->forAll(Square[] sq|
     @        sq->forAll(Square s| s.isMarked())) @*/

   /*@ fun boolean isWonBy(Square[][] sqs, Player p) =
     @   CJSet{0..2}->exists(int i| CJSet{0..2}->
     @     forAll(int j|sqs[i][j].isMarkedBy(p)))
     @   || CJSet{0..2}->exists(int i|CJSet{0..2}->
     @        forAll(int j|sqs[i][j].isMarkedBy(p)))
     @   || CJSet{0..2}->collect(int i|sqs[i][i]->
     @        forAll(Square s|s.isMarkedBy(p))
     @   || CJSet{0..2}->collect(int i|sqs[i][2-i])->
     @        forAll(Square s|s.isMarkedBy(p)) @*/
}
```

Fig. 4. Skeletal code with CleanJava annotations

invariants and pre and postconditions. However, the first two invariants are specific to the Java language and constraint the sizes of arrays. This is because the array size is not part of an array type in Java. As shown, OCL invariants are translated to CleanJava invariants [20], and pre and postconditions are translated to CleanJava intended functions. In general, pre and postconditions of the form **`pre:`** P **`post:`** Q are translated to an intended function of the form $[P' \rightarrow v_1, v_2, ..., v_n := E_i, ..., E_n]$, where P' is P written in the CleanJava syntax and v_i's and E_i's are derived from Q (see Section V for details). As shown, a concurrent assignment may have an optional condition or guard followed by an $\rightarrow$ symbol. This conditional concurrent assignment statement specifies a partial function that is defined only when the condition (P') holds. The example also shows that one can introduce mathematical functions (e.g., `isPristine`, `isGameOver`, and `isWonBy`) for the purpose of writing annotations.

4) Code Writing: Once a method is annotated with an intended function, the next step is to come up with working code—the method body. There are several possibilities here. It can be developed independently by referring to its pre and postconditions or the intended function. The intended function may be refined to working code in a stepwise refinement fashion. Yet another possibility is—if a detailed algorithm design was done and documented using a UML diagram such as a state machine diagram—to derive working code from a formal design model by systematically translating it. For example, it is straightforward to derive the following code for the `play()` method of the TicTacToe class from the behavior sate machine that describes its algorithm (see Section IV).

```
Player p = players[1];
while (!isWonBy(p) && hasEmptySquare()) {
  p = p == players[0] ? players[1] : players[0];
  Square sq = p.nextMove();
  sq.setPlayer(p);
}
```

5) Formal Verification: We verify the correctness of code by documenting each section of the code with an intended function and performing a functional program verification as described in Section II-B. We prove that the code is correct with respect to its intended function. If code was derived from a formally specified algorithm model such as a state machine and the algorithm was proved to be correct, the code may be correct by the way it was constructed provided that the algorithm model was transformed to code by following a set of transformation rules [21]. If a stepwise refinement was used to construct the code, the correctness proof may have already been performed as part of the refinement. In addition to intended functions and method bodies, we also need to prove the correctness of class invariants, if any. Essentially, we need to proved that each class invariant is established by the constructors of a class and preserved by all other methods of the class [20].

V. TRANSLATING OCL TO CLEANJAVA

An important component of our approach is translating OCL constraints to CleanJava annotations. We believe that this translation can be systematically done and even be automated by defining transformation rules. As an example, let's consider the invariant of the TicTacToe class shown below.

```
inv: squares[*,*].player->forAll(p|players->includes(p))
```

The constraint refers to two associations of class TicTacToe (`squares` and `players`) and an attribute of class Square (`player`). Remember that `squares` is the role name of a qualified association from TicTacToe to Square (see Figure 1 in Section II-A). If we know how these UML elements are reified in an implementation, we should be able to translate the OCL invariant to a CleanJava invariant by replacing UML/OCL elements with the corresponding Java/CleanJava elements. The following is one possible translation presented in the previous section.

```
inv: [squares->forAll(Square[] sqs|
      sqs->forAll(Square sq| !sq.isMarked() ||
      players->includes(sq.getPlayer())))]
```

However, a more direct and systematic translation would be to map each OCL construct to the corresponding CleanJava constructs. If there is no corresponding CleanJava construct, we can introduce a user-defined function for it (see below).

```
inv: [allPlaces(squares)->collect(Squares s| s.getPlayer())
     ->forAll(Player p|players->includes(p))] where
   CJSet<Square> allSquares(Square[][] sqs) = sqs->iterate(
     Square[] sq; CJSet<Square> r = new CJSet<Square>() |
     r.addAll(CJSet.fromArray(sq)))
```

In this translation, the reference to the qualified association end, `squares[*,*]`, is now translated to a user-defined function `allSquares` that, given a 2-dimensional array of squares, returns a set consisting of all the squares contained in the given array; the function is defined using the `iterate` collection operator. Also note that the dot notation in OCL when navigating an association (e.g., `squares[*,*].player`) is short for the `collect` iteration operator. Thus, it is translated to the CleanJava `collect` iteration operator.

The translation of pre and postconditions could be more involved depending on how they are written in OCL. This is because a functional program verification technique and notation is fundamentally different from an assertion-based technique and notation such as Hoare logic [11] and OCL. It is direct and constructive in that for each state variable such as a program variable one must state its final value explicitly. On the other hand, an assertion-based technique is indirect and constraint-based in that one specifies the condition that the final state has to satisfy by stating a relationship among state variables. The final value of a state variable isn't defined directly but instead is constrained and given indirectly by the specified condition.

As described in the previous section, pre and postconditions are translated to an intended function written using a conditional concurrent assignment. If there is a precondition, the translation produces a partial function of the form, $[P \rightarrow v_1, v_2, ..., v_n := E_i, ..., E_n]$, where P is the translation of the OCL precondition and v_i's and E_i's are derived from the OCL postcondition. For the translation of a postcondition, we can think of two different cases. If it is written in a constructive form, e.g, $x_1 = E_1$ and $x_2 = E_2$ and $\cdots$ and $x_n = E_n$, one possible translation would be $[x_i, x_2, ..., x_n := E_1', E_2', ..., E_n']$, where E_i' is a CleanJava translation of E_i. An example is the postcondition of the `getSquare` operation of TicTacToe class, `result = squares[i,j]`, which is straightforwardly translated to `[result := squares[i][j]]`. If a postcondition is not written constructively, its translation is more involved and complicate. There are several such postconditions in our TicTacToe example, including that of the `nextMove` operation of class Player, shown below.

```
context Player::nextMove(): Square
  pre: game.hasEmptySquare()
  post: not result.isMarked and
       game.squares[*,*]->includes(result)
```

However, it is also possible to translate these postconditions systematically and perhaps even automatically. One possibility is to use the `any` iteration operator that returns an arbitrary element of a collection that meets a given condition. Consider a postcondition $P(x_1, x_2, \cdots, x_n)$, written in terms of mutable state variables x_i's like class attributes and the return value. The new values of x_i's collectively have to satisfy the constraint P. Thus, the postcondition can be translated to:

```
[x1, x2, ..., xn :=
  T1->any(T1 x1'|
   T2->any(T2 x2'|
    ...
     Tn->any(Tn x2'|P'(x1, x2, ..., xn))))]
```

where P' is a CleanJava translation of P. For example, the pre and postconditions of the above `nextMove` operation can be translated to the following intended function.

```
[game.hasEmptySquare() ->
  result := Square->any(Square s| !s.isMarked() &&
    allSquares()->includes(s)) where
    allSquares() = /* ... */
```

VI. Discussion and Evaluation

There are a few interesting questions about translating OCL constraints to CleanJava annotations. OCL provides a special treatment for undefinedness of an expression and thus uses a three-valued (*true*, *false*, and *undefined*) propositional logic. This leads to an unpleasant consequence not only in correctness proof[1] but also in our translation of OCL constraints to CleanJava annotations. For example, the OCL disjunction operator (**or**) cannot be directly translated to the Java logical disjunction operator (||). In OCL, E_1 **or** E_2 is true even if E_1 is undefined as long as E_2 is true. In Java, however, the result of $E_1 \parallel E_2$ is an exception (i.e., undefined) if the evaluation of E_1 throws an exception. Operationally the equivalent Java code is:

```
boolean result = false;
Exception first = null;
try { result = E1'; }
catch (Exception e) { first = e; }
finally {
  if (!result) result = E2';
  if (!result && e != null) throw first;
}
```

There seems to be no simple and natural way of translating this OCL expression to CleanJava that is faithful to the standard OCL semantics. One possibility is to introduce a CleanJava-specific conjunction operator with the same semantics as the standard OCL, but its usefulness in general is questionable.

We said in the previous section that if a postcondition is written in a constructive form, e.g., $x = E$, we translate it to an intended function of the form, $[x := E]$. But what if E is also a mutable state variable, say y, to give a postcondition of the form $x = y$? The assertion states that x and y have an equal value in the final state. Thus, in addition to the intended

[1]For example, a well-known law of propositional logic, $A \Rightarrow B = \neg A \vee B$, doesn't hold in OCL [22].

function $[x := y]$, $[y := x]$ is also a correct refinement. In fact, there are numerous correct implementations including $[x, y := 0, 0]$. However, we learned that in most cases when one writes an OCL constraint like $x = y$ the intention was in fact $x = y$ **and** $y = y$@pre. In OCL, y@pre denotes y's initial value, and such a conjunct is needed because OCL doesn't provide a special construct for stating a frame axiom or property. Thus, we think our translation scheme is reasonable. If a postcondition is not written constructively, we used the `any` iteration operator to translate it. This allows us to systematically and possibility automatically translate OCL constraints. However, the `any` operator is similar to the μ operator in Z [13], and the resulting expression is not in a form that is easy to manipulate in verification using equational reasoning. Fortunately, however, our empirical study indicates that a significant fraction of OCL constraints is written constructively; e.g., 67% of OCL constraints for our tic-tac-toe example were written constructively.

We are currently elaborating and refining our approach as well as formulating the OCL-CleanJava translation rules. We are also assessing and evaluating our approach using more realistic case studies. The preliminary result is very promising in that we were able to systematically translate OCL constraints to CleanJava annotations and to prove the correctness of implementation code. In fact we found that an intended function often times provided a good guidance to a possible implementation. For example, we coded CleanJava user-defined functions as (private) helper methods, and an iteration operator such as `forAll` triggered an introduction of a loop in implementation code. The structure and constructs of a CleanJava annotation are frequently reflected in the implementation code, providing an additional assurance that the code conforms to its design.

VII. Conclusion

In this paper we proposed a new method that can complement testing as a practical software verification and validation technique. Our approach takes advantage of recent emphasis and advances on software modeling and systematically translates formally-specified design constraints such as class invariants and operation pre and postconditions written in OCL to code-level annotations written in CleanJava. The translated CleanJava annotations are refined to correct implementations in a stepwise refinement fashion or used for the correctness proof of the implementation code using a Cleanroom-style functional program verification technique.

We believe that our combination of OCL and CleanJava provides several advantages. CleanJava supports Cleanroom-style functional program verification, where a program is viewed as a mathematical function from one program state to another and a correctness proof is done by essentially comparing two functions, the function computed by the program and its specification. Since the technique uses equational reasoning based on sets and functions, it requires a minimal mathematical background, and unlike Hoare logic it supports forward reasoning, reflecting the way programmers informally reason about the correctness of a program. Thus, our approach will be more approachable to Java programmers and practitioners. Since OCL is part of the standard modeling language UML, it would be easier to adopt our approach and incorporate or integrate into existing object-oriented software development methods.

Acknowledgment

This work was supported in part by DUE-0837567.

References

[1] A. W. Brown, "Model driven architecture: Principles and practice," *Software and System Modeling*, vol. 3, no. 4, pp. 314–327, Dec. 2004.

[2] J. Warmer and A. Kleppe, *The Object Constraint Language: Getting Your Models Ready for MDA*, 2nd ed. Addison-Wesley, 2003.

[3] J. Rumbaugh, I. Jacobson, and G. Booch, *The Unified Modeling Language Reference Manual*, 2nd ed. Addison-Wesley, 2004.

[4] A. Tang and H. van Vliet, "Modeling constraints improves software architecture design reasoning," in *Proceedings of the Joint Working IEEE/IFIP Conference on Software Architecture 2009 and European Conference on Software Architecture 2009*, 2009, pp. 253–256.

[5] Y. Cheon, C. Yeep, and M. Vela, "The CleanJava language for functional program verification," *International Journal of Software Engineering*, vol. 5, no. 1, pp. 47–68, Jan. 2012.

[6] H. D. Mills, M. Dyer, and R. Linger, "Cleanroom software engineering," *IEEE Software*, vol. 4, no. 5, pp. 19–25, Sep. 1987.

[7] S. J. Prowell, C. J. Trammell, R. C. Linger, and J. H. Poore, *Cleanroom Software Engineering*. Addison Wesley, Feb. 1999.

[8] A. Stavely, *Toward Zero Defect Programming*. Addison-Wesley, 1999.

[9] Y. Cheon, "Functional specification and verification of object-oriented programs," Department of Computer Science, The University of Texas at El Paso, 500 West University Ave., El Paso, TX, 79968, Tech. Rep. 10-23, Aug. 2010.

[10] Y. Cheon and M. Vela, "A tutorial on functional program verification," Department of Computer Science, The University of Texas at El Paso, Tech. Rep. 10-26, Sep. 2010.

[11] C. A. R. Hoare, "An axiomatic basis for computer programming," *Communications of ACM*, vol. 12, no. 10, pp. 576–580,583, Oct. 1969.

[12] Z. Langari and A. B. Pidduck, "Quality, cleanroom and formal methods," *SIGSOFT Softw. Eng. Notes*, vol. 30, no. 4, pp. 1–5, May 2005.

[13] J. M. Spivey, *Understanding Z: a Specification Language and its Formal Semantics*. New York, NY: Cambridge University Press, 1988.

[14] A. M. Stavely, "Integrating Z and Cleanroom," in *LFM2000: Fifth NASA Langley Formal Methods Workshop*, Jun. 2000, pp. 141–150.

[15] A. Hamie, "Towards verifying java realizations of OCL-constrained design models using JML," in *6th IASTED International Conference on Software Engineering and Applications*, 2002.

[16] G. T. Leavens, "Tutorial on JML, the Java Modeling Language," in *ASE '07: Proceedings of the 22nd IEEE/ACM International Conference on Automated Software Engineering*. ACM, 2007, p. 573.

[17] L. Burdy, Y. Cheon, D. R. Cok, M. D. Ernst, J. R. Kiniry, G. T. Leavens, K. R. M. Leino, and E. Poll, "An overview of JML tools and applications," *International Journal on Software Tools for Technology Transfer*, vol. 7, no. 3, pp. 212–232, Jun. 2005.

[18] C. Avila, A. Sarcar, Y. Cheon, and C. Yeep, "Runtime constraint checking approaches for OCL, a critical comparison," in *Proceedings of SEKE 2010, The 22-nd International Conference on Software Engineering and Knowledge Engineering, July 1-3, 2010, San Francisco, CA*, 2010, pp. 393–398.

[19] D. S. Frankel, *Model Driven Architecture: Applying MDA to Enterprise Computing*. Wiley, Jan. 2003.

[20] C. Avila and Y. Cheon, "Functional verification of class invariants in CleanJava," in *Innovations and Advances in Computer, Information, Systems Sciences, and Engineering*, ser. Lecture Notes in Electrical Engineering, vol. 152. Springer-Verlag, Aug. 2012, pp. 1067–1076.

[21] K. Lano, *Model-Driven Software Development with UML and Java*. Course Technology, 2009.

[22] R. Hennicker, H. Hussmann, and M. Bidoit, "On the precise meaning of OCL constraints," in *Object Modeling with the OCL, The Rationale behind the Object Constraint Language*. London, UK, UK: Springer-Verlag, 2002, pp. 69–84.

An Open Source Platform for Collaborative Remote Usability Studies

Røder, Daniel L.[1] **and Frøkjær, Erik.**[2]
[1 2]Department of Computer Science (DIKU), University of Copenhagen, Denmark.

Abstract—In the field of usability testing, remote evaluation methods have been suggested as a way to combat the high costs incurred by traditional laboratory testing. The Distributed Usability Evaluation (DUE) framework is an asynchronous remote testing suite which has yielded good results in an industrial case study of production software. The framework allows users to send video/audio reports to a centralized server on which evaluators and developers can collaborate to find their optimal solutions. In this paper we present the latest development iteration of the framework, which brings about significant improvements to allow for studies with an extensive amount (>50) of participants. The updated framework is submitted to an expert evaluation by acknowledged usability experts and scientists which concludes that the framework holds a potential for doing extensive usability studies with minimal effort. Based on the promising results, the framework is now released as an open source project in an effort to assist others in conducting long-term studies involving many users.

***Index Terms*—Usability evaluation; remote usability testing; instrumentation; video/audio reporting; open source; collaboration.**

I. Introduction

THE software industry is becoming increasingly aware of the benefits of doing usability studies both in terms of how people perceive their products, and how efficient the products function. This has however been a long and slow journey as the methods most commonly used in the industry have a large demand for both time and person-hours to execute, leaving it in many cases a luxury of larger companies. As a response to these challenges, various "discount" usability methods have been introduced, spreading also to the field of remote usability testing.

In remote usability testing the test administrator and participant can be separated in space and time. According to Dumas [1] there are several advantages both in the logistics associated with conducting the test as well as making it easier to recruit users for studies. Remote methods has been explored since the mid 90'ies and different tools has since been made available to assist in the conduction of such studies [2], [3]. In some of the earlier studies, the technology was reported as a hindrance for the success of the methods, but with the rapid development in both hardware and software the boundaries of what is possible is continually moving [1].

Bruun et al. [4] recently published an article in which they do an extensive literature review in the field of remote usability testing. They recognize the distinction in remote usability studies between synchronous methods in which user and evaluator are only spatially separated, and asynchronous methods in which the separation is both spatial and temporal. While synchronous methods do deliver greater flexibility, it is just as time consuming as ordinary lab testing as the evaluator still needs to be present throughout the evaluation. The asynchronous methods are further subdivided into different categories depending on the technique used for gathering data from the users. From the overview provided by Bruun et al. it is apparent that textual data forms are the predominant technique employed by asynchronous studies, as they span methods such as automatic log data retrieval, online questionnaires and various collaboration tools.

We present the Distributed Usability Evaluation (DUE) framework for conducting asynchronous remote usability studies, which builds on the ideas behind the user-reported critical incident technique (UCI) [5], but expands this technique. The framework consists of a process to be followed during the evaluation as well as an open source toolset based on the process, which encompasses the full cycle of a usability study. The framework separates itself from commonly used remote evaluation techniques by using audio and video recorded from the users own workstation as basis for the evaluation. These reports are gathered on a centralized platform which provides functionality to strengthen communication and collaboration among different stakeholders. Following the UCI idea, the initial evaluation is done by the users themselves, thereby limiting the work load for the evaluator.

II. Process

The DUE framework is designed with the primary intention of enabling usability studies to be conducted without the extensive physical requirements incurred by traditional laboratory tests, while also minimizing the needed person-hours.

The process suggested by the framework calls for 4 different roles to participate in the evaluation:

User: The user is the source of data. They report usability issues on their own workstations and send them to the evaluation server.

Evaluator: Evaluates the data received by the users, categorizes them and assigns a rating based on severity.

Development Manager: Prioritizes the issues produced by the evaluator.

Developer: Changes the evaluated program in accordance with the issues, and closes the issue.

[1]**Email: daniel.lyng.roeder@gmail.com**
[2]**Email: erikf@diku.dk**

This division helps to clearly define responsibilities within the process, and also follows the practical approach adopted by many small to mid size companies. There is no implied limit or requirement as to how many people are participating in each role, but the workload will closely follow the number engaged in the user role. The associated toolset provides a separate interface for each of the four different roles, to further support this work process.

As stated in the definition of the roles, the users are alone responsible for reporting the usability issues. These reports are done via video and audio recordings from the users own computer. The user also provides a severity rating before the collected report is uploaded to an evaluation server. The user is thus working in his natural environment while the evaluation is running, which gives some unique advantages: Tests can run extended periods of time with minimal cost. Prolonged tests can help mitigate the learning curve effect of users working with new software. The user is in a stress free environment and will experience no pressure to perform at a certain level, as is the case with situated tests. The framework is also flexible enough to allow for the other roles to report issues, if they gain valuable insights through the process that the user themselves does not recognize.

III. Toolset

The process is supported by an open source toolset designed to assist both usability experts and novices in carrying out successful evaluations. The toolset consists of a client program to run on the user's workstation as well as a server to collect the reports generated, and support the evaluation process.

The clients primary function is to provide the video/audio reports generated by the user. This is accomplished by continuously recording all activity on the user's workstation as a screencast stored on the local machine. The client itself has only a minimal UI placed along with the windows of the application under evaluation. It stays on top of other windows, but reverts to a semi-transparent view in normal work situations, to avoid disturbing the user during normal work functions. The simple UI also serves to keep user training at a minimum, by providing a simple and intuitive interface that is easily understood and adopted by the users.

When the user indicates that an issue has been encountered, he will be prompted to describe the issue to the microphone. Video material from the last 30 seconds prior to the user marking an issue will be prepended to the explanation, thus not requiring the user to recreate the circumstances which brought fourth the issue. These time limits are based on the results obtained from a case study, which revealed these parts of the video to be enough for the evaluators to correctly classify the issues [6]. The video is then uploaded to the server for evaluation.

User reports uploaded to the server will be automatically imported to the evaluation system, and await further classification by the Evaluator role. Each role has it's own interface on the server which primarily means that the server automatically finds and promotes the issues ready for that particular role, but every role has access to the full database. In studies with more than one evaluator, this helps to mitigate the evaluator effect [7] as all data and all decisions made are kept on the server and accessible for everyone. To further support this notion of collaboration it is possible for every role to mark an issue as needing review by another role while adding a comment as well as sending an email with a direct link to an issue to other stakeholders. Practically this means that if e.g. a development manager does not agree with the classification assigned by an evaluator, she can voice her concerns and send the issue back for reevaluation to allow the evaluator to further explain his reasoning.

Currently the client program requires a Microsoft Windows environment to function also relying on Windows Media Encoder for the encoding of the screencast. The server runs on a normal AMP stack (Apache, MySQL, PHP) but requires Microsoft Silverlight for video playback in visiting browser.

IV. Results

The framework has been successfully tested in a case study with production software under active development, in which 16 people were assigned to the user role. The study showed that the framework did produce usable issue reports while keeping the requirements significantly lower than traditional methods [6]. Since this study, the framework has undergone an extensive redesign phase, building further on the aspects of collaboration, rationale capture and a general streamlining of the toolset to make it even easier to deploy and customize. These efforts have most notably resulted in a more structured view of the user reports, a tagging system and generally better access to issue details.

The updated framework was submitted to an expert evaluation among some of the worlds leading usability experts. All invited experts are established names within the scientific community within the area of HCI / Usability and most with ties to the industry as well. 31 invitations was sent, 15 responded positively and 7 evaluations were received. This low number is largely contributed to time limitations as evaluators were only given a week to complete the evaluation. The evaluation was designed to make the experts evaluate the ideas and concepts of the process rather than the actual implementation of the toolset. To accomplish this, they had to base their reviews on a prerecorded video presentation of the framework[1] rather than working directly with the toolset.

Respondents were very optimistic about the framework's ease of use as well as it's ability to be a persistent repository for all of the aggregated data through a study. A respondent writes:

> [R6] *"The strength is that it seems to be easy for the user to explain a problem"*

while another:

> [R4] *"Traceability of the data captured is the obvious strength of this framework"*

[1] Available at: http://youtu.be/Cb7ZwNrx-rM

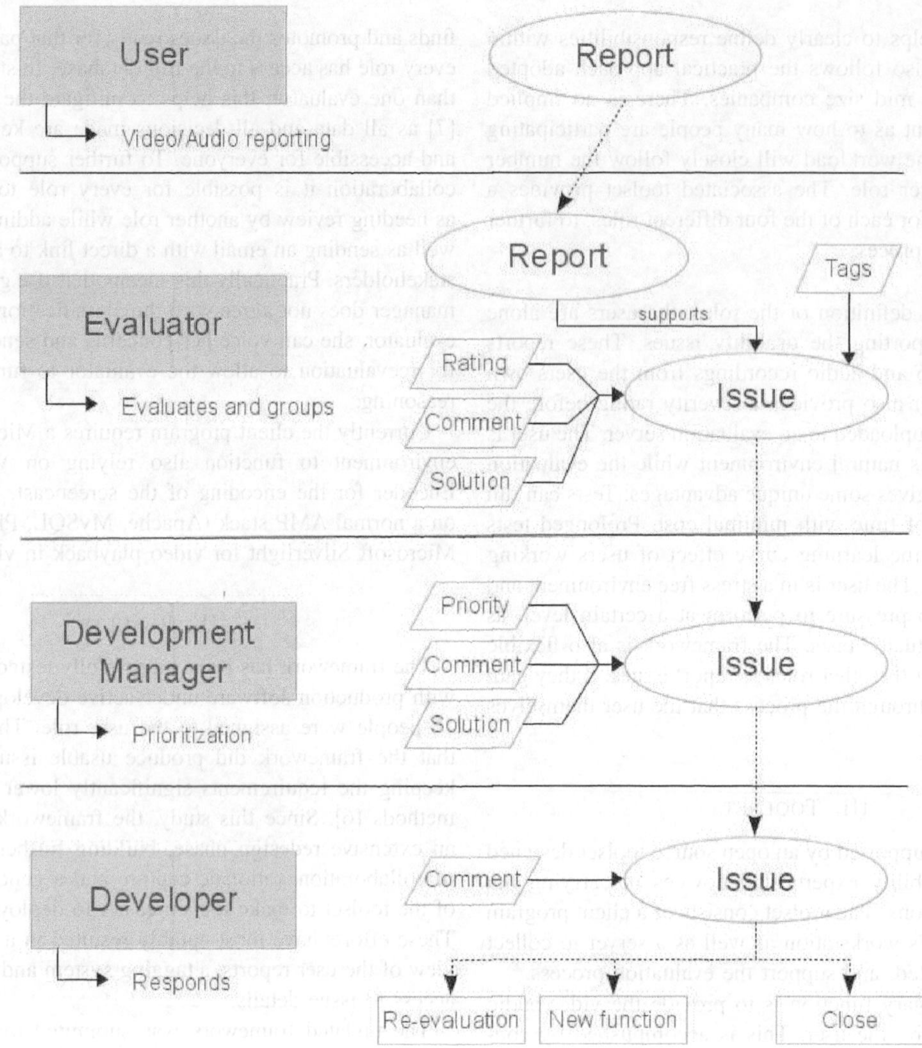

Figure 1. The four different roles of the process shown with their respective responsibilities, as well as the optional data elements available to each.

and along the same lines:

> [R2] *"The system also nicely stores the evaluation history which may be of remarkable value"*

The biggest concern being that the initial evaluation and classification was left to the end users, rather than an experienced evaluator. One respondent notes:

> [R2] *"The greatest weakness, in my mind, is that the evaluation is based on analysis made by users: users decide what usability problems / strengths are"*

This is an entirely valid concern, but is also a generic argument for all studies in which users are the subjects in the evaluation. Even for usability studies done in a laboratory environment, the results will be influenced by how well the user responds to the method employed. The DUE framework on the other hand has the advantage of being able to sample large groups of users, thereby increasing the chance that their combined reporting efforts are covering their concerns.

Another respondent suggests that the toolset should try to further capitalize on the users being involved in the process:

> [R7] *"...possibly it would be good to allow the user also to send off some comment together with the recording"*

which would further allow the users to act as responsible stakeholders. The toolset does indeed support letting the user send a textual comment along with the video, but it is not the default option. A feature of letting the users annotate the uploaded video as well as provide more detailed descriptions are planned for future development.

As a last question the respondents were asked if they themselves would be interested in using the framework in their professional work as scientists or business consultants, to which 5 out of 7 replied positively. Two of the respondents note that:

> [R1] *"Yes, I do lots of business usability consulting, I would be interested in getting access to DUE, and be happy to send you back the feedback from our work"*

Issue details:

Issue ID:	6 (send link to issue in e-mail)
Status:	prioritized, waiting for response
Report time:	14:09:30
User rating:	red
Occurrences:	3
User description:	
Tags:	new Usability Video interface

Evaluator:	role2
Category:	user interface problem
Evaluator rating:	red
Title:	Video only half screen
Comment:	The video is only half size
Suggestet solution:	disable multiscreen and increase bandwidth

Develop Manager:	role3
Priority:	1. MUST fix this.
Comment:	
Suggestet solution:	Go with the evaluator solution

Developer:	
Response:	
Comment:	

User video:

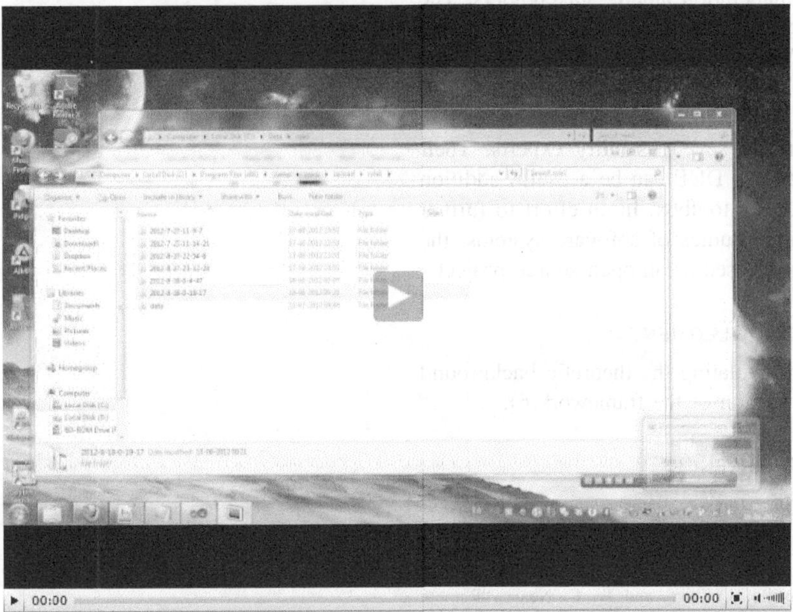

Supporting reports:

User	Date	Time	User rating	Report ID	User description	Evaluator description
role1	18 Aug 2012	00:25	red	10 view	no	yes
role1	18 Aug 2012	00:33	red	11 view	no	yes
role1	18 Aug 2012	00:38	yellow	12 view	no	yes

Figure 2. The issue details view of the server. At the top are all relevant data entered by any of the roles presented. In the middle the video uploaded by the user is directly available, and at the bottom all uploaded reports associated with this issue is listed.

> [R5] *"Yes, I think it might be interesting to experiment with, especially in relation to our work on user-reported usability problems"*

While the two voicing negative opinions:

> [R2] *"I find as a too big risk to trust that users can do valid evaluations (find and report valid usability problems & strengths) by themselves. I would do the analysis myself or let some other usability professional to do it"*

> [R3] *"I am rarely involved in developing the type of applications for which this was designed - I mostly work with 'tangible' products/prototypes ... also, I find it very important to observe users during their interaction with a system"*

This shows that the majority of the responding usability experts consider the toolset to be a potentially valuable supplement to their method palette when doing usability studies. As a consequence of this, a decision has been made to release the framework as an open source project to further develop the method and to gather more results from it's practical use. The expectation is that the DUE framework can find its place as a interesting supplement to methods already in use, by providing evaluations of a full software suite, with a large group of users. For instance a DUE evaluation can provide an overview of usability issues in a software suite, identifying areas suited for e.g. think aloud testing.

V. Conclusions

We have presented the DUE framework as a method for conducting asynchronous remote usability studies with automatic audio/video capture of usability issues aggregated from a large number of users working in their natural environment. These data are collected on a common repository with facilities encouraging collaboration among stakeholders. The framework has previously shown great potential in a case study of industrial software. With inspiration from this study the framework's associated toolset has been further streamlined and expanded. The revised framework has been submitted for an expert review among seven usability experts. Their response further indicates that DUE can be a useful addition to the usability professionals' toolbox. In an effort to further enable large scale usability studies of software systems, the framework is now being released as an open source project.

Acknowlegment

Lars Christensen for formulating the theoretic background and developing the first version of the framework[6].

References

[1] J. S. Dumas and J. E. Fox, *The Human Computer Interaction Handbook*, ch. 53, pp. 1221–1241. CRC Press, 3rd ed., 2012.

[2] M. Hammontree, P. Weiler, and N. Nayak, "Remote usability testing," *Interactions*, July 1994.

[3] H. R. Hartson, J. C. Castillo, J. Kelso, and W. C. Neale, "Remote evaluation: The network as an extension of the usability laboratory," *CHI*, 1996.

[4] A. Bruun, P. Gull, L. Hofmeister, and J. Stage, "Let your users do the testing: A comparison of three remote asynchronous usability testing methods," *CHI*, April 2009.

[5] J. C. Castillo, H. R. Hartson, and D. Hix, "Remote usability evaluation: Can users report their own critical incidents?," *CHI*, April 1998.

[6] L. Christensen and E. Froekjaer, "Distributed usability evaluation: enabling large-scale usability evaluation with user-controlled instrumentation," *NordiCHI*, pp. 16–20, 2010.

[7] K. Hornbaek and E. Froekjaer, "A study of the evaluator effect in usability testing," *HCI*, vol. 23, pp. 251–277, 2008.

Study of Data Imputation on the Predictive Value of Software Attributes in the ISBSG-10 Data Set

Adrian S. Barb
Information Science Department
Penn State University
Malvern, Pennsylvania 19335
Email: adrian@psu.edu

Kailasam Satyamurthy
Engineering and Management Departments
Penn State University
Malvern, Pennsylvania 19335
Email: kxs425@psu.edu

***Abstract*—With increased attention on reducing software cost, research has recently focused on developing new methods to measure software complexity that can be successfully applied for resource allocation, project complexity, and defect estimation. To help practitioners, a variety of public data sets were created and maintained to provide historical data for organizations that do not possess historical project data. However, due to their cross-company nature, such data sets contain missing values, and raise several practical estimation problems. This article explores the relevance of imputation on the predictive value of software attributes. We evaluated this on the International Software Benchmarking Standards Group release 10 (ISBSG-10) data set which is commonly used for software estimation. We build linear models for prediction, cluster results by the quality of prediction, and identify relevant predictors using association rule mining techniques.**

***Index Terms*—ISBSG, Software estimation, data mining, linear models, association rules.**

I. Introduction

Building accurate models for software prediction early in the life cycle of a project is the subject of many recent researches [1]. Such models are essential to the success of software projects, but still remain challenging to the software engineering community. They focus on providing cost estimates as a function of some variables measured early in the life cycle of the project [2], [3], [4], [5]. Early approaches were shown to provide low prediction accuracy [6], which in many cases are comparable to expert judgement methods of cost estimation [7], [8], especially in the case of un-calibrated algorithms with an emphasis on the fact that most models underestimate the time and cost of software development [9].

Many researchers have focused on providing computer-based algorithmic models for cost estimation, due to the fact that expert judgement exhibits large estimation variations [7]. To improve accuracy, recent approaches used data mining techniques [10], [11], [12] to extract knowledge hidden in historical software databases which are made available for the software community. Among the used data mining techniques, linear regression is most widely used in software estimation [13], [14]. Methods that use linear regression must use a set of dependent software project variables that can be used to accurately model the variation of the predicted variable with emphasis on predicting software attributes at each stage of a software life cycle. For an in-depth analysis of software estimation models and their replication, the reader is directed to [15], [16].

One major factor in prediction is the quality of the information in the historical data at hand. Many start-ups or small companies may have little historical project knowledge gathered to provide reliable effort estimates. To such issues, several groups have released public domain software development data with the purpose of helping companies build powerful and practical estimation models based on domain specific historical knowledge. One example is the International Software Benchmarking Standards Group [17]. This group defined a set of standards for data collection, and maintains a data set of cross-industry project data based on these standards. There are several issues about data completeness and quality in these data sets. For example, the ISBSG-10 data set has a large percentage of missing data which may result in smaller, varying sizes of training data [18]. This issue may lead to low replication accuracy of experiments [19] with low quality of the generated prediction models [20].

Techniques to ignore missing data such as list-wise or pair-wise deletions are the main reasons for training set reduction and they are shown to be suboptimal for treating missing values [21]. Similar results are obtained using mean or mode single imputation methods. Research shows that novel methods for data imputation may lead to significant improvement prediction. Among these, good results are shown using methods such as tree-based techniques [21], using maximum-likelihood or Bayes networks [22], or using hot-deck imputation with Euclidean distance and z-score standardization [23].

In this article, we describe an empirical study of the effects of data imputation on the predictive quality of linear models in software effort prediction. To accomplish our research goals, we hypothesize that the accuracy of project attributes using historical data increases with the percentage of imputed data in the training set. Specifically, we perform an in-depth evaluation of software attribute prediction using historical data from the ISBSG-10 data set by using linear models. These models are trained on imputed versions of the ISBSG-10 data set at two levels of missing data. We also analyze and compare the prediction power of the created models on the initial data using the adjusted R^2 statistical measure. This paper is

Algorithm 1 Predict Software Attributes

INPUT: ISBSG-10 data set
OUTPUT: adj-R^2 values for model and test data set

```
1: D ← preprocess(ISBSG-10)
2: DT ← impute(D)
3: result ← {}
4: for EACH set of attributes A ← {y, {X}|y ∩ X = ∅} do
5:     TR ← subset(DT, A)
6:     TR1 ← normalize(TR)
7:     TS ← subset(D, A)
8:     TS ← normalize_match(subset(D, A))
9:     lm ← y ~ X|train1
10:    p_res ← denormalize(predict(lm, subset(TR1, X)))
11:    R_res ← adj-R^2(p_res, subset(DT, X))
12:    p_tst ← denormalize(predict(lm, subset(TR, X)))
13:    R_tst ← adj-R^2(p_res, subset(DT, X))
14:    result ← result ∪ {R_res, R_tst}
15: end for
16: return result
```

organized as follows: Section II introduces the methodology, Section III presents our experimental, and we conclude our research in Section IV.

II. Methodology

To evaluate the effects of imputation on the predictive power of attributes in the ISBSG-10 data set we designed an experimental procedure that is described in Algorithm 1 and which was implemented in R [24]. First, in line 1 of the algorithm, we apply a preprocessing procedure to remove low quality and categorical attributes. This procedure is described in Section II-A. Then, as shown in line 2, we impute missing data at a predetermined level (30% or 50% in our study) using a procedure that we describe in-depth in Section II-B. Next, we exhaustively generate subsets of the imputed data with different sets of attributes as shown in line 4 of Algorithm 1 and explained in Section II-C. The generated subset is used to construct a linear model (line 9 of Algorithm 1 and Section II-D). Finally, we test our model on the original data as shown in line 10-13 in algorithm 1 and explained in Section II-E.

A. Data Preparation

In the first step of the experiment we preprocess the ISBSG-10 data set by removing the projects that are considered by the ISBSG Consortium as unsuitable for statistical analysis (data quality rating of C or D). We also retain only projects that report only the development team effort as measured by the attribute 'resource level'. Further, we transform some relevant categorical attributes to a binary representation. The list of these attributes include *Project Activity Scope*, *Application Type*, *Architecture*, *Development Techniques*, and *Primary Programming Language*. For example, the *Architecture* attribute was transformed into four binary attributes *Client-Server Architecture*, *Multitier Architecture*, *Standalone Architecture*, and *Web Architecture* with each generated attribute accepting true

TABLE I
Categorization of project attributes by phase of the project life cycle

Group	Project Attributes	Description
1	Defect, Test Effort, Total Effort	Post Completion
2	LOC, Project time, Work effort	Completion
3	Build and Implementation Effort	Mid project 2
4	Design, Plan, and Specify Effort	Mid project 1
5	AFP, Functional Size, Team Size	Initial Phase
6	All other project attributes	Input

or false values. After this preprocessing step, the resulting data set included 3146 projects with 64 attributes.

B. Imputation of missing data

Missing data is a common issue in the data preprocessing. For imputation of missing values in the ISBSG-10 data set, we used the Iterative Robust Model-based Imputation method [25]. One of its advantages is that can it handle mixtures of continuous, ordinal, and nominal variables including outliers. This method estimates the missing values by fitting a sequence of regression models and drawing values from the corresponding predictive distributions. Variables are sorted by the amount of missing values and their values are imputed in an iterative process starting with the most complete ones. For each type of attribute, a different type of imputation method is applied. For example, continuous variables are imputed using a robust least square regression, while categorical attributes are imputed with generalized linear regression and binary ones are imputed using logistic regression. For each attribute, the missing values are first initialized using k-nearest neighbor imputation and missing values are repeatedly imputed until the variation in values between two consecutive iterations is less than a threshold. Using this imputation method, we have constructed two data sets based on the ISBSG-10 data set: (1) a data set that contains only projects that have less than 30% missing data (TR_1) with a size of 285 projects and 60 attributes, and (2) a data set that contains only projects that have less than 50% missing data (TR_2) with a size of 1,245 projects and 60 attributes. Each of these data sets have no missing values.

C. Training data generation and processing

Once the training data set TR is generated, we scale all the continuous features into the range [0, 1] using a min-max normalization formula as shown below. Experiments show that the application of the min-max normalization procedure results in better prediction models [26].

$$TR_1[m_{i,j}] = \frac{TR[m_{i,j}] - min\,(TR[m_{*,j}])}{max\,(TR[m_{*,j}]) - min\,(TR[m_{*,j}])} \quad (1)$$

In this formula TR is a matrix with the form $TR[m_{i,j}]_{i=1,\ldots P;j=1,\ldots A}$ where m is the value of attribute j in project i, A is the number of project attributes, and P is the number of projects in the data set. Also, $TR[m_{*,j}]$ refers to all the project values values of the attribute j.

Fig. 1. Adjusted R^2 Scatter Plots for experiments that train models with (a) 30% of data and (b) 50% of data.

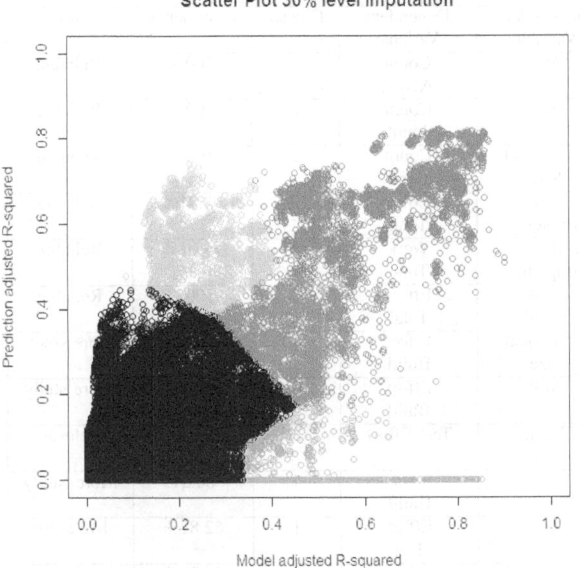

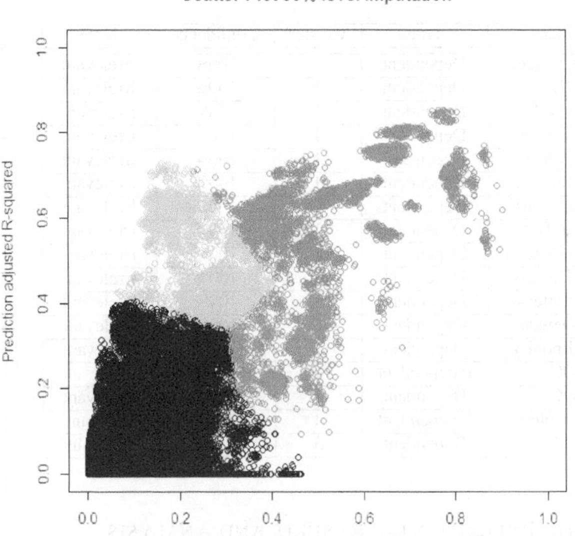

Further, we exhaustively generate combinations of attributes $\{Y, X = \{x_k\}\} \mid size(X) < 3,\ group(Y) < max(group(X))$ where Y is a dependent attribute and X is a set of independent attributes from TR to create linear models for prediction with a maximum size of three independent variables. The second filtering condition filters out all combinations of attributes for which the independent variables do not appear later in the life cycle of the product. For example, having a set where *AFP* is the dependent variable and *LOC* is the independent variable may have little meaning from the practical software prediction perspective since *AFP* is determined at the beginning of the project while *LOC* is the result of a project. To handle these cases, we assigned project attributes into six categories based on the time when they can be assessed over the life cycle of a software project. Using this grouping, for example, renders irrelevant the case where *AFP* is the dependent variable and *LOC* is the independent variable because *AFP* belongs to the fifth group, which is determined before group two in which *LOC* belongs. However, the reverse case where *AFP* is the independent variable and *LOC* is the dependent variable is considered relevant. After this process, we generated a number of 284,959 unique combinations of project attributes.

D. Linear Regression Models

For each attribute combination $\{Y, X = \{x_k\}\}$ we generate a training data set $TR_2[m_{i,j}] = TR_1[m_{i,j}] \mid j \in Y \cup X$ and we design a linear regression experiment as shown in the formula below:

$$Y^{pred} = \beta_0 + \sum_{j=1}^{\text{size(X)}} \beta_i m_{*j} \mid m_{*j} \in TR_2[m_{i,j}] \quad (2)$$

In this formula, β_o, β_i are coefficients of the linear regression and Y^{pred} is the response variable of the linear model when trying to predict the variable Y using the dependent variables X.

E. Model evaluation

Due to the fact that the model response Y^{pred} of the linear model is computed on min-max normalized data, we first de-normalize it so it is mapped in the initial attribute variables. We accomplish this using the equation below.

$$\begin{aligned} Y^{pred}_{dn} &= min\left(TR[m_{*,j}]\right) \\ &+ Y^{pred}\left(max\left(TR[m_{*,j}]\right) - min\left(TR[m_{*,j}]\right)\right) \end{aligned} \quad (3)$$

After the predicted attributes are de-normalized, we compute the prediction quality using adj-R^2 statistical measure as shown below. The use of the adj-R^2 has the advantage that that it copes better with the addition of irrelevant independent variables than its unadjusted version.

$$\text{adj-}R^2 = R^2 - \left(1 - R^2\right)\frac{P}{A - P - 1} \quad (4)$$

$$R^2 = 1 - \frac{\sum\left(TR[m_{*,Y}] - \overline{TR[m_{*,Y}]}\right)^2}{\sum\left(Y^{pred}_{dn} - TR[m_{*,Y}]\right)} \quad (5)$$

The resulted adj-R^2 will be used to compare results of the experiments across the two levels of data imputation.

TABLE II
RESULTS OF ASSOCIATION MINING TO EVALUATE THE RELEVANCE OF SOFTWARE ATTRIBUTES TO CLUSTERS.

Attribute	type	Cluster	Confidence	Note
Count Changed	Dependent	1	100%	Irrelevant
Count Deleted	Dependent	1	100%	Irrelevant
Count Interface	Dependent	1	100%	Irrelevant
Effort Design	Dependent	1	100%	Irrelevant
Effort Plan	Dependent	1	100%	Irrelevant
Effort Specify	Dependent	1	100%	Irrelevant
Elapsed Time	Dependent	1	100%	Irrelevant
Inactive Time	Dependent	1	100%	Irrelevant
Extreme Defects	Dependent	1	100%	Irrelevant
Major Defects	Dependent	1	100%	Irrelevant
Minor Defects	Dependent	1	100%	Irrelevant
Total Defects	Dependent	1	100%	Irrelevant
Count Enquiry	Dependent	1	93.8%	Irrelevant
LOC	Independent	1	89.83%	Irrelevant
LOC	Dependent	1	71.31%	Irrelevant
Effort Implem.	Independent	4	73.01%	Relevant
Effort Build	Dependent	3	60.03%	Unreliable

TABLE III
RELEVANT PROJECT ATTRIBUTES FOR PREDICTION

Independent Variable	Dependent Variable	Cluster	Confidence	Note
AFP	Count Added	2	100%	Reliable
AFP	Count Input	2	100%	Reliable
Functional Size	Count Input	2	100%	Reliable
Effort Implem.	Effort Total	2	93.71%	Reliable
Effort Implem.	Work Total	2	73.01%	Reliable
Effort Build	Effort Total	2	100%	Reliable
Functional Size	Effort Build	4	100%	More study
AFP	Effort Build	4	100%	More study
Team Size	Test Effort	3	78.01%	Irrelevant
*	Effort Build	4	60.31	More Study
AFP	Effort Test	1	62.82%	Irrelevant
Functional Size	Effort Test	1	63.78%	Irrelevant

III. Experimental Results and Analysis

We statistically evaluated the results of our experiments using the Wilcoxon paired test. When we compared the adj-R^2 of the generated models, the test shows, with a confidence of $2 * 10^{-16}$ that the experiment that uses 50% imputed data returns better models than the ones that use only 30% imputed data. However, this advantage does not translate into better predictions; the Wilcoxon test shows, with a confidence of $2.2 * 10^{-16}$, that predicting with 50% imputed data in training returns lower quality models than predicting with 30% imputed data in training sets. This pattern can be observed in Figure 1 which shows that, in general, the first experiment returns models for which both model and prediction adj-R^2 exhibit high density of scatter points on the top right of each plot.

We have further analyzed the patterns in 1 to identify the behavior of prediction models. To accomplish this, we have applied a k-means [27] algorithm to cluster the data. Due to the fact that the pattern of data is not fitted for clustering with euclidean distance, we have initially used a number of 15 clusters which were later merged using a agglomerative hierarchical clustering [27] based on the centroid distance. The result is shown in Figure 1 using different colors. In general, data was clustered in four clusters: (1) models that return low adj-R^2 for both training and for testing (represented by black color), (2) models that return good adj-R^2 for both training and testing (blue color), (3) models that return good training adj-R^2 but are not good predictors (red color), and (4) models with low training adj-R^2 which have good predicted power (cyan color). For training with 30% missing data there is a fifth cluster of models that have very good adj-R^2 in training but return very poor predictive models (green color).

We further investigated the assignment of models to each of these groups by evaluating groups of independent variable inside each group. We have applied the apriori algorithm [28] to a set of data with two attributes: maximum grouping of the independent variable and cluster number. We have used the following measures for the quality of generated associations: (1) *support* - the proportion of models that contain a pattern, confidence - the proportion of models that contain a pattern and belong to the same group, and lift - relevance of an association as compared with a random process. We have used the following apriori parameters: 10% level of minimum support and 90% level of minimum confidence. The result on the 30% imputed data set showed that using variables in the grouping 6 (input) for prediction returned models in *Cluster 1* (low adj-R^2 for both model and prediction) with a confidence of 99.65% and a lift of 1.0728. The rest of experiments that used input variables were located in *Cluster 5*. Similarly, for the 50% imputed data set we discovered that using the grouping 6 variables for prediction returned models in *Cluster 1* with a confidence of 100% and a lift of 1.0765. This demonstrate the fact the initial project variables such as *Project Activity Scope*, *Application Type*, *Architecture*, *Development Techniques*, and *Primary Programming Language* have a low predictive power of software effort and they are likely to negatively affect models where they are used as independent variables.

In the next phase of the analysis, we have removed all of the experiments that contain independent variables from grouping 1. This reduced the size of the data set to 9,687 models. A further comparative evaluation of training with 30% vs. 50% missing data, using the reduced data, showed a similar pattern as before in which, although it produces lower training adj-R^2, training with the 30% data set returns better predictive models with a high confidence of $2.2 * 10^{-16}$. Similar results are obtained when applying the Wilcoxon test to subsets of

Fig. 2. Percentage of models associated with each clustering group. In this figure, *Group*2 displays good models in both training and testing, *Group 3* displays good models only in training, while *Group 4* displays good models only for prediction

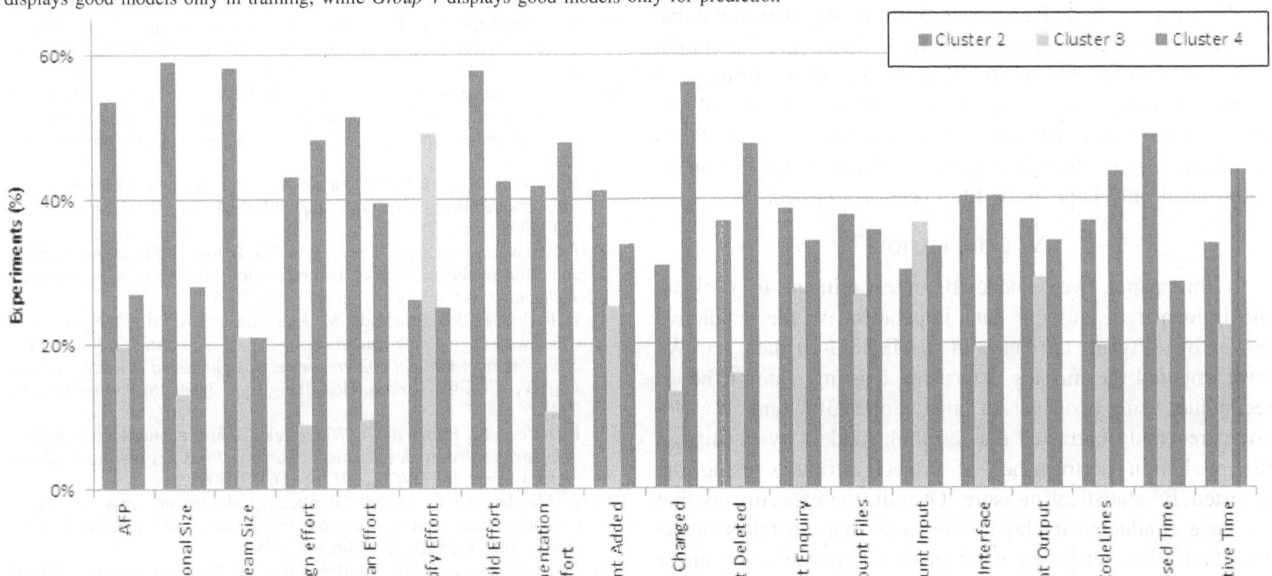

data in each cluster. This leads us to conclude that training with fewer imputed values has more predictive power than larger, more synthetic data sets. For this reason, the rest of the experiments will be performed only on the data set that uses 30% imputed data.

We have further applied the apriori association rule mining algorithm on the generated subset of data. For this experiment, we constructed the association rule antecedent from attributes of the linear model and the consequent from the cluster in which the model was assigned. We flagged each project attribute as independent or dependent. For example, the dependent variable *LOC* was encoded differently from the independent variable *LOC*. We were interested mostly in association rules for which the antecedent contained only one attribute while the consequent is a cluster, so we are able to evaluate the influence of each project attribute. The results are shown in Table II. From these results we learned, with 100% confidence, that defects cannot be predicted successfully using other software attributes. Similar results were obtained for predicting design, specify, and plan effort as well as for project timing values. *LOC* also returned irrelevant models but with a lower level of confidence. For example, using *LOC* as an independent variable, returned good models (cluster 4) in 5.06% of the cases and similar number of models that return good models with low prediction power (cluster 2). All of these models use *LOC* in conjunction with other attributes, such as functional points or effort related, which leads us to conclude that *LOC* has low predictive power but may improve the linear models in multivariate regression models. Also, trying to predict *LOC* with other software attributes returned results in cluster 5 which leads us conclude that *LOC* cannot be predicted with accuracy either.

With the accumulated knowledge we have repeated the experiment described in the previous paragraph on a 1,907 model data set that resulted from the removal of all of the irrelevant variables shown in Table II. In this experiment, we target the identification of pairs of independent-dependent variables and their assignment to clusters. For this we have used a minimum support level of 5% and a minimum confidence level of 50%. The results of this experiment are shown in Table III. For example, this table shows a good correlation between the *Count Added* and *AFP*. Predicting project additions and deletions can be reliably done using *AFP* (*Cluster 2*). This may have less practical relevance since the attributes mentioned above are constituents of *Functional Size* measure which is known to be correlated with *AFP*. However, since the project additions and deletions are not predicted but rather measured values, their intrinsic value is that they measure the validity of predictions made at the beginning of the project. We also found that the implementation effort is a good predictor of the total effort and can be used to allocate resources for the post completion life cycle of the project. The size of the team was determined to be a weak predictor of test effort because, although it returned good training models, its predictive power was limited (*Cluster 3*).

The last step of our experiment was targeted to the identification of attributes with best predictive power. For this, we have computed the percentage of occurrence of each independent variable to one of the clusters that promise good results. These results are shown in Figure 2. For example, this figure shows that using *AFP* as independent variable would return a 80.3% probability similar or better results in prediction than the value measured in training (*Cluster 2* and *Cluster 4*). Similar result were obtained when using *Functional Size* with a probability of 86.8%. *Team Size* also returns good results as independent variable but which is used only in conjunction with other independent variables. *Design Effort* and *Build Effort* show also good results although it can be determined only later in the life cycle of a project.

IV. Conclusion

In this paper, we conducted an experiment to evaluate the influence of missing data imputation on the predictive power of software attributes in the ISBSG-10 data set. We have imputed the missing data using existing state-of-the-art techniques using two levels of imputation at 30% and 50%. We compared and contrasted the resulting models by evaluating the prediction performance of project attributes using the adjusted R^2 statistical measure. Overall, the experiments that we have conducted in this article show that attributes in the ISBSG-10 data set have a weak predictive power using linear models and the majority of them return models that are unfit for predictions. Applying imputation to this data is likely to be unsuccessful, as our experiments show that the more imputed data is used in training, the less valuable are the models for prediction. One cause for this may be found in the cross-industry, cross-platform nature of this data set. This combined with the large quantity of data may affect the predictions. If project managers decide to use imputation, they need to use lower levels of imputed data, although the training results may show otherwise. Our results also give insight on which variables can be predicted with good accuracy such as *AFP* and *Functional Size* which reinforces the fact that current methodologies used for effort prediction are optimal, knowing the data at hand. Our future work includes the use of other data sets to increase the validity of the results. We will also expand our research to other imputation techniques to compare theirperformance of several methods given missing data.

References

[1] B. Boehm, C. Abts, and S. Chulani, "Software development cost estimation approaches - a survey," tech. rep., Annals of Software Engineering, 2000.

[2] R. Jensen, "An improved macrolevel software development resource estimation model," in *Proc. Fifth Conf. Int'l Soc. Parametric Analysts (ISPA)*, pp. 88–92, Apr. 1983.

[3] R. Park, "The central equations of the price software cost model," in *Proc. Fourth COCOMO Users Group Meeting*, Nov. 1988.

[4] B. Boehm, B. Clark, E. Horowitz, C. Westland, R. Madachy, and R. Selby, "Cost models for future software life cycle processes: Cocomo 2.0," in *Annals Of Software Engineering*, pp. 57–94, 1995.

[5] B. Boehm, "Safe and simple software cost analysis," *IEEE Software*, vol. 17, no. 5, pp. 14–17, 2000.

[6] C. F. Kemerer, "An empirical validation of software cost estimation models," *Commun. ACM*, vol. 30, pp. 416–429, May 1987.

[7] S. Grimstad and M. Jørgensen, "Inconsistency of expert judgment-based estimates of software development effort," *J. Syst. Softw.*, vol. 80, pp. 1770–1777, November 2007.

[8] Y. F. Li, M. Xie, and T. N. Goh, "A study of project selection and feature weighting for analogy based software cost estimation," *Journal of Systems and Software*, vol. 82, pp. 241–252, Feb. 2009.

[9] M. Jorgensen, "Regression models of software development effort estimation accuracy and bias," *Empirical Software Engineering*, vol. 9, no. 4, pp. 297–314, 2004.

[10] P. C. Pendharkar, G. H. Subramanian, and J. A. Rodger, "A probabilistic model for predicting software development effort," *IEEE T Software Eng*, vol. 31, no. 7, pp. 615–624, 2005.

[11] I. F. de Barcelos Tronto, J. D. S. da Silva, and N. Sant'Anna, "An investigation of artificial neural networks based prediction systems in software project management," *J. Syst. Softw.*, vol. 81, pp. 356–367, Mar. 2008.

[12] H. Park and S. Baek, "An empirical validation of a neural network model for software effort estimation," *Expert Syst. Appl.*, vol. 35, pp. 929–937, Oct. 2008.

[13] P. Sentas, L. Angelis, I. Stamelos, and G. Bleris, "Software productivity and effort prediction with ordinal regression," *Information and Software Technology*, vol. 47, no. 1, pp. 17 – 29, 2005.

[14] D. Rodríguez, J. J. Cuadrado, M. A. Sicilia, and R. Ruiz, "Segmentation of software engineering datasets using the m5 algorithm," in *Proceedings of the 6th international conference on Computational Science - Volume Part IV*, ICCS'06, (Berlin, Heidelberg), pp. 789–796, Springer-Verlag, 2006.

[15] R. Jeffery, M. Ruhe, and I. Wieczorek, "Using public domain metrics to estimate software development effort," in *Proc. Seventh Int. Software Metrics Symp. METRICS 2001*, pp. 16–27, 2001.

[16] E. Mendes and C. Lokan, "Replicating studies on cross- vs single-company effort models using the ISBSG database," *Empirical Softw. Engg.*, vol. 13, pp. 3–37, February 2008.

[17] The International Software Benchmarking Standards Group, "ISBSG repositories," 2007.

[18] B. Kitchenham and E. Mendes, "Why comparative effort prediction studies may be invalid," in *Proceedings of the 5th International Conference on Predictor Models in Software Engineering*, PROMISE '09, (New York, NY, USA), pp. 4:1–4:5, 2009.

[19] E. Mendes, C. Lokan, R. Harrison, and C. Triggs, "A replicated comparison of cross-company and within-company effort estimation models using the isbsg database," in *Proceedings of the 11th IEEE International Software Metrics Symposium*, (Washington, DC, USA), p. 36, IEEE Computer Society, 2005.

[20] C. Kirsopp and M. J. Shepperd, "Making inferences with small numbers of training sets," *IEE Proceedings - Software*, vol. 149, no. 5, pp. 123–130, 2002.

[21] B. Twala, "An empirical ccomparison of techniques for handling incomplete ddata using decision trees," *Appl. Artif. Intell.*, vol. 23, pp. 373–405, May 2009.

[22] J. L. Schafer and J. W. Graham, "Missing data: our view of the state of the art.," *Psychological Methods*, vol. 7, no. 2, pp. 147–177, 2002.

[23] K. Strike, K. El Emam, and N. Madhavji, "Software cost estimation with incomplete data," *Software Engineering, IEEE Transactions on*, vol. 27, pp. 890 –908, oct 2001.

[24] R Development Core Team, *R: A Language and Environment for Statistical Computing*. R Foundation for Statistical Computing, Vienna, Austria, 2011. ISBN 3-900051-07-0.

[25] M. Templ, A. Kowarik, and P. Filzmoser, "Iterative stepwise regression imputation using standard and robust methods," *Comput. Stat. Data Anal.*, vol. 55, pp. 2793–2806, Oct. 2011.

[26] A. Jain, K. Nandakumar, and A. Ross, "Score normalization in multimodal biometric systems," *Pattern Recogn.*, vol. 38, pp. 2270–2285, Dec. 2005.

[27] I. H. Witten and E. Frank, *Data Mining: Practical Machine Learning Tools and Techniques*. Morgan Kaufmann Series in Data Management Sys, Morgan Kaufmann, second ed., June 2005.

[28] R. Agrawal, H. Mannila, R. Srikant, H. Toivonen, and I. A. Verkamo, "Fast discovery of association rules," *Advances in knowledge discovery and data mining*, pp. 307–328, 1996.

Finding The Relationship Between Software Testing Effort And Software Quality Metrics

N. Yagci[1], **K. Ayan**[2]
[1] TUBITAK BILGEM, Gebze, Kocaeli, Turkey
[2] Computer Engineering, Sakarya University, Serdivan,Sakarya,Turkey

Abstract - *Software testing has very important role in Software Development Life Cycle for providing software quality and its role comes into prominence day by day. One of the jobs, which software test engineers perform, is executing the tests according to the test cases. But before the execution of tests starts, test manager has to schedule and plan and for this purpose he or she has to estimate the test effort accurate as possible. The accuracy of the estimation is very important for project success, because source and time planning is going to be actualizing according to this estimation. But so far the methods which have been used to estimate the test effort are too subjective or required too many efforts. In this article, we propose a new method for test effort estimation. Proposed method is about finding the relationship between software quality metrics and test effort execution then making the estimation according to this relationship.*

Keywords: Testing Effort Estimation, Software Quality Metric

1 Introduction and Previous Works

Software testing has growing importance in the software projects. Software developers used to test their own products so far, but nowadays many software companies embrace the independent testing team approach. In this approach, Testing team reports to the test manager not project manager. [1]. In this approach, test manager should organize time, source and budget planning. One of the jobs, which software test engineers perform, is executing the tests according to the test cases. [4] Test managers have to estimate the time which required for executing test cases.

Test effort estimation is estimation of test time and test source before the test execution starts. There are lots of methods for estimation test effort. The followings are prominent of these methods.

Taking the percentage of software development effort; this method is commonly used because of easy. In this method software effort is taken and test effort is calculated by dividing this number to a chosen number which project manager decides. (For example; Testing Effort = software test effort * ¼). But testing and coding are different professions, they requires different expertise.

Functional Point Analysis; this method is improved for specifying the project size. One of the initial design criteria for function points was to provide a mechanism that both software developers and users could utilize to define functional requirements. [3]

Test Point Analysis; Test point analysis (TPA) represents a test estimate preparation technique that can be used to objectively prepare estimates for system- and acceptance tests [2] However, it is important to note that TPA itself only covers black-box testing. Thus, it is often used in conjunction with FPA, which in return does not cover system- and acceptance tests. Consequently, FPA and TPA merged together provide means for estimating both, white- and black-box testing efforts. [2]

Use Case Points; Use cases in their most primitive forms are basically representative of what the user wants from a system. [9] Each scenario and its exception flows for each use case are input for a test case. Subsequently, the estimation calculations can commence. As the requirements become clearer further downstream, the estimates will also undergo revision. [9]

The common point of all these methods, a detailed work has to be done for estimating test effort. The team, that is going to make the estimation work, has to know very specific information about software under test and its documentations and to work for very long time. Getting the accurate estimation is only possible under these circumstances. But in these competitive world conditions, usually it is not possible to use these methods. There is no enough source and time. There is a strong need for handling test effort estimation in a short time without needing lots of input artifacts. Otherwise, tests seem to be executed in an unorganized way.

2 Proposed Approach For Estimating Test Effort And Case Study

Software quality metrics has been using since 1970 for measuring the software quality. Software quality metrics give us very important clues about software. [5] We claim that these metrics has also very important effect on test effort estimation. For examining this claim, we exercise a case study.

We take the software metrics in two bases.For description of these metrics; look up Appendix (Table 10 - Table 11).

Method Based Metrics;

Branches, Call_Pairs, ed(G), Edge_Count, ev(G), evgb4, id(G), iv(G), Lines_with_Nodes, MNT_SEV, Norm_v(G), Param_Count, pv(G), SLOC, vd(G), v(G), vgb10orevgb4

Class Based Metrics

Avg_v(G), Branches, Depth, ev(G), id(G), iv(G), Lack_Cohesion, Max_ev(G), Max_v(G), MNT_SEV, Norm_v(G), Parent_Count, pv(G), RFC, Sum_v(G), vd(G), v(G)

Finding the relationship between test effort and software quality metrics, makes possible to estimate the test effort easily, fast, reliable and objectively.

In this study, we have tried to examine the accuracy of the proposed method. We chose one of our programs which is developed by our software team. Software under test has software requirements and test cases which are documented according the software requirements. Choosing the test cases independent is important because that makes easy to see the difference.

Chosen test cases are; T1, T2, T3, T5, T6, T7, T9, T11, T13.

Method based metrics (Branches, Call_Pairs, ed(G), Edge_Count, ev(G), evgb4, id(G), iv(G), Lines_w_Nodes, MNT_SEV, Norm_v(G), Param_Count, pv(G), SLOC, vd(G), v(G), vgb10orevgb4) and class based metrics (Avg_v(G), Branches, Depth, ev(G), id(G), iv(G), Lack_Cohesion, Max_ev(G), Max_v(G), MNT_SEV, Norm_v(G), Parent_Count, pv(G), RFC, Sum_v(G), vd(G), v(G)) are used. After all test cases are executed, the coverage is saved for all test cases separately.

Table 1 shows method based coverage percentage of test case T1 as an example.

Table 1 Test Case-Method Coverage

Test Case No	Method Name	Coverage (Percentage)
T1	AdminPanel_ windows.Com monWorks.arr angeToolTip(DataGridView Dictionary,To olTip,DataGri dViewCellEve ntArgs)	85.71
T1	AdminPanel_ windows.Form s.FrmIntroduct ion.FrmIntrod uction()	100
T1	AdminPanel_ windows.Form s.FrmIntroduct ion.FillCombo Db()	100
	……………… ……	

After coverage work, Test case metric evaluation tables (Metric Based and Class Based) are composed.

An example calculation method metrics for a test case; It is assumed; Tn test case consists M1, M2, M3 methods and has the coverage percentage shows on the following table.

Table 2 Test Case-Method Coverage Example

Test Case No	Method Name	Coverage (Percentage)
Tn	M1	85.71%
Tn	M2	100%
Tn	M3	76%

The following table shows the v(G) metric value for M1, M2, M3 methods.

Table 3 Method-v(G) Metric

Method Name	v(G)
M1	5
M2	12
M3	3

The calculation of v(G) metric for Tn;

$$Tn_{v(g)} = \sum_{i=1..m} M_{i\ v(g)} * C_i \qquad (1)$$

$M_{v(g)}$ represents v(G) metric value of Method. C represents the Coverage Percentage

According to this formula, the following tables shows the results for T1, T2, T3, T5, T6, T7, T9, T11, T13 test case in method based calculation.

Table 4.1 Test Cases – Method Metrics

Test Case	Branches	Call_Pairs	v(G)	SLOC	vgb10or evgb4	vd(G)	id(G)
T1	59	144.54	43.73	779.01	0	6.26	26.64
T2	76	165.26	54.02	830.04	0	7.01	29.46
T3	69	156.46	49.51	802.61	0	6.62	27.61
T5	74	156.29	53.64	750.87	0	7.62	31.06
T6	77	162.31	54.93	762.83	0	7.29	30.27
T7	80	164.19	56.83	767.53	0	7.68	30.89
T9	130	221.78	87.63	1034.59	1.25	10.31	41.79
T11	67	127.1	46.72	648.48	0	6.03	25.35
T13	97	211.58	69.54	1031.33	0.44	9.61	39.56

Table 4.2 Test Cases – Method Metrics

Test Case	Edge Count	evgb4	ed(G)	ev(G)	iv(G)	Lines_w_Nodes	MNT_SEV
T1	1940.69	0	0	28.28	39.19	775.8	23.12
T2	2102.43	0	0	31.57	47.52	824.83	24.73
T3	2028.9	0	0	29.69	43.29	798.51	23.47
T5	1833.59	0	0	33.08	47.92	746.46	26.66
T6	1875.88	0	0	32.45	48.71	756.35	25.72
T7	1889.5	0	0	33.31	49.95	760.45	26.07
T9	2637.53	0.88	1.28	49.3	78.29	1024.65	33.78
T11	1575.69	0	0	26.41	42.96	645.05	20.54
T13	2663.86	0.44	0.73	44.34	63.78	1026.9	33.54

Table 4.3 Test Cases – Method Metrics

Test Case	Norm_v(G)	Param_Count	pv(G)
T1	5.04	27.77	28.28
T2	5.71	31.26	31.57
T3	5.39	27.63	29.69
T5	6.12	38.01	33.08
T6	5.89	33.56	32.45
T7	6.22	34.56	33.31
T9	8.39	54.65	44.94
T11	4.89	36.2	26.41
T13	7.78	52.09	41.7

An example calculation class metrics for a test case;

It is assumed; Tn test case consists C1, C2, C3 classes and has the coverage percentage shows on the following table.

Table 5 Test Cases-Class Coverage Example

Test Case No	Class Name	Coverage (Percentage)
Tn	Cl1	15.71%
Tn	Cl2	40%
Tn	Cl3	36%

The following table shows the v(G) metric value for Cl1, Cl2, Cl3 classes.

Table 6 Class-v(G) metric

Class Name	v(G)
Cl1	14
Cl2	12
Cl3	13

The calculation of v(G) metric for Tn;

$$Tn_{v(g)} = \sum_{i=1..n} Cl_{i\ v(g)} * C_i \quad (2)$$

$Cl_{v(g)}$ represents v(G) value of Class and C represents the Coverage Percentage

$$Tn_{vg} = 11,6794 \quad (3)$$

According to this formula, the following tables shows the results for T1, T2, T3, T5, T6, T7, T9, T11, T13 test case in class based calculation.

Table 7.1 Test Cases-Class Metrics

Test Case	Avg_v(G)	Branches	vd(G)	Depth	id(G)	ev(G)
T1	53.48	78.13	7.45	54.69	25.31	28.84
T2	60.19	88.1	8.2	61.26	28.37	32.13
T3	56.48	82.6	7.78	57.49	26.57	30.24
T5	61.5	89.37	8.7	64.16	29.77	33.75
T6	60.51	87.93	8.57	63.02	29.1	33.02
T7	62.19	90.37	8.8	64.74	29.86	33.88
T9	92.74	139.94	11.35	85.95	41.07	49.8
T11	51.12	75.83	6.38	48.82	24.5	28.42
T13	84.7	126.81	10.74	80.08	37.92	45

Table 7.2 Test Cases-Class Metrics

Test Case	iv(G)	Lack_ Cohesion	MNT_SEV	Max_ev(G)	Norm_ v(G)	Max_v(G)
T1	45.14	2727.15	20.39	31.7	6.01	119.94
T2	51.02	3055.72	22.74	34.99	6.63	140.22
T3	47.68	2867.14	21.35	33.1	6.29	129.71
T5	52.24	3208.11	24.28	37.08	7.02	136.31
T6	51.15	3143.82	23.77	35.88	6.91	136.79
T7	52.5	3230	24.38	36.74	7.1	141.69
T9	81.18	4292.54	32.13	86.49	9.2	220.82
T11	45.25	2540.94	19.4	38.41	5.22	100.04
T13	73.7	4069.21	29.61	75.76	8.76	198.66

Table 7.3 Test Cases-Class Metrics

Test Case	Parent_Count	pv(G)	RFC	Sum_v(G)	v(G)

T1	26.41	28.27	481.38	736.66	53.48
T2	29.7	31.56	546.3	839	60.19
T3	27.81	29.67	495.5	765.56	56.48
T5	31.08	33.08	657.52	954.11	61.5
T6	30.59	32.45	609.79	894.64	60.51
T7	31.45	33.31	620.19	912	62.19
T9	41.02	44.92	943	1425.19	92.74
T11	22.41	26.41	663.74	929.05	51.12
T13	38.4	41.7	818.45	1262.06	84.76

Meanwhile, a test team including four test engineers has involved to this study. While all of test cases are executed by all test engineers, test efforts are saved on test case based. Arithmetic average is calculated by using these efforts. Intention of using arithmetic average is minimizing human factor.

A calculation shows the following table.

Table 8 Test Cases-Test Execute Duration

Test Case	Tester1	Tester2	Tester3	Tester4	Arithmetic Average
T1	60	54	60	63	**59.25**
T2	31	25	29	44	**32.25**
T3	71	69	55	57	**63**
T5	26	67	53	64	**52.5**
T6	34	30	22	52	**34.5**
T7	48	49	56	66	**54.75**
T9	90	98	101	143	**108**
T11	31	22	34	36	**30.75**
T13	65	81	67	72	**71.25**
Sum	**456**	**495**	**477**	**597**	**506.25**

3 Results

All the results of the calculation normalized and ordered on method based, class based and test effort based.

Table 9 Test Cases Order Comparison

Method Based Metric Order	Class Based Metric Order	Test Effort Based
T9	T9	T9
T13	T13	T13
T7	T7	T3
T5	T5	T1
T6	T6	T7
T3	T3	T5
T2	T2	T6
T1	T1	T2
T11	T11	T11

As it can be seen from Table 9; the result of the first and last orders are the same for all the bases. The middle part of the table shows test cases that not have too many different results, so the order of them can be ignored.

4 Conclusion And Future Work

In this study, the relationship between software quality metrics and test effort is researched. Firstly test cases are chosen independently. Then chosen test cases are executed for the coverage calculation. At the same time, measurements for chosen metrics are taken for every method and class in the software under test. For showing the accuracy of proposed approach, chosen test cases are executed by a test team and test cases' execution times are saved. Then the order of test execution times and metric results are compared. In this comparison, it can be seen, software product metrics has very important effect at test execution time. The purpose of this study is showing test effort estimation can done by using test coverage and software quality metrics information. Estimation of test effort for a program can be very fast and objective by using this relationship.

For future work, we will try this method for more large scale projects and compare their results.

5 APPENDIX

a.Method-Based Metric Name;

Following metrics are calculated by method-based.

Table 10 Method Metrics Description

Metric Name	Description
Branches	An initial edge into a flow graph and coming out of any decision.
Call Pairs	Executable calls between methods
ed(G)	(ev(G)-1)/(v(G)-1)
Edge_Count	Edges represent the flow of control from one node to another on a flow graph.
ev(G)	Essential Complexity (unstructuredness indicator) [8]
evgb4	If ev(G)>4, value is True
id(G)	iv(G)/v(G)
iv(G)	Module Design Complexity [8]
Lines_with_Nodes	Lines of code with flow graph nodes
MNT_SEV	ev(G)/v(G)
Norm_v(G)	Normalized cyclomatic complexity (v(G) / nl) [7] nl= Number of lines for the module (physical count from start line to end line)
Param_Count	Formal parameter count of a method
pv(G)	All unstructured constructs except multiple entries into loops are treated as straight-line code in the module's flow graph. Pathological complexity is equal to the cyclomatic complexity of the reduced flow graph. [7]
SLOC	Line of Code contains only code
vd(G)	v(G)/(SLOC+MLOC)MLOC= Line of Code contains both code ad comment
vgb10orevgb4	if v(G)>10 or ev(G)>4 true

b. Class-Based Metric Name

Following metrics are calculated by class-based.

Table 11 Class Metrics

DescriptionMetricName	Description
Avg_v(G)	Average v(G)
Branches	An initial edge into a flow graph and coming out of any decision.
Depth	Depth (the level for a class) [6]
ev(G)	Essential Complexity

	(unstructuredness indicator) [8]
id(G)	iv(G)/v(G)
iv(G)	Module Design Complexity [8]
Lack_Cohesion	Lack of Cohesion of Methods [6]
Max_ev(G)	Maximum Essential Complexity [6]
Max_v(G)	Maximum Cyclomatic Complexity
MNT_SEV	ev(G)/v(G)
Norm_v(G)	Normalized cyclomatic complexity (v(G) / nl) [7] nl= Number of lines for the module (physical count from start line to end line)
Parent_Count	Formal parent count of a method
pv(G)	All unstructured constructs except multiple entries into loops are treated as straight-line code in the module's flow graph. Pathological complexity is equal to the cyclomatic complexity of the reduced flow graph. [7]
RFC	Response for a class [6]
Sum_v(G)	Sum of the v(G)
vd(G)	v(G)/(SLOC+MLOC) MLOC= Line of Code contains both code ad comment

6 Acknowledgement

The authors would like to thank Software Testing and Quality Evaluation Center (YTKDM in Turkish) of Scientific and Technological Research Council of Turkey (TUBITAK in Turkish) for funding this study.

7 References

[1] Cem Kaner, J. F. (1999). Testing Computer Software. In J. F. Cem Kaner, *Testing Computer Software* (p. 344). Wiley Computer Publishing.

[2] CISA, D. E., & Dekkers, T. (1999). Testpointanalysis: a method for test estimation.

[3] Heller, R. (2003). An introduction to function point analysis. *Q/P Management Group* .

[4] IEEE Std 829-1998, IEEE Standard for Software Test Documentation . (1998).

[5] Karl S. Mathias, J. H. (1999). The Role of Software Measures and Metrics in Studies of Program Comprehension. *ACM SE* .

[6] Kemerer, S. R. (1994). A Metrics Suite for Object Oriented Design. *IEEE Transactions on Software Engineering, VOL. 20, No:6* .

[7] McCABE, T. J. (1976). A Complexity Measure.

[8] McCabe, T. J., & Butler, C. W. (1989). Design Complexity Measurement and Testing.

[9] Nageswaran, S. (2001). Test Effort Estimation Using Use Case Points.

Examining the Performance of Java Static Analyzers

Kevin Daimi and Shadi Banitaan
Department of Mathematics, Computer Science and Software Engineering
University of Detroit Mercy,
4001 McNichols Road, Detroit, MI 48221
{daimikj, banitash}@udmercy.edu

Kathy Liszka
Department of Computer Science
The University of Akron
Akron, Ohio 44325-4003
liszka@uakron.edu

ABSTRACT

Static Analysis refers to the analysis of computer programs prior to executing them to reveal potential problems that need to be fixed before executing the programs. In this paper, five static analyzers for Java programs will be examined and compared using three Java programs, which are randomly selected from a collection available on the Internet.

Keywords

Static Analyzer, Java, Evaluation, Software Engineering

I. INTRODUCTION

Static analysis is becoming a critical component for software development. Currently, many software developers are appreciating the advantages of using static analyzers to improve software. Static analyzers function through using techniques from program analysis, model checking, and automated deduction [3]. Static analysis tools can also be used to automate the process of identifying violations of security rules [12].

Despite the popularity of static analysis tools for software flaws discovery, experimental assessments of the correctness and merits of the output of these tools are lacking. Ayewah et al. [2] examined the types of warnings generated and the classification of warnings into false positives, trivial bugs and serious bugs for FindBugs, a static analysis tool for Java programs. They stipulated some perception into why static analysis tools often uncover true but trivial bugs and some details about violations throughout the development lifecycle of software. They further added that there is little published information regarding the evaluation of these tools to verify their claims. It is understandable that companies may prohibit the publication of any experimental data for commercial tools. However, publishing such data for open source tools should not be a problem.

During software development, it is valuable to obtain early estimates of the defect density of software components to further improve the quality of software. Such estimates identify fault-prone areas of code requiring further testing. It is valuable to collect early estimates of fault density for software components throughout the process of software development. Nagappan et al. [13] presented an empirical methodology for the early projection of pre-release defect density based on the outcomes of static analysis tools. With the aid of two different static analysis tools, the discovered defects were used to predict the actual pre-release defect density for Windows Server 2003. They concluded that there was a strong positive correlation between the static analysis list of defects and the pre-release defect density list obtained through actual testing. There are a number of approaches for static analysis. Static analysis by Abstract Interpretation [15] is one such approach. The authors indicated that this approach offers a considerable assurance and evidence needed for supporting its findings. They demonstrated that static analysis must be able to scale and report few false positives without calling for expert interference.

As mentioned above, public information on evaluating static analyzers is scarce. An interesting study by Ware et al. [17] focused on evaluating the degree to which eight static analysis tools can isolate violations of a broad set of coding heuristics for increasing the quality and security of Java SE code. They revealed that a significant number of security violations were not detected by any tool. The resulting vulnerabilities can easily lead to various attacks. Note that three of the tools used in this study; CheckStyle, Findbugs, and PMD are further analyzed in our study below.

In this paper, four open source and one commercial static analysis tools are evaluated. Three levels of evaluation including general features, performance, and capabilities are exercised. For this purpose, three random programs available online, are used. To study the performance of each tool on unearthing various fault/violations categories and sub-categories, violations were temporarily inserted into these programs. Outcomes of these evaluations are summarized in various tables.

II. Static Analysis Tools Overview

The static analysis tools for Java studied in this paper are briefly described below.

A. *FindBugs*

FindBugs is an open source static analysis tool that digs into class or JAR files looking for potential problems through matching Java bytecodes against a list of known bug patterns [9]. The current version of FindBugs (2.0.2) requires JRE (or JDK) 1.5.0 or later to operate. However, it can analyze programs compiled for any version of Java, from 1.0 to 1.8. It is capable of identifying over 250 potential types of errors. FindBugs uses real bugs in software, extracts a bug pattern from those bugs, and develops possible detectors that can efficiently pinpoint that bug pattern. In other words, it is based on the concept of bug patterns [5]. The process is evaluated by trying the recommended detector on various test cases for that bug pattern [11]. In FindBugs, bugs are ranked from 1-20, and grouped into the following categories: scariest (rank 1-4), scary (rank 5-9), troubling (rank 10-14), and of concern (rank 15-20). It provides a flexible way for developers to share information and define and install plugins. It can be integrated with Eclipse, Maven, NetBeans, Hudson, and IntelliJ.

B. *PMD*

PMD is an open-source, rule-based, static source code analyzer that analyzes Java source code based on evaluative rules that have been extracted during a given execution [15]. This tool is equipped with a default set of rules which can be used to reveal common development bugs. PMD also supports custom analyses by allowing users the opportunity to develop their own (new) evaluative rules. It scans Java source code looking for potential problems including empty try, catch, finally, and switch statements, dead code, suboptimal code, overcomplicated expressions, and duplicate code. It can be integrated with JDeveloper, Eclipse, JEdit, JBuilder, BlueJ, CodeGuide, NetBeans/Sun Java Studio Enterprise/Creator, IntelliJ IDEA, TextPad, Maven, Ant, Gel, JCreator, and Emacs. Copeland [6] indicated that Junit tests can be kept in good order by using PMD].

C. *ESC/Java2*

The Extended Static Checker for Java version 2 (ESC/Java2) is a programming tool that endeavors to discover common run-time errors in JML-annotated Java programs by static analysis of the program code and its formal annotations. It allows users the flexibility to control the extent and types of checking that ESC/Java2 implements by annotating Java programs with specifically formatted comments called pragmas [8]. This implies that the ESC/Java2 tool tries to unearth common run-time errors in Java programs at compile time [10]. The approach used in ESC/Java2 comprises a range of techniques for statically checking the correctness of various program constraints. Extended static checking usually deploys an automated theorem prover [7]. ESC/Java2 can be integrated with the Mobius Program Verification Environment, used as a command-line tool with a simple Swing GUI front-end, or added as an Eclipse plugin.

D. *CheckStyle*

Checkstyle is an open source development tool, which aims to help programmers write Java code that follows some coding standard [4]. It automates the process of checking Java code resulting in coding standard enforcement. Checkstyle is highly configurable and can support many coding standards. A number of sample configuration files are supplied for well-known conventions, such as Sun Code Conventions. Historically, Checkstyle's main functionality evolved around checking code layout concerns, but since its internal architecture was modified starting in version 3, more checks for other purposes have been added. Currently, Checkstyle provides checks that uncover a number of issues including class design problems, duplicate code, or bug patterns like double checked locking. It supports loading a configuration from URL reference and can be integrated with Eclipse, IntelliJ

IDEA, NetBeans, BlueJ, tIDE, Emacs JDE, Jedit, Vim Editor, Maven, and QALab.

E. AppPerfect Java Code Test (AppPerfect)

AppPerfect Java Code Test is a commercial static Java code analysis tool aimed at automating Java code review and enforcing good Java coding practices [1]. AppPerfect Code Test analyzes both Java and Java Server Pages (JSP) source code using a large set of Java coding rules extracted from experts in the Java programming field. These rules are grouped into a number of functional areas such as security, optimization, and portability. AppPerfect analyzes Java code and furnishes detailed information about diverse metrics for the source code, such as number of code lines, comments lines, complexities of methods, and number of methods. It provides a number of reports to describe problems in the source code about through its user interface. These reports can be exported into various formats, such as HTML, PDF, CSV, XLS, and XML. AppPerfect Java Code Test supports IDE integration with most commonly used IDEs including Eclipse, NetBeans, IntelliJ, JBuilder and JDeveloper.

III. GENERAL FEATURES COMPARISON

In this section, the five tools are compared using Eclipse. The criteria used include the total number of violations found, run time, and memory usage. To this extent, three randomly selected large high complexity Java programs from *PlanetSourceCode* [14] are used. These programs include the following: 1. A Pong Game, 2. A Basic Calculator Application, and 3. Gtroids Arcade Shooter [14]. Other programs available on *PlanetSourceCode* can be included if needed. The aim of this random selection was to conclude unbiased comparison, and provide a set of programs for interested readers to look at when verifying the outcomes of this study. The results of the features comparison for the five tools based on the three programs are summarized in Tables 1-3. A blank row indicates the tool did not check the program for some reason. For the Checkstyle tool, violations refer to warnings.

By observing the tables 1-3 below, we conclude that AppPerfect is more optimized in terms of run-time and memory usage than the other tools. This should not cause any surprise as AppPerfect is a commercial tool. However, PMD was able to discover more violations than AppPerfect in two of the programs. Furthermore, Checkstyle was able to find many warnings and ESC/JAVA2 found more violations than AppPerfect in one of the programs.

IV. TOOLS RFORMANCE EVALUATION

Having analyzed the five tools based on the three criterions; violations, run-time, and memory, a deep-rooted evaluation will be carried out to reveal the actual performance of each tool with regards to various fault categories. For this purpose, various faulty codes are temporary injected in the three programs. The fault categories that will be used for this evaluation involves data faults, control faults, interface faults, measurement faults, duplicate code, and code convention violations. Each of these categories is further divided into subcategories. Detailed analysis is provided in tables 4-9 below. In these tables, “Y” indicates that the tool is able to catch such a fault. The performance of these tools and their analysis are based the examples that were selected. As the tables reveals, only the stated violations were investigated. It is possible that the performance will be different should other violations are exercised. It is worth noting that most of these faults/violations were flagged out immediately by Eclipse IDE for Java even before the tools were applied. This implies that, for these violations/examples, the Eclipse IDE for Java behaved as good as the tools above.

By examining tables 4-9 below, it is obvious that the commercial tool, AppPerfect, has the best capabilities. However, it failed to catch the “Variable assigned twice but never used between assignments” and “long variable name” faults. As it could be seen, PMD was able to catch them. Furthermore, both PMD and CheckStyle were able to find the “Variables/method/class/interface names have dollar signs” fault when AppPerfect failed to.

The evaluation of the tools presented in tables 4-9 is based on the number of faults discovered for each fault category. For the data faults, PMD performed the best among the reaming four tools followed by ESC/Java. With regards to control faults, CheckStyle and PMD were the best. However, CheckStyle did better. With regards to catching interface faults, PMD performed better than ESC.Java. Using “Classes with high Cyclomatic Complexity” as a criterion, only PMD was able to detect such a fault. None of the open source tools was able to uncover the duplicate code faults. Finally, PMD was superior with regards to code convention violations.

V. TOOL CAPABILITY ANALYSIS

The third evaluation deals with investigating the capabilities of each tool. The following five capabilities are employed for this purpose: test support, rule configuration, violation classification, auto fixing, and metrics analysis. Test support indicates whether the tool can provide test cases to test the program. Rule configuration implies that users can add, remove and modify rules. Violation classification deals with allocating faults to classes/types. Auto fixing refers to the automatic correction of some faults. Finally, Metrics analysis concentrates on extracting simple measurements (metrics). Table 10 summarizes the results of this evaluation. Using this table, it is evident that FindBugs and PMD satisfied three out of five capabilities. The two open source tools only lacked two capabilities as compared to the commercial tool.

TABLE I
TOOLS COMPARISON USING PROGRAM-1

Tool	Violations	Run Time (Sec.)	Memory (MB)
FindBugs	12	4	123
PMD	71	3	139
Checkstyle	982*	3	99
ESC/JAVA2			
AppPerfect	25	1	44

TABLE II
TOOLS COMPARISON USING PROGRAM-2

Tool	Violations	Run Time (Sec.)	Memory (MB)
FindBugs			
PMD	12	4	123
Checkstyle	2049*	2	105
ESC/JAVA2	498	3	194
AppPerfect	93	2	60

TABLE III
TOOLS COMPARISON USING PROGRAM-3

Tool	Violations	Run Time (Sec.)	Memory (MB)
FindBugs			
PMD	1593	6	226
Checkstyle	10495*	2	150
ESC/JAVA2	94	8	239
AppPerfect	564	5	108

TABLE IV
ANALYSIS USING DATA FAULTS

Violation	Tool Performance				
	PMD	FindBugs	Checkstyle	AppPerfect	ECS/Java2
Uninitialized local variable	N	N	N	Y	N
Variable declared but never used	Y	N	N	Y	N
Variable assigned twice but never used between assignments	Y	N	N	N	N
Undeclared variable	N	N	N	Y	Y
Assigning a variable to itself	Y	N	N	Y	N

TABLE V
ANALYSIS USING CONTROL FAULTS

Violation	Tool Performance				
	PMD	FindBugs	Checkstyle	AppPerfect	ECS/Java2
Unreachable code	N	N	N	Y	N
Empty try/catch/finally/switch blocks	Y	N	Y	Y	N
Empty if/while statements	Y	N	Y	Y	N
Method calls in loop	N	N	N	Y	N
Switch case does not cover all cases	N	N	N	Y	N
Array length in loop condition	N	N	N	Y	N
Empty for statement	N	N	Y	Y	N
Unnecessary do while loop	N	N	N	Y	N

TABLE VI
ANALYSIS USING INTERFACE FAULTS

Violation	Tool Performance				
	PMD	FindBugs	Checkstyle	AppPerfect	ECS/Java2
Mismatched parameter type	N	N	N	Y	Y
Mismatched parameter number	N	N	N	Y	Y
Unused parameter	Y	N	N	Y	N
Uncalled methods	N	N	N	Y	N
Unnecessary return	Y	N	N	Y	N
Unused imports	Y	N	N	Y	N
Unused public classes	N	N	N	Y	N
Unused public field	N	N	N	Y	N

TABLE VII
ANALYSIS USING MEASUREMENT FAULTS

Violation	Tool Performance				
	PMD	FindBugs	Checkstyle	AppPerfect	ECS/Java2
Classes with high Cyclomatic Complexity	Y	N	N	Y	N

TABLE VIII
ANALYSIS USING DUPLICATE CODE FAULTS

Violation	Tool Performance				
	PMD	FindBugs	Checkstyle	AppPerfect	ECS/Java2
Copied/pasted code (could imply copied/pasted bugs)	N	N	N	Y	N
Methods have same name	N	N	N	Y	N

TABLE IX
ANALYSIS USING CODE CONVENTION FAULTS

Violation	Tool Performance				
	PMD	FindBugs	Checkstyle	AppPerfect	ECS/Java2
Method names start with capital letter	Y	Y	Y	Y	N
Short method name	Y	N	N	Y	N
Long variable name	Y	N	N	N	N
Class name starting with lower case character	Y	N	Y	Y	N
Variable/method/class/interface names have dollar signs	Y	N	Y	N	N
For loops that could be while loops	Y	N	N	Y	N
If statement without curly braces	Y	N	Y	Y	N
Incomplete parts of for	N	Y	N	Y	N

TABLE X
TOOLS CAPABILITY ANALYSIS

Tool	Capability				
	Test Support	Rule Configuration	Violation classification	Auto Fixing	Metrics Analysis
PMD	Y	Y	Y	N	N
FindBugs	Y	Y	N	N	N
Checkstyle	Y	Y	Y	Y	Y
AppPerfect	Y	N	N	N	N
ESC/Java2	Y	Y	Y	N	N

TABLE XI
VIOLATION COVERAGE STATISTICS

Violation Category	Tool				
	PMD	FindBugs	Checkstyle	AppPerfect	ECS/Java2
Data Faults	3/5	0/5	0/5	4/5	1/5
Control Faults	2/8	0/8	3/8	8/8	0/8
Interface Faults	3/8	0/8	0/8	8/8	2/8
Measurement Faults	1/1	0/1	0/1	1/1	0/1
Duplicate Code Faults	0/2	0/2	0/2	2/2	0/0
Code Convention faults	7/8	1/8	4/8	6/8	0/8
Total Coverage	20/32	1/32	7/32	29/32	3/32

VI. VIOLATION COVERAGE STATISTICS

Statistics are very important for the analysis and presentation of the collected data. Table 11 demonstrates the fault coverage statistics based on the data collected from tables 4-9. The denominator represents the number of subcategories for the category in question and the numerator refers to how many fault subcategories the tool was able to successfully detect. Note that in Table 11, "32" represents the total number of violations/faults (total number of fault subcategories). Once again, PMD proved to be reasonable with regards to the total number of violations sub-categories. By excluding the commercial tool, it is clear PMD is the best and Checkstyle is second best.

VII. CONCLUSIONS

Static analyzers can locate potential problems in software code and facilitate good practices among software designers. In an attempt to assist software developers in selecting suitable static analyzers for their projects, five static analyzers were evaluated and compared. The result of this evaluation indicated that some of the open source tools can be good enough in discovering problems and are comparable to commercial ones. Based on the Java programs used and examples of faults introduced, it is concluded that PMD's performance proved to be the best. It is possible that different results might be produced when using more programs and introducing additional examples on further fault categories. Furthermore, it was interesting to discover that the Eclipse IDE for Java was able to unearth almost all the fault sub-categories immediately after typing the statements in prior to using any of the static analyzers.

Future improvements will concentrate on including more open source tools, expanding the fault categories, deploying more Java programs, and checking Java coding security.

ACKNOWLEDGEMENT

The authors would like to thank Xiaodan Lu and Xiaochen Zhang for their help.

REFERENCES

[1] AppPerfect Java Code test, AppPerfect Corporation, Available: http://www.appperfect.com/products/java-code-test.html.

[2] N. Ayawah, and W. Pugh, Evaluating Static Analysis Defect Warnings on Production Software, *in proc. 7th ACM SIGPLAN-SIGSOFT Workshop on Program Analysis for Software Tools and Engineering (PASTE'07)*, San Diego, California, USA, 2007, pp. 1-7.

[3] T. Ball, and S. K. Rajamani, The SLAM Project: Debugging System Software via Static Analysis, *in Proc. the 29th ACM SIGPLAN-SIGACT Symposium on Principles of Programming Languages (POPL'02)*, Portland, OR, USA, 2008, pp. 1-3.

[4] Checkstyle 5.6, Available: http://checkstyle.sourceforge.net, September 2012.

[5] B Cole, D. Hakim, D. Hovemeyer, R. Lazarus, W. Pugh, and K. Stephens, Improving Your Software Using Static Analysis to Find Bugs, *in proc. ACM SIGPLAN International Conference on Objected Oriented Programming, Systems, Languages, and Applications (OOPSLA'06)*, Portland, Oregon, USA, 2006, pp. 637-674.

[6] T. Copeland, *PMD Applied: An Easy-to-Use Guide for Developers*, Centennial Books, 2005.

[7] ESC/Java, Wikipedia, Available: http://en.wikipedia.org/wiki/ESC/Java, December 2012.

[8] ESC/Java2 Summary, Available: http://kindsoftware.com/products/opensource/ESCJava2, May 2012.

[9] FindBugs™ – Finds Bugs in Java programs, Available: http://findbugs.sourceforge.net , 2012.

[10] C. Flanagan, K. Leino, M. Lillibridge, G. Nelson, J. B. Saxe and R. Stata. "Extended Static Checking for Java," in *Proc. the Conference on Programming Language Design and Implementation*, Berlin, Germany, pages 234--245, 2002.

[11] D. Hovemeyer and W. Pugh. Finding Bugs is Easy, *ACM SIGPLAN Notices*, Vol. 39, No. 12, pp. 92-106, 2004.

[12] R. Krishnan, M. Nadworny, and N. Bharill, "Static Analysis Tools for Security Checking in Code at Motorola," *Ada Letters*, Vol. 28, No. 1, pp. 76-82, 2008.

[13] N. Nagappan, and T. Ball, Static Analysis Tools as early Indicators of Pre-Release Defect Density, *in Proc. the 27th International Conference on Software Engineering (ICSE '05)*, St. Louis, MO, USA, 2005, pp. 580-586.

[14] PlanetSourceCode, Available: http://www.planet-source-code.com.

[15] PMD, Available: http://pmd.sourceforge.net, May, 2012.

[16] A. Venet, and M. Lowry, Static Analysis for Software Assurance: Soundness, Scalability, and Adaptiveness, *in proc. Workshop on Future of Software Engineering Research (FoSER 2010)*, Santa Fe, New Mexico, USA, 2010, pp. 393-396.

[17] M. Ware, and C. Fox, Securing Java Code: Heuristics and an Evaluation of Static Analysis Tools, *in proc. SAW '08*, Tucson, Arizona, USA, 2008, pp.12-21.

Verification and Validation Experience of Safety-grade Optical Modem for Core Protection Calculator (CPC)

Jang Yeol Kim[1], **Kwang Seop Son**[1] , **Young Jun Lee**[1] , **Se Woo Cheon**[1], **Kyoung Ho Cha**[1], **Jang Soo Lee**[1], **Kee Choon Kwon**[1]
[1]Instrumentation and Control / Human Factors Division, Korea Atomic Energy Research Institute, 989-111 Daedeok-daero, Yuseong-gu, Daejeon, Republic of Korea 305-353

Abstract - *In general, an optical modem used in industry is composed of an integral system for the Transmitter/Receiver. However, a safety-grade optical communication modem in a nuclear safety system is composed of send-only service or receive-only service. A send-only optical modem of the control rod signal transmission is in charge of the transmitting function in the form of frequency-converted optical signals to the receive-only optical modem as frequency-converted optical signals in the range of an input voltage of 0V to 10V. The receive-only optical modem of the control rod signal receiving is in charge of the receiving function toward the Analog Input (AI) Gate through the Core Element Assembly Computer (CEAC) Analog Input (AI) Surge card in the form of frequency-converted optical signals to the sending-only optical modem as frequency-converted optical signals in the range of an input voltage of 0V to 10V. This paper describes the results of a software verification and validation for a send-only optical modem and receive-only optical modem, respectively. All tests were performed according to the test plan and test procedures. Functional testing, performance testing, event testing, and scenario-based testing for a safety-grade optical modem of a Core Protection Calculator in a Korea Standard Nuclear Power Plant as a thirty-party verifier was performed successfully.*

Keywords : Software, Qualification, Verification and Validation, System Test, Safety-grade Optical Modem, Core Protection Calculator

1 Introduction

A Plant Protection System mainly consists of a Reactor Protection System, Engineered Safety feature-Component Control System, and Core Protection Calculator. An optical modem is a communication modem. It's major function sending and receiving the control rod signal between the Core Protection Calculator (CPC) and Core Element Assembly Computer (CEAC), as shown in Figure 1.

In addition, the following items are among their functions as a convenience facility.

- A display the driving voltage status
- Failure status display function by a self-diagnosis
- Real-time monitoring function
- Console port for real-time monitoring
- Providing data storage for certain amount of time
- Display the input and output voltage

To distinguish between an optical modem for sending and receiving, respectively, the aim is to satisfy the licensing requirements of a unidirectional link and deterministic communication.

This paper describes the results of software verification and validation for a send-only optical modem and receive-only optical modem, respectively. This paper also describes the test environment, test components and items, a traceability analysis, and system tests as a result of system verification and validation based on Software Requirement Specification (SRS) for a safety-grade optical modem of a Core Protection Calculator (CPC) in a Korea Standard Nuclear Power Plant (KSNP), and Software Design Specification (SDS) for a safety-grade optical modem of a CPC in KSNP.

Following sections that detail each category of qualification, i.e. we will mainly focus on how the verification and validation of the optical modem software was conducted on a Core Protection Calculator (CPC).

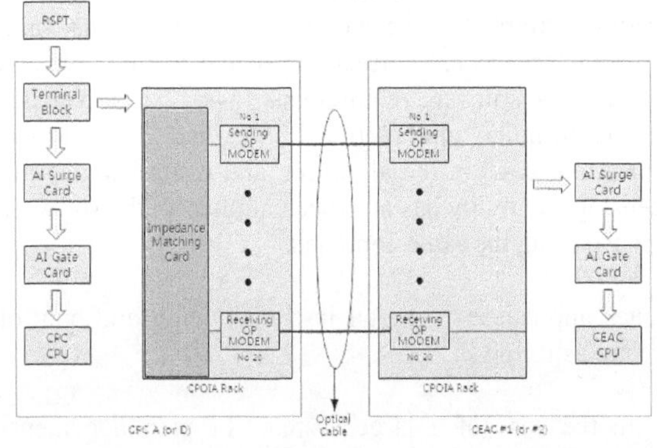

Figure 1. An overview of optical modem for sending and receiving of control rod signal.

2 Review of the licensing suitability

Largely, there are two regulatory frameworks USNRC based on the IEEE standard and IAEA-based IEC standard. In the process of developing this system, we met the USNRC based Code and Standard criteria. The criteria of safety-critical software qualification are based on the following Code & Standard framework where the most recent edition is used for each design output and verification. The thick line box in figure 2 is closely related to software qualification criteria [1].

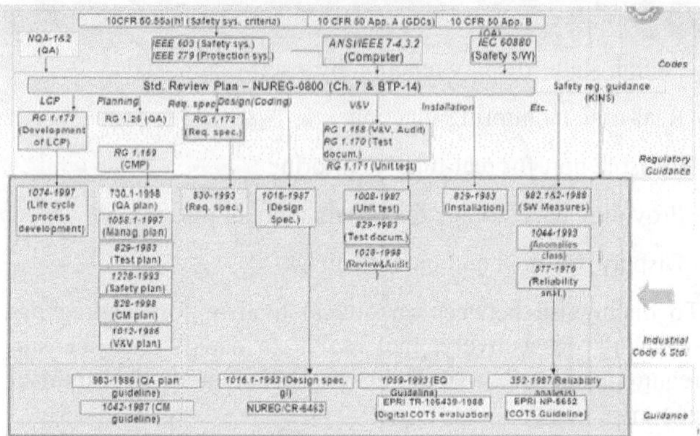

Figure 2. Code and standard framework for qualification of safety-critical system.

3 Well-structured qualification organization

The purpose of the licensing suitability review confirms whether the software requirements that coincide with the criteria of the software, performance and safety requirements defined in the safety-grade software requirement statement are suitable from a Code & Standard and technological viewpoint. According to the NUREG-0800 : SRP/BTP-14 criteria (USNRC, 1997), they must satisfy all the functionality and process characteristics.

Whether the contents described in the requirement specifications from the viewpoint of the functional and process characteristics are correct, consistent and complete is determined in the software requirement phase. It also verifies whether the formula, unidirectional link, and deterministic communication exist in the algorithm and control logic, etc. This licensing suitability has also been applied to the software design phase using the same approach.

Techniques applicable to digital instrumentation and control software are as follows.

In fact, in the case of a large system, 11 plan documents should be made in the planning phase. However, in the case of a small embedded system such as safety-grade optical modem, four planning documents are enough, such as a Software Quality Assurance Plan (SQAP), Software Safety Plan Description (SSPD), Software Verification and Validation Plan (SVVP), and Software Configuration Management Plan (SCMP), as shown in Figure 3.

To qualify for safety-critical software, the defined responsibilities among the assurance organizations are very important. The Development team is responsible for producing design output during the software life cycle. The Software Verification & Validation (SVV) and Software Safety Analysis (SSA) are responsible for a safety evaluation on the produced design output by the development team. First, prior to use a Commercial Off-The Shelf (COTS) software tool should be dedicated by quality assurance organization which is called COTS software dedication. The Software Configuration Management under Software Quality Assurance is responsible for configuration identification, status accounting, revision control, and version control on all of the design output and its verification results, respectively. The well-structured organization suggested in this paper is as shown in Figure 3 [1][2].

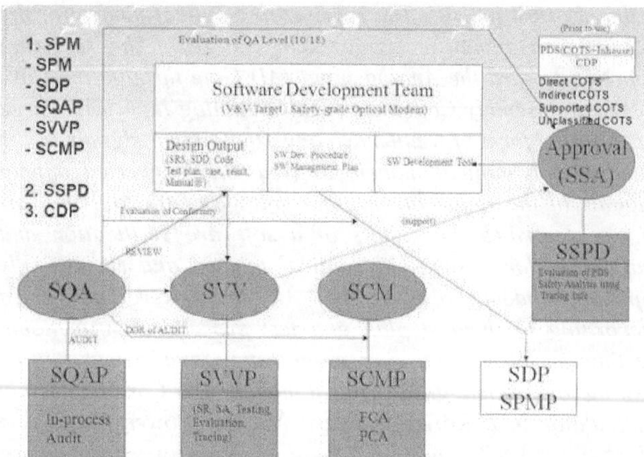

(SPM : Software Program Manual, SDP: Software Development Plan, SQAP: Software Quality Assurance Plan, SVVP: Software Verification and Validation Plan, SCMP : Software Configuration Management Plan, SO&MP : Software Operation and Maintenance Plan, SSPD : Software Safety Plan Description, CDP: Commercial Off the Shelf Dedication Plan, COTS: Commercial Off The Shelf Software, SQA: Software Quality Assurance, SVV: Software Verification and Validation, SCM: Software Configuration Management), SR: Software Review, SA: Safety Analysis, FCA: Functional Configuration Audit, PCA: Physical Configuration Audit)

Figure 3. Division of Responsibility of Well-structured qualification for safety-grade system

All of the designs and verifications were reviewed and evaluated to determine whether they meet the international standard criteria from licensing to compiling.

4 Methods and Results

In this section, the test methods and test results are described. Above all, in the case of embedded systems, it is important whether the system test results on the host environment are satisfied with target board. Functional tests, performance tests, event tests and scenario tests for a safety-grade optical modem have been performed. Coverage of the range value, boundary value, and equivalent value were also measured.

4.1 Verification test environment

Application firmware was developed under GNU /Linux Ubuntu 11.10 of AMD64 environments. To build a system test with the host environment, firmware was ported on a target board of an optical modem using USBISP. To measure the embedded software of a safety-grade optical modem, an AVR USBISP V3.0 and avrdude 5.10 utility were used as shown in Figure 4.

Figure 4. Verification test environments of safety-grade optical modem

4.2 Test components and test items

The methods for testing are shown here. An integration Test and System Test were carried out in order. We checked the coverage measurement for the statement coverage, and PATH coverage. The generations of test cases were made for the range value, boundary value, equivalent value, and error-injection value.

In the case of an embedded system, because it was difficult to set up a target testing environment, (for example, commercially available tools such as Cantata ++ and LDRA etc.), commercially available testing tools were partially used and the software quality evaluation function of LDRA was applied to the source code quality measurements mostly.

The test components and items are as shown in Table 1.

Table 1 Test components and test items for safety-grade optical modem of CPC

NO	Category	Test Components	Test Items
1.	Functional test	Initial setup	Variable of Hardware and Software - Optical Modem - LED - Timer - WDT etc.
		Optical signal translation	Voltage-Optical signal
			Optical signal - Voltage
		Data communication	Sending Only (Unidirectional)
			Receiving Only (Unidirectional)
		Status indication	POWER
			TX
			RX
			FAULT
		Setup	Gain, Offset
		Protocol	Protocol Analysis (Packet) CRC8
2.	Performance test	Accuracy	Accuracy ±0.05%
		Communication speed	- 4ms - 57600bps
3.	Event test	Fault injection	Power Fail, Abnormal State - Signal short - CRC - Timeout - Frame Error - Buffer overflow
4.	Scenario test	Continuous operation test	About three month burn-in test

In particular, the performance requirements listed above should satisfy the purchase order requirements of Korea Hydro and Nuclear Power Co. Ltd (KHNP), as follows.

- Response time should be less than 4ms.
- Full Range Accuracy within + 0.05% or better should be satisfied.
- Unidirectional buffering and deterministic communication should be satisfied.

4.3 Test results

For the initialization setup, the optical signal conversion capabilities, communication capabilities and accuracy, display status indication, parameter setup, and protocol was carried out in functional tests.

The Performance tests were carried out as follows;

- Response time : 4ms
- Accuracy of ± 0.05%
- 57600 bps transfer rate
- Communication time between ADC (Analog Digital Converter) and MCU (Main Control Unit)
- Communication time between MCU and DAC (Digital to Analog Converter)
- Optical modem transmitter Offset
- Gain adjustment between MCU and DAC
- TWI (Two Wire Interface) communication as an optical transmitter
- TWI communication as an optical receiver
- Communication between MCU of optical modem sender and external clock

- Communication between MCU of optical modem receiver and external clock
- Status of communication tracking between MCU of optical modem receiver and optical receiver component

The verification results of the performance test of a 57600 bps transfer rate and response time (4ms) among several performance tests are shown in Figure 5 and Figure 6, respectively.

To summarize the main points here, for all the software life cycles, V&V PASS/FAIL criteria were established as were V&V input criteria, and V&V Tasks and V&V exit criteria.

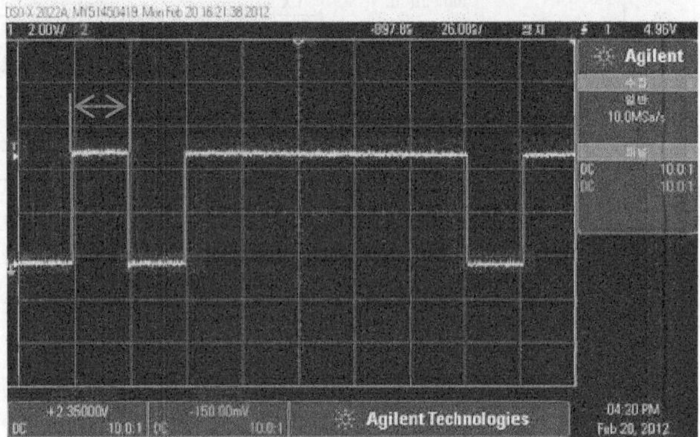

Figure 5 Verification result on transfer rate of 57600bps

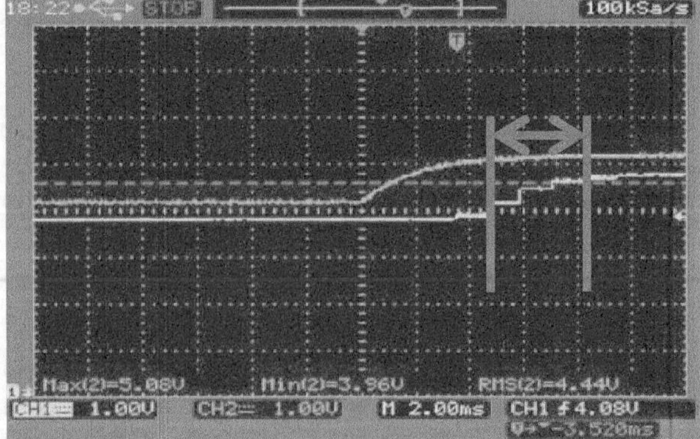

Figure 6. Verification result of 4ms response time

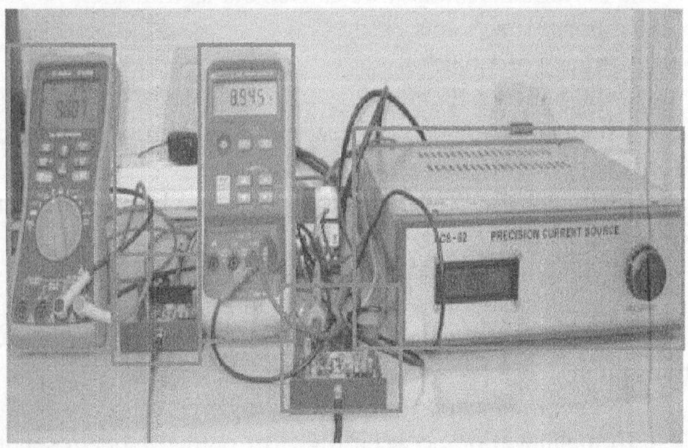

Figure 7 Continuous tests by triangular wave

Event tests were performed based on the error injection, and in particular, a signal short-circuit among several error injections has been tested successfully.

Signal source of triangular wave under the verification test oracle equipment were used, as shown in Figure 7. A scenario-based burn-in test was carried out for three month and two weeks continuously.

A test case generation, test procedure, and test execution were done, and finally, all the results from the testing were documented and reported.

The picture here demonstrates the integration and system test. Mainly, a functional test, performance test and, error-injection test were conducted.

5 Conclusions

All tests were performed according to the test plan and test procedures. Functional testing, performance testing, event testing, and scenario based testing for safety-grade optical modem of Core Protection Calculator in Korea Standard Nuclear Power Plant as a thirty-party verifier were successfully performed. We confirmed that the coverage criteria for a safety-grade optical modem of a Core Protection Calculator are satisfied using a traceability analysis matrix between the high-level requirements and lower-level system test case data set. To recap our points, we have completed verification for all software life cycles from the planning phase to system test phase. Unfortunately, we had some trouble in the beginning, and faced some difficult situations. However, we are thankful that communication and unification between the developers and verifiers helped us finish our project successfully.

6 References

[1] Jang-Yeol Kim, Soon-Gohn Kim, "Software Qualification Approach for Safety-critical Software of the Embedded System", The 2012 International Conference on Future Generation Communication and Networking (FGCN), Kangwondo Korea, December 16-19, 2012

[2] J. Y. Kim, Kee-Choon Kwon, "The Commercial Off The Shelf(COTS) Dedication of QNX Real Time Operating System(RTOS)," International Conference on Reliability, Safety and Hazard-2010, Mumbai India, December 14-16, 2010.

[3] J.Y. Kim, S.W. Cheon, J.S. Lee, Y.J. Lee, K.H. Cha, and Kee-Choon Kwon, "Software V&V Methods for a Safety Grade Programmable Logic Controller," International Conference on Reliability, Safety and Hazard-2005, Mumbai India, December. 1-3, 2005.

[4] K.H. Cha , J.Y. Kim, S.W. Cheon, J.S. Lee, Y.J. Lee, and Kee-Choon Kwon, "Software Qualificaiton of a Programmable Logic Controller for Nuclear Instrumentation

and Control Applications," 2006 WSEAS International Conferences(ISCGAV'06), Crete, August 2006.

[5] 10CFR 50 Appendix A,4/94, "General Design Criteria"

[6] ASME NQA-1-1997 "Quality Assurance Requirements for Nuclear Facility Applications"

[7] USNRC Reg. Guide 1.152, Rev. 02, 2006, "Criteria for Programmable Digital Computers System Software in Safety Related Systems of Nuclear Power Plants"

[8] USNRC Reg. Guide 1.172, Rev. 00, Jul. 1997, "Software Requirements Specifications for Digital Computer Software Used in Systems of Nuclear Power Plants"

[9] IEEE Std. 7-4.3.2-2003, "Standard Criteria for Digital Computers in Safety System of Nuclear Power Generating Stations"

[10] IEEE Std. 829-1998, "IEEE Standard for Software Test Documentation"

[11] IEEE Std. 1008-1987, "IEEE Standard for Software Unit Testing"

[12] IEEE Std. 1012-1998, "IEEE Standard for Software verification and validation"

Findings of Expert Validation and Review of the Technology Enhanced Interaction Framework

K. Angkananon[1], M. Wald[2], and L. Gilbert[2]
Electronic and Computer Science, University of Southampton, Southampton, UK

Abstract - *A Technology Enhanced Interaction Framework has been developed to support designers and developers designing and developing technology enhanced interactions for complex scenarios involving disabled people. Issues of motivation, time, and understanding when validating and evaluating the Technology Enhanced Interaction Framework were identified through a literature review and questionnaires and interviews with experts. Changes to content, system, and approach were made in order to address issues identified. A detailed analysis of the expert review and validation findings supported the view that the TEIF could help designers/developers design technology solutions in complex situations when disabled people are involved. The next step will be to run a motivating experiment to evaluate how and in what ways the framework helps designers/developers.*

Keywords: validation; expert review; user evaluation; framework; interaction

1 Introduction

This paper focuses on the findings of expert validation and review of the Technology Enhanced Interaction Framework (TEIF) adapted from and extending the work of Dix [1] and Gaines [2] to support technology developers and designers designing and developing technology enhanced interactions for complex scenarios involving disabled people. Previous papers have explained: the detailed rationale behind the TEIF and a comparison with existing Frameworks [3]; the development of a seven step prototype method and process [4] to help technology designers/developers understand and apply the TEIF; and an example of how the TEIF could be used to develop a mobile web solution [5]. An expert validation and review was designed and involved a renowned professor in Human Computer Interaction (HCI), three technology designer/ developer experts and three accessibility experts to confirm that the TEIF could help technology designers/developers design technology solutions in complex situations when disabled people are involved. The ways in which the TEIF helps technology designers/developers will be investigated in future work through user evaluations using modifications to the TEIF and its associated method and process based on the expert review. Section 2 explains the TEIF. Section 3 describes the example scenario. Section 4 presents part of the explanation of the technology solution. Section 5 explains the research methodology. Section 6 discusses the findings and Section 7 summarises conclusions and describes future work.

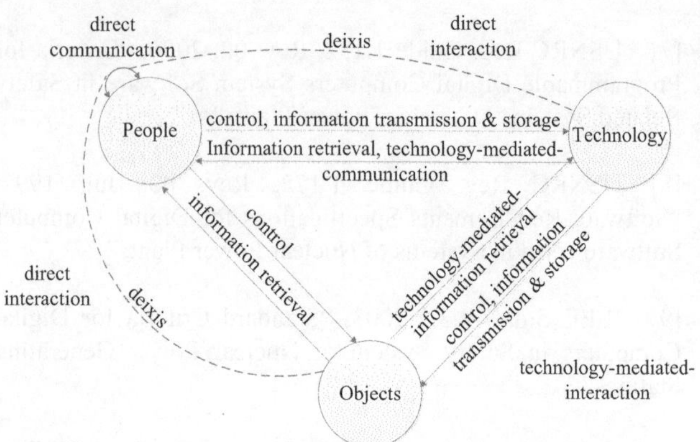

Figure 1 The Technology Enhanced Interaction Framework

2 Technology Enhanced Interaction Framework

The TEIF supports technology developers and designers designing and developing Technology Enhanced Interactions involving people, technology, and objects, and has seven main components as shown in Table 1 and an architecture shown in Figure 1. The seven step prototype method and process consists of: a scenario; requirement questions, answers, and explanation to gather requirements; technology suggestions based on the answers from the requirement questions; a scenario technology solution; interaction diagram; use case diagram and the seventh and last step is the explanation of the technology solution. The requirement question numbers are shown next to the relevant subcomponents in Table 1.

3 Technology Suggestion Table

Technology suggestions are provided to help design a technology solution to a scenario. Some of the technology suggestions for the example scenario are shown in Table 2. The technology suggestions are based upon an analysis of answers to the requirement questions. Note that the column furthest to the right (Total score) shows the number of scenario requirements met by each technology suggestion.

4 Example Scenario

The following scenario describes some problems faced by hearing impaired visitors at a museum and is used to provide experts and users with requirements for a technology solution to be developed using the Framework.

Table 1 Technology Enhanced Interaction Framework

Main Component	Main Component of Technology Enhanced Interaction Framework	
	Sub-component	***Example***
People	Role (3, 4, 11)	A person has a role when communicating with others (e.g. presenter, audience, peer). Roles normally come in pairs (e.g. speaker and audience, teacher and student or owner and visitor) and peer to peer (e.g. student and student or visitor and visitor).
	Ability/ Disability (5, 6, 7, 8, 9, 10)	People have abilities and disabilities which can affect their use of technology or understanding of language and which can lead to communication breakdown (e.g. physical, sensory, language, culture, communication, Information Technology (IT)).
Objects	Dimension	Objects have 2 dimensions (2D) or 3 dimensions (3D), and a 3D object may have a 2D representation.
	Property	Objects have colour, shape and size.
	Content (15)	Objects have content which is human readable (text, pictures, audio, video) and machine readable (QR code, AR tag, barcode, RFID tag, NFC).
Technology	Electronic (12,13, 19)	Electronic technology has stored information, is online (e.g. internet, phone network) or offline (e.g. not connected to the internet or phone network), and is mobile (e.g. smartphone) or non-mobile (e.g. desktop computer).
	Non-electronic	Non-electronic technology is used to store information in objects (e.g. writing with a pen on paper) and is mobile (e.g. pen) or non-mobile (e.g. full-size desktop typewriter).
	User Interface	People interact with technology through its user interface (e.g. touch screen, keyboard).
	Application or Service (14)	Electronic technology is an application (e.g. dictionary) or a service (e.g. weather forecast).
	Cost	Technology has cost (e.g. of hardware, software, maintenance).
Interactions and Communication	People-People (P-P) (11)	People communicate verbally (speak, listen, ask, answer) and non-verbally (lip-read, smile, touch, sign, gesture, nod). When communicating, people may refer (speak or point) to particular objects or technology – this is known as deixis.
	People-Objects (P-O) (11)	People interact with objects for two main purposes: controlling (e.g. touch, hold or move), and retrieving information (e.g. look, listen, read, in order to get information or construct personal understanding and knowledge).
	People-Technology (P-T) (11)	People control technology (e.g. hold, move, use, type, scan, make image, press, swipe) and transmit and store information (e.g. send, save, store, search, retrieve).
	People-Technology -People (P-T-P) (2)	People use technology to transmit information to assist communication with (e.g. send sms, mms, email, chat, instant message) other people.
	People-Technology -Objects (P-T-O) (2)	People use technology (e.g. point, move, hold, scan QR codes, scan AR tag, use camera, use compass) to transmit, store, and retrieve information (send, save, store, search, retrieve) to, in, and from objects.
Time/Place	Place	Same and different time and place yield four categories: same time (ST) and same place (SP), different time (DT) and same place (SP), different time (DT) and different place (DP), same time (ST) but different place (DP).
	Time	
Context	Location (16)	Location affects the use of technology (e.g. indoors, outdoors). For example GPS does not work well indoors.
	Weather Condition (17)	Weather condition may affect the use of technology (e.g. rainy, cloudy, sunny, windy, hot, cold, dry, wet). For example, the mobile phone screen doesn't work well in sunshine.
	Signal Type and Quality	Signal type can affect the quality of electronic technology (e.g. broadband, GPS, 3G, 4G).
	Background Noise (17)	Background noise can affect the communication particularly for hearing impaired people (e.g. background music, crowded situation).
	Lighting (17)	Light can affect the interaction (e.g. Inadequate light, too bright).
Interaction Layer	Culture (6, 7)	Cultural layer includes countries, traditional, language and gesture (e.g. "hello" is a normal greeting used in the culture).
	Intentionality (1)	Intention layer involves understanding, purpose and benefit (e.g. the intent is a greeting).
	Knowledge	Knowledge layer involves facts, concepts, procedures, and principles (e.g. how to spell the word "hello").
	Action	Action layer involves actions and behaviours (e.g. pressing the correct key and not hitting neighbouring keys).
	Expression	Expression layer describes how actions are carried out (e.g. whether action is correct, accurate, prompt).
	Physical	Physical layer is the lowest layer at which people interact with the physical world (e.g. the button is depressed and so sends the electronic code for the letter to the application).

Table 2 Technology Suggestions

Technology suggestions	**Which scenario requirements the technology meets**																
	1a.improve communication	2a.same time/ same place	3a.presenter-audience	6b. speaker speaks Thai	7b. presenter speaks Thai	9a. hearing impaired	11a. people people	11b. people - objects	12a.online technology	13a.mobile devices	14a.pre-prepared speech	16a. indoor	17a. noise	17e.inadequate lighting	18a. low cost solution	19a. work with smart phones	Total Score
Mobile web site	✓	✓	✓	✓	✓	✓	✓	✓	✓	✓	✓	✓	✓	✓	✓	✓	16
Pre-prepared caption/subtitle	✓	✓	✓	✓	✓	✓	✓	✓	✓	✓	✓	✓	✓	✓	✓	✓	16
Quick Response Code	✓	✓	✓	✓	✓	✓	✓	✓	✓	✓	✓	✓	✓	✓	✓	✓	16
Instant messaging	✓	✓	✓	✓	✓	✓	✓	×	✓	✓	✓	✓	✓	✓	✓	✓	15
Vibrating alert	✓	✓	✓	✓	✓	✓	✓	×	✓	✓	✓	✓	✓	✓	✓	✓	15
Speech recognition	✓	✓	✓	×	×	✓	✓	×	✓	✓	✓	✓	×	✓	✓	✓	12

Suchat Trapsin allocated some parts of his house to become the Museum of Folk Art and Shadow Puppets, in Thailand. There are exhibits of shadow puppets inside the museum, but there is no information provided in text format because Suchat normally explains the history and tradition in Thai by talking to visitors. He presents the same information in the same order every time. Chuty (who has been hearing impaired since birth) and her parents (who have some hearing loss due to their age) are local people who visit the museum. Suchat starts the talk by explaining about the exhibits. During the talk, Chuty and her parents find it very difficult to hear Suchat clearly. Chuty asks Suchat some questions about the exhibits. Suchat answers the questions, but Chuty misses some of the words. While Chuty and her parents are watching the shadow puppet show, they cannot hear the conversation clearly because of the background music which is part of the show. It is also fairly dark which makes lip-reading very difficult for them. Suchat would like to have a technology solution that makes it easier for Chuty and her parents to understand him. There is good Wi-Fi at the museum so he would like to use Chuty's and her parents' smartphones to keep his costs low.

5 Explanation of Technology Solution

The explantation of the technology solution is:

From the Scenario Technology Solution, Suchat has a role in the communication which is important because he can control technology to send an instant message to Chuty and her parents' phones to make them vibrate to let Chuty and her parents know when the conversation starts. The technology solution selected to enable this is instant messaging which was chosen over SMS. Instant messaging is suggested because it is free of cost using wireless and smartphones. Moreover, it can also vibrate Chuty's and her parents' smartphones which is better than turning lights in the room on and off to notify them as this may not be noticeable in sunlight. Captions can be of value to everybody, especially people with no useful hearing, and were selected as the solution of choice. Thai speech recognition is not very accurate for spontaneous speech and therefore as Suchat already knows what he plans to say the best solution is pre-prepared summary captions. As he presents his talk Suchat controls the changing pre-prepared captions on the mobile website using his smartphone. He has an application on his phone that can send a message to the webserver to display the next caption on the webpage that Chuty and her parents are looking at. This solution was chosen over using a pre-prepared captioned video as that would not have supported live face to face communication and interaction between Suchat and his visitors. Chuty and her parents ask spontaneous questions about some of the exhibits in the museum. Suchat will not have been able to pre-prepare the order of the captions. In this case, Suchat can introduce machine readable QR codes. QR codes were selected rather than other possible approaches (e.g. barcodes, RFID tags, image recognition, typing a code number) because they are simple, cheap, quick and work with smartphones using free software to provide a link to information on a mobile website.

6 Explanation of Technology Solution

6.1 Pilot Study

Validation and review of the framework by experts was undertaken using an online system before the next step of engaging with the users (technology designers/developers). The combination of online questionnaire on the system and interviewing were chosen because the experts need some time to complete the questionnaire, they can choose their preferred

Table 3 Pilot Study Findings

Category of changes	Result of changes
Content	
Spelling and grammar mistakes	Correct and more understandable
Rewrite instructions	Clearer
Rewrite descriptions	Clearer
Add explanation of the technology suggestion tables	Help respondents understand why technologies have ticks or crosses in cells corresponding to requirements
Improve content	Make it clear and understandable without assuming knowledge
Change the image tables to html tables	Make the table accessible, now can copy the content in order to make change, can link to the websites were provided, can provide explanations in tooltip
System	
Remove the logic and always display comment box and question	System processing was slow therefore logic didn't display question before user moved on to next question and processing icon at the top of page which was out of view unless scroll up
Choice, force entry to move on or just reminder	remind the respondents to provide the answer but allow blank entry

time and place and also can stop and return to the questionnaire whenever they want. Using the online questionnaire helps experts to see a prototype of the system so they can give more suggestions or comments about how to design the layout of the system. However, it might result in confusion between validating or reviewing the questionnaire and the system.

Therefore, in the analysis of the results it was important to note whether the comments were about the system or the framework. For example, in the pilot test respondents gave comments about the slow response of the online system, which is not an issue about the content. The online questionnaire makes it easy to analyse the data and read the comments compared to the paper based system but doesn't help when the expert requires clarification of the questions or misunderstands some points. Therefore, the study also used the interview methods to discuss with the experts about any unclear information. Having constructed the questionnaire, it is important to pilot it before giving it to experts to validate and review as it is difficult even for an experienced questionnaire designer to get a questionnaire completely right at the first time. To pilot the validation and review, one experienced accessibility expert and two experienced technology designers/developers took the online questionnaire through the system. Based on their responses changes were made to improve the questions, response times and layout as summarised in Table 3. The pilot study participants were shown all these changes and confirmed that they were satisfied with them.

6.2 Triangulation

Triangulation is a technique used to ensure the validity and credibility of the results [6-8] and methodological triangulation was used based on theory of existing frameworks, expert validation and review, and user evaluation. Validation is an important process particularly when an instrument is being developed to measure the construct in the context of the concepts being studied [6]. Without validation, untested data may need revision in a future study [9]. Checking reliability normally comes at the question wording and piloting stage as if an item is unreliable, then it must also lack validity [9, 10]. An expert review is a process asking the opinions, suggestions, feedback or comments from experts. For example, subject matter experts are asked to check content of questionnaires or appropriateness of wording and terminology of items [11].

The validation of the Technology Enhanced Interaction Framework was considered by two groups of experts: technology designer/developer experts and accessibility experts. The technology design experts focused on the main and sub-components while accessibility experts focused on checking the accessibility aspects. In addition the opportunity arose to discuss the TEIF with a professor who is world renowned in the HCI field. After the expert review and validation user evaluation involving real users (technology designers/developers) will be used to evaluate the Technology Enhanced Interaction Framework.

An important issue that can arise when users evaluate a new idea or concept using a prototype system is that they evaluate the system rather than the idea. Using a low fidelity prototype (e.g. paper) rather than a high fidelity prototype (e.g. a functioning website) can sometimes help the user focus on the idea rather than the system. However some users may find it more difficult to evaluate the potential of an abstract concept or idea than a concrete product [12].

7 Expert Validation and Review Findings and Discussion

If the majority of experts answer "Yes" to the questions this will be considered as a successful validation. The following sections describe the seven steps in validating and reviewing the Framework (section 7.1), method (section 7.2 and 7.3) and examples how to apply the Framework (section 7.4 - 7.7):

7.1 Validation and Review Technology Enhanced Interaction Framework (TEIF)

Table 4 Experts Validating TEIF

Questions	% of experts answering "Yes"	Successful validation
1. Are the instructions clear?	67%	Yes
3. Are the examples and explanations clear?	100%	Yes
5. Do you agree with the main and sub-components of the framework?	100%	Yes

The TEIF table was successfully validated by the experts (Table 4) but as a result of the comments from the three designer experts and the expert professor the following changes to the framework components are planned.

7.1.1 The "Objects" component

One expert suggested finding a better word than objects but it has not been possible to find a better word and so the definition and meaning of the word in the TEIF context will be explained in more detail. The TEIF has a consistent and clearly defined meaning of the word "Objects" but only a brief explanation was provided for the experts because of time limitation.

7.1.2 The "Weather Condition" sub-component

One expert found this "Oddly specific" and so more examples of how weather condition could affect technology interactions will be provided.

7.1.3 The "Examples" sub-heading

An expert suggested it was unclear what the examples were and what were the explanations and so the sub-heading will be changed to "Explanations and examples".

7.1.4 People being aware of other interactions

This aspect will be added as a sub-component to the context component as the professor suggested this might be something worth considering in the TEIF (e.g. between other people or between other people and technology or other people and objects).

7.1.5 Identity of an object

The identity of an object will be added to the sub-component "Property" as an example as suggested by the professor.

7.1.6 User Perception

An explanation will be provided that as pointed out by the professor, users may have the perception that technology (e.g. a robotic device triggered by the person walking past it) talking to them is a "Technology to People" interaction (T-P) whereas the TEIF categorises it as a "People – Technology-People" interaction (P-T-P).

7.1.7 Framework components as index for case based solutions

The Professor agreed that the framework components could be useful as an index for case based solutions. This aspect will be considered for the user evaluation.

7.1.8 Instructions

The majority of experts suggested proving more information about the purpose of the Framework. This participant information was provided through the email but some of the experts appear to have not read this carefully and so the information will be also provided in the start page of the online survey.

7.2 Validation and Review Scenario, Questions, and Answers

Experts wanted more detail in order to be able to answer requirement questions. This detail will be added into the scenario.

7.2.1 Part 1: Instructions in The Scenario, Questions, and Answers section

Two accessibility experts were unclear what "instructions" referred to (Table 5). Therefore, the wording will be changed to clarify this.

Table 5 Experts Validating Instructions part 1

Questions	% of experts answering "Yes"	Successful validation
1. Are the instructions clear?	67%	Yes

7.2.2 Part 2: Requirement questions and multiple choices Answers, and Explanations

7.2.2.1 Grammar/spelling/re-wording

There were many suggestions for improving the wording of the questions, multiple choices, answers and explanations and these will be used to improve this section.

7.2.2.2 Change multiple choices options and answers

Some experts found it unclear why choice 'f' was not also a correct answer to requirement Question 1 and so choice 'f' will be removed because this is not related to the component of the framework.

Question 1: what is the main purpose of technology solution?
(☐ Means can select more than 1 choice)

- ☐ a. improve communication and interaction
- ☐ b. make the service more interesting and exciting
- ☐ c. improve the service efficiency in term of time and easy to use
- ☐ d. improve the storage and retrieval information
- ☐ e. make the service more realistic and authentic
- ☐ f. improve users' experiences in using the service

One expert suggested another choice 'd' "mobile and non-mobile devices" to requirement question 13 even though the scenario stated a mobile was required and therefore the scenario wording will be improved to make this even clearer.

Question 13: what type of technology devices would be appropriate for the solution to the scenario? (O means can select only 1 choice)
O a. mobile devices
O b. non-mobile devices
O c. I don't know

Regarding requirement question 18 one expert stated there is no explanation why the low cost solution is required and another expert suggested there might be a lower cost technology than smartphones. To address this more explanation will be added into the scenario.

Question 18: does the customer require a low cost solution?
O a. yes
O b. no

7.2.3 Part 3: Questions, associated questions and multiple choices answers, and explanations

There were no questions, requirements, components or sub-components missing that would be relevant to the scenario (Table 6). Having the requirement numbers next to the sub-components did not help the majority of experts (Table 6). The framework is used to inform the method and processes but knowing the relationship between the requirements and the sub-components is not necessary to follow the method and processes. It is also difficult to move between the sections on an online survey to refer to the requirement numbers. One expert suggested putting the requirement numbers in the scenario but this would interrupt the flow of the scenario narrative. To address this issue the relationship will be explained more clearly and a way to make it easier to move between sections will be investigated.

Table 6 Experts validating instruction of part 3

Questions	% of experts answering "Yes"	Successful validation
60. Was it helpful to have the requirement numbers next to the sub-components in the Technology Enhanced Interaction Framework table shown in the previous section?	33%	No
62. Are there any questions, requirements, components or sub-components missing that would be relevant to the scenario?	0%	Yes

7.3 Validation and Review Technology Suggestion Tables

The technology suggestion tables were successfully validated (Table 7). The problem the experts had with the time required to validate all the information will not be a problem with the future user evaluation because they will only refer to a few technologies. The required grammar/spelling/re-wording changes will be made. Links to sources other than Wikipedia will be investigated. The problem one expert had understanding the "People to objects" column should be removed by the more detailed explanations that will be provided in the framework.

Table 7 Experts validating instructions of technology suggestion tables

Questions	% of experts answering "Yes"	Successful validation
1. Are the descriptions in the technologies tables clear?	67%	Yes
3. Do you agree that the ticks correctly identify the requirements met	60%	Yes

The professor's idea of the Technology Suggestions Table rating how well a technology meets the requirement rather than just showing a tick or cross had been considered when the framework was being developed but it was decided that this could be a refinement for future work.

7.4 Validation and Review Scenario Technology Solution

The Scenario Technology Solution was successfully validated (Table 8). The required grammar/spelling/re-wording changes will be made and the solution improved following the suggestions made. For example, it will be made clear that Chuty does not speak using Thai speech recognition at the same time as Suchat is talking.

Table 8 Expert validating scenario Technology Solution

Questions	% of experts answering "Yes"	Successful validation
1. Is the scenario solution clearly described?	83%	Yes
3. Does the solution meet the scenario requirements?	67%	Yes

7.5 Validation and Review Mobile Web Internet Diagram

The Mobile Web Interaction Diagram was successfully validated (Table 9). The numbering and re-ordering of actions will be improved following the suggestions made. For example, presenting concurrent as well as sequential actions.

Table 9 Experts validating Mobile Web Interaction Diagram

Questions	% of experts answering "Yes"	Successful validation
1. Does the Mobile Web Interactions diagram help understand the scenario solution?	100%	Yes

7.6 Validation and Review Use Case Diagram

The Use Case Diagram was successfully validated (Table 10). The login and logout functions will be added as suggested.

Table 10 Experts validating Use Case Diagram

Questions	% of experts answering "Yes"	Successful validation
1. Does the Use Case Diagram help understand the scenario solution?	100%	Yes

7.7 Validation and Review Chosen Solution and Explanations

The Chosen Solution and Explanations was successfully validated (Table 11). As suggested by the experts more information will be provided, the layout/presentation will be improved and the framework method and process will be broken down into easier smaller steps.

Table 11 Experts validating chosen solution and explanations

Questions	% of experts answering "Yes"	Successful validation
1. Is the explanation of how the solution was derived from the suggestions easy to understand?	100%	Yes
3. Do you agree that the framework with its associated questions and suggestions can help designers design technology to enhance interactions particularly in complex situations involving disabled people?	83%	Yes

8 Conclusions and Future Work

Issues of motivation, time and understanding when validating and evaluating the TEIF were identified through a literature review and piloting questionnaires and interviews. Changes to content, system and approach were made in order to address these issues. Future work will involve the implementation of a motivating user evaluation approach. The work undertaken so far confirms such a TEIF be developed based on existing frameworks, theories and principles. The results of the expert validation and review by the Professor, three technology designer/developer experts, and three accessibility experts following the methodology explained in section 6 supported the view that the TEIF could help technology designers/developers design technology solutions in complex situations when disabled people are involved. Future Work will be to run an experiment to determine how and in what ways the framework helps designers/developers using evaluation with designers using a motivating approach.

9 References

[1] A. J. Dix, "Computer supported cooperative work - a framework," *In Design Issues in CSCW Eds. D. Rosenburg and C. Hutchison.* , vol. Springer Verlag, pp. 23-37, 1994.

[2] B. R. Gaines, "A conceptual framework for person-computer interaction in complex systems," *Systems, Man and Cybernetics, IEEE Transactions on,* vol. 18, pp. 532-541, 1988.

[3] K. Angkananon, M. Wald, and L. Gilbert, "Technology Enhanced Interaction Framework," in *6TH Annual International Conference*, Singapore, 2013.(in press)

[4] K. Angkananon, M. Wald, and L. Gilbert, "Using the Technology Enhanced Interaction Framework for Interaction Scenarios involving Disabled People," in *2nd International Conference on Advances in Information Technology.*, Bangkok, 2013. (in press)

[5] K. Angkananon, M. Wald, and L. Gilbert, "Designing Mobile Web Solutions for Interaction Scenarios Involving Disabled People," in *Advances in Computer Science*, Phuket, 2013.

[6] L. Cohen, & Manion, L., *Research methods in education*: Routledge, 2000.

[7] H. Altrichter, A. Feldman, and P. S. Posch, B., *Teachers investigate their work; An introduction to action research across the professions*: Routledge, 2008.

[8] T. O'Donoghue and P. K., *Qualitative Educational Research in Action: Doing and Reflecting*: Routledge, 2003.

[9] H. Coombes, *Research Using IT*. New York: PALGRAVE, 2001.

[10] J. Bell, *Doing Your Reserch Project A guide for first-time researchers in education, health and social science*. England: Open University Press, 2010.

[11] C. Ramirez, "Strategies for subject matter expert review in questionnaire design.," presented at the the Questionnaire Design, Evaluation, and Testing Conference, Charleston, 2002.

[12] Y.-k. Lim, A. Pangam, S. Periyasami, and S. Aneja, "Comparative analysis of high- and low-fidelity prototypes for more valid usability evaluations of mobile devices," presented at the Proceedings of the 4th Nordic conference on Human-computer interaction: changing roles, Oslo, Norway, 2006.

An Approach to Configuration-based Generation of Validation Rules for Shipdex

Youhee Choi, Jeong-Ho Park, and Byungtae Jang
Industries IT Convergence Research Department
Electronics and Telecommunications Research Institute, Daejeon, KOREA

Abstract - *Shipdex protocol defines all technical documents including the ship equipment manuals in XML according to Shipdex document format. Data module, the smallest information unit of the Shipdex protocol shall be prepared based on S1000D XML schema and shall satisfy the fundamental S1000D XML schema rules and Shipdex standard as well. There are commercial tools that support validating whether these rules are met. However, when S1000D standard or Shipdex standard is modified, update by the validation tool developer and continuous maintenance as well are required as the tool has Shipdex rules inherent in it. In order to minimize such inconvenience, a scheme is proposed with which the Shipdex tool user can modify and add Shipdex rules easily.*

Keywords: Shipdex, S1000D, XML, validation

1 Introduction

These days, the shipbuilding industry requires ways to efficiently manage a vast amount of technical documents about various ship equipments mounted on the ship. In this respect, in aerospace and military field, the "S1000D International Specification for technical publication utilizing a common source database" is used for the procurement and production of technical publications[1]. Accordingly, some European shipping companies agreed to develop the Shipdex protocol that is a common and shared data exchange protocol based on ASD S1000D issue 2.3[2]. Both Shipdex and S1000D define a data module in XML format as the smallest independent information unit. Depending on the content to be described, various types of data modules are defined and each type has its own rules for defining data module. Some of these definition rules may be reflected in S1000D XML schema since Shipdex is based on S1000D XML schema. These rules can be easily verified using any schema-based verification tools. However, some of Shipdex authoring rules are different with the S1000D XML schema. In addition, there are rules that cannot be expressed with schema due to the limitations of XML schema expression. Because of this, in order to verify whether a data module has been generated in accordance with Shipdex protocol, it is necessary to verify the data module separately S1000D XML schema-based validation or using a Shipdex data module verification tool. From this perspective, there are many commercial tools to support S1000D authoring and verification, such as PTC's Arbotext CSDB for S1000D, CORENA S1000D solutions of CORENA and UltraCSDB S1000D suite of WebX Systems[4, 5, 6]. In comparison to S1000D, there are only a limited number of commercial tools specializing in Shipdex, such as Shipdex CSDB of CORENA and AMOS Shipdex Suite of SpecTec Group[7]. The tools, specializing in Shipdex, include Shipdex-specific rules that are different from S1000D. As these Shipdex rules are based on S1000D, any modifications to S1000D rules need to be reflected and Shipdex rules may also need to be modified accordingly or may be modified regardless of S1000D. However, as such modifications to the rules involve Shipdex rules inherent in the tool, update by the verification tool developer and continuous maintenance as well are required. In order to minimize such inconvenience, a scheme is proposed with which the Shipdex tool user can modify and/or add Shipdex rules easily. The proposed scheme can define a configuration file format for Shipdex rules, based on which tool-verifiable Shipdex rules can be automatically created and Shipdex data module can be verified by the user-defined Shipdex rules.

2 Related Studies

2.1 Shipdex

Shipdex defines technical documents of all equipment mounted on ship to be expressed on the basis of S1000D 2.3 XML schema. The data module types that the Shipdex protocol uses are Descriptive, Procedural, and Illustrated parts data (IPD). Descriptive data module is to represent descriptive information; Procedural data module represent procedural information; and IPD data module represent parts list and illustrated parts data. S1000D XML schema is defined for each data module type and different rules are applied to each type. Types of major rules defined in Shipdex are classified as follows:

- Rule for the number of digits of XML element value
- Rule for the format of XML element values
- Rule for the fixed values of XML elements
- Rule for the default values of XML elements
- Rule for the list of XML element values

· Rule for the condition for specific values of XML elements

· Rule for the occurrence (required/optional) of XML elements

· Rule for the subelements of XML elements

2.2 Classification of XML Validation Rules

XML validation rules can be divided into those that can be expressed on XML schema and those that cannot be[8]. In order to classify those that can be expressed on XML schema, it is necessary to analyze the syntax of XML schema. In XML schema, a data element can be declared either as a simple type or a complex type. According to the syntax that defines the simple type in the schema, Restriction element, among those that can be child elements of the simple type, is the element used for restricting the range of a value, which describes in the facet element the content to be restricted. Using the facet element, it is possible to express the rules for preparing XML data.

First of all, the rule for listing the items available for XML element values can be expressed according to the following syntax:

1) Expression that uses enumeration type for the facet element
- As the enumeration type should express the list of items that can be used as values, the rule should be configured to express these values as XML element values.
2) Expression that uses multiple pattern types with fixed values, for the facet element
- Pattern type can be used to define the format of XML value as well as fixed value. So, if several patterns with fixed values are defined, a rule for the list of possible XML element values can be configured.
3) When XML data value is a number, minExclusive, minInclusive, maxExclusive, maxInclusive types represent respectively the minimum value excluded, minimum value included, maximum value excluded and minimum value excluded. Therefore, these can form a rule for the list of values within the corresponding range.

Second, the rule for defining the format of XML element values can be expressed with various types of facet element.

1) Expression that uses pattern type for the facet element
- Basically, pattern type is used for defining the format of XML value, so it is applicable to the rule for defining the format of XML element value.
2) When XML data value is a number, the facet elements related to the format of digit expression such as totalDigits and fractionDigits can be used
- As totalDigits designates the total number of digits of a number, while fractionDigits designates the number of digits in the fractional part, they can be used to define the number of digits in numeric expression and thus can be included in the rule for defining the format of XML element value.
3) When XML data value is a character string, length, minLength, and maxLength indicate the total length, minimum length and maximum length of the character string respectively. Thus, they restrict the expression of the character string and can be included in the rule for defining the format of XML element value.

Third, the rule for defining the range of XML element value can be expressed as follows:

1) When XML data value is a number, minExclusive, minInclusive, maxExclusive, maxInclusive values designate respectively the minimum value excluded, minimum value included, maximum value excluded and minimum value excluded. Therefore, these can form a rule for defining the range of the element value.

Next, according to complexType definition syntax in the schema, elements that have properties or child elements can be declared. As complexType can have child elements, it is possible to express the rule about the relationship among XML elements. The rule for defining what elements and attributes can be included as XML subelements, can be extracted using minOccurs and maxOccurs attributes that indicate the frequency of occurrence of each element in XML document. Also, in case of the rule defining whether a XML element is required or optional, an XML element of which minOccurs is 0 that can be omitted as 0 indicates that it is optional. But, when minOccurs is 1 or higher, it indicates the XML element should be expressed at least once or more, the element can be considered as a required element. For an attribute of which 'use' value is 'required', it indicates that the corresponding attribute is a required attribute. Therefore, minOccurs and maxOccurs can be used for the rule for defining required attributes and optional ones.

3 Configuration-based Generation of Validation Rules for Shipdex

3.1 Configuration-based generation of validation rules for Shipdex

Figure 1 shows a conceptual diagram for automatically generating XML validation rules for Shipdex based on configuration files and then validating Shipdex XML data modules. The scheme shown in Figure 1 consists of Shipdex Rule Generation part where Shipdex rules are generated and Shipdex Rule Validation part where a data module XML file is validated based on the generated Shipdex rules. Schema Rule Generation part generates a XML schema file that represents Shipdex rules that can be expressed in XML schema based on the configuration file in which XML validation rules are defined. Non-Schema Rule Generation part where Shipdex rules that cannot be expressed in XML schema are generated as Shipdex rule objects. In the Shipdex Rule Validation part, XML files are validated based on the

XML schema generated based on Shipdex rules and according to the generated Shipdex rule objects, and the validation results are provided.

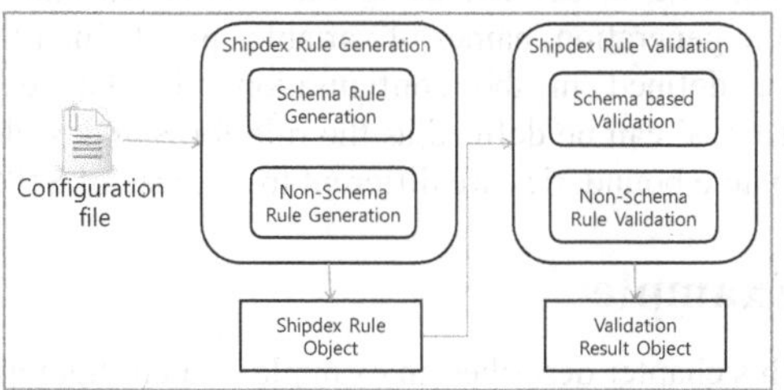

Figure 1. Conceptual Diagram of Configuration-based Shipdex Rule Generation and Validation

3.2 Definition of Configuration File Format for Defining Shipdex Rules

In order to generate Shipdex rules based on the configuration file, the rules need to be classified as schema-rules and non-schema rules. For Shipdex rules that can be expressed in XML schema, the content of S1000D xml schema file can be modified, when they are different from S1000D. In this case, if simpleType declaration needs to be added/modified and the corresponding element is not simpleType, an arbitary simpleType can be declared and defined. Also, if there is any pre-defined S1000D rule and it is not in violation of Shipdex rules, Shipdex rules can be added without deleting the existing rule. Shipdex rules that can be expressed in XML schema are classified as follows:

First, if the list of values that can be set for XML elements in Shipdex is different from the one in S1000D, the values can be expressed using enumeration type among facet elements of the restriction element on XML schema. In order to express this rule using configuration file, the following syntax is defined:

- Rule-Expr1 := Schema-Elem1 Sep Flag Sep Value-List
- Schema-Elem1 := <element-name> | [attribute-name] | <element-name>-[attribute-name]
- Sep := ;
- Flag := R | A
- Value-List := Value1, … , Value1
- Value1 := words

'Rule-Expr1' is expressed with 'Schema-Eleme1' to express XML element which the rule is to be applied, 'Sep' the separator, 'Flag' to indicate whether to replace the content of the existing XML schema or to add new content, and 'Value-List' to define the list of values of XML elements.

Second, the rule for XML elements with fixed values can be expressed in XML schema using the pattern type of the facet element, one of restriction elements. In order to express such rule based on configuration file, the following syntax is defined:

- Rule-Expr2 := Schema-Elem1 Sep Flag Sep Value
- Schema-Elem1 := <element-name> | [attribute-name] | <element-name>-[attribute-name]
- Sep := ;
- Flag := R | A
- Value := Programming-Language regular expression

'Rule-Expr2' differs from 'Rule-Expr1' in that it defines the value of XML element with 'Value'.

Third, in order to express the rule for Shipdex elements whose value boundaries are different from those of S1000D, the following syntax is defined:

- Rule-Expr3 := Schema-Elem1 Sep Flag Sep Value-Bound
- Value-Bound := minBound | maxBound | min-max-Bound
- minBound := >value2 | >=value2
- maxBound := <value2 | <=value2
- min-max-Bound := minBound & maxBound

'Rule-Expr3' has 'Value-Bound' to express the range of values, such as 'minBound' for the boundary of minimum value, 'maxBound' for the boundary of maximum value, and 'min-max-Bound' for the form in which minimum and maximum values are combined.

Fourth, those that are required elements or attributes in Shipdex but not in S1000D can be declared to have '1' for minOccurs value in the element declaration part or declared without minOccurs as its default value of 1 is applied when it is omitted. On the other hand, for the elements that are required in S1000D but optional in Shipdex, if minOccurs value set as 1 in S1000D schema is kept, it may be identified as an error at the time of schema validation. In order to prevent this, those elements should be declared with 0 for minOccurs value. In order to express this rule using the configuration file, the following syntax is defined:

- Rule-Expr4 := XML-Elem2,…,XML-Elem2
- XML-Elem1 := <element-name> | [attribute-name]

'Rule-Expr4' can express each required/optional XML elements or attributes regardless whether it is included in other XML elements or not.

Next, the rules that cannot be expressed in XML schema shall be classified:

First of all, the rules that cannot be expressed in XML schema are those with condition part. Depending on whether the condition is met or not, rules are classified into two types that occurrence characteristics of other XML elements can be changed and conditions about values of other XML elements can be applied. To expresses these types of rules, the following syntax is defined:

· Rule-Expr5 := Conditional-Part1 Sep Dependent-Part1

· Conditional-Part1 := Conditional-Expr1 | Conditional-Expr1 Logic-Op Conditional-Expr1

· Conditional-Expr1 := Conditional-Item1 | Conditional-Item1 Logic-Op Conditional-Item1

· Conditional-Item1 := Schema-Elem1 Op Value

· Dependent-Part1 := Conditional-Part1 | Dependent-List

· Dependent-List := Schema-Elem1, … , Schema-Elem1

· Schema-Elem1 := <element-name> | [attribute-name] | <element-name>-[attribute-name]

· Sep := ;

· Logic-Op := And-Op | Or-Op

· And-Op := &&

· Or-Op := ||

· Op := != | == | < | > | <= | >=

· Value := Programming-Language regular expression

In order to express XML validation rules that include a condition(s), 'Rule-Expr5' consists of 'Conditional-Part1' to define the conditional part, 'Sep' the separator, and 'Dependent-Part1' to express the part dependent on the conditional part. 'Conditional-Part1' is defined to be capable of expressing the rules with one conditional formula separately from those with multiple conditions identified by logical And/Or condition ('Logic-Op'). 'Conditional-Item1' is expressed with 'Schema-Elem1' to express XML element which a condition is to be applied, 'Op' the operator for comparison with the condition value, and 'Value' to express the value of the condition. 'Schema-Elem1' is defined to express XML element, XML attribute, and XML attribute specific to certain XML element. 'Value' is expressed in regular expression for the programming language of XML validation rule generation program. 'Dependent-Part1' is defined with 'Conditional-Part1' to express the rule that contains a condition about the value of other XML element that is affected by 'Conditional-Part1' of 'Rule-Expr5' or 'Dependent-List1' to express XML elements which occurrence characteristics can be changed. 'Dependent-List1' is defined to express the list of dependents as one or more 'Schema-Elem1' list.

Second, when each XML element includes different subelements in Shipdex from those in S1000D, it is difficult to apply the hierarchical structure of XML elements to XML schema if the definition of the hierarchical structure is complicated. In order to express such type of rule, the following syntax is defined:

· Rule-Expr6 := XML-Elem2 Sep1 XML-Elem1,…,XML-Elem1

· Sep1 := :

· XML-Elem2 := <element-name>

'Rule-Expr6' is expressed with the list of 'XML-Elem1' to express the rule for the list of elements to be or not to be included as subelements of 'XML-Elem2'. Each XML validation rule is defined using these syntaxes and, for its automatic generation, names of variables pre-defined for each rule are defined in the configuration file. For example, '%RULE1%' can be defined as the rule for Shipdex elements whose value boundaries are different from those of S1000D.

4 Example

This chapter describes an example of a configuration file for Shipdex and the generated XML schema file for Shipdex based on the configuration file and the validation result of an example Shipdex data based on the generated XML validation rule.

4.1 Example of Configuration File

Table 1 shows some of Shipdex rules that are not in compliance with the fundamental S1000D XML schema but can be expressed in XML schema.

Table 1. Some of Shipdex rules that can be expressed in XML Schema

XML element	Shipdex rule
<chapnum>	Shipdex™ protocol allocates the following fixed value for MICC: "H" - General sea vehicles SNS
	3 (1+2) alphanumeric characters
<itemloc>	Shipdex™ allows the use of the following values: • "A" Information related to items installed on the Product. • "B" Information related to items installed on a major assembly removed from the Product • "D" Information related to both locations A and B. No other combinations are allowed.
<orig>	The element <orig> is required for ASD S1000D™ but for the Shipdex™ Protocol Projects this element is optional and can be empty.

According to Table 1, the rule about the format of value can be applied to '<chapnum>'. The rule about items that can be used as values can be applied to '<itemloc>'. The rule about required elements in Shipdex but not in S1000D can be applied to '<orig>'.

Figure 2 shows an example of a configuration file defined based on the rule in Table 1, which is required by Shipdex and can be expressed in XML schema.

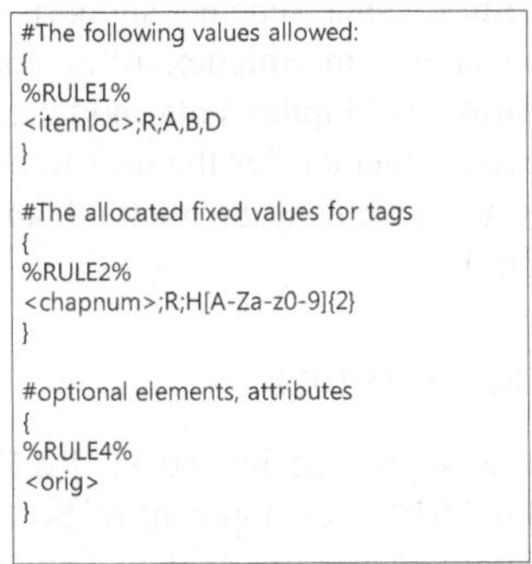

Figure 2. Example of configuration file defined for the rule that can be expressed in XML schema

Table 2 shows some of Shipdex rules that are not in compliance with the fundamental S1000D XML schema and cannot be expressed in XML schema.

Table 2. Some of Shipdex rules that cannot be expressed in XML Schema

XML element	*Shipdex Rule*
<warning>	The content of the element <warning> is given by a combination of the following subelements • element <para> • element <randlist> • element <symbol>
<note>	The content of the element <note> is given by a combination of the same subelements and attributes as used by element Warning except for the absence of the element <randlist> and <symbol>.
<refdm>	The elements <issno> and <dmtitle> in the <refdm> element shall not be used.
[issno]	The initial issue of a DM shall always be issue "001" and its issue status "new".

According to Table 2, The rule that each XML element includes different subelements in Shipdex from those in S1000D can be applied to '<warning>', <note> and <refdm>. The rule that is applied to '[issno]' is the rule that include a condition.

```
#unused elements
#owner element:unused element pairs
{
%RULE5%
<warning>:<seqlist>,<deflist>
<note>:<symbol>,<seqlist>,<deflist>,<randlist>
<refdm>:<issno>,<dmtitle>
}

#conditional values
{
%RULE1%
[issno]==001;[type]==new
}
```

Figure 3. Example of a configuration file defined for the rule that cannot be expressed in XML schema

Figure 3 shows an example of a configuration file defined based on the rule in Table 2 for the Shipdex rule that cannot be expressed in XML schema.

4.2 Example of XML Schema File Generation for Shipdex

The following is an example of XML schema generation for Shipdex. Figure 4 is an example of XML schema file generated for Shipdex, based on the rule for the case where XML element values of Shipdex are different from those of S1000D.

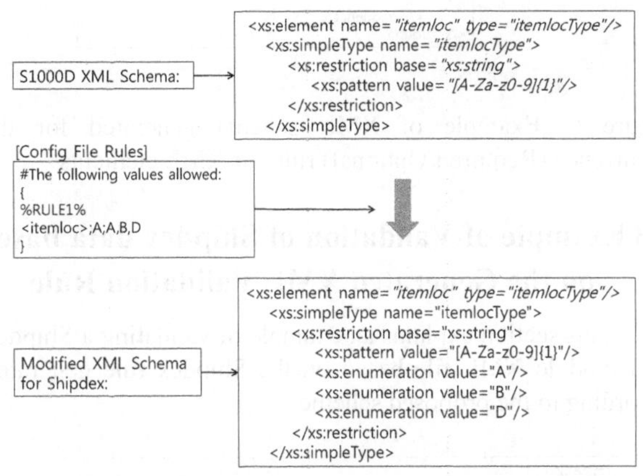

Figure 4. Example of XML schema generated for the rule about a list of XML element values

Figure 5 shows an example of XML schema file modified based on the rule for the case where XML elements have fixed values in pre-defined formats.

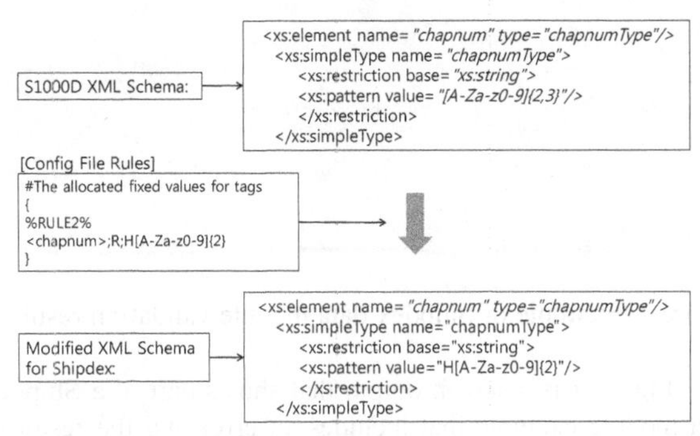

Figure 5. Example of XML schema generated for the rule for the format of XML element values

Figure 6 shows an example of XML schema file modified based on the rule for the case where an XML element which is required for S1000D but optional in Shipdex.

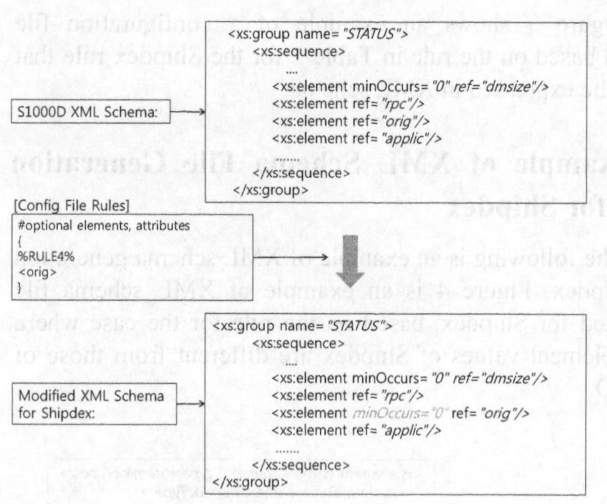

Figure 6. Example of XML schema generated for the occurrence (Required/Optional) rule for XML elements

4.3 Example of Validation of Shipdex data based on the Generated XML Validation Rule

This section explains an example of validating a Shipdex data module XML file based on the Shipdex rule generated according to the proposed scheme.

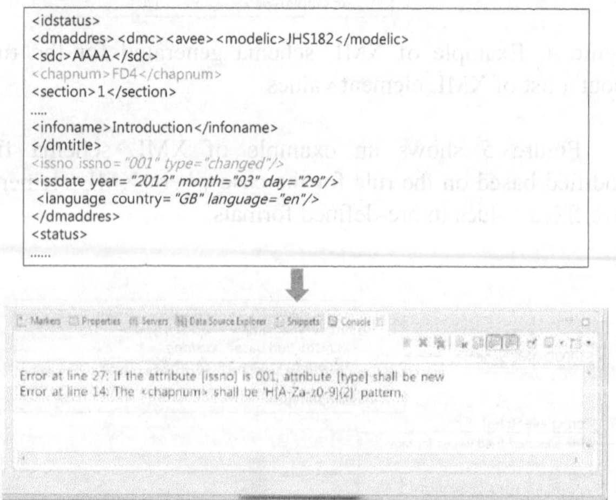

Figure 7. Example of Shipdex data module validation result

Figure 7 is a screen output that shows part of a Shipdex data module example that includes an error and the result of validating the data module using the proposed scheme.

5 Conclusions

In this paper, a scheme is proposed, in which the format of configuration file is defined to express Shipdex rules which are different from S1000D, Shipdex validation rules are automatically generated based on the configuration file, and Shipdex data modules can be validated through the user-defined Shipdex rules. This scheme supports the users to easily apply any changes in Shipdex rules and/or S1000D standards to validation of Shipdex data modules. It is needed in the future to devise a method for the user to easily generate configuration files, to implement this method, and to verify its effect as a CASE tool.

6 Acknowledgement

This work was supported by the IT R&D program of MKE/KEIT.[KI10038619, Development of Solution for Ship Safety Navigation based Maritime Ad-hoc Network].

7 References

[1] ATA, ASD, AIA, "S1000D: International Specification for Technical Publications Utilizing A Common Source Database", Issue 2.3, Air Transport Association, AeroSpace and Defence Industries Association of Europe, AeroSpace Industries Association[S], 2007.

[2] Shipdex Organization, http://www.shipdex.com

[3]W3C, "XML Tutorial", http://www.w3schools.com/xml/default.asp

[4] PTC, Arbotext CSDB for S1000D, Available: http://www.ptc.com/product/arbortext/csdb-for-s1000d/[retrieved: Apr., 2013]

[5] CORENA, CORENA S1000D solutions, Available:http://www.corena.com/what_we_offer/products/corena_s1000d/ [retrieved: Apr., 2013]

[6] Web-x, UltraCSDB S1000D suite, Available:http://www.webxsystems.com/. [retrieved: Apr., 2013]

[7] SpecTec, "How to implement and use Shipdex datasets", Sep., 2009. Available: http;//www.thedigitalship.com/. [retrieved: Apr., 2013]

[8] W3C, "XML Schema 1.1", Available: http://www.w3.org/XML/Schema/. [retrieved: Apr., 2013]

Experimental Evaluation of Static Source Code Analysis tools

Khalid Alemerien
Department of Computer Science
North Dakota State University
Fargo, ND, USA
Khalid.alemerien@my.ndsu.edu

Kenneth Magel
Department of Computer Science
North Dakota State University
Fargo, ND, USA
Kenneth.Magel@my.ndsu.edu

Abstract - **Code analysis is a substantial process to understand the source code. This needs effective, reliable, and accurate code analysis tools, but these tools may mislead the software developers because they might provide inaccurate measures. Therefore, there is a need to investigate empirically the features of these tools. This paper highlights the serious need to improve understanding of source code to support the development of reliable software in addition to achieve better understanding of how code analysis tools work. For this purpose, this paper presents an experiment, which is comparing between two static code metrics analysis tools. This paper provides significant evidence about the inconsistent values of metrics that are calculated by two code analysis tools for a given program. In addition, our paper shows how the tools are significantly different in terms of speed. Then, this paper discusses numerous of issues and causes of this difference such as unclear definition of code metrics.**

Keywords: static source code analysis, software metrics, code analysis tools, reliability, Measurement.

I. INTRODUCTION

The levels of quality, testability, and maintainability of software programs can be improved and measured through utilization of code analysis tools throughout the software development process. In the software development process [1][2][3], code metrics provide appropriate quantitative information about various aspects of software. Therefore, this information supports decision-making in different situations e.g. we can estimate how many test cases we need to cover each piece of code or whether a particular method is complex or not. In both situations, we need to measure the complexity of each method to determine if we need to divide that method to simple methods … and so forth. Therefore, the code analysis tools help to collect metrics from source code or during program runtime.

Basically, there are two kinds of code analysis: Static analysis and dynamic analysis [4]. On one hand, the static code analysis calculates the metrics based on source code without execution, such as the number of lines of code, number of classes, cyclomatic complexity, and so forth, but on the other hand, the dynamic code analysis calculates the metrics during the run-time of the program such as code coverage metrics. In this experiment, we focus on the static code analysis for Java and C++ programming languages.

Moreover, a variety of static analysis approaches have been incorporated into open source and commercial tools. Nowadays, there are many static code analysis tools, which are available as open source, freeware, and commercial such as *Understand* (commercial) [5] and *SourceMonitor* (freeware) [6]. This pool of tools makes a challenge for developers to decide which tool is better in terms of efficiency, comprehensibility, consistency, and accuracy. Since inadequate data have been published on the actual performance of these tools, there is no certainty that the output of the analysis process, using these tools, is accurate and precise. This leads us to ask the following question: To which degree code analysis tools are reliable to use during the software development process?

Mainly, these tools are widely used to improve overall the quality of decision making, but these decisions might be made based on unreliable or inaccurate data that are provided by code analysis tools. For that reason, there is a need to find evidence or proof to determine whether these tools are reliable or not, as well as explain why this difference exists.

In order to answer these inquiries and illustrate why there are differences between code analysis tools, we designed and performed a controlled experiment examining whether the metrics values collected by code metrics analysis tools are consistent, reliable, and accurate for Java and C++ programs or not. Moreover, we examine the efficiency of code analysis tools in terms of completion time needed to perform the code analysis process. In our experiment, we used *Understand* and *SourceMonitor* tools to analyze six object programs with two versions for each one.

Our findings show that software developers must be very careful when choosing any tool to help them comprehend the source code through understanding of how these tools calculate the metrics and grasp the metric definitions accurately. Moreover, our study assists developers with gaining insight into the static source code analysis tools through detailed quantitative evaluation. To our knowledge, we can say that this paper is the first to discuss this issue, which provides very important information to prove there is a difference between the results of these tools.

The rest of this paper is organized as the following. Section 2 presents related work. Section 3 describes the code metrics analysis tools. Section 4 presents our experiment design and results. Section 5 shows our results, and Section 6 presents conclusions.

II. RELATED WORK

Static code analysis is analysis of the source code, which is performed without actual code execution. Manually, it is a hard and time-consuming process to analyze the source code. Thus, we need automatic approaches to make the static analysis easier and less costly. In addition, the static analysis could be used during the software development process to improve the quality of code. Basically, a number of research studies have attempted to investigate the benefits, features, and performance of code analysis tools. Gomez et al. [4] evaluated the features of five static analysis tools in terms of buffer overflow. This study found that it is important to present the results in understandable manner as well as to provide data about the rules set that the tool enforces. Moreover, Zitser et al. [7, 8] evaluated five static analysis tools, presenting how to effectively detect buffer overflow in C programs. It is important to note that the Hoper's evaluation [9] focused on security aspects for 30 static analysis tools. Moreover, Emanuelsson and Nilsson [10] surveyed research articles, tools' manuals, and defect reports in order to identify the functionality provided by these tools. Furthermore, Ernst [11] compared, theoretically, static and dynamic techniques and he observed that there is a need for hybrid technique which incorporates the dynamic and static techniques in single tool.

There are research studies that evaluated the static analysis tools, but unfortunately they do not study the consistency and accuracy of results of the static analysis tools for specific object programs. To this end, we conducted a controlled experiment to evaluate the consistency and accuracy of metrics results of different static analysis tools for the same object programs. Therefore, the principle goal of our experiment is to apply different static code analysis tools to a set of open source programs. And then, we analyzed statistically the results, with focusing on our findings that provide software developers evidence whether the static analysis tools are accurate and consistent or not.

III. DESCRIPTION OF CODE ANALYSIS TOOLS

In order to be able to use the static analysis tools in effective way, we basically performed a comprehensive analysis of static analysis tools. Therefore, among various static code analysis tools [12], we have selected two tools to perform the static code analysis. These tools are *Understand* and *SourceMonitor*. Briefly, the main reasons behind choosing these tools are:

- These tools are used for analyzing the source code for both C++ and Java programming languages.
- These tools, basically, follow the same steps for performing the code analysis process.
- These tools are stand-alone applications, which mean you do not need the programming environment to make the code analysis process.
- *Understand* tool is a commercial tool and *SourceMonitor* is a freeware tool, which represents different development environments commercial and freeware.
- These tools can be used for analyzing different sizes of code.

A. Understand Tool

We have used *Understand* version 3.1. It is a commercial code analysis tool. It has many features such as: First, it is a cross-platform, which is used for different operating systems. Second, it supports 17 programming languages in different versions and or compilers. Third, it measures more than 50 metrics for statement, function/method, class, file, and project level. Fourth, it provides over 20 different graphs. Fifth, it shows the dependencies of code pieces. Finally, it generates a variety of output reports.

B. SourceMonitor Tool

We have used *SourceMonitor* version 3.3. It a freeware application, which is used to measure code metrics in terms of the number of lines of code, number of files, number of classes, number of functions, and methods. In addition, it helps to identify the relative complexity of methods/functions based on Cyclomatic Complexity (CC) and modified version of CC. Moreover, it measures the code metrics for source code written in Java, C, C++, C#, VB.NET, and others.

IV. THE EXPERIMENT

We wish to address the following research questions:

RQ1: Is the *SourceMonitor* tool more efficient than *Understand* tool in terms of completion time of the code analysis process.

RQ2: Are the values of metrics measured by *Understand* tool inconsistent with the values of metrics measured by *SourceMonitor* tool for a given program.

In order to address our research questions, we designed a controlled experiment. The following subtitles present, our object programs, independent variables, dependent variables and measures, experiment design, threats to validity, and data and analysis.

A. Object Programs

In our experiment, we used two programming languages, Java and C++ to investigate the features of code analysis tools such as pointing out the impact of programming language on the effectiveness of code analysis tools. We conducted our experiment on a variety of object programs in order to make our findings as generally representative as possible. The following existing software projects were used in our experiment. The C++ programs are 3Depict, CppCMS, and Thunderbird while the Java programs are Jtopas, Apatche_Ivy, and ApatcheMeter. We have chosen these to represent diversity of development contexts, programming languages, and code source size.

Apache_Ivy – is a popular dependency manager as well as it is a sub-project of the Apache Ant Project [13].

ApacheJmeter – is an open source software, which is developed to load functional tests behavior and measure the performance of static and dynamic resources [14].

Jtopas – is a Java library, which is used for the common problems of parsing text data [15].

Thnuderbird – is a free open source email and news client application developed by the Mozilla Foundation [16].

CppCMS – is an open source web application framework for the C++ programming language. It is used for Rapid Web Application Development [17].

3Depict – is an open source software for analysis of scientific datasets as well as a visualization application [18].

Table 1 shows, for each object program, a "Version" (the version numbers), "Programming Language" which is used for developing the program, "Size" (Number of Classes).

Basically, we classified our objects based on the number classes into three categories Large (>=1001 classes), Medium (501-1000 classes), and Small (<=500 classes).

B. Variables and Measures

1. Independent Variables

Our experiment manipulated one independent variable: A code metric tool. We used two code analysis tools, *Understand* (Commercial) and *SourceMonitor* (Freeware) tools, which represent two different software development environments.

2. Dependent Variables and measures

- *Completion time of the code analysis process*

To investigate our research questions we need to measure the efficiency of code analysis tools in terms of speed. Therefore, we use a metric, time of completion for the code analysis process for a given program.

- *Variance in Metrics values*

For each version of program, we collected the following metrics using both *Understand* and *SourceMonitor* tools: First, the number of lines of code, number of statements, number of functions (for C++), and number of methods (for Java), Second, percentage of comments to lines of code, Third, the maximum complexity and maximum depth of inheritance for overall functions/methods, Finally, the average complexity of functions for C++ or methods for Java.

C. Experiment Design

There were two types of data to be collected among this experiment: Time of completion the code analysis process and code metrics. Therefore, we obtained completion time of the code analysis process by running six object programs with two different versions for each program on both static analysis tools, *Understand* and *SourceMonitor*. Thus, we ran each version of program two times, one with *Understand* and another with *SourceMonitor*. For each version of program, we collected the following metrics using both *Understand* and *SourceMonitor* tools: First, the number of lines of code, number of statements, and number of functions (for C++)and methods (for Java), Second, percentage of comments to lines of code, Third, the maximum

TABLE 1
LIST OF OBJECT PROGRAMS USED IN THE EXPERIMENT

Subjects	Version	Programming Language	Size
Jtopas	7.0	Java	Small (~ 90)
	8.0		
Apache_Ivy	2.0.0	Java	Medium (~ 642)
	2.3.0		
ApacheJmeter	2.8	Java	Large (~ 1270)
	2.9		
3Depict	0.0.11	C++	Small (~ 113)
	0.0.12		
CppCMS	1.0.2	C++	Medium (~ 953)
	1.0.3		
Thunderbird	2.0.0.4	C++	Large (~ 5920)
	2.0.0.6		

complexity and maximum depth of inheritance for overall functions/methods, and finally, the average complexity of functions/methods. These metrics help us to investigate the impact of programming language, size of program, and the code analysis tools on the consistency of the output of code analysis tools.

The following steps demonstrate the overview of our experimental procedure:

1 – Run the code analysis tool
2 – Upload the object program.
3- Configure the tool settings for the object program.
4 – Choose the metrics that we need to measure.
5 - Repeat the steps 1-4 for all versions.

After the completion these steps that we described above, we obtained 24 log files which contains both completion time of the analysis process and the values of static metrics from both *Understand* and *SourceMonitor* tools for all program versions.

D. Threats to Validity

1. Internal Validity

First, the findings that we have obtained about the efficiency of code metrics analysis tools could be affected by potential faults in completion time calculations in our experiment tools. We addressed this threat by executing the tools on various sizes of C++ and Java programs. Second, the conclusions about the consistency of the values of code metric could be affected by unclear definition of each metric that was collected by analysis tools. To control this threat we reviewed carefully the definitions provided by the developers of tools for metrics and, moreover, we specified only the metrics which have the same definition in both analysis tools.

2. External Validity

The conclusions about the efficiency of code metrics analysis tools could be effected by this factor: Time calculation by the tools might be affected by execution of other system processes on the same machine that we used in our experiment. To address this threat we executed the analysis process more than one time in addition to we recorded the time manually.

E. Data Analysis

At the first, our hypothesis associated with RQ1 is: (H1) *the SourceMonitor analysis tool is faster than Understand analysis tool.* Also, the hypothesis associated with RQ2 is: (H2) *the code metrics that are measured by both Understand and SourceMonitor tools are different.*

We used ANOVA test to calculate the significance *p*. We used the R, it is a programming language, to perform statistical analysis and we used the BoxPlotter [19], it is an online tool, for drawing the Boxplots.

This section presents the collected data for all programs. We used Boxplots to show the results of the eight code metrics. Each boxplot contains two boxes showing the distribution of measurement scores for each of the two tools, across each of the versions of the object programs. The above box represents the scores of *Understand* tool while the lower box represents the scores of *SourceMonitor* tool.

So, we used the completion time of the code analysis process to accept/reject our hypotheses associated with RQ1 as well as we used the rest of metrics to accept/reject our hypothesis associated with RQ2. For each metric, this paper provides a Boxplot, which shows an overview of the collected data. Therefore, we present our research questions with their analysis granularity as the following.

1. RQ1: Efficiency of Code Analysis Tools

Our first research question assumes that the *SourceMonitor* tool is more efficient than *Understand* tool. For evaluating the efficiency of code analysis tools, we used the speed of tools in terms completion time as a measure of tool's efficiency. To test this hypothesis, we performed ANOVA test (df=1) for each tool per program, at a significance level (<0.001). Our findings show a significant difference between the tools with (p=0.0004547). Therefore, our hypothesis (*H1*) is supported. Fig. 1 shows the difference between the mediums of completion time of the two tools. To sum up, the *SourceMonitor* is more efficient than the *Understand*, as we previously assumed.

2. RQ2: Output Consistency of Code Analysis Tools

Our second research question assumes that there are differences between the values of metrics that are measured by *SourceMonitor* and *Understand*. For evaluating the

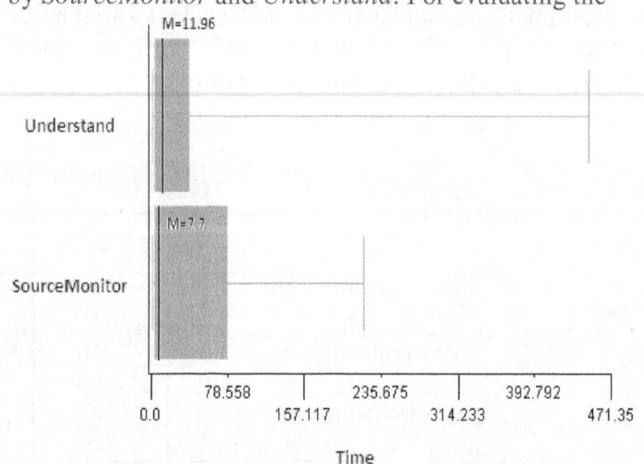

Fig.1. Completion Time of the Code Analysis Process in Seconds

consistency of values of the code metrics, we used seven metrics as the measures of output tools' consistency. To test this hypothesis, we performed ANOVA test (df=1) for each tool per program, at a significance level (<0.001). Our results are shown in the following subsections:

Number of lines

It is a code metric, which is used as a measure of program size. Boxplot in Fig. 2 shows the difference between the mediums of the two tools in terms of the number of lines for all programs. Statistically, from the ANOVA test, there is a significant difference between two tools with (p=2.2e-16). Therefore, our hypothesis (*H2*) is supported in terms of number of lines. To sum up, the results for each *SourceMonitor* and *Understand* are significantly different in terms of number of lines, as we previously assumed.

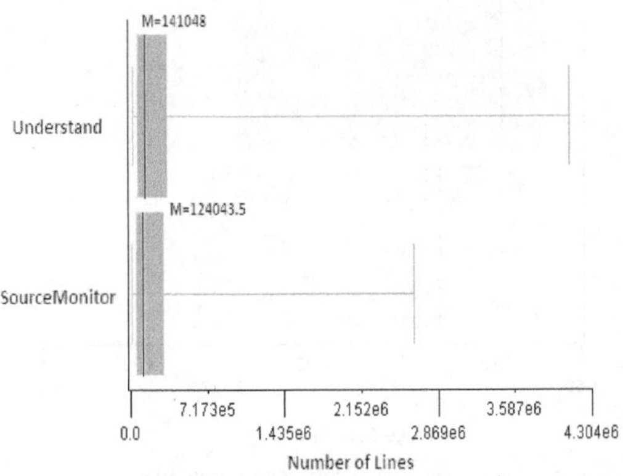

Fig. 2. Total number of lines for all programs

Number of statements

It is a code metric, which is used as a measure of program size as well. Boxplot in Fig. 3 shows the difference between the mediums of the two tools in terms of the number of statements for all programs. Statistically, from the ANOVA test, there is a significant difference between two tools with (p=1.2e-16). So, our hypothesis (*H2*) is supported in terms of number of statements. To sum up, the results for each *SourceMonitor* and *Understand* are different in terms of number of statements, as we previously assumed.

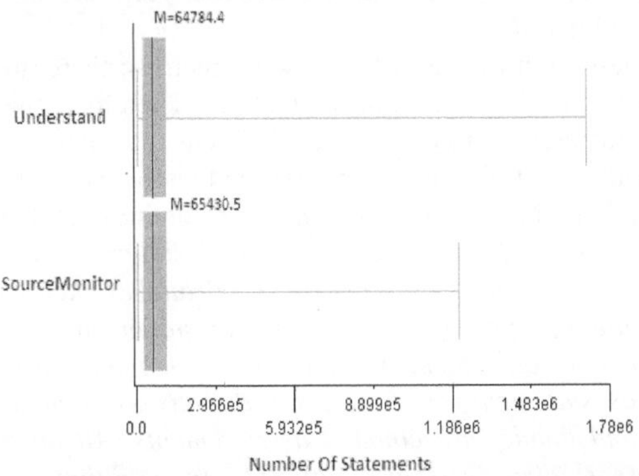

Fig. 3. Total number of statements for all programs

Number of functions (for C++) and methods (for Java)

It is a code metric, which is used as a measure of program size as well. Boxplot in Fig. 4 shows the difference between the mediums of the two tools in terms of the number of functions for all programs. Statistically, from the ANOVA test, there is a significant difference between two tools with (p=0.009386) at significant level (<0.01). Therefore, our hypothesis (*H2*) is supported in terms of number of functions. To sum up, the results for each *SourceMonitor* and *Understand* are significantly different in terms of number of functions, as we previously assumed.

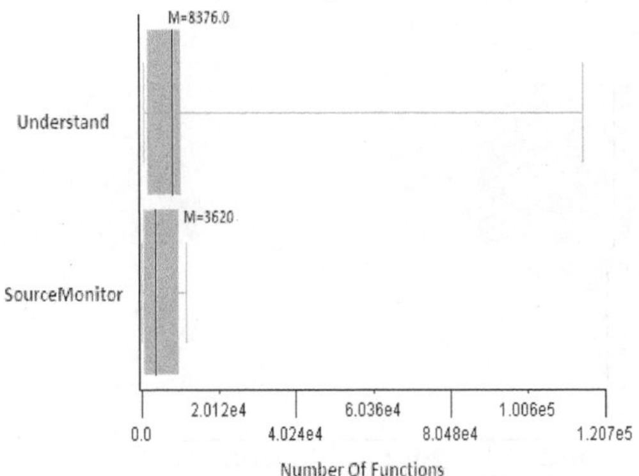

Fig. 4. Total number of functions for all programs

Percentage of comments to lines of code

It is a code metric, which is used as a measure of program size and readability as well. Boxplot in Fig. 5 shows the difference between the mediums of the two tools in terms of the percentage of comments to lines of code for all programs. Statistically, from the ANOVA test, there is a significant difference between two tools with (p=8.066e-07). Therefore, our hypothesis (*H2*) is supported in terms of percentage of comments to lines code. To sum up, the results for each *SourceMonitor* and *Understand* are significantly different in terms of percentage of comments to lines of code, as we previously assumed.

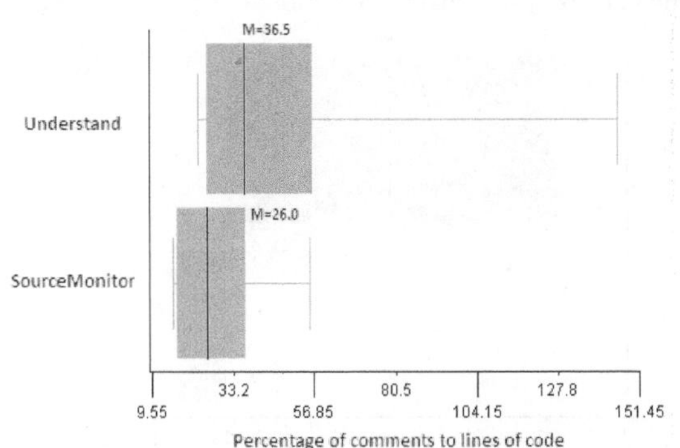

Fig. 5. Percentage of comments to lines of code for all programs

Maximum complexity

It is a code metric, which is used as a measure of the complexity of program. Boxplot in Fig. 6 shows the difference between the mediums of the two tools in terms of the maximum complexity for all programs. Statistically, from the ANOVA test, there is a significant difference between two tools with (p=4.92e-07). Therefore, our hypothesis (*H2*) is supported in terms of maximum complexity. To sum up, the results for each *SourceMonitor* and *Understand* are significantly different in terms of maximum complexity, as we previously assumed.

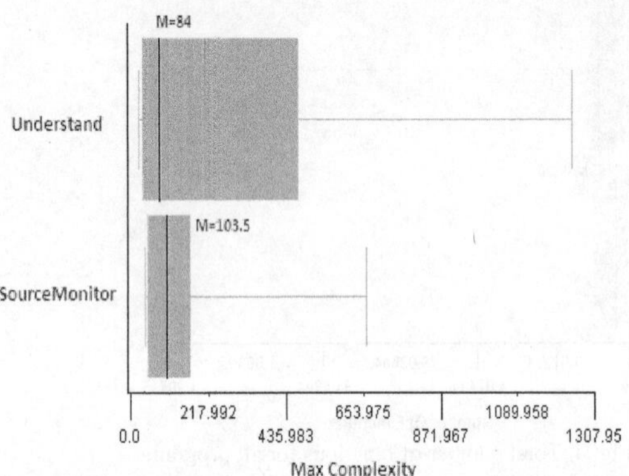

Fig. 6. The maximum complexity of functions/methods for all programs

Maximum depth of inheritance for overall functions/methods

It is a code metric, which is used as a measure of program complexity as well. Boxplot in Fig. 7 shows the difference between the mediums of the two tools in terms of the maximum depth of inheritance for each function or method cross programs. Statistically, from the ANOVA test, there is a significant difference between two tools with (p=0.0003803). Therefore, our hypothesis (*H2*) is supported in terms of maximum depth of inheritance. To sum up, the results for each *SourceMonitor* and *Understand* are significantly different in terms of maximum depth of inheritance, as we previously assumed.

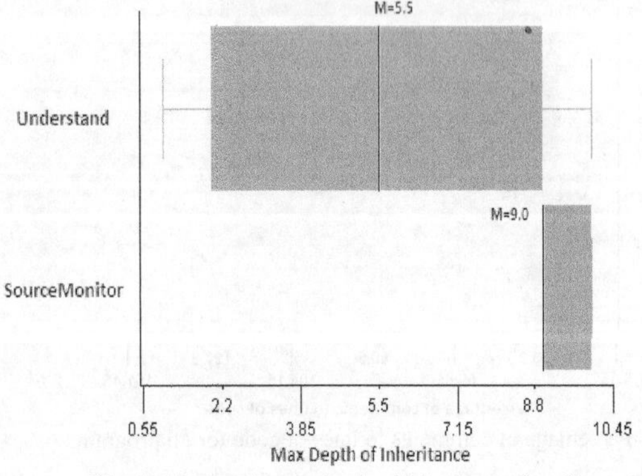

Fig. 7. The maximum depth of inheritance for all programs

Average complexity of functions/methods

It is a code metric, which is used as a measure the complexity of program as well. Boxplot in Fig. 8 shows the difference between the mediums of the two tools in terms of the average complexity of functions/methods for all programs. Statistically, from the ANOVA test, there is a significant difference between two tools with (p=0.000149). Therefore, our hypothesis (*H2*) is supported in terms of the average complexity of functions /methods. To sum up, the results for each *SourceMonitor* and *Understand* are significantly different in terms of the average complexity of functions/methods, as we previously assumed.

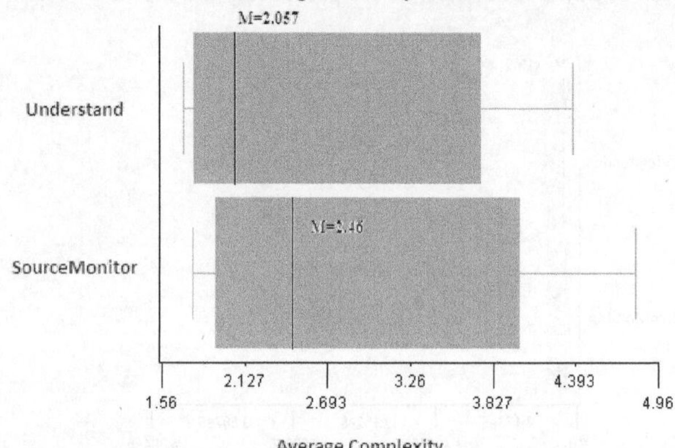

Fig. 8. The average complexity for all programs

To summarize this, all the observations for the seven code metrics in this experiment support our second hypothesis, which assumes that the values of metrics are significantly different.

V. DISCUSSION

Our results strongly support the conclusion that the values of code metric, were calculated by the code analysis tools, are different. This means some or all these values might be calculated in wrong way. Moreover, we attempt to demonstrate causes of these differences between the two tools as the following:

- Unclear definition of metrics: For some metrics, there are trivial differences in definition of metrics. Therefore, this kind of difference might cause different calculations, which leads the difference of metrics values between the two tools. For example, *SourceMonitor* [6] defines number of statements as "*In C++, computational statements are terminated with a semicolon character. Branches such as if, for, while and goto are also counted as statements. The exception control statements try and catch are also counted as statements. Preprocessor directives #include, #define, and #undef are counted as statements. All other preprocessor directives are ignored. In addition all statements between each #else or #elif statement and its closing #endif statement are ignored, to eliminate fractured block structures.*" By contrast, *Understand* [5] defines number of statements as "*Number of declarative plus executable statements.*"

- Errors in calculation of metrics: It might be exist in any of them. Consequently, we may not be able to say that, but we expect that. For example, the value of maximum depth of inheritance metric that was calculated by SourceMonitor is 9+ for all Java and C++ programs. By contrast, the values of maximum depth of inheritance metric using Understand are varying for object programs (1, 2, 5, 6, 9, and 10).
- Programming language: We noticed that the metrics were calculated for Java programs; have slight differences comparing with metrics of C++ programs for both tools. For example, the number of functions is significant different using both tools for any given C++ program in our experiment. By contrast, the number of functions is slight different using both tools for any given Java program in our experiment
- Structure organization of program: The analysis process may depend on how much the object program structurally organized.
- Different preprocessing steps: These steps might be varying from tool to another. For that, it might effect on the effectiveness of tool as well as the calculations.

Moreover, the *SourceMonitor* tool is more efficient than *Understand* tool.

Consequently, this difference among the results makes the code analysis tools unreliable enough. Therefore, the decision making under uncertainty, it needs more investigation about which tool is better. Moreover, decision makers have to specify the circumstances needed to choose the accurate tool.

VI. CONCLUSIONS

We have presented our study of two code analysis tools, which were used to analyze the source code of six programs in both C++ and Java programming languages. Furthermore, we used two versions per program. We found that there is a strong significant difference among the values of code metrics between two tools. Also we found that the *SourceMonitor* tool is more efficient than the *Understand* tool. Through the results are reported in this paper, we hope to provide valuable findings for practitioners, especially the developers of code analysis tools as well as the software developers in general.

For future work, we plan to conduct wider study that involves more tools and object programs. Also, we will attempt to examine the effectiveness of using various visualization techniques with code analysis tools. Furthermore, we plan to perform further studies to investigate analysis tools with different versions in order to examine the stability of these tools.

REFERENCES

[1] H.F. Li, W.K. Cheung, "An Empirical Study of Software Metrics," IEEE Transactions on Software Engineering, vol. 13, no. 6, pp. 697-708, June 1987, doi:10.1109/TSE.1987.233475

[2] H. B. Klasky, "A Study Of Software Metrics", issued by Graduate School-New Brunswick Rutgers, The State University of New Jersey, 2003.

[3] Q. Zoubi, I. Alsmadi, and B. Abul-Huda, "Study the impact of improving source code on software metrics," Computer, Information and Telecommunication Systems (CITS), 2012 International Conference on May 2012.

[4] I. Gomez, P. Morgado, T. Gomes, and R. Moreira, An overview on the Static Code Analysis approach in Software Development, Faculdade de Engenharia da Universidade do Porto, Portugal, 2009.

[5] (2013) Understand tool. [Online]. Available: http://www.scitools.com/

[6] (2013) SourceMonitor tool. [Online]. Available: http://www.campwoodsw.com/sourcemonitor.html

[7] M. Zitser, Securing Software: An Evaluation of Static Source Code Analyzers, Master's Thesis, Massachusetts Institute of Technology, Cambridge, MA, 130 pages, 2003.

[8] M. Zitser, R. Lippmann, and T. Leek, Testing static analysis tools using exploitable buffer overflows from open-source code, Proceedings of the 12th ACM SIGSOFT International Symposium on Foundations of Software Engineering, Newport Beach, CA, 97—106, 2004.

[9] T. Hofer, Evaluating Static Source Code Analysis Tools, Master's Thesis, Ecole Polytechnique Federale de Lausanne, Switzerland, 66 pages, 2010

[10] P. Emanuelsson, and N. Ulf, A Comparative Study of Industrial Static Analysis Tools (Extended Version), Linkoping University, Tech. Rep. 08-3, 2008.

[11] M. Ernst, Static and dynamic analysis: synergy and duality. MIT Lab for Computer Science, Cambridge, Workshop on Dynamic Analysis, ICSE'03 International Conference on Software Engineering Portland, Oregon 2003.

[12] (2013) List of code analysis tools. [Online]. Available: http://en.wikipedia.org/wiki/List_of_tools_for_static_code_analysis# C.2FC.2B.2B

[13] (2013) Apache_Ivy. [Online]. Available: http://ant.apache.org/i vy/

[14] (2013) Jmeter Apache. [Online]. Available: http://jmeter.apache.org/

[15] (2013) Jtopas. [Online]. Available: http://jtopas.sourceforge.net /jtopas/index.html

[16] (2013) Thunderbird. [Online]. Available: http://www.mozilla.org/en-US/thunderbird/

[17] (2013) CppCMS. [Online]. Available: http://cppcms.com/wikipp/en/page/main

[18] (2013) ThreeDepict. [Online]. Available: http://threedepict.sourceforge.net/

[19] (2013) BoxPlotter. [Online]. Available: http://illuminations.nctm.org/ActivityDetail.aspx?ID=77

An Efficient Regression Testing Technique For Test Case Prioritization

Mr.T.Prem Jacob[1], **Dr.T.Ravi**[2]
[1] CSE, Sathyabama University, Chennai, Tamil Nadu, India
[2] CSE, Srinivasa Institute of Engineering & Technology, Chennai, Tamil Nadu, India

Abstract - *Regression testing which is an expensive activity. Regression testing is used to verify the program correctness once it is modified. To ensure that the changes made to that program are correct and due to that change that has been made it should not affect the remaining portions in the program. If we execute all regression tests it will take more time to execute the excessive regression tests. Retest-all reruns all the test, consumes excess time. In regression testing selection technique selects the subset of test case from the test suite which reduces the time taken to retest the modified program .Since to make the regression testing to a cost effective manner the test cases are prioritized. We define an algorithm which provides maximum code coverage for a regression test suite.*

Keywords: Test case prioritization, regression testing, software testing, test suite reduction.

1 Introduction

Regression testing may be one way to improve the efficiency of the software development. Changes in the software happen continuously as the software product evolves overtime. Whenever the software gets some modifications testing must be done again to ensure all the features of the software are working properly [1].

As early as possible the Software developers try to detect the faults that occur in the system. We have to ensure that no bugs have been introduced in the software product due to the changes made. More time is required if all the test cases are executed from a test suite.

Researchers will be following different techniques for test suite minimization. The cost and the coverage of the code can be maintained according to some testing criteria.

By prioritizing the test cases the testing can be improved. Prioritization can also increase the fault detection rate [2]. We use code coverage prioritization techniques which treats all the faults equally.

2 Test Case Prioritization

The test cases can be prioritized in such a way that it should increase the effectiveness to meet certain performance goal. In the test process of regression testing the testers can prioritize the test case that has the highest priority which are executed earlier.

Two ways for prioritizing the test case

2.1 General

For a program P and T be the test suite. Test case in T are prioritized without having any knowledge of the modifications made to the program, so that P gets modified to the program P`[3].

2.2 Version specific

Test cases are prioritized by having the knowledge to the changes made to the program P.

Here in our work we use version specific technique. We proposed a technique here which achieves the code coverage for the modified code at a fastest rate as possible.

3 Problem Statement

Let the program be P.

Modified version of the program P be P`.

T be the test suite.

Test suite T is used for testing P.

When P gets modified to program P`we need to find T`, where test case T` is subset of T→ Which achieves the determined coverage of the code as earlier as possible and is given the highest priority in regression testing.

For this we need to identify the test that can able to execute the modified codes in the program earlier. At least once we have to execute the lines of code that gets modified as earlier as possible.

4 Regression test case selection algorithm

The regression test case selection algorithm we proposed here is version specific, we execute only the, modified lines. Our objective is to execute the modified code with minimum number of test case.

For selecting the test case used for performing regression testing we should require some knowledge on how a bug affects the system and how to fix it, the areas where frequent defects may occur like the area that undergone some code changes [4]. Due to some minor defect which can cause some major side effects.

For a sensitive defect that have been fixed which has no side effects. So the software tester has to balance all those aspects for creating an algorithm for selection of the test case for regression testing [6][7]. From the history of each test cases which tells the lines of code that are covered by the test case [15].

4.1 Algorithm

Step 1: Input to the algorithm is the number of test case.

Step 2: Store the line numbers covered by the test case and the modified lines.

Step 3: For each test case find the number of matches.

Step 4: Sort it in descending order.

Step 5: Select highest matched test case and execute.

Step 6: Repeat step 3 to 5 with modified lines of code.

Step 7: If all modified lines of code are covered STOP.

Table 1: Execution History

Test Case	Lines of code covered by the Test Case
T1	2,3,28,32,41,57,68,72
T2	1,8,28,30,48,58,67,70
T3	3,4,6,20,31,60
T4	1,2,3,7,18,31,38,42,55,67,71
T5	1,3,17,18,30,51
T6	2,4,15,31,41,59,60,76,79
T7	1,3,4,8,20,31,46
T8	1,3,7,17,20,55,61,76,78

Consider the test case T1 which covers the LOC 2, 3, 28, 32, 41, 57. The modified LOC are 2, 4, 8, 17, 31, 46, 55, 67, and 76. We need to identify the LOC modified in the test case and are executed which ensures the optimal code coverage [12].

In our problem we have six test case T1, T2, T4, T6, T7, T8 that have modified LOC. All the modified LOC has to be covered only if each test case gets executed, which is not provide the optimal solution for our problem.

In our proposed model which provide 100% coverage of code with minimum number of test case. T1 has one modified LOC which is 2. Similarly T2 test case has two modified LOC i.e. 8, 67.

Test cases T1 to T8 which are computed as in Table 1.

Table 2: Modified LOC

Test Case ID	Lines matched	Number of matches
T1	2	1
T2	8,67	2
T3	-	0
T4	2,31,55,67	4
T5	-	0
T6	2,4,31,76	4
T7	4,8,31,46	4
T8	17,55,76	3

From table 2 if there is any match found sort it by descending order .

Once sorted in descending order test case which has the maximum match are selected and executed which is shown in the table 2.

Table 3: Selected Test Case

Test Case ID	Number of matches	Matches found	Candidate
T4	4	2,31,55,67	1
T6	4	2,4,31,76	0
T7	4	4,8,31,46	0
T8	3	17,55,76	0
T2	2	8,67	0
T1	1	2	0

Set the value of the candidate be 1 for the selected test case.

Still now only T4 is selected, which covers 2,31,55,67. Lines of code [2, 4, 8, 17, 31, 46, 55, 67, 76] – [2, 31, 55, 67] = [4, 8, 17, 46, 76].

We need to implement only 4, 8, 17, 46, 76 LOC and T4 covers the LOC 2, 31, 55, 67.

Repeat the same procedure until all the modified LOC are covered.

Table 4: Select test case

Test Case ID	Number of matches	Matches found
T6	2	4,76
T7	3	4,8,46
T8	2	17,76
T2	1	8

After sorting in descending order, assign the candidate value as 1 for the selected test case as in table below.

Table 5: Rearrange and assign candidate value

Test Case ID	Number of matches	Matches found	Candidate
T7	3	4,8,46	1
T6	2	4,76	0
T8	2	17,76	0
T2	1	8	0

Since T7 covers these lines of code we need to implement only 17, 76.

i.e., [4, 8, 17, 46, 76] – [4, 8, 46] = [17, 76]

Table 6: Select Test Case and assign candidate value

Test Case ID	Number of matches	Matches found	Candidate
T6	1	76	1
T8	2	17,76	0

Since T6 covers these lines of code we need to implement only 17.

i.e., [17, 76] - [76] = [17]

Table 7: Assign candidate value

Test Case ID	Number of matches	Matches found	Candidate
T8	2	17	1

Since T8 covers these lines of code we have implemented all the lines of code.

i.e., [17] - [17] =0

5 Results and Conclusions

We have executed the test case T4, T6, T7, T8 out of six number of test case that have the modified lines of code. Simply if we run all the six test case which does not provides the optimal solution. So from our proposed model we have proved that by running only four test case we achieve maximum code coverage.

Hence we have achieved 60% saving of test cases by the proposed prioritization method. Since the cost for implementing this algorithm is less it will save the effort and cost to run the test cases.

6 References

[1] Adam M. Smith and Gregory M. Kapfhammer. "An empirical study of incorporating cost into test suite reduction and prioritization". In Proceedings of the 24th Symposium on Applied Computing, 2009.

[2] GregoryM. Kapfhammer. "A Comprehensive Framework for Testing Database-Centric Applications". PhD thesis, University of Pittsburgh, Pittsburgh, Pennsylvania, 2007.

[3] Hao Zhong, Lu Zhang, and Hong Mei. "An experimental study of four typical test suite reduction techniques". Information and Software Technology, 50(6), 2008.

[4] Sreedevi Sampath, Renee C. Bryce, Gokulanand Viswanath, Vani Kandimalla, and A. Gunes Koru. "Prioritizing user-session-based test cases for web applications testing". In Proceedings of the 2nd International Conference on Software Testing, Verification, and Validation, 2008.

[5] Boris Beizer , "Software Testing Techniques",2nd edition, Dreamtech publisher, New Delhi.

[6] Antoniol, G., Penta, M.D., and Harman, M., "Search-Based Techniques Applied to Optimization of Project Planning for a Massive Maintenance Project", Proc. 21st IEEE Int'l Conf. Software Maintenance ,2000.

[7] Deb, K., Agrawal, S., Pratab, A., and Meyarivan, T. , "A Fast Elitist Non-Dominated Sorting Genetic Algorithm for Multi-Objective Optimization: NSGA-II", Proceedings of the Parallel Problem Solving from Nature VI Conference,2000.

[8] Elbaum, S., Rothermel, G., Kanduri, S., and Malishevsky, A., "Selecting a Cost-Effective Test Case Prioritization Technique", Software Quality Control, vol. 12, no. 3, pp. 185-210,2004.

[9] Glover, F., and Kochenberger, G., "Handbook of Metaheuristics", Springer, 1st edition, 2003.

[10] Harman, M. (2007), "The Current State and Future of Search Based Software Engineering", International Conference on Software Engineering - Future of Software Engineering.

[11] Scott McMaster and Atif Memon. "Call stack coverage for GUI test-suite reduction". In Proceedings of the 17th International Symposium on Software Reliability Engineering, 2006.

[12] Zheng Li, Mark Harman, and Robert M. Hierons. "Search algorithms for regression test case prioritization". IEEE Transactions on Software Engineering, 33(4), 2007.

[13] Sebastian Elbaum, Alexey G. Malishevsky, and Gregg Rothermel. "Test case prioritization: A family of empirical studies". IEEE Transactions on Software Engineering, 28(2), 2002.

[14] David S. Rosenblum and Elaine J. Weyuker. "Using coverage information to predict the costeffectiveness of regression testing strategies". IEEE Transactions on Software Engineering, 23(3),1997.

[15] Kristen R. Walcott, Mary Lou Soffa, Gregory M. Kapfhammer, and Robert S. Roos. "Time-aware test suite prioritization". In Proceedings of the International Symposium on Software Testing and Analysis, 2006.

[16] Christian Murphy, Kuang Shen, and Gail Kaiser. "Automatic system testing of programs without test oracles". In Proceedings of the International Symposium on Software Testing and Analysis, 2009.

[17] JeffreyM. Voas. "PIE: a dynamic failure-based technique". IEEE Transactions on Software Engineering, 18(8):717–735, 1992.

[18] Monica Hutchins, Herb Foster, Tarak Goradia, and Thomas Ostrand. "Experiments on the effectiveness of dataflow- and controlflow-based test adequacy criteria". In Proceedings of the 16th International Conference on Software Engineering, 1994.

Security Requirements Engineering: Analysis and Prioritization

A. Daya Gupta[1], B. Shruti Jaiswal[2], and C. Anupriya Tewari[3]
[1,2,3]Computer Engineering Department, Delhi Technological University, Delhi, India

Abstract - *with the increase in the use of software system, security requirement engineering becomes an emergent area of study. Security requirements are constraints to a system which must be satisfied for consistent system. Most of the software engineering processes deals with security constraints during the design or implementation phases which may result into unnecessary constrained system. So the need for a new process arises which deals with security issues in requirement engineering phase and then take appropriate design decisions so that security mechanism used are optimal to some extent resulting in efficient secure system. Therefore the requirement engineers must discover security requirement along with functional and non functional requirement, so that security requirement can be dealt effectively. In this paper, we present a method for security requirement analysis and prioritization along with the other activities of security requirement engineering. Analysis is based on the technique of ontology that will automate the process and prioritization is based on risk analysis. The resultant system will be a cost effective in nature as well as it lay a foundation for further activities so that designer will adopt the most efficient technique for the implementation of security requirements.*

Keywords: Security Engineering, Security Requirements Analysis, Security Requirements Prioritization, Ontology, Risk Analysis

1 Introduction

Security engineering is a field of engineering which focuses on the security aspect of a system here we are talking about software systems. The security goals are traditionally classified into confidentiality, integrity and availability of information in an organization [24]. In early approaches, the security measures are taken during design phase, which could result in unseen constraints which can affect the cost and availability of the system and sometime failure of system. In response to this Software engineering community has proposed different methodology to elicit security requirements and then enforce measures to meet these requirements. Some of the proposals for eliciting security requirements are abuse case [4], misuse case [1, 2, 10, 11], common criteria [3, 14] and attack trees [5]. Also, methodologies like secure tropos extension of tropos methodology [19], intentional anti model extension of KAOS methodology with security requirement oriented construct [22] are also discussed. Also, there are proposals for security engineering which takes the risk and threats into consideration and then apply measures to enforce security on threats like OCTAVE [17], CORAS [16], and CRAMM [18]. Firesmith [6, 7] has given proposal to classify security requirements and identify them to mitigate threats that causes risk for a system. Methods like EBIOS [20], MEHARI [21], etc. are proposed for risk assessment and management.

In our previous work, we have proposed software engineering framework that integrates security engineering activities [15, 26] in SDLC. The process starts with the process of elicitation of security requirements along with functional and non functional requirements. These elicited requirements must be analyzed and prioritized so that proper design decisions can be taken [26]. This paper will focus on techniques for analysis and prioritization of security requirement. Process of analysis is based on Ontology and prioritization will be done using risk analysis.

Ontology is a formal, explicit specification of a shared conceptualization. Ontology consists of various domain specific concepts, their properties and relationships between them. Ontology is a hierarchical arrangement of knowledge related to a domain which can be used as a centralized dictionary. The domain relevant to our discussion is security. The advantage of using ontology as a tool for requirements analysis is that it allows the requirements engineers to analyze the requirements with respect to the semantics of the domain. The requirements are generally discovered and documented in natural language. Natural language statements may have different interpretations by different human engineers trying to analyze them, hence making the analysis difficult. Our approach of using ontology will overcome this problem as it helps in semantic analysis of the requirements. Our approach will also provide automation of the analysis process and will save human effort.

Risk analysis is important as it would tell what could possibly go wrong? What is the likelihood of it happening? How will it affect the project? So risk analysis is considered as an important factor. Further paper is organized as follows section 2 provides activities of security requirements engineering. Section 3 provides proposed framework for analysis and prioritization of security requirements; next section will provide a case study for illustration of proposed technique; and finally section 5 concludes the paper and provides the future scope for research.

2 Activities of Security Requirement Engineering

Security engineering framework proposed in our previous work consists of four main phase that are security requirements engineering, security design engineering, security implementation and security testing. Framework representing the overall procedure for Security Requirement Engineering is shown in Fig 1. Different activities in security requirement engineering are:

2.1 Requirements Discovery and Definition

Here our aim is to discover first the functional, non functional requirements and then security requirements which mitigates threats that affects the assets used by functional requirements. We have considered twelve types of security requirements as defined by Firesmith [6] and extended view point oriented method of Sommerville [12, 13] to define security requirements which are associated with functional requirements.

Different steps in this activity are:

- Identify various stakeholders of the system using view-point analysis [12, 13]. We have identified the various abstract classes of actors as direct and indirect actors. Direct actors are those who directly interact with the system such as human, software system and hardware devices. Indirect actors refer to Engineering personals who develop software and people who regulate application domain. For this paper our interest is in direct actor.

- Identify the functionality of each actor conceptualized in above step and also determine associated non – functional requirements, with assets on which the functional requirements are based.

- Identify the threats associated with each of the functional requirements or data which is used by the functionality. Threats are identified corresponding to functionality based on common criteria approach [3, 14] by filling the stakeholders profile which contains seven fields that define the whole function and actor relationship.

- Identify the security requirements to mitigate these threats using the threat database accessed by actor profile. For details refer [15].

2.2 Analysis and Validation of the Requirements

Analysis is not an easy task it comes with lot of problems as said by sommerville [13] due to change of requirements, stakeholder don't know what they really want, etc. If requirements will change, it will in turn affect everything. So analysis and validation needs special attention in security requirement engineering.

Analyze the identified security requirements for consistency and completeness. If any conflict occurs it must be resolved and must reach to an agreement to avoid any further conflicts.

Completeness Checking ensures inclusion of all necessary security requirements identified to protect the assets of an organization that are affected by threats. Here we check whether all the identified threats are mitigated by security requirements or not.

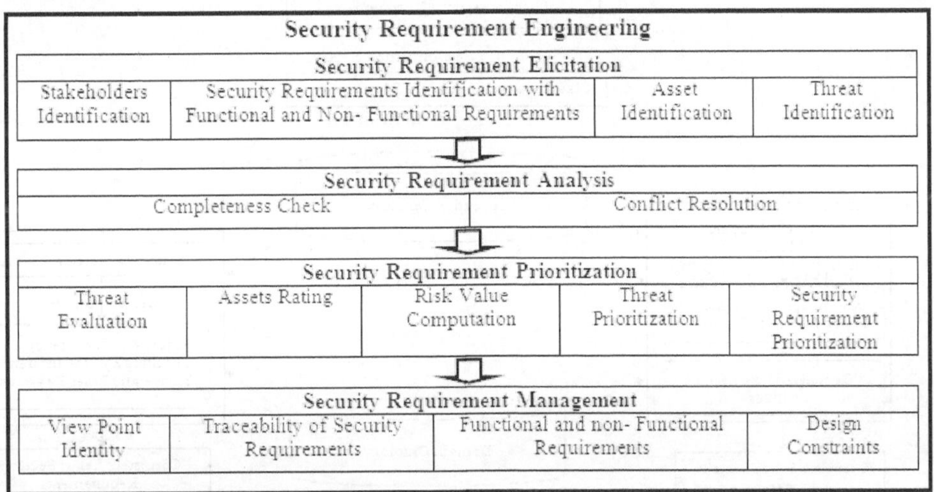

Fig 1. Framework for Security Requirements Engineering

Consistency Checking ensures that there are no contradictory security requirements. The two security requirements should not conflict. It ensures that two security requirements never conflict. Example, customer wants to authorize more number of customers to access the confidential data but want the cost incurred in providing privacy for individual and organizational data will get decreased. So, both of the requirements can't be satisfied simultaneously.

The steps involved in analysis of security requirements are discussed in the next section.

2.3 Prioritization of Security Requirements

Prioritize the security requirements so that it help the designers and other members involved in later phases to take design decisions. It tells about which security requiurement is more critical and need to be dealt first over other. The proposal devised for prioritization of security requirements is given in the next section

2.4 Management of the Requirements

Keep trace of each security requirements and its associated attributes such as requirement identity, view point identity, functional requirement, nonfunctional requirements, threats design constraint, other security requirement, design constraints. The techniques for requirement management presented in [12, 13] can be used for this activity. Details of this work will be dealt in the future.

3 Proposed Techniques for analysis and Prioritization

This section will be divided into two sub sections. The first part will cover the approach for security requirements analysis using ontology. And the next part deals with the steps involved in prioritization of security requirements using the concept of risk analysis.

3.1 Security Requirements Analysis Framework

We propose a framework for the analysis of security requirements that are discovered during security requirements elicitation. The framework is represented in Fig 2. Now various steps involved in the framework will be discussed.

Steps Involved in Analysis:

• *Creation of the Domain Ontology:* This is a major task, as it will serve as the main knowledge base for analysis. Ontology can be created using any of the various approaches available at present such as Methontology [26], OTK (On-To-Knowledge) [27], etc. Ontology will be constructed in hybrid fashion out of top down, bottom up and hybrid approaches because in the hybrid fashion, initially the ontology is constructed by a domain expert and further modifications can be made in it when needed. Protégé [30] is used for ontology development. Reason for using Protégé as a tool is that it is intuitive, easy to use, interactive, easily scalable and extensible due to plug-ins. And OWL (Web Ontology Language) is used for creation of our ontology.

• *Creation of the Application Ontology:* Application ontology will represent the elicited security requirements and their relationships. From the given set of elicited security requirements, application ontology can be created through following steps :

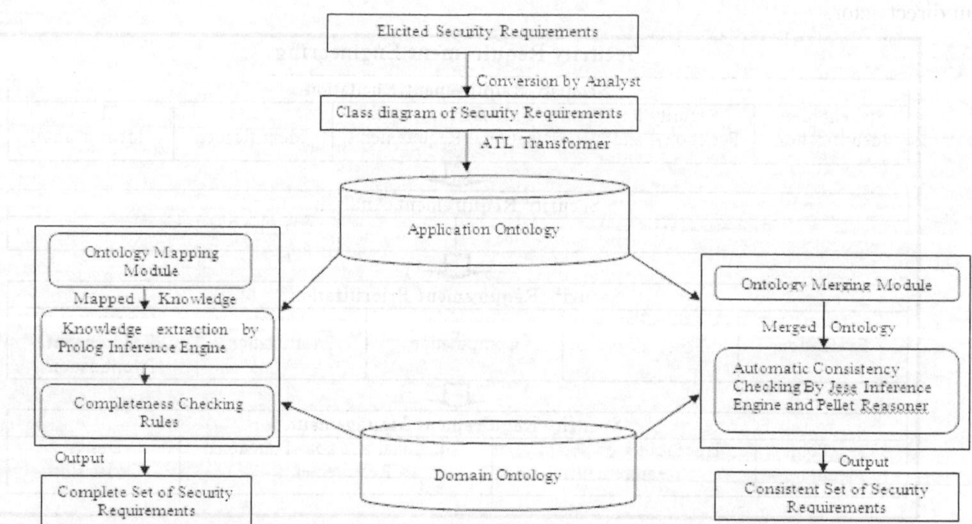

Fig 2: Ontology Based Security Requirements Analysis Freamework

i. Now classes will be converted into concepts of the ontology. As class consists of a class name, properties and relationships to other classes.

ii. Next properties of a class will become properties of corresponding concepts in ontology.

iii. The Subclass and Superclass inheritance relation will be maintained in the ontology, using Subclass and Superclass concepts.

iv. Other relations in the class diagram will be converted into properties in the ontology. For example: aggregation relation becomes PartOf property.

Various tools are available to automate the above task such as AToM3 [31], ATL [32], etc. tools can be used.

- *Mapping Application Ontology with Domain Ontology:* Ontology mapping module maps the classes and relationships in the application ontology with the corresponding classes and relationships of the domain ontology. The knowledge obtained through this mapping will serve as a knowledge base for the inference engine. The mapping process can be performed using existing ontology mapping algorithms [33]. The above tasks can be automated by tools such as OMEN [34], CROSI [35], etc.

- *Knowledge Extraction by the Inference Engine:* We can select any inference engine for querying and drawing out useful conclusions from the security requirements analysis process. In our proposal we are using the Prolog inference engine. Prolog Queries will be used to extract useful knowledge from the knowledge base. Here the knowledge base is the mapping result of the above step. For example, a Prolog query can be generated to obtain from the knowledge base, all the threats that can be mitigated by a particular security requirement.

- *Application of Completeness Checking Rules:* The following rules can be applied on the knowledge extracted by the inference engine for checking completeness of the security requirements:

i. If a concept c1 is related to concept c2 by relation R and the same concept c1 is related to concept c3 by the same relationship R in the domain ontology, then add the concept c3 to the given set of defined requirements and relate it to c1 by relation R (if it is not already in application ontology.)

ii. If c3 is already in the application ontology then just relate c3 and c1 with relation R.

iii. Repeat the above check for all the concepts of the application ontology.

For example, if we have *identification* and *privacy* as security requirements and *snooping* as threat concept in the application ontology and *snooping* is related to *authentication* in the domain ontology with relation "is mitigated by". Then *authentication* is added to our security requirements and it is related with *snooping* by "is mitigated by" relation.

- *Merging Application Ontology and Domain Ontology:* To merge the Application ontology with the Domain ontology we can use any existing ontology merging algorithm. The description of the algorithm is not given here because of the space constraints. Interested users can refer to [36].Various tools such as Chimaera [37] and PROMPT [29] are available for automated merging of ontologies.

- *Consistency Checking :* The above merging process makes consistency checking very easy for the analyst. To check consistency of the security requirements we run the merged ontology on the Protégé plateform. The recent versions of Protégé include *Jese Inference Engine* and *Pellet reasoner*[38]. The Jese Inference Engine automatically checks all the concepts for consistency and the Pellet reasoner automatically checks all the rules for consistency. The output of this step is the result phrase "consistent security requirements" or "inconsistent security requirements".

3.2 Security Requirements Prioritization Framework

As we have the list of security requirements, it's better to prioritize them. As prioritized list of security requirement would be helpful for designers and other members involved in later phases to take decisions. As it tells us about which security requirement is more critical and need to be dealt first over other.

The steps followed in security requirement prioritization are discussed in this section. Prioritization of security requirements will be done with the help of risk analysis. Risk is normally defined as the chance or likelihood of damage or loss [25, 39]. That is, it is a function of two separate components, the **likelihood** that an unwanted incident will occur and the **impact** that could result from the incident.

So risk can be calculated as :

Risk = (Probability of Occurrence of Threat * Impact of Threat Occurrence on Assets) (1)

Probability of Occurrence of Threat = Threat Rating and is represented by **TR**

Impact of Threat Occurrence on Assets = Summation of importance level of assets affected by threat, as one threat may affect more than one asset.

Represented by $\sum_{k=1}^{n} \text{IL}$ where n is the maximum number of assets affected. Hence (1) will become

$$\text{Risk} = \text{TR} * \sum_{k=1}^{n} \text{IL} \quad (2)$$

Steps involved in Security Requirement Prioritization

- Assign threat rating to each threats identified. Threat rating is the number which represent occurrence frequency of a threat in a system. The scale for threat rating is 1- 10. Assign lower value to threat whose occurrence frequency is low and higher to higher frequency threat.

- Assign assets a value in range of 1- 10, representing its importance to the organization. This importance level will show how much cost and resources are required to protect a praticular asset.

- List various assets affected by each threat.

- Calculate the risk value using (2).

- Now the threats will be prioritized based on risk value calculated in step4. Higher the risk value higher will be the priority of threat.

- Finally prioritize security requirements based on threats priority. For prioritization of security requirement following rules will be used:

  i. If the security requirement is mitigating single threat then in that case threat priority is simply assigned to security requirement and it acts as its priority.

  ii. If the security requirement is mitigating more than one threat in that case we add up all the corresponding threat priorities and assign the calculated value to the security requirement as its priority.

4 Case Study

The whole process of security requirement engineering is explained here with the help of a case study of "Railway Reservation System". It covers the full detail of the whole procedure that is from the identification of stakeholders to the final prioritization of security requirements.

- Various direct stakeholders or viewpoints involved are:
  - *i.* Traveler
  - *ii.* Railway Management
  - *iii.* Database

- List of functional and non functional requirements is listed in Table1. And, various assets involved are:
  - *i.* Traveler Information
  - *ii.* Ticket Information
  - *iii.* Credit Card/ Bank Details
  - *iv.* IT Infrastructure (Communication Channel, System Information, etc)
  - *v.* Employee and its Details

Various threats involved are identified using the concept of common criteria [3, 14]. We will be developing the repository of the threats. For extraction of threats from repository, one need to fill Actor Profiles that contains the seven fields as defined in [15]. All the threats identified are listed in Table1.

Various security requirements to mitigate threats are shown in Table 1.

Assigned asset importance level on the scale of 1- 10 are shown in Table 2.

Table 2 Asset Importance Level

ASSET	IMPORTANCE LEVEL (1- 10)
Traveller Information	7
Ticket Information	5
Credit Card	9
IT Infrastructure	4
Employee Details	6

Table 1. An Example "Railway Reservation System" Explaining our Process

Viewpoints	Services	Non Functional Requirements	Threats	Security Requirements
Traveler	1. Registration of Customer 2. Make Enquiry 3. Book Ticket 4. Cancel Ticket 5. Make Payment	1. Reliability 2. Response Time 3. Execution Time	1. Spoofing 2. Insider 3. Disclose Data 4. Privacy Violated 5. Change Data 6. Repudiate Receive	1. Authorization 2. Privacy 3. Non Repudiation
Railway Management	1. Update Data 2. Serve to Customer Request 3. Maintenance	1. Correctness 2. Response Time 3. Robustness 4. Scalable	1. Change Data 2. Privacy Violated 3. Social Engineer 4. Outsider	1. Integrity 2. Identification 3. Authentication
Database	1. Report Maintenance for Transaction	1. Reliability 2. Response Time 3. Integrity	1. Outsider 2. Impersonate	1. Security Auditing 2. Intrusion Detection

• Assigned threat rating values on the scale of 1 – 10 to various threats is given in Table 3.

Table 3 Threats with Threat Rating

THREAT	THREAT RATING (1 – 10)
Change Data	9
Repudiate Receive	5
Spoofing	5
Insider	3
Privacy Violated	7
Outsider	6
Disclose Data	4
Social Engineer	6
Impersonate	8

• Identify the assets affected by each threat. The identified assets corresponding to each threat is given in Table 4.

Table 4 Assets Affected by Threat

THREAT	ASSET THAT CAN BE AFFECTED
Change Data	Traveler Information, Ticket Information, Employee Details
Repudiate Receive	Credit Card Information
Spoofing	Credit Card Information
Insider	IT Infrastructure
Privacy Violated	Ticket Information, Credit Card Information, Traveler Information
Outsider	IT Infrastructure, Traveler Information, Employee Details
Disclose Data	Traveler Information, Ticket Information, Employee Details
Social Engineer	Traveler Information, Employee Details
Impersonate	Traveler Information, Employee Details

Once threats and assets affected are identified and valuated, risk valuation will be done and for above case study and computation of risk value is shown in Table 5.

Various security requirements to mitigate threats are already identified. Now the main part of our work comes into picture that is to prioritize these security requirements.

Table 5 Threat Priority

Threat	$TR * \sum_{k=1}^{n} IL$	Risk	Threat Priority
Change Data	$9 * \sum(7+5+6)$	162	8
Repudiate Receive	$5 * 9$	45	2
Spoofing	$5 * 9$	45	2
Insider	$3 * 4$	12	1
Privacy Violated	$7 * \sum(5+9+7)$	147	7
Outsider	$6 * \sum(4+7+6)$	102	6
Disclose Data	$4 * \sum(7+5+6)$	72	3
Social Engineer	$6 * \sum(7+6)$	78	4
Impersonate	$8 * \sum(5+6)$	88	5

Final computation of priorities is given in Table 6. As Security Requirement Authorization is mitigating three threats so for its priority we add the priority value of corresponding threats. And, in case of Privacy Security Requirement it is mitigating only one threat so whatever will be the priority value of threat it is directly assigned to security requirement.

Table 6 Priority of Security Requirements

Security Requirement	Threats Mitigated	Threat Priority	Security Requirement Priority
Authorization	Change Data Disclose Data Insider	8 3 1	12
Privacy	Privacy Violated	7	7
Non repudiation	Repudiate Receive Spoofing	2 2	4
Integrity	Social Engineer	4	4
Identification	Change Data Outsider	8 6	14
Authentication	Privacy Violated Outsider	7 6	13
Security Auditing	Impersonate	5	5
Intrusion Detection	Outsider	6	6

If in case two Security Requirements has same priority in that case designer will have to take decision which one to deal first. Throughout the computation higher number represent higher priority or higher value.

5 Conclusions and Future Work

In this paper we have presented techniques for analysis and prioritization of security requirement based on ontology and threat analysis respectively. This method is improvement over the method presented in [23], as it tries to quantify the value of risk value so that will get correct and consistent result. Further complexities in risk analysis are under processing which covers other factors then threat rating. Here analysis is done using the manual method of our previous paper [23] and will provide a detailed framework for it with proper example in our next paper. We are also developing a computer based tool to incorporate these techniques. Method block presented in [9] will be extended to incorporate the security characteristics also the CAME tool MERU [8] will be initiated in the construction of method which includes the security engineering.

6 References

[1] Alexander IF, "Modelling the interplay of conflicting goals with use and misuse cases". In: Proceedings of the 8th international workshop on requirements engineering: foundation for software quality (REFSQ'02), Essen, Germany, 2002.

[2] Alexander IF, "Misuse cases, use cases with hostile intent". IEEE Software, 2003, pp. 58–66

[3] Common criteria for information technology security evaluation. Technical report CCIMB 99–031, Common Criteria Implementation Board, 1999.

[4] John Mc Dermott, Chris Fox, "Using abuse case models for security requirements analysis." Department of Computer Science, James Madison University, 1999.

[5] Robert J. Ellison, "Attack Trees", Software Engineering Institute, Carnegie Mellon University, 2005.

[6] Donald G. Firesmith, "Engineering Security Requirements", Journal of object technology, 2003, vol 2, no.1, pp.53-68.

[7] Donald G. Firesmith, "Security Use cases", Journal of object technology, 2003, vol 2, no.3, pp.53-64.

[8] Gupta D. and Prakash N., "Engineering Methods from their Requirements Specification", Requirements Engineering Journal 2006, 3, pp.133 – 160.

[9] Prakash N., "On generic Method Models", Requirements Engineering Journal 2006, pp. 221 – 237.

[10] Sindre G, Opdahl AL, "Eliciting security requirements by misuse cases". In proceeding 37th Conference Techniques of Object-Oriented Languages and Systems, TOOLS Pacific 2000, pp 120-131.

[11] Sindre G, Opdahl AL, "Eliciting security requirements with misuse cases". Requirements Engineering 10, Springer-Verlag London Ltd, January 2005, pp. 34-44.

[12] Kotonya G., Sommerville I., "Requirement Engineering with viewpoints", 1995.

[13] Sommerville, I., "Software Engineering". Seventh edition 2003. ISBN - 8129708671. Pearson Education.

[14] M. Ware, J. Bowles, C. Eastman, "Using the common criteria to Elicit security Requirements with use cases", IEEE Computer Society, 2006.

[15] Agarwal A, Gupta D, "Security Requirement Elicitation Using View Points for online System", IEEE Computer Society, 2008.

[16] CORAS - http://www2.nr.no/coras.

[17] Alberts, Christopher and Dorofee, Audrey. *OCTAVE* Method Implementation Guide v2.0. Pittsburgh, PA: Software Engineering Institute, Carnegie Mellon University, 2001. http://www.cert.org/octave.

[18] The Logic behind CRAMM's Assessment of Measures of Risk and Determination of Appropriate Countermeasures available at www.cramm.com

[19] a) Paolo Giorgini, G.Manson, Haralambos Mouratidis. I.Philip, "A Natural Extension of Tropos Methodology for Modelling Security". In the workshop on Agent-oriented methodologies, at OOPSLA 2002.

b) Paolo Giorgini, G.Manson, Haralambos Mouratidis. I.Philip, "Modelling Secure Multi agent System". AAMAS - 2003.

[20] EBIOS- Expression of need and identification of security objectives, DCSSI, France, February, 2004.

[21] MEHARI- "Information Risk Analysis and management Methodology", V-3, Concepts and Mechanism, CLUSIF, October, 2004.

[22] A. van Lamsweerde, "Elaborating security requirements by construction of intentional anti-models", Proceedings of the 26th International Conference on software engineering (ICSE'04), IEEE Computer Society, Washington DC USA, 2004, pp. 148-157.

[23] Jaiswal S., Gupta D., "Security Requirement Prioritization", in the proceeding of SERP'09, pp. 673- 679.

[24] F. Benjamin, G. Seda, H. Maritta, S. Holger, "A comparision of security requirements engineering methods", in requirement engineering, 2010.

[25] Yogesh Singh, "Software Testing", Cambridge University Press, 2011, ISBN 1107012961, 9781107012967.

[26] Chatterjee K., Gupta D., De A., "A Framework for Security Design Engineering Process", in ICIP 2011, CCIS 157, pp. 287- 293.

[27] Fernandez M., Gomez-Perez A., Juristo N., "METHONTOLOGY: From Ontological Art Towards Ontological Engineering", *AAAI Spring Symposium on Ontological Engineering*, Stanford University, March 24-26th, 1997, pp 33-40.

[28] Sure Y., Tempich C., Vrandecic D., 2006. "Ontology Engineering Methodologies," in *Semantic Web Technologies: Trends and Research in Ontology-based Systems*, Wiley, 2006, pp. 171-187.

[29] Fridman N., Musen M., " PROMPT: Algorithm and Tool for Automated Ontology Merging and Alignment ", Stanford Medical Informatics, Stanford University, Stanford,2000.

[30]Protégé: http://www.protege.stanford.edu

[31] AToM3 tool Home page: http://atom3.cs.mcgill.ca.2002.

[32] Frédéric J., Allilaire F., Bézivin J., Kurtev I., "*ATL: a model transformation tool", in* Science of Computer Programming, 72, 2008. pp. 31-39.

[33] Falconer S.,Noy N.,Storeyl M., "Ontology Mapping - A User Survey", Stanford University, 2007..

[34] Mitra P., Noy N., Jaiswal A., "OMEN: A Probabilistic Ontology Mapping Tool", Workshop on Meaning coordination and negotiation at the Third International Conference on the Semantic Web (ISWC-2004), Hisroshima, Japan,2004.

[35]CROSI tool: http://www.aktors.org/crosi/

[36] Noy N., Musen M., "An Algorithm for Merging and Aligning Ontologies: Automation and Tool Support" , Sixteenth National Conference on Artificial Intelligence , 1999.

[37] McGuinness D., Fikes R., Rice J., Wilder S., "The Chimaera Ontology Environment", American Association for Artificial Intelligence, 2000.

[38] Evren Sirin a , Bijan Parsia a , Bernardo Cuenca Grau a,b ,Aditya Kalyanpur a , Yarden Katz Pellet: A Practical OWL-DL Reasoner.

[39] Aven, T.," Risk analysis and risk management. Basic concepts and principles" Reliability & Risk Analysis: Theory & Applications, 2009, vol 2, pp. 57-73.

Empirical Evaluation of Software Development Methodology Selection Consistency: A Case Study Using Analytical Hierarchy Process

Benson Moyo[1], Gonde, Peeps[2], Ndabezinhle Soganile[1], Gilbert Dzawo[1], Kudakwashe Madzima[1]
[1]Computer Science and Information Systems Department, University of Venda, Thohoyandou, Limpopo, South Africa;
{benson.moyo, ndabezinhle.soganile, gilbert.dzawo, kudakwashe.madzima} @univen.ac.za
[2]Computer Science Department, National University of Science and Technology, Bulawayo, Zimbabwe
peeps.gonde@nust.ac.zw

***Abstract** -When developing software, the selection of an appropriate software development methodology is an essential decision. The experience, knowledge, expertise, of the software developer and organizational development context are assumed to have a great influence in selecting a methodology. In this research, we examine factors affecting the selection of software development methodologies and the consistency in which the methodology selection process is carried out. Based on Analytical Hierarchy Process (AHP), we evaluate the consistency in software development methodology selection in a particular software development company. We investigate the importance of a number of factors by first soliciting the criteria from practitioners before methodology selection and then later observing the actual implementation of a software development methodology. The paper identifies the predictor variables for development methodology selection and the dynamics triggered by situational variables. The results of our findings as well as recommendations for further work are presented in this paper.*

Keywords: *Software development methodology, methodology selection consistency, AHP*

1 Introduction

One of the most critical decisions when developing software is the selection of an appropriate software systems development methodology. It is believed that a rich repository of systems development methodology exists [1]. Conversely, there is no universally accepted documented guide on how to select software systems development methodologies from a myriad of systems development methodologies in existence. Some empirical studies indicate that systems development methodologies are selected and used in practice [2]. It is possible to select, tailor and adapt systems development methodologies and/or methodology segments to specific systems development context [3],[4],[5]. The amount of expertise and time needed to select, tailor and match methodologies may present stumbling blocks. The experience, knowledge and expertise of the systems developer is assumed to have a great influence in selecting a methodology [6]. Naumann and Palvia[7] and Hughes[8] note that selection is biased towards experience and familiarity with the methodology.

Selecting systems development methodologies or a system development methodology from many available options is not only demanding, but also confusing as often selection criteria or guidelines might neither be clearly stated nor justified [3],[6]. Naumann and Palvia[7] posit that selecting a systems development methodology from the numerous existing methodology classes is a challenge with technical, social and financial consequences. Not only is the difficulty presented on the selection among methodology classes, but also on the instances of these methodology classes. Iivari *et al.*[9] presents a classification of methodologies in an effort to demystify the tenet of "methodology jungle" identified by Avison and Fitzgerald[10], however, the suitable methodology search space is a nondeterministic polynomial hard problem. Despite the complexity of selecting a suitable systems development methodology, it is prospected that an appropriate methodology should standardise the development process, organise work and resources and direct appropriately the perception of each member of the development team [11],[3].

2 Related work

This section overviews methodology models and frameworks proposed in literature.

2.1 Software development methodology selection

There is a growing literature on development of methodology selection theory, frameworks and models. It has been shown that a single systems development methodology is not sufficient to address the requirements and demands of all existing scenarios of systems development [11],[12],[13]. Avison and Fitzgerald [14] express the basis for methodology selection as the target problem domain. Yaghini *et al.* [15] propose a methodology selection framework based on a multi-faceted approach. Methodologies are first classified as hard or soft and then compared according to six basic features; the philosophy, systems development model, systems development scope, systems development tools, systems development background and participants. This model has limitations for example, it compares Soft Systems Methodology [16], and Structured Systems Analysis and Design Methodology (SSADM) which are methodology instances grounded on different paradigms [9], therefore they may not be viewed as competing as they have different philosophical assumptions. The criteria for determining the scope of each systems development phase is not precisely and explicitly stated in this model. Scope problems are inherent in a methodology as one of the dimensions of inconsistency [17]; therefore the selection framework might suffer from objectively scoping the phases. This model introduces only a set of six methodologies and it would be challenging to include any methodology not included in the list provided.

Naumann and Palvia[7] present a selection model centred on quantitative scoring method called Delphi to collaboratively evaluate and recommend essential methodology functions. The candidate methodology is selected based on the scores awarded to it. The drawback of this model is the subjectivity of the methodology function definition and the concentration on the system development techniques and neglecting the other methodology components. Cockburn [18] put forward a decision model based on evaluating appropriateness of each member of the Crystal methodology family instances to a target systems development problem domain. The stumbling block of this model is its being restricted to a limited methodology instances. Rashmi and Anithashree [13] recommend a selection framework for Rapid System Development (RSD) Methodologies built on a comparative analysis of a set of essential aspects of rapid development methodology instances under consideration. However, this selection is limited to Rapid System Development (RSD) Methodology family. Burns and Dennis [19] advocate for a two-dimensional framework for selecting the most suitable systems development methodology. This contingency strategy classifies projects in terms of project complexity and uncertainty factors [19]. The project complexity is determined by four aspects; the project size, the number of system users, the quantity of new generated information, and the complexity of generating new information [19]. On the other hand project uncertainty consist of three characteristics; the level of structure, the extent of users' knowledge on their duties and system developer's experience and expertise. The methodology selection process in this strategy involves a straightforward reading of the two dimensional array contents based on the level of complexity and uncertainty of the project. However, the drawback of this selection strategy is that it considers only two methodology instances. Yusof *et al.* [6] present yet another variation of selection criteria based on complexity and uncertainty, quality criteria and scope of methodology phases as key factors. The researchers select eight methodologies and state that they are the most common ones and in addition they give a formula for calculating the score for each methodology. Perhaps the drawback of this model is the determination of methodology scores. The approaches mentioned so far have a large likelihood of subjectivity when selecting a software development methodology.

Zhu [20] suggests three contingency approaches to software systems development methodology selection grounded on the dynamics of situational variables. The first strategy is "contingency at the outset" [20] and assumes contextual variables as static and thereby allows the selection of a methodology or methodologies prior to the development process and when chosen, a methodology or methodologies remain(s) invariant up to systems development project completion. The methodology and the contingency variables achieve a state of equilibrium throughout the development process.

The second strategy is "contingency with a fixed pattern" [20] which permits deterministic selection of systems development methodology or methodologies as the development process progresses. The possible future adjustments, variations and reconfiguration of the situational variables are considered predictable and follow some known archetype. The strategy assumes specific predictable expectations in different phases of a systems development life cycle. Systems development phases form decision points and allow the systems development methodology to be changed at each stage of systems development [21].

"Contingency along development dynamics" [20] is the third strategy which relies on selecting methodologies, or/and methodology fragments, tools and techniques into the development process as dictated by the dynamics of the evolving software systems development context. The strategy suggests a high level of uncertainty in the development process and therefore does not prescribe any set of systems development methodologies prior to any confrontation with particular contingency variable configurations at any point in time. This strategy allows multiple-decision points throughout the systems development process. In each stage, therefore it is assumed that new contextual features emerge that demand appropriate methodologies, or/and methodology fragments, tools and techniques to be employed. The suitability of systems development methodology is viewed as the achievement of equilibrium between the methodology and the situational variables. Therefore systems development methodology has to be adjusted from time to time in order to maintain development variables equilibrium.

2.2 Software systems development contingency variables

Systems development problem situations are different, some development environment are well-understood while some are ill-understood. These different systems development circumstances demand different methodologies to handle them if predictable results are expected. Even in single organisational settings the contingency variables configuration may differ on a software project to project basis. Carroll [3] found in a particular case study, that contingency factors affected the selection of methodologies throughout the development process. The contingent factors strategy suggests that each development situation demands an appropriately selected methodology from a portfolio of methodologies. However, the challenge is that there is no single repository with all the methodologies compared and contrasted, classified and analysed on their normative principles, strengths, weaknesses, and contextual appropriateness. Methodology engineering goes a step further to suggest selection of methodology fragments from a repository and construct an appropriate framework or adapt, configure or tailor methodologies to fit the specific systems development projects. However, experience and a high degree of expertise may be needed to apply this strategy. The derivations are more biased on theoretical deductions than empirical evidence which make them more of pieces of advice on what should be done.

Systems development contingency factors may be considered at both micro and macro levels. Micro-context level deals with specific localised and bounded systems development problem situation. The micro-context level dynamics may include how the methodology deals with the social, technical, management, and economic factors confined to a same development environment or a similar development environment. Organisational structure and culture, each systems development team member's previous experiences, existing knowledge, tacit knowledge, skills, culture, roles, rights and level of expertise constitute part of both social and technical contextual factors.

The macro-context level tends to be universal and may impact on micro-context level dynamics [22]. Ghaffarian [22] explains one of the reasons for the failure of the Effective Technical & Human Implementation of Computer-based Systems (ETHICS) methodology to propagate as probably the development context level dynamics. It is our contention that the development context is imperative when selecting a systems development methodology. Each methodology selection should be based on project to project specifics and the choice should be consistent and rigorous.

It is assumed that organisations should be able to select a systems development methodology that is best suited for a specific systems development project. Unfortunately, not much research has been performed to guide organisations in this regard. Research into contingent use of systems development methodology is relevant to organizations aiming at selecting suitable methodologies for specific projects, in specific organisations, with specific organisational cultures and political structures. The appropriate selection of a methodology is purported to reduce failure probability. It is also expected to increase systems development process efficiency, improve quality of developed systems, and deliver systems on schedule and within budgetary constraints. Organisations are aware of the software crisis and the implications of project failure on reputation, employee morale, costs and business continuity. This is probably one of the reasons of sticking to one proven and tested methodology to avoid uncertainty associated with a new methodology.

All illustrations, drawings, and photographic images will be printed in black and white. We recommend that you examine a printed copy of your paper (in black and white) and make the final adjustments before submission. All illustrations must be numbered consecutively

3 Methodology

In this work we endeavour to investigate consistency between what the practitioners say they do and what they really do. We aim to explore software systems development methodology selection consistency. Therefore we use the Analytic Hierarchy Process (AHP) as a rigorous subjective multi-criteria decision evaluation tool.

Given a set of software systems development methodologies, preference of one from the other can be established through knowledge solicitation techniques like observations, questionnaires or interviews and subjecting the data collected to a thorough statistical analysis. Selecting a software development methodology is a multi-criteria decision making process. AHP converts a multi-criteria decision making process into the solution of an Eigen value problem. Eigen values have their greatest significance in that dynamic problems tend towards a steady state under some mathematical operations. The appeal of AHP in the selection process is on its ability to verify consistency of subjective measures. Ratio scales are derived from paired comparisons and both quantitative and qualitative measures can be scientifically verified and validated. The ability to detect inconsistent judgements makes it a good candidate for selecting a software systems development methodology. New ideas and methodologies are viewed as prone to failure and risky. Learning from failures is not acceptable to organisations as failure may have a serious negative impact on reputation, employee morale, and continuity of business. The essence of AHP involves the construction of a square matrix expressing the relative values of a set of attributes. For example: What is the relative importance to the developers the market window of a software system as opposed to quality of the software system? What is more important responding to change over sticking to a plan? The fact that the human mind is capable of making a single pairwise comparison at any given time is taken advantage of in AHP. Each selection made is mapped onto a numerical value.

The structure of a problem is comprised of a hierarchy of components in terms of a goal, criteria, and alternatives. The priority setting of the criteria based on pairwise comparison allows the determination of the relative importance of the criteria within each level. The typical question is "How important is social issues interaction relative to technical issues?" The respondent selects from descriptive comparisons. The selection is then mapped into a numerical scale that expresses the intensity of importance. The values range from 1(Equal importance-when two activities contribute equally to the objective) to 9(Extreme importance-when evidence favouring one activity over another is of the highest possible order of affirmation). The numbers 2,4,6,8 represent intermediate values where a compromise has to be met. The reciprocal of each of these values is assigned to the other criterion in the pair. The weightings are then normalized and averaged in order to obtain an average weight for each criterion.

The case study was conducted in one registered Software Development Company in Zimbabwe from 2010 to 2012. The Company's core competency is in application software development and it permitted one of the research collaborators to participate. Within this period a total of four new software systems development projects are carried out and other activities involved client support services to already deployed systems. In the start of each project the researcher presents a questionnaire on the selection of development methodology. It solicits a simple pairwise comparison of organisational, project and systems development methodology characteristics. The interpretation of the responses is done using the AHP Fundamental Scale [24]. In case of group selection, a geometric mean is used to aggregate the individual choices into a single representative judgment [24].

The software methodology complex decision problem is structured as a hierarchy as shown in Figure 1. We assume three-tier architecture in decision making. The first layer entails the main goal (select the most appropriate software development methodology); second level has criteria and sub-criteria, and alternatives at the bottom layer. The stakeholders at criteria layer include the analysts (who are leading the proposals for development), management (who have to buy into the project for support), the programmers, and users (the clients of the system).

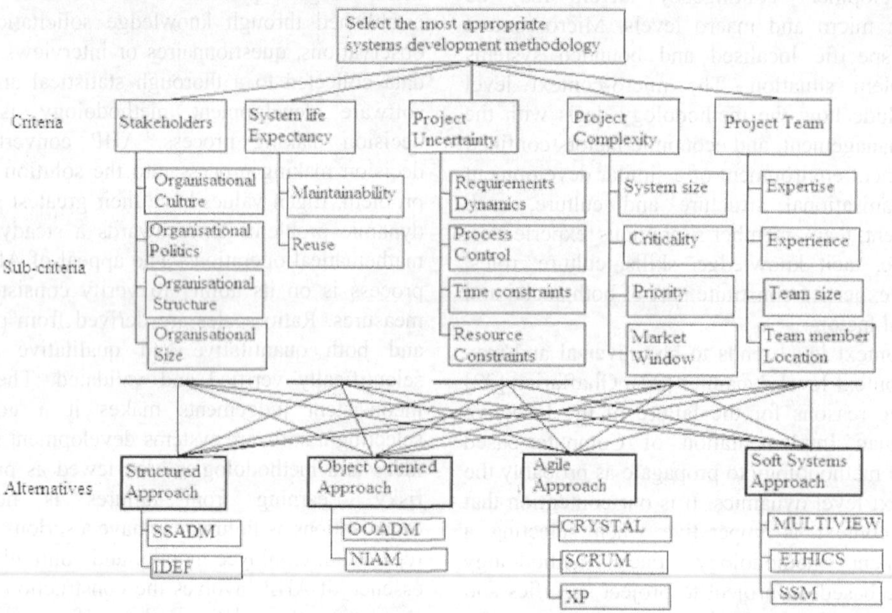

Figure 1: Problem decomposition

In Figure 2 we indicate the priority vector to guide the decision. At second layer the project team is the most significant factor in the selection of a software development methodology. It comes slightly ahead of stakeholders. During the study, resignations of a member of the team lead to change of software development methodology. Again expertise is relatively valued highest among experience, team size, and team distribution by location. The values may vary but fundamentally the importance of project team will show some strong intensity. Project complexity is relatively more significant than project uncertainty, however at one decimal place precision these have equal importance.

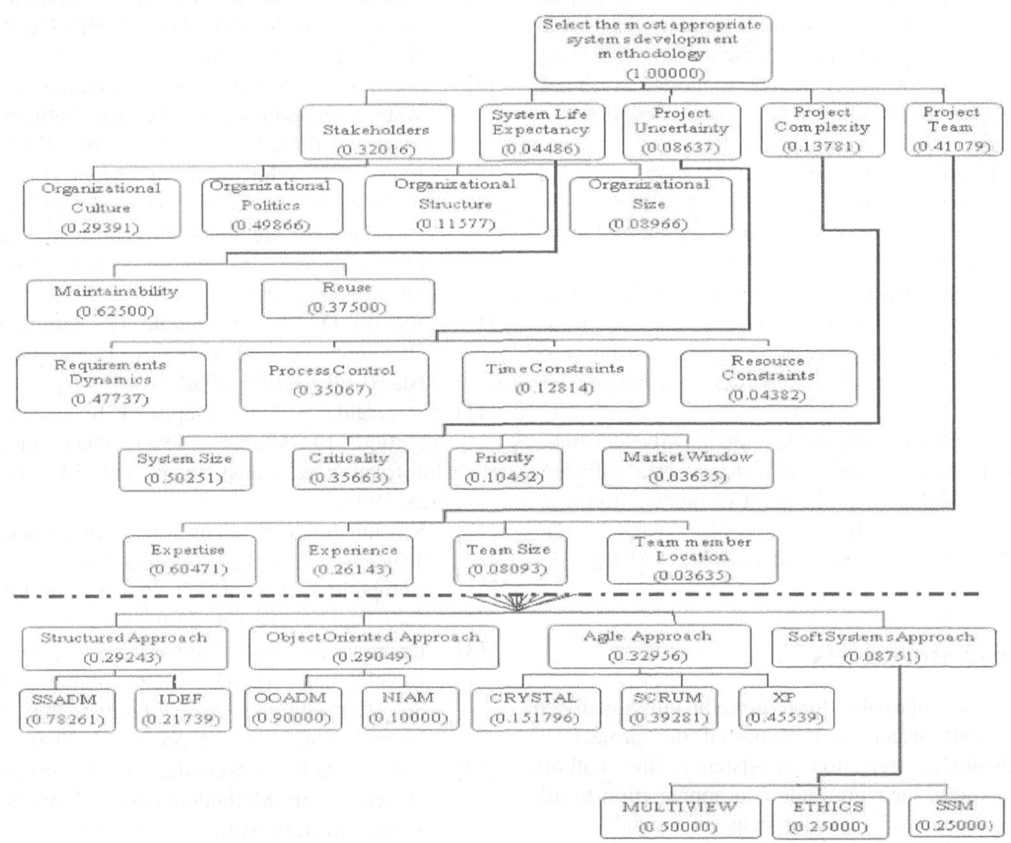

Figure 2: Priority vectors for goal, criteria and sub-criteria and alternatives

Alternatives are evaluated against each criterion. It is observed that structured methodologies may deal well with maintainability, organizational politics, and expertise; however, the stumbling block would be on handling requirements volatility. Object oriented handles well organizational politics, maintainability, expertise, moderate on requirements volatility. Agile methodologies deal well with organisational politics, team size, moderate on maintainability, and excellent on requirements dynamics. Lastly agile methodology is slightly more preferred than neither structured nor object oriented methodologies. However, expressing the decision values correct to one decimal place there is no difference in the appropriateness of these methodologies.

4 Discussion

The methodology selection is a fundamental exercise in and of itself. The use of AHP may expose consistency or inconsistency in the selection process of a software development methodology. The selection originates from the goal, trickles down to criteria, sub-criteria, and finally to the alternatives. There seem to be a praxis gap in the selection of a software development methodology due to the fact that a practitioner may strongly evaluate one alternative theoretically superior over another, however, practically recommends another.

5 Results and conclusions

An interesting observation is made during the implementation of a selected systems development methodology. An expert who is one of the well experienced members of the project team resigns from the company. The methodology initially selected is re-evaluated and dropped as part of response to contextual dynamics in systems development. Change in project characteristics may result in change or modification of a systems development methodology.

The AHP was applied to systematically and consistently evaluate the selection consistency of systems analysts who are basically tasked to select the most appropriate systems development methodologies amongst a myriad of existing alternative classes and instances of methodologies.

The study shows that there is need to investigate existence, adoption and use of systems development methodology selection frameworks. Our study contributes to the pool of knowledge in systems development in the following ways. Firstly, the conducted critical analysis of the prior literature on systems development methodology selection helps confirm the knowledge gap in this area. The important features for selecting a methodology are identified and the dynamics of the development process observed. Second, we investigated consistency in selecting methodology by the relevant actors. The suggested attributes can be used to understand the impact of systems development contextual variables on methodology selection.

One of the possible limitations in the study is that a single organization was considered. Generalization of the results of the study is limited as the study is based on a case study. Case studies are powerful to get the deeper understanding of a particular phenomenon in its actual settings but not for providing general predictor variables for the phenomenon. The findings are considered as a trigger to explore more in the area of systems development methodologies selection.

Further research work can be done on how the selection criteria are used. What are the criteria to select a software development methodology and change it or modify it during the development process? In the first place what is the threshold to change, tailor a selected software development methodology?

6 Acknowledgements

Although it is impossible to give credit individually to all those who participated and supported the project on software methodology selection consistency, the authors would like to express their gratitude and appreciation to all. This research is supported by the University of Venda.

7 References

[1] Jayaratna, N. "Understanding and evaluating methodologies, A systemic Framework", McGraw Hill, UK, 1994.

[2] Saeki, M. "A meta-model for method integration", Information and Software Technology, Vol. 39, pp. 925-932, 1998.

[3] Carroll. J. "The process of ISD methodology selection and use: a case study", in Claudio U. C., Riccardo. M., Marco de Marco, Marcello. M., Andrea C.(Eds.) Proceedings of the 11th European Conference on Information Systems, ECIS 2003, Italy 16-21 June, pp. 379-392, 2003.

[4] Goulielmos, M. "Systems development approach: transcending methodology", Information Systems Journal, Vol. 14, pp. 363-386, 2004.

[5] Barrow, R., Frampton, K., Hamilton, M., Crossman, B. "A Study of the In-Practice Application of a Commercial Software Architecture", IEEE, Proceedings of the 2005 Australian Software Engineering Conference, 2005

[6] Yusof, M.M., Shukur, Z., Abdullah, A.L. "CuQuP: A hybrid approach for selecting suitable systems development methodology", Information Technology Journal, Vol. 10, pp. 1031-1037, 2011.

[7] Naumann, J. D., and Palvia, S. "Selection Model for Systems Development Tools", MIS Quarterly, Vol. 6, No. 1, pp. 39-48, 1982.

[8] Hughes, J. "Selection and evaluation of information systems methodologies: The gap between theory and practice", IEEE Proc., Vol. 145, pp. 100-104, 1998.

[9] Iivari, J., Hirschheim, R., and Klein, H.K. "A Dynamic Framework for Classifying Information Systems Development Methodologies and Approaches", Journal of Management Information Systems, Vol. 17, No. 3, pp. 179-218, 2001.

[10] Avison, D.E. and Fitzgerald, G. "Information Systems Development Methodologies: Techniques and Tools", Blackwell, Oxford, 1988.

[11] Fitzgerald, B. "An Empirical Investigation into the adoption of systems development methodologies", Information & Management, Vol. 34, No. 6, pp. 317-328, 1998.

[12] Srivannaboon, S. "Toward a Contingency Approach: Tailoring Project Management to Achieve a Competitive Advantage", Proceedings PICMET, 9-13 July, Istanbul, Turkey, July 2006 .

[13] Rashmi, J., and Anithashree, C. "Rapid System Development (RSD) Methodologies: Proposing a Selection Framework", Engineering Management Journal, Vol. 21, No. 4, pp. 30-35, 2009.

[14] Avison, D.E., Fitzgerald, G. "Information Systems Development: Methodologies, techniques and tools", 4thedn, McGraw-Hill, London, 2006.

[15] Yaghini, M., Bourouni, A., Amiri, R.H. "A framework for selection of information systems development methodologies", Computer and Information Systems, Vol. 2, No. 1, pp. 1-9, 2009.

[16] Checkland, P.B. "Systems Thinking, Systems Practice", John Wiley, Chichester, England, 1981.

[17] Iivari J. and Maansaari J. "The usage of systems development methods: are we stuck to old practices?", Information and Software Technology, Vol. 40, pp. 501-510, 1998.

[18] Cockburn, A. "Agile software development, Agile software series", Addison-Wesley, Boston, 2002.

[19] Burns, R.N., Dennis, A.R. "Selecting the appropriate application development methodology", ACM SIGMIS Database, Vol. 17, No. 1, pp. 19-23, 1985.

[20] Zhu, Z. "Evaluating contingency approaches to information systems design", International Journal of Information Management Vol. 22, pp. 343–356, 2002.

[21] Khalifa, M., and Verner, J.M. "Drivers for Software Development Method Usage", IEEE Transactions on Engineering Management, Vol. 47, No. 3, pp. 360-369, 2000.

[22] Ghaffarian, V. "The new stream of socio-technical approach and main stream information systems research", Procedia Computer Science, Vol. 3, pp. 1499–1511, 2011.

[23] Saaty, T. L. "Decision making with the analytic hierarchy process", Int. J. Services Sciences, Vol. 1, No. 1 pp. 83-98, 2008.

The Impact of Non-Functional Attributes on the Analysis Operations of Feature Models

I. Achour[1], L. Labed[2], and H. Ben Ghazela[1]
[1]Computer Science Departement, Manouba University/ ENSI/ Lab. RIADI-GDL, Manouba, Tunisia
[2]Computer Science Departement, Tunis University/ ISG/ Lab. RIADI-GDL, Tunis, Tunisia

Abstract - *The functional aspect of a system is very important. In fact, it defines different features of the system, but it does not negate the reality of the non-functional aspects of it and that has an impact on this functional aspect. This aspect has been largely treated with classical systems but not enough with the product lines.*

So we had the idea to study the impact of non-functional attributes on the analysis operations of feature models.
In this work, we have resumed analysis operations of feature models listed in the literature. Moreover, we studied the effect of adding the non-functional attributes on these operations by giving examples. So this has enabled us to emphasize the presence of three types of constraints namely constraint value, constraint attribute-attribute and constraint feature-attribute.

Finally, we have deduced that some operations are not affected, others are affected and there is also the emergence of new one(s).

Keywords: Non-functional attributes, analysis operations, extended feature models.

1 Introduction

The consideration of non-functional attributes is crucial in features models. In fact, this models are the basis of our reference architecture. This is why we are interested in studying the impact of adding non-functional attributes (NFA) on analysis operations of features models. We based our work on the first challenge of Benavides [1] "Include feature attribute relationships for analyses on feature models and propose new operations of analysis leveraging extended feature models".
In this work, we will resume analysis operations described by Benavides [1] and we will present the effect of non-functional attributes on this operation and an example.
Section 2 concerns a short descriptive of the Extended Feature Model (EFM). In Section 3, we present the constraint on the attributes of the extended feature models. Section 4, deals with detailing the impact of non-functional attributes on the analysis operations of the feature models. Finally, Section 5 summarizes our work and outlines our prospects for future work.

2 Extended feature model

This model is a feature model (see figure 1). Each feature can be enriched by attributes. Each attribute has a type and a domain. Each feature can have three types of relations with their son (mandatory, optional, relation group that can be expressed by an alternative or an or-relationship). In addition, features can be connected by a relation of necessity (requires) or of exclusion (excludes) [1, 4].

3 Constraints on the attributes of the extended feature models

The NFA of the extended feature model may present constraints. These constraints are either attribute values or relations attribute-attribute or relations feature-attribute. And the presence of these constraints can influence the analysis operations of the extended feature models.
To explain these constraints, we present the following examples for each case:
-Value constraint: a feature with attribute run time must have value <= 10ms or belonging to the interval [10ms 5ms ..].
-Attribute-attribute constraint: a feature F1 with attribute accessibility (requires) a run time > 15ms of another feature F2.
-Feature-attribute constraint: a feature registration request (requires) a storage capacity >= 50 Mega Byte of feature archiving.

4 The impact on non-functional attributes on analysis operations of an extended feature models

Studying the impact of NFA on the analysis operations of feature model, we noticed that some operations are affected, others are not and there is also the emergence of new one(s). We list below the various operations [1] while quoting for each one its input, its output, its role, the effect of NFA and an example.

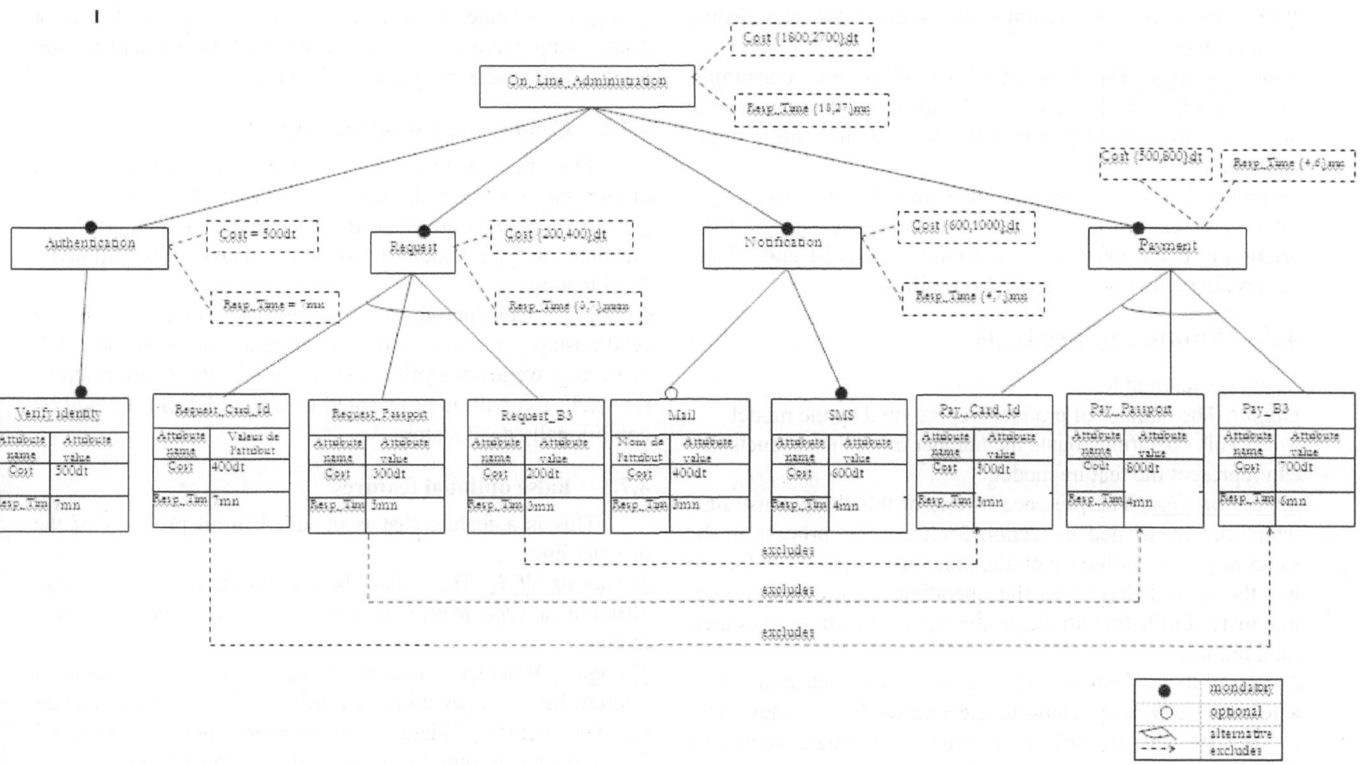

Figure 1: A sample of An Extended Feature Model

4.1 Void feature model

Input: Feature model
Output: Empty or not
Role: To see if the feature model present at least one product.
Impact of NFA: The presence of one of the three types of constraints can influence this operation in the sense that a constraint may omit the presence of a product. This is valid if the product that has the constraint is the only product in the model and its omission will cause the empty model.
Example: a1 is an attribute of a feature F1 connected by an exclude relation with an attribute a2 of a feature F2. Exclusion relationship between the two attributes is propagated to features F1 and F2 where a product P cannot present F1 and F2 at the same time.

4.2 Valid product

Input: Feature model and a product
Output: A product belong or not to the feature model.
Role: To see if the product belong or not to the list of all products representing the feature model.
Impact of NFA: The presence of one of the three constraints mentioned in section 3 may affect the validity of the product.
Example: In the feature model, the value of an attribute a1 should belong to the interval [min .. max]. If a product P1 has the attribute a1 with value less than min so the product P1 is invalid.

4.3 Valid partial configuration[1]

Input: Feature model and partial configuration
Output: Configuration invalid or not
Role: Check the validity of a partial configuration is to verify that the configuration has no contradiction as the presence of a *requires* relation between a feature in the set S and a feature in the set R (for the meaning of S and R refer to the explanation of the term configuration).
Impact of NFA: Configuration can have features with NFA. These are connected by constraints of type attribute-attribute or type feature-attribute and that causing contradictions.
Example: Let F1 a feature belonging to the set S connected by a relation *requires* to an attribute a2 of a feature F2 belonging to the set R. The *requires* relationship present a contradiction.

4.4 All products

Input: feature model
Output: All products are represented by the feature model

[1] Configuration: Given a feature model with a set of features F, a configuration is the pair (S, R), where S, R C F, where S is the set of features that can be selected and R the features that should not be presented with S ∩ R = Ø. Full configuration is represented by S U R = F and Partial configuration represented by (S U R) C F.

Role: This operation generates all products that the feature model can represent.
Impact of NFA: The presence of one of the three constraints mentioned in section 3 can vary the list of products generated and that by omitting products that do not meet these constraints.
Example: Let an attribute a1 of feature F1 connected by a relation of exclusion to an attribute a2 of feature F2. The relation of exclusion has spread to the features F1 and F2 and the product with both F1 and F2 is omitted.

4.5 Number of products

Input: Feature model
Output: The number of products represented by the model
Role: This operation counts the number of all the products that can represent the feature model.
Impact of NFA: The presence of one of this three constraints which are mentioned in section 3 affects this process in the same way as its influence on the previous operation. Indeed, it has the same behavior as the operation All products except that instead of listing all the products, the operation gives their total number.
Example: In the feature model, the value of an attribute a1 of a feature F1 should belong to the interval [min .. max]. If a product P1 with an attribute a1 with value greater than max then the product P1 is not counted.

4.6 Filter

Input: Feature model and configuration
Output: The set of derivatives of the feature model including the initial configuration
Role: From the feature model, this operation generates products that meet the initial configuration.
Impact of NFA: The presence of one of the three constraints mentioned in section 3 may affect this operation. In fact, some products including the feature model and the configuration can be excluded because of the constraints of their attributes. In fact, this has the same principle that operations *All products* and *Number of products*.
Example: We can adopt the same examples that the operations *All products* and *Number of products*.

4.7 Anomalies detection

The literature [1] postponed five analysis operations to detect anomalies in the feature model such as redundancies or contradictions.
Input: feature model
Output: information about the detected anomaly

4.7.1 Dead feature

This is a feature that does not appear in any product of the line products. This anomaly is caused by misuse of the *requires* and the *excludes* constraints of features.
Impact of NFA: The constraints of type attribute-attribute or type feature-attribute can make a dead feature.
Example: Whether a mandatory feature F1 connected by a relationship *excludes* with an attribute of an optional feature F2. So, F2 is necessarily a dead feature.

4.7.2 Conditionally dead features

This is a feature that becomes dead under certain circumstances such as the selection of another feature.
Impact of NFA: Here also, the constraints of type attribute-attribute or type feature-attribute can make a conditionally dead feature.
Example: Considering a feature F1 connected by a relationship *excludes* with an attribute of a feature F2. Assuming we always select the feature F1, the relationship of the exclusion will be propagated to feature F2. So, F2 will be conditionally dead feature.

4.7.3 False optional features

This is a feature that is included in all products of the product line.
Impact of NFA: Here also, the constraints of type attribute-attribute or type feature-attribute can make a false optional feature.
Example: Whether a mandatory feature F1 connected by a relationship *requires* with an attribute of an optional feature F2. The inclusion relation will be propagated to feature F2 that is always present. So, F2 is a false optional feature.

4.7.4 Wrong cardinalities

A group of features described as wrong cardinalities, is a group of cardinality that can not be instantiated. For example, we have an alternative of three features: A, B, and C. Which two are mutually exclusive and we have a cardinality <1..3>. So, the selection of three features is not possible.
Impact of NFA: Here also, the constraints attribute and attribute-relationship-attribute feature can present a wrong cardinalities.
Example: Considering an alternative of three features F1, F2 and F3, that has a cardinality <1 .. 3> and whose feature F1 is connected by a relationship *excludes* with an attribute of a feature F3. The exclusion Relationship will be propagated to the feature F3 and we cannot select both the three features F1, F2 and F3.

4.7.5 Redundancies

A feature model that contains redundancies is a feature model that represents the same information in many ways.
Impact of NFA: Here also, the constraints of type attribute-attribute or type feature-attribute may cause duplication.
Example: Considering a mandatory feature F1 connected by a relationship *requires* with an attribute of a mandatory feature F2. The inclusion relation is propagated to feature F2 which is already mandatory.

4.8 Explanations

Input: Feature model and an analysis operation
Output: An explanation of the operation answer

Role: Explanations are generally related to anomalies and are explanations of the cause of these anomalies.
Impact of NFA: Here also, the constraints of type attribute-attribute or of type feature-attribute may be the cause of the problem. Such as causing a dead feature.
Example: The cause of a dead feature may be an exclusion relation of the constraint of type attribute-attribute or of type feature-attribute.

4.9 Corrective explanations

Input: Feature model and an analysis operation
Output: A list of corrections to explanations
Role: This operation suggests a list of corrections to the anomalies identified.
Impact of NFA: Assuming that the constraints of type attribute-attribute or of type feature-attribute may be the cause of the problem, their removal may be a correction.
Example: Correcting a dead feature may be the deleting of the exclusion relation of the constraints of type attribute-attribute or of type feature-attribute.

4.10 Feature model relationships

Thum and al. [6] classifie the relationship between two feature models in four types: refactoring, generalization, specialization and arbitrary edit.
Input: Two feature models
Output: Information on how these two models are linked

4.10.1 Refactoring

A feature model is a refactoring of another, if they represent the same set of products even though they have different structures.
Impact of NFA: Here also, the constraints of type attribute-attribute or of type feature-attribute can influence the refactoring relationship between two feature models and that by altering or enhancing this relation
Example 1: an exclusion constraint of type attribute-attribute or of type feature-attribute of a feature model FM1 which has no equivalent in another feature model FM2. This varies the list of products of FM1.
Example 2: an exclusion constraint of type attribute-attribute or of type feature-attribute of a feature model FM1 has the same effect on the list of products as a relation of exclusion of two features.

4.10.2 Generalization

A feature model FM1 is a generalization of another feature model FM2, if all products of FM1 maintain and extend all products of FM2.
Impact of NFA: Here also, the constraints of type attribute-attribute or of type feature-attribute may affect the generalization of two feature models.
Example: Considering two identical feature models FM1 and FM2. Adding an exclusion constraint of type attribute-attribute or of type feature-attribute on feature model FM2, we will vary the list of products of FM2 by eliminating at least two products. Thus, FM1 is a generalization of FM2.

4.10.3 Specialization

A feature model FM1 is a specialization of another feature model FM2, if all products of FM1 is a subset of products of FM2.
Impact of NFA: Here also, the constraints of type attribute-attribute or of type feature-attribute can influence the specialization of two feature models.
Example: Considering two identical feature models FM1 and FM2. Adding an exclusion constraint of type attribute-attribute or of type feature-attribute on feature model FM1, we will vary the list of products of FM1 by eliminating at least two products. Thus, FM1 is a specialization of FM2.

4.10.4 Arbitrary edit

There is no relationship between the two feature models.
Impact of NFA: we believe that the constraints of the NFA did not affect this relationship. Indeed, the constraints alone can not make two feature models as arbitrary edit.

4.11 Optimization

Input: Feature model and objective function
Output: The product that meets the best to the criteria established by the objective function
Role: This suggests for a product a set of features that maximize or minimize the value of an attribute of a given feature.
Impact of NFA: This operation is only useful in the context of an extended feature model. Indeed, it is according to the values of the attributes and within both the constraints on features and constraints on the attributes that we select or omit some feature.
Example: Assuming that we have a cost minimization function we must choose the features with minimum cost: having an attribute with a minimum cost.

4.12 Core features

Input: Feature model
Output: The set of features present in all products of the product line.
Role: For a given feature model, this operation list all features that appear in all products of the product line. This is useful for determining the features that will be developed in the first place and which will form the reference architecture.
Impact of NFA: Here also, the constraints of type attribute-attribute or of type feature-attribute can make a feature as core feature and this by forcing its publication in all the products of the product line by the presence of a relationship *requires*.
Example: a mandatory feature F1 connected by a relationship *requires* to an attribute of an optional feature F2. The inclusion relation is propagated to feature F2 that is always present and belong to the list of core features.

4.13 Variant features

Input: Feature model
Output: The set of features not present in all products of the product line.
Role: For a given feature model, this operation list all features that do not appear in all products of the product line.
Impact of NFA: We think that the constraints of the NFA had no effect on this type of operation.

4.14 Atomic sets

Input: Feature model
Output: List of atomic sets.
Role: Giving a feature model, this operation lists the atomic sets. A set is a group of atomic features (at least one) considered as a single unit in some analysis. Intuitively, the mandatory features and their parents are grouped in an atomic set. This operation provides a lightweight version of the feature model that will make more efficient use of other analysis operations.
Impact of NFA : Here also, the constraints of type attribute-attribute or of type feature-attribute may influence the membership or not of a feature in an atomic set.
Example Giving a mandatory feature F1 connected by a *requires* relationship with an attribute of an optional feature F2. The inclusion relation is propagated to feature F2. So, F2 will be present in the same atomic set of F1.

4.15 Dependency analysis

Input: Feature model and a partial configuration
Output: New configuration
Role: From the feature model and the partial configuration, this operation generates a new configuration highlighting the features to include and exclude and taking into account the constraints of the feature model.
Impact of NFA: Here also, the constraints of type attribute-attribute or of type feature-attribute can influence the structure of the new configuration.
Example: Let a feature model FM, a partial configuration PC of FM and a feature F1 belonging to the set S. If F1 is connected by a *requires* relationship with an attribute of a feature F2. The inclusion relation is propagated to feature F2. So, F2 will belong to the set S of the new configuration.

4.16 Multi-step configurations

Input: Feature model, an initial configuration, a final configuration, a K step configurations to meet a global constraint and a function determining the cost of transition to a configuration from step T to step U.
Output: An ordered list of K configurations representing the different stages of transition from initial configuration to the final configuration.
Role: Based on various inputs, this operation offers an ordered list of K configurations representing the different stages of transition from initial configuration to the final configuration.
Impact of NFA: The constraint value influence the global constraint. Also, the constraints of type attribute-attribute or of type feature-attribute may influence the structure of intermediate configurations.
Example: If the feature model includes constraints related to attribute-attribute and to attribute-feature must be respected and this affects the list of configurations presented as a result.

4.17 Other operations

In this section, we include operations that have calculations based on the values of previous operations.

4.17.1 Homogeneity

Input: Feature model
Output: Homogeneity degree of of the feature model
Role: This is the complement of the ratio between the number of unique features (a feature is unique if it appears only in one product) in a product by the total number of products in the feature model. A feature model is more homogeneous than the number of unique features in a product is minimal.
Impact of NFA: The presence of attributes and their constraints affects indirectly the result of this operation since it affects the operation of calculating the number of products: *Number of products*.

4.17.2 Commonality

Input: Feature model and configuration
Output: The products percentage represented by the feature model and including the input configuration.
Role: This is the ratio of product including the input configuration by the total number of products of the feature model. This transaction enables us to classify the features that will be developed in the first place and decide who will be part of the basic architecture.
Impact of NFA: The presence of attributes and constraints affect indirectly the result of this operation since it affects the operation of calculating the number of products: *Number of products* and also the operation that gives the products of feature model including the initial configuration: *Filter*.

4.17.3 Variability factor

Input: Feature model
Output: The ratio of the number of products by 2^n which n is the number of features considered
Role: This is the ratio of the number of products by 2^n which n is the number of features considered. In particular, 2^n indicates the potential number of products represented by the feature model and assuming that any combination of features is allowed. Generally, the root and the features that are not leaves are not considered. A small factor indicates that the number of combinations is very limited compared to the total number of potential products.
Impact of NFA: The presence of attributes and constraints affecting indirectly the result of this operation since it affects the operation of calculating the number of products: *Number of products*.

4.17.4 Degree of orthogonality

Input: Feature model and a sub-tree
Output: Degree of orthogonality
Role: According to Czarnecki and al. [2], the degree of orthogonality is the ratio of the total number of products of the feature model by the number of products of the sub-tree knowing that only local constraints of the sub-tree are considered.
Impact of NFA: The presence of attributes and constraints affects indirectly the result of this operation because it affects the operation of calculating the number of products: *Number of products*.

4.17.5 Extra constraint representativeness (ECR)

Input: Feature model
Output: Degree of representativeness of the constraints of the tree
Role: This determines the degree of representativeness of the constraints of the tree. Mendonça and al. [5] defines Extra Constraint Representativeness (ECR) as the ratio of the number of features involved in the constraint (the repeated features are only counted once) by the number of features of the feature model.
Impact of NFA: The presence of attributes and constraints affects the result of this operation. En fact, it affects the operation of calculating the number of products: *Number of products* and also the number of features involved within the constraints (constraint of features and attributes).

4.17.6 Lowest common ancestor (LCA)

Input: Feature model and a set of features
Output: The feature being the lowest common ancestor of input features
Role: This determines the lowest common ancestor of input features. Mendonça. and al. [5] defines the lowest common ancestor (LCA) of a set of features as the common ancestor which is farthest from the root: LCA (FM {f1, ..., fn}).
Impact of NFA: We think that the attributes have no effect on this operation.

4.17.7 Root features

Input: Feature model and a set of features
Output: The set of features that are roots in the feature model.
Role: This determines the set of features which are the roots of the feature model. Considering l = LCA (FM {f1, ..., fn}) Mendonça. and al. [5] define the roots of all the features roots (FM,{f1,...,fn}) as the subset of the features of the son of l and ancestor of the set {f1,...,fn}.
Impact of NFA: We believe that the attributes have no effect on this type of operation.

4.18 Attribute values

Input: a product and attribute
Output: Values list of the attribute
Role: This is a new operation that lists all values of the attribute. This operation is useful if we want to do calculations on the values of an attribute for a given product.
Example: We can for a given product need the list values of the attribute cost to calculate the total cost.

5 Conclusion

In this work, we resumed analysis operations of feature models founded in the literature and we studied for each operation the impact of adding a NFA and basing ourselves on an example.
In fact, this work is only in its infancy and we are testing this impact on the Flame tool (FAMA Formal Framework) [3]. This will allow us to analyze the EFM and to add operations not yet taken into account.
Also, we plan to work more on the representation of NFA oriented quality.

6 References

[1] Benavides, D., Segure, S., and Ruiz-Cortés, A. 2010. Automated Analysis of Feature Models 20 years Later: a Literature Review. Information Systems. Elsevier. 2010. 35(6), (615-636). (Sept 2010). DOI= http://dx.doi.org/10.1016/j.is.2010.01.001

[2] Czarnecki, K. and Kim, P. 2005. Cardinality-based feature modeling and constraints: A progress report. In Proceedings of the International Workshop on Software Factories At OOPSLA 2005, 2005.

[3] Durán, A., Benavides, D., Segura, S., Trinidad, P., Ruiz-Cortés, A. 2012. FLAME: FAMA Formal Framework (v 1.0). Technical Report. Applied Software Engineering Research Group. ISA-12-TR-02. (March 2012). Seville, Spain.

[4] Gürses, Ö. 2010. Non-functional variability management by complementary quality modeling. Doctoral Thesis. Middle East Technical University.

[5] Mendonça, M., Wasowski, A., Czarnecki, k. and Cowan. D. 2008. Efficient compilation techniques for large scale feature models. In Proceedings of 7th International Conference of GPCE : the Generative Programming and Component Engineering, 13–22, 2008.

[6] Thüm, T., Batory, D. and Kästner, C. 2009. Reasoning about edits to feature models. In International Conference on Software Engineering, 254–264, 2009.

Determining Software System Type from Software Requirement Specification

A. Mrs Suneeta H Angadi[1], B. Dr Mohan S[2], and C. Dr G T Raju[2]

[1]Computer Science and Engineering, Anna University RNSIT, Bangalore, Karnataka, India

[2] Computer Science and Engineering, NGPIT, Coimbatore, Tamilnadu, India

[2] Computer Science and Engineering, RNSIT, Bangalore, Karnataka, India

Abstract - *Deciding type of software system appropriately helps in proactive software performance engineering with graph transformation approach. Further this task can be useful in performance analysis of software systems. Analysis carried out in requirement and design phases add value to implementation. In this paper idea of determining software system type based on software requirement specification is proposed.*

Keywords: Software Performance, Graph Transformation, Software Requirement Specification, Modeling

1 Introduction

Software Performance Engineering (SPE) deals with quantitative approach in constructing software systems [9]. Performance analysis can be considered as step in proactive performance engineering of SPE. Graph transformation approach for proactive performance analysis can reduce development time. With this reasoning in this paper the idea of software system type decision is given. This idea is result of study in graph transformation field. Also output of implementation is parameter of graph transformation process. In this section description of graph transformation, graph representations, graph transformation approaches, and graph transformation tools has been given.

1.1 Graph Transformation

Graph transformation defines rule based manipulation of graphs. It is the process of transforming one form of the graph into another form algorithmically. Graph is a pair (V(G), E(G)), where V(G) finite set of vertices and E(G) proper subset of { {V, V'} | V, V' ∈ V(G) , V'≠V } is set of edges. Number of vertices in a graph G is called size of G. All graphs are finite undirected with no multiple edges and self loops. Graphs describe complex data and object structures. And graph transformation defines dynamic evolution of structures. Process of graph transformation maps platform independent model to platform specific model, and this mapping will help developer with detailed implementation details possibly with constraint specification as well. This aids in through understanding of the system being developed. Graph transformations define rule based manipulation of graphs.

1.2 Graph Representations

Graphical notations are *entity relationship diagrams, control flows, message sequence charts, petri nets, automata, state charts* as shown in figure below.

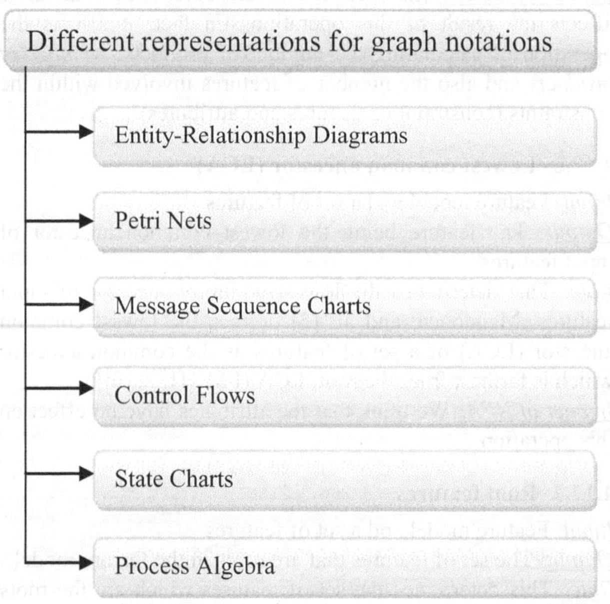

Figure 1.

Entity-relationship diagrams are *metalanguages* that describe entity types [1].

Control flow graphs or program graphs represent the control flow of programs used in the analysis of software [3]. The nodes of a control flow graph are statements of the program and the edges represent the control flow between the statements.

A Petri net is an abstract, formal model of information flow. Petri nets, mathematical modeling language for description of distributed systems [2]. Automata are simple mathematical and expressive formalism that allows one to model cooperation and synchronization between sub systems.

In state chart a state is represented by a rectangle and a transition between states is shown by a labeled arc [4]. Purpose of using state charts is to specify behavior of complex reactive systems. Other notations include type hierarchies, process algebras, data flow diagrams, parse trees, flow charts. Knowledge of different graphical representations is essential since it helps in transformation. Software system type must be known to decide type of the representation to adapt,. Towards this goal an attempt is made to check the type of software system to be developed from software requirements specification.

1.3 Graph Transformation Approaches

Approach can be for describing classes of graphs. Declarative approach for describing class of graph will check correctness of graph [5]. Computing by graph transformation can be used for visual modeling and specification, model transformation, concurrency and distribution, software development.

Graph transformation approaches include Node label replacement approach, Hyperedge replacement approach, Algebraic approach-Double Pushout, Single Pushout, High Level Replacement, Logical approach,Theory of 2-structures, Programmed graph replacement approach [7].

1.4 Automated Graph Transformation

Graph transformation systems, like PROGRES and Fujaba, support the automatic generation of executable code [8].

Rest of the paper is organized as section 2 gives information of related work, section 3 discusses implementation details, section 4 gives results details, conclusion of the work is done in section 5 and finally references are given in section 6.

2 Related work

Researchers have worked on various streams of graph transformations. Starting from identification of different notations, approaches, and tool design for transformation. Early traces of Graph theory area Contribution, towards transformation for software engineering was found around 1890's [6]. Then onward there are significant achievements in the field and graph representations have been adopted as software modeling notations. Graph transformation approaches have been used for giving mathematical reasons behind computation which is core of software being developed. Different approaches have been proposed. Then tools like Fujaba, Viatra, VMTS have been proposed for automating the task of graph transformations. But for all of these activities to be continued identifying type of software system is starting point. Hence we have come with a proposal of software, for identifying software system type from SRS.

3 Implementation details

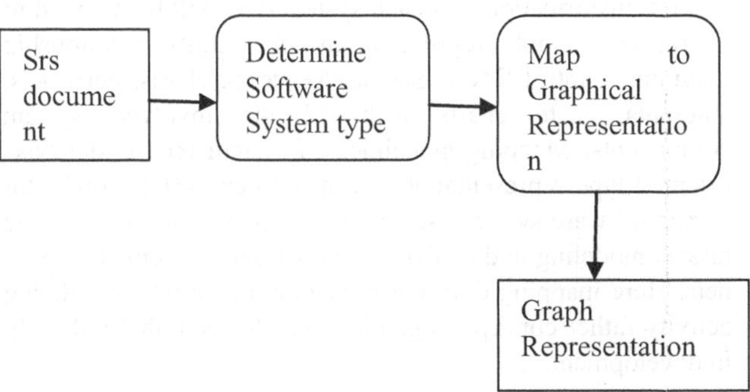

Figure 2.

Graph transformation helps in model transformation, and model transformation conveys idea of analyst and design specialist appropriately to developer. Hence graph transformation may reduce development time since model of system being developed is properly analyzed by means of theory of graphs. In order to adopt graph transformation approach deciding software system type is essential; because it helps in choosing graph representation from prominent graph representations. In this direction common software system types are system software and application software systems. Application software systems can be web applications, GUI based applications, object oriented applications, multiplatform applications, secure applications, distributed applications, mission critical applications, and distributed networking applications. A hint for identifying software system type can be *software requirement document (srs)*. Software requirement document states expected features of software being developed, from this we can derive possible graphical representation, and this representation will be mapped to conceptual graph [1]. Conceptual graph takes close to implementation details which give complete picture to the developer, and developer can accordingly develop the system. We have studied some Sample SRS, from them following factors were identified for software system identification,

Title of the software system being developed is one of the parameter for deciding software system type.

Detailed description of the software system in Scope section is another parameter for deciding the software system type.

Initially purpose of the srs was considered but it states purpose of srs itself, gist of software and intended user. This information will not help for system type decision, then hardware software requirement section was thoroughly analyzed but it cannot be generalized for system type determination. Then scope section as proper parameter for system type identification conclusion was derived. Sometimes in srs title itself system details will be present, this factor is also taken care in implementation. Dataflow diagram of our approach is as shown in figure 2,

After determining system type, for model transformation with graph transformation approach system type will be mapped to appropriate graph representation like entity relationship diagrams, control flows, message sequence charts, petri nets, automata, state charts with all the involved system components. Mapping guidelines- if system type is database oriented type representation is Entity Relationship graph, for parser software system use automata representation and if the task is modeling and analysis of concurrent systems use petri nets. Here mapping does not refer only to software modeling activity rather conceptual graph is also formed, that will help in development.

4 Results

The idea of software system type is implemented in Model View Controller with C# programming language. Implementation started with parsing of document, with the constraint that srs will be in document form.

Srs in document form was taken as input and parsing for scope keyword was logic, but appearance of scope keyword is not unique, it varies from one srs to another. Hence scope section itself is given as input. Then title of srs was considered as parameter for system determination. Also all srs may not be in document form they may be pdf form as well.

In the title of srs if words like *web/e/E based/online/hospital/hotel* are present then software system type will be data base oriented system.

If it is not possible to determine from the title system type then scope section details having keywords *controller, safe and efficient operation of all the components* was considered. If these words are present then it will be controller system. Some sample srs were given as input and system type was identified. Still implementation for large set of srs is in process.

5 Conclusion

Graph transformation helps in proactive software performance engineering since graph transformation oriented analysis decisions will correct design defects. Towards this goal choice of graphical representation is utmost important. An approach is proposed in this paper for identifying software system type. From that graphical representation is decided. Future work in this direction can be analysis of different representations, graph transformation approach analysis and tool/system analysis for model transformation in the form of framework.

6 References

[1] John F.Sowa,. "Relating Diagrams to Logic". http://staff.um.edu.mt/cabe2/lectures/webscience/docs/sowa_93.pdf

[2] James L Peterson "Petri Nets"

[3] Robert Gold " Control flow graphs and code coverage", Int. J. Appl. Math. Comput. Sci., 2010, Vol. 20, No. 4, 739–749.

.[4] Chris Fox and Arthorn Luangsodsai "And-Or Dependence Graphs for slicing State Charts" Dagstuhl Seminar Proceedings 05451 Beyond Program Slicing http://drops.dagstuhl.de/opus/volltexte/2006/493

[5] "A Declarative Approach to Graph Based Modeling", Jurgen Ebert, Angelika Franzke.

[6] Handbook of Graph Grammars and Computing by Graph Transformation,
Vol. 1 and Vol 2, H Ehrig, G Engles, H-J Kreowski and G Rozenberg

[7] Tutorial on Fundamentals of Algebraic Graph Transformation, Hartmut Ehrig, Ulrike Prange : TU Berlin Karsten Ehrig : U. Leicester

[8] "Search Trees for Distributed Graph Transformation Systems", Ulrike Ranger and Mathias L¨ ustraeten, Proceedings of the
Second International Workshop on Graph and Model Transformation

[9] "Response Time Estimation: a Study of Hospital Information Management System", Suneeta H. Angadi, Narasimha H Ayachit, Prakash. R.Patil, 2009 International Symposium on Computing, Communication, and Control (ISCCC 2009) Proc .of CSIT vol.1 (2011) © (2011) IACSIT Press, Singapore.

SESSION

SOFTWARE ENGINEERING AND MANAGEMENT + CODE REUSE + SOFTWARE MAINTENANCE METHODS + RELEASE PLANNING + SOFTWARE PRODUCTIVITY AND QUALITY

Chair(s)

TBA

On-Demand Source Code Generation & Scheduling Optimised Parallel Applications on Heterogeneous Platforms

K.A. Hawick and D.P.Playne
Computer Science, Massey University, North Shore 102-904, Auckland, New Zealand
email: { k.a.hawick, d.p.playne }@massey.ac.nz
Tel: +64 9 414 0800 Fax: +64 9 441 8181

March 2013

ABSTRACT

Scheduling applications tasks across heterogeneous clusters is a growing problem, particularly when new upgraded components are added to a parallel computing system that may have originally been homogeneous. We describe how automatic and just-in-time source code generation techniques can be used to make the best parallel decomposition for whatever resource is available in a heterogeneous system consisting of graphical processing unit accelerators and multi-cored conventional CPUs. We show how a high level domain specific language approach to our set of target simulation applications can be used to cater for a variety of different GPU and CPU models and scheduling circumstances. We present some performance and resource utilisation data illustrating the scheduling issue for heterogeneous systems in computational science. We discuss the future outlook for this code generation approach in software engineering.

KEYWORDS
software engineering; on-demand code generation; code reuse; computational science; simulation; GPUs.

1 Introduction

Scheduling application jobs [2,7] across heterogeneous parallel computing systems is a long standing problem in computational science, with renewed efforts and work reported for distributed systems [1,3,20,21] and grid systems. Cluster computing has also attracted a lot of scheduling research efforts [10,12,17,18]. As soon as it is given its first upgrade any computer cluster or systems typically becomes heterogeneous unless great care and planning moves are made to obtain exact replacement or upgrade components. Clocks speeds move on, memory speeds and capacities improve in performance and price performance and so do disk capacities. As nodes are added to any existing compute cluster there is firstly a strong temptation to upgrade with improved price performance or improved performance components. Secondly, as a system ages it may become effectively impossible to source the older

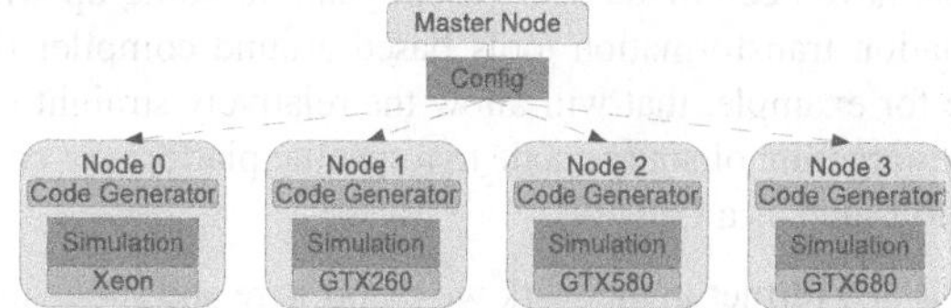

Figure 1: An illustration of a master node distributing a configuration file to four different nodes, each of which will generate code optimised to run it's specific hardware.

components, even if there is an intention to maintain the original systems' homogeneity.

This problem of managing a resource that inevitably becomes less homogeneous in nature with time is therefore common. In this paper we consider the particular issues concerning GPU-accelerated clusters that are growing in heterogeneity [26]. We describe how software engineering techniques such as automated code generation from a higher-level problem specification can improve code reuse and extend its lifetime.

Hybrid systems of multi-cored conventional CPUs as well as GPU-accelerated systems are also quite common and scheduling for highly heterogeneous environments is a particular challenge [4]. At the time of writing GPU systems are becoming widespread but we believe this issue of growing heterogeneity and other legacy system effects are still relatively new for GPU system owner/operators. The heterogeneous system effect will not go away and cannot be simply addressed as an economic issue. The pragmatic approach is to consider what ideas, terminologies, and software technologies and solutions are available to help quantify the scheduling inefficiencies and aid us to make better and effective use of heterogeneous resources as part of a managed process.

Many groups, like our own, will be working with a mix of optimisation goals. We are interested in parallel computing systems from an experimental computer science systems perspective as well as a computational science one. That means we actively collect disparate systems with different processors, CPU models, memory configurations and so forth as that gives us a wide range of experimental system data points with which to explore parallel algorithms, system capabilities, efficiencies, speed ups, cache effects and similar experimental systems effects. However, to make good use of the capital investment in such equipment we also like to keep our systems busy doing number crunching and running simulations and other science applications – when we are not deliberately reconfiguring them.

In this paper we discuss our ongoing work on scheduling dynamically generated applications codes on various parallel computing platform configurations. We are exploring the idea of applications software that is (re)compiled at run time for the particular platform that the scheduler deems appropriate and available. This is not new idea in general, and OpenCL [27] contains the notion of just-in-time compilation, particularly aimed towards heterogeneous systems [13]. Similarly, many attempts have been made over recent years to come up with compilation transformation tools based around compiler directive for example, that will allow the relatively straightforward re-targeting of source code to a specific platform or configuration such as a GPU [9].

We go a step further in the work we report here and show how some of the emerging domain-specific programming language technologies and ideas [8, 11, 14–16] can be used to tackle this issue. We show how numerical simulations - admittedly in a very specific applications domain - can be written in a high level language that can be used to generate highly optimised implementations for parallel paradigms and platforms. Specifically, we discuss how a set of field equation-based simulations that have been formulated in this way can be used to explore the idea of dynamically generating optimised parallel versions for different models or families of models of GPU devices or for multi-cored CPUs.

In this present paper we consider the new notion of dynamically interrogating the heterogeneous components of the cluster to determine which node or nodes best satisfy the parallelism capabilities that match the task as well as scheduling availability of the hardware resource in question. This model has restricted utility - it obviously involves an overhead to generate and compile the application code and the latency of carrying this out has to be weighed against the time to execute the task that is being optimised. Nevertheless we believe that for departmental resources in scenarios like ours, this model has great value.

The heterogeneity of GPU devices is hard to overcome due to the drastic change in architecture between different generations. To get the maximum performance out of a GPU, code must be specifically tuned to make best use of the device's specialized memory. Even a small change in memory patterns or problem decomposition can have a large impact on performance. While it is possible to write general GPU implementations that work on devices of all generations, these codes tend to be large, complex and still cannot fully utilize the device.

The novelty of our system comes from the software architectural notions shown in Figure 1. The assumption is that complex equation based code has been formulated in a high level form that is input to a source code generator. The output of the generator is conventional C/C++ source code that might have: embedded compiler directives; generated message passing calls; generated multi-threading management; or of most recent interest – specialist GPU kernel calls in CUDA or a similar language, also generated automatically. The resulting (human-readable) source code is then compiled in the usual way by the vendor or platform-specific tools and the job appropriately launched and run.

Dynamical source-to-source code generation is still a relatively unusual approach, with most reported work on generated code on-demand appearing in the mobile computing literature [6, 22]. In this paper we add to its novelty by doing it on-demand – effectively at run time, but with a high-level application-specific language specification of the core algorithmic aspects.

Our present article is structured as follows: In Section 2 we summarise the general problem of scheduling and lay out a notation for performance timing. We summarise the particular class of numerical simulations applications we use for our benchmarks and performance analysis in Section 3 and give a description of our prototype just-in-time source code generator in Section 4 and present some performance timing results in Section 5. We discuss the implications for scheduling applications on heterogeneous systems in Section 6 and offer some conclusions and areas for further work in Section 7.

2 Scheduling Systems

Scheduling jobs has been an important area of research throughout the history of computing. It is usual to split the subject from two usually different perspectives: firstly individual users or programmers aim to get a particular job to complete in the shortest time possible - either by having it start running as soon as possible in any given queue system and/or having it run on the fastest and most appropriate resource available. The organisation that owns and operates the resources usually has the possibly conflicting goal of having the resource be as well utilised as possible. Economic considerations can provide another axis of interest but in our discussion we focus only on the first two points.

We have realised that as a computer science research group we need to combine the two goals. Much of our "computer science" systems oriented research work involves experimenting with our systems, often deliberately reconfiguring them to try different combinations of processors, memory, accelerators, and communications system. When we are not doing this however we want to make it as easy as possible to deploy number crunching applications that will soak up as many compute cycles and other resources as possible while producing "computational science" outcomes in the form of completed numerical experiments and analysis and so forth. These two complementary aspects of computational science need to co exist and this present paper is a manifestation of some prototypical software management and scheduling analysis.

There are many good software systems for managing jobs on cluster computers. We focus here on the latency overhead issues concerned with giving a scheduler the additional capability of generating applications source code and compiling it "just in time" before running it in the usual way.

Suppose we have a number of compute jobs labelled by index j that are to be scheduled to run on the most appropriate of a set or resources index by r. Generally a scheduler or job management system will have one or more queues that are usually managed as first in first out streams of jobs. They need not of course be executed in the order of submission as there may be any number of economic and socio-political priority considerations in effect. The goals are either: to minimise the time to completion of all or some jobs; or to maximise the resource utilisation efficiency. Scheduling a homogeneous collection of resources is a relatively well known problem and often modern resources have the capability of running more than one job at once, with some degree of process level parallelism managed straightforwardly by the operating system software.

In the scenarios we consider in this paper, we are often interested in jobs that are being timed or benchmarked as part of an exploration of a resource configuration or as part of parallel algorithmic development work. Consequently we often want exactly one job running per resource at any given time, to minimise job-job interference through resource contention and so forth.

However in the heterogeneous systems we are interested in there is some extra information is available to the scheduler concerning the resources and their capabilities. They can be queries or polled dynamically to determine what their availability is, but they can (and need to) have a much richer and more detailed capability specification that would a plain ordinary CPU. These include floating point capability, number of GPU devices, number of low level cores per device and other parameters which as we find in our results can make an order of magnitude in difference in run time if not properly catered for.

Our approach to this problem has been to consider how much information can be made available to the scheduler about the application properties as well as the compute resources, and to consider how this information needs to be expressed and how it can best be matched by a smart scheduler.

3 Field Equation Examples

To focus on specific applications for which we can measure and demonstrate improved performance, we report on some simulation model calculations based upon a field equation formulation.

Three example field equations are used to evaluate the on-demand code generation system - the Heat (1), Ginzburg-Landau (2) and Cahn-Hilliard (3) equations. These equations were chosen for several reasons. First of all the

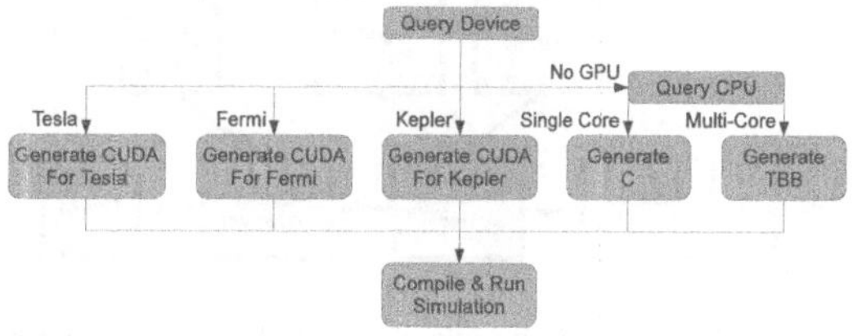

Figure 2: Code generator process to select a suitable processing device and generate code for the simulation.

code generation system used in this research is designed for field-equations that can be numerically simulated on N-dimensional regular lattices, using finite-difference methods and explicit Runge-Kutta integration methods [24]. These three equations all fit into this category and can be automatically generated.

$$\frac{\partial u}{\partial t} = \alpha\nabla^2 u \quad (1)$$

$$\frac{\partial \psi}{\partial t} = -\frac{p}{i}\nabla^2\psi - \frac{q}{i}\left|\psi\right|^2\psi + \gamma\psi \quad (2)$$

$$\frac{\partial \phi}{\partial t} = m\nabla^2\left(-b\phi + u\phi^3 - K\nabla^2\phi\right) \quad (3)$$

The three equations also have different computation intensities and memory halos. The the Heat equation is a very simple equation with a small memory halo and can be represented by a scalar field. The Ginzburg-Landau equation also has a small memory halo but requires a field of complex numbers to represent the field. Finally the Cahn-Hilliard equation is represented by a scalar field but requires the use of the biharmonic operator resulting in a larger memory halo. These equations are provided to the generator as ASCII representations in an equation file. An example ASCII representation of the Heat equation can be written as follows:

```
floating a;
floating[] u;
d/dt u = a * Laplacian{u};
```

The generator will then parse this file and combine it with the appropriate stencil and integration method as defined by the configuration file. This process is shown in Figure 3.

More details on the workings of our code generator and domain-specific field equation language are described in [19, 23] from the perspective of the applications domain. In what follows, we focus on the aspects of generation for different accelerator devices and capabilities.

4 Code Generation On-Demand

The Code Generation component of this system does not consider the problem of scheduling but will simply run the simulation on it's hardware as it sees fit. It assumes all scheduling

To launch a simulation on a machine, the master node sends the configuration file to the node and launches the code gen-

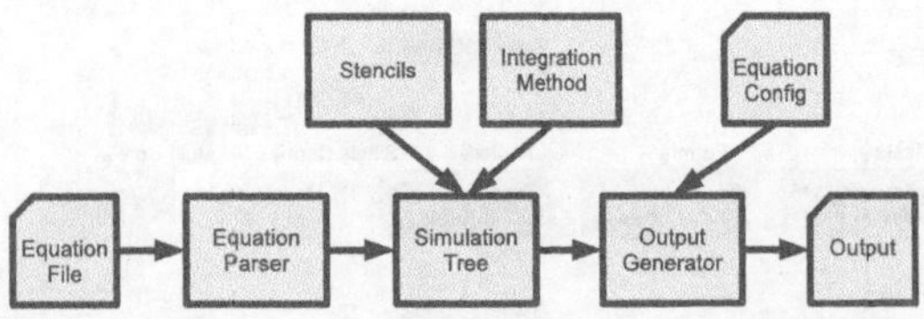

Figure 3: A diagram of the structure of the code generator. The generator take information on the equations, stencils and integration method to construct an abstract tree representation of the simulation. This tree and configuration is given to the output generator that produces code for a specific target language.

erator. This configuration file contains the details of the simulation, model parameters, numerical methods, time scale etc. When the code generator is launched it will first query the device to determine what computing resources it has available. First it will determine whether or not there is a suitable Graphical Processing Unit available.

If no GPU device exists the simulation must be run on the CPU in which case it will query the CPU to determine if it is a single- or multi-core CPU. The generator will then create a C implementation for a single-core or an implementation using Thread Building Blocks (TBB) [25] for a multi-core CPU. This is not a restriction of the generator, C and TBB were chosen simply due to previous experience with this language and library. Generators could easily be written for other languages or multi-threading libraries.

Listing 1: Code snippet of the Tesla implementation allocating texture memory and fetching values from texture memory for the point (ix,iy).

```
//Create texture
texture<float, 2, cudaReadModeElementType> texture_u;

//Create and bind array
texture_u.normalized = false;
texture_u.filterMode = cudaFilterModePoint;
cudaArray *array_u;
cudaChannelFormatDesc u_descriptor =
    cudaCreateChannelDesc<float>();
cudaMallocArray(&array_u, &u_descriptor, X, Y);
cudaBindTextureToArray(texture_u, array_u);

//Fetch values from texture memory
float u0ymlx = tex2D(texture_u, ix, yml);
float u0yxml = tex2D(texture_u, xml, iy);
float u0yx   = tex2D(texture_u, ix, iy);
float u0yxpl = tex2D(texture_u, xpl, iy);
float u0yplx = tex2D(texture_u, ix, ypl);
```

If a suitable NVIDIA GPU is available on the machine, the generator will run a small program to query the device(s) to determine their capabilities. The generator can be configured to find a suitable device to run the simulation. This includes selecting a device with sufficient memory for the simulation etc. If no suitable device is found to run the simulation, the generator will fall-back to using the CPU. If there is more than one suitable device, the generator will select the latest generation device. This process of querying the machine and generating code is shown in Figure 2.

The major difference in code generation lies between the Tesla and Fermi/Kepler generation cards. This is due to the introduction of L1/L2 cache in the Fermi and subsequent generation devices. Prior to this change in memory architecture, texture memory provided the best performance for the type of access pattern used by these simulation. The use of texture memory to fetch values from the field is shown in Listing 1. However, in later generations the higher bandwidth of L1/L2 cache provides the best performance (See Listing 2). This change in memory type requires some significant changes to simulation code. The difference between Fermi and Kepler devices is less as they are more similar architectures.

Listing 2: Code snippet of the Fermi/Kepler implementation fetching values from global memory through L1/L2 cache and calculating the heat equation for the point (ix,iy).

```
//Create global memory array
float *u0;
cudaMalloc((void**) &u0, X*Y*sizeof(float));

//Fetch values from global memory
float u0ymlx = u0[yml*X + ix];
float u0yxml = u0[iy*X  + xml];
float u0yx   = u0[iy*X  + ix];
float u0yxpl = u0[iy*X  + xpl];
float u0yplx = u0[ypl*X + ix];
```

Once the generator has determined the device it is going to run the simulation on. It can produce code tailored specifically for that device. This includes using different memory types, grid/block sizes based on the number and type of multiprocessors in that GPU etc. Currently this system only makes use of a single GPU however it can be extended to utilize mGPU machines including systems with multiple GPUs of different architectures.

The details of this code generation system is described in [24] but the general structure of the generator is shown in Figure 3.

There will be a slight overhead when running simulations using this code generation method. Obviously there will be some communication required to send the configuration file to the compute node, the configuration is a small file and the time to send it to the node is negligible. Copying the results back from the simulation may require more communication but this is dependent on the simulation not the code generator and thus is not considered.

The overhead comes about from the fact that rather than distributing and running a program, the nodes must read the configuration file and generate the code for the simulation. The exact generation time will vary based on the hardware and computational load of the node, the complexity of the equation and numerical methods and implementation of the generator. For the most part this generation completes in the order of seconds and generally much less than the run-time of the simulation. This generation time is discussed further in Section 5 below.

5 Results

The best way to assess the feasibility of the just-in-time code generation approach is to measure the performance attainable on different system configurations. Although one is normally interested in the scalability and how the performance of an application changes with the number of parallel components or with some measure of the problem size, in this paper we are especially interested in determining accurately the latency or overhead that arises from the code generation and recompilation. A reliable way to determine the "zero sized job" time is to plot run times with increasing job size and use a least-squares fit, weighted by the standard deviation on the completion times. the slope of such a fit gives us the normal indications of speed scaling, but more usefully here, the intercept - accurately extrapolates back to zero job size and gives us the latency overhead.

Figure 4 shows the compute time vs number of simulations steps run for a 1024x1024 cell sized Cahn Hilliard simulation, integrated using the RK2 integration method on four different nodes. These four nodes all have different compute devices - a Tesla GPU (GTX260), a Fermi GPU (GTX580), a Kepler GPU (GTX680) and a multi-core Xeon (X5675). Analysing the intercepts of these plots shows that the overhead of code generation is $\approx$ 1...6 seconds depending on the node.

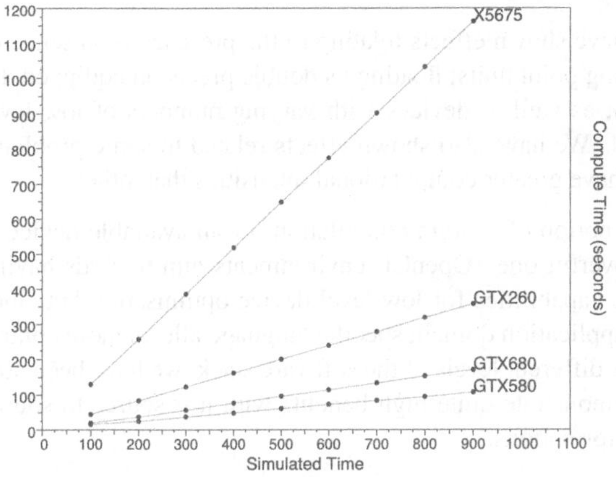

Figure 4: Plot of simulation time vs compute time for a Cahn-Hilliard simulation using RK2 numerical integration on a 1024x1024 field. Results shown for a GTX260, GTX 580, GTX680 and a four-core Xeon X5675.

Another comparison can be drawn between generic CUDA code and code that has been specifically targeted for a certain type of card. Obviously if all GPU cards were of the same generation, it would be much easier to create a general implementation that could run reasonably efficiently on all of them. However, to be able to run a simulation on all generations of card, the implementation must be built for the most general case. In this case we compare a Cahn-Hilliard simulation that can be run on any CUDA capable card and the implementations created by the code generator (Gen). It can be seen from Figure 5 that the generated code provides significant performance benefits over the general version.

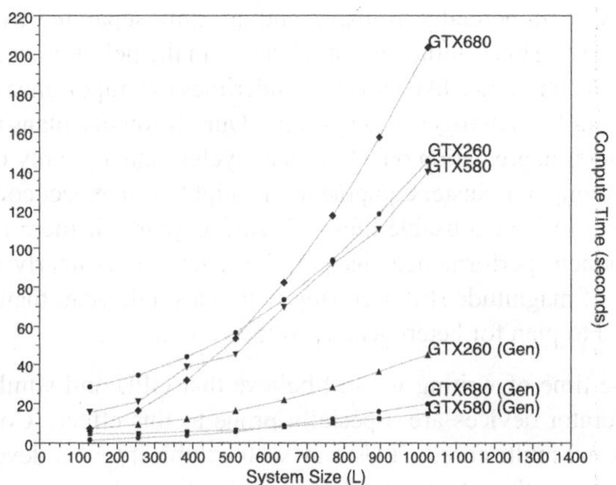

Figure 5: Comparison between code generated for specific devices (Gen) and device independent code. The simulation used to compare these implementations is a Cahn-Hilliard Simulation using RK2 (h=0.01) and system size of L={128...1024} run for a simulation time of 100.

Table 1 shows the performance variations of different devices computing the three example simulations using float and double data types.

Table 1: Performance variations (in seconds) across different devices. Accurate to $\pm 0.5s$

Precn.	Eqn.	TBB	Tesla	Fermi	Kepler
float	Heat	224s	57s	22s	18s
	TDGL	720s	114s	41s	32s
	CH	920s	133s	46s	30s
double	Heat	339s	119s	33s	44s
	TDGL	984s	305s	93s	129s
	CH	1161s	358s	106s	171s

As can be seen from the table, computing simulations with double precision requires more compute time. This increase in compute time is especially noticeable in the old (Tesla) and new (Kepler) generations of GPU.

6 Discussion

The code generation overhead times as shown in Figure 4 and from Table 1 are significant in absolute terms, but in relative terms and for the sort of numerical simulation job that might typically take more than a few minutes at least, and more likely take more than an hour, the overheads are not significant. The application codes were have focused one are have been shown to be good representative benchmark codes based on past work. The data suggest therefore that the dynamical code generation approach is quite feasible an practicable.

The different GPU models show quite significant variations in performance. These models are all still relatively recent - they are still commercially available and are only separated by a year or so. This is indicative of advances in the field for accelerator technologies like GPUs. It underlines the importance of planning for heterogeneous systems. Our University plans its computer depreciation on a four year cycles, and arguably for supercomputer cluster equipment one might even expect components to have a usable life-cycle of 5-6 years. It there are component performance changes as significant as nearly an order of magnitude still occurring within a single year, then it is vital to plan for heterogeneity in the system.

At the time of writing we still believe that GPU and similar accelerator devices are especially prone to this effect. Conventional multi-cored CPUs may well exhibit it too as developments in their technology are accelerating. It is entirely feasible to build 4, 6, 8, 16 cored CPU nodes in 2012, and its is likely that 32-cored CPUs will be commonplace and commodity priced by 2014. This same heterogeneity effect will quite likely influence even conventional cluster computer purchases and plans over that time-scale.

In this short present paper we have focused on a small class of numerical simulations that we already understand well and for which the code generation approach works well. Our code generation system obviously has greater scope than the issues discussed here. It allows relatively simple use of quite complex higher order numerical integration schemes with all the boilerplate communications and data structures management code generated automatically. This is useful to be able to experiment with different algorithms, but is beyond the scope of this present paper. Here we have just experimented with different GPU and multi-core tuning aspects rather than major algorithmic aspects.

We have seen in Figure 5 that we can obtain very good performance on GPU-accelerated nodes for this class of numerical simulation, but also that we can improve further by nearly an order of magnitude by tuning for the right device with the right properties. Furthermore as table 1 shows, the overheads accrued are insignificant next to the typical run times of production level jobs. There are a myriad of different GPU model available and this "horse for courses" approach is likely a good vendor strategy and will certainly persist to serve different market segments well. The area of floating point precision and precision capability available to each core will likely continue to be a major market segmentation aspect.

We believe the dynamic code generation approach could be incorporated into a more conventional scheduler software framework. What appears to need more work however is to develop a constraint specification language so that the user or the code generator can impart impart further information about the sort of compute resource that best suits the simulation. As we have commented, OpenCL encourages this notion within a limited scope at run time, but the notion of a domain-specific high level application language opens up this idea further to a greater range of device preferences.

We have not reported in the various scheduling heuristics [5] and other queue parameter tuning that could be done to optimise resource utilisation efficiency. The main point arising from our present work is that a scheduler with the extra information we have described about device specifics and the means to recompile a tuned application will be able to apply economic and other heuristics even more.

7 Conclusion

We have described how source code generation technologies can be used to schedule performance tuned parallel simulation applications on heterogeneous clusters of GPU-accelerated nodes and conventional multi-cored CPUs. Our data indicates that very significant performance enhancement comes from using specially tuned GPU-model specific codes instead of general versions.

We have been able to demonstrate these effects since we have focused on a well-defined set of field-equation based numerical simulation applications. The domain-specific high-level problem formulation works well on this class of problems and we believe could be extended to other application domain families that share common algorithmic and data structural elements

We have shown effects relating to the presence or absence of floating point units; floating vs double precision equipped devices; as well as devices with varying numbers of low level cores. We have also shown effects related to some problems that have greater computational intensities than others.

This notion of custom compilation for an available device is a powerful one. OpenCL environments aim towards having some capabilities for low level device optimisation but since our application domain specific language allows more control at the different levels of the software stack, we have been able to demonstrate quite high benefits with just source to source transformations.

We conclude that while GPUs are already known to greatly accelerate some problems, it is important to consider the particular device model and its availability in scheduling runs to give best turn-around run time and/or best resource utilisation. Allowing a scheduler access to the extra information available in a stack of automatically generated application source code opens up new scheduler optimisation potential especially for heterogeneous clusters. We believe there is scope for further work in incorporating these code generation and management ideas within the framework of existing cluster computing scheduler software systems and that this approach will be useful for improving utilisation of computational resources, particular for research groups like our own with mixed computer systems science and applied computational science goals.

References

[1] Abramson, D., Giddy, J.: Scheduling large parameteric modelling experiments on a distributed meta-computer. In: Proc. PCW '97 (September 1997)

[2] Adam, T.L., Chandy, K.M., Dickson, J.R.: A comparison of list schedules for parallel processing systems. Communications of the ACM 17(12), 685–690 (December 1974)

[3] Berman, F., Wolski, R., Figueira, S., Schopf, J., Shao, G.: Application-level scheduling on distributed heterogeneous networks. In: Supercomputing '96 (November 1996)

[4] Blazewicz, M., Brandt, S.R., Diener, P., Koppelman, D.M., Kurowski, K., Loffler, F., Schnetter, E.: A massive data parallel computational framework for petascale/exascale hybrid computer systems. arXiv 1201.2118v1, Poznan Supercomputing and Networking Center, poland (10 January 2012)

[5] Braun, T.D., Siegel, H.J., Beck, N., Boloni, L.L., Maheswaran, M., Reuther, A.I., Robertson, J.P., Theys, M.D., BinYao, Hensgen, D., Freund, R.F.: A comparison of eleven static heuristics for mapping a class of independent taks onto heterogeneous distributed computing systems. J. Parallel and Distributed Computing 61, 810–837 (2001)

[6] Carzaniga, A., Picco, G.P., Vigna, G.: Is code still moving around? looking back at a decade of code mobility. In: 29th IEEE Int. Conf. on Software Engineering (ICSE'07). pp. 9–20. Minneapolis, USA (20-26 May 2007)

[7] Casavant, T.L., Kuhl, J.G.: A taxonomy of scheduling in general-purpose distributed computing systems (May 1986)

[8] Chafi, H., Sujeeth, A.K., Brown, K.J., Lee, H., Atreya, A.R., Olukotun, K.: A domain-specific approach to heterogeneous parallelism. In: Proceedings of the 16th ACM symposium on Principles and practice of parallel programming. pp. 35–46. PPoPP '11, ACM, New York, NY, USA (2011), `http://doi.acm.org/10.1145/1941553.1941561`

[9] Chen, L., Liu, L., Tang, S., Huang, L., Jing, Z., Xu, S., Zhang, D., Shou, B.: Unified parallel c for gpu clusters: Language extensions and compiler implementation. In: Proc. 23rd Int. Workshop on Languages and Compilers for Parallel Computing (LCPC2010). pp. 151–165. No. 6548 in LNCS, Springer (2010)

[10] Fan, Z., Qiu, F., Kaufman, A., Yoakum-Stover, S.: Gpu cluster for high performance computing. In: Proc. Supercomputing (SC'04). p. 47. Pittsburgh, USA (6-12 November 2004)

[11] Fowler, M.: Domain-Specific Languages. No. ISBN 0-321-71294-3, Addison Wesley (2011)

[12] Gan-El, M., Hawick, K.A.: Parallel containers - a tool for applying parallel computing applications on clusters. In: Proc. Int. Conf. on Parallel and Distributed Processing Techniques and Applications (PDPTA'06). pp. 764–767. No. PDP3889, CSREA, Las Vegas, USA (26-29 June 2006), iSBN 1-932415-86-6

[13] Gaster, B., Howes, L., Kaeli, D.R., Mistry, P., Schaa, D.: Heterogeneous Computing with OpenCL. Elsevier (2012), iSBN 978-0-12-387766-6

[14] Ghosh, D.: Dsl for the uninitiated - domain-specific languages bridge the semantic gap in programming. Communications of the ACM 54(7), 44–50 (2011)

[15] Hawick, K.A.: Engineering internal domain-specific language software for lattice-based simulations. In: Proc. Int. Conf. on Software Engineering and Applications. IASTED, Las Vegas, USA (12-14 November 2012)

[16] Hawick, K.A.: Fluent interfaces and domain-specific languages for graph generation and network analysis calculations. In: Proc. Int. Conf. on Software Engineering (SE'13). IASTED, Innsbruck, Austria (11-13 February 2013)

[17] Hawick, K.A., James, H.A.: Trends in cluster computing scheduling and the missing cycles. In: Proc. Int. Conf on Parallel and Distributed Processing Techniques and Applications (PDPTA'05). pp. 732–738. CSREA, Las Vegas, USA. (27-30 June 2005)

[18] Hawick, K.A., James, H.A., Scogings, C.J.: 64-bit architectures and compute clusters for high performance simulations. Tech. Rep. CSTN-024, Computer Science, Massey University, Albany, North Shore 102-904, Auckland, New Zealand (April 2006), `http://www.massey.ac.nz/~kahawick/cstn/024/cstn-024.pdf`

[19] Hawick, K.A., Playne, D.P.: Automatically Generating Efficient Simulation Codes on GPUs from Partial Differential Equations. Tech. Rep. CSTN-087, Computer Science, Massey University, Albany, North Shore 102-904, Auckland, New Zealand (July 2010), `http://www.massey.ac.nz/~kahawick/cstn/087/cstn-087.pdf`

[20] James, H.A.: Scheduling in Metacomputing Systems. Ph.D. thesis, The University of Adelaide (1999), forthcoming

[21] Krueger, P., Chawla, R.: The stealth distributed scheduler. Proc. IEEE 11th Int. Conf. Distributed Computing Systems pp. 336–343 (1991)

[22] Lau, F.C.M., Belaramini, N., Kwan, V.W.M., Siu, P.P.L., Wing, W.K., Wang, C.L.: Code-on-demand and code adaptation for mobile computing. In: The Handbook of Mobile Middleware. Auerbach (2006)

[23] Playne, D.P., Hawick, K.A.: Auto-generation of parallel finite-differencing code for mpi, tbb and cuda. In: Proc. International Parallel and Distributed Processing Symposium (IPDPS); Workshop on High-Level Parallel Programming Models and Supportive - HIPS 2011. pp. 1163–1170. IEEE, Anchorage, Alaska, USA (16-20 May 2011), in conjunction with IPDPS 2011, the 25th IEEE International Parallel & Distributed Processing Symposium

[24] Playne, D.P.: Generative Programming Methods for Parallel Partial Differential Field Equation Solvers. Ph.D. thesis, Computer Science, Massey University (2011)

[25] Reinders, J.: Intel Threading Building Blocks: outfitting C++ for multi-core processor parallelism. No. ISBN 978-0596514808, O'Reilly, 1st edn. (2007)

[26] Samuel, T.K., Baer, T., Brook, R.G., Ezell, M., Kovatch, P.: Scheduling diverse high performance computing systems with the goal of maximizing utilization. In: Proc. 18th International Conf on High Performance Computing (HiPC). pp. 1–6. Bangalore, India (18-21 December 2011)

[27] Stone, J.E., Gohara, D., Guochun, S.: Opencl: A parallel programming standard for heterogeneous computing systems. Computing in Science & Engineering 12(3), 66–73 (May-June 2010)

Lights on the Impact of Requirements Interdependencies on Priorities during Release Planning Decisions

Bassey Isong[1], **Obeten Ekabua**[2], **and Ifeoma Ohaeri**[2]
[1]Department of Computer Science, University of Venda, Thohoyandou, Limpopo, South Africa
[2]Department of Computer Science, North-West University, Mmabatho, Mafikeng, South Africa

Abstract - *In market-driven software development, software release planning is both crucial and complex activity with a significant impact on the success or failure of software product development. However, the task of scheduling an optimal set of requirements for a particular release is not as easy as expected. This is because requirements prioritization is crippled by interdependencies. Consequently, release planning decisions are thwarted, prioritization is difficult, and interdependencies are complex and fuzzy. Furthermore, not much has been known about the nature of requirements interdependencies in release planning perspective in literature. Therefore, our objective in this paper is to bring into light the impact of interdependencies on priority of requirement and their complexity nature. In addition, an approach for intermediate representation of interdependencies is proposed.*

Keywords: market-driven, prioritization, interdependencies, requirements, release planning

1 Introduction

In market-driven software development, products are developed in several successive releases and planning the contents of the resultant product releases constitutes one of the most critical activities that determine a company's product success or failure [1]. During product planning and road-mapping, requirements evaluation and selection process is seen as a complex activity involving trade-offs between requirements from different origins and stakeholders. This is because market-driven development does not have specific identifiable customers and the requirements often need to be invented based on the 'assume' needs of several potential users [2]. Consequently, the software company bear all risk related to product development.

The goal of market-driven development is to achieve a competitive advantage by taking a reasonable market share, attract wide range of customers and amassing profits [3]. However, achieving favorable levels of revenue under conditions of scarce resources is a great challenge for software production intended for mass markets. The challenge is mainly dealt with product release planning – the process of planning for the next release, what should be and delivered when. The objective of release planning has been selecting subset of requirements that can yield optimal realization of products in a certain release within the constraints of fixed release date and resources available [4,5]. Achieving such an objective has been found to be particularly critical in the software product development [4].During the course of a project, many different decisions regarding product release plan has to be made. Release planning is considered a challenging and complex decision-making activity due to its size, the number of involved stakeholders, the variety of variables need to be taken into consideration for next releases (such as available resources, milestones, conflicting stakeholder views, available market opportunity, risks, product strategies, requirements interdependencies and costs) and so on [4]. Consequently, the problem of release planning has been described as "wicked" [6] and in particular, many of the identified challenges are stakeholder related [7]. When requirements originate from several stakeholders it often yields more requirements than can be implemented at once. This requires requirements to be prioritized so that the most significant ones are met by the earliest product releases.

Prioritization, a sub-problem of release planning is a crucial activity involving assigning priorities according to a set of criteria reflecting the views of a set of stakeholders, scheduling, resource planning and requirements interdependencies [8]. However, determining priorities for requirements has proved to be difficult and most requirements cannot be treated independently since they are related to and affect each other in complex ways [4]. This however makes it difficult, if not impossible for requirements to be planned based on priority only [9]. With the nature of the relationship, decisions made on one or many requirements may affect other requirements in ways not anticipated for during development [1]. In fact, the challenge with requirements interdependencies tends to grow in time. As such, requirements interdependencies have to be taken seriously in order to make good decisions about the importance of requirements during the process of prioritization which in turn facilitates quality product release plan.

Planning a product release inevitably involves dealing with all categories of interdependencies. With the complex nature of release planning, requirements interdependencies is seen as an important research area since little attention has so far been gained in existing literature. Research in this area has been focused mostly on specific problem or a development activity which does not specifically address release planning problems [9]. Thus, our objective in this paper is to bring into light, the nature of prioritization and interdependencies challenges during product release planning. In addition, this paper tries to propose an approach to represent interdependencies between requirements that will add to the facilitation of the selection of optimal subset or requirements that add values to customer needs within the constraints of fixed release date and available resources.

The remaining part of the paper is organized as follows: section 1 is the introduction, section 2 gives a description of requirements prioritizations and its challenges, section 3 describes requirements interdependencies and their fuzziness nature. Accordingly, section 4 presents the impact of interdependencies on priority, section 5 gives the details of the proposed interdependencies representation while section 6 is the paper conclusion..

2 Requirements Prioritization

With the proliferation of markets for packaged software, market-driven software development is gaining increased momentum against bespoke software development [3]. Stated by [10], the difference between them is characterized by stake-holding and schedule constraints. This means market-driven software development involves wide markets with large potential customer based outside the company and more stakeholders within the company [10]. Consequently, large volume of requirements is produced which are continuous and often cannot be implemented at once. However, the challenge is often how to select the correct set of requirements that are valuable for the customers, and can be implemented within budget for an organization to become more successful in the market in upcoming releases. If a subset of the requirements should be selected, the decision makers must understand the relative priorities of the requested requirements.

Sommerville [11] defined requirements prioritization as the activity during which the most important requirements for the system are discovered. This activity is a vital step towards making good decisions concerning product planning for multiple releases as it help to establish the importance of requirements and their implementation and testing order throughout the development lifecycle. With requirements prioritization, software engineers can focus on a subset of all the requirements, and implement them in the earliest product releases [12]. Generally, the process of selecting the right set of requirements for a product release is dependent on how well the organization succeeds in prioritizing the requirements candidates. In market-driven software development, how to prioritize large number of requirements is one of the greatest challenges which negatively affect release planning decisions.

Requirements prioritization is an important requirements engineering activity that originates from limited product development resources. It is triggered when customer expectations are high, timelines short, and resources limited, prompting a limited set of requirements with most critical functionality to be implemented and delivered as early as possible in one product release while meeting the needs of the customers and reach the markets in time [12].

Unfortunately, requirements prioritization has been recognized as a very challenging activity. In existing literature, it has been described as an easy task, of medium difficulty, while some authors considered it one of the most complex requirements activities, with no effective and systematic methods to perform in most software organizations [13]. Accordingly, Karlsson et al [14] stated that requirements prioritization requires domain knowledge and estimation skills in order to be successful. In practice, determining the priorities for requirements has proved to be difficult and not easy to define the aspects on the basis of which prioritization decisions should be based [8]. This is because priority itself is a term that is ambiguous and a complex amalgam of different aspects such as importance, penalty, cost, time and risk where each aspect is an extremely multifaceted concept [21]. For instance, importance could be combination of implementation urgency, requirement importance for the product architecture, strategic importance for the company, etc. [8, 21].

In addition, it has been found that decision-makers ought to consider multiple aspects before deciding the implementation scheduling of the requirements [21]. However, dealing with these multiple aspects of priority is difficult in practice and is challenging for decision makers to determine which aspects are important in making prioritization decisions [4]. Also, it is sometimes difficult to get real information on those aspects and not only do prioritization depends on the chosen aspects, but also on the selected stakeholders [8]. To make the issues more complicated, priorities may vary as a function of time [7]. Requirements depend on each other and priorities are always complex in relative where the importance in one release or to a certain customer may not be as important in the next release or to another customer – fuzziness nature [4].

There are several techniques of requirements prioritization that exist in the literature which are categorized based on determining the absolute importance of the candidate requirements while others are based on relative and require a person to determine which requirement is more important. In other words, they are *methods* based on giving values to different factors of requirements and *negotiation approaches* [14].These include the analytic hierarchy process (AHP), binary search tree creation, greedy-type algorithms, cumulative voting, the 100-dollar Test, numerical assignment (grouping), Theory-W, requirements triage, Wiegers' Method, ranking, top-Ten requirements, planning games, other common sorting methods [12, 15]. The pitfalls with these approaches include not scalable, do not takes into account different stakeholder view points and release planning with effort constraints [15]. Lastly, their basic model is fixed and does not permit any requirements changes, complete priorities or constraints. Other techniques aimed at supporting release planning, in particular when several stakeholders are involved are EVOLVE [16] and Quantitative WinWin [17]. More information about the list of techniques that supports release planning refer to Svahnberg et al [18].

3 Requirements Interdependencies

Like a system, requirements do not exist in isolation instead they are related to and affect each other in complex ways. Requirements interdependency is a special aspect of requirements traceability with a specific interest on the relationships between individual requirements. Studies have shown that during the RE process, most developed individual requirements cannot be treated separately during software development due to the cost and value relationship between them [19]. This however, affects several other development activities in an uneven manner such as release planning. For instance, requirements may affect each other by either: constrains how other requirements can be implemented, affects the cost of implementing other requirements, or increases or decreases the customer satisfaction of other requirements [19]. Moreover, a study by [9] has shown that only roughly 20% of the requirements are responsible for 75% of the interdependencies out of which a few requirements are singular where bespoke development has more feature-related dependencies and market-driven product development have more value-related dependencies.

Though, less work has been done in the area of requirements interdependencies, few strategies for identifying and managing interdependencies exist. Dahlstedt and Persson [19] in their studies identified three types of requirements dependencies: structural, constraints, and cost-value interdependencies. The classification was aimed at understanding the relationship between requirements. Each interdependency type is categorized into: ***Structural*** (Refined_to, Change_to, and Similar_to), ***Constraining*** (Requires, and Conflicts_with) and lastly, ***Cost/Value*** (Increases/Decreases_cost_of and Increases / Decreases_value_of) dependencies. The study recommends that *requires*, *similar_to*, *conflicts_with*, and the entire *cost/value* category should be used to group requirements in order to avoid costly mistakes during release planning.

In another study, Carlshamre et al [9] discussed several alternatives aimed at minimizing the time required in carrying out the analysis and proposed a classification scheme for interdependencies: *functional related* (AND, REQUIRES) and *value related* (ICOST, CVALUE) for bespoke and MDRE respectively. Others are OR and TEMPORAL dependencies. In addition, to facilitate release planning a simple visualization method was applied for the ease of interdependencies identification. In a similar study, Johan et al [20], also work on automated similarity analysis which uses language tools to analyze sets of requirements. The technique was aimed at supporting requirement engineers to identify requirements duplicates and interdependencies and was evaluated based on Carlshamre et al [9]. Results obtained shown that the technique only identified similarities between requirements with a correct classification of up to 16% of the actual interdependencies.

4 Requirements Interdependencies Impacts on Prioritization

It is clear that most individual requirements cannot be treated in isolation during software development due to the complex relationships between them. However, though requirements interdependencies tends not to be problematic as such, the manner they affects a number of other development activities and decisions, makes them problematic and complex [9,19]. These activities include release planning, testing, change management, requirements design and implementation, etc [19]. In market-driven development, interdependencies among requirements are value-related which affects prioritization negatively which in turn affects release planning decisions in an unintended manner. For instance, the selection process during release planning is achieved through prioritization and its implementation cost estimation. Nonetheless, the selection is not always possible as expected due to the fact that requirements are related to and affect one another in a complex way. In essence, choosing one requirement may involve selecting many other requirements as well. For example, selecting a highly prioritized requirement **R1** may require that a costly but lowly prioritized requirement **R2** be chosen as well. Consequently, **R1** cannot be implemented without implementing **R2** first.

All this poses a serious challenge to many organizations where requirements are treated by bundling related requirements without considering the cost-value complexity relationships among them. In the release planning point of view, interdependencies play a major role but they are hardly ever identified clearly due to issues relating to multiple stakeholding [9]. In literature, interdependencies have been described as complex and fuzzy in nature [9]. Therefore, knowledge and the comprehension of these relationships are indispensable to avoid selecting a set of requirements that can lead to costly mistakes. One approach is the intermediate representation of these dependencies using the graph theory approach of impact analysis.

5 Requirements Interdependencies Identification Approach

The priority of requirements is a major determinant in release planning but is often crippled by requirements interdependencies. In release planning, interdependencies between requirements play a vital role though ignoredv by most software engineers. This lack of explicitness makes them complex to identify and managed coupled with their fuzziness nature [9]. Therefore, in order to identify explicitly the nature of interdependencies and support human decisions during the course of release planning, an intermediate representation is indispensable. We propose an approach based on [9], utilizing dependency graph theory which we referred to as requirements dependency graph (RDG). The representation is simplified by the computation of both in-degrees and out-degrees for each requirement, **R**. With this representation, reasoning about possible and good ways of partitioning or scheduling a set of requirements in a release plan can be supported. This will go a long way to offer clear and fast identification of all forms of dependencies (such as singular, clusters or highly dependent requirements [9]) at a quick glance. These are discussed as follows:

Definition 1: **[Dependency Type (DT)]**
Based on Carlshamre et al [9], we therefore classify these interdependences into six types: AND, REQUIRES, TEMPORAL, IVALUE, ICOST and OR. And r is defined in the following way:

Definition 2: **[RDG]** Given set of requirements for selection in the next release, RP and let **G < V, D, DT >** represent the RDG, where V is a finite set of nodes representing the requirements R and D = V × V × DT represents the set of various edges with dependency types: DT ={AND, REQUIRES, TEMPORAL, IVALUE, ICOST, OR}. Computation of the numbers of DT is described as follows:

Definition 3: **[Out-degree]**
The out-degree of $R \in v$ is the number of DT emanating from that node. The out-degree of v is computed by $|A(v)|$.

Definition 4: **[In-degree]**
The in-degree of $R \in v$ is the number of DT incident on that node. The in-degree of v is computed by $|I(v)|$.

A typical example is illustrated in Fig.1 and the corresponding in-degrees and out-degrees for each R are presented in Table 1. The representation in Fig.1 is simple and easy to understand how requirements relate with one another. The nodes are the requirements while the edges are the dependencies types. By representing requirements in this manner, it is possible to draw important conclusions associated with release planning from just a glance at the graph. Based on the representation on Table 1, singular requirements (e.g. R8), clustered (e.g. R6) and heavily depended requirements (e.g. R9) can be easily identified.

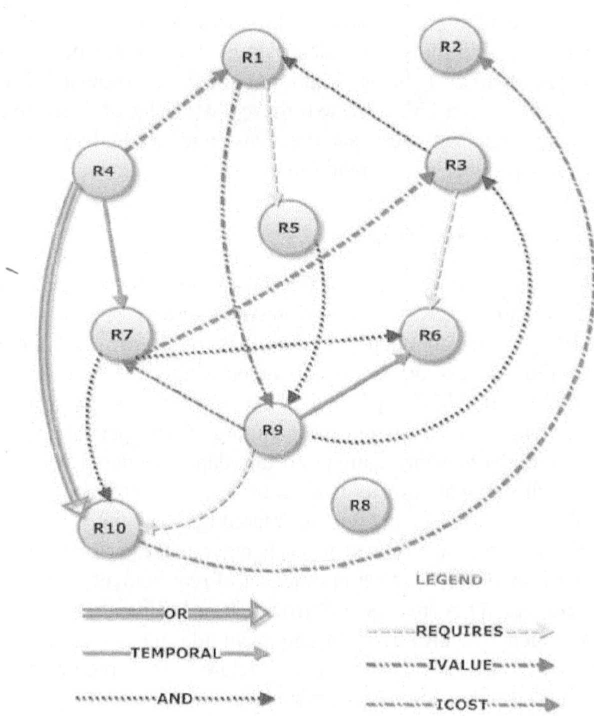

Fig. 1. Requirements dependency graph

Table 1: RDG In-degrees and Out-degrees

R ε v	*A(v)*	*I(v)*
R1	2	2
R2	-	1
R3	2	2
R4	3	-
R5	1	1
R6	-	3
R7	3	2
R8	-	-
R9	4	2
R10	1	3

With these representation and based on the recommendations in [9], requirements having no relationship with any other requirements (i.e. singular requirements) can be scheduled for any release as "top-off" depending on the amount of available development resources from an interdependencies perspective. Accordingly, requirements having many relationships to many other requirements should be scheduled for early release, in order to reduce risk. Lastly, clustered requirements can be scheduled for any release as long as all involved requirements are scheduled for the same release.

Unfortunately, one of the issues with the representation is how to represent large volume of requirements. Market-driven development often has large requirements and it will be challenging representing them this way. This however calls for automation of the dependencies. We however recommend more research in this area in order to explore more possibilities of identifying interdependencies in requirements. This is important because knowing how requirements are affected will make a whole lot of differences in speeding up more accurate cost and schedule analysis during product release planning.

6 Conclusions

Release planning is one of the most severe challenges faced by organizations where incremental systems development strategies are common practices. It is the determinant factor of the success or failure of a company's product in the market. In this paper, we have explored some of the challenges faced by release planning in the perspective of requirements prioritization and interdependencies. Literature has shown that priority and requirements interdependencies play major role in release planning, but the fact that requirements are related to each other makes it difficult, if not impossible to select optimal set of requirements based on priority. This makes prioritization a difficult task and interdependencies fuzzy in nature. In addition, much has not been known about the nature of requirements interdependencies. As a contribution of this paper, we have proposed the intermediate representation of requirements using a directed graph. With this representation, requirements relationships can easily be identified. This will assist decision makers in deciding on which requirements to be scheduled in the next release that is capable of achieving higher business value.

7 References

[1] Regnell, B. and Brinkkemper, S. "Market-Driven Requirements Engineering for Software Products," in Engineering and Managing Software Requirements, Berlin Heidelberg: Springer, 2005, pp. 287-308.

[2] Sawyer, P.: Packaged software: Challenges for RE. In Proceedings of the Fifth International Workshop on Requirements Engineering: Foundations for Software Quality(REFSQ 2000), Stockholm, Sweden, 137–142, 2000

[3] Karlsson, L., Dahlstedt, A.G., Natt, J., Regnell, B. and Persson, A.: Challenges in Market-Driven Requirements Engineering - an Industrial Interview Study, Proceedings of Eighth International Workshop on Requirements Engineering: Foundation for Software Quality, 2003, pp. 101-112.

[4] Carlshamre, P. "Release Planning in Market- Driven Software Product Development: Provoking an Understanding", Springer, pp. 139-151, 2002

[5] Ruhe, G. "Software Release Planning" University of Calgary 2500 University Drive NW Calgary, AB T2N 1N4, Canada, 2004.

[6] A. Ngo-The and G. Ruhe, "A systematic approach for solving the wicked problem of software release planning," Soft Computing - A Fusion of Foundations, Methodologies and Applications, vol. 12, pp. 95-108, 2008.

[7] Lehtola, L. and Kauppinen, M."Suitability of Requirements Prioritization Methods for Market-driven Software Product Development," Software Process Improvement and Practice, vol. 11, pp. 7-19, 2006

[8] Lehtola, L. Kauppinen, M. and Kujala, S. Requirements Prioritization Challenges in Practice, Springer, 2004, pp. 497–508

[9] Carlshamre, P. et al.: An industrial survey of requirements interdependencies in software product release planning. In: Proceedings of the 5th International Symposium on Requirements Engineering, Toronto, Canada, 2001, pp. 84-91

[10] Sawyer, P., Sommerville, I. and Kotonya, G. Improving Market-Driven RE Processes. Proc International Conference on Product Focused Software Process Improvement, 1999

[11] Sommerville, I. *Software Engineering*, 5th edn. Addison-Wesley: Wokingham, England. 1996

[12] Wiegers, KE. *Software Requirements.* Microsoft Press: Redmont, DC. 1999

[13] Lehtola, L. and Kauppinen, M. Suitability of Requirements PrioritizationMethods for Market-driven Software Product Development, Softw. Process Improvement Practices, 2006

[14] Karlsson L, Berander P, Regnell B, Wohlin C. *Requirements prioritisation: An experiment on exhaustive pair-wise comparisons versus planning game partitioning.* In Proceedings of Empirical

Assessment in Software Engineering (EASE2004), Edinburgh, Scotland, 2004

[15] Karlsson, J., Wohlin, C and Regnell, B.,"An Evaluation of Methods for Prioritising Software Requirements", Information and Software Technology 39 (1998), pp. 939-947

[16] Greer, D. and Ruhe, G. Software release planning: an evolutionary and iterative approach, Information and Software Technology 46 (2004) 243–253

[17] Ruhe G., Eberlein, A., and Pfal, D. Quantitative WinWin: a new method for decision support in requirements negotiation. Proc of the Int Conf on Software Engineering and Knowledge Engineering, pp 159–166. 2002

[18] Svahnberg, M. et al. "*A systematic review on strategic release planning models*". Journal of Information and Software Technology 52, 2010, pp. 237–248

[19] Dahlstedt, Å.G., Persson, A.: Requirements Interdependencies: State of the Art and Future Challenges, Proceedings of the 9th International Workshop on Requirements Engineering: Foundation for Software Quality, 2003, pp. 71-80

[20] Natt och Dag, J. Regnell, B., Carlshamre, P.; Andersson, M. and Karlsson, J., A feasibility study of Automated Natural Language Requirements Analysis in Market-driven Development, Requirements Engineering, 2002, p 20-33

[21] Berander, P. and Andrews, A.: "Requirements Prioritization," in Engineering and Managing Software Requirements, A. Aurumand C. Wohlin, Eds. Berlin: Springer, 2005, pp. 69-94..

Towards a Software Domain Metric based on Semantic Web Techniques

F. Edgar Castillo-Barrera[1], Héctor G. Pérez-González[1], and S. Masoud Sadjadi[2]
[1]School of Engineering, Universidad Autónoma de San Luis Potosí, San Luis Potosí, México
[2]School of Computing and Information Sciences, Florida International University (FIU), Miami, USA

Abstract

The reuse of software remains a major objective in the software industry. An important task in order to accomplish this goal is to classify the software based on the application domain for which it was done. This action facilitates their possible assembly with other programs based on the same vocabulary and domain. In this paper we describe a software domain metric which is measured based on semantic web techniques. This metric is independent of lines of code, binary and executable code of the software, and the programming language. Our approach is based on a lightweight ontology of CORBAL-IDL language and SPARQL queries. The ontology captures the vocabulary and its relation. This is encoded using OWL DL, supported by the Pellet reasoner to check the ontology component consistency. The populated ontology is queried using SPARQL. These queries look for matching words based on a vocabulary which describes a domain. We use an example and a prototype (a semantic framework called Chichen-Itza) to show the feasibility of our approach.

1. Introduction

The IEEE Standard 610.12-1990, Standard Glossary of Software Engineering, defines a Metric as: "A quantitative measure of the degree to which a system, component, or process possesses a given attribute". This quantitative measure is not always possible to apply based on lines of code. For example, Software Components are sold without source code. Another example is the concept of abstract attributes, for which there are not direct ways of measuring them or to quantify them. In this work we focus on attributes based on "the domain or context" which allows us to determine if a software component or application was done for a specific domain. Information about the domain can be used to determine if it is possible to assemble two software componentes, for example. Crnkovic and Larsson [8] define Component-Based Software Engineering (CBSE) "as an approach to software development that relies on software reuse". The goal of CBSE is the rapid assembly of complex software systems using pre-fabricated software components. In order to achieve this aim, methods for verifying the matching among components based on its domain are necessary.

In this work, we propose a software metric based on semantic web techniques (Ontologies, Reasoners and Semantic queries) in conjunction with the *Chichen-Itza* framework to mitigate this problem. We propose an approach for measuring such indicators. This approach looks for matching words in *a CORBA-IDL++ file* using and Ontology populated with *words based on a vocabulary for a specific domain*. For each application, artifact or software component it is neccesary to make a file in CORBA-IDL++ and a file with the vocabulary of the domain. CORBA-IDL++ is an extension of CORBA-IDL language which we made it for this purpose. Our method for measuring is able to check matching words in differente languages and it can recognize a word within another.

Our method for measuring, can only be applied if the application, artifact or software components can be described as methods and parameters. Binary, Executable, and Source Code are not required. In this work, we consider the following definition: *"A component is a reusable unit of deployment and composition that is accessed through an interface"*[8]. In practice, we have noted that problems related to interface incompatibility are frequent. In particular, incompatibility with the semantics of operation parameters and interface operations (behavioral contracts [4]). We consider that the use of a semantic matching approach (a software component ontology) could help to detect domain based on the vocabulary of the domain before the component-based system is deployed. The rest of the paper is structured as follows. In Section 2 we present our proposal to measure the vocabulary in a specific domain. In Section 3 we explain the Semantic Web Framework called Chichen Itza and semantic web techniques (Ontologies and SPARQL queries). Section 4 shows an example about our semantic approach in the ATM domain. In Section 5 we draw some concluding remarks. Finally, acknowledgments are given in Section 6.

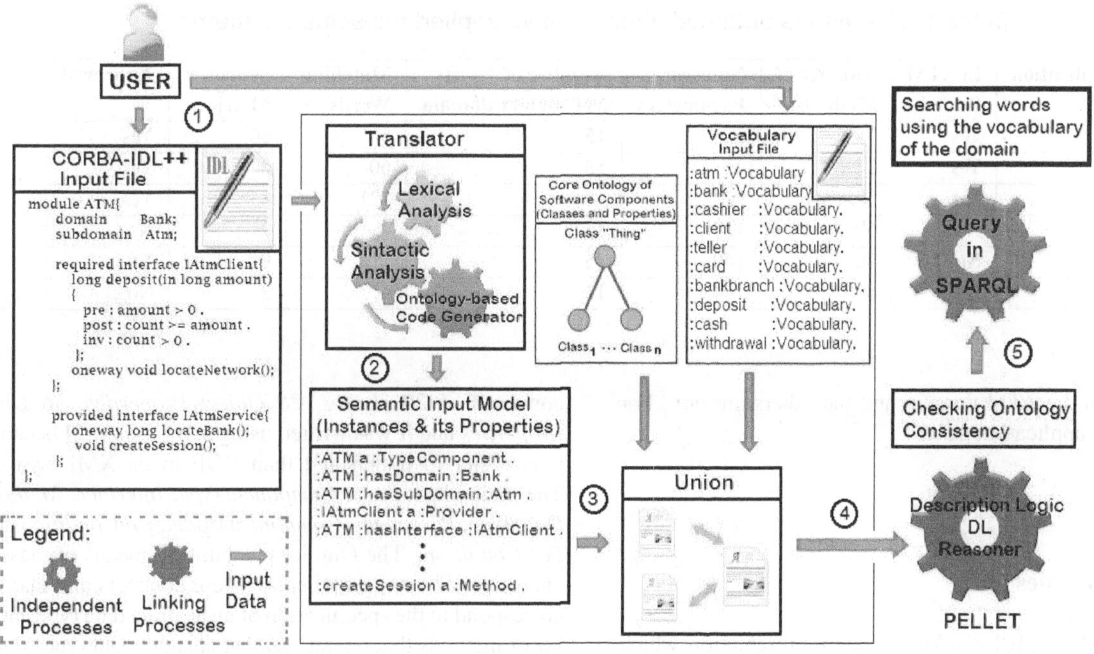

Figure 1. Process to measure the Vocabulary Domain.

2. A Metric based on Semantic Web Techniques

2.1 How to measure?

The measurement process takes place in five steps as shown in Figure 1. In the first step, the user must create an input file written using the language of CORBA-IDL++ (which is an extension of the language of CORBAL-IDL) where it must specify the methods or instructions with its parameters. It is also necessary to have a file with the vocabulary of the domain to check, which must be as complete as possible.

In the second step it is necessary to translate the input file written in CORBA-IDL++ into the language RDF. On having applied the translator, a file with extension n3 is generated.

Phase 3 will need to join the generator file by the translator in n3 with the file the vocabulary of the domain and the ontology of CORBA-IDL developed to the prototype of Chichen-Itza in just one project (which will be called le ontological project).

In phase 4, we have to apply the Pellet Reasoner to the ontological project created in the previous phase.

It is at this stage where the reasoner verifies the consistency of the ontology. If the consistency is right we can ensure that the ontology does not have problems of inconsistencies, so we can apply Semantic queries without problems of computability and decidability [13].

Finally, in phase 5 the user has to apply a query made in SPARQL to search the vocabulary in the ontological project and thus with this to have how many words matched with the language used in the application. With this information, we can apply the semantic metric.

2.2 What is the Metric?

The most common definition of Metric is: "quantitative measure of degree to which a system, component or process possesses a given attribute". The metric proposed tries to give a quantitative measure of degree to which a system possesses an attribute based on a specific domain or context. The formula that appears below calculates the percentage to which a program belongs in a specific domain:

$$MDom = \frac{\#matching\ words\ input\ vocabulary}{\#identifiers\ (\#methods + \#parameters)} * 100$$

In order to calculate this, we have to know the number of matching words, the number of methods and parameters. We want to point out that the words defined in the input vocabulary file have to be as complete as possible. In table 1 we have calculated the metric for 6 applications, 3 of

Table 1. The results obtained after we have applied the semantic metric

Application	In ATM Domain	Number of Methods	Number of Parameters	Number of Words Vocabulary domain	Matching Words	Semantic Metric	Approved
A	**Yes**	7	5	**15**	8	66	Yes
B	**Yes**	25	46	**15**	60	84	Yes
C	**Yes**	50	92	**15**	121	85	Yes
D	**No**	60	127	**15**	4	2	No
E	**No**	70	140	**15**	1	0.5	No
F	**No**	80	204	**15**	6	2	No

them are in the ATM domain and the others are not. For example in application A:

$$MDom = \frac{8}{(7+5)} * 100 = 66$$

2.3 Ontologies

An ontology [10] is a knowledge representation which defines the basic terms and relations comprising the vocabulary of a topic area, as well as the rules for combining terms and relationships used to define extensions to the vocabulary. In our case, the domain area is CORBA-IDL language.

2.4 SPARQL Query Language

SPARQL is a query language for the Resource Description Framework (RDF). We have selected it because this is a W3C Recommendation [18]. We use Web Ontology Language (OWL-DL) [19] which extends RDF and RDFS. We selected OWL DL language because we can assure that all conclusions given by the Reasoner are computable and decidable.

3 Chichen Itza: a Semantic Web Framework

Chichen Itza [1] is a Semantic Web Framework which allows the management of semantic models (Ontologies) in memory, verify its consistency (Reasoners) and execute semantic queries in SPARQL language. Chichen Itza consists of a friendly visual editor where the users can edit, save and load their ontologies and queries. This framework was programmed in Java language [11] and is portable to other plataforms. The Chichen Itza framework is shown in 2

3.1 A CORBA-IDL Ontology

A CORBA-IDL Ontology was created for verifying information about the input domain models. This ontology consisted of *20 classes*, *28 Object Properties*, *36 Data Properties* and it was written using *n3 notation* [3] because it is easier to understand than RDF in its XML syntax. The main classes are: *ComponentType*, *Interface*, *Method*, *DataType*, *Parameter*, *ComponentModel*, *PreCondition* and *PostCondition*. The Ontology is built by means of classes and relations among concepts. These concepts and classes correspond to the specification of an abstract data type and a set of methods that operate on that abstract data type. Each method is specified by an *interface*, *type declarations*, a *pre-condition*, and *post-condition* [8]. The interface of a method describes the syntactic specification of the method. Interfaces define the methods used in contracts. The typing information describes the types of input and output or both parameters and internal (local) variables. All of the above is represented in our ontology (class Type, class Parameter, etc.). The most important part to consider in our ontology are the Conditions (Pre and Post). The Pre-condition describes the condition of the variables prior to the execution of the method whose behavior is described by the Post-condition.

3.1.1 Evaluating the ontology created

The ontology developed has been evaluated in an informal and formal way. Regarding the former, the ontology was evaluated by the developers using the *Pellet* reasoner [14] to check the consistency of the ontology. The second evaluation applied to the ontology is based on the work of Gómez-Pérez [2] who establishes five criteria: (*consistency*, *completeness*, *conciseness*, *expandability* and *sensitiveness*). The number of concepts and their relations among them, allow us to check the ontology consistency with less steps than other kind of ontologies.

3.2 Domain Verification based on Vocabulary

Our approach about matching words is based on interfaces as contracts by Szyperski [16]. Interface specifications are contracts between a client of an interface and a

[1] Chichen Itza is the name of a large city built by the Maya civilization

provider of an implementation of the interface. A contract states what the client needs to use the interface. It also states what the provider requires to implement to meet the services promised by the interface. Such a match is validated for sytactic and functional semantic aspects. In the first case, it is checked whether the provided interface includes at least the same list of methods defined in the required interface. We follow a structural approach whereby the names of the interface operations can be different but the types of the parameters and the order of the paramenters must be compliant. Conditions defined for each method have to be matched with the same variable, logic operator and value. We verify restrictions and assumptions at construction time, in a completely static manner, prior to the testing stages. Semantic verification is the process which uses Semantic Web Techniques (Ontologies and SPARQL queries) to guarantee compliance with contractual agreements. The semantics of an operation are described in an interface (contract). The only task for the user before applying our model is to define the vocabulary of his domain and semantics. He introduces his model into the framework by means of a file or by the menus that allows to do an automatic evaluation by using the Pellet reasoner [14] which checks inconsistencies. Chichen Itza transforms his vocabulary from a text file into an ontology instances and its relations. The instances are created from classes defined in the software component ontology.

3.3 Extending CORBAL-IDL vocabulary with Semantics

CORBA(Common Object Request Broker Architecture)[17] is a standard created by the Object Management Group (OMG)[7] that enables software components written in different computer languages to work among them by means of their interfaces. These interfaces are described using the *Interface Definition Language (IDL)*. In our semantic model, we need to receive the interface written using the concepts and properties defined in the CORBA-IDL ontology. For the reasons above, we have decided to use the keywords of the CORBA-IDL with elements of the ontology and supported with Chichen Itza framework. For example, *ComponentType*, *Interface*, *Method*, *Parameter* and *hasNumParameters* are keywords. Part of the semantic ATM-IDL vocabulary. It is showed below.

```
:Atm         a :ComponentType .
:Bank        a :ComponentType .
:IAtmClient a :Interface .
:IAtmClient   :hasMethod :deposit .
:IBank       a :Interface .
:IBank        :hasMethod :withdrawal .
:deposit     a :Method .
:withdrawal a :Method .
:amout       a :Parameter .
:idClient    a :Parameter .
:deposit       :hasNumParameters  2 .
:withdrawal    :hasNumParameters  3 .
```

In the code above we would like to emphazise that there are some instaces of clases (*Atm* and *Bank*), some classes (*ComponentType*, *Parameter*, *Interface* and *Method*), object property *hasMethod* and just one data type property (*hasNumParameter*). In particular, the notation *:deposit :hasNumParameters 2* means that the method deposit has exactly 2 parameters.

3.4 The Pellet Reasoner

Pellet [14] is an open-source Java based OWL DL reasoner. In our verification process we use Pellet for checking the consistency of the ontology. We have selected the Pellet reasoner because it gives an explanation when an inconsistency is found. It is also possible to check for restrictions.

3.5 Domain verification using SPARQL queries

For more complex checking we can apply other actions such as: production rules [9]. We decided to explore semantic queries in SPARQL [15] instead of production rules. The second step after the reasoner has checked the ontology consistency is to apply a SPARQL query. We defined specific queries that evaluate matching words in methods and parameters identifiers. Such queries are completely transparent to the user who only needs to provide the file produced in n3 by the translator. We have used Jena API [12] and Java language [6] for programming and NetBeans IDE 7.0 [1]. SPARQL is similar to the database SQL but for ontologies. Besides, we can use variables in the queries, filtering information, and if statements. Lines are linked by variables which begin with a question mark. The same name of variable implies the same value to look for in the query. The *Jena API* allowed us to use SPARQL queries in our framework programmed in Java language. The query which verifies the *matching words with the name of the methods* is showed below.

```
PREFIX      : <http://www.ejemplo.org/#>
PREFIX  rdf: <http://www.w3.org/1999/02/
                          22-rdf-syntax-ns#>
PREFIX  owl: <http://www.w3.org/2002/07/owl#>
SELECT ?Vocabulary  ?MatchMethod WHERE
 {
   ?Vocabulary  rdf:type  :Vocabulary  .
   ?Interface :hasMethod ?Method .
   BIND( if(regex(str(?Method),
                 str(?Vocabulary), "i"),
```

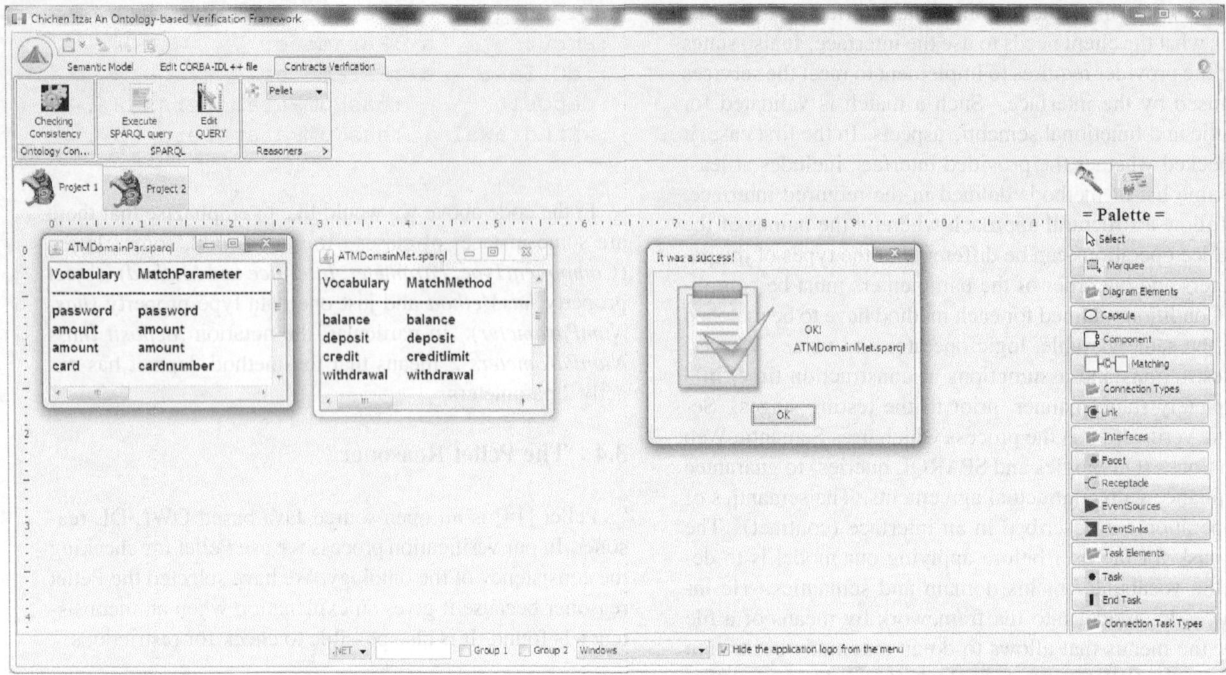

Figure 2. Chichen Itza Framework: two queries in SPARQL were used by looking for matching words

```
              ?Method, " ")  AS ?MatchMethod)
  FILTER (  ?MatchMethod != " "  )
}
```

An additional benefit of using ontologies and SPARQL queries has been the extra information (metadata) to offer support for writing the CORABA-IDL++ file.

4 Example: Automated Teller Machine

ATM is a machine at a bank branch or other location which enables customers to perform basic banking activities. The component model used for describing the ATM was written using UML 2 notation [5], and is shown in figure 3. The vocabulary of the input file is created by the user or expert in the domain of ATM. He selects which words are used in that domain. In our example, for each component is neccesary to create an input file written in CORBA-IDL++.

```
:bank                     a :Vocabulary .
:Atm                      a :Vocabulary .
:cashier                  a :Vocabulary .
:client                   a :Vocabulary .
:bankbranch               a :Vocabulary .
:teller                   a :Vocabulary .
:card                     a :Vocabulary .
:money                    a :Vocabulary .
```

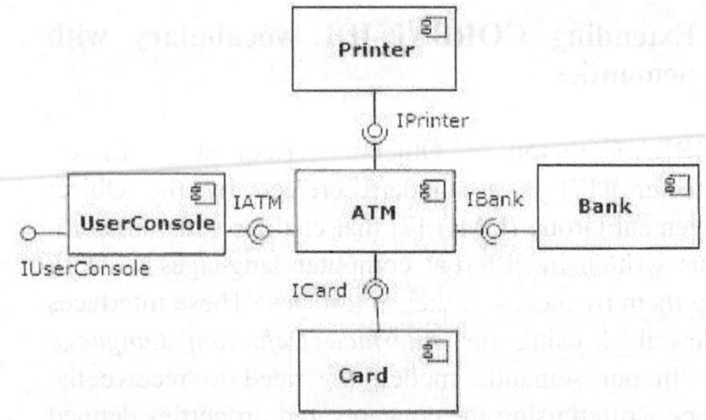

Figure 3. UML ATM Component-based system

```
:amount                   a :Vocabulary .
:password                 a :Vocabulary .
:balance                  a :Vocabulary .
:deposit                  a :Vocabulary .
:withdrawal               a :Vocabulary .
:credit                   a :Vocabulary .

module ATM{
       domain      Bank;
       subdomain   Atm;
```

```
        provided interface IAtmService{
            oneway void locateBank();
                    long createSession();
                    long balance();
                    long creditLimit();
        };
        required interface IAtmClient{
          long deposit(in short amount,
                       in short numclient);
          void withdrawal(in short cardnumber,
                          in char password,
                          in short amount);
          void locateNetwork();
        };
};
```

5. Conclusions

In this paper we have presented and described a software metric for measuring the percentage that belongs to an application of a specific domain based on a vocabulary used in that domain. In comparision with other metrics, this metric tries to measure an abstract attribute based on the vocabulary of a specific domain. This measure is based on an Ontology, a Reasoner, and a set of SPARQL queries which allow us an easy way to check matching words. This model can be extended and enriched with more attributes that rely on semantics. The Ontology was expressed in a logic-based language (OWL DL). Using this language we can assure the query will not have problems of computability and decidability. The OWL DL ontology proposed is checked with the Pellet reasoner. The use of a domain ontology allows us to search for specific words using intelligent techniques such as SPARQL queries. Extending the ontology with no functional properties (Quality of Services attributes), Design Patterns and Object properties (*hasInvoke*, *hasResponse*, etc.) for measuring the behaviour are key points for our future work.

6 Acknowledgments

This material is based upon work supported by the National Science Foundation under Grant No. OISE-0730065.

References

[1] E. Armstrong, J. Ball, S. Bodoff, D. B. Carson, I. Evans, K. Ganfield, D. Green, K. Haase, E. Jendrock, J. Jullion-ceccarelli, and G. Wielenga. The j2ee TM(tm) 1.4 tutorial for netbeans TM(tm) ide 4.1 for sun java system application server platform edition 8.1.

[2] S. Bechhofer, C. A. Goble, and I. Horrocks. Daml+oil is not enough. In *SWWS*, pages 151–159, 2001.

[3] T. Berners-Lee, D. Connolly, and S. Hawke. Semantic web tutorial using n3. In *Twelfth International World Wide Web Conference*, 2003.

[4] A. Beugnard, J. Jézéquel, N. Plouzeau, and D. Watkins. Making components contract aware. *Computer*, 32(7):38–45, 1999.

[5] M. Bjerkander and C. Kobryn. Architecting systems with uml 2.0. *Software, IEEE*, 20(4):57–61, 2003.

[6] P. J. Clarke, D. Babich, T. M. King, and B. M. G. Kibria. Model checking and abstraction. *ACM Transactions on Programming Languages and Systems*, 16:1512–1542, 1994.

[7] O. CORBA and I. Specification. Object management group, 1999.

[8] I. Crnkovic and M. Larsson. Building reliable component-based software systems. Artech House computing library, Norwood, MA, 2002.

[9] A. C. del Río, J. E. L. Gayo, and J. M. C. Lovelle. A model for integrating knowledge into component-based software development. *KM - SOCO*, pages 26–29, 2001.

[10] T. Gruber. Toward principles for the design of ontologies used for knowledge sharing. pages 907–928. 1995.

[11] Java.net. Flamingo. http://java.net/projects/flamingo/, 2010.

[12] Jena. Jena a semantic web framework for java. 2000.

[13] J. Z. Pan and E. Thomas. Approximating owl-dl ontologies. In *Proceedings of the National Conference on Artificial Intelligence*, volume 22, page 1434. Menlo Park, CA; Cambridge, MA; London; AAAI Press; MIT Press; 1999, 2007.

[14] B. Parsia and E. Sirin. Pellet: An owl dl reasoner. In *In Proceedings of the International Workshop on Description Logics*, 2004.

[15] J. Pérez, M. Arenas, and C. Gutierrez. Semantics and complexity of sparql. *The Semantic Web-ISWC 2006*, pages 30–43, 2006.

[16] C. Szyperski, D. Gruntz, and S. Murer. *Component software: beyond object-oriented programming*. Addison-Wesley Professional, 2002.

[17] S. Vinoski. Distributed object computing with corba. *C++ Report*, 5(6):32–38, 1993.

[18] W3C. http://www.w3.org/consortium/. 1994.

[19] W3C. Owl web ontology language, 1994.

A Template-Based Approach to Modeling Variability

Soheila Bashardoust Tajali, Jean-Pierre Corriveau and Wei Shi
School of Computer Science, Carleton University
Colonel By Drive
Ottawa, CANADA
1-613-520-2600
{sbtajali, jeanpier, wei_shi}@scs.carleton.ca

ABSTRACT

Arnold and Corriveau have recently described ACL/VF, a non-state-based quality-driven approach to software specification that enables the requirements of stakeholders to be validated against the actual behavior of an implementation under test. Simultaneously, in recent years, the software product line (SPL) approach, initiated by Parnas back in the 1970s, has emerged as a promising way to improve software productivity and quality. The problem we address here can be summarized in one question: how can ACL/VF support product lines? The solution we propose adopts Cleaveland's template-based general approach to variability. We first explain how to go from the traditional feature diagram and feature grammar used in SPL to a) ACL domain contracts capturing commonalities between the requirements contracts of a domain and b) variability contracts capturing how features and their relationships (captured in a feature grammar) can affect these domain contracts. Domain and variability contracts are then captured in XML files and we rely on XSLT to specify how variability is to be resolved in order to generate a specific member contract.

Keywords— Variability, XSLT Template, Generators, Feature Diagrams

Contact author for SERP 2013 paper: J-Pierre Corriveau

1. ON GENERATIVE APPROACHES TO VARIABILITY

In recent years, the software product line (SPL) approach [7, 8, 9] initiated by Parnas back in the 1970s [17] has emerged as a promising way to improving software productivity and quality. A product line, which corresponds to a *domain*, arises from situations when we need to develop multiple similar products. A *commonality* is a property held across this domain, whereas a *variant* (or *variability*) is a property specific to certain *members* of this domain. Most importantly, Zhang and Jarzabek [20] remark that "the explosion of possible variant combinations and complicated variant relationships make the manual, ad hoc accommodation and configuration of variants difficult." Thus, it is generally agreed that a variability mechanism that supports automated customization and assembly of product line assets is required. Consequently, a significant amount of work has focused on the creation of *generators* to automate going from a model of variability to a specific member of a family of products. Let us elaborate.

With respect to terminology, we will adopt the one of Czarnecki and Eisenecker [9]: In System Family Engineering (or equivalently, Software Product Lines), *members* of a *domain* share a set of common *features*, as well as possibly possessing their specific ones. Commonalities, we repeat, refer to the characteristics that are common to all family members, while variabilities distinguish the members of a family from each other and need to be explicitly modeled and separated from the common parts. Conceptually, a feature is a *variation point* in a space of requirements (the domain) and has several *variants* (also called feature values) associated with it. The two main processes of SPL engineering are a) domain engineering (for analyzing the commonality and variability between members) and application engineering (for generating individual members of the domain).

Domain engineering rests on the creation of a domain model via feature modeling [9]. Conceptually, application engineering then consists in defining a specific *configuration* of feature values and generating from the domain model and from this configuration the corresponding member (of the domain). Thus, SPL engineering is a model-driven activity involving both the modeling of commonalities and variabilities of a domain, and the generation of a member of this domain from this model. Many languages and approaches have been proposed for modeling variability (see [4] and [18] for recent in-depth reviews). As for approaches to generation, they can be separated into two categories, each including many proposals:

- *transformational* methods, which define explicit mappings between semantic elements of a source model and those of a target model.
- *generative* approaches, which build a target model from what amounts to a parameterized source model and a configuration list (that supplies specific values for these parameters).

It has been argued that generative approaches correspond to a more powerful semantic approach to the production of a target model than transformations [7, 9]. This paper focuses on the creation of a particular generator. We first introduce the specific problem we address, then overview the solution we propose for it.

2. PREMISES

A quality-driven approach to software development and testing demands that, ultimately, the requirements of stakeholders be validated against the actual behavior of an Implementation Under Test (hereafter IUT). That is, there needs to be a systematic (ideally objective and automated) approach to the validation of the requirements of the stakeholder against the actual behavior of an IUT [3]. Unfortunately, such systematic approach to validation remains problematic [5, 11] and, in practice, testers mostly carry out only extensive unit testing [6, 16].

In order to validate the requirements of a stakeholder against the actual behavior of an IUT, it is necessary to have a specification language from which tests can be generated and executed 'against' an actual IUT (as opposed to a model of the latter). Arnold and Corriveau have described at length elsewhere [1] such an approach and its corresponding tool, the Validation Framework (hereafter VF [2]).

The VF operates on three input elements. The first element is the Testable Requirements Model (hereafter TRM). This model is expressed in ACL, a high-level general-purpose requirements contract language. We use here the word 'contract' because a TRM is formed of a set of contracts, as illustrated shortly. ACL is closely tied to requirements by defining syntax/semantics for the representation of scenarios, and design-by-contract constructs [15] such as pre and post-conditions, and invariants (rooted in [12, 13]).

The second input element is the candidate IUT against which the TRM will be executed. This IUT is a .NET executable (for which no source code is required).

Bindings represent the third and final input element required by the VF. Before a TRM can be executed, the types, responsibilities, and observability requirements of the TRM (see example below) must be bound to concrete implementation artifacts located within the IUT. A structural representation of the IUT is first obtained automatically. The binding tool, which is part of the VF, uses this structural representation to map elements from the TRM to types and procedures defined within the candidate IUT. In particular, this binding tool is able to automatically infer most of the bindings required between a TRM and an IUT [1, 2, 3]. Such bindings are crucial for three reasons. First, they allow the TRM to be independent of implementation details, as specific type and procedure names used with the candidate IUT do not have to exist within the TRM. Second, because each IUT has its own bindings to a TRM, several candidate IUTs can be tested against a single TRM. Finally, bindings provide explicit traceability between a TRM and IUT.

Once the TRM has been specified and bound to a candidate IUT, the TRM is compiled. Upon a successful compilation, all elements of the TRM have been bound to IUT artifacts. The result of such a compilation is a single file that contains all information required to execute the TRM against a candidate IUT. The validation of a TRM begins with a structural analysis of the candidate IUT, and with the execution of any static checks (e.g., a type inherits from another). Following execution of the static checks, the VF starts and monitors the execution of the IUT. The VF is able to track and record the execution paths generated by the IUT, as well as execute any dynamic checks, and gather user-specified metrics specified in the TRM. The execution paths are used to determine if each scenario execution matches the grammar of responsibilities corresponding to it within the TRM.

The key point of this overview is that once a TRM is automatically bound to an IUT, all checks are automatically instrumented in the IUT whose execution is also controlled by the VF. This enables verifying that actual sequences of procedures occurring during an execution of an IUT 'obey' the grammar of valid sequences defined in ACL scenarios. Most importantly, no glue code (that is, code to bridge between test specifications and actual tests coded to use the IUT) is required.

The problem we address in this paper can be summarized in one question: how can ACL/VF support domain engineering and application engineering? In the specific context of ACL/VF, this question can be broken down into two more immediate ones:

1) how can ACL (i.e., the requirements modeling language) be 'augmented' to support some modeling of variability?

2) how can such augmented ACL models be used, together with some specification of a configuration of feature values, to generate a domain *member* contract, that is, the set of contracts associated with a specific member of a domain?

An answer to these questions requires that the reader first get a basic understanding of the syntax and semantics of ACL. To this end, we give below a short self-explanatory example:

```
Namespace My.Examples
{
/*Each ACL contract is bound to one or more
types of the IUT. An ACL contract may define
variables, which will be stored and updated
by the VF. */
Contract ContainerBase<Type T>
/* The variable size tracks the number of
elements in a container according to the ACL
model. It is NOT associated or dependent on
any similar variable(s) in the IUT. */
{  Scalar Integer size;
```

```
/*An observability is a query-method that is
used to request state information from the
IUT. That is, they are read-only methods
that acquire and return a value stored by
the IUT. An observability thus defines some
data that the IUT MUST be able to supply to
the VF for the VF to properly monitor the
IUT.*/
  Observability Boolean     IsFull();
  Observability Boolean     IsEmpty();
  Observability T ItemAt(Integer index);
  Observability Integer     Size();
Responsibility new()
{ size = 0;   Post(IsEmpty() == true)
      }
Responsibility finalize()
{ Pre(IsEmpty() == true);  }
Invariant SizeCheck
{ Check(context.size >= 0);
   Check(context.size == Size())       }
/* The next responsibility defines pre- and
post- conditions for addition. It is not to
be bound but rather to be extended by actual
responsibilities. The    keyword    'Execute'
indicates where execution occurs. */
Responsibility Add(T aItem)
{ Pre(aItem not= null);
   Pre(IsFull() == false);  Execute();
   size = size + 1;
  Post(HasItem(aItem));            }
/*This    responsibility    extends    Add.    It
therefore    reuses    its    pre-    and    post-
conditions of Add. */
Responsibility  InsertAt(Integer    index,  T
aItem)
     extends Add(aItem)
{      Pre(index >= 0);     Execute();
       Post(ItemAt(index) == aItem);    }
/*    other    responsibilties    for    adding,
removing, searching, etc. are ommitted here.
/*
Scenario AddAndRemove
{ once Scalar T x;
   Trigger(Add(x) | Insert(dontcare, x)),
   Terminate((x          ==          Remove())        |
(RemoveElement(x));   }
}
/* The Export section defines the types used
in   this   contract,   as   well   as   their
constraints. */
Exports
{ Type tItem conforms Item
      { not context;    not derived context;
      } } }
}  //end of contract ContainerBase
```

This single TRM has been applied to several simple data structures (e.g., different kinds of arrays and linked lists) implemented in C# and C++/CLI, with and without coding errors, in order to verify that ACL/VF indeed detects responsibility and scenario violations. This ability to bind the same TRM against several distinct IUTs may mislead some readers to believe ACL/VF already handles some form of variability. In fact, it does not: all the IUTs that can bind to this TRM can do so specifically because there is **no** variablity in the TRM they must conform with. In other words, regardless of their differences at the level of code, all the IUTs that can bind to this TRM can do so because they have been adapted to support the observabilities required by this TRM.

So the question remains: how can ACL/VF be augmented to support variability? As previously mentioned, many languages and approaches have been proposed for modeling variability. But few are relevant to this work due to a fundamental restriction we are faced with: neither the ACL nor the VF can be modified. That is, given the ACL/VF is an experimental tool of over 250,000 lines of code, which is still undergoing testing, we decided to support variability in ACL contracts *without* altering the syntax or semantics of ACL, or the working of the ACL compiler, or the modus operandi of the VF.

To achieve this goal, we adopt Cleaveland's [7] template-based general approach to variability, captured in Figure 1.

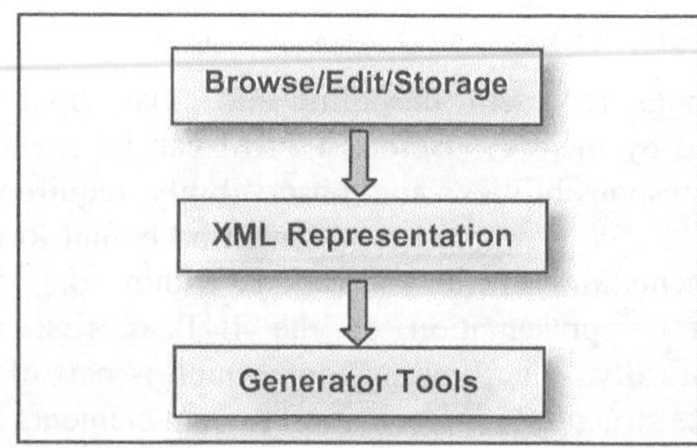

Figure 1: Cleaveland's Generative Approach

In a nutshell, following this approach, modeling variability is a task that ultimately must produce an XML representation of variabilities and commonalities of the domain. It is this representation that is used to generate a specific member of the domain. The advantage of choosing XML is that it makes available the much wider world of XML technologies and tools. In particular, XSLT is a standard transformation language for transforming between XML languages or to other text-based languages. That is, XSLT is readily usable for creating a generator. Czarnecki [10] explains (in the specific context of code generation):

"In a template-based generative approach (a) an arbitrary text file such as a source program file in any programming language or a documentation file is instrumented with code selection and iterative code expansion constructs. The instrumented file called template needs a template processor. A template processor takes a template file and a set of configuration parameters as inputs and generates a concrete instance of that template as output".

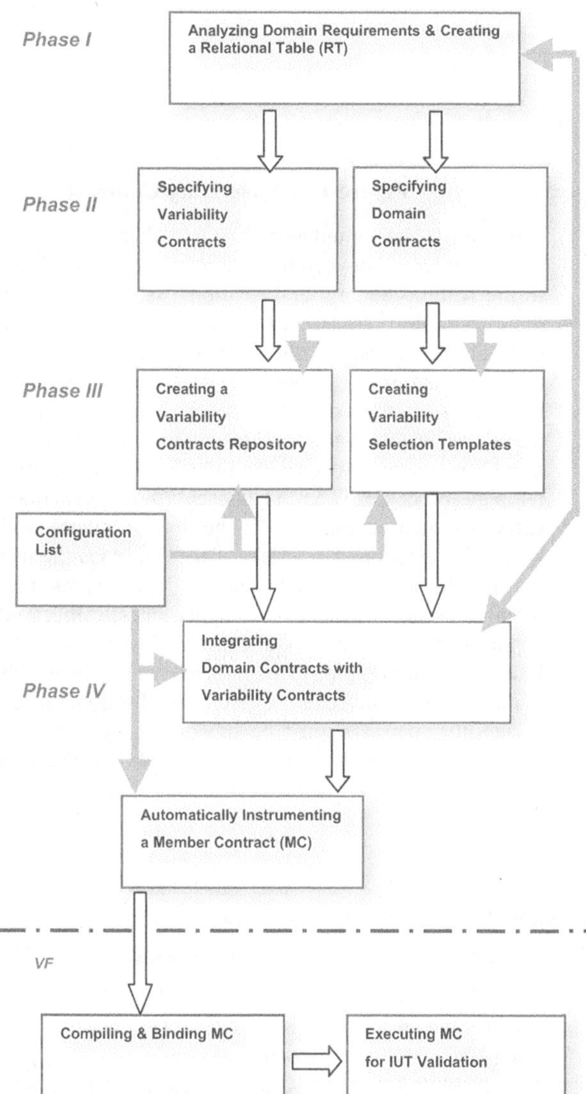

Figure 2: Overview of our Generative Approach

In contrast, a programming language based generative approach, such as Czarnecki and Eisenecker's [9] C++ metaprogramming, typically uses advanced programming techniques (such as partial template specialization in C++) that are not only hard to master and problematic to debug (leading to complex generators), but also do not offer as much semantic flexibility as an XML based approach. For these reasons, the generative approach we propose (see Figure 2) for tackling variability in ACL adopts a template-based approach rooted in XML. In the rest of this paper, we overview the different steps identified in Figure 2 (in which the white arrows show the evolution from one artifact to another, and the blue arrows on the right of the figure indicate where user input is required, in contrast to those on the left that show where the configuration list is used).

3. DETAILS

In Phase I of our approach, the domain engineer first identifies commonality and variability in the domain at hand. This analysis of the domain leads to the production of a *feature model* [9]. The syntax and semantics of this model are that of FODA [14] and similar notations [see 9 for a review]. A feature diagram captures variation points and their variants. Here, for example, variation point VP1, "Length Type", has two variants VP1-1 "Variable" and VP1-2 "Fixed". It captures the fact that containers can have a variable length or fixed length, where length is number of elements.[1]

While a feature diagram is a good starting point for domain analysis, it is crucial to understand that the complexity of a generative approach lies first and foremost in its handling of interactions between features and feature values, which are captured in a *feature grammar* [9]. Consequently, it is unfortunately often the case that the processing of such a feature grammar is entirely manual (e.g., [18]). In contrast, in our solution, the feature interactions identified by the domain engineer are captured in a table whose use is automated. We call such a table a feature grammar table, or equivalently a feature relational table (RT). Table 1 (next page) presents a few of the rows of the large RT developed for one of our case studies. Rows 1 and 11 of the complete table [4] are examples of how to define the exact relationship between a variation point and its variants. For example, row 1 below states that VP0 has two mutually exclusive variants VP0-1 and VP0-2. It also states that if the configuration list (defining a specific member of the domain through a specific set of variants) includes one of the variants of VP-0, there are no conditions to verify and this variant can be taken as the value of VP0 (for further verification of the feature grammar, as well as subsequent generation). Rows 13 to 21 in the complete table [4] deal with feature interactions proper. Row 13 below, for example, states that if VP31 is assigned any one of its valid variants in the configuration list, then VP30 must also appear in this configuration and must be set to variant LC-Type. VP30 is an optional feature

[1] We also refer to VP0 (whether a container is key-based or not), VP4 (whether a container is circular, VP4-1 or not, VP4-2), and VP5 (whether a container allows 2-way, VP5-1, or 1-way traversal, VP5-2).

capturing whether or not the container keeps track, via a counter, of the number of its elements. VP31 merely captures the type of this counter.

Rows 18 and 19 illustrate how multiple valid combinations of variants are handled: one action is associated with a circular container supporting two-way traversal (row 18) and another action is used for a circular container supporting only one-way traversal (row 19). The key point to be grasped is that all such valid combinations of features and variants must be explicitly captured in this feature grammar (according to specific syntax and semantics defined in [4] and similar to FODA).

In Phase II of our approach, first, the commonalities of the domain at hand are captured in ACL contracts forming the *domain contracts*. These contracts are merely ACL contracts augmented in Phase III with plugIn labels (see Figure 3) marking where variability (and thus the generator) may modify such contracts. In Figure 3, we are simply indicating that *IsFull* may be affected by the variant chosen for VP1. (Several variation points may affect the same element of an ACL contract.)

The feature diagram and relationship table of phase I also lead, in Phase II, to *variability contracts* (via algorithms we have developed for this specific purpose [4]). The idea is to capture how each variant of a variation point affects the domain contract. Without going into (syntactic and semantic) details (given in [4]), a portion of such a variability contract is shown in Figure 4. Intuitively, if length is variable (VP1-1), then the *IsFull* observability necessarily returns false, otherwise (VP1-2), it returns whether the actual size of the container has reached the maximum size.

```
Observability Boolean IsFull()
    {       //plugin_VP1();     }
```

Figure 3: Variability in a Domain Contract

```
Variation VP1 <Length-Type> [1..1] outof 2
{case "Variable":
   plug-in: VP1-1 //Container has variable length
   Refine-a: Observability
   Boolean IsFull(){ value = false; }
 case "Fixed":
   plug-in: VP1-2 //Container has fixed length
   Refine-a: Observability
   Boolean IsFull() { value = (size() == max_size()); }
}
```

Figure 4: A Variability Contract

It must be emphasized that there is a direct correspondence between the features and variants identified in the feature diagram and relational table of Phase I, and these variability contracts (as well as the plugIn labels of domain contracts). Conceptually, variability contracts define the actions to be performed (by the generator) on the template (i.e., the domain contracts in our work) when a particular feature value is present in a configuration list input to generate a specific member of the domain. A template processor (i.e., our chosen kind of generator) can carry out such actions only if the domain contracts define where these actions are to take place (and thus the need for the plugIn labels we introduced). That is, as in other template-based generative approaches, the artifact capturing the domain model must be *instrumented* (to use Czarnecki's terminology) to indicate where in it template manipulations can occur. Then, both the domain and the variability contracts must be transformed into their XML equivalents in order to be made usable by the template processor. This is what Phase III of our approach tackles:.

Table 1: A portion of a Relation Table for Sequential Containers

No	Related VP(s) Var(s)	Related VP & Var Types	Related VP & Var Names	Relation: Rule# Constraints & Actions	Relation: <depends>, <requires>,<excludes> Constraints and Actions in Contracts
1	VP0 VP0-1 VP0-2	Var. point Variant Variant	"Is-key-based" "True" "False"	Rule 1, 2: VP0 ←X VP0-1 VP0 ←X VP0-2	VP0 <depends>VP0-1, VP0-2 Cond = - Action = variant
11	VP31 VP31-1 VP31-2 VP32-3	Var. point Variant Variant Variant	"LC-Type" "int" "short" "long"	Rule 1, 2: VP31 ←X VP31-1 VP31 ←X VP31-2 VP31 ←X VP31-3	VP31<depends>VP31-1, VP31-2, VP31-3 Cond = - Action = variant
13	VP31 VP31-1 VP31-2	Var. point Variant Variant	–	Rule 7: If(VP31 !=null && VP31 ==VP31-1 ||	VP31 <requires>VP30? = VP31 Cond1 = (VP30? == LC-Type)

<table>
<tr><td></td><td>VP31-3
VP30</td><td>Variant
Var. point</td><td></td><td>VP31 ==VP31-2 ||
VP31 ==VP31-3)
IMPLIES
VP30?==LC-Type</td><td>Action = variant1</td></tr>
<tr><td>18</td><td>VP4
VP4-1
VP5
VP5-1</td><td>Var. point
Variant
Var. point
Variant</td><td>_</td><td>Rule 5:
If(VP4==VP4-1)
IMPLIES
VP5 == VP5-1</td><td>VP4-1<requires>VP5-1
Cond1="VP5==Twoway"
Action= variant1</td></tr>
<tr><td>19</td><td>VP4
VP4-1
VP5
VP5-2</td><td>Var. point
Variant
Var. point
Variant</td><td>_</td><td>Rule 5:
If(VP4==VP4-1)
IMPLIES
VP5 == VP5-2</td><td>VP4-1<requires>VP5-2
Cond2="VP5==Oneway"
Action= variant2</td></tr>
</table>

a) The variability contracts of Phase II are transformed (again according to specific algorithms) into an XML-ready repository of these contracts.

b) Everywhere in the domain contracts where a plugIn label is used, a *variability selection template* is inserted. Given our specific approach to template processing, in our work these variability selection templates take the form of XSLT style sheets as explained at length in [4].

Finally, in order for these selection templates to be able to use the information of the variability contract repository, we still need to augment the domain contracts with XSLT code to bridge to the variability contract repository. At the end of phase III, both the variability contracts and the domain model have been transformed into XML-based artifacts that serve as input to the template-based generator, which also requires a configuration list specifying the exact list of feature values (i.e., the configuration) to be used to generate a specific member of the domain. Phase IV of our approach deals with the generation of such a member contract, that is, of an ACL contract corresponding to the specific input configuration list at hand. In a nutshell, the configuration list, as well as the variability contracts and selection templates (compiled using both an XML and an XSLT compiler) are integrated. The resulting ACL contract can then serve as input to ACL/VF so that it can be compiled and tested.

4. CONCLUSION

The main contribution of this work is a domain-independent generative process we propose for obtaining ACL member contracts from ACL-based domain and variability contracts. It is worth repeating that this process is comprehensive inasmuch as it addresses how the two traditional artifacts of domain engineering, namely a feature diagram and a feature grammar, can be evolved into domain and variability contracts whose XML equivalents serve as inputs (along with a configuration list) to the proposed generative process, which generates a member's contract (that can be compiled and run in ACL/VF).

ACL/VF is still an experimental model-based testing tool at this point in time, with advantages and drawbacks that its creators have discussed elsewhere [3]. We chose it to illustrate the power and generality of the template-based approach to generation advocated by Cleaveland [7]) for two main reasons:

1) It's a textual requirements language and ACL/VF already produced an XML equivalent of the ACL contracts specified by a user [1]. (Dealing with a visual language is somewhat more complex.)

2) The semantics of ACL are sufficiently comprehensive to tackle domain modeling and yet, most importantly, almost all of ACL's semantic elements (e.g., responsibilities, scenarios, observabilities, etc.) are relevant to variability.

Furthermore, we stress that, in contrast to many existing generative approaches, we have not only defined the artifacts relevant to the generative process but, most importantly, we also specified elsewhere [4] detailed algorithms to go from the more abstracts artifacts to those directly used by the generator. In fact, these algorithms inherently define traceability between the different artifacts of Figure 2. In turn, such traceability is essential to support an iterative approach to domain and application engineering. We also emphasize that, in contrast to many existing approaches (e.g., [18]), these algorithms do not assume that the user only inputs valid configurations. Such an assumption is a gross oversimplification: in our opinion, 'enforcing' that a configuration does respect the rules of a feature grammar must be automated, as is the case in our solution. Similarly, our work does not depend on any notion of the 'semantic correctness' of a feature diagram, feature grammar or domain contract supplied by a user. Such notion appears quite problematic [1].

Finally, the validation of our solution for the generation of an ACL member contract from domain contracts, variability contracts and a configuration specific to that member rests two extensive case studies. Both case studies [4] pertain to containers, reflecting the fact that the use of off-the-shelf component (COTS) libraries is pervasive in current software development processes. The first case study focuses specifically on sequential containers (such as arrays, lists, stacks and queues). This choice was straightforward given existing work [9, 19] on feature modeling across a large set of such container libraries (including those found in the Standard Template Library of C++). In other words, we wanted to avoid the all-too-frequent 'toy' example in favor of a realistic example based on public domain libraries. For our second case study, our focus was specifically on exercising more of the mechanisms we had developed for variability contracts. To do so we decided to tackle another facet of the STL, namely associated containers (such as dictionaries, multisets, etc.). The point we want to emphasize is that having an actual code base to take inspiration from for domain modeling eliminated the risk of creating an artificial domain conveniently scoped to work with our proposal. But this choice also meant tackling the modeling of some of the complexities of actual industrial code.

We have now turned our attention to the modeling of variability in design patterns, a radically different domain, in order to demonstrate that our proposal is not domain dependent.

5. REFERENCES

[1] Arnold, D.: “Supporting Generative Contracts in .Net”, Doctoral dissertation, School of Computer Science, Carleton University, April 2009.

[2] Arnold, D.: “Validation Framework and Another Contract Language”, http://vf.davearnold.ca/, last accessed in October 2012.

[3] Arnold, D., Corriveau, J.-P., Shi, W.: “Modeling and Validating Requirements using Executable Contracts and Scenarios", SERA 2010: 311-320.

[4] Bashardout-Tajali, S., Generative Contracts, Doctoral Dissertation, School of Computer Science, Carleton University, December 2012.

[5] Bertolino, A.: “Software Testing Research: Achievements, Challenges and Dreams”, In IEEE – Future of Software Engineering (FOSE ’07), Minneapolis, pp. 85-103, May 2007

[6] Binder, R.: *Testing Object-Oriented Systems*, Addison-Wesley Professional, Reading, MA, 2000.

[7] Cleaveland, C.: “Program Generators with XML and Java”, Prentice-Hall, Upper Saddle River, NJ, ISBN-10: 0130258784, Jan. 2001.

[8] Coplien, J., Hoffman, D., Weiss, D.: “Commonality and Variability in Software Engineering”, Bell Labs, IEEE Software, pp.37-45, Dec. 1998.

[9] Czarnecki, K., Eisenecker, U.W.: “Generative Programming: Methods, Tools, and Applications”, Addison-wesley, Boston, MA, 2000.

[10] Czarnecki, K., Bednasch, T., Unger, P., Eisenecker, U.: “Generative Programming for Embedded Software: An Industrial Experience Report”, In Don Batory et al., editors, Generative Programming and Component Engineering: ACM SIGPLAN/SIGSOFT Conference, GPCE 2002, LNCS 2487, Pittsburgh, PA, USA, pp. 156-172, October 2002.

[11] Grieskamp, W.: “Multi-Paradigmatic Model-Based Testing”, Technical Report #MSR-TR-2006-111, Microsoft Research, August 2006.

[12] Helm, R., Holland, I. M., Gangopadhyay, D.: “Contracts: Specifying Behavioural Compositions in Object-Oriented Systems”, In Proceedings of the ACM European conference on object-oriented programming systems, languages, and applications, Conference (OOPSLA'90), pp. 169-180, October 1990.

[13] Holland, I. M.: “Specifying reusable components using Contracts”, In Proceedings of the 6th European Conference on Object-oriented Programming (ECOOP ’92), pp. 287-308, 1992, LNCS/615.

[14] Kang K., Cohen S., Hess J., Novak W., Peterson A.: “Feature-Oriented Domain Analysis (FODA) Feasibility Study”, Technical report, CMU/SEI-90-TR-021, November 1990.

[15] Meyer, B.: “Design by Contract”, In *IEEE Computer*, vol. 25, no. 10, pp. 40-51, IEEE Press, New York, October 1992.

[16] Meszaros, G.: “xUnit Test Patterns: Refactoring Test Code”, Addison-Wesley Professional, ISBN-10: 0131495054, 2007.

[17] Parnas, D.L.: “On the Design and Development of Program Families”, IEEE Trans. Software Engineering, vol. 2, no, 1, pp. 1-9, March 1976.

[18] Tawhid, R.: “Integrating Performance Analysis in Model Driven Software Product Line Engineering”, Doctoral dissertation, School of Computer Science, Carleton University, May 2012.

[19] Tian, B., Corriveau, J.-P.: “On Facilitating the Reuse of C++ Graph Libraries”, In Proceedings of the IASTED International Conference on Software Engineering, part of the 23rd Multi-Conference on Applied Informatics, Innsbruck, Austria, pp. 7-12, February 2005.

[20] Zhang, H., Jarzabek, S.: “XVCL: A Mechanism for Handling Variants in Software Product Lines”, Special issue on Software Variability Management of Science of Computer Programming, Vol. 53, No. 3, pp. 381–407, December 2004.

Software Maintenance Risk Management Process – A Case Study

Vinicius Miana[1], Calebe Bianchini[1], Selma Melnikoff[2] and Marcelo Martins[2]
[1]FCI, Mackenzie University, São Paulo, SP, Brasil
[2]POLI, Universidade de São Paulo, São Paulo, SP, Brasil

Abstract - *Software Maintenance risk management differs in many aspects from software development risk management. Although it is the longest and the riskier phase on the software life cycle, differently from software development where many processes and models were established, very few processes have been developed to deal with software maintenance. Because it deals with systems that are already in production, software maintenance presents much more sources of risks. In this paper, we go through the software maintenance process identifying the main sources of risks and defining a process that can help mitigate those risks. Finally, we present a case study where this process was applied and some of the results are shown.*

Keywords: software evolution, risk management

1 Introduction

Software maintenance encompasses all activities enacted after software deployment that aim to modify it [1]. Many studies have shown that the costs associated with software maintenance have grown as time goes by [2]. Since it is not as attractive as new software development, software maintenance was not studied and researched in the same depth as development and therefore very few models were developed to deal with it [3].

In this work a software maintenance risk management model is developed using the following work as reference: Bennet [1], Polo [2] and Webster [3]. This paper is divided in 6 sections. The first one introduces the subject. On the second section software maintenance and its state of the art is presented. The third section presents software risk management and its existing models. On the fourth section a proposal for software maintenance risk management is presented. The fifth section presents a case study and finally the sixth section presents the conclusions of this work.

2 Software Maintenance

Software maintenance is the modification of a software product after its deployment with the objective of correcting errors, enhancing performance and other attributes or adapting the product to changes in the environment IEEE [4]. Pressman [5] categorized software maintenance into four types:

- Adaptive: changes in software environment;
- Perfective: new user requirements;
- Corrective: error correction;
- Preventive: to prevent problems in the future.

Pressman [5] also believes that software maintenance should be viewed from 3 main perspectives:

- The activities involved in software maintenance and software engineering impact on the efficacy these activities;
- The costs related to software maintenance;
- Problems that usually happen during software maintenance.

Regarding software maintenance activities, Pressman [5] distinguishes structured software maintenance and unstructured software maintenance and highlights the following activities on structured software maintenance:

- Design evaluation;
- Maintenance approach planning;
- Design change;
- Re-coding;

Revision: which may imply on re-changing the design and re-coding depending on whether the desired results are met or not.

Regarding software maintenance costs, there is a concern with growing costs in various studies [2], however it was observed that intangible costs are often not taken into account. These are the main intangible costs in software maintenance [5]:

- Customer dissatisfaction with unmet requirements or on the delay on meeting them;
- Quality reduction as result of some changes introducing latent errors;
- Problems caused in a development effort when programmers are forced to stop what they were doing to work on software maintenance activities.

Regarding usually found problems in software maintenance, the following arises [5]:

- Impossibility to trace software evolution: changes not documented;

- Impossibility to trace the process in which the software was created;
- Difficulty to understand code written by someone else;
- Difficulty in finding the code's author for clearing doubts;
- Inexistent or bad quality documentation;
- Difficulty in changing the software: software design does not take into account possible future changes.

The considerations mentioned earlier are very important when we are defining maintainability, which is the easiness that software can be understood, corrected, adapted and/or enhanced, and it is influenced by the following factors [5]:

- Skilled personnel availability;
- Capacity to understand system structure;
- Easiness to manipulate the system;
- Use of standard programming languages;
- Test case availability;
- Code debugging mechanisms availability;
- Availability of adequate environment for conducting maintenance.

Bennett [1] introduces a software maintenance life cycle model, which allows distinguishing software regarding its age and maintainability. This model is called a software-staged model and it divides software product life cycle into 5 different stages counted from its deployment:

- Initial Development: in this stage software is exactly as it was and it was deployed. Software will be in this staged until its first maintenance is executed;
- Evolution: in this stage the application is adapted to constant changes in user requirements and operational environment;
- Service: as time goes by, changes in software corrupts the initial architecture and members of the original development team leave until you get to a point where making changes becomes so hard, either due to lack of knowledge in the current team or due to the need of large architectural changes, that is no longer possible to evolve the software. In this stage only small tactical changes are undertaken;
- Phase-Out: in this stage no changes are made in the software. Users must work around software problems;
- Close-Down: in this stage, the software is disconnected and users are directed to a substitute.

3 Software Risk Management

Before starting with software risk management, we shall define software risk: Software Risk is a measure of the probability of loss and its impact related to a software project, process or product [6].

Risk Management is a general procedure for resolving risk and has two main components [7]:

- Risk Assessment defines risk by identifying hazards, evaluating their potential effects and the likelihood of their occurrence.
- Risk Control is the process of developing risk resolution plans, monitoring risk status, implementing risk resolution plan and correcting deviations from the plan [6].

The risk management process can be divided into 6 elements, three related to risk assessment: identification, analysis and prioritization and three related to the control: planning, monitoring and resolution of risks [6]. According to Boehm [7], risk management can be classified in the following way:

- Risk assessment
  - Risk identification
  - Risk analysis
  - Risk prioritization
- Risk Control
  - Risk Management Planning
  - Risk resolution
  - Risk monitoring

The risk identification process encompasses activities that lead to the identification of the hazards that may threat the software product, process or project. Software Risk Identification may use methods involving one or more of the listed below [6]:

- Checklists – use of lists as a reminder of possible risk areas;
- Interviews – use of group interview session where people may talk about their concerns, doubts, problems and uncertainties related to the software;
- Meetings – use of periodic meetings to discuss project risks;
- Revision – use of plan, procedure and work products review;
- Forms – use of standard risk management form to input routinely found risks;
- Survey – use of questionnaires as a faster way than interviewing people about their perceived risks;
- Working Group – use of brainstorming, meditation, modeling, simulation and other group activities.

The risk analysis process consists on quantify each hazard identified on the Risk Identification Process by calculating its occurrence probability and impact. By using a probability/impact matrix, risks can be classified as critical, high, moderate, low or negligible [3]. This process encompasses the following activities: grouping similar and related hazards, determining which may have an impact on risk, determining sources of risk, using risk analysis techniques and tools, estimating risk exposure, evaluating risk against criteria, ranking risk according to its severity [6].

The risk planning process consists of all activities and methods used to develop risk resolution alternatives [8]. This process encompasses the following activities: development of risk scenarios for high-severity risks, development of risk resolution alternatives, selection of risk resolution approach, development of risk resolution action plan, and establishment of variables to be monitored with threshold values for warning [6].

The risk monitoring process consists of activities of risk measurement and indicator tracking, which may indicate that a risk resolution plan must be executed. Tracking indicators may anticipate the loss occurrence, giving more alternatives to mitigation [6].

The risk resolution process consists of activities that aim to reduce risk to an acceptable level. The activities in this process include: response to a notification of triggering event, execution of a risk resolution plan, report of progress against the plan, and correction of deviations from the plan [6].

4 Software Maintenance Risk Management

Using software maintenance and software risk management concepts, we developed a software maintenance risk management model. As stated in many references ([1],[2].[3], [7], [8], [9], [10]), most of software maintenance environments present some factors that increase risks in software maintenance. These factors were used as premises when developing this model and are listed below:

- The deployment of risk management process will be in a environment with no previous risk management culture;
- The software to be maintained were developed by other people;
- Documentation either does not exist or is outdated or has bad quality;
- Languages and platforms used in many modules are old.

Given these premises, we used Hall [6] risk management model and added activities proposed by Charette [8] for cultural adjustment of personnel and good software maintenance practices proposed by Weber [11]. The use of the premises was important to create a process that can be applied in an organization that already performs software maintenance activities and needs to have its software maintenance risk management process improved. The work of Hall [6], Charette [8] and Weber [11] was integrated into one single model after a careful review of their proposal. Additional elements were added based on author's experience and redundancies eliminated. Finally, the proposed model was checked against the IEEE Std 1219-1998 Standard [4] which defines software maintenance, to make sure that correct naming was used and that the process would conform to the standard.

Software Maintenance Risk Management should fit into the Software Maintenance Process [4], with the following changes:

- Team preparation: through training and mentoring, the team will be better prepared to find and communicate risk found in their activities;
- Communication: risk communication strategies should be established and periodic meetings should take place to evaluate those risks;
- Problem Classification: the process of receiving new functionality and bug fixing requests should be redesigned to take into consideration that the risk involved in these activities when prioritizing them;
- Documentation: a task-force should be defined to produce, enhance and update all maintained software documentation. The documentation activities should be prioritized according to the degree of changes made in each software and/or module. Also, when modifying any part of the code, the maintenance team should enhance and correct/update its existing documentation;
- Tests: an automated test policy should be established, this tests would expedite the maintenance process and ensure that any corrections and changes made on the software did not cause an error somewhere else.

The changes mentioned earlier were implemented first, by adding extra activities in the following IEEE Std 1219-1998 [4] Process:

4.1 Problem/modification identification, classification, and prioritization

- For every problem/modification identified, the risks associated to them should be evaluated. It should be considered the risk of doing the change against the risk of not doing it. When not performing a modification or fixing a problem, we have a risk of loosing customer base by not attending some desired/expected requirements. On the other hand, some modifications may bring distortions to the system architecture making it more difficult to perform future maintenance and reducing system life. Another risk that must be taken into consideration is an excessive maintenance cost that must be compared with the cost of replacing the solution. When prioritizing modifications, the risk involved in each one of them must be used as reference when defining what must be done immediately, what will be postponed and what will not be done;
- A mitigation plan must be established and the team should be prepared to act if a loss occurs;
- To identify risks, we suggest using the taxonomy proposed by Webster [3].

4.2 Analysis, Design, Implementation

- When performing analysis, design and implementation activities, the team must pay attention to the risks already listed in previous activities and also to new ones not previously identified. All identified risks should be entered in the risk matrix and monitored by the team that is performing the maintenance;
- During these activities, updating and enhancing documentation should be done as a measure to reduce future maintenance risk.
- System Test and Acceptance Test:
- Tests should be automated for faster and more reliable execution.

Then there were few activities that would not fit into the IEEE Std 1219-1998 [4] proposed phases and they should be executed as specified below:

4.3 Team Preparation

- This phase prepares the team to changes in their daily activities, introducing them to risk management paradigms;
- In this phase, training in risk and in the proposed process should be given to the whole team.

4.4 Documentation

Documentation can be the most important ally or enemy when maintaining a legacy system. Due to that, the proposed process has documentation activities in the analysis, design and implementation, but also a documentation taskforce. This taskforce should perform search, organization, consolidation, complementation and correction activities on the existing documentation. These activities even though not directly related to risk management they are verify important for providing resources that will allow a more precise assessment of maintenance risks.

5 Case Study

In order to test the proposed model, a case study was developed. It was chosen to apply it in an legacy university crm system that has a web interface and as it was complex enough to have maintenance issues and simple enough to have results easily monitored.

The application was developed using the JAVA language and was very recent. As it had tough deadlines and integration requirements with other systems, some developed in Natural/Adabas which are old and have many documentation issues, the project was deployed very fast and faced constantly changing requirements moving it fast to the Evolution stage. Complying with the activities proposed in the process was very time consuming and we face challenges both from user expectations and developer hastiness. With weekly deployments, sometimes more problems emerged when a simple change was performed. It was hard convincing developers to apply the process and we decided to count new bugs per week and use it as metric to show progress. Since the system was recently developed, we did not face any challenges with use of old technologies or corruption of architecture coherence. With bug tracking system in place and version control using cvs, we could easily recover the statistics before the process was implemented and be able to show a reduction in new bugs per week with few weeks of implementation.

Regarding the implementation of the proposed activities, we made the following findings:

5.1 Problem/modification identification, classification, and prioritization

Associating risk for every problem/modification identified was easy in most cases. At the end of the week, all problems and changes requests were discussed and maintenance team evaluated the risk. Webster's taxonomy was used and helped raising the right issues and making the meeting more productive [3]. This extra task didn't make the meeting much longer than usual and helped bringing consciousness of the impact of changes to the development team, making them more careful. In general terms, we could also say that better decision were made in the Problem/modification identification, classification, and prioritization activities.

Before, starting working on a new release, the code was tagged in the source control software, allowing going back as a mitigation step. Also, to prevent problems when larger architecture changes were made, the whole cvs tree was backed up. During this study, sometimes it was necessary to move back to the previous compiled version; however we didn't face situations where we had to roll back source code.

5.2 Analysis, Design, Implementation

Finding risks during analysis, design and implementation activities was not very successful in the beginning, as the team was not used to do that and differently than in a meeting there is no driver of the discussion, developers are working on the own. We perceived that they were afraid to present the risks as they felt as showing weakness on their work. It took strong persuasion to improve that and we still feel it is not working as well as it should.

Documentation activities also were hard to implement, developers didn't like doing that and were always in a hurry, not having time to document. Regular documentation activities during Analysis, Design and Implementation were only made after few weeks of micro-managing this topic.

Choosing correct tools and environments could help the team not only writing down analysis, design and implementation documents, but also could generate automatically some architecture design and source-code [12]. Furthermore, these tools could help finding and reusing components already developed and available in a common repository [13].

5.3 System Test and Acceptance Test

Slowly, Junit tests were developed and helped a lot during System tests.

5.4 Team Preparation

A PowerPoint presenting this process and some literature regarding risk was presented to the maintenance team to prepare them to the changes in the process. After that, these changes were discussed individually with each member of the maintenance team to make sure they really understood how the team would perform from that point.

5.5 Documentation

Due to lack of resources, we were not able to implement the documentation taskforce.

After analysing the data, we found that the quantitative results were inconclusive. Many variables may have had an effect on bug reduction, including that as time passed, requirements became better known and more stable. Nevertheless, the experience of implementing this process gave to the developer team a greater level of conciousness regarding maintainance risks. That led to more carefully designed, documented and coded software. The weekly release meetings after risk was brought to the table made developers more careful before making bold movements of, for instance, changing a database structure.

From that experience, we perceive the following challenges, when implementing the proposed process:

Change resistance:

- In many cases, the additional activities proposed by the process may be seen as bureaucratic and pointless, making necessary a strong convincing work to make people adopt this new way of working;
- Aiming to make this argument stronger, metrics that allow monitoring the progress and seeing the benefits to clients, team and company when adopting the process should be implemented;
- Management must be convinced before anyone else to adopt risk management as a priority. An implementation of risk management process should not be started without total support from management.

Lack of skills in the team:

- The adoption of risk management demands higher skills than what is usually found in maintenance teams. In most cases, this problem can be reduced by the proposed training, however many times it involves more basic education in software engineering matters;
- The adoption of a process implies in discipline and skills. When there are no previous processes in place, this may mean a big leap in skills needed;
- As it is not as attractive as new software development, maintenance most often has less experienced professionals.

Difficulties to access information:

- Documentation activities present a enormous challenge, since, in many cases, there is no documentation or it is outdated and the team that developed the system is no long available;
- To gather this information it is often necessary to read source-code which is often obscured by many patches brought by the changes in the software;
- Users themselves could be a great source of information, since they supposedly know well the business rules that were automated by the system.

To face to those challenges, many measures must be adopted, the study of those measures is the objective of future work in this area. One approach to deal with this problem with lower overhead might be documenting directly in the source-code using annotations [14].

6 Conclusions

During the development of this work we came across significant differences between software maintenance and software development. These differences make risk management also very distinct when dealing with software maintenance versus software development. Even though maintenance is responsible for 90% of software costs in its life cycle, very few studies were developed on software maintenance risk management. Maintenance process and practices were studied as way of analyzing its risk factors, which helped adding risk management practices in the process. Similarly current software development risk management work and software maintenance work were studied. All this information was compiled and helped generating the proposed software maintenance risk management process.

During the development of this process and on its trial in the case study, many challenges were found and they were highlighted in this paper. It was verified that the most impacting risk factors in software maintenance are the lack of skills in maintenance personnel and the lack of documentation. The proposed process aims to mitigate, at least partially, these risks. Specific risk mitigating measures that should be taken still rely on management experiences and can not be defined in a generic risk management process, as the one we proposed.

As we verified in our case study and on the literature, the implementation of risk management process as this has a great impact on diminishing problems related to schedule, costs and meeting customer needs in software maintenance activities. However, for better results, it is required to start taking maintenance in consideration from the first conceptual sketch of a new system and during the software entire life-cycle.

As future work, we hope to enhance the software risk management process, identify most common risks, metrics to help identifying them as soon as possible and include in the maintenance process activities that help mitigating those risks. On another research line, a very interesting research subject would be the definition of characteristics and metrics that could be used to evaluate software regarding its maintainability and its maintenance risk.

7 References

[1] BENNETT , K; RAJLICH, V. Software maintenance and evolution: a roadmap. Proceedings of the Conference on The Future of Software Engineering table of contents. Limerick, Ireland. p. 73 – 87. ISBN:1-58113-253-0. Publisher ACM Press New York, NY, USA, 2000.

[2] POLO, M. Advances in Software Maintenance Management: Technologies and Solutions. Idea Group Publishing. Loughborough, UK. 2002.

[3] WEBSTER, K. et al. A Risk Taxonomy Proposal for Software Maintenance. 21st IEEE International Conference on Software Maintenance (ICSM'05). p. 453-461, Budapest, 2005.

[4] IEEE. IEEE Std 1219-1998: Standard for Software Maintenance. Los Alamitos, CA USA. IEEE Computer Society Press, 1998.

[5] PRESSMAN, Roger. Software Engineering – A Practicioner's Approach. London, England. Mc-Graw Hill Book Company, 6th Edition. 2004.

[6] HALL, E. M. Managing risk : methods for software systems development. Addison-Wesley , 5th Edition, ISBN 0201255928. Boston, 2002.

[7] BOEHM, B. IEEE Tutorial on Software Risk Management. New York, NY USA. IEEE Computer Society Press, 1989

[8] CHARETTE, R.N; ADAMS, K.M; WHITE, M.B. Managing risk in software maintenance. IEEE – Software. V. 14 N. 3, p. 43-50. May/June, 1997.

[9] BUCLEY, J. et al. Towards a taxonomy of software change. Journal of Software Maintenance: Research and Practice. V. 1 – 389. John Wiley & Sons, Ltd., 2003.

[10] RUIZ, F. et al. Utilización de Investigación-Acción en la Definición de un Entorno para la Gestión del Proceso de Mantenimiento del Software. In: 1er. Workshop en: Métodos de Investigación y Fundamentos Filosóficos en Ingeniería del Software y Sistemas de Información. (MIFISIS'2002). Madrid, 2002.

[11] WEBER, R. et al. Fit for Change: Steps towards Effective Software Maintenance. 21st IEEE International Conference on Software Maintenance (ICSM'05). p. 26-33, Budapest, 2005.

[12] BEZERRA, V. et al. Designing object oriented systems using stereotypes and patterns. Proceeding of IADIS WWW/Internet 2006. 1ed.Murcia: IADIS, 2006, v. 1, p. 162-166. 2006.

[13] LUCRÉDIO, D. et al. ORION – A Component-Based Software Engineering Environment. The Journal of Object Technology (JOT), v. 3, n.4, p. 51, 2004. URL : http://dx.doi.org/10.5381/jot.2004.3.4.a4

[14] BEZERRA, V. et al. Requirements oriented programming in a web- service architecture. IADIS www/Internet Proceedings. Lisboa: IADIS, 2010. v. 1. p. 287-292.

Test Case Prioritization Related to Code Quality

Savas Ozturk[1], Nurhan Yagci[1], Mehmet Aktas[2], Mehmet Ozbek[1], Furkan Paligu[1]
[1] TUBITAK BILGEM, Gebze, Kocaeli, Turkey
[2] Computer Engineering, Yildiz Technical University, Davutpasa, Istanbul, Turkey

Abstract - *Regression testing, which is a type of testing that determines whether a change in one part of the software affects other parts of that software, can effectively be done when the execution of test case scenarios are scheduled based on pre-defined priorities. Test case prioritization, one of the regression test methods, deals with scheduling the execution of test case scenarios so that the testing can be done quickly and efficiently. In this paper, we investigate methodologies to find high-risk test case scenarios based on software metric measurements. We introduce a novel metric named Quality Risk Ratio (QRR), which denotes the amount of risk for a module. The key idea of our approach is the evaluation of testing importance for each module covered by test cases. Experimental results show that our fast and practical approach gives approximately the same prioritization results as risk-based analysis, which is a conventional and subjective method.*

Keywords: *Test Case Prioritization, Regression Testing, Software Metrics*

1 Introduction

When the test execution phase starts, there usually is a time constraint for the test engineers. As a result, the test engineers frequently do not have enough time to run all the test cases for all the test life cycles. Regression testing is a way of testing software to find new (functional and non-functional) faults after changes have been made in software. Because a change made in one part of the software may cause new faults in the other parts of the software, the test engineer retests the unchanged parts of the software and checks the software to see whether it works as it previously did and whether the new features caused new faults. Regression testing is important, albeit an expensive process.

There are four methodologies that are available for regression testing [1]:

- **Retest All:** In this technique, the test cases that are no longer applied to the modified version of the program are discarded and all the remaining sets of test cases are used to test the modified program.

- **Regression Test Selection:** The retest all technique takes time and effort as all test cases are used to test the software again, so it may be quite expensive. This technique is much better as it uses information about the program, the modified program, and the test cases to select a subset of test cases for testing.

- **Test Suite Reduction:** This technique uses information about the program and the test suite to remove the test cases which have become redundant with time as new functionality is added.

- **Test Case Prioritization:** In this technique, test cases are assigned a priority. The priority is set according to some criterion and test cases with the highest priority are scheduled first.

Regression testing usually takes place under very tight time constraints and high stress factors. The retest all methodology may become impossible to apply in these circumstances. Therefore, prioritizing test case scenarios has become a feasible way to manage. Today, test case prioritization studies carry out analysis based on the errors caught in previous tests. However, it may not be sufficient to test the modules that have the mistakes. We argue that the fixing done to correct such mistakes may possibly affect another module. Recent studies have shown that the resulting number of errors encountered in the testing phase is associated with the quality of the software code [2,3,4]. This indicates that better quality code will ease the burden on software testing.

In this paper, we investigate test case prioritization techniques prior to any testing based on the static code analysis that can be done without having to run the code. In this approach, we have determined 20 different software metrics and the most critical code module of an enterprise software project. Then, we associated the test case scenarios with this code module and investigated the benefits that will be provided as a result of an improvement in the code quality (such as a reduction in the number of errors). We have compared the results of the proposed approach against a risk-based test case prioritization, which is a technique that requires certain specialized work experience.

2 Related Work

Among the several studies in the literature, coverage-based prioritization techniques come one step to the fore [5]. There exist four different techniques towards coverage-based test case prioritization in Software Engineering literature: 1) Total function coverage prioritization, 2) Additional function coverage prioritization, 3) Total binary-diff function coverage prioritization, and 4) Additional binary-diff function coverage prioritization [6,7,8].

The total function coverage prioritization sorts the test case scenarios by function coverage. If multiple test case scenarios cover the same number of functions, they are sorted randomly.

Additional function coverage prioritization combines feedback with coverage information. This technique iteratively selects a test case scenario that yields the greatest function coverage. Then, it adjusts the coverage information on subsequent test case scenarios to evaluate them considering the functions that are not yet covered. This process is repeated until all functions are covered by at least one test case scenario. If multiple test cases cover the same number of functions that have not yet been covered, they are ordered randomly. When all functions have been covered, this process is repeated on remaining test case scenarios until all have been sorted.

Total binary-diff function coverage prioritization uses modification information, but without feedback. It sorts test case scenarios in the order of their coverage of functions that differ textually. If multiple test cases cover the same number of differing functions, they are ordered randomly. When all test case scenarios that cover differing functions have been ordered, the remaining test case scenarios are ordered using total function coverage prioritization.

Additional binary-diff function coverage prioritization uses both feedback and modification information. It iteratively selects a test case scenario that yields the greatest coverage of functions that differ, then adjusts the coverage information on subsequent test cases to indicate their coverage of functions not yet covered, and then repeats this process until all functions that differ and that have been covered by at least one test case have been covered. If multiple test cases cover the same number of differing functions that have not yet been covered, they are ordered randomly. Then, additional binary-diff function coverage prioritization is applied to the remaining test cases.

One potential goal of test case prioritization is increasing a test suite's rate of fault detection. To formally illustrate how rapidly a prioritized test suite detects faults, the Average Percentage of Faults Detected (APFD) metric is introduced in order to measure how quickly a test suite detects faults during the testing process [6]. An increased rate of fault detection can provide earlier feedback on the system under a regression test and let developers begin locating and correcting faults earlier. This metric, however, assumes that all test cases and fault costs are uniform. In practice, test cases and fault costs can vary, and in such cases, the previous APFD metric and techniques designed to improve APFD can be unsatisfactory. So, this metric is updated for assessing the rate of fault detection of prioritized test cases, APFDC, that incorporates varying test cases and fault costs [9].

APFD studies require the gathered fault information for each test case. Inputs, outputs and artifacts of the selected prioritization method is dependent on the project or program structure. There exist different inputs of the test case prioritizing. Some of these include the length of the code, the complexity of the code, the number of functions, the complexity of the functions, the number of errors, and the test execution history [10,11]. Srivastava et al. [12] and Srikanth et al. [13] presented requirement-based test case prioritization. One potential weakness of these approaches is the fact that requirement properties are often estimated and are subjective values [5]. Ma and Zhao investigate the change in the fault proneness and complexity of the modules when code is updated [14]. Although they attempt to derive a result from program structure, it still requires fault information from the previous tests. The focus of this study lays on obtaining prioritization without requiring fault information of previous tests, requirements, and risks.

A major percentage of software projects suffer from quality problems. Software testing provides visibility into product and process quality. Software projects are usually developed in an undisciplined way such that there may exist a gap in requirements, such as a formal fault database, design documents, or technical solution documents. In this case, code quality may be used to derive an opinion about the most critical sections of the code. There is a strong correlation between complexity, which is one of the most important indicators of software quality and the number of faults, security bugs, and the amount of untested portions. All of the faults cannot be removed completely as methods are needed to at least ensure the quality of the software, but the costs for fault handling should at least be possible to be decreased considerably by obtaining early estimates of the fault content that can be expected in a particular software system [16].

Software metrics are key "facts" that project managers use to understand their current position and to prioritize their activities in order to reduce the risk of schedule over-runs on software releases. To this end, software metrics help us to control our software projects. They enable us to better estimate and predict the quality of our projects in the future. This study can be said to be first among existing studies at employing code quality metrics for test case prioritization without needing the list of previous faults detected.

3 Proposed Work

Defects cause high costs when detected at acceptance tests and they often cause unaffordable costs when they are observed after products are delivered to the customer. One of the main concerns of software engineering is to prevent defects before delivering to the customer, before acceptance, and even before system tests.

A well-managed project ensures measurements on code and watches trends whenever the project is underway. However, for many projects measurement has been considered a luxury. This study proposes a model that combines metric measurements and coverage rates of each method and class in order to reach a priority idea. We assume we are informed about the relationship between modules and test cases; in other words, we query which method or class is tested by which test and the amount of coverage as well. If it is lacking, test case definitions may be helpful for collecting coverage information by testing all the software, but it is expensive and may be time consuming.

Fig.1 summarizes our approach using an example. First, the coverage matrix is constructed. Second, the Quality Risk Ratio (QRR) is calculated for each method and class. Next, the Priority Factor (PF) for each test case for methods and classes is found, respectively. Finally, we sort PF values in descending order and get an updated test case list.

Coverage Matrix

	T1	T2	T3
M1	45	12	45
M2	67	56	0
C1	23	17	90

Quality Risk Ratio

	vG	LOC	QRR
M1	45	62	25
M2	67	56	75
C1	23	17	0

Priority Factor

Approach	T1	T2	T3
Method-based	341	768	78
Class-based	897	938	0

Prioritization

T2
T1
T3

Fig. 1 Proposed Prioritization Steps

QRR is the percentage quality risk for a method or class and calculated according to Eq. (1) and Eq.(2).

$$Td_j = \Sigma\left(MV_{ij} - Thr_j\right) \qquad (1)$$

$$QRR_i = \Sigma \left(\left(MV_{ij} - Thr_j\right) \;/\; Td_j * 100\right) * C_j \qquad (2)$$

For Eq. (1) and Eq. (2); i is the method or class numerator, j is the metric type, Td_j is the raw risk value of the method or class, MV_{ij} is the measured metric value, Thr_j is the threshold value of the selected metric, and C_j is the defined weight coefficient for the selected metric. MV_{ij} - Thr_j is assumed as zero if Thr_j is bigger than MV_{ij}.

Selected metrics, preferred thresholds, and the defined weighting coefficients are listed in Table 1. The metrics are split into two groups according to the level: Method-level metrics and class-level metrics(a.k.a. Object Oriented Metrics). The sum of weighting coefficients of the both groups is 1(one). The coefficients can be set according to the project type or according to the preferences of the evaluator. In this study, the coefficients are balanced due to their importance and previous skills.

Table 1 Selected Software Metrics [17]

Metric	Metric Code	Metric Level	Threshold	Coefficient
Cyclomatic Complexity	v(G)	Method	10	0.20
Essential Complexity	ev(G)	Method	4	0.20
Module Design Complexity Metric	iv(G)	Method	7	0.10
Global Data Complexity Metric	gdv(G)	Method	4	0
Lines of Code	Code	Method	30	0.20
Lines of Comment	Comment	Method	10	0.10
Lines Left Blank	Blank	Method	10	0.05
Lines of Mixed Code and Comments	mixed	Method	10	0.05
Maximum v(G)	MAXV	Class	10	0.20
Maximum ev(G)	MAXEV	Class	4	0.20

Average v(G)	AVGV	Class	10	0.10
Sum v(G)	SUMV	Class	70	0.05
Depth of Inheritance	DIT	Class	7	0.10
Lack of Cohesion of Methods	LOCM	Class	75	0.05
Number of Children	NOC	Class	3	0.05
Response for a Class	RFC	Class	100	0.05
Weighted Methods per Class	WMC	Class	14	0.05
Coupling Between Objects	CBO	Class	2	0.05
Fan-in	fanin	Class	1	0.05
Public Data	pubdata	Class	0	0.05

Table 2 shows an example calculation for QRR in detail. There are three methods in the example and the effect of cyclomatic complexity is calculated. MethodB is the most critical method to be improved because it handles approximately 10% of the risk of all of the projects, taking only v(G) into consideration. These calculations are repeated for other method-level metrics. The totals of the weighted values for each method give the QRR value of the method.

Table 2 An Example for QRR Calculation Based On v(G)

v(G) Threshold	10			
v(G) Coefficient	0.125			
	MethodA	**MethodB**	**MethodC**	**TOTAL**
Measured v(G)	15	23	7	
Difference = Measured - Threshold	5	13	0	18
Normalized Diff. = (Difference / Total Difference)	27.8	72.2	0	100%
*Weighted = Normalized Diff. * Coefficient*	**3.48**	**9.02**	**0**	**12.5%**

QRR_i is related to the amount of metrics exceeding thresholds and how far the method is from the threshold when it exceeds the threshold. Three example methods are listed in Table 3. When considering the relationship between MethodD and MethodE, only the Line of Code (LOC) metric measurement exceeds the threshold for both, and the QRR value is affected according to the amount of LOC only. The metric measurements of MethodF seem on the border, but the QRR is calculated as 0 because of no excess. Although MethodF seems worse than MethodD when looking at the overall, exceeding the threshold at one of the metrics is penalized. Defining the thresholds is an important decision point for a project.

Table 3 An Example Of QRR Comparison

	LOC	ev(G)	v(G)	iv(G)	QRRi
Thresholds	30	4	10	7	7
MethodD	32	3	3	3	11.5
MethodE	45	3	3	3	25.4
MethodF	30	4	10	7	0

After calculating the QRR for each method and class and sorting them in descending order, we have two groups of risky sections of the code, one for methods and one for classes. The QRR value represents the percentage of quality risk load of the pointed method or class. For example, if the QRR of a class is 20, then we can reduce quality problems of the project 20% by reducing the metric values under the thresholds for that class. The sum of the QRRs for each group will always be 100, but the most hazardous parts of the code will be viewed more clearly by this technique. Efficient usage scenarios for the QRRs can be developed. For example, a development team may have a goal to handle QRRs below 10, which means that quality will remain almost equally balanced.

QRRs and coverage are combined by multiplication. For each test case, the PF is a product of QRR and coverage (Eq. (3))

$$PF_m = \sum QRR_i * PC_i \qquad (3)$$

For Eq. (3); i is the method or class numerator, m is the test case numerator, PC is the Percentage Coverage of method or class i , QRRi is the QRR value of method or class i, and PFm is the Prioritization Factor of test case m.

Finally, we have a numeric value for each test case. The more PF a test case has, the more risky it is. Sorted PF values give the prioritization order of the test cases.

Calculation of the QRRs is automatically performed in seconds as soon as code is checked in. This operation ensures instantaneous code quality as soon as any change in the software is caught and warns the team against potential damage. Combining coverage and QRRs is also easily obtained. As in other related work, there are numerous ways for prioritization, but it when time matters this model seems to be the fastest among the conventional methods although a subjective step for coverage calculation remains.

4 Experiments and Discussion

4.1 Selected Application

We selected a 4 KLOC desktop application for comparing the proposed model and a risk based prioritization written in C# which contains file operations, database operations, windows services, and GUI operations.

4.2 Coverage Matrix

In this study, test team has written 14 test cases that cover the main functionalities of the application. While tests are executed, coverage ratios (the amount of code covered when a test case is run) are noted using McCabe IQ test utility. Coverage values are normalized in that the method which is covered completely by executing a test is marked as 100 whereas if it is not hit at any time coverage is noted as 0 and partially covered methods have a coverage value between 0 and 100. Coverage of a class is calculated by addition of all the methods' coverage values of the class. Coverage computation is performed once while testing. We assume that test cases-methods matrix and test cases-classes matrix will be provided for future studies.

4.3 QRR Calculation

Metric measurements are collected and the QRR values are calculated according to Eq.(2) as stated in the previous section. Calculated QRR values of methods are listed in descending order in Table 4. As the selected project is small in size and as it is a well-managed project, the list has become short. It can be seen that by refactoring with only a few methods will make this project perfectly qualified. Almost half of the quality risk is collected using only one method and this method does not seem complex.

Table 4 Sorted List of Method-Based QRRs

		Size	Complexity		
Method Name	**QRR**	**LOC**	**ev(G)**	**v(G)**	**iv(G)**
Forms.FrmMeasurement.SaveButton()	**45.79**	86	1	13	10
CommonWorks.createCheckBox(CheckedListBox,AdminPanel_windows.ToolType)	**10.00**	13	5	5	5
Forms.FrmMeasurement.btnSave_Click(object,EventArgs)	**10.00**	22	5	5	5
MeasurementTool.Understand.WriteFile()	**3.95**	46	1	6	2
Forms.FrmProject.Save(AdminPanel_windows.Project)	**2.11**	38	1	8	6
Forms.FrmConfigurationItem.Save(AdminPanel_windows.ConfigurationItem)	**1.58**	37	1	8	6
Forms.FrmPcfCreator.CreatePcf(string)	**1.58**	41	1	6	5

Calculated QRR values of classes are listed in descending order in Table 5. Although most metric values of *Service1Client* seem normal, it is third in order because of fan-in threshold excess. This is the only class which exceeded fan-in threshold.

Table 5 Sorted List of Class-Level QRRs

Class Name	**QRR**	**sum**	**Avg**	**max**	**max**	**NOC**	**DIT**	**RFC**	**WMC**	**CBO**	**LOCM**	**Fan-**	**Pub**
FrmMeasurement	**31**	46	3.3	13	5	0	2	22	22	2	100	1	0
CommonWorks	**10**	18	3	5	5	0	1	8	8	0	100	0	0
Service1Client	**5**	8	1	1	1	0	2	9	8	0	0	2	0
ProjectSummary	**1.5**	43	2.2	3	1	0	2	46	46	0	100	1	0
Measurement	**1.3**	40	2.2	3	1	0	2	40	40	0	100	1	0
MainForm	**1.1**	48	1.8	4	1	0	2	36	36	1	100	1	0
Result	0.8	23	2.1	3	1	0	2	27	27	0	100	1	0

4.4 Prioritization Ordering

The method and class QRR tables give us information about the most critical methods and classes. After combining QRR and coverage information, the PF table was constructed as Table 6. Prioritization orders are listed in two categories: Method-based and Class-based.

Table 6 Prioritization Factors and Prioritized Test Case Orders

	Method-based		Class-based	
	PF	Ordered	PF	Ordered
TC1	45	*TC12*	2158	*TC12*
TC2	105	*TC10*	2608	*TC10*
TC3	75	*TC9*	2174	*TC9*
TC4	120	*TC14*	2476	*TC14*
TC5	33	*TC13*	2860	*TC13*
TC6	67	*TC4*	2546	*TC11*
TC7	56	*TC2*	2564	*TC5*
TC8	90	*TC8*	2675	*TC8*
TC9	260	*TC3*	2543	*TC2*
TC10	390	*TC6*	2791	*TC7*
TC11	0	*TC7*	5070	*TC6*
TC12	406	*TC1*	3017	*TC4*
TC13	507	*TC5*	1580	*TC3*
TC14	523	*TC11*	1580	*TC1*

4.5 Risk-Based Evaluation

In order to see the benefits of this work, we have compared the proposed approach with a legacy prioritization method. Risk based test case prioritization is a widely used technique, but it requires skill and domain expertise for a specific project. Risk is the product of damage and probability for damage to occur (see Fig. 2). Risk analysis assesses damage during use, usage frequency, and determines the probability of failure by looking at defect introduction [18].

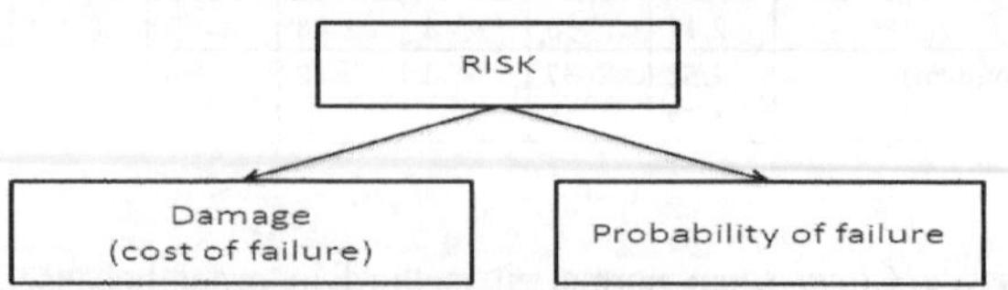

Fig. 2 Intentional task allocation; a) auction-based b) market-based

We have evaluated the risk analysis by brainstorming with three domain experts in a meeting.. We used risk-based testing, but in an ad hoc fashion based on experts' personal judgment. The experts asked some questions and noted the estimations on the impact of failure of the test cases and the probabilities of test case failures. The impact and probability is graded as numbers from 1 to 5 and the product of impact and probability gives the risk factor of the selected test case as seen in Table 7.

Fig. 3 summarizes the prioritization results by grouping test cases in three categories. Grouping is done according to the similarity of the scores of test cases for each category. For example, in the method-based category, TC12, TC10 and TC9 have values of 4060, 3901 and 2605 respectively and are grouped together where there is a big difference with the second group (TC14:523 and TC13:507). It may be possible to split risk-based results into three groups and other results into four groups according to the neighborhood of the values. When test suite reduction is needed, the last group of test cases can be eliminated.

Table 7 Risk-based Prioritization

	Impact (Damage)	Probabilit y	Product of Impact and	Ord. Pri.
TC1	2	5	10	*TC12* *TC10* *TC9* *TC4* *TC13* *TC1* *TC3* *TC14* *TC5* *TC8* *TC2* *TC6* *TC7* *TC11*
TC2	3	2	6	
TC3	3	3	9	
TC4	3	5	15	
TC5	2	4	8	
TC6	2	2	4	
TC7	2	2	4	
TC8	2	4	8	
TC9	4	4	16	
TC10	4	4	16	
TC11	3	1	3	
TC12	4	4	16	
TC13	4	3	12	
TC14	3	3	9	

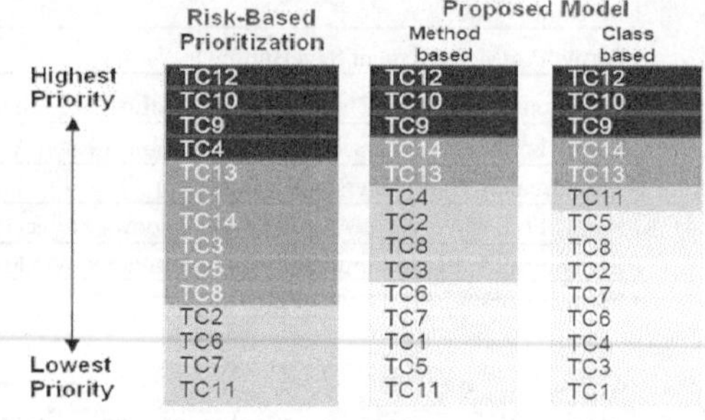

Fig. 3 Comparison of Risk-Based Prioritization and Proposed Model

It can be clearly seen that first three test cases in the orders are the same. TC11 has the least importance according to the risk-based and method-based sorting because of *Main* class which has auto-generated code we can't eject from the code. For method-based calculation, we don't make calculations for auto-generated code, so it gives better results. Consequently, it can be said that our model is reliable at finding the most and the least important test cases. This approach can be applied to either test case prioritization or test suite minimization. Reliability of method-based prioritization is better than a class-based one as well because it may contain some auto-generated code which affects code quality in a negative way. Also, some discussions on object oriented metrics bring uncertainty to a class-based approach. Another advantage of the method-based approach is its more sensitive nature. As soon as code is changed, the prioritization order is updated. Maybe the need for the coverage matrix can be seen as a limitation here, but it is enough to provide it at the beginning regression tests. We ignore the changes in the coverage matrix once it is created, because updating the matrix may become an unworthy task due to its sustaining very few changes.

Metric selection is another issue to be well thought out. It depends on the type of project, the culture of the organization, the programming language, etc. For example, if the code is developed in Cobol or Fortran, Halstead metrics can be taken into account [17]. Metric coefficients should be set according to the project's requirements as well.

5 Conclusion

Test case prioritization is one of the most used techniques in regression testing. This study proposes a test case prioritization model which is based on quality metrics such as size, complexity, and object orientation. The model uses the measurements of approximately 20 metrics of code and creates a novel metric named QRR, which clearly shows methods and classes which should be refactored. After combining QRR results with the test cases' code coverage, two alternative prioritization orders are taken: Method-based and Class-based. In order to validate our model, we compared results with well-known, risk-based analysis results which are based on domain expertise. Comparisons show that our model, which does not require any prior knowledge about the code or application, and which does not require any expertise about domain or requirement information, gives approximate results with legacy techniques in seconds. This model not only prioritizes the test cases, but also prioritizes the problematic methods and classes for refactoring as well. Future work will be based on extending the metric set and including factors like test duration to the prioritization problem.

6 Acknowledgement

The authors would like to thank Software Testing and Quality Evaluation Center (*YTKDM in Turkish*) of Scientific and Technological Research Council of Turkey (*TUBITAK in Turkish*) for funding this study.

7 References

[1] Rothermel, G., Elbaum, s., Malishevsky, A., Kallakuri, P. and Xuemei Qiu, *"On test suite composition and cost-effective regression testing"*, ACM Transactions on Software Engineering and Methodology (TOSEM) Volume 13 Issue 3, July 2004, Pages 277 – 331

[2] K. Bogdan,Al-Yami, A., *"Automated Regression Test Generation"*, Proceedings of the ACM SIGSOFT International Symposium on Software Testing and Analysis ISSTA98, 1998.

[3] Kaner, C., *"Exploratory Testing"*, Florida Institute of Technology, Quality Assurance Institute Worldwide Annual Software Testing Conference,Orlando, FL, 2006.

[4] Chhillar, U., Bhasin, S., *"Establishing Relationship between Complexity and Faults for Object-Oriented Software Systems"*, IJCSI International Journal of Computer Science Issues, Vol. 8, Issue 5, No 2, September 2011

[5] Yoo, S., Harman, M., *"Regression testing minimization, selection and prioritization: a survey"*, Journal of Software Testing, Verification and Reliability, 2012; 22: 67–120

[6] Elbaum, S., Rothermel, G., Kanduri, S., Malishevsky, A., *"Selecting a Cost-Effective Test Case Prioritization Technique"*, Journal of Software Quality Control, Volume 12, Issue 3, September 2004, Pages 185-210

[7] Malishevsky, A.,Rothermel, G. and Elbaum, S., *"Modeling the Cost-Benefits Tradeoffs for Regression Testing Techniques"* ,Proceedings of the International Conference on Software Maintenance (ICSM'02), 2002.

[8] Catal, C., Mishra, D., *"Test case prioritization: a systematic mapping study"*, Software Quality Journal, July 2012

[9] Malishevsky, A.,Ruthruff, J.,Rothermel, G., and Elbaum, S., *"Cost-cognizant Test Case Prioritization"*, Technical Report TRUNL-CSE-2006-0004, Department of Computer Science and Engineering, University of Nebraska –Lincoln, 2006.

[10]Do, H.,Rothermel, G., *"A Controlled Experiment Assessing Test Case Prioritization Techniques via Mutation Faults"*, Proceedings of the IEEE International Conference on Software Maintenance, pages 411-420, 2005.

[11] Jones, J., Harrold, M., *"Test-Suite Reduction and Prioritization for Modified Condition/Decision Coverage"*, In Proceedings of the International Conference on Software Maintenance, 2001.

[12] Srivastava, P.R., Kumar, K., Raghurama,G., *"Test case prioritization based on requirements and risk factors"*, ACM SIGSOFT Software Engineering Notes 33(4) (2008)

[13] Srikanth H, Williams L, Osborne J., *"System test case prioritization of new and regression test cases"*, Proceedings of the International Symposium on Empirical Software Engineering. IEEE Computer Society Press: Silver Spring, MD, 2005; 64–73.

[14] Ma, Z., Zhao, J., *"Test Case Prioritization based on Analysis of Program Structure"*, 2008 15th Asia-Pacific Software Engineering Conference

[15] Schneier, B., *"Testimony of Bruce Schneier"*, Committee of Homeland Security, U.S. House of Representatives - Jun 25, 2003

[16] Wohlin, C., Xie, M., *"Fault Content Estimations:A Pragmatic Approach using Design Metrics"*, Proceedings International Workshop on Empirical Studies of Software Maintenance", pp. 43-47, Bari, Italy, 1997.

[17] McCabe Software, *"All Metrics Thresholds in McCabe IQ"*, http://www.mccabe.com/pdf/McCabe%20IQ%20Metrics.pdf

[18]Schaefer, H., *"Test Management is Risk management:Risk Based Testing"*, White Paper, http://pi.informatik.uni-siegen.de/stt/25_1/01_Fachgruppenberichte/TAV/TAV22P3Schaefer.pdf

An Eclipse Plug-In for Generating Database Access Documentation in Java Code

Paul L. Bergstein and Aditya Gade
Dept. of Computer and Information Science, University of Massachusetts Dartmouth, Dartmouth, MA, USA
pbergstein@umassd.edu, agade@umassd.edu

Abstract – *Enterprise applications typically consist of a web layer, the business logic layer, and a relational database. However, the interaction between these various layers is not sufficiently captured by the current generation of IDE (Integrated Development Environment). For example, current Java IDE's do not evaluate the relationship of classes with the database, or how a particular java method interacts with database tables and columns. We report here our progress in developing an Eclipse plug-in that helps the programmer document the interactions between Java code and relational databases. A primary motivation is to facilitate code maintenance in the face of database modifications.*

Keywords: Software maintenance, software documentation, CASE tools.

1 Introduction

Modern tools have simplified the development of enterprise applications by bridging gaps across various technologies like file systems, relational databases, messaging, and web services. However, this has also led to challenges in maintenance and enhancement of enterprise applications. An enterprise application usually consists of a web layer, the business logic and relational database, often enhanced with frameworks like Struts and Hibernate for web and persistence. However, the interaction between these various layers is not sufficiently captured by the current generation of IDE (Integrated Development Environment). For example, the Eclipse IDE provides support for syntax and debugging of java classes, but it does not evaluate the relationship with the database, or how a particular java method interacts with database tables and columns. For example, it does not flag a warning where an SQL query might be formed incorrectly. Similarly, the Visual Studio .NET would not flag a warning if an XPath applied on an XML document does not correspond to a valid value according to the schema. This makes it very difficult to maintain and enhance applications written by a third party, since a change in code may break some other layer, and the problem will become known only after extensive testing.

Our goal is to develop a framework that will help programmers in bridging the gap between different technologies used in an enterprise application. However, this is very substantial initiative and we have so far focused our efforts on developing a suite of tools to support development and maintenance of database applications using Java in the Eclipse environment. We report here our recent progress in developing a plug-in tool for generating documentation of the interactions between Java code and relational databases.

The obvious benefit of the documentation is to facilitate code maintenance in the face of requirement changes or database modifications. Certain database accesses may be fairly well self-documenting, e.g. by a simple statically defined SQL statement. However, there are many other situations where additional documentation can greatly enhance understanding the code dependencies on a database. Consider for example a query string that is built dynamically from SQL fragments which may be taken from user input, stored in variables, or passed as parameters from other methods. Furthermore, the point in the code where the query is executed may be far removed from the place where the query string is built. Even in a situation where a query is statically defined and used immediately, it may take some effort to determine which database elements are being read or written if the query is complex.

With our tool, the developer may use our "find and document" interface to locate each database access of interest in their Java source code and selectively generate documentation where desired, in a manner similar to the familiar "find and replace" function of a word processor. Alternatively, they may choose to automatically generate documentation of all database access with a single click on the "Document All" button. Our tool also provides considerable flexibility in specifying search criteria and scope as well as documentation style.

2 Background

We have previously reported [1-3] our development of tools to provide a visual mapping of java code-to-database and code-to-code (via database) couplings. We have implemented our tool as a fully integrated plug-in to the popular Eclipse development environment. Developers can view the database and the project at various levels of granularity and easily find the types of coupling they are most interested in. For example, users can choose to view couplings of code to anywhere in the database, to a particular table in the database, or to a specific column in a table. Similarly, they can adjust the granularity of their project view between the project, class, and method levels. Search facilities enable users to quickly identify important dependencies. For example, when a method that stores information in the database is modified, it is easy to find all of the methods (or classes or projects) that retrieve the same information and might be affected.

The database access of an application is discovered by our visualization tool through a combination of static and dynamic code analysis, or by processing user supplied java annotations. The static and dynamic code analysis approaches each have their relative advantages and disadvantages, but share some common characteristics. Both approaches have the advantage of automatic discovery that makes them suitable for maintaining legacy applications where the database access is not well documented. However, neither is 100% effective in finding all possible interactions between the application and the database.

The static code analyzer uses the Sun java compiler API [4] and the Compiler Tree API [5] to parse the java source and walk the abstract syntax tree. It looks for string literals that are included either directly or after assignment to String variables in calls to the *execute*, *executeQuery*, and *executeUpdate* methods of the JDBC *Statement* class. The analyzer attempts to identify column and table names occurring in select, from and where clauses and record these dependencies in the coupling repository.

The code analyzer considers certain string concatenations including some concatenations that are built from a combination of string literals and variables to detect simple cases of dynamic SQL generation in the code. However, static analysis in general is a hard problem and it will never be possible to detect all couplings to the database that may occur at runtime, possibly dependent on user input.

The main component of the dynamic analyzer is a JDBC bridge driver that logs the database accesses to the coupling data repository. Our driver acts as a bridge between the application and the "real" driver that communicates with the user's database. The implementation is conceptually simple. Most of the methods in our driver classes simply pass requests on to the underlying "real" driver and return whatever data is returned from the real driver. The main exception is in the Statement class methods (e.g. execute, executeQuery, executeUpdate) that take SQL statements as arguments. These methods receive only complete, valid, fully formed SQL statements as arguments (unless there are errors in the application) even if they have been built dynamically. The SQL statements processed in the JDBC driver are parsed to determine the database elements that are being accessed and the coupling information is recorded in the repository.

The main drawback to the dynamic analysis approach is that it will only find database accesses that occur during testing with the bridge driver in place. Therefore the success of this technique is highly dependent on the developer's ability to generate adequate test cases.

In [3], we describe an extension of our previous work to allow the developer to explicitly supply the database access information in the form of java annotations to replace or supplement the code analysis tools. We chose annotations rather than comments since they are easier to process by machine. For legacy projects, or when the developer hasn't completely documented the database access, code analysis is still extensively used to obtain the necessary information. Our plan was to further enhance the system by adding a tool to inject the access information obtained through static and dynamic code analysis into the source code in the form of java annotations in order to automatically document the code. We realized, however, that annotations are more verbose and harder to read than ordinary comments, and decided to use comments for generated documentation. In the future, we plan to add an option to generate documentation in the form of annotations.

3 Results

Figure 1 shows the overall architecture of the system. The system uses annotation processing as well as both static and dynamic analysis of the java code to find database couplings. The results of all analysis methods are combined in the coupling data repository. For every code-to-database coupling that is detected, there is an entry in the repository. Each coupling entry in the repository includes the code location (class, method, file, and line number), the database element (database, table, and column), the SQL statement type (select, insert, update, etc.) and the type of access (read, write, or read/write). The statement type does not necessarily determine the access type. For example, a field occurring in the *set* clause of an update statement indicates a write access, but a field occurring in the *where* clause of the same statement indicates a read access.

In order to detect changes over time, the repository also records the first time and last time that a coupling is detected. Also, each time the tool is run, the structure of the database is checked using the JDBC metadata API, and any structural changes are recorded in the repository.

The user interface, implemented as an Eclipse plug-in, displays the results to the user, allows easy navigation to code based on its database coupling, and allows the user to generate documentation using the "Find and Document" feature. Figure 2 shows the details of the Find and Document interface, with all the option nodes expanded. The simplest form of the Find and Document interface is shown in the screenshot of Figure 3, where all option nodes are collapsed.

The user can select the scope of the search from the drop down menu under the search node. Available options are to search the current file, the current project, or the entire workspace. In the Data Elements section, the user can choose to search only for code that accesses a particular database, column, or table, or they can choose all databases, all tables, or all columns. The dropdown menus are populated with the names of databases, tables, and columns that appear in the repository.

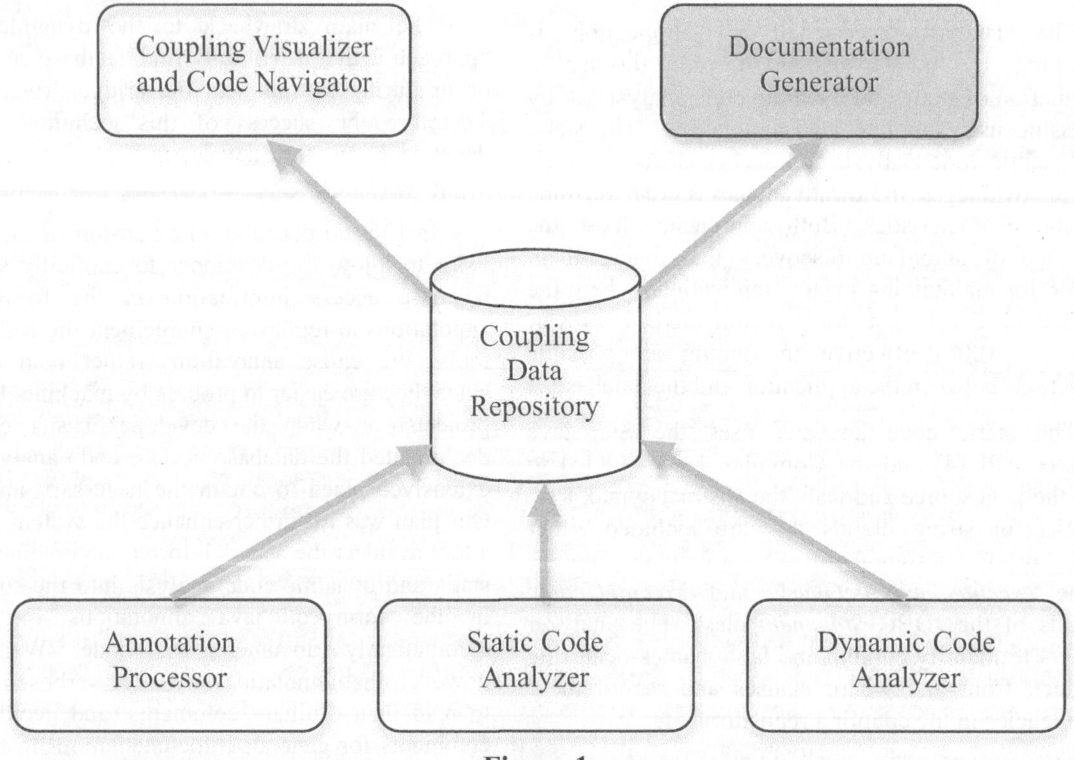

Figure 1

The user may also choose to find and document database access only of a certain type (read, write, or read/write) or by a particular type of SQL statement (select, insert, update, or delete). Note that the tool will find the place where an SQL statement is executed, which may be far removed from the place where the SQL string is declared or built.

Several options are available to customize the generated documentation, including comment style, a prefix to be included in comments, and if the dynamic code analyzer was employed, the option to include recently executed SQL statements.

Listing 1 contains a fragment of code from a web application for managing stock portfolios that has been documented by the documentation generator. The generated documentation is highlighted in bold font. In this case, the documented code that executes the query is only removed from the code where the query string is built by a few lines. Even so, the documentation makes it easier to see which database elements are accessed, and the included sample query is much easier to read than the code used to build the query string.

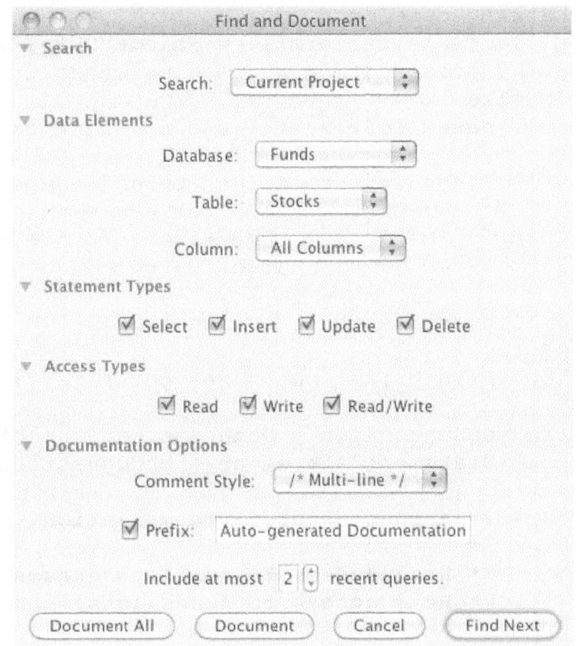

Figure 2

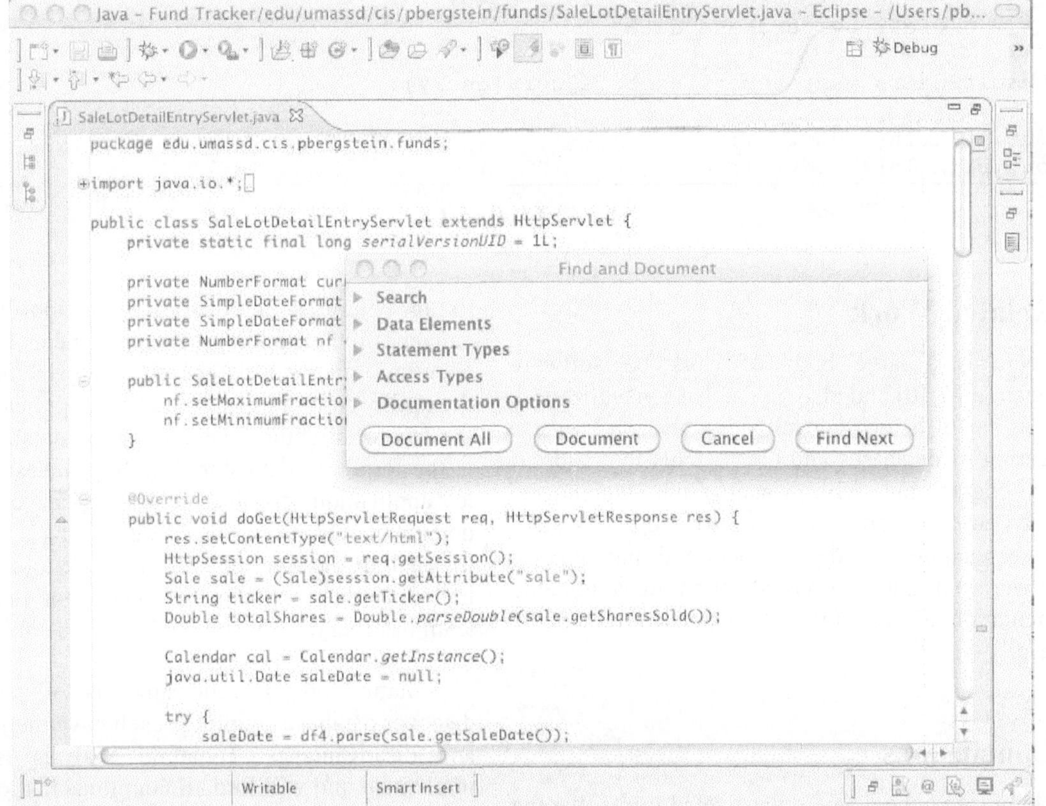

Figure 3

```
String dateCondition;
  if (sale.getTerm() == Sale.SHORT_TERM)
    dateCondition = " and purchase_date > '" + cutOffDate + "' ";
  else
    dateCondition = " and purchase_date <= '" + cutOffDate + "' ";

  String query = "select purchase_date, shares, round(adjusted_basis/shares, 2), " +
                 "lot from purchases p, lots l where p.pnum = l.pnum" +
                 " and ticker = '" + ticker + "' and snum = 0" + dateCondition +
                 "order by purchase_date";

  Connection dbConnection = null;
  try {
    PrintWriter out = res.getWriter();

    dbConnection = Database.getConnection();
    Statement statement = dbConnection.createStatement();

    /* Auto-generated Documentation
     *
     * Read access to funds.purchases: purchase_date, pnum, ticker
     * Read access to funds.lots: shares, adjusted_basis, lot, pnum, snum
     *
     * Examples:
     *   select purchase_date, shares, round(adjusted_basis/shares, 2), lot
     *     from purchases p, lots l
     *     where p.pnum = l.pnum and ticker = 'FB' and snum = 0
     *       and purchase_date <= '2012-03-01'
     *     order by purchase_date
     */
    ResultSet rs = statement.executeQuery(query);

    out.println("<html>");
    out.println("<body>");
```

Listing 1

4 Related Work

There is a large body of work on software visualization [6-10] and also on database visualization. There is also a good deal of work on reverse engineering of databases and CASE tools that support reverse engineering with visualization techniques. However, we are not aware of any other system designed to support the development and maintenance of software through the visualization or automated documentation of program code dependencies on the database.

5 Conclusions

Many researchers have investigated to resolve the dependencies between different technologies involved in an enterprise application. Our tool significantly enhances understanding of dependencies between java code and relational databases. The principal benefit is the ability to more easily maintain application code in the face of structural changes to the database, changes in the format of data stored in the database, or changes to application requirements. We have tested our documentation generator by generating documentation for each of the five tools in our system (see Figure 1), including the documentation generator itself, and our team has found the results to be very useful.

Static and dynamic analysis of java code to discover database couplings each have their advantages and disadvantages. Dynamic analysis is easier to implement and will find all couplings that occur during testing. Static analysis is harder to implement and cannot identify couplings that only occur dynamically (e.g. based on user input). However, static analysis may identify couplings that are missed during the testing phase. By combining the results of static and dynamic analysis in a coupling data repository, we get the combined benefits of each. The repository also allows for tracking of changes over time so that areas of code that may be affected by a change could be flagged for the developer.

6 Future Work

In the near term, we intend to continue testing our system on a wider range of database applications, particularly other projects under development by our team, and student projects developed in our database courses. We will continue to refine the functionality and user interface based on feedback from our users.

In the long term, we plan to extend this tool to handle additional languages and technologies. For example, we plan to extend our java code analyzers to support JSP by analyzing the java snippets embedded in JSP pages, so that we can document couplings of JSP code to the database. This would also allow the visualization tool to display couplings between the presentation layer (JSP) and business logic code that occur through the database in a typical J2EE environment. If all these dependencies between the various layers of a J2EE application can be documented and visualized, the task of maintaining and enhancing such applications would be greatly facilitated. Eventually, we would also like to support additional programming languages such as C# and C++ and add support for ODBC applications.

7 References

[1] Paul L. Bergstein, Priyanka Gariba, Vaibhavi Pisolkar, and Sheetal Subbanwad. An Eclipse Plug-In for Visualizing Java Code Dependencies on Relational Databases. In *Proceedings of the 2009 International Conference on Software Engineering Research and Practice (SERP'09)*, Pages 64-69, July 13-16, 2009, Las Vegas, Nevada. CSREA Press ISBN 1-60132-129-5.

[2] Paul L. Bergstein and Ashwin Buchipudi. Coupling Detection to Facilitate Maintenance of Database Applications. In *Proceedings of the 2011 International Conference on Software Engineering Research and Practice (SERP'11)*, Pages 289-94, July 18-21, 2011, Las Vegas, Nevada. CSREA Press ISBN 1-60132-201-1.

[3] Paul L. Bergstein. Documenting Java Database Access with Type Annotations. In Proceedings of the 2012 International Conference on software Engineering Research and Practice (SERP '12), Pages 459-465, July 16-19, 2012, Las Vegas, Nevada. CSREA Press ISBN 1-60132-231-3.

[4] Java 6 Compiler API http://today.java.net/pub/a/today/2008/04/10/source-code-analysis-using-java-6-compiler-apis.html

[5] Compiler Tree API http://java.sun.com/javase/6/docs/jdk/api/javac/tree/index.html

[6] G. C. Roman and K. C. Cox. A taxonomy of program visualization systems. *IEEE Computer*, Vol. 26(12), Pages 11-24, 1993.

[7] Blaine A. Price, Ian S. Small, and Ronald M. Baecker. A Principled Taxonomy of Software Visualization. *Journal of Visual Languages and Computing*, Vol. 4, Pages 211-266, 1993.

[8] Jonathan I. Maletic, Andrian Marcus, and Michael L. Collard. A task oriented view of software visualization. In *Proceedings of the First International Workshop on Visualizing Software for Understanding and Analysis (VISSOFT)*, Pages 32-40, 2002.

[9] Christian Collberg, Stephen Kobourov, Jasvir Nagra, Jacob Pitts, and Kevin Wampler. A system for graph-based visualization of the evolution of software. In *Proceedings of the 2003 ACM symposium on Software visualization*, Pages 77-86, 2003. ACM Press.

[10] M. D. Storey, K. Wong, F. D. Fracchia, and H. A. Müller. On Integrating Visualization Techniques for Effective Software Exploration. In *Proceedings of IEEE Symposium on Information Visualization*, Pages 38-45, 1997.

A Decision Model for Monitoring Project Status with Earned Value Management Indicators.

Maria Teresa Baldassarre, Nicola Boffoli, Danilo Caivano, Giuseppe Visaggio
Department of Informatics, University of Bari
SER&Practices Spin Off
Bari, Italy
{baldassarre, boffoli, caivano, visaggio}@di.uniba.it

***Abstract*— Project management is the discipline of planning, organizing, motivating, and controlling resources in order to fulfill specific goals. Project managers are required to monitor and control project execution, i.e. verify actual progress and performance of the project with respect to the project plan and timely identify areas in which changes may be required. Earned Value Management (EVM) is a valuable technique for determining and monitoring project status. It indicates performance variances based on measures related to work progress, schedule and cost information. The technique involves systematically collecting a set of indicators during project execution. As so, a manger may strive to systematically use all the indicators during a project, and, without an appropriate guideline, correctly interpret the values collected. In this paper we propose a classification of the EVM indicators in five conceptual classes and present an interpretation model that managers can adopt as checklist for monitoring EVM values and predict project status. The model has been applied in an industrial case study to monitor project status and guide project manager decisions.**

***Index Terms*—Earned Value Management, decision model, project monitoring**

I. INTRODUCTION

In the last decade project management has always more been recognized as primary competence by several sectors, including software engineering. Project management is the discipline of planning, organizing, motivating, and controlling resources in order to fulfill specific goals, whereas a project is a temporary effort with a defined start and end point, usually time and budget constrained, carried out to meet unique goals and objectives and deliver results that provide added value and innovations to current practices on time and within budget [1, 2] conforming to certain quality expectations.

A project management lifecycle includes five process groups known as: initiating, planning, executing, monitoring and controlling, closing (Fig.1) [2]. Planning is an essential component of the lifecycle as project managers are called to define project plans where they estimate how acceptable results will be delivered within time, budget and other resource constraints. Since plans are made based upon assumptions (effort for tasks, productivity of teams, learning effect on staff) that are especially variable in immaterial domains such as software engineering, successful project completion requires that managers continuously monitor and control the execution and progress of the activities with respect to the plan and adopt corrective actions whenever necessary. This is mostly true in software contexts where, being human-centered it is difficult to predict factors such as productivity and performances, and therefore project duration and costs. Studies in literature have reported that 18% of software projects are prematurely canceled, while up to 53% turn out to be over budget and take longer time than expected [8]. As so, monitoring and controlling processes are critical activities. For this reason, when carrying out a project it is crucial for a project manager to be able to determine the project status with respect to each milestone.

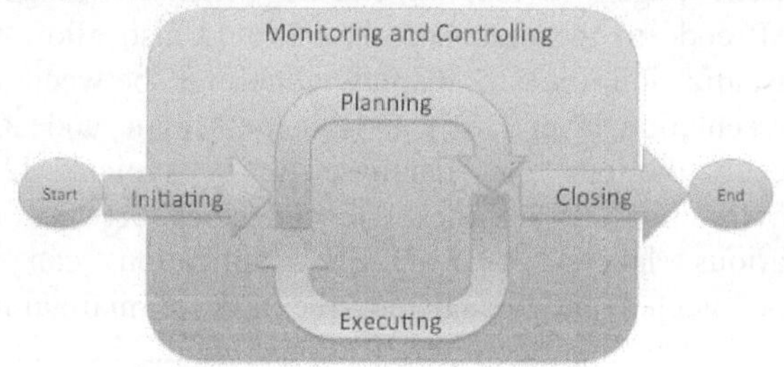

Fig.1: Project Management Lifecycle Processes

Questions a manager is expected to answer during project execution are: what is the real status of the project? How far along is the project? What part of the budget has been spent? How much work has been done and what is left to do? In monitoring a project it is also necessary to accurately relate cost to performances, so questions to answer may be: if you spent 30% of the budget does that mean that you are 30% complete? If you are 30% complete, have you spent 30% of the budget? What % is complete with respect to the forecast? Without a proper and formal approach or technique for answering such questions, determining the status of a project, monitoring its costs and performances at any point in time can be quite difficult and risk to be error prone and not reflect the actual state.

One of the most accredited techniques for project monitoring and control is Earned Value Management (EVM) [3]. It has been adopted in past on behalf of organizations like NASA and DoD [4, 5, 6, 7] as means for assuring an effective risk analysis and correct execution of a project in accordance with budget and time restrictions. In recent years it has become an integrated part of the PMBOK [2]. There are also several evidences of the success of this technique for project monitoring and control [9, 10, 11].

The approach consists in collecting a set of indicators that capture information on cost, schedule, technical performance and scope related to the work done up to a point in time (i.e. the earned value) and comparing them to the project plan, i.e. what the project manager had estimated would have been the progress of the project at that time. This comparison gives the manager an idea of how far or near the project execution is to the project plan, and whether it is deviating or not. Depending on the results of the indicators the manager must decide on which actions to undertake, if any, on the remaining activities to get the project back on track, i.e. on schedule and within budget before its conclusion. Although the concept of EVM is quite easy and straightforward to understand, from a practical point of view its adoption may turn out to be trivial for a manager as he is called to collect and interpret indicator values in order to readily make decisions and take action before its too late. In this sense there is little support in literature on decision support tools that guide data collection and interpretation as pointed out in other studies as well [12, 13, 14, 15].

Given this gap, our intention in this paper is to clarify the meaning of EVM indicators and provide guidance for their interpretation. Our contribution is therefore twofold:

- organize the EVM indicators in conceptual categories each with a specific meaning and scope;
- provide a decision model able to guide project managers in interpreting EVM indicator values and making the most appropriate decisions on the project execution.

The proposed solutions have been validated in a real industrial case study. Here, the conceptual classes and decision model have been used to apply and interpret the EVM indicators during monitoring and control activities of the entire project, in order to support decision making.

The rest of the paper is organized as follows: in the next section a classification of EVM indicators in conceptual classes is provided, as well as the decision model we propose for interpreting EVM values. Section 3 presents the application of our model in an industrial case study where managers adopted the model for monitoring project performances. Finally conclusions are drawn.

II. Our proposal: Classification of EVM Indicators and Decision Model

Execution of any project requires going through three essential phases (Fig.2) that can be identified as: (i) define work; (ii) schedule & budget; (iii) measure performance. In "define work", the activities of the project are identified and a work breakdown structure (or similar) is developed. It is a hierarchical outline that breaks the project down into a list of tasks, used to manage the project's price, estimation, scheduling and performance. WBSs determine the resources (i.e. materials, labor, costs and contracts) needed to complete project phases. This structure should be detailed so the work can be categorized into individual elements of work.

Next, in the "schedule and budget" phase, the project manager defines how the activities of the WBS are organized, he defines the project plan, schedules the activities and fixes the milestone checkpoints. In this phase techniques such as Pert or Gantt diagrams, as well as critical path method (CPM) are most likely to be used to define the project plan and obtain execution plan based on project restrictions like resources, time and budget. Furthermore, work responsibility is assigned to the owners who are accountable for managing resource allocation and cost baselines, which allow to spread the budget across the project's length. Scheduling also consists of arranging work packages into logical frameworks that define the project milestones.

As the project is executed, performances must be constantly measured, controlled and monitored. So, this is where "monitoring and controlling processes" are called into action. Performance measurement is the process of identifying specific means by which any given performance could be improved, then setting goals and modifying processes to reach those goals. In short, performance measurement is about increasing efficiency and streamlining existing processes. To do so, a full and accurate assessment of the present level of performance must first be made. In particular, monitoring and control are the set of processes necessary to track and review the work carried out, manage the project progress and performances; control changes and carry out actions able to mitigate risks, verify aspects related to project execution, identify the state of the project and identify areas that require particular attention and supervision.

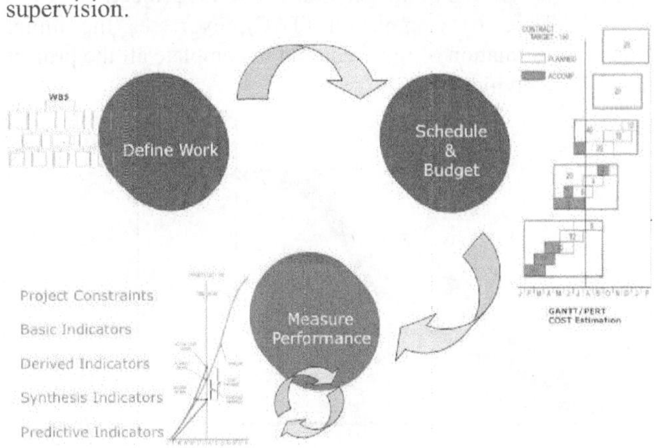

Fig.2: Essential phases for project execution

Literature offers several approaches for measuring project performances such as: GQM-QIP [16], Plan Do Check Act (PDCA) [17], TQM [18], and EVM. While the first four approaches are more specific for measuring performances in terms of project goals, EVM is more appropriate for monitoring and controlling activities as it allows to check the progress state of the project, i.e. the amount of work done up to a point in time (milestone) compared to the planned value. Performance measurement defines how success or failure is determined on a project. In the case of Earned Value Management, performance measurements focus on cost and schedule management.

The idea behind EVM is that it prevents rather than cures by identifying and solving problems early, as soon as they arise. It acts as an early alarm for signaling trends and detours from the original project plan, allowing the manager to readily take action, make corrections and get the project back on track, in line with schedule and budget restrictions. It is important to adopt the technique constantly throughout the project in order to detect variances when they are small and easy to correct, instead of discovering unpleasant surprises at the end of the project, when the situation is unrecoverable and the project is bound to fail or be canceled. The technique is made up of several indicators that may generate confusion for a project manager having to systematically collect, measure, analyze and interpret them during the project lifecycle. As so, we have proposed a classification of the indicators and organized them in conceptual categories.

A. EVM Conceptual Categories

The categories identified reflect the general meaning of the indicators and their application with respect to project progress. The classification consists of five categories:

1) Project Constraints

When defining the project plan the project manager must take into account the project constraints such as budget available, resources that can be assigned to the project activities, and time restrictions. In this sense, two relevant indicators that represent this information are:

- Budget At Completion (BAC), expresses an initial estimation of budget allocated to the project;
- Time At Completion (TAC), expresses the initial estimation of time required to complete all the project activities.

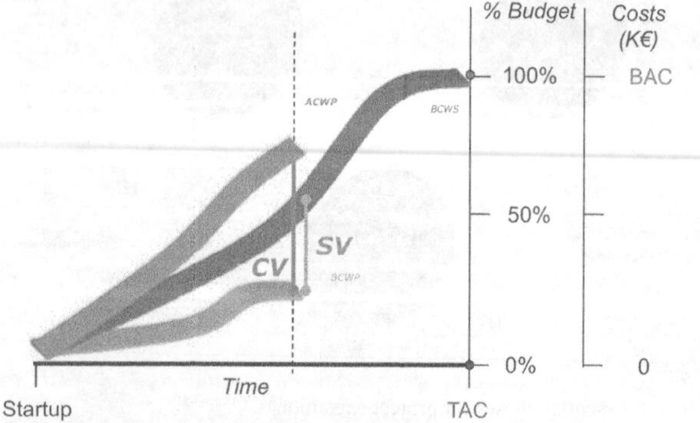

Fig.3: EVM indicators

Both these indicators (Fig.3) are fixed and established when the project plan is defined.

2) Basic Indicators

This category is made up of three indicators that express the earned value of the project at a certain point in time, generally in correspondence to a milestone established in the project plan. A graphical representation is provided in Fig.3, more precisely:

- Budgeted Cost of Work Scheduled (BCWS): also referred to as planned value, is the amount of money budgeted to complete the scheduled work of the data date. It is the monetary value of all the work scheduled. This value is determined early in the plan and establishes the baseline against which performance is measured;
- Budgeted Cost of Work Performed (BCWP): also referred to as earned value, is the budgeted cost of work that has actually been performed in carrying out a scheduled task at a certain time point, usually related to a milestone;
- Actual Cost of Work Performed (ACWP): represents the actual cost sustained for carrying out the project up to a specific milestone. This is a final data value, usually provide by a management/accounting system to keep track of the production.

3) Derived Indicators

This category comprises two indicators that are obtained from the basic ones. They express variances between planned values and actual ones collected with respect to the milestone check points, in absolute values:

- Cost Variance (CV = BCWP-ACWP): expresses the difference between the cost of the work performed in accordance to the project plan carried out to a point in time (BCWP) and the actual cost sustained. Depending on whether the variance is positive, negative, or zero, the project is interpreted as being under, over, or in line with the forecasted budget;
- Schedule Variance (SV= BCWP-BCWS): expresses the difference between the cost of the work carried out up to a certain point in time and the cost of work that should have been done according to the project plan (BCWS). Based on the value of this indicator, project managers have an idea of whether it is early on schedule (SV>0), late (SV<0), or on time (SV=0).

4) Synthesis Indicators

These indicators are indexes that express synthetic information in percentages. More precisely, Cost Performance Index (CPI) and Schedule Performance Index (SPI) are indicators of how closely accomplished work is on budget and on schedule.

- Cost Performance Indicator (CPI=BCWP/ACWP) is an index showing the efficiency of the utilization of the resources on the project. It shows how many dollars (or other type of currency) worth of work is being accomplished for every dollar spent. If CPI is less than 1.0, means that the project is overspending as the budgeted costs are lower than the actual ones; if CPI is more than 1.0, the project is actually saving money.
- Schedule Performance Indicator (SPI=BCWP/BCWS) shows how the work is progressing compared to the original schedule. If SPI is more than 1.0, the work performed is more than the work that was scheduled, making the project ahead of schedule; if SPI is less than 1.0, the project is lagging and needs to catch up; SPI ratio of 1 means everything is proceeding precisely as per schedule.

Both of these formulas begin with the Earned Value (BCWP), which is the value of the work already accomplished. SPI and CPI ratios help managers evaluate the project at any point and make changes. For instance, if the SPI is tending towards 1 and higher, it indicates that the current time and plan is now more favorable for the project than the time and plan were when the project was initiated. The management may want to study the changed scenario and re-evaluate the project goals and objectives in the light of the new environment. CPI ratio provides a uniform platform on which to compare projects irrespective of their size. If a company has multiple projects going on simultaneously, and would like an update on the status of the various projects, the CPI ratio is one of the best means available to provide that information.

Operatively, it is recommended for a manager to first calculate these two synthesis indicators to have an idea of the project status and whether there is a deviation (either positive or negative) from the baseline and then go into detail by considering the derived indicators (SV and CV) which provide a quantitative (absolute value) evaluation of the deviation.

5) Predictive Indicators

This category includes two indicators that express the estimate at completion (EAC) which forecasts the value of the project with respect to time and cost when the project is complete. It should be noted that the EAC can be calculated in a number of different ways and is only an indicator of what the project's cost/time will be at the end of the project. Each project needs to be evaluated to determine which EAC formula best fits the project's size and complexity. Studies show that EACs based on CPI and SPI values tend to be significantly higher and are also more accurate [19, 20], as so we have adopted the following formulas for calculating these indicators:

- Estimate At Completion – Cost (EACC = BAC/CPI): expresses the amount of money estimated to be spend at the end of the project given its progress;
- Estimate At Completion – Time (EACT = TAC/SPI): estimates the end time of the project given the current state of progress of the project.

It is clear that although BAC and TAC are fixed at the beginning of the project, the EAC values most likely change compatibly and conformingly as the synthesis indicators change during project execution.

B. Decision Model

The concept of granularity is very important in the application of EVM and interpretation of the collected values. Indeed, SPI, CPI, SV and CV measured at a project level (high granularity) are useful for top management, portfolio/program managers, but turn out to be almost insignificant for a project manager who, without any other information, is not able to make any considerations or valuable interpretations. On the other hand, if the indicators are calculated with respect to an individual sub-project, phase, task (low granularity), rather than the overall project, it is possible to: monitor the actual state of the sub-project, phase, task compared to the project plan; designate budget/resources saved on an activity to mitigate risks related to other late or over budget activities, allowing to optimize project performances. The level of granularity as well as milestone checkpoints, with respect to which entity and how often EVM indicators are to be collected, should be defined at project start, taking into account the critical points and risk factors and eventually, if necessary, can be varied during execution.

Since the amount of data collected at each milestone checkpoint during the entire project is considerable, its interpretation can in turn become quite challenging for a project manager and for the entire management team involved in analyzing the data, identifying weaknesses, avoiding problems from occurring and promptly acting when they arise. For this reason, as practical support to the EVM technique we have provided a decision model (Fig. 4) to use at each milestone checkpoint. The model basically guides monitoring activities step by step as collected values are reported in the form and compared to baseline values. Secondly, interpretation guidance is provided allowing to optimize project management by using/re-allocating available resources at their best, verifying critical points and mitigating delays or over budget risks.

CHECKLIST MILESTONE N.X

Date dd/mm/yyyy

Name of monitor: Signature: ______________

Indicator to collect	Baseline Value	Collected Value
1. What is the expected cost of the work carried out (BCWP) up to this moment?	BCWP=BCWS	
2. What is the cost for the work carried out up to this moment (ACWP)?	ACWP=BCWP	
3. What is the variance between planned costs and actual costs (CV=BCWP – ACWP)?	CV>=0	
4. What is the variance between the actual and planned state of work (SV=BCWP – BCWS)?	SV>=0	
5. What are the performances in terms of execution costs for the task being considered (CPI=BCWP/ACWP)?	CPI>=1	
6. What are the performances in terms of execution times of the task being considered (SPI=BCWP/BCWP)?	SPI>=1	
7. What is the overall duration estimated for executing the task considered (EACT)?	EACT<=TAC	
8. What is the estimated overal cost for executing the task considered (EACC)?	EACC<=BAC	

INTERPRETATIONS

- If the task is under budget (CPI>1) and late in execution (SPI<1), it is necessary to involve more resources using the available budget not spent yet (CV).
- If the task is under budget (CPI>1) and early in execution (SPI>1) designate part of the budget not spent (CV) and the resources assigned to this task to make up for the delays in the execution of other project tasks.
- If the task is over budget (CPI<1) and early in execution (SPI>1) it is the case to reduce the resources assigned to the task in order to gain the extra budget spent (CV) compared to the planned.
- If the task is over budget (CPI<1) and late in execution (SPI<1) verify if it is possible to recover extra resources assigned to other tasks that are currently on time or early compared to the plan, in order to recuperate the extra budget spent (CV) until this moment compared to the project plan.
- If the project satisfies times (SPI=1) and cost (CPI=1) there are no initiatives to undertake. The project execution is compliant to its plan.

To this date, the estimated duration of the project is:	EACT=TAC/SPI=______________
To this date, the estimated overall cost of the project is:	EACC=BAC/SPI=______________

Fig. 4: Decision model for interpreting EVM indicators

This data is used by those who are responsible of managing work in order to understand cost and schedule performances throughout the project lifecycle. The main goal is to point out (cost and schedule) issues early providing the maximum time to minimize their impact and provide an effective manner for developing recovery plans and improvement actions where necessary.

III. Case Study

The classification and decision model have been applied in an industrial case study. The project was a nationally funded project that involved the University of Bari and a large Italian IT company. The project is called E-MARK. It focused on designing and developing a solution able to automate marketing processes through use of technologies that make use of traceable information on the internet. In practice, the project developed innovative models and techniques supported by tools able to guide: Internet search of information to characterize the target market of a product/service and define the placement of its competitors; identification of the desirable properties of a product/service that are a source of attraction for consumers/users; definition of the user profile of a product/ service; identification of correlations between product/service properties and consumer/user profile; promotion of a product/ service

Project monitoring and control was carried out with EVM indicators. In particular, project managers used the proposed classification of conceptual classes as reference to systematically collect the values during project execution. Furthermore, they adopted the decision model illustrated in the previous section to guide interpretation of collected values. in the next paragraphs we will provide detail of the project monitoring progress

The project was organized in four work packages and nine activities. The granularity selected for applying the indicators related to each activity at fixed milestones.

In Fig.5 the planned effort and costs with respect to each project activity are reported. They are compared to the actual values collected during the project. Furthermore, Fig.6 shows the values of EVM indicators for every activity. In the following we report the results of the interpretations carried out, after applying the decision model to the EVM indicators collected.

WP	ACTIVITIES	PLANNED PERSON/DAYS	PLANNED COST	PLANNED SOLAR DAYS	ACTUAL PERSON/DAYS	ACTUAL COST	ACTUAL SOLAR DAYS
	A1	48	€ 8.151,60	18	40,07	€ 8.005,36	18
	A2	9,6	€ 1.630,32	3,6	8,01	€ 1.601,07	3,6
WP1	A3	81,6	€ 13.857,72	30,6	60,1	€ 12.008,04	27
	A4	14,4	€ 2.445,48	5,4	12,02	€ 2.401,61	5,4
WP2	A5	48	€ 8.151,60	18	20,03	€ 4.002,68	9
	A6	91,2	€ 15.488,04	34,2	76,13	€ 15.210,18	34,2
WP3	A6				16,03	€ 3.202,14	7,2
	A7	144	€ 24.454,80	54	120,20625	€ 24.016,08	54
	A7				12,02	€ 2.401,61	5,4
	A8	33,6	€ 5.706,12	12,6	28,05	€ 5.603,75	12,6
	A8				4,01	€ 800,54	1,8
WP4	A9	9,6	€ 1.630,32	3,6	4,01	€ 800,54	1,8
		480	€ 81.516,00	180	400,68	€ 80.053,60	180

Figure 5: descriptive statistics of planned and actual values for E-MARK

ACTIVITY	% of progress	BCWP	BCWS	SV	ACWP	CV	SPI	CPI	EACC	EACT
A1	10%	8.151,60	8.151,60	0,00	8.005,36	146,24	1,00	1,02	80.053,60	6,00
A2	12%	9.781,92	9.781,92	0,00	9.606,43	175,49	1,00	1,02	80.053,58	6,00
A3	27%	23.639,64	22.009,32	1.630,32	21.614,47	2.025,17	1,07	1,09	74.532,66	5,59
A4	30%	26.085,12	24.454,80	1.630,32	24.016,08	2.069,04	1,07	1,09	75.050,25	5,63
A5	35%	34.236,72	28.530,60	5.706,12	28.018,76	6.217,96	1,20	1,22	66.711,33	5,00
A6	54%	41.980,74	44.018,64	-2.037,90	43.228,94	-1.248,20	0,95	0,97	83.939,70	6,29
A6	58%	49.724,76	47.279,28	2.445,48	46.431,09	3.293,67	1,05	1,07	76.116,54	5,70
A7	88%	61.952,16	71.734,08	-9.781,92	70.447,17	-8.495,01	0,86	0,88	92.693,64	6,95
A7	91%	74.179,56	74.179,56	0,00	72.848,77	1.330,79	1,00	1,02	80.053,60	6,00
A8	98%	77.032,62	79.885,68	-2.853,06	78.452,52	-1.419,90	0,96	0,98	83.018,54	6,22
A8	99%	79.885,68	80.700,84	-815,16	79.253,06	632,62	0,99	1,01	80.870,47	6,06
A9	100%	81.516,00	81.516,00	0,00	80.053,60	1.462,40	1,00	1,02	80.053,60	6,00

Figure 6: EVM indicator values for the entire project

The TAC (initial estimation of project duration) is 6 months, while BAC (initial estimation of project cost) is €81.516,00. The first activity (A1) required 18 solar days, according to the plan, and a total of 40 person/days (p/d) compared to 48 planned with a lower cost. This data is confirmed by the EVM indicators for this activity. From the collected data, consulting the decision model it can be seen that the conditions are: CV > 0, under budget, so the project is spending less than planned; SV=0, schedule according to plan; CPI>1, project costs are lower than planned; SPI = 1, execution times are according to plan.

In 18 solar days, the first activity requested a lower budget than expected to be completed. As so the expected project duration remains the same (EACT <= TAC) while the expected costs are lower, €80.053,60 (EACC).

In A2, descriptive statistics show that actual values are lower than planned ones. Indeed, the EVM indicators show that the trend in A1 is confirmed in A2 as well. As so, the project was proceeding correctly and project managers decided to designate the extra budget to future activities, if necessary, that may have been late on schedule.

In A3, the activities were carried out in less time wrt planned (27 solar days, and 60 p/d, compared to 30 solar days and 81 p/d planned). The conditions and interpretation of the decision model are as follows: CV > 0, under budget, so the project is spending less than planned; SV>0, activities ahead of plan; CPI>1, project costs are lower than planned; SPI > 1, activities are executed in less time than planned. In accordance to the interpretation of the decision model, project managers decided to designate part of the budget not spent and the resources assigned to this task to make up for the delays in the execution of other project task that may have occurred in the following milestone control points of the project.

In A4 the trend of EVM indicators confirms the results of the previous phases as they satisfy the baseline values of the decision model.

As it appears from both the descriptive statistics and from the EVM values, A5 was carried out with a significant less effort and cost than planned, i.e. 20 p/d and €4.002,68 instead of 48 p/d and a planned cost of €8.151,60. So up to this point, the project was ahead of schedule and certainly below estimated costs.

In A6, when the milestone checkpoint was carried out, the project was behind schedule and not yet completed. At this point the EVM indicators pointed out a situation where CV<0, over budget as more than expected was being spent; also, SPI<1 and CPI<1, i.e. project cost and effort were higher than planned. Furthermore this situation impacted the overall estimated project cost and budget (EACT > TAC and EACC>BAC). Managers decided to adopt as improvement action that of designating part of the resources that had been saved in the previous phases and placing them on this one. As so, staff that had terminated activities in advance and had the required skills were placed in this activity. Also, part of the budget saved in the previous phases was also shifted onto this one. This improvement action had positive effects, as at the next milestone checkpoint the EVM indicators were within baseline values. More precisely, as it can be seen from the descriptive statistics (highlighted row) an extra 16 p/d were necessary with an extra budget of €3.202,14 to complete the activity. Nonetheless, having recovered both budget and resources from previous activities, the overall budget and effort for the project were not impacted. Indeed, the EVM indicators related to A6 are inline with the baseline values. This was possible because manager decisions in previous checkpoints were taken in order to prevent difficulties in further activities.

In A7 another delay occurred. After a period of 54 days, the activity was not completed. This situation is confirmed by the EVM indicators for A7 (Fig.6 first row) which are below the threshold values. Once again, managers acted promptly reallocating resources from previous activities or from activities that were ahead of schedule and below budget, and shifted them to A7. This choice impacted positively on the EVM indicators collected and the next milestone checkpoint. Indeed, as it can be seen from Fig.6, the second row of A7 shows positive values, that satisfy the baselines (CV>0, under budget; SV=0, in line with the plan; CPI>1 and SPI=1). Overall, the delay accumulated in this activity was compensated by the effort and budget saved in some of the other project activities. Furthermore, since the delay (extra effort and cost needed) for A7 was not higher than the effort and costs saved in previous activities, the overall project indicators of EACC and EACT returned to be congruent with the threshold values.

For what concerns A8, as it can be seen in Fig.5, after 12.6 days it was not completed. Further 1.8 days were necessary to conclude. Consequently, the activity requested more effort and cost than planned, i.e. 32 p/d and a total cost of €6.404,00. The EVM indicators have been reported for both milestone checkpoints (at the planned termination of the activity, first row, and at its actual termination, second row). The trend appears to be similar to that of A6 and A7 as there was a further delay in the execution of the activity turning out in a request for further resources (effort and cost) than planned. After having carried out improvement actions, the indicators show that: CV >0, under budget so the project until this point is spending less than planned; SV < 0, the project is still behind schedule, in spite of the improvements made; CPI >1, project costs are less than planned; SPI < 1, execution times are higher than expected. So, although the activity was completed spending less budget, it requested more effort because the resources recuperated in the previous activities had all been spent to face critical situations that arose in previous checkpoints. This impacted the EACT prevision indicator as it consequently turned out to be slightly higher than the expected threshold.

A9 requested less resources in terms of performances and cost to be carried out, and consequently indicators SPI and CPI returned to satisfy the baselines. Consequently, following to the improvements made in the previous activities and milestone checkpoints, indicators EACC and especially EACT returned to be within the thresholds and the project finished on time.

Having collected EVM values during milestones with a granularity related to activities rather than work packages or entire project, allowed the project managers to appropriately monitor and control the general trend of performance indicators and readily act to recuperate delays accumulated during the project. Indeed, the resources saved in on-schedule/budget activities were allocated on other critical off-schedule/budget ones. As so, delays were mitigated by improvement actions without impacting on the overall final project cost and effort, which by the end of the project turned out to be within the expected thresholds. Deviations from the plan in some activities were successfully recovered in other ones by readily reallocating budget and effort to face problematic situations pointed out during monitoring checks. Having adopted a decision model to guide the interpretation of indicators turned out to be helpful as it simplified the entire monitoring and control process during project execution.

IV. Discussion and Conclusions

Earned Value Management technique is easy to understand, and, in theory, also to apply. Nonetheless, there are several critical factors that should be taken into account: collecting cost values at a low level of granularity requires ad advanced level of management control, as costs must be broken down conformingly to the level of detail chosen; determining the percentage of completion of an activity requires "structured processes" and careful evaluations. Consequently several applications of EVM are done at project termination when it is obviously no longer productive or useful. Furthermore, it is difficult to apply EVM in distributed project due to the common problems related to monitoring and control processes in distributed/dislocated sites. Finally, it is not appropriate for monitoring costs other than personnel/consultancy ones such as equipment costs, determining only a partial control of the project status.

EVM allows to achieve an objective evaluation of risk and project status and, at the same time, provides useful indicators that allow to change management strategies, increasing or decreasing resources assigned to activities based on performances, in order to improve and optimize the general progress of the project in terms of cost and time.

Tracking earned value is of little value if the estimating and analysis capability that it provides is not used to operatively manage the project. Furthermore, reporting real project status systematically, at regular intervals provides an opportunity to serve as early alarm and address potential problems readily, before it is too late and avoid cost overrun and schedule slippage. For this reason it is important that project managers adopt this approach and use the decision model for conducting project monitoring and interpreting the indicators collected in specific milestones and granularity entities, fixed at the beginning of the project, in order to prevent problems from occurring and promptly act when they arise.

EVM is not the silver bullet for project monitoring and control, however it surely provides a higher level of control on the project execution. Moreover, the use of the decision model provided supports its application and systematic adoption during the entire project. This technique, given its features is more appropriate for medium to large structured contexts rather than small and agile ones.

We are currently refining the decision model so it can be better tailored to any task, activity, phase, of a project and therefore be adapted to any desired level of granularity according to the project needs. It is also being implemented in a decision support system tool, as the model has been formalized in decision tables. This solution will provide automated support to project managers allowing them to monitor and control EVM values with less effort.

Our future work will therefore include validation of the decision support system, as well as application of the automated decision model in real project case studies for collecting further evidence.

REFERENCES

[1] A.B. Pyster, R.H.Thayer, "Software engineering project management 20 years later", IEEE Software, 22(5), pp.18-21, 2005

[2] PMI, A Guide to the Project Management Body of Knowledge (PMBOK® Guide) - Fifth Edition, Project Management Institute, ISBN: 9781935589679, 2013.

[3] PMI, Practice Standard for Earned Value Management, Pensylvania, 2005.

[4] NASA, Earned Value Management Web Site - http://evm.nasa.gov/

[5] DoD 5000.2-R, "Mandatory Procedures for Major Defense Acquisition Programs (MDAPS) and Major Automated Information System (MAIS) Acquisition Programs", April 2002

[6] "The Earned Value Management Maturity Model", Version 0.0, Initial Public Draft, Management Technologies", September 2000. http://www.mgmt-technologies.com/evmtech.html

[7] The Program Manager's Guide to Software Acquisition Best Practices, Version 2.1, DoD Software Program Manager's Network, April, 1998.

[8] R.A.Marshall, "The contribution of earned value management to project success on contracted efforts: a quantitative statistics approach within the population of experienced practitioners", Project Management Institute, 2006.

[9] A. Jaafari, "Time and priority allocation scheduling technique for projects", International journal for project management, 14(5), pp.289-299.

[10] E. KimW.Wells, M.Duffey, "A model for effective implementation of earned value management methodology". International journal for project management, 21(5), pp.375-382

[11] M.Raby, "Project management via earned value", Work study 49(1), 2000, pp6-10.

[12] P.Donzelli, "A decision support system for software project management", IEEE Software, 23(4), 2006, pp.65-75

[13] M.N.Garcia, L.A Quintales, F.J.Penalvo, M.J.Martin, "Building knowledge discovery-driven models for decision support in project maangement", Decision Support Systems, 38(2), 2004

[14] M.M.Nkasu, K.H.Leung, "A resources scheduling decision support system for concurrent project management", Int.Journal of production research, 35(11), 1997, pp.3107-3132

[15] M.Plaza, O.Turetken, "A model based DSS for integrating the impact of learning in project control", Decision Support Systems, 47(2009), pp.488-488.

[16] V.R.Basili, F.E.McGarry, R.Pajerski, MV.Zelkowitz, "Lessons learned from 25 years of process improvement: the rise and fall of the NASA software engineering laboratory", Proceedings 24th ICSE 2002, pp.69-79.

[17] N.R.Tague, The Quality Toolbox, Second Edition, ASQ Quality Press, 2004, pp. 390-392.

[18] C.R.Matthews, "Linking the supply chain to TQM", Quality Progress, November 2006.

[19] D.S.Christensen, "Project advocacy and the estimate at completion problem", Journal of Cost Analysis, Spring 1996.

[20] M.J Christensen, H.R.Thayer, The project managers guide to software engineering best practices", IEEE Computer Soc, 2001, ISBN:0-7695-1199-

Software Engineering Practices for Minimizing Technical Debt

Vinay Krishna[1], **Dr. Anirban Basu**[2]
[1]Product Development, Cegedim Software India Pvt Ltd, Bangalore, India
[2]Department of CSE R&D, East Point College of Engineering & Technology, Bangalore, India

Abstract - *Often we find it difficult to incorporate any changes in a software project during later phases of its development, or during post-delivery maintenance. Primary reason for this is inflexibility in design and code which makes it difficult for changes to be incorporated. This inflexibility substantially increases the cost of making changes and this metaphor has been termed as Technical Debt [1]. While Technical Debt cannot be eliminated completely, its burden needs to be reduced. Many practitioners, especially from agile community, have suggested some practices to avoid or eliminate Technical Debt. This paper discusses methods for relief from Technical Debt and proposes seven software engineering practices that a developer can follow to minimize Technical Debt. These practices have been used and found to be effective when implemented in projects as discussed here.*

Keywords: Technical Debt, Code improvement, Refactoring, Technical Credit, Living Budget

1 Introduction

Most software projects suffer from one major technical challenge [1]: introduction of unnecessary complexity in design and code, knowingly or unknowingly [2]. System requirements mature with time, business requirements change with market dynamics and evolution of technology warrants complete requirements development. Incorporating desired changes at a late stage of software development require modification to the design and code. For meeting customer's expectations without any disruption in the schedule, developers make quick and dirty changes in design and code. Such unplanned changes done by the developer add complexity to the code. There are also situations when developers unknowingly make the code messy by not abiding to the prescribed coding standards, by incorporating changes in a hurry and by making over commitments without understanding the ramifications. Whether it is inadvertent or deliberate, such changes cause stiffness in code and gradually a situation is reached when making further changes in the code becomes extremely difficult. This state of dogmatism in code is named as **Technical Debt** [1].

Although, IT community understand the ill effects of Technical Debt little has been done to minimize it. Software engineers, who are key players in software development, can play an important role in minimizing it. This paper discusses ways of reducing the burden of Technical Debt by introducing robust software engineering practices and discipline. The practices proposed in this paper have been implemented in real life software projects and data collected shows that the proposed techniques can substantially reduce the Technical Debt. An earlier version of the work was presented in ICSEMA 2012 [3].

2 Background

According to James Higgs [4], "All projects incur Technical Debt, and that's not a bad thing". He has explained different grades of Technical Debt and how we can overcome it. As per Gartner [5] total Technical Debt in the global IT industry in 2010 was $500 billion and it is expected to grow to $1 trillion in 2015. This is not only alarming but appalling.

Practitioners from the software development community have suggested many good practices to reduce Technical Debt [2] [4] [6] [7]. As described in Table 1 these practices can be classified into 3 groups: Practices to Identify, Practices to Classify and Practices to Reduce.

TABLE 1

Category	Description
Identification [2][4][7]	Contains practices to identify Poor code quality Insufficient code coverage Inadequate documentation
Classification [2][4][6][7]	Contains practices to Classify Knowingly/Unknowingly Short term/Long Term Prudent and Reckless Debt Strategic/Non-strategic 4 grades of debt
Reduction [2][7]	Contains practices to Reduce by Refactoring Test Driven Development Code reviews/ Audit Pair programming Continuous Integration Best Practices/ Coding Standard Evolutionary design

Practices related to Identification provide the developer ways to identify Technical Debt in the code whereas the practices in the Classification category help in understanding the reason. Reduction practices are used to reduce the debt identified. However, we find that although the practices suggested to identify, classify and reduce Technical Debt are effective to some extent but not enough to reduce Technical Debt in real life software projects. This paper proposes software engineering practices which have been found to be more effective in practical situations.

3 Software Engineering Practices for Reducing Technical Debt

Although the benefits of Test Driven Development and other good practices [8] are well established, developers feel that effective methods [9] are still missing to reduce Technical Debt. With experience on working on several projects, we were able to identify seven software engineering practices discussed below that can be used to reduce the Technical Debt. These practices are discussed along with situations where it can be applied.

3.1 Practice1: Determine one's living budget

Description: One must know his/her living budget. A minimal output in a day that needs to be produced to meet the deadlines is defined here as "*living budget*" and needs to introduced in Work Management Plan. The concept of "Living Budget" is clarified as follows. When one plans his/her development work, one must estimate and plan for self-code review and refactoring. So if one plans for z hours of work in a day (normally z=8) one should plan to spend x hours for development and y hours for review and refactoring the code. The value of x and y should be determined by the developer as below,

$$1 \text{ day} = z \text{ hrs}$$

$$1 \text{ day development} = \underbrace{x \text{ hrs development} + y \text{ hrs review and refactoring}}_{\text{LivingBudget}}$$

where *x hrs + y hrs = z hrs*

Recommendation: One should include time for code review and refactoring in work plan. Sprint planning practice of Scrum have been found to be useful as team availability is planned in advance including daily hours available for each team member. Besides, we suggest following approaches:

i) Efficiently utilize extra/free time

In some projects we get extra time either due to early completion of assigned tasks or due to some other reasons. In such situations, this time should be used for Technical Debt reduction and extra time used efficiently without ignoring steps suggested in Practice 1.

ii) Self-organize

One must be able to manage his living budget, and keep track of all time and delivery commitments. We should update code regularly and keep monitoring so that undesirable practices do not recur, Team members should be empowered in task selection, estimation etc. There are many Scrum practices such as Daily standup and retrospective which help to achieve these.

3.2 Practice 2: Smell one's own code

Description: Code should be reviewed to find out where it has defects and unwanted code exists. Steps should be taken to reduce/remove unwanted code in these areas, even if it means avoiding certain situations due to over anticipation. This is well understood and easy to do, but very hard to follow. Normally developer finds very less time or no time to review/smell his own code since he always struggles to meet the deadlines. Following Practice 1, i.e., "Determine one's living budget", helps to plan for this activity.

Recommendation: For following this practice, first define coding standards and best practices and make the team aware of these. A check list should be created and developer should use it to make sure that defined coding standard and best practices have not been ignored. As it is a manual process and hard to follow it is advisable to identify some code analysis tool that can be used to find out deviation from standards and best practices. However we still need to apply manual effort to review the code in order to refactor it.

3.3 Practice3: Make optimal use of Technical Credit

Description: Introducing anticipated inflexibility in design and code is termed here as *Technical Credit*. This adds complexity to design and code which may not be required eventually. This is very important aspect in coding and unless one is sure about future needs, one should not introduce flexibility by mere anticipation

Recommendation: We need to encourage all members in the development team to discuss all issues in order to avoid guessing customer requirements and over anticipation. The following approach is recommended:

i) Start Refactoring the Technical Credit portions

The portions of the code having Technical Credit are to be found. Refactoring to improve the code should start after that. More attention should be given to the portions where additional code has been written due to anticipation. These are portions with Technical Credit

We should refactor only one part at a time until it is improved and look for reduction in Technical Debt. Refactoring on one part will show this better than refactoring on several parts of the code at the same time.

3.4 Practice 4: Find the causes for un-necessary complexity in design and code

Description: If one introduces additional complexity in the code to cover some un-practical scenarios, it is necessary to deal with these and get to the causes. Introducing unnecessary complexity makes the code more complex and rigid and increases Technical Debt. It is better to remove such additional complexity as early as possible. Such inadvertent additions in code complexity can happen due to several reasons as discussed below.

Recommendation: We suggest the following two approaches:

i) Take help from others in design and coding related obstacles
We have found that frequently we spend time on issues which have already been solved by someone else or can be done quickly by a person with the necessary expertise but we avoid seeking help from them. Pair programming is the best option to avoid such situation. However if we cannot practice pair programming, we need to encourage open communication
ii) Stop Keeping up with Joneses
Avoid blindly following others' designs, patterns, codes and libraries unless one really needs them. Ask suggestions from all but accept the best one suitable.

3.5 Practice5: Follow Best Practices and Coding Standards

Description: Use recommended Coding Standards/Guidelines. This is the best way to get code back on track. If one portion of the code e does not adhere to the standards/guidelines, one needs to modify it.
Recommendation: Define the best practices and Coding Standards and share them with the team. Check if any third party tool can be used for review and to quickly find out deviations or shortcuts.

3.6 Practice6: Increase productivity with Quality in mind

Description: Always focus on quality and not on speed. Never measure productivity in terms of quantity but in terms of quality and importance.
Recommendation: Test driven development is one of best practices to increase the code quality. Maintaining product backlog with proper order is also a good practice to get important items done first. Continuous integration is another good practice, as we make changes in our code apart from unit testing. Always do an integration testing to make sure it didn't break others code.

3.7 Practice7: Learn continuosly

Description: Learn techniques continuously and apply it to improve code. Plenty of resources are available to enhance one's knowledge.

Recommendation: Impart proper training to the team on code refactoring and share good resources with them. Encourage continuous learning and experience sharing within the team. There is always scope for improvement and continuous learning helps. Never give up on learning emerging coding standards, best practices, refactoring techniques etc.
Discuss in the team technical updates, any new special defect or fix that has been encountered or used by anyone and keep the meetings less formal and encourage team member to share his/her experience/learning.

4 Application on Projects

Although SQALE method [10] has been proposed, measurement of Technical Debt is not easy. We have chosen the following metrics for the purpose of measuring Technical Debt:

- Number. of defects found in production
- Mean time taken for enhancement
- Mean time taken to fix production defects

We compared the values of these metrics on internal projects which are part of customer support system for one payroll product. We analyzed projects which were showing increase in Technical Debts and came out with the practices proposed in this paper. The proposed practices were applied in subsequent projects and the results clearly brought out the advantages of the proposed practices.

We chose projects which are in same category, of same size (approx. 1500 Man-hours) and were related to IT service management for one payroll product. This was done to have better control on any new change requested by the customer requiring some complex workflow to implement. We were experiencing lots of difficulties due to severe defects during all phases of development and even post-production. Defects were of various types: wrong interpretation/assumption by developer, in-adequate unit testing, hurry-burry approach, lack of self-planning etc. The projects chosen for analysis were:

CR001: This is used to create and manage request for new column creation and analyzing the impact and contain workflow that it require to pass along with SLA.
SW01: This is used to create and manage request for new worksheet creation. This also contains workflow that it requires to pass along with SLA.

4.1 Observations

The above seven practices were applied along with the prevalent practices mentioned in Table 1.The results are summarized below in three sub sections.

4.1.1 Results without applying Technical Debt reduction techniques

In project CR001, we observed large number of defects reported and number of changes that came during release and production. We also found that effort was high in both for fixing defects and for implementing the new changes, see Figure 1.

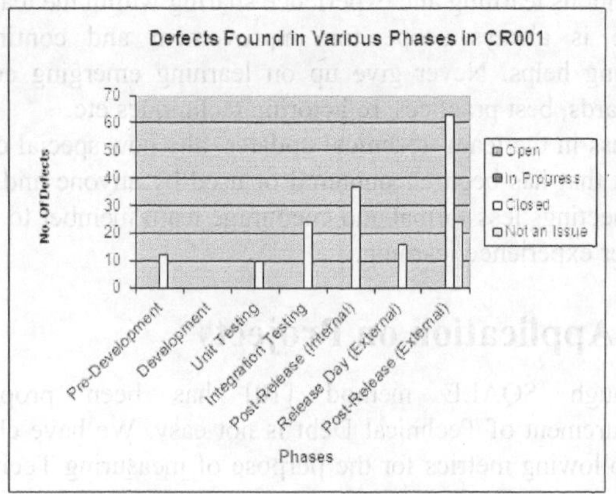

Figure 1. Defects in CR001 without applying technical debt techniques

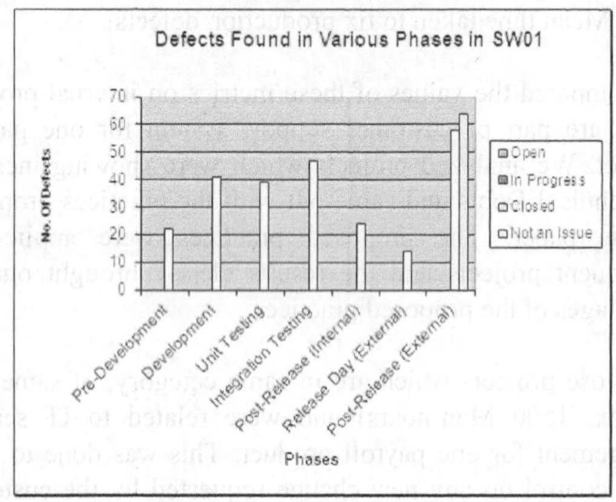

Figure 2. Defects in SW01 after applying practices in Table 1

Do not end a page with a section or subsection heading. Keep footnotes to a minimum. Proper usage of the English language is expected of all Camera-Ready papers.

4.1.2 Results with application of techniques mentioned in Table 1

We analyzed the situation in CR001 and we decided to apply identification and reduction methods mentioned in Table 1 in project SW01. We used Test-Driven Development approach without any automation tool [7]. On comparing CR001 data with SW01 data (see Figure1 and Figure 2), we observed rise in number of defects found prior to Post-Release phase especially during development, Unit testing and Integration testing phases. Nevertheless, during Post-Release phase, we found increase in number of "Not an Issue" (potential candidate for new change due to wrong interpretation/assumption) by 182% and slight decrease by 6% in number of defects found There were signs of improvement as shown in Figure 2 but not to our expectations for the number of defects found in Post-Release phase.

4.1.3 Results with application of Technical Debt reduction practices of Table 1 and seven practices proposed here

It was therefore decided to apply the proposed seven practices in subsequent projects: JTC001 and LTC001.

JTC001 is used to create and manage request for new type of leave creation and for analyzing the impact and contain workflow that it requires to pass along with SLA.

The results of application of the practices on projects JTC001 and LTC001 are shown in Figure 3 and Figure 4.

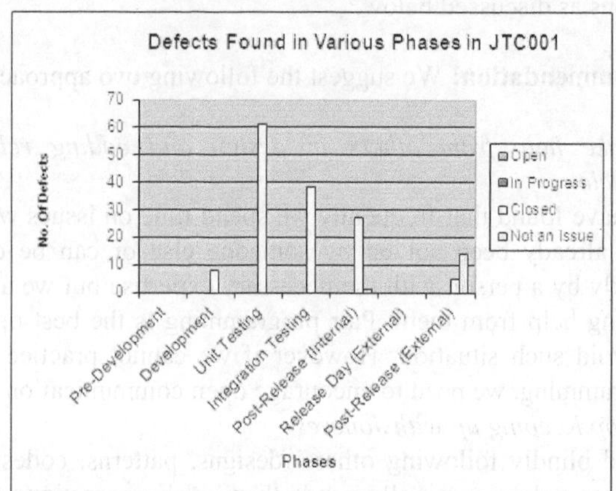

Figure 3. Defects in JTC001 after apllying proposed practices

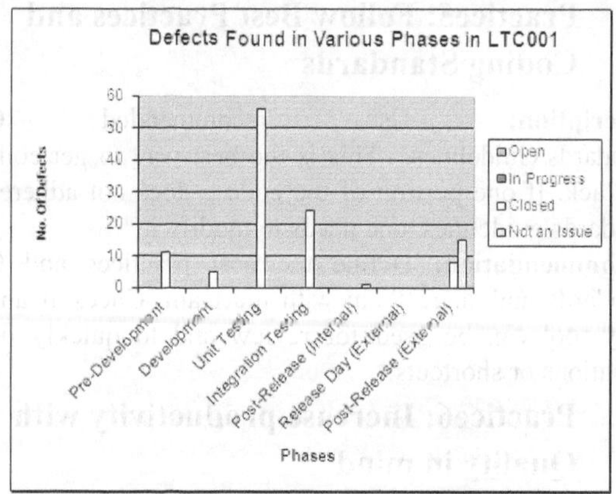

Figure 4. Defects in LTC001 after applying proposed practices

On comparing the parameters obtained in JTC001 and LTC001 with that for CR001 and SW01, we found significant reduction in defects count and number of "Not an Issue" in post-production phase while we observed significant rise in defects count during Unit testing and Integration testing phases.

In case of JTC001 and LTC001 we also observed significant reduction in total number of defects and in changes required in production as shown in Figure 5.

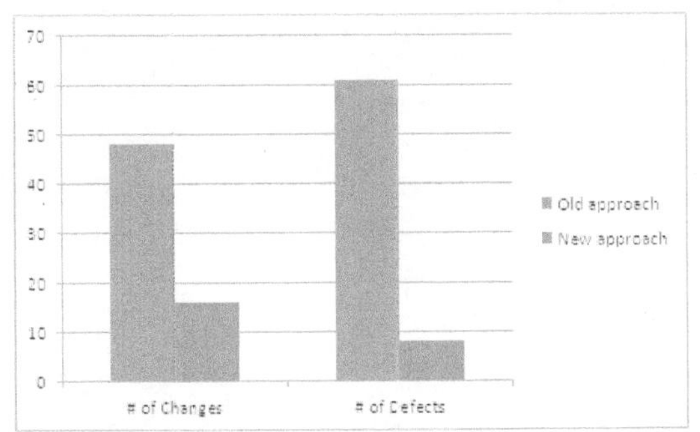

Figure 5. Improvement at production after applying proposed practices

We saw improvement, as in Figure 6, in terms of time taken to adopt new changes as well as the time for fixing the defects.

These observations clearly brought out the advantages of applying the seven practices proposed here in reducing Technical Debt. The proposed practices are being applied in more number of projects.

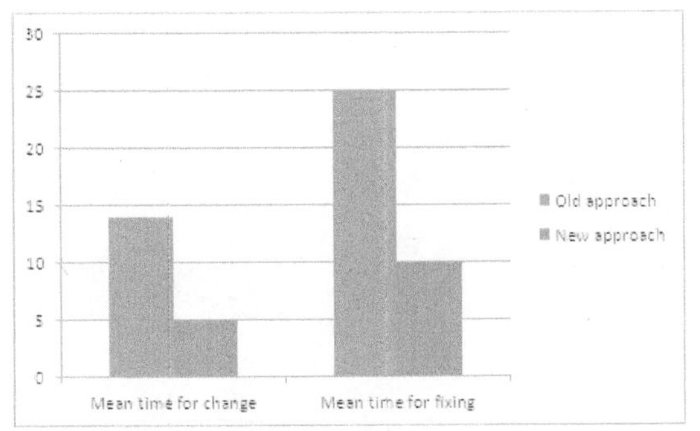

Figure 6. Improvement at production (meantime) after applying proposed practices

5 Conclusions

It is really hard to eliminate Technical Debt completely and it is not easy. It is abundantly clear that large amount of debt can lead to failure or substantial loss in terms of extra effort and rework needed to make changes to meet customer expectations. As a developer we should minimize Technical Debt as much as possible. This paper suggests software engineering practices to reduce Technical Debt. The practices have been found to be effective based on the authors' practical experience on application on real life projects. The seven software engineering practices proposed in this paper are being applied on more projects of different categories and sizes to check their robustness.

6 References

[1] W. Cunningham, The WyCash Portfolio Management System, OOPSLA, 1992;http://c2.com/doc/oopsla92.html

[2] S. McConnell, Technical Debt, 2007; http://blogs.construx.com/blogs/stevemcc/archive/2007/11/01/technical-debt-2.aspx

[3] V. Krishna and A. Basu, "Minimizing Technical Debt: Developer's Viewpoint", in Proc ICSEMA 2012, Chennai, Dec 2012

[4] J. Higgs, The Four Grades of Technical Debt, 2011; http://madebymany.com/blog/the-four-grades-of-technical-debt

[5] Gartner, Press Release, 2010 ; http://www.gartner.com/it/page.jsp?id=1439513

[6] M. Fowler, Technical Debt Quadrant, 2009; http://www.martinfowler.com/bliki/TechnicalDebtQuadrant.html

[7] T. Theodoropoulos, Technical Debt Part1-4, 2012; http://blog.acrowire.com/technical-debt/technical-debt-part-1-definition

[8] V. Krishna, My Experiments with TDD, ScrumAlliance, 2010; http://www.scrumalliance.org/articles/357-my-experiments-with-tdd

[9] D. Laribee, Using Agile Techniques to Pay Back Technical Debt, MSDN Magazine, December 2009; http://msdn.microsoft.com/en-us/magazine/ee819135.aspx

[10] J. Letouzey, The SQALE Method, January 2012; http://www.sqale.org/wp-content/uploads/2010/08/SQALE-Method-EN-V1-0.pdf

SESSION

AGILE SOFTWARE METHODS

Chair(s)

TBA

Agile Project-Based Teaching and Learning

Dagmar Monett
Computer Science Dept.
Faculty of Cooperative Studies
Berlin School of Economics and Law, Germany
Dagmar.Monett-Diaz@hwr-berlin.de

***Abstract*—Agile courses in university settings aim to prepare students to face the ever increasing demands from the software industry, where Agile has become mainstream. This proves the teaching and understanding of Agile in such settings is of the utmost importance. This is why Agile is no longer just a part of the software engineering curriculum in Computer Science but a standalone course in most cases, though with increasing challenges for both faculty and students. This article presents yet another example case of the design, planning, development and evaluation of an agile project-based course. The reason for addressing the Agile teaching is twofold: not only are the Agile theory and practice taught and experienced in class, but also the teaching itself, and consequently the learning, has been adapted to changing requirements and priorities in each edition of the course. Making it project-based allows students to work with realistic projects through which they learn Agile more effectively, in collaborative and self-organizing teams. These insights, as well as settings and experiences over a total of 4 years, are addressed in this article.**

***Keywords*—Agile, eXtreme Programming, teaching, project-based learning.**

I. Introduction

There are lots of strong reasons for including Agile principles in CS education [1]. Positive experiences that go from *project-based* Computer Science (CS) courses using Agile [2, 3] over *Agile teaching* [4] to *Agile instructional design* [5] have had a common denominator: the practices, the values and the methods of the agile software development are essential; Agile is a current mainstream in the software industry [6] and educational environments are profiting from this, too. Meanwhile, project-based learning has proven to be very attractive in tertiary teaching: students learn the discipline via a realistic project, they pursue questions and connect them to activities that are part of the project, they construct knowledge and autonomously work towards a final product, as well as they master the curriculum standards with academic rigor [7].

The module *Project Management* is part of the CS education during the third semester at the Berlin School of Economics and Law (BSEL). By successfully passing this module, dual studies CS students can obtain 14 ECTS-credits,[1] which are assigned by considering the following proportion: a 20% of them goes to the sub-module *Project and Quality Management*, a 30% goes to the sub-module *Multidisciplinary Lab using Agile techniques*, and a 50% goes to the sub-module *Practice Transfer*, where students are at their enterprises and where they should apply gained knowledge in software engineering in general and in Agile and project management in particular. Credit hours, however, were never intended to be a measure of student learning, as Laitinen argues in [8]. She brings forward the argument that there should be found "what students are expected to –and actually do– learn", as well as the measurements to meaningfully assess what they have learned, not only concerning time-based units. By introducing Agile project-based techniques in CS assignments and by accurately defining both the learning goals and their evaluation forms, as it is further presented in this article, a positive step in this direction is achieved.

Much of the Agile courses in university settings have a common goal: to prepare students to face the ever increasing challenges in the software industry. Jaccheri and Morasca define in [9] five main roles that industry can play in software engineering education from the point of view of the university teacher: industry as students, as teachers, as researchers, as customers, and as former students. Three of these roles are well-identified in the mentioned module *Project Management*:

- Industry as teachers: the sub-module *Project and Quality Management* runs parallel to the sub-module *Multidisciplinary Lab using Agile techniques*. The first sub-module is taught by an industry specialist in close collaboration with the latter's teacher.
- Industry as customers: a real customer, who presents a problem to the students and who is available for consulting, is simulated in the Lab, if it is not possible to invite "a real" one. The concrete problem that is selected and the algorithm for solving it are also present in many industrial applications.
- Industry as former students: there are a Faculty Technical Commission and a Faculty Commission for Cooperative Studies at the BSEL both integrated by several industry partners, former dual studies students some of them, that discuss and approve the curriculum and other teaching and learning issues. Part of the faculty is composed of former BSEL students as well.

Two of the most important advantages of the program that prepare CS students for their further professional life are: firstly, students from the Faculty of Cooperative Studies are dual studies students and work in German companies from their first career's semester on. This means, they gain practical experience in real industry scenarios from the beginning of their studies on. Second, the sub-module *Multidisciplinary Lab using Agile techniques* (Lab using Agile, for short) provides them with several hard skills like specifying, designing, implementing and testing software, as well as communicating,

[1] European Credit Transfer and Accumulation System. One credit point is equivalent to 30 hours of study.

presenting, and working in a team, to name a few soft skills. Furthermore, both advantages successfully minimize new hires' common frustrations, as addressed in [10].

The Lab using Agile uses an interdisciplinary approach from the viewpoint of different cross-disciplinary topics addressed there. Perhaps these are reasons why the course has been favorably received by both faculty and students. Its careful design and planning, as well as its constant adaption to changing teaching and learning requirements has proven extremely effective in project-based courses. The remainder of this paper describes aspects for the Lab using Agile in detail.

II. Agile and XP Techniques

One of Agile's most used methodologies is eXtreme Programming (XP), which has also been very popular in CS teaching [11–15]. For example, Stapel and colleagues propose in [15] a XP lab design property system for teaching a project-based XP course to CS master students, emphasizing in XP practices as part of a closed block course. Their work inspired the study summarized in this paper, which recommends a change from a weekly course to a blocked one. However, not only the course design, its type and the students' level, but also the blocks' duration, the XP iteration lengths, the team sizes, and the project content, among others indicators, differentiate their research from the one presented in this paper. Valuable insights from other works evaluating Agile in education environments also influence the findings presented here.

Pair programming is no longer extrinsic to CS education. In [16], for example, a case study concludes that pair programming is an effective approach for mastering computer programming together with cooperative learning principles. The authors extensively review the literature about the advantages and disadvantages of pair programming as a teaching-learning strategy, too. In [17], the authors additionally comment about the benefits of pair programming when practicing it in graduate software engineering class projects. Furthermore, several works have been published concerning both the strengths and weaknesses of pair programming but from the perspective of the Agile community.

The rest of the XP techniques are also introduced to the students in the Lab using Agile, both theoretical and practically. The students are, however, undergraduate students with little programming experience. In fact, they have only attended a few semesters at the university. Nevertheless, they learn quickly how to develop software with the aid of Agile, they solve a concrete real problem working in teams and they gain experiences by simulating a working day at an enterprise as part of the course project.

Differentiated supervision and guidance allow for better reactions to problems that might arise when introducing Agile or simply when working with others. In the Lab using Agile, individual and general coaching is offered as well. The faculty coaches individuals and teams in the course and is able to monitor progress and development anytime. Thus, continuous feedback can be provided to the students, to the teams and to the entire group. In reciprocation, students should be capable of presenting different stages of working software, and they should discuss with faculty in the role of (simulated)

TABLE I. Course schedule: teaching blocks and semester credit hours.

Block 1	Block 2		Block 3		Block 4
Day 1	*Day 2*	*Day 3*	*Day 4*	*Day 5*	*Day 6*
6 SCH	8 SCH (PC Lab)	8 SCH (PC Lab)	8 SCH (PC Lab)	8 SCH (PC Lab)	6 SCH
	16 SCH		16 SCH		
44 SCH					

TABLE II. Course schedule: teaching blocks and Agile cycles.

Block 1	Block 2		Block 3		Block 4
Day 1	*Day 2*	*Day 3*	*Day 4*	*Day 5*	*Day 6*
Syllabus Intro I	Intro II Planing game 1 Iteration 1 (Incremental teamwork)		Release 1 Planing game 2 Iteration 2 (Incremental teamwork)		Release 2 Conclusion

customers, acceptance criteria for their software products. In the coaching sections, it is expected that students come with concrete questions they have prepared in advance about any topic they need advice on.

III. Course Schedule

Table I shows the course schedule for the Lab using Agile in teaching blocks and semester credit hours (SCH, 1 SCH meaning what follows 45 minutes of teaching time). The course is divided into four teaching blocks for a total of 44 SCH. Blocks 2 and 3 take place in a PC Lab. They are mainly intended for teamwork. In the Fall 2009 and 2010 editions of the course, three XP iterations were programmed for respective three product releases. However, in the Fall 2011 and 2012, only two XP iterations and their respective releases were planned, in response to the course appraisals administered at the end of the previous terms. More on this respect can be found in Section VI-B.

Table II shows the same course schedule but in teaching blocks and Agile cycles. Both *Syllabus* and *Intro I* at Day 1 conform Block 1 and refer to an introductory section, which states the purpose and goals of the course, as well as the theory about the algorithms selected to solve the customer problem. *Intro II* at Day 2 refers to an introduction to Agile and to XP. Days 2 and 3 are two continuous calendar days from Block 2, as well as days 4 and 5 are from Block 3. *Iteration 1* starts with *Planing game 1* and takes between three and four weeks until *Release 1* is accomplished, with only the first two days at the university. This similarly occurs for *Iteration 2*, whose *Release 2* takes place at the end of the course, at Day 6. The *Conclusions* are mainly based on the presentations of the final product releases and on the teacher's feedback concerning the projects as a whole. In [15], to name one crucial difference to this work, the block course has no interruption at all: the (very short) iterations are continuously located in the course time frame.

Incremental teamwork in blocks 2 and 3 means students become more independent while working in a team. Students not only do work incrementally on different tasks without interruption while planning and developing software: they also apply Agile techniques that make them more independent.

They progressively need lesser coaching from faculty for mastering activities that are more complex with time. In order to cope with these challenges, the course schedule includes more time for programming and less for other didactic exercises, also in a progressive way.

IV. Learning and Teaching Goals

Faculty should be aware of both the coarse and the fine-grained learning goals for a course, in order to break down those goals and to focus on the content to be taught. The former, the coarse-grained learning goals, are often defined in the curriculum in a general way. The latter ones help faculty to plan and to draw up in detail what students need to master and the ways of achieving and evaluating that. By defining thoroughly the fine-grained learning goals of the Lab using Agile, faculty creates the course syllabus without difficulty, and individual blocks and days are planed easier. This does not require a straightforward, additional effort for the conception of all these teaching materials, but the time saved later pays dearly the invested one.

The second block of the Lab using Agile is dedicated to the first experiences with the XP practice, especially at Day 2. The fine-grained learning goals of the second block (B2) for the firsts double credit hours (2 SCH each, i.e., $1\frac{1}{2}$ hours) are:

After completion of the second block, the students will be able...

B2.1 (2 SCH): *...to identify and to describe software requirements using story cards; to assess their priorities; to coordinate and to discuss their inclusion in the current iteration; and to plan and to schedule related activities for the first XP iteration.*

B2.2 (2 SCH): *...to meet and to participate in "stand-ups" or daily meetings; to develop software programming in pairs.*

B2.3 (2 SCH): *...to discuss and to formulate rules for working in a team; to discuss and to formulate rules for the work of several teams in a room.*

B2.4 (2 SCH): *...to develop software working in teams.*

Didactic exercises worked out in this block include organizational aspects that allow for better collaborative work when applying XP, since this is essential to Agile [18]. Rules for working in a team are then to be discussed by the students, for example, and each project group could present its set of rules using a flip chart in one of the sessions.

Teaching screenplays were used to better schedule the sequence of concrete teaching and learning activities to be included into a class, as well as the time required to complete them. They were planned using a sandwich structure, i.e., by combining passive and active learning units, and are like lesson plans or teaching worksheets that describe the teaching roadmap for a class or for part of a class in detail. For example, the teaching screenplay for the first double credit hour from block B2 is shown in Table III. It corresponds to the fine-grained learning goals defined above for the first double credit hour of that block, i.e., for B2.1.

TABLE III. Example Teaching Screenplay for the Double Credit Hour B2.1.

90 min.	Entry	5 min.	**Start** – *passive unit* Welcoming (oral) Contents and time schedule (flip chart)
	Working phase	20 min.	**Content 1** – *passive unit* Motivation (oral) Learning goals (flip chart) Planning game (flip chart, blackboard) Story cards (blackboard)
		3 min.	**Brainstorming** – *active unit* Collect examples (plenum)
		20 min.	**Content 2** – *passive unit* Project description (hand outs) Project goals (blackboard) Project requirements (hand outs) Requirements for 1st release (blackboard)
		2 min.	**Introduce exercise** – *passive unit* Planning game: method, time management (oral)
		35 min.	**Knowledge transfer** – *active unit* Planning game 1st iteration (teamwork, coaching) Define story cards Set priorities Discuss realization
	Exit	5 min.	**End** – *active and passive unit* Questions, feedback (oral) Conclusions (oral) Short about the next double SCH, i.e., B2.2 (oral)

TABLE IV. Example Teaching Screenplay for a Double Credit Hour with Teamwork.

90 min.	Entry	2 min.	**Start** – *passive unit* Welcoming (oral) Goals and time schedule (flip chart)
	Working phase	83 min.	**Teamwork and coaching** – *active unit* Incremental software development (by students) Individual team coaching (by faculty) Questions, feedback (team-oriented)
	Exit	5 min.	**End** – *passive unit* Conclusions (oral) Short about the next double SCH (oral)

19 such teaching screenplays are needed for blocks 1 to 3, i.e., one screenplay as in Table III for each double SCH. However, much of them are only an outline like the one presented in Table IV. All teaching screenplays can be adjusted and adapted depending on the concrete class' rhythm when developing the course projects, which is just an expression of the Agile project-based teaching. An extra column could be added to the screenplays, too, for comments on self reflection and on self assessment after completing the scheduled exercises and activities.

V. Project Requirements

The general project description was formulated as follows: *Solve the traveling salesman problem (TSP) using a meta-heuristic algorithm in the context of an XP project. Wanted is a software product with a graphical user interface (GUI) that includes menus and controls to define settings and that visualize results, as well as with a graphical window to show both the cities and the optimization process in real time.*

Students should use metaheuristics algorithms, like genetic

algorithms (GA) and ant colony systems (ACO), to solve instances of the TSP. They should test their programs using 2-dimensional, symmetric TSP instances of geographical problems from TSPLIB [19], as well as they should report both their findings and the software development using Agile in a research paper of at least five pages, following the guidelines for two-column conference proceeding in IEEE style.

Software requirements are defined by the customer (real or simulated) at the beginning of each XP iteration, depending on the focus the software development in that phase is centered around. Only those requirements related to the GUI development, for instance, are defined, specified, planned, and prioritized in the same planning game. Those requirements concerning the data and the algorithms to process them are defined in another planning game. Whether to start with the GUI or with the logic was discussed with the students. For many of them it was more important and attractive to have a working product with options and other components to present to the customer in the different releases, into which other functionalities could be added onto.

In Fall 2012, the first release, at the beginning of the third block (see Table II), was an "individual" meeting of each team with faculty playing the roles of *customer* and *coach*. The second release, in the last course's block, was a "public" meeting (all teams, in plenum), where faculty played both the *customer* and the *evaluator* roles. Each team presented a software prototype in the former, as well as it addressed the main aspects related to other Agile methods and techniques. In the latter, the final release, a formal oral presentation of about 35 minutes gave insights about the final product, about the project development, and about the experiences and lessons learned during the project completion.

Emphasis was also put on project management tools for collaborative work. The students had the opportunity, at least in the last two editions of the Lab using Agile, to test and to use several new tools (for them), like Redmine[2] and Trello[3], for instance.

VI. Course Evaluation

The composition and the size of the class, together with other information related to the last four editions of the course, are presented in Table V. The number of students answering a customized, anonymous questionnaire at the end of the semester is given in parenthesis for each course edition.

In the Falls 2009 and 2010, the course was offered weekly and there were a total of three XP iterations (and therefore, a total of three releases). No special didactic methods were applied at that time. In each of both editions, a different algorithm was considered to solve the TSP problems, i.e., ACO in Fall 2009 and GA in 2010. Students had difficulties especially when programming in the class, since the time available each week was minimal. They also had problems that prevented them completing their projects on time.

In the Falls 2011 and 2012, however, the course was divided in four presence blocks, as it is presented in Table I. Both editions of the course scheduled only two XP iterations,

TABLE V. Characteristics of the last four course editions.

Fall	Group size	Female prop.	Weekly/ Blocks	Agile iter.	Algo-rithm	Special didactic	Special coaching
2009	30(30)	1	w	3	ACO	–	–
2010	30(30)	2	w	3	GA	–	–
2011	24(24)	–	b	2	ACO	++	+
2012	28(19)	2	b	2	ACO	++	++

as derived from students' feedback in the former courses. The algorithm used for solving TSP was the same in both cases (i.e., ACO). Both editions included several special didactic methods not applied before, as well as a close team coaching by the professor, more intensive in Fall 2012. Additionally, the faculty was coached in Fall 2012 by an external training coach, expert in didactic in higher education.

A. Evaluating Learning

Each student can earn at most 100 points, which are then converted to a grade-point system in the German grading scale, as usual. A final student's grade is the team grade to which they belong. It is determined using a percentage system with 20% for each of the following areas: first release, second release, research paper, software program, and project management.

For assessing the releases and the team presentations, an evaluation form was designed by the faculty. It considers key components like presentation skills, content, timing, confidence, quality, and so on. The research paper was evaluated according to guidelines for scientific events. What to consider for both its content and structure was previously discussed with the students. Last but not least, the software program should satisfy all requirements, the teams should submit an executable version out of bugs, and the main software features and their functioning should be shown in the final presentation, without forgetting the project management aspects related to the project as a whole.

B. Evaluating (not only) Teaching

By the term's end, a questionnaire independent of formal faculty evaluations was administered to students. The questions catalogue with their descriptive scale values is shown in Table VI. The questions are grouped in four major topics, these corresponding to the course requirements in particular, to teaching in general, to how students learned, and to Agile.

Students could also provide an overall evaluation of the course, including what they liked the most, what they did not like at all, as well as further suggestions and comments.

VII. Results and Discussion

Figure 1 shows a polar line chart with an area layer divided in four sectors that depend on the four general questionnaire topics mentioned so far. The question P is not included since it refers to different scenarios (two or three releases).

The plotted data are computed using the following formula,

[2]Redmine (at http://redmine.org) is a project management web application.
[3]Trello is a board-based collaboration tool. See more at http://trello.com/.

TABLE VI. QUESTIONS CATALOGUE WITH DESCRIPTIVE SCALE VALUES.

Id.	Question	Descriptive scale values and index			
		4	3	2	1[a]
A	What do you think about the required time for the course	too high	normal	too low	abstention
B	How were the requirements concerning the course assignments/tasks?	too high	realistic	too low	abstention
C	How did you find the problem that was selected to be solved (i.e. TSP)?	motivating	neutral	dissuasive	abstention
D	How did you find the algorithm that was selected to solve the user problem?	motivating	neutral	dissuasive	abstention
E	How was the introduction on the course goals and topics?	very good	normal	very bad	abstention
F	How did the teacher/on-site customer respond to the questions, how was her feedback?	very good	normal	very bad	abstention
G	Do you feel as if you would have learned something during the course?	very much	normal	very little	abstention
H	How did the course form your interest on the working field?	motivating	neutral	dissuasive	abstention
I	Did you enjoy Agile practices, especially XP?	very much	normal	very little	abstention
J	Do you think you have improved your programming skills when participating in the XP project?	very much	normal	very little	abstention
K	And how about your social skills? Did you improve them?	very much	normal	very little	abstention
L	Do you think that using XP improves the productivity of small teams?	very much	normal	very little	abstention
M	Do you think that using XP improves the quality of the code?	very much	normal	very little	abstention
N	Do you think that Pair Programming speeds up the developing process?	very much	normal	very little	abstention
O	How did you find the planning game at the beginning of each iteration?	very helpful	normal	irritating	abstention
P	How was the division in two (Fall 2011, Fall SS2012) / three (Fall 2009, Fall 2010) releases?	excessive	adequate	insufficient	abstention

[a] The scale index with value 1 is reserved for abstentions, for each question, so that students can leave questions unanswered.

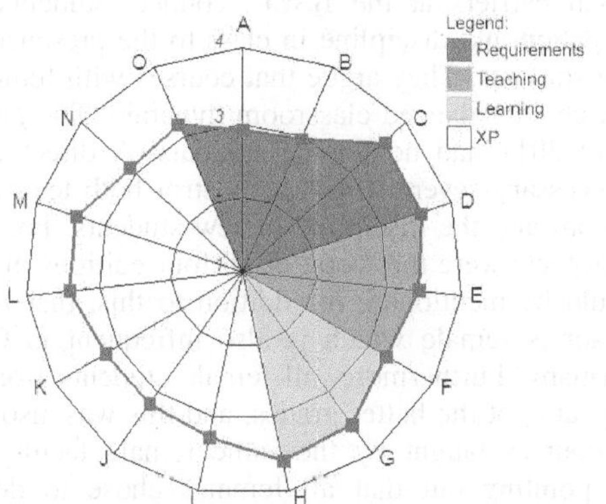

Fig. 1. Questionnaire results averaged for the four editions of the course.

which represents a weighted average for each question i:

$$y = \frac{\sum_{j=1}^{4} (5 - j) \cdot v_{ij}}{N} = \frac{4 \cdot v_{i1} + 3 \cdot v_{i2} + 2 \cdot v_{i3} + v_{i4}}{103}$$

N being the total number of students responses over the four years ($N = 103$) and v_{ij} being the sum of all responses multiplied by a scaling of the descriptive scale value j, for each question. For example, question A refers to the required time for the course and it has the descriptive scale values *too high*, *normal*, *too low*, and *abstention* (see Table VI). The number of total responses were 13, 70, 18, and 2 for each descriptive value, respectively. Thus, $y = 2.9126$ in the polar line chart for question A, which means that a substantial number of all students considered the required time as normal.

The rest of the plotted data can be read in a similar way: most students found the requirements concerning the course assignments (question B) to be realistic, the TSP and solving it with the selected metaheuristic (questions C and D) were motivating, and so on. All in all, the students' feedback was very positive in general, particularly regarding Agile.

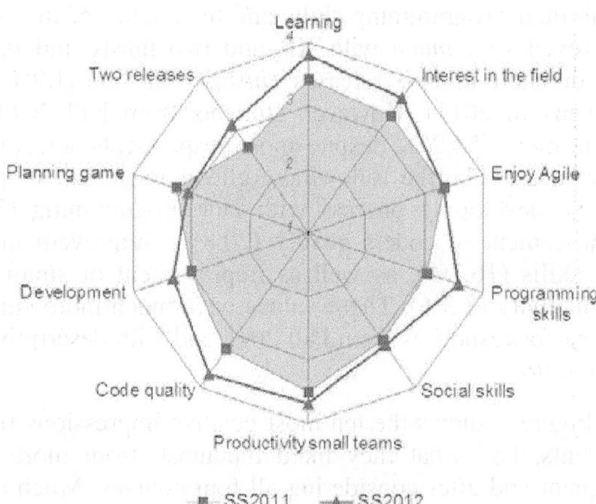

Fig. 2. Questionnaire results comparing Fall 2011 and Fall 2012 in detail.

Figure 2 shows a polar line chart with a polar area layer and a polar line layer comparing in detail some data for the Fall 2011 and for the Fall 2012, respectively. Only the questionnaire topics "how students learned" and "Agile techniques" are considered. In the figure, *Learning* refers to the question with identifier *G*, *Interest in the field* to *H*, *Enjoy Agile* to *I*, *Programming skills* to *J*, *Social skills* to *K*, *Productivity small teams* to *L*, *Code quality* to *M*, *Development* to *N*, *Planning game* to *O*, and *Two releases* to *P*, respectively, as specified in Table VI. The corresponding values are listed in Table VII, which includes the relative percentage of responses for each descriptive scale value, for each question, not including the abstentions for being irrelevant. Such details give more information than the weighted average when comparing both courses.

The main differences between the settings for Falls 2011 and 2012 concern the presence of female students (none in 2011) and the team coaching (more intensive in 2012), as it is presented in Table V. The questionnaire results, however, differ strongly in several aspects: almost all results for questions *G* to *P* show remarkable changes from Fall 2011 to Fall 2012. In the

TABLE VII. FALL 2011 AND 2012 COMPARED FOR GENERAL LEARNING AND AGILE DATA.

Question Id.	Fall 2011				Fall 2012			
	rel. %			glb. %	rel. %			glb. %
G	45,8	50	4,2	3,4	62,5	16,7	0	3,8
H	33,3	62,5	4,2	3,3	50	29,2	0	3,7
I	54,2	29,2	12,5	3,3	29,2	45,8	4,2	3,3
J	29,2	50	16,7	3,0	50	25	4,2	3,6
K	25	58,3	16,7	3,1	29,2	33,3	16,7	3,2
L	58,3	33,3	8,3	3,5	54,2	25	0	3,7
M	45,8	33,3	20,8	3,2	58,3	20,8	0	3,7
N	33,3	33,3	33,3	3,0	29,2	45,8	4,2	3,3
O	33,3	58,3	8,3	3,2	16,7	54,2	4,2	3,0
P	16,7	37,5	41,7	2,7	12,5	62,5	4,2	3,1

latter, for example, most students feel they learned *very much* during the course (62.5%). One year before, more than half (54.2%) of the students considered learning between *normal* and *very little*. Similarly, for students in Fall 2012 the course is much more *motivating* than for their peers in 2011, they think their programming skills and the quality of the code are improved *very much* with XP, and two thirds find *adequate* the division in two releases (*insufficient* for 41.7% of the students in 2011). However, students from Fall 2011 enjoy Agile more (54.2%) despite more respondents selecting *very little* to describe the following Agile characteristics: speeding up the developing process with pair programming (33.3%), improvement of code's quality (20.8%), improvement of social skills (16.7%), as well as improvement of small teams' productivity (8.3%). These values were much more smaller or absent for responses from Fall 2012 and with descriptive scale *very little*.

Figure 3 shows the ten most positive impressions from the students, i.e., what they liked the most, from more to less frequent and after considering all four courses. Much of them refer to both Agile and XP. Pair programming was the most mentioned with a total of 12 occurrences. Both its benefits and practice were well accepted by the students. Working in a team and applying XP to implement a motivating algorithm was also very important for the students, as well as the chance to improve their programming skills in such a course project.

The students also had the possibility to mention what they did not like at all, as well as the opportunity to suggest changes to be considered in new editions of the course. Some typical responses were the following ones: it is too much work that has to be done for too few credits (there should be assigned more credits points for such a lab), the time pressure is too high (more time should be allocated for both programming and teamwork in the class), it is difficult to work in a room with too many teams at the same time (fewer teams should work in the same room).

The overall evaluation of the course in the four editions was as follows: About 80% of all students evaluated the course as *very positive* (18,45%) and *positive* (61,16%). A neutral evaluation was given by 18,45% of the students, mainly from the Fall 2011. Two students from the same year evaluated the course as *negative*, for a 1,94%. No student evaluated the course as *very negative*.

A subjective explanation of the negative results could be

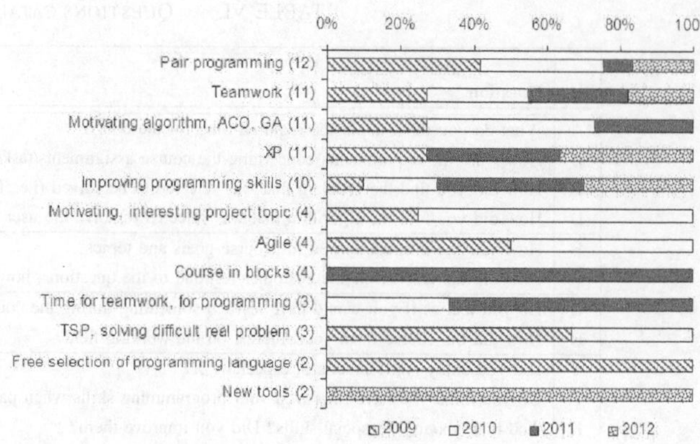

Fig. 3. Most mentioned positive comments.

related to gender aspects, although no factual evidence is available. For years, usual comments between faculty staff, not only from Computer Science but also from the other three technical carriers at the BSEL, connect students' attention, participation and discipline in class to the presence or lack of female students. They argue that courses with female students have a better balanced classroom dynamic. The group attending Fall 2011 had no female students. A direct intervention was necessary several times to control both teamwork in the classroom and the discipline of few students. For that group, these aspects were the worst of all four editions of the course. It should be mentioned, in addition to this, that the teaching professor is female which is also infrequent in CS, at least in Germany. Furthermore, all female students from the other three years got the better grades, and this was also the case in other courses taught by the same female faculty. It is also worth pointing out that all females chose to do their two student research projects with this female teacher and their final grades were the highest possible scores. This supports Shaikh's conclusion in [20]: "the presence of female faculty in CS is also an important source of mentoring".

Another possible reason is the observed students' behavior during the course assignments and exercises. Most students were somehow resistant to participate in didactic exercises involving traditional methods other than the ones they use to work with while frontal teaching. Open feedback asked at the end of some blocks confirmed the argument that, when exercises were not directly related to programming activities for their projects, students were *wasting their time*. They could not see the potential advantages class games or student debates or think-pair-share might have on long-term learning. In Fall 2012, already knowing the difficult situations that arose in Fall 2011, students were instructed in advance about the goals and benefits of such kind of supporting exercises. Appropriate advise was also given by an expert coach. The working environment and the relations student–faculty were more relaxing and productive in 2012, in general.

The final grade in the module considers 30 points (from 100) for the Lab using Agile. The averaged final grades from all four editions of the course were:[4] Fall 2009, 27.82 (6); Fall 2010, 26.79 (7); Fall 2011, 28.92 (5); and Fall 2012,

[4]The number of teams is given in parenthesis. Each team is composed of 4 to 5 students, as a rule.

29.43 (7) points from 30. All in all, the grades were more than satisfactory: all students earned the required credits and the final grades were good despite the students' lack of participation and the difficult situations from the Fall of 2011. Most of the lost points were on scientific writing and not on the programs. The developed software programs were successful working products that satisfied the defined requirements and they were finished on time. Furthermore, the most XP values and practices were well understood by the students and were consequent applied during the project realization.

VIII. Conclusions

In this paper, the most significant differences between Agile weekly and block courses at the BSEL were presented. The combined use of all XP practices is very effective when developing Agile based-projects in these courses. Pair programming and whole team proved the most enjoyed by the students. However, students' engagement is higher in block courses because they have more time to concentrate and to participate in active learning tasks that need more time to complete. Students exploit the XP practices better when they work without interruption and when the teaching process is adapted accordingly. They are more able to improve their skills in planning and discussing, in analyzing and creating software, in evaluating and presenting results, as well as in working in teams in block courses than in weekly ones.

Since Agile's success in the software industry, it has been a constant in the CS curriculum at educational environments. Yet it is of utter importance not only how students learn Agile, but also how to teach it effectively. Teaching screenplays could help faculty in alleviating the conception and use of teaching materials. These roadmaps could describe the fine-grained learning goals of Agile teaching in detail. They proved to be very useful when used in Agile block courses.

Future work will be related to the introduction of other practices and techniques, for example from Scrum. The use of more tools to support the Agile development in the classroom is planned too. They should value individuals and interactions, working software, customer collaboration, and response to change, as Agile software development encourages.

References

[1] O. Hazzan and Y. Dubinsky, "Why software engineering programs should teach agile software development," *SIGSOFT Softw. Eng. Notes*, vol. 32, no. 2, pp. 1–3, March 2007.

[2] G. Perera, "Impact of using agile practice for student software projects in computer science education," *International Journal of Education and Development using ICT*, vol. 5, no. 3, pp. 85–100, 2009.

[3] A. Schroeder, A. Klarl, P. Mayer, and C. Kroiß, "Teaching Agile Software Development through Lab Courses," in *Proceedings of the IEEE Global Engineering Education Conference, EDUCON'2012*, Marrakesh, Morocco, April 2012, pp. 1–10.

[4] V. Razmov and R. J. Anderson, "Experiences with Agile Teaching in Project-Based Courses," in *Proceedings of the American Society for Engineering Education, ASEE Annual Conference & Exposition*, Chicago, Illinois, USA, 2006.

[5] D. Lembo and M. Vacca, "Project Based Learning + Agile Instructional Design = EXtreme Programming based Instructional Design Methodology for Collaborative Teaching," Dipartimento di Informatica e Sistemistica Antonio Ruberti, Sapienza Università di Roma, Italy, Tech. Rep. 8, 2012.

[6] , "7th Annual State of Agile Development Survey," VersionOne, Inc., Atlanta, GA, USA, Tech. Rep., 2013.

[7] J. Thomas, "A Review of Project Based Learning," Prepared for The Autodesk Foundation, San Rafael, CA, USA, Tech. Rep., 2000.

[8] A. Laitinen, "The Curious Birth and Harmful Legacy of the Credit Hour," *The Chronicle of Higher Education*, January 21 2013, available online at http://www.scoop.it/t/higher-education-and-more/curate.

[9] L. Jaccheri and S. Morasca, "On the Importance of Dialogue with Industry about Software Engineering Education," in *Proceedings of the 3rd Intl. Summit on Software Engineering Education, SSEE'2006*. New York, NY, USA: ACM, 2006, pp. 5–8.

[10] R. Conn, "Developing Software Engineers at the C-130J Software Factory," *IEEE Software*, vol. 19, no. 5, pp. 25–29, September/October 2002.

[11] A. Goldman *et al.*, "Being Extreme in the Classroom: Experiences Teaching XP," *Journal of the Brazilian Computer Society*, vol. 10, no. 2, pp. 4–20, 2004.

[12] K. Keefe and M. Dick, "Using Extreme Programming in a capstone project," in *Proceedings of the 6th Conference on Australasian Computing Education, ACE'2004*. Australian Computer Society, Inc., 2004, pp. 151–160.

[13] M. Müller and W. Tichy, "Case Study: Extreme Programming in a University Environment," in *Proceedings of the 23rd International Conference on Software Engineering, ICSE'2001*. IEEE Computer Society, 2001, pp. 537–544.

[14] A. Shukla and L. Williams, "Adapting extreme programming for a core software engineering course," in *Proceedings of the 15th Conference on Software Engineering Education and Training, CSEE&T'2002*. Covington, Kentucky, USA: IEEE Computer Society, 2002, pp. 184–191.

[15] K. Stapel, D. Lübke, and E. Knauss, "Best practices in extreme programming course design," in *Proceedings of the 30th International Conference on Software Engineering, ICSE'2008*. New York, NY, USA: ACM, 2008, pp. 769–776.

[16] E. Mentz, J. van der Walt, and L. Goosen, "The effect of incorporating cooperative learning principles in pair programming for student teachers," *Computer Science Education*, vol. 18, no. 4, pp. 247–260, December 2008.

[17] S. Xu and V. Rajlich, "Pair Programming in Graduate Software Engineering Course Projects," in *Proceedings of the 35th ASEE/IEEE Frontiers in Education Conference, ICSE'2008*. IEEE, October 2005, pp. 7–12.

[18] K. Beck *et al.*, "The Agile Manifesto," The Agile Alliance, Tech. Rep., 2001.

[19] G. Reinelt, "TSPLIB - A Traveling Salesman Problem Library," *RSA Journal on Computing*, vol. 3, pp. 376–384, 1991.

[20] S. A. Shaikh, "Participation of Female Students in Computer Science Education," *Learning and Teaching in Higher Education (LATHE): Scholarship of Inclusive Curricula*, vol. 3, pp. 93–96, 2008.

Study of Agility in Mobile Application Development

Vanessa N. Cooper and Hisham M. Haddad

Department of Computer Science
Kennesaw State University
Building 11, MD# 1101
Kennesaw, GA 30144

Abstract - Not only has Agility infiltrated enterprise and consumer mobile application development, but it has also become an integral part of most IT departments and the standard for younger generation developers. Despite the numerous benefits of Agile development, software developers often find out that there are also several pitfalls to avoid during mobile application development. In this study, we explore the potential pitfalls of incorporating agility into the development of mobile applications. The motivation behind this work stems from professional and personal experience of the primary author. As a junior software developer in the mobile application age, the primary author has experienced first-hand the demands of a "we want it now" market.

Keywords: agile development effects, mobile computing.

I. Introduction

The year is 2013. Mobile development is the hottest software skill for the youth. Social media is how everyone communicates; people now have the option to digitally share photos and daily schedules with their friends and family. Almost all software requires substantial consumer interactivity. The entire world now revolves around how quickly consumers have access to what they want. We are living in the "We Want It Now" era.

Smart, mobile devices are the fastest growing computing platform with an estimated 1.6 billion device users by the end of 2013 (compared to only 2 billion PC users) [7]. Even though the mobile industry is a massive, mobile computing is still relatively new. Since there are not many open-source mobile examples to follow many developers must quickly adapt to the environment and the ever-changing list of mobile devices and their respective operating systems. Developers have scrambled to find a suitable development methodology to accommodate for the fast-growing craze, and the Agile methodology has quickly become an industry-standard.

So why has Agility been adapted, and what exactly is agile development? Agile software development is a group of methods, which surround the idea of flexible, iterative, and incremental development with the intent to develop high quality applications. Agile development places great emphasis on scope creep and change control where changing requirements is the most faced challenge in the software industry. Furthermore, frequent and rigorous testing ensures that a high-quality product will be delivered to the consumer coupled with heavy customer involvement and short-term feedback. Ideally, Agile software development methods are good practice, allowing the construction of a highly collaborative product, and accommodate fast development with short-term feedback. That's the primary reason that many developers are now embracing agile development, especially for mobile application development.

Other reasons why most customers obsess over the constant tweaks of their mobile apps lie within the profit margin and popularity of this new craze. Figure-1 [17] shows the total number of applications and downloads over a 2-year period between June 2008 and June 2010. The growth appears to be almost exponential. Figure 2 [16] outlines some estimated figures of mobile application sales and revenue. With these statistics, it's easy to understand why businesses are rushing to brand themselves in the mobile application industry.

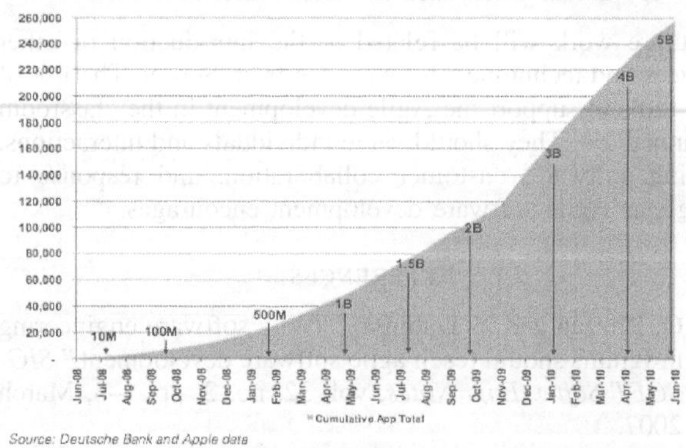

Figure-1: Growth of Mobile Applications.

The case against incorporating agile development into mobile computing does not lie within the pros and good practices but within the cons and loopholes that many consumers manipulate. When we combine the interactive nature of mobile applications, our situation becomes very slippery. Because of heavy customer involvement throughout the development process, there are often frequent changes to business needs, especially when increment results showcase unintended results. Those disappointments are quickly uncovered when customers review a demo of their increments. The idea of short cycles to complete use cases leads some to rush through development. This in turn leads to low quality software, which will require multiple sprints to complete. In addition, business investors sometimes mistake the iterative and incremental process of Agility as an opportunity to alter and negotiate new business needs. In this study, we will explore the potential pitfalls of incorporating agility into the development of mobile application.

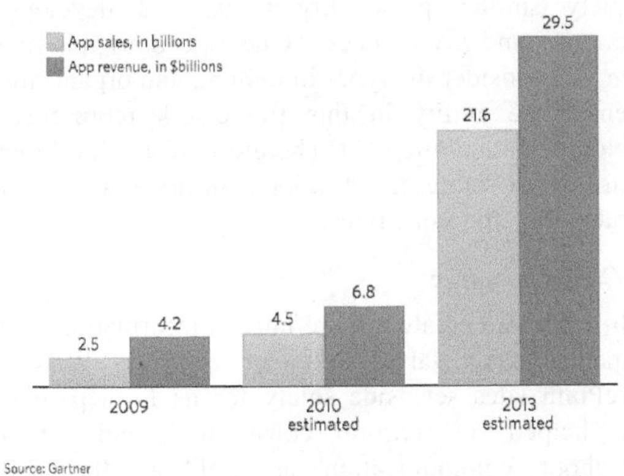

Figure-2: Sale and Revenue from Mobile Applications.

II. Agility In Mobile Computing

The problem with Agile development is the lack of quality results and experience in mobile application development despite being driven by a software development methodology. There are two main talking points related to the effects of agility in mobile computing: social issues and the development environment factors.

A. SOCIAL ISSUES

Social issues, integral part of all teams, often dictate the flow of a development environment through instruction, production, and efficiency. The immersion of technology into our daily lives has broken many culture and communication barriers among civilization, and many companies are globalizing for maximum profits. Figure-3 shows how these factors easily blend together on a social front. Here, we address the impact of social issues on mobile development.

A.1 Globalization

The integration of outsourcing into Agile is another hazard that seems to affect mostly all corporate IT departments. The primary author has interned at a few corporate companies, and each company had development teams in India. Those teams were also responsible for daily stand-ups and sprint tracking. There is a great effort on management to coordinate development teams across multiple time zones and continents. What makes project management easier across continents is the designation of project leaders for Quality Assurance (QA) and development per site. Having a project manager per site also decreases the lack of information from superiors but it also likely increases the costs dramatically. However, it is important to point out that it is still possible for a lack of information whenever you have project managers and development leads at other sites.

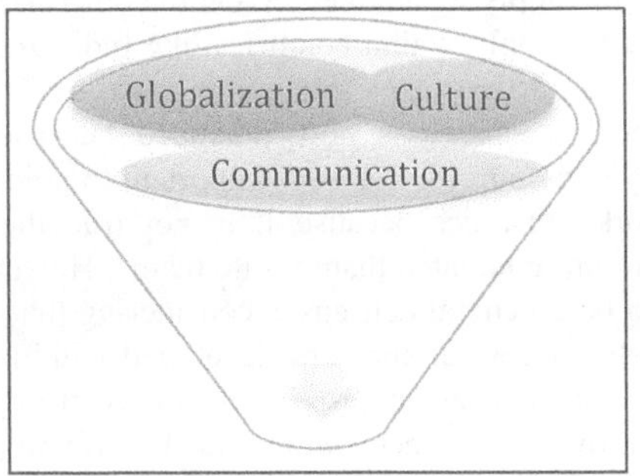

Figure-3: Social Issues.

The ability of an organization to adapt to unexpected changes is critical to achieving and maintaining a competitive advantage [15]. Outsourcing does not particularly benefit from the Agile process because of difficulties in relationship building and coordination through communication. Poor work dynamics in the workplace often lead to lower levels of trust and a lack of team effort [10]. Lower levels of trust often mean that US developers are constantly double-checking source code from other sites, and offshore sites are constantly questioning or clarifying why something is being done a certain way. Furthermore, offsite testers may attempt to test a product that caters to their own culture even when they are a very small percentage of the mobile application's users. The primary author has experienced this constant push and pull in the workplace, and it seems to be unanimous in all of the companies.

In the US, onsite location is normally seen as the main branch and the offsite location is normally known as the supplementary branch. What happens in most cases is that US developers are responsible for the bulk of software development, whereas the offsite employees perform the testing on development. This opens a multitude of issues. For one, the process of playing catch-up and getting familiar with different parts of the system can be quite time consuming and labour intensive for both onsite and offsite locations. The "training period" ends up attributing to even more meetings, which further takes away from development time. In addition, onsite and offsite employees typically use a mobile device differently. When we also consider the distance to servers and download speeds, it is easy to see how testing the mobile application can become very tedious and lacklustre in performance.

There have also been constant complaints of more thorough code reviews for source code developed by the teams in offsite locations. If this were a common occurrence, one would ask why companies continue to endure this painstaking task. Despite the high demand of software developers in the US, there is still a large shortage of supply within the US. On the other hand, there is an ample supply within countries like India and China. Whereas in earlier years, outsourcing was practiced for economical means, it is now practiced because of the necessity of resources. It is very important to point out the poor work dynamics because it is not true that onsite teams are more talented than offsite teams. However, that seems to be a general consensus considering that most of the widely successful apps are developed within the US. We believe that an improvement of work dynamics improves the general perception and the effectiveness of quality development, and that will ultimately contribute to all sites in a very positive way.

A.2 Culture

Culture is also another underestimated factor in the corporate world. In this study we focus on two subcultures: organizational culture and personal culture. Organizational culture is especially important because it lays the foundation of unspoken rules and business laws within an organization. Though some unspoken rules are not strictly enforced, it does play into the work dynamics of a group. For example, Company A may expect all software developer employees to eat lunch together on Fridays; however, this could be problematic to a software developer whom works remotely on Fridays. This affects team and relationship building within a mobile development team. Fitting into the work culture is increasing becoming just as important as the mobile software developer's skills.

Most job postings have began to list details about regular company events and desired personality traits of potential employees. These factors often dilute the options of available software developers seeking employment. Some developers also feel the pressure to fit into a particular work culture, which could ultimately negatively affect their overall work performance. By definition, Agile is a culture and approach to software development. With increasing flexibility for the customer, more restrictions and difficulties are often placed on the mobile application developers. The combination of the Agile methodology and the company dynamics often overcomplicates the simplicity of a software developer's primary function in an organization.

In discussing personal culture, one must also consider language, subcultures, and religious backgrounds. Some sites celebrated holidays that the other teams at different sites did not and this could affect the sprint in either planning or development. Though these days can be substituted, it is a clear indication of different values and customs. Cultural members always socially construct the meanings and purposes of their activities. Enculturation thus refers to gaining an implicit sense of those meanings and purposes [11]. Therefore it is very important to have a unified approach to development and the understanding of how business operations should take place within a certain environment. When you compare developers from different countries such as China, India, and the US, you must also take into account their educational systems, uniquely similar personality traits, and development experience and preferences. "One size does not fit all" when you consider the types of culture, and organizational or enterprise agility in this framework represents the developmental culture [11]. Therefore, if the development culture is not stable, the development process will surely operate along the same lines.

A.3 Communication

In efforts to create a more unified information source, companies have started to create company Wikis and SharePoint sites set aside solely for its IT departments. This helped to ensure consistency and structure throughout communication as well as the mobile application development process. Software changes, story specifications, and other guidelines could be added for quick reference. In Agile, development is done in increments and those short increments are quickly out-dated. This is very useful because the information can be easily changed, and information becomes irrelevant rather quickly. In addition to that, operating systems, standards, and features change daily in the mobile world. Incidentally, software developers are often spending a lot of their time updating Wiki's, Sharepoint sites, and other information mediums in order to keep some sense of consistency for the development team.. When you compound this with the Agile structure of daily stand-up meetings, sprint planning, and other meetings, the development is left with significantly less time for actually completing development. So, what does that mean for those whom create the services and products for consumers in a "We Want It Now" era? This means that there should be very little time between asking and receiving. This also means that consumer complaints and feedback should be quickly addressed and fixed without much delay or contemplation. Agile greatly impedes this.

B. DEVELOPMENT FACTORS

Most of us understand how a finished product or current service must be maintained by the producer in order to keep the consumer happy. However, let us also apply this same logic to a stakeholder and a software developer during the beginning stages of planning new software. Now, let's picture that the stakeholder is the consumer, and the software developer is the producer. Is it smart to handle this consumer the same as we would with a finished product? Is our decision dependent on the idea of how a service should be planned and developed, or is it based on the idea of ensuring that we also satisfy the consumer within the best of our means? Figure-4 displays the factors that must be considered when understanding how to create business agreements if Agility is a requirement.

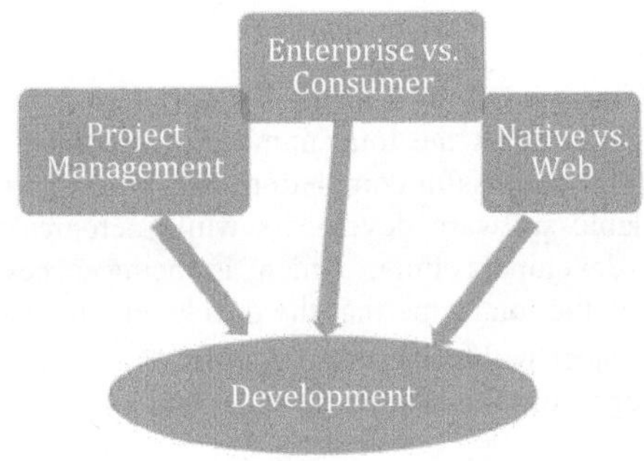

Figure-4: Development Environment.

B.1 Project Management

In the primary author's internships, she has discovered that each company also used VersionOne, which is a type of project management software catering to Agile software development. We believe that VersionOne is an excellent software utility; however, it should be noted that it is also new software that employees must learn to use properly for accurate use. It is unclear if there is a general consensus as to how that learning curve is built into the software developer's schedule. She also notes that software training is normally completed during the software developer's own desk time.

The reason we point this out is that each company normally uses a daily, 6-hour capacity rule under the Agile methodology. All of this information is tracked in VersionOne and reviewed by product management during sprint closing and retrospectives. These 6 hours are for development, testing, and documentation tasks; it does not include meetings or product training. This also means that a two-week (or 10 day work week) sprint would actually involve 1 day set aside for previous sprint closing and the current sprint planning, and the remaining 9 days would be available for actual development at 6-hours per day. A developer would then enter 54 hours for availability in their capacity for the sprint. If we consider the fact that developers are actually in office for 80 hours during that 2-week period, is it economically feasible for the company to afford the 26-hour net loss per mobile developer per week in the name of Agile?

B.2 Enterprise vs. Consumer

Most mobile applications tend to be enterprise or consumer applications. There is a huge difference between these types of applications. Consumer applications are geared toward the general public and do not have huge list of documentation; this is because developers determine which features are very valuable in the consumer market and implement those features due to the response from software releases. Great examples of mobile consumer applications would be Facebook, Twitter, and LinkedIn. All of these sites started as web interfaces and were migrated to mobile because it has become a key device for consumers. Most of these companies quickly took the corporate approach to incorporating mobile apps by attempting to brand themselves and build more personal relationships with their customers through its presence on mobile [15]. Consumer applications use a lot of prototyping procedures to ensure that the look and feel of the application flows well for the average consumer. Under Agile, the design team will complete the prototyping process before major development is began and that leaves developers with the simple task of coding all functionality for the those exposed features in the interface. In this case, agile is a great choice because of the less general development process.

On the other hand, mobile enterprise applications target businesses and corporations and require very specific user requirements. Most of these applications are related to information security, monitoring, and constant contact. Customer feedback is initiated throughout the development process rather than post-release. These types of applications are great under the Waterfall model because of its thorough documentation and unchanging requirements. Under Agile, there is a much longer development process because of constant changes made from customer feedback and many meetings despite the specifics of the documentation. For an enterprise-scale application, this could extend the development process to several years before a final product is completed. In addition, Agile can have devastating affects on the team morale and focus. Some software developers often find more excitement in working on various projects in shorter time intervals. The Agile approach leads architects to plan for the quickest solution rather than a long-term, more sustainable approach. Though code may be developed quicker, it is also more prone to security issues and inconsistent results and will hence require more changes over the life of the product as well as development.

B.3 Native vs. Web

When you consider all of these factors, companies must consider how much they are willing to invest in third-party software as well as the learning curve for new mobile application developers in a native platform environment. Even though most companies expect for developers to "hit the ground running", they must be very realistic about skill level, the number of available software developers, and the overall budget of a mobile application. In addition, with third party software, features are less likely to change per release of the native OS, and this can often quickly outdate a mobile application. Table-1 outlines the development and social issues which occur during the use of Agility in mobile computing.

Social Issues	• Personal culture impact on development • Poor work dynamics in the workplace • Consistent and unified information
Development Factors	• Very restrictive project management • Lack of fixed user requirements • Lack of available software developers • Choosing the wrong development platform

Table-1: Social Issues and Development Factors.

Another important concept is to understand the importance of the chosen platform when considering Agile. During the rush to create mobile applications, most companies also have begun to realize the huge shortage of mobile application developers well versed in object-oriented programming languages such as C++, Java, and Objective-C. For native mobile applications, iOS uses Objective-C, Android uses Java, and Windows Phone uses C++. Native platform development allows for better performance, seamless user interfaces, and it is great for branding. However, with more options and being free of a standard cross-platform API, it means that developers are option expected to do more but in the same amount of time. For very experienced mobile application developers, this may not be a huge problem. The key thing to remember is that there is a very large shortage of experienced developers, and there is also much more demand than available supply for mobile application developers overall.

However, there are certainly several web developers available to increase their skill sets in order to remain valuable in this sifting market. Since the third party software normally requires JavaScript or HTML, it doesn't does require much of a learning curve for web developers delving into the software development world. This has sparked a large market for web-based, cross-platform software kits. The names PhoneGap and Titanium Studio are very familiar to companies whom want a quick and dirty mobile application to get their mobile branding kicking. Though there is a higher cost of the software and tools for development through third party software, it also offers a quicker turnover rate for development for most companies. Mobile applications, developed under a web-based platform, work great with the Agile development process, mainly because of the limited amount of choices. With cross-platform software, you don't have as many options and the mobile applications tend to be very simple. From a developer standpoint, it could be viewed as a relief because it reduces the likelihood of "changing requirements" under Agile development.

III. MATHEMATICAL MODEL

The main factors to consider in the mathematical model are the social and development issues. Both of these impact the timeline and budget of a mobile application development project. My formula uses money and time to determine if Agile is worthwhile pursuit for project management and developers. If the total result is negative, then Agile should be avoided; however, if the final result is positive, then Agile should not have any detrimental effects on the project and the development phase.

In Figure-5 below, t denotes a sprint in a particular project. N denotes the total number of projected sprints required for successful completion. X denotes the number of available software developers while c represents the current developers time, which is being accessed. P represents the total time that the developer can contribute to the project within the current sprint. $\propto$ represents the total budget for the software development project.

$$\propto + \sum_{t=0}^{n} \sum_{c=0}^{x} p$$

Figure-5: Determining Agility feasibility.

Though this formula seems simple and straightforward, it is often ignored for the sake of creating a highly customizable, customer friendly type application. Even though that it is the ultimate goal of delivery satisfaction, it ignores the necessity for standards and documentation to guide project managers and software developers.

IV. DISCUSSION

Since we cannot operate without some type of structure, we must also consider if there is a more suitable methodology for software development. Surprising, Agility is not a new approach to software development; it's just that newer programming generations are being rapidly exposed to the methodology. Another thing to consider is the difference in the business world. Simply put, most companies have 'learned their lessons' from the old way of doing things and are desperately seeking for a better way of doing things. "Early software projects were late, over budget, and had low quality". [8]. So naturally, companies have diverted their focus to on-time, under budget, and higher quality software. In order for them to determine if a product meets all of the above, then heavy involvement is necessary throughout the entire planning and development of their software.

A. Waterfall vs Agile

There are two other priorities that can wreak havoc for a mobile development team: the second principle on welcome changing and the agile manifesto statement on "Responding to change over following a plan". Business investors sometimes mistake the iterative and incremental process of Agile development as an opportunity to alter and negotiate new business needs. This is a problem if the new business need is drastically different from the original plan. Before Agile development, there was primarily the Waterfall Model. In the Waterfall model, there were "well-defined phases" [3]. Since the Waterfall Model was a sequential, the "requirements were expected to be clear before going to the next phase of design" [2]. Under the Waterfall method, most consumers felt trapped and were forced to commit to the documentation before development. Under Agile, the consumer now has the option to change requirements and documentation, even if it occurred in the last stages. In the Waterfall model, the "rigid structure" ensured that the "quality of the project was maintained" [2]. Though Agile claims, "working software is the primary measure of progress", it does not address the need for high-quality software.

B. Globalization

Unfortunately, more problems arise when more people are involved. Multiple working styles, work schedules, and opinions weigh into this fact; the complexity of satisfying every single person becomes a constant struggle. In mobile application development, one person may swipe the screen for a specific function, whereas another individual may quickly tap. Incorporating more functionalities and options dependent upon user touch quickly adds to the mountain of problems already persistent in any software development project.

C. Continuously Changing Requirements

Another significant argument is that the lack of commitment during planning will ultimately disrupt the development process through numerous changes. Overhead and continuous changes will always be prominent problems when using Agile methodology in mobile computing. This is definitely a problem when stakeholders favour flexible and ever-changing requirements, whereas the developer requires a more structured and detailed approach. When developers are required to constantly tweak or re-design a use case requirement, they may never proceed to the next requirement. When stakeholders fail to see progress, the developer may appear to be wasting time versus actually spending unnecessary time on changed requirements that should have finalized beforehand. Using Figure-5's formula, one can calculate the project failure caused by the addition of sprints caused by continuous changes.

D. Lack of Documentation

Agility also requires short development cycles; this is mandated through the priority of "working software over comprehensive documentation". Unfortunately, this also causes most to rush through development by producing modules of the system rather than focusing on the system as a whole according to the missing comprehensive documentation. Ultimately, this also increases the likelihood of low quality software. If this is the case, then why is there a need to rush in adopting the Agile methodology into software development? The answer to that question can be further explored by reviewing the Twelve Principles of Agile Software shown in Table-2 [1].

1. Our highest priority is to satisfy the consumer through early and continuous delivery of valuable software.
2. Welcome changing requirements, even late in development. Agile processes harness change for the consumer's competitive advantage.
3. Deliver working software frequently, from a couple of weeks to a couple of months, with a preference to the shorter timescale.
4. Business people and
5. The most efficient and effective method of developers must work together daily throughout the project.
6. Build projects around motivated individuals. Give them the environment and support they need, and trust them to get the job done.
7. conveying information to and within a development team is face-to-face conversation.
8. Working software is the primary measure of progress.
9. Agile processes promote sustainable development. The sponsors, developers, and users should be able to maintain a constant pace indefinitely.
10. Continuous attention to technical excellence and good design enhances agility.
11. Simplicity--the art of maximizing the amount of work not done--is essential.
12. The best architectures, requirements, and designs emerge from self-organizing teams.
13. At regular intervals, the team reflects on how to become more effective, then tunes and adjusts its behaviour accordingly.

Table-2: Agile Principles.

E. Prototyping vs. Development

Understanding the difference between prototyping and development is also essential for determining if Agile should be used for mobile application development. Since prototyping is technically apart of the planning process, then it should definitely be done beforehand to appropriately distribute the workload for developers and allow focus on actual requirements. Some customers have taken it upon themselves to focus more on the "look and feel" rather than the core functionality. Though both are very important, one must understand the actual process of prototyping so that it does not delay actual software development. During most mobile application development projects, a developer will attempt to demonstrate a core function of the application through incremental development. Most customers respond to these changes as rapid throwaway prototyping results because of the relatively short two to three week increment cycles. Prototypes are "instruments" [9], and they are not products or components of the software product.

F. General Consensus

Without sounding negative, the authors think of Agile software development as being the parent that desperately seeks to win over their children by not teaching them about delayed gratification. The explanation may be somewhat exaggerated, but many software developers are now being forced to accept these realities. The main argument against Agile methods is the asserted lacks of scientific validation for associated activities and practices, as well as the difficulty of integrating plan-based practices with Agile ones [6]. Table-3 outlines the discussed pitfalls of using Agility in mobile application development.

Agile Pitfalls:
• Lack of fixed user requirements lead to constant changes and tweaks during development. • Confusion between mobile app prototyping and development. • Globalization introduces many culture and communication problems during development. • Project management tends to micromanage development time

Table-3: Issues with Agility in Mobile Computing.

V. Conclusion

Despite the numerous downloads and high profits made in the mobile industry, we must also ask ourselves if Agile-driven software is better software. We must also ask if the standard of quality software has also changed with the change in generation. Sturdy code functionality is being replaced every day by user-friendly, pretty functionality. The usability factor seems to be the only extreme positive in favour of incorporating Agility into mobile application software development. As we have discussed in our findings, using Agility in mobile computing is a very slippery slope. The fast-paced development is definitely desired for the "we want it now" era, but the pitfalls greatly outweigh the long-term effects on the development process.

References

[1] T. Way, S. Chandrasekhar, and A. Murthy. The Agile Research Penultimatum. Software Engineering Research and Practice, CSREA Press, (2009), page 530-536.

[2] S. Balaji and M. Murugaiyan, Waterfall Vs V-Model Vs Agile: A Comparative Study. International Journal of Information Technology and Business Management, June 2012, Volume 2, Number 1, page 26-30

[3] B. Madhu, M. Jigalur, and V. Lokesha, A Study on Agile Software Testing: Emergence and techniques. African Journal of Mathematics and Computer Science Research. Volume 3 Number 11, page 288 - 289

[4] P. Maher and J. Kourik, Agile Software Development in Evolving Business Environments: Integrating Modern Techniques into Computer Science Curricula. ASBBS Annual Conference: Las Vegas. February 2011, Volume 18 Number 1, page 248-254

[5] G. Galal-Edeen and M. Seyam, Traditional versus Agile: The Tragile Framework for Information Systems Development.

[6] A. Spataur. Agile Development Methods for Mobile Applications. (2010).

[7] J. Dehlinger and J. Dixon, Mobile Application Software Engineering: Challenges and Research Directions. (2011).

[8] R. Shriver and D. Birckhead, Delivery Business Value with Lean and Agile. Dominion Digital.

[9] B. Boehm, T. Gray, and T. Seewaldt, T. Prototyping vs. Specifying: A Multi-Project Experiment. IEEE Transactions on Software Engineering Volume 10 Issue 3, May 1984, page 290-302

[10] S. Chinbat and A. Agahi, Lessons Learned in Virtual Teams from Global Software Development. (2010).

[11] J. Iivari and N. Iivari, The relationship between organizational culture and the deployment of agile methods. In Special Section on Best Papers from XP2010, Information and Software Technology. Volume 53 Issue 5, page 509-520

[12] D. Batra. Modified Agile Practices for Outsourced Software Projects. Communications of the ACM. Sep2009, Volume 52 Issue 9, page 143-148.

[13] A. Ganguly, R. Nilchiani, and J. Farr, Evaluating agility in corporate enterprises. International Journal of Production Economics. Volume 118 Issue 2, page 410-423.

[14] D. Fernandez and J. Fernandez, Agile Project Management – Agilism versus Traditional Approaches. Journal of Computer Information Systems. Winter2008/2009, Volume 49 Issue 2, page 10-17.

[15] V. Jyothi and R. Nageswara Rao, Effective Implementation of Agile Practices – Incoordination with Lean Kanban. International Journal on Computer Science & Engineering. Jan2012, Volume 4 Issue 1, page 87-91.

[16] C. Foresman. Apple responsible for 99.4$ of mobile app sales in 2009. http://arstechnica.com/apple/2010/01/apple-responsible-for-994-of-mobile-app-sales-in-2009/

[17] AB Mobile Apps. Developing a Mobile Application for Small Business. http://www.abmobileapps.com/developing-a-custom-mobile-application-for-a-small-business/

A Model-Based Agile Process for DO-178C Certification

David J. Coe and Jeffrey H. Kulick
Department of Electrical and Computer Engineering
University of Alabama in Huntsville, Huntsville, Alabama, USA

Abstract - *Increasing complexity has driven aerospace companies to consider the use of Agile processes for development of safety-critical systems. For other domains, Agile processes have been shown to improve cost, schedule, and quality metrics. Airworthiness certification under the Federal Aviation Administration (FAA) guidelines imposes unique challenges that require adaptation of Agile processes. The FAA's mission is maintaining safety within the National Air Space, and the certification process that the FAA has adopted is a process-oriented standard RTCA DO-178C. Here we present a Model-Based Agile Process (MBA process) that will allow companies to benefit from some of the efficiencies inherent in Agile methods while maintaining compliance with airworthiness certification requirements. Model-based requirements capture using the Unified Modeling Language (UML) facilitates iterative and incremental capture, refinement, and verification of requirements using executable requirements models, maintaining the Agility of the requirements elicitation process.*

Keywords: RTCA DO-178C, RTCA DO-331, Model-Based Agile Process, MBA Process, safety critical systems

1 Motivation

Modern aircraft have become increasingly dependent upon computers for control of critical functions including engines, brakes, flight controls, navigation, and communications. The F-35 Joint Strike Fighter has approximately 9.5 million lines of code on board and a total of 24 millions lines of code for this system [1]. Late software releases for the F-35 have resulted in delays in testing, training, and delivery, and they have contributed to cost overruns. While delays and overruns have been common in the development of complex military systems, increased hardware and software complexity is also appearing in civilian aircraft systems.

The Boeing 787 Dreamliner is an example of a civilian aircraft that is projected to have over 6 million lines of code with major subsystems such as engines, flaps, and landing gear all incorporating network connections that will allow engineers to log half a terabyte of data per flight [2-3]. The added capabilities and complexity have resulted in significant cost with software development and integration issues resulting in delivery delays and reports of over 200,000 hours expended during the Federal Aviation Administration (FAA) airworthiness certification effort not counting the recent battery fire issues [4-5].

To cope with cost, schedule, and quality issues, the aerospace industry has started to explore the use of Agile methodologies for the development of safety-critical aerospace software systems. Agile processes offer a number of advantages in comparison to traditional Waterfall-based methods including higher quality, lower cost, higher productivity, and improved schedule performance [6]. An open question has been the compatibility of Agile methods with the FAA airworthiness certification process. Below we discuss the airworthiness certification process, principles of Agile development and the potential conflicts with the certification process, and our modified Agile process that addresses the areas of concern.

2 Airworthiness Certification

The FAA currently utilizes the RTCA DO-178C standard for certification of airborne software [7]. Rather than mandating a particular process, DO-178C requires that any development process used for airborne software satisfy a list of process-oriented objectives, with the specific subset of required process objectives dictated by the criticality of the software to safe operation of the aircraft. Some examples of DO-178C process objectives include end-to-end traceability, change control and configuration management, and requirements-based testing.

A safety analysis process is used to determine the criticality of the software's function in the context of the overall system. It is important to note that safety is an emergent property of the system as whole, and that

Table 1 – Design Assurance Levels and DO-178C Process Objectives [7,10]

Category	Failure Condition Description	Design Assurance Level (DAL)	Number of Required DO-178C Process Objectives
Catastrophic	Failure condition results in multiple fatalities with probable loss of aircraft	A	71/30
Severe	Failure condition would significantly reduce the ability of the crew and/or aircraft capabilities required to compensate for adverse operating conditions	B	69/18
Major	Failure condition would reduce the ability of the crew and/or aircraft capabilities needed to compensate for adverse operating conditions	C	62/5
Minor	Failure condition has no significant impact on safety margins or crew workload	D	26/2
No Safety Effect	Failure condition has no impact on safety	E	0/0

the safety of a component cannot be established outside of the context of its use [8]. Thus, system-level requirements are an input to the safety analysis process. While no particular safety process is mandated, SAE ARP4761 is an example of a commonly used safety process that includes Functional Hazard Analysis (FHA), Fault Tree Analysis (FTA), Failure Modes and Effects Analysis (FMEA), and Common Cause Analysis (CCA) [9].

Two key results emerge from the safety analysis process. First, the safety analysis establishes the Design Assurance Level (DAL), which dictates the specific DO-178C process objectives that must be satisfied by the software development process and the level of rigor that must be demonstrated for each objective. The safety analysis also identifies safety requirements that the software product itself must demonstrably satisfy as part of the verification process. As summarized in Table 1, the number of required process objectives that must be demonstrated dramatically increases from DAL E up to DAL A as does the number of the objectives requiring independence. In Table 1, xx/yy indicates that xx objectives must be satisfied with yy of them satisfied with independence.

Designated Engineering Representatives (DERs) are the FAA's embedded representatives within the development teams. DERs are in a unique position in that they represent the FAA while being paid by the company developing the product. The role of the DER is to use their engineering background and aviation safety certification experience to provide feedback to the team regarding the team's compliance with DO-178C. The DER also interacts directly with the FAA to facilitate the certification process.

3 Agile Development Principles and Airworthiness Certification

As shown in Table 2, the term Agile development encompasses a family of processes that embrace a common set of core principles enumerated by the Agile Manifesto [11]. Examples of commonly used Agile processes include Scrum and Extreme Programming. Below we briefly examine potential sources of conflict between the principles of Agile development and DO-178C certification requirement

Table 2 – Guiding principles of Agile development versus DO-178C principles [11].

Agile principle	DO-178C principle
Individuals and Interactions	Processes and Tools
Working Software	Comprehensive Documentation
Evolving Requirements via Customer Collaboration	Rigorous Requirements Specification
Responding to Change	Following a Plan

3.1 Individuals and Interactions versus Processes and Tools

Agile processes emphasize face-to-face communication as the best way to convey information. No rigorous process is outlined for the method of communication nor are there any requirements to capture the result of the communication. Components may be added or deleted at any time without an impact analysis as to what the addition or deletion will have to already existing software.

DO-178C, however, requires clear commitments to processes and tools. The very first step in a DO-178C project is the PSAC – Plan for Software Aspects of Certification. This detailed plan outlines the roles of other plans and processes in the certification process. For each tool used the level of quality of the tool must be examined, particularly if the output will not be subsequently inspected such as by peer review [12]. For example, a tool that verifies the output is correct and agrees with regression runs, must itself be developed to the same level of rigor as the system itself. In other words, a DAL A product requires a DAL A tool if the outputs of the tool are trusted without verification.

3.2 Working Software versus Comprehensive Documentation

Proponents of Agile processes believe that working software is the best documentation of product requirements and design, and that it is also the best measure of progress. Alternatively, in Waterfall development, artifacts such as Software Requirements Specification and Software Design Documents must be maintained throughout the development lifecycle otherwise the information contained within such artifacts may begin to diverge significantly from the actual product, thereby reducing the end value of the documentation artifacts to future maintenance and enhancement efforts. For certification under DO-178C, however, the development team must demonstrate that the required subset of process objectives has been satisfied.

Failure to maintain adequate documentation of compliance with process objectives can lead to costly delays, even when the software is working error free. For example, the FAA requires documentation that shows end-to-end traceability for DAL A through DAL D software. End-to-end traceability means that a requirement must be forwards/backwards traceable through the design, the source code, the object code, and the associated requirements-derived tests. Delivery of the Airbus A400M military transport was delayed due to a subcontractor's inability to demonstrate artifact traceability for the aircraft's full authority digital engine controller to the European Aviation Safety Agency (EASA) [13]. While the EASA aircraft certification process is different than the FAA process, both agencies require traceability.

3.3 Evolving Requirements via Customer Collaboration versus Rigorous Requirements Specification

Agile methods emphasize customer collaboration as the best means of eliciting product requirements. Requirements documents do a poor job of capturing product requirements in no small part because the majority of customer requirements knowledge is internal, never documented information that may emerge in the form of new requirements when a customer gets to see and interact with an implementation of the product [14]. In addition, requirements specifications for complex systems may entail thousands of potentially conflicting requirements that are elicited over extended periods of time, in some cases years. In an ideal Agile development scenario, the customer works closely with the development team in an iterative fashion to identify, prioritize, and refine product requirements and to develop a set of acceptance tests that will be used to verify successful implementation of those requirements by the end of each increment. By delivering working, tested software frequently, Agile processes have a tremendous advantage with their ability to elicit early feedback from the customer.

For applications subject to DO-178C certification, the iterative nature of Agile requirements elicitation impacts the safety analysis process. The safety analysis process requires as an input a rigorous requirements specification. Early and accurate determination of the DAL is critical since it determines the process objectives that must be satisfied for airworthiness certification. For example, Modified Condition/Decision Coverage (MC/DC) testing using requirements-derived tests is required only for DAL A software. Late determination that the software must be developed to DAL A standards may mean that insufficient schedule and budget remain to satisfy the additional process objectives associated with DAL A.

3.4 Responding to Change versus Following a Plan

Planning activities are part of Agile processes with the most detailed plans constructed just for the next increment. This is necessary because of the iterative nature of Agile requirements elicitation. It allows for great adaptability since the periodic re-planning activity gives the customer the opportunity to add, delete, modify, or reprioritize requirements.

Extensive planning, however, is a key element required for DO-178C certification. Project planning begins with completion of the Plan for Software Aspects of Certification (PSAC). The PSAC document is a comprehensive plan that states in detail how the development teams plans to approach development of the product to achieve all required process objectives. In addition to the PSAC, more detailed supporting planning artifacts are required including a Software Development Plan, a Software Verification Plan, a Software Configuration Management Plan, and a Software Quality Assurance Plan.

4 Model-Based Engineering and DO-178C Airworthiness Certification

The FAA recently adopted several new supplements to DO-178C to address certification issues related to *model-based engineering*, *object-oriented technologies*, *formal methods* and *tool qualification*. Model-based methodologies are of great concern to the FAA because it is unclear what role any simulation results derived from the models should play in the determination of airworthiness. The believability of the simulation results is in part a function of the fidelity of the model to the actual system. Models, however, can be constructed at different levels of abstraction to capture high-level requirements or various aspects of the architectural design, for example.

The certification of products developed using model-based methodologies is discussed extensively in RTCA DO-331, the recently released model-based development supplement to RTCA DO-178C [15]. DO-331 does provide some flexibility in how model-based methodologies may be used. A specification model may be used to explore the consistency and correctness of the modeled requirements. A design model may be used to verify various architectural details. It is acceptable to include a specification model with no design model, a design model with no specification model, both a specification model and a design model, or neither type of model (i.e. use no model-based methods).

DO-331 does provides a substantial opportunity to introduce Agile methods by distinctly separating the requirements processes and artifacts from the design process and artifacts by *mandating* that any specification model be distinct from any design model that is used for certification. As a result of this separation, any model from which delivered code was synthesized is considered a design model, not a specification model. DO-331 also stipulates that all top-level requirements must be in textual form.

5 The Model-Based Agile Process (MBA)

We propose a new software development process that combines key advantages of both agile development processes and model-based engineering methodologies to produce a Model-Based Agile (MBA) process capable of satisfying FAA-mandated process objectives for software of all Design Assurance Levels. A key element of the MBA Process is the use of an Agile-style iterative and incremental approach to requirements elicitation, capture, and verification. Provided that an appropriate modeling tool is used that admits executable specification models (again, DO-331 forbids synthesizing deliverable code from specification models), one can start by developing use cases and iteratively refine them into executable models. These executable models will bring to bear the advantages of agile requirements elicitation while facilitating the complete capture of a set of requirements for a system before the detailed design and testing is begun.

As with a traditional agile process, the development team works closely with the customer to identify requirements and to develop acceptance tests that will be used to verify the correctness of the requirements as captured in the specification model. The acceptance tests are executed on the specification model, and the results used to verify correctness, completeness, and consistency of the specifications. It should be understood that the test cases used to exercise and test the requirements model would most likely not be directly applicable to any subsequent design model without substantial refinement due to their lack of detail. For example, messages might only contain message types for exercising the specification model while design model messages will require detailed values in the message body for exercising any design model.

For the MBA Process, we propose the use of a Unified Modeling Language (UML) tool such as IBM's Rhapsody to capture these requirements as they emerge from face-to-face interactions with the customer. Requirements capture via UML has been shown to be an effective means of communicating requirements information among stakeholders. Moreover, the Rhapsody tool allows the construction of executable UML models using non-synthesizable components of UML such as sequence diagrams. Commercial UML tools such as Rhapsody also provide interfaces to industry standard textual requirements management tools such as IBM's DOORS. This allows the developers to maintain traceability from the top-level textual requirements to the specification model as mandated by the FAA.

In our MBA process, the initial iterations are focused only on eliciting, capturing, and refining requirements for input into the safety analysis process. Once the customer and the team are satisfied that all requirements have been identified and verified, the safety analysis is performed to determine the DAL and identify any safety requirements. The safety requirements are integrated into the UML specification model and verified during the next iteration. A test coverage analysis on the model can be performed to ensure adequate testing of the specification model to the required DAL. Since only design models can be used for code generation, future iterations will focus primarily on implementation of the captured requirements.

As with our previous modifications to the requirements elicitation process to enable agile development of safety critical systems, the design process may be similarly modified to accommodate construction of the optional design model, if desired. The forced separation of specification models and design models permits the use a different modeling tool for the design model including one that is more amenable to code synthesis and formal verification, if desired. Once the textural requirements and specification model are completed, then the implementation of the requirements can proceed piecemeal with testing and verification of each unit, component, subsystem, and system in turn.

6 Impacts of the MBA Process on Certification

The first part of the safety process, which occurs primarily during the requirements phase, is the functional hazard analysis. This process is applied to the aircraft functions, not to the components design, which has not taken place at this time. The proposed agile requirements process can be extended to permit incremental functional hazard analysis as subsystem components are elicited. Since no design is taking place at this time, the safety processes that follow design processes, such as FEMA, will not be done prematurely.

Concomitantly, if the design proceeds using agile processes, it is possible, but not as clear, that incremental FMEA and FTA analysis will be possible. The problem is that analysis at this level is intended to generate additional safety requirements, if necessary, and these probably should not be developed piecemeal. However, development within a given component or subsystem may be made small enough so that incremental FMEA and FTA analysis is possible.

One must also keep in mind that DO-331 also stipulates additional required process objectives specific to model-based methodologies that include verification of simulation cases (scenarios), simulation procedures, and simulation results with explanation of any discrepancies for both specification models and design models if present. The decision to use model-based methodologies impacts other process objectives as well. For example, if both a specification model and a design model are developed, one must establish forwards/backwards traceability starting with the top-level text requirement through the specification model, design model, source code, object code, and requirements derived tests. Configuration management and change control must be extended to include the modeling and simulation tools themselves and the set of tool configuration options selected.

7 Conclusions

The proposed Model-Based Agile process should facilitate the use of agile methodologies in the development of safety-critical systems. Moreover, the MBA process was developed specifically to be compatible with the FAA-accepted RTCA DO-178C airworthiness certification standard for airborne software and the RTCA DO-331 model-based engineering supplement. Given the relatively recent release of DO-178C and DO-331, it remains to be seen what consensus will emerge among practicing DERs as to what evidence will be considered an acceptable demonstration of satisfying the model-based engineering process objectives when it comes to certification of an actual aircraft.

To validate the MBA process, the authors are currently planning on developing a small safety critical system, such as an Unmanned Aerial System and ground controller, using this Model-Based Agile process to produce the artifacts necessary for FAA certification. This work will be conducted in collaboration with local DERs to ensure that acceptability of the process and process artifacts to a practicing DER.

8 References

[1] Michael J. Sullivan, "JOINT STRIKE FIGHTER: Restructuring Added Resources and Reduced Risk, but Concurrency Is Still a Major Concern", GAO-12-525T, Tuesday, March 20, 2012.

[2] Robert N. Charette, "This Car Runs on Code", IEEE Spectrum online, posted February 2009, http://spectrum.ieee.org/green-tech/advanced-cars/this-car-runs-on-code

[3] Matthew Finnegan, "Boeing 787s to Create Half a Terabyte of Data per Flight, Says Virgin Atlantic", *Computerworld UK*, Published 14:27, 06 March 13, http://www.computerworlduk.com/news/infrastructure/3433595/boeing-787s-create-half-terabyte-of-data-per-flight-says-virgin-atlantic/

[4] Bloomberg Business Magazine, "The 787 Encounters Turbulence", posted June 18, 2006, http://www.businessweek.com/stories/2006-06-18/the-787-encounters-turbulence

[5] W.J. Hennigan, "Boeing Dreamliner to undergo federal safety review", *Los Angeles Times*, 11 Jan. 2013, http://articles.latimes.com/2013/jan/12/business/la-fi-boeing-dreamliner-review-20130112

[6] David F. Rico, "What is the ROI of Agile vs. Traditional Methods? An analysis of XP, TDD, Pair Programming, and Scrum (Using Real Options)", http://davidfrico.com/rico08gpdf.htm

[7] RTCA DO-178C, "Software Considerations in Airborne Systems and Equipment Certification", December 13, 2011.

[8] Nancy G. Leveson, *Safeware: System Safety and Computers*, Addison-Wesley, Boston, 1995, p. 151.

[9] SAE ARP4761, "Guidelines and Methods for Conducting the Safety Assessment Process on Civil Airborne Systems and Equipment", Issued 1996-12.

[10] SAE ARP4754, "Certification Considerations for Highly-Integrated or Complex Aircraft Systems", Issued 1996-11

[11] Agile Manifesto, viewed March 14, 2013, http://agilemanifesto.org

[12] RTCA DO-330, "Software Tool Qualification Considerations", Issued December 13, 2011.

[13] Craig Hoyle, *Flight International*, 8 May 2009, http://www.flightglobal.com/news/articles/europrop-boss-reveals-origins-of-a400m-engine-crisis-326189/

[14] David F. Rico, "Why Agile Methods Work in Lieu of Big Up Front Requirements, Architectures, and Designs", http://davidfrico.com/agile-requirementspdf.htm

[15] RTCA DO-331, "Model-Based Development and Verification Supplement to DO-178C and DO-278A", December 13, 2011.

IEEE std 829-2008 and Agile Process– Can They Work Together?

Ning Chen

Department of Computer Science, California State University, Fullerton, California, USA

Abstract - IEEE **Standard for software and system test documentation** (i.e., IEEE std 829-2008) is a comprehensive guide that specifies a common framework for planning the testing activities. The agile process is known for its promotion of frequent delivery of working software over comprehensive documentation and responding to change over following a plan. Although the IEEE std 829-2008 has strong association with the traditional waterfall development process, it does offer flexibility that allows user to combine or eliminate some of the test documentation content topics. Furthermore, it does not prohibit short-term and incremental planning. The underlining philosophies of the test standard and agile process are not at odd. This paper attempts to investigate whether they can be married and work together to great effect.

Keywords: IEEE std 829-2008, Agile

1 Introduction

One measurement of the importance of testing is the cost associated with it. Some industry survey reveals that between 30 and 50 percent of the cost of development is spent on testing [1]. Since any modification of the software, even a simple change, may inadvertently break the whole software, testing will not stop even after the end of the development. For this reason alone, having quality test documents during and after the development phase to support testing activities becomes essential. Instead of inventing quality test documents, one can easily find templates from IEEE std 829-2008 [2] that offers a general framework for needed test documents. Professionals coming from traditional waterfall development camp embrace IEEE std 829-2008 wholeheartedly due to the fact that the standard indeed has a deep root in the waterfall community. Time moves on and nowadays, agile process with a philosophy of working software over extensive documentation comes into the picture [3]. The arrival of agile stirs up two important questions. The first question is that do we still need to have standard test documents when using agile as the development and testing process? If the answer for the first question is affirmative, we have a follow-up question on hand– can IEEE std 829-2008 and agile development/testing process work together? This paper starts with a review of IEEE std 829-2008 and agile development and testing process. An analysis and comparison of IEEE std 829-2008 and Agile is followed. Our answer to the question we raised is affirmative. We, then, propose a way of integrating IEEE std 829-2008 to a variant of agile (Scrum) with some insights we contemplated. The paper ends with a conclusion section that summaries with our findings, insights and suggestions.

2 What is IEEE 829-2008?

We start our discussion on IEEE829-2008 with one of its main goals of "establish(ing) a common framework for test processes, activities, and tasks in support of all software life cycle processes, including acquisition, supply, development, operation, and maintenance Processes." [2] As we noted in the introduction, the goal of establishing a common framework for test processes, activities, and tasks is the key that motives us to see whether this common framework can work with the agile development and testing process. The standard comes with 132 pages in length and is not that easy to comprehend. We feel that the entry point of unwrapping this not-so-small document is the understanding of the consequence-based integrity level scheme promoted by the standard. The standard says that there are four integrity levels:

Level 4–Catastrophic
Level 3–Critical
Level 2–Marginal
Level 1–Negligible

The descriptions of level are:

Level 4 (Catastrophic) -Software must execute correctly or grave consequences (loss of life, loss of system, environmental damage, economic or social loss) will occur. No mitigation is possible.

Level 3 (Critical) - Software must execute correctly or the intended use (mission) of system/software will not be realized causing serious consequences (permanent injury, major system degradation, environmental damage, economic or social impact). Partial-to-complete mitigation is possible.

Level 2 (Marginal) – Software must execute correctly or an intended function will not be realized causing minor consequences. Complete mitigation possible.

Level 1 (Negligible) - Software must execute correctly or intended function will not be realized causing negligible consequences. Mitigation not required.

Most readers will not have any difficulty on accepting this consequence-based integrity level scheme, after all, the descriptions are very easy to understand and they are quite reasonable and acceptable. In terms of what documents are required at each level, the standard says that:

Level 4: 10 test documents
Level 3: 10 test documents
Level 2: 8 test documents
Level 1: 7 test documents

It is a bit surprising to see that there is not too huge difference between levels. No difference (counting number of documents) between Level 4 and Level 3. The main difference between Level 3 and Level 2 is the adding of two so-called Master Test Plan and Master Test Report. The adding of the master plan and report probably is due to the desire to give stakeholders some long-term (in the context of time) and global (in the context of scope) view and awareness of what's going on. The difference between Level 2 and Level 1 is the adding of a so-called Level Interim Test Status Report. The adding of the interim report most likely is driven by the idea that the stakeholders may need to know the status of the project more frequently (shorter time period). Although the small difference as the level goes up is a bit unusual, the increased frequency of reporting and the more long-term planning and broader view as level goes up are quite expected.

What are those 10 documents (maximum number for Level 3 and 4)? The standard specifies the following:

Master Test Plan (MTP)
Level Test Plan (LTP)
Level Test Design (LTD)
Level Test Case (LTC)
Level Test Procedure (LTPr)
Level Test Log (LTL)
Anomaly Report (AR)
Level Interim Test Status Report (LITSR)
Level Test Report (LTR)
Master Test Report (MTR).

All users of the standard have no problem on forming an intuitive understanding of the term "plan, design, case, procedure, log, and report." The term "master" is also quite straightforward. The only curiosity one may have is on the definition of "level." What is the definition of the term "level"? Is it related to the term "integrity level" in some way? A careful reader of the standard may soon find the following:

(T)he word "Level" is replaced by the organization's name for the particular level being documented by the plan (e.g., Component Test Plan, Component Integration Test Plan, System Test Plan, and Acceptance Test Plan).

After further readings, a reader may encounter the following:

Other possible examples of levels include operations, installation, maintenance, regression, and nonfunctional levels such as security, usability, performance, stress, and recovery. Any one of the example levels may be more than one level for an organization; e.g., Acceptance testing may be two levels: Supplier's System and User's Acceptance test levels.

At this point, most of the readers of the standard can easily come to the following realizations:

1. We are not talking about 10 documents – it actually is 10 different *kinds* of documents. Depending on the actual project (and the replacement of the term Level by other terms such as Component, Integration, System, and Acceptance), the total number of documents may easily explodes.

2. For those who are familiar with the V model shown in Fig. 1 [4], they may immediately feel that IEEE829-2008 maps to the V model almost perfectly. For example, in the V-model, it talks about Unit (component) testing, Integration testing, System testing and Acceptance testing that mirror to the Level Test Plan/Design/Case/Procedure/Log/Report mentioned in the IEEE 829-2008 directly.

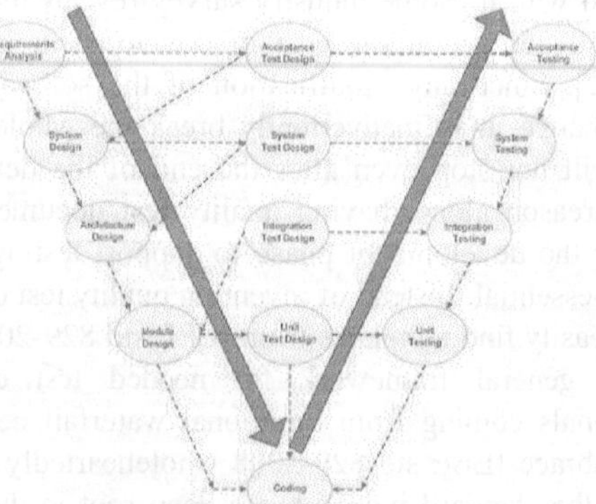

Figure 1. The V-Model [4]

To end our discussion on IEEE 829-2008 in this section (and to provide convenience to the readers of this paper), we decide to include a brief description of those 10 different kinds of documents as follows:

Master Test Plan (MTP) - There can be only one MTP for a project. The MTP identifies how many levels of test are required

Level Test Plan (LTP) - it covers scope, approach, resources and schedule of the testing activities and identifies the items being tested, the features to be tested, the testing tasks to be performed, the personnel responsible for each task, and the associated risks.

Level Test Design (LTD) - it specifies features to be tested, approach refinements, test identification, feature pass/fail criteria and test deliverables.

Level Tests Case (LTC) - it identifies inputs/outputs for each test.

Level Test Procedure (LTPr) - it covers the description of the steps to be taken to execute the test cases.

Level Test Log (LTL) - it provides a chronological record of relevant details about the execution of tests.

Anomaly Report (AR) - it documents any event that occurs during the testing process that requires investigation.

Level Interim Test Status (LITSR) - it summarizes the results of the designated testing activities and optionally to provide evaluations and recommendations based on these results.

Level Test Report (LTR) - it summaries the results of the designated testing activities and to provide evaluations and recommendations based on these results.

Master Test Report (MTR) - it summarizes the results of the levels of the designated testing activities and to provide evaluations based on these results.

3 What is Agile?

Like most researchers in software engineering, we start our discussion on Agile by quoting the Agile Manifesto [2]:

Individuals and interactions *over processes and tools*
Working software *over comprehensive documentation*
Customer collaboration *over contract negotiation*
Responding to change *over following a plan*

The Agile method of software development is built on a series of iterative development cycles where a set of features or user requirements are the basis for each iteration. The process is repeated until all requirements are delivered in the released software. The Agile framework is based upon the Value and Principles of the Agile Manifesto

We also would like to quote the Twelve Principles of Agile [5]:

1. *Our highest priority is to satisfy the customer through early and continuous delivery of valuable software.*
2. *Welcome changing requirements, even late in development. Agile processes harness change for the customer's competitive advantage.*
3. *Deliver working software frequently, from a couple of weeks to a couple of months, with a preference to the shorter timescale.*
4. *Business people and developers must work together daily throughout the project.*
5. *Build projects around motivated individuals. Give them the environment and support they need, and trust them to get the job done.*
6. *The most efficient and effective method of conveying information to and within a development team is face-to-face conversation.*
7. *Working software is the primary measure of progress.*
8. *Agile processes promote sustainable development. The sponsors, developers, and users should be able to maintain a constant pace indefinitely.*
9. *Continuous attention to technical excellence and good design enhances agility.*
10. *Simplicity--the art of maximizing the amount of work not done--is essential.*
11. *The best architectures, requirements, and designs emerge from self-organizing teams.*
12. *At regular intervals, the team reflects on how to become more effective, then tunes and adjusts its behavior accordingly.*

Next we would like to summarize some insights reported in literatures on the agile process from several aspects:

From the aspect of Test Documentation [6]:

- *Agile is not an excuse to not providing test documentation.*
- *Agile does say that huge volume of test documentation most likely is counter-productive.*
- *From the Manifesto – "Valuing working software over documentation" does not mean that test documentation is not valuable.*
- *Agile encourages test documenting early and often.*

From the aspect of testing [1]:

- *To get working software, it must be tested.*

- *To know if it was tested properly, there should be some test documentation.*

From the aspect of processes and plans [7]:

- *Agile means that individuals should make conscious decisions that react to changing situations. They should not just follow rigid plans.*

From the aspect of timing of the documentation [7]:

- *In agile we write test case for each iteration. We get feedback from stakeholders and then write test cases for the next iteration.*

4 Is it possible integrating IEEE 829-2008 to Agile Process?

At a first glance, we may conclude that IEEE 829-2008 is an alternative expression of the V-model and demands great number of documents. Since the V-model follows purely the waterfall process, integrating a waterfall model to an agile process is, of course, futile. This first glance, in our opinion, is a fallacy. A careful analysis reveals that there is a time-line expression embedded in the V-model. The left leg of the V implies a sequence of events that happened at a sequenced time line. The bottom of the V indicates the midpoint of the process and the right leg, again, shows a sequence of events in a time-line manner. Does the IEEE 829-2008 dictate any time-line fashion? The answer is no. The IEEE 829-2008 does tell us *what* documents to produce [8][9][10]. Nonetheless, it never tells us *when* to produce those documents, nor it tells us *how* to produce those documents. One may still argue that IEEE 829-2008 is so heavily documentation oriented. There is no hope of integrating it into the agile process in which we value simple or even no test documents. Again, we believe this argument is a fallacy too. Clearly, a careful reader can find the following description that shows the flexibility of the standard [2]:

Users of this standard may choose to add, combine, or eliminate whole documents and/or documentation content topics based on the needs (and integrity level) of their individual systems.

As for the argument that agile tends to end up with simple or even no test document, our counter argument goes as follows: Since any software project eventually ends up with spending 30 to 50% of its resource and budget on testing, a decision to produce (using any process) simple or even no test documents does not make business sense. Lastly we wish to argue that the IEEE 829-2008 focuses mainly on *what* to produce, not on *when* to produce, and not on *how (in the context of process)* to produce test documents. On the other hand, the Agile Process focuses mainly on *how* to produce, for sure, not on *what* to produce. We really don't see any inherent barriers in integrating *what* and *how* together to achieve a greater effect. Our answer to the question asked in the title of this paper – "IEEE std 829-2008 and Agile Process– can they work together?" therefore is affirmative.

5 Our attempt on integrating IEEE 829-2008 to Agile Process

Of course, the devil is in the details. As a reader of this paper, you may demand to see the details on integrating IEEE 829-2008 to an agile process. We present our attempt as follows. For simplicity, in this paper we focus our attempt on one variant of agile process (i.e., Scrum) only. Figure 2 [11][12][13] shows a typical Scrum process.

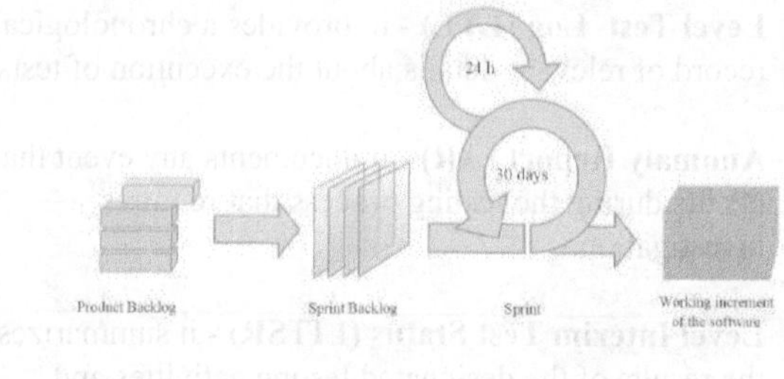

Figure 2 Scrum Process [13]

First we would like to briefly describe the Scrum Process. The main difference between Scrum and traditional waterfall or V model is that the Scrum development is done in time-boxed efforts called Scrum sprints. At the beginning of each Scrum sprint, the team conducts a sprint planning on the goal of the sprint driven by some user stories or requirements. The duration of the Scrum sprint typically varies from two weeks to a month. The important rule is that the team keeps a very close interaction at a 24-hour cycle called daily Scrum meeting and stand up. The goal of each Scrum sprint is to produce some working software. The desire of producing working software at the end of every Scrum sprint implies that each Scrum sprint needs to go through all phases of the software development life cycle. Since the testing is part of the software development life cycle, it becomes clear that testing must be one of the activities performed in each Scrum sprint. Agile promotes the iterative code development. Can test and test documentation also be iteratively done? We think the answer is affirmative. We argue that iterative test activities (in which planning and developing test documents are continuously refined and logging and reporting are continuously performed) can tag along with iterative code development seamlessly. Even after accepting the iterative test activities, a critic may still complain the excess number of documents required by IEEE 829-2008. How about the 10 different kinds of test documents (shown below again for convenience) specified in IEEE 829-2008?

Master Test Plan (MTP)
Level Test Plan (LTP)
Level Test Design (LTD)
Level Test Case (LTC)
Level Test Procedure (LTPr)
Level Test Log (LTL)
Anomaly Report (AR)
Level Interim Test Status Report (LITSR)
Level Test Report (LTR)
Master Test Report (MTR).

How do you weave those 10 kinds of test document development into Scrum sprints? Our attempt starts at the Level Test related documents first and address the Master Test Plan and Report later.

Level Test Plan (LTP)
Initially LTP can be roughly drafted at the first sprint planning meeting. In most sprints, level test plans may include ***unit test plans, integration test plans, system test plan*** and ***acceptance test plan.*** The main reason for having a complete set of level test plans (unit, integration, system, acceptance) in most sprints is that the goal of each sprint is to deliver a potentially shippable product by the end of each sprint. A shippable product indeed needs to go through, at least, unit test, integration test, system test and acceptance test [14]. Will a complete set of level test documents bogs down the sprint? We don't think so. In early sprints, although we need to work on a complete set of level test plans, every one of them, in fact, is very simple to begin with. Again, the rationale is that development plans are iterative and test plans will be developed iteratively as well. Those level plans are reviewed at every sprint retrospective meeting and revised as necessary.

Level Test Design (LTD)
Level test designs include unit test designs, integration test designs, system test design and acceptance test design.

Level Test Case (LTC) and Level Test Procedure (LTPr)
Level test designs include unit test cases and procedures, integration test cases and test procedures, system test cases and test procedures and acceptance test cases and test procedures.

Level Test Log (LTL) and Anomaly Report (AR)
Level test logs and anomaly reports may include unit test logs and anomaly reports, integration test logs and anomaly reports, system test logs and anomaly reports and acceptance test logs and anomaly reports. LTL and AR are continuously created, reviewed, and revised as needed during sprint.

Level Interim Test Status Report (LITSR)
Created and updated daily following daily scrum.

Level Test Report (LTR)
Level test reports may include unit test reports, integration test reports, system test reports and acceptance test reports. Most of those reports can be created and revised prior to sprint review meeting.

How about the **Master Test Plan (MTP)**? We propose that a Master Test Plan can be produced early in the project at sprint 0 to start the process. Later on, we could use the Master Test Plan to tie the Level Test Plans generated from each sprint together to create a final version of the Master Test Plan and Report. Sure enough, some of our readers may point out that what we have attempted is just to compress the whole testing life cycle into one individual Scrum sprint. Doing so will simply bog down each Scrum sprint and is totally against the sprite of Agile. There are two arguments to respond to such a criticism. First, if iterative code planning and development can be accepted/tolerated why not iterative test planning, design, and reporting? Second, if it becomes apparent that resources need to be reserved for other high priority tasks, we may also consider to combine some type of test documents which is certainly allowed by IEEE 829-2008. For example, in some small-size projects, one may combine Level Test Plan (LTP), Level Test Design (LTD) and Level Test Procedure (LTPr) into one document. Level Test Log (LTL) and Anomaly Report (AR) also can be merged.

6 Conclusions

In this paper our main goal is to convince our readers that integrating a testing standard such as IEEE 829-2008 to an agile process *should* be done and *can* be done. First, why it *should* be done? Our premise on "*should* be done" is purely based on business reasoning and is not related to what development process used (waterfall or agile). Any modern software product development requires, at the minimum, some testers' participation. In some large organizations, having a separate department or team that works on software quality assurance is also not that uncommon. Furthermore, it is an industry consensus that testing eventually may consume 30 to 50% of all resources spent. Having spent and committed such a large portion of resources and personnel on testing but not demanding the ultimate fruit of testing (i.e., test documents) is simply beyond any business sense. If the premise on demanding quality test documents is valid, the desire to have standardized test documents (such as documents specified in

IEEE 829-2008) becomes not that to understand. In this globalization era insisting on one-of-kind, ad-hoc approach, in most business scenarios, proves fatal. The argument on "*can* be done" is a bit challenging due to some ill perceptions from both agile and waterfall communities. Our main defense is to point out that IEEE 829-2008 is *NOT* a mirror image of the V model. The standard does not have embedded time-line as in the V model and it mainly focuses on the notion of "what to produce." The agile process, on the other hand, mainly focuses on "how to produce." Integrating "what to produce" and "how to produce" is actually natural and logical. We further support our argument by providing an attempt in which we integrated IEEE 829-2008 documents to Scum agile process. The corner stone of this integration is hinged on the fact that at the end of each Scrum sprint a potentially shippable product is created. This fact implies that we should start a complete set of level test documents at the beginning of each sprint and incrementally improve them very similar to what we have done on the iterative development of source code.

7 Acknowledgement

The author would like to thank

1.the class of cpsc545 of the Master of science in Software Engineering (MSE) program at California State University, Fullerton for contributing some of insights mentioned in this paper.

2. the MSE research and development fund for partial supports.

8 References

[1] Burnstein, Ilene. "Practical Software Testing". NY: Springer-Verlag, 2003

[2] IEEE 829-2008 IEEE Standard for Software and System Test documentation

[3] Agile manifesto. Retrieved from http://agilemanifesto.org/

[4] The V-Model (Software Development). Retrieved from http://en.wikipedia.org/wiki/VModel_%28software_development%29

[5] 12 Principles of Agile software Development. Retrieved from http://www.agilityspeaks.com/capabilities/aboutus/agile-development/

[6] *Lisa Crispin, article titled "Agile Documentation"*, 03/02/2011. Retrieved from http://www.stickyminds.com/sitewide.asp?Function=edetail&ObjectType=COL&ObjectId=16698&tth=DYN&tt=siteemail&iDyn=2

[7] Janet Gregory, Lisa Crispin, Book - Agile Testing: A Practical Guide for Testers and Agile Teams, Jan. 2009, Addison-Wesley Professional

[8] Glazer, H., J. Dalton, D. Anderson, M. Konrad, S. Shrum. "CMMI or Agile: Why Not Embrace Both!" Software Engineering Institute. November 2008.

[9] Curran, C. "Are Agile and CMMI Compatible?" CIO Dashboard. 25 June 2010. Retrieved from http://www.ciodashboard.com/it-processes-and-methodologies/agile-cmmi-compatible

[10] Shelton, C. "Agile and CMMI: Better Together". ScrumAlliance. 9 July 2008. Retrieved from http://www.scrumalliance.org/articles/100-agile-and-cmmi-better-together

[11] Agile Scrum. Retrieved from http://en.wikipedia.org/wiki/Scrum_(development)

[12] "Inside the Inbox". Retrieved from http://www.ecircle.com/blog/2011/08/04/enare-effectively-integrating-marketing-tools/

[13] Scrum (Development). Retrieved from http://en.wikipedia.org/wiki/Scrum_%28development%29

[14] Ship it! - Scrum's "Potentially Shippable" Product Increment. Retrieved from http://agilemakingprogress.blogspot.tw/2011/03/ship-it-scrums-potentially-shippable.html

Managing a Global Software Project under an Agile and Cloud Perspective

Giulio Concas[1], **Katiuscia Mannaro**[1] **and Luisanna Cocco**[1]
[1]Department of Electrics and Electronics Engineering, University of Cagliari, Piazza d'Armi
Cagliari, Italy

Abstract - *Nowadays Lean-Kanban approach is perhaps the fastest growing Agile Methodology in software engineering. At the same time Cloud Computing (CC) is a technological phenomenon that is becoming more and more important in these last years. In our opinion Small and Medium Enterprises (SMEs) can increase their competitiveness by taking advantage of CC, and we think that it is very important to study and assess its impact on SMEs' management processes. In this paper we proposed an effective tool to support strategic initiatives to the software development for the companies that develop software using agile methodologies and distributed resources. We used System Dynamics to model and simulate the software development: it allowed us to highlight in a very efficient way the interaction among several factors present in the software project.*

Keywords: System Dynamics, Modeling, Simulation, Agile Processes, Global Software Development, Cloud System

1 Introduction

Nowadays, software engineering involves people collaborating to develop software and in this context many challenges, such as geographic, cultural, linguistic and temporal [4], [18], meet into Global Software Development (GSD). Some problems are related to the issues about the communication for information exchange, coordination of teams, and activities.

Normally, the distance and the lack of overlapping working hours create a negative impact on software projects, indeed problems in the knowledge transfer and, as a consequence, communications gaps or ambiguity on technical aspects must be resolved.

Cultural diversities may bring to an unequal distribution of work, lack of trust and fear, from which cost increases, poor skill management and reporting issues may arise. Linguistics and temporal diversities can instead lead to issues in knowledge transfer, communication and project visibility.

In our opinion, Cloud Computing (CC) allows us to deal with better all these problems.

CC is a delivery model for software, platforms and infrastructures. Cloud providers have got the possession of physical location, hardware, and system maintenance. Enterprise users access cloud services via the Internet from anywhere and at any time. Users usually pay a subscription fee, and can run a single instance of system on a robust infrastructure.

Indeed, Cloud services are delivered from a "multi-tenant" system; there is a single instance of software running, but many individual or enterprise customers use this system along with their own necessities.

In this paper we proposed a tool for managing an agile development environment on cloud platforms. This tool may support companies with distributed resources to take strategic decisions, no matter whether the choice involves outsourcing development or supplier networks. Software engineering involves people collaborating to develop better software. Therefore, we use collaboration tools all along the product life cycle to let us work together, stay together, and achieve results together.

This management tool is based on a model that we built by using an analysis of feedback loops among the components of the process, such as requirements, iterations, releases and so on, and through workflows and delays, in order to control their dynamics. We used System Dynamics to model and simulate how effective are Cloud-based software development environments for Global Software. We assumed a development process based on Scrum agile methodology and simulated the agile software development process on Cloud platform using a commercial tool available on the market: Vensim.

The proposed model helps managers to highlight all the factors that influence the software development in the companies with distributed resources. Indeed, in our opinion, our tool can be useful to improve all the activities linked to the software development. It allows us easily to highlight and focus all the elements that influence and compromise the success of a software project. Consequently, it allows us to discover, and then, to correct problems or conditions that could compromise the success of the project.

The remainder of the paper is organized as follows. Section 2 presents a brief description of some key software concepts of the two studied software development approaches and the Section 3 presents some related works. Finally Section 4 describes the details of the simulation model and Section 5 gives some final considerations of our research, and the recommendations for future works.

2 Optimizing the Software Development with Agile Methodologies and Cloud.

In this section we take a look at the considered software development approaches.

Scrum is presently the most used Agile Methodology (AM) [1], while the Lean-Kanban approach is perhaps the fastest growing AM. Scrum and Lean-Kanban have been proposed as two possible solutions to quickly respond to changing customer requirements, without compromising the quality of the code.

Specially in real-life software projects having up-front planning and budgeting, waterfall-like approaches are still very used. The Waterfall model was introduced by Royce in 1970. This software approach requires that all process phases (planning, design, development, testing and deployment) are performed in a sequential series of steps.

Each phase starts only when the previous one has ended. It is possible to step back to the previous phase, but it is not possible to go back in the process, for instance in order to accommodate a substantial change of requirements. This methodology requires defining a stable set of requirements only during the phase of requirements definition, and feedbacks to previous stages are not easily introduced.

Agile Methodologies, so named in 2001 in the Agile Manifesto [20], have been introduced in response to rigid and hard methodologies to follow. Among them, Scrum and Lean-Kanban are Agile process tools [8] based on incremental development. They both use pull scheduling and emphasize on delivering releasable software often.

The original term Scrum comes from a study by Takeuchi and Nonaka [19] that was published at 1986 in the Harvard Business Review. In 1993 Jeff Sutherland developed the Scrum process at Easel Corporation, by using their study and their analogy as the name of the process as a whole. Finally, Ken Schwaber [15] [16] formalized the process for the worldwide software industry in the first published paper on Scrum at OOPSLA 1995. Scrum [17] is a simple agile framework, adaptable also to contexts different from software development [12].

Adopting Scrum implies to use timeboxed iterations and to break the work into a list of smaller deliverables, ordered according to a priority given by the Product Owner. Changes to requirements are not accepted during the iteration, but are welcomed otherwise. Scrum projects are organized with the help of daily Scrums: 15 minutes update meetings, and monthly Sprints, or iterations, which are designed to keep the project flowing quickly.

Generally, at the end of every iteration the team releases working code, and a retrospective meeting is held also to look for ways to improve the process for the next iteration.

Lean software development is a translation of Lean manufacturing [6] to the software development domain. The Lean approach emphasizes on improving the value given to the customer, by eliminating the waste (Muda) and considering the whole project, avoiding local optimizations.

Kanban is a Japanese term that translated literally means visual (Kan) and card or board (ban). Adopting Kanban means to break the work into work items, to write their description on cards, and to put the cards on a Kanban board, so that the flow of work is made visible to all members of the team, and the Work in Process (WIP) limits are made explicit on the board. The Kanban board provides a high visibility to the software process, because it shows the assignment of work to the developers, it communicates priorities and highlights bottlenecks. One of the key goals of Lean-Kanban approach is to minimize WIP, so that only what is needed is developed, there is a constant flow of released work items to the customer, and developers focus only to deliver a few items at a time. So, the process is optimized and lead time can be reduced.

In a nutshell, Scrum and Lean-Kanban approaches are both agile processes aiming to quickly adapt the process by using feedbacks loops.

In Lean-Kanban the feedback loops are shorter, and the work does not flow through time-boxed iterations, but flows continuously and smoothly. Kanban is less prescriptive than Scrum and it is able to release anytime, while Scrum will release new features only at the end of the iterations. Moreover, in Scrum it is not possible to change the requirements in the middle of the sprint.

A common definition of Global Software Development is a software development process at geographically separated locations. For this reason, GSD involves communication for information exchange, coordination of teams, activities and artifacts so they contribute to the overall objective, and finally control of teams. Many challenges meet into GSD [4], [18] these are geographic, cultural, linguistic and temporal. The distance and the lack of overlapping working hours create a negative impact on software projects, create problems in the knowledge transfer, and as a consequence communications gaps or ambiguity on technical aspects may occur. Cultural diversities may bring to an unequal distribution of work, lack of trust and fear, from which cost increases, poor skill management and reporting issues may arise. Linguistics and temporal diversities can instead lead to issues in knowledge transfer, communication and project visibility. The GSD can be facilitated using the Cloud.

CC is a delivery model for software, platforms and infrastructures. Cloud providers have got the possession of physical location, hardware, and system maintenance.

3 Related Work

Our model stemmed from two works about Global Software Development.

In [4], Hossain, Babar, Paik, and Verner discuss the use of Scrum practices in GSD projects, and identify key challenges, due to global project distribution that restricts the use of Scrum. In [18] instead, the authors present the challenges encountered in globally dispersed software projects and propose to exploit Cloud Computing characteristics and privileges both as a product and as a process to improve GSD.

In a more and more globalized world the relationship between culture and management of remote work is an avoidable issue to face. So, they exploit CC proposing both a product and a process to manage the many challenges in terms of culture, management, outsourcing, organization, coordination, collaboration, communication, development team, development process and tool.

In [1] a practical experience in the application of some agile software development practices, as Scrum model, to Azure application development is described. Azure Services Platform is an application platform on the cloud and it offers PaaS capabilities, which allow application to be built and consumed from both on-premise and on-demand environments. This paper starts from several questions about the interactions between cloud computing and agile software development and it attempts to discuss their potential advantages. In fact the authors show how setting up a development environment on the Azure platform helps enhance the agile practices.

Our work is based on a simulation technique used to study and analyze the software development. The used technique is known as System Dynamics.

The System Dynamics approach was introduced by Jay W. Forrester [7] of the Massachusetts Institute of Technology during the mid-1950s, and is suitable to analyze and model non-linear and complex systems containing dynamic variables that change over time.

System dynamics modeling has been used in similar research on software development process, where there are multiple and interacting software processes, time delays, and other non--linear effects such as communication level, amount of overtime and workload, schedule pressure, budget pressure, rate of requirement change, and so on. In the field of the Agile Methodologies, many system dynamics models were introduced. The main goals of these researches aim to better understand the agile process and to evaluate its effectiveness. Most of the performed research was made on Extreme Programming (XP), or generic AMs. Other processes such as Scrum, however, are almost absent.

For example, Chichaly in [2] investigated when AMs may work by using System Dynamics modeling, and comparing AMs with a traditional waterfall process. In [21] the author explored whether agile project management had a unique structure, or would fit within the generic conceptually formed system dynamic project management structures.

An analysis of factors that impacts on productivity during agile web development and maintenance phases was conducted by Xiaoying Kong et al. [10]. Another analysis published in [9] gives both theoretical insights into the dynamics of agile software development, and practical suggestions for managing these projects.

4 A Tool for the Global Agile Software Development on Cloud Environments

In this section, we describe a tool proposed to analyze and study the efficiency of a Cloud development environment used for Global Software Development. Since the collaboration among team members is an essential factor in GSD, this tool using Cloud resources is perfect to enable the facilitation, the automation and the control of all the development process.

The development methodology adopted in this environment set up using On-Demand resources is an Agile methodology known as Scrum methodology.

On the contrary of collocated software development, in GSD the distance among team entails difficulties in the coordination and the control due to problems which stem from many challenges in terms of culture, management, outsourcing, organization, coordination, collaboration, communication, development team, development process and tool among distant teams from each other.

We propose a tool that uses a simplified version of the Scrum approach in an On Demand development environment, in order to obtain a structure easy to understand and to modify during the whole life cycle of a software project.

According to SD modeling, and as reported in [11], our model is represented in terms of level variables, flow variables and auxiliary variables.

The tool proposed, shown in Fig.1, describes the development of a generic software project gone ahead by a small team of developers. In order to simplify the model, all the phases of planning, design, coding, unit testing and similar have been merged into just one development phase, represented by the requirements development rate valve.

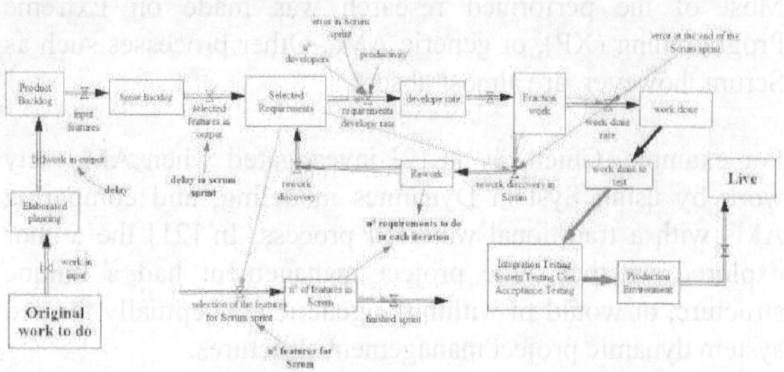

Figure 1.Tool for Cloud Software Development Environment .

The project software is modeled through a specific number of requirements, defined as a set of functionalities to be implemented. Therefore, the initial stock of requirements, which are represented by the level variable called "Original Work to Do", evolves in a stock of developed requirements which are represented by the level variable called "Live".

For the purpose of modeling a planning phase, which matches the real planning phases in the software development, we introduced in the tool some variables which represent the time spent in planning. They were modeled as delays in the software project development, which influence project outcomes and determine the system development speed.

On the contrary of traditional development environments, in Cloud development environments, the infrastructure is readily available, and system maintenance and system updates of the cloud server will be bear by the cloud providers and not by the developers.

The values of these variables will be linked to the set up of the Cloud development environment, in order to customize it as a function of their own needs.

The time and effort spent at the beginning of project development lifecycle are modeled by the following auxiliary variables: *setting up infrastructure hardware and software licenses, deploying skilled resources to setup, manage and certify the software development and deployment infrastructure, building applications from multiple locations when teams geographically distributed are added*.

Some of these variables just cited, were taken from the work of Dumbre et al. [1] and all are reported in Fig.2.

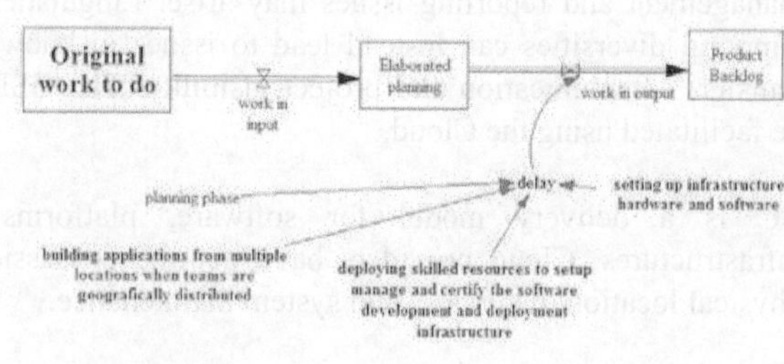

Figure 2. Tool for Cloud Software Development Environment: Delay.

In addition to these variables, another variable for planning and creating the Backlog is taken into account. This variable is indicated as *planning phase* and it models the role of the Product Owner.

Indeed, Scrum prescribes roles, such as the role of the Product Owner. This role is given to a single person, who represents the customer's interest, prioritizes the requirements in the backlog, and answers to questions about requirements.

Moreover, Scrum prescribes a Sprint Planning Meeting, a Sprint Retrospective Meeting and Scrum of Scrums meeting, respectively, to plan the Sprint, to plan the iteration at the end of every sprint and to coordinate more teams which work at geographically separated locations.

As regards the modeling of the software development phase, as well known, the life cycle of the software project depends on the productivity of the developers and on the error made by them (see Fig. 1), but also by the uncertain customer requirements. Therefore, the fewer errors there are during the process, the sooner the project will be finished.

In according to [2], we modeled the auxiliary variable *productivity*: it represents the productivity of the developers. We take into account only these factors that in our opinion can be considered very relevant to the software development processes. However further factors can be easily introduced.

The factors taken into account are: the *personnel experience*, the *personnel turnover*, the *communication complexity*, the *amount of overtime and workload*, the *schedule pressure*, and the *budget pressure* (see Fig. 3).

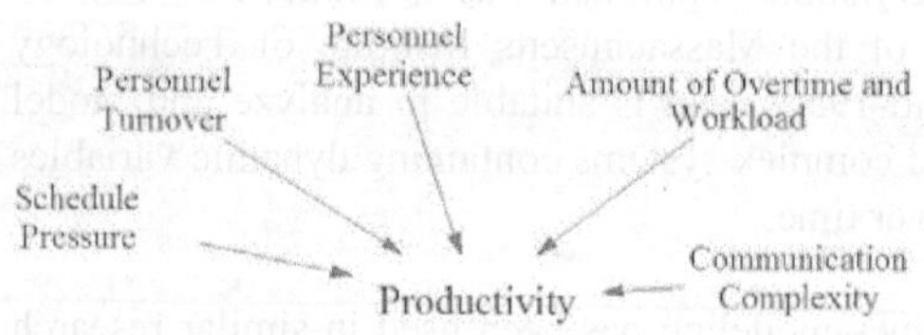

Figure 3. Tool for Cloud Software Development Environment: Productivity.

So for example in Fig. 3 the *personnel experience* auxiliary variable contributes to the value of the *productivity* variable introducing a multiplicative factor that takes into account the knowledge of the current domain by developers. The *schedule pressure* auxiliary variable contributes to the value of the *productivity* variable introducing a multiplicative factor that takes into account the effect of the project falling behind the time schedule. Finally, for example the *communication complexity* auxiliary variable contributes to the value of the *productivity* variable by introducing a multiplicative factor that takes into account the effect present primarily in large project teams, where a large number of involved people increases the number of communication paths.

For each iteration, only a fraction of the requirements, in the level variable called "Selected Requirements", is completed. This is because a fraction of the work is done incorrectly due to three types of error: *effect of uncertain customer requirements*, *problem in the software design*, *bug introduced during the development*.

Only the *bug introduced during the development error passes through the rework discovery in Scrum* valve. The two other errors can be discovered only at the end of the iteration.

Note that the requirements have the same size and weight and before to be developed are subdivided in different Sprint backlogs. Each backlog includes a random number of features, extracted from a Gaussian distribution. These Sprint backlogs are developed during short fixed-length iterations.

As requirements are implemented, they flow into the level variables "Integration Testing", "System Testing" and "User Acceptance Testing" stock. If the tests are successfully passed, then the requirements are accepted and considered completed. Consequently, the accepted requirements flow into the level variable called "Production Environment". Otherwise, a rework must be performed. This rework entails a delay due to the time needed for the correction. From "Production Environment" level variable the requirements flow into the "Live" level variable and the work is finished.

As we have already said, in our model, the time to finish the work "Original Work to Do" is affected by two main effects: delays and errors.

In Cloud system, Production and Testing environments are accessible anytime and anywhere. Any team member and user can work and build applications referring just to one location, with no need to coordinate multiple locations. In this way, significant time and effort will be saved, and users will use all their resources for creating value for their business.

Indeed, little time and efforts are spent to write verbose installation scripts or release notes, and for the setup of system testing, integration testing and user acceptance testing, with the aim to obtain a product released under rigorous test and validation. The deployment process is simplified, there is no need of any separate packaging efforts; to pass from development environment to testing environment, and from here to production environment does not require any additional step.

Prototypes and demos can be made accessible immediately to customers for eliciting feedback in a short time. The code can pass from one environment to another without writing deployment script to set up the application in the respective environments. All these activities have been modeled by two variables: *creating and managing different test environments* and *creating and managing production environment prototyping and demos* introduced when the requirements are moved from *work done to test* to a different testing environment, and then are deployed to *production environment* (see Fig. 4).

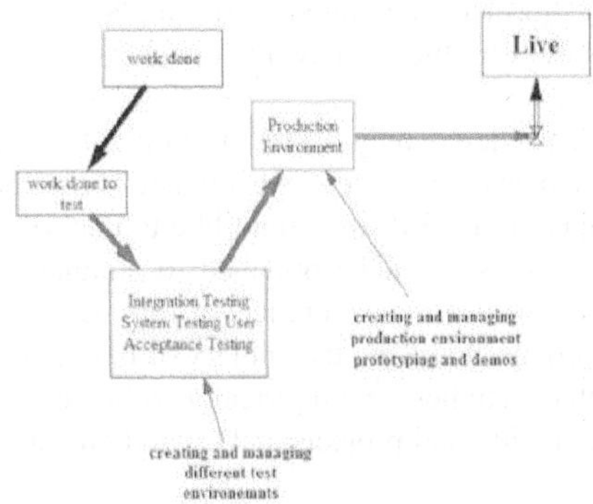

Figure 4. Tool for Cloud Software Development Environment: Test Environments.

All the variables described above represent time and effort spent in the development process.

5 Final Considerations and Future Work

In recent years, a new way to distribute and use the information and the communication technologies are heavily gaining ground at the expense of the traditional information and communication technologies. This new technology is the Cloud Computing.

This work analyzes and studies this new technology applied to the Software development process.

So, we propose a model based on System Dynamics for highlighting the efficiency of the Cloud Platforms for Global Software Development.

We underline that the modeled software development process is based on agile methodologies. In particular, we applied a Scrum process, and hence an agile methodology able to manage better the software development with respect to the heavy and prescriptive traditional methodologies to develop as can be Waterfall process.

The realized model is a simple tool, this can be customized and used in order to follow the software development among its geographically distributed teams.
Such a development environment allows to reduce the costs and the time with respect to an environment set up On-Premise, and hence a traditional environment.
We developed a simplified model to describe all the significant factors that, in our opinion, enter during the life cycle of a software project. However, further factors can be easily introduced, and hence, the model can be easily customized to analyzing and studying real software project management.
The modeled real development environment is very complex, and so, the model has been simplified. In addition, given the lack of experimental data, our goal is only to propose a tool to be used to help the software companies to plan and develop a software project.
Moreover our study has been carried out under some limiting assumptions that could threaten its validity. The proposed model needs to be further elaborated and validated, for example by adding new variables or new relationships among factors.
This work must be considered only a starting point. Indeed, given the lack of data available, here we do not show the results obtained simulating it. But, we would like to underline that very interesting results could be obtained to simulate it with real data from real software development experience.
Therefore, the tool proposed will be the subject of our future work, that will include studies to empirically validate the model using data from GSD real projects and carried on using Cloud environments.

6 References

[1] Amit Dumbre, Satha Priya Senthil, Sidharth Subhash Ghag: Practising Agile software development on the Window Azure platform, White Paper, May 2011.

[2] Carina Andersson, Lena Karlsson, Josef Nedstam, Martin Host, Bertil I Nilsson: Understanding Software Processes through System Dynamics Simulation: A Case Study, Proceedings of the Ninth Annual IEEE International Conference and Workshop on the Engineering of Computer-Based Systems (ECBS'02).

[3] Chichakly Karim: Modeling Agile Development: When is it Effective?. Proceedings of the 2007 System Dynamics Conference. Boston, MA. Print.

[4] Collabnet: Reinforcing Agile Software Development in the Cloud. Why the Cloud is Advantageous for Agile, and for Accelarating its Enterprise-wide Adoption, White Paper, 2011.

[5] Emam Hossain, Muhammad Ali Babar, Hye-young Paik, June Verner: Risk Identification and Mitigation Processes for Using Scrum in Global Software Development: A conceptual Framework, 2009 IEEE.

[6] Marc I. Kellner and Raymond J. Madachy and David M. Raffo: Software process simulation modeling: Why? What, How?. Journal of Systems and Software, vol. 46, pages 91--105, (1999).

[7] James P. Womack, Daniel T. Jones, Daniel Roos: The Machine That Changed the World : The Story of Lean Production. Harper Perennial, (November 1991).

[8] J.W. Forrester: Industrial dynamics. Cambridge, MA: MIT Press, (1961).

[9] Henrik Kniberg and Mattias Skarin. Kanban and Scrum making the most of both. Managing Editor: Diana Plesa. Enterprise software development series. InfoQ. USA. ISBN 978--0--557--13832--6 (2010).

[10] Kim E. van Oorschot, Kishore Sengputa, Luk N. van Wassenhove: Dynamics of Agile Software Development. Proceedings of the 27th International Conference of the System Dynamics Society, July 26--30, (2009) Albuquerque, New Mexico, USA.

[11] Kong Xiaoying, Liu Li, Lowe David: Modelling an Agile Web Maintenance Process. (2005).

[12] Luisanna Cocco, Katiuscia Mannaro, Giulio Concas, and Michele Marchesi: Simulating Kanban and Scrum vs Waterfall with System Dynamics, XP2011

[13] M. Marchesi, K.Mannaro, S. Uras, M. Locci: Distributed Scrum in a Research Project Management Agile Processes. In Software Engineering and Extreme Programming, Lecture Notes in Computer Science, Volume 4536/2007, pp. 240-244, (2007).

[14] Raffaele Giordanelli, Carlo Mastroianni, The Cloud Computing Paradigm: Characteristic, Opportunities and Research Issues, RT-ICAR-CS Aprile 2010.

[15] SalesForce: Agile Development Meets Cloud Computing for Extraordinary Results at Salesforce.com, White Paper, 2008.

[16] Schwaber Ken: Agile Project Management with Scrum, Microsoft Press,Redmond, WA, (2004).

[17] Schwaber Ken: Scrum Development Process, White Paper, (1997).

[18] Scrum Alliance, http://www.scrumalliance.org

[19] Sajid Ibrahim Hashmi, Victor Clerc, Maryam Razavian, Christina Manteli, Damiani Andrew Tamburri, Patricia Lago, Elisabetta Di Nitto, Ita Richardson: Using Cloud to Facilitate Global Software Development Challenges, 2011 IEEE.

[20] Takeuchi H. and Nonaka I.: The New New Product Development Game, Harvard Business Review, January-February (1986).

[21] URL: http://agilemanifesto.org/

[22] Warren W. Tignor: Agile Project Management. International Conference of the System Dynamics Society, Albuquerque, NM 2009, July 26- July 30, 2009.

[23] Yash Talreja: Lean Agile Methodologies Accentuate Benefits of Cloud Computing, 2010

SESSION

SOFTWARE ENGINEERING AND EMBEDDED SYSTEMS

Chair(s)

TBA

Video Processing for Motion Tracking of Safety Critical Systems

Travis Cleveland, David J. Coe, and Jeffrey H. Kulick
Department of Electrical and Computer Engineering
University of Alabama in Huntsville, Huntsville, Alabama, USA

Abstract - *The authors have been developing a laboratory for teaching safety critical software development. The laboratory currently utilizes an HO model train system, which provides for easy understanding of the operational and safety requirements. In earlier years, mechanical, magnetic and optical sensors have been used to provide location data to the scheduling and safety software. However, this approach has grown to the level that over 1000 wire segments need to be maintained for correct operation. This paper discusses the use of video tracking software to significantly reduce the number of electrical contacts subject to failure, and to provide more flexibility to the system as the track layout changes.*

Keywords: RTCA DO-178C, motion tracking, safety critical systems, software safety, real-time embedded systems

1 Motivation

The Department of Electrical and Computer Engineering at The University of Alabama in Huntsville has been teaching a course in safety critical software design for the past two years [1]. The students have been developing a software controller for a model train system shown in Figure 1 below.

During the course, students perform a functional hazard analysis and assign Design Assurance Levels, as described in Table 1, to the various functions as in typically found in a DO-178C aircraft safety analysis [2-3]. During this analysis, the students determined that the scheduler is a Design Assurance Level A (DAL A) component since it can cause train crashes and thus (model) loss of life. To reduce the DAL assurance level so that assurance artifacts requirements are moderated, students developed a parallel safety monitoring system that is much simpler in design and complexity so that the scheduler can be DAL C while the monitor is DAL A. In normal railroad parlance, this monitor logic is called *vital logic*.

The train scheduler hardware utilizes DCC control protocols, and each locomotive has a DCC decoder. Control signals are provided by a computer controlled Digitrax controller system [5]. Within the DCC controller system, contact with the rails from the locomotive wheels provides occupancy data for the scheduler software. For the DCC controller system, the track is divided up into individually power able sections although the DCC system uses DCC commands to control the speed and direction of the locomotives and power is never removed by the DCC system. In the current design there are 24 distinct track sections.

During the safety analysis, it is determined that the scheduler software in and of itself is unlikely to be developed to DAL level A and using standard FTA analysis a second safety system is developed to ensure safe operation. This safety system is much smaller in code size but contains additional sensors and software. The original version of the safety system was developed using CTI hardware components and in the past year a new student team replaced that system with an Arduino-based safety controller.

The safety system, which is entirely independent of the DCC controller system, has a power management capability for each of the 24 DCC track sections. A relay control board allows the safety systems to independently power down each of the 24 track sections as needed to prevent a collision. Each safety section is monitored either by a set of optical sensors that straddle the track as shown in Figure 2 or magnetic sensors that are located in the middle of the track. The photographs in Figure 3 below show the complexity of wiring required for the DCC track sections and the wiring associated with the safety monitor's optical and magnetics occupancy sensor systems.

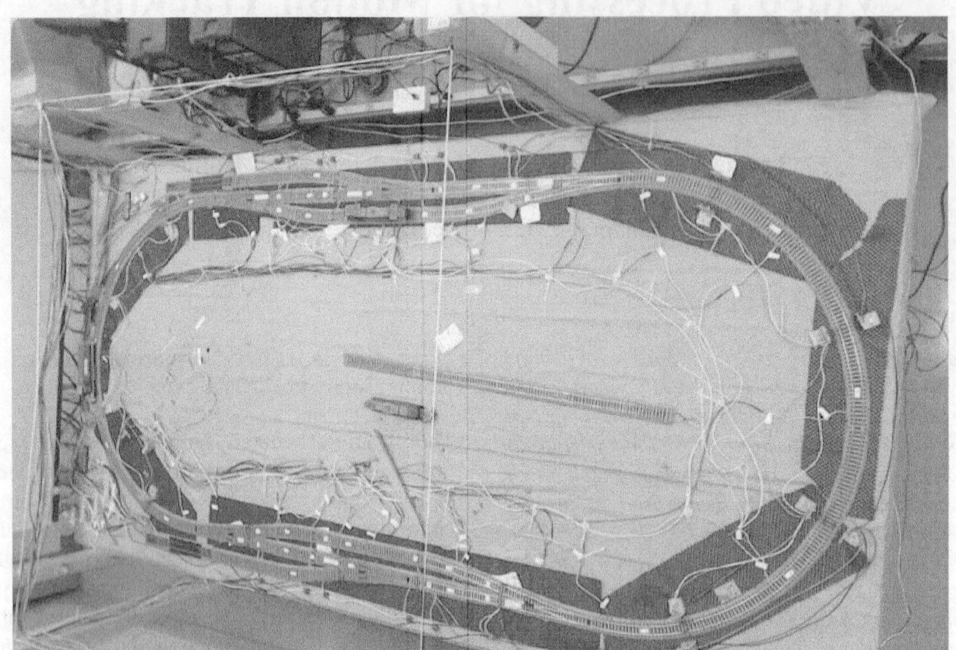

Figure 1 – Camera-eye view of model train system used for safety critical software design course.

Table 1 – Aircraft Design Assurance Levels [2,4]

Design Assurance Level	Category	Description
DAL A	**Catastrophic**	Failure condition results in multiple fatalities with probable loss of aircraft
DAL B	**Severe**	Failure condition would significantly reduce the ability of the crew and/or aircraft capabilities required to compensate for adverse operating conditions
DAL C	**Major**	Failure condition would reduce the ability of the crew and/or aircraft capabilities needed to compensate for adverse operating conditions
DAL D	**Minor**	Failure condition has no significant impact on safety margins or crew workload
DAL E	**No Safety Effect**	Failure condition has no impact on safety

During the past year it was decided that the large number of wires for the safety system was a significant safety risk. Each DCC track section requires at minimum two wires to provide power to any train and 4 wires for sensor data. Each wire goes through a number of wiring blocks, relay blocks, and power management blocks requiring over 1000 discrete wires. Thus, to reduce the risks associated with the large number of wires, we have sought ways to simplify the safety monitor's occupancy sensing. Efforts are underway to replace the optical/magnetic sensor system and its associated 700+ wires by a video camera system that only has a few wires linking the cameras to the safety management computer. Once the computational workload is better understood, we expect to port the safety system software to a dedicated pcDuino platform [6].

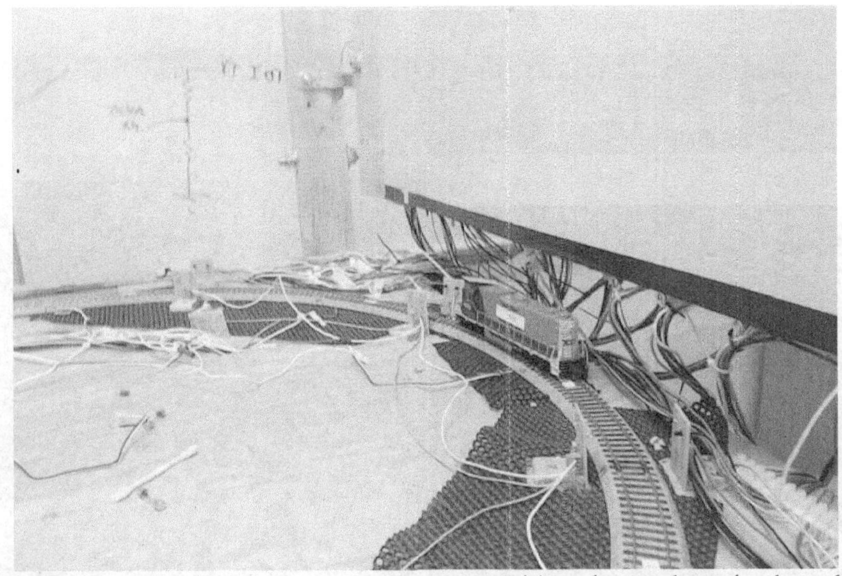

Figure 2 – Photograph showing optical sensors positioned at track section boundaries

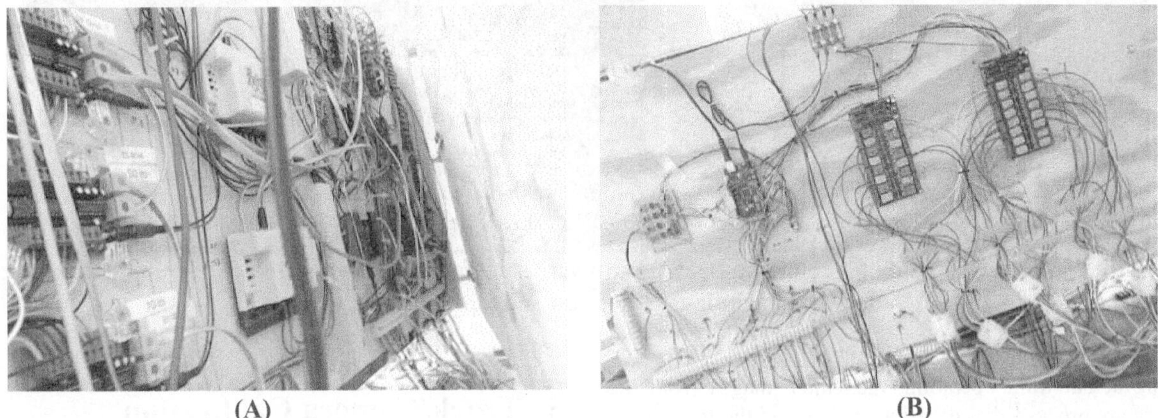

(A) (B)

Figure 3 – Photographs of (A) DCC controller and safety system occupancy sensor wiring and (B) relays for controlling power distribution to each track section.

2 Train Tracking System

The safety system currently uses a Logitech 1080p web camera connected by USB to the safety management computer. Figure 1 is a photograph of the entire track layout as captured by the camera. Custom locomotive tracking software has been developed using OpenCV computer vision libraries that will process images collected by the camera and output a continuous stream of track section occupancy data in the form of data pairs consisting of the locomotive identification number and the track section number currently occupied by that locomotive. Colored tags have been added to each locomotive to facilitate tracking and locomotive identification. Figure 4 below is a screen shot of the locomotive tracking application showing both the track layout and the filtered image revealing only the tracking tags. Note that in the model train layout, the DCC controller wiring for each track section is currently visible to the camera unless it is blocked from view by white paper during development of the locomotive tracking software. The DCC controller wiring will eventually be rerouted underneath the table surface. The algorithms used for locomotive tracking are described below.

Figure 4 – Screen capture of locomotive tracking software showing track layout (lower left) and locomotive tracking tags (top left and top right).

During actual train operation, the video images from the camera are processed as described below and the location of the occupancy blocks are recorded. As the software algorithms are completed, an Nvidia GPU processor will be used to accelerate processing of the images to reduce the error between computed locomotive position versus the actual locomotive position. Finally, the completed algorithms will be ported to the pcDuino and included GPU. For debugging purposes, the tracking data is currently printed to the screen continuously. In the production version of the software, in addition to being used by the safety critical software, tracking data will be made available via a socket connection for possible use by the scheduling system.

3 Track/Camera Calibration Procedure

The first step in the tracking process is to map the pixel data to track section boundaries. The calibration process develops a map of the locations of the track safety sections by using the video system and a manually controlled locomotive. The locomotive is positioned at the ends and middle of each safety section and the video coordinate of the individual block is recorded. Because the camera may move from session to session, a calibration run is performed at the beginning of each session to obtain the correct location of the track on the video frame. Figure 5 (left) shows the track sections as identified by the calibration process with track sections overlaid onto the track layout photograph using an alternating sequence of colors. Figure 5 (right) shows the actual location of the locomotive as it traverses the track under DCC control.

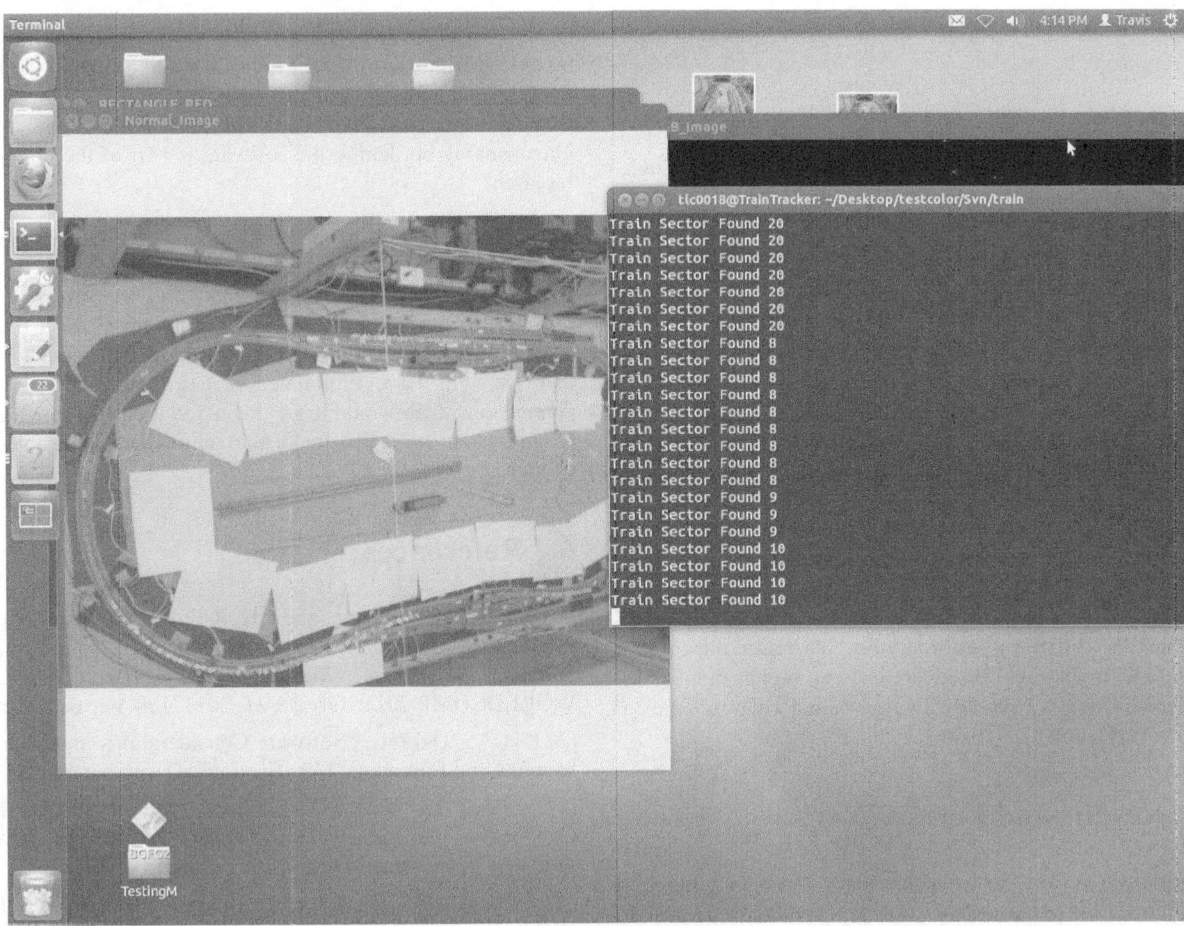

Figure 5 – System state post calibration process (left) showing the track sections marked in alternating color scheme and (right) tracking data showing locomotive as it traverses the track under power

4 Locomotive Tracking Algorithms

The goal of the locomotive tracking system is to at any time be able to identify the track section occupied by any particular locomotive and produce a continuous stream of locomotive tracking data indicating the current position of each locomotive. Our solution was to use a color-based tracking scheme to locate and track colored markers positioned on the top of each locomotive, with one marker positioned at the front of the locomotive and one marker at the rear. The locomotive tracking system must (1) capture an image, (2) analyze the image, (3) track any locomotives, and (4) report the positions of the locomotives. The OpenCV computer vision libraries facilitate image capture and subsequent processing. Below we describe image analysis and locomotive tracking in more detail.

4.1 Image Analysis

The image coming into the system from the camera is a color image. Once an image is captured, a function is used to convert the RGB image over to the HSV spectrum to simplify color processing. The program then extracts out for each color a mask that is only of that color (eg. red). During this masking phase the color is also searched for centers of mass using a moments function. The centers of mass are then pushed onto a vector where further calculation can occur. The masked image is then used as the main image to display as a debug aid where all the colors that the system can see are displayed.

4.2 Locomotive Tracking

After all the colors are found and marked, the system goes through each one and depending on the current mode,

Debug Mode or Tracking Mode, perform one of two operations.

Debug Mode - In Debug Mode, the system ignores all colors that are not orange since the train is marked in orange. The user is instructed to calibrate the track by using a single orange mark on a Train and track it around all possible paths in the system (See Calibration). The Path is then built over a system of grid cells and each location is marked with the sector number. The more times the train is allowed to travel over each sector the more accurate the sector locations will be because it is averaging samples over multiple image frames.

Tracking Mode - In Tracking Mode, the system will look at the (X,Y) coordinates of each of the centers of mass in the system. It will then determine where they are in relation to a defined grid set up. Currently the grid is the full size of the image and each pixel gets a marked grid cell location. When the (X,Y) coordinates are returned, the system checks the sector number of that particular grid cell. If it was not marked on calibration, the system will check the surrounding cells for a sector number. Therefore the current center of mass may be ignored if no sector number is marked. This has been tested and does not seem to have an adverse effect on the system.

5 Results and Future Work

A prototype system has been completed and is running on a Pentium workstation. Real time processing of the video images of multiple locomotives has been achieved at model train velocities in the range of 5 inches per second for a single locomotive. Figure 5 (right) above shows locomotive track sector position as it traverses track under DCC control.

We are currently planning to port this to the processor that is going to run the safety monitor software. Although the current safety system utilizes an Arduino, the plan is to port it to a dedicated processor, the pcDuino from Sparkfun. Although the pcDuino is substantially slower than the Pentium [7], we are investigating speedups including removing pixels from consideration where the locomotives cannot exist. However, one goal of this project was to include the ability to detect non-locomotive objects on the track such as model livestock and vehicles. Determining how to increase the scope of the search with out unreasonably burdening the software is part of the ongoing research.

Upon completion of this project, we will have demonstrated that the traditional approach to modeling safety critical systems with extensive sensors and miles of wire may be replaced with video processing. This should make it much easier for others to replicate our instructional setup given that we will have eliminated a large number of wire connections that would have been required. The video-based system will also make the setup more amenable to change.

6 References

[1] D.J. Coe, J.S. Hogue, and J.H. Kulick, "Software Safety Engineering Education," *2011 International Conference on Software Engineering Researchand Practice (SERP'11)*, WORLDCOMP 2011, July 18-21, 2011, Las Vegas, NV

[2] RTCA DO-178C, “Software Considerations in Airborne Systems and Equipment Certification”, December 13, 2011.

[3] SAE ARP4761, “Guidelines and Methods for Conducting the Safety Assessment Process on Civil Airborne Systems and Equipment”, Issued 1996-12.

[4] SAE ARP4754, “Certification Considerations for Highly-Integrated or Complex Aircraft Systems”, Issued 1996-11.

[5] Link to Digitrax Controller Board, http://www.digitrax.com/products/stationary-decoders/ds64/

[6] Link to pcDuino Development Board, https://www.sparkfun.com/products/11712

[7] Katie Roberts-Hoffman and Pawankumar Hedge, “ARM Cortex-A8 vs. Intel Atom: Architectural and Benchmark Comparisons”,
http://www.ee.unlv.edu/~meiyang/ecg700/readings/ARM%20Cortex-A8%20vs.%20Intel%20Atom.pdf

Strengthening Interrupt Controls in Embedded Systems by Cooperation between Windows CE and REMON

Shigeki Nankaku [1], **Hisao Koizumi**[2]. **and Akira Fukuda**[3]
[1]Computer Science, Osaka Electro-Communication University, Shijyonawate, Osaka, Japan
[2]Science and Engineering, Tokyo Denki University, Ishisaka, Hatoyama, Hiki, Saitama, Saitama
[3]Information Science and Electrical Engineering, Kyushu University, Nishi-ku, Fukuoka, Japan

Abstract - *Many recent embedded system products have sophisticated display functions. Microsoft Windows Embedded CE (hereafter referred to as 'Windows CE') is a widely used embedded OS with a simple GUI design. However, Windows CE has threaded interrupt processes, and therefore it has problems in handling processes for which a strict interrupt response time is requested. We have developed Real-Time Embedded Monitor (REMON) for controlling Interrupt Service Routine (ISR) processes. When using REMON, it is possible to improve the real-time characteristics of the interrupt processes. This paper proposes a system that combines Windows CE and REMON and utilizes the advantages of both to create an embedded system having both sophisticated display functionality and excellent responsiveness to interrupts.*

Keywords: Embedded Systems, Interrupt, Interrupt Service Routine, HMI, Windows

1 Introduction

It is vital for embedded systems to be able to send a response to changes in an external environment within a set period of time, such as in the case of mobile phones where it is necessary to respond to an incoming call while creating an email. Changes in the external environment are detected by a wide variety of sensors and are communicated to the CPU using interrupts.

Interrupts are functions of the CPU, and the mechanism used by the CPU hardware is to place interrupt signals in the interrupt signal lines and call the Interrupt Service Routine (ISR). An ISR is software that is used to respond to changes in an environment. Conceptually, interrupts can be considered as a method by which hardware calls software. In other words, it is possible for hardware to process responses to changes in the embedded system environment by calling the ISR and returning the results.

There are various types of environmental changes, and there is also a wide variation in the times at which these changes occur. Multiple changes can occur simultaneously. The priority of a response depends on the type of change involved. As a result, concurrency is sought in ISRs in order to permit multiple interrupts with priorities attached.

Because ISRs directly handle hardware, such as when prohibiting/permitting hardware-level interrupts to attain exclusive control, knowledge of time restrictions for processes and hardware is required when designing ISR systems. Furthermore, as the ISR directly processes hardware, it has a major influence on the system as a whole [1]-[4].

Normally, hardware is encapsulated and virtualized using a real-time operating system (RTOS). This eliminates the need for most of software that makes up the embedded system to directly handle hardware. Furthermore, the ISR is encapsulated in the same way using the RTOS.

In an RTOS environment, processes are executed using tasks and threads (hereafter referred to as 'threads'). The RTOS provides a variety of functions to threads, such as exclusive control and communication, known as system calls. Threads are able to process interrupts in concurrent using functions also provided by the RTOS [5]-[7].

Many recent embedded systems such as car navigation systems have sophisticated display devices. Microsoft Windows Embedded CE (hereafter referred to as 'Windows CE') is a widely used embedded OS with a simple GUI design.

However, Windows CE has threaded interrupt processes, and therefore it has problems handling processes for which a strict interrupt response time is requested. Although it is possible to directly embed interrupt processing into the Windows CE kernel, since the processing is performed in a state where interrupts are disabled by the kernel, problems such as lower interrupt response times and difficulty in predicting the interrupt response time may arise.

ISR controls are vital in embedded systems in order to enable them to respond to changes in the external environment. We have researched the interrupt scheduler

Real-Time Embedded Monitor (REMON) as a means of controlling interrupts in embedded systems [8]-[10].

As REMON provides the same functionality as an RTOS semaphore for each ISR, it is possible for the ISR to execute exclusive control without using disable interrupt/enable interrupt (DI/EI). The result is that, by shortening the interval in which interrupts are prohibited, the interrupt responsiveness of the embedded system is enhanced, i.e. using REMON improves the real-time characteristics of the embedded system.

REMON provides an independent execution environment for each ISR in which each ISR has a state. Where execution is paused, the state is referred to as a 'wait state'. REMON uses the fact that ISR has a 'wait state' and that ISR can use a semaphore.

REMON is highly versatile and can also be applied to RISC-type CPUs, which do not have hardware-interrupt priorities. Furthermore, it records the interrupts that occur and their frequency so its drop rate for interrupts will be low even when they are occurring at a high frequency. REMON also has ISR control functions such as ISR stack overflow detection. In addition, there is little fluctuation in the processing time for ISR execution, making real-time design simple.

However, the objective of REMON is to control ISRs, and it does not have the sophisticated display functions and human interface (HMI) functionality integrated into Windows CE.

In this paper, we propose, through the link-up of Windows CE and REMON, a method to improve the interrupt response of embedded systems with sophisticated display functionality.

With the proposed system, both REMON and Windows CE are simultaneously loaded on one CPU. High-priority interrupts are processed by REMON, and low-priority interrupts are processed by Windows CE.

Currently, REMON prohibits low-priority interrupts, whereas Windows CE always permits high-priority interrupts. As a result, switching from Windows CE to REMON is always possible.

The proposed system makes it possible to handle processes for which a strict response time is requested and those which Windows CE has traditionally been unable to handle. Furthermore, in the proposed system, it is possible to use sophisticated display features using the functionality of Windows CE.

2 Interrupt Processing by Windows CE and REMON

2.1 What are interrupts?

In this paper, an interrupt is defined as a function that uses changes in a specific terminal within the CPU as a trigger for the CPU to suspend its current activities and to start the execution of a program specified in advance , i.e. the ISR.

Interrupts are functions contained by all CPU hardware. Using an interrupt, it is possible to switch from the executing program to a different program.

The computer system switches control from the application program to the OS using periodic interrupts from a timer device.

In an embedded system, changes in the external environment are detected by various sensors which notify the CPU by issuing an interrupt. The CPU can use this interrupt to execute a process that responds to the change.

Figure 1 show an example of a connection where the sending and receiving of packets is communicated by the network controller to the CPU via an interrupt signal pin.

2.2 Interrupt Processing by Windows CE and Related Issues

Windows CE is a 32-bit RTOS for embedded devices. It is compatible with multiple CPU architectures such as ARM, MIPS, SuperH and x86. Furthermore, as the supported application programming interface (API) is a subset of the Windows API, it has high software productivity and is used by a wide variety of devices such as portable AV players, point-of-sale registers, car navigation systems, video projectors and thin client terminals.

In Windows CE, when a device driver is loaded, a thread that processes interrupts, known as the interrupt service thread (IST) starts(Figure 2). The IST has a higher priority than normal threads. When the IST starts, a system call known as WaitForSingleObject, which waits for the generation of an event provided by Windows CE, is issued straight away and the IST goes into a wait state. When an interrupt is generated, the ISR searches the interrupt number for that interrupt (Figure 2). After notification of the interrupt number from the ISR, the Windows CE kernel generates an event responding to that interrupt number and releases the wait state of the IST. When this happens, IST will process the interrupt.

In Windows CE, an important issue in interrupt processing is that latency may occur because the interrupt is executed by a thread. Therefore, it is difficult to predict the interrupt

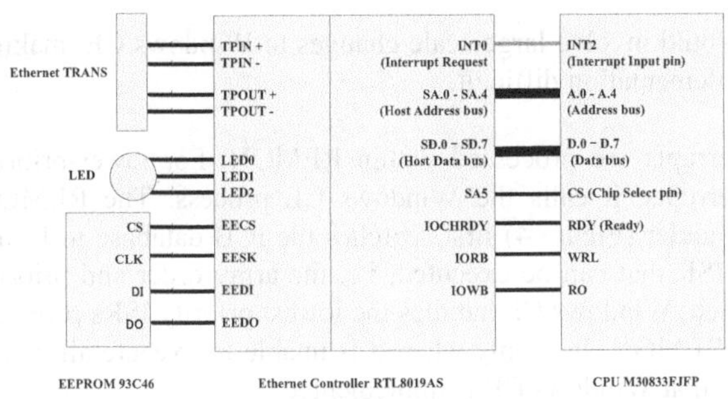

Fig. 1 Use of interrupt signals

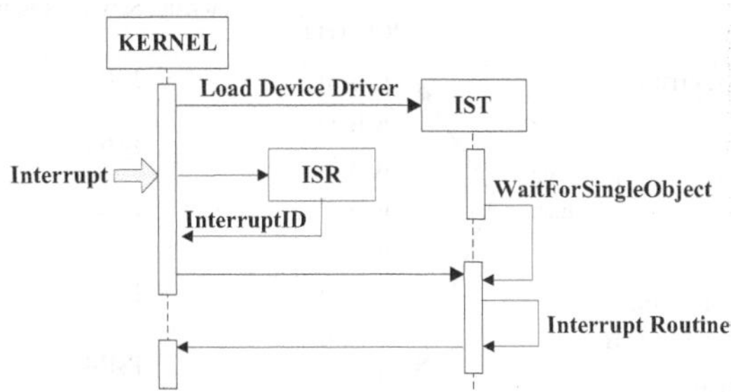

Fig. 2 Interrupt processing in Windows CE

response time and to handle processes for which a strict interrupt response time is requested.

In order to improve the response to the interrupt in Windows CE, it is possible to process the interrupt within the ISR (Figure 3). However, this approach poses a problem, as interrupt processing occurs in an interrupt-prohibited state, because other high-priority interrupts may be delayed. It also does not resolve the issue of predicting the interrupt response time.

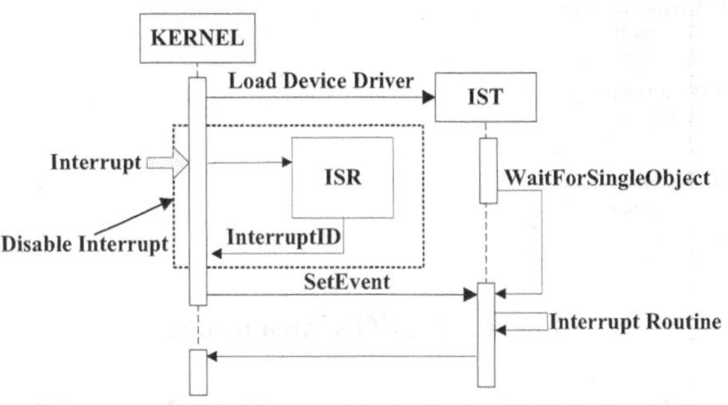

Fig. 3 System in which interrupt processing occurs in the ISR

2.3 Interrupt processing by REMON

REMON, by virtue of having a separate execution environment and state for each individual ISR, can provide each ISR with the same functionality as an RTOS semaphore [8]-[10]. By applying an independent execution environment to an ISR, REMON can associate each ISR with an interrupt control block (ICB, Figure 4). When pausing the execution of an ISR, the execution environment, including the CPU register data, is stored in the ICB, and when restarting the ISR, this data is retrieved.

A stack is allocated to each ISR for use as the local data area for the ISR.

In REMON, each ISR has an independent execution environment, and it is therefore possible for each ISR to restart execution in an arbitrary order. By using REMON, the ISR can be executed with minimal delay. In addition, it is possible to attain exclusive control without using DI/EI. Furthermore, through the use of semaphore provided by REMON for synchronization, it is possible to coordinate the operation of multiple ISRs.

2.4 Issues in the use of semaphore by ISR and the use of semaphore by REMON

Unrelated processing is not delayed in mutual exclusion through semaphores that are used in embedded systems with a RTOS. If an ISR can also use semaphores, the previously described issue does not occur. However, an ISR cannot use semaphores if REMON is not used.

If an ISR requests the acquisition of a semaphore at a time the semaphore is locked by another ISR, the ISR stops executing and saves the context data, which refer to data required for restarting the execution. The restart sequence is not related to the sequence in which the ISRs were stopped, as the restart of a stopped ISR is performed through the release of the semaphore by another ISR. Because ISRs use semaphores, an ISR must be stopped and restarted in a free sequence.

When REMON is not used, ISRs share one stack, where the context is saved. When an ISR is pre-empted, the context data are saved in the stack. As data are restored in the reverse order in which they have been saved in the stack, ISRs are only restarted in the reverse order in which they have been pre-empted.

REMON assigns each ISR an individual storage place for its context, thus enabling the use of ISR semaphores.

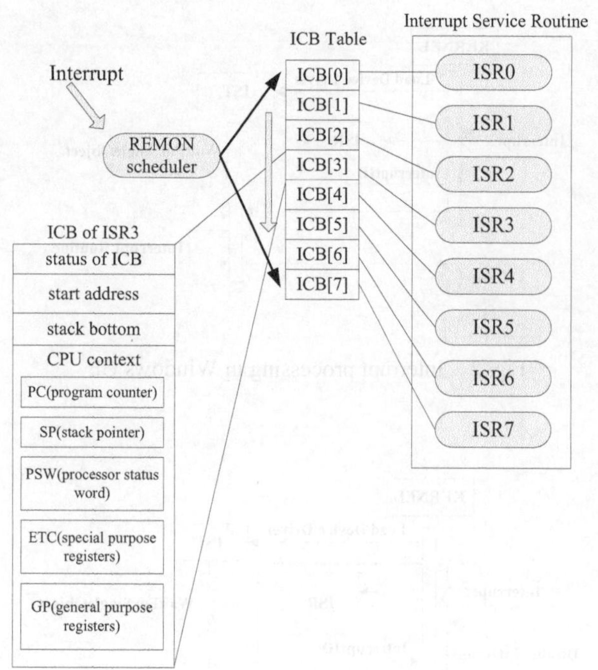

Fig. 4. REMON Architecture

3 Cooperation between Windows CE and REMON

Here we propose a new embedded system that cooperate Windows CE and REMON. We hope that, by combining the sophisticated display capabilities of Windows CE and the interrupt-control functionality of REMON, the new system can be effective as an embedded system that has advanced display functionality and can process interrupts within strict response times.

There are several methods of combination of REMON and Windows CE and each is described briefly below.

3.1 Method involving replacement of the Windows CE interrupt handler by REMON

With this method (Figure 5), the Windows CE interrupt process can be freely started from REMON. However, the structure in which the interrupt is processed by IST does not change, and this does not promise much improvement in the interrupt response

3.2 Method that calls Windows CE from REMON

With this method (Figure 6), all interrupts from the hardware are received by REMON and high-priority time. Furthermore, it would involve large-scale changes to Windows CE, making implementation difficult.

interrupts are processed within REMON. For lower-priority interrupts, it calls the Windows CE process. The REMON scheduler (Figure 4) first searches the ICB database to locate an ISR that can be executed, i.e. the array order and priority match. Windows CE handles the lowest priority ISRs received by REMON. It is only when it is unable to execute all of the ISR that Windows CE is implemented.

With this method, it is also possible to monitor Windows CE. This method also allows REMON and Windows CE to be developed separately.

However, this method of linking REMON and Windows CE has a disadvantage in that it further complicates the already complicated Windows CE interrupt sequence. In addition, the Windows CE interrupts are also delayed.

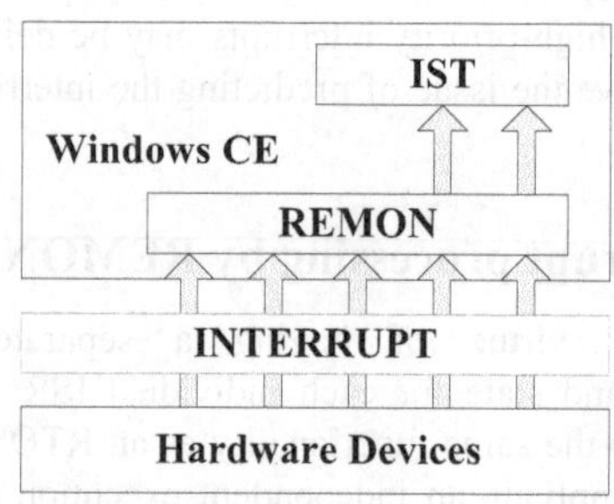

Fig. 5. Method where Windows CE interrupt handler is replaced by REMON

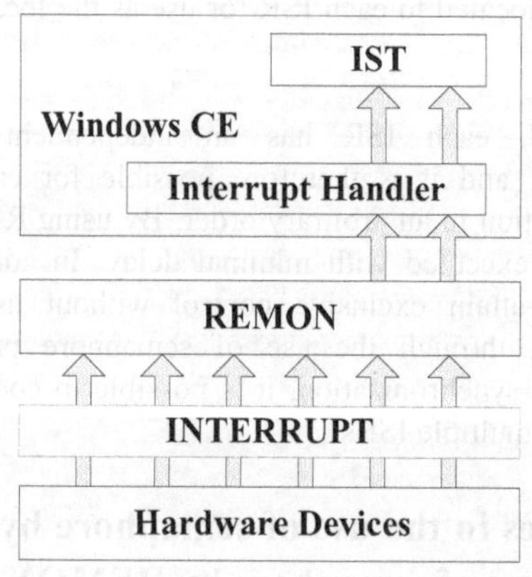

Fig. 6. Method where Windows CE is called from REMON

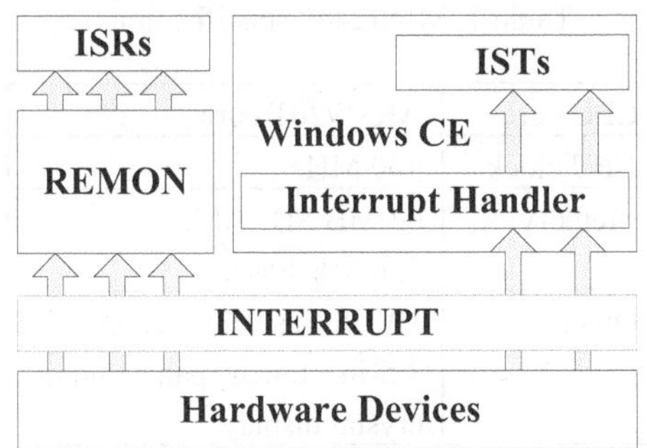

Fig. 7. System that separates on the basis of the interrupt level

3.3 Method to separate Windows CE and REMON interrupts using interrupt priority

With this method (Figure 7), the interrupts to be processed by REMON and Windows CE are separated. While REMON is executing high-priority interrupts, low priority interrupts are prohibited. As a result, the interrupts processed by Windows CE are prevented from hindering the execution of the high-priority interrupts processed by REMON. Furthermore, since Windows CE never prohibits interrupts and always allows high-priority interrupts, it is always possible to switch to REMON for any high-priority interrupts that occur while Windows CE is executing.

Figure 8 shows the operation of ISR and IST, using CPU interrupt priority, when the interrupts processed by REMON and Windows CE are separated. CPU interrupt priority is a function included in the CPU hardware that can set the priority of interrupts. It is also possible to prohibit/allow interrupts from the software on the basis of priority. Figure 9 shows the transitions in Windows CE and REMON when using a method that separates interrupts on the basis of priority.

Figure 10 shows the sequence of processing interrupts when high-priority interrupts occur in a system that uses interrupt priority to separate interrupts. The figure shows that REMON is called when a high-priority interrupt occurs. If other high-priority interrupts occur, REMON is called, but REMON is not called for low-priority interrupts, Windows CE is called.

Figure 11 shows the interrupt operating sequence when a low-priority interrupt is generated in a system that separates interrupts on the basis of priority.

These are processed by Windows CE, with the same interrupt process operation as that previously used by Windows CE.

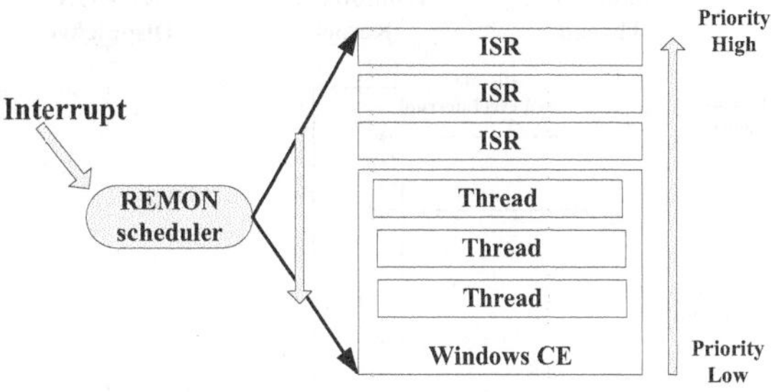

Fig. 8. Windows CE–REMON architecture

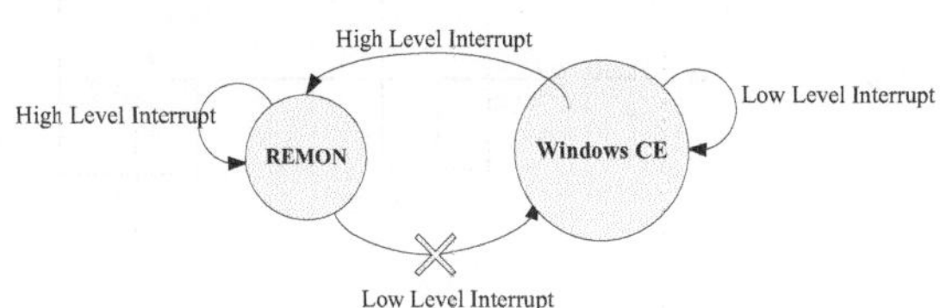

Fig. 9. State transition for Windows CE and REMON interrupts

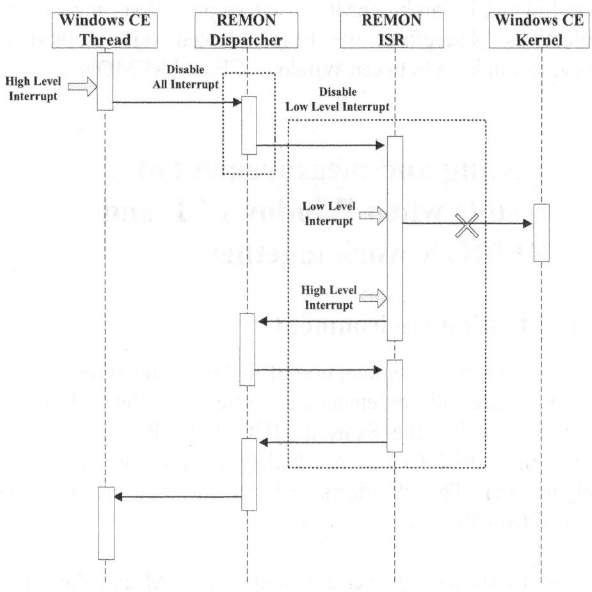

Fig. 10. Operation when a high-priority interrupts occurs

When a low-priority interrupt is generated, Windows CE is called. Further, when high-priority interrupts that are processed by REMON are generated, REMON is called.

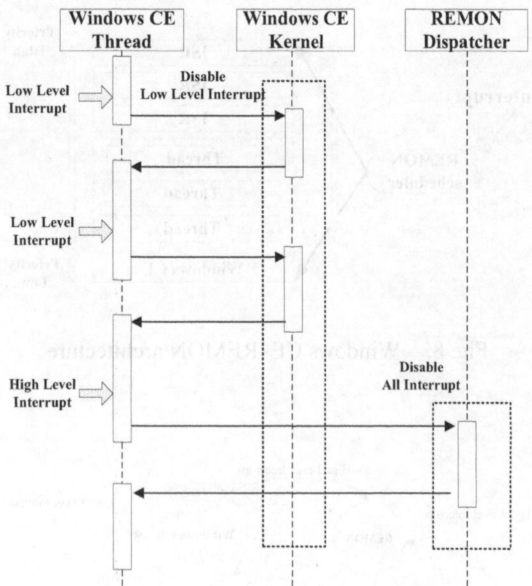

Fig. 11. Operation on occurrence of low priority interrupts

This method (Method 3.3) of creating a combined Windows CE–REMON system, using interrupt priority to separate Windows CE and REMON interrupts, best meets our objectives. Therefore, we have adopted this method to provide a link-up between Windows CE and REMON.

4 Testing and measurement of results when Windows CE and REMON work together

4.1 Testing environment

In order to test the combination of REMON and Windows CE, we have created an embedded system on the MINI2440 (Table 1), using the Samsung S3C2440 ARM architecture CPU, the ARM CPU most widely used by Windows CE (Figure 12). The Windows CE version used is Windows Embedded CE6.

Figure 13 shows the interrupt model in ARM and the ARM interrupt control register. In ARM, two levels of interrupts, known as IRQ and FIQ, are present. As FIQ processes at a faster speed than IRQ, ARM uses a banked register in which a part of the register can be switched. As FIQ has a banked register, it can process at faster speeds than IRQ.

FIQ is not used by Windows CE and is used only as an interrupt executed by REMON.

Table 1. MINI2440 specifications

CPU core	ARM920T core
CPU clock	400 MHz
Memory	64 MB SDRAM, 256 MB Flash
Other	10/100Base-T Ethernet 3.5-in. touch panel liquid crystal display

Fig. 12. Test environment MINI2440

Reset
Undefined
Software Interrupt
PrefetchAbprt
DataAbort
FIQ
IRQ
ARM Exception

Register [CPSR]

-	I	F	T	M

I : IRQ Disable
F : FIQ Disable

Fig. 13. ARM interrupt model

Table 2. Test environment MINI2440

	Interrupt response speed (µs)
Windows CE	32.09
REMON–Windows CE	4.58

4.2 High-speed ISR switchover

FIQ is not used by the Windows CE kernel. By using REMON for FIQ interrupts, the efficiency of interrupt processing can be increased.

When the REMON ISR is initiated by temporarily disabling IRQ interrupts, the embedded system can process interrupts at high speeds without the interrupt overhead of Windows CE.

When processing interrupts with a strict interrupt response time, it is necessary to switch to ISR at high speeds when an interrupt occurs. Furthermore, if the interrupt that occurs has a low priority, it must return processing promptly. For this reason, the embedded system is constructed in such a way that switchover uses the FIQ banked register and can switch with the minimum amount of processing.

4.3 Measurement results

We used a logic analyser to measure the time from when the interrupt was generated until the time processing started for Windows CE alone and for the combined embedded REMON– Windows CE system. As the logic analyser conducted sampling using 800 MHz signals, the minimum measured unit was 0.25 ns. Measurements showed the mean value for each and every 100 calculations. The results are shown in Table 2.

While processing interrupts with Windows CE had a response time of 32.09 μs, this was reduced to 4.58 μs

when processing interrupts with the combined embedded REMON–Windows CE system. Thus, we were able to attain a sufficiently practicable interrupt response time.

5 Conclusions

By combining Windows CE and REMON, it has become possible to handle and process strict interrupt response times that could not be processed with Windows CE alone. Furthermore, we believe that realizing exclusive control of interrupt processing has led to an improved level of reliability in regard to interrupts.

Issues to be examined in the future include the reinforcement of the interrupt control functionality of Windows CE through sharing the interrupts of Windows CE and REMON. We also plan to apply this to other real-time operating systems.

6 References

[1] Shigeki Nankaku : “Guarantee of interruption response time in embedded systems”, Systems, Control and Information, The Institute of Systems, Control and Information Engineers, Vol.51, No.9 pp.388-392 (2007) (in Japanese)

[2] Ministry of Economy, Trade and Industry Japan: Embedded Software Industry Survey Report 2010, (2011)

[3] ED LIPIANSKY : "EMBEDDED SYSTEMS HARDWARE FOR SOFTWARE ENGINEERS", WILEY IEEE PRESS, (2012)

[4] Julio Sanchez and Maria P. Canton : "EMBEDDE SYSTEMS CIRCUITS and PROGRAMMING", CRC Press, (2012)

[5] Phillip A. Laplante and Seppo J. Ovaska : "Real-Time Systems Design and Analysis 4TH EDITION", WILEY IEEE PRESS, (2012)

[6] Alan Burns and Andy Wellings : "Real-Time Systems and Programming Languages", ADDISON-WESLEY, (1997)

[7] Giorgio C. Buttazzo : "Hard Real-Time Computing Systems", Springer, (2011)

[8] Shigeki Nankaku : “Development of the simple interrupt monitor REMON”, Proceedings of Electronics, Information and Systems Conference Electronics, Information and Systems Society, pp.447-448 (2009) (in Japanese)

[9] Shigeki Nankaku, Hisao Koizumi, Akira Fukuda: “Control of Stack Overflow of ISRs for Embedded Systems without MMU”, Proceedings of Electronics, Information and Systems Conference Electronics, Information and Systems Society, pp. 254-259 (2012) (in Japanese)

[10] Shigeki Nankaku, Kiminori Mizushino, Hisao Koizumi, Akira Fukuda : “Interrupt Scheduler REMON for Embedded Systems”, The Institute of Electrical Engineers of Japan, Transactions on Electronics, Information and Systems Society, Vol.133 No.2 pp. 316-325 (2013) (in Japanese)

Independent Verification and Validation of Software for Weapon Management System of a High Performance Aircraft

Sudha Srinivasan, Rekha.R, Dr.K.Karunakar
IV&V, Aeronautical Development Agency, Bangalore, Karnataka, India

Abstract - *The failure of safety critical embedded software is unacceptable be it for safety, security or economic reasons. The risk of software failure in complex embedded systems is overcome by using the Independent Verification and Validation (IV&V) technique. The process of IV&V and its planning needs to be initiated early in the development life cycle of the weapon management system for a high performance aircraft. In the present context, the aircraft has so far achieved successful integration and release of Air-to-Ground weapons and Air-to-Air close combat missiles. The above functionalities are achieved by complex embedded software systems which constitute the weapon management system for which advanced IV&V techniques have been used to remove errors during development phase. The methodology used for performing IV&V of software for weapon management system has been discussed in this paper.*

Keywords: Independent Verification and Validation, Safety Critical Embedded System

1 Introduction

Software IV&V is a systems engineering process employing rigorous methodologies for evaluating the correctness, quality and safety of the airborne embedded systems throughout the software development life cycle. It provides for the early detection and identification of risk elements. The program is then able to take actions to mitigate these risks early in the life cycle.

The IV&V Program plays a key role to identify, understand and mitigate risks associated with the safety critical systems, increase the probability of success of the mission as a whole while reducing software errors, development cost and development time.

The weapon management system is a high integrity software system which manages the integration, preparation, selection and firing of Air-to-Ground Weapons and Air-to-Air Close Combat Missiles.

In this paper, the method used for performing the IV&V of the weapon management system of a high performance aircraft which is categorized as an airborne safety critical embedded system is discussed. The importance of carrying out the compiler validation, evolving the coding standards and performing the independent verification and validation of the Programmable Logic devices, INSITU software, device driver software and acceptance test software for hardware is discussed apart from the method used for performing the IV&V of the application software of the embedded system. The architecture and system details of the weapon management system is however not discussed in this paper since this paper emphasizes on the work carried out for the IV&V of weapon management system , which can be followed as a generic approach for performing the IV&V of any safety critical airborne embedded system.

Outline of this paper is as follows: section 2 describes the Independent Verification and Validation, Section 3 describes IV&V of application software, Section 4 describes the IV&V of hardware related software, Section 5 describes the coding standards and compiler validation and Section 6 summarizes this paper.

2 Independent Verification & Validation

In the modern high performance aircraft, when the initial design was perceived, many safety and mission critical functions were planned to be implemented in software which amounted to many embedded software systems.

In order to ensure safe flight and error free performance, the technique of IV&V was adopted and has pioneered in the country from the year 1990 in order to bring out new techniques and new methods to evaluate complex systems.

The three types of independence required for an effective verification and validation process identified for the IV&V of weapon management system software are:

Firstly , Technical independence where the members of the IV&V team are not involved in the development of the software and this team works with an unbiased approach in learning about the system requirements, proposed solutions for building the system, and problems encountered. Technical independence of the IV&V team is crucial in the team's ability to detect the subtle software requirements, software design, and coding errors that frequently escape detection during development testing and Software Quality Assurance reviews.

Secondly, Managerial independence where the IV&V team independently decides the areas of the software or system to be analyzed and tested, the IV&V techniques to be conducted, schedule of tasks (within the framework of the system schedules) and technical issues to act upon. The IV&V team provides its findings in a timely fashion to the development team who act upon the reported discrepancy and findings.

Thirdly, financial independence is achieved with the budget being allocated by programme management and controlled at high level such that IV&V effectiveness is not compromised. This independence helps in usage of appropriate tools and preventing the delays of IV&V analysis and timely reporting of the results.

The focus of the IV&V objective is accomplished by providing value-added, high quality, technical assurance that the safety critical system being used is meeting its requirements in terms of the technical, safety, security, and reliability objectives of that mission.

3 IV&V of Application Software

Incremental approach is followed for the IV&V of the application software of the weapon management system. The IV&V of the software life cycle artifacts for the application software are carried out incrementally for each weapon integrated to the aircraft. Regression analysis and testing is carried out when there is a change in requirements. Finally the IV&V with the integration of all the weapons is carried out.

Figure 1 represents the independent verification and validation process which is followed for the application software of the weapon management system.

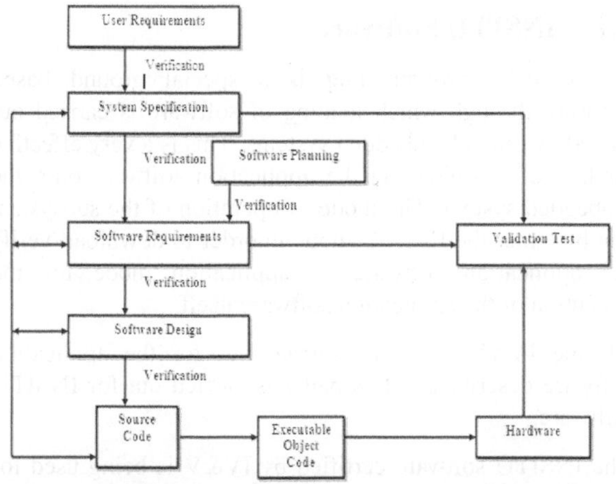

Figure 1: IV and V Process

The IV&V of application software begins early in the life cycle, when the user requirements are captured and continues till the system testing is completed successfully without errors. As a part of the IV&V activity in the software requirements phase, the correctness of the allocation of system requirements to software is checked along with the correctness, completeness, non-ambiguity and testability of the software requirements.

Concurrently with software requirements IV&V, software system test planning is initiated. All the proposed testing for the system to ensure comprehensive testing and planning of appropriate resources are carried out. The Software Requirement Specification (SRS) and Interface Requirement Specification (IRS) documents supplied by the development team are analyzed and traceability to the system requirements documents are checked in order to ensure completeness.

The software design IV&V activities occur after the software requirements have undergone the software IV&V process and the software design or an increment of the software design is completed.

The software IV&V tasks of traceability, evaluation and interface analysis provide assurance that software requirements are not misrepresented, incompletely implemented or incorrectly implemented. By verifying that the software design meets its software requirements, the software design IV&V activity also supports validation that the software design meets system requirements. Code walkthrough is another opportunity to find and remove errors that can cause unnecessary costs and delays from advancing poor code into any of the test activities. Code validation is accomplished through unit test described below:

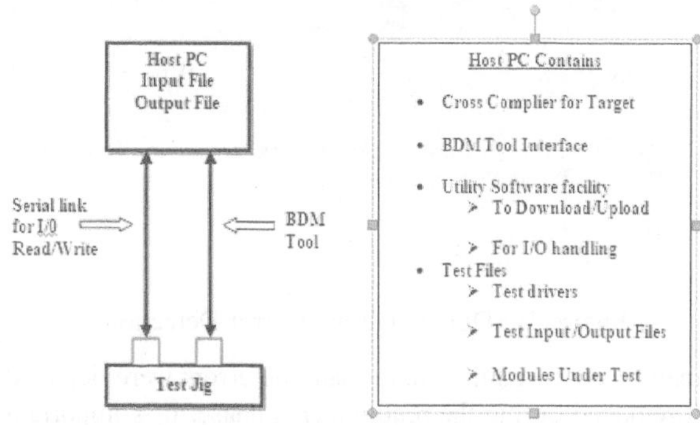

Figure 2: Test setup for Unit Testing

Unit testing is the test of the software elements at the lowest level of development. Since the weapon management software is a safety critical software, unit testing is performed on the target as shown in figure 2.

In order to ensure coverage, test tools are used for unit testing and the output of the tool such as the coverage chart shown in Figure 3 is released as evidence to the designers.

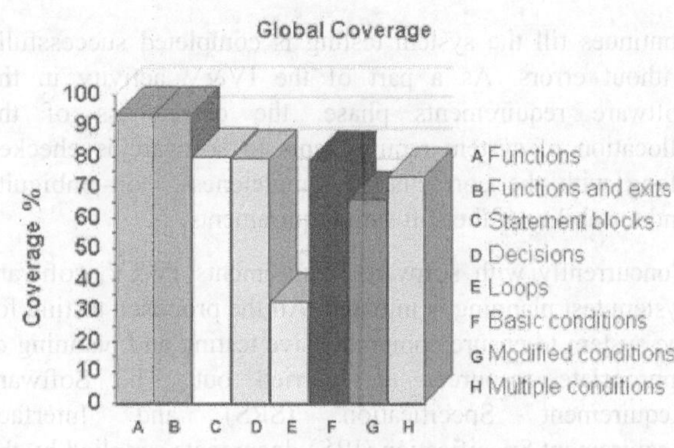

Figure 3: Coverage Chart

Appropriate regression testing with identified parameter setting is performed whenever changes are made in software.

System testing, in the context of software IV&V, involves the conduct of tests to execute the completely integrated system.

Figure 4 shows the plot of the number of errors detected by IV&V at each stage of the software development life cycle (SDLC) for one of the subsystems having about 20000 lines of code of the weapon management system.

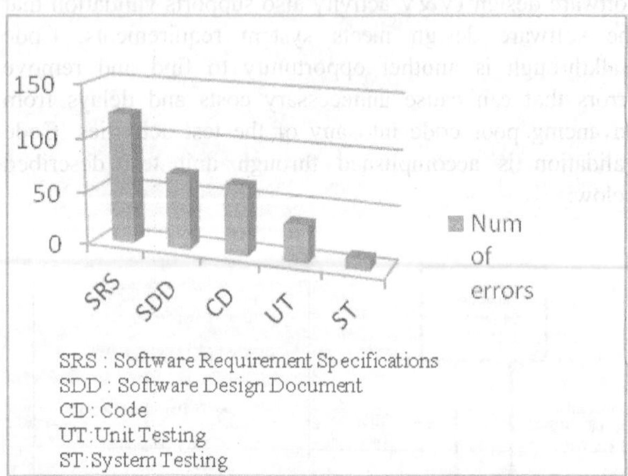

Figure 4: SDLC Stage-wise Error Detection

It may be observed that more than 100 errors were detected and removed during the requirements phase. It is important to note that the stringent IV&V process followed to catch errors in the early phases of the software life cycle has resulted in reduced errors during system testing resulting in saving of time and cost.

The recommendations provided by the IV&V team, serves as the basis for obtaining certification of this system for flight from the certification agencies. The techniques used for the IV&V of application software include analysis, walkthroughs, simulations, reviews, checklists and defect tracking of the software system.

4 IV&V of Hardware Related Software

For Safety Critical systems, extensive test and evaluation of all the software present in the embedded system is essential. Thus, besides the independent verification and validation of the application software, the IV&V of all the software pertaining to the hardware is performed. This includes the IV&V of INSITU software, IV&V of software for acceptance test of the hardware, IV&V of device driver software, and IV&V of Programmable Logic Devices.

Table 1 shows the Size (approximate lines of code -LOC) of the software and the number of errors uncovered by IV&V in each of the hardware artifacts of one of the subsystems of the weapon management system.

Table 1 : Software size and errors detected

Hardware Artifact	Approx. LOC	Num of Errors
INSITU Software	10000	40
Acceptance Test Software	11000	93
Device driver Software	4000	57
Programmable hardware	1209	11

The IV&V activities carried out for each of the hardware artifact of the weapon management system listed in the table is discussed below:

4.1 INSITU Software

INSITU programming is a special ground based software through which loading of software is carried out for safety critical embedded systems. This is a very effective method of downloading the application software onto the embedded system. The mode of operation of the subsystem can be either the INSITU mode in order to download/verify the application software or application mode for the execution of the application software itself.

All the IV&V activities carried out for the application software described in this paper is carried out for INSITU Software.

The INSITU software certified by IV&V is being used for downloading of application software and also for the checksum verification of the weapon management system. This is proved to be an efficient and time saving method.

4.2 Software for Acceptance Test of Hardware

The IV&V of software for the acceptance test of hardware is a very important activity since the application software is ported onto this validated hardware. Carrying out the acceptance test of hardware before testing the application software on target, enables clear bifurcation of errors encountered during development and testing of the embedded system.

The verification and validation of the software used for the acceptance test of all the hardware components present in the unit under test are performed. The activities carried out include, study of the data sheets of each of the hardware components and memory mapping, verification of software requirement specification, software design, code analysis of the acceptance test software and test / analysis of the coverage of each test. For example: Testing of the Flash memory involves the loading, verification and checksum calculation of the entire Flash contents.

The tests conducted are specific to the hardware design of the particular unit under test and the IV&V team participates in the final acceptance test of the hardware.

4.3 Device Driver Software

Device drivers act as translators between the device and programs that use the device. IV&V of device drivers of each device is carried out. Each device has its own set of specialized commands that its device driver software contains. The device driver accepts the generic commands from a program and translates them into specialized commands for the device.

The activities for IV&V of device driver software included the study of the devices used, analysis of software requirements for each of the devices, analysis of the device driver design document, code analysis, preparation of test plan for testing each of the device driver functions, preparation of test matrix table for all the functional test cases and preparation of test drivers for each unit level function for each of the devices.

Figure 5: Device Driver Test Setup

Figure 5 shows the device driver test setup with a Host PC having compiler and BDM tool which is used to download the software and to access the RAM to see the results. It is connected to the Background Debug Mode (BDM) port of the unit under test.

The test set up for testing of device driver software is established based on the devices used and the test approach involves the following steps:

STEP 1: Identification of inputs: The necessary input parameters are identified as per the functional requirements.

STEP 2: Test driver: The test driver is custom written for testing identified drivers.

STEP 3: Development of Test Matrix: After the code analysis, based on the functionalities, the test cases are generated manually.

STEP 4: Test Execution: The test cases are executed on the unit under test.

STEP 5: Result analysis and generation of report: The result obtained after the execution of the test cases is compared with the expected output and Pass / Fail criteria is recorded.

The IV&V report with the observations documented is released for all the activities carried out for the device driver software.

4.4 IV&V Of Programmable Logic Devices

The application of Programmable Logic devices has become widespread, especially in mission/safety critical applications and hence the means to verify and validate their design and functionality is essential.

The IV&V of the requirements of Programmable Logic Devices involves analysis of requirements, traceability of requirements to hardware specifications, check for missing requirements, ambiguous requirements, duplication of requirements and correct functional partitioning.

Programmable hardware designs that are primarily designed at the behavioral and the structural level using Very high speed integrated circuit Hardware Description Language (VHDL) are good candidates for IV&V methods. IV&V involves understanding & analysis of design and verification of correct implementation of every requirement.

IV&V of VHDL source code includes checking the entity declarations, architecture declarations, structural and behavioral functionality, and verification of Pin numbers against the hardware schematics.

IV&V testing of VHDL code comprises of preparation of test cases to be tested on the simulator, generation of test benches for running the simulation, execution of tests on the simulator, analysis of actual test results against the expected results, preparation of test report with simulation results captured as waveforms. Further, testing on target is carried out to ensure correctness.

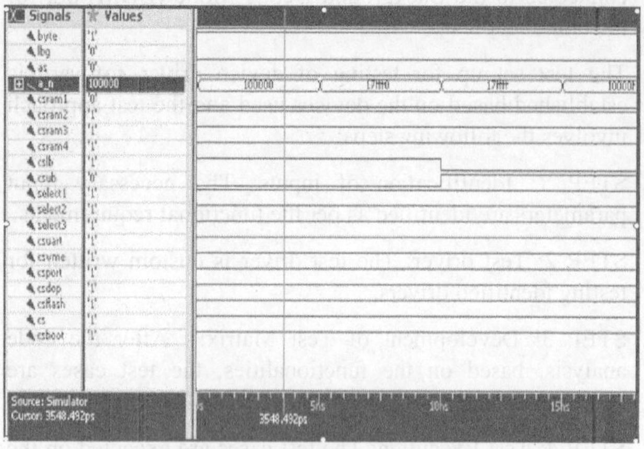

Figure 6: Simulation Results

The report is then released to the designers and the regression testing is again carried out for the corrected version. Figure 6 shows the simulation results for a sample test case.

5 Coding Standards and Compiler Validation

The general-purpose languages like Ada and C , which were developed to meet a number of different needs makes the supporting compilation system and run-time environment too large to be used with confidence on safety-critical applications.

It is not considered safe to use these languages in its complete form for safety critical applications. The use of the programming language is restricted to a well-defined and analyzable subset which does not contain complex and non-deterministic features of the language. For the weapon management system software, the safe subset was defined by the IV&V team which was followed for the design and development of the software system.

The compiler has direct effect on the final code that is produced and the compilation process could introduce faults or unsafe features into the object code. Thus, it is necessary to take steps to ensure that the conversion to object code does not introduce errors or undesirable machine level features.

In order to find compiler code generated faults and to provide the level of confidence required for safety critical software, compiler validation is carried out before the compiler is used for the development of software of safety critical systems like the weapon management system.

6 Summary

IV&V is a valuable tool for increasing software quality and reliability. Verification, Validation, and Certification are essential in the life cycle of any safety critical embedded system.

Independent Verification and Validation (IV &V) is important, especially in software, as the complexity of software in systems has increased and planning for IV&V is necessary from the beginning of the development life cycle.

It is also very important to perform the Compiler Validation, IV&V of Programmable Logic devices , INSITU software , Device Driver software and software for acceptance test of hardware apart from the IV&V of application software as brought out in this paper. Many errors are detected during these phases and subsequently they are removed from the system.

IV&V stands tall in the software life cycle of an embedded application and is very closely linked with certification because it is a major component in support of certification.

Shouldering the responsibility of correcting the design/development mistakes on one hand and working hand in hand with the designer to produce every evidence to certification agencies on the other hand is a major challenge of an IV&V specialist.

7 References

[1]Dr.K.Karunakar. "Software Testing Effective Methods, Tools and Techniques". Tata McGraw Hill, pp. 261 "Testing of Embedded Software Systems used in Aerospace Applications".

[2]Audit Report on Independent Verification and Validation of Software Released by Assistant Inspector General for audits "National Aeronautics and Space Administration". NASA IG-03-011,A-02-005-00, March 2003.

[3]Wallace Dolores R. "Software Verification and Validation An Overview". Software IEEE , vol. 6, issue 3, pp. 10-17, 1989.

[4] Arthur James D. "Evaluating the Effectiveness of Independent Verification and Validation" , vol. 32, issue 10 pp. 79-83., 1999.

[5] IEEE Standard for Software Verification and Validation Link: https://standards.ieee.org/findstds/standard/1012-1998.html

SESSION

POSTERS AND SHORT PAPERS

Chair(s)

TBA

An Effective Method to Test Sensor Applications

Hwan-Cheol Joeng and Jang-Wu Jo
Department of Computer Engineering, Dong-A University

Abstract - *The common way of testing sensor application is to build a test board, connect sensors to the board, and test sensor applications on the board. This paper introduced the problem of existing approach to test sensor applications, and proposed our approach to solve it. In the existing approach, it's impossible to apply the techniques of automatic test data generation. In other words, users cannot manage test data of sensor applications. This paper proposed sensor reading generator through which users can manage test data.*

Keywords: *Sensors, SW testing, Sensor applications, Embedded SW*

1 Introduction

Sensors can be defined as devices that sense external stimuli, and change them into electrical signals[1]. In addition to the above basic functions, sensors can convert electrical signals into digital signals. The digital signals are then processed and analyzed by micro processors. For the purpose of precise processing and efficient analysis, the digital signals can be interfaced to communicate with computers which are called as Central Control Unit[2]. Software that run on the Central Control Unit are called sensor applications, which receive sensor readings(digital signal) from sensors, process and analyze them precisely[3].

Recently, sensors are more and more widely used in many areas, such as in automotive applications[4], medical applications[5], and marine application[6] etc. Due to defects in the sensor software, a lot of accidents have been reported: Naro launch failure, AUDI A6's SW defects of deceleration sensor, BMW's SW defects of injection pump, Hyundai's SW defects of air bag[7].

In this paper, we survey how to test sensor applications and introduce some problems of current testing methods. We also propose an effective method to test sensor applications, that can manage test data of sensor applications without using sensor data from real sensors..

Section 2 gives a motivation of this research. In section 3, we propose an effective method to test sensor applications where users can manage sensor readings without real sensors, which is possible by sensor reading generator. We discuss related works and conclude in Section 4.

2 Background

The current method for testing the sensor application is to build an board-level system and run the application on that board[3]. The board-level system which has the same environment as the target system needs to be built and sensors need to be connected to the board-level system.

Fig.2 shows the block diagram of board-level system, including test-board, sensors, and a kind of communications. The test data of sensor applications on the test-board is sensor readings. The problem of this approach is that the range of test data is limited, because sensor readings represent the environment of sensors and environment has to be changed to get different sensor readings.

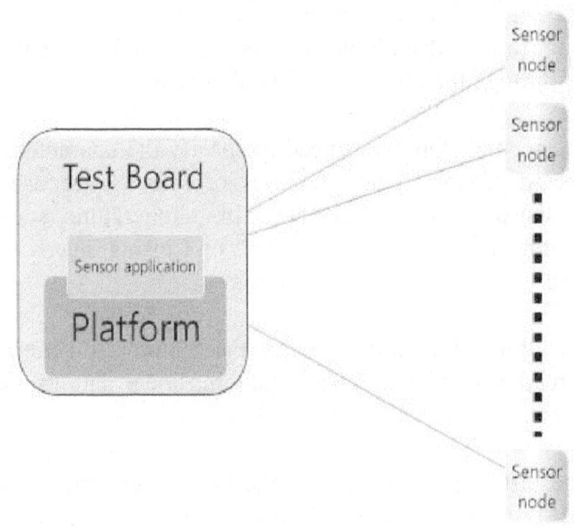

Fig. 1 Structure of testing sensor applications

3 Our Approach

The goal of our approach is as following. 1) On the view of programmers of sensor applications, programs need not to be changed in case of using our approach. Without modification of sensor applications, sensor readings can be replaced by sensor readings generated by our sensor reading generator. 2) Sensor reading generator is capable of generating any value of the range of the sensor. 3) Sensor readings from multiple sensors can be also generated at the same time.

Fig.2 shows the process of generating sensor readings without using real sensors. At the bottom of Fig.2, sensor reading generator consists of four steps to generate artificial sensor readings.

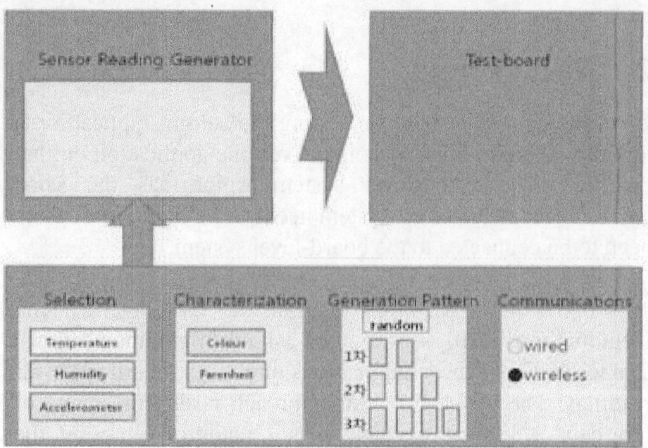

Fig. 2 Sensor reading generator

At the step of sensor selection, users select a sensor that they want to use. If multiple sensors are needed, you can add sensors through the repetition of the first step.

At the second step, users need to specify the characteristics of selected sensors. Characteristics of sensors are used to define sensors. As an example of temperature sensors, temperature unit, such as Fahrenheit or Celsius, needs to be specified.

At the third step, users specify the pattern of generating sensor readings, such as random pattern, linear pattern, curve pattern etc.

At the last step, users specify the kind of communications between test-board and sensor reading generator. Two kinds of communications, such as wired or wireless one, are included. The details of wire communication include serial, parallel, internet, and CAN(Controller Area Network) and those of wireless one include wifi, Bluetooth, mote, and RFID.

4 Conclusion

This paper introduced the problem of existing approach to test sensor applications, and proposed our approach to solve it. In the existing approach, it's impossible to apply the techniques of automatic test data generation. In other words, users cannot manage test data of sensor applications.

This paper proposed sensor reading generator through which users can manage test data. In the future research, we will apply techniques of test data generation, such as branch-coverage or path coverage, to sensor reading generator.

5 Acknowledgement

This work was supported by 2012 Academic Industry Co-innovation Project from Busan Techno Park.

6 References

[1] Namki Min, “Introduction to sensors”, Dong-il press, 2013

[2] A. Feng, et. al, “Embedded system for sensor communication and security”, IET Information Security, Vol. 6, Iss.2, 2012

[3] H. Ramamurthy, et. al, “Wireless Industrial Monitoring and Control Using a Smart Sensor Platform”, IEEE SENSORS JOURNAL, Vol. 7, NO. 5, 2007

[4] M. H. Salah, et. al, “A smart multiple-loop automotive cooling system – model, control, and experimental study”, IEEE/ASME Trans. Mechatronics, Vol. 15, NO. 1, 2010

[5] M. E. Cater, T. O'Reilly, “Promoting interoperable ocean sensors the smart ocean sensors consortium”, Proc. OCEANS 2009, MTS/IEEE Biloxi – Marine Technology for Our Future, Oct. 2009

[6] M. Rusu, et. al, “Distributed e-health system with smart self-care units”, Proc. IEEE Fifth Int. Conf. on Intelligent Computer Communication and Processing, 2009

[7] S.I. Cha, “The Present and Prospect of Software Testing Industry”, communications of KIISE, vol.28, no.11, 2010

[8] Williarm C. Hetzel, “Program test methods”, Prentice-Hall, 1973

[9] B Korel, “Automated software test data generation”, IEEE Transations on Software Engineering, Vol. 16, 1990

[10] Phil McMinn, “Search-based software test data generation: asurvey”, Software Tesing, Verification and Reliability, John Wiley & Sons, 2004

Towards Cycle-Accurate Performance Predictions for Real-Time Embedded Systems

Konstantinos Triantafyllidis, Egor Bondarev, Peter H.N. de With
Eindhoven University of Technology
5600 MB, Eindhoven, The Netherlands
{k.triantafyllidis, e.bondarev, p.h.n.de.with}@tue.nl

Abstract— **In this paper we present a model-based performance analysis method for component-based real-time systems, featuring cycle-accurate predictions of latencies and enhanced system robustness. The method incorporates the following phases: (a) instruction-level profiling of SW components, (b) modeling the obtained performance metrics in MARTE-compatible models, (c) generation, schedulability analysis and simulation of a system model, (d) architecture improvement based on the analysis results. Our proposed method incorporates both the schedulability analysis and the simulation technique, complementing the advantages and eliminating the limitations of the individual steps. Moreover, the cycle-accurate performance metrics initiated by our method lead to accurate performance predictions for an autonomous navigation robot system, with only 6% deviation (or less) from the actual performance metrics.**

Component-based development has become an adopted practice in the real-time systems domain, since it enables rapid system prototyping and development of a system from existing blocks. Real-time systems are normally characterized by hard performance requirements, such as throughput, latency, etc. Therefore, at the early composition phases, reliable assessment methods are required to accurately evaluate and predict the performance of a designed system. Such analysis should consider the complete set of influencing factors, starting with intrinsic properties of hardware blocks (e.g. cache hierarchy) and ending with behavior of system tasks over the SW/HW topology and parameter-dependent workload. Another challenge comes from the limitations of analysis mechanisms, which are normally classified into two categories: analytical methods and simulation techniques. The former does not provide a detailed execution timeline, while the latter cannot guarantee a proper prediction of worst-case situations.

In the past decade, several methods addressing the problems of SW/HW component modeling, predictable assembly and evaluation of real-time systems have been proposed by the research community. Cortellessa *et al.* [2] have proposed a comprehensive approach for SW/HW component modeling, composition and consequent simulation of an assembly behavior. Klobedanz *et al.* [3] have discussed a performance analysis approach based on the AUTOSAR model. Both approaches do not provide platform-independent models with cycle-level accuracy. Bondarev *et al.* [4] have proposed a solution for design and performance analysis of conventional CBSE embedded real-time systems based on ROBOCOP components. This approach does not support detailed modeling and simulation of network-related primitives. Finally, Thiele *et al.* [6] presented an analytical method targeting worst-case latencies without predictions on detailed execution behavior.

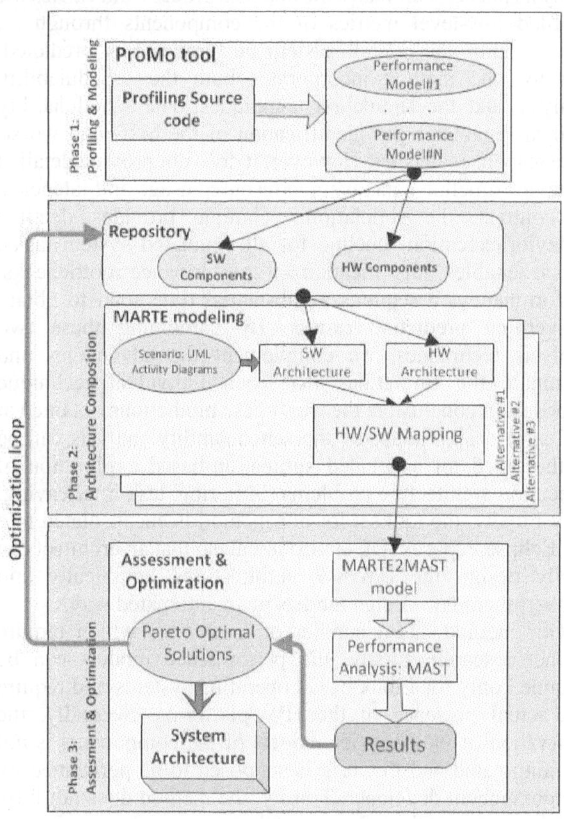

Fig.1: Analysis and design-space exploration method for RT systems

In this paper, we present our ongoing work on the ProMARTES method for analysis and design space exploration of real-time component assembly, see Fig. 1. The method consists of the following three phases. The *Profiling and Modeling* phase aims at profiling and automated generation of cycle-accurate performance models (MARTE compatible) for individual components at component development time. The *Architecture Composition* phase includes component selection, composition, SW/HW mapping and automated generation of a system model based on defined workload scenarios. The composition can be performed for a number of architectural alternatives. The *Analysis and Optimization* phase enables prediction of system performance properties (latency, resource use, throughput, robustness, etc.) by schedulability analysis and simulation of the system model. The results are validated against the requirements, leading to follow-up design iterations. Each iteration searches for an optimal architecture by tuning the allowed *factors of freedom* (hardware topology, SW/HW mapping, scheduling policies, etc.).

The proposed ProMARTES method features a number of *benefits*. Firstly, the involved component profiling technique provides cycle-accurate performance metrics [1]. Our tooling chain offers automated generation of component performance models compliant with the UML-MARTE profile. Secondly, the established pipeline, generating models at different analysis phases, automates the analysis process and carries the profiled low-level metrics of the components through all phases, until the overall system performance is predicted. Thirdly, the method incorporates both the schedulability analysis and the simulation techniques. The schedulability analysis enables rapid identification of the best- and worst-case response latencies. However, it does not provide detailed behavior timeline data, average resource usage and latencies. In contrast, the simulation technique provides detailed behavior/execution timeline for all simulated system tasks, which enables identification of performance bottlenecks. Unfortunately, it requires a substantial time span to obtain converging prediction results. By combining these two analysis techniques, we complement the advantages and eliminate the limitations that each individual technique imposes. In conclusion, the worst-case predictions obtained at the early design phase by the schedulability analysis can be further used for a detailed simulation-based exploration of execution architecture problems (buffering, task interleaving, etc). Finally, the tool set for our method is encapsulated into the Eclipse Papyrus IDE environment, so that an architect can easily design the HW/SW architectures graphically and convert them into design models in an automated way.

Our method has a number of *limitations* which require further research. Firstly, the performance models can be obtained only for Linux-based operating systems and require the actual presence of the HW platforms. Secondly, the generation of the behavior models of the components is not yet automated and this task is supposed to be performed by the component developer. Thirdly, the method does not fully take into account the influence of the memory-, bus- and cache behavior on the performance of the system. For more accurate performance prediction, a cycle-accurate platform simulator needs to be integrated into the method. Moreover, due to the increasing popularity of applications that can be executed on a GPU, it would be valuable to support the modeling and the performance analysis of GPU-based systems. For analysis of network-related activities, ProMARTES does not incorporate the delays at the low OSI layers (transport, data link, physical), which reduces the accuracy of predictions on communication delays. We plan to integrate a more sophisticated network simulator for most of the OSI layers. Finally, manual composition of the architecture alternatives during the design space exploration is time-consuming and limits the space of possible alternatives. We are developing an engine for automated generation of architecture alternatives, which enables faster and broader exploration of possible design choices.

To *validate* our method, we have applied it to the real-world problem of an autonomous navigation robot system [5]. The system is composed of a robot and a remote processing node which communicate through a wireless network. The SW of the system is delivered by ROS, and it is based on four SW components. The navigation task is performed by 7 parallel tasks which characterize the behavior of the system. The most critical tasks of the navigation process are the `GM:Map` (composes the map of the environment) and the `MB:Nav` (transmits the control commands to the robot). Both tasks are periodic and characterized by hard real-time deadlines. We have composed the system and measured the actual latencies of the two critical tasks. Subsequently, we have compared these actual latencies to the predicted latencies, obtained by schedulability analysis and simulation techniques. The simulation predictions have shown a deviation of 1-2% compared to the actual response-time delay for the worst-case execution time (WCET) and 6-8% for the average-case execution time (ACET) of the two tasks. The predictions from schedulability analysis have shown that the predicted WCET is 8% higher than the actual WCET of the two tasks. The latter, increased, deviation can be explained by the fact that it cannot be ensured whether the system has reached the worst-case scenario during the actual execution. Moreover, we have applied a robustness test to check if the proposed architecture is still schedulable under overload conditions. To this end, we have increased the frequency of the robot's control loop by 10%. The system simulation has shown that the system still satisfies the hard real-time requirements with 3% increase of the WCET for the `MB:Nav` task. By examining the actual response-time delays, we have proven that also the actual system implementation satisfies the real-time requirements of the autonomous navigation robot.

The improved prediction accuracy of our framework is that our proposed method incorporates both the schedulability analysis and the simulation technique, which are complementary to each other in strength and eliminating the individual limitations.

REFERENCES

[1] K. Triantafyllidis *et al.*, "Low-Level Profiling and MARTE-Compatible Modeling of Software Components for Real-Time Systems".

[2] V. Cortellessa, *et al.*, "Integrating Software Models and Platform Models for Performance Analysis".

[3] R K. Klobedanz *et al.*, "Timind Modeling and Analysis for AUTOSAR-Based Software Development - A Case Study" .

[4] Bondarev et al., "CARAT: a toolkit for design and performance analysis of component-based embedded systems".

[5] K. Triantafyllidis *et al.*, "Performance Analysis Method for RT Systems: ProMARTES for Autonomous Robot", submitted to FDL.

[6] L. Thiele, "Performance analysis of distributed embedded systems".

A Study on Traceabilty for Model-based Testing of Automotive Embedded System

Kabsu Han
Intelligent system R&D Center
Korea Automotive Technology Institute
Daegu, Republic of Korea
kshan@katech.re.kr

Insick Son and Jeonghun Cho
School of EE,
Kyungpook National University,
Daegu, Republic of Korea
{mesque, jcho}@ee.knu.ac.kr

***Abstract*—Traceability is a potential ability for traces to be established and used. Traceability is thereby an attribute of a source, a target and trace links. Traceability is researched for a long time and commercial tools are widely used. But actual practices are searched hardly even model-based development and testing are adopted. This paper present traceability fundamental and practical case study for model based testing that the model represents the requirements.**

Keywords-Model-based testing; Test automation; Traceability; Requirement management; Automotive embedded system;

I. INTRODUCTION

The traceability was recognized to discuss the problem of software engineering in 1968 [3]. Traceability was pointed as an issue of interest in software engineering. In 1980s, traceability was founded as a requirement in lots of national and international standards for software and system development. But the actual practice of traceability are hardly documented, even model-based development and testing are widely used. This paper introduces the concept of model-based testing and provides traceability fundamental. Also, practical requirements tracing with commercial tools are described.

II. MODEL-BASED TESTING

Model-based testing automates the design of test cases and the assurance of traceability using model of SUT (system under test), shown as Fig. 1 [1][2]. In detail, hundreds of test cases will be generated automatically, test designer describes abstract model of SUT that is based on requirements. After that model-based testing tool generates test cases from the model of SUT and executes test cases automatically.

III. TRACE AND TRACEABILITY

In a software and system engineering area, the trace can be defined like below.

1) A specified triplet of element comprising : a source, a target and a trace link which connecting a source and a target. When more than a source and a target are associated by a trace link, such as a sub-pair of a source and a target, the sub-pair are treated as a single aource or a target.

2) The action of folloing a trace link from a source to target.

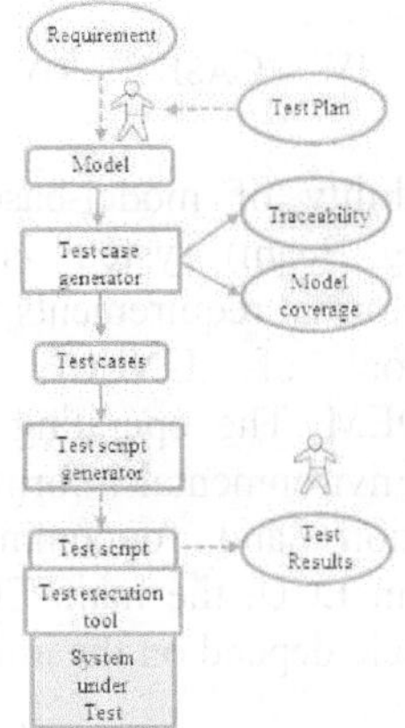

Figure 1 Model-based Testing

The trace can either be atomic or chained. The traceability is the potential ability for traces. To assure the traceability, each of the sources, targets and trace links have to be acquired and stored. After that, software and system engineering activities and task can be traced, shown as Fig. 2. The traces exist within specific development and maintenance life cycles. Also, the trace can be reused in different life cycles. The requirement s traceability is the ability to describe and follow the requirement lifecycle in forwards and backwards direction. The tracing is the activity of either establishing or using traces. The tracing can be divided into 3 types, manual, automated and semi-automated.

1) Manual tracing – traceability is eshtablished by human tracer. Traceability creation and maintenance with drag and drop user interfaces are used in requiremnt management tools commonly.

2) Automated tracing – traceability is established via automated tools and methods. Typically, traceability creation and trace link maintenance are automated.

3) Semi-automated tracing – traceability is established via combination of automated tools and human activities. For example, automated tools sugguest candidate trace links and human tracer verify them.

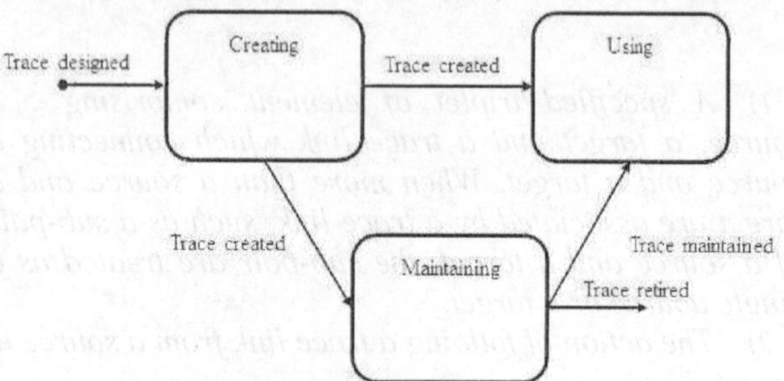

Figure 2 Traceabilty model

IV. Case Study

To test traceability of model-based testing, ADB (Adaptive Driving Beam) system is adopted. Model described from informal requirements that are a parts of vehicle regulation of UNECE and functional requirement of OEM. The operating requirements are shown as Fig.3. Environmental information, e.g., wheel speed, illumination and oncoming vehicle, are transferred to main ECU, the main ECU controls each front lamp of vehicle depend on the information.

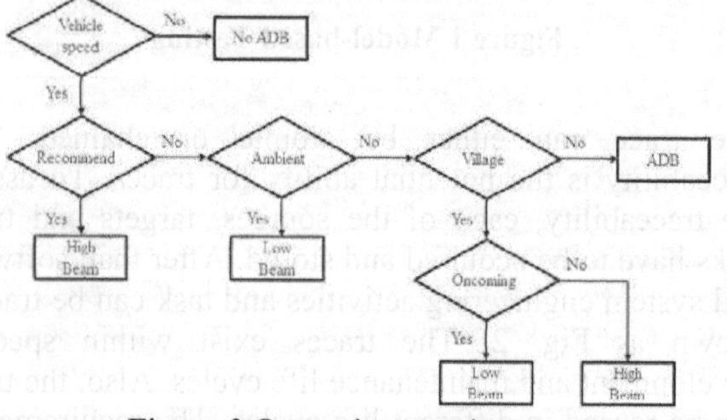

Figure 3 Operation requirements

Generation of abstract test with transition-based notation is based on the number of inputs and the number of state. The model is designed with MATLAB/SIMULINK and V&V (Verification and Validation) are used for requirements traceabilty, shown as Fig. 4. V&V provides trace links via MS-word, Excel and Rational Doors. The model with traceability is more helpful to understand the system functionalities. Also, the modification of some requirements can be verified and validated via traces.

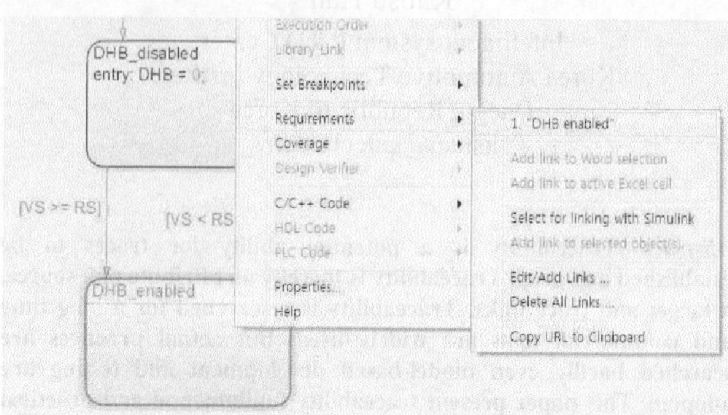

Figure 4 semi-automated tracing

V. Conclusion

To test traceability for model based testing, semi-automated tracing is considered. MATLAB/Simulink with V&V is applicable to trace the requirements for manual and semi-automated tracing. To provide automated tracing, more research is needed. Automated tracing between requirements and model will be very helpful for model based testing.

Acknowledgement

This research was financially supported by the Ministry of Education (MOE) and National Research Foundation of Korea (NRF) through the Human Resource Training Project for Regional Innovation. (NO. 2011-05-대-05-024)
This research was supported by the MKE (The Ministry of Knowledge Economy), Korea, under the CITRC (Convergence Information Technology Research Center) support program (NIPA-2013-H0401-13-1006) supervised by the NIPA (National IT Industry Promotion Agency).

References

[1] M. Utting, B. Legeard, Practical model-based testing, 1st ed., vol. 1. Elsevier: San Francisco, 2007, pp.19–35.

[2] M. Panek, "Model-baseddevelopment and testing in embedded automotive systems", Testwarez, 2008.

[3] J. Huang, O. Gotel, A. Zisman, Software and Systems Traceability. Springer, 2012.

SESSION

LATE BREAKING PAPER: SOFTWARE ENGINEERING + MAINTENANCE, LEGACY CODES, METRICS, COLLABORATIVE WORK, SOFTWARE PROCESS IMPROVEMENT AND MODELS, SOA, CASE STUDIES

Chair(s)

Prof. Hamid Arabnia

Emerging and Innovative Techniques and Methodology in Software Engineering for Systems Maintenance and Development

Maureen Ann Raley
University of Alabama in Huntsville
P.O. Box 6904
Arlington, VA 22206 USA
Telephone: 571-357-3797

Abstract

When undertaking a substantial upgrade to a heavily used, widely distributed network, it is important to have a realistic status of the system at all times to ensure all resources required are available and in place. Our previous research examined the utility of atomic and information theory metrics to identify potential risks and predict project progress to completion. These metrics were derived from an information system inventory database. Our results demonstrated it was possible to predict the behavior of future maintenance projects in one hardware or software environment using the data from a different environment assuming both projects require similar labor and scheduling. We were also able to identify risks during the project so that mitigation could be effected. We propose future work using metrics derived from inventory databases for risk assessment that introduces internal and external contingencies that could impact the success of the systems maintenance effort.

Keywords

Distributed systems; maintenance phase upgrade; project management metrics; entropy metrics; information theory metrics; COTS-based systems.

1.0 Introduction

An essential activity in project management is risk assessment and management. Risk identification and mitigation is critical when dealing with the maintenance and upgrade of a large geographically distributed computer system. The assessment involves mitigation of issues that adversely impact delivering a system on time and within budget that meets its goals. When the system also must continue functioning during system maintenance or upgrade, it is essential to ensure that system availability, data integrity, system security, and system performance are not compromised [1] [2].

Collecting and continuously monitoring measurement data (metrics) can help management gain insight into the project status and plan for contingencies to keep the project on track. As the complexity of a project increases or if the project is conducted under atypical circumstances with geographically diverse facilities, risk assessment becomes even more critical. Monitoring effectiveness of the processes and to identify and manage the critical risks in the processes is essential under these circumstances.

2. 0 Background

With systems that are largely software-based, most research in the area of risk analysis has focused on the development and maintenance of software source code to determine software reliability, complexity, dependability, coupling, cohesion, and maintainability. Various traditional and object-oriented software engineering metrics have been employed to analyze quality and used as part of risk assessment [1] [3] [4] [5] [6]. Additionally, metrics measuring the amount of disruption or entropy in the software have been the subject of research [3] [7] [8] [9] [10]. Other research [5] [11] [4] [6] has focused at the architectural level on the interactions between the commercial or commodity off-the-shelf (COTS) components and involved the use of component dependency graphs in the risk determination of COTS components integrated into a large system.

Systems which are a combination of commercial hardware, commercial software, and customized code, known as COTS-based systems, have come into common use, because few organizations can spare the resources to replicate commercial software and hardware. Use of COTS-based systems, however, introduces, fundamentally different approaches between it and the conventional software development and maintenance lifecycle [12] [13]. Because the introduction and increasing use of COTS-based systems are relatively recent occurrence, a substantial amount of research has not yet been conducted to determine appropriate tools and metrics. Requirements definition and system integration remain the principal topics of interest [14]; however, risk management and the development and use of system maintenance metrics is still in its infancy.

We conducted research to examine the maintenance phase in upgrades of COTS-based widely geographically distributed systems and to develop and analyze metrics to predict risks that could affect successful project completion [1].

One focus of our research was to predict the behavior of future upgrades. Our analysis of systems status was performed using information from an inventory database. To our knowledge, only a few previous research efforts involving inventories and inventory modeling have been published.

We examined two primary areas: Maintenance Phase Behavior Analysis, in which we compare and predict behavior in different environments and Maintenance Phase Risk Assessment, using both simple inventory-based metrics and information theory-based metrics. The data we examined was from inventory database that was collected during a massive nationwide distributed computer systems upgrade by a very large United States entity.

3. 0 Discussion

We examined data from an inventory database that had been collected and recorded into the database on a weekly basis

The data shown in Table 3.1 included both software and hardware upgrades on three different types of computer systems. These systems were mainframes (Type 1) and client computers, workstations, desktop computers, and laptops (Type 3). Data was also collected over the first 12-weeks for servers and related network equipment (Type 2).

We used the Type 2 data along with the Type 1 and Type 3 data in our statistical analyses that forms part of our Maintenance Phase Behavior Analysis. However, due to space limitations, and since fewer weeks of the Type 2 data was available, we have not included the Type 2 data in our graph-based analyses, in both the Maintenance Phase Behavior Analysis and in the Maintenance Phase Risk Assessment.

Table 1 - Data Examined by Our Research

Data Set	Maximum Total Units	Average Total Units	Weekly Data Collection Duration
Type 1 INFO	2875	2767	1 year
Type 1 OPS	6412	4530	1 year
Type 2 INFO	3728	3660	12 weeks
Type 2 OPS	38,814	35,985	12 weeks
Type 3 INFO	37,429	36,826	1 year
Type 3 OPS	648,463	595,006	1 year
Units distributed throughout the continental U.S. • Type 1 - Mainframes and associated software • Type 2 - Servers, routers, hubs, switches and associated software • Type 3 - Clients, workstations, and associated software			
INFO – Information Systems Division		OPS – Operations Division	

There were two categories of applications for each system type: Information Systems (INFO), which provided support functions similar to a generic Information Technology (IT) activity, in that INFO personnel kept the network, software, and hardware functioning. Additionally, INFO personnel developed in-house data mining and data analysis programs, as well as the hybrid COTS-based systems.

The second application category was Operations (OPS), which performed the activities associated with the agency's mission. OPS personnel were the users of the system.

We primarily examined three categories of inventory data for our research. Because of the nature of the inventory, a unit was the smallest element and could be either hardware (one computer) or software (one application or program). Within the inventory database, as part of project planning, all units were assigned categories indicating how each would be handled during the project upgrade. Compliant (C) units were those units that had been processed and were in compliance of the project goals, capable of functioning as expected within the distributed system. Replace (R) units were to be removed from inventory and replaced with new units. No Effect (N) units were units that did not impact the project upgrade.

3.1 Inventory Stability Metric

We developed the Inventory Stability metric to gauge the movement of units into and out of the inventory, as well as changes in inventory as initial inaccuracies in unit count were corrected.

The inventory stability and unit accuracy is critical to assessing project progress when the inventory database is used to track the number of units in the categories that indicate the type of maintenance performed. The inventory stability metric had as input the weekly changes in the number of units that:

- Are in compliance with maintenance goals (C)
- Have no effect on the project and will not be subject to maintenance activities (N)
- Will be replaced with new units, then removed from inventory and disposed (R)
- Will be isolated to stand-alone status, rather than modified or replaced (I)

Graphical analysis of our results from the Information Systems (INFO) and Operations (OPS) data on the same Type stations tend to be similar. This could occur because the hardware platform (computer) is similar and some, but not all, of the software is similar.

INFO is similar across system Types, possible because these systems are centrally located and have the same type of characteristics. OPS is very different across types. This could possibly be attributed to logistics issues, as the OPS offices are small and dispersed across very widely separated locations, sometimes many hundreds of miles. The scale of the effort for OPS differed greatly among the system Types ranging from 6412 units for Type 1 to 648,463 units for Type 3 systems. There were very few mainframes in the field and a very large number of laptops, workstations, and client computers. Additionally, Type 1 mainframe hardware required limited modifications, while most of the Type 3 hardware platforms were replaced with new equipment.

The Inventory Stability metric indicated high activity and continuous fluctuation within all datasets. Most of the graphs are characterized by alternating weeks of high activity with weeks of low inventory movement. High levels of inventory activity can serve as a warning to management to ensure incoming and outgoing logistics are well planned and closely monitored to avoid bottlenecks in the project.

3. 2 Project Progress Metric

We developed the Project Progress metric to measure progress toward goal within time constraints and to assess the risk of not achieving goal when the time line must be met. Any project, particularly a large one, needs to closely monitor timeline and approach to goal because time is the one resource that cannot be replaced. Accurate oversight of subordinate offices is critical. Inputs to the Project Progress metric are the units that:

- Have been or will be modified (M)
- Still need to be modified (NM)
- Will be replaced with new units, then removed from inventory (R)
- Will be isolated to stand-alone status, rather than modified or replaced (I)

The project progress metric gives insight to magnitude and frequency of movement within each maintenance category, measures progress toward the goal, and assesses the risk of not achieving the goal when the time line must be met.

Graphical analysis of our Project Progress metric showed that the Type 1 INFO and OPS projects were fairly similar and this also held true for the Type 3 INFO and OPS. The Project Progress metric for the Type 1 and Type 3 INFO projects, was very different [1]. This could be because the Type 1 project was significantly less complicated and smaller in scope than the Type 3 effort. Additionally, management direction for Type 1 systems was consistent, but was highly changeable for Type 3 systems, particularly regarding whether to modify or replace a large number of the systems. Location was not much of a factor with INFO systems, as the systems were centrally located.

Project Progress metric also indicated a very different result for OPS data among Type 1 and Type 3 [1]. Again, management direction for Type 1 systems was fairly consistent, while it was inconsistent for Type 3 systems, particularly regarding the modify or replace decision, which changed several times over a few months. Additionally, OPS systems faced significant logistical issues over widely separated geographical locations. Further, the magnitude and scope of the projects for Type 1 systems and Type 3 systems differed greatly.

Based on our initial analysis of maintenance effort, upgrading the centrally located mainframe systems tended to take less effort and ran more smoothly than upgrading the physically smaller and widely dispersed commodity systems that frequently had been individually customized, unlike the mainframe systems

4. 0 Summary

We developed both simple (atomic) metrics and information theoretic (entropy) metrics suites from data that is available in most inventory databases. We found the introduction of categories that characterized the final disposition of the hardware and software units had to be done before we could develop and use the metrics; however, categorization of this nature would be necessary before beginning the project to determine the scope of the work to be undertaken.

We also found that to use the metrics to predict behavior and perform trend analysis among different projects, we had to normalize the input data to account for the vastly different numbers of the units in the different projects.

We developed new information theoretic or entropy metrics to measure inventory stability and project progress. We found that the simple (atomic) metrics suite was complementary to the information theoretic (entropy) metrics suite. The information theoretic aspect of the metrics allows a better analysis of activity "spikes" and the magnitude of change than provided by simple atomic metrics. A better understanding of inventory stability and project progress by using these metric formulations would enable project managers monitor activity levels throughout the project to identify areas for resource allocation. Knowing where and when to allocate resources, particularly if the resources are scarce or the activity is time critical, can affect the success or failure of the project.

We performed a very large study of system upgrades on different platforms and environments using real data from a very large entity. To our knowledge, the size of our inventory system upgrade study is unprecedented. During this study, kinds of similarities and differences between different platforms and environments were identified. A better understanding of variations in upgrades in different environments should help managers predict upgrade schedules and know when to allocate resources.

Our research showed it is possible to predict the behavior of upgrades in one kind of hardware or software environment using information collected in a different hardware or software environment, when the labor and scheduling assumptions are the same. Due to the large scale of this research, the results of our analysis have great significance.

The results from our research can be important to any large distributed upgrade and have applications to government agencies and large companies. These results can determine the status of project completion and help identify difficulties or aberrations within the project, so are thus able to provide insight to management when determining what resources need to be allocated to projects. This research has particular utility for time critical upgrades, such as those needed to recover from directed intrusion by foreign governments or hostile agents or to interdict hacking. It also has potential use in non-time critical maintenance, when software or hardware reaches the end of its useful life.

The intrinsic characteristics of inventory databases required us to return to basic statistical assumptions and definitions to perform statistical analysis on this data. An alternative would be to analyze this data using Markov chains. These have been used in the past in Operations Research publications to perform inventory optimization and behavior prediction [17].

Another alternative would be to use decision-tree induction techniques (data mining, machine learning) that are not limited by restrictions associated with statistical models. These techniques examine patterns in data to produce multivariate classification models [18] [19] [20]. During our research, we have also considered other normalization methods for analyzing dynamic, fluctuating inventory databases.

5.0 REFERENCES

[1] M. A. Raley. Metrics for Risk Determination in Large-Scale Distributed Systems Maintenance, University of Alabama in Huntsville, Huntsville, Al, May 2008

[2] M. A. Raley and L. H. Etzkorn, "Case Study: Lessons Learned During a Nationwide Computer System Upgrade," in ACM SE 2004, Huntsville, AL, 2004.

[3] A. E. Hassan and R. C. Holt, "Studying the Chaos of Code Development," in International Workshop on Principles of Software Evolution, Helsinki, Finland, 2003, p. 11.

[4] T. Wang, A. Hassan, A. Guedem, K. Abdelmoez, K. Goseva-Popstojanvoa, and H. H. Ammar, "Architectural Level Risk Assessment Tool Based on UML Specifications," in 25th International Conference on Software Engineering, Portland, OR, 2003, pp. 808-809.

[5] A. Ibrahim, S. M. Yacoub, and H. H. Ammar, "Architectural-Level Risk Analysis for UML Dynamic Specifications," in 9th International Confrence on Software Quality Management (SQM 2001), Loughborough University, Leicestershire, England LE11 3TU, 2001, pp. 179-190.

[6] S. M. Yacoub, B. Cukic, and H. H. Ammar, "Scenario-Based Reliability Analysis of Component-Based Software," in Tenth International Symposium on Software Reliability Engineering (ISSRE '99), Boca Raton, FL, 1999, pp. 22-31.

[7] S. K. Abd-El-Hafix, "Entropies as Measures of Software Information," in International Conference on Software Maintenance (ICSM '01), Florence, Italy, 2001, pp. 110-117.

[8] E. B. Allen, "Measuring Graph Abstractions of Software: An Information-Theory Approach," in Eighth IEEE Symposium on Software Metrics (METRICS '02), Ottawa, Canada, 2002, pp. 182-193.

[9] N. Chapin, "Entropy-Metric for Systems with COTS Software," in Eighth IEEE Symposium on Software Metrics, Ottawa, Canada, 2002, pp. 173-181.

[10] C. E. Shannon, "A Mathematical Theory of Communication,"The Bell System Technical Journal, vol. 77, pp. 379-423, 623-656, 1948.

[11] S. M. Yacoub, H. H. Ammar, and T. Robinson, "Dynamic Metrics for Object Oriented Designs," in Sixth IEEE International Symposium on Software Metrics, Boca Raton, FL, 1999, pp. 50 - 61.

[12] R. W. Selby and V. R. Basili, "Analyzing Error-Prone System Structure," IEEE Transactions on Software Engineering, vol. 17, pp. 141-152, 1991.

[13] B. Boehm, "Forward," in International Conference on COTS-Based Software Systems (ICCBSS), Redondo Beach, CA, 2004, p. 215.

[14] X. Franch, N. Maiden, and B. Boehm, "Do We Need Requirements in COTS-based Software Development?," in Third International Conference, ICCBSS 2004, Redondo Beach, CA, 2004, p. 8.

[15] M. D. Martin, J. O. Lenz, and W. L. Glover, "Uncertainty Analysis for Program Management," in A Decade of

Project Management: Project Management Institute, 1981.

[16] M. M. N. El Agizy, "Multi-Stage Programming Under Uncertainty," in Industrial Engineering and Operations Research, Berkeley: CA, 1965.

[17] M. M. N. El Agizy, "Dynamic Inventory Models and Stochastic Programming," IBM Journal of Research and Development/IBM 2750, vol. 13, 1969.

[18] H. M. Olague, L. H. Etzkorn, W. Li, and G. Cox, "Assessing Design Instability in Iterative (Agile) Object-Oriented Projects," Journal of Software Maintenance and Evolution, vol. 18, p. 30, July/August 2006.

[19] J. R. Quinlan, C4.5: Programs for Machine Learning. San Mateo, CA: Morgan Kauffman Publishers, 1993.

[20] W. C. Navidi, Statistics for Engineers and Scientists. New York, NY: McGraw-Hill, 2006.

Novel Visual and Analytical Methods in Repurposing Legacy Scientific Code – A Case Study

Submitted to The 2013 International Conference on Sofware Engineering Research and Practice

Christopher S. Oehmen, Darren Curtis, Aaron Phillips
Computational and Statistical Analytics Division
Pacific Northwest National Laboratory
Richland, WA USA
{Christopher.Oehmen, Darren.Curtis, Aaron.Phillips}@pnnl.gov

Elena S. Peterson (Contact Author)
Computational Science and Mathematics Division
Pacific Northwest National Laboratory
Richland, WA USA
Elena.Peterson@pnnl.gov

Abstract— Scientific computing is dominated by team-authored legacy code that has evolved over decades with the purpose of capturing the evolving understanding of a scientific discipline. Accumulated deprecated code, various optimization techniques, and evolving algorithms lead to convoluted source code that is impractical to reverse engineer using mainstream methods. This prevents codes from being truly repeatable or understandable, which are two of the most essential needs in scientific computing. We refactored a long-standing implementation of a common biosequence alignment algorithm in an effort to reproduce its salient behaviors in usable form. Because of the sheer size and complexity of this code base, we developed custom tools to visualize and manipulate the source code behavior under a variety of conditions. We present a case study of extracting and refactoring the algorithmic core and a novel process of discovery/prototyping/testing using a combination of openly available and custom-built tools. The result is a reduction in code size of over 2 orders of magnitude while reconstructing the key protein alignment function in BLAST.

Keywords- code reuse; bioinformatics; scientific computing; visualization; program understanding

I. Introduction

Scientific computing has unique needs in terms of software development, including the frequent absence of up-front requirements, constantly changing algorithms that reflect progress in understanding, and authorship that can include large geographically dispersed collaborative teams with fluid membership and nonstandard coding styles. Driving such a software development environment is an underlying scientific discipline that evolves rapidly in terms of fundamental understanding that must be captured by the code. This leads to an organic style of software development in which code must be modified more quickly than it can be standardized. A second concern for many scientific applications is the need for optimization, which often leads to hard-coded (and often undocumented) code regions that are initially only for testing, but that are eventually absorbed into the functional core.

Along with the need for an organic code development process, scientific computing also has a driving need for repeatability since the professional credibility of its users relies on the ability of others to reproduce important results. However, this is often very hard to realize in an organic development environment. We present here a case study for refactoring one such code: Basic Local Alignment Search Tool (BLAST [1])—one of the most commonly used biological sequence analysis algorithms, having tens of thousands of citations for the original publication and a variety of applications and services built using the BLAST computational core.

BLAST is a large-scale legacy code that is of central importance to the biology community. BLAST was originally developed in the late 1980's to address the need for comparing genes and proteins based on the text that describes the sequence of chemical subunits in them. The BLAST algorithm was originally published in 1990 and with its related papers has been cited over 100,000 times for use in applied research such as drug discovery and biomarkers research, and decades of fundamental research into molecular processes that give species and communities the capacity to survive. The BLAST algorithm has become so fundamentally important to biological sciences that increasingly large datasets are being analyzed using BLAST. In fact, typical sequencing platforms that are mostly responsible for the influx of new sequences to analyze are increasing their throughput more quickly than Moore's Law—leading to a situation in which the need for computing is outpacing the underlying hardware improvements. This

The Department of Homeland Security sponsored the production of this material under DOE Contract Number DE-AC05-76RL01830 for the management and operation of Pacific Northwest National Laboratory. A portion of this work was supported by the Signature Discovery Initiative, Laboratory Directed Research and Development program at Pacific Northwest National Laboratory, operated for the DOE by Battelle under contract DE- AC06-76RLO-1830.

motivates a need for parallel implementations of BLAST such as ScalaBLAST [2].

However, BLAST was not implemented as a library, so using it as the algorithmic core of ScalaBLAST and other parallel implementations is challenging because of its lack of external API and problematic because of the possibility of unintentional side effects when modifying the BLAST core. As with most scientific software, the low-level details of how BLAST is implemented have been left out of publications. Even with the large corpus of publications on the details of BLAST, there are many implementation-level details that must be *discovered* to create a repeatable BLAST compute core. Our goal was to re-implement the BLAST functionality necessary to drive protein comparison calculations (the *blastp* operating mode) so that we would have complete transparency and understanding of the implementation details, and so that we could be certain that our generalized parallel implementation did not introduce unwanted side effects into the serial BLAST core when driving it with our parallel ScalaBLAST control layer. A second motivation for refactoring the BLAST core is to create a domain-agnostic (i.e. non-biological) string analysis platform. The utility of such a platform has been previously demonstrated in domains such as cyber security [3].

However, in order to use BLAST on data from non-biology domains, the user must map their data into text sequences. This mapping requires converting the data space of a generic domain into the specific amino acid frequencies that occur naturally in biology. If this mapping is not done accurately, it can significantly impact performance and accuracy. This constraint on character frequency that is imposed by using the biological code without modifications makes use of BLAST on non-biological datasets over-constrained in most cases, hence our desire to achieve a domain-agnostic version of the code.

II. The BLAST Algorithm

BLAST was devised to address a fundamental question in biosequence analysis—calculating the statistical confidence behind the assertion that two biosequences are derived from a common ancestor. Biosequences are linear sequences of chemical subunits.

At the heart of the BLAST algorithm is a process of text alignment between two sequences—pairwise alignment. The goal of pairwise alignment is to discover regions of two sequences that have a high degree of similarity (see Figure 1).

```
String 1: HTNSILPWWFLRSTEAGGESLLQSDFMNT
String 2: FRDVVAPPLFLRSTEAGGESRFLLQSDF
Alignment
String  1: PWWFLRSTEAGGES--LLQSDF
Consensus: P  FLRSTEAGGES  LLQSDF
String  2: PPLFLRSTEAGGESRFLLQSDF
```

Figure 1. Example of text strings and a local alignment.

Local alignment is calculated efficiently using a staged process where each level is designed to reduce the overall search space that must be examined by the code to identify alignments.

The functions that perform these tasks are captured in a large code base having a high degree of complexity. Table 1 illustrates some of the attributes of the source code for the version of the NCBI BLAST toolkit that was frozen as the basis for ScalaBLAST (BLAST 2.2.13).

Table 1 Serial BLAST source code attributes*

Number of lines of code	1.5 Million (with comments)
Number of statements	Nearly 800,000
Number of files	1953
Number of functions	Over 25,000
% lines that are comments	19 (mostly terse source code revision history)

*figures obtained using SourceMonitor from Campwood Software

Not all of the functionality in the original code was needed for our applications but extracting the necessary functionality from the code base required analysis of the entire toolkit to discover which segments of the code were needed for our refactoring.

III. Software Extraction

A. Generalizing the BLAST algorithm for non-biological use

ScalaBLAST was originally built on top of BLAST, and was later modified to be more tightly integrated with the BLAST libraries via the use of BLAST data structures and "API". The tight integration caused ScalaBLAST to become unstable as new versions of BLAST were released. In the biology community, BLAST is considered a software library, but has a very volatile API. Therefore efforts to adapt ScalaBLAST to new versions of BLAST resulted in large programming overhead. To gain stability in ScalaBLAST, the version of BLAST was frozen. This had the advantage of making ScalaBLAST maintainable, but the disadvantage of being unable to compare results with newer releases of BLAST. This presents a problem in the biology community, as BLAST is widely considered the gold standard for sequence alignment.

BLAST is designed to process DNA and protein sequences only. The heuristics and algorithms have been crafted using assumptions from the biology domain. In particular, the statistical models used by the algorithms are based on existing DNA/protein populations. To give the reader an appreciation of the scope of the influence of the statistical models [4] on the software as a whole, there is a 55 page paper summarizing the statistics that heavily influence nearly every algorithm or heuristic[8].

Because of the complexity of the BLAST source code distribution, we searched for existing alternatives to the BLAST library as the basis for refactoring our code. We considered several programs, including Biopython, Bioperl, and Seqan. These tools did not help as they are based on many of the same biological assumptions as BLAST and in some cases are just wrappers that call the BLAST routines underneath.

We attempted to create our own version of BLAST based solely on research papers describing the BLAST algorithms and heuristics. But our results from ground-up BLAST refactoring differed significantly from the open source BLAST due to a large number of undocumented algorithmic details. The sophistication and importance of the underlying statistical model were beyond our ability to replicate effectively.

The complexity of the codebase and various optimization techniques precluded a brute force method of reading and understanding directly from source code. In addition, understanding of the code is complicated by optimization techniques that confound code analysis. These include heavy use of C pointers, use of the 'register' keyword, C structs comprised of void * pointers, heavy use of #ifdef, and a "super-global" data structure that is constructed, extended, and significantly modified throughout the code. Of course standard issues such as a complicated build system, lack of test code, and undocumented API also existed.

B. Software Archeology

Attempting to understand the BLAST code base resulted in what is commonly called "software archeology" [5]. Digging through the layers of the code allowed us to identify some of the key issues that we would need to address to re-engineer this code. Since BLAST was developed over a period of decades, there has been a "layering" affect in the API. Functions that were once part of the API were wrapped with new functions as requirements changed. These were in turn wrapped with even newer function calls, some of which simply reorder arguments from other parts of the API. These API layers make it extremely difficult to locate key functionality, as it may be hidden under 10 or 20 layers of the call-stack. The BLAST code also shows signs of complete functionality replacement over time and both the original and improved functions are left in the code. This results in having to actually run and debug the software to determine which piece of code is operational. This "abandoned code" and code bloat added to the complexity of detailed understanding.

IV. Non-Intrusive Methods

A. Commercial Software Attempts

In an attempt to gain an understanding of the overall structure of BLAST (and eventually the underlying details), we used several pieces of commercial software. These included SourceMonitor, Starlight [6], KCacheGrind, Visustin, and DDD.

We used SourceMonitor to perform static analysis on BLAST and gathered metrics on the entire code base. In particular, the cyclomatic complexity provided by SourceMonitor proved to be extremely high on average in BLAST. There are over 50 files in the BLAST code base that have a cyclomatic complexity greater than 100 [7].

Starlight is a tool for visualization and exploration of data networks. We used it to visualize a static representation of the potential BLAST call stack. We developed a structure containing every function call in the BLAST code base, and used Starlight to view the resulting associations. We found almost all functions tightly-coupled with the system as a whole. This technique was useful for identifying clusters of functions that make up specific functionality or heuristics.

We used Valgrind in combination with KCacheGrind to analyze the function call tree at run-time and gained a high-level understanding of the portions of code that were exercised during a given run of BLAST. KCacheGrind is an interactive tool that allowed us to explore multiple aspects of the code, including the call tree, function names, call frequency, looping structures, code coverage, and functionality discovery. A portion of the tree traversed during a run is shown in Figure 2. Each box in Figure 2 represents a single function and the line between the boxes is the number of times the path was traversed during the Valgrind (callgrind) snapshot.

Other tools such as Visustin for static analysis of control flow structures and Visual Studio's debuggers only confirmed the complexity of the problem but did not provide any useful additional analysis.

We were able to use the information gathered from KCacheGrind in conjunction with GDB to walk through the code at run-time. We set breakpoints at the beginning and end of every function that KCacheGrind identified as being executed. While this gave us a better understanding of the run-time behavior of BLAST, the complicated control flow structures and "super-global" data structure proved to be too cumbersome for basic debugging. This led us to the use of DDD as a way to visualize the data structures at run-time. DDD is a wrapper around GDB, with the added benefit of visualizing C data structures. Unfortunately, the size and complexity of the data structures again proved too cumbersome for the tool. In addition, since the "super-global" data structure in BLAST is constructed of multiple levels of structs of (void *) pointers, DDD was unable to dynamically display the structure in its entirety because it did not know how to cast the structure to the correct type.

These commercial applications gave us various hints as to the depth and complexity of the code although they did not individually or collectively provide an easy way to understand the functionality and data flow in BLAST.

B. Custom-built debugging tool: GdbShell

In order to track changes to the "super-global" data structure throughout the program run we used GDB to step through the code. We combined GDB with Graphviz to create a visualization of the data structure and the changes that had been made to it. To more easily control the GDB process we wrote a Perl wrapper as a scripting engine for automated GDB control. This allowed us to set breakpoints at an arbitrary number of specific points of interest in the code, and walk through them automatically. We call this tool GdbShell.

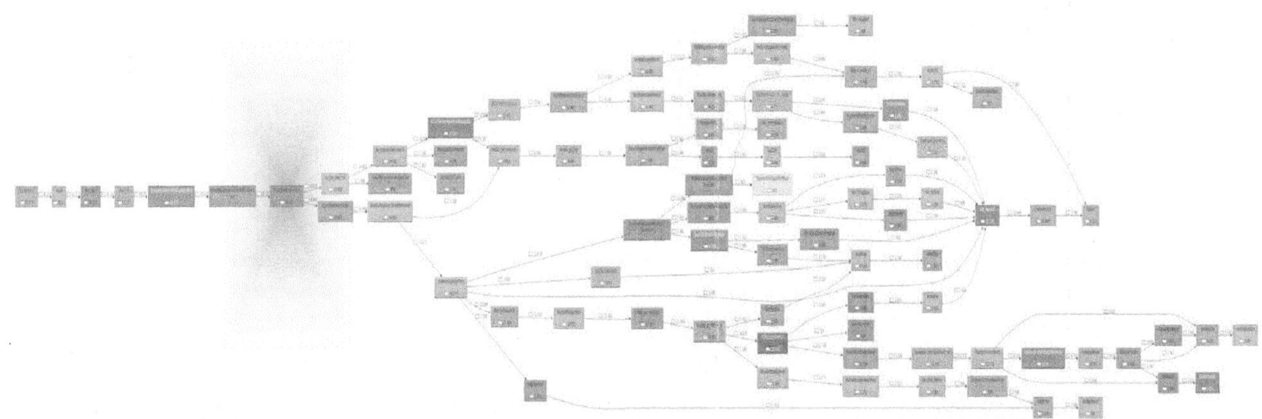

Figure 2. Illustration of a small part of the BLAST call tree using KCacheGrind.

GdbShell provides the ability to display the changes to a data structure between two points in a program. This involves setting a breakpoint, asking GDB for a text representation of a given structure, parsing that text for nested structures and finally recursively parsing the GDB responses for additional nested structures. After the data structure had been completely traversed, GdbShell saves it as a snapshot of the data structure. GdbShell continues debugging until another breakpoint is reached. Then another snapshot of the same data structure is captured and compared to the previous one. This comparison involves searching for parts of the structure that had been added or deleted between breakpoints, as well as modifications to the internal values of any part of the data structure. A color-coded image is created based on which portions of the data structure were added, deleted, or modified, shown in Figure 3. The colors for Figure 3 are coded to signify:

- White - no change between breakpoints
- Green - new structures created
- Blue - modified structures (with OLD and NEW)
- Yellow - custom code had to be written to view data structures (e.g. pointers to arrays of pointers to arrays of integers representing 5-bit packed ASCII characters) between breakpoints.
- Purple/Orange – legend showing the breakpoints used to create the image.

GdbShell did not originally have the ability to display complicated dynamically allocated structures such as a pointer to an array of pointers to arrays that represent a two-dimensional matrix. We enhanced the functionality by developing a framework that supports a simple plug-in architecture using a visitor pattern for each unique data structure. When a new data structure is discovered, custom Perl code can be written to convert GDB representation of the data into a human-readable ASCII representation.

GdbShell provided the necessary tools and processes for understanding the BLAST code in a practical timeframe. Without adding the features of automation and the ability to quickly add custom analysis of new data structures the process of detailing the complicated data flows and data structures would have been technically possible but not practical.

V. PROTOTYPING WITH A "DISCOVERY CYCLE"

After using non-intrusive methods to determine where the algorithms of interest were located, and the sequence of the related function calls, we used GdbShell to discover what the algorithms did and how they affected the data structure and then prototyped what we learned in Perl. Perl allows for rapid development, includes object orientation, and works well with text-based problems like BLAST.

This cycle involves using KCacheGrind to isolate portions of the code and GdbShell to gain an understanding of data structures (how they changed, and which boundary conditions caused these changes). Once we gain an understanding of a particular feature, we implement it in our Perl prototype. We attempted to "checkpoint" the code in between heuristics, to ensure that each individual piece of our prototype was producing comparable results to the corresponding BLAST heuristic. If the results differed at these checkpoints, we investigated by hand using old-fashioned "intrusive" methods such as printfs and exit statements. This allows for comparison of data structures at diverging points which then is fed into the prototype discovery cycle.

VI. TESTING AND VERIFICATION

Our goal was to abstract, extend, and simplify the overall algorithm, while producing comparable results without simply copying the BLAST source code into our prototype. It was essential for us to understand all the details of how the code works.

BLAST is a heuristic chain, meaning that the overall algorithm consists of multiple heuristics, each of which is designed to perform some amount of data reduction on the overall data space. The input data given to BLAST can

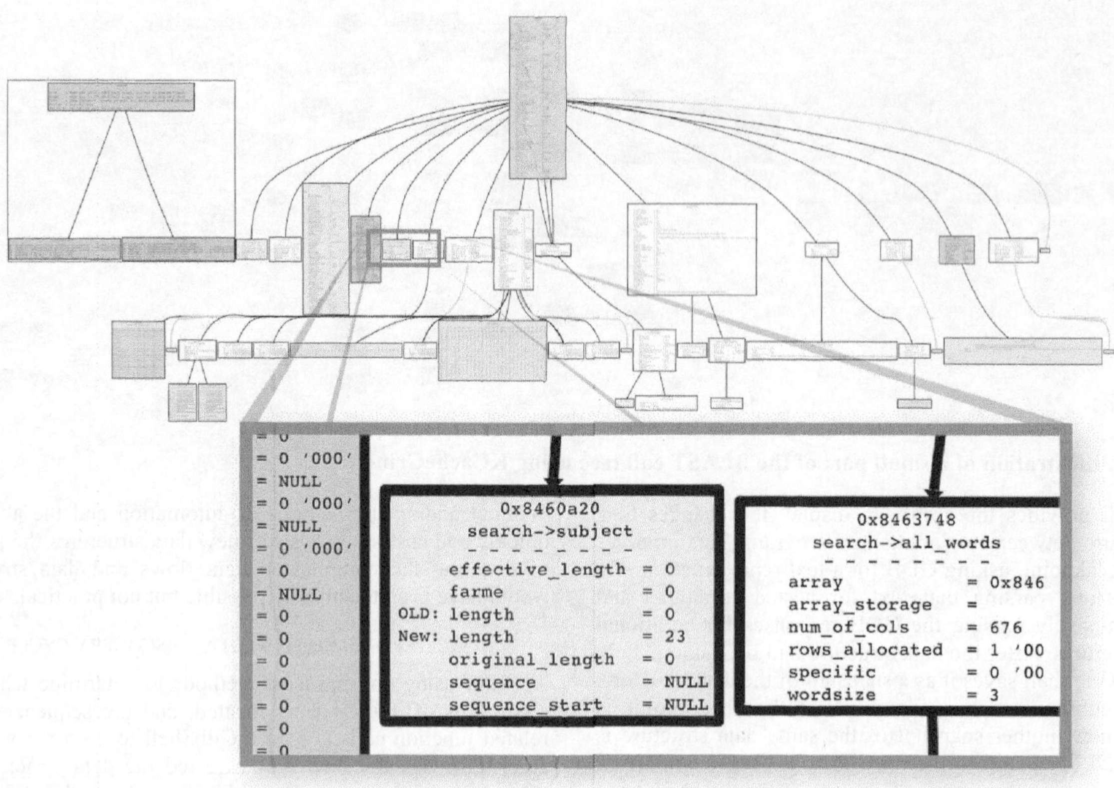

Figure 3. Visualization of the "super-global" data structure that is passed between many BLAST functions as a pointer. The functions create, destroy, and modify portions of the structure dynamically. For example, the blue box in the zoomed area shows that the 'length' field was 0 at the first breakpoint and is now 23 at the second breakpoint. The hex value, 0x8460a20, is the memory address of the 'subject' pointer in the global search struct.

influence the underlying statistical models, which in turn influence each of the data reduction heuristics. Such a combination of heuristics creates a data-dependent decision making process wherein a subtle statistical change at one layer of the heuristic can propagate through other layers resulting in very different output. This cascading dependency is illustrated in Figure 4. In addition, each heuristic is so finely tuned for performance that there are too many boundary conditions to exercise all combinations with a reasonable set of test data.

Because of the large amount of boundary conditions and dependencies in the heuristics, we needed a large, diverse data set to test the overall process with. And we were much more concerned with accuracy than speed during the prototyping phase so individual tests could take minutes to hours and there were hundreds or thousands of tests in order to exercise all boundary conditions. To get around this accuracy/time conundrum, we developed a simple test framework on a large cluster (Olympus - 179th on the top 500 list). This allowed us to quickly create tests that used a large data set, exercise relevant code, and combine results in real time in order to compare the aggregate results of our prototype and BLAST. This allowed us to terminate large test runs if we discovered a difference/problem early in the run, or if it was obvious that a recent change did not improve results. At the end of a test run (and in real time), we gathered statistics regarding the accuracy of our prototype, where any problems were located in the code, as well as the details of the individual problems.

For a more detailed test, we used a whole yeast species genome which has 5753 proteins. This whole genome was compared against itself, which should result in a strong alignment between each protein and itself, followed by a collection of lower scoring alignments to more distantly related proteins, followed by a large collection of statistically insignificant alignments, which are useful for our purposes of exposing all the details of how alignments are calculated. Using this detailed dataset to test as much as possible of the operational code regions, we evaluated the performance using the following metrics: (1) the fraction of proteins for which non-self top-hits had the same identity in both our code and the NCBI implementation; and (2) the average number of hits in agreement between the two methods before a difference is found. The first metric assesses one of the most important functions of the BLAST code, namely the ability to recognize highly similar but non-identical proteins to a query. Many

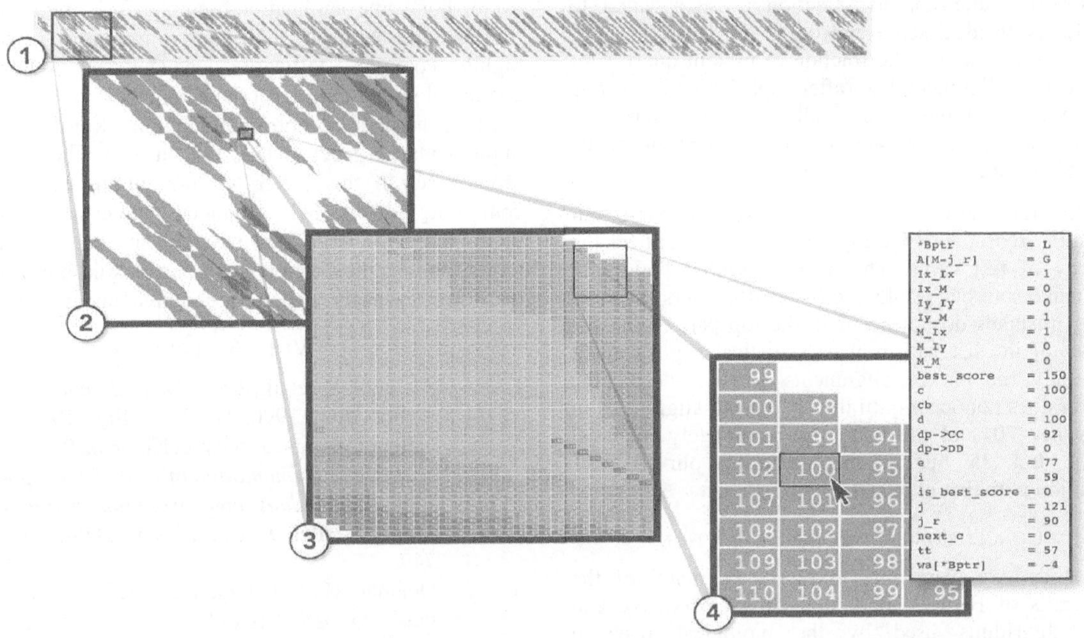

Figure 4. Hierarchical visualization of (1) coverage of the global alignment space sampled by the BLAST heuristic; (2) detail of this region -covered alignment space is shown in red, untouched space is white and represents saved computation and storage; (3) represents an area that is being explored by an Affine Gap heuristic; (4) shows a border case where the scores are too low to continue exploring. The tan box has the actual C language variables representing the data used to calculate the value in the cell at the mouse pointer (cell with value 100).

users really only want the top (non-self) hit or the top few, so getting the first non-self hit is the first metric we used. The second metric assesses the quality of the complete hit list. For a given protein query, all of the target proteins that have a significant alignment are returned by the BLAST method. This list is sorted by score and a statistical measure that is calculated by the code. When multiple hits have identical score and statistical measure, they appear in the list in random order. This creates difficulties when comparing two results because things can be in a different order, but still correct because there is no correct order for a collection of alignments that have identical scores. We solved this problem by sorting alphabetically on unique protein names within identical score blocks for both our runs and NCBI BLAST runs before calculating our performance statistics. This ensured that differences that are not resolvable by either code did not count against our results.

Using this procedure, our code achieved the same non-self top hit as NCBI BLAST for 5707 of 5753 proteins (99.2% of proteins tested). This is an encouraging result that suggests we are in agreement the vast majority of the time when alignments are strong alignments (and therefore less likely to be influenced by decision making at the statistical fringe). Table 2 illustrates the performance of our method using a variety of metrics that explore all hits for each protein instead of just the top non-self hits.

Table 2 Comparison of refactored BLAST vs. NCBI BLAST

Cutoff value 'x'	AHBM	AHBM %	Fraction identical
500	386.7	0.77	.45
400	311.9	0.78	.45
300	237.2	0.79	.45
200	162.3	0.81	.46
100	86.00	0.86	.51
50	45.44	0.91	.58
25	23.71	0.95	.68

For each cutoff value 'x', only the top 'x' alignments for each protein were considered. The 'Average Hits Before Mismatch' (AHBM) value was calculated by locating the first discrepancy between NCBI and our BLAST implementation for each protein. If there was no discrepancy and a protein had fewer than 'x' alignments, the value of the first mismatch was counted as 'x'. Ideal performance for this metric is to have an AHBM value equal to 'x', meaning that the end of all lists was reached without a discrepancy. A value of 0 would be the worst case, meaning that on average, lists varied at the top hit location. AHBM% is a second representation of this metric that expresses the same score as a fraction of the 'x' value. In this case, 1.0 is an ideal score and 0.0 is the worst possible score. The third measure is the fraction of protein queries for which the entire alignment list (after alphabetically sorting within score-invariant blocks) had all the same alignments with the same scores in the same order to that produced by NCBI BLAST for the given cutoff value.

This validation shows two significant results. First, our implementation reproduced the top non-self alignment for the vast majority of test cases. This is an essential feature to capture to make sure our results are relevant to users. Second, on average, mistakes do not occur in the top part of the list (*i.e.* the part of the list with highest statistical significance), and when only the top 25 alignments are considered, the average error does not occur until the 23rd or 24th alignment. In addition, nearly 70% of the lists were completely identical through the top 25 hits when comparing our BLAST implementation with that of NCBI.

VII. Conclusions and Future Directions

In this study, we were able to reproduce many of the essential details of BLAST, one of the most pervasive and significant algorithms used by the biological research community. Because of the complexity of the code, we used a combination of commercial products and custom-designed tools to understand the original implementation enough to refactor it. Without automating the "discovery cycle" and prototyping and testing smaller sections of code we would not have been able replicate the outcome to any degree of certainty. Standard tools and processes did not apply to this particular set of constraints so new tools were developed and applied. These tools were built specifically for this effort but are in the process of being abstracted for general use. They could provide other developers attempting to re-construct functionality of code where traditional methods don't work.

Our testing and validation has shown that we have captured many of the essential core heuristics of the NCBI BLAST implementation, but the differences between them have led us to discover further undocumented details in the BLAST source code that would need additional development for us to replicate.

We must point out that the NCBI BLAST code we used was extremely fast and robust which is a testament to the dedicated developers and their attention to detail. Because our emphasis was on correctness and not performance, we have not introduced optimization into our implementation. Much of the complexity in the NCBI BLAST core is due to hand-optimization of code segments. It is not yet clear how much of this must be captured to reproduce both the performance and the results of the BLAST core. However, our intention is to have a complete implementation of correctly refactored code, then proceed with our own optimization on a much smaller, more formally designed codebase that can be easily maintained and extended to non-biology data domains.

We believe that our experience refactoring the BLAST source code is representative of the complexities of maintaining and refactoring legacy scientific codes and for other multi-author codes that have a similar development cycle. For some applications, emphasis on performance and the evolving nature of the underlying algorithms can lead to highly complex software dependencies. When this is combined with a long-term development cycle for which there is a large number of contributors, gaining transparency into the implementation-level details of an algorithm can become prohibitive. In this paper we present an example of how combining off-the-shelf products with custom analysis can yield some of the transparency needed for more fully understanding these implementation details but acknowledge that further work is needed for complete understanding.

VIII. References

1. Altschul, S., et al., *Basic local alignment search tool.* J. Mol. Biol., 1990. **215**(3): p. 403-410.
2. Oehmen, C. and J. Nieplocha, *ScalaBLAST: A scalable implementation of BLAST for high-performance data-intensive bioinformatics analysis.* Trans. Parallel Distributed Sys., 2006. **17**(8): p. 740-749.
3. Oehmen, C., E. Peterson, and S. Dowson, *An organic model for detecting cyber events*, in *Proc. Sixth Annual Workshop on Cyber Security and Information Intelligence Research*, F. Sheldon, et al., Editors. 2010, ACM: Oak Ridge, TN.
4. Altschul, S., et al., *The estimation of statistical parameters for local alignment score distributions.* Nucl. Acids Res., 2001. **29**(2): p. 351-361.
5. Hunt, A. and D. Thomas, *Software Archaeology.* IEEE J. Software, 2002. **19**(2): p. 20-22.
6. Risch, J., et al., *The STARLIGHT Information Visualization System*, in *IEEE International Information Visualization Conference (IV '97)*. 1997: London, England.
7. McCabe, T. and C. Butler, *Design Complexity Measurement and Testing.* Commun. ACM, 1989. **32**(12): p. 1415-1425.
8. [ftp://ftp.ncbi.nlm.nih.gov/blast/documents/ developer/ scoring.pdf

Use of Closures to Engineer Software for a Family of Numerical Simulation Models

K.A. Hawick and E.P. Clarkson
Computer Science, Massey University, North Shore 102-904, Auckland, New Zealand
email: k.a.hawick@massey.ac.nz; elliot.clarkson@gmail.com
Tel: +64 9 414 0800 Fax: +64 9 441 8181

June 2013

ABSTRACT

Closures offer powerful capabilities for encapsulating adaptive parts of a simulation program into dynamical data structures. We investigate the use of closure mechanisms for managing different simulation models in a lattice simulation framework implemented in both the Java and Groovy programming languages. We present results based on compiled Java with fixed model definitions as well as with user input of models at runtime expressed in dynamical Groovy. We discuss performance and other tradeoff issues as well as the potential for highly compact and reusable software components in what would otherwise be quite a complex software system.

KEY WORDS
closures; software engineering; on-demand code generation; code reuse; computational science; simulation.

1 Introduction

Developing fast and memory efficient simulation software is time consuming and demanding of a lot of domain-level as well as programmer expertise. programming languages offering mechanisms for maximising code reuse and allowing frameworks or libraries that can be used by short and compact domain-specific language calling-fragments are potentially very attractive providing computational efficiency can be maintained.

The Groovy programming language [39] is a relatively new system that is now widely available. Groovy [2, 25] builds upon Java [13] and makes use of a number of the standard Java data structures and libraries to extend the language to support generics [5], closures and other features [6, 23, 28] helpful in establishing internal domain-specific languages(DSLs) [11, 17, 32] for various application areas including graph or network systems [4, 18] and simulation modelling [16].

Closures [7, 35] are not new and have been available in effect in declarative programming languages [31, 41] for some time but it is not until relatively recently that efficient and compact syntax notations for them have become widely available in modern high-level imperative paradigm programming languages such as Ruby, Lua [22], Terra [8] or Groovy.

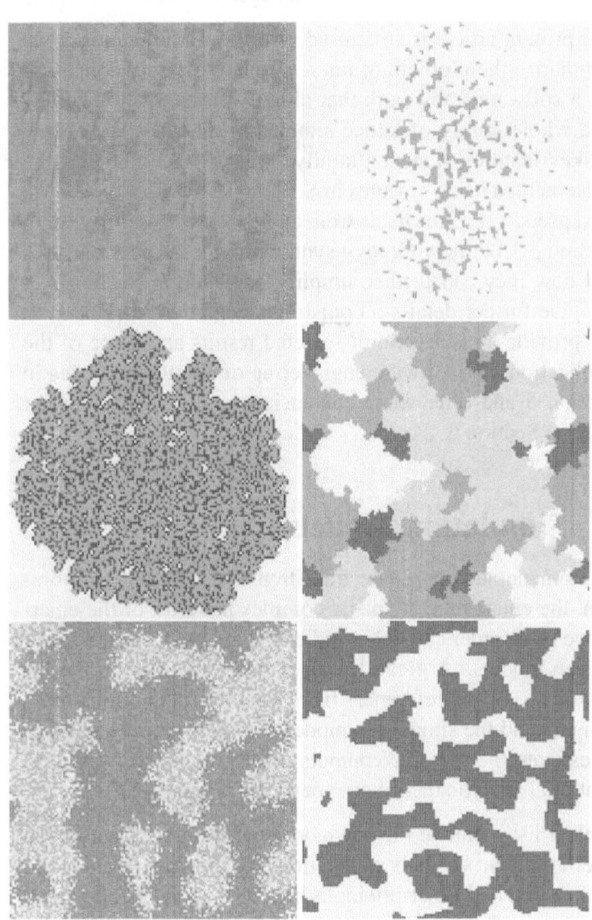

Figure 1: Some of the family of lattice simulation models that can be generated by the closures framework: Prisoners' Dilemma; Diffusion Gas; Epidemic; Sznajd Opinion; Cyclic Layering; Schelling Segregation.

Other projects such as X10 [14, 37] are investigating mechanisms to support high performance yet high level programming language constructs for simulations [33] and various language paradigms such as functional [38], object-oriented languages [3] and dynamic [34] and scripting languages [27] have various features that support this goal.

In this present paper we focus on a class of lattice oriented simulation models that can be used as a whole family to investigate critical and phase transitional phenomena. Figure 1 shows snapshots of some of the family of lattice simulation models that can be accommodated within our closure based simulation framework. Other related families of models include multi agent systems for artificial intelligence and artificial life investigations [29] where a large number of agents is needed to probe multi scale phenomena both spatially and temporally. Computer simulations where a trajectory through model space is needed are notorious for requiring a numerical sampling and average over many independent "runs" and this further emphasises the need for a simulation framework that is computationally efficient. Our models are aimed at routinely running in excess of 10^6 individual agents or cells.

Our present article is structured as follows: In Section 2 we summarise the problem of interest to us – namely constructing a software framework that allows fast simulation of any of a whole family of lattice simulation models. We review the key features of such a family and show how they can be implemented using closures in Section 3. We discuss how we used pseudo closures made from anonymous classes in Java in Section 3.1 but how Groovy syntax provides proper closures and how they can further simplify our code in Section 3.2. We give further details on our implementation in Section 4. We provide a discussion of selected results and some of the implications for software engineering of simulation codes in Section 5 and offer some conclusions and areas for further work in Section 6.

2 Simulation Models

Phenomena such as phase transitions, relaxation, equilibration, the emergence of spatial complex patterns, or the emergence or disorder can al be studied using lattice oriented simulation models. A great deal of work is available in the literature ([17] and references therein) concerning critical phenomena and the simulation model that must often be used to investigate the systems computationally rather than by conventional analytic theory or experimental approaches.

Table 1 lists some of the key models used in this work with a brief comment on their applications arena and a reference to a more detailed description. In brief these models all follow the pattern of requiring a set of scalar variables that comprise the model state to be initialised (usually in a random pattern) on a spatial lattice and then evolved according to some local update formula.

In our investigations of such models, we need to study them as a whole class rather than just solely as individual systems of interest. As a consequence of this it is necessary to manage them within a unified framework so as to be able to effectively compare like with like and minimise assumptions and coding errors. In fact this opens up great potential for savings of software engineering effort. The models we focus on in this present paper can be formulated as follows.

A lattice structure of the regular form $\sigma_i \in \mathcal{L}$ where the N model variables are indexed by $i = 0, 1, ..., N-1$ and may be scalars or sometimes vectors of more than one degree of freedom. In fact many of the models we focus on have a simple integer variable that can take on some number Q different states. In the case of the Ising magnetism model $Q = 2$ and the only; two allowable states are the quantum spin values "up" and "down." The Potts model extends this to some arbitrary number Q of pseudo spin variables. The Sznajd opinion model can use the same structure to represent Q allowable different opinions. The Kawasaki and diffuse models can use Q different atomic species held in the same way. We can right $\mathcal{S} = \sigma_i$ to represent a particular state of the whole model, with a definite and specific value for each of the N site variables σ_i.

Model Name	Application Arena	Reference
Ising	Magnetic Materials	[20]
Q-State Potts	Materials Science	[19]
Kawasaki	Materials Science	[24]
Sznajd	Opinions and Sociology	[40]
Axelrod	Culture Dissemination	[1]
Reichenbach	Cyclic Predator-Prey	[36]
RPSLS	Cycles and Parity	[15]
Rabbit-Fox CA	Predatory-Prey Cycles	[21]
Conway GoL	Complex System	[12]
Forest Fire	Ecology & Damage	[9]
Eden	Cancer Growth	[10]
Epidemic	Disease Spread	[30]
Langton Ant	Complex Growth	[26]
Random Walk	Growth & Information	[30]
Self-Avoiding	Constrained Growth	[30]

Table 1: Models that use discrete cell types of finite number of states and which can be modelled on the Bravais lattices in two dimensions and with different cell neighbourhoods.

The lattice $\mathcal{L}$ itself can have any geometry we can suppose and typical examples are square or simple cubic (SC), but this can be extended to hyper-cubic lattices of the form $N = L^d, d = 2, 3, 4, ...$ with a length L and dimension d. In practice, we can also implement other structures such as triangular and hexagonal lattices in two dimensions, or the common crystallographic structures found in real three dimensional substances such as face centred cubic (FCC), body-centred cubic (BCC) or hexagonal close-packed (HCP) lattices.

The notion of locality is very important to the model family we discuss. In most cases the model time evolution can be written in the form:

$$\begin{aligned} \mathcal{S}_t &\rightarrow \mathcal{S}_{t+1} \\ \sigma_{i,t} &\rightarrow \sigma_{i,t+1} = \mathcal{F}(\sigma_{i,t}, \sigma_{\mathcal{N}(i),t}) \end{aligned} \quad (1)$$

where we use $\mathcal{N}(i)$ to denote a **localised** neighbourhood of sites around site i. This is an important restriction and the locality of interactions - namely that the new value of site i is obtained through a formula that depends only upon nearby site values - imposes a realistic spatial structure and causality time and length scales on the model. It also provides the basis for incorporating parallelism into the model computations as it allows a simple geometric decomposition and allows sites in the whole system to be allocated in some sort of spatial patching to different processors - real or virtual.

Some models are stochastic - that is the formula for updating individual sites has a random or thermal term in it. Our framework is able to supply random fields in the form of pseudo-randomly generated variates from one of several different generator algorithms.

The framework then must manage the site variables in terms of their initialisation and time evolution. The framework must also manage the spatial geometry mapping of i to space in the form of x, or x, y, z or if using a higher dimension $d > 3$ then to appropriate hyper-coordinates in the d-dimensional space. The locality and neighbourhood being used can also be varied. So for instance, it is often revealing to vary a model from using nearest neighbour to next nearest, or Moore neighbourhood or some other structure such as neighbourhoods defined by a radial distance of proximity.

In summary, the simulation is specified by: Model $(\mathcal{M}, Q)$; Lattice Geometry $(\mathcal{L}, L, d)$; Neighbourhood $(\mathcal{N})$. Each of these parameters can be usefully managed and specified using the closure and pseudo-closure mechanisms we describe below.

3 Closures

Closures are embedded code fragments that "close over the embedding scope" and are thus able to combine code locality of reference and scope with access to key variables that are set up in the embedding source code. The closure mechanism is particularly useful in the context of our simulation framework for a family of models. Closures allow us to reuse many of the services, and data structures in effect for a simulated model but still keep the details of the particular chosen model defined locally in a manner that is easy to read for the programmer and subsequent developer. This is particularly important for an ongoing project where new models are added later - and could not practically have been formulated all at once at the start of the project.

Attempts have been made to use simulation objects and an object-oriented architecture [35] for simulation model frameworks but it is not trivial to separate out all the necessary apparatus for each model without introducing significant memory or speed inefficiencies. More significantly it does not necessarily aid development and addition of brand new models conceived on an ongoing basis in the same way that the closures mechanism allows.

3.1 Pseudo-Closures in Java

We first developed our simulation framework using Java, which does not have a fully developed closures syntax and mechanism. It does however allow anonymous classes which can be stored in a data structure such as a HashMap as we illustrate below in Figure 2.

```
public interface Evolver{public void evolve(int n);}
...
HashMap<Model, Evolver> map = new HashMap<>();
..
map.put( Model.ISING, new Evolver(){
  // evolve using Metropolis Ising dynamics:
  public void evolve(int steps) {
    for(int ender=step+steps; step<ender; step++){
      for(int site=0;site<N;site++){
        int k = neighbourHood.randomSite();
        int currentValue = spin[k];
        int newValue =
          (spin[k] + 1 + rng.nextInt(Q-1) ) % Q;
        // pick possible (different) new value
        int nbonds = 0;
        for( int kn : neighbourHood.list(k) ){
          if( kn != NONE ){
            nbonds+=currentValue==spin[kn]?-1:+1;
            nbonds+=     newValue==spin[kn]?+1:-1;
          }
        }
        if( ferromagnetic ){
          if( nbonds >= 0 ||
            rng.nextDouble() <
            metropolis( nbonds, currentValue) )
          spin[k] = newValue;
        }
        else{
          if( nbonds <= 0 ||
              rng.nextDouble() <
              metropolis(-nbonds, currentValue) )
            spin[k] = newValue;
        }
      }
    }
  }
});
```

Figure 2: Inserting a closure with evolve(int) method into HashMap of models – example shown is for the Ising $Q = 2$ state model - generalised for Potts model case with arbitrary number of states Q and ferro or antiferromagnetic coupling cases.

Figure 2 shows how a type-parameterised Java generic data structure – in this case a `HashMap` – was used to hold the collection of Java pseudo-closures that close around the various `evolve()` method implementations for each simulation model. We used a Java enumeration to specify the allowed different models $\mathcal{M}$. The Ising model is one such and its *evolve()* method shown in explicit detail. In essence these lines of code shown are all that is needed to implement a particular model using the other data variables (such as L, d, N, σ_i) and structures in scope at the time. Service level methods to pick random lattice sites in a random order, or to gather the neighbours for a particular site (independent of the lattice geometry and chosen neighbourhood) are part of the support framework.

This was a useful Java capability to be able to exploit and it helped to significantly reduce the number of lines of source code for our simulation and in particular for a new model and incrementally incorporate it into our framework.

3.2 Closures in Groovy

The Groovy language builds on top of Java and provides compact, explicit closure syntax and mechanisms, an example of which is given in Figure 3.

```
// Minimal closure
{ println "Hello, World!" }

// Closure demonstrating accessing variables
// in enclosing scope
def greeting = "Hello"
def printGreeting = { name ->
  println greeting + ", " + name + "!"
}

// Prints "Hello, Ken!"
printGreeting("Ken")
```

Figure 3: A demonstration of closure syntax in Groovy

3.2.1 Resolving variables in Groovy closures

Groovy offers three keywords which provide handles to implicitly available objects used to resolve references. Just as `this` in Java refers to the enclosing class, `owner` in a Groovy closure refers to either `this` or the surrounding closure. `delegate` is a user-settable handle which is used similarly and normally points to the same object as `owner`. By default, references to variables are resolved to `owner`, and then `delegate` if this is unsuccessful (though this behavior can be changed.) This mechanism is important as it provides a way for closures to maintain their own symbol table, and thusly opens the door to allow closures to become a collection of both code and data in a manner analogous to class instances.

3.2.2 Closures as Pseudo-objects

If a separate object is created for each closure to use as a delegate and the resolve strategy is set to have the closure look nowhere else for variable references, it is possible to treat closures as pseudo-objects, each with their own namespace.

To take this approach even further, Groovy provides a mechanism to override the default behavior when a referenced property cannot be located. If the coder attempts to write to a variable that does not exist, it is possible to have it be created and stored for later use. Figure 4 shows an example implementation of this technique, whereupon variables referenced for reading are first searched for in the accompanying map. If the reference cannot be resolved, the search is 'passed upwards' to another scope - whatever was passed in the constructor for the `ClosureScope` object.

4 Groovy Implementation

We discuss the models in terms of tick closures that implement a single time-step on a model. A tick closure embodies

```
class ClosureScope {
  def bindingEnv
  def vars = Collections.synchronizedMap([:])

  public ClosureScope(bindingEnv) {
    this.bindingEnv = bindingEnv
  }
  def propertyMissing(String name) {
    vars[name] != null ? vars[name] :
      bindingEnv."\${name}"
  }
  def propertyMissing(String name, value) {
    vars[name] = value
  }
}
...
cls = {
  x = "I am stored in the map!"
  println x
}
cls.resolveStrategy = Closure.DELEGATE_ONLY
cls.delegate = new ClosureScope(this)
cls()
```

Figure 4: Using Groovy's propertyMissing hook to store newly-referenced variables in a map.

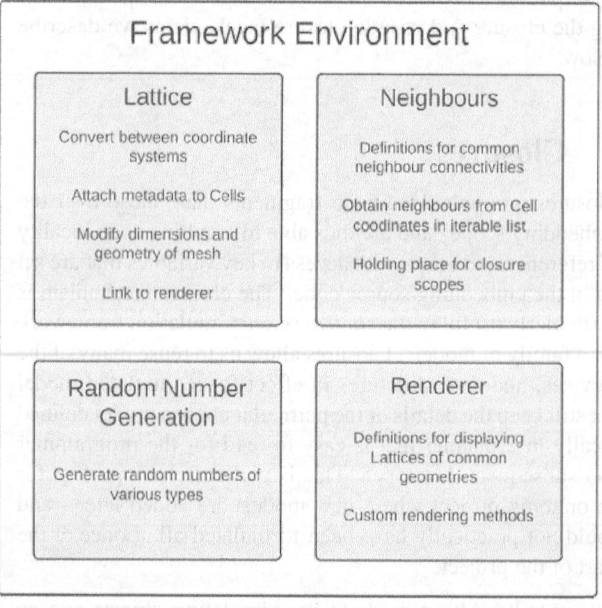

Figure 5: The resources available to the developer for rapid prototyping through the framework.

precisely the particular model $\Updownarrow \in \{\mathcal{M}\}$ we wish to run. The chosen neighbourhood $\setminus \in \{\mathcal{N}\}$ is specified by the chosen neighbours closure.

The Groovy implementation was designed to allow the coder to completely and concisely define a model by using a combination of sensible, predefined closures, and custom-made closures that would cater to its idiosyncrasies. Figure 5 shows the main facilities available to the developer within the framework. The dynamic nature of the Groovy environment means that it is relatively straightforward to add other capabilities for new models. This practice is especially useful for Cell objects, where it is a simple matter to add a new property to each cell in a lattice, such as temperature, height, attractive force, or whatever else the simulation might call for.

It is worth noting that when the choice between optimization and coder-friendliness had to be made, the choice was to lean to coder-friendliness in an effort to make the crafting of new models as simple as possible. The Groovy implementation was designed to be a rapid development tool for quickly prototyping new models, which could later be remade using other, more specialised code outside of the framework.

Addition of a new model therefore requires only the construction of an appropriate new 'tick' closure, which would be called for every iteration of evolution. This tick closure would later be called by the support framework, and code inside the tick closure has full access to all framework functions through instances of classes in the enclosing scope.

```
def tick = {
  lattice.buffer.eachWithIndex { cell , k ->

  def aliveNeighbours = neighbours(k).findAll( {
     lattice.cell(it).state == ALIVE
  } ).size()

    if( cell.state == ALIVE &&
      (aliveNeighbours==2 || aliveNeighbours==3) )
      cell.state = ALIVE
    else cell.state = DEAD
  }
  lattice.update() // Copy buffer to current lattice
}
```

Figure 6: A Groovy tick closure for Conway's Game of Life

Figure 6 shows a tick closure defined for the Conway game of life model. Not the concision of this and in particular how easy it is to set up for example the live neighbour count using existing framework apparatus. Other models in the simulation family can be encoded with similar concision.

Closures are also utilised for neighbour calculation. It is thus easy to substitute the *neighbours()* closure to quickly apply existing algorithms to unusual neighbourhoods; for example, taking neighbours from only an area below the cell in question - as shown in Figure 7.

5 Results & Discussion

Neighbours can be dynamically generated, but we have found that resolving variables in neighbour closures takes a significant amount of processing power. This is consistent with neighbours being called a lot and highlights this as an area for optimisation. Some sacrifice of dynamical freedom for performance is likely justified for a production model run. For model development purposes and where a relatively small prototype model would only be run for short times, it is still acceptable.

```
// A Closure to find neighbours below the cell:
def nBelow = { k ->
  def results = [] as ArrayList
  def x = l.toX(k)   // Convert to Euclidean coords
  // Get the 3 horizontal cells one below this one
  (-1..1).each {
    results << l.toK([x[0] + it, x[1]-1])
  }
  return results
}
// Override the neighbours closure
def neighbours = nBelow
```

Figure 7: Replacing the neighbours closure with something unusual for a new model - in this case a spatially asymmetric halo gathering neighbours only from below the cell.

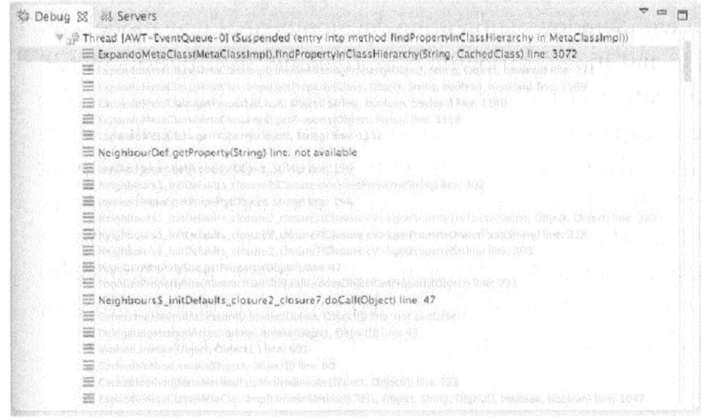

Figure 8: Method calls involved in resolving references in pseudo-object closures

Figure 8 shows a stack trace of the method calls involved in resolving references in the pseudo-object closures. Every time a property is requested that is not present in the *metaClass*, program flow is caught by *propertyMissing*, which searches a map for the desired property. The overhead involved in such a large quantity of method calls quickly adds up, especially when these properties are referenced for every cell every iteration (a likely situation.)

In principle, it would be possible to interface directly with the appropriate *metaClass* to avoid this overhead. However, this runs the risk of having the coder accidentally overwriting some important variable that is part of the inner workings. A hybrid approach may be appropriate, whereupon *propertyMissing* modifies the *metaClass* itself, but only when it is safe to do so. This would prevent further calls to *propertyMissing* the next time the property is referenced as the *metaClass* would return the desired value, saving time. This tradeoff between security/safety and efficiency is a general aspect of Groovy that justifies further investigation.

Figure 9 shows the multi window development environment enabled by the dynamical approach with available diagnostics, console, model properties and development windows supporting new model closures.

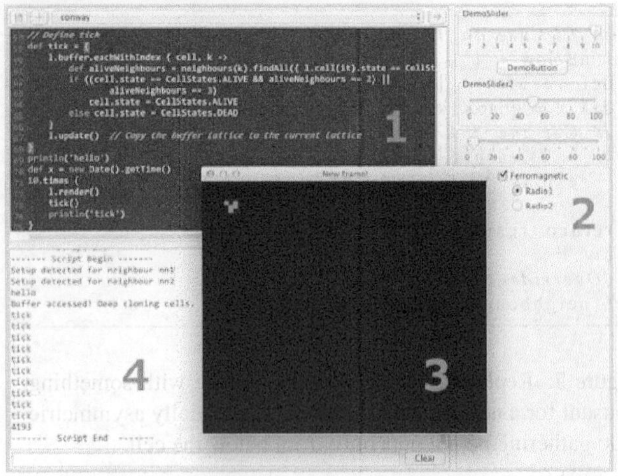

Figure 9: Screen shot of the development environment in action with windows supporting development of new model closures and model properties (1), dynamic user interfaces (2), and Lattice visualisation (3). A debugging panel (4) is also open, capable showing the output from the currently open script and also accepting input in the form of a read-eval-print loop. This allows the coder to enter commands which modify the loaded code to test how the model behaves in response to changes such as hot-swapping out the active neighbours closure for something different mid-run, or to probe values of variables such as the properties of individual cells.

6 Conclusion

We have implemented a lattice-oriented simulation framework in both Java and in Groovy. In Java we have been able to use anonymous objects containing appropriate methods defining the time-evolutionary behaviour of particular models, which can be stored in an appropriate data structure for access at runtime. Similarly, we can package the appropriate methods for accessing nearest, next-nearest, Moore neighbourhoods for each different lattice geometry using the same mechanisms.

This does help code clarity, keeping the requisite apparatus for geometry all in one part of the program and the individual model details also relatively localised within the source code.

The Groovy closure syntax helps extend this and enables further source code reduction. The closure mechanism helps considerably in an architectural case such as the simulation model family where it is non-trivial nor optimal to separate every model into a separate class/object. Closures have allowed us to maximise model code locality while appropriately still closing over other data structures and variables within the simulation framework.

However, we encountered some speed deficiencies with our Groovy implementation. It appears that further optimisation is necessary to avoid too much overhead from some of the dynamical calls Groovy inserts. In particular, the neighbours cross-indexing and gathering routines are used so heavily it would be worthwhile trading off some dynamic call flexibility to maintain their performance.

Generally we have found Groovy and its syntactic mechanisms for Closures a useful tool for reducing lines of code and code complexity for the sort of family of applications that we experimented with. There is scope for a revised system that takes the best from both pure Java and a Groovy implementation and gives a hybrid that gives good performance but retains much of the dynamic calling capabilities.

We have focused on Java/Groovy as this allowed us to leverage development with a large existing code base. There is also however scope for attempting the architecture we have discussed using other modern languages that also support closures. The general notion of how one derives an optimal mix of closures and objects that approximate pseudo version of one another has great promise for further software engineering investigations. Finally, we note that this approach provides very good support for a research software project where new unknown models are added incrementally and by definition, the complete specification is open ended.

Acknowledgments

Thanks to B.Kennedy, S.Innes, M.Fraser and J.Scogings for useful comments and assistance in exercising the preliminary implementations described.

References

[1] Axelrod, R.: The dissemination of culture: a model with local convergence and global polarization. J. Conflict Resolution 41, 203–226 (1997)

[2] Barclay, K.A., Savage, J.: Groovy for Programming - An Introduction for Java Developers. Morgan Kaufmann (2006)

[3] Barros, F.J.: A compositional approach for modeling and simulation of bio-molecular systems. In: Proc. 2012 IEEE Winter Simulation Conference (2012)

[4] Bergmann, G., Ujhelyi, Z., Rath, I., Varro, D.: A graph query language for emf models. In: Proc. Int. Conf. on Model Transformation (ICMT 2011). pp. 167–182. No. 6707 in LNCS, Zurich, Switzerland (27-28 June 2011)

[5] Bracha, G.: Generics in the java programming language. Tech. rep., Sun Microsystems (July 2004)

[6] Burgin, M.: Basic classes of grammars with prohibition. arXiv 1302.5181, UCLA, USA (February 2013)

[7] Clarke, E.M.: Programming language constructs for which it is impossible to obtain good hoare axiom systems. J. ACM 26(1), 129–147 (1979)

[8] DeVito, Z., Hegarty, J., Aiken, A., Hanrahan, P., Vitek, J.: Terra: A multi-stage language for high-performance computing. In: Proc. 34th ACM Conf. on Programming Language Design and Implementation. pp. 1–11. Seattle, Washington (16-22 June 2013)

[9] Drossel, B., Schwabl, F.: Formation of space-time structure in a forest-fire model. Physica A: Stat. Mech and its Applications 204, 212–229 (1994)

[10] Eden, M.: A two-dimensional growth process. In: Proc. Fourth

Berkeley Symposium on Mathematics, Statistics and Probability. vol. 4, pp. 223–239. Univ. California Press, Berkeley (1960)

[11] Fowler, M.: Domain-Specific Languages. No. ISBN 0-321-71294-3, Addison Wesley (2011)

[12] Gardner, M.: Mathematical Games: The fantastic combinations of John Conway's new solitaire game "Life". Scientific American 223, 120–123 (October 1970)

[13] Gosling, J., Joy, B., Steele, G.: The Java Language Specification. JavaSoft Series, Addison Wesley Longman (1996), iSBN 0-201-63451-1

[14] Hannig, F., Roloff, S., Snelting, G., Teich, J., Zwinkau, A.: Resource-aware programming and simulation of mpsoc architectures through extension of x10. In: Proc. 14th Int. Workshop on Software and Compilers for Embedded Systems (SCOPES'11). pp. 1–8. Schloss Rheinfels, St. Goar, Germany (27-28 June 2011)

[15] Hawick, K.A.: Complex Domain Layering in Even Odd Cyclic State Rock-Paper-Scissors Game Simulations. In: Proc. IASTED International Conference on Modelling and Simulation (MS2011). pp. 129–136. No. 735-062, IASTED, Calgary, Alberta, Canada (4-6 July 2011)

[16] Hawick, K.A.: Engineering domain-specific languages for computational simulations of complex systems. In: Proc. Int. Conf. on Software Engineering and Applications (SEA2011). pp. 222–229. No. CSTN-123, IASTED, Dallas, USA (14-16 December 2011)

[17] Hawick, K.A.: Engineering internal domain-specific language software for lattice-based simulations. In: Proc. Int. Conf. on Software Engineering and Applications. IASTED, Las Vegas, USA (12-14 November 2012)

[18] Hawick, K.A.: Fluent interfaces and domain-specific languages for graph generation and network analysis calculations. In: Proc. Int. Conf. on Software Engineering (SE'13). IASTED, Innsbruck, Austria (11-13 February 2013)

[19] Hawick, K.A., Johnson, M.G.B.: Bit-packed damaged lattice potts model simulations with cuda and gpus. In: Proc. Int. Conf. on Modelling, Simulation and Identification (MSI 2011). pp. 371–378. IASTED, Pittsburgh, USA (7-9 November 2011)

[20] Hawick, K.A., Leist, A., Playne, D.P.: Regular Lattice and Small-World Spin Model Simulations using CUDA and GPUs. Int. J. Parallel Prog. 39(CSTN-093), 183–201 (2011)

[21] Hawick, K.A., Scogings, C.J.: A minimal spatial cellular automata for hierarchical predator-prey simulation of food chains. In: Proc. International Conference on Scientific Computing (CSC'10). pp. 75–80. WorldComp, Las Vegas, USA (12-15 July 2010)

[22] Ierusalimschy, R.: Programming with multiple paradigms in lua. In: Proc. Workshop on Functional and Constraint Language Programming (WFLP'09). pp. 1–12. No. 5979 in LNCS, Springer (2010)

[23] Kabanov, J., Hunger, M., Raudjarv, R.: On designing safe and flexible embedded dsls with java 5. Science of Computer Programming 76, 970–991 (2011)

[24] Kawasaki, K.: Diffusion constants near the critical point for time dependent Ising model I. Phys. Rev. 145(1), 224–230 (1966)

[25] Konig, D., Glover, A., King, P., Laforge, G., Skeet, J.: Groovy in Action. Manning (2007), iSBN 978-1-932394-84-2

[26] Langton, C.G.: Studying artificial life with cellular automata. Physica D 22, 120–149 (1986)

[27] Li, D., He, S.: Javascript closure: Conceptm usage and application. Computer Science Applications and Education 13, 463–468 (2013)

[28] Lienhardt, M., Lanese, I.: A reversible abstract machine and its space overhead. In: Proc. IFIP Int. Conf. on Formal Techniquesfor Distributed Systems. pp. 1–17. No. 7273 in LNCS, Stockholm, Sweden (13-16 June 2012 2012)

[29] Lytinen, S.L., Railsback, S.F.: The evolution of agent-based simulation platforms: A review of netlogo 5.0 and relogo. In: Proc. Fourth Int. Symp. on Agent-Based Modelling and Simulation (2012)

[30] Meakin, P.: Fractals, Scaling and Growth far From Equilibrium. No. ISBN 0-521-45253-8, Cambridge University Press (1998)

[31] Merunka, V.: Instance-level modeling and simulation using lambda-calculus and object-oriented environments. In: Enterprise and Organizational Modeling and Simulation - 7th International Workshop (EOMAS 2011). London, UK (20-21 June 2011)

[32] Miller, J.A., Han, J., Hybinette, M.: Using domain specific language for modeling and simulation: Scalation as a case study. In: Proc. 2010 Winter Simulation Conference. pp. 741–752 (2010)

[33] Milthorpe, J., Rendell, A.P., Huber, T.: Pgas-fmm: Implementing a distributed fast multipole method using the x10 programming language. Concurrency and Computation: Practice and Experience POnline, 1–16 (2013)

[34] Ozik, J., North, M.: Modeling endogenous coordination using a dynamic language. In: Proc. Simulating Interacting Agents and Social Phenomena: The Second World Congress, Agent-Based Social Systems 7 (2010)

[35] Reddy, U.S.: Objects as closures: Abstract semantics of object-oriented languages. In: Proc. ACM Conf. on Lisp and Functional Programming. pp. 289–297. ACM (1988)

[36] Reichenbach, T., Mobilia, M., Frey, E.: Coexistence versus Extinction in the Stochastic cyclic Lotka-Volterra model. Phys. Rev. E 74, 051907–1–11 (2006)

[37] Saraswat, V., Bloom, B., Peshansky, I., Tardieu, O., Grove, D.: Report on the programming language x10. Tech. rep., IBM, Thomas J. Watson Rresearch Center, USA (2010), `http://x10-lang.org/`

[38] Steele, C.S., Bonn, J.P.: Fast functional simulation with a dynamic language. In: Proc. High Performance Extreme Computing (HPEC 2012). pp. 1–3. IEEE, Waltham, MA, USA (10-12 September 2012)

[39] Strachan, J.: Weblog (August 2003), `http://radio-weblogs.com/0112098/2003/08/29.html`

[40] Sznajd-Weron, K., Sznajd-Weron, J.: Opinion evolution in closed community. Int. J. Modern Physics C 11(6), 1157–1165 (2000)

[41] Todd, A.B., Keller, A.K., Lewis, M.C., martin G. Kelly: Multi-agent system simulation in scala: An evaluation of actors for parallel simulation. In: Proc. Int. Conf of Parallel and Distributed processing and Applications (PDPTA'11) (2011)

A Case Study in the Model-Driven Development of CorkBoard – a WebApp for Collaborative Work

Andrew Harnage, Doug Flagg, Amber Whittemore, Devon M. Simmonds
University of North Carolina Wilmington
601 South College Road, Wilmington, NC 28403
{cah5854, dgf4958, arw5194, simmondsd}@uncw.edu
SERP '13

Abstract

We report on the model-driven development of CorkBoard - a project designed to provide a mechanism for small groups of persons to work collaboratively. We narrowed the most important software functions that a group would need for project success to: notification, communication, organization, accountability, and management. By focusing on these five topics, we believed we could create a WebApp that would serve as a positive environment for a group and facilitate the process of achieving success. Ultimately, we gained invaluable knowledge and experience in planning, estimation, scheduling, settings goals, meeting deadlines, and working in teams through the progression of the CorkBoard project. We present our results and lessons learned in the process.

Keywords: CorkBoard, Collaboration, WebApp, Model Driven Development, Communication.

1. Introduction

Working within a group can be a daunting task. This is true whether group members are familiar with each other or are meeting for the first time. Professional and institutional workgroups encounter multiple conflicts during the creation, progression, and completion of a project. For example, scheduling and personal conflicts arise; members may be unavoidably absent from work at a time when projects still need to be completed on time. Organizational and communicational issues also occur when members are forced to use multiple sources for communication and data sharing. Additionally, responsibilities and tasks are not always well defined, allowing for an uneven distribution of work and lack of accountable on the part of some project members.

Users, whether they are professional, scholastic, or casual, use applications in the hopes of simplifying and condensing otherwise complex tasks. Too often, applications are built with unnecessary functions, confusing controls, or too many operations, taking away from the application's main purpose. These faults can force users to spend extra time learning the functionality of the application, instead of utilizing it for its intended purposes. Users need easy to use applications, without large learning curves.

To aid individuals engaged in collaborative projects and provide software that minimizes unnecessary functionality and complexity, we designed a Web application called ***CorkBoard***. WebApp's are a popular category of applications spawned by the Internet. WebApp's have evolved into sophisticated computing tools that provide both stand-alone software and integrated business applications [1, 20]. CorkBoard provides functionality to aid scheduling, communication, organization, and distribution of work within groups of individuals.

Our motivation for the project was three-fold. First we wanted to test our model-driven development (MDE) skills. Secondly, we wanted to test these skills by developing software that would be useful and third, we wanted to engage in Web-based development given the growth and reach of the Internet and associated technologies. Model-driven engineering (MDE) [11 – 13] is an approach to software engineering that shifts the development philosophy from a code-centric approach to an approach where models become indispensable first class entities in the software lifecycle. MDE is especially appealing as if enables a reduction in some of the accidental complexities [14] that arise in software development when code-centric approaches are used. Modeling for CorkBoard was done using UML [15] class, activity, sequence, state and use case diagrams.

Several collaborative software are available [16 – 18], however, we have found several of these applications to be very complex, difficult to use, and containing unnecessary functionality. In addition, we wanted to gain personal experience developing this kind of software. In contrast to some of the available applications, CorkBoard was designed to be simple, reducing unnecessary functionality, while being a productive program that is easy to navigate and that focuses on small teams. Small teams [2] have been found to be more effective and productive than a single individual toiling away at a project [3]. We focus on these small groups, facilitating their effort to produce a successful.

2. Project Plan

Given the project goal of developing collaborative software with a small learning curve, we began the software engineering process with project planning. Planning was done to define the scope, assess risks, estimate required resources and schedule project activities. The key emphasis of the project was to create a unified accountability system to allow for development of a group project. Planning enabled us to lay a foundation for performing, observing and having control over later software lifecycle activities such as design, implementation and testing.

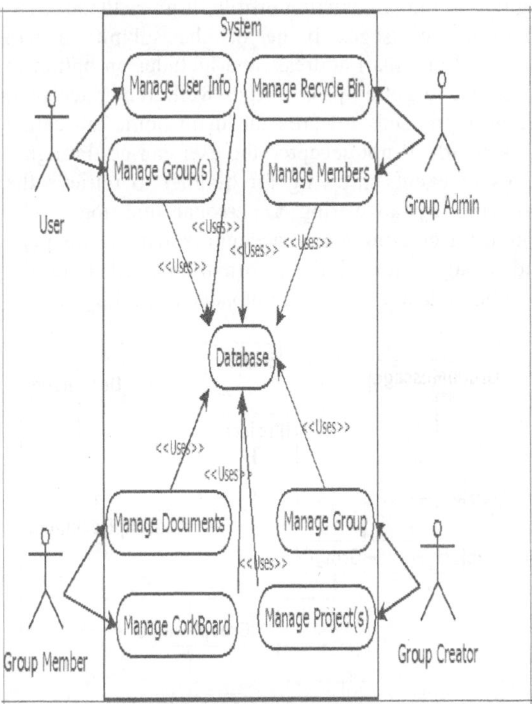

Figure 1: Use Case Diagram

The foremost purpose of the UML use case diagram (UCD) is to visually associate users with the services or processes provided by the system [7, 19].

In Figure 1 our actors, e.g. Group Admin, Group Creator, User, and Group Member, each have specific needs, roles and responsibilities. For example, the Group Creator responsibilities include creating and updating roles for other users. These roles are stored in the database. Users differ from Group Members because users are persons that haven't been accepted into a group. Group Creator, Group Admin's, and Group Members and general users form an inheritance hierarchy users being the most abstract. As such, the group Creator has the most authority and the users the least.

2.1 Project Scope

Table 1: Risk Assessment

Risk	Prob.	Impact	Priority	Actions
Loss of Project Member	2	8	10	Divide work up among remaining members
Hardware Breaks, Loss of Information	5	3	7	Backups are on Dropbox and on other members computers
Change in Deadlines	5	5	3	If a member finishes work early then that person will help the others

The scope of the CorkBoard software is reflected in the Use Case diagram shown in Figure 1. The services provided by the software include managing projects, managing groups, and managing documents. These software features are meant to enable project members to keep their work organized, with functions to ensure that other members are up-to-date on deadlines and other constraints. The WebApp is meant to be easy to learn and navigate by providing users with pictures, colors, and tools to customize and organize the information and data for the project.

2.2 Risk Plan

Ignoring risks because they are improbable and not worth analysis has proven to be highly risky in itself [5]. Table 1 shows the 3 risks that we identified for the project. The probability, impact and priority are on a scale of 0 to 10 with 0 being the lowest chance and 10 being the greatest. The first risk that we identified was the possibility of losing a project member. This risk would have the greatest impact on our group if it happened. Hardware breaks and changes in deadlines were the most probable risks.

2.3 Project Estimates and Schedule

Project planning included the development of a work breakdown structure (see Figure 2) and assigning responsibilities to project team members. Tasks are defined for the product as a whole or for individual functions [4]. The work breakdown structure (WBS) was used to create a list to keep track of each group member's responsibility. The WBS allows for an easy transition to project responsibilities by taking the main ideas of what a group will need and developing it. WBS is a vehicle for breaking an engineering project down into subproject, tasks, subtasks, work packages, and so on. It is an important planning tool which links objectives with resources and activities in a logical framework [6].

CorkBoard

Preliminary Group Setup	Project Planning	Software Requirements	System Design	Testing and Control	Deployment
Determine the Project	Create a Schedule	Functional Capabilities	Client Side		Increase or Decrease Capabilities
Initialize Roles and Responsibilities	Estimate Resources	Nonfunctional Capabilities	Server Side		Function Testing
Hold the First Official Meeting	Assess Risks				Reliability and Security Testing
	Assess Issues, Constraints, and Limitations				Update Changed Specifications or Functions

Figure 2: Work Breakdown Structure (The First two Layers)

3. Software Design & Development

The design class diagram for the software is shown in Figure 3. The figure lists all the types of Objects we thought we would need to complete the project. We thought it would be important to use classes and inheritance to minimize code duplication.

By having an inheritance hierarchy we allow for the possible code to be reused in the current modle of the system [11]. Picture, StickyNote, Tape and Tac are all instances of BoardObject and each of can be used as many times as the user would like. Each of the BoardObjects has their own unique attributes related to what the user applies to it. StickyNotes will have a particular message a User wants along with the ability to change the color and it will have the location (x and y points) of the StickyNote.

As you go down the hierarchy of GroupMember's we are applying more specific roles to each particular User. GroupMember's can upload documents, put objects on the CorkBoard, Chat and update their own My Workspace page. GroupAdmin's can appoint other members to Admins, change the Admin tab, use the Calendar and Recycling bin and let Users into the group. Finally the GroupCreator is the first member to create a group and has the ability to remove members, give a group name, delete a group and override changes for roles in the group.

Several state diagrams were developed for the CorkBoard software. The state diagram shown in Figure 4, focuses on either creating a new account or logging in into an existing profile. It gives the user the additional messages if he or she submits a bad password or Email address, and includes an option to retrieve a forgotten password as well. When accepted the user proceeds towards the main home tab called CorkBoard. If not accepted the user can go through a series of events allowing for him/her to retrieve the password by answering a personal question. The option for creating a new account is also on this page and a page with all the information needed for the member's database will be uploaded accordingly.

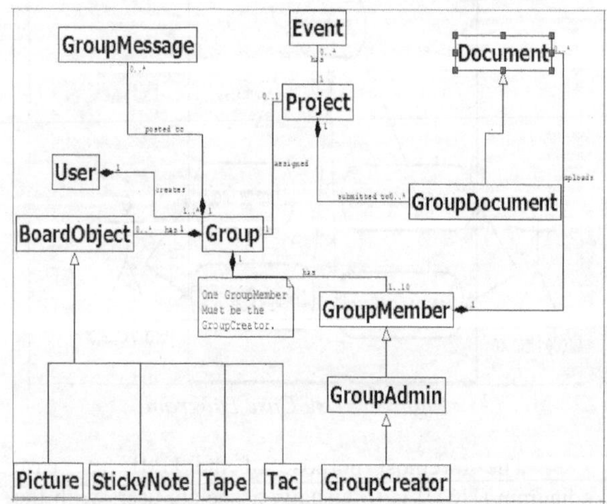

Figure: 3 Design Class Diagram

Architecture models describe the environment, but not the relationship between other systems in the environment [8]. These models are important because they show how the data moves through the system, which helps analyst understand what's going on [4,8]. Architecture is intended to develop a recommended practice for architectural description, allowing for communication of system-level and software-level architectural information between parties [9].

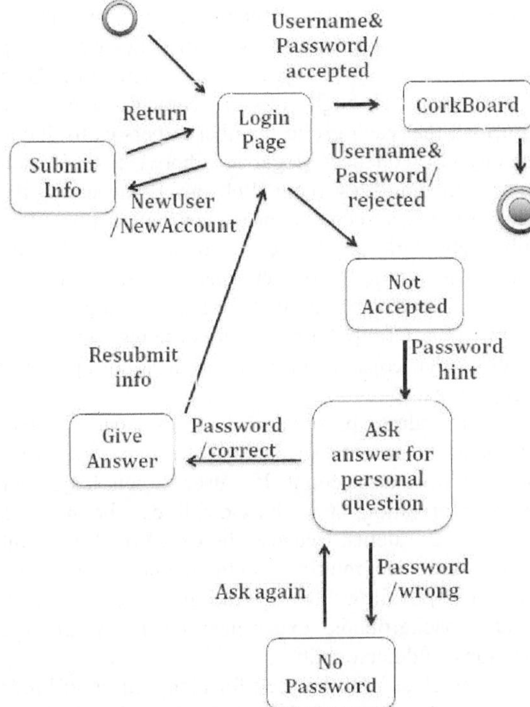

Figure 4: State Diagram for Login Page

Figure 5 shows our Shared Repository Architecture for the software identifying the major software subsystems. The Shared Repository Architecture boasts several advantages including:

- Efficient way to share large amounts of data
- Sub-systems need not be concerned with how data is produced Centralised management e.g. backup, security, etc.
- Sharing model is published as the repository schema

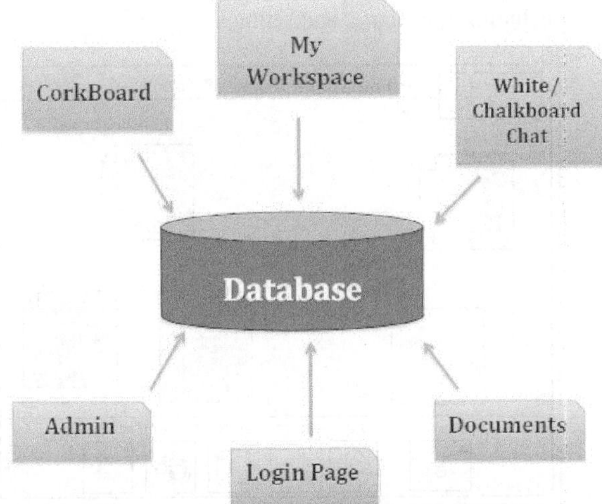

Figure 5: Shared Repository Architecture

4. Results

CorkBoard is a customizable group board where individuals can notify the group on due dates, and post reminders, pictures, and other important information. The CorkBoard WebApp consists of four main tabs as shown in Figure 6: CorkBoard, WhiteBoard, Documents, and My Workspace. An additional Admin tab will be visible to group creators and administrators. As Figure 6 shows, CorkBoard is a customizable group board where individuals can notify their group of due dates, reminders, pictures, and other important information.

Figure 6 is what the user would see as soon as their user and password are accepted in the login page. In this tab users can attach 'board objects' to the CorkBoard. These board objects are guaranteed to be seen by all of the members of the group, as the opening tab is always displayed immediately following user login. By using simple text and color schemes we've given each 'tab' its own personality.

Whiteboard tab is an advanced group chat system that allows members to communicate to one another. The Documents tab will list each member's submissions to the project. Here, members can also download these files to their personal computer. The My Workspace tab allows members to upload documents for personal viewing until they are ready to share their personal documents with their group through the Documents tab. Here, members can also save personal notes and reminders. For the administrators of the group, the Admin tab allows him or her to change certain aspect of group, projects including appearance and settings.

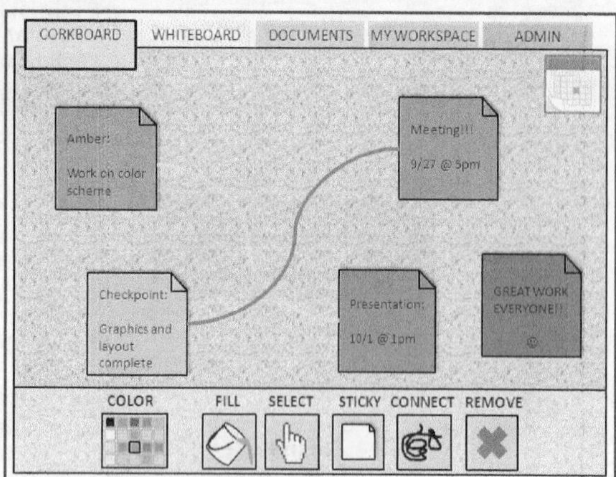

Figure 6: CorkBoard Home Tab

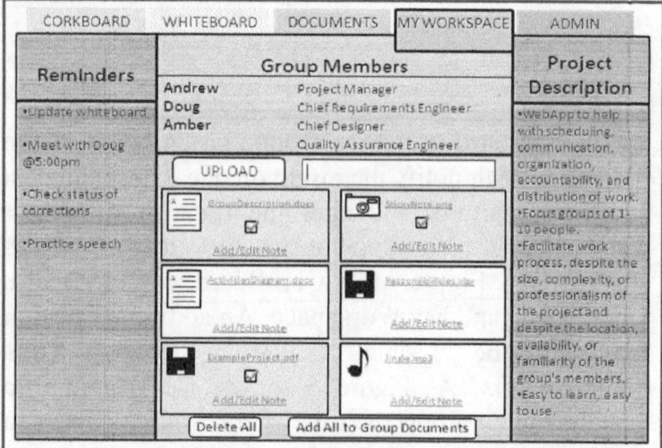

Figure 7: My Workspace Tab

5. Discussion and Lessons Learned

What sets the CorkBoard program apart from other group organizing software is the level of customization and organization automatically implemented within this WebApp. Without the ability to share ideas, the small group will likely suffer or fail. Through the CorkBoard, members can set priority on more important tasks, as well as be alerted of higher priority changes or jobs. Accountability is also automatically implemented within our system. Through timestamps on each user's last login and uploads, members are able to track a particular person's progression through their responsibilities.

We experienced several challenges in undertaking this project. Firstly, software engineering often requires that engineers learn new technologies, techniques and tools. in the CorkBoard project, only one group member was experienced with programming in C#, the others of us had to learn on the fly. A second challenge common to software engineers that we faced is the challenge of balancing competing interconnected concerns sometimes expressed as information management. In our case we had to manage and balance a number of features including a calendar, databases, and real-time updates. Managing all of these elements was a learning experience in itself. So too was, managing timing and scheduling which proved to be a complicated process with members being involved in multiple non-related endeavors resulting in schedules colliding much of the time.

Appropriate ethical practices are important in fostering a viable software engineering community in the long term. We address issues of ethics by making users agree to our copyright agreement (End User Agreement). Through this agreement, users are informed that each group member is personally liable for any consequences (legal or otherwise) that result from uploading files to our WebApp. By accepting the terms of this agreement, users consent to uploading only their work, and agree not to share files they do not own without proper permissions. In this agreement, we also state that we are not liable for lost information. Group Administrators are responsible for ensuring that copyrighted material does not appear in their groups.

To address personal and group security, users are asked to provide an email address and password upon creating an account. If a user forgets his or her login information, a backup email can be used to recover these items. Because the CorkBoard is meant to accommodate multiple group members, we hope our WebApp allows for a wide array of users with diverse backgrounds, experience levels, geographic locations, and personalities.

CorkBoard can be used for many different kinds of projects and it would have helped us if we had this software at any stage of our team effort, from inception to actually creating the final program. We believe this program will be very useful to future group projects as being able to communicate, plan, and design before and after coding begins is central to good software engineering groups.

We are currently making the final changes to the software which should be fully functional before this paper comes to publication.

References

1. Georgia M. Kapitsaki, Dimitrios A. Kateros, Christos A. Pappas, Nikolaos D. Tselikas, and Iakovos S. Venieris. 2008. Model-driven development of composite web applications. In *Proceedings of the 10th International Conference on Information Integration and Web-based Applications \& Services* (iiWAS '08), Gabriele Kotsis, David Taniar, Eric Pardede, and Ismail Khalil (Eds.). ACM, New York, NY, USA, 399-402. DOI=10.1145/1497308.1497380 http://0-doi.acm.org.uncclc.coast.uncwil.edu/10.1145/1497308.1497380

2. Ryoko Yamaguchi, Nathan Bos, and Judy Olson. 2002. Emergent leadership in small groups using computer-mediated communication. In *Proceedings of the Conference on Computer Support for Collaborative Learning: Foundations for a CSCL Community* (CSCL '02), Gerry Stahl (Ed.). International Society of the Learning Sciences 138-143.

3. Sonal Panse, "Small Group Communication: Effective Team Communication," Buzzle.com, http://www.buzzle.com/articles/small-group-communication-effective-team-communication.html, Accessed 11/2/12

4. Roger Pressman, "Software Engineering A Practitioner's Approach Seventh Edition," 2010, McGraw-Hill, pp. 732

5. Ed Perkins, "Risk Based Decision Making," 2011, IEEE-USA Today's Engineer Online, URL: http://www.todaysengineer.org/2011/Aug/risk-management.asp, Accessed 3/7/13.

6. "The work breakdown structure in software project management," **Robert C. Tauseworthe**, Journal of Systems and Software, Volume 1, September, 1984 Pages 181-186, http://dl.acm.org/citation.cfm?id=2305981

7. Neil Maiden and Suzanne Robertson. 2005. Developing use cases and scenarios in the requirements process. In *Proceedings of the 27th international conference on Software engineering* (ICSE '05). ACM, New York, NY, USA, 561-570. DOI=10.1145/1062455.1062555

8. Ian Sommerville, "Software Engineering, 6th Edition," 2001, Pearson Education Limited, pp. 151-155

9. "Software Engineering Standards," James W. Moore, 1998, IEEE Computer Society Press Order Number BP08008, pp. 128-130

10. "Integration-Ready Architecture and Design, Software Engineering with XML, Java, .NET, Wireles, Speech, and Knowledge Technologies," Jeff Zhukl, The Press Syndicate of the University of Cambridge, 2004, pp. 5

11. R. France and B. Rumpe. Model-driven evelopment of complex software: A research roadmap. In *FOSE '07: 2007 Future of Software Engineering*, pages 37.54,Washington, DC, USA, 2007. IEEE Computer Society.

12. B. Selic. The pragmatics of model-driven development. *IEEE Software*., 20(5):19.25, 2003.

13. Simmonds, D. M., Reddy, Y. R., Song, E. and Grant, E. "A Comparison of Aspect-Oriented Approaches to Model Driven Engineering", in Proceedings of the International Conference on Software Engineering Research and Practice, (SERP), 2009.

14. Fred Brooks, "No silver bullet: Essence and accidents of software engineering," *IEEE Computer*, 20(4):10-19, April 1987.

15. The Object Management Group (OMG). Unified Modeling Language: Superstructure. Version 2.2, Final Adopted Specification, OMG, http://www.omg.org/uml, February 2010.

16. Brian J. McNely. 2007. Agency, invention, and sympatric design platforms. In *Proceedings of the 25th annual ACM international conference on Design of communication* (SIGDOC '07). ACM, New York, NY, USA, 49-54. DOI=10.1145/1297144.

17. Gabriele D'Angelo, Fabio Vitali, and Stefano Zacchiroli. 2010. Content cloaking: preserving privacy with Google Docs and other web applications. In *Proceedings of the 2010 ACM Symposium on Applied Computing* (SAC '10). ACM, New York, NY, USA, 826-830. DOI=10.1145/1774088.1774259

18. Anita Z. Schwartz. 2007. UD dropbox 2.0: collaboration magic. In *Proceedings of the 35th annual ACM SIGUCCS fall conference* (SIGUCCS '07). ACM, New York, NY, USA, 305-309. DOI=10.1145/1294046.1294118

19. Tao Yue, Lionel C. Briand, and Yvan Labiche. 2013. Facilitating the transition from use case models to analysis models: Approach and experiments. *ACM Trans. Softw. Eng. Methodol.* 22, 1, Article 5 (March 2013), 38 pages. DOI=10.1145/2430536.2430539

20. Suman Jana and Vitaly Shmatikov. 2011. EVE: verifying correct execution of cloud-hostedweb applications. In *Proceedings of the 3rd USENIX conference on Hot topics in cloud computing* (HotCloud'11). USENIX Association, Berkeley, CA, USA, 11-11.

21. "Project-Based Software Engineering, An Object-Oriented Approach," Evelyn Stiller, Cathie LeBlanc, 2002, Addison-Wesley, pp. 217-219

An Object Oriented Runtime Complexity Metric based on Iterative Decision Points

Amr F. Desouky[1], **Letha H. Etzkorn**[2]
[1] Computer Science Department, University of Alabama in Huntsville, Huntsville, AL, USA
[2] Computer Science Department, University of Alabama in Huntsville, Huntsville, AL, USA
SERP'13

Abstract - *Software metrics are used to measure the quality of a software system. Such metrics indicate the level of desired quality present in a system. However software metrics have traditionally been captured at compile time, rendering useful results, but often times inexact, as the complete source code differs from the executing subset. For this reason, static metrics can fall short of measuring the true operational behavior of object oriented programs. In this paper, we present an investigation into the runtime boundary behavior of Rhino 1.7R4 – an open source implementation of JavaScript, in which we introduce a new runtime metric that measures the quality of complexity based on iterative decision points. We call this the "runtime boundary" as we are instead measuring object oriented quality at runtime; normal performance metrics collected at runtime are typically neither object oriented nor focused on quality. Finally, we validate the metric by comparing it to bug data.*

Keywords: Object Oriented Runtime Metrics, Complexity Measurement, Object Behavior, and Software Engineering.

1 Introduction

Object oriented software metrics have traditionally analyzed the quality of software systems at compile time [5]. Static, compile time measurements must consider the entire source code, since it's not known at compile time which sections of code will actually execute. Therefore, static metrics have some degree of inaccuracy. However, some previous work [1, 2, 3, 4] has proposed a shift from the compile time boundary to runtime, allowing software complexity to be measured solely on a program's runtime behavior. This approach of measurement yields improved accuracy as non-executed code is ignored during metric computation. For instance, consider a metric which determines the quality of complexity based on the number of method invocations achieved per object. To compute such a metric outside the runtime boundary (that is, at compile time) will prove inadequate as the exact number of calls made to a given method cannot be fully determined at compile time, primarily since program execution typically relies on external arguments such as user input, which is often irregular. These Runtime boundary metrics are object oriented, which differentiates them from typical performance metrics which are largely not focused on objects. Also, they examine quality factors such as complexity (or cohesion) at runtime, whereas typical performance metrics clearly focus on performance.

In this paper, we propose a new object oriented runtime complexity metric based on *iterative decision points*. A decision point is a conditional expression which can alter the control flow of the program resulting in the execution of a particular branch – sequence of code, over another [1]. Iterative decision points on the other hand are control structures which execute a code fragment repeatedly based on a single decision point. Common examples of iterative decision points are for loops, do-while, and while loops. To the best of our knowledge, object oriented runtime complexity metrics based on iterative decision points have never been examined before.

The remainder of this paper is organized as follows: Section 2 describes background information and related work. Section 3 defines our runtime complexity metric. Section 4 outlines the experimental design and analyzes results compared to bug data. And finally, section 5 concludes the paper and outlines future work.

2 RELATED WORK

While a large contribution has been made to static metrics, a limited body of work has been conducted in the field of Object Oriented Runtime Metrics. Mitchell et. al. [3] investigate whether objects of a class exhibit different behavior at runtime from a coupling perspective. They introduce a runtime object-level coupling metric based on Chidamber and Kemerer's widely accepted CBO metric [5]. The authors conclude objects of the same class at the runtime boundary do exhibit different behavior than static metrics.

Mitchell et. al. [4] measure the quality of a software design using runtime object oriented metrics. The authors show that although some degree of correlation exists between runtime metrics and static metrics, runtime metrics capture properties not found in static metrics.

Mathur et. al. [1, 2, 6] present runtime metrics based on (1) decision points and (2) memory occupied by an object at runtime; both provide quality measurements of complexity. The former of the two counts the number of decision points executed per object for all selection structures: if, if-else, if-else-if, and switch – as well as repetition structures: for, while, and do-while. However, each decision point is only counted once, irrespective of the number of iterations. Our proposed metric is different because we are considering the number of iterations per decision point as a complexity metric itself.

3 RESEARCH APPROACH

Chidamber and Kemerer [5] have defined complexity: "The complexity of the class relates to simplicity, in that the more complex the class, the less simple the class". For instance, a class comprised of inheritance, control structures, boolean logic, and methods, is more complex than a simple hello world class with a single method. To expand on this, a class with *1+n* looping iterations is intuitively more complex than a class with only *1* looping iteration. The extra cycles require CPU overhead to fetch, decode, and execute all instructions inside the loop, as well as memory, cache and register resources. Moreover, each additional cycle carries the risk of impeding performance in the event of a branch misprediction, ultimately resulting in penalties i.e., lost execution time. We use this intuitive understanding in defining our runtime complexity metrics.

Metric Name	Definition
RuNFA	Runtime Number of Functions Accesses for all instances of a class. Object Instances that do not access a function are not considered.
RuNOI	Runtime Number of Object Instances per class
RuNLI	Runtime Number of Looping Iterations for all instances of a class
RuCIDp-A	Runtime Complexity based on Iterative Decision Points $RuCIDp-A=\frac{RuNLI}{RuNFA}$
RuCIDp-B	Runtime Complexity based on Iterative Decision Points $RuCIDp-B=\frac{RuNLI}{RuNOI}$
RuCIDp-C	Runtime Complexity based on Iterative Decision Points $RuCIDp-C=\frac{ln(RuNLI)}{RuNFA}$

Table 1. Runtime Metric Definitions

Consider the following example:

```
class Example
{
    void funct_1(int n) {
        while (n < 10) {
            n++;
        }
    }

    void funct_2(int n) {
        for (int i = 0; i < n; n++) {
            continue;
        }
    }

    void funct_3(int n)
    {
        do
        {
            n++;
        }
        while (n < 10);
    }

    void funct_4(int n) {
        for (int i = 10; i > n; n--) {
            continue;
        }
    }
}
```

Figure 1. Program Example

Table 2 shows the runtime behavior of Figure 1 by assuming the number of looping iterations for a particular function of an object instance.

Class Example				
Object Instances	funct_1	funct_2	funct_3	funct_4
1	10	20	0	0
2	0	0	0	0
3	2000	40	0	80
4	10	0	0	100
5	0	0	0	30

Table 2. Runtime Results from Figure 1

In reference to Table 2, we compute our metrics as follows:

RuNFA	$_{Count}\,\boldsymbol{Object\ Instances}\,(1,3,4,5) = 4$
RuNOI	$_{Count}\,\boldsymbol{Object\ Instances}\,(1,2,3,4,5) = 5$
RuNLI	$\sum_{iterations}(funct\_1, funct\_2, funct\_3, funct\_4)$ $= 10 + 20 + 2000 + 40 + 80 + 10 + 100 + 30$ $= \mathbf{2290}$

Table 3. Metric Computation Example

$$RuCIDp - A = \frac{RuNLI}{RuNFA} = \frac{2290}{4} = 572.5$$

$$RuCIDp - B = \frac{RuNLI}{RuNOI} = \frac{2290}{5} = 458$$

$$RuCIDp - C = \frac{\ln(RuNLI)}{RuNFA} = \frac{\ln(2290)}{4} = 0.83$$

4 Experimental Study

In this section, we perform four case studies as a validation benchmark for our suggested metrics. For our case study, we used Rhino 1.7R4. The purpose of our validation is to determine whether *RuCIDp-A, RuCIDp-B,* and *RuCIDp-C* are good quality measures for object oriented complexity at runtime. We employ Pearson Product-Moment Correlation Coefficients to determine a correlation between the presence of bugs per class and our complexity metrics *RuCIDp*-A, *RuCIDp*-B, and *RuCIDp*-C. Our hypotheses for all three metrics are:

H0: *RuCIDp* has measurable impact in predicting the presence of bugs per class

H1: *RuCIDp* has no measurable impact in predicting the presence of bugs per class

4.1 Rhino

Rhino is an open source software package which serves as a JavaScript implementation written in Java. We selected a subset of 10 Rhino classes and modified them to compute our metrics. We chose these classes because they were the classes that mapped to bugs. Tags were applied to each repetition structure to track the Runtime Number of Iterations (*RuNLI*). In addition, each constructor was marked to track the Runtime Number of Object Instances (*RuNOI*) for a particular class. However, any object instance that did not access a loop was not counted. Finally, we tagged each function containing a loop to measure the Runtime Number of Functions Accessed (*RuNFA*). We used Rhino's comprehensive Test Suite comprised of over 180 test cases to fully exercise all components of Rhino [10].

4.2 Case Study 1

In our first case study, we analyze the presence of bugs and *RuNLI*. A normality test indicated the data was normal, so we employed Pearson's correlation. The results of the Pearson's correlation were not significant. However, an observation of the data set does show a number of bugs increasing with the number of loop iterations.

4.3 Case Study 2

In our second case study, we consider the correlation between the presence of bugs and *RuCIDp-A*. A test for normality shows *RuCIDp-A* data as not normal. The results of the Pearson's correlation were not significant. See Table 4.

Pearson's Correlation	
Pearson	-0.004
p-value	0.99

Table 4. Case 2 Pearson's Correlation

4.4 Case Study 3

Our third study considered the correlation between the presence of bugs and $RuCIDp - B$. A test for normality shows data as not normal. The results of Pearson's correlation were not significant. See Table 5.

Pearson's Correlation	
Pearson	-0.463
p-value	0.178

Table 5. Case 3 Pearson's Correlation

4.5 Case Study 4

Our final case study considered the correlation between the presence of bugs and $RuCIDp$-C. We compute the numerator using a natural logarithm function in order to stabilize the variance sample of $RuNLI$ because of the high iteration count. Log transformation is an accepted data transformation technique convenient for transforming extreme ranges into a normal distribution [9]. A test for normality shows $RuCIDp$-C data as normal. Thus, we employ Pearson Product Correlation. The results show a fairly large (according to the Hopkins scale) correlation [8] of $RuCIDp$-C with bugs, while a measure of p-value also indicates a statistical significant correlation at the 90% confidence level.

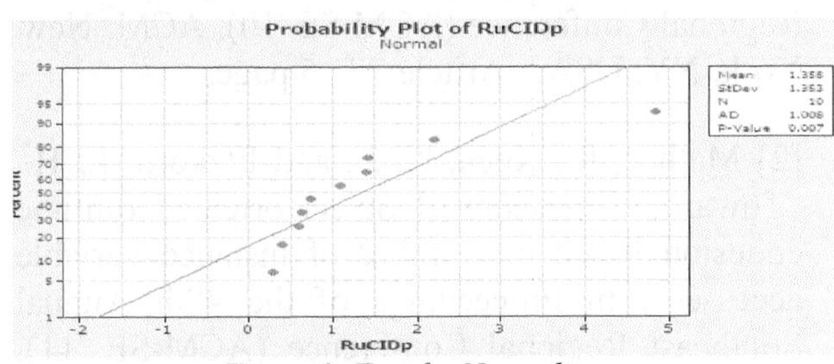

Figure 2. Test for Normality

Pearson's Correlation	
Pearson	-0.606
p-value	0.064

Table 6. Case 4 Pearson's Correlation

5 Conclusions & Future Work

In this paper, we presented an experimental study into the runtime boundary behavior of Rhino 1.7R4 for computing our runtime metric. We observed a fairly large negative correlation and statistical significance at the 90% confidence level. The negative characteristic of the correlation was unexpected. However, we note that the correlation was relatively strong. We conjecture that perhaps software with a large number of loops receives extra attention from the programmer earlier on, and perhaps in some cases this could overcome problems related to any additional complexity through loop execution. Further study on different software packages is required.

This kind of situation would not have been seen in a static, compile-time examination of the program, because all loops would have been considered equal. Since our approach works dynamically, the execution of different loops could in fact be different.

Future work includes examining the runtime complexity behavior of self-iterative functions (i.e. recursion) and bugs using *RuCIDp-C*.

6 References

[1] Mathur, R., Keen, K. J., and Etzkorn, L. H., Towards an object-oriented complexity metric at the runtime boundary based on decision points in code. In Proceedings of the 48th Annual Southeast Regional Conference (ACM SE '10). ACM, New York, NY, USA, , Article 77 , 5 pages.

[2] Mathur, R., Keen, K. J., and Etzkorn, L. H., “Towards a measure of object oriented runtime cohesion based on number of instance variable accesses”. In Proceedings of the 49th Annual Southeast Regional Conference (ACM-SE '11). ACM, New York, NY, USA, 255-257.

[3] Mitchell, A., Power, J. F., “Using Object-Level Run-time metrics to Study Coupling Between Objects”, 2004 International Conference on Software Engineering Research and Practice (SERP’04), Las Vegas, NV, June 21-24, 2004, 532-537.

[4] Mitchell, A., Power, J. F., “An empirical investigation into the dimensions of run-time coupling in java programs”. In 3rd Conference on the Principles and Practice of Programming in Java, Las Vegas, Nevada, June 16-18 2004.

[5] Chidamber, S. R., and Kemerer, C. F., “A metrics suite for object-oriented design”. IEEE Transactions on Software Engineering, 20(6):467{493, June 1994.

[6] Keen, K. J., Mathur, R., Etzkorn, L. H., “Towards a Measure of Software Intelligence Employing a Runtime Complexity Metric”, Software Engineering and Applications, SEA 2009, November 2009.

[7] Etzkorn, L. H., “A Metrics-based Approach to the Automated Identification of Object-Oriented Reusable Software Components,” PhD Dissertation, University of Alabama in Huntsville, 1997.

[8] Stein, C., Etzkorn, L., Gholston, S., Farrington, P., Utley, D., Cox, G. and Fortune, J., (2009) “Semantic Metrics: Metrics Based On Semantic Aspects Of Software”, Applied Artificial Intelligence,23:1,44 — 77

[9] Osborne, J., (2002). Notes on the use of data transformations. Practical Assessment, Research & Evaluation, 8(6). Retrieved February 13, 2013 from http://PAREonline.net/getvn.asp?v=8&n=6

[10] www.mozilla.org

The Influence of Human Aspects in Software Process Improvement: a Brazilian Public Company Study

Regina Albuquerque [1], **André Bibiano** [1], **Rosilene Fernandes** [1], **Daniel Araújo** [1], **Andreia Malucelli** [1], **and Sheila Reinehr** [1]

[1] Post-graduate Program in Informatics, Pontifícia Universidade Católica do Paraná – PUCPR, Curitiba, Paraná, Brasil

Abstract - *This study discusses issues related to factors that can influence the success of Software Process Improvement (SPI) initiatives and seeks to contribute to the understanding of these factors, focusing especially on human aspects in the adoption of these initiatives. The study is quantitative, based on a survey approach, and was conducted at a public information technology (IT) company that aims at reaching Maturity Level G of the MR-MPS-SW Model (Reference Model for Brazilian Software Process Improvement). The results are analyzed taking into account four basic hypotheses, organized based on four human factor categories: inertia and resistance to negative experiences; lack of evidence of benefits; imposition; and, restricted resources.*

Keywords: Human Aspects, Software Process Improvement, MPS.BR. MR-MPS-SW.

1 Introduction

Software development companies have focused their attention on SPI (Software Process Improvement). According to Vavpotic and Bajec [1], this interest is due to the fact that SPI includes a wide variety of approaches and practices that seek to improve the quality and reliability of software products, customer satisfaction and a return on investment in software development.

A number of standards and models with the best software development practices, such as the CMMI [2] and the reference models of the MPS.BR program [3] have been developed for these purposes. The CMMI family, composed of models that scale process improvements into maturity levels, is widely known and used worldwide. The MPS.BR (Brazilian Program for Software Process Improvement) was created in Brazil in 2003 and is widely used to improve software processes all over the country, with over 400 companies evaluated at different maturity levels. Its improvement principles are also based on maturity levels.

There are several studies that discuss the aspects involved in successfully adopting this kind of improvement program, including motivation, resources and professional training [4]. According to [5], observing previous experiences, identifying what went right and wrong, can be very useful for understanding which motives led to success and which led to the failure of a given approach. This information is important to managers of SPI programs in order to prevent possible problems and make adequate planning for a successful implementation.

In this context, it is important to understand the factors that can influence the success of improvement initiatives, especially human factors. The present study was conducted at a Brazilian public information technology company, analyzing human aspects in the implementation of the improvement program based on the MR-MPS-SW reference model [3]. The study is quantitative and the survey method was used to gauge the perceptions of the workers during the implementation of this program.

The article is organized as follows: Section 2 presents the theoretical framework of critical factors in the success of SPI; Section 3 presents the research method and structure; Section 4 shows the main results and also includes a discussion; and Section 5 contains the conclusions of this study.

2 Theoretical Framework

2.1 Main factors of the success of SPI program

Despite the development and availability of a series of standards and improvement models for over two decades, there are still problems and they remain difficult to adopt. For this reason, studies have been conducted in an attempt to identify and analyze factors that influence the implementation of SPI programs [6].

In [7], the authors conducted a study to investigate the factors and their impact on SPI programs in order to offer recommendations to professionals and researchers in this field. They analyzed the perception of SPI managers in companies with different maturity levels (evaluated maturity, evaluation of maturity and no evaluation) located in the United Kingdom and in multinational companies. The factors with the greatest impact, in the opinion of the managers, were: i) reviews; ii) standards and procedures; iii) training and mentoring; and iv) an experienced team. In more mature companies they found internal leadership, inspections, executive support and the quality of internal processes.

In [8], the authors presented the results of an empirical study on what demotivates software professionals from lending their support to SPI programs. The study used data derived from focus group discussions at 13 companies in the

United Kingdom involving 200 software professionals, providing the views of managers of this type of program and identifying problems that these professionals face when there is no motivation for SPI. These issues include some human factors such as: i) resistance to change; ii) lack of evidence of process improvement; iii) imposition; iv) restricted resources; and, v) commercial pressures.

In [9], the authors reported the results of a qualitative study using the procedures of Grounded Theory. The data were collected during open interviews with 21 participants from 11 different companies in Pakistan. The aim of the study was to identify the factors that were successful in software improvement in small and large companies with a web domain. The result was a set of success factors of SPI initiatives. In the view of the participants, these factors were: automated tools, client support, communication, company vision, cost benefit analysis, support from the staff, gradual approach, support from the senior administration, consultancy in SPI, function of the implementer, SPI measures, supportive policies, adaptation of processes, application of existing knowledge regarding SPI, SPI awareness programs, targets and benefits of SPI, success of the company, the most mentioned by the participants being the support of the senior administration, benefits and targets of SPI and the success of the company.

In [10], the authors reported the results of a study of 81 software development companies in Santa Catarina State, Brazil, comparing micro and medium size businesses to medium and large size companies, taking into account factors that might influence the adoption of SPI programs. The study showed that the group of medium and large size companies found the model bureaucratic, while half of the smaller companies cited a lack of financial resources as a reason for not adopting SPI programs. The study also found that each group had different interests in adopting SPI. While the smaller companies had less knowledge of the existing models, made less use of them and were more concerned with expanding their market, the larger companies were concerned with customer satisfaction.

2.2 The Importance of the Human Factor in the Activities of Organizations

Considering human aspects and seeking to understand and manage them can be a differential for the success of the activities developed by organizations. For this reason, they have become the object of study in recent years [11]. When analyzing SPI, one of the main characteristics is to understand and evaluate the needs and expectations of each user to organize them following a technical formality [12].

Software Engineering, according to [13], "is a domain that is highly driven and guided by knowledge, in which the factors of success are related to experience in accordance with the data collected from people involved in the following phases: project, construction, testing and implementation". It is necessary to harness the knowledge of each collaborator and convert it into something that the organization can use, which according to [14] is knowledge management.

In this view of knowledge, according to [15] and [16], tacit knowledge is highly personal and depends on the action and commitment of each individual within a given context, including cognitive elements, where human beings create models and establish analogies. It is important to verify that in accordance with the authors in [14], it is necessary to understand how the creation of knowledge takes place within a work environment and also that "the creation of organizational knowledge is a spiraling process that begins at the individual level and keeps moving up, extending the communities of interaction that cross frontiers between sections, departments, divisions and organizations".

In [8], the authors stated that many collaborators end up not accepting practices that even logic, evidence or experience suggest that they should. This can happen for a number of reasons, such as established personal practices (since people learn to develop programs that work and establish some personal practices) and previous bad experiences with new techniques or tools. Consequently, the workers end up thinking that new practices do not bring them any benefits.

According to some studies, software developers are resistant to initiatives when they feel they are being imposed. According to [8], improvement programs initiated at the corporate level are not conducted consultatively and do not involve the developers in decision making.

Furthermore, in the studies reported in [17] and in accordance with Rainer et al. [7], the developers wanted some evidence of the direct benefits of implementing the improvement processes before they would agree to take them on. Most of the studies showed that resources dedicated to implementing SPI were a critical factor to their success [18]. Moreover, according to [17], software developers of all the participating groups of the software development company are highly motivated by people, experience and the tools dedicated to the software improvement program.

Kitson and Masters [19] conducted a study in which they separated the practitioners of improvement processes into three hierarchical groups and saw that, due to having collected data from managers and developers, who had questions that were faced in a daily analysis, there was a high level of reliability in the range of accuracy and validity of data. This separation is important because, according to [13], this perspective enables differences to be detected in the perception of the participants from the companies in question.

3 Research Method

This is a quantitative study using the survey method. Forza [20] describes three types of survey-based research: exploratory, descriptive and confirmatory or theory testing. Using these definitions, this study could be classified as confirmatory because it has an understanding of the research theme and aims to confirm hypotheses concerning the influence of the human factors listed in the previous section.

The study followed the script proposed by [20]: (i) related to a theoretical level; (ii) project the survey; (iii) conduct a pilot test; (iv) collect the data; (v) prepare data analysis; (vi) produce a report. The procedures for each state will be described in the following topics.

3.1 The Importance of the Human Factors in the Activities of Organizations

3.1.1 Phase I: Relate to a theoretical level

The aim of this study is to understand the different perceptions of workers at a public company during the implementation of Level G of the MR-MPS-SW. The MRMPS-SW model is divided into 7 maturity levels, ranging from A to G; with A being the highest level of maturity. At each level, there are associated processes and expected results. Level G, the first level of the model, is composed of Project Management (PM) and Requirements Management (RM) processes.

The objective of the study was delineated in accordance with the Goal-Question-Metric paradigm and stated as: Analyze the implementations of an improvement program based on the MR-MPS-SW reference model for the purpose of investigating and understanding the factors involved in relation to human aspects from the viewpoint of the information technology manager, analysts and programmers in the context of a public software development company. From the theoretical context presented in Section 2 of this study, the human factors that served as a basis for the definition of four hypotheses were identified, for the purposes of achieving the goals of this study, as shown in Table 01.

TABLE 01: HYPOTHESES

Human Factors	Hypotheses
Inertia and resistance to negative experiences.	H1: It is harder for workers who have been at the company for longer to accept the activities involved in the process.
Lack of evidence of benefits	H2: The workers can see no benefits from adopting the SPI.
Imposition	H3: The more technical workers in the organization believe that they are less involved in the software process improvement.
Restricted resources	H4: The workers believe that the resources allocated to SPI programs (training, staff and equipment) are insufficient.

3.1.2 Phase II – Designing the Survey

In this stage, the target public was defined, along with the sample and data collection method. The target public of the study was professionals in the field of software development who are involved in SPI. The size of the sample was approximately 300 people. The data collection method that was chosen was a questionnaire to be distributed locally.

3.1.3 Phase III – Conducting the pilot test

To validate the questionnaire, 14 questionnaires with 12 closed questions were distributed in the company's development sector. All of these questionnaires were returned, with contributions from the management of the development sector and the management responsible for the implementation of the MPS.BR program. Following an analysis of the results of the pilot test, some questions suggested by the managers were added and two questions were altered because the respondents had difficulty in understanding them, which could compromise the results.

3.1.4 Phase IV – Collecting the data to test the theory

After the adjustments to the questionnaire, 90 of them were distributed during two workshops promoted by the managers in charge of implementing the MPS.BR program, of which 63 were returned completed

3.1.5 Phase V – Analyzing the data

The first step of the data analysis was to verify whether all 63 questionnaires could be considered valid, i.e., with all the questions answered. All the questionnaires proved to be valid for the study and the responses were tabulated. A detailed analysis will be given in the following section.

3.1.6 Phase VI – Producing the report

Following the tabulation of the data, a report was produced with the perceptions gauged through data analysis, highlighting whether or not the hypotheses of the study were validated. The resulting graphs are included in this study.

4 Results and Discussion

In this section, the results are presented and discussed. They are organized into 4 factors: i) inertia and resistance to negative experiences; ii) lack of evidence of benefits; iii) imposition; and iv) restricted resources.

4.1 Inertia and resistance to negative experiences

To analyze the first hypothesis, H1, the respondents were asked to characterize their profiles according to how long they had been working at the company: the newer workers, who had been at the company for less than ten years, and the older workers, who had been there for over ten years. They were then asked about their experience in other SPI programs and what they thought of this experience.

The results showed that 59% of the workers had been at the company for less than ten years and 41% are more experienced. Regarding experience in SPI, 30% of the newer workers had already been involved in such a program and 42% of the older workers. In both categories, the workers considered their experience in SPI as positive.

From these results, the conclusion is that hypothesis H1, in which the older workers of an organization find it more difficult to adapt to SPI programs is confirmed. Another finding is that resistance was not detected among the less experienced workers.

4.2 Lack of evidence of benefits

To analyze the second hypothesis H2, questions were asked about the direct and indirect benefits, motivation and the continuity perspective in the eyes of the workers in order to gauge whether they saw any benefits to be gained by adopting this type of program. It should be mentioned that this question generated many responses since the workers could see more than one benefit or motivation.

The results showed that only 2% of the respondents thought that the program would bring no improvements, while the others found some type of improvement, with the most outstanding benefits being: increased quality (79%) and the accuracy of estimates (68%). Regarding to the motivation perceived by the respondents for the organization adopting the MPS.BR program, the most expressive motivations were improved products/company projects (78%) and improved company management (57%). The continuity perspective of the improvement program has an expressive percentage of respondents who believe that the program will continue, as a result of its proven benefits (71%).

These results show that the influence of this factor does not apply to the implementation of the organization under study, as its workers see benefits, motivations and continuity perspectives because the benefits of this type of program have been proven to them. This becomes more evident in terms of the quality of products and project management. Therefore, hypothesis H2 was not confirmed.

Other factors that were highlighted by the respondents in their answers to this open question concerning the continuity of the program were: political issues, understanding of benefits, results obtain and the commitment of those involved.

4.3 Imposition

To analyze the third hypothesis, a question was asked that characterized the role of the respondent in the software development process of the organization in order to obtain the point of view of the more technical workers.

The workers were characterized as technical and managerial. The technical workers were those who worked as analysts, designers, developers and/or software development supporting staff. The managerial roles were business analysts, project managers and project leaders. The sample included 23 technical respondents, accounting for 37% of the total number of interviewees. There were 40 respondents employed in operational or managerial positions, representing 63% of the total number of interviewees.

It was observed that 52% occupy a technical position and had no opportunity to participate in the improvement program. This can be partially related to the fact that at G Level, the focus is on management practices.

Concerning the degree of knowledge of the MR-MPS-SW model, there is a low level of knowledge of the model in both groups. Among the technical staff, nobody had a high degree of knowledge of the model, a considerable number (78%) have low knowledge and 4% of these workers have no knowledge of the model. As for the managerial positions, 3% have in-depth knowledge of the model and 73% have a low level of knowledge.

These results led to the conclusion that hypothesis H3 that workers with a more technical role in the organization believe that they are less involved in software process improvement is confirmed. However, it is important to point out that this is a result that is coherent with the level of the model that is being implemented. As mentioned above, Level G focuses more intensely on managerial practices. This is inevitable because it has a more direct effect on managerial rather than technical activities.

4.4 Restricted resources

For the fourth hypothesis H4, the respondents were asked two questions. The first dealt with whether the human resources made available were sufficient. The second had to do with possible obstacles that would be faced in this type of program. Multiple choices were permitted and an open field was provided for the respondents to include other obstacles that they felt deserved to be mentioned.

The results showed that 54% of the respondents claimed that the amount of resources allocated to the process was less than required and that the workers viewed this lack of resources as an obstacle to the implementation of the program. There were some factors that stood out: lack of tools (52%) and lack of training (44%).

The results showed that, in the opinion of the respondents, there were insufficient resources for the successful implementation of the SPI program. Therefore, the conclusion is that hypothesis H4 that workers believe that the resources allocated to the SPI program (training, staff and equipment), was confirmed.

Other obstacles to the MPS.BR at the company were identified by the respondents, such as organizational culture (6%) and resistance to change (5%).

5 Final Considerations

This article presented the results of a quantitative study concerning human factors that can influence the success of a software process improvement process in the environment of a Brazilian public information technology company, where the implementation process is progress, i.e., there is yet to be an official evaluation.

The factors that the study sought to explore were resistance, lack of benefits, imposition and restricted resources. These factors gave rise to four research hypotheses. An analysis of the collected data showed that the hypotheses related to resistance and evidence of benefits were not confirmed, while the hypotheses regarding imposition and restricted resources were confirmed.

The adoption of the MPS.BR by the organization in question is well regarded and eagerly awaited by the workers no matter how long they have been working at the organization or what position they hold. The study showed that a very important factor to the success of the adoption of this type of program, although it is often not given the priority it deserves, is the allocation and availability of resources such as training, number of staff involved, availability of adequate equipment and communication to all the participants throughout the implementation process.

Some other factors that could influence process improvement programs were obtained through responses to the open questions asked in this survey. These factors included political issues, understanding of benefits and results obtained/commitment of those involved regarding the continuation of the program and factors of organizational culture, in addition to resistance to change, which were identified as obstacles to successfully implementing the MPS.BR.

For future studies, this study could be expanded in the same organization, involving new variables identified during the course of this study in response to the open questions. This further study could examine whether this behavior applies after the official evaluation of the MPS.BR.

6 References

[1] Vavpotic, D.; Bajec, M. "An approach for concurrent evaluation of technical and social aspects of software development methodologies" in Information and Software Technology, July 2008.

[2] SEI – Software Engineering Institute. "Standard CMMI® Appraisal Method for Process Improvement (SCAMPISM) A", Version 1.2: Method Definition Document. 2006.

[3] SOFTEX – Associação para Promoção da Excelência da Excelência do Software Brasileiro –. "MPS.BR – Melhoria de Processo do Software Brasileiro: guia geral", Agosto 2012.

[4] Viana, Davi., Conte, T., Vilela, D., Santos, G., Prikladnicki, R., "The Influence of Human Aspects on Software Process Improvement: Qualitative Research Findings and Comparison to Previous Studies" in 16th International Conference of Evaluation & Assessment in Software Engineering (EASE 2012), in Universidad de Castilla-La Mancha - Ciudad Real - Spain , Published by IET Conference Publications pp. 121 - 125.

[5] Kasse, T.; McQuaid, P. A. "Factors Affecting Process Improvement Initiatives" in The Journal of Defense Software Engineering, August 2000.

[6] Nizam, M. H. ; Ahmad, N. R. and Hassan, N. H. "Resistance Factors in the Implementation of Software Process Improvement Project in Malaysia" in Journal of Computer Science 4 (3): 211-219, 2008.

[7] Rainer A.; Hall, T. (2002), "Key success factors for implementing software process improvement: a maturity-based analysis" in The Journal of Systems and Software 62 (2002) 71–84.

[8] Baddoo, N.; Hall, T. (2003), "De-motivators for software process improvement: an analysis of practitioners views" in The Journal of Systems and Software vol.66 pp.23–33.

[9] Sulayman, M.; Urquhart, C.; Mendes, E. and Seidel, S. "Software process improvement success factors for small and medium Web companies: A qualitative study" in Information and Software Technology 54 (2012) 479–500, Contents lists available at SciVerse ScienceDirect, 2012.

[10] Schoeffel, P.; Benitti, F. B. V. "Factors of Influence in Software Process Improvement: a Comparative Survey Between Micro and Small Enterprises (MSE) and Medium and Large Enterprises (MLE)" in IEEE Latin America Transactions, vol. 10, nº. 2, march 2012.

[11] Santos, D.V., Vilela Júnior, D.C., Souza, C., Conte, T., "Aspectos humanos que afetam um programa de melhoria de processo de software - Uma análise qualitativa" in XIV CIBSE (Congresso Ibero-Americano em Engenharia de Software), RJ-Brasil.

[12] Sommerville, Ian. "Engenharia de Software" São Paulo – Pearson Addison Wesley, 2007.

[13] Desouza, K.C. "Barriers to Effective Use of Knowledge Management Systems in Software Engineering" En: Communications of the ACM, vol. 46, n.1, p. 99-101, jan. 2003.

[14] Nonaka, I.; Takeuchi, H. Criação de conhecimento na empresa. 16ª ed. Rio de Janeiro: Campus, 1997,358p.

[15] Coser, M. A., Carvalho, H. G., Kovaleski, J. L. "A gestão do conhecimento no apoio à gestão de requisitos em software". XIII SIMPEP - Bauru, SP, 2006.

[16] Parreiras, F.S.; Bax, M.P. "A gestão de conteúdo no apoio à engenharia de software". In: Anais Congresso Brasileiro de Gestão do Conhecimento, KMBrasil 2003, São Paulo, SP, Brasil, 12 a 14 de Novembro 2003.

[17] Baddoo, N., Hall, T. (2002), Motivators of software process improve-ment: an analysis of practitioners' views. Journal of Systems and Software 62, pp. 85–96.

[18] El Emam, K., Fusaro, P., Smith, B., "Success factors and barriers for software process improvement". In: Messnarz, R., Tully, C. (Eds.), Better Software Practice for Business Benefit: Principles and Experience. IEEE Computer Society, Los Alamitos, CA, pp. 355–371, 1999.

[19] Kitson, D.H., Masters, S.M., "An analysis of SEI software process assessment results: 1987-1991". In: 15th International Conference on Software Engineering, Baltimore, Maryland, May 17–21, 1993.

[20] Forza, C. "Survey research in operations management: a process-based perspective" in International Journal of Operations & Productions Management; 2002;22,2; Academic Research Library pg 152, 2002.

[21] Basili V.R.; Selby R.W "Paradigms for Experimentation and Empirical Studies in Software Engineering" in Reliability Engineering and System Safety vol.32 pp 171- 191, 1991.

Methodology for ontology development in support to the MPS model for software

Alessandro Viola Pizzoleto,
Hilda Carvalho de Oliveira
Statistics, Applied Mathematics and Computer Science
Institute of Geosciences and Exact Sciences
Universidade Estadual Paulista, Unesp
Rio Claro, Brasil
alessandropizzoleto@gmail.com, hildaz@rc.unesp.br

Abstract*— This paper proposes the use of enterprise ontologies as a complementary tool to support the adoption of software process quality models. The model selected for this work was the Reference Model MPS for software development (RM-MPS-SW), which is part of the Brazilian Software Process Improvement Program (MPS.BR). The RM-MPS-SW was developed focusing micro, small and medium-sized enterprises (MSMEs), although it is completely suited to large organizations. In this context, this work presents a methodology for the ontology development on the levels G and F of the RM-MPS-SW. Concepts of the PMBOK (Project Management Body of Knowledge) are included to support adherence to its principle by software companies. The inclusion of BSC (Balanced Scorecard) indicators approximates the model with the strategic planning of the company. The intention is that this methodology can be used as a basis for the representation of the other MPS-SW levels and other software process models.

Keywords*—Software process model, Quality model, Enterprise ontology, MPME, MPS.BR, MPS-SW, PMBOK, BSC

I. INTRODUCTION

Currently, in the software development market there are important and well-known international processes quality models such as CMMI (Capability Maturity Model Integration) and ISO 9000. Some countries adopt their own models, such as Mexico with MoProSoft (Process Model for Developing and Maintaining Software) and Brazil with the RM-MPS-SW (MPS Reference Model for Software). Both of them use as references CMMI model and ISO/IEC standards: 12207 and 15504. Both MoProSoft as the RM-MPS-SW aim national and international recognition as a model applicable to the software industry. For this, a project titled RELAIS (Latin American Software Industry Network) was created focusing on the approximation of these two models [2].

These quality models are usually written in formal language, designed for software development companies regardless of size, features and stakeholders profiles. Typically, the processes models are defined in maturity levels that establish evolutionary stages for process improvement. These levels define where companies should focus their efforts to implement processes improvements.

For the implementation and management of these quality models in enterprises, great efforts are required for the appropriate understanding of its principles, the appropriate strategy definition and dissemination of knowledge in order to obtain the commitment from all those involved. Major organizational restructuration is required, as well as financial investments in professional team training and hiring specialized consultants. Companies should also reserve funds for certification implementation and its maintenance, considering the developments at specific levels of the model.

For micro, small and medium-sized enterprises (MSME) these challenges are bigger due to diverse technical and financial restrictions. These companies often do not have well defined and properly documented processes. There are difficulties in defining dedicated teams to the comprehension and implementation of the process quality model. The level of details to be considered in the real working environment of software companies requires dedicated workers and it directly affects other services and projects. In general, the costs are relatively high for the MSME. However, it is important that MSME be encouraged to use quality models that give them advantages in the competitive market. The vast majority of the software development market is composed of MSME. In Brazil, they constitute 99.1% of the number of companies in the software market [1].

The textual form of these models covers a wide range of information in breadth and depth (processes, attributes, requirements, specific elements, etc.). Usually there is usually a large number of dependencies between the information at the same level and among all levels of maturity. Due to this diversity, and high amount of content and interdependencies, standardizing the understanding of everyone involved in implementation, consulting and certification of these models is very complex.

In this direction, this paper proposes an alternative representation for organizing the content of software process models, with the intention of simplifying and standardizing the comprehension of these models.

The process model considered for this work was the Reference Model MPS-SW (RM-MPS-SW). This model was developed focusing on MSME. However the MPS-SW is completely suitable to large organizations that have sufficient resources to invest in software process improvement. This model is part of the Brazilian Software Process Improvement Program (MPS.BR). The Program provides funds raised by SOFTEX (Brazilian Association for Promoting the Software Export) for MSME groups to implement the MPS-SW model [2]. Section 2 presents detailed information about RM-MPS-SW, including the seven maturity levels, from A to G. This paper considers the two lower levels: G and F.

The alternative considered in this work to represent the contents of the MPS-SW quality model was ontology-based, more specifically enterprise ontology [3]. An enterprise ontology is a formal and explicit specification of a shared concept among the community of people in a company or part of it. According to Dietz [5], this kind of ontology must satisfy the following parameters: coherence, comprehensiveness, consistency, conciseness and essence. Some additional comments are presented in section 3.

The methodology for creating the ontology on levels G and F of the MPS-SW Model is presented in section 4. This methodology is meant to serve as the basis for representation of other MPS-SW levels and other process models. The methodology considers concepts and terminology of the PMBOK (Project Management Body of Knowledge) and they can be inserted in the ontology to support adherence to its principle by software companies. The set of indicators of the MPS-SW model is reinforced by inclusion of indicators of three perspectives of BSC (Balanced Scorecard).The aim is to contribute to the rapprochement with the strategic planning of software development companies, considering the progress of implementation of the MPS-SW model.

II. MPS Reference Model for Software

The MPS.BR program is coordinated for the Association for Promotion of Brazilian Software Excellence (SOFTEX), which has the support of other institutions such as: Ministry of Science, Technology and Innovation (MCTI), Studies and Projects Finance Organization (FINEP), Brazilian Micro and Small Business Support Service (SEBRAE) e Inter-American Development Bank (IDB).

The MPS model is currently made up of four components, as illustrated in Fig. 1: (1) MPS Reference Model for Software (MPS-SW); (2) MPS Reference Model for Services (MPS-SV); (3) Assessment Method (MA-MPS); (4) Business Model (MN-MPS). Each model consists of a set of normative documents (guides) with general and specific descriptions. The guides contemplate the processes involved, processes attributes (AP) and expected outcomes (RAP).

The RM-MPS-SW describes "outcome" as being the transformation on a feedstock in the product during the execution of the process. Already an "expected outcome" (RAD) is the successful execution of the process in reaching its purpose.

The RM-MPS-SW includes internationally recognized practices for implementation and evaluation of processes meeting the business needs of the software industry. Processes are described in terms of its purpose and a set of expected outcomes (RAP), which are used for certification. The execution of the processes is related to the definition of roles, represented by people with the following responsibilities: (1) perform the process, (2) monitor the performing process, (3) audit to certify that the process is performed correctly and the requirements are archived (4) validate that the process complies with the requirements imposed by the enterprise internal policy. The process is made up expected outcomes (RAP), which should be documented. For certification of the company at one specific level of maturity all, the objectives and the expected outcomes defined for that level must be attended.

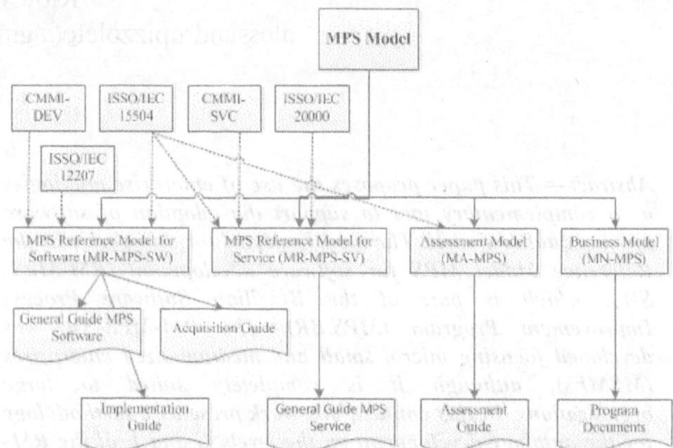

Fig. 1. MPS model components which are part of program MPS.BR [2].

In general, the MPS-SW defines seven levels of maturity: A (Optimization), B (quantitatively Managed), C (Defined), D (Largely Defined), E (Partially Defined), F (Managed), and G (Partially Managed). The level "G" is the first level and "A" the highest level of maturity. This paper aims at the representation ontological of levels G and F.

The processes of level G determine more appropriate mechanisms to be used in critical management processes: Project Management (GPR) and Requirements Management (GRE). On the level F are set out processes in support of the software development that ensure the quality of products and process, as well as manage product configurations. These processes deal with quantitative indicators about the performance of all processes. On the level F the organization is still dependent on the knowledge of a particular professional. At the higher levels, the new processes already incorporate the knowledge.

Each level has a set of cumulative processes and their attributes to achieve the business objectives and model. The entire process is composed by RAP, which should be documented. For the company to obtain certification in a certain level of maturity, all objectives and all are defined in the guides for that level must be attended. The Table I shows the processes and their attributes (AP) that must be attended at each level of maturity. There are nine AP, identified as: - AP 1.1: the process runs; - AP 2.1: the process is managed; - AP 2.2: the work products of the process are managed; - AP 3.1: the process is defined; - AP 3.2 : the process is implemented; - AP 4.1: the process is measured; - AP 4.2: the process is controlled; - AP 5.1: the process is the object of incremental improvements and innovations; - AP 5.2: the process is continuously optimized.

It is important to observe that the MPS-SW model is fully compatible with the CMMI-DEV. There is a correspondence established between the seven levels of the MPS-SW and the five levels of the CMMI-DEV. In addition to the independent certification processes of each model, there is a specific process for evaluations MPS-SW complementary to evaluations CMMI-DEV. Additionally, there is a process of joint evaluation: MPS-CMMI.

TABLE I - Processes and attributes of the RM-MPS-SW levels.

Levels	Processes	Process Attributes
A		AP 1.1, AP 2.1, AP 2.2, AP 3.1, AP 3.2, AP 4.1, AP 4.2, AP 5.1, AP 5.2
B	Project Management - GPR (new outcomes)	AP 1.1, AP 2.1, AP 2.2, AP 3.1, AP 3.2, AP 4.1, AP 4.2
C	Decision Analysis and Resolution - DRU Risk Management - GRI Development for Reuse - GDE	AP 1.1, AP 2.1, AP 2.2, AP 3.1, AP 3.2
D	Requirements Development - DRE Product Design and Construction - PCP Product Integration - ITP Verification - VER Validation - VAR	AP 1.1, AP 2.1, AP 2.2, AP 3.1, AP 3.2
E	Human Resources Management - GRH Process Establishment - AMP Process Assessment and Improvement - DFP Project Management (new outcomes) - GPR Reuse Management - GRU	AP 1.1, AP 2.1, AP 2.2, AP 3.1, AP 3.2
F	Measurement - MED Acquisition - AQU Configuration Management - GCO Quality Assurance - GCA Project Management Portfolios - GPP	AP 1.1, AP 2.1, AP 2.2
G	Project Management - GPR Requirement Management - GRE	AP 1.1, AP 2.1

III. ENTERPRISE ONTOLOGY

Enterprise ontology is a research line that has origins in the Enterprise Project [3], from the inclusion of new concepts of the TOVE project [3]. Enterprise ontologies describe concepts and relationships that exist in an enterprise domain. The objective is to improve and replace the existing modeling methods to a structure of methods and tools that meet the enterprise modeling and change management.

Enterprise ontology is intended to supply a common vocabulary to be used by developers and users. It allows the reuse of knowledge about the organization, the drafting of a first version of the requirements and the identification of those responsible for system information. An enterprise ontology is a guide to acquiring knowledge since from one or more organizations. This kind of ontology supports identifying professionals with the right skills to compose project teams, discussing matters related to the organizational environment and guiding the execution of a task.

Enterprise ontologies make easy the development of systems that manipulate the knowledge of the organization. They provide the development of generic tools, reducing the effort required to build integrated development environments to specific software to different organizations. Moreover, foster the integration between the tools that manipulate knowledge related to ontology, through shared databases created from its ontological structure.

According to Uschold and King [3] the building of an enterprise ontology is based on four stages: (1) identification of proposal of the ontology, in order to determine the level of formality of the ontology description; (2) construction of ontology, capturing, encoding and integrating appropriate knowledge since from existing ontologies (when possible); (3) evaluation of ontology throughout the process; (4) formal documentation (definition of constants, predicates and axioms), reviewing the of scope identifying stages and formalization.

Blomqvist [6] presents a model of build an enterprise ontology that direction, but structuring it more simply. This method consists of five basic stages: (1) requirements analysis, considering the scope and use cases; (2) iterative construction, with middle-out approach, to covet the requirements specifications; (3) implementation, with appropriate tool; (4) assessment of clarity, consistency and usability; (5) maintenance.

According to Blomqvist [6] the development of an enterprise ontology may be manual or automatic. In this first stage of the work, efforts were devoted to the definition of a methodology for the manual construction based on the RM-MPS-SW (levels G and F).

IV. METHODOLOGY FOR THE LEVELS G AND F OF THE RM-MPS-SW

In this section we propose a methodology for the levels G and F of the RM-MPS-SW, with support from the models of enterprise ontology of Uschold and King [3] and Blomqvist [6]. The methodology consists of five primary stages: (1) design of the organizational structure of the model and defining the scope of the ontology; (2) requirements specification, by modeling of the quality model elements using middle-out approach and by supplementing this with the expert knowledge, PMBOK and BSC; (3) implementation of the ontology, with the specification of additional information (alpha release); (4) evaluate the clarity, consistency and usability by business users and experts to generate a beta release; (5) Maintenance, aiming new releases with necessary changes, improvements and knowledge inclusion from experts and companies that use the ontology.

In order to specify the requirements in stage 2 should be used class diagrams using UML (Uniform Modeling Language). Due to the complexity of the correspondence between text structures and the model composed by class diagrams, it is recommended to use Design Patterns for support. The Stage 2 includes three steps: (2.1) supplementation of the requirements specification with elements that represent the experts' knowledge in the model; (2.2) supplementation of the requirements specification with concepts and terminology from PMBOK; (2.3) supplementation of the requirements specification with indicators of the BSC model.

In relation to the step 2.2, it is observed that the generic format of process quality models do not provide information on how to execute and deliver the expected outcomes (RAP) in order to prove their adoption. This can be mitigated by using additional information from the PMBOK. On the other hand, with respect to step 2.3, it is observed that the MPS-SW includes a measurement process that is responsible for managing indicators, from the level F. These indicators are defined and used to support decision making related to projects and processes, besides checking the efficiency of the model in the company. The measurement process does not have concepts that provide the definition of indicators related to knowledge. Thus, it is recommended that the BSC indicators are considered on the following perspectives: customer, internal processes and learning and growth (The financial perspective may not be used).

During all stages checks should be made to assess the coverage of the elements considered, inconsistencies (see partitions and circularities) and semantic errors. In relation to the documentation, all stages generate documents, which must be arranged in order to compose the ontology documentation.

The following subsections show how these stages were implemented for the levels G and F of the RM-MPS-SW.

A. *Stage 1: Organizational Structure of the Model*

In stage 1 the structures of the thirteen guides of the RM-MPS-SW were analyzed and a common structure among them was observed. Fig. 2 shows the structure of these guides, according to the concepts presented in section 2. Each level has several processes and each process has its capacity. Each process can have multiple results. For each level there are capacities that are represented by a set of attributes described in terms of expected outcomes (RAP). Every component provides information related to theoretical basis, purpose and requirements.

Verifications were made on the structure and guides of the levels G and F, which comprise the scope of the ontology.

B. *Stage 2: Requirements Specification of the Model*

In step 2, all the structural features of the G level content were analyzed, so that class diagrams were gradually being built using the middle-out approach (from the principal elements). Similarly, a diagram was constructed for level F, relating it to the level G. Approximately 130 classes were defined for each level. The support of Design Patterns was required to assist in modeling. For example, the Creational Design Patterns following were used: Abstract Factory, Factory Method, and Builder.

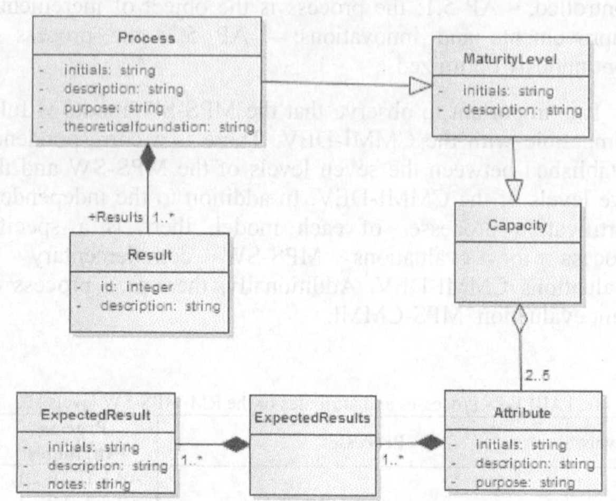

Fig. 2. Organizational structure of the RM-MPS-SW including levels G and F.

Thus, it was possible to classify the processes considered, observing the interdependencies and the information that compose the RAP. Fig. 3 shows a class diagram evidencing some interdependencies between the levels G and F.

For all text from the guides of the levels G and F was checked if there were classes and corresponding relationships.

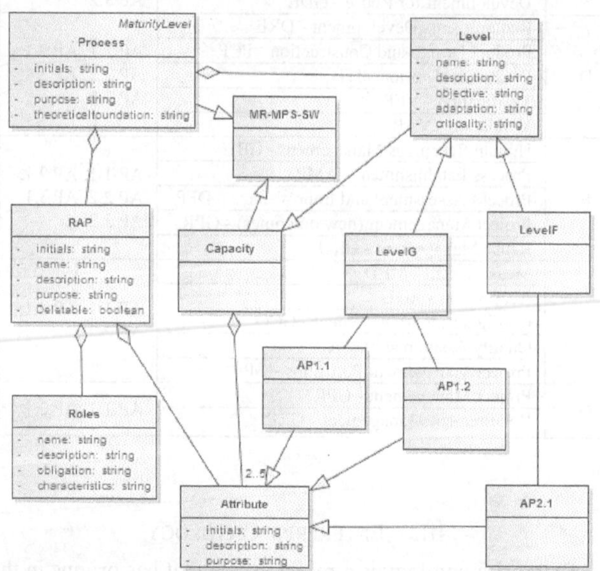

Fig. 3. Class diagram showing interdependences between levels G and F.

In step 2.1 the focus was to identify the parts of the texts where there was identification of documents to be generated, but there was no information about the characteristics of these documents. To facilitate the understanding of the characteristics of such documents, information was collected through personal interviews with experts in the model (implementers and evaluators). Such characteristics have been added to the class diagram and their interdependencies defined. Examples of these documents types: matrix qualification (information on the capacities of employees), matrix of physical resources, etc.

In step 2.2, the focus was to identify the parts of the text where could be added PMBOK concepts. It is emphasized that the PMBOK have 47 PM processes, and these processes are scattered among five process groups and ten knowledge areas, which are found in almost all areas of projects. Then, a strategy was defined for the cross-checking of information between the processes of levels G and F of the MPS-SW Model and processes of the PMBOK. The first action was to analyze the 47 PMBOK processes and determine which of them were directly related to the processes of the level G. The same was done with the processes of the level F. The second action was to define which related processes would be used to complement the RAP of each level. As an example, Table II shows the PMBOK processes consistent with the results of the Project Management (GPR1 and GPR 2), which are part of the levels G and F. The concepts of each of the PMBOK process that was selected were added to the class diagrams.

TABLE II - Results of the Project Management process x PMBOK processes.

Result RM-MPS-SW	PMBOK Process
GPR 1	Develop Project Charter.
	Collect Requirements.
	Define Scope.
	Create WBS.
GPR 2	Create WBS.
	Define Activities.
	Estimate Activity Resources.
	Estimate Activity Durations.
	Estimate Costs.

In step 2.3 the BSC concepts on intangible indicators were considered. It was analyzed how these concepts could complement the measurement process (MED) of the level F. This process is responsible for measuring, so it generates indicators for all other processes. The concepts of the three perspectives recommended in step 2.3 were added to class diagrams to complement the MED process. The example shown in Table III considers the transformation of an intangible asset in a tangible asset to the Requirement Management process (GRE). The column "how to measure" aims to help companies capture a tangible value, which will be used to define weights for decision making. Example of values for the "indicator": 0-2 doubts - no changes; 3-5 doubts - prepare training for the analyst.

TABLE III. Example to turn an intangible indicator into tangible.

Process	Indicator	how to measure
GRE 1 – Project requirements	Assess the quality of the requirements.	Number of questions regarding to the understanding of the requirement.
		Number of rework in code writing.
		Number of generated versions.

After steps 2.2 and 2.3, it was necessary to verify the correspondence among the information in the class diagrams, the PMBOK processes and the BSC indicators. Thus, a cross-reference table was defined using spreadsheet software. In this table were included all classes and relationships of class diagram represented in column form. On the other hand, information from the guides, personal interviews, PMBOK concepts and BSC indicators were represented in line form. All data were compared. Due to the complexity and large volume of data, this correspondence was conducted through a modular strategy The first step was to compare data in diagrams with the texts of the levels G and F, including the processes that evolve from level G to F. Subsequently, comparisons were made with the PMBOK processes and then with the intangible indicators of BSC used for the process MED. Finally, checks were made with the information from the individual interviews.

C. *Stage 3: Implementation of ontology of the Model.*

The ontology development started in Stage 3 from the class diagrams defined in the previous step. The language used was OWL (Web Ontology Language), which includes descriptions of classes with their properties and relationships. According to the World Wide Web Consortium (W3C), this language was designed to be used by applications that require processing of the elements that compose the information. The ontology editor Protégé v4.1 was selected, which is considered to as a knowledge-based framework. The Protégé v4.1 ontology editor was selected, which is considered to as a knowledge-based framework. Protégé is a tool freeware, open source and self-explanatory, without the need to investment in training. Three Protégé plug-ins were used: (1) OWLViz, which visually shows the aggregation of classes; (2) FACT++, which is a classifier of ontology terminologies used to verify the integrity of the components; (3) OWLViz, which allows viewing and comparing the hierarchy of classes, facilitates navigation gradually between the classes and allows the comparison between class hierarchies.

The ontology is basically composed of the following components: superclasses, subclasses and objects properties. The main classes of the diagrams defined in stage 2 corresponded to superclasses and subclasses. The abstract classes and relationships were used as objects properties. The subclasses were related to each other through the objects properties, according to the relationships of the class diagrams. Fig. 4 shows the superclasses of ontology. For example, the subclasses of "adaptation" represent all adaptations that may occur in the company in each of the maturity levels of the model. The superclass "work product" represents all documents which are generated from the execution of processes (results). Information about the hierarchy of the ontology subclasses were derived from the relationships between the subclasses of the diagrams. Some of these relationships were represented by objects properties, as shown in Fig. 5. The names assigned to objects properties are intuitive to users. Each of the objects properties contains a description that shows its association with the subclasses.

The relationships between the subclasses represent the network of interdependencies between the processes of the model. The visualization of the ontology in OWL allows software development company identify where efforts should be concentrated. The company can also identify higher-level processes and how they can be related to each other, expanding the vision of current "window" of the RM-MPS-SW. Optionally, the company may invest efforts in processes of the upper levels, depending on the degree of interdependence and costs. Fig. 6 shows the visualization of the interdependence between the levels G and F of the model MPS-SW. The same systematic way was applied to other processes.

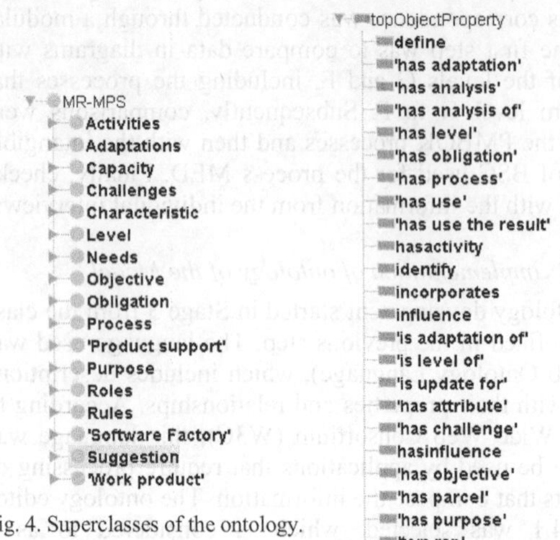

Fig. 4. Superclasses of the ontology.

Fig. 5. Objects properties of the ontology.

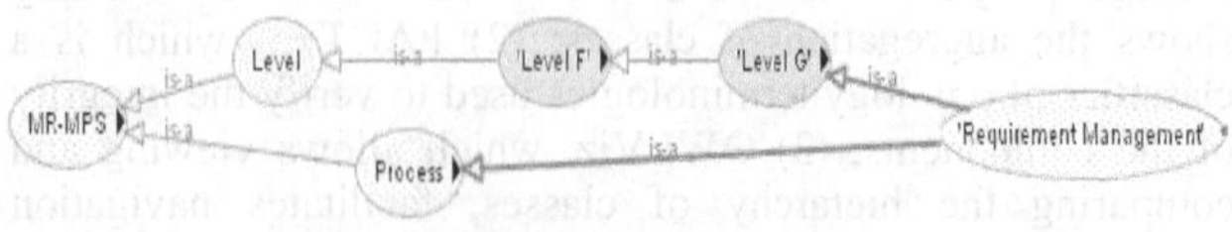

Fig. 6. Interdependence between the levels G and F.

It is important to emphasize that during the process of ontology development, all terms used in the ontology were defined in Portuguese and in English. Moreover, additional information was introduced in the ontology, with explanations of the terms used, as shown in Fig. 7. The goal is to provide a "dictionary" so that the user can get explanations while he navigates through the ontology. It is noteworthy that the information that was collected through personal interviews with experts at the model is also documented.

A strategy using cross-references was conducted to verify coverage of all class diagrams in ontology development.

D. *Stage 4: Evaluation of the Ontology Model*

The previous stage resulted in an alpha version of the ontology, edition 1.1 (v1.1). The stage 4 consisted of the evaluation of this ontology by people involved with the RM-MPS-SW. The purpose of this evaluation was to generate a set of recommendations for the generation of a beta version, which could be available for use. This evaluation was planned and executed as a process of usability testing. The following documents were developed: test plan, evaluator´s guide, participant´s orientation guide, document for notes during testing, questionnaire to collect participants' opinions and consent for use of image.

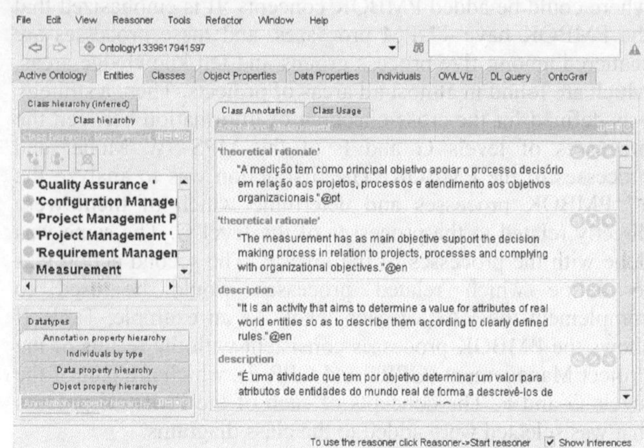

Fig. 7. Example of additional information for level F.

E. *Stage 4: Evaluation of the Ontology Model*

The previous stage resulted in an alpha version of the ontology, edition 1.1 (v1.1). The stage 4 consisted of the evaluation of this ontology by people involved with the RM-MPS-SW. The purpose of this evaluation was to generate a set of recommendations for the generation of a beta version, which could be available for use. This evaluation was planned and executed as a process of usability testing. The following documents were developed: test plan, evaluator´s guide, participant´s orientation guide, document for notes during testing, questionnaire to collect participants' opinions and consent for use of image.

The preparation of the test structure aimed to allow to the user to navigate through the ontology and perform some functionalities on an increasing scale of difficulty. It is noteworthy that despite the ontology be navigable through the Protégé system was not the target of evaluation. This information was clearly conveyed to participants at the beginning of the tests. A brief guidance regarding the use of Protégé was given to participants who did not report use problems.

Three classes of participants were defined: beginners, project managers and/or quality managers, implementers and/or evaluators. Table IV presents the basic profile of these participants regarding knowledge required. The tests were conducted with nine participants: four beginners, two project managers, a manager of quality and two implementers and evaluators.

The tests resulted in a large amount of data that were analyzed using the Morae Recorder and Morae Manager systems. Table V shows the positive points that were indicated by the participants after the tests. One of the participants, who is implementer and evaluator, pointed out that the ontology is a useful tool for training of implementation staff on the MPS-SW model. A list of recommendations was generated from the results. These recommendations were implemented in v1.1, generating a beta release. For example, a superclass "Questions" was created from the suggestions of the participants during the testes. This class also includes clarifications to many doubts of a team of model implementation.

TABLE IV. Basic profile of the participants of usability testing.

Classification	Knowledge
Beginner	Knowledge in the area of Software Engineering
Project Manager / Quality Manager	Knowledge in the area of Software Engineering
	Knowledge of the business policy
Implementers. / Assessors	Academic training solid: specialization, master's or PhD concluded
	Solid knowledge in software engineering with a focus on software process
	Minimum experience of six years in the area of Software Engineering
	MPS Reference Model Implementation Exam (P2-MPS.BR)
	MPS Assessment Method Course (C3-MPS.BR)
	MPS Assessment Method Exam (P3-MPS.BR)
	Experience Minimum of three years proven project management software or proven experience of implementing software processes in which the organizational unit was certified with some level of maturity of the RM-MPS-SW

TABLE V. Positive aspects indicated by the participants.

Positive points	Number of answers	% of answers
Easy of locating the information desired	8	89%
Rapid access to information coming	4	44%
Simple language	7	78%
Detailed information	4	44%
Visualizing the flow of information of the process	7	78%
None of the registered alternatives	0	0%
Others: "Useful tool for training"	1	11%

F. Stage 5: Maintenance of ontology of the model.

The result of stage 4 was a beta release (v1.2) of the enterprise ontology for the levels G and F of the RM-MPS-SW. This version is available in three free international repositories (file "MR-MPS-SW.owl"): (1) www.daml.org/ontologies; (2) owl.cs.manchester.ac.uk/repositor; (3) protegewiki.stanford .edu/wiki/Protege_Ontology_Library.

This beta release can be used by software development companies interested in implementing the G and F levels of the RM-MPS-SW. The aim is to contribute to the implementation of the Model, as well as to collect suggestions for changes, improvements and inclusion of new knowledge.

V. CONCLUSION

The main objective of this paper was to present a methodology for the development of an enterprise ontology for the levels G and F of the MPS-SW model. This model is part of the Brazilian Software Process Improvement Program (MPS.BR). It was developed focusing on micro, small and medium-sized enterprises (MSME), although it can be implemented in large organizations. The MPS-SW model is fully compatible with the CMMI-DEV and there a correspondence established between their levels. Some of the PMBOK processes and BSC indicators were integrated into the ontology to support the implementation of the model. That methodology comprises four stages and can be applied to other levels of the MPS-SW model as well as to other process quality models.

In the direction of future projects, workflows are being developed from the ontology for levels G and F of the MPS-SW, with tools for Business Process Management (BPM). Considering the development of an ontology for all levels of the model, there are studies aimed at evaluating a integrated and modular way to build the ontology of the MPS-SW. The intention is to minimize the size and complexity of the ontology. Comparisons between the modular process and the process presented in this paper should be made. One line of research in this project is directed at mechanisms for automating the ontologies development for software quality models.

REFERENCES

[1] ABES - Brazilian Association of Software Companies. Brazilian Market of Software, 2011. Available in: http://central.abessoftware.com.br/ Content/UploadedFiles/Arquivos/2012_Publicacao_Mercado_ABES.pdf

[2] SOFTEX - Association for Promotion of the Excellence of the Brazilian Software, website of MPS.BR program: Brazilian Software Process Improvement Program, 2013. Available in: http://www.softex.br/ mpsbr.

[3] M., Uschold, M., King. Towards a methodology for building ontologies. Artificial Intelligence Applications Institute, University of Edinburgh, 1995.

[4] T. Gruber, "A translation approach to portable Ontologies specifications." Knowledge Acquisition, California, vol. 5, n. 2, pp. 199-220, 1993.

[5] J. Dietz. Enterprise Ontology: Theory and Methodology. Springer, 2006.

[6] E. Blomqvist, "Fully automatic construction of enterprise ontologies using design patterns: Initial method and first experiences". On the move to meaningful internet systems 2005: CoopIS, DOA, and ODBASE. Springer Berlin Heidelberg, pp. 1314-1329, 2005.

A method and a tool for evaluating the quality of an SOA

R. Belkhatir[1], **M. Oussalah**[2], **and A. Viguier**[2]
[1]Department of computing, University of Nantes, Nantes, Loire-Atlantique, France
[2]Research/Development Department, BeOtic, Rezé, Loire-Atlantique, France

Abstract - *During these last years, Service Oriented Architecture (SOA) has known a meteoric rise and more and more companies are lured by this technology and its strengths (reusability, costs benefits and productivity increase) because of an improved control of the business expectations. This technology could bring a lot of benefits but there may also appear some major complications while disrupting the company organization to adopt it. First and foremost among these, is the risk of not being able to answer favorably to expectations in terms of quality of services. As these risks are distributed through all the services, the question of evaluating SOA has recently arisen. In this light, before adopting SOA, it is fundamental to evaluate the quality of the architecture to set up. This paper presents a tool enabling the assessment of a software oriented architecture based on a model called SOAQE allowing architecture decomposition with the aim of evaluating it easier. The SOAQE model, validated by the software engineering community, served as a basis for the elaboration of this new generation of tools returning results under textual and graphical forms for a better understanding of data.*

Keywords: Software architecture paradigms. Service oriented architecture. Quality attributes

1 Introduction

Recently, more and more companies focus on SOA solutions for developing their architecture. However, because of the complex nature of the financial issues that this technology involves, there exists a real need in assessing the coherence of the project and the quality of the architecture chosen. This would essentially allow:

(i) Controlling different costs.

(ii) Bringing much more credibility to the project.

(iii) Distinguishing itself from the competition.

(iv) Leading to certifications (standards).

(v) Preventing any future significant potential threat including project failures that such evolution could potentially lead to.

Moreover, increases in terms of software size make the development more complex to handle, and this same complexity makes any form of predictability or estimation (cost and quality) extremely difficult. There exists a need to first build a predictive model of quality. We propose in this article a new semi-automated method for evaluating SOAs, called SOAQE (for Service Oriented Architecture Quality Evaluation). This method considerably overcame shortcomings observed so far such as lacks of pertinence and accuracy. The McCall model, which describes software quality and led to the international standard for the evaluation of software quality, the ISO/IEC 9126-1:2001 [1] (which has recently been updated to the SQuaRE standard ISO/IEC 25010:2011 [2]) serves as a basis for our work. Correlatively, we work with a model that can be defined by a set of views and each view is divided in several factors, criteria and metrics. Our experimentations led us to implement a tool called the SOAQE tool (Flex Client/Java Server application), which, based on the SOAQE model, allows quantifying numerically the quality of the architectural point of view branch and all the attributes of its structure. We deal with some state of the art works in the next section then we present the case study from the BeOtic Company in Section 3. Section 4 introduces the SOAQE tool which supports our model and Section 5 is devoted to the discussion. Finally, section 6 concludes this paper.

2 State of the art works

The software engineering community first developed methods such as GQM (Goal/Question/Metrics) [3] consisting in a few steps:

1. Define goal of measurement

2. Devise suitable set of questions

3. Associate metric with every question.

The limits of such methods appeared quickly: the fact that the process cannot be automated because the different goals of measurement and the questions/metrics resulting from these goals are exclusively set by stakeholders (human intervention) distorts results because stakeholders are not able to cover all the possible requirements to evaluate the quality. We have then seen emerge very similar methods like

ATAM or SAAM [4] which propelled software architecture evaluation to a standard stage for any paradigm. However, several major concerns have been raised with these methods [4]; in particular their cost in terms of time (a lot of steps to perform the whole process) and money because of the hand operated nature of the evaluations conducted. And again, the major lack concerned the results of the evaluations supported with these methods: lots of deficiencies concerning the requirements of the architecture because the process is still not automated. The scale of the task has brought the academic world to tackle these issues and to try to develop a more formal and generic approach than different existing methods to evaluate SOAs [4]. New efforts to evaluate SOA are being undertaken in different aspects using different tools and methods like [5] in which they applied attack graphs for SOA security metrics. But the majority of these kinds of researches are just a proposal or they are about some certain aspects of evaluation or using different techniques [6]. From a global perspective, current methods of evaluation are too vague when it comes to giving accurate measures to quality. Our work differs from those existing insofar as we wish to obtain a precise quantitative measurement for each quality factor with our model.

3 Case study

This section describes an extract of a case study of an existing BeOtic's project (http://www.beotic.com/). This case study has not a purpose of validating our method that we already explained in details in a past paper [7] but illustrating it.

3.1 Requirements

For our case study, we collected data from an existing project of the BeOtic Company. These confidential data include code from the service oriented architecture of one of the clients of the company. More exactly, the company implemented its own tool called BeoMetric for collecting metrics from the code (LOC, CR, CCN...); functioning as JMetric (http://sourceforge.net/projects/jmetric) and we had the chance to gather XML files regrouping the values of the metrics considered for each method, class and package of the client project.

3.2 Method use

One of our past works [7] is dedicated to the realization of the SOAQE model. In [7], we consider that the architectural point of view of an SOA is composed by three main factors (dynamism, reusability and composability) affected by different coefficients according to their importance for SOA (see figure 1).

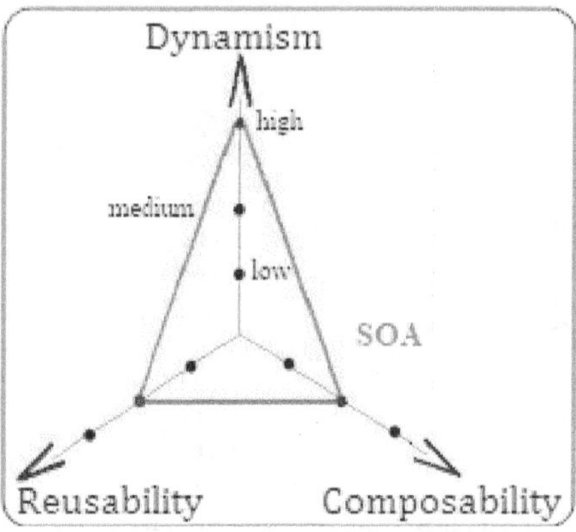

Figure 1: SOA interest points

And each of these factors is composed by the same six criteria (Loose coupling, upgradability, communication abstraction, owner's responsibility, explicit architecture and expressive power) to which we allocate a different weight according to the factor considered (see figure 2).

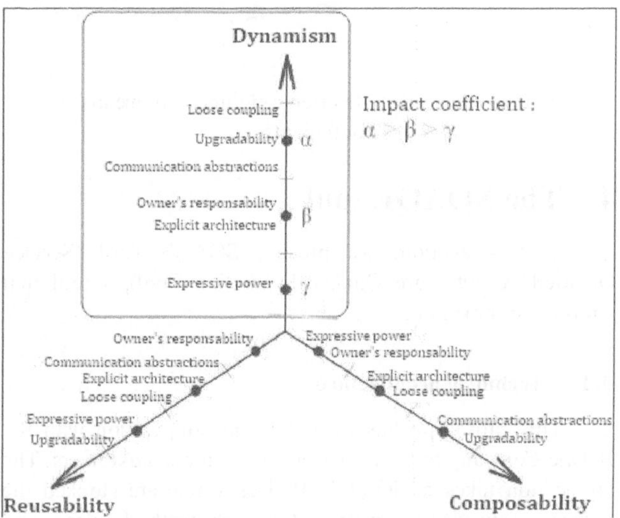

Figure 2: Expression of reusability, composability and dynamism perspectives.

Our first work prompted us to study closely the loose coupling criterion for which we defined its constituent metrics. The aggregation of the values of these metrics allows obtaining a finite value for the loose coupling criterion (see figure 3). Therefore, we wish to incorporate to the SOAQE model, the metrics obtained after applying the BeoMetric module to the submitted architecture in order to get a final mark for the quality of the architecture. The current state of our research works allows us to work exclusively on the path indicated with a blue circle on figure 3 (the loose coupling criterion).

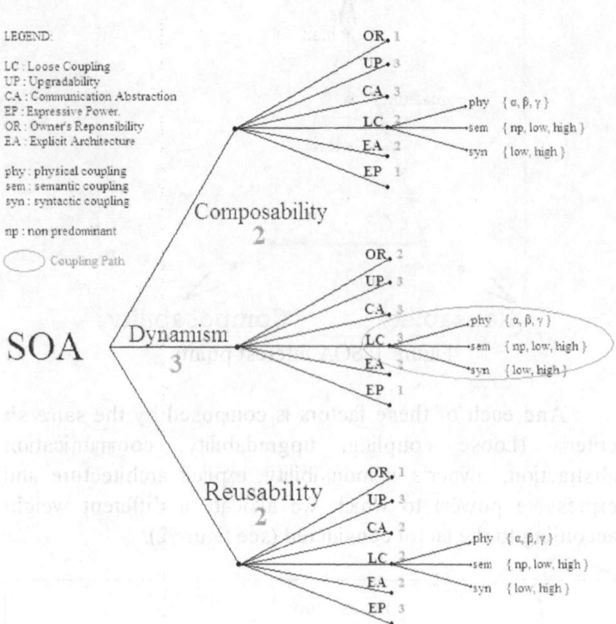

Figure 3: SOA attributes tree weighted with means of coefficients.

4 The SOAQE tool

In this section, we present SOAQE Tool (Service Oriented Architecture Quality Evaluation Tool), a tool that supports our method.

4.1 Technical architecture

This prototype has been built in cooperation with the BeOtic Company to be used as a service for its customers. The application takes as input XML files where are stocked the values of twenty-six metrics for each method, class and package of the architecture submitted. All these values are then stocked in a SQL database to facilitate data retrieving for the application. The server has been built using Java and the server and the database communicate together via the DAO technology. The client of the application has been implemented using Flex and communicates with the server using Blaze DS. Figure 4 describes the architecture of the SOAQE tool.

4.2 General organization

The first step of the application consists in displaying in a data grid the set of metric values retrieved from the SQL database. According to the user's choice, these values can be displayed for the classes or the packages of the source code. This is to allow the user to compare the metrics desired for the evaluation before launching it. As show in figure 5, we implemented for the application a cube stack for the visualization of the results and improved ergonomics.

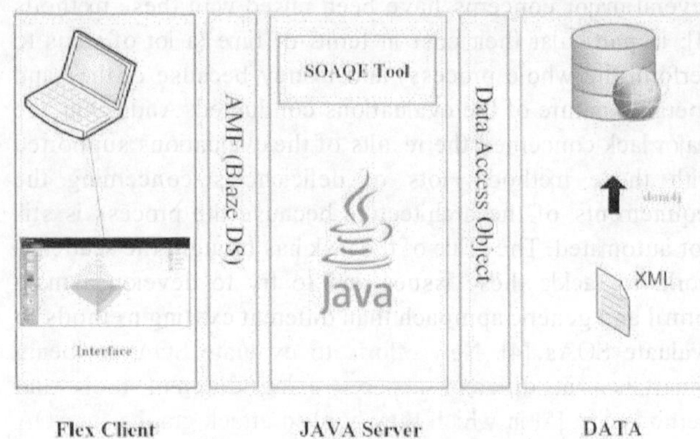

Figure 4: Architecture of the SOAQE tool.

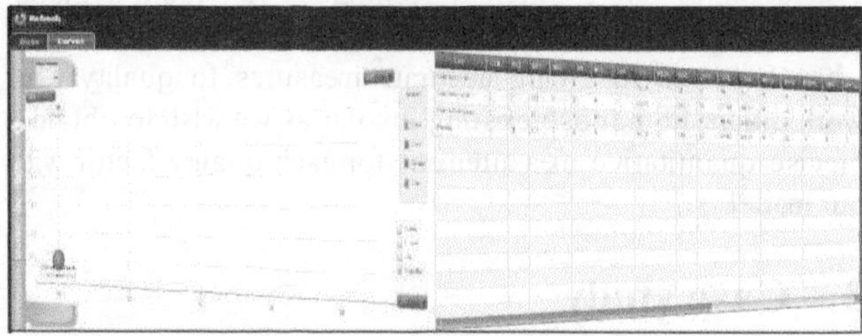

Figure 5: Graphical visualization of the metric values.

In this light, the user can see, in addition to the data grid, the behavior of the metric values with the help of a scatter plot composed by three axes corresponding to the classes or packages that the user chooses for the comparison. We also implemented another module where, this time, the user can visualize the evolution of the metric values for each class in the architecture through colored curves (see figure 6).

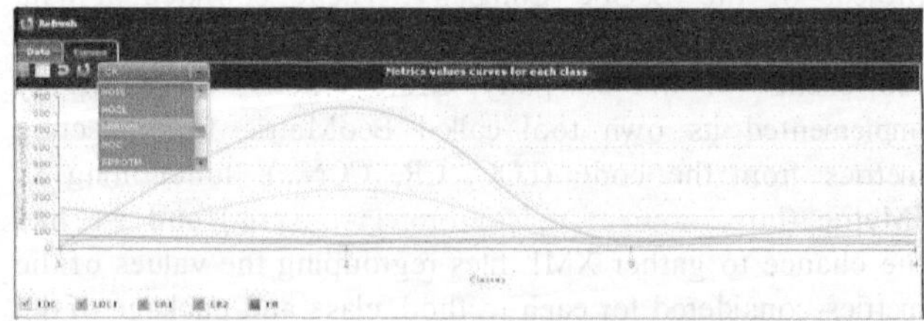

Figure 6: Curves module of the SOAQE tool.

Before launching the evaluation of the architecture submitted, the user can set the tree view of the part of the architecture being evaluated (organized under points of view, factors, criteria and the metrics which has been displayed from the database in the previous phase). The structure of the arborescence is set with a panel under the form of a data grid where is first displayed a default tree corresponding to the most complete declination of the architecture for the architecture point of view we concluded in a past work [7].

Nevertheless, we offered the possibility to the user to be totally free with his evaluation; this is why it is still possible:

(i) To modify the attributes selected in the default arborescence.

(ii) To add new attributes.

(iii) To delete existing attributes

It has been concluded in past works that only factors and criteria must have corresponding weights because the latter have not the same importance according to the point of view considered. The figure 7 is an overview of this control panel.

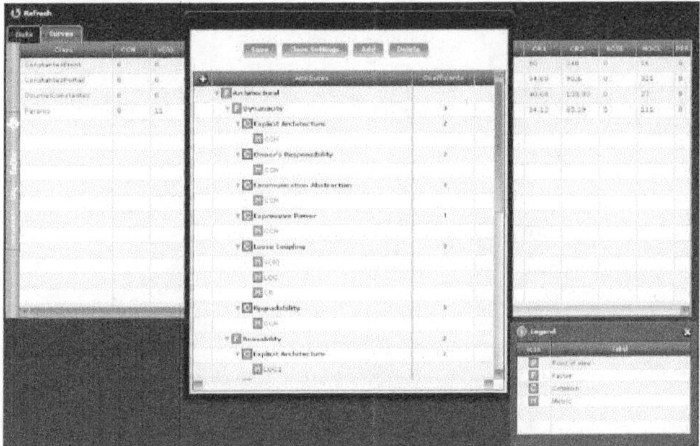

Figure 7: Control Panel

By clicking on the save button, the new arborescence the user created is directly stocked in the SQL database for the next step of the application: the evaluation. Correlatively, the panel closes and a new "Launching the evaluation" button appears. This new operation consists in obtaining a finite value for the quality of the architecture submitted.
(Because the graphics rendering of the results is not only textual, the BeOtic Company asked us to not disclose any overview of the graphics rendering to avoid any potential leaks.)

5 Discussion

Our proposition offers a new way of evaluating the quality of a service oriented architecture since the process is semi-automated and allows save time and money contrary to all existing works trying evaluating the quality of an SOA [3, 4, 5, 6]. The model in which the tool is based has always been validated by the software engineering community [7] and allows obtaining real, accurate and immediate results for the quality evaluation of the SOA. This tool has been implemented to avoid major project fails. Indeed, we can now know if it makes sense to swing towards SOA technology for the company involved and this is exactly where the BeOtic Company has an interest in the project because the company is specialized in IT auditing and software distribution. Nevertheless, we worked on this project as architects and the work for the architectural point of view is not finished as there still are criteria which have not been decomposed in aggregations of metrics. So even if the tool works well and the results obtained are correct, it is still possible to bring new elements to the current work. This is why we chose to let the user free to modify the default arborescence proposed for new research results which are going to be revealed with future works. We first designed a work rather restricted but when the prototype considerably evolved, we added new functionalities to have the most configurable tool possible for the user.

6 Conclusion

In this paper, we present a model, the SOAQE model that allows splitting and evaluating the quality of a service oriented architecture. The method is based on two main steps:

(i) The division of the architecture into four levels of attributes (points of view, factors, criteria and metrics).

(ii) The calculation of the quality mark.

The SOAQE tool has been implemented according to the SOAQE model [7] in order to allow evaluating any SOA considered according to our method. Further step concerns the deep study of new criteria for the architectural point of view. Correlatively, to obtain a model and a tool which can evaluate in a complete way the quality of any SOA, it is essential to be able to split the whole architecture in a combination of several attributes. Another part of the perspectives concerns research on new points of view; we already started a bit with the business one.

7 References

[1] J.P. Carvallo, X. Franch "Extending the ISO/IEC 9126-1 Quality Model with Non-Technical Factors for COTS Components Selection" In *Proceedings of the 2006 international workshop on Software quality* (WoSQ '06). ACM, New York, NY, USA, 9-14.

[2] W. Suryn, A. ABran, A. April, "ISO/IEC SQuaRE: The second generation of standards for software product quality" (2003)

[3] V.R. Basili, G. Caldiera, H. Dieter Rmbach, "The Goal Question Metric Approach" Chapter in Encyclopedia of Software Engineering, Wiley, 1994

[4] P. Clements, R. Kazman and M. Klein, "Evaluating Software Architectures: Methods and case studied", Addison-Wesley, 2002 – 323 pages

[5] J. Magott, M.Woda "Evaluation of SOA security metrics using attack graphs", IEEE 2008, pp 277-284.

[6] D.Cotroneo, C.Di Flora, S.Russo "Improving Dependability of Service Oriented Architectures for Pervasive Computing", Proceedings of The Eighth IEEE International Workshop on Object-OrientedReal-Time, 2003.

[7] R. Belkhatir, M. Oussalah, and A. Viguier, A Model Introducing SOAs Quality Attributes Decomposition. ;In Proceedings of SEKE. 2012, 324-327.

Training Users of Accounting Information Systems for their Satisfaction, Decision-making, and Competitiveness

J.M. Medina, Y. Loera, K. González, and A. Mora

Facultad de Comercio y Admón., Universidad Autónoma de Tamaulipas. Cd. Victoria, México

Abstract - *Information technologies are rapidly changing the world. Therefore, more scientific research that can contribute to the development of our understanding regarding information technology is needed. In particular, research that addresses the role of accounting information systems is urgently needed as financial problems in all types of organizations are common worldwide. For this reason, this research is aimed at determining the impact that training in the operation of Accounting Information Systems has on their users regarding Satisfaction, Decision-making, and Competitiveness. A questionnaire was administered to 92 users. The positive impact that training has on competitiveness (financial performance, market share and customer satisfaction) is highlighted.*

Keywords: IT, Decision-making, Competitiveness, User Satisfaction

1 Introduction

Accounting is the engine that moves an enterprise forward, and helps it face its competitors' efforts, trade agreements, fiscal issues, etc. The accounting's aim is to mirror an enterprise's estate, financial statement, and outcomes. Decision makers in a company benefit from this information when they receive it. For example, they can decide on what direction they can give to the company or what policies they can develop. Similarly, information related to accounting is also beneficial for an enterprise's partners as a good performance of the company can determine the benefits they will obtain from it.

However, in order to achieve the above mentioned and with the support of the information technology (IT), the accounting information systems (AIS) have emerged which have widely facilitated these activities. Training, though is needed to obtain a competitive advantage, users' satisfaction, and more informed decision-making. This study seeks to link these elements in the operation of the informatics applications/systems.

To achieve this aim, a transversal study is proposed. A questionnaire was administered to 92 users of these AIS in 46 enterprises located in the central region of Tamaulipas (Mexico). After that, a regression analysis was conducted using the SPSS software package version 18, from which the results are derived. Finally, the hypothesis is answered and the main contributions to knowledge are discussed.

2 Literature review

2.1 Training

Training is defined as an educational act and a systematic effort made by enterprises in order to increase the potential of their three main areas such as cognitive, psychomotor, and affective. In other words, training is the action aimed at developing workers' aptitudes, attitudes, and skills so they can perform their job effectively. Chiavenato [2] considers it as a short-term educational process, which is systematically applied and organized through which people develop competences such knowledge, skills and attitudes according to predefined aims.

Nevertheless, small enterprises offer less training to their employees. Moreover, small organizations tend to prefer in situ training to that provided by companies devoted to it [13]. The lack of time, high costs, slowness and scarcity of information are frequently cited reasons for not offering external training. Compared to large companies, small ones have less capability to make up for the temporal losses in productivity which can be present in the formation stages. In other words, small companies are less able to allow their employees to be absent or replace them when they are in training. Several studies show that employee training has a positive impact on the enterprises' performance. These studies usually establish the hypothesis that training helps employees improve their productivity level, which is then translated into a better organizational performance [1].

2.2 Satisfaction

The need to assess the effectiveness of information systems (IS), coupled with the difficulty of operationalizing economy based variables have accelerated the search for easily measurable variables, in this case, user satisfaction and system use [4]. There have also been attempts to measure users' satisfaction with information as a substitute for IS total effectiveness in the organization [16]. Even then, user friendliness and interface are both associated with IS satisfaction, but the lack of positive benefits leads to a decrease in the use and eventual disappearance of the system or even the IS department [4].

The IS user's satisfaction and performance is an important assessment parameter [21], this variable has been the research object since the 1970's; despite this, there is not an understandable theoretical assessment. The scale developed by Ives, Olson and Baroudi [10] is one of the most popular. No doubt, satisfaction has been a widely researched topic; however, the analyses conducted correspond to particular contexts. Therefore, such studies share the belief that they need further research due to the complexity of the concept and the multidisciplinary nature of the elements they contain. The lack of agreement in the conceptual definition of the user satisfaction variable leads to a situation in which there are many operationalizations and definitions. It refers to a positive orientation that an individual has towards an information system [9], an attitude/feeling that he or she has as a result of a transaction [23], affected by a variety of factors in a situation and associated with the perception of an application.

Having reviewed the literature, the hypothesis for these variables is now introduced:

H_1. Training is an influential factor in the AIS users' satisfaction.

2.3 Decision-making

Decision-making is defined as the selection of a course of action from several alternatives; it is at the center of planning. Sometimes, managers view decision-making as their main task, as they constantly have to decide what to do, who does it, when to do it and even how to do it [22]. The IT includes all the range of operations and decision-making activities. This is both a beneficial aspect and a difficulty, Eisenhardt [5] argued that little research on decision-making had been undertaken until the late 1980's; other scholars such as Teng and Calhoun [20] state the potential effect of information technology on decision-making at all levels has been captured by the IT researchers from the beginning of the informatics era; since the world is moving towards open and global markets, the need to have access to timely, reliable and easy information will be essential for effectiveness in decision-making processes [7]. For this reason, managers of enterprises need to determine the extent to which IT helps in the achievement of decision-making aims.

The IT decisions have the potential to change individuals, businesses and societies at large. However, they need to be made in an accurate, fast and timely manner. Arguably, technologies help improve productivity, and decision-making [8]. Research has found that IT can change the hierarchy in decision-making activities, which lowers the cost of information acquisition and distribution [14].

H_2. Training is an influential factor in the IT users' decision-making processes.

2.4 Competitiveness

Competitive advantage is a phenomenon that occurs when a firm experiences returns that are superior than those of its competition (rents) [12]. The classical conception of competitiveness was very similar to competition as it denoted rivalry among economic agents. If understood like that, a high concentration of enterprises with scarce differentiation attributes can occur. However, what is needed is to defeat the competitors through competitive advantage. Therefore, competitiveness should be addressed beyond competition since competitive advantage is not only about defeating competitors, but defeating them with superior qualities. Another approach adopted by the Organization for Economic Cooperation and Development [18] defines competitiveness as the capability that an enterprise, industry, region, or nation has to generate revenue and high employment rates in a sustainable manner when international competition exists.

Generally speaking, competitiveness is considered to be meant success. Competitiveness can be considered a multi-dimensional variable with a series of variables that need to be adopted jointly in order to be measured [15]. On the way to meet that aim, it is important to recognize that competitiveness does not rule out cooperation, particularly from a national perspective. But even more significant is the fact that this aim requires entrepreneurs to be willing to construct companies which can build their way on their own. This way starts by giving priority to the domestic market, as the internationalization requires them to face the demanding world market challenges [19].

In addition, Lavon and Todd [12] state that those organizations that refuse to invest in IT are likely to miss the opportunity to improve their efficiency and effectiveness. If such companies operate in a highly competitive environment, which is the current tendency as a result of globalization, then they will be more likely to fail in the market in which they operate. The need that small and medium sized enterprises (SME's) have to address the concept of competitiveness is evident. The addressing of such a concept can allow them not only to face competition, but also to survive over time.

H_3. The training of AIS' s users is an influential factor in the enterprise's competitiveness.

3 Method

All today's IT, which were unimaginable a few years ago, have made a significant progress in the study, treatment, analysis and outcomes of large amounts of information in all knowledge areas. That is to say, the methodological limitations are no longer a critical issue for those who seek empirical evidence. On the other hand, a clear definition of the dependent variable enhances the reliability of the results obtained; otherwise, the research becomes speculative only.

For this study, the definition and operationalization of the variables were carried out as follows:

- Dependent variables: Satisfaction (trust in the accounting information system, feelings of efficiency and effectiveness) and Competitiveness (financial performance, market share, innovation levels in products/services, customer satisfaction).
- Independent variables: Trainig (updating in informatics, continuous program, personal skills).

The empirical part of this project took place in the central region of the Mexican state of Tamaulipas. The process followed to meet the stated aim started with the state-of-the-art review of the variables to test, mainly in scientific journals, prestigious books and official websites. A questionnaire was designed which included 10 open ended and 88 five point Likert scale items. The open ended items were about demographics and the Likert scale items covered the variables under study. The questionnaire was piloted with 12 enterprises, and resulted in the elimination of 10 items which lacked the minimum recommended statistical loading. Therefore, the final version of the questionnaire included 78 items. For this study, only four variables are considered, with 5 items for Satisfaction, 4 for Decision-making, 3 for Competitiveness, and 3 for Training.

According to the National System of Entrepreneurship Information (http://www.siem.gob.mx), a total of 1463 SMEs were registered in in the state of Tamaulipas (in Mexico, small enterprises are those which have between 11 and 50 employees and medium- sized enterprises are those with a range of 51 and 250 employees). The region under study has 365 SMEs. Unfortunately, managers/leaders' participation in research continues to be poor. Therefore, the final version of the questionnaire was administered to 46 enterprises (92 valid questionnaires for their analysis). Those people who make the most use of information in enterprises such as the manager, owner and the person in charge of the computers department answered two questionnaires per enterprise. Two masters' students who have an active professional live and two undergraduate students provided support in the data collection process. The respondents were given a week to return the completed questionnaires so they could have the freedom and sufficient time to answer it appropriately. The researched enterprises represented different types of enterprises as the study was transversal in nature. Based on the data collected, the analysis of results is presented mainly using descriptive statistics and regression analysis with the help of the SPSS software package version 18.

Results

The first step was to analyze the descriptive data of the respondents in order to obtain a profile of them. The analysis reveals that 67% of the AIS users are females. Therefore, it is recommended that the training provided be *accessible* to all the participants, especially female participants, in terms of knowledge acquisition and skills development. The most predominant age group of the respondents is that between 21 and 30 years (87%). That is to say, while their age suggests that they are likely to embrace IT, they are also in need of continuous training. 52% of the AIS users are accounting assistants, 39% are accountants, 7% are administrative staff, and 2% are data entry operators.

In the hypothesis assessment, reliability degrees of each of the variables measured with the Cronbach's Alpha: Training=.733, Satisfaction=.933, Decision-making=.929 and Competitiveness=.701. In order for a variable to be considered acceptable, its value needs to be greater than 0.7 [17]. If so, it indicates that the questionnaire is valid; and its results can be interpreted as reflecting the current reality.

It is important to indicate that according to Chin [3]: R (Relation) represents the *path coefficients*, which should obtain a value of 0.2 if they are to be considered significant, with above 0.3 being an ideal value. R^2 on the other hand, indicates the variance explained by the variable within the model. This should be equal or greater than 0.1, as lower values provide little information even if they are significant. Similarly, the significance should be lower than 0.05 ($p<0.05$). Of the three dependent variables, only one meets the previous requirements; and therefore, it is the only one accepted as true as the summary provided in Table 1 shows.

Hypothesis	R	R^2	Sig	Remark
H_1. Training ➔ Sat.	0.221	0.048	0.393	Rejected
H_2. Training ➔ DM	0.229	0.052	0.394	Rejected
H_3. Training ➔ Com.	0.362	0.131	0.050	Accepted

Table 1. Hypotheses Testing Summary

Sat. : Satisfaction, DM : Decision-making, and Com.: Competitiveness

Figure 1 shows the tested research model, which includes a graphical representation of the data as stated on table above. It also includes the levels of relation between the independent and dependent variables with their respective hypothesis.

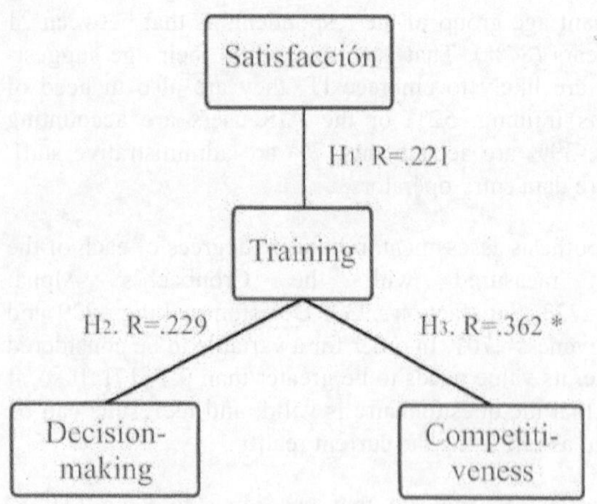

Figure 1. Tested Research Model

This figure shows that of the three stated hypotheses, only one (H_3) is accepted. Therefore, the following conclusions are drawn:

H_1: Rejected; although it achieves an R=.221 level, which is greater than recommended, it falls behind the variance explained (R^2), with only .048 and with little significance (it is greater than 0.05, achieving 0.393) (See Table 1). This may mean that the training program provided to the AIS users is not working effectively for their satisfaction. This is especially true for the little confidence that users have in the data they enter and obtain. In other words, users do not clearly perceive efficiency in the operation of the AIS. Two situations might explain this. Either there is a lack of training or the training provided is inadequate.

H_2: Rejected; even though it achieves an R=.229 level, which is greater than recommended, it falls behind the variance explained (R^2), with only .052, and with little significance (it is greater than 0.05, achieving 0.394) (See Table 1). This can also be interpreted that the training received by the AIS users is not helping them make good decisions. In other words, the AIS is not providing them with relevant information than could be useful for their decision-making practices.

H_3: Accepted; it achieves a level of R=.363, which is greater than recommended, the explained variance (R^2) achieves acceptable levels of .131 and with a significance of 95% of reliability (lower than or equal to 0.05, achieving 0.05) (See Table 1). This suggests that training always has an impact somewhere in the organization. In this case, it appears that training has an impact on competitiveness. That is to say, the AIS users seem to believe that their organization is obtaining a market gain, a certain degree of innovation, a higher level of profit margin, and above all, a higher level of customer satisfaction. They seem to attribute all these benefits to the training they receive in the operation of these IT.

4 Conclusions

The world is rapidly changing and creating large amounts of information which have not been exploited sufficiently by institutions. This is so even though it is widely known that information exists in both the physical world by which we are surrounded and the mental world of the human thoughts also known as *the computer limbo,* as information is created, stored, managed, and organized for its own benefit and that of the human capital. The accounting information systems have become essential in organizations as they are the main generators of information for their users which can later be used in a wide range of activities of the administrative process.

The aim of this study was to determine the degree of influence that Training, has on the Users of the Accounting Information Systems of the Small and Medium Sized Enterprises for their Satisfaction, effective Decision-making, and Competitiveness. With the support of the review of the literature, the three stated hypotheses have been answered. Now, answers to the stated aims and the research questions will be provided next.

In that context, it is important to recall that the training provided to the users of the accounting information systems is of paramount importance. However, in this case, it is only having a positive influence on the competitive levels of the organizations. Unfortunately, there are other aspects of organizations such as customer satisfaction that are equally, or even more, important. In particular, the results show that users satisfaction is an aspect that is not being successful. Therefore, it is highly recommended that organizations should make every effort to attempt to maintain the AIS users' motivation so they can remain productive and can make contributions to the organizations. Failing to perceive the usefulness of the information generated by the AIS can lead to a lack of trust in the AIS processes. Therefore, if the AIS users do not trust the AIS, they will be very unlikely to take advantage of all the benefits that these technologies can bring to themselves as users and to the enterprise at large.

Similarly, the procedures followed during the decision-making processes also need to be further assessed. The AIS users seem to be under using the information generated by the AIS as they consider it insufficient for their decision-making practices. They seem to believe that they need a wider range of alternatives at their disposal that can assist them in their decision-making practices, which unfortunately the AIS is not providing them. Further research can have this as a starting point as the worldwide tendency is the emphasis placed on the importance of empowering employees so they can make their own decisions, especially, if based on information generated by the AIS.

Likewise, it is important to recognize that training is being perceived by the organizations and their employees as valuable for their competitiveness development efforts. This was reflected in their confidence that the organization is making progress in terms of financial performance, market share, and customer satisfaction thanks to training. Therefore, the training in the operation of the AIS that they have received has had a direct impact on competitiveness, which is an important variable for the development of positive relationships between different parties such as users, organization, and technologies.

5 References

[1] Betcherman, G.; N. Leckie; K. McMullen. "Barriers to Employer-Sponsored Training in Canada", *Réseauxcanadiens de recherche en politiques publiques*, Ottawa, p. 28, (1998)

[2] Chiavenato, I. *"Las etapas de evaluación de un proceso de capacitación, Administración de Recursos Humanos"*. 8va edición, Mc Graw Hill, México, (2007).

[3] Chin, W.W. "Issues and Opinion on Structural Equation Modeling". *MIS Quarterly*, 22(1), pp. vii-xvi, (1998)

[4] DeLone, W.; E. McLean. "The DeLone and McLean Model of Information Systems Success: A Ten-Year Update". *Journal of Management Information Systems*, 19(4), pp. 9-30, (2003)

[5] Eisenhardt, K.M. "Making Fast Strategic Decisions in High-Velocity Environments". *Academy of Management Journal*, 32(3), pp. 543-576, (1989)

[6] Escobar, I.; E. Tamayo. "*Contabilidad*". EDITEX. Madrid, (2008)

[7] Hamill, J.; R. Deckro; J. Kloeber. "Evaluating Information Assurance Strategies". *Decision Support Systems*, 39(3), pp. 463-484, (2005)

[8] Hubbard, T. *"Information, Decisions, and Productivity On-Board Computer* and *Capacity Utilization in Trucking"*. University of Chicago and NBER. DRAFT. September, (2001)

[9] Ishman, M. "Measuring Information Success at the Individual Level in Cross-Cultural Environments". *Information Resources Management Journal*, 9(4), pp. 16-28, (1996)

[10] Ives, B.; M. Olson; J. Baroudi. "The Measurement of User Information Satisfaction". *Communications of the ACM*, 26(10), pp. 785-793, (1983)

[11] Koontz, H.; H. Weihrich; M. Cannice. *"Administración. Una Perspectiva Global y Empresarial"*. 13a. Edición, McGraw Hill, México, (2008)

[12] Lavon, G.; M. Todd. *"Information Technology and Its Role in Creating Sustainable Competitive Advantage"*, 6(1). Consulted: jul 5, In: [http://www.jimsjournal.org/pi.html], (2011)

[13] Leckie, N.; A. Léonard, J. Turcotteet; D. Wallace. *"Pratiques des ressources humaines perspectives des employeurs et des employés"*. Statistique Canada, Ottawa, (2001)

[14] Malone, T.W. "Is Empowerment Just a Fad? Control, Decision Making, and IT". *MIT Sloan Management Review*, 38(2), pp. 23-35, (1997)

[15] Mayer, T.; J. Mucchielli. "Hierarchical location choice and multinational firms' strategy: a nested logit model applied to Japanese investment in Europe". *Multinational Firms: The Global and Local Dilemma*, London: Routledge, pp. 133-158, (2002)

[16] Miller, J.; B. Doyle. "Measuring the Effectiveness of Computer-Based Information Systems in the Financial Services Sector". *MIS Quarterly*, 11(1), pp. 107-124, (1987)

[17] Nunnally, J.C. *"Psychometric Theory"*. McGraw Hill Editorial, New York, U.S.A., (1978)

[18] OECD (Organisation for Economic Co-operation and Development). *"Industrial Competitiveness"*. París, (1997)

[19] Rozzo, C. "Internacionalización y Competitividad". *Política y Cultura.* No. 2, México, pp. 307-318, (1993)

[20] Teng, J.; K. Calhoun. "Organizational Computing as a Facilitator for Operational and Managerial Decision Making: An Exploratory Study of Managers' Perceptions". *Decision Sciences*, 27(4), pp. 673-710, (1996)

[21] Torkzadeh, G.; X. Koufteros; W. Doll. "Confirmatory Factor Analysis and Factorial Invariance of the Impact of Information Technology Instrument". *Omega*, 33(2), pp. 107-118, (2005)

[22] Weihrich, H.; M. Cannice; H. Koontz. *"Management: A Global & Entrepreneurial Perspective"*. McGraw Hill. Edition 11th, (2010)

[23] Wilkin, C.; B. Hewitt. "Quality in a Respecification of DeLone and McLean's IS Success Model". In: M. Khosrowpour (Ed.). *Proceedings of IRMA International Conference.* Hershey, PA: Idea Group Publishing, pp. 663-672, (1999)

Dynamic Registration Forms

Troy Johnson, Joshua Edinborough, Matthew Binder, Andrew Bryant, Blayne Dennis, Roger Lee
Department of Computer Science, Central Michigan University, Mt Pleasant,USA
Software Engineering & Information Technology Institute, Central Michigan University, Mt Pleasant, MI

Abstract - *User registration for events has been made easier via the use of web applications. Similarly, administrative systems often accompany them providing event coordinators with the ability to manage the registration data of users who register via web form. Many web applications that exist make the management of registered users' data easier to manage. However, the creation of unique registration forms for each new event is often lacking in most systems; this often places undue stress on companies and organizations providing the online registrations, requiring significant development time to create unique registration forms. In this paper, we present a method for minimizing this development time by providing a system for dynamic, self-service form creation for event coordinators. This method uses a scheme for event data storage requiring minimal database tables in MS SQL, control and form generation in C#, and provides client access to registration data. The system is intended to minimize form creation time and provide ease-of-use for system administration, event coordinators, and end-users. Our test results demonstrate that the designed system is successful in these regards as well as being responsive, secure, and accessible in its performance.*

Keywords: registration, dynamic, forms, generation

1 Introduction

Event registration has been made more efficient by the internet. Online registrants can now provide their registration information to a web site holding the registration form for the particular event, and event coordinators may easily view this data. These interactive web applications leverage the ubiquity of the internet and advances in web development to provide more customized access [3] and more cost-effective solutions for creating, distributing, and managing event registration. Event coordinators are connected to their end-users (or registrants) via authenticated access to event information on these sites. The credentials of the user of the system will identify the user as either an event coordinator or end-user; if the user is a qualified event coordinator, they may complete a variety of management tasks associated with an event. These tasks will often include creating the events, manually adding event registrants, and managing registrant data from completed forms.

Registration forms for events, distributed as web forms to end-users, include a variety of field types and requirements for completion. Forms may utilize one or more of the following field types: Text input boxes for information such as names and other short text; drop-down menus with designated options to collect information such as birth month, for example; check-box lists in which multiple options may be selected, etc. These fields may or may not be required for submission of the registration form to be successful. Event coordinators will likely find systems that are made to fit their needs based on the type of event they are creating and/or the network used by their potential registrants to maximize exposure. Many of these systems are fairly inflexible in their ability to allow the event coordinators to customize the registration forms. Often, the fields that need to be filled out by registrants are pre-determined with little to no variability. This poses a problem for coordinators who wish to vary the fields and requirements for registration. With such rigidity, the event coordinator must make do with the forms already created or have systems developers to manually create new forms, requiring hours of development time as custom code must be created to display and handle the new registration forms.

An alternative to these problems would be to implement a dynamic registration form application. Such a program would remove the need for hard-coding to be done, shift the task of designing the form to the event coordinator by providing a self-serve system, and allow registrants to also access the newly created forms to register for the event.

2 Related Work

Systems often allow event coordinators to create new events, propagate a URL address to event attendees to access the registration form, and view attendee data. However, each event will most likely require unique fields and registration data to be obtained. As a result, system developers may be required to develop unique registration forms for said events, or else event coordinators must be limited in their abilities to adapt forms. This is inconvenient for both the developers and the event coordinators. This, among others, represents key problems that exist in such systems, and solutions providing dynamic form creation must address them.

Systems lacking dynamic form creation often require significant development time to update or create new web registration forms. For example, the Office of Information Technology (OIT) at Central Michigan University (CMU), where our solution was implemented, typically requires 20-40 hours of development time for such tasks. Automation of the form creation process is possible via a system using pertinent form creation data stored in a database and an interface for interacting with said system, hence, allowing the user to create and store new form information. The new form data may then be retrieved dynamically and used to generate a subsequent web form. In his system for generating forms dynamically in various languages, Burget [2] helps to alleviate the need to create unique, hard-coded registration forms in order to accommodate the variety of needs of clients. In Burget's system, a client will request the form they wish to fill out and a language to present the form in. Burget makes use of three databases: First, a template database holds the layout information for each unique form. Second, a question database contains data regarding each field held in a forms layout to be used in the construction of the form. Lastly, a language database holds counterpart text for the data held in the question database used to convert the form to other languages. Ravishankar [5] addresses this problem further. Their system configures an application server to dynamically generate web forms, delivered to users, by retrieving field data from XML documents and user information from their requests. Users logging in as an administrator are qualified for a variety of options including the editing of form information to be stored in further XML documents. They may also update subscriber information after having added subscriber profiles. This implementation offers the capabilities of dynamic form creation and editing of both form data and subscriber accounts by client users (or coordinators), hence, reducing effort on the part of systems administrators. Data, however, is stored in a variety of sources. Data for form field markups, validation of fields, form structures, subscriber-specific data for a given form, and subscriber information are all stored in separate XML documents or data sources, hence, requiring extensive data source setup. Also, while access is flexible and available to systems administrators and event coordinators, end-user completion of registration forms is unavailable.

Another problem to address is the responsibility placed on the organizations and systems administrators to create web registration forms for their clients. Dynamic form creation is intended to alleviate this responsibility and make the task a self-service action for the event managers (clients of the systems administrators). For this to be possible, a web-based solution is ideal as access is made more readily available for end-users. Also, the system must analyze and store data provided by the client users to create forms to their specifications. Solutions such as that of Burget's do not wholly minimize system administrators' creation of this content as form templates must be created by administrators. Similarly, Revishankar's methods do not offer a complete solution for all three types of users: systems administrators, event coordinators, and end-users.

Ultimately, dynamic form creation systems can be streamlined to directly deliver the web forms to both event coordinators for approval and end-users for use and then store their provided data for viewing by event coordinators. Kirkpatrick [4] presents a system by which web forms may be created dynamically from stored data and then used by end-users to store their form data. The data storage design in this system stores data such as field types and requirements, and allows forms to be dynamically generated and delivered to users. Class files are used, if present, or dynamically created for forms of various fields and types to use this information to generate and deliver web forms. The software component uses response data for a form and saves it in an output table containing fields identical to those of the form. This solution addresses the dynamic generation of the forms and reduces development time by eliminating the need for unique HTML file creation. Similarly, it stores resulting response data to be viewed later by coordinators. The system, however, does not specifically address the need for this dynamic form creation and delivery process to be managed mostly by the clients who wish to have the forms made.

While methods exist that address various problems to be solved by an effective dynamic form creation, our system addresses the need for an easy-to-use, fully automated system for self-served registration form creation by client users while also allowing consumption by end-users. Moreover, our system will address problems regarding excessive data storage for such a system and provides greater accessibility.

3 Methodology

The dynamic form implementation presented here aims to reduce down-time related to the creation of unique registration forms for events. It does so by providing a self-serve system for client users to manage form creation and registered users via an easy-to-use interface presented uniformly in a variety of web browsers. The system provides access to systems administrators (OIT), event coordinators (client users), and event registrants (end-users).

During the event creation and following registration form creation processes, both client users and OIT are involved in the access of data. The use case diagram below depicts the interaction each actor has with the system during form creation.

A client user uses basic web forms to provide request information to the control software regarding event data, field alterations, and registration users. The control software accesses the database to select and manipulate event data, and it uses the form generation object to build forms to be displayed to the user's browser. The OIT users are able to access the system as well via OIT web forms, allowing them to manage events and event administrators as well as verifying and approving event registration data as provided by client users.

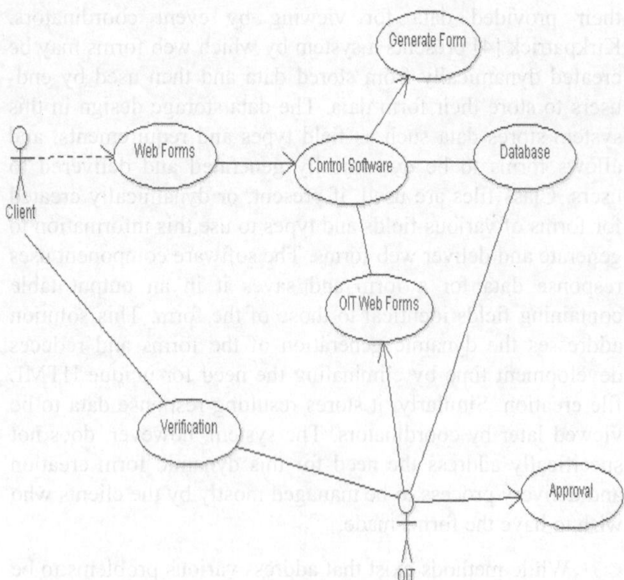

Figure 1: Use Case Diagram

4 Dynamic Form Storage

Storage of pertinent registration form data is done in a database implementation in MS SQL. In order to maintain the dynamic creation and alteration of form content, generic database practices were implemented in a relatively small number of tables; most major data exists in one or two different tables with rows identifying where the data belongs.

Figure 2: Database Diagram

As can be seen in figure 2, events are stored in table '410Event'. Each row in this table relates to multiple rows in '410Info'; this table designates form fields for the registration form for the event with columns for the field name and input type. In '401List', various options and their values are held and relate to specific field types such as check boxes, radio options, selectable menus, and alike. Each row in '410Info' may relate to many options in '410List'. These tables allow for the generation and creation of event registration forms by the event coordinators. End-users, however, will create data to be stored in the remaining two tables. Once registered, the end-user's registration information is store in '410Registration', a table whose rows designate a registration for an event in '410Event' as designated in the foreign key field 'EventId'. Each field of the registration form that is completed by the end-user creates gathered registration data stored in '410Gathered'. Each entry in this table corresponds to one registration in '410Registered' and stores 'Information' for a field as defined by '410Info'. This relational database uses a small number of tables to store all necessary event registration data to be used by event coordinators as well as end-users. User profile and log in information for both, however, are separately stored, authorized, and created by the system in which this program extends.

4.1 Form Generation and Control

Interactions between the database and web clients is controlled by the control software, implemented in C#. This portion of the system initiates requests to and from the database after receiving information from the web client and OIT web forms. This portion is also responsible for calling the form generator when needed; the form generator, also implemented in C#, is responsible for creating the physical manifestation of the even registration form, both temporary test and final versions.

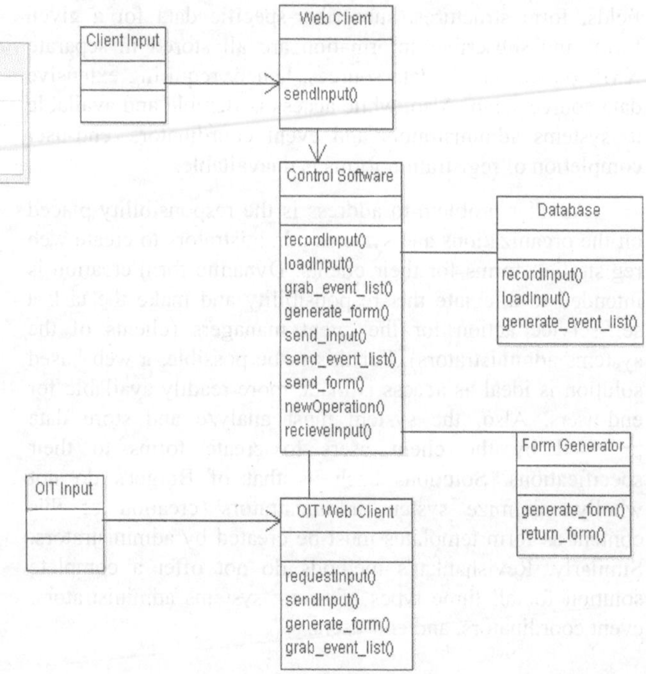

Figure 3: Object Model

Figure 3 depicts the relation between the various objects within the system. Clients will input data into simple forms created to collect all necessary information the request type being pursued by the client: these actions may include creating a new event, modifying the event registration form, editing the list of users who may access the registration form, and viewing registered users. Once received and processed via a scripting language, the control software object controls access to the database to collect and edit its contents. Using fetched data, the control software relies on the form generator to create output to be returned to the client's web browser. OIT clients (or systems administrators) also use a similar process for checking event data correctness, generating temporary forms, and approving final form creation and subsequent distribution back to the client.

4.2 Registration Form Creation Process

The system described facilitates registration form creation by providing an interactive process between client users and OIT. This process involves a few key steps to be completed by one or both user types:

1. Client users inputs and uploads event information via client web forms.

2. The event is placed in the OIT event queue for verification.

3. OIT edits and checks the data for correctness and generates a temporary form.

4. OIT sends the temporary form to the client for verification.

5. Client verifies the form or requests changes (back to step three if needed).

6. OIT approves and distributes the finalized form to the client.

4.3 Implementation

To complete the described system the user interface, control software, and database required implementation. A web implementation was used to deploy access to all user types, providing greater ease of access. Hence, HTML web pages containing forms and menus were coded to create a user interface that client-users, end-users, and OIT can interact with at all stages of the registration form creation process. The Control Software and Form Generation aspects were coded in C#, in accordance with OIT standards documentation, to mediate interaction between users providing requests via web forms and the database containing all event information. The database to hold said information was implemented as an MS SQL database.

5 Results

Upon implementation of the described system in a testing environment, various performance tests on the user interface and overall system, as well as functional tests, provided positive results that the system was successful. While limited, the testing environment allowed many tests to be performed. A development machine was used to deploy the site with the database living on the same server; deployment on this machine allowed testing to occur internally only. Specific test cases were used to test the performance of the system in regards to ease-of-use, response time, availability, and security. The following test cases provided feedback:

- Client attempts verification before completely filling our form.
- OIT attempts to approve a form when the database communication has failed or experienced and error.
- OIT attempts to approve an unverified form.
- Client attempts to start a new form before finishing an old one.
- Client attempts to start a new form before the old one has finished processing.

These test cases, as well as more general ones, provided the results that described the function of the site. Teams of users were used to test the site, using some or all of the above test cases, and they provided feedback via questionnaire. These users required no knowledge of the system and its expected behaviors, as to test the system more accurately from a perspective like that of a production environment. Each of the following categories was tested and users were asked to rate each "poor", "fair", or "good":

	Result
Administrative Interface	
Ensure no unauthorized access	Good
Events properly created; access granted to event organizer	Good
Event start/end dates enforced	Good
End-User Visual Display	
Ensure access without authentication	Good
Ensure required fields are truly required	Good
Ensure page loads all fields	Good
Drop-down menus properly populate	Good
Event Organizer Display	
Custom field addition	Good
Drop-down list item addition	Good
Required field addition	Good
Field order save/recovery	Good
Data Access Layer	
All data access calls perform as expected	Good
Data storing as expected	Good
Entity models properly reflect database schema	Good

From the team results, also, we found that the developed system proved to be responsive in its test environment. Responsiveness was determined by measuring response times of the systems after various user requests. The threshold for wait times without providing any feedback were set to 1 second, based on human perceptual abilities; any waiting time longer should provide a dialog giving an estimated wait time [6]. These test results demonstrate the success of our system in this regard based on team testing and questionnaire responses.

6 Conclusions

By providing a web-based system for client-users, end-users, and OIT to interact in the dynamic registration form creation process, this system is able to facilitate the creation of unique event registration forms to be filled out by registrants. Some systems exist, at present, which alleviate the down-time and development time required to create unique registration forms for unique events by removing the need to hard-code forms in HTML or alike. However, many lack ease-of-use, full automation, or storage of registrant information, and may also be unnecessarily complex. Our system implements web-based forms for users to submit requests for various steps in the form creation process including event creation, form generation, form approval, and event registration. These requests are handled by the control software and form generator, implemented in C#, to handle authentication, database manipulation, and form generation from data. A minimal, generic database was used and implemented in MS SQL to store all event information in, primarily, a few tables. Implementation in a testing environment and subsequent tests show that the system achieves its intended purpose, while being easy-to-use, responsive, and secure. Future studies may be done on implementing a potentially more efficient object database in order to create a more flexible system. Also, while initial testing seems to indicate success and potential release as an alpha version, further testing should be done in a production environment to allow for stress tests to be placed on the system. The current design and implementation seems to be an ideal solution for organizations wishing to minimize administrative development time for event form creation for unique events by allowing event coordinators to more easily manage their own content.

7 References

[1] Bruegge, Bernd, and Alleng H. Dutoit. Object-Oriented Software Engineering: Using UML, Patterns, and Java. Upper Saddle River: Prentice Hall, 2004. Print.

[2] Burget, Brenda. "Method and system for dynamically generating web forms in a variety of languages." U.S. Patent No. 6,557,005. 29 Apr. 2003.

[3] Ginige, A., & Murugesan, S. (2001). Web engineering: An Introduction to Multimedia, IEEE, 8(1), 14-18.

[4] Kirkpatrick, Mark A., Wendy Jennings, and Mauricio Lopez. "Method, System, and Apparatus for Presenting Forms and Publishing Form Data." U.S. Patent No. 7,469,270. 23 Dec. 2008.

[5] Ravishankar, Geetha, et al. "Application server configured for dynamically generating web forms based on extensible markup language documents and retrieved subscriber data." U.S. Patent No. 7,346,840. 18 Mar. 2008.

[6] Nielsen, J., & Hackos, J. T. (1993). Usability engineering (Vol. 125184069). San Diego: Academic press.

Software Reuse: The State Of Art

Abdullah A. Al-Baity[1], Kanaan Faisal[2], and Moataz Ahmed[3]
Faculty of and Computer Science, King Fahd University of Petroleum and Minerals (KFUPM), Dhahran, Saudi Arabia

Abstract - *this paper surveys the different approaches to software reuse found in the research literature. It describes and compares the different approaches and makes generalizations about the field of software reuse.*

In this survey we will present the definitions of software reuse and will demonstrate the cases where software reuse are valuable. Then, the different approaches of software reuse are mentioned with an examination of the effectiveness of each approach. Subsequently, the advantages and disadvantages of each approach are presented. After that, we will study the difficulty of implementing a software reuse process. Finally, the open areas of research in this field are highlighted.

Keywords: Software Reuse, Architecture, COTS, Design Patterns, Requirement, and Product Line

1 Introduction

This paper will make a breadth survey about the different approaches of software reusability.

Let us start with the basic definitions. We have two different terms related with Software Reusability Development.

1.1 Software Development with Reuse: Software development with reuse is the use of existing software or software knowledge to construct new software. Reusable assets can be either reusable software or software knowledge. In this survey we will focus on this part of reuse the software development with reuse [1].

1.2 Software Development for Reuse: Software Development for Reuse is a process of producing potentially reusable components. We know clearly the difficulties that are faced when trying to reuse a component that is not designed for reuse. The process of developing potentially reusable components depends solely on defining their characteristics such as language features and domain abstractions [2].

However, both terms are overlapped related to the whole Reuse process.

Reusability is a property of a software asset that indicates its probability of reuse. Software reuse's purpose is to improve software quality and productivity. Reusability is one of the major software quality factors. Software reuse is of interest because people want to build systems that are bigger and more complex, more reliable, less expensive and that are delivered on time [1].

1.3 Software Reuse Benefits [3]:

• *Increased dependability:* Reused software, that has been tried and tested in working systems, should be more dependable than new software.

• *Reduces Process Risks:* If software exists, there is less uncertainty in the costs of reusing that software than in the costs of development. This is an important factor for project management as it reduces the margin of error in project cost estimation.

• *Effective use of specialists:* Instead of application specialists doing the use of specialists same work on different projects, these specialists can develop reusable software that encapsulate their knowledge.

• *Standards compliance:* Some standards, such as user interface standards, can be implemented as a set of standard reusable components. For example, if menus in a user interfaces are implemented using reusable components, all applications present the same menu formats to users.

• *Accelerated development:* Bringing a system to market as early as possible is often more important than overall development costs. Reusing software can speed up system production because both development and validation time should be reduced.

1.4 Software Reuse Problems [4]:

• *Increased maintenance costs:* If the source code of a reused software system or component is not available then maintenance costs may be increased as the reused elements of the system may become increasingly incompatible with system changes. Lack of tool support CASE toolsets may not support development with reuse.

• *Not-invented-here syndrome:* Some software engineers sometimes prefer to re-write components as they believe that they can improve on the reusable component. This is partly to do with trust and partly to do with the fact that writing original software is seen as more challenging than reusing other people's software.

• *Creating and maintaining a component library:* Populating a reusable component library and ensuring the software developers can use this library can be expensive. Our current techniques for classifying, cataloguing and retrieving software components are immature.

• *Finding, understanding and adapting reusable components*: Software components have to be discovered in a library, understood and, sometimes, adapted to work in a new environment. Engineers must be reasonably confident of finding a component in the library before they will make routinely include a component search as part of their normal development process.

1.4 Software Reuse Activity [4]: The reuse activity is divided into six major steps performed at each phase in preparation for the next phase. These steps are:

Studying the problem and available solutions to the problem and developing a reuse plan or strategy; Identifying a solution structure for the problem following the reuse plan; reconfiguring the solution structure to improve reuse at the next phase; acquiring, instantiating, and/or modifying existing reusable components; integrating the reused and any newly developed components into the products for the phase, and evaluating the products.

2. Software Product Line (SPL):

The study of software product lines addresses the issues of engineering software system families, or collections of similar software systems. The objective of a software product line is to reduce the overall engineering effort required to produce a collection of similar systems by capitalizing on the commonality among the systems and by formally managing the variation among the systems. This is a classic software reuse problem [5].

2.1 Basic Software Product Line Concepts [6]:

Software product lines can be described in terms of four simple concepts, as illustrated in the figure below:

Software asset inputs: a collection of software assets – such as requirements, source code components, test cases, architecture, and documentation – that can be configured and composed in different ways to create all of the products in a product line. Each of the assets has a well-defined role within a common architecture for the product line. To accommodate variation among the products, some of the assets may be optional and some of the assets may have internal variation points that can be configured in different ways to provide different behavior.

Decision model and product decisions: The decision model describes optional and variable features for the products in the product line. Each product in the product line is uniquely defined by its product decisions - choices for each of the optional and variable features in the decision model.

Production mechanism and process: the means for composing and configuring products from the software asset inputs. Product decisions are used during production to determine which software asset inputs to use and how to configure the variation points within those assets.

Software product outputs: the collection of all products that can be produced for the product line. The scope of the product line is determined by the set of software product outputs that can be produced from the software assets and decision model.

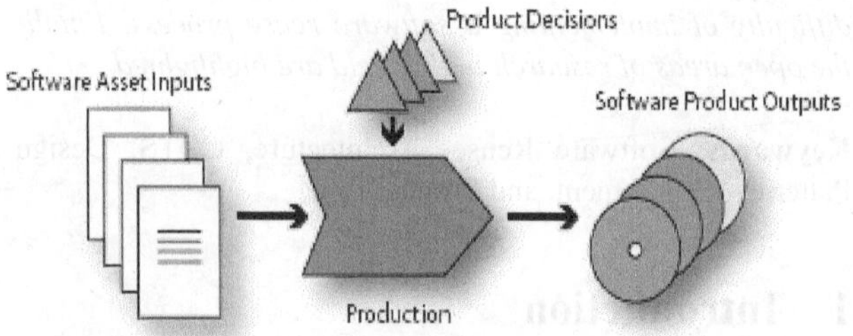

Figure 1: Basic Software Product Line Concepts

2.2 Software Product Line Challenges:

However, the predominant challenges, in most software product lines, are:

a) The management of variability required to facilitate the product differences. This is due to the fact that industrial software product lines can easily incorporate thousands of variable features and configuration parameters for product customization. Managing this amount of variability is extremely complex. One of the reasons for this high complexity is that, due to continuous evolution of the product line, a large number of new variable features and configuration parameters are introduced but at the same time obsolete variability is not removed. This increasing complexity results in a combinatorial explosion of variants [7].

b) With single systems, software engineers can maintain a single point of view throughout the development process (i.e., focused on the implementation of the single system). In contrast, with software product lines, software engineers must take different points of view at different times in order to effectively develop the software family[5].

However, there are several tools exist for support Software Product Line development and maintaining such as ConExp, sunifdef and DMS [5].

3 Commercial of the Shelf (COTS):

A commercial-off-the-shelf (COTS) product is a software system that can be adapted to the needs of different customers without changing the source code of the system [3].

When a software system is developed around a COTS product[8], it is called a "COTS-solution system." If a system includes a large proportion of COTS products it is called "COTS- intensive systems ", "COTS-integrated systems"[2], or "COTS-aggregate systems" [9].However, the term "a COTS-based system" is generally used for all purposes [8].

3.1 COTS-Solution System:

A COTS-solution system is a single product or suite of products, usually from a single vendor, that can be tailored to provide the system's functionality. Vendors offer such solutions if a consistent and well-bounded range of end-user needs exists throughout a broad community, justifying the vendors' costs for developing the products or suites of products.

Significant tailoring is required to set up and use these products, and the ability and willingness of an organization to understand and adopt the processes supported by the products are often key factors in success or failure. COTS-solution systems are commonly found in such well-established domains as personnel management, financial management, manufacturing, payroll, and human resources. Typical software vendors in this area include PeopleSoft, Oracle, and SAP.

COTS-Solution Systems usually require extensive configuration to adapt them to the requirements of each organization where they are installed. Once the configuration settings are completed, a COTS-solution system is then ready for testing. Testing is a major problem when systems are configured rather than programmed using a conventional language [9].

3.2 COTS-Integrated Systems:

COTS-aggregate systems are systems in which many disparate products (from different and sometimes competing vendors) are integrated to provide a system's functionality. Such systems are created if operational procedures are sufficiently unique to preclude the possibility of a single

COTS product solution, if the constituent technologies are immature, if the scale of the system is large enough to encompass several domains, or simply because different products provide distinct pieces of functionality to form the complete system. Systems with these characteristics include software support environments, large information systems, and command-and-control systems. Often, the COTS products and other components are combined in ways or to degrees that are unprecedented [3].

3.2.1 Challenges of COTS-Integrated System:

While adapting these components we did not care to identify whether the causes of our problems were with the functionality of the COTS products, their architecture, or in fact the functionality or architecture we desired, so it is somewhat difficult to button-hole the problems easily. [10].

3.3 Main Processes for Evaluation and Selecting COTS Software [11]:

Based on previous studies, several processes for evaluating and selecting COTS software are shared by existing methods for COTS software selecting. These processes can be ordered as iteratively, sequentially, or overlapping. However, the common processes for evaluating and selecting COTS software can be classified in terms of four general processes.

Supporting Process : This process consists of set of activities that support other processes of the valuation and selection. This process begins with planning for an evaluation and selection COTS software; the tasks that might be completed during this activity include forming the evaluation and selection team (e.g. technical experts, domain experts, end users, etc.), identifying stakeholders (e.g. integrators, (funding customers, business owners, etc.), define the goals and objectives, etc .Documentation is also performed during this process.

Preparation Process: The main purpose of this process is to collect and prepare the information that required for further detail evaluation.

Evaluation Process: This process plays a vital role to determine how well each of the COTS software alternatives achieves the evaluation criteria.

Selecting Process: The outputs of the evaluation process are several kinds of data such as facts, checklists, weights, opinions. Those kinds of data should be consolidated and interpreted into information.

3.4 COTS Products Problems [8]

Incompatibility: COTS component may not have the exact functionality required; moreover, a COTS product may not be compatible with in-house software or other COTS products; *Inflexibility:* usually the source code of COTS software is not provided, so it cannot be modified; *Complexity:* COTS products can be too complex to learn and to use imposing significant additional effort; *Transience:* Different versions of the same COTS product may not be compatible, causing more problems for developers.

4. Software Requirement Reuse

Much of the effort of building complex software systems goes into understanding, specifying, and validating system requirements. For mission- and safety critical systems, requirements errors represent a major source of development problems. Prior work in product-line engineering has shown that we can substantially increase productivity while decreasing errors by systematically re-using (rather than re-creating) the work products for families of systems where system requirements are sufficiently similar. Embedded software for commercial product lines like printers, mobile phones, or flight-control systems are typically families in this sense [12].

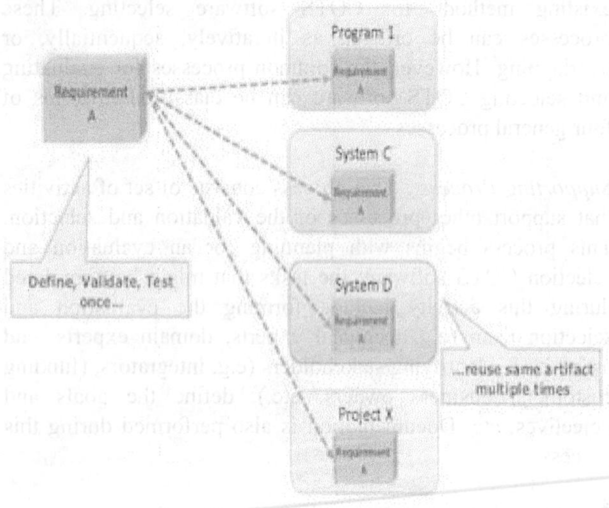

Figure 2: implementation of Requirements Reuse.

The systematic requirements reuse to develop software requires two specific actions. First, to define the adequate way to model and to store specifications in the phase of development for reuse. Second, to define a process to compare and to adapt the reusable requirements in the phase of software development with reuse [13].

4.1 Requirement Representation for Reuse

The best and the common classification and retrieval techniques show limited utility in representing requirements for reuse. Some different alternatives based on knowledge representation, analogical reasoning to reuse the requirements from a knowledge base has been proposed are based on meta-models, evolutionary development and formal methods all of which emphasize the process for development and maintenance the reusable requirements [13].

4.2 Comparing and Adapting Requirement

Comparing and adapting requirements means that it should be established an equivalence relation between requirements models and the sufficient condition to determine the similarity between the requirements models, and it should be established a process to compare requirements so that it supports software. One technique is to reuse domain descriptions and task specifications. And the other is to apply techniques based on artificial intelligence to support the structural and semantic matching when retrieving requirements [13].

4.1 Benefits of Requirement Reuse

Requirements need not be re-Validated with stakeholders repeatedly; ensure consistency of requirements & business rules within organization or Program; test Cases/Test coverage is already available and can be reused; reduce requirements work for subsequent uses.

However, the main obstacle reported for adopting requirements reuse is poor quality of existing requirements. Having unstructured, incomplete, outdate existing requirements makes it difficult to reuse them going forward. Developing techniques to analyze the inventory of and refactor existing requirements can help practitioners better adopt and benefit from reuse.

5. Code Reuse

In computer science and software engineering, reusability is the likelihood a segment of source code that can be used again to add new functionalities with slight or no modification. Reusable modules and classes reduce implementation time, increase the likelihood that prior testing and use has eliminated bugs and localizes code modifications when a change in implementation is required.

The evolution of programming languages is tightly coupled with reuse in two important ways. First, programming languages have evolved to allow developers to use ever larger grained programming constructs, from ones and zeroes to assembly statements, subroutines, modules, classes, frameworks, etc. Second, programming languages have evolved to be closer to human language, more domain focused, and therefore easier to use. Languages such as Visual C++, Delphi, and Visual Basic clearly show the influence of software reuse research [1].

To reduce programming effort and shorten time-to-market, programmers can find and reuse existing solutions for their prototypes. Source code search engines have been developed to locate implementations that are highly-relevant to a feature specified by a programmer (e.g., via a natural-language query). Existing search engines often return packages that match only a small subset of the desired features, and developers have to invest considerable effort to integrate features from several different packages and projects. Under these circumstances, the cost and effort required for a programmer to comprehend and integrate the returned source code can significantly reduce the benefits of reuse [14].

But, code, which is executed from other developer, has a problem hard to understand and reuse because of missing and insufficient document, the existing system developer's absence. And that code causes decline in performance. It also needs much time and costs in order to solve these problems [15].

5.1 Code Reuse Benefits [16]

Reusing code saves programming time, which reduces costs. Sharing code can help prevent bugs by reducing the amount of total code that needs to be written to perform a set of tasks. Relatedly, separating code into specialized libraries lets each be tuned for performance, security, and special cases. Delegation of tasks into shared modules allows offloading of some functionality onto separate systems. Proper and efficient reuse of code can help avoid code bloat. Bloated code contains unnecessary duplication and unused instructions.

5.1 Code Reuse Drawbacks [16]

There are other potential drawbacks to code reuse, often very dependent on the situation and implementation:

5.1.1 Performance might become a factor:

Depending on the platform and programming language, a library or framework might perform slower than desired. In some situations it might be beneficial to build a specialized one-time solution instead of using a common library. APIs accessed over a network will sometimes be slower than solving a problem within the local system. The system of modularity itself might create a bottleneck. For example, extra process initialization or shared library management can create overhead.

5.1.2 Loss of control over 3rd party solutions might have negative repercussions.

For example, there might be lack of support, desired feature enhancements might not get added, or security might not be fully tested. Outside the technical considerations, there might also be licensing and liability issues. When not well implemented or when taken too far, code reuse can eventually cause code bloat. Ironically, adding modularity can eventually lead to lingering APIs and libraries which go unused. In very large systems it's not uncommon to lose track of how every component is used. Over time a component my become useless, but linger in the system. This, however, is not so much an inherent drawback of code reuse as it's a problem of implementation.

6. Design Reuse

Broadly speaking, design reuse appears promising for at least three reasons. First, since designs address early phases of system development, many of the up-front (and hence most costly) errors can be avoided. Second, reuse of familiar designs can improve the understand ability of a system, making it easier to evolve and maintain. Third, design reuse promotes code reuse: often much of the infrastructure to support a design can be shared among applications that share that design.

It is perhaps not surprising then, that some of the more impressive examples of reuse today involve a strong component of design reuse. Prominent examples include specialized frameworks such as user interface toolkits, application generators (such as Visual Basic), domain specific software architectures, and object-oriented patterns [17].

6.1 Framework Reuse

A software framework is an abstraction in which software providing generic functionality can be selectively changed by user code [clarify], thus providing application specific software. A software framework is a universal, reusable software platform used to develop applications, products and solutions. Software frameworks include support programs, compilers, code libraries, an application programming interface (API) and tool sets that bring together all the different components to enable development of a project or solution [18].

6.1.1 Framework Reuse Benefits [18]

Application frameworks offer a variety of advantages:

Using code which has already been built, tested, and used by other programmers increases reliability and reduces programming time. Software development teams can be split between those who program the framework and those who program the final complete application. This separation of tasks lets each team focus on more specific goals and use their individual strengths. Frameworks can provide security features which are often required for a common class of applications. This provides every application written with the framework to benefit from the added security without the extra time and cost of developing it. By handling "lower level" tasks frameworks can assist with code modularity. Frameworks often help enforce platform-specific best practices and rules. Frameworks can assist in programming to design patterns and general best practices. Upgrades to a framework can enhance application functionality without extra programming by the final application developer.

6.1.1 Framework Reuse Drawbacks [18]

There can be negative consequences to using a framework:

Performance can sometimes degrade when common code is used. This sometimes occurs when a framework must check for the various scenarios in which it is used to determine a path of action. Frameworks often require a significant education to use efficiently and correctly (i.e. some have a high learning curve). Functionality which needs to bypass or work around deficiencies in a framework can cause more programming issues than developing the full functionality in the first place. Bugs and security issues in a framework can affect every application using that framework. Therefore it must be tested and patched separately or in addition to the final software product.

6.2 Architecture Reuse [17]

The other broad area of related work is software design reuse, a topic that is receiving increasing attention from researchers and practitioners in areas such as module interface languages, domain-specific architectures, software reuse, codification of organizational patterns for software, architectural description languages, formal underpinnings for architectural design, and architectural design environments. Collectively these efforts are attempting to establish an engineering basis for architectural design, and make principles and techniques of architectural design more widely accessible.

6.2.1 Software Architecture and Architecture Styles [17]

An architectural style provides a specialized architectural design vocabulary for a family of systems, and typically incorporates a number of idiomatic uses of that vocabulary and design rules for system composition. From the point of view of a designer, architectural style is important for several reasons:

It limits the design space, thereby simplifying design choices. It allows a designer to exploit recurring patterns of organization, such as topological configurations, , or even specific organizations of components (such as the MVC pattern in object-oriented systems). It provides a context within which certain kinds of design integrity can be enforced, such as the fact that no cycles are allowed. It permits specialized analyses such as detection of deadlock. And finally, as we detail in the next section, it provides a basis for supporting reuse of architectural building blocks and patterns.

6.3 Design Patterns

A design pattern is a general reusable solution to a commonly occurring problem within a given context in software design. A design pattern is not a finished design that can be transformed directly into source or machine code. It is a description or template for how to solve a problem that can be used in many different situations. Patterns are formalized best practices that the programmer must implement themselves in the application. Object-oriented design patterns typically show relationships and interactions between classes or objects, without specifying the final application classes or objects that are involved. Many patterns imply object-orientation or more generally mutable state, and so may not be as applicable in functional programming languages, in which data is immutable or treated as such.

6.3.1 Design Patterns Goals:

• To support reuse of successful designs, to facilitate software evolution (add new features easily, without breaking existing ones), in short, we want to design for change.

6.3.2 Types of Design Patterns

Creational Patterns: To create objects rather than developer instantiate it.

Structural Patterns: to compose group of objects in larger structures.

Behavioral Patterns: To defines communication & flow between objects.

7. Conclusions

From the 1960s to the 1990s, most new software was developed from scratch, by writing all code in a high-level programming language. The only significant reuse or software was the reuse of functions and objects in programming language libraries. However, costs and schedule pressure meant that this approach became increasingly unviable, especially for commercial and Internet-based systems. Software reuse is possible at a number of different levels:

1. The abstraction level: At this level, you don't reuse software directly but rather use knowledge of successful abstractions in the design of your software. Design patterns and architectural patterns are ways of representing abstract knowledge for reuse.

2. The object level: At this level, you directly reuse objects from a library rather than writing the code yourself. To implement this type of reuse, you have to find appropriate libraries and discover if the objects and methods offer the functionality that you need. For example, if you need to process mail messages in a Java program, you may use objects and methods from a JavaMail library.

3. The component level: Components are collections of objects and object classes that operate together to provide related functions and services. You often have to adapt and extend the component by adding some code of your own. An example of component-level reuse is where you build your user interface using a framework. This is a set of general object classes that implement event handling, display management, etc. You add connections to the data to be displayed and write code to define specific display details such as screen layout and colors.

4. The system level: At this level, you reuse entire application systems. This usually involves some kind of configuration of these systems. This may be done by adding and modifying code (if you are reusing a software product line) or by using the system's own configuration interface. Most commercial systems are now built in this way where generic COTS (commercial off-the-shelf) systems are adapted and reused. Sometimes this approach may involve reusing several different systems and integrating these to create a new system. By reusing existing software, you can develop new systems more quickly, with fewer development risks and also lower costs. As the reused software has been tested in other applications, it should be more reliable than new software.

However, there are costs associated with reuse:

1. The costs of the time spent in looking for software to reuse and assessing whether or not it meets your needs. You may have to test the software to make sure that it will work in your environment, especially if this is different from its development environment. *2.* Where applicable, the costs of buying the reusable software. For large off-the shelf systems, these costs can be very high. *3.* The costs of adapting and configuring the reusable software components or systems to reflect the requirements of the system that you are developing. *4.* The costs of integrating reusable software elements with each other (if you are using software from different sources) and with the new code that you have developed. Integrating reusable software from different providers can be difficult and expensive because the providers may make conflicting assumptions about how their respective software will be reused.

How to reuse existing knowledge and software should be the first thing you should think about when starting a software development project. You should consider the possibilities of reuse before designing the software in detail, as you may wish to adapt your design to reuse existing software assets.

8. References

[1] William B. Frakes and Kyo Kang, "Software Reuse Research: Status and Future", IEEE TRANSACTIONS ON SOFTWARE ENGINEERING, VOL. 31, NO. 7, JULY 2005.

[2] Muthu Ramachandran School of Computing Leeds Metropolitan University " Software Reuse Guidelines", ACM SIGSOFT Software Engineering Notes Homepage archive volume 30 Issue 3, May 2005.

[3] Sommerville, Ian , "Software engineering / Ian Sommerville". — 9th ed.

[4] Dr. Parvinder S. Sandhu, Aashima and Priyanka Kakkar, Shilpa Sharma, "A Survey on Software Reusability" International Conference on Mechanical and Electrical Technology (ICMET 2010).

[5] Charles W. Krueger , "Software Product Line Reuse in Practice" , Conference 2000 IEEE.

[6] http://www.softwareproductlines.com.

[7] Felix Loesch and Erhard Ploedereder "Optimization of Variability in Software Product Lines" , 11th International Software Product Line Conference 2007 IEEE.

[8] Daniil Yakimovich, "A COMPREHENSIVE REUSE MODEL FOR COTS SOFTWARE PRODUCTS",University of Maryland, College Park, 2001.

[9] *Santiago Comella-Dorda, John Dean, Grace Lewis, Edwin Morris, Patricia Oberndorf, and Erin Harper, "A Process for COTS Software Product Evaluation", TECHNICAL REPORT CMU/SEI-2003-TR-017 ESC-TR-2003-017.*

[10] David Wile, Robert Balzer, Neil Goldman, Alexander Egyed, Marcelo Tallis and Tim Hollebeek, "Adapting COTS Products The Fine Line between Development and Maintenance", 26th IEEE International Conference on Software Maintenance in Timişoara.

[11] Feras Tarawneh, Fauziah Baharom, Jamaiah Hj. Yahaya, and Faudziah Ahmad, "Evaluation and Selection COTS Software Process: The State of the Art", International Journal on New Computer Architectures and Their Applications (IJNCAA) 1(2): 344-357 The Society of Digital Information and Wireless Communications, 2011 (ISSN: 2220-9085)..

[12] Oscar L´opez Villegas and Miguel A´ ngel Laguna, "Requirements Reuse for Software Development", University of Valladolid, Technological Institute of Costa Rica 2002.

[13] Stuart R. Faulk , "Product-Line Requirements Specification (PRS): an Approach and Case Study", Conference 2001 IEEE.

[14] Collin McMillan, Negar Hariri, Denys Poshyvanyk, and Jane Cleland-Huang, "Recommending Source Code for Use in Rapid Software Prototypes", Conference Publications 2012 IEEE.

[15] Jong-Ho Lee, Nam-Yong Lee,and Sung-Yul Rhew , "OBJECT-ORIENTED REFACTORNG PROCESS DESIGN FOR THE SOFTWARE REUSE",Conference Publications 2001 IEEE.

[16] http://docforge.com/wiki/Code_reuse.

[17] Monroe, Robert T. and Garlan, David, "Style-Based Reuse for Software Architectures" ",Conference Publications *Tepper School of Business.* (1996).

[18] http://docforge.com/wiki/Framework.

[19] Erich Gamma, Richard Helm, Ralph Johnson and John Vlissides " Design Patterns: Elements of Reusable Object-Oriented Software techniques".

Empirical Validate C&K Suite for Predict Fault-Proneness of Object-Oriented Classes Developed Using Fuzzy Logic.

Mohammad Amro[1], **Moataz Ahmed**[1], **Kanaan Faisal**[2]

[1]Information and Computer Science Department, King Fahd University of Petroleum and Minerals, Dhahran, Saudi Arabia

Abstract Empirical validation of software metrics suites to predict fault proneness in object-oriented (OO) components is essential to ensure their accuracy in practical industrial. In this paper, we empirically validate the Chidamber and Kemerer (CK) metrics suite metrics for their ability to predict software quality in terms of fault-proneness: we explore the ability of these metrics suites to predict fault-prone classes using defect data for six versions of Rhino, an open-source implementation of JavaScript written in Java. We conclude that the C&K suite contain similar components and produce statistical models that are effective in detecting error-prone classes. Analyzing Fuzzy Logic models across six Rhino versions indicates these models may be useful in assessing quality in OO classes produced using modern highly iterative or agile software development processes.

Keywords- fault-prone; fuzzy logic; software quality; prediction model

1 Introduction

Several Object-Oriented metrics have been developed by researchers to help evaluate software design quality [1-3] . While a measure may be correct from a theoretical perspective, it may not be of practical use in software industrial[4, 5]. Metrics may be difficult to collect or may not really measure the intended quality properties of software. Empirical validation is necessary to determine the usefulness of a metric in assessing open source software quality. Open source tools are becoming ever more important for the user these days. Many companies are using this kind of software in their own work. Therefore, many of these projects are being developed rapidly and are quickly becoming very large. However, because open source software is usually produced by volunteers, and the development approach employed is quite different from the usual methods applied in commercial software development especially for level of testing, the quality and reliability of the code needs to be investigated. Various kinds of code measurements can be quite helpful in obtaining information about the quality and fault-proneness of the code.

In this paper, we describe how we calculated and validated the object-oriented metrics suite given by Chidamber and Kemerer [3] for fault-proneness detection from the source code of the open source Mozilla Rhino JavaScript written in Java[6].

2 Chidamber and Kemerer's (CK) Metrics

Chidamber and Kemerer originally defined the CK metrics suite in 1991. In 1994, they published another paper containing revised definitions of some of the metrics [3]. In this research, all CK metrics are selected to be validated its ability to predict the fault, in total CK suite continue six metrics which describe in Table 1.

TABLE 1: CK SUITE METRICES [3, 7]

Metric	*Description*
DIT	Depth of Inheritance Tree (DIT) it measure the general classes, which are expected to be reused by other classes, are usually at a high level in the inheritance hierarchy.
WMC	Weighted Methods per Class Number of Methods per Class is a measure of software size, and hence an indicator of complexity
RFC	Response for Class is a measure of coupling. It counts the number of methods that are immediately available to and potentially used by a class.
CBO	Coupling Between Objects (CBO) is a measure of coupling, counting the number of other classes to which a class is coupled. A class A is said to be coupled to another class B, if class A accesses methods or variables defined by class B. large CBO value often indicates a high degree of dependency on other classes
LCOM	Lack of Cohesion of Methods
NOCL	Number of Children is measure the complexity of an inheritance hierarchy .It counts the number of immediate subclasses derived from the current class.

3 Experimental Evaluations

3.1 Datasets:

We chose the Mozilla Rhino project to examine in this study because it was a real open source project and because of the availability of fault data for several versions of the project, Rhino is an open source implementation of JavaScript. The development team of Rhino consists of three programmers. All in separate locations delivering the java implementation with a varying cycle time from two to 16 months. In this study, we analyzed 14R3, 15R1, 15R2, 15R3, 15R4, and 15R5. Error data exists for Rhino in the online Bugzilla website[8]. We Collect the Rhino fault data form a published work done by *Hector M et al[5]*. Figure 1 shows the statistic for selected Rhino versions that had been investigate during the study.

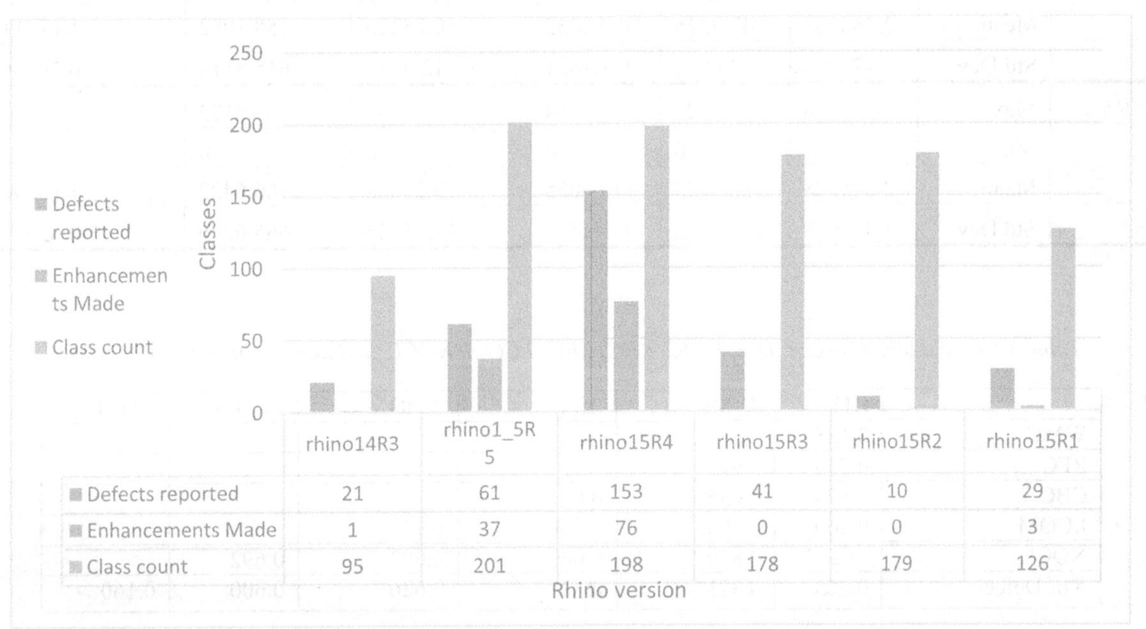

	rhino14R3	rhino1_5R5	rhino15R4	rhino15R3	rhino15R2	rhino15R1
Defects reported	21	61	153	41	10	29
Enhancements Made	1	37	76	0	0	3
Class count	95	201	198	178	179	126

Figure 1: Defects reported and enhancements made per Rhino version.

Table 2 shows the descriptive CK metrics statistics for the Rhino datasets which extracted by using commercial tool named METAMATA.

Table 2: THE DESCRIPTIVE STATSTICS FOR THE DATASETS

version	Statistics	DIT	WMC	RFC	CBO	LCOM	NOCL
14R3	Max	6	464	165	59	2681	2
	Min	1	0	0	0	0	1
	Mean	2.506494	109.4805	26.66234	10.22078	115.3377	1.012987
	StdDev	1.154207	123.0208	33.43517	11.28182	420.9545	0.113961
15R1	Max	6	688	202	65	3305	3
	Min	1	0	0	0	0	1
	Mean	2.578431	122.6765	28.87255	10.89216	112.8627	1.019608
	StdDev	1.120787	140.9371	37.09919	11.98424	460.8304	0.19803
15R2	Max	7	732	203	69	4126	3
	Min	1	0	0	0	0	1
	Mean	2.779817	139.7064	29.23853	10.21101	141.2477	1.027523
	Std Dev	1.480477	167.6788	38.70709	12.13128	546.7883	0.213382
15R3	Max	7	730	206	76	4524	3
	Min	1	0	0	0	0	1
	Mean	2.841121	144.1402	29.96262	10.4486	152.1308	1.065421
	Std Dev	1.486731	169.6414	40.12408	12.59697	594.096	0.315362
15R4	Max	7	764	205	77	4951	3
	Min	1	0	0	0	0	1
	Mean	2.756757	147.5225	30.32432	10.25225	158.1982	1.117117
	Std Dev	1.472266	173.6812	41.31831	12.5274	615.8118	0.398605
15R5	Max	6	922	214	67	5172	6
	Min	1	0	0	0	0	1
	Mean	2.825688	156.1193	31.66055	10.25688	166.6422	1.155963
	Std Dev	1.470979	181.4662	41.41484	11.65746	665.6276	0.626192

Table 3:Correlations between: DIT, WMC, RFC, CBO, LCOM, NOCL, and number of Defects reported

	DIT	WMC	RFC	CBO	LCOM	NOCL
WMC	0.188					
RFC	0.349	0.941				
CBO	0.829	0.535	0.671			
LCOM	0.460	0.904	0.838	0.757		
NOCL	-0.267	0.859	0.667	0.093	0.692	
# of Defects	0.325	0.371	0.328	0.626	0.600	0.160

In order to get most relevant independent variables to the dependent variable, we used Pearson's Correlation Coefficients (PCC), indicates the strength and direction of a linear relationship between two variables. Table 3 shows the PCC between number of Defects and each of the CK metrics. From the table, there is a significant correlation between number of Defects and the CK metrics. Table 3 shows that, there highly correlations between CBO, LCOM and WMC metrics and number of Defects.

3.2 Prediction Accuracy Measures

The term prediction accuracy in this paper means how well a predictive model constructed using known data can predict the outcomes of unknown data. This paper evaluates and compares the Rhino software Fault-Proneness prediction models quantitatively, using the described below prediction accuracy measures. For all the used measures the lower the error measure, the better is the performance.

- Root-mean-square error (*RMSE*) shows differences between values predicted by a model and the values actually observed from the thing being modeled.

$$RMSE = \sqrt{\frac{\sum_{i=1}^{n}(f(x_i) - y_i)^2}{n}} \quad (1)$$

- Normalized root-mean-square error (*NRMSE*): to normalize the RMSE to the range of the observed data.

$$NRMSE = \frac{RMSE}{f(x)_{\max} - f(x)_{\min}} \quad (2)$$

- MRE is a normalized measure of the discrepancy between actual values and predicted values.

$$MRE = \frac{|y - f(x)|}{y} \quad (3)$$

- Mean magnitude of relative error (*MMRE*) :

$$MMRE = \frac{1}{n}\sum_{i=1}^{n} MRE_i \quad (4)$$

4 Result and Discussion

This section describes the experiments conducted in our study. In the conducted experiments, we training the model using one time all CK metrics and other with only high correlated metrics CBO, LCOM and WMC. We repeated the experiment more than one time to produce reliable results. Figure 2 and 3 show the result for two error measures (NRMSE, MMRE) for fuzzy Mamdani model.

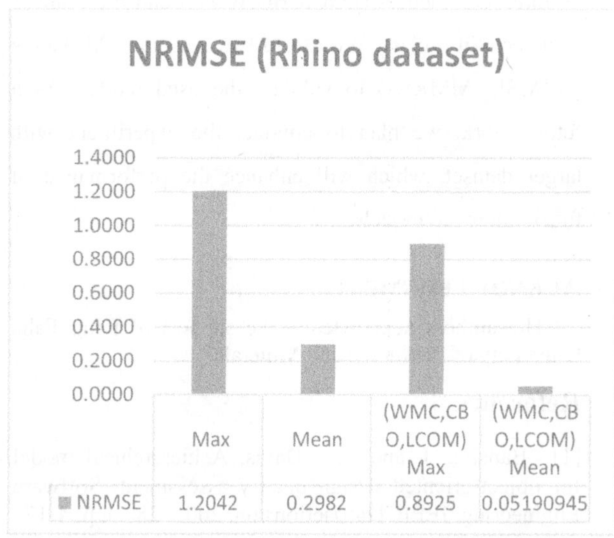

Figure 2: NRMSE error measures using Mamdani model

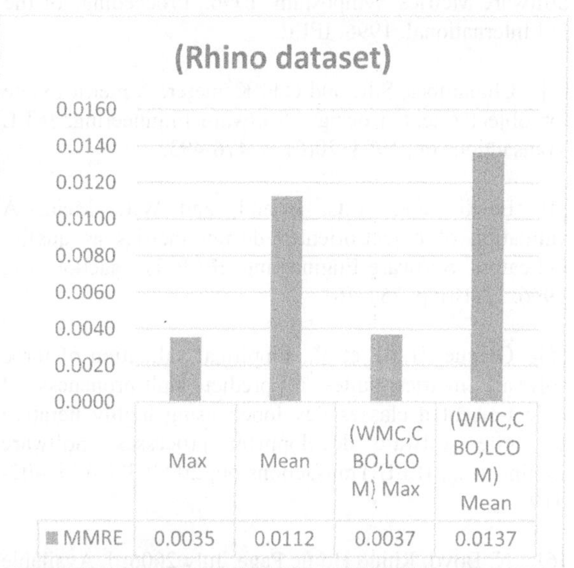

Figure 3: MMRE error measures using Mamdani model

5 Conclusion and Future Work

In this paper, we conducted the experiments to evaluate the performance of the fuzzy inference systems models to predict Fault-Proneness of Object-Oriented Classes Developed Using CK metrics. As shown in table 3, there is significant correlation between the measure provided by three CK metrics (LOC,CBO,WMC) and the number of defects in a class. We use to two Accuracy Measures (NRMSE ,MMRE) to validate the used model. As a future work, we plan to conduct the experiment with larger dataset, which will enhance the performance of fuzzy inference models.

ACKNOWLEDGMENT

The authors acknowledge the support of King Fahd University of Petroleum and Minerals.

Reference

[1] Bansiya, J. and C.G. Davis, A hierarchical model for object-oriented design quality assessment. Software Engineering, IEEE Transactions on, 2002. 28(1): p. 4-17.

[2] Brito e Abreu, F. and W. Melo. Evaluating the impact of object-oriented design on software quality. in Software Metrics Symposium, 1996., Proceedings of the 3rd International. 1996. IEEE.

[3] Chidamber, S.R. and C.F. Kemerer, A metrics suite for object oriented design. Software Engineering, IEEE Transactions on, 1994. 20(6): p. 476-493.

[4] Basili, V.R., L.C. Briand, and W.L. Melo, A validation of object-oriented design metrics as quality indicators. Software Engineering, IEEE Transactions on, 1996. 22(10): p. 751-761.

[5] Olague, H.M., et al., Empirical validation of three software metrics suites to predict fault-proneness of object-oriented classes developed using highly iterative or agile software development processes. Software Engineering, IEEE Transactions on, 2007. 33(6): p. 402-419.

[6] N. Boyd. Rhino Home Page. July 2006;]. Available from: http://www.mozilla.org/rhino/.

[7] Yu, P., T. Systa, and H. Muller. Predicting fault-proneness using OO metrics. An industrial case study. in Software Maintenance and Reengineering, 2002. Proceedings. Sixth European Conference on. 2002. IEEE.

[8] Database, B. Mozilla Foundation. July 2004; Available from: https://bugzilla.mozilla.org/.

Template Generation in a Tiered Architecture

Practical C# class templates from DDL statements

James duPuis, Daniel Riehl, Roger Lee
Department of Computer Science
Central Michigan University
Mount Pleasant, MI, USA
{dupui1jp, riehl1dl, lee1ry}@cmich.edu

***Abstract*— Business applications are often written as tiered applications with tiers dedicated to presentation, business logic, and data access. Much research has been done to show the benefits of structuring applications with tiered abstractions, but this process often means developers spend considerable time creating similar abstractions for different business and data objects. In this paper, we present an application that preforms automated code generation by parsing T-SQL DDL statements to create stored procedures and C# .NET data access classes, and classes to mimic business logic templates. Our research showed that by using this application some of the mundane tasks programmers who write multi-tiered applications face could be automated.**

Keywords—tiered architecture; three tiered architecture

I. Introduction

Applications driven by relational database management systems have become ubiquitous in today's society. These applications cover a range presentation options from web interfaces to mobile applications. Perhaps even more diverse than the presentation of data is the range of domains that these applications are used in. Everything from healthcare records, call detail, to social media relies on storing data in a relational database. Software engineers who design and maintain these applications are faced with the same challenge, selecting an architecture model to map the persistent data from the application to a database and vice versa. This research attempts to automate coding of templates for database centric applications using a custom application named tier-gen.

II. Background

Engineers have many models to refer to when selecting architectures to map objects to a RDBMS. Choices range from spaghetti code to tiered architectures to automation tools such as object-relational mapping (ORM) such as Microsoft's ADO.NET Entity Framework or rapid application development (RAD) tools such Iron Speed.

A. N-Tier Architecture

In an n-tiered, or multi-tiered, architecture the applications logic is split into distinct and separate layers. These systems gained popularity as client server architectures became pervasive in the 90s [1]. Each layer encapsulates a set of functionality, possibly calls to some persistent storage mechanism, or UI. Often the terms layer and tier are used interchangeably [1]. Layers have no knowledge of the adjacent layers, with the exception of the calls placed between them [2] [1]. Layering or tiers are a very common method to deal with complex systems in computing. In the same way the specific methods can break down large programs logic into smaller more comprehensible components, layering can break down an application's logic into simpler modules [1].

Perhaps the most common example of layers in computing is the OSI reference model describing communication over a network. The OSI model defines 7 layers which abstract different services for network communication include: application semantics, reliable or effective data transfer, routing, and electrical signaling [3]. This reference model was popularized due to its ability to break up the intricate requirements of network communication into simpler to manager layers.

Besides simplifying a complex system, tiered architectures provide other benefits. Black box abstraction is a tangible benefit. For example, a developer can create a new application protocol without any more than a rudimentary knowledge about network routing or electrical signaling. Similarly, the layers can be maintained and deployed separately [1]. Regressing to the previous example, if while creating a protocol a developer discovered a bug in his device TCP implementation, it is possible that the bug could be fixed without adversely affecting the services running adjacent OSI layers.

Layered implementations are not without their shortcomings. There are times when a change to one layer cascades throughout all layers who consume its services. This is a classical problem with tiered applications and databases. If a database is changed to include another column, each layer that deals with that particular table must be changed. Additionally, each layer will have a performance impact as it deals with its abstraction [1]. The overhead of the abstraction has the potential to surpass any benefits provided.

B. Three Tier Architecture

Three tiered architectures became very popular towards the end of the 20th century [2]. The rise of the web fueled organizations to migrate their client server applications to web applications. This amounted to a new user interface but the same business logic. This coincided with explosive growth of object oriented programming languages such as Java and Microsoft's .NET framework [1].

The three tied architectural defines three layers: data access, business logic, and presentation [2]. These tiers can also be referred to as data source, domain, and presentation [1]. The organizations who had implemented a three tiered architecture in their client server applications were able to use the same business logic and data access layers with a new presentation layer for their web pages. Those without the abstractions had to retool their applications, sometimes from the ground up.

The data access layer is responsible for storing data in persistent storage, typically a RDBMS. Messaging systems and transaction monitors can also appear in this layer, but are less common [1]. The business objects are responsible for implementing an organizations policies and procedures. Examples include validation of input from the presentation layer or performing calculations. The presentation layer is responsible for presenting the information the end user in a pleasant manner [2].

A purely implemented three tiered architecture should only allow communication between adjacent tiers. This guideline is not often followed closely in reality [1]. Consider a web interface (presentation layer) that lists the unfiltered entries from a table (data access layer). There is little use for a business access layer here, with the exception of preforming any calculations based on persistent values, or simply providing a common internal representation between the presentation and data access interfaces. In cases similar to this, it is possible for the presentation layer to make a direct call to the data access layer.

How the different layers are programmatically represented can vary depending on the complexity of the project and design choices. It is possible that the different layers are represented by methods, but in object oriented code, it is more likely to see them as separate classes, or even packages [1].

III. OBJECTIVES OF REASEARCH

Our research aims to automate part of the development process by generating general purpose templates. These templates are indented to provide broad CRUD operations.

The process of creating templates for business objects is often quite repetitive. Typically when mapping a relational table to an object, each column with become a property, or possibly a private member with public set and get methods, depending on the preferred coding style. There are also common database calls, it is almost assured that an application will view, modify, and add records to particular tables within a database. Assuming the persistent storage is a RDBMS and the tables were created before other coding was started, it is possible that an algorithm could produce code templates representing the tables. This is often the case with a three tiered design, that the database and data access are designed first [2]. Both templates for business objects and rudimentary data access could be generated. The business object template could mimic the table by providing properties for the columns. The data access template could generate basic CRUD stored procedures to interact with the database as well as calls to the procedures that use the business objects as parameters.

The more explicit the DDL design is the more information can be gleaned from it for template generation. Consider different column attributes, there are attributes to define keys to enforce referential integrity, uniqueness, allow unknown values, or default values. This data can all be read by an application able to parse the input and then generate templates taking it into account. Uniform templates can provide many advantages.

Depending on implementation, code reuse is inherent to a tiered architecture [1]. Consider the business needs of a banking organization. It is possible that the bank designs their systems for mobile customer access, ATM access, and access via web interface. These applications all must perform similar tasks, authenticating users, checking balances, and recording transactions. It is possible that these applications could share common modules providing access to mutual business and data access layers. The by changing the user interface the code can take on a completely new form. When a new technology ultimately supplants web and mobile applications, the bank's developers need do nothing more than retool the presentation layer. Similarly, when code is modified in the business logic layer, it might be possible to replace that module across all applications with little distribution or affect to the other layers.

IV. METHODS – TIER-GEN

Tier-gen is an application written in C# that attempts to transform Transact-SQL (T-SQL) DDL, specifically CREATE TABLE statement's into templates for a tiered architecture. Executing the application will run the user through a series of simple questions including: path to DDL script, connection string parameters, what namespace output should be generated in, and lastly the output type. There are two options for output, just to generate C# classes, or to also generate a class library DLL. The rough outline of the programs logic follows these four steps: parse user input, create stored procedures and GRANT EXECUTE statements for table access and manipulation, create C# data access classes to call the stored procedures, create C# business objects to represent the tables, and finally create a base classes and generic abstractions. The base classes and abstractions always generated are displayed in Figure 1.

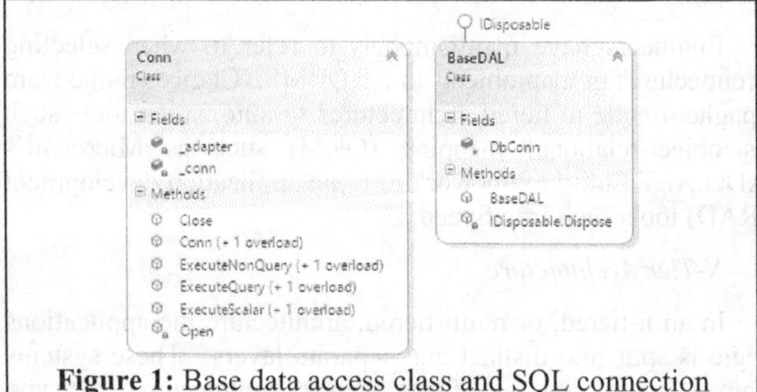

Figure 1: Base data access class and SQL connection abstraction

A. Parsing DDL

The input script may contain a variety of T-SQL statements, however, only CREATE TABLE statements will be processed others are discarded. Since only create statements are parsed, not all column attributes are if they are passed as subsequent ALTER TABLE statements. That is, in figure 2, the two samples would result in different output from tier-gen.

```
/* Sample 1 */
CREATE TABLE Foo
(
        Bar INT NOT NULL IDENTITY,
        Val         CHAR(1) NOT NULL
)

ALTER TABLE Foo
ADD CONSTRAINT FooPk PRIMARY KEY (Bar)

/* Sample 2 */
CREATE TABLE Foo
(
        Bar INT NOT NULL IDENTITY PRIMARY KEY,
        Val         CHAR(1) NOT NULL
)
```

Figure 2: Example SQL DDL statements

For all practical purposes, the two samples will result in the same structure. However, as tier-gen parses the script, the ALTER TABLE statement is discarded.

Microsoft's .Net framework provides an SQL parser that was used for this process. The ScriptDom and ScriptDom.Sql objects inside the Microsoft.Data.Schema namespace were taken advantage of. This greatly simplified the process of analyzing user input.

B. Output

The code for two objects is always generated as shown in Figure 1. The class Conn is an abstraction that all data access objects make use of. This class holds the connection string. This is the only object in the project that actually integrates with the database. The second object is BaseDAL with is the class that all data access classes will derive.

1) SQL Script

Part of tier-gen's output is in the form of an SQL script. Five stored procedures are generated for each table in the input. The following lists each procedures function: return all tuples in the table, return one tuple based on a primary key, insert a tuple, delete a tuple based on its primary key, and to update a tuple based on its primary key. Before each CREATE PROCEDURE statement is a check that will drop any existing procedures with the computed name. One of the parameters tier-gen prompts the user for is the username to use in the connection string. This allows tier-gen to not only embed a connection string, but generate GRANT EXECUTE after each procedure. This has the potential to simplify the developer or DBA's job by providing explicit security settings for the user account, or roll based access. That is, the user defined in the connection string does not need the ability to delete, drop or even select from a table, only execute a stored procedure.

2) C# Classes

For each table in the input, two C# classes are generated. The two classes will be named the table name followed by DAL and the table name followed by BLL, for the data access and business logic respectively.

The business logic is a shell that represents a single tuple in the associated table. Each column is represented by two parts, a private member and a public property. The SQL data types are mapped to compatible data types in C#. Different column attributes are taken into consideration such as if the column allows nulls. If the column is nullable, then the data type selected must allow nulls. With reference types, such as strings, allowing null values is implicitly handled since null is a valid state for a variable. With value types such as integer, long and decimal this is not the case. An integer in C#, or other value type, can never have the value null. However, a nullable integer, or int? is a valid data type that allows the null value. If a length was defined for a variable, such as a VARCHAR, the setter for the corresponding property will perform a check to verify that the value is within the bounds of the field. If the value is outside the bounds an ArgumentOutOfRangeException is thrown.

Two constructors for each business object are built. The first is an empty default constructor waiting for information to be added to it. The second constructor takes one parameter, a DataRow from the System.Data namespace. It indexes the DataRow by column name, assigning values to all the member variables which are publicly accessible through the properties.

The data access files provide methods that make the parameterized queries to the stored procedure. The UPDATE, DELETE, and INSERT calls all accept a business object as a parameter, and call the procedure using the data from the business object. There are two SELECT methods made available by the class, one to return a single object based on the tables primary key, and a second that would return a collection of business objects representing all rows in that table.

Tier-gen is auto documenting. As the C# code is generated, tier-gen does its best to use XML documentation to explain the classes, methods, properties and members generated. Since the applications output is C#, it is assumed that the developers will be using some flavor of Visual Studio. XML documentation integrates with Visual Studio to provide IntelliSense integration [4]. This should aid developers who are familiar with the SQL schema, but unfamiliar with tier-gens output get started with a project.

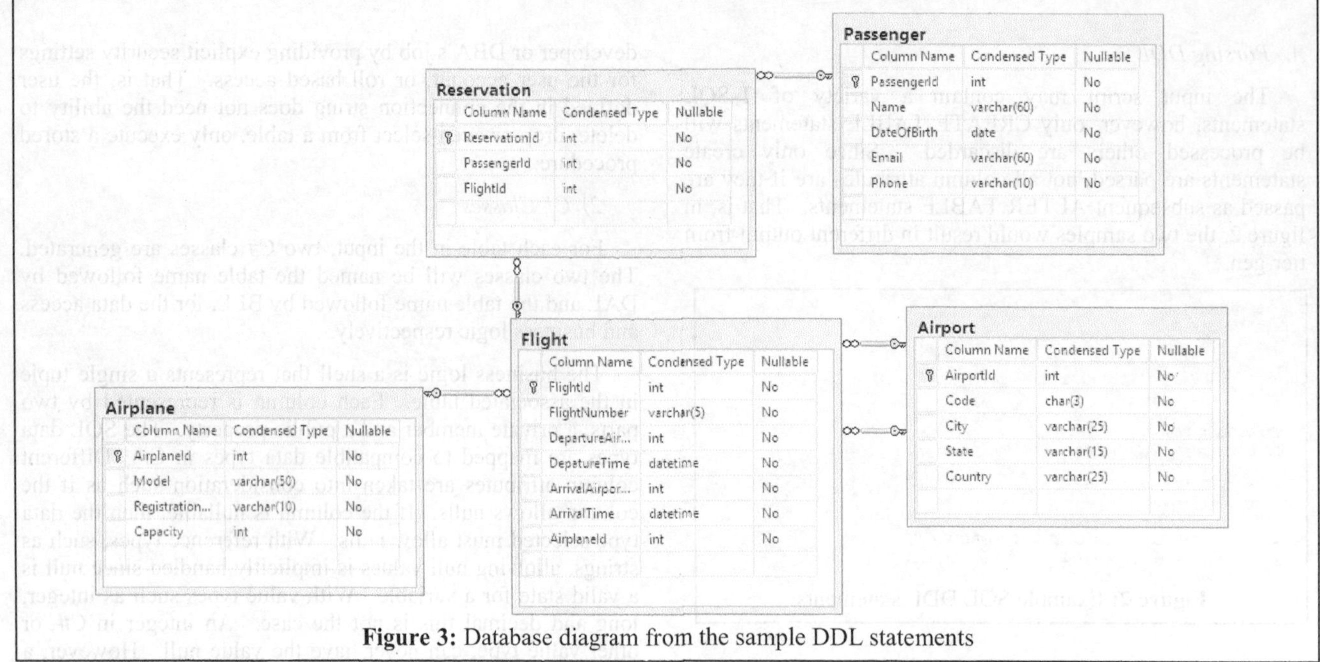

Figure 3: Database diagram from the sample DDL statements

3) *Class Library*

In addition to generating the C# libraries, the application can also generate a dynamic-link library or DLL. The DLL is the compiled C# classes. While this option does produce working code there are notable drawbacks. When the classes are compiled, the business logic layer is in effect sealed. It is very unlikely that this layer should be sealed without modifications, after all, this is where an organization or projects custom business rules are supposed to be implemented. However, it's possible this feature could be useful for extremely simple applications or proof of concept templates.

Another reason a DLL is given as an output option is to make the developer considers building a class library, instead of directly embedding the class files in a project. There are scenarios where multiple applications will use the same database. For example, it is possible a mobile application will need many of the same features as a web application, connecting to the same database and same business rules. In this case it might be possible to build a DLL contains these database calls and business objects, effectively creating an abstraction for both applications to use.

As the parser analyzes input, results are stored internally in two object types; one class represents a SQL table and the other a column. The table data type contains a collection of columns. Each column has properties such as its name, SQL data type, the corresponding C# data type, if it is part of a primary key, if it is an identity field, if it allows nulls, and its length, if applicable. For primitive C# data types such as integers and decimals, when tier-gen converts the SQL data type to a C# data type, it checks some of these properties such as whether or not the field is nullable to select the correct data type. That is, column defined as "VALUE INT NULL" in a DDL statement should not be represented as an "int" in C#, but an "int?" indicating that the value accepts null. This is not needed for none primitive types such as strings, which will accept null values by default.

V. Results of Research

Instead of analyzing the output by reviewing the code produced by tier-gen, we decided to review how useful the output was to make a simple sample application. This seemed to be the most effective analysis the application, trial by fire. If the programs output does not prove to decrease development time with an academic application, it seems to reason that it real world value would be very limited at best.

A. *Airplane Reservation System*

For test data a simplistic five table airplane reservation system was used. The five entities provided included: airplane, airport, passenger, flight, and reservation. Figure 3 provides an abbreviated database diagram to show relationships between the tables.

All tables used in the sample schema include the identity column attributes which is SQL Server's auto numbering mechanism [6]. While some of these columns might have natural primary keys, such as RegistraionNumber in the Airplane table, the use of identities is a simple way of forcing the DBMS to maintain the unique row identifier [6]. While this is not always the case, identities are used very frequently. Researchers from Singapore and China evaluated nine PHP and MySQL applications finding that 89.47% of tables made use of MySQL's AUTO_INCREMENT column attribute, which is that DBMS' auto numbering mechanism [5].

1) *Preforming CRUD Operations*

The .NET framework provides many features that allow developers to make use of the output of tier-gen without further extending it. Figure 4 provides an overview of the class diagrams for the two classes generated to represent and access the Airplane table. Recall that one object is generated to represent the Airplane business object, AirplaneBLL and another to represent the data access, AirplaneDAL. AirplaneBLL has public members and properties for each of the columns in the table. The class also has a default constructor that is overloaded to also accept a DataRow object to populate the object's members. The data access class is derived from the BaseDAL class. It provides the same five methods all DAL classes provide, to return a single AirplaneBLL based on a primary key (Get), to return all AirplaneBLL objects (GetAll), to insert a AirplaneBLL object (Add), to delete a AirplaneBLL object (Remove), and to modify a AirplaneBLL object (Update).

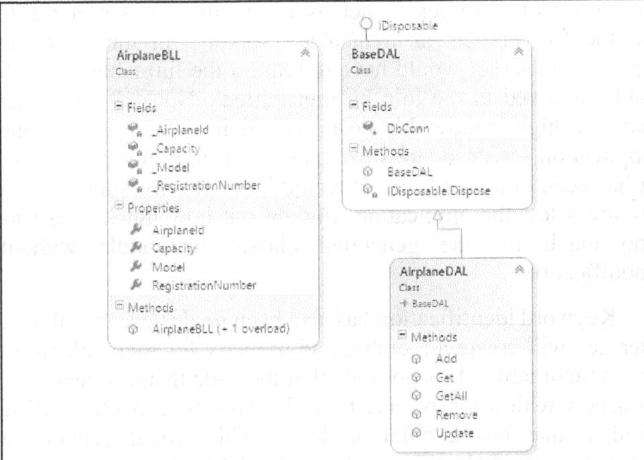

Figure 4: Example class diagrams for the AirplaneBLL and AirplaneDAL objects.

The .NET framework makes using the default methods and objects very simple. As mentioned earlier, it is not unlikely for a presentation layer call to reach the data access layer. In ASP.NET, one of Microsoft's web application frameworks, the task is trivial, requiring only two controls, an ObjectDataSource to point the application and the method call, and a GridView or similar graphical control to display the results. Figure 5 demonstrates a working example, both code and the output, after adding the generated code to an application.

```
<asp:GridView runat="server" ID="airplanegridview"
DataSourceID="AirplaneObjectDataSource" />
<asp:ObjectDataSource ID="AirplaneObjectDataSource" runat="server"
TypeName="Test.AirplaneDAL" SelectMethod="GetAll">
</asp:ObjectDataSource>
```

AirplaneId	Model	RegistrationNumber	Capacity
4	Boeing 747	B4799	200
5	Boeing 727	B2709	200
6	Cessna 525	CA452	12

Figure 5: Code and example view from sample database.

Using the operations to update, delete, and insert data require more code, but are still simple operations. Consider adding a new airplane, this requires creating an AirplaneBLL object, populating its properties and then passing it to AirplaneDAL to be inserted into the database. Ignoring the presentation layer controls, and assuming the method in figure 6 is fired after user input to the presentation controls has completed, the code in figure 6 is able to perform this task.

```
/// <summary>
/// User wants to add an airplane
/// </summary>
protected void AddPlane_Click(object sender, EventArgs e)
{
    var plane = new Test.AirplaneBLL() {
        Capacity = Convert.ToInt32(CapacityTextBox.Text),
        Model = ModelTextBox.Text,
        RegistrationNumber = RegistrationNumberTextBox.Text
    };
    using (var db = new Test.AirplaneDAL())
        db.Add(plane);
}
```

Figure 6: Code sample populating an AirplaneBLL and passing it to the AirplaneDAL class

2) *Complex Joins*

The CRUD operations performed by the generated code are straight forward and simple to understand. However, applications are rarely limited to such simple operations and data displays. Consider the following tasks in SQL: filtering a data set with a where clause, merging multiple data sets with the JOIN keyword, viewing distinct values, and preforming aggregate calculations. Listing how to perform an object version of a corresponding SQL query is beyond the scope of this document, but a simple example illustrating should illustrate some of the possibilities. For the example consider the following SQL query:

```
SELECT  AD.Code, DepatureTime, AA.Code, ArrivalTime, Name, Email,
DateOfBirth, Phone
FROM    Flight AS F
INNER JOIN Reservation AS R ON F.FlightId = R.FlightId
INNER JOIN Passenger AS P ON R.PassengerId = P.PassengerId
INNER JOIN Airport AS AD ON F.ArrivalAirportId = AD.AirportId
INNER JOIN Airport AS AA ON F.ArrivalAirportId = AA.AirportId
INNER JOIN Airplane AS A ON F.AirplaneId = A.AirplaneId
WHERE   FlightNumber = @value
```

Figure 7: Sample SQL JOIN for the sample schema

The query is preforming joins across each table in the database, using the airport table twice for destination and departure airports. Selection is used to limit the columns returned in the results. Finally @value is used to signify that the flight number is a variable that filters what flight's roster is shown. The same results can be retrieved from the tier-gen output, without modification. Starting with version 3.5 of Microsoft's .NET Framework, the Language Integrated Query or LINQ was included. One of LINQ's many features is preforming SQL like query expressions on enumerable datasets. The example in figure 8 demonstrates how a developer could produce a similar output as the previous figure, without modifying tier-gen's output.

VI. Evaluation and Limitation of Templates

There is a great deal of work that could be done experimenting with DDL statements with non-auto numbering primary keys, foreign keys, and also tables without primary keys. tier-gen targets applications with identity fields as the primary key, the usefulness of the templates was not evaluated with natural primary keys. Additionally, experimentation was not done on tables without primary keys, it is likely that these tables would not produce useful, or even possibly useable code.

The easy way out was taken with foreign key enforcement as well, leaving the enforcement to the DBMS to handle. While this is a valid solution, it could be worked into the business logic as well. That is, a setter in a business object that represents a foreign key could check to verify that the primary key exits.

```
var results =
from f in (new FlightDAL()).GetAll()
join r in (new ReservationDAL()).GetAll() on f.FlightId equals
r.FlightId
join p in (new PassengerDAL()).GetAll() on r.PassengerId equals
p.PassengerId
join ad in (new AirportDAL()).GetAll() on f.DepartureAirportId equals
ad.AirportId
join aa in (new AirportDAL()).GetAll() on f.ArrivalAirportId equals
aa.AirportId
join a in (new AirplaneDAL()).GetAll() on f.AirplaneId equals
a.AirplaneId
where f.FlightNumber == SearchTextBox.Text
select new
{
    Leaving = ad.Code,
    DepartureTime = f.DepatureTime,
    Arriving = aa.Code,
    ArrivalTime = f.ArrivalTime,
    Name = p.Name,
    Email = p.Email,
    DOB = p.DateOfBirth,
    Phone = p.Phone
};
```

Figure 8: Example of using LINQ to preform SQL like queries on tier-gen's enumerable datasets.

Researching other methods of handling foreign keys does not end at referential integrity. In the sample application, the business class representing Reservation contained three values, all integers, even though two values were foreign keys, one representing a flight, the other representing a passenger. While this is the most straightforward method to automate these classes, it might not be the most useful output for the developer to consume. For example, the ReservationBLL object tier-gen generated could include an integer to represent its own primary key, and then replace the other two integers with a PassengerBLL and FlightBLL objects.

Recall tier-gen's input and part of its output is T-SQL, a SQL extension language that is proprietary to Microsoft SQL Server. No provisions are made for handling other SQL extensions such as PL-SQL. The output SQL script contains CREATE PROCEDURE statements that are untested with other RDMSs other than Microsoft SQL. Many organizations expect applications to be portable from one platform to another, despite the fact that this is a rare occurrence [1]. There are multiple options to solve this problem, everything from writing a custom SQL parser, to integrating with an open source or commercial .NET SQL parser, both which are readily available. Some of the open source libraries available for SQL parsing require extensive grammars to be written, which is on reason they were not used during implementation.

The scalability of the application is concerning, especially if the DAL templates are not expanded and the DLL is used. Consider SQL joins. It is possible to produce results similar to joins using collection of the business objects and Microsoft LINQ.

There are further concerns about the applications scalability. In the sample applications used to test tier-gen has one characteristic in common, they dealt with small datasets. In the real world this is often impractical. It is likely that out of the box the DLL produced by tier-gen would perform extremely poorly with large dataset. The main reason the application would scale so poorly can be seen in the sample applications example using LINQ. This example requires all the data in each table to be pulled to the device the application is running from. Consider a web application where it is common for a server to act as an application server while another server acts as a database server. In this case the application server would have to request the full table for each table involved in the join be transmitted. Not only does this have a high bandwidth cost and high CPU cost for the application server, it stops the database from preforming a task it has been optimized for. It would be worth investing time in to stress test the application, finding out how much data was too much for the generated classes to handle without modification.

Keyword identification has also been neglected. Recall that tier-gen will create a member and property for each column in in an input table. It is possible that the code that has generated conflicts with a C# reserved word. That is, consider a table student that has a column class. This would generate a property named class inside the studentBLL object, resulting in invalid code due to the conflict between the class property and the C# reserved word class.

VII. Conclusions and Further Study

There are many short comings that tier-gen suffers from as outlined in the previous example. Additionally, further research should be done in both the areas of foreign key representation, natural primary keys, and large datasets. The project is Microsoft centric. The application must be run on a Microsoft operating system with particular libraries, in addition to those provided by default in .Net, for the SQL parsing. If during the code conversion process a table or column is named with a C# reserved word, the output code will not compile and a DLL will not be generated.

Tier-gen is not a complete project, and is far from being ready to work on large scale systems. A full evaluation of the usefulness of these templates would likely span a semester. More time and effort is needed to implement other features and to test which design tradeoffs. However, tier-gen did provide a simple framework for working with small applications. The following aspects would be interesting to further investigate:

- Can this technique be used with architectures other than a multi-tiered architecture?
- Is it possible to address the shortcomings listed in the templates evaluation?

References

[1] Fowler, M. (2003). *Patterns of Enterprise Application Architecture*. Addison-Wesley Professional

[2] Anderson, E. B. (1998). The Tracks of My Tiers. *ENT*, vol. 3 iss. 3, pp. 22.

[3] Day, J. (1983). The OSI reference model. *Proceedings of the IEEE*, vol. 71. Iss 12, 1334-1340.

[4] Randolph, N. David, G. Anderson, C. Minutillo, M. (2010). *Professional Visual Stuido 2010*. Wiley

[5] Zhang, H., Tan, H., Zhang, L., Lin, X., Wang, X., Zhang, C., Mei, H., (2011). Checking enforcement of integrity constraints in database applications based on code patterns. *Journal of Systems and Software*, vol 84, iss 12, 2253-2264

[6] Ben-Gan, I. (2005). Should I use identity or not? Sometimes another approach works better. *SQL Server Magazine*, vol 7, iss 12, 30

The Proposal of Smart Phone Camera Application Which Realize a Person's Super Deformation

Hideaki Hashimoto , Takayuki Fujimoto
Graduate School of Engineering, Toyo University
Kujirai2100, Kawagoe-City, Saitama, Japan
s36d01210025@toyo.jp, me@fujimotokyo.com

Abstract – *Today, Japanese animation is a digital contents which represents Japan, and it become worldwide that me really proud of. Also, Print Club (Purikura), the picture-taking machine which you could add some hand drawing or grafttii, and "unique effect camera app" become really popular in Japan. So we know there are some market of add-effect picture. In this paper, we propose the camera app which makes two heads high picture of person as a effect. By this system, you could take two heads high picture pretty easy without using any special systems.*

Keywords: Smart phone, Camera application, Image processing, Super deformation,

1 Introduction

In resent years, Japanese anime and the word "Kawaii" Really pointed out as culture. Because of this, we changed our mind anime for entertainment and we really proud as Japanese representative culture. Popularity of anime have the factor of not only by interesting story. The other factor is the Super deform character, chibi chara. Chibi chara iis tow heads high character and it really influenced to anime. Also, "Print Club", the picture-taking machine which you could draw some grafitti, and adding-effect apps become popular because you could make any effect on your picture. In addition, because of SNS become really popular, users wanted to use their picture as icon, but they don't want some one realize who is the person in the picture. We know there is amarket. In this paper, we propose the camera apps which make two head high character picture by adding deform effect to your picture. By this system, you could easily make Cibi chara picture by only using one camera apps.

2 Purpose

Purpose for this paper is propose of camera apps which you could easily make two head high picture by only taking a picture. It is not difficult system as exist image treatment applications. It is a smart phone apps.

3 Background

3.1 What is Chibi chara

Chibi chara is the character which drawed by Super deform and usually two heads high. Japanese animator, Gen Sato, said Chibi chara is shrinked to twenty-four heads high by exaggerated expression. In general, people thinks SD series (BANDAI) is the beginning Gundam, the giaut machine anime, was maded for realistic figures so they couldn't develop market except realistic figures and DVDs. However they put Gundam into Doraemon, humor two head high anime, and it success because Doraemon spread support from 5th graders or up to kids or up. Cute two head high characters also spred support from teenager girls. Again, using of Chibi chara is not only for anime or comics. It appered in commercial, ar ads, for apply uses.

Figure 1. Chibi chara

Source : http://upload.wikimedia.org/wikipedia/commons/

Figure 2. SD (Super deform) Gundam

Source : http://userdisk.webry.biglobe.ne.jp

3.2 What is deform

Deform means transform realistic picture or paiintings to different touch drawings and shows you different expression. This word come from Freach, but this word doesn't have a mean simplify or exaggerate. Comics or anime, caricature, and recent arts are world wide expressing technique, but because of tequnique is incomplete, if the drawing doesn't balanced, it couldn't accept as deformed. Only intentionally works are called deform. Egypt's wall painting is good example. Compare to real human body, the paintings are ridiculous, but the paintings are intentionally. In the other hands, Pablo Picasso leave his deform painting.

3.3 What is Avatar

In computing, an avatar is the graphical representation of the user or the user's alter ego or character. It may take either a three-dimensional form, as in games or virtual worlds, or a two-dimensional form as an icon in Internet forums and other online communities. It can also refer to a text construct found on early systems such as MUDs. It is an object representing the user. The term "avatar" can also refer to the personality connected with the screen name, or handle, of an Internet user.

4 Mechanism of a system

4.1 Abstract of system

The mechanism of this system is explained in full detail below.

① A photographic subject is photoed in blaubok.

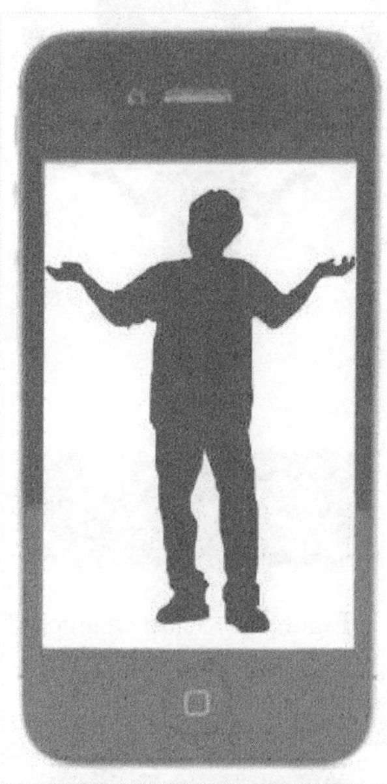

Figure 3. A photograph is taken by blaubok.

② The position of a photographic subject's neck is specified.

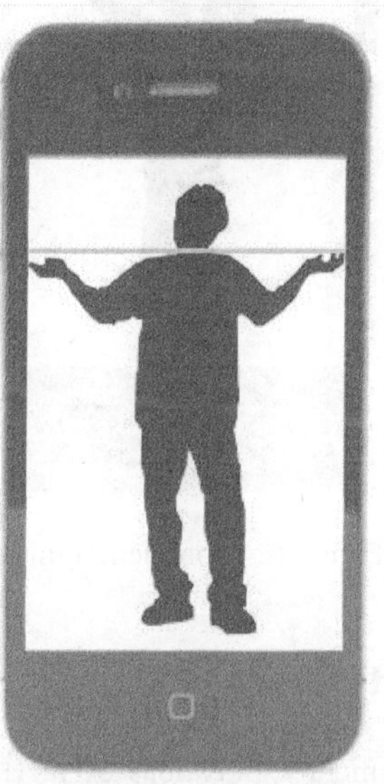

Figure 4. Position setup

③ A scale change of the ratio of the head and the body is made.

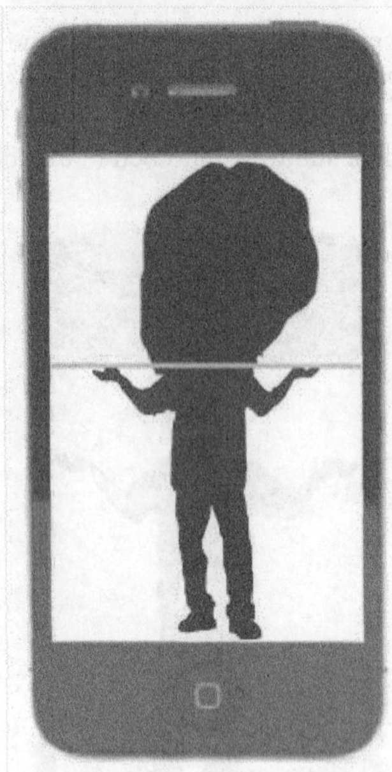

Figure 5. Scale change

④ Finished super deform character

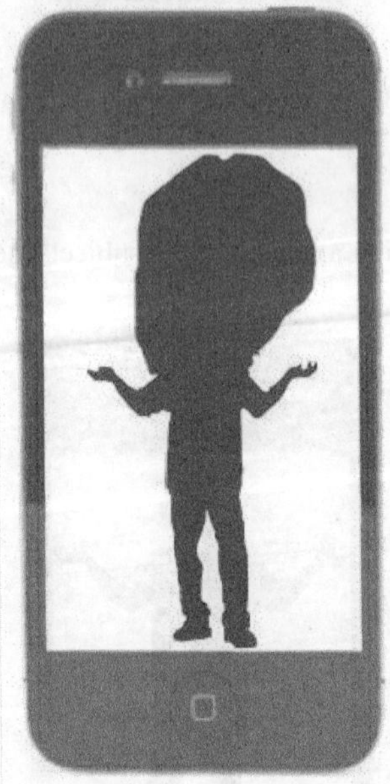

Figure 6. Completion image

4.2 Validity

Now, many camera applications exist. However, the most adds what changes a color tone, and a frame. This system divides a screen into two, the upper part and the lower part, and changes the magnification of size automatically for every area. The existing smart phone application does not exist but it can be said that this research is fresh. Moreover, since it is called smart phone application, a display cannot say that operation is easy in the small existing graphics editing application. Furthermore, since a smart phone is familiar and cheaper than a common computer, many younger age groups own. It can be said that this system by which a user with little knowledge of IT can also give super deformation processing of a person easily with feeling which uses a camera function also has validity.

5 Consideration

In this research, the person was photoed and the smart phone camera application which can be easily formed into an anime character (formation of the two-animal body) was proposed.

In the middle of development, for a certain reason, much more research and development will be furthered towards utilization from now on, and it is considered now that whether there is any sense of incongruity in the ratio after a feeling of use and processing would like to solve the problem which arose. In the existing smart phone camera application, there is nothing that the two-animal body makes form into an anime character the person who took a photograph, and it can be said that this system is fresh.

Moreover, unlike the existing graphics editing application, since it is automatic processing with camera application, everyone can do super deformation processing of a person easily. Therefore, it is thought that this research has validity and is in demand.

6 Associated research

As related application "HENGAO camera ", "Stretch Cam", a "comics camera", etc. exist. "although not passed, the camera " has the center line which divides the right and left of a screen, and it unites with the center of the face of the person who photos this line, and displays 2 par turn of the face which combined only the left-hand side of the face after photography, and the face which combined only right-hand side. Thereby, right-and-left asymmetry of man's face is made intelligible, and the difference in an impression is enjoyed. The step and the usage of photography are close to this system. After taking a photograph of "Stretch Cam" like fundamental camera application, it chooses the range of a photograph and makes every direction of a photograph expand and contract by pinch out [with a finger / pinch in and]. After a "comics camera" chooses the frame containing a comment, it can be photoed, and also it gives an effect to the taken photograph, and becomes a result like comics of Japan. Although such camera applications which process it like exist mostly, the application which carries out super deformation processing of the person like this research does not exist. And it can be said that this research is fresh. [making a person form into an anime character easily with smart phone camera application] [no one but / this / research]

7 Conclusion

In this research, research was advanced on the theme of "the proposal of smart phone camera application which realizes a person's super deformation (wearing out character-izing). Moreover, it is because it thought that the smart phone camera application with which there are many users using what SNS had spread in recent years and gave effect processing to the icon picture with an own portrait, a comics camera, etc., and they make a person form into an anime character was in demand.

8 References

[1] G. SATOU, "Chibi chara no egaki kata jinbutu hen", Graphics sya, 2003-8

[2] G. SATOU, "Chibi chara no egaki kata doubutu/mono hen", Graphics sya, 2003-8

[3] "Asahi key word, 1990-4, Asahi shinnbun sya

[4] Nikkei business, 1992-7-13, Nikkei BP sya

[5] K. OOTANI, R. KASHIWAZAKI, A.TAKAI, Y. TAKAI, "Anime ni okeru jinnbutu kao gazou no moe innshi tokutyou hyouka to kennsaku bunrui system" 'Eizou media', 113-118, 2010-2-15

An Interface Generator For Customizable Fuzzy Expert System

Tongjun Ruan, Robert Balch
Reservoir Evaluation and Advanced Computational Technologies Group
Petroleum Recovery Research Center of New Mexico Tech.
801 Leroy Pl, Socorro, New Mexico 87801

Abstract- *The Interface Generator is a tool which allows user to define an interface by input some information and generates the data input interface for defined fuzzy expert system. Testing shows that it can successfully accept and store interface definitions from users and dynamically generate the data input interface for defined fuzzy expert system.*

Key words: Interface Generator, Interface definition and Fuzzy Expert System

1. Introduction

REACT group started a new project in January, 2005 to create a user definable and customizable fuzzy expert system tool (CFES)[1] to dramatically speed local and regional play analysis and to reduce subsequent drilling risk. In the previous projects, Risk Reduction with Fuzzy Expert Exploration Tool (FEE Tool)[2,3], the users were only able to input the location information and information about the prospect, while all the rules, the fuzzy membership type used, the number of fuzzy sets, and so on have already been defined in the system and are not changeable to users. The goal of the new project is to develop a more customizable expert system, in which the users without computer science background will be able to define/adjust the system including the variables, the rules and the fuzzy sets used in the inference engine. Hence, the expert system will be more individualized and fit the needs of different users better.

In the customizable fuzzy expert system, since the user can define a new Fuzzy Expert System similar to FEE Tool and add or reduce or modify the variables of the system, the data input interface should be automatically changed to reflect the changed variables of the defined system. Interface Generator was designed to implement the functions.

2. System architecture

The Interface Generator consists of three major modules. They are storage module, question definition module and interface generation module. Below figure, figure 1, is the architecture for the interface generator.

The storage module includes binary file, binary input/output engine and question/group management sub-module. A binary file is utilized to store the definition of the interface. Binary I/O engine is a set of read and write procedures created to operate binary file to load or save question records. The question/group management groups the questions to groups. It also provides the functions to create, update and delete questions and groups.

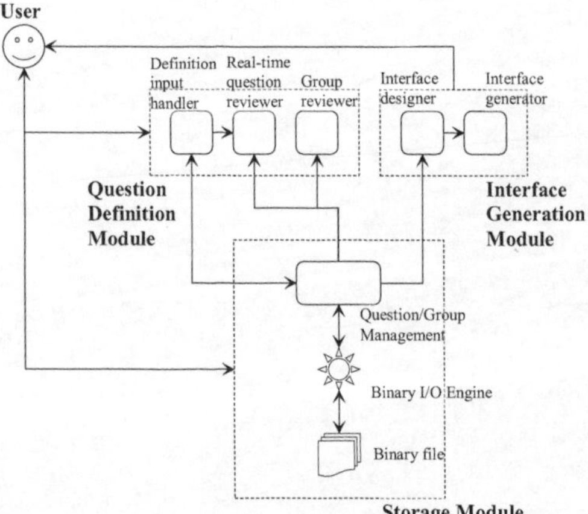

Figure 1. Three dish lined rectangles represent the three major modules of the system. The right table shows the corresponding source files for each module.

Question definition module accepts the inputs from users and provides the corresponding reviewers. Definition input handler sub-module handles the user inputs and sends the update message to real-time question reviewer sub-module, which adjusts the dynamic interface reviewer in real-time. To review a group interface, group reviewer sub-module is implemented.

Interface generation module creates the final interface by the information from question/group management sub-module. For each group, interface designer calculates the display heights of all questions. The accumulation of the heights is calculated to design how many pages are required to display all the questions in that group. Then the locations are calculated for all questions. Interface generator sub-module then creates the multiple tabs (an example is shown in figure 2), which contain all the questions in all groups.

3. Interface Definition

The graphic user interface could be very various. We focus on a 'question-answer' structure, which is used by the previous project (FEET).

The "question-answer" structure consists of following terms:

- Group----- a system may have several groups
- Step ------a group may have several steps
- Step title---question name
- question body---state the question
- variable name----user defined variable
- component type--------provide components (radio button, List and/or Numerical field, etc) to let user input the their answers
- unit --------------the unit of variable value, like "ft", " %", etc.

Fig. 2. shows FEET interface for data input. There are three groups: Trap, Formation and Regional assessments.

Question definition module visualizes the active question data from question/group management sub-module. It processes the user requirements and adjusts the dynamic interface reviewer in the real time. This module includes input process, real time question reviewer and group reviewer sub-modules.

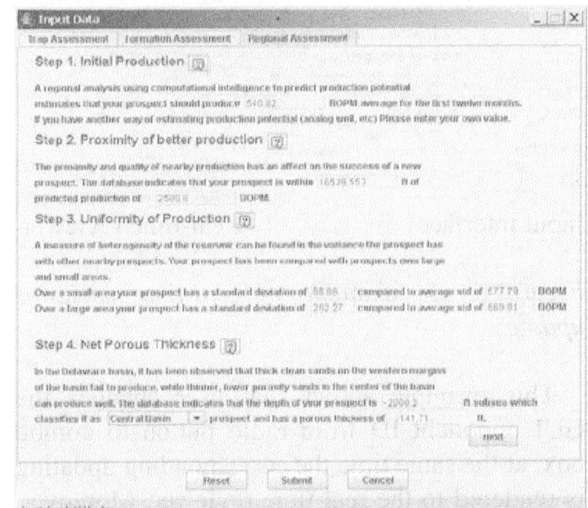

Figure 2. a 'question-answer' interface from FEET.

Input process sub-module accepts, validates the user inputs and creates a record data for the current active question. The inputs are question title, question description, unit, GUI component parameter and GUI component ID. The first three are the normal string inputs, which is collected from text fields or text area. The GUI component ID is collected from a combo box. Currently the system supports three types of answers for the question. They are :

1. text field,
2. radio button group
3. combo box.

GUI parameter is a comma separated string, which specifies the labels of GUI object.

This sub-module is also responsible for informing the real-time reviewer sub-module to update the reviewer based on the modification given by user. An example of real-time reviewer updating is shown in figure 3.

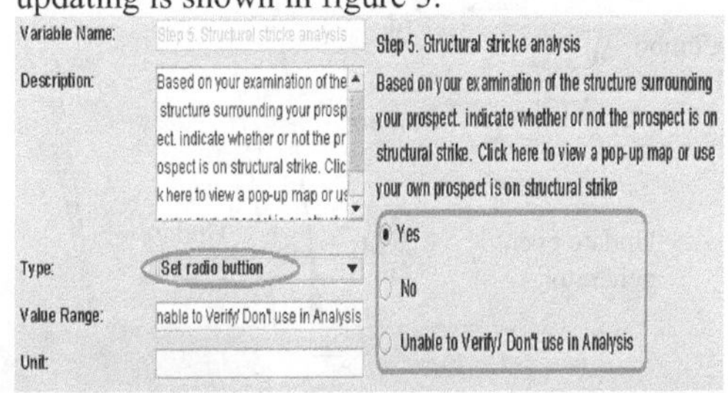

Input interface Real-time reviewer

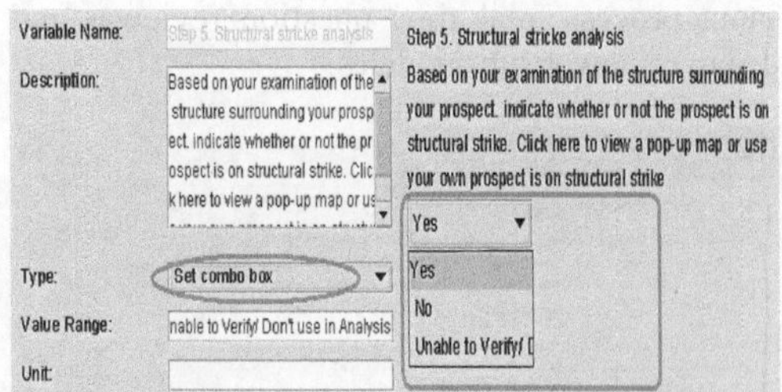

Input interface Real-time reviewer

Figure 3. An example of real-time reviewer update.

This example shows that user changes the GUI opponent ID from radio button to combo box, at the same time the corresponding updating is rendered to the real-time reviewer. Moreover, even a single character modification would be reflected in the reviewer.

Since the input process sub-module and the real-time reviewer sub-module are implemented in two separated panels, the special event handling processes are designed to achieve communication between them. The user input actions are collected in input process panel by implementing the system event listeners, which include keyboard listener and combo box listener. Since the events are not transparent between panels, reviewer panel can not be notified by listener the system events. To notify reviewer panel the modifications on real-time, an update event is defined. This event is generated and broadcasted out from the input process panel when the validated modification is accepted. A special event listener is implemented in the reviewer panel to accept the update event and to notify reviewer to update. (see fig. 4)

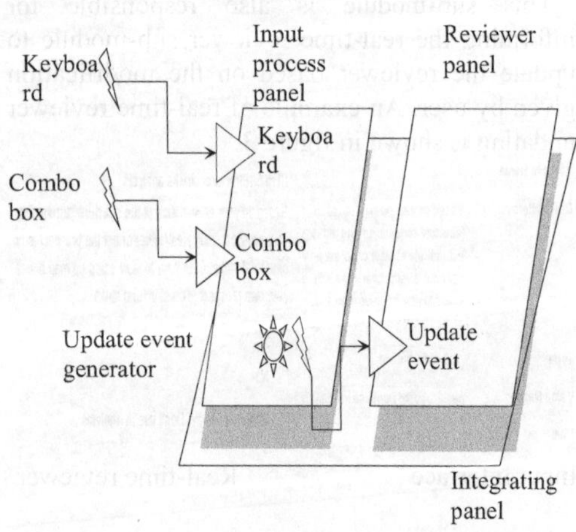

Figure 4. Event handling for the question definition module, where keyboard and mouse events are system defined events, update event is user defined event.

Group reviewer sub-module shows the reviewer for all the questions in one group. It is a combination of question reviewers.

4. Interface Generation

The interface generated from the group list is a dialog with multiple tabs. Each tab shows a question group. There can be an undefined number of questions in a group, so displaying them within one fixed size window is not always possible. In this case, questions can be distributed in a set of grouped windows. Since the questions in a group constantly update as dynamic GUI component, dimension calculation and alignment algorithms were designed to achieve optimal window sizes, based on the computed sized of the question box and set them in corresponding positions by distributing them across virtual pages.

Figure 5 shows the screen shots of an example of a tab designed and generated by interface generating module.

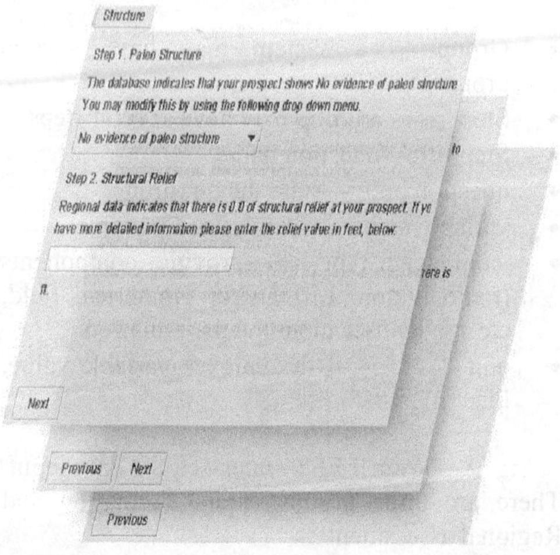

Figure 5. A tab containing multiple visual pages.

The algorithm to distribute questions to visual page groups (VPGs) is shown in below pseudo code:

```
VPG QuestionDistribution( group, tabheight, tabwidth){
    accumulateheight = 0;
    initialize the first element of VPGs;
    for each question(i) in group {
        if ( 0 == accumulateheight ) {
            add question(i) to current VPG;
        } else {
            curheight = calheight(question(i),
tabwidth);
            accumulateheight += curheight;
            if ( accumulateheight <= tabheight ) {
                add question(i) to current VPG;
            } else {
                new a VPG
                add question(i) to the new VPG;
                accumulateheight = curheight;
            }
        }
    }
}
```

The algorithm is achieved by function *QuestionDistribution*, which takes questions in a group and the expected dimension of tab as inputs, has visual page groups as output. The basic idea of the algorithm is to place the questions within a rectangle specified by tab dimension, and monitor the increase of the height. If an overflow happens, a new VPG is created to hold the new questions and the question causes the overflow.

A function was also designed, *calheight* in above pseudo code, to dynamically calculate a height of a question. The height of a question depends on the tab width and the question specification, which includes the question title, question description and the type of answers of that question. Function *calheight* calculates the total height required to display all the components of the question, at the same time sets the local offsets for each component. The function was implemented largely based on the function *getPreferredSize* of JAVA AWT component.

After questions of a group are distributed to VPGs, the corresponding offsets should be assigned to the questions according to the VPGs id. For each question in VPG(i) the offset is calculated and set as:

Offset(i) = XMargin + tabwidth × i,
YOffset(i) = YMargin, where XMargin and YMargin are the margins in both directions, see figure 6.

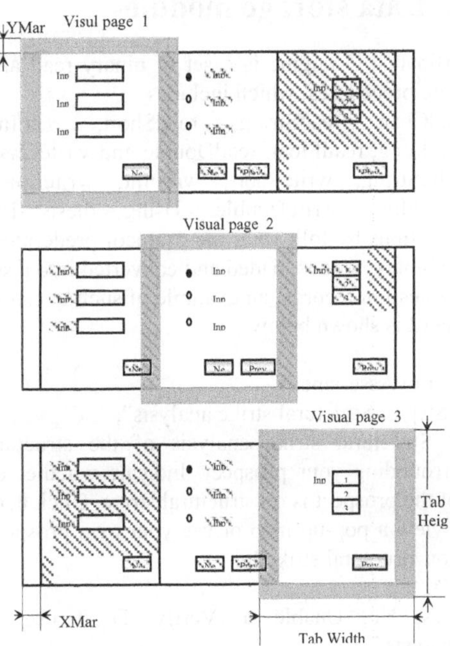

Figure 6. An example of distributing question in visual pages. Each visual page shows only questions in corresponding VPG. The objects within the green rectangle including the rectangle are a tab page visible to user each time.

When a tab for a group is displayed, a current visual page ID, *id*, is stored. Based on *id*, interface generator sub-module finds the questions in VPG(*id*), and displays them in the tab. Moreover, in order to page among visual pages, the visibilities of two buttons are also carefully controlled. If the *id* equals one, only the 'next' button should be visible. If the *id* equals the number of VPGs, only the 'previous' button should be visible. Otherwise, both buttons are visible.

After set positions of the visible GUI components, interface generator sub-module defines the event handling process for each component. For example, the clicking of the next button should increase the *id*, and it makes the next visual page active. On the contrast, the clicking of the 'previous' button leads previous visual page active.

5. Data storage module

Binary I/O engine is a set of binary read and write procedures, which includes readChar, readString, readShort, readInt, readLong, readFloat, readDouble and writeChar, writeString, writeShort, writeInt, writeLong, writeFloat, writeDouble. Using these I/O operations by following the protocol predefined, the binary code is loaded and converted into a set of question records, an example of such question record is shown below:

{"Trap Assessment",
"Step 5. Structural strike analysis",
" Structural strike analysis of the structure surrounding your prospect. Indicate whether or not the prospect is on structural strike. Click here to view a pop-up map or use your own prospect is on structural strike",
"2",
"Yes, No, Unable to Verify/ Don't use in Analysis",
""
}.

The question record includes the following attributes: group name, question title, question body, GUI component id, and GUI component parameter list and unit description. The example of such record is shown in figure 3.b. In this example, the group name is "Trap Assessment", the question title is "Step 5. Structural strike analysis", the question body is "Step 5. Structural strike analysis...", GUI id is 2, which means it is a radio button group, the GUI parameters are "Yes, No, Unable to Verify/ Don't use in Analysis ", which decides the descriptions of radio buttons, and unit is empty.

Figure 7 shows the corresponding GUI for that question.

The question record includes the following attributes: group name, question title, question body, GUI component id, and GUI component

Step 5. Structural stricke analysis

Based on your examination of the structure surrounding your prospect. indicate whether or not the prospect is on structural strike. Click here to view a pop-up map or use your own prospect is on structural strike

- (•) Yes
- ( ) No
- ( ) Unable to Verify/ Don't use in Analysis

Figure 7. Corresponding GUI for that question

The question record includes the following attributes: group name, question title, question body, GUI component id, and GUI component parameter list and unit description. The example of such record is shown in figure 3. In this example, the group name is "Trap Assessment", the question title is "Step 5. Structural strike analysis", the question body is "Step 5. Structural strike analysis...", GUI id is 2, which means it is a radio button group, the GUI parameters are "Yes, No, Unable to Verify/ Don't use in Analysis ", which decides the descriptions of radio buttons, and unit is empty.

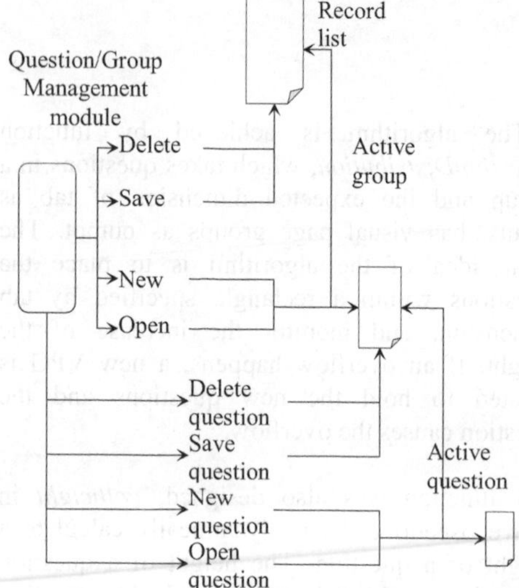

Figure 8. The functions of question/group management sub-module. Group operations: New, Open, Save, Delete. Question operations: New, Open, Save, Delete.

By using the 'group name' and 'question title' the question/group management sub-module groups the questions in groups. It also provides user the functions to create, update and delete questions and groups. The basic functions of question/group management sub-module are shown in figure 8.

"New group" and "Open group" operations make an active group, on which three operations can be performed. 'New question' and 'Open question' operations create or open an active question of the current active group. An active question is the input of the question definition module.

6. Test Result

When the initial functions of Customizable Fuzzy Expert System were implemented, we tried to define and implement Delaware FEE tool, [2,3] .

Totally, three groups, 5 pages and 17 questions were defined using the interface definition module presented above.

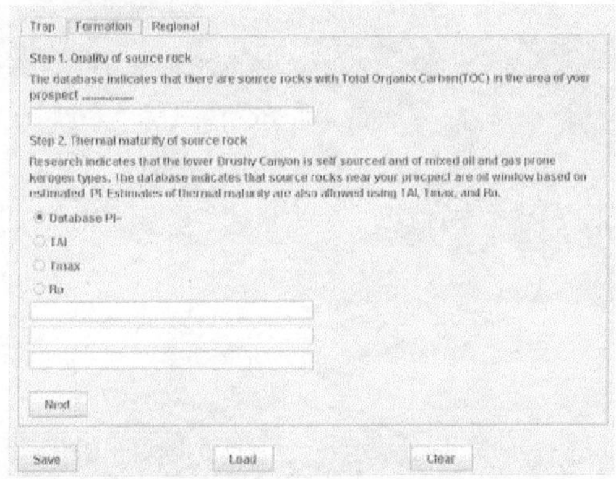

Figure 9. Generated Interface

Figure 9. shows the generated interface. Input values in the interface will be saved into a file. Since the number of variable and names are changeable, the file will store the variable definition defined by user and the value, i.e. {variable definition, value}. The inference engine accesses them by the variable name and inference based on these values.

7. Conclusion

The Interface Generator was design and implemented based on the frame of FEE Tool interface[2,3].

It consists of three modules: Interface Definition, interface generation and Storage. Interface definition module dynamically generates one step interface to let user review the defined interface during defining the step.

Data storage module provides the function of data management, which follows the protocol predefined. Question record was designed as an element exchange between Data storage module and other modules.

Interface generation module generates a combined tabbed pane. Each group will be put into one tab. The number of pages will be automatically decided by the number of steps and the size of each step.

The interface generator has been written in Java. Testing shows that this tool can successfully accept and store interface definitions from users and can dynamically generate an interface for an expert system based on the questions defined by a user.

Reference :

[1] R.S. Balch, R.F. Broadhead, and T. Ruan, A Customizable Fuzzy Expert System for Regional and Local Play Analysis , First Annual Report to the Department of Energy, 2007.

[2] Ruan, T., Balch, R.S., and Schrader, S.M.: “A Fuzzy Expert System for Oil Prospecting in the Lower Brushy Canyon of SE New Mexico”, IEEE International Conference on Information Reuse and Integration, Las Vegas, NV August 15-17,2005.

[3] R.S. Balch, R.F. Broadhead, and T. Ruan, *Risk Reduction with a Fuzzy Expert Exploration Tool*, Fifth Annual Report to the Department of Energy, 2004.

Lessons Learned: Porting Java Applications to Android

G. Hsieh, D. Paruchuri, C. Steward, E. Nwafor and D. Gadam

Department of Computer Science, Norfolk State University, Norfolk, Virginia, USA
ghsieh@nsu.edu, [d.paruchuri, c.c.steward, e.c.nwafor, d.gadam]@spartans.nsu.edu

Abstract – *Android has become the world's most popular mobile platform. It provides a very powerful Android runtime and application framework that enable application developers to efficiently create innovative and feature-rich apps in Java. This attribute is very attractive to application developers who are familiar with Java and may wish to port some existing Java applications to Android. However, there are significant differences between Android's Java and the Java SE environments. In addition, Android apps need to be designed and implemented with more care in order to meet the more stringent resource and performance constraints for mobile devices than those assumed for the Java SE environment. As a result, porting non-trivial Java applications from the SE to Android environments may not be as easy and straightforward as one may assume. In this paper, we discuss our experiences and lessons learned in our efforts to port two Java-based applications/systems - each utilizing an extensive set of open-source Java libraries - to Android from the SE environment.*

Keywords: *Android, Java, application porting.*

1 Introduction

Android has become the world's most popular mobile platform [1]. It has gained widespread acceptance since the announcement of the Open Handset Alliance in late 2007 [2]. Seeing a tremendous growth of internet usage and search in mobile devices, Google acquired Android, Inc. in 2005.

Android powers hundreds of millions of mobile devices in more than 190 countries around the world. It's the largest installed base and fastest growing of any mobile platform [3]. There are more than one hundred different makes of Android devices on the market currently, including smartphones and tablets, from more than fifteen manufacturers worldwide [1].

Android is also an open-source platform optimized for mobile devices. It is made available through the Android Open Source Project (AOSP) [4] which is led by Google, Inc. Android builds on the open-source Linux kernel, and its openness has made it very attractive for consumers and developers alike.

In addition, Android truly is a complete stack, from boot loader, device drivers, and libraries, to software APIs, included applications, and SDK [5]. Figure 1 shows the system architecture for the Android platform [6].

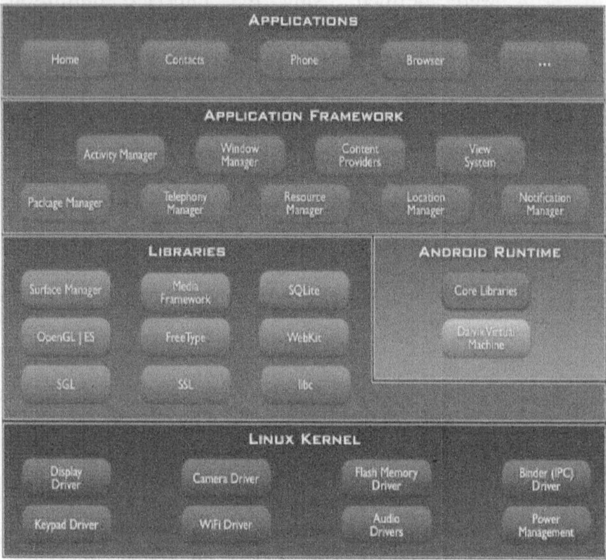

Figure 1. Android platform architecture

Android applications are typically written in Java. The application framework provides a tightly integrated part of the platform SDK and APIs that allow for high-level interaction with the system from within applications (e.g., accessing network data) [5]. Beneath the application framework is the middleware layer which contains the Android runtime and system libraries.

Android's runtime environment is similar to the Java runtime environment (JRE) provided by Sun/Oracle. First, it provides a core library which bundles all classes that are part of the specific Java platform, including language utilities, networking, concurrency, etc. Second, the runtime environment provides a Java virtual machine (JVM), called *Dalvik*, for running Java applications [5].

Android's integrated support for Java application development and deployment makes it very attractive to application developers, especially those who are familiar with Java and who may wish to port some existing Java applications from the SE to Android environments.

However, it is important to note that Android's Java is not equal to Sun/Oracle's Java SE. First, Android's core libraries do not bundle the same packages as in Java SE. Second, Dalvik is a JVM optimized for mobile platforms which accepts a different bytecode called Dalvik executable (*Dex*). This requires that the regular Java bytecode produced by a standard Java compiler needs to be translated into Dex code in advance such that the latter can be executed by Dalvik VM on Android.

These two major differences can have varying degrees of impact when attempting to port existing Java applications from Java SE to Android environments. Some may be able to reuse many existing Java libraries with Android applications while the bytecode translation is merely a procedural issue that is automatically taken care of by Android SDK.

On the other hand, porting of more complex and larger scale applications may not be as easy and straightforward due to these two major differences in the Java platforms. There are also additional Java language/API-level differences which require the modification of Java application code. For example, the entry point to a Java program on Java SE is its *main*() method, while an Android app is not allowed to have a main() method. Another example is that Android does not support the AWT or Swing widget toolkits that are standard in Java SE for developing graphical user interfaces in Java.

Furthermore, Android apps need to be designed and implemented with more care in order to meet the more stringent resource and performance constraints for mobile devices than those assumed for the Java SE environment. For example, the application may need to be restructured or optimized in order to reduce the memory and storage requirements, or to improve the response time by performing tasks asynchronously.

Hence, porting of complex and larger scale Java applications/libraries from Java SE to Android environments can be very challenging. In some situations, it can be too difficult or impossible without major redevelopment, and thus it no longer qualifies as a "porting" effort.

In this paper, we present our experiences and lessons learned in our efforts to port two non-trivial Java applications (libraries) from Java SE to Android environments, hoping to invite more systematic and comprehensive discussion and information sharing among software engineering professionals on this interesting topic of "to port, or not to port".

Both of our efforts are related to the self-protecting security framework research program which began in 2005 at Norfolk State University [7] [8] [9] [10] [11] [12]. The fundamental concept underlying this framework approach is the use of a variety of XML-based open standards that are commonly used for web services security [13], including eXensible Access Control Markup Language (XACML) [14] for expressing access control policies.

This self-protecting security framework approach can be applied in a general-purpose fashion by using XACML as the container for all related information. Or it can be applied in a domain-specific fashion to use an open XML-based standard, such as Clinical Document Architecture (CDA) [15] for electronic health/healthcare information, as the container for all related information.

For experimentation and demonstration purposes, we have continued to develop prototype software for the self-protecting security frameworks [7] [9] [16] [17]. Our prototype software is written primarily in Java and it involves extensive processing of XML documents.

One of our objectives is to provide similar self-protecting security for apps and documents on Android. Our first effort was centered on the open-source XACML Java libraries, both Version 1.2 and 2.0, implemented by Sun/Oracle [18]. We successfully ported, after some difficulty, the Version 1.2 of Sun's XACML Java library which has been used for our prototype software on Java SE. However, we abandoned porting the Version 2.0 after running into so many problems.

Our second effort began with the open-source Model-Driven Health Tools (MDHT) Runtime Jars for Java (Release 1.0) [19], which has been used for developing our initial prototype Personal Health Record (PHR) application for the Java SE environment [16]. We successfully ported, after a period of trial and error, a subset of the Jars to meet the needs for our PHR application. Equipped with the ported MDHT Runtime Jars, we next attempted to port our PHR Java application code to Android. Due to the reasons mentioned above, we ended up practically redeveloping the PHR application as a native-architecture Android app throughout [17].

The remainder of the paper is organized as follows. In Section 2 we provide an overview of Android's Java application architecture and runtime environment, focusing on the implications for porting Java apps. In Section 3 we discuss the activities, results, and experiences in our case studies of porting efforts. In section 4 we conclude the paper with a summary.

2 Android Java

In this section, we discuss some of the most common and important factors affecting the degree of reuse of existing Java libraries or applications for Android. These factors include the Android core libraries and Dalvik VM which combine to form the Android Runtime, and the structure and performance considerations for Android apps which affect the scope of restructuring of Java application code.

2.1 Android Core Libraries

Android's Java core library implementation is based on Apache Harmony [20] which is an open source Java SE implementation by the Apache Software Foundation. Although Harmony is the basis for Android's core Java library, they are not exactly the same.

The Android core library implementation includes only those Harmony packages that are useful for Android mobile devices. It also includes Android-specific implementation of Java SE, replacing comparable packages in Harmony.

As a result, not all of Java SE runtime library is implemented in Android. The degree of potential reuse of existing Java apps or libraries is significantly determined by what is supported, partially supported, or not supported at all by Android's core Java library.

One obvious example is the user interface toolkits. Android provides its own user interface components that are optimized for mobile devices, and does not support AWT or Swing which are considered the standard user interface components for desktops. Thus, an existing Java SE app which uses AWT or Swing will need to have its user interface re-developed to replace AWT or Swing with Android's own user interface components.

As mentioned earlier, XML processing is fundamental to our self-protecting security framework approach and prototype implementation. Again, Android provides most, but not all, of the many XML support classes in Java SE.

Android supports both Document Object Model (DOM) and Simple API for XML (SAX) parsing of XML documents, and includes all core Java classes that those parsers require. On the other hand, the Java API for XML Binding (JAXB) is missing from Android completely [5].

2.2 Dalvik VM

Dalvik VM [21] is in charge of executing Java applications running on Android. It is developed through an open-source project with support from Google. Dalvik is optimized for mobile devices which have limited resources and power comparing with the desktop environment.

For efficiency considerations, Dalvik does not interpret Java bytecode directly. Instead, it uses the custom Dex bytecode. The *.class* files produced by a Java compiler needs to be converted to this Dex format. This conversion can be easily done by the Android SDK took, *dx*. So it is not necessary to have the source code for a Java library in order to use it in an Android application.

The main difference between the Dalvik and Oracle/Sun Java bytecodes is in the packing of code [22]. With Dex, all the classes of the application are packed into a single Dex file, as shown in Figure 2 [21]. In addition, all the classes in the same Dex file share the same constant pools for strings, fields, methods, etc.

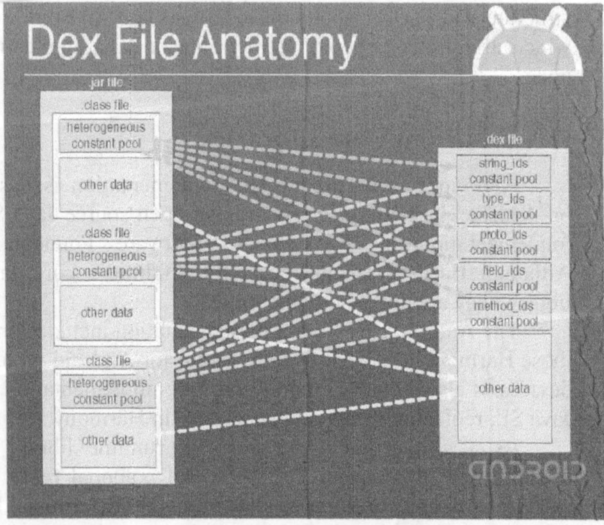

Figure 2. Dex file anatomy

The Dex approach helps reduce duplication of internal data structures and cuts down on the file size. On the other hand, classes from the same Dex file are loaded by the same class loader instance. In other words, these classes cannot be loaded using different class loader instances [22] as what can be done with Java SE. This restriction can pose a problem for porting those Java applications or libraries which require the manipulation of multiple classloaders.

This also means that all the classes in the same Dex file belong to the same namespace, and thus duplicated names across multiple Java classes can be a problem for Dex even when they are fine for the Java SE environment.

2.3 Android Applications

As mentioned earlier, Android applications are typically written in the Java programming language. Unlike applications on most other systems, Android applications don't have a single entry point (there's no *main*() function, for example) [23].

Android applications are composed of one or more application components. There are four types of application components: activities, services, content providers, and broadcast receivers. An *activity* is an application component that provides a screen with which users can interact in order to do something, such as dial the phone or view a map. Thus, it is commonly used by Android apps which provide user interfaces.

An activity is created as a subclass of the public class *android.app.Activity* (or an existing subclass of it). The lifecycle of an activity is managed by implementing callback methods that the system calls when the activity transitions between various states, such as when it is being created, stopped, resumed, or destroyed [23].

In summary, the structure of Android Java applications is quite different from that of Java SE. Thus, some restructuring of the application code is required when porting existing Java SE apps to Android.

Furthermore, Android apps need to be designed and implemented with more attention towards performance than typical Java SE applications, in order to meet the more stringent resource and energy requirements for mobile devices.

In Android, the system guards against applications that are insufficiently responsive for a period of time by displaying an "Application Not Responding (ANR)" alert and may even force the non-responding application to close [24]. It is critical to design responsiveness into the application so the system never displays an ANR alert to the user.

Android applications normally run entirely on a single thread (by default the "UI thread"). This means anything the app is doing in the UI thread that takes a long time to complete can trigger the ANR alert because the app is not giving itself a chance to handle the input event or intent broadcasts. Therefore, any method that runs in the UI thread should do as little work as possible on that thread. Potentially long running operations should be done in a worker thread, which can be most effectively created with the *AsyncTask* class [24].

Again, an existing Java app code may need to be restructured for performance consideration, as we have done for the Android version of our PHR prototype application.

2.4 Android SDK

The Android SDK [25] provides the API libraries and developer tools necessary to build, test, and debug apps for Android. The recommended IDE is Eclipse with the ADT (Android Developer Tools) plugin.

Since we have been using Eclipse IDE for Java Developers for our prototype software development, Android's Eclipse+ADT IDE is very convenient for us. To test our Android apps and libraries, we used a variety of Android device emulators, smartphones, and tablets.

3 Case Studies

In this section, we discuss our efforts, results, and experiences in two cases: 1) porting Sun's XACML Java libraries and a sample application; and 2) porting MDHT Runtime Jars for Java and our prototype Personal Health Record application.

3.1 Sun XACML Jars and Sample App

Oracle/Sun Lab released its Version 1.2 of XACML Java Library in July 2004 and Version 2.0 in July 2010 [18]. We have been using the Version 1.2 of the *sunxacml* library for our prototype software. As a matter of fact, we have extended the library to add new features and conventions for our self-protecting security framework approach.

As we were already planning to upgrade our prototype software to leverage the Version 2.0 of sunxacml, we first attempted to port this version to Android in late 2011. After running into so many problems with this version, we went back to the Version 1.2 of sunxacml with which we had more knowledge and experiences.

In the end, we managed to port the Version 1.2 of sunxacml library to Android. However, the process was not easy, nor straightforward. The main challenges were due to the fact that the sunxacml library requires a set of Java core (java.* or javax.*) classes that were not supported by Android runtime.

The sunxacml Version 1.2 release contains the source, data files, documentation, and the produced libraries. The main library, *sunxacml.jar*, for producing and reading XACML documents is 191 KB in size. The source needed to build sunxacml.jar is contained in a */src/sunxacml* folder which contains 243 files in 23 subfolders taking up a total space of 1.14 MB. The distribution also contains a *samples.jar* (7 KB in size) which includes a sample program called *simplePDP* that can be run to demonstrate XACML applications while using sunxacml.jar. The source and XML data files needed to build samples.jar and run simplePDP are contained in a */sample* folder which contains 22 files in 4 folders taking up a total space of 104 KB.

To port Sun's Version 1.2 XACML Java API library (sunxacml.jar) and its sample application (simplePDP) to Android, we undertook the following major activities:

(1) Set up a new Android application project also called *simplePDP*, using the Eclipse-integrated Android SDK (r6 or newer). The project target was set for Android API Level 6 (Android 2.0.1 Release 1) which was released in December 2009 and represented the Android platform that was broadly supported by Android devices in 2010-2011 timeframe.

(2) Set up the source for the simplePDP application project. This step was quite straightforward as sunxacml already used the same Apache Ant build tool and a very similar project structure as required by the Eclipse-integrated Android SDK.

(3) Restructure the code for the simplePDP class. The original class for Java SE contains a *main*() method which is not allowed for an Android application. Thus, we created a new *simplePDPActivity* class, which extends the Android Activity class, to serve as the entry point and to provide a user interface for the Android simplePDP app.

The relevant initialization code contained in the main() method was implemented inside the *onCreate*() method for simplePDPActivity, such that the necessary and equivalent initialization functions can be performed when the activity is created after the app is launched by the user. Also contained in the onCreate() method is the code to start an instance of the modified simplePDP class which no longer contains a main() method. Note that the sample program contains six other helper classes for the simplePDP class. Those classes did not require any code modification for Android.

(4) Restructure the file I/O. The sample application for sunxacml takes two XML files as input to produce another XML file as output. On Java SE, the input files are stored under the */sample/policy* and */sample/request* folders, respectively, within the project's file structure, and they can be easily accessed by using *java.io* APIs on the same Java SE host.

For Android, we prefer to have these input files distributed with the app such that no separate file transfer or configuration actions are required. To accomplish this goal, we have not found a working solution other than including these files as resources or assets for the app such that they can be packaged and installed as part of the app.

Unfortunately, this solution requires a different set of APIs, namely *Resources* or *AssetManager* classes, instead of the *java.io.File* class, to access the contents. This posed a problem for the sample application as it relies on File operations extensively. Instead of modifying the app code to use AssetManager operations everywhere and thus causing more widespread changes, we chose to isolate the changes within the onCreate() method by adding the code to read the contents through the AssetManager and then store them into files on internal storage. The references to the internal files (e.g., fully-qualified file names) are then used in the rest of the application in the same way as before.

(5) Bundle the missing core Java libraries. With all the preparations done, we proceeded to build and run the app using the Eclipse-integrated Android SDK. After fixing application-level errors, a compilation or execution could still fail due to "unresolved symbol" compilation errors or "NoClassDefFoundError" runtime errors, both indicating that some core Java classes were needed but missing from the Android runtime.

To resolve these types of errors, we chose to bundle the missing core Java classes with the app itself, instead of extending the core runtime library for Android platform, to facilitate our porting and experimentation efforts without modifying Android platform releases. We also used an iterative process to find appropriate solutions if possible. For each missing core Java class or package, we first used online resources, such as findJAR.com [26], to find available Jar(s) that contain the missing element. After further investigation, we next added such a Jar to the list of external libraries used to build the simplePDP app. Then we proceeded to build and run the app with the added external Jar which in turn might need additional Jars that were missing from Android runtime. This process was repeated until there was no core Java class that was apparently missing. After a working set was assembled, we next worked to reduce the memory and storage requirements for the app by eliminating redundant or extraneous classes from the working set.

For the sunxacml 1.2 Java API library and sample app, we added three additional Jars: xml-apis.jar, jndi.jar, and jndi-properties.jar, which combine to take 290 KB in size.

(6) Work around the "Conversion to Dalvik format failed with error 1" problem. According to the error message, this error indicates an "ill-advised or mistaken usage of a core class (java.* or javax.*) when not building a core library. This is often due to inadvertently including a core library file in your application's project, when using an IDE (such as Eclipse)." On the other hand, the Android app building tool does provide a --core-library option which can be set to suppress this error message and allow the build to proceed even when core classes are present in the application project. However, the ADT plugin for Eclipse does not allow this option to be set through Eclipse. It is interesting to note that the Android Maven Plugin does allow this option to be set through Maven.

For our porting effort, we needed to include these missing core library files (e.g., xml-apis.jar) in our application's project. However, we did not want to change our build tool from Ant to Maven. Therefore, we modified the default *build.xml* file to set this --core-library option through a custom shell script that we developed. Using this approach, we managed to work around the problem with a relatively simple custom solution. However, it was not ideal as it required modifying the default build file, and running the final application packaging tool through the command line interface outside of Eclipse.

In summary, we managed to port Sun's XACML v1.2 Java Library and sample application to Android. The size of the Android application package (.apk) file is about 187 KB.

Our efforts to port the Version 2.0 of Sun's XACML library and sample program did not succeed. One major reason for our difficulties was due to the fact that the Version 2.0 library was re-implemented using the JAXB technology.

JAXB is very powerful as it provides a fast and convenient way (using automation tools) to bind XML schemas and Java representations, making it easy for Java developers to map Java classes to XML representations [27]. On the other hand, it also adds a great deal of complexity to the runtime environment. As an indication, the size of the source-only release of Version 2.0 Sun XACML library is already approximately 570 KB in size.

Since JAXB was not supported by Android's runtime core library, it was very challenging and time-consuming trying to bundle all missing core classes (e.g., *java.xml.bind*) and their dependencies in the application's project. As a result, we abandoned this approach after putting in a good amount of effort without ever gaining enough confidence that this approach could work from both functional and performance viewpoints. For example, the size of the none-functional .apk file had already reached a size of approximately 500 KB for the same "application".

3.2 MDHT Runtime Jars and PHR App

Our interests in MDHT runtime Jars and personal health record applications centered on our efforts in developing the self-protecting security framework and associated prototype software for securing electronic medical records [8] [28] [16] [17].

As mentioned earlier, our approach leverages the CDA which is an XML-based document markup standard that specifies the structure and semantics of a clinical document. For our prototyping effort, we chose to leverage the runtime Jars provided by the open-source MDHT project which was initiated, by the Veterans Health Administration in April 2008 in collaboration with IBM as the co-lead of the project, to promote interoperability in healthcare infrastructure.

The MDHT runtime distribution contains JAR files with generated Java code from template models, plus all necessary dependencies for Eclipse-based modeling framework and code generation facility. It is intended for application developers who are using MDHT Java libraries created from models (e.g., CDA), not for creating or editing model specifications.

We first implemented a prototype PHR application for the Java SE environment [16]. This application used the MDHT runtime distribution Release 1.0, which became available in September 2011 timeframe, for processing CDA documents. Although the MDHT runtime release contained 24 Jar files with a total size of 9.68 MB, it was not an issue for the prototype PHR application running on Java SE.

With our interest in providing self-protecting security capability for Android, we undertook an effort to port the MDHT runtime Jars to Android. The first major roadblock we encountered was due to the duplicated file names. Each of the Jar files contained a text file named *plugin.xml* and/or another text file named *plugin.properties*. Given the duplicated file names, the Eclipse-integrated Android SDK would fail to build an Android application with these Jars in the application's project.

To work around this problem, we chose to delete these files from all of MDHT runtime Jars, as they were descriptor files used for describing how the plugin (Jar) extends the Eclipse platform, etc. [29]. After the files with duplicated names were removed from the Jars, the Android application could be built successfully. Note that the file removal could be easily accomplished by using the Java *jar* command without modifying or recompiling any source files.

Since our focus was on using the MDHT Java libraries that were already created from models (and not on creating or editing the models themselves), we believed that the impact of removing these types of descriptor files would not be significant for our purposes. Our experiences in running the Android application with the modified Jars seemed to confirm this assumption, as we have not observed any side effect due to the removal of these descriptor files.

After resolving the major roadblock caused by duplicated file names, we undertook optimization effort to reduce the number and total size of the Jars required for our application which did not need all the capabilities provided by all the Jars collectively. We used an iterative and (more or less) a trial-and-error approach to select the minimal subset of Jars that we needed for our Android application. It turned out that the final subset contained 11 (vs. 24 originally) Jars with a combined size of 4.35 MB (vs. 9.68 MB originally). This optimization effort and results were very beneficial to our prototyping program as they helped to reduce the application's runtime memory and persistent storage consumption on Android devices.

Our Java SE personal health record prototype application had GUI-based user interfaces that allow users to enter, view, modify, encrypt, and digitally sign their records maintained in CDA documents. These user interfaces were implemented using Swing.

To develop a similar PHR application for Android [17], we used the final subset of modified MDHT Jars to provide the same CDA processing functions. However, we did major restructuring of our application level code for both functional and performance considerations.

First, we restructured the code based on Android's application architecture. The Android PHR application now consisted of five Android activities plus additional helper classes. These activities allowed us to organize the code in a very modular fashion, and they provided the main and submenu user interfaces for starting the app, entering data, viewing data, editing data, and emailing data, respectively.

Second, we developed the user interfaces for our Android PHR application using the View-based components for Android.

Third, we implemented the Android PHR application with multi-threading capabilities in order to improve user responsiveness and avoid the much dreaded ANR problem. We used the AsyncTask construct to execute potentially long-running operations (e.g., encrypting or saving a CDA document which could be large) in separate threads away from the UI threads.

Fourth, we used the SAX-based XML parser for the Android PHR application, in contrast with our using the DOM-based XML parser for the Java SE based PHR application. This approach allowed us to conserve memory usage when parsing large CDA documents. However, it did add a great deal more complexity in our application code in order to handle the SAX events asynchronously. In addition, the CDA structure is very flexible and hence complex, and it is difficult to use SAX-based parser to extract information from CDA documents [30].

The MDHT runtime Jars were implemented using the in-memory, DOM-based programming model, and it did a very good job of hiding the low-level details and complexity from the application developers. Using the SAX-based parser, the application developers had to handle the low-level details themselves and this increased the application programming complexity significantly. To save time, we implemented only a subset of the data fields for the Android based PHR application.

In summary, we managed to migrate our PHR app from Java SE to Android. For performance consideration, we used multi-threading and memory-efficient parsing of XML documents. In the end, we practically redeveloped it as a native-architecture Android app which bears little resemblance with the Java SE based PHR app, while reusing the MDHT runtime Jars.

4 Summary

In this paper, we presented our efforts, results, and experiences in porting two Java applications/libraries from Java SE to Android environments. These software packages involved open-source Java libraries for processing XML-based documents.

Overall, we found these experiences very educational, as we encountered numerous problems along the way, including those caused by the differences in the core Java runtime library and virtual machine, IDE restrictions, etc. We were able to overcome those problems in all cases except the one involving the sunxacml v2.0 library. In addition, we learned important lessons in dealing with the more stringent resource and performance constraints for mobile devices which are not the same as desktops. Using techniques such as multi-threading and event-driven XML parsing helped to improve the resource and performance aspects; on the other hand, they added more complexity and required more effort in developing the applications.

We like to close the paper with the following observations:

(1) Migrating Java applications from Java SE to Android is more complicated than what might be assumed, except for small and trivial programs perhaps. Minimally, the app needs to be restructured to conform to Android's application model (e.g., activity versus main() method).

(2) The complexity increases if the application has extensive user interfaces implemented with AWT or Swing.

These user interfaces need to be practically rewritten using Android's View components.

(3) Third-party Java libraries could be a problem, especially if they use many of the core Java libraries (java.* or javax.*) that are not supported by Android.

(4) Files for initialization, configuration, or information could present a problem. Android has different classes and APIs to handle "resource" type of content which are treated differently from "files". Duplicated file names could cause additional problems.

(5) For performance and resource usage considerations, Android implementations may require more efficient or user-responsive techniques such as multi-threading and asynchronous/event-driven processing.

(6) Do not ignore the fact that Android-powered mobile devices are not the same as desktops, let alone servers. Be careful not to overload Android devices with apps requiring heavy-weight processing or storage.

5 Acknowledgement

This research was supported in part by U.S. Army Research Office, under contract no. W911NF-12-1-0081, and U.S. Department of Energy, under grant no. DE-FG52-09NA29516/A000.

6 References

[1] "Android," android.com, [Online]. Available: http://www.android.com/. [Accessed 27 May 2013].

[2] "Open Handset Alliance," [Online]. Available: http://www.openhandsetalliance.com/. [Accessed 27 May 2013].

[3] "Android, the world's most popular mobile platform," [Online]. Available: http://developer.android.com/about/index.html. [Accessed 27 May 2013].

[4] "Android Open Source Project," [Online]. Available: http://source.android.com/. [Accessed 27 May 2013].

[5] C. Collins, M. G. Galpin and M. Kaeppler, Android in Practice, Manning Publications Co., 2011.

[6] "Android Architectural Diagram," [Online]. Available: http://developer.android.com/images/system-architecture.jpg. [Accessed 27 May 2013].

[7] G. Hsieh and E. Nwafor, "A Self-Protecting Security Framework for CDA Documents," in *Intl' Conf. on Security and Management (SAM'13)*, Las Vegas, NV, 2013.

[8] G. Hsieh, "Towards Self-Protecting Security for e-Health CDA Documents," in *Proc. Int'l Conf. on Security and Management 2011 (SAM'11)*, Las Vegas, NV, 2011.

[9] G. Hsieh and M. Masiane, "Towards an Integrated Embedded Fine-Grained Information Protection Framework," in *Proc. 2011 Int'l Conf. on Information Science and Applications (ICISA'11)*, Jeju Island, Korea, 2011.

[10] G. Hsieh, R. Meeks and L. Marvel, "Supporting Secure Embedded Access Control Policy with XACML+XML Security," in *Proc. 5th int'l Conf. on Future Information Technology (FutureTech'10)*, Busan, Korea, 2010.

[11] G. Hsieh, K. Foster, G. Emamali, G. Patrick and L. Marvel, "Using XACML for Embedded and Fine-Grained Access Control Policy," in *Proc. 4th Int'l Conf. on Availability, Reliability and Security (ARES'09)*, 2009.

[12] G. Hsieh, G. Patrick, K. Foster, G. Emamali and L. Marvel, "Integrated mandatory access control for digital data," in *Proc. SPIE 2008 Defense + Security Conf.*, Orlando, FL, 2008.

[13] E. Bertino, I. D. Martino, F. Paci and A. C. Squicciarini, Security for Web Services and Service-Oriented Architectures, Springer-Verlag, 2010.

[14] "eXtensible Access Control Markup Language (XACML) Version 2.0," OASIS, 2005. [Online]. Available: https://www.oasis-open.org/committees/tc_home.php?wg_abbrev=xacml. [Accessed 31 May 2013].

[15] R. H. Dolin, L. Alschuler, C. Beebe, P. V. Boyer, D. Essin and E. Kimber, "The HL7 Clinical Document Architecture, Release 2," *J. Am Med Inform Assoc.*, vol. 13, no. 1, pp. 30-39, Jan-Feb 2006.

[16] D. Gadam, "Generating CDA Documents and Embedding XML Security," M.S. Thesis, Department of Computer Science, Norfolk State University, Norfolk, VA, March 2012.

[17] D. Paruchuri, "Developing a Personal Health Record Application for Android Platform," M.S. Thesis, Department of Computer Science, Norfolk State University, Norfolk, VA, April 2013.

[18] "Sun's XACML Implementation," [Online]. Available: http://sourceforge.net/projects/sunxacml/. [Accessed 27 May 2013].

[19] "Model-Driven Health Tools (MDHT)," [Online]. Available: https://www.projects.openhealthtools.org/sf/projects/mdht/. [Accessed 27 May 2013].

[20] "Apache Harmony," [Online]. Available: http://harmony.apache.org/. [Accessed 29 May 2013].

[21] D. Bornstein, "Dalvik VM Internals," Google, 29 May 2008. [Online]. Available: https://sites.google.com/site/io/dalvik-vm-internals/2008-05-29-Presentation-Of-Dalvik-VM-Internals.pdf. [Accessed 29 May 2013].

[22] G. Paller, "Understanding the Dalvik bytecode with the Dedexer tool," 2 Dec 2009. [Online]. Available: http://www.slideshare.net/paller/understanding-the-dalvik-bytecode-with-the-dedexer-tool. [Accessed 29 May 2013].

[23] "Application Fundamentals," [Online]. Available: http://developer.android.com/guide/components/fundamentals.html. [Accessed 30 May 2013].

[24] "Keeping Your App Responsive," [Online]. Available: http://developer.android.com/training/articles/perf-anr.html. [Accessed 30 May 2013].

[25] "Get the Android SDK," Android Developers, [Online]. Available: http://developer.android.com/sdk/index.html. [Accessed 31 May 2013].

[26] "findJAR.com," [Online]. Available: http://www.findjar.com/index.x. [Accessed 31 May 2013].

[27] "Lesson: Introduction to JAXB," [Online]. Available: http://docs.oracle.com/javase/tutorial/jaxb/intro/. [Accessed 31 May 2013].

[28] G. Hsieh and R.-J. Chen, "Design for a secure interoperable cloud-based Personal Health Record service," in *IEEE 4th Int'l Conf. on Cloud Computing Technology and Science (CloudCom'12)*, Taipei, Taiwan, 2012.

[29] "FAQ What is the plug-in manifest file (plugin.xml)?," eclipse.org, [Online]. Available: http://wiki.eclipse.org/FAQ_What_is_the_plug-in_manifest_file_(plugin.xml)%3F. [Accessed 31 May 2013].

[30] Keith Boone, The CDA Book, Springer, 2011.